Acquisitions Editor: Paul Donnelly
Assistant Editor: Gladys Soto
Editorial Assistant: Jodi Hirsh
Editorial Director: James Boyd
Marketing Manager: Patrick Lynch
Production Editor: Anne Graydon
Production Coordinator: Carol Samet
Associate Managing Editor: David Salierno
Managing Editor: Dee Josephson
Manufacturing Buyer: Kenneth J. Clinton
Manufacturing Supervisor: Arnold Vila
Manufacturing Manager: Vincent Scelta
Design Director: Pat Smythe
Cover Design: Maureen Eide
Composition: Omegatype Typography, Inc.
Cover Photo: T. del Amo/H. Armstrong Roberts, Inc.

Library of Congress Cataloging-in-Publication Data

Sinkey, Joseph, F.
    Commerical bank financial management in the financial-services
industry / Joseph F. Sinkey, Jr.
    992 p.   cm.
    Includes bibliographical references and indexes.
    ISBN 0-13-521048-8
    1. Bank management.   I. Title.
HG1615.S57   1998
332.1'2'068—dc21   97–35594
                                                                  CIP

Prentice-Hall International (UK) Limited, London
Prentice-Hall of Australia Pty. Limited, Sydney
Prentice-Hall Canada, Inc., Toronto
Prentice-Hall Hispanoamericana, S.A., Mexico
Prentice-Hall of India Private Limited, New Delhi
Prentice-Hall of Japan, Inc., Tokyo
Simon & Schuster Asia Pte. Ltd., Singapore
Editora Prentice-Hall do Brasil, Ltda., Rio de Janeiro

Printed in the United States of America

10 9 8 7 6 5 4 3 2 1

Fifth
Edition

COMMERCIAL BANK FINANCIAL MANAGEMENT

In the Financial-Services Industry

Joseph F. Sinkey, Jr.

*Professor of Banking and Finance
and The Edward W. Hiles Chair
of Financial Institutions*

*Terry College of Business
The University of Georgia, Athens*

PRENTICE HALL   Upper Saddle River, New Jersey 07458

This book is dedicated to the memory of my parents:
Dorothy Fagan Sinkey
(Alzheimer's patient)
May 5, 1915–October 30, 1997
and
Joseph F. Sinkey, Sr.
June 4, 1915–June 20, 1982 (Father's Day)

Brief Contents

Contents

Preface

"Bank financial management" and "financial-services industry," the two major themes of this book, are captured by the title: *Commercial Bank Financial Management in the Financial-Services Industry.* First, the book's approach to bank management is financial in the sense that it reflects modern corporate financial management as opposed to simply describing what banks do. This means that maximizing shareholder value, risk-return tradeoffs, and risk management are key concepts. Second, because banks operate in the *financial-services industry* (FSI) and not in the more narrowly defined banking industry, they must have an expansive view of (1) where they are going and (2) how they are going to get there. A prerequisite is to know where the bank is today, especially in terms of its profitability, liquidity, and comprehensive risk-based capital requirements. With declining franchise value in the traditional business of funding loans with deposits in order to be competitive in the FSI of the twenty-first century, banks must have strategic, technological-based visions of ways to add value.

Several centuries B.C., Heraclitus, the Greek philosopher, achieved literary immortality and aptly anticipated *modern banking* in the FSI when he said:

> All is flux, nothing stays still. Nothing endures but change.

The sources of flux in banking, which have been numerous and sometimes volatile, include

- *Competition*
- *Consolidation*
- *Information technology*
- *Product and geographic expansion*
- *Re-regulation* (including deposit-insurance reform)
- *Volatility* of *interest rates, exchange rates,* and *commodity prices*

Combined with rational self-interest, these driving forces of change generate financial innovation. Schematically,

Forces of Change + Rational Self-Interest → Financial Innovation

where rational self-interest refers to the pursuit of *profitable investment opportunities.* This model represents a framework for analyzing change and the important role of financial innovation in banking and the FSI.

One of the most important innovations in banking has been the development of *tools for managing risk.* Because risk management is arguably the critical component of bank financial management, it is a major focus of this book. Risk-management techniques range from traditional methods such as *asset-liability management* (ALM) and borrower *credit analysis* to more sophisticated *on-* and *off-balance-sheet* techniques such as *duration* analysis, the use of *derivatives* in the form of *futures, forwards, options,* and *swaps* for *hedging,* and the removal of risk through *securitization.* Securitization, which is the process of packaging loans for sale as securities, reflects one of the important "-izations" that is fundamentally changing banking and the FSI. Other important "-izations" include the *globalization* of world financial markets, which because of the domination of U.S. financial-services firms can, without too much exaggeration, be called *Americanization;* the *institutionalization* of savings into pension and mutual funds; and the *privatization* of formerly state-owned enterprises.

The ability to adapt to change will determine who survives in the financial-services industry. For some large U.S. banks, adaptation in the early 1990s took the form of corporate restructurings including dividend cuts, reorganizations, and major charges against earnings (e.g., for losses on commercial real-estate loans). The consolidation trend in banking and the FSI, which has been going on for years, accelerated during the mid-1990s marked by the megamerger of Chase Manhattan Bank and Chemical Bank in 1996 to form the largest bank in the United States.

Corporate restructurings and mergers are designed to make firms into the "lean, mean fighting machines" that we so often hear about; corpulent banks will be gobbled up by competitors. Banks that take on too much risk and miscalculate their downside vulnerability will find that market forces and *prompt corrective action* by regulators (as required by the FDIC Improvement Act of 1991) will prevent them from becoming "zombies"—the antithesis of the 1980s when numerous savings-and-loan associations (S&Ls) and commercial banks failed. Also, banks that sell their products without *full disclosure,* whether they be mutual funds sold to consumers or derivatives products sold to corporate clients, will find limitations on *caveat emptor* ("let the buyer beware").

Dealing with commercial banking from a finance perspective and applying principles of financial management to banking in the rapidly changing financial-services industry, as this book does, is an approach that is crucial today because of the dramatic changes occurring in the competition for financial services. To be successful, bank managers must be able to respond quickly and rationally to these changes. Former principles, like the "3-6-3 rule" (i.e., money in at 3%, out at 6%, and on the golf course by 3 P.M.), do not apply in today's dynamic environment. The theory and practice of financial management provide a framework that highlights the importance of making decisions that add value creators and eliminate value destroyers. Banks that achieve these objectives will thrive.

Structure of the Fifth Edition

Just as downsizing has affected the corporate world, it has affected the size of the fifth edition. Down from 25 chapters to 20, the book is more efficient. Following two introductory chapters that provide an overview of banking and its risks, the book continues in six parts and 18 chapters:

- Bank performance and financial management (chapters 3–5)
- The risks of banking and their management (chapter 6–9)
- Managing the lending function and securitization (chapters 10–12)
- Managing bank capital (chapters 13–14)

- The federal safety net and ethics in banking (chapters 15–17)
- Financial innovation, information technology, and corporate restructuring in banking (chapters 18–20).

The Brief Contents on page **v** provides a structural overview of the book; whereas the Contents, beginning on page **vii**, provides detailed information for each chapter.

Major Changes in and Themes of the Fifth Edition: A Top-Ten List

In the spirit of David Letterman's top-ten list and as a device for keeping the description of changes and themes manageable, consider the following top-ten items for the fifth edition of this book:

10. Chapters—and fewer of them—designed to be more user friendly by including Learning Objectives, a Chapter Theme, and *two* lists of Key Concepts, Ideas, and Terms (one at the beginning of each chapter and a more detailed one at the end).

9. An acronym glossary to make the arcane world of ALM, LIBOR, CAMEL, and FDIC less confusing.

8. Author and subject indexes to make it easy to find who, what, where, and when.

7. New end-of-chapter questions, problems, cases, and projects to test learning comprehension and challenge research, writing, and analytical skills.

6. A complete analysis and description of the role of bank regulation, deposit insurance, and the federal safety net.

5. The interweaving throughout the book of the critical role that financial innovations such as information technology, securitization, and derivatives play in bank financial management.

4. A clear treatment of the important distinction between accounting and market measures of bank performance.

3. Understanding that a comprehensive measure of a bank's capital adequacy must take account of all of a bank's risk exposures, including credit risk, interest-rate risk, liquidity risk, foreign-exchange risk, and sensitivity to market risk.

2. Understanding that maximizing shareholder value requires bankers to develop strategic plans and policies, risk-management techniques, and corporate checks and balances that are designed to add value creators and eliminate value destroyers.

And, drum-roll, please

1. The addition of a new chapter on ethics in banking—not by accident the thinnest chapter in the book, because the thinnest book in the world is: *Ethics for Bankers, Lawyers, and Regulators.**

What Banks Do and How They Are Special

Are commercial banks special or different from other business firms? To be a player in the financial-services industry, a company needs a different mix of assets from those of a nonfinancial corporation. Banks have very few tangible assets like

---

*in Letterman-wit fashion

factories and machinery. Offices, furniture, computers, and software programs are the "hard" assets of banking. In contrast, banks use lots of intangible assets, like reputational capital, technical expertise, customer relationships, market presence, trade names, and deposit-insurance guarantees.

Banks use their real and intangible assets to produce such financial products and services as loans and checking accounts, items that appear on a bank's balance sheet. In addition, they produce items that do not appear on their balance sheets (e.g., loan commitments, letters of credit, and interest-rate swaps); these are known as off-balance-sheet activities or OBSAs. These activities generate "contingent claims" on a bank's balance sheet. The interest and fees paid for these products and services, whether on or off the balance sheet, are the "sales" of banking. Like any other business, banks expect to make a profit by having sales exceed costs. In addition, because business success is usually judged by value, banks strive to maximize their equity or net asset values by undertaking only positive net-present-value projects. Unlike most other businesses, however, banks are heavily regulated and have access to deposit insurance and the discount window. If anything makes banks special, regulation and deposit insurance do.

For Whom the Bell Tolls

This book is designed for both academic and practitioner markets and for anyone interested in the financial management of commercial banks in the financial-services industry. As a college textbook, upper-division undergraduates and MBA students are the intended audiences. In addition to bank management courses, the book can be used in courses dealing with the management of financial institutions. Doctoral students and practitioners will find the book to be both a good background text and a useful reference.

Auxiliary Teaching Materials

The *Instructor's Manual and Test Bank* that accompanies this book has answers to all of the end-of-chapter questions and problems and a comprehensive test bank of objective and other questions. In addition, it contains chapter outlines, transparency masters, pedagogical suggestions, and updated chapter information if available. My preferred approach to teaching a bank-management course is to supplement it with a bank-management simulator. The one I have used for over 20 years is the Stanford Bank Game (Version 11).

Acknowledgments

Since I started teaching banking at The University of Georgia in 1976, I recognized and thought about the need for a banking textbook based on the concept of financial and risk management. This vision was realized with the first edition of *Commercial Bank Financial Management* (1983). Through the second, third, fourth, and now the fifth edition of the book, the vision has continued.

Writing a book and revising it four times means fewer hours to devote to loved ones. I thank Joanne, my wife, and Alison and Jessica, my daughters, for their love, patience, encouragement, and understanding. When Jessica was very young, she thought that I lived upstairs in my home office. As an honor student at Georgia Southern University, Jessica understands effective time management. Alison, a 1996 graduate of the Terry College of Business of The University of Georgia, has embarked on a career in banking with the Factoring Division of SunTrust Banks in

Atlanta. Joanne, a devoted wife and mother, continues her work as a community and church volunteer. Lately, she has come to learn and appreciate why her husband, a native of Latrobe, Pennsylvania, the home of Arnold Palmer, loves golf so much. More than that, she has taken up the game and appreciates the challenge of the skill level, focus, and mental toughness it takes to play golf. Finally, Joanne's chocolate-chip cookies have become famous among my students. Last spring when she was writing a check at a local grocery store, she asked the clerk if he wanted to verify her identification. Looking at the check, he said, "Are you Dr. Sinkey's wife?" Joanne affirmed that she was, and he said, "That won't be necessary and, by the way, your chocolate-chip cookies are great." Manolis Kipreos, a native of Greece and a good student during my spring quarter 1997 banking class, was the clerk.

I thank James Don Edwards, Interim Dean, and Albert W. Niemi, former Dean, of the Terry College of Business, and James A. Verbrugge, Head of the Department of Banking and Finance, for providing an environment conducive for research and writing. Elaine Dunbar was helpful and efficient in preparing parts of the manuscript. As usual, Joanne Sinkey provided valuable proofreading. Scott McGarity and Matej Blasko provided important research assistance and comments on draft chapters. Tom Arnold and Dave Carter also read and commented on various chapters. I am especially thankful for the detailed comments on the new chapter on ethics provided by my colleagues Warren French and Jeffry Netter and by my long-time friend and mentor, Edward J. Kane of Boston College. Mataj Blasko constructed the author and subject indexes.

Six reviewers contracted by the publisher provided valuable comments and suggestions on the manuscript for the fifth edition. In alphabetical order, they are:

- Scott W. Barnhart, Clemson University
- David R. Durst, University of Akron
- Jocelyn D. Evans, Georgia State University
- Brian Gibson, Iowa State University
- James E. McNulty, Florida Atlantic University
- Robert C. Winder, Christopher Newport University

I thank each of you for taking the time to read and comment on the portions of the manuscript you reviewed.

Finally, pay special attention to the list of people on page ii. They are the Prentice Hall people who worked on this project. A special thanks to Paul Donnelly, Anne Graydon, Gladys Soto, and Jodi Hirsh; they tried their best to keep me on schedule.

If I have inadvertently omitted anyone from the acknowledgments for this edition, I apologize in advance. *Mea culpa, mea culpa, mea maxima culpa.* Individuals who provided valuable assistance on the previous four editions of the book are too numerous to mention. They are acknowledged in the prefaces of the earlier editions.

—Joseph F. Sinkey, Jr.
Athens, Georgia
October 1997

About the Author

Joseph F. Sinkey, Jr., is Professor of Banking and Finance and holds the Edward W. Hiles Chair of Financial Institutions, Department of Banking and Finance, Terry College of Business, The University of Georgia, Athens, Georgia. He received his Ph.D. in economics from Boston College in 1971 and his B. A. in economics from St. Vincent College, Latrobe, Pennsylvania, in 1966. From 1971 to 1976, he was a financial economist with the Division of Research of the Federal Deposit Insurance Corporation, Washington, D.C. He joined the faculty of The University of Georgia in 1976 as an associate professor and was promoted to full professor in 1983. From 1985 to 1992, he held the Georgia Bankers Association Chair of Banking.

Professor Sinkey has distinguished himself as a teacher, author, and researcher. He was recognized for superior teaching at The University of Georgia Honors Day in 1984 and 1985 and by the Georgia Finance Club in 1984. He is the author of six previous books: *Commercial Bank Financial Management,* published in 1983, 1986, 1989, and 1992; *Application of Classification Techniques in Business, Banking, and Finance,* a coauthored research book published by JAI Press, Inc., in 1981; and *Problems and Failed Institutions in the Commercial Banking Industry,* a research book published by JAI Press, Inc., in 1979. Professor Sinkey has written numerous articles, chapters, and book reviews for various banking and finance publications. He is an associate editor and the book review editor for the *Journal of Banking and Finance,* a former associate editor for the *Journal of Financial Research,* and an ad hoc reviewer for major banking and finance journals.

In addition to his teaching and research duties, Professor Sinkey has served as a consultant to industry and government, testified before the United States Senate, and been an expert witness in cases involving banking and financial matters. Professor Sinkey has taught at various banking schools across the country including the School for Bank Administration, The Michigan Graduate School of Bank Management, The Management School of Bank Marketing, The School for Executive Development, and the Georgia Banking School. His international experience includes teaching, seminars, paper presentations, and speeches in Bratislava (Slovakia), Byblos (Lebanon), Istanbul, Jerusalem, London, Lyon, Montevideo, Oslo, Phnom Penh, Rome, Seoul, Taipei, Tours, and Vilnius (Lithuania).

Professor Sinkey has been married to Joanne Marie Forsyth since 1970, and they have two daughters—Alison, 23, and Jessica, 20. His nonacademic interests include golf, tennis, duplicate bridge, long-distance running, theater/cinema, travel, and freelance writing. A hole-in-one in 1986 and a completed marathon (26 miles 385 yards in 3:34:51) in 1978 mark his accomplishments in these areas. Becoming a life master in duplicate bridge, lowering his golf handicap, and writing a book about life in and beyond the Latrobe Restaurant are his post-retirement goals.

P A R T

I

INTRODUCTION TO BANK FINANCIAL MANAGEMENT IN THE FINANCIAL-SERVICES INDUSTRY

This part of the book contains two chapters: Chapter 1 provides an introduction to banking in the financial-services industry (FSI). The major themes of the chapter are the functions of a financial system, the major players in the FSI, the fundamentals of financial intermediation, the risks of banking, and dimensions of bank competition and how regulation shapes them. The decline of banking, described as "The End of Banking as We Know It," furnishes a starting point for distinguishing between the gathering of deposits to fund loans, the traditional business of banking, and modern banking, which goes beyond the customary geographic and product markets of old-line commercial banking. Although traditional commercial banking has been in relative decline over the past quarter century, commercial banks still are the most important players in the U.S. financial system. Appendix A to chapter 1 provides a detailed list of sources of banking information and a few tips on researching on the Internet and writing reports as "executive summaries." Appendix B contrasts and compares three alternative models of bank industry linkage: (1) the Japanese model, or *keiretsu* approach; (2) the German model, or universal-bank approach; and (3) the Anglo-American model, or capital-markets approach.

Chapter 2 presents three alternative ways of viewing a bank: (1) as a consolidated balance sheet or portfolio, (2) as an information processor with similarities to communications firms, and (3) as a regulated financial-services firm. The chapter mainly develops the portfolio concept by highlighting a bank's sources and uses of funds and its risk management.

CHAPTER

1

OVERVIEW OF BANKING AND THE FINANCIAL-SERVICES INDUSTRY

Contents

LEARNING OBJECTIVES

- ■ To understand the functions of a financial system

- ■ To understand the role, importance, and risks of banking

- ■ To distinguish between direct and indirect finance

- ■ To understand the "decline" of banking

- ■ To distinguish between traditional commercial banking and modern banking

- ■ To understand the dimensions of bank competition and how regulation shapes them

CHAPTER THEME

This chapter presents an introduction and overview of banking and the **financial-services industry** (FSI). The primary function of a financial system is resource allocation. **Financial-services firms** (FSFs) act as intermediaries in the allocation of financial resources. As financial markets become more complete, **direct finance** tends to reduce the importance of certain financial institutions and the process of **indirect finance.** This phenomenon, driven in part by deregulation, financial innovation, and technological change, has led to the decline of the business of funding loans with deposits—traditional commercial banking. To survive in the FSI, banks must adapt to this changing environment. A financial-management perspective emphasizes the importance of understanding the risks of banking and how to manage them. Both **market and regulatory discipline** monitor and restrict bank risk taking. Explicit price, user convenience, and public confidence are the primary dimensions of bank competition.

KEY CONCEPTS, IDEAS, AND TERMS

- Bank holding company (BHC)
- Credit risk
- Dimensions of bank competition (price, confidence, convenience)
- Direct finance versus indirect finance (intermediation)
- Discipline (market and regulatory)

- Financial markets
- Financial-services firm (FSF)
- Financial-services industry (FSI)
- Financial system (core functions)
- Globalization
- Institutionalization
- Interest-rate risk

- Intermediation versus disintermediation
- Liquidity risk
- Pass-through finance
- Regulatory dialectic (struggle model)
- Risk management
- Securitization

THE FUNCTIONS OF A FINANCIAL SYSTEM[1]

The primary function of a **financial system** is resource allocation. To accomplish this task, financial systems perform six basic, or core, functions:

1. They clear and settle payments (a payments system)
2. They aggregate (pool) and disaggregate wealth and flows of funds so that both large-scale and small-scale projects can be financed
3. They transfer economic resources over time, space, and industries
4. They accumulate, process, and disseminate information for decision-making purposes
5. They provide ways for managing uncertainty and controlling risk
6. They provide ways for dealing with incentive and asymmetric-information problems that arise in financial contracting

Although financial institutions come and go, these six core functions are relatively unchanging. Moreover, as financial innovation and competition among institutions generate greater efficiency in the performance of a financial system, institutional form tends to follow function.

To see the importance of commercial banks to a financial system, consider each of the six functions in the form of a question focusing on the importance of banks. For example, do banks clear and settle payments? Do they pool funds? For commercial banks, the answer to each of the six questions is: Yes! This is not to deny that other financial institutions perform some of these functions also. The important point, however, is that commercial banks perform all of these functions and that they have been adapting their institutional forms to follow the evolution of the individual functions.

FINANCIAL-SERVICES FIRMS AND THE FINANCIAL-SERVICES INDUSTRY

A financial system can be viewed in terms of a *financial-services industry* (FSI) consisting of *financial-services firms* (FSFs). The major players in the FSI include the following:

Banks: Commercial and investment, both domestic and foreign

Thrift institutions: Savings and loans (S&Ls), savings banks, and credit unions

---

[1] This section draws on Merton [1995].

Insurance companies: Life and property and casualty

Pension funds: Private and government

Finance companies: Consumer and commercial

Mutual funds: Money market, bond, stock, and so on

Nonfinancial corporations (NFCs): Subsidiaries of NFCs such as General Motors Acceptance Corporation (GMAC), General Electric (GE) Capital Services, and AT&T Universal

Because all these companies provide financial services, they can be described as financial-services firms, or **financial intermediaries** (FIs).[2] In addition, because the industries in which these companies operate have become less compartmentalized, their fusion or coming together has marked the birth of the FSI. The structural changes occurring in the FSI can be described as its "-ization."

The "-ization" of the FSI

Four phenomena, or innovations, describe the "-ization" of the FSI: institutionalization, securitization, globalization, and privatization. **Institutionalization** refers to the growing pool of savings held by nondepository institutions such as mutual funds and pension funds. **Securitization** refers to the process in which financial intermediaries pool and package loans (e.g., mortgages) for sale as securities. If the lenders, such as banks, also service the loans, then they collect interest and principal payments for a servicing fee, and they pass the proceeds on to investors, hence the terms **pass-through finance** and mortgage-backed securities.

Globalization refers to the growing interconnection among financial markets and financial institutions throughout the world. New York, London, and Tokyo provide the financial axis on which the world of global banking and finance rotates. In the United States, the traditional spokes emanate from the hub on Wall Street in New York City to Boston, Chicago, San Francisco, and Los Angeles, whereas new banking and financial centers can be found in Atlanta, Charlotte (NC), and Columbus (OH).

Privatization refers to the conversion of formerly state-owned enterprises into private companies. Financial institutions, as resource allocators, play a major role in privatization efforts. Normally, we think of privatization as occurring in transforming economies such as Russia and Eastern and Central Europe following the collapse of communism, or in the developing economies of Western Europe when the socialists lose political power. The assets of many failed S&Ls being taken over by the U.S. government during the thrift crisis of the 1980s and later being put back in the private sector, a mess that cost U.S. taxpayers about $160 billion not counting interest, provides another example of privatization.

The Role of Banks in the FSI

Within the FSI, banks, S&Ls, and credit unions are known as depository institutions. Financial-services firms that are not in this category are called nondepository institutions. The view that commercial banks operate in the FSI means that their role will look diluted in this framework. Nevertheless, commercial banks are still the kingpins of the FSI. Bear and Maldonado-Bear [1994] expand upon this theme:

---

[2] The existence of financial intermediaries, including commercial banks, can be explained because financial markets are imperfect and incomplete. As markets become more efficient and more complete, the foundations of all intermediaries are eroded. In the never-never land of a theorist's mind, perfect and complete markets would relegate banks to a "Jurassic Park" for financial intermediaries.

Commercial banking is the cornerstone of America's financial system. How it is set up and how it operates are matters not only of enormous economic significance but also of legal, political, social, and ethical significance. How American banking fares determines in some consequential degree how every American citizen fares—as well as a sizable number of people living in other nations. (p. 239)

TYPES AND CLASSES OF COMMERCIAL BANKS

Because commercial banks are so important to America's financial system, let's look at the various types and classes of commercial banks in the United States (Table 1-1 and Box 1-1). The birth of a bank begins with a charter obtained at either the national or the state level. Charters for national banks are granted by the **Office of the Comptroller of the Currency** (OCC), while those for state banks are granted by state governments, including the District of Columbia. Although a state bank has the option of joining the **Federal Reserve System** ("the Fed"), a national bank does not. A Fed-member bank must be insured by the **Federal Deposit**

TABLE 1-1   Types and Classes of Commercial Banks

Charter (federal or state agency)
- National bank (Office of the Comptroller of the Currency, OCC)
- State bank (50 states & D.C.)

Federal regulation (agency)
- National bank (OCC)
- State member bank (Federal Reserve)
- State-insured nonmember bank (FDIC)
- State noninsured bank (state regulator only)
- Bank holding company (BHC) (Federal Reserve)
- Banks or BHCs with 500 shareholders or more (Securities and Exchange Commission (SEC)

Structure or organizational form
- Unit bank
- Branch bank
- Holding-company bank
- One-bank holding company (OBHC)
- Multibank holding company (MBHC)

Type of business
- Wholesale bank (e.g., engaged in global wholesale finance)
- Retail bank (e.g., credit-card bank)
- Wholesale/retail bank (all things to all customers)
- Private bank (for individuals with high net worth)
- "Shadow" bank (e.g., pawnshops, check-cashing outlets, etc., for individuals with little or no net worth)

Geographic market
- Community (local) bank
- Regional bank
- Superregional bank
- Multinational ("money-center") bank

Federal Reserve size classes (by assets)
- Ten largest banks
- Banks ranked 11th through 100th
- Banks ranked 101st through 1000th
- Banks not ranked among the 1000 largest ("community banks")

BOX 1-1

THE LEGAL DEFINITION OF A BANK AND THE NONBANK BANK

The 1970 amendment to the Bank Holding Company Act of 1956 defines a commercial bank as an institution that "(1) accept[s] deposits that the depositor has a legal right to withdraw on demand and (2) engages in the business of making commercial loans." In the 1980s, prior to the passage of the Competitive Equality Banking Act of 1987, organizations were chartered that engaged in one of these activities but not both. They were called *nonbank banks* or *limited-service banks;* those that did not make commercial loans were also known as consumer banks. By using this loophole, these organizations avoided being regulated by the Federal Reserve as bank holding companies (BHCs). Companies such as Merrill Lynch, Sears, Shearson/American Express, E. F. Hutton, Gulf &

Western, Prudential-Bache, Household International, Parker Pen, and J. C. Penney jumped on the nonbank-bank bandwagon.

To attempt to level the playing field in the FSI, the Competitive Equality Banking Act of 1987 banned further establishment of nonbank banks. Although the 160 or so existing nonbank banks were grandfathered, their activities were restricted such that they could not cross-market products and services with their parent companies, and after 1988 they were limited to annual growth of 7 percent. Bona fide trust companies and consumer banks were exempted from these restrictions, and because of the thrift crisis, nonbank banks were not excluded from bidding on failed S&Ls with assets of $500 million or more.

Insurance Corporation (FDIC). Before the crises in deposit insurance (both state and federal), a state charter could be obtained without FDIC insurance; today such an occurrence would be highly unlikely but legally possible. As a result, de facto chartering power for state banks is effectively controlled by the FDIC.

Organizational form, business orientation, and geographic reach represent three additional ways for classifying banks. The dominant organizational form in commercial banking is the **bank holding company** (BHC), an organization that owns one or more banks. With money- and capital-market instruments (e.g., commercial paper and corporate bonds) crowding banks out of the wholesale market, the business focus of commercial banking has turned more toward small businesses, consumers, and nontraditional banking products such as investment banking, mutual funds, and insurance.[3] Although technology has permitted even the smallest banks to have a wide geographic reach, most banks operate in limited geographic areas defined by towns, counties, states, or regions. In contrast, multinational banks have worldwide reach.

Although pawnshops have been around for centuries, consumer advocacy groups, like the Consumer Federation of America, have recently brought attention to these businesses as "shadow banks."[4] In addition to pawnshops, which numbered about 10,000 in the United States in 1994 (the number doubled since 1986), some 5,000 check-cashing stores and 7,500 rent-to-own stores are included in the category

---

[3] Only a few states allow banks to underwrite insurance. In 1990, Delaware passed a bill to permit banks to underwrite and sell insurance (Garcia [1990]). The legislation permits a bank to set up an insurance unit or division provided that the bank's reserves or surplus capital are not used to fund the insurance unit. The insurance unit's capital, however, cannot be counted toward meeting the bank's capital requirements. Insurance agents argue that consumers would be at a disadvantage buying insurance from bankers who also sell loans and mortgages. Szego [1986] discusses the increasing interaction between banking and insurance and their complementarity.

[4] According to the Consumer Federation of America, "Americans who can least afford it pay the most for financial services." Fees of 25 percent per transaction and triple-digit interest rates are not uncommon.

of shadow banks. They provide high-cost financial services to the less affluent members of society. Although one in five Americans has no relationship with a bank, some consumers prefer to have it that way. Others simply have no alternative but to deal with shadow banks, which provide money transfers, high-rate mortgages, and rent-to-own items such as televisions and furniture. Shadow banks are easily identified by their neon and chrome storefronts, in sharp contrast to the glass and steel facades of the modern commercial bank.

To blunt criticism from consumer-advocacy groups and politicians, some commercial banks began offering "lifeline banking" in the early 1980s. Defined as a limited package of retail banking services offered at a relatively low fixed monthly cost, lifeline banking has been offered to low-income depositors and senior citizens. Lifeline banking has evolved to "basic banking" (the term preferred by bankers), and this type of account or service is generally available to all depositors.

BANK HOLDING COMPANIES: THE DOMINANT ORGANIZATIONAL FORM

Because bank holding companies (BHCs) are the dominant organizational form in U.S. banking, they deserve closer scrutiny. Using total deposits as the focal variable (total assets, total equity capital, or total revenues would provide similar pictures of domination), Table 1-2 reflects the dominance of BHCs among banks and also among federally insured depository institutions, and shows how that dominance has increased from 1984 to 1994. For example, at year-end 1994, BHCs had almost 67 percent of deposit market share among depository institutions, up from 61 percent in 1984. Among banking organizations, BHCs are even more dominant, controlling 93 percent of total deposits, up from 87 percent in 1984. The number of banks a BHC controls determines its classification as a one-bank holding company (OBHC) or a multibank holding company (MBHC). As Table 1-2 shows, the average deposit size of an MBHC more than doubled from 1984 to 1994, going from slightly less than $1 billion in total deposits to a little more than $2 billion. To put a perspective on this distribution, the merger of Chase Manhattan and Chemical Banking in 1996 resulted in a BHC with over $200 billion in total deposits and over $300 billion in total assets.[5]

Panel A of Figure 1-1 presents an example of a BHC's organizational structure. A BHC's nonbank subsidiaries or affiliates are restricted from engaging in nonbanking activities not approved by the Fed. The role of the parent company is to supply various financial, legal, accounting, and other services to its subsidiaries, for which it receives fees and interest revenue. In addition, the parent, as owner of the subsidiaries, is entitled to receive tax-deductible dividends from its subsidiaries. These dividend payments, however, are limited by federal and state laws. For example, the Fed requires approval for any dividend declaration by its members that exceeds a bank's combined net profits for the current year and the two previous years. If the parent company is an operating company (not just a "shell"), then it

---

[5] Table 1-2 also reveals that independent banks and OBHCs lost deposit market share over the years 1984 to 1994, while federal savings banks and state savings banks gained market share. The demise of the S&L industry is captured by the decline in market share from 26.5 percent (1984) to 4.4 percent (1994) and the decline in the number of S&Ls from 2882 (1984) to 776 (1994).

TABLE 1-2 The Distribution of Federally Insured Depository Institutions by Type of Institution, 1984 and 1994

1984

Type of Institution	Number of Firms	Percent of Total	Deposits (billions of dollars)	Percent of Deposits	Mean Deposits per Firm (millions of dollars)
Banking organizations	11,342	38.0	1,613.7	61.4	142.3
Independent banks	5,698	19.1	209.9	8.0	36.8
One-bank holding companies	4,926	16.5	467.7	17.8	94.9
Multibank holding companies	718	2.4	936.1	35.6	1,303.7
Thrift institutions	3,414	11.4	929.8	35.4	272.3
Savings and loan associations	2,882	9.6	697.5	26.5	242.0
Federal savings banks	264	0.9	121.6	4.6	460.6
State savings banks	268	0.9	110.7	4.2	413.0
Credit unions	15,126	50.6	84.1	3.2	5.6
Total	**29,882**	**100.0**	**2,627.6**	**100.0**	**87.9**

1994

Type of Institution	Number of Firms	Percent of Total	Deposits (billions of dollars)	Percent of Deposits	Mean Deposits per Firm (millions of dollars)
Banking organizations	7,898	36.1	2,382.7	71.7	301.7
Independent banks	2,634	12.0	170.0	5.1	64.5
One-bank holding companies	4,464	20.4	523.0	15.7	117.2
Multibank holding companies	800	3.7	1,689.6	50.9	2,112.1
Thrift institutions	2,058	9.4	684.5	20.6	332.6
Savings and loan associations	776	3.5	147.2	4.4	189.7
Federal savings banks	756	3.5	357.5	10.8	472.9
State savings banks	526	2.4	179.8	5.4	341.8
Credit unions	11,927	54.5	254.0	7.6	21.3
Total	**21,883**	**100.0**	**3,321.2**	**100.0**	**151.8**

Note: The data in this table are, to the extent possible, aggregated within categories. Thus, banks that are part of the same multibank holding company are aggregated into one banking organization. Banking organizations and thrift institutions that are affiliated are counted separately, as are any combinations of the three different types of thrift institution that are under common ownership. "Chain banking" organizations—banks owned by an individual or a group of individuals but not legally affiliated—are not consolidated, owing to data limitations. (Data may not sum to totals, and calculations may not yield the percentages shown, because of rounding.)

Source: Federal Reserve Bulletin (January 1996), p. 5.

generates other sources of revenue besides dividends. Panel B of Figure 1-1 shows the cash flows associated with a BHC.[6] After interest and other expenses are paid, the parent company usually has negative taxable income. When a BHC files a consolidated tax return, this negative taxable income reduces federal income taxes.[7]

BHCs were developed primarily to circumvent geographic restrictions, especially in states that restricted branching, or for tax purposes or both. Because the BHC organizational form cannot be used to circumvent product restrictions

---

[6] When parent debt is invested in subsidiaries as equity, the procedure is referred to as "double leverage." Chapter 14 provides more details.

[7] Two additional tax considerations encouraged the expansion of BHCs: (1) the opportunity to avoid local taxes by establishing subsidiaries in states or municipalities outside the institution's headquarters area, and (2) the opportunity to avoid federal income taxes by conducting foreign operations through separately chartered subsidiaries rather than through foreign branches (i.e., "tax havens," such as the Caribbean islands). Under present tax laws, since only repatriated income from subsidiaries is subject to U.S. tax, the incentive is to establish subsidiaries in low-tax countries and to repatriate as little income as possible.

Panel A. The structure of a bank holding company

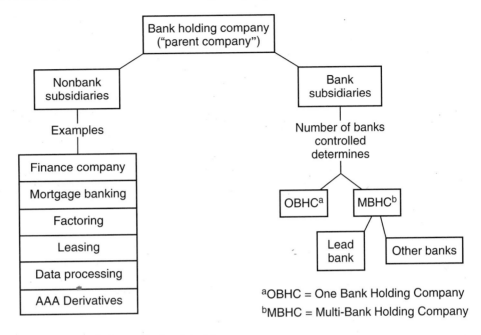

Panel B. The cash flows of a bank holding company

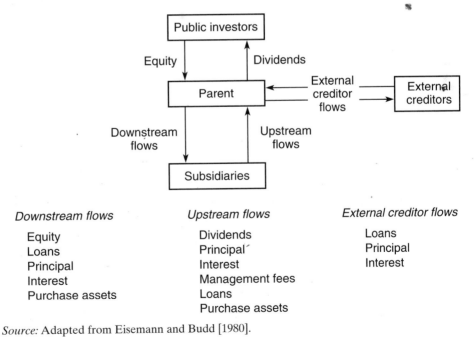

Source: Adapted from Eisemann and Budd [1980].

FIGURE 1-1 **The Structure and Cash Flows of a Bank Holding Company**

per se, it offers no direct advantage over any other organizational form. However, if an approved nonbanking activity is a relatively riskier undertaking, placing it in a nonbank sub can be used in an attempt to isolate bank subs from the increased risk exposure.

The Diversity and Capitalization of Large BHCs

Panel A of Table 1-3 shows how diverse large BHCs can be with respect to total assets, banks controlled, branches, and number of employees. If you have seen one BHC, you have not seen them all. Citicorp (473 branches), Chase Manhattan (475), and First Chicago NBD (742) represent wholesale/retail shops without the extensive brick-and-mortar branches of First Union (1,977 branches), NationsBank (1,948), BankAmerica (1,923), Wells Fargo (1,580), and Banc One (1,503). In contrast, J. P. Morgan and Bankers Trust are organizations geared toward "global wholesale finance"; their focus on trading and investment banking requires substantially fewer banks, branches, and employees.

TABLE 1-3 The Diversity and Capitalization of Large Bank Holding Companies

Panel A. The Diversity of Large BHCs (June 30, 1996)

Company (State)	Total Assets	Banks	Branches	Employees
Chase Manhattan (NY)	$ 322 bil.	2	745	68,828
Citicorp (NY)	267	7	473	87,700
BankAmerica (CA)	239	14	1,923	78,300
J. P. Morgan & Co. (NY)	199	2	4	15,390
NationsBank (NC)	192	6	1,948	62,137
First Union (NC)	140	12	1,977	45,353
Bankers Trust (NY)	115	3	0	5,427
First Chicago NBD (IL)	114	10	742	34,445
Wells Fargo (CA)	108	1	1,580	41,548
Banc One (OH)	97	56	1,503	51,200
Total	$1,793 bil.	113	10,895	428,328

Panel B. The Ten Largest BHCs in Terms of Market Capitalization

Rank/Company	Market Capitalization	
	June 28, 1996	Ratio to Total Assets
1. Citicorp	$ 39.8 billion	12.3%
2. Chase Manhattan	30.7	11.5
3. BankAmerica	27.6	11.5
4. NationsBank	24.7	12.4
5. Wells Fargo & Co.	22.9	21.2
6. First Union Corp.	17.1	12.2
7. J. P. Morgan & Co.	15.5	7.8
8. Banc One Corp.	14.8	15.3
9. Norwest Corp.	12.5	16.1
10. First Chicago NBD	12.4	10.9
Total/Average	$218.0 billion	13.3%

Note: Number of banks and branches controlled are domestic only. Market capitalization is computed by multiplying the banking company's common shares outstanding by the closing price on the indicated date. The capital ratio is market capitalization divided by the BHC's total assets in Panel A. Norwest's total assets were $77.8 billion.

Source: Adapted and compiled from company quarterly reports, call reports, and *The Wall Street Journal* for closing prices.

At one time, total assets and total deposits were the benchmarks for ranking banks. Today, market capitalization is the key. Panel B of Table 1-3 shows the ten largest U.S. BHCs in terms of market capitalization as of midyear 1996. Citicorp, with $39.8 billion, topped the list, more than triple the capitalization of 10th-ranked First Chicago NBD. Relative to total assets, the capital ratios of large BHCs show substantial variation, ranging from a high of 21.2 percent for Wells Fargo to a low of 7.8 percent for J. P. Morgan. The average ratio was 13.3 percent. Because market capitalization as measured in Table 1-3 equals the product of the BHC's common stock price and the number of shares outstanding, it ignores the value of preferred stock, if any.

INTERMEDIATION VERSUS DISINTERMEDIATION AND INDIRECT FINANCE VERSUS DIRECT FINANCE

The traditional role of depository institutions has been to gather deposits and make loans—the **intermediation** function, also known as indirect finance because the process involves an intermediary between economic units that need funds and those that supply them. When an intermediary is not involved, the funding process is called direct finance and is illustrated by the issuance of commercial paper or corporate bonds by borrowers directly to investors. When the process of securitization is employed, pass-through finance occurs.

When the intermediation function is disrupted, **disintermediation** occurs, or a shift from indirect finance to direct finance. Disintermediation has occurred on both sides of bank and S&L balance sheets as they have lost deposits to other FSFs, especially mutual funds, and as they have lost loans to the instruments of direct finance described above (e.g., commercial paper).

The Creation and Characteristics of Financial Claims (Contracts)

A financial claim (contract) is an asset to the holder and a liability to the issuer. When a financial intermediary is involved, the three relevant parties are

- The depositor, or creditor
- The intermediary, or bank
- The borrower

Table 1-4 provides a schematic and balance sheets ("T-accounts") that show the relationships among the parties.[8] The person or enterprise agreeing to make future cash payments is the issuer of an obligation and has incurred a liability, e.g., a bank issuing a certificate of deposit or a borrower agreeing to repay a loan. In contrast, the owner of a claim, the investor, expects to receive cash payments and holds a financial asset, e.g., a depositor expecting payments of interest and principal or a bank expecting loan repayments. When a bank makes a loan or investment, it acts

---

[8] In a perfect capital market (i.e., one without any frictions or imperfections such as transaction costs, regulations, lack of coincidence of wants, etc.), financial intermediaries would not exist, and lenders and borrowers would contract directly.

TABLE 1-4 The Intermediation Process and the Creation of Financial Claims or Contracts

Panel A. The Players

Depositor:	Has a claim on the bank, an asset for the depositor.
Bank:	Issues a claim against itself, a liability of the bank.
Bank:	Makes a loan to a borrower, an asset for the bank.
Borrower:	Issues a claim against itself, a liability of the borrower.

Panel B. A Schematic View

Intermediary

$ \qquad $

Borrower ← **Bank** ← **Depositor**

Acts as "delegated monitor"
of the borrower for the depositor

The bank has a claim on the borrower, which is an asset to the bank and an obligation of the borrower.	The depositor has a claim on the bank, which is an asset to the depositor and a liability to the bank.

Panel C. Marginal T-Accounts

The Borrower		The Bank**		The Depositor	
Cash(+) or DDA*(+)	Debt(+) (loan)	Loan(+)	Deposit(+)	Cash(−) Deposit(+)	

Notes: *DDA = demand-deposit or checking account. The depositor simply substitutes one asset (cash) for another (deposit) while the bank and the borrower "create" both assets and liabilities for themselves. **When disintermediation occurs, banks lose loans to instruments of direct finance or lose deposits to competitors, e.g., mutual funds. When banks securitize loans, they originate loans and then sell them, thereby removing risk from the balance sheet.

as an agent for the depositor;[9] the borrower simultaneously issues a claim against itself in the form of a promise to repay the debt plus interest (hence the term "promissory note" or any promise to pay).

Intermediation involves separate financial contracts (e.g., deposits and loans) in which the bank assumes the variable cash flows and timing differences between the two contracts. The uncertain net cash flows associated with the underlying contracts capture the risks of banking. Innovations in contracting technologies, such as floating-rate loans and securitization, provide tools for managing these risks.

The Financial Cornerstones: Debt and Equity Claims

Financial claims come in two basic forms: debt and equity. These two instruments are the financial cornerstones of capital markets and firms' balance sheets. A fixed or variable dollar claim is called a debt instrument (e.g., a fixed- or floating-rate

---

[9] One theory of financial intermediation, due to Diamond [1984], says that banks act as "delegated monitors" (agents) for their depositors (principals). If banks make relatively safe loans, then depositors' funds will be protected from credit loss. Even though a bank may be insured, its managers have a fiduciary responsibility to the FDIC and taxpayers to engage in safe-and-sound banking. Nevertheless, moral-hazard and risk-shifting problems exist for insured depositories (Hovakimian and Kane [1996]).

loan); a residual claim on the earnings of an enterprise represents equity (e.g., common stock). Hybrid claims such as preferred stock and convertible bonds have characteristics of both debt and equity.

Because all other financial contracts derive their values from either debt or equity, we use the term derivatives to describe such innovations as futures, options, and swaps. The development of these innovative contracts has been described as financial engineering and is referred to as innovations in contracting technologies. Because of these developments, financial claims can have many distinguishing traits. Nevertheless, four common characteristics for distinguishing among financial claims are the following:

- Risk
- Liquidity
- Maturity
- Denomination (size)

These four factors provide key insights into why commercial banks are the kingpins of the FSI. First, they provide credit-risk diversification and other risk-management services. Second, they are the major providers of liquidity to the economy. Third, they provide maturity flexibility in terms of checking accounts, CDs, lines of credit, short-term loans, and long-term loans. Fourth, they provide denomination divisibility in terms of savings accounts, large CDs, small loans, and large syndicated loans.

The Pricing of Financial Assets

A fundamental principle of financial economics is that the price of any financial asset equals the present value of its expected future cash flows. Because the cash flows are expected, they are uncertain and therefore risky. The size, timing, and riskiness of cash flows determine the value of financial assets. In pricing financial assets, an inverse relation exists between risk and value. Risky assets have relatively low values, whereas safe assets have relatively high values. The basic risks associated with bank financial assets are default or credit risk, interest-rate risk, and liquidity (or resale) risk.[10]

The Role and Function of Financial Markets and Securitization

Financial markets perform two basic economic functions: (1) They transfer funds from those economic units that have surplus funds to those that need them (usually to buy tangible assets), and (2) they transfer funds in such a way as to redistribute or shift risk among those seeking and those providing funds. In short, the two principal functions of financial markets are funds transfer and risk shifting. As intermediaries, banks also perform these two functions. These functions, whether performed by financial institutions or markets, provide three important economic services: (1) They determine the prices of financial assets through the interaction of buyers and sellers; (2) they provide liquidity by offering investors the opportunity to sell (liquidate) their financial assets; and (3) they reduce search and information costs, **or transactions costs.**

---

[10] These risks, which are the basic risks of banking, are discussed in detail later in this chapter and throughout the book.

Financial markets also provide a mechanism for trading financial assets. Some financial assets are created and subsequently traded on organized financial markets or exchanges. The more developed an economy is, the more organized its financial markets tend to be. Assets that are not bought and sold on organized exchanges trade in over-the-counter (OTC) markets. Most bank loans share three characteristics that make them similar to OTC-type contracts:

- They are customized
- They are privately negotiated
- They lack liquidity and transparency

These traits make bank loans rather difficult to quantify and manage, which creates the potential for the mispricing of bank stocks. Securitization, pooling and packaging bank loans for sale as securities, and the development of secondary markets for bank loans have made bank loans more liquid and less opaque and reduced the potential for mispricing bank equities. Both of these innovations shift risk from loan originators to investors. Another risk-shifting technique is the floating-rate loan, which requires borrowers to bear some of the risk of rising interest rates. If interest rates decline, borrowers receive the benefits.

Why Do Financial Intermediaries Exist?

Because financial markets are far from being complete and perfect, financial intermediaries (FIs) exist. The existence of inefficiencies in direct financing permits FIs to exist. Fundamentally, direct finance is unable to solve the double-coincidence problem: The financial claims sold by debtors (deficit-spending units) must have the exact characteristics (risk, liquidity, maturity, and denomination) desired by creditors (surplus-spending units). Financial intermediaries that can solve this problem have the potential to exist. To survive, however, FIs must be able to make an economic profit. The profitable ones have developed the financial capital, human resources, and reputational capital that permit them to have lower information, contracting, and transacting costs or better revenue-generating functions or both than other players in the FSI. These advantages can be traced, in varying degrees, to potential benefits associated with specialization, firm size (economies of scale), and the diversity of the firm's activities (economies of scope).

THE END OF BANKING AS WE KNOW IT?[11]

Much has been written about the decline of banking and its loss of market share to mutual funds, commercial paper, and corporate bonds. Table 1-5 shows the levels, changes, growth, and market shares of total assets for selected financial sectors in the United States for the years 1978 and 1995. The declining market shares for U.S. banks and thrift institutions suggest "the end of banking as we know it."

Since market share is only one aspect of an industry's performance, and not a very good one at that, it is important to understand exactly what is meant by the "decline" of banking and whether or not it means the end of banking as we know it. Although commercial banks' relative share of the total assets held by all finan-

---

[11] This section has the same title as the three-part series from *The Wall Street Journal* (July 7–9, 1993). Banking, of course, is not ending; it is changing. Boyd and Gertler [1994] and Kaufman and Mote [1994] describe the changes.

TABLE 1-5	Levels, Changes, Growth, and Market Shares of Total Assets for Selected U.S. Financial Sectors, 1978 and 1995

Panel A. Total Assets ($ trillions end of period)

Industry	1978	1995	Change	Annual Growth (%)
Commercial banking	1.2	3.5	2.3	6.5
U.S. banks	1.1	3.1	2.0	6.3
Foreign banks	0.1	0.4	0.3	8.5
Thrift institutions	0.7	1.2	0.5	3.2
Savings and loans	0.5	0.7	0.2	2.0
Savings banks	0.1	0.2	0.1	4.2
Credit unions	0.1	0.3	0.2	6.7
Life insurance cos.	0.4	1.5	1.2	8.1
Other insurance cos.	0.1	0.5	0.4	9.9
Private pension funds	0.3	0.7	0.4	5.1
Finance companies	0.1	0.6	0.6	11.1
Mutual funds	0.05	0.8	0.7	17.7
Money-market funds	0.01	0.5	0.5	25.9
Sec. brokers & dealers	0.03	0.2	0.2	−11.8
Total	2.88	9.6	6.7	7.3

Panel B. Market-Share Percentages: Then (1978) and Now (1995)

Industry	1978	1995	Selected Ranks 1978	Selected Ranks 1995
Commercial banking	41.4%	36.4%		
U.S. banks	37.9	32.3	1	1
Foreign banks	3.4	4.2		
Thrift institutions	24.1	12.5		
Savings and loans	17.2	7.3	2	4/5
Savings banks	3.4	2.1		
Credit unions	3.4	3.1		
Life insurance cos.	13.8	16.7	3	2
Other insurance cos.	3.4	5.2		
Private pension funds	10.3	7.3	4	4/5
Finance companies	3.4	6.2		
Mutual funds	1.7	8.3		3
Money-market funds	0.3	5.2		
Sec. brokers & dealers	1.0	2.1		
Total	100.0%	100.0%		

Memo: At year-end 1995, federally related mortgage pools totaled $1.6 trillion and asset-backed securities issuers had total assets of $0.6 trillion.

Note: Totals may not sum due to rounding.

Source: Flow of Funds Accounts: Flows and Outstandings, Board of Governors of the Federal Reserve System.

services firms has declined, the dollar or absolute share has continued to grow because the size of the pie has grown (Panel B, Table 1-3). In this respect, banks are not stagnant nor in decline. Moreover, in terms of product and geographic expansion, banks are moving into the twenty-first century by diversifying with new products and expanding into regional, national, or global markets.

Funding loans with deposits has been and still is the core business of commercial banking. The erosion of this core business captures the essence of the decline of banking and explains what analysts mean when they talk about the end of banking as we know it, i.e., in the narrow sense of funding loans with deposits. Because a strategy based solely on this core business has limited growth opportunities, many bankers are looking to expand into other businesses, such as investment banking, insurance, mutual funds, data processing, and information services. These narrow and broad views capture the basic distinction between traditional banking, which is in decline, and modern banking, which offers greater growth opportunities. Although "community banks," those with total assets under $1 billion, may find it difficult to tap many of the growth opportunities of modern banking, the need for basic banking services in rural markets suggests that many of them will survive. The delivery systems of modern banking are becoming more and more electronically based (electronic banking) as evidenced by international large-dollar payment systems, globalized ATM networks, and worldwide acceptance of credit cards. Home banking on the Internet (chapter 18) is one of the exciting developments in this area.

The consolidation of the banking industry refers to the decline in the number of commercial banks (e.g., from some 14,500 banks in 1984 to about 9,500 at the beginning of 1997).[12] Many people regard this shrinkage as a symptom of the decline of banking. However, when an overbanked system is opened to greater competition, such a phenomenon is not unexpected. For many years regulation and lack of technological developments acted as shelters for commercial banks and thrift institutions, providing a protected environment that permitted many of them to exist without diversified portfolios. At various times deflation in energy, farm, and commercial real-estate prices decimated these portfolios, contributing to the thrift and banking debacles of the 1980s and early 1990s.

In the late 1970s and early 1980s, the combination of volatile interest rates, greater competition, and technological advances made interest-rate and geographic restrictions obsolete. For depository institutions to compete with money-market mutual funds in the early 1980s, Regulation Q interest-rate ceilings had to be removed; the timing, however, was extremely bad, especially for thrift institutions. Although the 1990s started with a recession, financial distress, and a credit crunch, declining interest rates permitted depository institutions to recover with record profits by 1993 and continued strong performances over the next three years.

Table 1-6 presents some thoughts about banking's decline by bank regulators, consultants, and bankers. The fundamental question focuses on whether banking is a competitive vehicle to attract savings and investment from the American public. More specifically, when banks raise certificate of deposit (CD) rates, will consumer deposits flow back to banks? Have banks lost customer relationships along with the outflow of CDs? Think of the basic bank-customer relationship as consisting of deposits, loans, and other financial and information services.

Because the environment of the FSI is dynamic, banking as we have known it is changing. This does not mean that banks are dead. To survive, however, they must adapt to the changing environment of the FSI. On balance, the reports of banking's death are greatly exaggerated (Boyd and Gertler [1994] and Kaufman and Mote [1994]).

---

[12] Note that these figures do not conflict with those in Table 1-2, as they are for the number of banks; whereas the figures in the table are for the number of banking organizations, which declined from 11,342 (1984) to 7,898 (1994).

TABLE 1-6 "The End of Banking As We Know It?"

Panel A. What the End of Banking Could Do

- Weaken the Fed's ability to influence the economy through monetary policy
- Increase the size and complexity of risks the Fed must get under control in a financial crisis
- Hurt small- and medium-sized businesses that depend primarily on banks for loans and financial advice
- Reduce access to traditional banking offices by spurring consolidation among the nation's numerous commercial banks
- Because of the outflow of assets and deposits from the banking system, pose a wider range of risks associated with the $7 trillion market in financial derivatives, i. e., new financial products (futures, options, and swaps) that link banks, investment firms, and corporations in efforts to hedge against changes in interest rates, stock prices, commodity prices, and currencies

Panel B. Some Thoughts by Banking Experts

Alan Greenspan, chairman of the Fed
  "Public policy should be concerned with the decline in the importance of banking. The issues are too important for the future growth of the economy and the welfare of our citizens."
Eugene Ludwig, comptroller of the currency
  "I think that banks play a fundamentally important role in society that is less well filled by others. I see a decline in the banking system as a shifting of risk—rather than an elimination of risk—to the public from the government."
Edward Crutchfield, chairman, First Union
  "We'll live or die on our customer service."
William Issac, former chairman FDIC
  "The banking industry is becoming irrelevant economically, and it's almost irrelevant politically."
Andrew Hove, former chairman FDIC
  "Will banks be able to attract the money back as loan demand increases? I think they will, but you wonder."
Economic Policy Institute (a liberal think tank)
  Solution: Impose bank-type regulation over the "parallel" financial system of nonbank financial-services firms that perform bank functions.

Source: "The End of Banking As We Know It" (a three-part series), *The Wall Street Journal* (July 7–9, 1993), pp. 1+.

THE ROLE OF BANK REGULATION AND SUPERVISION

Because commercial banks are more heavily regulated than their nonbank competitors, many bankers view the playing field as slanted in favor of the competition. To evaluate this charge, let's consider the role and degree of bank regulation and supervision in the United States. In 1984 a former U.S. bank regulator proposed the following strength-in-banking equation:[13]

$$\text{New Powers} + \text{Firm Supervision} \rightarrow \text{Strength in banking} \qquad \textbf{(1-1)}$$

This framework can be applied to either established financial systems or developing ones. In general, the trade-off in equation (1-1) is a direct one. The more powers

---

[13] Sinkey ([1992], pp. 165–166) provides additional details.

and freedom banks are given, the greater is the need for firm supervision (e.g., monitoring and risk-based pricing) if strength in banking is to be maintained. The supervision can originate from financial markets or regulators or both (i.e., market versus regulatory discipline). Regarding market discipline, the chief executive officer of a major U.S. banking company recently stated: "We believe financial institutions should be operated as if there were no regulators for supervision, no discount window for liquidity, and no deposit insurance for bailouts." This view means that bank managers take seriously their fiduciary responsibilities to their depositors and other creditors. For this approach to work, market participants must penalize bank managers who violate that trust (e.g., by engaging in unexpected risk taking).

The Principal-Agent Relations in a Regulated Financial System

In a regulated environment, a government guarantee (in the form of deposit insurance) may give depositors confidence in banks, but at the same time it may cause banks to shirk their responsibilities—a moral-hazard problem. *Moral hazard* refers to behavior that is altered by the existence of insurance (e.g., greater risk taking by insured depositories). Table 1-7 depicts the principal-agent relations in a regulated financial system. If the government guarantee is credible and protects all bank debt, market discipline may fail to exist. In this case, regulatory discipline must prevent excessive risk taking by monitoring bank behavior. In a regulated banking system, market and regulatory discipline should complement each other.

Techniques for Managing the Guarantee Business

Since bank regulators and supervisors supply guarantees (either explicit or implicit) that banks are safe and sound, they can be viewed as operating a guarantee business. Merton and Bodie [1992] describe three interrelated methods available to a guarantor (e.g., bank regulator or deposit insurer) to manage its business:

- Monitoring the value of the collateral
- Restricting the kinds of assets acceptable as collateral
- Charging risk-based premiums

In practice, bank regulators use combinations of monitoring, asset restrictions, and risk-based pricing to manage their guarantees (i.e., to achieve firm supervision). Some of the specific weapons that bank regulators and deposit insurers use to promote safe-and-sound banking include on- and off-site bank examinations, risk-based

---

TABLE 1-7   The Principal-Agent Problems of Regulated Financial Institutions

Principal	(monitors →)	**Agent**
Taxpayers	→	President/Congress
President/Congress	→	Regulators/Deposit Insurers
Regulators/Deposit Insurers	→	Insured depositories
Insured depositories	→	Borrowers
*Lenders (depositors) and equity holders (owners)	→	Financial intermediaries

*Market discipline occurs when lenders and equity holders monitor bank risk taking and impose costs on borrowing institutions. The linkages running from taxpayers to insured borrowers reflect the relations of regulatory discipline.

capital requirements, risk-based deposit-insurance premiums, cease-and-desist orders, removal of bank officers and directors, prompt corrective action, and CAMEL ratings (C = capital adequacy, A = asset quality, M = management, E = earnings, and L = liquidity). These weapons provide the ingredients for the firm-supervision component of the strength-in-banking equation.

Entry and Exit Rules

One of the requirements of a competitive market is freedom of entry and exit. The reregulation of U.S. banking, which began in 1980, permitted greater freedom of entry (e.g., by permitting existing banks to enter new product and geographic markets) but failed to allow economically insolvent banks and thrifts to exit (e.g., lack of prompt corrective action or an effective closure rule). The result was a financial disaster because both the bank and thrift deposit-insurance funds went bankrupt and had to be bailed out by the U.S. Treasury (i.e., U.S. taxpayers). The **FDIC Improvement Act** of 1991 attempts to provide for a more orderly exit of weak depositories by requiring "prompt corrective action" for such institutions.

Viewed in terms of a weakness-in-banking equation, the lesson for either a developed or a developing economy is unmistakably clear:[14]

$$\text{New Powers} + \text{Forbearance} \rightarrow \text{Weakness in banking} \qquad \textbf{(1-2)}$$

Forbearance (short for capital forbearance or, more generally, lax supervision) refers to the unwillingness on the part of the U.S. regulatory troika (Federal Reserve System/FDIC/Office of the Comptroller of the Currency, OCC) to close banks and thrifts *before* their economic net worths were exhausted. This practice means that economic insolvency (market value of assets < market value of liabilities) occurs before bank closure, which is a regulatory decision. The longer the lag between economic insolvency and closure, the greater is the risk of loss to the FDIC and taxpayers. The prompt-corrective-action provision of the FDIC Improvement Act of 1991 attempts to provide firmer supervision for this regulatory shortcoming.

THE REGULATORY DIALECTIC (STRUGGLE MODEL)

Kane [1977] describes the battle between bank regulators and bankers as a "regulatory dialectic," or struggle model. His idea builds on philosopher Hegel's concept of change as consisting of three stages: (1) thesis, (2) antithesis, and (3) synthesis. When thesis and antithesis clash, a synthesis results. The synthesis becomes a new thesis, only to be confronted by a new antithesis, resulting in a new synthesis. The struggle is an ongoing one because regulation acts as a tax that bankers try to avoid.

The nature of the struggle originates in the different objectives of regulators and bankers. Regulators typically focus on safety, stability, and structure (competitiveness), whereas bankers focus on maximizing some variable, such as wealth, profits, or size or engaging in expense-preference behavior. When their actions are constrained, bankers look to circumvent restrictions by searching for loopholes in laws and regulations. Regulators react by trying to close loopholes, and the ongoing

---

[14] The case of de novo S&Ls, discussed by Lindley, Verbrugge, McNulty, and Gup [1992], is a good example of this weakness.

battle resembles a dialectic. To the extent that the struggle stimulates financial innovation (as a way of circumventing restrictions), the regulatory dialectic also explains the process of financial innovation.

The benefits and costs of regulation are difficult to measure because the benefits can be short term but the full costs are incurred over a much longer period. For example, the full costs of U.S. deposit insurance and regulatory restrictions, born in the 1930s, did not become apparent until 50 years later. Laws and regulations must be analyzed carefully for their good intentions and their unintended evils.

THE RISKS OF BANKING

Bankers manage portfolios of assets and liabilities and the accompanying information flows. The key portfolio risks of banking are **credit risk, interest-rate risk, and liquidity risk.** These specific risks generate variability in banks' cash flows—a common general definition of risk in finance. Excessive risk taking and adverse economic conditions are the ingredients for bank failure. Chronologically, the typical failure scenario unfolds with excessive credit or interest-rate risk taking (bad policies), followed by unexpected inflation or deflation, which brings public recognition of the excessive risk taking (bad publicity) and precipitates a bank liquidity crisis. Although banks with good policies usually can withstand bad publicity, banks with bad policies cannot. The techniques for managing guarantees—monitoring, asset restrictions, and risk-based pricing—are the same tools lenders need for managing the portfolio risks of banking.

Credit Risk

Credit or default risk refers to the uncertainty associated with loan repayment. Because most of a bank's earning assets are in the form of loans, problems with loan quality have been the major cause of bank failure. Symptoms of poor loan quality include high levels of nonperforming loans, loan losses, and examiner-classified loans (i.e., substandard, doubtful, and loss: Sinkey [1978]). A high proportion of loans relative to total assets and rapid growth of the loan portfolio are potential early-warning signals of loan-quality problems, which may indicate potential failure.[15] In contrast, high-performance banks tend to have high-quality loan portfolios as characterized by low levels of nonperforming loans and loan losses.

Interest-Rate Risk and the Fisher Effect

Because most depository institutions borrow short and lend long, they take on interest-rate risk. Variable-rate loans and off-balance-sheet activities in the form of hedging instruments (e.g., interest-rate swaps) are techniques for managing interest-rate risk. The S&L crisis in the United States effectively began in 1966 with the first of a series of interest-rate spikes culminating with the peak rates of 1980 to 1982. Over this period, unanticipated inflation wreaked havoc with S&L portfolios because they consisted mainly of long-term, fixed-rate loans funded with short-term, variable-rate deposits. With less of a maturity imbalance, commercial banks were not as adversely affected by unanticipated inflation.

---

[15] According to a study by Salomon Brothers, "the best single predictor of future asset quality is the rate of loan growth" (*The Economist* [May 2, 1992], p. 3).

Expected inflation works its way into nominal interest rates through the **Fisher effect** or equation, that is,[16]

$$\text{Nominal interest rate} \approx \text{Real interest rate} + \text{Expected inflation} \qquad \textbf{(1-3)}$$

The exact Fisher effect includes a cross product or interaction term between the real rate and expected inflation. For example, if the real rate is 4 percent and expected inflation is 4 percent, then the nominal rate is $0.00816 = 0.04 + 0.04 + [0.04 \times 0.04]$ or 8.16 percent. The nominal rate based on the approximate Fisher effect is only 8 percent = 4 percent + 4 percent. Don't be surprised if you see the Fisher effect, expressed in dollar terms, written as:

$$(1 + R_N) = (1 + R_R)(1 + E[\Delta P/P]) \qquad \textbf{(1-4)}$$

where R_N = nominal rate, R_R = real rate of interest, and $E[\Delta P/P]$ = expected inflation. To illustrate, and using the numbers from above, if you borrow \$1 at a real rate of 4 percent and expected inflation of 4 percent, you agree to repay $\$1.0816 = 1.04 \times 1.04$. In other words, your nominal rate of interest is 8.16 percent. The compensation to the lender consists of \$0.04 as a real return, \$0.04 for expected inflation, and \$0.0016 for the effect of inflation on the real return. Solving equation (1-4) for R_N, we get:

$$R_N = R_R + E[\Delta P/P] + (R_R \times E[\Delta P/P]) \qquad \textbf{(1-5)}$$

where the third term on the right-hand side of equation (1-5) is the cross-product item omitted from equation (1-3).

The Fisher Effect, Monetary Discipline, and Economic Growth and Development

Inflation, foreign-exchange exposure, and capital scarcity represent three critical problems in the financial and strategic management of companies, especially in developing countries. Whereas capital shortages are chronic in developing countries, inflation and currency devaluation tend to be episodic events driven by undisciplined monetary policy. In this kind of unstable financial environment, it is difficult to estimate expected inflation and maintain a sound currency. Because lenders are hurt by unexpected inflation, the development of financial markets slows, retarding the pace of economic development. With an unsound currency, both domestic and foreign trade suffer. If a country has monetary discipline, frequently associated with an independent central bank and a commitment to maintaining stable prices, it can create a financial environment more conducive to promoting economic growth and development.

Liquidity Risk

Banks need liquidity for two reasons: (1) to meet deposit withdrawals, and (2) to fund customer loan demand. Bank liquidity can be stored in the balance sheet by holding liquid assets such as T-bills or short-term, high-quality loans, or it can be purchased in federal-funds and CD markets. The latter method requires a bank to maintain its creditworthiness and reputational capital and to have a market presence, whereas the former forfeits the higher yields associated with less liquid assets. The

---

[16] The real rate of interest can be viewed as being determined by (1) the time preference for consumption (savings) and the productivity of capital (investment), or (2) the supply and demand for loanable funds. In an environment without inflation or deflation, real and nominal interest rates would be the same. The ex post real rate can be approximated as the difference between the nominal rate and actual inflation.

development of securitization has increased the ease with which banks can sell loans and generate liquidity.

External Conditions: The Risks of Price-Level and Sectoral Instabilities

Character, capacity (cash flow), capital (net worth), collateral, and conditions (economic) capture the five Cs of credit analysis.[17] Although economic conditions play a crucial role in the safety and soundness of financial institutions, banks have no direct control over this factor (e.g., deflation has been especially harmful in disrupting borrowers' abilities to repay loans). To illustrate the importance of economic conditions, consider the following counterfactual propositions for the U.S. economy: a level of price stability that avoided the interest-rate spikes of 1966, 1969–1970, 1974, and 1980–1982 and absence of sectoral deflations in energy, farm, and commercial real estate. Under this scenario, without the international debt crisis, the bank and thrift problems of the 1980s and early 1990s would have been substantially reduced, if not eliminated.

This fictional tale highlights the connection between the behavior of monetary policy and the conditions under which borrowers and lenders contract.[18] The essence of the connection is the uncertainty associated with future interest rates and prices. Clearly, reducing this uncertainty would increase financial stability.[19] Absent such monetary reform, lenders must price credit and interest-rate risks carefully, diversify, and be liquid.

Problem Banks: Identification, Enforcement, and Closure

The bank regulator's supervision problem can be viewed in terms of identification and enforcement. The critical issue in the United States in the 1980s and early 1990s has been the lack of an effective bank closure rule—an enforcement problem. Because most closed banks in the United States were identified prior to closure as problem banks, identification of problem institutions has not been the culprit. Nevertheless, without an accounting system to capture the economic value of banks' on- and off-balance-sheet activities, an effective closure rule will be difficult to implement. Although the "prompt-corrective-action" mandate of the **FDIC Improvement Act** (1991) attempts to remedy this deficiency, it also gives regulators considerable flexibility in designing the enforcement rules and action. Based on past experience, this may mean business as usual and ineffective regulatory discipline. On balance, however, the cumulative effects of explicit risk-based pricing of deposit insurance (1993), more refined risk-based capital requirements, and FDICIA may be enough to overcome the shortcomings of the past.

Recapitulation and Lessons

Credit risk and interest-rate risk are the critical risks faced by depository institutions. Securitization enables banks to remove risks from their balance sheets, but

---

[17] Chapters 6 and 11–14 analyze bank management of credit risk and ways to conduct credit analysis.

[18] Schwartz [1987], a noted monetary historian, writes: "The critical condition that will determine the safety and soundness of financial institutions in the future, as it has in the past, is the price level environment in which they operate. . . . Stabilizing the price level will do more for financial stability than reforming deposit insurance or reregulation" (p. 13).

[19] In a fiat money system, as Schwartz ([1987], p. 14) notes, the crux of the problem is monetary authorities operating without formal constraints. An alternative monetary mechanism is a currency board as described in Schuler, Selgin, and Sinkey [1991] and Schuler [1992].

it simultaneously erodes their traditional business of funding loans with deposits. Although the mismanagement of credit and interest-rate risks has been the leading cause of U.S. bank and thrift failures, a mismanaged system of regulation and deposit insurance and the interest-rate and price volatilities of the years 1966 to the early 1990s are intricately interwoven in the fabric of the U.S. bank and thrift crises. To attempt to avoid the problems that have plagued the U.S. banking system, developed and developing countries need to maintain a stable economic and financial environment, to regulate banks in a way that does not restrict their diversification opportunities, and if they provide deposit insurance, to price it properly (e.g., on the basis of risk exposure).

THE DIMENSIONS OF FINANCIAL-SERVICES COMPETITION AND THE ROLE OF REGULATION IN SHAPING THEM

Financial-services firms and their regulators compete for business in three basic areas: explicit price, user convenience, and public confidence.[20] As regulated firms, banks typically have faced restrictions with respect to price, place, and product, among other things. These restrictions limit the ability of regulated FSFs to compete, and they fundamentally shape all aspects of the financial-services business, but especially the price, convenience, and confidence functions.

The Price Function

Interest rates on loans and deposits (and prices for other financial services) are the explicit prices of banking. Government-imposed ceilings on bank interest rates, if effective, restrict competition and result in market distortions. In 1933, the U.S. government imposed deposit-rate ceilings on banks and prohibited payment of interest on demand deposits (checking accounts). For years the ceilings were not binding, because market interest rates remained low. However, when the U.S. economy began facing a series of increasingly severe interest-rate spikes, beginning in 1966 and peaking in 1980–1982, the costs and distortions of the ceilings began to take a heavy toll in terms of disintermediation and discrimination against small savers. The current regulatory environment permits banks to compete more freely for loans and deposits on the basis of interest rate—the price dimension. On balance, the techniques of monitoring, asset restrictions, and risk-based pricing are more efficient tools for attempting to limit bank risk taking than interest-rate controls.

The Convenience Function

The convenience function for a financial-services firm can be described in terms of four elements:

- The organization's geographic reach (e.g., number of branches or ability to transfer funds electronically)
- The number of products and services offered (e.g., a "universal" bank versus a "narrowly defined" bank)
- The average cost of accessing the bank's facilities
- The quality of the product and services (e.g., speed and reliability)

---

[20] This section draws on Kane [1986] and Sinkey [1992].

Although the cost and quality of an individual FSF's products and services are mainly a function of its internal environment and operations, regulations indirectly affect the cost of doing business and contribute to shaping this component of the convenience function. In contrast, geographic and product restrictions directly affect user convenience by limiting the scope of an FSF's geographic reach and its product offerings. To the extent that these restrictions limit firms' ability to diversify, they increase (bank) riskiness. Nevertheless, because asset restrictions are among the tools for managing guarantees, the basic question is: What businesses should regulated firms (banks) be in and who should decide (bankers, regulators, or lawmakers) what those businesses are? Given prompt corrective action and other regulatory reforms, a freer market solution is to let bankers decide what their businesses should be.

The Confidence Function

If we abstract from government guarantees for the moment, confidence in a financial institution should be a function of its net worth or capital adequacy (capacity to absorb losses), stability of earnings (an indicator of its riskiness), liquidity, and the accessibility, reliability, and cost of information about its operations, management, and so on. In general, market participants will have less confidence in firms with low net worth, highly variable earnings, illiquid assets, and weak managers. In an efficient market, disclosure of the components of a firm's confidence function would permit market participants to judge the safety or riskiness of financial institutions.

Because banks administer the payments mechanism and provide transactions services, supply backup liquidity to the economy, and serve as a conduit for monetary policy, most governments provide some form of guarantee or safety net for banks (e.g., in the form of deposit insurance or as a lender of last resort or both).[21] A government guarantee then becomes a critical component in establishing public confidence in banks and the banking system. However, if the government guarantee is too strong (e.g., 100% deposit insurance), it can create its own set of problems in the form of moral hazard, being too big to fail and too reliant on regulatory discipline to the exclusion of market discipline.

Recapitulation and Lessons

Price, convenience, and confidence represent three key layers of financial-services competition. In trying to achieve a financial system that is safe, stable, and competitive (too safe and too stable mean less competitive), regulators play a major role in shaping these three aspects of bank competition. Countries trying to develop efficient and safe banking systems need to understand how regulation shapes these functions and what trade-offs are involved.

Chapter Summary

Financial systems perform six basic or core functions:

- Clearing and settling payments (a payments system)
- Aggregating (pooling) and disaggregating wealth and flows of funds so that both large-scale and small-scale projects can be financed
- Transferring economic resources over time, space, and industries

---

[21] Corrigan [1987] is one of the leading proponents of the specialness doctrine. Sinkey ([1992], pp. 19–21) provides a summary of alternative views on this issue.

- Accumulating, processing, and disseminating information for decision-making purposes
- Providing ways for managing uncertainty and controlling risk
- Providing ways for dealing with incentive and asymmetric-information problems that arise in financial contracting

Because commercial banks perform all of the functions, they are vital to any financial system. This is not to deny, however, that other financial institutions also perform the same or similar functions. Commercial banks have been adapting their institutional forms, epitomized by the bank holding company, to follow the evolving functions of the financial system.

A U.S. financial system described as the financial-services industry (FSI) includes depository institutions such as commercial banks, savings and loans (S&Ls), savings banks, and credit unions and nondepository institutions including insurance companies, pension funds, finance companies, mutual funds, and subsidiaries of nonfinancial corporations such as General Motors Acceptance Corporation (GMAC) and General Electric Capital Services. All of these companies can be described as financial-services firms (FSFs) or financial intermediaries (FIs). In addition, because the industries in which these companies operate have become less compartmentalized, their fusion or coming together has marked the birth of the FSI, an industry marked by -ization (e.g., securitization). The view that commercial banks operate in the FSI means that their role will look diluted in this framework. Although discussions of the decline of banking and the end of banking as we know it have been topical recently, commercial banks are still the kingpins of the FSI in the United States.

When the intermediation function is disrupted, disintermediation occurs, or a shift from indirect finance to direct finance. Disintermediation has occurred on both sides of bank and S&L balance sheets as they have lost deposits to other FSFs, especially mutual funds, and they have lost loans to instruments of direct finance (e.g., commercial paper and corporate bonds).

Financial markets perform two basic economic functions: (1) They transfer funds from those economic units that have surplus funds to those that need them (usually to buy tangible assets); and (2) they transfer funds in such a way as to redistribute or shift risk among those seeking and those providing funds. In short, the two principal functions of financial markets are funds transfer and risk shifting. As intermediaries, banks perform these two functions, which create credit risk, interest-rate risk, and liquidity risk—the dilemmas of bank risk management.

In the process of transferring funds and distributing risk, financial markets and institutions provide three important services: (1) They determine the prices of financial assets through the interaction of buyers and sellers; (2) they provide liquidity by offering investors the opportunity to sell (liquidate) their financial assets; and (3) they reduce search and information costs of transacting or exchanging financial assets (transactions costs). In addition to providing funds transfer and risk shifting, banks justify their existence by providing liquidity and reducing search and information costs.

Strength in banking requires a balance of banking powers and firm supervision. In practice, bank regulators use combinations of monitoring, asset restrictions, and risk-based pricing to manage their guarantees (i.e., to achieve firm supervision). Freedom of exit based on "prompt corrective action" is an essential component of any system of bank regulation and supervision. Nevertheless, Schwartz [1987] suggests that stabilizing interest rates and prices will do more for financial stability than reforming deposit insurance or reregulation. Moreover, with advances in monitoring technology and increases in the liquidity of bank assets through securitization, market discipline will increasingly supplant the need for regulatory discipline.

The inability of lenders, regulators, and deposit insurers (as principals) to adequately monitor the actions and information of agent borrowers (including banks) captures the central principal-agent problem of a regulated financial system. Although market discipline is an alternative to regulatory discipline, most market economies rely on both forms to control bank risk taking. Ideally, market and regulatory discipline should complement each other to promote a safe-and-sound banking system.

Countries striving to develop efficient banking and financial systems should learn from the mistakes of the United States. To attempt to avoid these problems, developing countries need to maintain a stable economic and financial environment, to regulate banks in a way that does not restrict their diversification opportunities, and if they provide deposit insurance, to price it properly (e.g., based on risk exposure).

List of Key Words, Concepts, and Acronyms

- Asset prices
- Bank holding company
- Confidence function
- Convenience function
- Credit or default risk
- Dimensions of bank competition
- Expected inflation
- FDIC Improvement Act (FDICIA)
- Federal Deposit Insurance Corporation (FDIC)
- Federal Reserve System
- Federal safety net
- Financial intermediary

- Financial markets
- Financial-services firms (FSFs)
- Financial-services industry (FSI)
- Fisher effect
- Five Cs of credit analysis
- Globalization
- Institutionalization
- Interest-rate risk
- Interest rates (nominal versus real)
- Liquidity risk
- Office of the Comptroller of the Currency (OCC)
- Pass-through finance

- Price function
- Privatization
- Prompt corrective action (PCA)
- Regulation
- Regulatory dialectic (struggle model)
- Securitization
- Techniques for managing the guarantee business
- Transactions costs
- Types and classes of commercial banks

Review Questions

1. What is the most basic task that a financial system performs, and what are the six relatively unchanging functions that it executes?
2. Carefully distinguish between the following pairs of terms:
   a. Intermediation versus disintermediation
   b. Direct finance versus indirect finance
   c. Depository institution versus nondepository institution
   d. Real rate of interest versus nominal rate of interest
   e. Confidence function versus convenience function
   f. Regulatory discipline versus market discipline
3. What is the FSI and who are the major players in it?
4. Distinguish among the various types and classes of commercial banks. What is the dominant organizational form in commercial banking? What were the driving forces in the development of this organizational form?
5. Describe what is meant by the "-ization" of the FSI.
6. Describe the dollar flows, claims, and T-accounts involved in the process of financial intermediation.

7. What are the financial cornerstones of financial markets and firms' balance sheets? What innovations have been derived from these building blocks?

8. What are four common characteristics of financial claims? What do banks do with respect to these claims?

9. Why do financial intermediaries exist?

10. What are the agency relations and problems of regulatory discipline?

11. Explain the strength-in-banking equation. Who proposed it?

12. Discuss "The end of banking as we know it." When will it occur? Why is it happening?

13. What are the techniques for managing the guarantee business? Do banks use these techniques for making and monitoring loans, and how do the techniques relate to the five Cs of credit analysis? Distinguish among the identification, enforcement, and closure of problem banks.

14. What are the key risks faced by bank managers? What have been the primary causes of bank failures? S&L failures?

15. What is the Fisher effect or equation? What determines the real rate of interest? In an environment without inflation or deflation, what is the relation between real and nominal interest rates?

16. What is the ongoing struggle depicted by the regulatory dialectic?

17. According to Bhattacharya and Thakor [1993], "the big questions" that have puzzled financial-intermediation researchers are:[22]
    a. Why do we have financial intermediaries?
    b. Why do banks routinely deny credit rather than charge higher prices?
    c. What is the role of banks in maturity transformation?
    d. Should banks be regulated? If so, how?
    e. What is the role of financial intermediaries in the overall allocation of capital and how is this role affected by capital market microstructure?
    f. What are the major unresolved issues?
    Form discussion groups to exchange ideas about these questions.

18. Go to the library (or the Internet) and browse through some of the sources of banking information listed in Appendix A of this chapter. *The American Banker* is the best source for keeping abreast of daily developments in banking and the financial-services industry.

Problems

1. If you borrow $1000 for one year when the real rate of interest is 4 percent and expected inflation is 6 percent, how much must you repay at the end of the year and what are the components of the compensation to the lender?

2. If the nominal rate of interest is 25 percent and the real rate is 5 percent, what is the expected inflation rate approximately and more exactly?

3. If expected inflation is 5 percent but actual inflation turns out to be 10 percent, who benefits? What happens in the opposite case? What kind of contract can be used to shift the underlying risk?

---

[22] For each one of these key questions, Bhattacharya and Thakor [1993] list at least two related smaller questions. Their Table 1 (pp. 4–5) provides the details.

APPENDIX A

SOURCES OF BANKING INFORMATION

Newspapers
American Banker
Banking Week
Barron's (weekly)
National Thrift News
The New York Times
The Wall Street Journal
Regional and local papers

Magazines
Business Week
The Economist
Forbes
Fortune
The Money Manager

**Trade publications
(practitioner oriented)**
ABA Banking Journal
Bank Asset/Liability Management
Bank Auditing and Accounting Report
Bank Credit Card Observer
Bank Directors Report
Bank Expansion Reporter
Bank Financial Quarterly
Bank Financial Strategies
Bank Fraud
Bank Insurance and Protection Bulletin
Bank Loan Report
Bank Management
Bank Marketing
Bank Mergers and Acquisitions
Bank Operating Report
Bank Personnel Report
Bank Rate Monitor
Bank Security Report
Bank Software Review
Bank Tax Report

The Banker
The Banker's Magazine
Banker's Monthly
Bankers' Research
Banking Issues and Innovation
Banking Law Report
Banking Literature Index
Banking Strategies
Banking World
Bankrisk
Financier, The Journal of Financial Affairs
The Independent Banker
Issues in Bank Regulation
Journal of Commercial Bank Lending
The Magazine of Bank Administration
The Mortgage Banker
Mutual Savings Banks Journal
Private Banking
Real Percentgram
Real Estate Review
Savings Institutions
Secondary Mortgage Markets

Academic journals
The Banking Law Journal
Financial Management
The Financial Review
Global Finance Journal
Journal of Accounting, Auditing, and Finance
Journal of Bank Research (ceased publication in 1986)
Journal of Banking and Finance
Journal of Finance
Journal of Financial and Quantitative Analysis
Journal of Financial Economics
Journal of Financial Intermediation
Journal of Financial Research
Journal of Financial Services Research

Journal of Futures Markets

Journal of International Financial Markets, Institutions, and Money

Journal of Money, Credit, and Banking

Review of Financial Studies

Government publications

Annual Reports (FDIC, OCC, FRS, etc.)

Congressional Hearings, Reports, and Staff Studies usually may be obtained by writing the Chief Clerk of the committee in question.

Bank Structure and Competition (Annual, FRB of Chicago)

Federal Home Loan Bank Board *Journal*

Federal Reserve Bulletin and the Monthly/ Quarterly Reviews of the District Federal Reserve Banks *Treasury Bulletin*

Cases

Intercollegiate Case Clearing House
  Soldiers Field Post Office
  Boston, MA 02163

Check bookstores and libraries for case books on commercial banking.

Computer tapes (report of condition and report of income, i.e., balance-sheet and income-expense data, respectively, for commercial banks).

National Technical Information Service, U.S. Department of Commerce

Standard and Poor's Compustat Service, Inc.

Commercial-bank computer simulations

Stanford Bank Management Simulator, Stanford University

BankSim, American Bankers Association/ FDIC

Asset/Liability Management: A Model for Commercial Banks, Olson Research Associates (Silver Spring, Maryland)

Miscellaneous

Bankers Desk Reference

Polk's Bank Directory

Notes on Research, the Internet, and Writing Cases and Reports

The Internet and various on-line sources and search procedures available in libraries and school computer labs (or in your home) are convenient, valuable, and easily accessible sources of banking information. Most major banks, their regulators, and other financial services have home pages on the Internet, or you can search by key words. In most cases your research problem will be not scarcity of information but too much information. To prepare your writing skills for the business world, you should attempt to write executive summaries that get to the heart of an issue or problem. Get in the habit of using bullets to highlight major points, and headings and subheadings to give your reports structure.

APPENDIX B

MODELS OF BANK-INDUSTRY LINKAGES[23]

The bank-industry linkages in the United States, Japan, and Germany represent three alternative ways of relating financial economics and real economics (i.e., banks and industry). The Japanese *keiretsu* and German *Hausenbanken* (universal bank) foster closer relations between banks and industry, while the U.S. approach relies on

---

[23] This section draws on Smith and Walter [1993].

capital markets and a well-developed banking system but one that is separated from commerce (i.e., nonbanking businesses cannot own a bank in the United States).

The Japanese Model, or *Keiretsu* Approach

In pursuit of economic growth, the Japanese model attempts to provide a high degree of leverage to industrial firms. The approach builds on a strong, centralized banking and credit system in which firms are encouraged to rely on relationships with banks, suppliers, agents, and customers to maximize their borrowing (e.g., for government-authorized projects). Banks own shares in businesses, which also own shares in the banks. Although cross-holdings tend to be nominal, the practical effect links dissimilar companies together for mutual support and protection. These cross-shareholding groups, called *keiretsu,* provide a unique approach to corporate control based on continuous surveillance and monitoring by the managers of affiliated firms and banks.

The *keiretsu* approach resulted in a single-minded pursuit of industrial objectives based on a management-bank-government consensus. Although effective early in providing for reconstruction following World War II, the Japanese system has demonstrated at least three weaknesses in the 1980s and 1990s:

- Near-total bureaucratization of the system, which has dampened initiative and innovation and made subsequent changes difficult
- Loss of control of the price-setting mechanism to powerful nonmarket forces with adverse effects on efficiency and equity
- Deterioration of banking standards and quality-and-safety controls resulting from inefficiencies and corrupt practices

Smith and Walter [1993] conclude that the more powerful and successful a banking system is in fostering industrial development, the more difficult it is to alter or control later.

The German Model, or Universal-Bank Approach

The German model is a broad-based one built on four interrelated elements that link universal banks and industrial companies:

- The *Hausbank* approach to providing financial services (i.e., reliance on only one principal bank)
- Bank ownership of equity shares
- Bank voting rights over fiduciary (trust) shareholdings
- Bank participation on supervisory boards

The Hausbank relationship results in companies accessing both capital-market services (new issues of stocks and bonds, mergers and acquisitions, etc.) and bank-credit facilities through their "universal bank." Hausbank credit facilities to client firms are "insured," for which the borrower pays a fee. In addition, Hausbank loans are viewed as quasi-equity for the bank, because if financial difficulties arise, the Hausbank may convert the debt to equity and take control. In general, the Hausbank is deeply involved in its corporate clients' business affairs, with the relationship considered a two-way street based on loyalty. By providing all of the financing needed to start a business (e.g., seed capital, initial public offerings of stock, bond underwritings, and working capital), German banks gain Hausbank standing.

Although German universal banks' ownership of equity in all companies is not large (less than 1% in 1989), concentration is much greater in some larger companies, which comprise a major portion of the holdings of large banks. An unusual feature of the German system is that the voting rights of the shares held in custody by universal banks are typically exercised through proxy voting. Thus, banks have a degree of control over industrial enterprises that usually is larger than their own proportionate share ownership.

The previous three elements of the Hausbank relationship are cemented by bank representation on supervisory boards. Under German law, board members must act in the interest of the firm and its shareholders. In addition, bank board members provide advice on questions of financial management and capital markets. Supervisory board members are concentrated among the largest German firms.

On balance, in the German model, bank-industry linkages involve strong surveillance and monitoring by banks of industrial firms and the potential for a high degree of control in maximizing shareholder value, because banks have an equity stake and fiduciary obligations with respect to shares held in custody.

The Anglo-American Model, or Capital-Markets Approach

The Anglo-American approach relies on capital markets (direct finance) and a well-developed banking system (indirect finance) for allocating financial resources using debt and equity instruments. The discipline of an informed marketplace replaces centralized control of capital allocation and pricing. Asset prices, interest rates, and financial innovation, as described earlier in the chapter, play a critical role in allocating financial resources in a market economy.

Smith and Walter [1993] conclude that attempts to impose the Anglo-American model on developing or transforming economies runs the risk of public disillusionment and rejection of market-based reforms in general. They suggest a three-stage approach, beginning with the Japanese model, followed by the German model as a pragmatic intermediate step, and finishing with the capital-markets approach. Given the lack of an accounting, financial, and legal infrastructure in developing countries, where financial transparency is low and information costs are high, their recommendation has intuitive appeal.

Selected References

Bear, Larry A., and Rita Maldonado-Bear. [1994]. *Free Markets, Finance, Ethics, and Law.* Englewood Cliffs, NJ: Prentice-Hall.

Berger, Allen N., and Gregory F. Udell. [1993]. "Securitization, Risk, and the Liquidity Problem in Banking." In Michael Klausner and Lawrence J. White, eds., *Structural Change in Banking.* Homewood Hills, IL: Irwin Publishing, pp. 227–294.

Bhattacharya, Sudipto, and Anjan V. Thakor. [1993]. "Contemporary Banking Theory." *Journal of Financial Intermediation* 3, pp. 2–50.

Boyd, John H., and Mark Gertler. [1994]. "Are Banks Dead? Or, Are the Reports Greatly Exaggerated?" Research Department, Federal Reserve Bank of Minneapolis (May).

Buser, Stephen A., Andrew H. Chen, and Edward J. Kane. [1981]. "Federal Deposit Insurance, Regulatory Policy, and Optimal Bank Capital." *Journal of Finance* 36, pp. 775–787.

Corrigan, E. Gerald. [1987]. *Financial Market Structure: A Longer View.* New York: Federal Reserve Bank.

Diamond, Douglas. [1984]. "Financial Intermediation and Delegated Monitoring." *Review of Economic Studies* 51, pp. 393–414.

Eisemann, Peter C., and George A. Budd. [1980]. "An Approach to Capital Planning at Bank Holding Company Parents." Working Paper, Georgia State University.

"The End of Banking As We Know It?" (a three-part series). [1993]. *The Wall Street Journal* (July 8–9), p. 1+.

Frankel, Allen B., and Paul B. Morgan. [1992]. "Deregulation and Competition in Japanese Banking." *Federal Reserve Bulletin* (August), pp. 579–593.

Garcia, Beatrice E. [1990]. "Delaware Bill Opens Insurance to Banks." *The Wall Street Journal* (May 21), p. A5.

Grant, James. [1992]. *Money of the Mind: Borrowing and Lending in America from the Civil War to Michael Milken.* New York: Farrar Straus Giroux.

Hovakimian, Armen, and Edward J. Kane. [1996]. "Risk-Shifting by Federally Insured Commercial Banks." Working Paper 5711, National Bureau of Economic Research.

Kane, Edward J. [1977]. "Good Intentions and Unintended Evils . . ." *Journal of Money, Credit, and Banking* (February), pp. 55–69.

———. [1986]. "Competitive Financial Reregulation: An International Perspective." Paper presented at the 1986 Conference of the International Center for Monetary and Banking Studies, August.

Kaufman, George G., and Larry R. Mote. [1994]. "Is Banking a Declining Industry? An Historical Perspective." *Economic Perspectives,* Federal Reserve Bank of Chicago, (May/June).

Lindley, James T., James A. Verbrugge, James E. McNulty, and Benton E. Gup. [1992]. "Investment Policy, Financing Policy, and Performance Characteristics of De Novo Savings and Loan Associations." *Journal of Banking and Finance* (April), pp. 313–330.

Merton, Robert C. [1995]. "A Functional Perspective of Financial Intermediation." *Financial Management* (Summer), pp. 23–41.

Merton, Robert C., and Zvi Bodie. [1992]. "On the Management of Financial Guarantees." *Financial Management* 21, pp. 87–109.

"Privatization: The Lessons of Experience." [1992]. Country Economics Department, The World Bank.

Schuler, Kurt. [1992]. "Currency Boards." Unpublished doctoral dissertation, George Mason University, Fairfax, VA.

Schuler, Kurt, George Selgin, and Joseph F. Sinkey, Jr. [1991]. "Replacing the Ruble in Lithuania: Real Change versus Pseudoreform." In *Policy Analysis,* Cato Institute (October 28).

Schwartz, Anna J. [1987]. "The Lender of Last Resort and the Federal Safety Net." *Journal of Financial Services Research* 1, pp. 1–17.

Sinkey, Joseph F., Jr. [1978]. "Identifying Problem Banks: How Do the Banking Authorities Measure a Bank's Risk Exposure?" *Journal of Money, Credit, and Banking* 2, pp. 184–193.

———. [1979]. *Problems and Failed Institutions in the Commercial Banking Industry.* Greenwich, CT: JAI Press.

———. [1992]. *Commercial Bank Financial Management in the Financial-Services Industry.* New York: Macmillan.

Smith, Roy C., and Ingo Walter. [1993]. "Bank-Industry Linkages: Models for Eastern European Economic Restructuring." In Donald E. Fair and Robert J. Raymond, eds., *The New Europe: Evolving Economic and Financial Systems in East and West.* Dordrecht, Netherlands: Kluwer Academic Publishers, pp. 41–60.

Szego, Giorgio P. [1986]. "Bank Asset Management and Financial Insurance." *Journal of Banking and Finance* (June), pp. 295–307.

"World Banking Survey." [1992]. *The Economist* (May 2), pp. 1–50.

CHAPTER

2

SOURCES AND USES
OF BANK FUNDS
AND THE RISKS
OF BANKING

Contents

LEARNING OBJECTIVES

■ To understand a bank as a portfolio or balance sheet

■ To understand a bank's sources and uses of funds

■ To understand the components of a bank's income-expense statement

■ To understand the risks of banking

■ To distinguish between economic "values" and accounting "numbers"

■ To understand banks as information processors and regulated firms

CHAPTER THEME

Three ways of viewing a bank are:

- As an information processor
- As a regulated firm
- As a portfolio or balance sheet

If you understand these three ideas, you will have a good grasp of the modern bank. The financial-management approach of this book stresses the portfolio or balance-sheet concept. Because risk-management strategies are time-dependent, place-dependent, and data-dependent, information and **information technology** play crucial roles to banks as information processors. Moreover, as bank technology and information flows have improved, geographic and many product restrictions have become obsolete and have necessitated a rethinking and reshaping of the role of bank **regulation.**

Although the traditional business of gathering deposits to fund loans is in relative decline, it still represents the heart of a bank's balance sheet. These **sources** (deposits) and **uses** (loans) **of banks' funds** generate **income-expense statements,** which have three key components:

1. **Net interest income** (NII) = interest income minus interest expense
2. **Provision for loan losses** (PLL)
3. **Net noninterest income** ("burden") = noninterest income minus noninterest expense

These three components highlight the basic risks of banking and the financial-management perspective of this book. Specifically, net interest income maps into

interest-rate risk, liquidity risk, and prepayment risk; the provision for loan losses maps into **credit risk** or loan quality; and "burden" maps into the generation of fee or noninterest income (product-development risk) and the control of operating or noninterest expenses (operating risk). These factors capture the way bankers look at risk, and they link with the financial-management view of risk as variability in earnings because they are the source of the variability (e.g., bad loans). On balance, the essence of modern banking is the measuring, managing, and accepting of risk and the heart of bank financial management is **risk management,** a major theme of this book.

KEY CONCEPTS, IDEAS, AND TERMS

- Accounting "numbers" (book value)
- Balance sheet (portfolio)
- Core deposits
- Equity capital
- Federal funds
- Income-expense statement
- Information technology and processing
- Managed liabilities
- Net interest income (NII)
- Net interest margin (NIM)
- Opportunity cost
- Regulation
- Return on assets (ROA)
- Risk management
- Safekeeping (risk-control) function
- Sources and uses of funds
- Transactions function

INTRODUCTION

Etymology refers to the linguistic history of a word. The word *bank* traces to the French word *banque* (chest) and the Italian word *banca* (bench). The earliest known banks, temples, operated as places to store wealth. They were among the first places where a need for money and money-changers emerged.[1] These early meanings capture the two basic functions that banks perform:

1. Chest: the **safekeeping,** or **risk-control function**
2. Bench: the **transactions function,** including intermediation or two-way funds rental

A chest, such as a gold, jewelry, cedar, or hope chest, is a place to store valuables. A bank's chest is its portfolio of assets and liabilities. In concrete and steel, a bank's chest is its vault; the vault, however, is only a hollow shell. The heart of a bank is its portfolio, or balance sheet, including off-balance-sheet items. Bank portfolios generate the accounting lifeblood of banking: earnings net of expenses and taxes. A bank's economic lifeblood is its cash flow, defined as net earnings plus any non-cash outlays (e.g., provision for loan losses or PLL). The variability of accounting earnings or cash flow reflects a bank's riskiness.

Depositors' and other creditors' funds are stored (invested) for safekeeping in a bank's portfolio of earning assets. If it helps you sleep better, think of a bank's portfolio as safely tucked away in its vault at night. However, if you want to understand bank financial management, think of a bank's liabilities as stored in financial assets representing claims on the earnings of households, business firms, and governments. The difference between a bank's assets and its liabilities represents its net asset value or total equity capitalization.

---

[1] Because "money" is named after Rome's moon goddess and goddess of warning, Juno Moneta, Kane [1994] notes that the formative role that temples played in primitive banking is permanently enshrined in the etymological root of the English word for "money."

BANKS' EVOLUTION FROM MONEY CHANGERS TO INFORMATION PROCESSORS

In twelfth-century Italy, *banca* (bench) referred to the table, counter, or place of business of a money changer. This meaning suggests the transactions and trading functions of a modern bank. More generally, the transacting "benches" of modern society include the supermarket checkout counter/scanner, the platform of a convenience/gasoline/lottery store, and the shopping program on your cable TV station. The usual means of payment at these benches are cash, check, or credit/debit card—means of payment supplied, but not exclusively, by banks. Banks have benches themselves in the form of the new-accounts desk, the teller's window, the loan officer's desk, the trading desk for securities and derivative instruments, and the proverbial hole-in-the-wall—the ATM. In addition, bankers still make "house-calls" at businesses (wholesale, commercial, or merchant banking) and will be "on call" for wealthy individuals (private banking). These benches provide bank customers with access to the safekeeping and transactions functions of banks.

In providing safekeeping, transactions, and trading functions, banks monitor information for themselves and for customers' accounts, especially borrowers. This monitoring requires banks to collect, analyze, store, retrieve, and update information. In this regard, banks are similar to communications firms in that both are entities that establish networking relationships through which they process and transmit information. Banks employ five separate information technologies to keep information flowing smoothly:[2]

1. *Communications:* Banks build internal and external networks to make information flow cheaply and in timely fashion to decision makers who need it.

2. *Data Processing:* Banks use computer software to analyze data in customer-information files as they estimate creditworthiness, service accounts, and monitor activities.

3. *Advisory Services:* Banks exercise risk management and other control and monitoring activities on their own balance sheets and on those of their customers. Since banks want their employees and their customers to make sound decisions, they work to reduce their own operating costs and to generate fees from customers. To achieve this, banks stand ready to provide internal and external decision makers with software-supported advice at critical points in the decision-making process.

4. *Executing Decisions:* As agents, banks execute customer transactions directly (e.g., in check clearing and settlement) and indirectly (e.g., in establishing and carrying out the investment policies of a proprietary mutual fund).

5. *Tax and Regulatory Avoidance and Compliance:* By studying the law and attempting to minimize the burdens compliance places on their bottom lines (think of the "regulatory dialectic"), bankers enhance their profitability.

These five technologies have affected some familiar characteristics of a bank, including its physical appearance and the technological organization of its work flow, its products and business plans, its ownership structure, and its relationships with

---

[2] These technologies are described by Kane [1994].

government officials.[3] To visualize the technology embodied in appearance and work flow, think of a how a bank's front office, back rooms, and communication media have evolved.[4] Specific products have expanded and business plans and risk-management systems are a must.

The organizations that control the majority of bank loans and deposits are the large publicly held corporations known as bank holding companies (BHCs, chapter 1). In the twenty-first century, these financial-services firms will strive to be "virtual banks," which according to Citicorp/Citibank means ability to serve customers "anywhere, any time, (in) any way." The Internet, for example, will permit you to bank from your home similarly to home-shopping networks but with your personal computer rather than your telephone. Innovations related to **information technology** will pave the way for further advances in electronic banking (e-banking), and electronic money (e-money), which go hand in hand.

Regarding the potential diffusion of e-money/e-banking in the United States, Alan Greenspan, chairman of the Federal Reserve, expressed a cautious view in 1996:

> . . . electronic money is likely to spread only gradually and play a much smaller role in our economy than private currency did historically. Nonetheless, the earlier period affords certain insights on the way markets behaved when government rules were much less pervasive. These insights, I submit, should be considered very carefully as we endeavor to understand and engage the new private currency markets of the twenty-first century.

It is interesting to note that in Europe and other developed countries that are less wedded to the check as a means of payment, e-money/e-banking have been adopted more quickly than in the United States. On balance, Greenspan's message is not new: *Payment habits change slowly.*

BANKS AS REGULATED FIRMS

The concept of a regulated financial-services firm represents another way to view a bank. The myriad of regulations and restrictions that banks face was introduced in chapter 1; part 6 of this book provides the details. The important point for this chapter is that bank portfolios and information processing are affected by the intense way banks are regulated.

The view that banks are special because of the important roles they play in clearing and settling payments, determining the money supply, and providing liquidity to the economy is reason enough for most people to accept at least some regulation of banking. Specialness, however, is a matter of degree as nonbank financial institutions have made substantial inroads in the provision of payment, transaction, and liquidity services. To maintain confidence in the banking system, regulators and deposit insurers promote safe-and-sound banking practices. As a

---

[3] To vividly capture the cumulative effect of changing information technology, Kane [1994] suggests that we travel back to those "days of yesteryear" and compare the typical frontier bank (found in a Clint Eastwood movie or a Lone Ranger TV series) with a modern bank.

[4] An important information-processing issue is whether banks should use outside sources to handle systems integration and manage data-processing centers. This issue of "outsourcing" is analyzed in chapter 18.

result, bank relationships with U.S. government officials are pervasive as chartering, examining, and regulating are conducted on both the federal and state levels. Because most state deposit-insurance funds collapsed during the 1980s or early 1990s, insuring deposits has become the sole domain of the FDIC. Because the combination of deposit insurance and the Fed's liquidity facility ("the discount window") provides a federal safety net (guarantee) for banks, bank regulation does have its benefits.

BANKS AS PORTFOLIOS: TWO-WAY FUNDS RENTAL AND RISK CONTROL

Bank portfolios and their financial management can be viewed in terms of **two-way funds rental** and risk control. The former is simply another name for the financial-intermediation process. Banks rent funds from depositors and other creditors and then turn around and rent the funds to households, businesses, or governments as borrowers. The rental fees, of course, are interest rates. Because some borrowers default and because interest rates change, banks face two basic risks: credit risk and interest-rate risk. When these risks are mismanaged or when creditors think they are mismanaged (rumors of financial distress), banks must have liquidity to meet deposit withdrawals. In addition, banks need liquidity to meet the loan demands of their best customers. Thus, a third basic uncertainty banks face is liquidity risk. Also, since borrowers tend to refinance their loans when interest rates decline, banks encounter prepayment risk. Liquidity risk and prepayment risk arise from the options embedded in financial contracts (i.e., deposit contracts and loan contracts). Controlling bank risk focuses on managing credit risk, interest-rate risk, and liquidity risk such that shareholder value (or some other objective function) is maximized.

Because balance sheets generate revenues and expenses, a bank's income-expense statement goes hand in hand with its balance sheet or its sources (deposits) and uses (loans) of funds. These two statements are easily and compactly represented by:

$$\text{Balance sheet: } A = L + NW \qquad \textbf{(2-1)}$$

where A = total assets, L = total liabilities, and $NW = A - L$ = net worth, total equity capital, or net asset value; and

$$\text{Income-expense statement: } P = R - C \qquad \textbf{(2-2)}$$

where P = profits, R = total revenues, and C = total costs.

The critical variables in (2-1) and (2-2) are (1) a bank's net worth and (2) its profits or net income.

BANK BALANCE SHEETS: SOURCES OF FUNDS

Let's begin with how banks raise funds. Like other firms, banks use debt and equity to fund their assets. Most of a bank's liabilities are in the form of various kinds of deposits such as checking accounts, savings accounts, or certificates of deposit. Because **core deposits** and **managed liabilities** ("purchased funds") are two common and mutually exclusive ways of classifying bank liabilities, we begin with these two generic categories. Together they account for about 90 percent of bank funding. The remaining 10 percent of bank assets are supported by equity capital.

Core Deposits: What Are They and Why Are They Important?

Core deposits are gathered in local markets and typically have lower interest costs than purchased funds. Another important feature of core deposits is their relative stability compared to "hot money," or funds purchased in national or international money markets. Because they are a stable and relatively low-cost source of funds, bankers like to have lots of core deposits, and banks that have lots of them are more valuable than those without them, all other things being equal.

Although definitions may vary, core deposits have four common components:

1. *Demand-deposit accounts or DDAs.* These sources of funds are simply checking accounts that do not pay interest. Although DDAs are non-interest-bearing liabilities of the bank, they are not expense free because they generate processing costs. To help cover these operating expenses, banks usually charge fees related to account activity or account balances or both. Many students are familiar with the charge for "insufficient funds" and fees for usage of another bank's ATM. By meeting certain requirements, customers may purchase "free checking." "Purchase" is the operative word here as reflected by the quip: There is no such thing as a free lunch. Customers pay for free checking by maintaining minimum balances or using other banking services/products such as a credit card, a mortgage, or a certificate of deposit.

2. *Other checkable balances.* This deposit category refers to interest-bearing checking accounts. They first became available in the early 1970s and were known as "negotiable orders of withdrawals," or NOW accounts.[5] From 1933 to 1980, commercial banks could not pay interest on demand deposits. The Depository Institutions Deregulation and Monetary Control Act (DIDMCA) of 1980 permitted all depository institutions to offer NOW accounts, or interest-bearing checking accounts.

3. *Savings accounts.* Historically, this deposit category was dominated by passbook savings accounts and included such marketing devices as Christmas-club accounts. The key savings vehicle today is the money-market-deposit account, or MMDA. Commercial banks introduced these accounts to compete with money-market accounts offered by retail brokerage firms. Merrill Lynch's "cash-management account," or CMA, was the pioneering instrument. Whereas CMA-type accounts are true interest-bearing checking accounts, bank money-market accounts are savings accounts on which a limited number of checks can be written (as of this writing only three per month).

4. *Small time deposits.* Time deposits (TDs) are segmented by denomination or size, where the critical value is $100,000, the current level of the FDIC deposit-insurance ceiling. Small time deposits are less than $100,000, whereas large time deposits exceed $100,000. A time deposit is simply a deposit account that pays interest for a fixed term during which the funds cannot be withdrawn before maturity without either advance notice or an interest penalty or both. Time deposits are

---

[5] The innovation of NOW accounts was pioneered by mutual savings banks in Massachusetts in 1974 as a way of competing with commercial banks.

sometimes referred to as "investment accounts" but are most commonly known as (time) certificates of deposit, or simply CDs. Retail and wholesale CDs are also known as "small" and "large" (also called "jumbo") CDs, respectively.

Core Deposits: Who Has Them?

Table 2-1 shows the composition and growth of core deposits for all insured commercial banks for the years 1985 to 1995. Composition is expressed as a percentage of total assets (Panel A), whereas growth is measured on an annual basis

TABLE 2-1 The Composition and Growth of Core Deposits for All Insured Commercial Banks, 1985–1995

PANEL A. CORE DEPOSITS AS A PERCENTAGE OF TOTAL ASSETS

| Year | *Type of Domestic Core Deposit* | | | | |
	DDAs	*Other Checkable*	*Savings*	*Small TDs*	*Total*
1985	15.5%	4.6%	16.4%	16.8%	53.3%
1986	15.9	5.2	17.5	15.8	54.4
1987	15.3	6.0	18.3	15.1	54.7
1988	14.2	6.2	17.6	16.2	54.2
1989	13.5	6.1	16.3	18.4	54.3
1990	12.8	6.2	16.6	20.0	55.6
1991	12.6	6.7	18.0	21.3	58.6
1992	13.2	7.6	20.3	19.2	60.3
1993	13.9	8.2	20.9	17.0	60.0
1994	13.5	7.8	19.6	15.3	56.2
1995	12.7	6.6	17.5	16.1	52.9
Memo: 1995 level	$545B	$283B	$751B	$691B	$2270B

PANEL B. THE ANNUAL GROWTH RATES OF CORE DEPOSITS, MANAGED LIABILITIES, EQUITY CAPITAL, AND TOTAL ASSETS, 1985–1995

Year	*Core Deposits*	*Managed Liabilities*	*Equity Capital*	*Total Assets*
1985	10.28%	9.17%	9.77%	8.91%
1986	11.79	3.06	7.56	7.66
1987	−0.76	6.09	−0.66	2.00
1988	5.48	2.26	8.77	4.33
1989	5.75	5.20	4.18	5.35
1990	7.57	−6.16	6.68	2.63
1991	5.25	−6.18	5.98	1.33
1992	5.09	−6.03	13.78	2.20
1993	1.49	12.29	12.56	5.67
1994	−0.16	17.64	5.26	8.08
1995	3.96	10.61	12.06	7.60
Memo: 1995 level	$2292B	$1380B	$349B	$4293B

Note: DDAs are demand-deposit accounts. "Savings" include money-market-deposit accounts. In the next-to-last column in Panel A, *TD* stands for time deposits.

Source: Data are from the *Federal Reserve Bulletin* (June 1994), pp. 547 and 560, and (June 1995), pp. 484 and 496.

(Panel B). Comparing 1985 with 1995, we see that the core-deposit profile for the average commercial bank was as follows:

| | *Percentage of Total Assets* | |
Source	1995	1985
DDAs	12.7	15.5
Other checkable	6.6	4.6
Savings	17.5	16.4
Small TDs	16.1	16.8
Total core deposits	52.9	53.3

With assets growing at roughly 5 percent over this period (Panel B of Table 2-1), the industry has experienced only a slight decline in its core-deposits funding. Within this total, DDAs are down the most, whereas small TDs are down slightly, with checkable and savings up. Contrary to the previous chapter's discussion of the decline of banking, core deposits reveal that the industry is holding its own in terms of proportional funding, and as Panel B of Table 2-1 shows, except for 1987 and 1994, core deposits have continued to grow.

The important financial-management implication of core deposits is that they provide a relatively stable and lower cost of financing than alternative sources of bank funds. A bank that can fund more of its total assets with core deposits will have an interest-cost advantage over competitors with lower proportions of core deposits, all other things being equal. Additionally, it will be an attractive takeover target for a bank looking for core deposits.

Core Deposits by Bank Size

In 1994, the Federal Reserve introduced new size classifications for commercial banks. On the basis of total assets, the four size groups are:

1. The ten largest banks
2. Banks ranked 11th through 100th
3. Banks ranked 101st through 1000th
4. Banks not ranked among the 1000 largest

These four classes will be referred to as "ten largest," "large," "medium," and "small."[6] They also can be described as multinational or "money-center" banks (the ten largest), superregional banks (large), regional banks (medium), and community banks (small). At the time the Fed announced the use of these size classes, the number of small or community banks totaled about 10,000. As of this writing (1997), the number of community banks is about 7,000. The numbers of banks in the other three groups are perforce constant at 10, 90, and 900. The composition of and rankings in all four groups have been subject to considerable variation because of consolidation associated with mergers and failures.

---

[6] Unless otherwise indicated, these four terms are used throughout this chapter and throughout the book when referring to bank size classes. Table 1-3 (chapter 1) shows the ten largest BHCs (not banks) in terms of total assets (Panel A) and total market capitalization (Panel B).

The composition of core deposits for the four size classes described above for the years 1985 to 1995 reveals the following average profiles:

	As a Percentage of Average Assets				
Size Class	*DDAs*	*Other Checkable*	*Savings*	*Small TDs*	*Total*
Ten largest	11	3	12	5	31
Large	16	5	17	14	52
Medium	15	7	22	20	64
Small	13	11	22	31	77

These data clearly show an inverse relationship between bank asset size and total core deposits, and except for DDAs, this relationship holds for each of the components. It is also interesting to note that the *median,* or "middle," ratio of core deposits to total assets (as opposed to the *mean* ratio of 53%) is in the range of 64–77 percent. The reason for this nonsymmetrical distribution is that low values of the ratio for the biggest banks (30% or lower) drag the mean down.

Managed Liabilities (Purchased Funds): The Antithesis of Core Deposits

Managed liabilities, or "purchased funds," are the "hot money" of bank funding. As the antithesis of core deposits, managed liabilities are volatile, rate-sensitive funds gathered in national or international money markets. They can be measured as the sum of deposits in foreign offices, large time deposits in domestic offices, federal funds purchased and securities sold under agreements to repurchase (RPs or repos), demand notes issued to the U.S. Treasury, subordinated notes and debentures, and other borrowed money. To tap these sources of funds on a continuous basis, banks must maintain their creditworthiness and presence in these markets.

The data in Table 2-2 reveal a strong direct relationship between bank asset size and the use of managed liabilities to fund bank assets, the opposite of the relationship with respect to core deposits. Specifically, consider the following representative values:

Bank Size Class	*Managed Liabilities to Assets (%)*
Small	13
Medium	20
Large	32
Ten largest	49

An important element in explaining this relationship is the lack of access by small- and medium-sized banks to national and international money and deposit markets. Perhaps as a reflection of more conservative bank management in the early 1990s, the use of managed liabilities by all banks declined from 35.7 percent of total assets in 1989 to 28.2 percent in 1993. Since then, however, the figure has rebounded to 32.1 percent (1995).

The decline of managed liabilities over the years 1990 to 1992 reflects such factors as the slowdown in the economy, the crisis in commercial real-estate lending,

TABLE 2-2   The Use of Managed Liabilities by Insured Commercial Banks, 1985–1995 (as a percentage of average consolidated assets)

Definition: Managed liabilities consist of the sum of deposits in foreign offices, large time deposits in domestic offices, federal funds purchased and securities sold under agreements to repurchase, demand notes issued to the U.S. Treasury, subordinated notes and debentures, and other borrowed money.

| | *Bank Size Class* | | | | |
Year	*Ten Largest*	*Large*	*Medium*	*Small*	*All Banks*
1985	59.32	41.85	25.88	13.70	35.49
1986	57.37	42.56	25.67	13.43	35.07
1987	56.79	43.29	26.00	13.14	35.13
1988	56.34	44.27	27.51	13.34	35.74
1989	56.24	43.81	27.62	13.53	35.69
1990	54.74	41.50	25.93	13.24	34.24
1991	53.18	35.42	23.40	12.17	30.99
1992	50.76	32.53	19.97	10.53	28.65
1993	49.17	31.69	19.64	10.06	28.23
1994	46.16	32.83	22.86	10.81	29.57
1995	47.89	35.64	24.69	12.04	32.06
Median	54.74	41.50	25.93	13.24	34.24

Note: Size class refers to the 10 largest banks, the 11th through 100th largest banks, the 101st through 1,000th largest banks, and banks smaller than the 1,000 largest.

Source: Data are from the *Federal Reserve Bulletin* (June 1996), pp. 496–505.

voluntary contractions in bank lending, and increased monitoring of lending by bank examiners. The voluntary and involuntary contracts of bank lending, of course, reduced the need for funds. Over the next three years, however, managed liabilities rebounded and grew at double-digit annual rates ranging from 10.6 percent (1995) to 17.6 percent (1994).

Panel B of Table 2-1 shows the annual growth of managed liabilities for all insured commercial banks for the years 1985 to 1995. The volatility of the growth rates reflects the fact that purchased funds are used to fund loans, the demand for which varies considerably over the business cycle. In contrast, core deposits (Panel B, Table 2-1) reveal more stable but declining growth rates. These characteristics are reflected in the standard deviation of the growth rate for managed liabilities (7.6%) compared to the standard deviation of the growth rate for core deposits (3.7%).[7] The greater variability of managed liabilities compared to core deposits explains why managed liabilities are called "volatile" and core deposits "stable."

Gathering Deposits in Foreign Countries

Deposits in foreign offices show a strong and direct relationship with bank size for two reasons: (1) Most of the funds are managed liabilities, and (2) most small banks

---

[7] As an exercise, brush up on your statistics and compute these standard deviations from the data in Panel B of Table 2-1. To four places, you should get 7.6334 percent (managed liabilities) and 3.7490 percent (core deposits). Recall that the standard deviation is a measure of dispersion or variability of a distribution or list of numbers.

TABLE 2-3 Deposits in Foreign Offices of U.S. Commercial Banks Ranked by Size of Bank, 1985–1995 (as a percentage of average assets)

| Year | Bank Size Class | | | | |
	Ten Largest	Large	Medium	Small	All Banks
1985	34.60	11.85	2.00	0.07	12.28
1986	32.43	10.45	2.07	0.06	11.27
1987	32.60	10.14	1.96	0.04	11.02
1988	31.49	9.68	2.04	0.04	10.41
1989	30.08	8.63	2.09	0.06	9.68
1990	29.66	7.84	1.65	0.07	9.26
1991	28.47	6.69	1.76	0.08	8.55
1992	27.16	6.20	1.56	0.07	8.37
1993	25.51	6.78	1.44	0.08	8.32
1994	26.10	8.05	1.69	0.09	9.39
1995	28.36	8.12	1.71	0.11	10.27

Note: Size classes refer to the 10 largest banks, the 11th through 100th largest banks, the 101st through 1,000th largest banks, and banks not ranked as the 1,000 largest.

Source: Data are from the *Federal Reserve Bulletin* (June 1996), pp. 496–505.

do not have foreign offices. The 10 largest banks tend to fund at least 25 percent of their total assets with deposits gathered in foreign countries, whereas large banks finance less than 10 percent of their total assets with foreign deposits. Medium-sized banks use less than 2 percent; community banks use less than 0.2 percent. Table 2-3 shows deposits in foreign offices of U.S. commercial banks ranked by bank size for the years 1985 to 1995.

The debt crisis in less-developed countries (LDCs) in the 1980s and the problems with commercial real estate loans in the late 1980s and early 1990s explain, in part, why the percentage of assets financed by deposits in foreign offices has been declining steadily since 1985, especially at the 100 largest banks. On balance, as banks have become more conservative about their lending policies and practices, they have become less aggressive in their acquisition of managed liabilities.

Recapitulation

Banks have two generic funding sources: core deposits and managed liabilities, or purchased funds. Core deposits are gathered in local markets, have slightly lower interest costs, and tend to be relatively stable. In contrast, managed liabilities are gathered in national and international money markets. Since these markets are more competitive, the funds cost more; and since purchased funds seek the highest interest rate (all other things being equal), they are more volatile than core deposits. Thus, if you have seen the right-hand side of one particular bank's balance sheet, you have not seen them all. Nevertheless, across our four size categories, we can conclude that small- and medium-sized banks use relatively more core deposits to finance assets, whereas the 100 largest banks use relatively more managed liabilities to finance their assets. The use of purchased funds requires banks to maintain their creditworthiness and presence in money and deposit markets.

BANK BALANCE SHEETS: USES OF FUNDS (TOTAL ASSETS)

At year-end 1995, all insured commercial banks held total assets of $4.3 trillion. Across the size groups shown in Table 2-4, the following relative positions existed at year-end 1985 and year-end 1995:

Size Group	Percentage of Industry Total Assets		
	1995	1985	Change
Ten largest	25.3	25.1	0.2
Large banks (90)	32.2	26.0	6.2
Medium banks (900)	26.4	24.8	1.6
Small banks (9000+)	16.0	24.1	−8.1

These data indicate that the 10 largest banks are *not* increasing their control over total banking assets; in fact, their degree of concentration has been essentially the same from 1985 to 1995. Small or community banks have experienced the greatest loss of industry assets. In contrast, large and medium banks have increased the total assets under their control on both an absolute and a relative basis. These data suggest that the decline of banking, narrowly defined, is the decline of community banking. The growth rates shown in Table 2-4 confirm this conclusion. For the years 1985 through 1995, total assets for all banks grew at an annual rate of 4.9 percent. Across the four size groups, the ranked growth rates were 7.19 percent (large banks), 5.54

TABLE 2-4	Average Net Consolidated Assets by Bank Size Class, 1985–1995 ($ billions)				
Year	All Banks	Ten Largest	Large	Medium	Small
1985	2,572	646	668	638	620
1986	2,775	681	735	710	649
1987	2,922	691	802	771	659
1988	3,048	685	870	839	654
1989	3,187	693	940	892	662
1990	3,338	725	995	938	681
1991	3,379	717	1,006	961	695
1992	3,442	775	1,003	966	698
1993	3,567	818	1,082	975	689
1994	3,863	949	1,204	1,032	679
1995	4,149	1,051	1,338	1,094	666
Annual Growth	4.90%	4.99%	7.19%	5.54%	0.72%

Note: Size classes refer to the 10 largest banks, the 11th through 100th largest banks ("large"), the 101st through 1,000th largest banks ("medium"), and all banks not ranked as the 1,000 largest ("small").

Source: Data are from the *Federal Reserve Bulletin* (June 1994), pp. 498–506, and (June 1996), pp. 496–505.

percent (medium banks), 4.90 percent (the 10 largest banks), and 0.72 percent (community banks). In terms of growth of total assets, banking has not been declining in absolute terms, and within the industry growth rates have varied by size class.

Specific Uses of Bank Funds: Interest-Earning, Fee-Based, and Nonearning Assets

Bank uses of funds can be grouped into two traditional categories of assets: those that earn interest income and those that do not earn interest income, or interest-earning and non-interest-earning assets. Of course, because banks also generate noninterest income, or fees, the fact that an asset is classified as non-interest-earning does not necessarily mean that it does not generate any revenue. Non-interest-earning assets, which can be split into fee-based assets and nonearning assets, exist for operational, regulatory, or fee-income reasons. Examples of non-interest-earning assets include (1) required reserves held on deposit with the Federal Reserve or as vault cash; (2) cash balances needed for check clearing or other operational needs; (3) originated or purchased servicing rights on mortgage loans; (4) fixed assets, such as buildings, computers, and furniture. All other things being equal, banks want to minimize their holding of nonearning assets.

For the years 1985 to 1995, Table 2-5 shows that, on average, banks' non-interest-earning assets began at 13.3 percent of total assets in 1985 and were at about the same relative level in 1995 (13.5%). The figure, however, had dropped to 11.3 percent at year-end 1993. Across the four size categories, non-interest-earning assets increase with bank size. For example, the 10 largest banks had non-interest-earning assets of 23 percent in 1995, whereas the other three classes held 11.7 percent (large), 9.9 percent (medium), and 8.3 percent (small). Reserve requirements may explain some of this relation. For example, banks with net transaction accounts[8] greater than $51.9 million face reserve requirements of 10 percent, whereas those with less than $51.9 million have only a 3 percent reserve requirement. In the absence of legal reserve requirements, banks could have higher levels of earnings assets if their prudent level of reserves were lower than the legal requirements. One reason that bankers talk about an unlevel playing field is that the reserve-requirement tax is not imposed on nondepository institutions such as mutual funds or securities firms.

Bank Interest-Earning Assets: Loans and Investment Securities

Bank interest-earning assets consist of loans and securities. Three general categories of bank loans are the following:

1. Commercial-and-industrial (C&I) loans
2. Real-estate loans
3. Consumer loans

As Table 2-5 reveals, loans are the major interest-earning asset held by the banking industry, 58 percent in 1995, down slightly from 60 percent in 1985. The relative

---

[8] Net transaction accounts include all deposits against which the account holder is permitted to make withdrawals by negotiable or transferable instruments, payment orders of withdrawal, and telephone and preauthorized transfers for the purpose of making payments to third persons or others, other than money-market deposit accounts and similar accounts that permit no more than six preauthorized, automatic, or other transfers per month, of which no more than three may be checks. Accounts subject to such limits are savings deposits. *Federal Reserve Bulletin* (p. A9) shows reserve requirements for depository institutions.

TABLE 2-5   Components and Growth of Selected Balance-Sheet Items for All Banks, 1985 and 1995

	1985		1995	
Item	*% of Assets*	*% Growth*[a]	*% of Assets*	*% Growth*[a]
Earning assets	86.68	8.92	86.48	7.75
Loans & leases	59.59	7.93	58.38	10.61
C&I loans	22.16	2.16	15.20	12.27
Real estate	15.88	13.98	25.00	8.28
Consumer	11.04	15.81	12.11	9.99
Credit card	2.64	28.19	4.73	12.35
Loss reserves[b]	0.94	9.13	1.27	0.45
Securities	16.84	15.96	21.94	0.60
Investment acct.	15.62	14.06	19.38	−1.54
Trading account	1.22	41.40	2.55	18.52
Nonearning assets	13.32	4.62	13.52	6.59
Interest-bearing liabilities	72.85	NA	71.87	NA
Deposits	61.52	7.94	56.29	6.46
Non-interest-bearing liabilities	20.88	NA	20.12	NA
Total liabilities	93.74	8.86	91.99	7.22
Equity capital	6.27	9.79	8.01	12.06
Memo				
Comm. RE loans	NA	NA	9.01	5.82
Other RE owned	0.26	NA	0.19	NA
Managed liabilities	35.49	9.17	32.06	10.61
Average net consolidated assets (bils.)	$2,572	8.92	$4,149	7.60

Note: [a]Growth from previous year. [b]Loss reserves are for 1986 and include the allocated transfer-risk reserve.
Source: Data are from the *Federal Reserve Bulletin* (June 1994), pp. 485, 497–499, and (June 1996), pp. 484 and 496. Figures may not add up due to rounding.

amount of total loans varies by bank size but not in a linear fashion. For example, based on 1995 data, the figures are 56.6 percent (community banks), 62.2 percent (medium), 62.7 percent (large), and 50.0 percent (10 largest).

Within the three major loan categories, C&I lending for all banks dropped from 22 percent of total assets in 1985 to 15 percent in 1995, an indication of loan disintermediation. Consumer loans rose slightly, from 11 percent of total assets in 1985 to 12 percent in 1995, whereas real-estate lending increased from 16 percent of total assets in 1985 to 25 percent in 1995. One of the major reasons for the increase in bank real-estate lending was the savings-and-loan crisis of the 1980s—commercial banks entered the market to take up the slack created by the demise of hundreds of S&Ls.

The securities that banks hold are divided into those held for investment purposes and those held for trading purposes. The critical difference between the two is that the investment account does not have to be marked to market, whereas the trading account must be marked to market. The securities held in trading accounts tend to be actively traded. The kind of securities that might be held in either account include the following:

- U.S. Treasury
- U.S. government agency

- Corporate obligations
- Government-backed mortgage pools
- State and local government

Banks can use the most liquid of these securities (e.g., Treasuries) to generate funds by selling them and agreeing to buy them back—repurchase agreements (RPs, or repos). The counterparty to an RP does a reverse repo and supplies the funds.

Table 2-5 shows the total securities and the investment and trading-account components held by all banks at year-end 1985 and 1995. Within our four size groups, the relative holdings of total securities (as a percentage of total assets) in 1985 and 1995 were as follows:[9]

Size Group	1995	1985	Change
Ten largest banks	19.5%	9.3%	10.2
Large banks (90)	18.6	11.5	7.1
Medium banks (900)	23.1	19.4	3.7
Small banks (9000+)	30.5	27.5	3.0

The increased holdings of securities by commercial banks over these years can be traced to several factors:

- The introduction of risk-based capital requirements in 1987
- A more favorable interest-rate environment
- Reduced loan demand
- Prodding by bank examiners to improve loan quality

Most banks hold securities in their investment accounts. Over the years 1985 to 1995, except for the 10 largest banks, most banks held substantially less than 1 percent of their assets in trading accounts. For the 10 largest banks, trading-account assets increased from 3.5 percent in 1985 to 10.3 percent in 1993 before declining to 8.9 percent in 1995.

Credit Risk, Provision for Loan Losses, and Reserves for Loan Losses

Credit or default risk is the uncertainty associated with borrowers' repayment of their loans. Most of the securities that banks hold are free of default risk or close to it. Bank loans, however, carry varying degrees of default risk. In anticipation of some borrowers' defaulting, banks set aside part of their earnings, through an expense account called *provision for loan losses* (PLL), to attempt to cover such contingencies. In effect, a bank earmarks capital or earnings (the PLL expense provision) for future loan losses. Like bad debt losses in other businesses, a bank's PLL is part of the expense of making loans. It is, however, a noncash outlay that flows into the reserves for loan losses.[10] The loan-loss reserve, also called the allowance for loan losses (ALLL), is an estimate of future loan losses, a valuation reserve. When loans are charged off, they deplete the loan-loss reserve; the provision is an inflow that augments the stock or level of the reserve. The periodic provision (usually quarterly) is an important discretionary managerial activity that is driven by sufficiency of the loan-loss reserve.

---

[9] These data, not shown in Table 2-5, are from the *Federal Reserve Bulletin* [June 1994], pp. 500–507.

[10] Technically, the allowance for loan loss or loan-loss reserve is a "contra-asset," which when deducted from "gross loans" gives "net loans." Net loans represent the principal that lenders think they can collect.

It is helpful to think of the loan-loss reserve as the water level in a bathtub, where the level reflects the reserves needed to cover future loan losses. The level, which is the focal variable, can be raised by turning on the PLL spigot. It is lowered by loans that are charged off, represented by water going down the drain. Gross charge-offs go down the drain, however, because recoveries are made on some of these bad loans; only net loan losses deplete the level of the reserve. Think of recoveries as a small part of the drainage that is pumped back into the tub through the overflow valve, or simply think of only net charge-offs going down the drain.

Table 2-5 shows that all banks held, on average, loan-loss reserves of 1.3 percent of their total assets in 1995, up from about 1.0 percent in 1985. An overall industry minimum for the loan-loss reserve is 1 percent of a bank's total assets. Within size groups and over time, however, the ratio varies. For example, the 10 largest banks held reserves of 1.45 percent of total assets in 1995 compared to an average ratio of 2.5 percent for the years 1987 to 1992. The 90 next-largest banks, which suffered less from the LDC debt crisis, held loan-loss reserves of 1.3 percent in 1995 compared to an average 1.67 percent for the years 1987 to 1992. For medium-sized banks, the figures were 1.23 percent (1995) compared to 0.9 percent (1985); for small banks, the figures were 0.9 percent (1995) compared to 0.7 percent (1985). On balance, a reasonable range for loan-loss reserves as a percentage of total assets for the late 1990s is 1–2 percent.

A bank builds up its reserve, or allowance for loan losses, by "turning on the PLL spigot." Remember, however, that the loan-loss reserve is the key variable. The PLL spigot needs to be turned on because the loan-loss drainage is larger than expected; the inflow can be cut back or turned off completely if losses are smaller than anticipated. Table 2-6 shows bank PLLs (as a percentage of average assets) for the years 1985 to 1995. The PLLs from 1985 to 1992 were relatively high, reflecting the poor loan quality associated with LDC debt, commercial real-estate loans, and to a lesser extent, farm loans. The breakdown of PLL by size class in Table 2-6 can be used to describe how these credit-risk problems affected banks

TABLE 2-6 Loan-Loss Provisions by Bank Size, 1985–1995 (as a percentage of average assets)

Year	All Banks	Ten Largest	Large	Medium	Small
1985	0.69	0.73	0.63	0.59	0.82
1986	0.81	0.79	0.79	0.74	0.89
1987	1.30	2.15	1.55	0.78	0.67
1988	0.65	0.40	0.57	0.74	0.56
1989	0.98	1.45	1.18	0.74	0.49
1990	0.97	0.77	1.27	1.11	0.52
1991	1.03	1.21	1.19	1.06	0.51
1992	0.78	1.12	0.78	0.76	0.43
1993	0.47	0.64	0.47	0.46	0.26
1994	0.28	0.26	0.32	0.32	0.19
1995	0.30	0.11	0.39	0.43	0.23

Note: Size classes refer to the 10 largest banks, the 11th through 100th largest banks, the 101st through 1,000th largest banks, and banks not ranked among the 1,000 largest. The loan-loss provision includes provision for allocated transfer risk.

Source: Data are from the *Federal Reserve Bulletin* (June 1994), pp. 501–507, and (June 1996), pp. 496–505.

differently over this period. For example, problems with farm loans for small banks were reflected by the 0.8 percent (1985) and 0.9 percent (1986) PLL ratios. Problems with LDC loans, which first surfaced in 1982, were not properly allocated for until 1987 and 1989. In those two years, the 10 largest banks took LDC hits of 2.15 percent and 1.45 percent, respectively. To put these percentages into perspective, note that in 1987 Citicorp's PLL for LDC debt (mainly Brazilian debt) was $3 billion.[11] To a lesser extent, the 90 large banks also were affected by the LDC debt crisis because they took hits of 1.55 percent (1987) and 1.18 percent (1989). In the early 1990s, when the crisis in commercial real-estate lending was at its height, PLLs of over 1 percent of total assets were common, except for the smallest banks.

To summarize, bankers increased their PLLs so they could write down loans closer to market values. When they do a better job of matching accounting income with economic income, the divergence between book and market values of loans is minimized or eliminated.[12]

Federal Funds and Repurchase Agreements as Sources and Uses of Bank Funds

The term **federal funds** refers to excess reserves that banks trade among themselves in the interbank market. Technically, federal funds (or "Fed funds") are unsecured advances of "immediately available funds" from excess reserves held at Federal Reserve banks. Although some nonbank institutions participate in the Fed-funds market, for the most part it is an interbank market. When a bank advances Fed funds, it sells excess reserves. Rather than expanding its balance sheet, the bank simply shifts assets from a non-interest-bearing account (reserves) to an interest-earning account, Federal funds sold. If the counterparty is another bank, it receives or buys the funds and incurs a liability, Federal funds purchased. If the Fed funds are purchased to make a loan or buy a security, then the transaction expands the bank's balance sheet. If the purchase is used to repay an existing debt, the transactions merely change the composition of the bank's liabilities. Fed funds are not explicitly protected by deposit insurance.

Because most Fed-funds transactions are overnight (24-hour maturity), they are the most liquid earning asset banks hold. Over weekends, Fed funds have a 72-hour maturity. When Fed-funds transactions are arranged for longer periods of time, which is rare, they are called "term Fed funds." Banks that fund their balance sheets with large purchases of Fed funds take on substantial liquidity risk. If the banks encounter financial distress, federal funds, which are unsecured and not protected by deposit insurance, will not be rolled over.[13] Under such circumstances, the bank is usually forced to replace the lost Fed funds with discount-window borrowings, which must be secured. Because the Federal Reserve does not permit borrowing under distressed conditions over the long run, the bank must find replacement funds or sell assets or both. If it doesn't, it will be closed when the Fed calls its loan. The economic failure of a bank (either cash-flow or real net-worth insolvency) typically occurs *before* the bank is closed by bank regulators.

---

[11] Musumeci and Sinkey [1990a] and [1990b] analyze the market's reaction to Brazil's debt moratorium, and Citicorp's reserve decision, respectively.

[12] The concepts of book and market values and accounting and economic income are discussed in greater detail later in this chapter and in part 2 (chapters 3–5).

[13] Sinkey [1979] describes several cases in which this problem occurred (e.g., Franklin National Bank of New York in 1974).

The rate of interest for Fed funds is known as the *federal-funds* or *Fed-funds rate*. It is a key money-market rate. Although the Federal Reserve tries through monetary policy (e.g., open-market operations) to influence the Fed-funds rate, the rate is not "administered" like the Fed's discount rate but is a market rate determined by the supply and demand for excess reserves. To the extent that the Fed can influence the supply and demand of excess reserves, it affects the Fed-funds rate.

Federal Reserve Surveillance of the Discount Window

Because administered rates, like the Federal Reserve's discount rate, are usually below market rates, why don't bankers always borrow from the discount window? The reason is that the discount window is intended to be a liquidity facility for maintaining a safe-and-sound banking system and not a pure arbitrage game for member banks. To this end, the Fed conducts surveillance of discount-window borrowing. In addition, the managers of the discount windows at the 12 Federal Reserve banks frequently act as informal money brokers by informing the "street" about banks that have reserves to sell or buy.

Secured Liquidity Trading

Similar to Federal funds, repurchase agreements, also known as repos, RPs, or buyback agreements, play a major role in bank liquidity management. In contrast to Fed-funds transactions, repurchase agreements are secured arrangements backed by pledged securities. As a liability, a repurchase agreement is a contract to sell and subsequently buy back securities at a specified date and price. Although term contracts can be arranged, most repos are very short-term contracts similar to Fed-funds transactions (e.g., overnight). The difference between the selling price and the buyback price represents the return to the seller. For example, suppose a bank sells a security at a price of 97.99 (converted from 32nds) and buys it back the next day at a price of 98. The one-day cost is $0.01/97.99 = 0.000102$, which, using a 360-day year, converts to an approximate annual rate of 3.67 percent ($= 0.000102 \times 360$).

The counterparty in an RP contract simply takes the opposite side of the transaction, called a "reverse repurchase agreement." The counterparty agrees to purchase securities and resell them back at an agreed price at a later date. Based on the example above, it buys at 97.99 and resells the next day at 98 for an annual yield of 3.67 percent. In the case of default (failure to repurchase), the buyer has the pledged securities as collateral.

The major players in the RP market are the Federal Reserve, nonbank dealers, dealer banks, and nondealer banks.[14] Any bank or FSF can engage in an RP arrangement, and some banks offer "retail repos" in small denominations. At the wholesale level, the Fed arranges RPs with dealers, dealers contract among themselves, and dealers transact with nondealers (e.g., Orange County, California).[15]

From an accounting perspective, since Fed funds and repurchase agreements serve similar functions, they are listed together on bank "call reports" (balance sheets). In general, federal funds sold and reverse RPs, which are interest-earning assets, decrease as bank size increases. In contrast, federal-funds purchases and

---

[14] Recent data indicate RP activity by commercial banks at more than $90 billion a day. Counting S&Ls and other financial institutions, RP transactions swell to almost $200 billion a day. Money-market mutual funds used about $73 billion in repos a day in 1994. These data do not include repo transactions by Wall Street securities firms, which are not tracked by the Fed.

[15] In December 1994, Orange County filed for protection from creditors under Chapter 9 of the federal bankruptcy code. The county's investment manager used RPs and derivatives (e.g., "inverse floaters") to construct a highly levered and risky investment fund.

repurchase agreements, which are sources of funding, tend to increase with bank size. If we combine these positions, banks are net users of Fed funds and RPs because they buy more funds than they sell. The Fed and other financial institutions provide the balance of funds. Within the banking industry, the 1,000 largest banks are, on average, net users, whereas small banks are, on average, net providers of funds. This pattern leads to a reallocation of funds from small banks to large ones, or from rural areas to metropolitan areas.

Recapitulation

Eighty-five to 90 percent of a bank's assets (uses of funds) are classified as interest-earning assets. The remaining, or noninterest-earning, assets are needed to support bank operations, are required by law as reserves, or are used to generate noninterest or fee income. The bulk of a bank's earning assets, in the range of 50–65 percent of total assets, are in the form of loans. The major types of bank lending are commercial and industrial (C&I) loans, real-estate loans, and consumer loans. Loans are the major source of credit risk for banks, and in anticipation of loan defaults, banks regularly set aside portions of their earnings, through the PLL provision, to establish reserves for loan losses. Securities, the other major category of bank interest-earning assets, serve as investments, trading accounts, especially by the 1,000 largest banks, or liquidity instruments through repurchase agreements. In contrast to repos, which are secured, federal funds are unsecured excess reserves traded in an important interbank market known as the federal-funds market. Surveillance of the Federal Reserve's discount window prevents banks from arbitraging this liquidity facility, which is intended to provide a safety net for banks' short-term liquidity problems.

BANK CAPITAL (NET ASSET VALUE)

The difference between a bank's total assets and total liabilities represents its net asset value (NAV), more commonly referred to as bank equity capital (K) or **net worth** (NW). In symbols,

$$NAV = K = NW = A - L \qquad \textbf{(2-3)}$$

This net asset value represents the owners' equity interest in the bank. As a buffer or cushion for absorbing losses, more bank capital is regarded by analysts and regulators as better than less, all other things being equal. In this regard, some bankers interpret FDIC as "*F*orever *D*emanding *I*ncreased *C*apital." Because additional equity capital dilutes earnings and control, bank managers and owners might be less enthusiastic about the need for increased capital. When bankers think they have too much capital, they frequently execute stock repurchase plans, sometimes to the chagrin of bank regulators.

Table 2-5 shows that at year-end 1985 the average bank had a capital-to-asset ratio of 6.3 percent; by the end of 1995, the ratio was 8.0 percent. Across size groups, the capital-to-asset ratio decreases as banks get larger. For example, at year-end 1995, the ratios were 9.97 percent for small banks, 8.64 percent for medium banks, 7.77 percent for large banks, and 6.41 percent for the 10 largest banks.[16] To the extent that larger banks may have greater access to money, capital, and labor markets, they should be able to operate safely with less capital. Without

---

[16] These data, not shown in Table 2-5, are from the *Federal Reserve Bulletin* [June 1996], pp. 496–505.

qualification, however, the more risk exposure a bank faces, the more capital it should have, all other things being equal.

SOURCES OF BANK REVENUE: INTEREST AND NONINTEREST INCOME

Banks generate income or revenue in two ways:[17]

1. Interest income from loans, securities, and federal funds sold
2. Fees and services charges, called noninterest income, related to such products and services as loan originations, loan servicing, deposit-account activity, credit-card annual fees, and fees for safety deposit boxes

Panel A of Table 2-7 shows the major sources of bank income for the banking industry for 1995. During that year, the industry generated total income of $386.9 billion, 78.3 percent of which came in the form of interest income ($303 billion). Seventy-five percent of the interest income for all banks came from the loan portfolio. Total revenues were 9.32 percent of total assets, consisting of 7.30 percent in interest income and 2.02 percent in noninterest income.

Across our four size groups, revenue generation (per dollar of assets) varies considerably. For example, for 1995 the figures were:[18]

	1995 Income (% of total assets)		
Size Group (number)	*Interest*	*Noninterest*	*Total*
Ten largest	6.44	2.68	9.12
Large banks (90)	7.40	2.38	9.78
Medium banks (900)	7.71	1.84	9.55
Small banks (8000)	7.79	1.38	9.17

Two relationships are evident from these data: (1) Interest income (as a percentage of total assets) varies inversely with bank size, and (2) noninterest income (as a percentage of total assets) varies directly with bank size.

BANK COSTS: INTEREST AND NONINTEREST EXPENSES

Like bank revenues, bank expenses are described and measured in terms of interest and noninterest items. Interest expenses, of course, vary considerably with the interest-rate cycle; in contrast, noninterest expenses are a relatively stable percentage of a bank's assets. Because deposits are the major source of bank funding, interest paid on deposits is the major interest expense. Panel B of Table 2-7 shows that during 1995, all banks paid $105.4 billion in interest on deposits, which

---

[17] Although "selling" financial products and services is important in banking, the term "sales" is not commonly used. When "sales" is used in this book, it refers to the sum of a bank's interest and noninterest income or revenue. Sales per dollar of assets, called the "turnover ratio" for nonfinancial corporations (NFCs), exceeds one (i.e., sales > assets) for NFCs, whereas the typical bank has an "asset utilization" of about 10 percent (sales < assets).

[18] These data, not shown in the text, are from the *Federal Reserve Bulletin* [June 1996], pp. 495–505.

TABLE 2-7   How Banks Generate Income and Incur Expenses

Panel A. Interest Income and Noninterest Income (data for 1995)

Source of Income	$ Billions	% of Assets
Loans	227.5	5.48
Securities	51.1	1.23
Gross FFS and reverse RPs	9.8	0.24
Other	14.6	0.35
Total interest income	303.0	7.30
Service charges on deposits	16.1	0.39
Fiduciary activities	12.9	0.31
Foreign-exchange gains/fees	2.7	0.09
Trading income	3.6	0.17
Other	48.6	1.14
Total noninterest income	83.9	2.02
TOTAL INCOME	386.9	9.32%

Panel B. Interest and Noninterest Expenditures (data for 1995)

Expense Item	$ Billions	% of Assets
Deposits	105.4	2.54
Gross FFP and RPs	18.4	0.44
Other	24.5	0.59
Total interest expense	148.4	3.58
Salaries and benefits	64.1	1.54
Premises and fixed assets	19.8	0.48
Other	67.4	1.62
Total noninterest expense	151.2	3.64
TOTAL EXPENSE (excluding PLL)	299.6	7.22

Memo: Efficiency ratio = total expense (excluding PLL)/total income = 299.6/386.9 = 7.22/9.32 = 77.4 percent. For 1995, PLL was $12.6 billion, bringing total expense to $312.2 billion and raising the efficiency ratio to 80.7 percent.

Note: FFS stands for gross federal funds sold; RPs stand for repurchase agreements; FFP stands for federal funds purchased. Figures may not add up due to rounding.

Source: Data are from the *Federal Reserve Bulletin* (June 1996), pp. 495–497.

amounted to 2.54 percent of total assets. The payment by banks of $161.4 billion in total interest for deposits in 1990 and of $79.2 billion in 1994 illustrates how sensitive bank interest expenses are to the interest-rate cycle. These expenditures were 4.83 percent of total assets in 1990 and 2.05 percent in 1994.

Across our four bank size classes, deposit-interest expenses as a percentage of assets in 1995 were 2.43 percent for the ten largest banks, 2.29 percent for large banks, 2.56 for medium banks, and 3.20 percent for small banks.[19]

---

[19] The data in this paragraph and the next one, which are not shown in tabular form in the text, are from the *Federal Reserve Bulletin* [June 1996], pp. 495–505.

In 1995, the banking industry paid total interest expenses of $148.4 billion, or 3.58 percent of total assets, compared to $204.7 billion in 1990 (6.13 percent of assets). Across the four size groups, total interest expenses as a percentage of total assets in 1995 were 3.76 percent for the 10 largest banks, 3.62 percent for large banks, 3.46 percent for medium banks, and 3.38 percent for small banks. Competition and the composition of sources of funds result in a direct relation between size and relative interest expense. The higher interest expenses for the larger banks result from their higher costs for "other" sources of funding, which include capital notes, "other borrowed money," and miscellaneous items. For example, for 1995 the cost of these funds for the 10 largest banks was (relative to total assets) 1.03 percent, compared to the 0.59 percent for all banks, as shown in Panel B of Table 2-7.

Salaries and employee benefits are the major noninterest expenses incurred by banks. In 1995, all banks spent $64.1 billion on such compensation, or 1.54 percent of total assets. The 10 largest banks spent 1.58 percent of their total assets on wages. The corresponding expenditures for large, medium, and small banks were 1.47 percent, 1.44 percent, and 1.80 percent, respectively.

Panel B of Table 2-7 shows that during 1995, all banks spent $151.2 billion on total noninterest expenses, or 3.64 percent of total assets. Although the ratio of noninterest expense to total assets for all banks has been trending upward since 1985, when it was 3.21 percent, this ratio was less volatile than the ratio of interest expense to total assets. During 1995, the 10 largest banks incurred noninterest expenses amounting to 3.32 percent of their total assets. The corresponding figures for large, medium, and small banks were 3.79 percent, 3.69 percent, and 3.80 percent, respectively. Taking this ratio as a crude measure of operating efficiency, it suggests operating-cost economies of scale per dollar of assets for the 10 largest banks. The measure is crude because all other things are *not* equal or held constant.

The memo item in Table 2-7 shows another measure of bank overall efficiency: the ratio of total expense (excluding the provision for loan loss) to total income. For 1995, the figure for all banks was 77.4 percent; for 1985, it was 85.9 percent—clearly a favorable trend for the banking industry. The efficiency ratios for 1995 for our four size groups were 82.3 percent (ten largest banks), 75.8 percent (large banks), 74.9 percent (medium banks), and 78.3 percent (small banks). Compared to 1985, when the efficiency ratios were 87.2 percent (10 largest banks), 85.6 percent (large banks), 85.4 percent (medium banks), and 85.1 percent (small banks), all bank classes have shown considerable improvement in their overall operating efficiency.

A BANK'S INCOME-EXPENSE STATEMENT

If we combine the income and expenses items described above and add loan-loss provisions, taxes, and nonrecurring items, we have the ingredients to construct a bank's income-expense statement. Panel A of Table 2-8 shows the major components of a bank's income-expense statement, and Panel B presents income-expense data for 1995 for all banks. Beginning with Panel A, the difference between a bank's gross or total interest income and gross or total interest expense is called its **net interest income** (NII). For a traditional bank engaged in funding loans with deposits, NII represents the bread and butter of the business. It has the major task of

TABLE 2-8   A Bank's Income-Expense Statement

Panel A. The Major Components

1.	Gross interest income
2.	Gross interest expense
3. $(=1-2)$	Net interest income (NII)
4.	Loss provisions or provision for loan losses (PLL)
5. $(=3-4)$	NII after provision for losses
6.	Noninterest income
7.	Noninterest expense
8. $(=6-7)$	Net noninterest income ("burden")
9. $(=5+8)$	Pretax net operating income
10.	Gains/losses on investment account securities
11. $(=9+/-10)$	Income before taxes
12.	Taxes
13.	Extraordinary items
14. $(=11-12-13)$	Net income
15.	Cash dividends declared
16. $(=14-15)$	Retained income

Panel B. Example for All Banks for 1995

Item	$ Billions	% of Assets
1.	303.1	7.30
2.	148.4	3.58
3. $(=1-2)$	154.7	3.73 (= net interest margin or NIM)
4.	12.6	0.30
5. $(=3-4)$	142.1	3.43
6.	83.9	2.02
7.	151.2	3.64
8. $(=6-7)$	−67.3	−1.62
9. $(=5+8)$	74.8	1.81
10.	0.4	0.01
11. $(=9+10)$	75.2	1.82
12.	26.3	0.63
13.	0.0	0.00
14. $(=11-12-13)$	48.9	1.18 (= return on assets or ROA)
15.	31.1	0.75
16. $(=14-15)$	17.8	0.43

Note: For almost all banks, net noninterest income (item 8) is negative because noninterest expense (item 7) exceeds noninterest income (item 6). Because it is negative, net noninterest income has been referred to as a bank's "burden." Taxable-equivalent NIM in 1995 was 3.79 percent.

Source: Data in Panel B are from the *Federal Reserve Bulletin* (June 1996), pp. 495–497. Figures may not add up due to rounding.

covering the bank's loan-loss provision, net noninterest income ("burden"), securities losses, taxes, extraordinary items, and dividends. Except for dividends, deducting these items gets you to a bank's bottom line, or net income (accounting net profits).

Getting to a Bank's Bottom Line Begins with the Net Interest Margin (NIM)

As an exercise let's walk through Panels A and B of Table 2-8 to see how to get to a bank's bottom line. Panel A supplies the words and terminology, and Panel B provides dollar data for all banks and ratios relative to total assets. Line 3 gives us NII, the bread-and-butter item. When we compare this to a bank's total, average, or earning assets, we get the bank's **net interest margin,** or NIM, which measures a bank's "spread" per dollar of assets. As line 3 in Panel B shows, in 1995, all banks had an NIM of 3.73 percent. In general, NIMs vary inversely with bank size. For 1995, the NIMs were 2.68 percent for the 10 largest banks, 3.79 percent for large banks, 4.25 for medium banks, and 4.41 percent for small banks. One reason for this inverse relationship is that larger banks operate in more competitive markets, which means they must pay more for funds and cannot charge as much for loans. Because the numerator components of NIM are both interest sensitive, NIM does not vary much over an interest-rate cycle. However, since bankers like to price loans and deposits in their own self-interest, which should be aligned with shareholder interests, we tend to observe the following movements in bank loan and deposit rates: During an upswing in interest rates, we expect loan rates to rise faster than deposit rates; during a downswing in rates, deposit rates drop faster than loan rates. Of course, variable-rate instruments that are tied to some market rate of interest, such as a T-bill rate or LIBOR, will move with market rates.

Provision for Loan Loss (PLL)

The PLL is an important discretionary variable that bankers can use to manipulate their accounting earnings. For example, overly conservative bankers may understate their current accounting earnings by building loan-loss reserves above industry norms. In contrast, overly aggressive bankers may overstate current accounting earnings by keeping loan-loss reserves relatively low. The PLL for all banks in 1995 was only 0.3 percent of industry assets; in 1987, however, when money-center banks were taking their LDC hits, it was 1.30 percent. During the height of the crisis in commercial real-estate lending (1989–1991), the PLL averaged about 1 percent of assets.

Net Noninterest Income: A Bank's "Burden"

Items 6 and 7 combine to generate a bank's net noninterest income. Because the variable is constructed as noninterest income minus noninterest expense, and because for most banks the latter exceeds the former, net noninterest income is negative for most banks.[20] For this reason, it can be regarded as a bank's **burden.** For 1995, all banks had a burden of −$67.3 billion, or (dropping the negative sign) 1.62 percent of assets. In general, burden tends to decrease with bank size. The burden figures as a percentage of total assets for 1995 were 1.16 for the 10 largest banks, 1.41 percent for large banks, 1.85 percent for medium banks, and 2.42 percent for small banks. Because noninterest expenses exhibit only modest economies of scale, the ability of larger banks to generate more noninterest income per dollar of assets explains why burden decreases as bank size increases. For example, in 1995,

---

[20] An example of a bank with a positive "burden" is Bankers Trust (New York). It, however, is a nontraditional bank engaged in "global wholesale finance" with active trading and derivatives businesses.

the figures for noninterest income per dollar of assets were 2.16 percent for the 10 largest banks, 2.38 percent for large banks, 1.84 percent for medium banks, and 1.38 percent for small banks. The components of noninterest income for all banks for 1995 were as follows:

Component	Billions	Percentage of Assets
Service charges on deposits	$16.1	0.39 (0.25)
Fiduciary (trust) activities	12.9	0.31 (0.30)
Foreign-exchange gains and fees	2.7	0.07 (0.18)
Trading income	3.6	0.09 (0.28)
Other	48.6	1.17 (1.15)
Total noninterest income	$83.8	2.02 (2.16)

The sum of these items matches line 6 in Panel B of Table 2-8. The figures in parentheses are the percentages for the 10 largest banks, which show that their biggest relative advantage comes from trading income. The components of "other" noninterest income include such items as other fee and noninterest income, gains (losses) on other foreign transactions, and net gains on real estate owned, sale of loans, and buildings and fixed assets.

Return on Assets (ROA)

Line 9 in Table 2-8 shows a bank's pretax net operating income. Netting out gains/losses on investment account securities produces pretax income. Deducting taxes and extraordinary items generates net income. This figure as a percentage of assets is **return on assets** or ROA, the key accounting measure of overall bank performance. All banks in 1995 had an ROA of 1.18 percent, substantially above the 1985 ROA of 0.69 percent. The low ROA in 1987 was due mainly to the large PLL hits taken for LDC debt problems by the 100 largest banks, especially the 10 largest banks.

Looking at ROAs over time and across size classes, we observe the following picture of bank performance:

	Return on Assets (ROA)	
Size Group	1995	1985
Ten largest banks	0.88%	0.46%
Large banks (11–100)	1.31	0.74
Medium banks (101–1000)	1.28	0.85
Small banks (not among the 1000 largest)	1.21	0.72
All banks	1.18%	0.69%

If we focus on all banks, the difference between ROA in 1995 and 1985 amounts to 49 basis points. The more favorable interest-rate environment in 1995 led to an NIM of 3.73 percent, which was 20 basis points higher than the 1985 NIM of 3.53 percent. Improved loan quality resulted in a PLL that was 39 basis points lower in 1995 compared to that in 1985, and the reduction in burden saved 37 basis points. Since these three items sum to 96 basis points (> 49), obviously other factors adversely affected ROA. Since ROA is on an after-tax basis, we can look at taxes for the remaining difference. In fact, taxes for 1995 took a much bigger bite out of bank earnings than they did in 1985, a difference of 41 basis points (0.22 percent for 1985 compared to 0.63 percent for 1995, as a percentage of assets).

Dividends and Additions to Retained Earnings

Because returns to shareholders consist of dividends and price appreciation of their shares (capital gains), lines 14 and 15 are crucial to them. Of course, real earnings or economic income drive stock prices, not accounting or book earnings. A bank's net income has two resting places: shareholders' pockets by means of dividend payments or the bank's equity capital account by means of additions to retained earnings. This split is affected by several factors. First, bank regulators have rules that restrict bank dividend payments (i.e., to encourage the retention of earnings and improve capital adequacy, all other things being equal). Second, additions to retained earnings are the only internal source for augmenting a bank's capital. And third, since dividend payments are subject to double taxation, some shareholders may want banks to retain a higher portion of their net income in anticipation of the market valuing the bank more highly because of its improved capital adequacy, all other things being equal. In 1995, all banks paid $31.1 billion in cash dividends to their shareholders while adding $17.8 billion to retained earnings. These figures were 0.75 percent and 0.43 percent of assets, respectively; by definition, they sum to the ROA of 1.18 percent. The 1985 ROA for all banks of 0.69 percent was split into 0.33 percent (dividends) and 0.36 percent (addition to retained earnings).

Dividing the dividend-to-asset ratio by ROA (= net income/assets) generates the dividend-payout ratio = dividends/net income, or deflating both figures by the number of shares outstanding gives dividend per share (DPS) relative to earnings per share (EPS). Because of earnings variability, the payout ratio tends to be inherently unstable. Deflating by total assets, as done in Table 2.8, provides a more stable foundation. In 1995, all banks had a dividend-payout ratio of 63.5 percent (= 0.75/1.18). The ratios for the 10 largest banks, large banks, medium banks, and small banks in 1995 were 64.8 percent, 64.9 percent, 67.9 percent, and 51.2 percent. The comparable figures for 1985, which demonstrate the instability of DPS/EPS, were 47.8 percent (all banks), 52.2 percent (10 largest), 35.1 percent (large banks), 47.1 percent (medium banks), and 59.7 percent (small banks).

Recapitulation

Bank income-expense statements have four key components:

1. Net interest income (NII) = interest income minus interest expense
2. Provision for loan losses (PLL)
3. Net noninterest income ("burden") = noninterest income minus noninterest expense
4. Taxes

If we exclude taxes, the first three components highlight the risks of banking and the financial-management perspective of this book. Specifically, NII reflects interest-rate risk and liquidity risk, PLL captures credit risk or loan quality, and "burden" reflects the generation of noninterest income and the control of operating or noninterest expenses. The financial-management tasks of bankers are to control these risks and manage operations.

BANK FINANCIAL STATEMENTS AND TRANSPARENCY[21]

Webster's Collegiate (tenth edition) defines **transparency** as "easily detected or seen through: obvious . . . readily understood." "Clear" is the key synonym. In the context of FSF accounting, "truer" or "fairer" (clearer) pictures of firms' risk exposures capture the major benefit of transparency. Richard Breeden, former chairperson of the Securities and Exchange Commission (SEC), said that bank financial statements should be stamped: "Once Upon a Time," suggesting that they are "fairy tales" regarding the risks embodied in them. Recent examples of once upon a time include the discrepancies between market values and book values of commercial real-estate loans, loans to less-developed countries (LDCs), energy loans, and farm loans. More recently, questions about the transparency of banks' derivatives activities have been raised. As noted in chapter 1, bank loans and over-the-counter (OTC) derivatives share three characteristics that make them similar:

- Customized
- Privately negotiated
- Lacking liquidity and transparency

These traits make bank loans and OTC derivatives activities rather difficult to quantify and manage, which creates the potential for mispricing bank stocks.

Transparency is also an important issue for other FSFs, such as insurance companies (e.g., adequacy of reserves) and thrift institutions (e.g., exposure to interest-rate risk). In addition, if regulators are to be held accountable for their decisions, transparency is a must. Without it, regulators will have difficulty determining when to take prompt corrective action against problem depository institutions.

The transparency issue boils down to **market value accounting** (MVA) versus **book value accounting** (BVA), which can be analyzed in terms of itemization and valuation principles.

Itemization Principles

When we itemize things, we set them down in detail or by particulars. We make a list. A balance sheet is a list of assets (A), liabilities (L), and net asset value (A-L). An income-expense statement is a list of revenues (R), costs (C), and net income (R-C). The **itemization principle** refers to the procedures that govern what entries do or do not need to be recognized or "booked" in the body of each financial statement. Market value accounting attempts to make bank financial statements as transparent or clear as possible by recognizing and attempting to measure all critical risks.

Valuation Principles

Valuation procedures determine the worth or value assigned to itemized entries. Economists think of value in terms of **opportunity cost** or fair market value, where *fair* presumes no time pressure for quick sale and no hidden information. Two clarifying points for valuation under MVA are helpful. First, fair market values are established under "normal" marketing periods, which means orderly liquidation by a highly motivated seller. Under conditions of financial distress, typically described

---

[21] This section draws on Kane [1993], especially with respect to the issues of regulatory accountability and market-value accounting (MVA) versus book-value accounting (BVA).

as a "fire sale," values of assets are impaired, and such impairments are likely to affect different assets differently. Second, the practice of MVA depends on appraisal methods, such as replacement value or income methods, and related information. Examples include comparable prices found in arm's-length transactions observed in secondary markets or values determined by discounting projected (pro forma) cash flows.

Except in depository institutions, the BVA method of corporate accounting uses the lower of historical cost (possibly amortized) or market value. In 1938, federal bank regulators persuaded accountants to adopt "intrinsic value accounting" for banks, thrifts, and credit unions. This approach values financial assets and liabilities at cost, unless they are sold off, and reserves only for "probable losses that have been incurred and can be reasonably estimated." Valuing at cost is akin to offering our weight and height at birth as "reasonable estimates" of our adult size.

Economic "Values" versus Accounting "Numbers"

Let's begin with a very simple bank to illustrate the difference between the economist's MVA and the accountant's BVA and to spotlight the key risks of banking—credit risk, interest-rate risk, and liquidity risk—and the value of government guarantees. Assume that a bank funds a $100,000 fixed-rate bond with $90,000 in deposits and $10,000 in equity. The bond has an annual coupon rate of 7.5 percent and matures in five years, whereas deposits currently cost 6 percent but reprice (mature) every year. The bank's financial statements are easy to establish:

$$\text{Balance sheet: } \$100{,}000 = \$90{,}000 + \$10{,}000$$

and

$$\text{Income-expense statement (year-end): } \$100{,}000 \times .075 - \$90{,}000 \times .06 = \$2{,}100$$

Excluding any unbooked intangible assets (e.g., government guarantees or customer relationships), MVA and BVA would agree that this simple bank has a net worth of $10,000 and net income of $2,100 at the end of the first year.

Comparative-Statics Experiments

To illustrate the difference between MVA and BVA, let's assume that interest rates double immediately after the deposits are gathered and the bond purchased. Comparable bond yields are now 15 percent, and new deposits cost 12 percent. How will the bank's financial statements change? Under historical-cost accounting, and assuming the bank elects not to reserve for the paper capital loss on the bond, two effects result: (1) The book values of the asset, the liability, and the bank's book net worth ($10,000) remain unchanged; (2) current and future incomes are booked at 7.5 percent when the opportunity cost is 15 percent. The bank's accounting net income for the first year will be $2,100, but after that deposits will cost 12 percent and net income will be $-\$3,300(= 100{,}000 \times 0.075 - 90{,}000 \times 0.12)$ per year for the next four years.

Under MVA, the bank would mark its balance sheet to market. In this case, the market value of the bond, $74,859 (= the present value of the promised payments of $7500 per year for five years and $100,000 at maturity, both discounted at the market rate of 15 percent), is recorded on the MVA books. In this case, the bank's real net worth is $-\$15,141 \ (= \$74{,}859 - \$90{,}000)$. This procedure lets the bank "accrue" future income on the bond at 15 percent, consisting of the 7.5 percent coupon plus 7.5 percent average annual price appreciation in the bond.[22]

It is useful to think of the bank's economic profit (loss) in this example as a holding-period return consisting of coupon, or interest, income plus a capital gain or loss. When interest rates doubled, the bank had an immediate (paper) capital loss of −$15,141. At the end of the year, the bank had net income of $2,100 and (paper) price appreciation in the value of the bond from $74,859 to $78,588 (see footnote 19). During years two through five, the bank has net income per year of −$3,300, plus capital gains due to the price appreciation of the bond (again see footnote 19).

Risk Implications

Continuing with the previous example, suppose that depositors decided to withdraw their funds when interest rates doubled. Banks can either store liquidity in their balance sheets or purchase it in the marketplace. Stored liquidity won't work in this case because the bank has liabilities of $90,000 and assets worth only $74,859. If depositors demand payment, they will get only 83.2 cents on the dollar $(= 74,859/90,000)$.[23] If the bank can purchase funds in the marketplace (recall that the bank is insolvent under MVA), the funds will cost 12 percent (the going market rate) while earning only a fixed 7.5 percent for the next five years.

The liquidity problem the bank faces is not the inherent cause of its financial difficulties. The fundamental cause of the bank's dilemma is the maturity or duration imbalance of its asset-liability structure, which exposes it to interest-rate risk. By borrowing short and lending long, the bank is vulnerable to an increase in interest rates. The bank has a liability that reprices every year whereas its asset reprices only every five years. To hedge this risk, the bank could have tried to match the rate sensitivities of its assets and liabilities or used off-balance-sheet activities such as interest-rate futures, options, or swaps.

Using fixed-income instruments such as bonds or mortgages is the easiest way to illustrate the different valuation effects of MVA and BVA. The same principle, however, applies to a bank's credit risk. For example, suppose that a borrowing firm's creditworthiness deteriorates. Because the firm's cash flows are riskier, the bank must discount them at a higher rate of interest for the purpose of determining the market value of the loan. If the bank marks to market, it will follow the procedures described above for valuing the bond in the face of an increase in interest rates. If it sticks to BVA and does not reserve for the increased probability of loan default, the bank, in effect, ignores the enlarged credit risk.

The Role of Government Guarantees

The federal safety net of deposit insurance and access to discount-window borrowing represents a guarantee to insured depositories. The guarantee, G, takes the form of an unbooked intangible asset, one that becomes more valuable as the bank's risk increases. Based on MVA, a bank with a credible guarantee has the following balance sheet:

$$A + G = L + K \qquad\qquad \textbf{(2-4)}$$

---

[22] At the beginning of years 2–5, the bond has market values of $78,588, $82,876, $87,807, and $93,478, respectively. Of course, at the end of the fifth year (maturity), the bond pays $100,000. The increasing market value of the bond illustrates how the bank accrues future income.

[23] Alternatively, if a secondary market existed for the bank's deposit debt, the depositors could sell their claim of principal ($90,000) plus interest $(0.06 \times 90,000)$ for $85,178 $(= [90,000 + 5400]/1.12)$ and recover 94.6 cents on the dollar.

The unbooked asset, *G,* has an offsetting entry as an unbooked liability on the guarantor's balance sheet. Because the Fed requires collateral to borrow at the discount window (i.e., its loans are secured), the contingent claim falls on the FDIC's balance sheet. In the example above, the bank's liquidity problem could have been solved by borrowing at the discount window. In the case of a forced liquidation of the bank, however, the deposit insurer would have been forced to pay the difference between the market value of the bank's assets and depositors' claims. When an insured bank is closed because $A - L < 0$, liability holders are protected such that $A + G = L$. The amount of protection, *G,* comes from the net worth or reserves of the deposit insurer, called the deposit-insurance fund. One way to determine the real net worth of a bank or of a deposit insurer is to apply MVA to its balance sheet (see Kane and Yu [1994]).

Recapitulation

The objective of MVA is to make financial statements more transparent. When underlying risks change because of changes in creditworthiness or interest rates, bank asset values and cash flows change. By recording asset values at historical cost, BVA ignores these changes and obscures the valuation process. Greater transparency and its accompanying accountability can lead to better decision making by both bank managers and their regulators.

Chapter Summary

This chapter has explored three alternative ways of viewing commercial banks:

- As a portfolio or balance sheet
- As an information processor
- As a regulated firm

The traditional business of banking is to fund loans (the primary use of funds) with deposits (the primary source of funds). **Core deposits, purchased funds,** and **equity capital** are banks' sources of funds. Bank income-expense statements have four key components:

- Net interest income (NII) = interest income minus interest expense
- Provision for loan losses (PLL)
- Net noninterest income ("burden") = noninterest income minus noninterest expense
- Taxes

Excluding taxes, the first three components highlight the risks of banking. Specifically, NII captures **interest-rate risk** and **liquidity risk,** PLL reflects **credit risk,** or loan quality, and "burden" combines the generation of fee or noninterest income and the control of operating or noninterest expenses. The risk-management aspect of the business of banking and the financial-management theme of this book involve managing and controlling these risks and operations.

This chapter also emphasized the importance of market value accounting (MVA), and compared it to book value accounting (BVA). In this framework, the federal safety net applied to commercial banks (and other insured depositories) was analyzed. It results in a **government guarantee,** *G,* that enters a bank's balance sheet as an unbooked intangible asset, that is, $A + G = L + K$. The offsetting entry, an unbooked liability on the deposit insurer's balance sheet, may cause a deposit insurer to go bankrupt if insurees are not closed before their economic net worths are exhausted. This notion helps explain the S&L mess and the banking problems of the 1980s and early 1990s.

List of Key Words, Concepts, and Acronyms

- Balance sheet (portfolio)
- Book value accounting (BVA)
- Burden (net noninterest income)
- Core deposits
- Credit risk
- Etymology (transactions and safekeeping functions)
- Federal Deposit Insurance Corporation (FDIC)
- Federal funds

- Federal Reserve System
- Federal safety net
- Funds (sources and uses)
- Government guarantee (*G*)
- Income-expense statement
- Information technology and processing
- Interest-rate risk
- Itemization principle
- Liquidity risk

- Managed liabilities (purchased funds)
- Market value accounting (MVA)
- Net income (profits)
- Net interest income (NII)
- Net interest margin (NIM)
- Net worth
- Return on assets (ROA)
- Risk management/control
- Transparency

Review Questions

1. Trace the functional role of banks beginning with ancient Rome and the etymology of the word bank and ending with the notion of a regulated financial-services firm operating as an information processor in the FSI.
2. Describe and discuss the importance of information technologies to banks and financial-services firms in general.
3. How do banks raise funds and how does this financing vary with bank size? Carefully define and distinguish between core deposits and managed liabilities.
4. What are a bank's major uses of funds?
5. Distinguish between a bank's provision for loan loss and its loan-loss reserve.
6. How do banks generate revenue and how does this generation vary with bank size?
7. What are the major expenses banks incur and how do they vary with bank size?
8. What are the major components of a bank's income-expense statement and how do they map into the major risks of banking? What can managers do to minimize, reduce, or transfer these risks?
9. What is "burden" and why is it important? How does it vary with bank size?
10. Briefly but carefully distinguish between the following pairs of terms:
    a. MVA versus BVA
    b. Itemization principles versus valuation principles
    c. Economic "values" versus accounting "numbers"
11. Explain the federal safety net and the government guarantees associated with it. How do these guarantees enter the balance sheets of the insurer and the insuree?

Problems

1. Complete the following bank balance sheet:

Reserves	?	Deposits	88
Securities	30	Net Worth	?
Loans	?		
Other	?		
Total	100		100

Assume that the bank keeps no excess reserves and that required reserves equal 5 percent of total deposits. The bank lends 55 percent of its total sources of funds.

2. If the bank in the previous question faces the following revenue and cost functions, find its net income, addition to retained earnings, ROA, and ROE. Reserves and other assets generate no income. Securities earn a return of 0.07 whereas loans earn 0.10. Deposits cost 0.06, PLL equals 0.01 of total loans, noninterest income equals 0.001 of total assets, and noninterest expense equals .002 of total deposits. The bank's tax rate is 0.25 and its dividend-payout rate is 0.40. The bank has no gains or losses from securities or other transactions. Show all the components of the bank's income-expense statement.

3. If the bank in the previous two questions experiences growth in earning assets and deposits of 10 percent, what will its balance sheet be at the end of this second period but before the second period's retained earnings are added? Assume that the first period had zero growth except for the addition to retained earnings found in problem 2. Assume that the second period's PLL equals net loan charge-offs and that the addition to retained earnings is stored as excess reserves.

4. Assume that a bank funds a $100,000 fixed-rate bond with $90,000 in deposits and $10,000 in equity. The bond has an annual coupon rate of 7.5 percent and matures in five years, and deposits currently cost 6 percent but reprice (mature) every year. Assume that immediately after the deposits are gathered and the bond purchased, all interest rates drop by 100 basis points. Comparable bond yields are now 6.5 percent and new deposits cost only 5 percent. Show the bank's financial statements on book and market value bases before and after the rate change.

5. Using the bond from the previous problem after the rate change, find its market value at the end of years 1, 2, 3, 4, and 5.

6. Assume that a bank manager faces a dilemma: Borrow federal funds at 5 percent per annum (nominal rate), or undertake a one-month repurchase agreement in which T-bills are sold at $1000 and repurchased at $1004. Compute effective annual rates and advise.

Selected References

Boczar, G. E., and Samuel H. Talley. [1978]. "Bank Holding Company Double Leverage." Washington, DC: Board of Governors of the Federal Reserve System.

Debussey, Fred W. [1978]. "Double Leverage in Bank Holding Companies." *Bankers Magazine* (March–April), pp. 86–90.

Eisenbeis, Robert A. [1983]. "Bank Holding Companies and Public Policy." In George J. Benston, ed., *Financial Services.* Englewood Cliffs, NJ: Prentice-Hall, pp. 127–155.

English, William B., and Brian K. Reid. [1993]. "Profits and Balance-Sheet Developments at U.S. Commercial Banks in 1993." *Federal Reserve Bulletin* (June), pp. 483–507.

Federal Reserve Bulletin (various issues). Washington, DC: Board of Governors of the Federal Reserve System.

Garcia, Beatrice E. [1990]. "Delaware Bill Opens Insurance to Banks." *The Wall Street Journal* (May 21), p. A5.

Graven, Kathryn. [1990]. "First Fidelity and EDS Set Software Accord." *The Wall Street Journal* (September 4), p. B4.

Kane, Edward J. [1989]. *The S&L Insurance Mess: How Did It Happen?* Washington, DC: The Urban Institute Press.

———. [1993]. "Measuring the Current Value and Periodic Performance of a Financial Institution." Lecture Notes for MF159, Nos. 93–11 and 93–12, Boston College.

———. [1994]. "Changing Information Technology and the Endless Re-Engineering of Banking and Banking Regulation." Working Paper, Boston College (May 10).

Kane, Edward J., and Min-eh Yu. [1994]. "How Much Did Capital Forbearance Add to the Tab for the FSLIC Mess?" Working Paper, Boston College.

Musumeci, James J., and Joseph F. Sinkey, Jr. [1990a]. "The International Debt Crisis and Bank Loan-Loss Reserve Decisions: The Signalling Content of Partially Anticipated Events." *Journal of Money, Credit, and Banking* (August), pp. 370–387.

———. [1990b]. "The International Debt Crisis, Investor Contagion, and Bank Security Returns in 1987: The Brazilian Experience." *Journal of Money, Credit, and Banking* (May), pp. 209–220.

Sinkey, Joseph F., Jr. [1979]. *Problem and Failed Institutions in the Commercial-Banking Industry.* Greenwich, CT: JAI Press.

Szego, Giorgio P. [1986]. "Bank Asset Management and Financial Insurance." *Journal of Banking and Finance* (June), pp. 295–307.

PART

II

THE BIG PICTURE: STRATEGIC AND FINANCIAL MANAGEMENT AND THE MEASUREMENT OF BANK PERFORMANCE

Where is the bank today? Where is it going? How is it going to get there? To see the big picture, top management and directors must address these questions, which capture the basic thrust of strategic planning and risk management. From a financial-management perspective, bank strategic planning, at either the business or corporate level, should focus on a single idea: managing value. This approach looks for *value added* in particular products, companies, and markets. Since value added is a symmetrical concept, managing value means looking for value destroyers as well as value creators. Conceptually, the difference between the two equals the bank's equity value. To maximize this value, managers need to maximize value creators and minimize value destroyers.

Let's consider how you, as a student, might apply this framework to your upcoming professional life. Where are you today? Where are you going? How are you going to get there? Why should a company want to hire you? Let's view these questions in terms of value added. What do you, as a would-be college graduate, perhaps without any meaningful work experience outside of summer jobs, have to offer? The bottom line is: You have to sell yourself! For example, you highlight your training (e.g., as a finance major), your strong work ethic (e.g., as reflected by your 3.0+ GPA and the fact that you learned time management and earned spending money by working 30 hours a week while carrying a full academic load), your enthusiasm, and your knowledge of the company from studying its financial reports, products, and strategic focus. And, most importantly, you emphasize your integrity and character—sell yourself as a good citizen! If you convey this kind of positive attitude, employers will recognize your potential to add value to the company and want to hire you.

Chapter 3 focuses on alternative ways of determining where the bank has been and where it is today in terms of *market valuation* and *accounting performance.* Accounting and economic models of value and performance provide frameworks for the analysis. Since the accounting model is easy to use, it presents a convenient way to attempt to answer difficult questions about a bank's value and its performance. To determine real or economic value, however, is a more relevant and more challenging task. It requires discounting a bank's future net cash flows at rates that reflect the riskiness of those cash flows. The economic model of the firm, as opposed to the accounting model, is the proper framework for analyzing financial decision making. The terms *cash flow, time,* and *risk* capture the important dimension of the discounted-cash-flow method for analyzing investment opportunities. Nevertheless, accounting data provide useful information for comparing bank performance over time and across peer groups or competitors. Pro forma or forecasted financial statements indicate where the bank is going.

Chapter 4 focuses on bank corporate strategy in the financial-services industry by emphasizing managing value and risk. The chapter highlights where the bank is going and how it is going to get there. Chapter 5 looks at the first stage of implementing a bank's strategic plan, bank asset-liability management (ALM) and bank risk-management systems. This chapter explains and illustrates the technique of ALM as the coordinated management of the bank's on- and off-balance-sheet items. Bank ALM can be viewed as the first step in moving the bank in its desired strategic direction. Chapter 5 also expands on the important innovation of *securitization,* which manages risk, assuming no recourse, by removing risk from the lender's balance sheet.

ACCOUNTING AND ECONOMIC MODELS OF BANK VALUE AND PERFORMANCE

Contents

LEARNING OBJECTIVES

- To understand modern finance in the real world
- To distinguish between accounting and economic models of bank valuation and performance
- To understand the notion of "hidden capital" in banks
- To understand bank financial statements and ratio analysis
- To understand bank return-on-equity decomposition analysis
- To understand variability of return as a measure of risk

CHAPTER THEME

How do you value a bank? How do you measure a bank's safety and its financial performance? The consolidation, restructuring, and failures in banking have increased interest in and the importance of these basic questions. Bank consolidation means mergers and acquisitions, which means that both buyers and sellers, if they are to maximize their shareholders' values, must know how to value banks. Bank restructurings, which have taken the form of dividend cuts, various charges against earnings (especially for bad loans), and reductions in employees ("downsizing"), have made bank shareholders, managers, and employees nervous about their investments and their jobs. Numerous bank failures resulted in a crisis in deposit insurance during the 1980s and early 1990s, which heightened the concerns of bank depositors and other creditors about bank safety and confidence in the banking system.

    This chapter focuses on answering basic questions about bank valuation, safety, and performance. To put the fundamental concepts of financial management in perspective, we begin with a look at modern finance in the real world and then contrast and compare the accounting and economic models of the firm. Next, the chapter focuses on accounting and market measures of value and performance in banking. The return-on-equity (ROE) model and its decomposition analysis provide an accounting framework for measuring bank performance and explaining ratio analysis. Because thousands of community banks in the United States lack market data, the ROE accounting model provides a comprehensive framework for evaluating the performance of these banks. In contrast, only several hundred bank holding companies (BHCs) have actively traded debt and equity for which market data are available. For these banking firms, both market and accounting measures of bank performance are relevant. Return on assets (ROA) and its variability, as captured by the standard deviation of ROA(σ), provide the best accounting measures of a bank's return and overall riskiness. These two factors and a bank's capital ratio (CAP) can be combined to generate a risk index (RI) such that $RI = [E(ROA) + CAP]/\sigma$, where $E(ROA)$ = expected ROA. This risk index is appealing because it includes ROA (the most widely accepted accounting measure of overall bank performance), the variability of ROA (a standard measure of risk in financial economics), and book capital adequacy (an industry standard for bank safety and soundness).

KEY CONCEPTS, IDEAS, AND TERMS

- Accounting model of the firm
  $(P_0 = EPS \times P/E)$
- Asset utilization (AU)
- Bank valuation
- Constant-growth model
  $(P_0 = D_1/[r - g])$
- Discounted cash flow (DCF)
- Earnings per share (EPS)
- Economic model of the firm
- Equity multiplier (EM)
- Hidden capital
- Loan-loss reserve (LLR)
- Market-to-book ratio
- Market value
- Price-earnings ratio (P/E)
- Profit margin (PM)
- Provision for loan loss (PLL)
- Return on assets $(ROA = PM \times AU)$
- Return on equity
  $(ROE = ROA \times EM)$
- Risk index (RI)
- ROE decomposition analysis
- Standard deviation (of ROA)
- Statistical market value accounting model (SMVAM)

INTRODUCTION

Newsweek has an engaging column called "Conventional Wisdom Watch." In its issue of November 19, 1990 (p. 6), the focus of the watch was "banking stability," which brought the esoteric topic of **bank valuation** to the man and woman on the street. The magazine prefaced its up-and-down arrows with the following words:

> Scrutinized by regulators trying to avoid another S&L disaster, ailing banks have shut off the loan tap. Now smart billionaires are trying to buy them cheap.

On November 19, 1990, *Newsweek* saw the conventional wisdom (CW) in U.S. banking as follows:[1]

Banks		Conventional Wisdom
Citicorp	▼	Suckered by Trump and joins Manny Hanny, Chase in Layoff City
Continental	▲	Old CW: First of the big failures. New CW: First of the big cheap stock buys.
New England	▼	Whatever happened to Yankee prudence? Reams of bad paper.
J. P. Morgan	▲	By invitation only. Old money; it skipped the 1980s.
Wells Fargo	▲	Stock undervalued, so take a tip from Buffet and buy, buy, buy.
FDIC	▼	Everyone knows it doesn't have the cash to cover a depression.

---

[1] Manny Hanny refers to Manufacturers Hanover Bank, which has since been acquired by Chase Manhattan Bank ("Chase"). Continental was acquired by BankAmerica, and Bank of New England failed. Citicorp, J.P. Morgan, and Wells Fargo are thriving as of this writing.

Approaching the twenty-first century, the market's valuations (May 1997) of these banks, compared to their values near year-end 1990, were as follows: Citicorp's stock price had increased almost twelvefold to $117 per share as "layoff city" has been profitable; Continental Bank was acquired by BankAmerica in 1994; Bank of New England was declared insolvent on January 6, 1991, and taken over by Fleet/Norstar on April 23, 1991 (in between, the FDIC arranged for the company to be operated as a "bridge bank"); J. P. Morgan has remained the steady flagship bank it has always been; and Wells Fargo apparently was undervalued, because its stock price has since jumped more than fivefold to $275 per share.

Regarding the FDIC, everyone knew then, and still knows today, that it does not have the insurance reserves to cover depression-type bank failures. No insurance company, public or private, can cover the catastrophic losses associated with such failures. It is the job of macroeconomic (monetary and fiscal) policies to prevent a severe economic collapse. Thanks mainly to lower interest rates, but with some minor accolades to variable-rate deposit-insurance premiums and better enforcement of problem-bank situations, the FDIC has moved from insolvency (a $7 billion insurance fund deficit at year-end 1991) to viability (a $25.8 billion fund balance at midyear 1996).

This chapter goes beyond conventional wisdom to highlight **accounting and economic models** of bank valuation and performance.[2]

MODERN FINANCE IN THE REAL WORLD

The essence of corporate finance is the acquisition of assets and the funding of those assets. Commercial bankers as *lenders* and providers of *risk-management services* need to know something about how client managers select investment opportunities and how they finance those opportunities. By knowing more about how borrowers conduct the *financial management* of their businesses, lenders are better able to assess their own risk exposure and better able to determine the products and services their client firms need (e.g., cash-management services, lines of credit, derivatives products, etc.). This knowledge permits banks to conduct the financial management of their own businesses more effectively.

When bankers make loans, they make "incomplete transactions." Specifically, until the loans are repaid, the bankers' job is not done—the transaction is incomplete. While loans are outstanding, domestic lenders face *credit, liquidity,* and *prepayment risks,* and depending on how the loan is priced, possible *interest-rate risk.* International or cross-border lenders incur additional perils in the form of *sovereign* or *country risk* and *foreign-exchange risk.* The uncertainties associated with these risks drive the variability of bank returns and play critical roles in determining bank market values.

Joel Stern, a leading financial consultant with a belief in the fundamental tenets of modern finance, has this to say about the acceptance of modern finance across the boardrooms of corporate America: "The majority of our corporate directors and senior executives remain blissfully ignorant of, if not actively hostile toward, the central tenets of modern finance."[3] According to Stern, this ignorance is best

---

[2] Chapter 2 established some basic differences between market value accounting (MVA) and book value accounting (BVA).

reflected in the adherence by corporate America to the **"accounting model of the firm,"** which says that stock prices are determined primarily by reported earnings, in particular, **earnings per share** (EPS). In its most simplistic form (as a strawman), this approach relates value to a multiple of the firm's EPS:

$$\text{Stock price} = \text{earnings per share} \times \text{price-earnings ratio}$$

or,

$$P = EPS \times P/E \tag{3-1}$$

where P represents the current stock price, EPS the firm's earnings per share, and P/E the industry **price-earnings ratio.** Given the firm's EPS, the accounting model says that industry-wide P/E ratios determine stock prices. For example, a firm with an EPS of $5 in an industry with a P/E multiple of 10 would sell for $50. To maximize stock price, managers need only to maximize EPS. The way some managers, stock analysts, and investors concentrate on a company's short-term earnings prospects suggests that Stern's claim has some validity.

THE ECONOMIC MODEL OF THE FIRM AND DISCOUNTED CASH FLOW

If the accounting model doesn't determine real value, then what does? In modern finance, **discounted cash flow (DCF)** determines economic, real, or **market value.** Stern refers to this alternative to the accounting model as the **economic model of the firm.** According to this view of valuation, the market value of a company's common stock (similar to the value of any other security or project that generates an earnings or cash-flow stream) is equal to the present value (PV) of its expected future cash flow (CF) discounted at interest rates (r) reflecting investors' required rates of return for investments of comparable risk. In symbols,

$$PV = CF_1/(1 + r) + CF_2/(1 + r)^2 + \cdots + CF_n/(1 + r)^n \tag{3-2}$$

When will the accounting model and the economic model give the same estimate of value? At least two conditions are required:

1. The firm's reported or accounting earnings would have to equal its cash flow
2. The firm would have to be a typical or average one in the industry such that the industry-wide P/E ratio adequately captured its riskiness

These two conditions highlight the fundamental determinants of value: (1) risk and (2) return on investment (i.e., cash flow). Holding all other things constant, as cash flow (return) increases, value increases; as risk increases, value decreases. Because it is difficult to increase return without taking on additional risk, risk-return trade-off dominates financial decision making.

Even without managers' overt attempts to manipulate their reported earnings, the chances that reported earnings will equal cash flow are remote. Regarding risk, the accounting model implies that one risk fits all. Just as one size fits all seldom works in selecting clothing (the baggy look notwithstanding), it seldom

---

[3] *Six Roundtable Discussions of Corporate Finance with Joel Stern* (edited by Donald H. Chew, Jr.). Westport, CT: Quorum Books, 1986, p. 2. This section and the next three draw on these roundtable discussions.

works in evaluating risk. Each firm, in effect, has a unique P/E ratio tailored to the riskiness of its **cash flows.** Thus, only when the firm's cash flows are of average risk would the application of the industry-wide P/E be appropriate for capturing its riskiness. On balance, careful analysts don't buy valuations from the one-risk-fits-all rack.

A COMPROMISE MODEL BASED ON REAL EARNINGS AND AN ADJUSTED P/E RATIO

Suppose that a firm's accounting earnings were equal to its real earnings (or that accounting earnings were marked up or down to reflect real earnings) and that an adjustment was made to the industry P/E ratio to reflect the firm's unique risk profile. In this case, we would have a better estimate of the firm's value as captured by

$$P = EPS* \times P/E \times K \qquad (3\text{-}3)$$

where the new terms are $EPS*$ = current economic or real earnings and K ($K > 0$) is an adjustment factor that marks the industry P/E ratio either up or down to reflect the firm's unique risk profile.[4] For example, consider the firm described earlier with a price per share equal to $50 = 5×10. Suppose that this firm's economic earnings per share are only $4 and that its $K = 0.9$; then its value per share becomes $4 \times 10 \times 0.9 = 36. The lower real earnings and greater risk result in a lower valuation of the firm. In contrast, suppose the firm has real earnings of $6 per share and that its $K = 1.5$; then its value per share equals $6 \times 10 \times 1.5 = 90. Higher real earnings and greater safety (lower risk) make this firm more valuable. Finally, suppose that real earnings equal $7 per share and $K = .714$; then the price per share would be almost $50 ($7 \times 10 \times .714 = 49.98). The higher earnings and greater risk illustrate the risk-return trade-off.

This compromise valuation model, although an improvement over the pure accounting model of the firm, falls short of rivaling the economic model on two counts:

1. It fails to value real earnings over the *life* of the firm. Think of it still as a snapshot, rather than a movie.

2. Although it makes some adjustment for risk, the process is incomplete because it does not discount cash flows at the appropriate required rate of return.

THE ECONOMIC MODEL, MARKET EFFICIENCY, AND "LEAD STEERS"

The cattle drive was an obligatory part of the Western movies of yesterday. Once the director made this commitment, the stampede scene was a must. The stampede usually was started by the bad guys, or by an approaching thunderstorm. To regain control of the herd, the good guys had to head off the lead steers, which they always did just before the thundering herd approached the cliff. Great drama for

---

[4] The use of an adjusted P/E ratio or "K-factor" is a component of the valuation process used in *The Stanford Bank Game* (Parker and Beals [1996]). Specifically, the approximate valuation model is bank stock price equals the bank's "smoothed" EPS times the industry P/E ratio times the bank's unique K-factor, where K is an average of 12 components designed to capture such bank characteristics as liquidity, interest-rate risk (GAP), capital adequacy, credit risk, dividend policy, etc.

a ten-year-old in 1954. The good guys succeeded because they reached the lead steers and because it was in the script.

In writing his finance script, Joel Stern has introduced the notion of "**lead steers**" as an important determinant of economic value, and as an important concept for understanding **market efficiency.** In Stern's parlance, "lead steers" are sophisticated investors who dominate financial markets. They have achieved this dominance because they have seen the "finance light" and are thereby able to distinguish between accounting illusion and economic reality in setting stock prices. As a result, they reward "value-maximizing behavior" by buying the stocks of companies whose managers read and practice the finance gospel, and by selling the stocks of the accounting-model heathens. By focusing on economic value, the lead steers ensure that companies' securities (whether debt or equity) are properly priced. In effect, lead steers do not select their risk evaluations from the one-risk-fits-all rack. They attempt to estimate future cash flows and discount those flows at interest rates reflecting the timing and riskiness of the future flows. They in effect engage in what the "street" calls **fundamental analysis**—they attempt to value companies by analyzing their fundamentals. These fundamentalists can be contrasted to chartists or technicians, who attempt to predict future stock prices by analyzing the movements and patterns of historical stock prices.

To summarize, the three essential ingredients of valuation for fundamentalists are *cash flow* ("money"), *time,* and *risk.* Bigger and safer cash flows received sooner are more valuable than smaller and riskier cash flows received later. Lead steers recognize the importance of these factors and act accordingly. In the marketplace, the lead steers are large institutional investors such as pension funds, mutual funds, insurance companies, securities firms, and the trust departments of large commercial banks.[5]

MARKET MEASURES OF VALUE AND RETURN AND THE MARKET VALUE OF EQUITY[6]

Suppose that as an investor you bought 100 shares of a major bank holding company (BHC) at the beginning of 1992 at a price of $10 per share and that you sold the shares two years later at $40 per share. Because the company was engaged in corporate restructuring and was under regulatory pressure to improve its capital adequacy, it did not pay any common-stock dividends over your two-year holding period. Thus, your investment return consisted entirely of capital gains. Your compound annual rate of return, r, can be found by solving the following present-value (PV) equation for r:

$$PV = FV/(1 + r)^2 = \$10 = \$40/(1 + r)^2$$

where $PV = \$10$ (your investment), future value (FV) = $40 (your selling price), and the exponent ^{2} reflects your two-year holding period. You shouldn't need a handheld calculator to see that $r = 1.00$, or 100 percent per year, because $10 = 40/(1 + r)^2 \rightarrow (1 + r)^2 = 40/10 = 4$. Taking the square root of both sides, $1 + r = 2$,

---

[5] Potential advantages of institutional ownership include (1) improved liquidity, (2) reduced volatility of stock prices, and (3) reduced likelihood of takeover.

[6] The data in this section roughly reflect Citicorp's accounting and market performance for the two-year period January 1, 1992, to December 31, 1993. By the end of 1996, Citicorp was trading in the low 90s and paying a dividend of $1.80 per share; as of August 25, 1997, its 52-week high was 141.5.

and therefore $r = 1$, or 100 percent. Needless to say, you earned a handsome rate of return. Your net total dollar return *before* taxes and transactions costs is $4,000 − $1,000 = $3,000, where $4,000 = 100 × $40 and $1,000 = 100 × $10. Of course, if this was your only investment, you were not diversified.

How risky was this investment? In terms of earnings volatility, the firm's accounting earnings had been unstable, with losses reported in 1987 and 1989. More relevant, however, were future earnings prospects, which in 1991 suggested higher and less volatile earnings. With an equity beta greater than 1.0 (see Box 3-1 for a review of beta), if the stock market rose, the investment would "beat" the market. In terms of firm-specific risk, insolvency risk was minimal, because, as the largest BHC in the United States at the time and a major player in world financial markets, this firm would not have its too-big-to-fail safety net pulled out from under it. Investments with a taxpayer subsidy are a relatively safe bet, all other things being equal.[7] Any firm's total market value of shareholders' equity equals its market price per share times the number of shares issued or outstanding. With approximately 372 million shares of common stock outstanding at year-end 1991, and 412 million shares at year-end 1993, the company's total market value of equity rose from $3.72 billion to $16.48 billion, an increase of $12.76 billion.

BOX 3-1

PRICING CAPITAL ASSETS AND BETA

Capital asset pricing theory provides a method for determining asset prices based on the asset's contribution to portfolio risk. The main idea underlying this framework, one version of which is known as the capital asset pricing model (CAPM), is the distinction between diversifiable and nondiversifiable risk. The former, also called unique, specific, residual, or unsystematic risk, can be diversified away; the latter, also known as market or systematic risk, cannot be eliminated. The CAPM measures systematic risk using β (beta), which can be viewed as an index of risk. Beta is defined statistically as follows:

$$\beta_j = Cov(j, m)/Var(m) = \rho_{j,m}\sigma_j\sigma_m/\sigma_m\sigma_m$$

where $Cov(j, m)$ is the covariance between the return on the jth asset or security and the return on the market portfolio, and $Var(m)$ is the variance of the return on the market portfolio. The covariance term equals the product of the correlation coefficient and the respective standard deviations, that is, $\rho_{j,m}\sigma_j\sigma_m$. The variance of the return on the market portfolio is the square of the standard deviation or $\sigma_m\sigma_m$.

According to the CAPM, the expected risk premium on a risky investment is

$$r - r_f = \beta(r_M - r_f)$$

where r_f is the risk-free rate. Expressed in terms of the required rate of return, the CAPM says the following:

$$r = r_f + \beta(r_M - r_f)$$

In words, the required return equals the risk-free rate plus the risk premium, which equals beta times the market risk premium. For investments that are more volatile than the market portfolio, $\beta > 1$, and the investments are called "aggressive." In contrast, for investments that are less volatile than the market, $\beta < 1$, and the investments are called "defensive." If an investment's return moves exactly with the market and the return has the same variability as the market's return, then $\beta = 1$. The common stocks of major domestic BHCs tend to have betas that are close to 1.0, with the multinational BHCs having betas slightly greater than 1.0, and smaller regional BHCs having betas less than 1.0.

---

[7] Bank failures such as USNB of San Diego (1973), Franklin National of New York (1974), Continental Illinois of Chicago (1984), and Bank of New England (1991) provide counterexamples showing that investments in bank stock are not always relatively safe bets.

During 1992 and 1993, this company, which you owned a small portion of, earned accounting after-tax profits or net income of $722 million and $2,219 million, respectively. With stockholders' equity (book value) of $8,358 (1992) and $10,459 (1993), the BHC's accounting ROE, defined as net income/total shareholders' common equity, was $722/$8,358, or 8.6 percent for 1992 and $2,219/$10,459, or 21.2 percent in 1993. A firm's total shareholders' common equity consists of three parts (data in millions for the BHC):

Component of Common Equity	1993	1992
Common stock	$412	$392
Surplus	3,898	3,598
Retained earnings	6,149	4,368
Total	$10,459	$8,358

Dividing by the number of shares outstanding, we get the BHC's book values per share of $21.32 (1992) and $25.39 (1993). At the time you bought the common stock (year-end 1991), the book value per share was $7,738/372 = $20.80.

The Market-to-Book Ratio

Although high ($40) or low ($10) stock prices have little meaning in themselves, putting the adage "buy low, sell high" into practice will make you financially secure and qualified for early retirement. To judge value or performance, however, we need a benchmark. One such standard for common stocks is the ratio of a firm's *market value per share* to its *book value per share,* commonly referred to as the **market-to-book ratio.**[8] Using information from the previous example, we see that the BHC's market-to-book ratios for year-end 1991 and 1993 were $10/$20.8 = 0.48 and $40/$25.4 = 1.6. The ratio of 0.48 means that the BHC, according to the dollar votes of the stock market, was worth 52 percent less than past and present shareholders had put into it. Two years later, when the ratio was 1.6, the company was worth 60 percent more than past and present shareholders had put into it. A more cynical way of looking at this is the following: At a market-to-book ratio of 0.48, management will turn an investor's dollar into 48 cents; at a ratio of 1.6, it turns $1 into $1.60.

To summarize, a market-to-book ratio greater than 1.0 implies that the firm is creating value, whereas a ratio less than 1.0 suggests the firm is destroying value. Alternatively, investing $1 in a firm with a market-to-book ratio less than 1.0 generates less than $1 in market value, whereas investing in a firm with a market-to-book ratio greater than 1.0 creates more than $1 in market value.

The Price-Earnings Ratio

The price-earnings ratio measure equals the ratio of *market price per share* to *earnings per share* (EPS), commonly referred to as the price-earnings or P/E ratio. It is meaningful only for firms with $EPS > 0$; otherwise it is undefined. An important

---

[8] The market-to-book ratio, sometimes referred to as the *q* ratio, should not be confused with *Tobin's q,* which measures the total market value of a firm's assets (debt plus equity) relative to the estimated replacement cost of its assets.

caveat is that as $EPS \rightarrow$ zero, the P/E ratio $\rightarrow$ infinity. If we exclude firms with very low EPS, the higher a firm's P/E ratio is, the more highly its earnings are valued by investors. If we focus on our BHC, its P/E ratio for 1991 was undefined, because the firm had negative accounting earnings. For 1993, the BHC had an EPS of $4.11 and a P/E ratio of $40/4.11 = 9.7$.

The **constant-growth model** provides valuable insight for interpreting P/E ratios. This simple model says that the present value (P_0) of a share of common stock equals the expected (constant) dividend, D_1, divided by the difference between investors' required rate of return, r, and the expected rate of dividend growth, g. For $r > g$, the constant-growth model is as follows:

$$P_0 = D_1/(r - g) = D_0(1 + g)/(r - g) \qquad \textbf{(3-4)}$$

If we divide this equation by expected earnings per share for the next period, EPS_1, this generates the basic determinants of a firm's P/E ratio:

$$P_0/EPS_1 = [D_1/EPS_1] \times [1/(r - g)]$$

The first term on the right-hand side of this equation is the firm's expected **dividend-payout ratio** (DPS/EPS). All other things being equal, the higher the payout ratio is, the more valuable the firm is. In addition, the higher the expected growth rate is, the more valuable the firm is. In contrast, the riskier the firm is, as captured by a higher required rate of return, the less valuable the firm is. Of course, because in the real world all other things are *not* held constant, the determinants of value depend on the interaction of expected dividend payout, risk, growth, and other factors not captured by the simple constant-growth model.

Dividend Yield

A stock's dividend yield is its expected dividend divided by its current stock price, or D_1/P_0. During 1990, two years prior to its corporate restructuring, our sample BHC (Citicorp) paid an annual cash dividend on its common stock of $1.74. Using its year-end 1990 stock price of $12.625, we find that its dividend yield was an unsustainably high 13.8 percent ($= 1.74/12.625$). During 1991, the annual dividend was only $0.75 per share, and the stock closed the year at $10.375, for a dividend yield of 7.2 percent ($= .75/10.375$), again a payout rate the company could not sustain. During 1992 and 1993, the BHC did not pay any common stock dividends. Although the moral-suasion weights are unknown, both managerial discretion and regulatory coercion led the firm to eliminate its dividend. In 1994, with regulatory permission, the dividend was reinstated at 15 cents per share per quarter paid June 17, 1994. On January 17, 1995, the dividend was raised to 30 cents per quarter ($1.20 per share annually), resulting in an annual yield of 2.9 percent ($= 1.20/40.75$).[9] By year-end 1996, with its stock price around $90 per share and an annual dividend of $1.80, Citicorp's dividend yield had dropped to 2 percent, a yield comparable to those of its major competitors, for example, BankAmerica (2.5%) and Chase Manhattan (2.7%).

In general, a trade-off exists between the potential for a high dividend yield and the potential for price appreciation in a stock. When a company experiences financial difficulties, it may have to cut or eliminate its dividend. For example, Citi-

---

[9] Citicorp's dividend increase, announced on January 17, 1995, made its dividend yield more competitive with the returns of other major BHCs in the United States. On January 18, 1995, other major BHCs headquartered in New York City had dividend yields of 4.67 percent ($= 1.6/34.25$, Chase Manhattan), 4.65 percent ($= 1.76/37.875$, Chemical Banking, acquired by Chase in 1996), and 5.03 percent ($= 3.00/59.625$, J. P. Morgan). Outside NYC, BankAmerica had a dividend yield of 3.84 percent ($= 1.60/41.625$).

corp's annual dividend went from \$1.74 (1990) to \$.75 (1991) to \$.00 (1992 and 1993). As it restructured and reduced its financial problems, however, its stock price appreciated from \$10 per share to \$40 per share, and then to \$90 per share (1996). In 1994, it reinstated its dividend at a low level and then made it more competitive at \$1.20 (per share per annum) in 1995 and \$1.80 in 1996.

Returning to the simple constant-growth model (equation 3-4) provides insight regarding a company's dividend yield and valuation. Assuming a firm with a steady expected growth in dividends and assuming $r > g$, the model can be rearranged as follows:

$$\text{Dividend yield} = D_1/P_0 = r - g$$

Because the yield depends on the difference between r and g, the yield may be high because investors expect r to be high (a high-risk stock) or because g is low (a low-growth stock) or both. During its period of financial distress, Citicorp had an abnormally high dividend yield because it was a risky firm with limited near-term growth options. As it restructured and grew, this situation reversed itself.

HIDDEN CAPITAL AND THE RELATIONSHIP BETWEEN MARKET AND BOOK VALUE OF EQUITY

When accounting net worth—**book value**—and economic net worth (market value) diverge, "hidden" or unbooked capital exists (Kane and Unal [1990]). Hidden capital has two sources:

1. Differences between the market values (MV) and book values (BV) of *on-balance-sheet items*

2. Neglect of *off-balance-sheet items* that **generally accepted accounting principles** (GAAP) do not permit to be formally booked

Under a system of perfect market value accounting with formal booking and precise estimates of off-balance-sheet items and exact estimates of on-balance-sheet items, practices absent from GAAP, hidden capital would not exist.

Kane and Unal [1990] have developed a clever way of estimating a firm's hidden capital, which they call the **statistical market value accounting model,** or SMVAM. In its simplest form, SMVAM relates the market value of a bank's (or any firm's) equity (MVE) to its book value of equity (BVE) as follows:

$$MVE = a + b(BVE) + e \qquad \textbf{(3-5)}$$

where a and b are estimated regression coefficients and e represents an approximation error or random-disturbance term. Equation (3-5) can be estimated over time or cross-sectionally. Mechanically, it is easy to see that if $a = 0$ and $b = 1$, then market and book values of equity or net worth do not diverge, except for random disturbances that, on average, are expected to be zero.

Figure 3-1 provides some pictures to assist you in understanding hidden capital and SMVAM. Panel A shows the relationship between market value and book value when $a = 0$ and $b = 1$. It's the familiar one-to-one relationship captured by a 45-degree line out of the origin. This picture says that (1) when book value of equity is zero, market value of equity is zero; (2) for each dollar increase in book value of equity, market value of equity increases by one dollar. Panel B shows actual estimated relationships for 1987 and 1988 for a sample of large bank holding

Panel A. Intercept equals zero, and slope equals one [*a* = 0, *b* = 1]

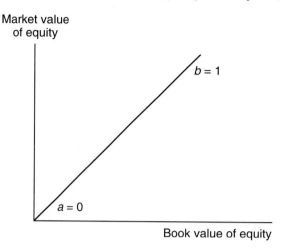

Panel B. Estimated relationships for 1987 and 1988 for 128 BHCs

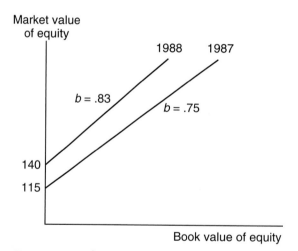

Source: Kane and Unal [1990] developed SMVAM.

FIGURE 3-1 The Relationship between Market Value and Book Value of Equity Using the Statistical Market Value Accounting Model (SMVAM)

companies (BHCs). In 1987, if book value was zero, then the average sample BHC had a total market value of equity of $115 million; and if book value of equity increased by one dollar, then the average BHC's market value of equity increased by only 75 cents. To interpret the results for 1988, simply substitute $140 million for $115 million and 83 cents for 75 cents.

Getting the Economic Message of SMVAM

Going beyond the statistics and pictures of SMVAM, the economic interpretation of hidden capital is the important message. Consider the intercept first. Suppose that a bank is book-value insolvent ($A - L < 0$) but still trading in the marketplace at a positive market value. Since it's dead but still living, let's call it a *zombie institution.* As an exercise draw an SMVAM diagram for a zombie. The only requirement is that $a > 0$, that is, there is positive unbooked net asset value. The federal safety net (chapter 1) is a strong candidate for such a source of hidden capital for a zombie. For 1987 and 1988, Panel B of Figure 3-1 reveals a positive intercept ($a > 0$), suggesting that positive effects from hidden capital were supporting bank market values (e.g., from the unbooked government guarantees behind the federal safety net of FDIC insurance and the Fed's discount window). The change in the intercept ($25 = 140 - 115$) from 1987 to 1988 suggests a further increase in unbooked capital as a source of bank capital. When the intercept is negative ($a < 0$), then unbooked assets and liabilities serve as a net drain on bank capital.[10]

When the slope coefficient of SMVAM equals one ($b = 1$) and the intercept is constant, changes in accounting values of booked assets and liabilities are perfect (or unbiased) estimates of changes in market values of those items. If the estimated intercept is greater than one ($a > 0$) when $b = 1$, then a premium exists because a one-dollar change in the book value of equity results in more than a one-dollar change in the market value of equity. In contrast, if $a < 0$ and $b = 1$, then a discount exists because a one-dollar change in the book value of equity results in less than a one-dollar change in the market value of equity. The discount is due to negative hidden capital.

What about situations in which $a = 0$, but $b \neq 1$? When the estimated slope coefficient is less than one, a one-dollar change in book value results in a less than a one-dollar change in market value. The discount suggests accounting overvaluation of changes in booked assets and booked liabilities relative to market valuations. From 1987 to 1988, although the estimated slope coefficient moved closer to one from 0.75 to 0.83, it still was significantly different from one.[11] When $b > 1$, a premium exists because a one-dollar change in book value results in more than a one-dollar change in market value. The premium can be interpreted as a reward for the present value of future growth opportunities not captured by assets in place. Only when $b = 1$ will changes in booked accounting values be fully reflected in changes in market values of equity.

Hidden Capital and SMVAM Recapitulation

If the book value of bank's capital was a perfect or an unbiased estimate of its market value of equity, then **hidden capital** would not exist. The statistical test for this condition is that $a = 0$ and $b = 1$, called a joint hypothesis. In this case, the equation $MVE = a + b(BVE)$, called the Statistical Market Value Accounting Model, or SMVAM, is a straight line out of the origin ($a = 0$) with a slope of 45 degrees ($b = 1$). When one or both of these conditions are not met, book value estimates of a bank's market value of equity capital are *biased* estimates. An intercept bias can be traced to the neglect of off-balance-sheet items by GAAP. The existence of a slope bias results in either a premium (when $b > 1$) or a discount (when $b < 1$) from the book value of bank equity. A slope bias can be traced to misvaluation of the items on a bank's balance sheet (e.g., loan portfolio). Another important lesson from SMVAM is that the existence of government guarantees permits book-value insolvent or zombie financial institutions to still have positive market values.

---

[10]For the 25 largest BHCs from 1975 to 1981, Kane and Unal [1990] found negative intercepts based on their estimates.

[11]The *t*-statistic of 6.3 is significant at the 5 percent level or better.

READING BANK FINANCIAL STATEMENTS AND RATIO ANALYSIS

Shortly after the failure of Franklin National Bank of New York in 1974, Harry Keefe, a well-known analyst of bank stocks, remarked: "People who can read a balance sheet were out of there long ago." For a person who founded a firm that analyzes bank stocks, the statement was a judicious one to make because you want to convince your customers and would-be clients that your firm really does know how to analyze bank financial statements. Being able to read bank financial statements also is important to bank owners, directors, managers, uninsured creditors, regulators, and deposit insurers.

Reading financial statements can be viewed as a form of fundamental analysis. An important part of this reading is the construction of ratios and analyzing them over time (trend analysis) or against competitors (peer-group or cross-sectional analysis). This kind of investigation is known as ratio analysis. Four general categories of ratios are derived from financial statements:

- Profitability
- Liquidity
- Leverage
- Activity (also described as turnover or efficiency)

For banks, leverage is described as "capital adequacy," and an important fifth category, loan quality, must be analyzed. The latter is captured by such ratios as those of nonperforming loans to total loans, loan-loss reserves to total loans, and loan-loss provisions to total revenue.

Analyzing Financial Statements: Approaches and Caveats

Although numerous approaches exist for analyzing bank financial statements, this chapter focuses on a traditional method known in corporate finance as the "du Pont model." The technique is described here as **return-on-equity decomposition analysis.** The first stage of the analysis links accounting **return on equity** (ROE) with **return on assets** (ROA) and the **equity multiplier** (EM = Assets/Equity) through the following identity:

$$ROE = ROA \times EM \qquad (3\text{-}6)$$

Since the components of the model are ratios, one must not overlook the component parts. For example, just as a P/E ratio may be high because a bank has very low EPS, accounting ROE can be high because a bank has very little equity. Thus, a ratio is simply a convenient way of collapsing two pieces of information into one. In the process, no new information is gained, and existing information may be obscured unless there is careful analysis.

Ratios by themselves have limited information content. We need a standard or norm against which to judge them. Accordingly, in evaluating financial statements, either for banks or their clients, we analyze trends in performance and make comparisons with similar firms over time. To the extent that ratio analysis uses only current and historical accounting data, it is not forward looking. Through the use of forecasted financial statements, however, the technique can be made forward looking, called *pro forma* analysis. In addition, ratios frequently are used with various statistical methods to attempt to predict corporate bankruptcy, for commercial loan surveillance, and as early-warning systems for distressed financial institutions.[12]

Although bank accounting values do not fully and completely reflect market values, analysis of bank financial statements is an important part of measuring bank performance for several reasons. First, accounting models of valuation and performance are easy to use and popular. Second, because 7000 or so banks in the United States do not have actively traded shares of equity, keeping score on the basis of accounting data, although it's second best, is the only game in town. To not be fooled by accounting data, however, it is necessary to attempt to adjust bank asset values and earnings for risk, especially for credit and interest-rate risks. Estimates of loan quality derived from on-site bank examinations reflect regulators' attempts to measure banks' credit risk. Examiners classify loans and other assets into five risk categories: safe or nonadversely classified, special mention, substandard, doubtful, and loss. Risk-based capital requirements also attempt to adjust for bank risk, but they do not go far enough because they fail to fully capture interest-rate risk.

Focusing on the accounting model of valuation (*EPS* $\times$ *P/E*) encourages managers to attempt to manipulate accounting earnings. There are three ways of doing this:

1. Changing accounting methods
2. Manipulating managers' estimates of costs
3. Shifting the period when expenses and revenues are included in results

Judgment plays an important role in the third technique. Moreover, banking and property-and-casualty (P&C) insurance are two industries where the opportunity for judgment in accounting matters can have a major effect on earnings. For example, banks must make a provision to cover expected loan losses, and P&C insurers must establish reserves to cover expected claims on current policies. Prior to the 1986 Tax Reform Act, large banks (assets over $500 million) could deduct provisions for loan losses from profits in the year they were added to reserves, rather than in the year loans were charged off.[13] Under the 1986 tax law, large commercial banks are permitted to deduct loan losses only when the loans become partially or wholly worthless. Regardless of the tax treatment, bank managers must make a judgment on the probability of loans being repaid. In addition to earnings manipulation, bank accounting data also are subject to window dressing (e.g., with respect to end-of-period liquidity positions through federal funds and securities transactions).

OVERALL BANK PERFORMANCE: A RISK-RETURN FRAMEWORK

Figure 3-2 depicts a risk-return framework for conceptualizing overall bank performance. Return on equity (ROE) and its variability are the key elements of the approach. The decomposition of the two elements provides insights regarding bank risks and returns. On the return side, ROE splits into **return on assets** (ROA) and

---

[12]Altman, Avery, Eisenbeis, and Sinkey [1981] provide examples of applications of classification techniques in business, banking, and finance.

[13]Greenawalt and Sinkey [1988] and Scheiner [1981] present evidence regarding bank accounting choices and income smoothing.

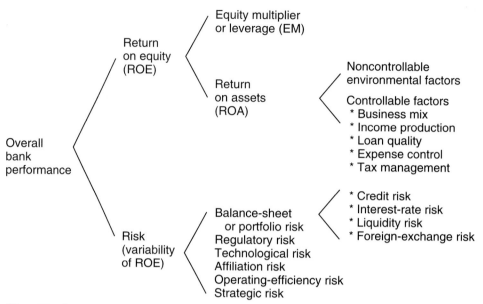

(Note: The first four controllable factors are those suggested by Gillis, Lumry, and Oswald [1980], pp. 70-71.)

FIGURE 3-2 **A Risk-Return View of Overall Bank Performance**

the **equity multiplier** (EM). Controllable and noncontrollable factors determine ROA. Think about the supply-and-demand conditions banks face in their geographic and product markets as noncontrollable elements. Factors that banks have some degree of control over include business mix, income production, loan quality, expense control, and tax management.

The risk component of Figure 3-2 highlights the six generic risks banks/BHCs face:

1. Portfolio or balance-sheet risk, including the risk of off-balance-sheet activities (OBSAs)
2. Regulatory risk
3. Technological risk
4. Affiliation risk
5. Operating-efficiency risk
6. Strategic risks (i.e., issues of market strategy and corporate control)

Portfolio and operating risks have the most direct effect on the variability of earnings. The key portfolio risks of banking are credit risk, interest-rate risk, liquidity risk, and foreign-exchange risk. These risks should determine how much capital a bank should have on hand. In addition, the amount of capital a bank holds should depend on whether it uses OBSAs to speculate rather than to hedge.

Because of the numerous risks banks face, it is convenient to have a comprehensive measure of a bank's risk exposure. The regulatory approach is to use risk-based capital requirements and CAMEL ratings, where C = capital adequacy, A = asset quality, M = management, E = earnings, and L = liquidity. In finance, variability of earnings is a preferred measure of risk (e.g., the standard deviation of EPS). This chapter proposes the variability of ROA, as captured by its standard deviation, σ_{ROA}, as a comprehensive measure of a bank's risk exposure. The coefficient of variation (*CV*) of ROA, the ratio of σ_{ROA} to average ROA, provides a relative measure of risk exposure.

THE RETURN-ON-EQUITY MODEL[14]

Return on equity (ROE) measures profitability from the shareholder's perspective. Accounting ROE, however, should not be confused with investment profitability (or return) as measured by dividends and stock-price appreciation. Accounting ROE measures bank accounting profits per dollar of book equity capital. It is generally defined as net income divided by average equity. Because ROE can be decomposed into a leverage factor (the equity multiplier, or EM) and return on assets (ROA), it can be expressed as shown in equation (3-6) as $ROE = ROA \times EM$. Return on assets (ROA), defined as net income divided by average or total assets, measures bank profits per dollar of assets. The equity multiplier (EM) is average assets divided by average equity, the reciprocal of the capital-to-asset ratio. It provides a gauge of a bank's leverage $(1 - 1/EM = \text{debt-to-asset ratio})$ or the dollar amount of assets pyramided on the bank's base of equity capital. The equity multiplier provides the leverage that makes ROE a multiple of ROA. For example, a bank with an ROA of 1 percent and an equity multiplier of 10 generates an ROE of 10 percent. The EM of 10 implies an equity-to-asset ratio of 1/10, or 10 percent, or a debt-to-asset ratio of 90 percent.

All-Equity and All-Debt Banks

Although banks financed with either all equity or all debt do not exist in the real world, these two notions are useful for illustrating how leverage affects ROE. First, consider an all-equity bank. Its $EM = 1$ because assets are financed totally by equity. With $EM = 1, ROE = ROA$. If an all-equity bank had an ROA of 1 percent, its ROE would be 1 percent. Second, consider an all-debt bank. Its EM would be undefined, because division by zero is impossible, theoretically infinite leverage. As a compromise, consider a bank with a regulatory minimum ratio of equity to assets of 3 percent. Its EM would be 1/0.03 or 33.33. If this highly leverage bank could return 1 percent on assets, its ROE would be $0.01 \times 33.33 = 0.3333$, or 33.33 percent.

Stage Two: Profit Margin (PM) and Asset Utilization (AU)

The second stage of ROE decomposition analysis (referred to in corporate finance as "du Pont analysis") splits ROA into two components: (1) **profit margin,** denoted by PM, and (2) **asset utilization,** denoted by AU. In symbols

$$ROA = PM \times AU \qquad (3\text{-}7)$$

where *PM* equals net income divided by total revenue (interest revenue plus noninterest revenue), and *AU* equals total revenue divided by average total assets. By splitting *ROA* into these two components, we can pinpoint the variables that underlie ROA performance. Profit margin reflects profits per dollar of total revenue (sales), whereas asset utilization expresses total revenue (sales) per dollar of assets. A bank with a 10 percent profit margin and a 10 percent asset utilization has an

---

[14]Cole [1972] appears to have been the first to apply this framework to banks.

ROA of 1.0 percent. The variables and components of the ROE model are summarized in Table 3-1.

The ROE model contains three alternative measures of profitability: (1) return on equity, (2) return on assets, and (3) profit margin. Because the ratios *ROE, ROA,* and *PM* all have the same numerator (net income), the different denominators (i.e., average or total equity capital, average or total assets, and total revenue) simply provide alternative perspectives on the measurement of profitability. Accounting ROE measures profitability from the owners' perspective. Its primary shortcoming as a measure of bank performance is that ROE can be high because a bank has inadequate equity capital. In addition, a bank with negative book equity (book insolvency) and positive profits would show a negative return on equity, whereas a bank with negative book equity and negative profits would show a positive return on equity. By splitting ROE into ROA and EM, we can resolve this dilemma. Thus, ROA is the preferred accounting measure of overall bank performance. It measures how profitable all of a bank's (on-balance-sheet) assets are employed. By splitting ROA into PM and AU, we focus on the third measure of profitability, PM, and on asset utilization, AU, or "total asset turnover." (Because banks do not generate sales volumes greater than their total assets, as most nonfinancial corporations do, "asset utilization" describes the ratio better than "asset turnover.") Given a bank's ability to generate revenue (sales) as measured by AU, the profit-margin component of the ROE model focuses on a bank's ability to control expenses.

The ROE decomposition analysis described above and summarized in Table 3-1 highlights the usefulness of the ROE model for analyzing bank performance.

Components of the ROE Model for Commercial Banks, 1985–1995

Panel A of Table 3-2 shows ROE decomposition analysis for the U.S. banking industry for the years 1985 to 1995. The highlighted year (1987) was the profitability nadir for U.S. banking in the post–World War II era. In that year some 13,000 commercial

---

TABLE 3-1 The ROE Model

Return on Equity = Return on Assets × Equity Multiplier

$$= ROA \times EM$$

$$= \text{Profit Margin} \times \text{Asset Utilization} \times \text{Equity Multiplier}$$

$$= PM \times AU \times EM$$

$$\frac{\text{Net Income}}{\text{Average Equity}} = \frac{\text{Net Income}}{\text{Operating Income}} \times \frac{\text{Operating Income}}{\text{Average Assets}} + \frac{\text{Average Assets}}{\text{Average Equity}}$$

$$= \frac{\text{Net Income}}{\text{Average Assets}} \times \frac{\text{Average Assets}}{\text{Average Equity}}$$

$$= \frac{\text{Net Income}}{\text{Average Equity}}$$

Note: Four pieces of accounting information are needed to start ROE decomposition analysis: (1) net income, (2) total operating income or "sales," (3) average assets, and (4) average equity capital (excluding debt capital). The first two pieces of information are flow variables from the income-expense statement; the last two are stock variables from the balance sheet. To make the stock and flow variables more compatible, use average balance-sheet figures. The inverse of the equity multiplier is the familiar capital equity-to-asset ratio, excluding debt capital from the numerator.

TABLE 3-2	Return-on-Equity (ROE) Decomposition Analysis

Panel A. All Insured Commercial Banks, 1985–1995

Year	ROE	ROA	EM	AU	PM
1985	0.1108	0.0069	16.06	0.1085	0.0636
1986	0.0983	0.0062	15.85	0.0992	0.0625
1987	**0.0129**	**0.0008**	**16.12**	**0.0982**	**0.0081**
1988	0.1161	0.0071	16.32	0.1050	0.0676
1989	0.0733	0.0047	15.60	0.1157	0.0406
1990	0.0729	0.0047	15.51	0.1126	0.0417
1991	0.0771	0.0051	15.11	0.1037	0.0492
1992	0.1266	0.0091	13.91	0.0942	0.0966
1993	0.1534	0.0120	12.78	0.0900	0.1333
1994	0.1465	0.0115	12.74	0.0879	0.1308
1995	0.1472	0.0118	12.47	0.0932	0.1266

Panel B. ROA by Bank Size Class for Selected Years

Size Class	1985	1987	1995
Top ten	0.0046	−0.0080	0.0088
Banks 11–100	0.0074	−0.0009	0.0131
Banks 101–1000	0.0085	0.0062	0.0128
All other banks	0.0072	0.0058	0.0121

Note: The equity multiplier (EM) is calculated as ROE/ROA, and the profit margin is calculated as ROA/AU, based on the identities $ROE = ROA \times EM$ and $ROA = AU \times PM$.

Source: ROE, ROA, and AU are from the *Federal Reserve Bulletin* (June 1994), pp. 499–509, and (June 1996), pp. 495–505.

banks had an aggregate net income of only $2.3 billion, or less than $180,000 per bank. Relative to industry assets of $2.775 trillion, the ROA was 0.0008, or 0.08 percent. With an equity multiplier of 16.12, the industry's ROE was a measly 1.29 percent.

As Panel B of Table 3-2 shows, the 100 largest banks, but especially the 10 largest banks, had a disastrous 1987, as reflected in the group's negative ROA. The negative aggregate profits for these banks in 1987 can be traced directly to the international, or LDC (LDC = less-developed country), debt crisis. During 1987, the 10 largest banks reported aggregate losses of $5.53 billion, which were driven by massive provision for loan losses (PLL) expected losses on LDC debt. Citicorp, for example, took the lead by biting the LDC bullet with a $3 billion PLL. Other banks with LDC exposure followed Citicorp's lead. Banks ranked 11 to 100 had less LDC exposure, but as a group they recorded a loss on net income of $72 million, or $800,000 per bank on average. The rest of the industry was profitable in 1987 but not as profitable as in 1985. For example, the ROA for all other banks (some 10,000) declined from 0.72 percent in 1985 to 0.58 percent in 1987.

Although industry profitability rebounded in 1988, it was more appearance than reality, because earnings were overstated because inadequate PLLs were taken. In 1989, another, but much smaller, LDC haircut was needed, and in 1989, 1990, and 1991 the crisis in commercial real-estate lending reduced bank earnings. The problems in commercial real estate were more widespread than the LDC debt crisis, which mainly hit the 10 largest banks.

The years 1993, 1994, and 1995 were banner years for the banking industry because record profits were earned, and except for the 10 largest banks, ROAs greater than 1 percent were the norm rather than the exception. Excluding the 10 largest banks, the average bank had the following ROE profile:

$$ROE = ROA \times EM = 0.0125 \times 12.67 = 0.1584$$

with ROA consisting of

$$ROA = PM \times AU = 0.1389 \times 0.0900 = 0.0125$$

The improved profitability of the banking industry in the mid-1990s can be traced to several important factors:

- Improved loan quality
- Lower and more stable interest rates
- Enhanced generation of fees and other noninterest income
- Improved operating efficiency

By far, improved loan quality has been the critical factor. Without sour loans, banks do not need massive provisions for loan losses that deplete their earnings. A stable but modestly growing economy provides an environment in which borrowers have greater prospects of being able to repay their loans. Combing the third and fourth points captures the burden, or net noninterest income component of banking, the factor that bank managers are continually trying to improve to reduce the burden.

The equity multiplier, which links ROA to ROE ($= EM \times ROA$), reflects market and regulatory pressures for banks, especially the largest ones, to reduce their leverage and meet risk-based capital requirements. Like ROA and ROE, profit margin (PM) captures the variability of bank net income over recent years and reflects the recent surge in bank earnings. In contrast, AU has been fairly steady but trending downward over recent years, mainly because of shrinking interest revenues associated with declining interest rates.

ROE Decomposition Analysis: Stage Three

To recap, the first two stages of ROE decomposition analysis are as follows:

$$\text{Stage 1: } ROE = ROA \times EM$$

and

$$\text{Stage 2: } ROA = PM \times AU$$

Figure 3-3 presents stage 3 of the analysis. Because it is more detailed, it cannot be summarized as compactly as the first two stages. The idea in stage 3 is to determine the cause of the good or bad performance uncovered by the first two stages of analysis. As with the first two stages, trend and peer-group analyses are the *modus operandi.*

To illustrate, let's consider the ability of banks to generate noninterest revenue (noninterest sales) per dollar of assets. In 1985, the figure for the average insured commercial bank was 1.22 percent; by 1995 it was 2.02 percent. If we focus on the effectiveness of banks in controlling noninterest expenses per dollar of assets, the figures were 3.21 percent for 1985 and 3.64 percent for 1995. Combining these two measures, we get a net noninterest margin (burden) per dollar of assets of −1.99 percent in 1985 compared to −1.62 percent in 1995. Clearly, the

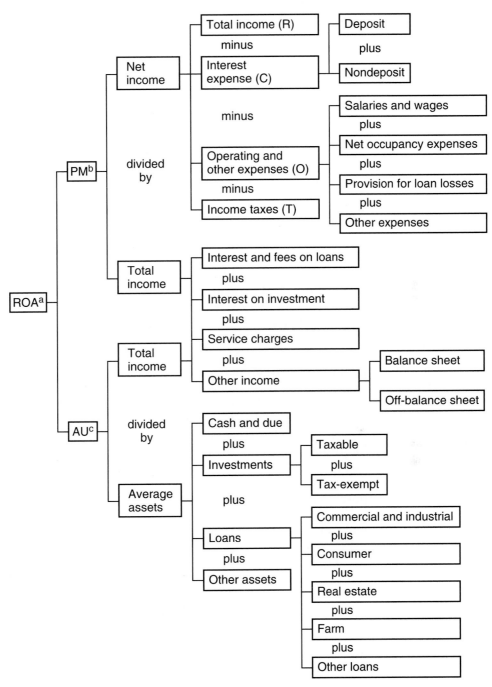

^a ROA = Return on Assets; ^b PM = Profit Margin; ^c AU = Asset Utilization.

FIGURE 3-3 **ROE Decomposition Analysis: Stage 3**

reduction in burden was due to the ability of banks to generate more noninterest revenue per dollar of assets rather than to their ability to control noninterest expenses.

In conducting any stage of ROE decomposition analysis, it is important to compare oranges with oranges and apples with apples to ensure valid peer-group comparisons. For example, consider the components of net noninterest income per dollar of assets for the following bank size categories for 1985 and 1995:

	1985			1995		
Bank Size Class	*Noninterest Income*	*Noninterest Expense*	*Net*	*Noninterest Income*	*Noninterest Expense*	*Net*
Ten largest	1.33%	2.68%	−1.35%	2.16%	3.32%	−1.16%
Banks 11–100	1.40	3.17	−1.77	2.38	3.79	−1.41
Banks 101–1000	1.28	3.55	−2.28	1.84	3.69	−1.85
All other banks	0.84	3.43	−2.59	1.38	3.80	−2.42
All banks	1.22	3.21	−1.99	2.02	3.64	−1.62

If we compare 1995 with 1985, all four bank classes improved their net noninterest margins. In absolute terms, the basis-point improvements were 19 (10 largest), 36 (banks 11–100), 43 (banks 101–1000), 17 (banks not ranked among the 1000 largest), and 37 for all banks. The corresponding percentage improvements were 14.1 percent, 20.3 percent, 18.8 percent, 6.6 percent, and 18.6 percent. If we focus on the data for 1995, size has a definite advantage in enabling banks to generate noninterest income per dollar of assets, but the 10 largest banks do not have an advantage over banks ranked 11–100. Noninterest expenses per dollar of assets show less variation with size, except for the 10 largest banks. The net effect is that net noninterest margin increases (becomes less negative) as bank size increases. For 1995, the 10 largest banks had a 126 basis-point edge in net noninterest margin compared to banks not ranked among the 1000 largest (i.e., −1.16 − [−2.42] = 1.26).

How can bank managers, bank directors, investors, stock analysts, and other interested parties use the information generated by ROE decomposition analysis and ratio analysis? Consider the data on net noninterest margins described above and the way bank managers and their directors might use the information. Suppose that a bank that is not among the 1000 largest has a 1995 burden of −3% = 1% − 4%. Its peer banks (a more exact size matching would be better) have an average profile of −2.42% = 1.38% − 3.80%. Because the bank's burden is higher when both its revenue generation and expense controls are lacking, it should concentrate on improving both of these measures. Specific areas to analyze would be fee schedules, products offered, salaries and wages, and the components and size of other expenses. Regarding other expenses, they are a major component of noninterest expenses, as shown by the following data for 1985 and 1995:

	1985		1995	
Bank size class	*Other Expense*	*% Noninterest Expense*	*Other Expense*	*% Noninterest Expense*
Ten largest	0.84%	31.3%	1.24%	37.3%
Banks 11–100	1.11	35.0	1.84	48.5
Banks 101–1000	1.34	37.7	1.85	50.1
All other banks	1.24	36.1	1.56	39.7
All banks	1.13	35.2	1.62	44.5

Table 3-3 shows the kinds of items typically included in a bank's "other expenses."

TABLE 3-3	Examples of "Other Expenses" for a Community Bank

Expense Category	Monthly
Advertising	900.00
Bank travel	350.00
Business development	275.00
Cost of insuring deposits—FDIC	275.00
Directors' fees	—
Equipment maintenance	725.00
Postage	1,300.00
Express and freight	500.00
General insurance	1,100.00
Machine rentals	700.00
Legal service	350.00
Examinations	700.00
Credit report costs	−200.00
Professional services—other	400.00
"The Club" expense	1,000.00
Stationery and supplies	1,700.00
Small fixtures	150.00
Dues—social clubs	125.00
Dues—business clubs	150.00
Publications and subscriptions	75.00
Telephone and telegraph	1,300.00
Cafeteria	175.00
Charitable contributions	200.00
Data processing	2,500.00
Miscellaneous expense	400.00
Other losses	200.00
Reserve for bond losses	—
Total other operating expenses	15,350.00
Total operating income	79,750.00
Other/operating income	19.25%

Note: The figures shown are not representative because they reflect data for a bank that was financially distressed at the time.

How Getting to a Bank's Bottom Line Varies with Bank Size

Chapter 2 showed how to get to a bank's bottom line, its net income or after-tax profits. Table 3-4 shows how banks in four different size classes get to their bottom lines. Since the basic business of banking is funding loans with deposits, net interest income is the key variable in this process.[15] Net interest income (think of dollars) or net interest margin (percentage) has the enormous task of covering a bank's **provision for loan loss** (PLL), its burden (i.e., net noninterest income =

---

[15]The major exceptions to this are the largest banks and their holding companies. For example, the business focus of Bankers Trust of New York is "global wholesale finance" with a heavy dose of derivatives.

TABLE 3-4   Getting to a Bank's Bottom Line in an ROA Format (income and expenses as a percentage of average net consolidated assets)

Panel A. How Banks Got There in 1985

	Ten Largest Banks	Banks 11–100	Banks 101–1000	Banks under Top 1000
Interest income	9.49%	9.19%	9.61%	10.29%
Interest expense	6.75	5.89	5.75	6.04
NIM	2.74	3.30	3.86	4.25
PLL	0.73	0.63	0.59	0.82
NIM after PLL	2.01	2.67	3.27	3.43
Nonint. income	1.33	1.40	1.28	0.84
Nonint. expense	0.68	3.17	3.55	3.43
Burden	−1.35	−1.77	−2.27	−2.59
Sec. gains/losses	0.06	0.05	0.05	0.08
Pretax income	0.71	0.95	1.05	0.91
Taxes	0.25	0.21	0.21	0.20
Net income	0.46	0.74	0.85	0.72
Cash dividends	0.24	0.26	0.40	0.43
Retained income	0.22	0.48	0.45	0.30
Memo: ROE	9.59%	13.48%	12.99%	8.70%

Panel B. How Banks Got There in 1995

	Ten Largest Banks	Banks 11–100	Banks 101–1000	Banks under Top 1000
Interest income	6.44%	7.40%	7.71%	7.79%
Interest expense	3.76	3.62	3.46	3.38
NIM	2.68	3.79	4.25	4.41
PLL	0.11	0.39	0.43	0.23
NIM after PLL	2.57	2.40	3.82	4.18
Nonint. income	2.16	2.38	1.84	1.38
Nonint. expense	3.32	3.79	3.69	3.80
Burden	−1.16	−1.41	−1.85	−2.42
Sec. gains/losses	0.03	0.02	−0.01	0.00
Pretax income	1.44	2.01	1.96	1.76
Taxes	0.55	0.71	0.68	0.55
Net income	0.88	1.31	1.28	1.21
Cash dividends	0.57	0.85	0.87	0.62
Retained income	0.31	0.46	0.41	0.59
Memo: ROE	13.78%	16.87%	14.86%	12.13%

Note: Figures may not add up because of rounding and exclusion of "extraordinary items," items between pretax income and net income. *NIM* = net interest margin, *PLL* = provision for loan losses or loss provisions, and burden = net noninterest income = noninterest income − noninterest expense.

Source: Federal Reserve Bulletin (June 1996), pp. 498–505.

noninterest income − noninterest expense), its taxes, and its dividend, not to mention the additional task of having something left over (i.e., retained earnings) to maintain a bank's capital adequacy. The component parts of bank profitability vary by bank size. Table 3-4 shows what this variation looked like for 1985 and 1995. Study these two panels to see how banks of different sizes get to their bottom lines and to see how temporal changes in interest rates, technology, operations, products offered, and competition affect a bank's bottom line.

BANK RISK AND THE VARIABILITY OF RETURN ON ASSETS (ROA)

Loan quality or the lack of it is the primary driver of bank earnings and return on assets (ROA). If we want to capture the overall risk of a bank, the variability of ROA provides a comprehensive measure that captures not only credit risk but also interest-rate risk, liquidity risk, operating risk, and any other risk that is realized in bank earnings. The standard deviation of ROA (over time or cross-sectionally) is a good measure of the variability of ROA. Box 3-2 provides a primer on measures of dispersion such as standard deviation. Table 3-5 shows ROA and its variability for the banking industry by size class for the years 1985 to 1995. Two things are clear from the ROA data:

1. ROA declines as bank size increases, although the decline from "all other banks" to the "next 900" is minuscule (on average only two basis points for the 11-year period).

2. The variability of ROA increases with bank size whether measured on an absolute (standard deviation) or relative (CV) basis.

BOX 3-2

MEASURES OF DISPERSION: STANDARD DEVIATION AND THE COEFFICIENT OF VARIATION

The standard deviation, σ, is defined as the square root of the sum of squared deviations from the mean, weighted by the probability of the event occurring. Thus, for some variable x that is observed n times, its variance (the square of the standard deviation or σ^2), is defined as follows:

$$\sigma^2 = [1/n]\left[x_i - \sum x_i/n\right]^2$$

where $\sum x_i/n$ is the (equally weighted) mean of x. The square root of this calculation is the standard deviation (s.d.) of the variable x. It is a measure of the dispersion of the distribution of the variable x. A relative measure of dispersion is the coefficient of variation (CV), defined as the ratio of the standard deviation to the mean. Consider the following simple hypothetical ROA examples (Table 3-3 contains real ROA data by bank size):

	ROA	
Year	Bank Stable	Bank Volatile
1990	1.0%	1.0%
1991	1.0	−1.0
1992	1.0	0.75
1993	1.0	−0.75
1994	1.0	0.5
1995	1.0	−0.5
1996	1.0	0.25
Mean *ROA*	1.0%	0.04%
s.d. of *ROA*	0.0	0.32%
CV of *ROA*	0.0	8.00

Because Bank Stable has no variation in its ROA, it shows zero dispersion in terms of s.d. and CV. In contrast, Bank Volatile shows a highly variable *ROA,* which is captured by its s.d. of 0.32 percent (around its mean of 0.04 percent) and a CV of 8.0.

TABLE 3-5   Return on Assets (ROA) and Its Variability by Bank Size Class, 1985–1995

Year	All Banks	Top Ten	Next 90	Next 900	All Others
1985	0.69%	0.46%	0.48%	0.74%	0.72%
1986	0.62	0.47	0.72	0.73	0.55
1987	0.08	−0.80	−0.09	0.62	0.58
1988	0.71	1.07	0.51	0.67	0.68
1989	0.47	−0.19	0.47	0.71	0.83
1990	0.47	0.48	0.23	0.51	0.74
1991	0.51	0.61	0.47	0.60	0.77
1992	0.91	0.61	1.05	0.92	1.04
1993	1.20	1.13	1.26	1.21	1.19
1994	1.15	0.91	1.23	1.29	1.16
1995	1.18	0.88	1.21	1.28	1.21
Mean	0.73	0.47	0.69	0.84	0.86
s.d.	0.34	0.55	0.44	0.27	0.23
CV	0.46	1.15	0.63	0.32	0.27

Note: s.d. = standard deviation; *CV* = coefficient of variation (s.d./mean).
Source: ROA data from the *Federal Reserve Bulletin* (June 1994), pp. 499–509, and (June 1996), pp. 495–505.

These findings, which suggest that after the fact, larger banks are both less profitable and riskier than smaller banks, are consistent with the conventional wisdom that smaller banks are more risk averse than larger ones. One should not interpret this conclusion as inconsistent with the fundamental risk-return principle of financial management, which is an *ex ante* or expected relationship. If a bank's historical ROA does not match its expected ROA, this does not mean that managers anticipated both lower ROA and greater variability of ROA as a result of their decisions.

A RISK INDEX FOR BANKS[16]

Let's take ROA, EM, and the **standard deviation** of ROA and combine them in a risk index (RI) for banks. The empirical form of this risk index is as follows:

$$RI = [E(ROA) + CAP]/\sigma_{ROA} \qquad \text{(3-8)}$$

where $E(ROA)$ = expected return on assets, CAP = the inverse of EM or the bank's ratio of equity capital to total assets, and σ_{ROA} = the standard deviation of ROA.[17] From an accounting perspective, equation (3-8) is appealing because it includes ROA (the most widely accepted accounting measure of overall bank performance), the variability of ROA (a standard measure of risk in financial economics), and book capital adequacy (an industry standard for bank safety and

---

[16]This risk index, which is due to Hannan and Hanweck [1988], has been applied by Liang and Savage [1990], Eisenbeis and Kwast [1991], Sinkey and Nash [1993], and Nash and Sinkey [1997].

[17]Using the symbols from equation (3-8), Hannan and Hanweck ([1988], pp. 204–205) derive the upper bound of probability of book-value insolvency, p, as $p \le .5\sigma^2/[E(ROA) + CAP]^2$. We emphasize that this p expresses the probability of book-value insolvency, which, in many instances, significantly differs from market-value solvency. In terms of RI, the probability of book-value insolvency can be expressed as $1/[2(RI)^2]$.

soundness). The resultant risk index is a measure, expressed in units of standard deviations of ROA, of how much a bank's accounting earnings can decline before it has a negative book value. Intuitively, RI gauges the thickness of the book-value cushion a bank has available to absorb accounting losses. Therefore, a lower RI implies a riskier bank; a higher RI implies a safer bank.

Let's think about the intuitive appeal of RI and use a couple of extreme cases to illustrate its use. First, consider a bank with a high expected ROA, a strong capital position, and stable earnings (ROA). Its RI will be a relatively high value. In contrast, a bank with negative expected earnings, minimum capital, and highly variable earnings will have a low RI. If we call these two institutions Strong Bank and Weak Bank and put some numbers on them, the RIs could be as follows:

	Strong Bank	*Weak Bank*
$E(ROA)$	0.02	−0.02
CAP	0.10	0.03
σ_{ROA}	0.001	0.007
RI	120.0	1.43
$Pr(BVE < 0)$	0.0035%	24.5%

The last line in the profiles is the upper-bound probability of book-value insolvency or $Pr(BVE < 0)$, which equals $1/[2(RI)^2]$ (see footnote 17). Not surprisingly, the Strong Bank has a very small chance of exhausting its book equity, whereas the Weak Bank has a substantial chance of exhausting it. Moreover, the Weak Bank is very vulnerable. For example, if its E(ROA) drops below −2.99 percent, all other things being equal, it becomes book value insolvent.

Let's consider some more realistic inputs for the risk index by using data from Table 3-3 and appendix A of this chapter. To estimate expected ROA, we will extrapolate from the most recent actual ROA and let E(ROA) equal it. Thus, the inputs will be ROA and EM for 1995, with σ_{ROA} based on the 11 years of ROA. The analysis will be for the 10 largest banks, the next 90 largest, the next 900 largest, and all other banks. We can make a very educated guess as to what the rankings of the RIs will be, because we have learned that ROA and EM (the inverse of CAP) tend to decrease as banks get larger and that σ tends to increase as banks get larger. These configurations suggest that RI will decrease with bank size. The exact data are as follows:[18]

	Risk Index	$Pr(BVE < 0)$
Top ten	13.2	0.29%
Banks ranked 11–100	20.4	0.12%
Banks ranked 101–1000	36.6	0.04%
Banks not ranked among the 1000 largest	48.6	0.02%

If it seems strange that this framework suggests that the nation's largest banks, on average, are more vulnerable to failure than the average community bank, keep two

---

[18]As an exercise, use the data from Table 3-3 and the appendix to reproduce these figures. Ignore rounding error.

points in mind: (1) The probability of book-value insolvency for the average bank in each size class is very low—less than 0.5 percent; (2) we are dealing with book values and not market values.

To summarize, indices such as the bank risk index are useful because they collapse several pieces of information into a single number. In this regard, an index is similar to a ratio that collapses two pieces of information into one. In either case, we gain some informational economies but we also lose some detail. The bank index presented here is interesting because it employs two key measures of banking performance, ROA and CAP, and a common measure of risk in finance, the standard deviation of a return distribution.

THE PROFITABILITY OF OTHER FINANCIAL-SERVICES FIRMS

In their bread-and-butter business of borrowing and lending, commercial banks compete with

1. Other depository institutions (i.e., savings banks, S&Ls, and credit unions)
2. Nondepository financial-services firms (e.g., life insurance companies, finance companies, pension funds, and mutual funds)
3. The financial subsidiaries of nonfinancial corporations such as GMAC, Ford Credit, and GE Capital

In addition, banks compete with the branches of foreign banks operating in the United States and with the basic instruments of direct finance: commercial paper and corporate bonds. Beyond the bread-and-butter business, because the biggest banks provide investment-banking services and derivatives products, they also compete with investment banks both domestic and foreign.

Table 3-6 presents ROE profiles for three groups that compete with commercial banks: savings banks (Panel A), life insurance companies (Panel B), and securities firms (Panel C). For comparison, Panel D repeats ROE, ROA, and EM for commercial banks. To the extent that the data are comparable, what emerges is a competitive profile for commercial banks. If we focus on ROA, commercial banks have been beating both savings banks (handily; no great accomplishment given the S&L crisis) and life insurance companies, and doing it with comparable or less leverage. Shifting to the ROE figures for securities firms, we find that commercial banks have lower ROEs mainly because they have less leverage (not shown) than securities firms. Although the ROEs for the largest banks were quite volatile prior to 1992 (because their ROAs have been volatile), they have not been as volatile as ROE for securities firms. For example, the after-tax ROEs for securities firms from 1988 to 1991 were 6.3 percent (1988), 4.6 percent (1989), −0.4 percent (1990), and 12.8 percent (1991).

DECISION-MAKING LESSONS FROM HISTORICAL BANK PERFORMANCE

Although it is interesting to know where a bank has been and where it is today in terms of financial performance, where is it going and how is it going to get there are the interesting and difficult questions of managerial decision-making. Since most

TABLE 3-6 Profitability and Leverage Measures for Financial-Services Firms Other than Commercial Banks

Panel A. FDIC—Insured Savings Institutions

	1996[a]	1995	1994	1993
Return on equity	11.92%	9.41%	8.28%	9.24%
Return on assets	1.00%	0.77%	0.66%	0.70%
Equity multiplier	11.92	12.22	12.55	13.20

Panel B. Life Insurance Companies

	1994	1993	1992	1991
Return on equity	11.50%	13.92%	13.14%	13.37%
Return on assets	0.70%	0.80%	0.75%	0.75%
Equity multiplier	16.43	17.32	17.43	17.86

Panel C. Securities Industry

	1994	1993	1992	1991
Return on equity[b]	3.30%	27.10%	22.80%	23.70%
Est. after-tax *ROE* ($t = 0.3$)	2.31%	18.97%	15.96%	16.59%

Panel D. Commercial Banking

	1996[a]	1995	1994	1993	1992
Return on equity	14.43%	14.72%	14.65%	15.34%	12.66%
Return on assets	1.18%	1.18%	1.15%	1.20%	0.91%
Equity multiplier	12.23	12.47	12.74	12.78	13.91

Note: [a]Through June 30, ratios annualized. [b]Average pretax *ROE*. The equity multiplier is either the ratio of total assets to total equity capital or is derived as the ratio *ROE/ROA. ROA* and *EM* not available for securities firms.

Source: Panel A from *The FDIC Quarterly Banking Profile* (Third Quarter, 1996); Panel B from *Best's Aggregates & Averages—Life Health;* Panel C from *Securities Industry Yearbook,* 1995; and Panel D from *Federal Reserve Bulletin.*

of the remaining 17 chapters of this book address these where-to-go and how-to-get-there questions, these issues come later. At this stage, however, let's draw some lessons based on the data presented in this chapter. The key lesson is the importance of loan quality. Without it, bank earnings are depleted because of loan losses and can fluctuate in a helter-skelter fashion. During the 1980s and early 1990s, problems with bad loans related to energy, farm, LDC, and commercial real-estate lending devastated commercial banks and pushed the FDIC into de facto insolvency. Since then, both the industry and the FDIC have recovered and look quite strong going into the twenty-first century.

On balance, banks that mismanage credit risk do not maximize shareholder value. For financial institutions with severe maturity imbalances such as traditional S&Ls, interest-rate risk is the key uncertainty. For multinational banks, these two risks and foreign-exchange risk must be managed successfully. Beyond these three risks, management of operations (noninterest expense) and generation of fee and noninterest income are critical. These two factors are combined in the measures of net noninterest income, or a bank's burden. Successful bankers are those who know how to take and manage risk for profit.

Chapter Summary

The heart of financial management is the allocation of capital across alternative investment opportunities, and the financing of those opportunities or growth options. The economic model of the firm, as opposed to the accounting model, is the proper framework for analyzing financial decision making. Cash flow, time, and risk capture the important dimension of the discounted-cash-flow method for analyzing investment opportunities. This chapter has focused on accounting and economic models of value and ways to measure a bank's value and its performance. Because accounting data are readily available and relatively easy to use, accounting measures of value and performance present a convenient way to answer difficult questions about a bank's value and its performance. To determine real or economic value is a more challenging task because it requires discounting a bank's future net cash flows at a rate that reflects the riskiness of those cash flows. For bank holding companies with actively traded equity securities, stock markets provide estimates of their underlying net asset values. For the thousands of community banks in the United States, no such estimates are readily available. In either case, however, we can think about a bank's per share equity value (P_0) as determined by

$$P_0 = EPS^* \times P/E \times K$$

where EPS^* = real or economic earnings and K ($K > 0$) is an adjustment factor that marks the industry P/E ratio either up or down to reflect the firm's unique risk profile. This formulation improves on the accounting model of the firm, which describes value as a markup of the firm's accounting EPS by the industry P/E ratio. Without adjusting for the riskiness of a firm's cash flows (as captured by the adjustment factor, K), meaningful net asset values cannot be determined.

Accounting data provide useful information for comparing bank performance over time and across peer groups or competitors. An important framework in this regard is the return-on-equity (ROE) decomposition model. Its first two stages are as follows:

$$\text{Stage 1: } ROE = ROA \times EM$$

and

$$\text{Stage 2: } ROA = PM \times AU$$

This framework provides a starting point for decomposing a bank's accounting performance using ratio analysis. Return on assets (ROA) is the best and most comprehensive accounting measure of a bank's overall performance. The variability of ROA, as captured by its standard deviation, provides a good measure of riskiness. A risk index based on E(ROA), CAP, and σ_{ROA} provides a convenient way for collapsing three important measures of bank performance into a single number.

Focusing on a bank's profit margin highlights the critical components of, and the way to get to, a bank's bottom line: net interest income, provision for loan losses, net noninterest income or burden (noninterest income minus noninterest expense), capital gains and losses, and taxes. What's left over can be paid out to shareholders as dividends or retained to bolster the bank's capital adequacy.

The major lesson of this chapter is that successful bankers are those who know how to take and manage risk for profit. The risk that has caused the greatest fluctuation in bank earnings has been credit risk.

Key Words, Concepts, and Acronyms

- Accounting model of the firm $(P_0 = EPS \times P/E)$
- Asset utilization (AU)
- Bank valuation
- Book value
- Cash flow
- Constant-growth model $(P_0 = D_1/[r - g])$
- Decomposition analysis (of ROE)
- Discounted cash flow (DCF)
- Dividend-payout ratio
- Dividend yield

- Earnings per share (EPS)
- Economic model of the firm
- Equity multiplier (EM)
- Fundamental analysis
- Generally accepted accounting principles (GAAP)
- Hidden capital
- Investment banking (bank)
- "Lead steers"
- Market efficiency
- Market-to-book ratio
- Market value

- Off-balance-sheet activities
- Price-earnings ratio (P/E)
- Profit margin (PM)
- Return on assets $(ROA = PM \times AU)$
- Return on equity $(ROE = ROA \times EM)$
- Risk index $(RI = [E(ROA) + CAP]/\sigma_{ROA})$
- Standard deviation (of ROA)
- Statistical market value accounting model (SMVAM)

Review Questions

1. Why is it important to be able to measure a bank's value, safety, and performance?
2. What is the essence of corporate finance? Distinguish between direct finance and indirect finance. What roles do investment bankers and commercial bankers play in these alternative methods of finance?
3. Distinguish between the accounting and the economic models of the firm. What would be a reasonable compromise between these two approaches?
4. Who are "lead steers" and what role do they play in financial markets? What are the potential advantages of lead-steer ownership? Where do lead steers search for information?
5. What are the three essential ingredients of valuation?
6. Briefly but carefully identify and explain the importance of each of the following terms:
   a. investment return
   b. market-to-book ratio
   c. price-earnings ratio
   d. constant-growth model
   e. dividend-payout ratio
   f. earnings per share
   g. dividend yield
7. What is "hidden capital" and its relationship to market value and book value?
8. Explain the statistical and economic significance of SMVAM. What's the basic economic message of SMVAM?
9. Who needs to know how to read bank financial statements and what are the various approaches for doing so? What is ratio analysis and what are the key ratios used in such analysis?
10. Explain the various stages of ROE decomposition analysis. What's the purpose of doing this type of investigation?

11. What is the best and most comprehensive accounting measure of bank performance? How can this variable be used to measure overall bank risk exposure? What's behind the variability of ROA?

12. What three measures of bank performance make up the risk index (RI) described in this chapter? What's the intuitive appeal of RI?

Problems

1. Alan, an accountant, says that the Bank of Boulder is worth $50 per share because it earns $5 per share in an industry in which the average *P/E* ratio is 10. Fred, a financial economist, says Alan's estimate undervalues the bank's equity because its conservative managers have understated *EPS* by overallocating for potential loan losses. Fred also notes that the bank ranks above average among its peers in terms of capital adequacy. If Fred, without double counting, claims that *EPS* are understated by $1.50 per share and that the industry P/E should be marked up by 20 percent, what is his estimate of the per share equity value of the bank?

2. Angie, a CPA, says that the Bank of Biloxi has a per share equity value of $100 = $10 × 10 based on the accounting model of *EPS × P/E*. Construct an argument for Faye, a financial economist, that estimates the bank's value at no more than $50 per share.

3. During the first quarter of 1995, Bankers Trust of New York had net income of −$157 million, $35 million of which was for nonrecurring severance-related costs. During the first quarter of 1994, the bank had net income of $164 million. Common shares outstanding on these dates were 74,407,758 and 86,315,789. As of April 20, 1995 (Jessica Sinkey's 18th birthday), Bankers Trust was paying a quarterly dividend of $1 per share and its stock price closed at 53 and ¼. Around this time a benchmark *P/E* ratio for a U.S. money-center bank was 8.5. Over the previous 52 weeks, Bankers Trust's stock had a high of 74 and a low of 49 and ¾.

   a. Use the accounting model to estimate the value of Bankers Trust's common stock as of the first quarter of 1994 and 1995. How would you apply the economic model to this valuation problem?

   b. What was the bank's dividend yield as of the first quarter of 1994 and 1995? Is the yield sustainable?

4. During the first quarter of 1995, Citicorp (New York) had net income of $829 million compared to $553 million a year earlier. Common shares outstanding on these dates were 484,795,322 and 471,681,416. As of April 20, 1995 (Jessica Sinkey's 18th birthday), Citicorp was paying an annual dividend of $1.20 per share, and its stock price closed at 46 and ⅝. Around this time a benchmark P/E ratio for a U.S. money-center bank was 8.5. Over the previous 52 weeks, Citicorp's stock had a high of 47 and ¾ and a low of 36 and ¼.

   a. Use the accounting model to estimate the value of Citicorp's common stock as of the first quarter of 1994 and 1995. How would you apply the economic model to this valuation problem?

   b. What was the bank's dividend yield as of the first quarter of 1994 and 1995? Is the yield sustainable?

5. Suppose that your guesstimates of the parameters of the constant-growth model for Bankers Trust and Citicorp are as follows:

	Bankers Trust	Citicorp
Current dividend	4.00	1.20
EPS/DSP growth rate	5.5%	11%
Required rate of return	15%	12%

a. Using the constant-growth model, what values are implied for these two stocks? How do they compare with the values reported in problems 3 and 4?

b. Suppose that Bankers Trust cannot sustain its dividend at $4 per share and cuts it to $2 per share per annum. As a result of its restructuring, its EPS/DPS growth is revised to 12 percent and its required return drops to 14 percent. How is the company valued now?

c. How realistic are any estimates based on the constant-growth model? How do the franchise values of Bankers Trust and Citicorp differ? What are Value Line's projections for these two companies?

6. Given the following information for the average credit-card bank (CCB) and the average non-credit-card bank (non-CCB), calculate risk indices and probabilities of book-value insolvency for each:

	ROA	CAP	σ_{ROA}
Average CCB	0.0403	0.1065	0.0141
Average non-CCB	0.0130	0.0732	0.0050

The data are for the years 1989 through 1993. What do you conclude about the riskiness and performance of these two groups?

7. The Bank of New England was declared insolvent by the Comptroller of the Currency on January 6, 1991. By year-end 1989 or sooner, the bank was probably insolvent on a market-value basis, and this translated into a 99 percent probability of book-value insolvency. Assuming that its expected ROA at the end of 1989 was −0.02 and that CAP was 0.03, what would its standard deviation of ROA (σ_{ROA}) have to be?

8. Consider the following data for Mogen David Bank for 1995:

Net income	$ 1,296,000
Interest revenue	9,937,000
Noninterest revenue	3,901,000
Total assets	184,879,000
Total equity	10,451,000

a. Compute the first two stages of ROE decomposition analysis.

b. Compute the bank's RI and PR($BV < 0$) if its $\sigma_{ROA} = 0.0075$ and $E(ROA) = ROA$ (1995).

c. What kind of bank do you think it is? Money center? Regional? Community? How would you answer this question if the data were in billions instead of millions?

9. If a bank has noninterest revenue of $4,499 million and noninterest expense of $3,580 million, what is its burden and what, if anything, is different about it?

10. If a bank has net income of $1,296 million, and pays a total dividend of $612 million, what is its payout ratio? If the bank has 200 million common shares outstanding with a book value of $50 per share and a market-to-book ratio of 1.4, find its dividend yield and market price per share of common stock.

11. If the Bank of Banks County has pretax net income of $1,906 and after-tax net income of $1,296, what is its tax rate?

12. If the Unleven Bank has $ROE = ROA$, what is its EM? What's strange about this bank?

13. Bet-the-Bank Bank has an EM of 50 and an ROA of 0.005. What is its ROE? What's different about its ROE profile? If the bank's standard deviation of ROA has been 0.01 over the past decade, what are its RI and PR($BV < 0$)?

14. Unpredictable Bank has had ten years of *ROA* as follows: (0.01, 0.005, 0.0025, 0.0, −0.0025, −0.005, 0.01, 0.011, 0.005, −0.005). Find its standard deviation of *ROA* (σ_{ROA}), *RI,* and *Pr*(*BV* < 0) if *E*(*ROA*) equals a weighted average of its last three *ROA*s with weights of 0.5 (most recent), 0.3, and 0.2. The bank's *CAP* is 0.02.

15. The Zombie S&L has *E*(*ROA*) = −0.05, *CAP* = 0, and σ_{ROA} = 0.002. How viable is this institution?

16. If Morgan Stanley, a major investment bank, has a *P/E* ratio of 9 and a price per share of $51, find its *EPS*. If it pays a dividend of 70 cents per share, find its payout ratio and its dividend yield. If Morgan expects to earn 2 percent on assets next year, and has a *CAP* of 0.10 and σ of 0.001, what are its *RI* and *Pr*(*BV* < 0)?

17. Ahmanson, a major West Coast S&L holding company, recently traded at $29.375 and had *EPS* of $3.26. What is its *P/E*? How does its *P/E* compare with Morgan Stanley's *P/E* from the previous question? How valid is it to make such a comparison?

18. Using the data in appendix A, update the *ROE* decomposition analysis for the size groups shown and write a report on your findings. The *Federal Reserve Bulletin* (usually the June issue) has the data.

19. Extra credit: As a research project, collect data on market values and book values (either over time for a single BHC or cross-sectionally for several BHCs) and run a simple linear regression of market value against book value. Write a brief report on your findings. Appendix B provides some additional tests you might try.

**APPENDIX
A**

RETURN-ON-EQUITY DECOMPOSITION ANALYSIS BY BANK SIZE, 1985–1995

This appendix presents ROE decomposition analysis by bank size for the 11-year period 1985 to 1995. The size classes, which are the standard ones used in the text, include the 10 largest banks (Table A3-1), banks ranked 11 to 100 (Table A3-2), banks ranked 101 to 1000 (Table A3-3), and banks not ranked among the 1000 largest (Table A3-4). Table A3-5 presents comparisons of the first two stages of ROE decomposition analysis by bank size for 1985 and 1995.

TABLE A3-1	Return-on-Equity (ROE) Decomposition Analysis for the Ten Largest Banks, 1985–1995

Identities: $ROE = ROA \times EM$ and $ROA = AU \times PM$

Year	ROE	ROA	EM	AU	PM
1985	0.0959	0.0046	20.84	0.1082	0.0425
1986	0.0946	0.0046	20.56	0.0977	0.0471
1987	−0.1811	−0.0080	22.64	0.1039	−0.0770
1988	0.2328	0.0107	21.76	0.1158	0.0924
1989	−0.0392	−0.0019	20.63	0.1301	−0.0146
1990	0.1013	0.0048	21.10	0.1264	0.0380
1991	0.0435	0.0022	19.77	0.1117	0.0197
1992	0.1091	0.0061	17.88	0.1027	0.0594
1993	0.1675	0.0113	14.82	0.1021	0.1107
1994	0.1386	0.0091	15.23	0.0871	0.1045
1995	0.1378	0.0088	15.66	0.0860	0.1023

Note: The equity multiplier (EM) is calculated as ROE/ROA and the profit margin is calculated as ROA/AU.

Source: ROE, ROA, and *AU* are from the *Federal Reserve Bulletin* (June 1994), p. 501, and (June 1996), p. 499.

TABLE A3-2	Return-on-Equity (ROE) Decomposition Analysis for the 11th Largest to the 100th Largest Banks, 1985–1995

Identities: $ROE = ROA \times EM$ and $ROA = AU \times PM$

Year	ROE	ROA	EM	AU	PM
1985	.01348	0.0074	18.21	0.1059	0.0699
1986	0.1271	0.0072	17.65	0.0961	0.0749
1987	−0.0169	−0.0009	18.78	0.0957	−0.0094
1988	0.1552	0.0081	19.16	0.1015	0.0798
1989	0.0881	0.0049	17.98	0.1160	0.0422
1990	0.0429	0.0024	17.87	0.1112	0.0216
1991	0.0834	0.0051	16.68	0.1017	0.0500
1992	0.1518	0.0104	14.60	0.0937	0.1110
1993	0.1688	0.0126	13.40	0.0887	0.1420
1994	0.1628	0.0123	13.23	0.0871	0.1412
1995	0.1687	0.0131	12.88	0.0978	0.1339

Note: The equity multiplier (EM) is calculated as ROE/ROA and the profit margin is calculated as ROA/AU.

Source: ROE, ROA, and *AU* are from the *Federal Reserve Bulletin* (June 1994), p. 503, and (June 1996), p. 501.

TABLE A3-3	Return-on-Equity (ROE) Decomposition Analysis for the 101st Largest to the 1000th Largest Bank, 1985–1995

Identities: $ROE = ROA \times EM$ and $ROA = AU \times PM$

Year	ROE	ROA	EM	AU	PM
1985	0.1299	0.0085	15.28	0.1089	0.0780
1986	0.1109	0.0074	14.99	0.0997	0.0742
1987	0.0953	0.0064	14.89	0.0973	0.0658
1988	0.1000	0.0067	14.92	0.1022	0.0655
1989	0.1094	0.0074	14.78	0.1102	0.0671
1990	0.0744	0.0051	14.59	0.1085	0.0470
1991	0.0860	0.0061	14.10	0.1025	0.0595
1992	0.1222	0.0092	13.28	0.0902	0.1020
1993	0.1485	0.0121	12.27	0.0847	0.1428
1994	0.1545	0.0129	11.98	0.0877	0.1471
1995	0.1486	0.0128	11.61	0.0955	0.1340

Note: The equity multiplier (*EM*) is calculated as ROE/ROA and the profit margin is calculated as ROA/AU.

Source: ROE, ROA, and *AU* are from the *Federal Reserve Bulletin* (June 1994), p. 505, and (June 1996), p. 503.

TABLE A3-4	Return-on-Equity (ROE) Decomposition Analysis for All Banks Not Ranked among the 1000 Largest Banks, 1985–1995

Identities: $ROE = ROA \times EM$ and $ROA = AU \times PM$

Year	ROE	ROA	EM	AU	PM
1985	0.0870	0.0072	12.08	0.1113	0.0647
1986	0.0682	0.0056	12.18	0.1014	0.0552
1987	0.0710	0.0059	12.03	0.0959	0.0615
1988	0.0821	0.0069	11.90	0.0986	0.0700
1989	0.0964	0.0083	11.61	0.1064	0.0780
1990	0.0854	0.0074	11.54	0.1049	0.0705
1991	0.0897	0.0077	11.65	0.0997	0.0772
1992	0.1196	0.0107	11.18	0.0905	0.1182
1993	0.1337	0.0125	10.70	0.0845	0.1479
1994	0.1208	0.0116	10.41	0.0827	0.1403
1995	0.1213	0.0121	10.02	0.0917	0.1319

Note: The equity multiplier (*EM*) is calculated as ROE/ROA and the profit margin is calculated as ROA/AU.

Source: ROE, ROA, and *AU* are from the *Federal Reserve Bulletin* (June 1994), p. 507, and (June 1996), p. 505.

TABLE A3-5   ROE Profiles across Bank Size Classes, 1985 and 1995

Panel A. Return on Equity (ROE = ROA × EM)

Bank Class	1985	1995
All banks	0.1108	0.1547
10 largest	0.0959	0.1675
11–100	0.1348	0.1688
101–1000	0.1299	0.1485
Under 1000	0.0870	0.1337

Panel B. Return on Assets (ROA = ROE/EM)

Bank Class	1985	1995
All banks	0.0069	0.0121
10 largest	0.0046	0.0113
11–100	0.0074	0.0126
101–1000	0.0085	0.0121
Under 1000	0.0072	0.0125

Panel C. Equity Multiplier (EM = ROE/ROA)

Bank Class	1985	1995
All banks	16.06	12.78
10 largest	20.84	14.82
11–100	18.21	13.40
101–1000	15.28	12.27
Under 1000	12.08	10.70

Panel D. Asset Utilization (AU = ROA/PM)

Bank Class	1985	1995
All banks	0.1085	0.0899
10 largest	0.1082	0.1021
11–100	0.1059	0.0887
101–1000	0.1089	0.0847
Under 1000	0.1113	0.0845

Panel E. Profit Margin (PM = ROA/AU)

Bank Class	1985	1995
All banks	0.0636	0.1346
10 largest	0.0425	0.1107
11–100	0.0699	0.1420
101–1000	0.0780	0.1428
Under 1000	0.0647	0.1479

Note: The equity multiplier (*EM*) is calculated as *ROE/ROA* and the profit margin is calculated as *ROA/AU*.

Source: *ROE, ROA,* and *AU* are from the *Federal Reserve Bulletin* (June 1994), pp. 501–507, and (June 1996), pp. 499–505.

HIDDEN CAPITAL AND APPLICATIONS OF THE STATISTICAL MARKET VALUE ACCOUNTING MODEL (SMVAM)

To further illustrate the use of Kane and Unal's [1990] SMVAM, consider the following cross-sectional regressions for 128 bank holding companies (BHCs) for year-end 1987 and 1988:

Date	Intercept	Slope	R^2
12/87	115	0.75	0.86
	(2.5)	(7.3)	
12/88	140	0.83	0.93
	(3.4)	(6.3)	

These regression results stand behind Panel B of Figure 3-1 in the text. The figures in parentheses are *t*-statistics. They test the intercept for significant difference from zero by dividing the estimated intercept by its standard error (e.g., for 1987, $2.5 = 115/46$) and test the slope coefficient for significant difference from one, in either direction, by subtracting the estimated slope coefficient from one and dividing by its standard error (e.g., for 1987, $7.3 = [1 - .75]/.034$). Recall that SMVAM's joint null hypothesis is: ($a = 0, b = 1$). R^2 measures the overall strength or goodness of fit of the regression equation; it ranges between 0 (nothing explained) and 1.00 (everything explained).

When Kane and Unal applied SMVAM to a sample of bank stocks over the period 1975 to 1985, they concluded that movements in the amount and sensitivity of hidden capital at the largest bank holding companies in the United States during the interest-rate peak of 1978–1982 were consistent with the hypothesis that during this period

> ... increases in the unbookable value of FDIC guarantees and enhancements in franchise values fed by technological change and relaxations of regulatory restrictions cushioned a sharp decline in the valuation ratio for their net bookable assets. (p. 135)[19]

Subsample Tests and Alternative Specifications of SMVAM

The 128 BHCs used to estimate SMVAM consist of three types of banks: (1) money-center or multinational banks, (2) superregional banks, and (3) regional banks. Because the relations between market value and book value may differ among these groups, SMVAM was reestimated for 1987 for each group separately with the following results:

---

[19]Kane and Unal ([1990], Table 1, pp. 120–121) present quarterly estimates of SMVAM from 1975-I through 1985-III for large, medium-sized, and small BHCs. Their estimates show $a < 0$ and $b > 1$ was a common occurrence for the 25 largest BHCs from 1975 through 1980.

Group	Number of Banks	Intercept	Slope	R^2
Money center (11 largest)	11	−206	0.77	0.87
		(−0.26)	(1.16)	
Superregional ($10B to $34B)	28	30	1.02	0.89
		(0.12)	(−0.13)	
Regional (total assets equal to or less than $10B)	89	−6	1.04	0.92
		(−0.31)	(−0.63)	
Pooled	128	115	0.75	0.86
		(2.5)	(7.3)	

Again the figures in parentheses are *t*-statistics, testing for differences from zero (for the intercept) and from one (for the slope). Clearly, the pooled equation masks the diverse relations across the groups. In the two regional groups, from a purely statistical perspective, the intercept and slope coefficients are not significantly different from zero and one. Although the same can be said for the money-center equation, the *t*-statistic for the slope coefficient (1.16) has some statistical significance. The money-center slope ($b < 1$) reflects the discount applied to book equity of the money-center group.

Estimates of SMVAM for 1988 show how quickly the relations between market and book values can change:

Group	Number of Banks	Intercept	Slope	R^2
Money center (11 largest)	11	−167	0.85	0.94
		(−0.23)	(0.98)	
Superregional ($10B to $36B)	28	−173	1.25	0.95
		(−0.83)	(1.68)	
Regional (total assets equal to or less than $10B)	89	92	0.83	0.87
		(4.09)	(2.51)	
Pooled	128	140	0.83	0.93
		(3.4)	(6.3)	

In this set of results, the money-center equation has changed the least. The equations for the two regional groups, however, have changed substantially. The superregionals show a larger and more significant premium as reflected by the slope coefficient, and off-balance-sheet activities now act as a drain on capital. The 87 regional BHCs (total assets equal to or less than $10 billion) show the most dramatic shift, going from an acceptance of SMVAM's joint hypothesis ($a = 0, b = 1$) in 1987 to its rejection in 1988. Economically the change resulted in a discount on recorded equity and an increase in the value of federal deposit-insurance guarantees.

Kane and Unal [1990] also test SMVAM under a quadratic specification such that

$$MVE = a + b_0 BVE + b_2 (BVE)^2 + e_Q$$

If we use the quadratic equation on the three groups of banks in both years, only the 89 regional BHCs in 1988 showed a significant result. Specifically,

$$MV = 0.55 + 0.65 (BV) + 0.00072 (BV^2), \ R^2 = .91$$
$$(2.8) \quad (5.5) \qquad (6.2)$$

This finding indicates that for 1988 the relation between market values and book values for regional banks was a nonlinear, or quadratic, one.

Caveat

Kane and Unal's [1990] SMVAM is not quite as easy to apply as this appendix may suggest. More refined analysis requires more than the simple regressions presented here. Nevertheless, as Shakespeare noted, simplicity does have its beauty, and SMVAM's beauty lies in the insights it provides about hidden capital, how it arises, and how to interpret it.

Selected References

Altman, Edward I., Robert Avery, Robert A. Eisenbeis, and Joseph F. Sinkey, Jr. [1981]. *Application of Classification Techniques in Business, Banking, and Finance.* Greenwich, CT: JAI Press.

Citicorp Annual Report (various years). New York: Citicorp.

Cole, David W. [1972]. "The Return-on-Equity Model for Banks." *The Bankers Magazine* (Summer), pp. 40–47.

Collins, M. Cary, David W. Blackwell, and Joseph F. Sinkey, Jr. [1995]. "The Relationship between Corporate Compensation Policies and Investment Opportunities: Empirical Evidence for Large Bank Holding Companies." *Financial Management* (Autumn), pp. 40–53.

"Conventional Wisdom Watch." [1990]. *Newsweek* (November 19), p. 6.

Eisenbeis, Robert A., and Myron L. Kwast. [1991]. "Are Real Estate Depositories Viable? Evidence from Commercial Banks." *Journal of Financial Services Research* (March), pp. 5–24.

Federal Reserve Bulletin (various issues). Washington, DC: Board of Governors of the Federal Reserve System.

Gillis, Harvey N., Rufus W. Lumry, and Thomas J. Oswald. [1980]. "A New Approach to Analyzing Bank Performance." *The Bankers Magazine* (March/April), pp. 67–73.

Greenawalt, Mary Brady, and Joseph F. Sinkey, Jr. [1988]. "Bank Loan-Loss Provisions and the Income-Smoothing Hypothesis: An Empirical Analysis, 1976–1984." *Journal of Financial Services Research* (December), pp. 301–318.

Hannan, Timothy H., and Gerald A. Hanweck. [1988]. "Bank Insolvency Risk and the Market for Large Certificates of Deposit." *Journal of Money, Credit, and Banking* (May), pp. 203–211.

Kane, Edward J., and Haluk Unal. [1990]. "Modeling Structural and Temporal Variation in the Market's Valuation of Banking Firms." *The Journal of Finance* (March), pp. 113–136.

Liang, J. Nellie, and Donald T. Savage. [1990]. "The Nonbank Activities of Bank Holding Companies." *Federal Reserve Bulletin* (May), pp. 280–292.

Nash, Robert C., and Joseph F. Sinkey, Jr. [1997]. "On Competition, Risk, and the Hidden Assets in the Market for Bank Credit Cards." *Journal of Banking and Finance* (January), pp. 89–112.

Parker, George G. C., and Terry Beals. [1996]. *The Stanford Bank Game* (Version 11). San Franciso: Human Resources West.

Scheiner, James H. [1981]. "Income Smoothing: An Analysis of the Banking Industry." *Journal of Bank Research* (Summer), pp. 119–123.

Sinkey, Joseph F., Jr., and Robert C. Nash. [1993]. "Assessing the Riskiness and Profitability of Credit-Card Banks." *Journal of Financial Services Research* 2, pp. 127–150.

Six Roundtable Discussions of Corporate Finance with Joel Stern. [1986]. (Edited by Donald H. Chew, Jr.) Westport, CT: Quorum Books.

CHAPTER

4

MANAGING VALUE AND RISK: BANK CORPORATE STRATEGY AND STRATEGIC PLANNING IN THE FINANCIAL-SERVICES INDUSTRY

Contents

LEARNING OBJECTIVES

■ To understand the importance of a bank's corporate strategy and strategic plan

■ To understand alternative managerial motives

■ To understand the concept of economic value added

■ To understand managing value and risk and their effects on bank performance

■ To understand a bank's strategic business plan

■ To understand a bank's framework for risk management

■ To understand a bank's strategy for corporate control

CHAPTER THEME

A bank's overall **corporate strategy** and strategic plan need at least three critical components: (1) a **business plan,** (2) a framework for **risk management,** and (3) strategies for **corporate control.** These components provide a solid foundation for **managing value** and **risk.** A bank's business plan, as a corporate strategy for operating and competing in the financial-services industry, reflects the traditional approach to **strategic planning.** Part of the plan is deciding what products and services to produce and how to price them. The modern strategic approach also includes a framework for risk management and strategies for competing in the market for corporate control (i.e., a plan for the buying and selling of companies). The risk-management component fits the modern idea of the basic business of banking as measuring, managing, and accepting risk. The bank's objective is to manage value and risk by maximizing those items that create value and minimizing or eliminating those that destroy value. This approach highlights **economic value added** or **EVA.** A bank's corporate strategy and strategic-planning efforts can be viewed in terms of its **risk index** ($RI = [E(ROA) + CAP]/\sigma_{ROA}$, chapter 3), where planning and corporate control are designed to enhance $E(ROA)$ by adding value, whereas risk management concentrates on reducing the variability of ROA (σ_{ROA}) and strengthening capital adequacy (CAP).

KEY CONCEPTS, IDEAS, AND TERMS

- Business plan
- Corporate control
- Corporate strategy
- Economic value added (EVA)
- Managing value
- Risk index ($RI = [E(ROA) + CAP]/\sigma_{ROA}$)
- Risk management
- Strategic planning

JUSTICE HOLMES AND WHERE AM I GOING?

Supreme Court Justice Oliver Wendell Holmes was riding on the (then great) Pennsylvania Railroad when the conductor, a young man, approached him to check his ticket. Mr. Holmes began searching for his ticket among the various pockets of his three-piece suit. The conductor, sensing the man's frustration and recognizing him as Justice Holmes, said: "Sir, I am sure that the great Pennsylvania Railroad will be glad to transport you to your destination, where you may purchase another ticket." Justice Holmes looked up at the conductor in exasperation and said: "The problem, my young man, is not where is my ticket, but where am I going?"

The punchline of this story reflects one of the three questions managers, as corporate strategists, must ask about their companies: Where is the company going? As part of the trinity of strategic management and corporate planning, the critical questions are

- Where is the company today?
- Where is the company going?
- How is the company going to get there?

Whereas the first question can be viewed as a "situation audit," the second and third questions involve corporate vision and execution.

In assessing a company's future in the financial-services industry, managers of financial-services firms must address these questions. Moreover, they need to think about their answers in terms of managing value. Executives are rewarded for **adding value** to their companies. Chapter 3 provided some basic techniques for valuing a bank, measuring its risk exposure, and evaluating its accounting performance. This chapter expands on these themes in the broader context of corporate strategy. When we think about where the bank is going we focus on what opportunities exist to create (or destroy) value. Specifically, what businesses (e.g., securitization, mutual-funds management, financial-advisory services, investment banking, derivatives, insurance) should the bank enter or exit? Given these decisions, how can the businesses be managed such that they add value to the company? Implementation is the name of the game here. It requires generating positive net cash flows from existing or new businesses—the heart of the process of creating value.

THE CORPORATE OBJECTIVE: MANAGING VALUE

Copeland, Koller, and Murrin [1990] suggest that strategic planning at either the business or the corporate level must focus on a single idea: managing value. The heart of this concept is the notion of value added, which is symmetrical, because companies may have both **value creators** and **value destroyers.** The difference between the two can be viewed as net equity value. For companies with multiple businesses, value can be added by eliminating a business unit that destroys value or by adding one that creates value. The key to maximizing shareholder value reduces to a simple dictum:

> Add value to the company's existing businesses, which may mean getting out of unprofitable businesses (i.e., eliminating value destroyers).

The narrow or traditional view of strategic planning emphasizes business strategy in terms of gaining market share and increasing current earnings (the accounting model of the firm). In contrast, a broader view of strategic planning, the one advocated by Copeland, Koller, and Murrin, stresses both business and corporate strategies. A business plan focuses on products and prices, revenues and costs, and other day-to-day activities. In contrast, a corporate plan focuses on the market for corporate control. For companies that have only one business, the two strategies are the same; however, for companies with multiple businesses, such as large bank holding companies, both business and corporate strategies are needed. Because a particular business in a multibusiness company may be a takeover target, the entire company may be a takeover candidate. Planning for business units means managing value on the basis of the economic model of the firm where the focus is on discounted future cash flows. Copeland, Koller, and Murrin stress that without an ongoing focus of managing value from a cash-flow perspective, "a strategy that wins in a product or service market may lose in the market for corporate control" (p. 24).

COMMERCIAL BANKS AND VALUE MAXIMIZATION

The American Bankers Association (ABA) is the major trade organization for commercial banks. At the ABA's 1996 annual convention in Honolulu, Hawaii, Alan Greenspan, chairman of the Federal Reserve, was the leadoff speaker. His opening remarks were as follows:

> You may well wonder why a regulator is the first speaker at a conference in which a major theme is *maximizing shareholder value.* I hope that by the end of my remarks this morning it will be clear that we, the regulators, share with you ultimately the same objective of a *strong and profitable banking system.* Such a banking system knows *how to take and manage risk for profit.* The problem is what, if anything, regulators should do to constrain the amount of risk bankers take in trying to meet their *corporate objectives.* I have given considerable thought to this issue over the years, and today I would like to address this theme once again. (p. 1, emphasis mine)

The fact that the objective of modern finance was a major theme at a banking convention does not mean that the principles of modern finance are practiced on a widespread basis in U.S. banking. Nevertheless, the mere existence of this theme at an ABA convention is encouraging. Perhaps even more promising is finding regulators and bankers on the same page with respect to the most appropriate corporate objective for banks.

ALTERNATIVE MANAGERIAL MOTIVES

Models of managerial behavior typically assume that decision makers are attempting to optimize some variable such as utility, wealth, or profits. The assumption here is that managers are attempting to maximize the value of the firm and are focusing on managing value by adding value. Managers may have other motives, such as maximizing firm size, maximizing sales, or achieving personal fame and fortune. Given these alternative motives, bankers with monopoly power (i.e., control over price) tend to hire more staff, pay higher wages, and be less conscious of costs in general. In other words, they exhibit expense-preference behavior[1] and

---

[1] Evidence of expense-preference behavior has been found for both banks and S&Ls. For example, Edwards [1977], Glassman and Rhoades [1980], Hannan and Mavinga [1980], and Rhoades [1980] present evidence for banks, and Verbrugge and Goldstein [1981] and Verbrugge and Jahera [1981] present evidence for S&Ls.

perhaps a quest for what Hicks [1935] described as "the best of all monopoly profits: a quiet life" (p. 8). In a more competitive market, however, expense-preference behavior and other suboptimal maximizing would be competed away. As the financial-services industry (FSI) approaches the year 2000, managers of financial-services firms (FSF) will find it difficult to lead a quiet life.

ECONOMIC VALUE ADDED (EVA) AND EXECUTIVE COMPENSATION[2]

To measure managerial performance, Stern, Stewart & Co., a consulting firm, developed a joint measure of profitability and high-quality growth called economic value added (EVA™). Managers with EVA on their minds focus attention on the critical problem of allocating and managing capital, the fundamental task of modern finance. Since economic value added encourages managers to seek profitable growth, it discourages them from myopically focusing on the accounting model and current earnings. EVA can be defined as:

EVA = [Return on Capital − Cost of Capital] × Capital Invested at the Margin

Or, in symbols,

$$EVA = [r - k]K = rK - kK \qquad \textbf{(4-1)}$$

where r is the return on capital, k is the cost of capital, and K is capital invested at the margin. By removing the brackets in equation (4-1), we can describe EVA, at the margin, as the level of earnings management generates: (rK) minus the level of earnings investors require for bearing the risk associated with the investment (kK). The sign of EVA is determined by the difference between the return on capital (r) and its cost (k). When the return exceeds the cost, managers are adding value to the firm. In the opposite case, they are not adding any value to the firm. When managers have undertaken all projects for which $r > k$, managers have maximized the value of the firm because EVA, at the margin, is zero.[3] Figure 4-1 summarizes how EVA works, and some examples follow in the next paragraph.

The intuitive appeal of EVA, which gets at the heart of the benefit-cost foundation of modern finance, can be demonstrated by the following example. Consider a firm with a 10 percent cost of capital (k) and the following schedule of investment-opportunity returns (r): (0.15, 0.12, 0.10 0.08, 0.05). If each project costs $100 million ($K$), the schedule of EVA ($ millions) is (5, 2, 0, −2, −5). The value of invested capital is maximized when $r = k = 0.10$. At this point, EVA is zero. Investment beyond that point destroys value rather than creating it.

The linkages among EVA, profitable growth, and equity share price are straightforward. First, the use of EVA as a performance measure encourages managers to expand the company, but not at the expense of profitability, because $r > k$. Expansion continues as long as projects return more than they cost. When $EVA = 0$, the company stops its economic growth until new profitable projects can be discovered. The linkage between EVA and share price is also a direct one. In an efficient market, the economic model of the firm ensures that market value, as reflected

---

[2] This section draws on *Six Roundtable Discussions of Corporate Finance with Joel Stern* edited by Donald H. Chew, Jr., [1986]. Also see "Debate" [1997], Hamel [1997], and "Valuing Companies" [1997].

[3] Because EVA is a marginal concept in the value-maximization framework, it is similar to the case of profit maximization, where profits are maximized at the output at which marginal revenue equals margin cost and marginal profit is zero. In the case of value maximization, this point is reached when $r = k$ and $EVA = 0$.

Case 1: Value Added (Value Creation)
$$EVA > 0 \rightarrow r - k > 0 \rightarrow rK - cK > 0$$
Case 2: No Value Added (Value-Maximization Point at K*)
$$EVA = 0 \rightarrow r - k = 0 \rightarrow rK - cK = 0$$
Case 3: Value Subtracted (Value Destruction)
$$EVA < 0 \rightarrow r - k < 0 \rightarrow rK - cK < 0$$

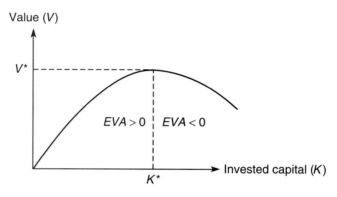

FIGURE 4-1 Economic Value Added (EVA)

by share price, equals the present value of future net cash flows. This value will be maximized when $EVA = 0$. Highly valued companies will be those whose managers have demonstrated to the market the ability to invest capital that earns a return greater than the opportunity cost of capital.

Figure 4-2 shows the relation between estimates of EVA (as captured by the spread, $r - k$) and a measure of market value (as captured by ratio of market value to book value). The observations are for the members of the Dow-Jones Industrial Average and for three components of the insurance industry: life insurance companies (LIFE), multiple-line companies (MULTI), and property-and-casualty companies (P&C). If we ignore the cross-industry comparisons, the evidence is clear: Firms that add value by investing in projects whose returns exceed their costs of capital are rewarded by the marketplace with higher market-to-book ratios. The location of LIFE, MULTI, and P&C in the southwest quadrant of Figure 4-2 suggests that the relative performance of the insurance industry in the early 1980s had room for improvement. Nevertheless, the insurance firms were not alone, because one-half of the members of the Dow-Jones Industrial Average (DJIA) were in the same quadrant. Perhaps the managers of these firms were relying too much on the accounting model of the firm rather than the economic model.

EVA and a Bank's Risk Index

The three components of a bank's risk index (RI) are $E(ROA)$, CAP, and σ_{ROA}. Recall from the previous chapter that $E(ROA)$ is the bank's expected return on assets, CAP is the reciprocal of the bank's equity multiplier or the bank's ratio of equity capital to total assets, and σ is the standard deviation of ROA. To generate RI, the relation among the variables is

$$RI = [E(ROA) + CAP]/\sigma_{ROA} \tag{4-2}$$

Because the components of RI are accounting-based measures, it suffers from all the shortcomings of such yardsticks. It should be clear, however, that bank managers who employ EVA-based decision making (let's call them "EVA banks") will have higher expected accounting earnings, stronger book capital positions, and reduced

FIGURE 4-2 Creating Value: The Relationship between EVA and Market Value

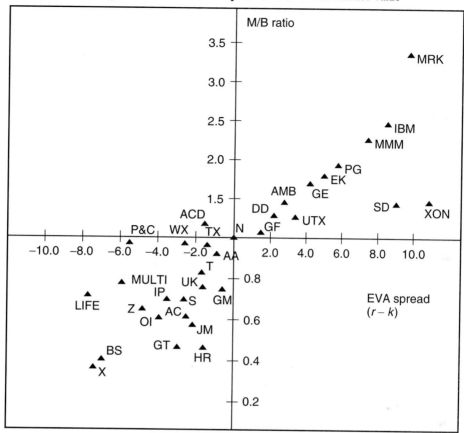

DJIA Legend

ACD	Allied Chemical	HR	Int'l Harvester
AA	Aluminum Co. of Amer.	IP	Int'l Paper
AMB	American Brands	JM	Johns-Manville
AC	American Can	MRK	Merck & Co.
T	American Telephone	MMM	Minnesota Mining
BS	Bethlehem Steel	OI	Owens-Illinois
DD	DuPont	PG	Procter & Gamble
EK	Eastman Kodak	S	Sears, Roebuck
XON	Exxon Corp.	SD	Standard Oil (C)
GE	General Electric	TX	Texaco, Inc.
GF	General Foods	UK	Union Carbide
GM	General Motors	X	US Steel Corp.
GT	Goodyear Tires	UTX	United Technologies
IBM	Int'l Business	WX	Westinghouse E
N	Inco Limited	Z	Woolworth (F.W.)

M/B ratio = Market-to-book ratio
EVA = Economic value added
r = Return on capital
k = Cost of capital

Source: Sweeney and Plyler (1984), Exhibit A, p. 23. DJIA data from Marakon Associates (1980). Reprinted by permission of LOMA.

variability of *ROA*, all other things being equal. On balance, EVA banks should have high values of *RI* (recall that higher is better for *RI*). However, a bank having a high *RI* does not mean that it is an EVA bank.

Rewarding Executives for Adding Value

Behavior can be conditioned by the carrot or the stick or some combination of the two. For example, the behavior of corporate executives can be shaped by the carrot of incentive compensation and by the stick of their potential removal from office (i.e., being fired or asked to resign by the board of directors).[4] Executive-compensation packages, including incentive clauses, are determined by negotiations between the executive (e.g., the chief executive officer, CEO, or the chief financial officer, CFO) and the compensation committee of the board of directors. Stern, Stewart & Co. contend that EVA-based compensation plans are doubly desirable because they encourage a favorable allocation of capital and high prices for investors. Specifically, such plans provide incentives for managers to

- Increase the efficiency of assets in place
- Expand assets as long as the rate of return on new projects exceeds the cost of capital
- Contract or redeploy underperforming assets

Because the last incentive can lead to downsizing and layoffs, displaced employees, especially those without an equity interest in the company, may become disgruntled with EVA-based plans. In this regard, Steward [1986] argues that executive compensation plans should be designed to[5]

- Build morale
- Retain good managers
- Promote decisions that will benefit shareholders

Because executive compensation is not independent of shareholder value,[6] the board of directors and the board's compensation committee (as shareholders' agents) must understand the economics of executive compensation and provide value-maximization incentives to managers. Economic value added (EVA) is a measure that links incentive compensation to the goal of enhancing shareholder value.

FINANCIAL MANAGEMENT AND MODERN CORPORATE STRATEGY

Let's think of a company's overall corporate strategy as consisting of three critical ingredients:

- A strategic business plan
- A framework for risk management
- A strategy for corporate control

---

[4] The executives of bank holding companies and insured depositories also face the threat of being removed from office by their regulators or deposit insurers.

[5] From Steward, in *Six Roundtable Discussions of Corporate Finance with Joel Stern* [1986], edited by Donald H. Chew, Jr., p. 2

[6] *Ibid*, chapter 6, pp. 265–320.

The old view of strategic planning tended to focus on a business plan as the only factor in strategic management. The influence of modern finance has added risk management and corporate control to create a triad of modern corporate strategy. This section focuses on these three aspects of overall corporate strategy as applied to commercial banks and other financial-services firms.

Strategic Business Planning in the Financial-Services Industry

Because banks produce financial services and products, they need strategies for operating and competing in these markets. In effect, they need a strategic business plan. Given the removal of geographic and product restrictions in banking and the ongoing fusion of the financial-services industry, this type of planning is crucial. Product development, marketing, and selling, especially cross-selling, are important ingredients of a bank's business plan as defined here. These aspects of planning are vital if a company is to be a successful deliverer of financial services. The three questions of the planning trinity

- *Where is the bank today?*
- *Where is the bank going?*
- *How is the bank going to get there?*

provide a framework for describing and analyzing the process of strategic planning.

In the jargon of strategic planners, the overall process of determining where the organization is today is sometimes called the *situation audit,* a prerequisite for planning. The cornerstone of the situation audit is SWOT analysis, where SWOT is the acronym for

- *Strengths*
- *Weaknesses*
- *Opportunities*
- *Threats*

The elements of SWOT (call them the SWOT team) underlie the planning process. The situation audit and the SWOT analysis assist managers in identifying alternative courses of action and evaluating them. The idea is to build on or exploit strengths and opportunities and to correct or eliminate weaknesses and threats; strengths and weaknesses are typically perceived as internal factors, whereas opportunities and threats are external factors.

Once the managers know where their institution is and what it is worth, they can decide where it should be going. In effect, a target for the organization is established. Typically, this target has a five-year time horizon, and in some instances the time horizon may extend to seven or ten years. Whatever the time horizon, the strategic plan is not a one-shot deal put on the shelf to gather dust; it is subject to annual readjustments. Thus, strategic plans should not be rigid and static; they should be flexible so that they can adapt to changing SWOT conditions and other dynamic factors.

In establishing where a financial institution is going, an articulated corporate vision is essential.[7] In essence, this vision is an image of what the organization should look like, say, five years hence. It should contain more than platitudes about

---

[7] This chapter ends with descriptions of the corporate visions of three major BHCs: Banc One (Columbus, OH), Bankers Trust (NY), and Citicorp (NY).

quality, pieties about competitiveness, and lengthy digressions into forecasts and projections. Instead, the corporate vision or master strategy should identify customers and services representing the bank's priorities and tell how the bank wishes to be positioned in those markets identified as having high priority. In short, the statement of vision is the blueprint for where the organization is going and how it will get there.

The articulation of a master strategy or vision statement is the responsibility of the chief executive officer (CEO), who must establish the importance of the planning process and the need to plan. Given a bank's long-run strategic target, which should be viewed as multidimensional, the CEO needs to focus on the alternative strategies that will best exploit the company's unique SWOT conditions. In brief, how is the bank going to move in the direction of its desired target? At this stage, what-if analysis, scenario planning, computer models, simulations, or other planning tools and techniques can be used to evaluate alternative strategies. Once an overall plan and specific strategy have been developed, they must be implemented and monitored. The monitoring part is important because the dynamic nature of the planning process requires annual revisions.

The Process and Definition of Strategic Planning

By focusing on how to answer the three basic questions of strategic planning, we get a clearer idea about the *process* of strategic planning. Strategic planning is, in effect, a thought process or way of thinking about the future of one's business and how to *add value* to it. To put it more formally, consider Drucker's [1974] definition of the strategic-planning process:

> . . . the task of thinking through the mission of the business, that is, of asking the question "what is our business and what should it be?" This leads to the setting of objectives, the development of strategies and plans, and the making of today's decisions for tomorrow's results. This clearly can be done only by an organ of the business that can see the entire business; that can make decisions that affect the entire business; that can balance objectives and the needs of today against the needs of tomorrow; and that can allocate resources of men and money to key results. (p. 611)

More succinctly, Kane ([1984], p. 725) says, "Allowing for alternative futures is the stuff of strategic planning." Although the "stuff" of strategic planning is complex and requires detailed information flows, managers must avoid getting bogged down in picayune details. They must look at the overall "forest" and not at the individual "trees" and certainly not at the myriad "leaves." Accordingly, strategic planners should foresee the overall effect of their financing and investment decisions. In addition, by exploring alternative futures, they are better prepared for surprises and for how to react to them.

Another View of Strategic Planning: Bobby Knight on General Patton   Bobby Knight and General George Patton are two renowned strategic planners in two vastly different games. Knight is the unpredictable and volatile but highly successful basketball coach at Indiana University. If we ignore Knight's personal shortcomings, he is successful because his teams win *and* most of his players graduate and become productive citizens. Patton, who also was unpredictable and volatile, was a highly successful U.S. general in World War II. Knight, who coached at West Point from 1965 to 1971 (six seasons, with a record of 102–50 and three National

Invitational Tournament bids), also is a student of military history. In a 1984 interview, Knight had these words on Patton, the military strategist:[8]

> Patton had an incredible ability to see *what to do* and *how to do it.* . . . I admire him because of his ability to grasp what he was confronted with and then beat it . . . he recognized *opportunities* and *developed strategies*—we'll use this road because it takes us here and that one *can't*—and the way he was willing to get down in the mud and direct tanks. (p. 62, emphasis mine)

Patton knew how to SWOT the enemy long before some business-school whiz coined the term. To some managers, the competitive nature of the FSI of the twenty-first century may look like a war in which they wish to surrender. To others the battle cry will be: "We have not yet begun to fight!"

A Take-No-Prisoners Approach to Bank Expansion   Another ex-military person, Hugh L. McColl, Jr., chairman of NationsBank of Charlotte, NC (formerly NCNB Corporation), has been making banking news in the area of corporate control (chapter 19). His corporate vision for NationsBank reflects the organization's name—he wants NationsBank to be a national and international franchise. In 1989, NCNB, offering $39 per share, attempted a hostile takeover of C&S Corporation, Atlanta. C&S fought off the takeover attempt and merged with Sovran to form C&S/Sovran. When Sovran's commercial real-estate loan portfolio turned sour shortly after the merger and its shareholders complained about low earnings for 1991, McColl was back with a friendly merger offer. The marriage of NCNB with C&S/Sovran created, at the time, the second-largest BHC in the United States, with total assets of $116 billion and a franchise extending from Washington, D.C., to Miami to west Texas. As of year-end 1996, NationsBank was the third-largest BHC in the United States.

McColl, a former marine who once used a dummy hand grenade as a paperweight on his desk, created an image of NCNB as the "Citicorp of the South." Under his tenure, NCNB gobbled up almost 30 competitors across the South and Southwest. In 1996, NationsBank moved away from its "southern U.S. strategy" with the acquisition of Boatsmen's Bancshares of St. Louis. On August 29, 1997, however, NationsBank made another major move in the south, when it agreed to buy Barnett Banks (FL) and push its total assets to almost $300 billion. McColl views the U.S. banking system as "archaic . . . locked in space and time, mollycoddling smaller and weaker banks" (*The Atlanta Constitution* [June 27, 1991], p. B8). McColl's objective is to become large enough to compete with Japanese and German banks. Given the globalization of world financial markets, McColl says banks have two choices: Buy or be bought. McColl, whose image has softened a bit recently, also has NationsBank known as a leading company in employee benefits (e.g., paternity leave). He uses a marine analogy regarding treatment of employees: "We were always told to feed the troops first and to lead from the front" [*ibid*].

The Objectives and Techniques of Strategic Planning

Although managing value and adding value should be the objectives of strategic planning (as suggested by Copeland, Koller, and Murrin [1990] and as

---

[8] In other parts of the interview, Knight has some less flattering words to say about Patton; see *Playboy* [August 1984].

TABLE 4-1 Ranking the Objectives of Strategic Planning		
Objectives	*Past*	*Future*
Provide a competitive return on assets and equity	1	1
Increase market share	2	3
Survive in a more competitive environment	3	2
Improve prestige in financial community	4	8
Reduce portfolio risk	5	6
Achieve a competitive advantage	6	5
Have new technology for customers' use	7	4
Have new technology for internal use	8	7

Source: Gup and Whitehead [1983].

pushed by the ABA as a theme at its 1996 annual convention), managers of financial institutions are not prone to express their strategic objectives in this context. Based on a survey by the Federal Reserve Bank of Atlanta, Table 4-1 reveals the planning objectives expressed by some managers of financial institutions. The number one objective was generating a competitive ROA and ROE. Focusing on these accounting measures of performance is misdirected, however, because competitive ROEs and ROAs may not result in adding value to the firm. Other objectives that boards of directors and CEOs considered important in the planning process were survival, market share, and technology for internal use.

Table 4-2 shows a ranking of the most important techniques used in strategic planning. Of the 16 techniques reported, the top five were

1. Portfolio analysis (i.e., evaluating the composition and value of current and future portfolios)
2. "Brainstorming"
3. Simulation models

TABLE 4-2 Techniques of Strategic Planning	
Techniques	*Rank*
Portfolio analysis	1
Brainstorming	2
Corporate financial simulation models	3
Cash flow	4
Market research	5
Conferences	6
Risk and decision analysis	7
Futuristic projections	8
Panel consensus	9
Product Information Market System (PIMS)	10
External on-line data banks	11
Product life cycle	12
Leading indicator analysis	13
Time series analysis	14
Econometric analysis	15
Regression analysis	16

Source: Gup and Whitehead [1983].

4. Cash-flow analysis

5. Market research

Although managing value and adding value were not listed as objectives of strategic planning, two of the top five techniques, portfolio analysis and cash-flow analysis, suggest that managing and adding value are important techniques of strategic planning. Thus, although the accounting model in the form of ROE and ROA appears at the top of the list of strategic-planning objectives, two of the top five planning tools are oriented toward market valuation or the economic model of the firm. Nevertheless, finding the accounting model at the top of the list is consistent with three interrelated facts: (1) The overwhelming majority of banks are small community banks whose stocks are not actively traded; (2) given infrequent trading, the true values of community banks are less certain; and (3) with uncertain true values, bank managers naturally look at accounting proxies like ROE and ROA to convey information about changes in value.

A Marketing Approach

Because many observers of the financial-services industry view it as becoming increasingly a market- and customer-driven business, the **five Ps of marketing** are interesting to consider as a strategic-planning framework:[9]

1. Product

2. Place

3. Price

4. Promotion

5. People

To judge the success of a bank's business planning, one can address the following kinds of questions: Are we (the bank) producing the products and services our customers want and need? Are we in the best places for doing the kinds of business we want to do? Are we setting our prices appropriately? Are we getting the most out of our advertising dollar? Are bank employees eager to support bank promotions?

Given the people factor, if a bank has the appropriate products, locations, prices, and promotions, it will be well on its way to maximizing shareholder value.

SWOT Analysis

Bank managers must know how their organizations stack up in terms of their strengths, weaknesses, opportunities, and threats, or SWOT. Various frameworks exist for conducting SWOT analysis. For example, what is the bank's SWOT with respect to adding value, its risk index, the five Ps of marketing, or the four success factors shown in Table 4-3?

If SWOT analysis can be tied to customers, products, and delivery systems, it can be a very useful planning technique. To illustrate, money-market mutual funds grew tremendously during the late 1970s and the 1980s by exploiting technological and regulatory opportunities to become viable competitors for consumers' savings. The 800 telephone number and less-regulated production processes were key factors in their success. In the FSI, chances to add value will be available to those players who are able to deliver innovative products in a timely fashion, products that

---

[9] This framework is a traditional marketing paradigm that I first heard applied to banking by a representative of Mellon Bank (Pittsburgh, PA) at a conference on bank strategic planning in the early 1980s.

TABLE 4-3 Strategic Success Factors for Banks

- General Management
  - Management quality (the M in CAMEL ratings)
  - Management evaluation and motivation (EVA)
  - Risk management (a bank's risk index, RI)
  - Responsiveness to change (financial innovation)
- Marketing
  - Product offerings (investment banking, insurance, and mutual funds)
  - Customer service (supermarket banking, 24-hour banking via the Internet)
  - Segmentation (new products, such as home equity loans)
  - Marketing skills (cross-selling)
- Technology/Operations
  - Technological readiness (securitization and derivatives)
  - Distribution (electronic funds transfer, ATMs, and Internet banking)
- Finance
  - Capital access (nondeposit sources of funds and securitization)
  - Pricing (floating-rate loans)
  - Asset-and-liability management (ALM)

Source: Adapted from Arthur Andersen & Co. [1983]. Exhibit 1, p. 5. Parenthetical inserts mine.

exploit market opportunities opened up by technology (e.g., the Internet) and competitive reregulation.

Success Factors in Bank Strategic Planning

New Dimensions in Banking: Managing the Strategic Position, a joint study by the Bank Administration Institute (BAI) and Arthur Andersen & Company, identified four strategic success factors for banks:

1. General management
2. Marketing
3. Technology/operations
4. Finance

Although these elements were identified as important success factors for bank strategic planning in the early 1980s, they are still relevant today as bankers plan to enter the twenty-first century. Table 4-3 provides additional detail regarding each of the success factors, with examples or potential measures supplied for each subcategory.

A Planning Approach for Small Banks

Managers of small banks may feel overwhelmed by the task of developing a strategic plan. However, once they start *thinking,* rather than *feeling,* about the project, the task will appear more manageable. Dunahee [1983] has suggested an approach and a framework for small banks to follow to get the planning process started. The first step is to organize the planning process (Figure 4-3) by appointing an officer to shepherd staff and data through (1) the planning schedule and (2) the thinking through of the plan. Figure 4-3, Panel A, presents a sample planning schedule in which steps, deadlines, and responsibilities are specified. Figure 4-3, Panel B, summarizes the process of thinking through a brief sample plan. Dunahee suggests organizing the logical flow of the plan into a series of questions about the

FIGURE 4-3 A Planning Approach for Small Banks

Panel A. The planning schedule

Step	*Deadline*	*Responsibility*
(1) Preparation for planning day	August	Planning officer (manager of product development)
(2) Planning day	September	All senior vice presidents, the CEO, and the president
(3) First draft of plan	October	Planning officer
(4) Middle-management input	October	Sampling of line and staff officers
(5) Final draft of plan	November	Planning officer
(6) Communicate plan Officer dinner meeting Branch, dept. meetings	November	Everybody
(7) Develop action plans	December	Branch managers and department heads
(8) Develop budgets	December	Branch managers and department heads
(9) Follow-up action plans and budgets	Quarterly	CEO

ORGANIZE PLANNING by appointing an officer to shepherd staff and data through a process like this—then think it through as shown in Panel B.

Panel B. Thinking planning through

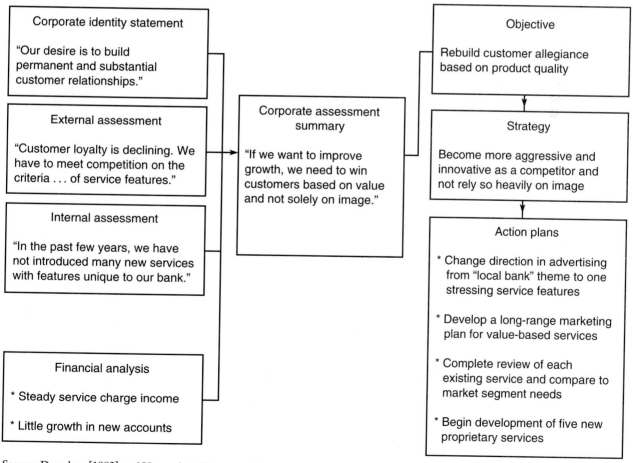

Source: Dunahee [1983], p. 189; reprinted by permission.

bank's performance and future. Only when the answers to the questions are in dispute are research and analysis needed. This approach emphasizes thinking, which is the focus of the planning process, and urges smaller banks to match their desire for data with their resources.

If community bankers will put their thoughts about the future of their organizations and businesses down in writing and review them with management teams at least once a year, they will be on their way to preparing for alternative futures—the stuff of strategic planning.

A Framework for Risk Management[10]

Fluctuations in interest rates, exchange rates, and commodity and real-estate prices are not something new. However, beginning with the interest-rate peak of 1966 (the prime rate hit 6 percent), managers of U.S. financial-services firms have been buffeted for over three decades by greater volatility of underlying rates and prices. Deflation in energy prices, agricultural prices, and real-estate prices resulted in major credit-risk problems for U.S. commercial banks in the 1970s, 1980s, and 1990s. Inflation and rising interest rates over the years 1966 to 1982 were the catalysts for the savings-and-loan crisis. Similar problems in less-developed countries (LDCs) generated massive loan losses for large U.S. banks during the 1980s—the international debt crisis. In 1994 and early 1995, unexpected inflation and exchange-rate volatility wreaked havoc with the derivatives deals and trading profits of large banks, especially Bankers Trust of New York.

Clearly, fluctuations in economic and financial variables destabilize the corporate strategies and performance of banks *and* their client customers. Thus, it is crucial that banks have a framework for risk management and for selling risk-management services to clients. Risk management can be conducted on a bank's balance sheet through adjustments in portfolio composition, or off the balance sheet by using a host of risk-management weapons derived from the technology of financial engineering. These off-balance-sheet tools of risk management are known as derivatives contracts or activities, or simply as "derivatives."

As presented here and consistent with the approach of Froot, Scharfstein, and Stein (FSS, [1993, 1994]), a bank's risk-management strategy must be integrated with its overall corporate strategy. According to FSS [1994], a risk-management framework rests on three pillars (p. 92):

- *Making good investment decisions creates corporate value.* For traditional banks, this means making good loans and investments; for nontraditional banks, it means this *plus* making good investment decisions regarding their nontraditional activities, e.g., investment banking, mutual funds, insurance, derivatives.
- *Generating enough cash flow internally is the key to making good investments.* Companies that do not generate enough cash flow internally tend to cut investment more substantially than their competitors do. In banking, generating enough cash flow internally plays a critical role in maintaining a firm's capital adequacy. Adequate capital, in turn, is a prerequisite for expansion and making good investments. With respect to costs and control, banks with inadequate capital are subject to higher deposit-insurance premiums, greater regulatory scrutiny, and possible takeover by outsiders.

---

[10] This section draws on the framework for risk management found in Froot, Scharfstein, and Stein [1993] and [1994]. My analysis differs from their approach only in terms of its application to banks and other financial-services firms.

- *Because cash flow can be disrupted by adverse movements in external factors such as interest rates, exchange rates, and commodity prices, a company's ability to invest can be jeopardized.* Banks are especially sensitive to adverse changes in interest rates and adverse movements in the underlying commodity prices faced by their borrowers.

Understanding these three points is doubly important to bankers because it permits them to better comprehend not only their own risk-management problems but also those of their client borrowers. And, since credit risk is the major risk banks face, a risk-management framework that highlights the cash flows and investment opportunities of borrowers and would-be borrowers provides the appropriate focus for making lending decisions.

FSS [1994] conclude that a company's risk-management program should have as its sole objective:

> to ensure that the company has the cash available to make value-enhancing investments (p. 92).

From a lender's perspective, if a company has such cash available, it perforce has funds to repay its lenders. Timely repayment of loans, of course, is a lender's ultimate objective. FSS's view of the linkage between cash flow and value-enhancing investments is not new, because the work of Nobel-prize winners Franco Modigliani and Merton Miller established this foundation of modern finance years ago. It can be restated as the primacy of the investment decision (over the financing and dividend decisions).[11] Alternatively, the key to creating value rests on the left-hand side of the balance sheet, which has two components in a market-value context:

> The value of assets in place and the present value
> of future growth opportunities (PVGO).

In this view, the focus of corporate strategy is maximizing the value of assets in place and adding value by tapping future profitable growth opportunities.

The goal of enhancing company value leads bank managers to focus on the same basic questions of risk management:

- Which credit, interest-rate, or currency risks should they hedge and which ones should be left unhedged?
- What kinds of instruments and asset-liability-management strategies are available and appropriate for the bank's operating environment and competitive circumstances?
- Should the bank's risk-management strategy be affected by its competitors' strategies?

In a sterile academic world, one might argue that risk-management strategies do not matter. A modern synthesis, however, views risk management, like the treatment of financial policy, as critical in terms of "*enabling* companies to make valuable investments" (FSS [1994], p. 93). This enabling process of risk management guarantees that a company's supply of funds will equal its demand for funds and thereby permit the company to make value-enhancing investments.

Guidelines for Bank Managers

As risk managers and sellers of risk-management products, bank managers need to think about risk-management issues. The following list, which is not intended

---

[11] In the real world, no one takes seriously the views that the financing and dividend decisions are irrelevant. In terms of priorities, however, the investment decision ranks as more important.

to be exhaustive and which follows FSS [1994], presents some (adaptive) guidelines for how bank managers can think about risk-management issues.

- The nature of banking and financial services makes it imperative that financial-services firms (FSFs) engage in risk management. Because FSFs do not have major investments in plant and equipment, they lack "hard assets" as collateral for securing sources of funding. Their investments are more in the form of human and reputational capital rather than physical capital. These "softer" or intangible assets include such items as skilled underwriters, experienced calling officers, brand-name recognition, market share, government guarantees, and valuable core deposits. Thus, because of the nature of their investments, FSFs may have to be even more active about managing risk.

- Financial-services firms in the same industry should not necessarily have the same hedging strategy. All commercial banks, for example, face interest-rate risk, but as noted in chapter 3, one risk does not fit all. Thus, unexpected changes in interest rates affect the cash flows and investment opportunities of banks differently. The key ingredient in risk management is understanding how a bank's cash flows and investment opportunities are affected by all the risk exposures a bank faces.

- Even banks with adequate capital and conservative lending policies can benefit from hedging. The fundamental question here is would the bank be more valuable if management took on more leverage and adopted a more aggressive lending policy, and then used derivatives markets to hedge the greater risk taking?

- Multinational banks and superregional banks with growing international exposure must recognize that foreign-exchange risk affects both their cash flows and their investment opportunities. A comprehensive risk-management strategy requires banks to understand the nature of their globalized operations, which can be viewed as a weighted average of their domestic and foreign businesses. Thus, these businesses have cash flows and investment opportunities that must be analyzed and understood jointly to conduct effective risk management.

- Banks should not ignore the risk-management strategies of their competitors. The development of the financial-services industry means looking not only at what other banks are doing but also at what other FSFs are doing. If a bank's competitors are not hedging, should the bank follow the pack and also not hedge? Suppose that several banks are considering establishing nationwide franchises and only one of them is engaging in hedging activities. Although external shocks weaken its competitors, the hedging bank's cash flows will be protected at precisely the time when its competitors' weaknesses can be exploited.

- Finally, to echo the words of Charles Sanford [1994], chairman of Bankers Trust Corporation of New York, senior management needs to be "the risk manager of risk managers." This means that risk-management strategies and the selection of specific derivatives should *not* be delegated to financial specialists in the bank. Since the educational gap between younger, "hotshot" financial engineers and older senior managers can be great, it is even more imperative that Sanford's advice be heeded.[12]

Recapitulation

Since the basic business of banking is the measuring, managing, and accepting of risk, it is imperative that bankers have a framework for risk management. Such a program offers two avenues for enhancing the value of the bank: First, by hedging their own risk exposures, banks can reduce the variability of firm value

---

[12] Regarding the use of specific derivatives instruments, details of which are explained in the next chapter, Sanford [1994] emphasizes that top management needs to understand two key aspects of their use: First, different cash-flow requirements exist for different instruments (e.g., exchange-traded futures that must be marked-to-market). And second, the nature of the payoff or profit profiles of the derivatives contracts must be considered. Futures and forwards are "linear" contracts that have symmetrical payoff patterns, whereas options are "nonlinear" contracts that have asymmetrical profit profiles.

and enhance the value of the bank. And second, by selling risk-management services to client borrowers, banks generate fees and help ensure that borrowers will have funds to repay loans, and take advantage of growth opportunities. To do a good job of selling risk-management services to their corporate clients, bankers must understand the risks, cash flows, and investment opportunities these customers face.

On balance, a bank's framework for risk management should be part of its overall corporate strategy for enhancing the value of the bank.

Strategies for Corporate Control[13]

The wave of consolidation in banking and the financial-services industry and the debate about who can own a bank require financial-services firms to have strategies for competing in the **market for corporate control,** which refers to the market for buying and selling companies. In mergers and acquisitions (M&A) the dictum is:

Gobble or Be Gobbled

Banks that effectively manage their cash flows and investment opportunities will be in a position to gobble rather than be gobbled. The corporate strategy is to determine how the company can add value to existing businesses, and to add new businesses that create value. Adding value is the name of the planning game. Moreover, when business and corporate strategies are successful, they maximize shareholder value. If shareholder value is maximized, then nothing exists for corporate raiders to take because existing management has done its job. Managers who have failed to maximize firm value must waste energy, money, and time trying to prevent their companies from being taken over.

THREE CORPORATE VISIONS: BANC ONE, BANKERS TRUST, AND CITICORP

This section describes the corporate visions of three major U.S. bank holding companies: Banc One of Columbus, Ohio, a prominent "superregional" BHC and a new member of the 10 largest BHCs in the United States; Bankers Trust Corporation of New York, a traditional New York money-center bank that embarked on a strategy of "global wholesale finance," a substantial departure from its origins as a commercial bank; and Citicorp (New York), a major U.S. bank holding company and one of the world's leading financial-services firms.

Banc One, Columbus, Ohio

When John G. McCoy took control of Banc One in 1959, he envisioned building a high-quality "Tiffany" bank, not merely a big "Woolworth" bank, out of an also-ran with $140 million in assets (Wysocki [1984]). McCoy's approach to planning was to thrust "zealots" together with "implementers" and "controllers" and let them engage in "gentle confrontation" to establish Banc One's corporate vision and execution plan. One of the leading zealots at Banc One was John F. Fisher, who led the bank's push into consumer banking and who helped the bank gain its

---

[13] Chapter 19, which deals with consolidation in the FSI, deals with corporate-control issues and bank mergers in detail.

reputation as a pioneer in consumer banking. As an innovator, Banc One was not afraid to break with tradition, because it played a major role in launching Merrill Lynch's cash-management account. McCoy, who retired as CEO in 1984, managed Banc One by hiring people who were exceptional at something and giving them ample room to operate.

Although John G. McCoy was succeeded in 1984 by his son, John B. McCoy, Banc One's corporate vision remains intact. The vision, however, has expanded beyond the Midwest. The younger McCoy's rules for expansion by acquisition are

> Keep existing management in place, consolidate back-office operations, build up the retail business, and never buy a bank more than one-third the parent company's size. (Hirsch [1990])

In 1989, Banc One acquired MCorp's 20 failed banks in Texas. The deal, which McCoy opposed until subordinates convinced him otherwise, was an FDIC-assisted transaction that cost Banc One only $500 million. The original terms of the deal gave Banc One a 7.2 percent interest in the failed banks, with the FDIC holding the rest. Over the next five years, however, in accordance with the agreement, Banc One bought out the FDIC's position with profits from Banc One, Texas. Following the MCorp acquisition, Banc One embarked on building a retail branch network in Texas by buying zombie S&Ls. At the beginning of 1991, Banc One was the fifth-largest bank in Texas and the 15th largest in the United States, with total assets of $40 billion. Without its Texas operations, Banc One ranked as the 24th-largest U.S. bank. By the end of the first quarter of 1995, Banc One was the eighth largest BHC in the United States, with total assets of $87.8 billion, $18 billion of which came from its Texas operations, which had jumped from fifth largest to third in the Lone Star State. One year later, Banc One had total assets of $96 billion.

Size is not Banc One's only strength, however, because it has consistently been one of the most profitable banks in the United States. Because cost efficiency is one of the characteristics of high-performance banks, Hirsch reported that Banc One's top management was embarrassed when it hosted analysts in MCorp's executive suites decorated with $2.5 million of paintings and sculptures. Moreover, MCorp's atrium lobby, with marble floors, granite arches, and $8 million dollars of cherrywood paneling, probably caused some blushing too. Such expense-preference behavior does not add to shareholder value. Hirsch describes Banc One's corporate headquarters as "nondescript," a fact that is no doubt greatly appreciated by Banc One's shareholders.

Two cornerstones of Banc One's corporate culture are discipline and efficiency. At Banc One's headquarters in Ohio, Hirsch describes these two rules: "Employees who have a glass of wine, or any other alcoholic beverage, at lunch are told not to return in the afternoon. They also aren't allowed to drink coffee at their desks" (p. 2). When John B. McCoy took over for his father, he refused a vice president's request to lift the no-coffee-at-desk ban. Although John G. McCoy was said to patrol the building at night to make sure that desks were neat, his son has not gone that far. Moreover, not all of the rules at Banc One's corporate headquarters are enforced in its branch offices.

To summarize, a company's corporate vision comes from its CEO. Quality, discipline, and efficiency have been the hallmarks of the McCoy vision for Banc One. Although the boundaries of the vision have expanded from father to son, the vision has been clear and steady.

The Focus of Bankers Trust[14]

In 1987, Charles S. Sanford, Jr., became chairman of Bankers Trust Corporation, New York. Following his company's derivatives debacles of 1993 and 1994, he resigned on April 16, 1996.

Because he viewed banking as a dead-end industry, Sanford's vision for Bankers Trust was "global wholesale finance" based on the business of risk management. Viewing itself as a model of the modern investment bank, Bankers Trust relied heavily on the creation, sale, and trading of derivatives and a collective hubris in which the bank's sellers and traders believe they were good enough to beat the other players. Until April 1994, the strategy was the darling of Wall Street. The bank earned a net profit of over $1 billion in 1993 and was flying high. Since then, however, Bankers Trust has plunged back to earth. Its 12-month stumble reached a nadir on March 13, 1995 (not a Friday, just a black Monday) when its stock price dropped 16 percent, almost $10 a share, to close at $51.625, some 33 percent below its 52-week high. The adverse market reaction was to the news of a projected first-quarter loss of $125 million due to serious losses in Latin America and on derivatives transactions.

Before this, Bankers Trust was battered by a series of complaints by corporate clients about high-pressure and possible deceptive sales practices associated with derivatives products. As a result of these complaints, Bankers Trust settled out of court with Gibson Greetings Inc., agreeing to accept only $6 million for a $20-million debt but denying any guilt or wrongdoing. In addition, Bankers Trust was fined $10 million by the Securities and Exchange Commission and signed an "unusual enforcement agreement" with the Federal Reserve Bank of New York to improve its supervision of the sale of risky derivatives to corporate clients. Finally, based on its own internal probe, Bankers Trust reassigned five executives involved in soured derivatives deals. These events notwithstanding, Bankers Trust decided to battle Procter & Gamble in the courts over derivatives liability regarding their deals.

When things go wrong, the critics come out of the woodwork. *The Economist* referred to Bankers Trust's corporate strategy as "blurred vision." Reporting for *The Wall Street Journal,* Knecht [1995] quoted one former executive as saying

> Charlie (Charles Sanford) caused a mass hypnosis that led everyone to believe that derivatives were the new paradigm of the financial world. Some of us thought that derivatives were a good business, but that we could not rely on them forever. Charlie thought they were the be-all and end-all.

Critics contend that the focus on derivatives led Bankers Trust to neglect developing long-term customer relationships. Prior to his retirement in early 1996, Mr. Sanford attempted to rebuild relationships by appointing a high-level committee to focus on increasing them.

What does the future hold for Bankers Trust? Will the company downsize its derivatives business and risk a takeover? Will it shift gears and attempt to become a financial conglomerate? Will it attempt to maintain its derivatives vision but without the problems that plagued it in the mid-1990s? Whatever course the bank

---

[14] This section draws on Knecht [1995], Kaplan [1995], and "Bankers Trust: Blurred Vision," *The Economist* (April 8, 1995).

follows, we can expect it to reflect Mr. Sanford's philosophy, as expressed in a commencement address at the University of Georgia in 1989:[15]

> The real risk in life turns out to be the refusal to take a risk. Risk, properly conceived, is often highly productive rather than something to avoid.

Citicorp/Citibank as Innovator

On September 1, 1984, John S. Reed, at the age of 45, became chairman of Citicorp. He succeeded Walter B. Wriston. Both of these men have been described as having "wide, expansive, and visionary minds," which no doubt is one of the reasons why Citicorp has been a leader of banking changes on the technological, regulatory, and competitive fronts. Innovative and adaptive managers and planners are key ingredients in the strategic-planning process and in getting companies to change. On his rise to the top, Reed, a technocrat with an MIT engineering degree, was responsible for cleaning up Citibank's back-office problems and developing a systems approach to the operations of its proposed national consumer and electronic banking network. Like Wriston, Reed has continued Citicorp's innovative and expansionary ways, which include a plan to make the organization a worldwide force in investment banking, insurance, and information processing, in addition to its traditional banking activities. One of Citicorp's strategies has been to challenge or circumvent regulations that impede its progress. Citicorp's approach to potential opportunities is reflected in the following statement by Wriston regarding the possibility of Citicorp's acquiring Continental Illinois during the Chicago bank's 1984 liquidity crisis: "We're always interested in anything. We've had people studying all the possible scenarios."[16]

An Alternative View of Citibank's Innovativeness

On August 30, 1984, the editorial page of *The Wall Street Journal* carried a story (Stabler [1984]) that lauded the stewardship of Walter Wriston as the innovative leader of Citicorp/Citibank. The article, which appeared three days before Wriston's retirement, compared the innovative changes introduced by Citibank (described as an "avalanche") to the glacierlike movements of the industry as a whole.

On September 26, 1984, Clark Bass, chairman of the First National Bank of McAlester, Oklahoma, sent the following letter to the editor of *The Wall Street Journal,* published under the heading of "Performance Audit."

> Only time will determine the accuracy of your glowing article concerning the stewardship of Walter Wriston in the banking industry. . . . Negotiable certificates of deposit and variable-rate loans are no big deal. We even have these out here in the boondocks and have had for years. However, third world loans we don't have. The only reason the "Great Crisis" Mr. Wriston mentioned has not already occurred is that the taxpayers have put up billions of dollars in order for banks like Mr. Wriston's to avoid a great crisis. One of these days the taxpayers are going to rebel against such practices, and then and only then will the true value of his leadership be determined.

As you can see, Chairman Bass has a different view of Wriston's stewardship. Most community bankers *probably* would support the view from 235 East Choctaw

---

[15] As reported by Knecht [1995].
[16] *American Banker* [April 29, 1984], p. 22.

rather than the one from Wall Street. Although Citicorp/Citibank has been an innovator, when Mr. Bass raises the question of taxpayer subsidies to bail out third-world lenders (which is a different issue), he is right on target.

Citicorp's View of Winning the Financial-Services Battle

What will it take to be competitive in the FSI? One view of a potential winning game plan is presented in Table 4-4. The strategy was formulated by George Vojta, a former Citicorp executive. His nine-point program, expanded to ten elements here, can be grouped into two broad categories, focusing on

1. Financial management
2. Customers, products, and markets

The financial-management factors emphasize the importance of consistent earnings and a portfolio of earning assets that is maturity (or duration) balanced or

---

TABLE 4-4   What It Will Take to Win the Battle for Financial Services in the Twenty-First Century: A Top-Ten List

1. *Profitability.* A winner will make a reasonable profit during any phase of the business and interest-rate cycles. Earning assets will be duration matched or hedged using derivatives.
2. *Liquidity and Securitized Assets.* A winner will liquidate assets when they no longer suit the bank's book or risk profile. Because of securitization, assets will not be held to maturity.
3. *Positive Margin.* A winner will earn an adequate return on capital even with lower spreads whereas losers will likely have too much capital earning unacceptable returns.
4. *Increased Productivity.* A winner will commit to lower nonfinancial costs; develop new, less costly modes of electronic distribution; and achieve higher productivity. Lower margins will dictate that only cost-efficient producers survive.
5. *Market Segmentation.* A winner will effectively identify, segment, organize, and manage discrete and diverse market segments in order to serve particular sets of customers more efficiently.
6. *Complete and Competitive Product Lines.* A winner will achieve product superiority in whatever market segments it competes in. The consumer will select the best products on the market, regardless of whether banks or nonbanks deliver them.
7. *Structuring Integrated Businesses.* A winner will organize and effectively use subsidiary businesses as an integrated unit. The key to effective strategic management is to know which businesses create value (EVA) and which ones destroy value.
8. *Restructuring Compensation Policies.* A winner will pay people who get successful results. Hierarchical compensation structures will be a thing of the past as commissions play a greater role.
9. *Market Position.* A winner will select a market niche it can defend against all comers, which will be especially important for community banks and smaller institutions to survive against bigger players.
10. *Electronic Banking, Fees, and Customer Service.* A winner will have to walk a tightrope in balancing electronic delivery systems and the fees to support such systems while still trying to maintain quality services for customers.

Source: The first nine points are adapted from Vojta [1983].

hedged, flexibility to permit portfolio restructuring, maintaining ROE in the face of lower spreads by increasing asset utilization, and increasing productivity by controlling overhead costs and rewarding productivity in people. The key elements with respect to customers, products, and markets stress the importance of segmentation and positioning in markets, complete and competitive products, and development of integrated businesses for the FSI.

Citicorp and Capital Adequacy: A Rethinking[17]

"Be capitalized or beware" is a traffic sign on the road to survival in the financial-services industry. On December 18, 1990, Citicorp's top management sent a memo to its employees stressing the importance of capital adequacy in the 1990s. In part the memo stated: "The notion of low capital balanced by a broadly diversified business is simply not accepted in today's world" (Loomis [1991], p. 90). It's not that the Wriston/Reed leadership ever thought that capital was not important; however, Citicorp did have a rather cavalier attitude toward it. Less kindly, one might say that Citicorp's management thought that its organization was so large and diversified and so good at what it did (the hubris or ego factor) that it could get along with less capital than its competitors. In addition, unlike Banc One, Citicorp also was a bit cavalier about controlling its costs, which in the 1980s rose by 20 to 25 percent in some years. Citicorp's 1990 memo also called for "less bureaucracy" and fewer "inefficiencies."

To implement its new "capital-awareness-and-efficiency strategy," Citicorp cut its 1990 dividend from $1.78 per share to $1.00 (later the dividend was eliminated and then restored; chapter 3), reduced the number of employees by about 8,000, and attempted to cut $800 million from its $10 billion in expenses. When the industry's largest bank, and one of its most innovative players, has to announce a turnaround strategy based on strengthened capital and cost efficiency, it reflected poorly on Citicorp's leadership and planning and demonstrated, at the time, the weakened condition of the banking industry. As the industry approaches the twenty-first century, no bank can ignore the warning sign: Be capitalized or beware.

Citicorp's Shifting Corporate Focus: International Business and Global Reach

Early in 1995, John Reed announced (Kraus [1995]) that Citicorp, with $250 billion in assets, would shift the focus of its *corporate banking business* more toward clients with global reach, implying less emphasis on the purely local and the purely domestic business of corporate banking. The shift in focus, which took 12–18 months to complete, led Citicorp to concentrate on a select group of some 1000 companies worldwide, resulting in a corporate banking business with "a smaller asset sheet, smaller risks, and better growth." As part of his corporate philosophy, Reed wants a more "centralized strategy" with respect to corporate banking, which in the past has been described "as a group of semi-autonomous entities that were free to expand as opportunities arose." This new approach calls for corporate banking to develop areas where it can bring a "substantial advantage" to the table rather than be a "me-too-product bank" in an industry with clear overcapacity.

Citicorp does not plan, however, on scaling back its international consumer banking and related operations, such as credit cards. Over recent years, consumer banking, domestic and international, has accounted for well over one-half of

---

[17] Chapter 3 documents Citicorp's financial decline in the late 1980s and early 1990s and its strong rebound since then.

Citicorp's earnings. With income from consumer banking expected to grow twice as fast as income from corporate banking, Citicorp is looking for products and markets with the greatest potential to add value to the company.

Recapitulation

Banc One, Bankers Trust, and Citicorp have different corporate visions and different approaches to attempting to add value for their shareholders. The common denominator in their corporate strategies, however, is a financial-management approach to modern corporate strategy: a business plan, a framework for risk management, and a strategy for corporate control.

BANKING AND THE RAILROAD SYNDROME

A popular analogy has been to compare banks (and other FSFs) with the transportation revolution faced by U.S. railroads following World War II. The ill fate of the railroads was established when they failed to see that they were operating in the transportation industry and not in the railroad industry. Bankers who fail to recognize that they are operating in the *financial-services industry* (FSI) and not in the banking industry will eventually suffer the same fate as the railroads, or at best, wind up as the caboose on the FSI express. To put it more elegantly, consider John Naisbitt's statement from his book *Megatrends* [1982]:

> Unless banks reconceptualize what business they are in, they will be out of business. In the next few years, we will witness many bank mergers and bank failures. When I was a young person growing up with the memories of the Depression all around me, bank failures meant the end of the world. Today bank failures only mean that, like the railroaders, some bankers are just waiting around for their virtue to be rewarded. There will still be abundant banking services available from many kinds of institutions. (p. 92)

Chapter Summary

In managing value and risk, banks need a business plan, that is, a corporate strategy for avoiding the **railroad syndrome.** A business plan for operating in the financial-services industry deals in part with what products and services to produce and how to price them. It reflects the traditional approach to strategic planning. The modern approach also includes a framework for risk management and strategies for competing in the market for corporate control (i.e., a plan for the buying and selling of companies). The risk-management aspect fits the modern idea of the basic business of banking as measuring, managing, and accepting risk. The bank's objective is to manage value and risk by maximizing items that create value and minimizing or eliminating those that destroy value. Economic value added (EVA) is a device for measuring firm performance and rewarding executives.

On balance, a company's overall corporate strategy needs to include a business plan, a framework for risk management, and strategies for corporate control.

Key Words, Concepts, and Acronyms

- Adding value
- Business plan
- Corporate control
- Corporate strategy
- Economic value added (EVA)
- Financial-services industry (FSI)

- Five Ps of marketing
- How is the bank going to get there?
- Managing value
- Markets (for products and services versus for corporate control)

- Railroad syndrome
- Return on assets (ROA)
- Return on equity (ROE)
- Risk management
- Strategic planning

- Strengths, weaknesses, opportunities, and threats (SWOT)
- Value (creators and destroyers)
- Where is the bank going?
- Where is the bank today?

Review/Discussion Questions

1. What are the three important questions of strategic planning and how do they relate to managing and adding value? Do all managers attempt to maximize the value of the firm? What are some alternative managerial motives?

2. What is the market for corporate control? Does the regulation of banks restrict this market? If so, how?

3. How can managers manage value and add value to their companies? Is this process different for banking companies? Discuss this process with respect to the major trends/issues facing banks as they approach the year 2000.

4. What is economic value added (EVA)? How can it be used to measure managerial performance? What evidence exists regarding EVA and firms' market values?

5. What are the three critical ingredients of a company's overall corporate strategy? Carefully explain each component.

6. What are the three pillars of a risk-management framework for any company, and how do these factors relate to a risk-management program for banks? What should the objective of risk management be? What is the major risk banks face and the objective related to the underlying banking function?

7. What are some guidelines for bank managers in the area of risk management?

8. Identify those who made the following statements. Discuss the statements and how they are interrelated, if at all.
   a. Top management must be "the risk manager of risk managers."
   b. "The real risk in life turns out to be the refusal to take a risk. Risk, properly conceived, is often highly productive rather than something to avoid."
   c. "The best of all monopoly profits is the quiet life."

9. What is strategic planning? What is SWOT? How can they be combined?

10. Contrast and compare the corporate visions of NationsBank, Banc One, Bankers Trust, and Citicorp. How innovative have these companies been?

11. What are the revealed objectives and techniques of strategic planning? Do these results suggest that bankers adhere more to the accounting or the economic model of the firm?

12. What business are banks in? What is the "railroad syndrome" and what do banks have to do to avoid it?

13. Long ago Heraclitus said: "All is flux, nothing stays still. Nothing endures but change." More recently King Whitney, Jr., former president of Personnel Laboratory Inc., said: "Change has considerable psychological impact on the human mind. To the fearful it is threatening, because it means that things may get worse. To the hopeful it is encouraging, because things may get better. To the confident it is inspiring, because the challenge exists to make things better." Discuss how you think bankers and other players have reacted to the changing environment of the FSI.

14. According to Greenspan [1996], regulators and banks have a common interest. What is it?

15. If a firm is insolvent, how can EVA be used to reward its executives?

Problems

Given the following data,

	Banc One		Bankers Trust		Citicorp	
Year	ROA	CAP	ROA	CAP	ROA	CAP
1995	1.44%	8.9%	0.21%	4.57%	1.34%	7.22%
1994	1.10	8.23	0.61	4.73	1.41	6.41
1993	1.59	8.77	1.30	5.56	0.89	5.86
1992	1.46	8.09	1.12	4.91	0.34	4.60
1991	1.17	7.61	1.05	4.87	-0.42	3.84

1. Conduct a "situation audit" for all of these companies by computing their risk indices (chapter 3). How do the BHCs compare?
2. Relate your results from the previous question to the corporate visions described in the text for each of the BHCs.

Given the following data,

	Banc One		Bankers Trust		Citicorp	
Year	X1	X2	X1	X2	X1	X2
1995	2.10%	4.13%	2.07%	2.84%	3.41%	4.41%
1994	1.87	4.53	2.34	2.80	3.27	4.40
1993	2.14	5.02	3.95	3.71	3.99	5.13
1992	2.17	4.95	3.42	3.44	3.87	4.81
1991	2.01	4.06	3.88	3.41	3.30	5.18

where X1 = noninterest income as a percentage of average assets
X2 = noninterest expense as a percentage of average assets

3. Compute the burden (net noninterest income) for each BHC and compare and discuss the relative efficiency of their operations in terms of noninterest income and noninterest expense. How do these data relate, if at all, to the company's corporate visions as discussed in the text?

Selected References

Arthur Andersen & Co. [1983]. *New Dimensions in Banking: Managing the Strategic Position*. Chicago: Bank Administration Institute.

"Bankers Trust: Blurred Vision." [1995]. *The Economist* (April 8), pp. 67–68.

Collins, M. Cary, David W. Blackwell, and Joseph F. Sinkey, Jr. [1995]. "The Relationship between Corporate-Compensation Policies and Investment Opportunities: Empirical Evidence for Large Bank Holding Companies." *Financial Management* (Autumn), pp. 40–53.

Copeland, Tom, Tim Koller, and Jack Murrin. [1990]. *Valuation: Measuring and Managing the Value of Companies*. New York: John Wiley & Sons.

"Debate: Duking It Out Over EVA," *Fortune* (August 4, 1997), p. 232.

Drucker, Peter F. [1974]. *Management: Tasks, Responsibilities, Practices*. New York: Harper & Row.

Dunahee, Michael H. [1983]. "Small Banks Can Have Better Plans without Big-Bank Staffs." *ABA Banking Journal* (October), pp. 187–189.

Edwards, Franklin R. [1977]. "Managerial Objectives in Regulated Industries: Expense-Preference Behavior in Banking." *Journal of Political Economy* (February), pp. 147–162.

Froot, Kenneth A., David S. Scharfstein, and Jeremy C. Stein. [1993]. "Risk Management: Coordinating Corporate Investment and Financing Policies." *The Journal of Finance* (December), pp. 1629–1658.

Froot, Kenneth A., David S. Scharfstein, and Jeremy C. Stein. [1994]. "A Framework for Risk Management." *Harvard Business Review* (November–December), pp. 91–102.

Glassman, C. A., and S. Rhoades. [1980]. "Owner vs. Manager Control Effects on Bank Performances." *Review of Economics and Statistics* (May), pp. 263–270.

Greenspan, Alan. [1996]. Speech before the Annual Convention of the American Bankers Association, Honolulu, Hawaii (October 5).

Gup, Benton, and David D. Whitehead. [1983]. "Shifting the Game Plan: Strategic Planning in Financial Institutions." Federal Reserve Bank of Atlanta *Economic Review* (December), pp. 22–33.

Hamel, Gary. [1997]. "Killer Strategies," *Fortune* (June 23), pp. 70+.

Hannan, T. H., and F. Mavinga. [1980]. "Experience Preference and Managerial Control: The Case of the Banking Firm." *The Bell Journal of Economics* (Autumn), pp. 671–682.

Hicks, J. R. [1935]. "Annual Survey of Economic Theory: The Theory of Monopoly." *Econometrica,* pp. 1–20.

Hirsch, James S. [1990]. "Growing Ambition: Fast-Rising Banc One." *The Wall Street Journal* (December 26), pp. 1–2.

Iida, Jeanne. [1994]. "Top Bank Executives' Cash Compensation Soared with Profits." *American Banker* (June 21), pp. 3–5, 22.

Kane, Edward J. [1983]. "The Metamorphosis in Financial-Services Delivery and Production." In *Strategic Planning for Economic and Technological Change in the Financial-Services Industry.* San Francisco: Federal Home Loan Bank, pp. 221–239.

———. [1984]. "Strategic Planning in a World of Regulatory and Technological Change." In Richard C. Aspinwall and Robert A. Eisenbeis, eds., *Handbook for Banking Strategy.* New York: John Wiley & Sons, pp. 725–743.

Kanter, Rosabeth Moss. [1983]. *The Change Masters: Innovation for Productivity in the American Corporation.* New York: Simon & Schuster.

Kaplan, Daniel. [1995]. "Bankers Trust Stock Dives 16 Percent on Projection of $125M Loss." *American Banker* (March 14), pp. 1, 24.

Knecht, G. Bruce. [1995]. "Bankers Trust Risk Apostle Faces Tough Strategic Play." *The Wall Street Journal* (April 18), p. B1.

Kraus, James R. [1995]. "Citi Shifting Corporate Focus to Clients with Global Reach." *American Banker* (February 23), pp. 1, 6.

Levit, Theodore, and Scott Cunningham. [1979]. *Marketing Myopia in the Trust Business.* Washington, DC: American Bankers Association.

Loomis, Carol J. [1991]. "Citicorp's World of Troubles." *Fortune* (January 14), pp. 90–99.

Marakon Associates. [1980]. "The Role of Finance in Strategic Planning." New York: Business Week Conference on Strategic Planning.

Naisbitt, John. [1982]. *Megatrends.* New York: Warner Books.

Peters, Thomas J., and Robert H. Watermann. [1982]. *In Search of Excellence.* New York: Harper & Row.

Prasad, Rose M., and S. Benjamin Prasad. [1989]. "Strategic Planning in Banks: Senior Executives' Views." *International Journal of Management* (December), pp. 435–441.

Reimann, Bernard C. [1989]. *Managing for Value: A Guide to Value-Based Strategic Management.* Oxford, OH: The Planning Forum in association with Basil Blackwell, Cambridge, MA.

Rhoades, Stephen. [1980]. "Monopoly and Expense-Preference Behavior." *Southern Economic Journal* (October), pp. 419–432.

Sanford, Charles S., Jr. [1994]. "Financial Markets in 2020." Federal Reserve Bank of Kansas City *Economic Review* (First Quarter), pp. 19–28.

Sheehan, Timothy J. [1994]. "To EVA™ or Not to EVA: Is That the Question?" *Journal of Applied Corporate Finance* (Summer), pp. 85–87.

Six Roundtable Discussions of Corporate Finance with Joel Stern. [1986]. Edited by Donald H. Chew, Jr. Westport, CT: Quorum Books.

"Stern Stewart EVA™ Roundtable." [1994]. *Journal of Applied Corporate Finance* (Summer), pp. 46–70.

Stewart, G. Bennett III. [1994]. "EVA™: Fact and Fantasy." *Journal of Applied Corporate Finance* (Summer), pp. 71–84.

Sweeney, John C., and David B. Plyler. [1984]. *Creating Shareholder and Policyholder Wealth: Strategic Financial Planning and Capital Allocation for Life Insurance Companies.* Report No. 59 (June). Atlanta: Life Office Management Association.

Taylor, Jeremy F. [1990]. *The Process of Change in American Banking.* New York: Quorum Books.

"Valuing Companies," *The Economist* (August 2, 1997), pp. 53–55.

Verbrugge, James A., and Steven J. Goldstein. [1981]. "Risk, Return, and Managerial Objectives: Some Evidence from the Savings-and-Loan Industry." *Journal of Financial Research* (Spring), pp. 45–58.

Verbrugge, James A., and John J. Jahera. [1981]. "Expense-Preference Behavior in the Savings-and-Loan Industry." *Journal of Money, Credit, and Banking* (November), pp. 465–476.

Vojta, George J. [1983]. "New Competition and Its Implications for Banking." *The Magazine of Bank Administration* (July), pp. 34–44.

Wysocki, Bernard J. [1984]. "Executive Style." *The Wall Street Journal* (September 11), pp. 1, 12 (first of a five-part series).

5

ASSET-LIABILITY MANAGEMENT (ALM) AND TECHNIQUES FOR MANAGING INTEREST-RATE RISK

Contents

LEARNING OBJECTIVES

■ To understand the importance of and techniques for bank asset-liability
management (ALM)

■ To understand the maturity imbalance of banks' balance sheets in terms
of rate-sensitive assets (RSAs) and rate-sensitive liabilities (RSLs)

■ To understand accounting and economic measures of ALM performance

■ To understand interest-rate risk and its components: price risk and
reinvestment risk

■ To understand unexpected changes in interest-rate risk as the source of
ALM uncertainty

■ To understand ALM risk profiles as pictures of banks' exposure to
interest-rate risk

■ To understand how to hedge interest-rate risk using on- and off-balance-
sheet methods

CHAPTER THEME

Because the business of banking involves the measuring, managing, and accepting
of risk, the heart of bank financial management is risk management. One of the
most important risk-management functions in banking is **asset-liability management**

(ALM), broadly defined as the coordinated management of a bank's balance sheet to allow for alternative interest-rate, liquidity, and prepayment scenarios. Three techniques of ALM are (1) on-balance-sheet matching of the repricing of assets and liabilities, (2) off-balance-sheet hedging of on-balance-sheet risks, and (3) securitization, which removes risk from the balance sheet. The key variables of ALM include accounting measures such as **net interest income** (NII) or its ratio form **net interest margin** (*NIM = NII*/average assets) and an economic measure: the market value of a bank's equity. Planning and controlling for how a bank's NIM and stock price react to **unexpected changes in interest rates** is the task of ALM. **Risk profiles** provide useful pictures for visualizing this sensitivity and for understanding the ALM process. Practical aspects of ALM focus on the rates, volumes, and mixes of **rate-sensitive assets** (RSAs) and **rate-sensitive liabilities** (RSLs) over the short run. Simulation models permit ALM managers to estimate the effects of different portfolio strategies and different interest-rate scenarios on accounting and economic variables. In addition, strategic choices regarding products, markets, and bank structure need to be linked to ALM.

KEY CONCEPTS, IDEAS, AND TERMS

- Asset-liability management (ALM)
- Asset-liability management committee (ALCO)
- Assets repricing before liabilities (ARBL)
- Gap (maturity and duration)
- Interest-rate contracts (IRCs: futures, forwards, swaps, options)

- Interest-rate risk: Price risk and reinvestment risk
- Liabilities repricing before assets (LRBA)
- Liability management (LM)
- Liquidity risk
- Market value of equity (MVE)

- Net interest income (NII)
- Net interest margin (NIM)
- Prepayment risk
- Rate-sensitive asset (RSA)
- Rate-sensitive liability (RSL)
- Risk profile
- Unexpected changes in interest rates

INTRODUCTION

Allowing for alternative futures is the stuff of strategic planning. Allowing for alternative interest-rate, liquidity, and prepayment scenarios is the heart of asset-liability management (ALM). Because ALM can be viewed as the first step in moving a bank in its desired strategic direction, it plays a critical role in determining the major component of a bank's cash flow: net interest income (NII). In a study for the Bank Administration Institute, Binder and Lindquist [1982] found strong agreement among bankers that the **asset-liability management committee,** or **ALCO,** is "the single most important management group and function in the bank." As banks move into the twenty-first century, ALM retains that critical position.

ALM AS COORDINATED BALANCE-SHEET FINANCIAL MANAGEMENT: A THREE-STAGE APPROACH

The importance and function of ALM can be viewed in terms of the three-stage approach to balance-sheet financial management presented in Table 5-1.

TABLE 5-1 Coordinated Balance-Sheet Management: A Three-Stage View of ALM

Stage I (General)

Asset management	Liability management
	Capital management

Stage II (Specific)

Reserve-position management	Liability management, LM ("purchased funds")
Liquidity management	Reserve-position LM (federal funds)
Investment/securities management	Generalized or loan-position LM (CDs)
Loan management	Long-term debt management (notes & debentures)
Fixed-asset management ("brick and mortar")	Capital management (common equity)

Stage III (Balance sheet generates the income-expense statement, given interest rates and prices)

$$\text{Profit} = \text{Interest revenue} - \text{interest expense} - \text{provision for loan loss} + \text{noninterest revenue} - \text{noninterest expense} - \text{taxes}$$

Policies to achieve objectives:

1. Spread management
2. Loan quality
3. Generating fee income and service charges
4. Control of noninterest operating expenses
5. Tax management
6. Capital adequacy

Definition: ALM involves a global or general approach (Stage I) that requires coordination of the various specific functions (Stage II). The process in Stage II focuses on planning, directing, and controlling the levels, changes, and mixes of the various balance-sheet accounts, which generate the bank's income-expense statement (Stage III). From an accounting perspective, the key variables of ALM are net interest income (NII) or net interest margin (NIM), return on assets (ROA), or return on equity (ROE); from an economic perspective, the key variable is the market value of equity (MVE). To achieve the objectives of ALM, managers focus on the six policies listed above.

Stage I reflects a global or general approach that focuses on the coordinated management of a bank's assets, liabilities, and capital.

Stage II identifies specific components of a bank's balance sheet used in coordinating its overall portfolio management.

Stage III shows that, given interest rates and prices, a bank's balance sheet generates its income-expense statement.

Except for the management of fixed physical assets such as "brick and mortar," all of a bank's earning assets play a crucial role in ALM.[1] The interest rates, volumes, and mixes of these asset categories are the critical elements of the asset-management component of ALM. Bank asset management can be described in terms of reserves, liquidity, investment securities, and loans. An important distinction, addressed later in the chapter, is between assets that are rate sensitive and those that are not rate sensitive. This sensitivity can be described in terms of the effective time to repricing or duration. By definition, reserves and other liquid assets

---

[1] Couched in terms of risk management, chapters 6 through 12 focus on detailed explanations of each of these aspects of bank asset management.

reprice quickly, whereas longer-term, fixed-rate loans and securities do not reprice quickly.

The liability-management (LM) aspect of ALM can be viewed in terms of two functions.[2] First, reserve-position LM focuses on the use of very short-term instruments to meet deposit withdrawals or to temporarily meet loan demand. Repurchase agreements (securities sold under agreement to repurchase, known as "repos" or "RPs") and purchases of federal funds (excess reserves traded overnight among banks) are the basic instruments of reserve-position LM.[3] This LM method generates short-term sources of funds to complement liquidity stored in a bank's balance sheet. This technique, which permits a bank to hold higher-yielding, less-liquid assets, mainly affects the composition of a bank's balance sheet. However, a bank that attempts to use federal funds to finance a permanent expansion of its assets incurs substantial liquidity risk. Failure to maintain its creditworthiness will jeopardize the bank's ability to roll over the funds.

The second type of LM is generalized, or loan-position, LM. It focuses on a permanent expansion of a bank's balance sheet to meet profitable investment opportunities, especially customer loan demand. Large certificates of deposit (CDs) are the primary instrument of this technique. Large, creditworthy banks purchase such funds by selling their CDs in either domestic or international money markets. Large CDs are negotiable instruments that trade in secondary markets. In contrast, funds gathered in local markets are known as core deposits (e.g., checking and savings accounts); secondary markets do not exist for these instruments. To tap funds outside local markets, smaller or lesser-known banks can use the technique of brokering deposits, whereby a large, retail brokerage firm such as Merrill Lynch will sell the bank's CDs. Since investors in brokered CDs may lack information and confidence in the issuing bank, brokered deposits typically are raised in amounts under the federal deposit-insurance ceiling of $100,000. The basic differences between purchased funds and core deposits are the higher cost and greater variability of purchased funds ("hot money") compared to core deposits.

Both types of LM involve an active rather than a passive approach to attracting sources of bank funding. The maturity, risk, and other characteristics of the underlying instruments distinguish the two approaches. As with bank assets, an important distinction is between liabilities that are rate sensitive and those that are not rate sensitive. This sensitivity can be described in terms of the effective time to repricing or duration. By definition, federal funds purchased, repos, and money-market accounts reprice quickly whereas longer-term, fixed-rate CDs do not reprice quickly.

Because of the short-term nature of ALM, long-term debt and equity capital are not day-to-day instruments of ALM. They are shown in Table 5-1 to give a complete picture of a bank's balance sheet. Nevertheless, to the extent that a bank can raise additional long-term sources of funds, it can lengthen its average asset maturity, and all other things being equal and assuming a positively shaped yield curve, it can increase its interest revenue.

Stage III of coordinated bank-balance-sheet management shows a bank's income-expense statement as generated by its balance-sheet (and off-balance-sheet) activities, given interest rates and prices. This stage, in effect, is a product of the quality of the balance-sheet decisions made by bank managers. It serves to highlight the

---

[2] This distinction comes from Kane [1979]. Chapter 8 provides more detail on LM as a technique for generating sources of bank funding.

[3] Reserve-position LM also can be described as "money-desk" LM because it focuses on daily funds management. The two basic instruments of money-desk LM differ in that repos are secured transactions whereas federal-funds transactions are unsecured.

policies bankers need to achieve their objectives. These policies, shown as a part of Stage III because of their linkages to the income-expense statement, focus on spread management, loan quality, generation of noninterest income, control of noninterest operating expenses, tax management, and maintaining the bank's capital adequacy.

THE OBJECTIVES AND FOCAL VARIABLES OF ALM

Because net interest income (NII) is the bread and butter of banking, the objectives of ALM usually are expressed in terms of a target NII (or target net interest margin, NIM) and minimization of the variability of NII or minimization of the variability of the bank's **market value of equity.** As a practical matter and from a strategic-planning perspective (chapter 4), the goal of ALM also can be expressed generally as maintaining a competitive return on assets (ROA) and minimizing its variability (σ_{ROA}). Although return on assets and its variability depend on a bank's NIM and its variability (σ_{NIM}), the most critical historical determinant of a bank's profitability has been not **interest-rate risk** but credit risk. Nevertheless, viewed in terms of a bank's risk index (RI),

$$RI = [E(ROA) + CAP]/\sigma_{ROA} \qquad \textbf{(5-1)}$$

ALM plays a key role in determining *RI,* because $E(ROA)$, *CAP,* and σ_{ROA} all depend on NIM and its variability.

MEASURING BANK ALM PERFORMANCE: NET INTEREST MARGIN AND ITS VARIABILITY

To capture ALM accounting performance across banks and over time, the industry standard is net interest margin (NIM), defined as net interest income (NII) divided by average total assets.[4] Because NII equals interest income minus interest expense, NIM can be viewed as the "spread" on earning assets, hence the term "spread management." Also, remember that NII has the major task of covering a bank's provision for loan losses, net noninterest expense (burden), nonrecurring losses, taxes, and dividends. To summarize,

$$NIM = \text{Net interest income/Average total assets} \qquad \textbf{(5-2)}$$

where net interest income = interest income − interest expense.

Net Interest Margin and Bank Size

Table 5-2 shows that net interest margins vary inversely with bank asset size. The data, which are for 1985 and 1995, use average net consolidated assets to calculate NIM; NIM(TE) refers to NIM stated on a tax-equivalent basis.[5] For comparative

---

[4] Because the denominator of NIM is a "stock" variable, it should be measured as an average to make it more compatible with the flow variable (NII) in the numerator. NIM also can be computed using average "earning" assets.

[5] Because interest income or revenue can be calculated on a tax-equivalent (TE) basis, *NII* and *NIM* also can be expressed that way. To measure interest income on a tax-equivalent basis, divide tax-exempt interest income by $(1 - t)$, where t is the bank's marginal tax rate, and add it to taxable interest income. For example, if a bank with $t = .30$ has total interest income of $1,000 consisting of $800 of taxable interest income and $200 of nontaxable interest income, its tax-equivalent interest income is $800 + $200/0.7 = $1,086. If total interest expense = $800 and average assets = $5,000, $NIM = 200/5,000 = 0.04$, and $NIM(TE) = 286/5,000 = 0.0572$.

TABLE 5-2 Net Interest Margins and Bank Size, 1985 and 1995

Panel A. Net Interest Margins for 1995

Bank Class	NIM	NIM(TE)	ROA
Ten largest	2.68%	2.70%	0.88%
11–100	3.79	3.84	1.31
101–1,000	4.25	4.33	1.28
Not among 1,000 largest	4.41	4.55	1.21
All reporting banks	3.73	3.79	1.18

Panel B. Net Interest Margins for 1985

Bank Class	NIM	NIM(TE)	ROA
Ten largest	2.74%	3.01%	0.46%
11–100	3.30	3.75	0.74
101–1,000	3.86	4.39	0.85
Not among 1,000 largest	4.25	4.71	0.72
All reporting banks	3.53	3.96	0.69

**Panel C. The Variability of NIM and ROA
for All Reporting Banks, 1985–1995**

Year	NIM	ROA
1985	3.53%	0.69%
1986	3.44	0.62
1987	3.42	0.08
1988	3.54	0.71
1989	3.51	0.47
1990	3.46	0.47
1991	3.61	0.51
1992	3.90	0.91
1993	3.90	1.20
1994	3.79	1.15
1995	3.73	1.18
Mean	3.62%	0.73%
Standard deviation	0.17%	0.34%
Coefficient of variation	0.05	0.46

Note: NIM = net interest margin, NIM(TE) = tax-equivalent NIM, and ROA = return on assets.

Source: Federal Reserve Bulletin [June 1996], pp. 495–505.

purposes, the last column presents return on assets (ROA). Panel A shows the NIMs for 1995. The smallest banks (i.e., those not among the 1,000 largest, about 9,000 banks) had, on average, a 173 basis point advantage over the 10 largest banks (4.41% vs. 2.68%). As Panel B shows, this advantage is up from the 151 basis points edge in 1985 (4.25% vs. 2.74%). If we focus on any of the groups and compare the improvements in NIM and ROA between 1985 and 1995, it is easy to see that increases in NIMs did not account for all of the increases in ROAs. For example, the average bank saw an improvement in ROA of 49 basis points, whereas NIM increased by only 20 basis points. For the 10 largest banks, the contrast is even greater, because NIM actually declined by 6 basis points, whereas ROA improved by 42 basis points. In general, the interest-rate environment for the years 1985 through 1995 was favorable for banks of all sizes.

The Variability of NIM and ROA

Panel C of Table 5-2 clearly shows that NIM is substantially less variable than ROA. The data are for the years 1985 through 1995 for all reporting banks. Over this period, the typical commercial bank had an average ROA of 0.72 percent with a standard deviation of 0.34 percent, compared to an average NIM of 3.62 percent with a standard deviation of 0.17 percent. The coefficients of variation (CV) show the relative variability more directly as the CV of ROA is 0.46 (= 0.34/0.72) compared to 0.05 (= 0.17/3.62) for the CV of NIM. Recall that a higher *CV* indicates greater variability. In this case, ROA was more than nine times as variable over the years 1985 to 1995. As the bread and butter of banking, net interest margin has been abundantly and consistently available for bankers to consume.

TWO FACES OF ASSET-LIABILITY MANAGEMENT: ACCOUNTING AND ECONOMIC PERSPECTIVES[6]

Although accounting numbers (like NIM) are important, bank managers need to cut through accounting veils to see the economic effects of their decisions. In ALM, the same need arises. To demonstrate the importance of the accounting numbers and to show the economic effects of ALM decisions, this section presents two faces of ALM: an **accounting model** and an **economic model.**

The Accounting Model and Interest-Rate Sensitivity

The accounting model of the firm focuses on reported earnings per share (EPS) in the short run as the key determinant of value. Net interest income (NII) and net interest margin (NIM), the lifeblood of a bank's accounting earnings, are the focal variables of ALM from the accounting perspective. In this context, the ALM objective is the minimization of risk, as reflected by the variability of NII or NIM, for a target level of NII or NIM. Alternatively, the objective can be viewed as to maximize NII or NIM for a given level of risk.

The following simple formula captures the relationship between changes in interest rates (Δr) and the change in net interest income (ΔNII):[7]

$$\Delta NII = \Delta r \,[GAP] = \Delta r \,[RSA - RSL] \qquad \textbf{(5-3)}$$

---

[6] This section draws in part on "Overview of Interest-Rate Risk: An OCC Staff Paper," Multinational Banking Department, OCC [December 1989], and on Rose [1989].

[7] An equation for the percentage change in *NIM* is $\Delta NIM/NIM = [GAP/EA][\Delta r/NIM]$, where EA = earning assets. *GAP* as presented here and in equation (5-3) can be interpreted as an average. Both of these equations, however, are simplifications of more complex relationships. To see the complexity, set up an equation for *NII* and note the assumptions needed to arrive at equation (5-3). See Rose [1982] and Hayes [1980].

where GAP = the difference between rate-sensitive assets (RSA) and rate-sensitive liabilities (RSL) over a particular time horizon (e.g., 90 days).[8] The relationships among RSA, RSL, and GAP are as follows:

- When $RSA - RSL > 0$, a bank is said to have a positive GAP
- When $RSA - RSL < 0$, a bank is said to have a negative GAP
- When $RSA - RSL = 0$, a bank has a zero GAP

To the extent that banks borrow short and lend long, they have negative maturity gaps. Table 5-3 provides a catalog of ALM terminology.

Equation (5-3) assumes that the unexpected change in the interest rate is the same for both assets and liabilities. If the changes are not the same, formula (5-3) modifies to

$$\Delta NII = \Delta r_A[RSA] - \Delta r_L[RSL] \tag{5-3a}$$

where the subscripts A and L stand for assets and liabilities, respectively.

Equation (5-3) should be viewed in terms of expected and unexpected changes in interest rates that give rise to expected and unexpected changes in net interest income. Suppose that interest rates increase by 200 basis points, but the ALCO expected only an increase of 100 basis points. A positive-gap position would produce a windfall gain from the unexpected rise in rates. Suppose, however, that the bank has a negative-gap position of 100. Given the change in rates, net interest income will change by -2 ($= 0.02 \times -100$), consisting of an expected decline of 1 and an unexpected decline of 1. All other things being equal, the bank will report lower earnings and lower book value of equity capital. If stockholders and market analysts have the same expectations as the bank, then they will be disappointed by the bank's performance.

To summarize, the accounting model of ALM focuses on the sensitivity of reported earnings to unexpected changes in interest rates as driven by unexpected changes in net interest income. Mismanagement of interest-rate risk, as the thrift crisis has proven, first manifests itself in reported earnings and, if unchecked, results in liquidity and solvency problems.

The Economic Model and the Market Value of Bank Equity

Although the accounting model of ALM or management of interest-rate risk is important, it is not complete, because it ignores how changes in interest rates affect the market value of the bank's equity (broadly defined to include the value of unbooked equity associated with off-balance-sheet activities or OBSAs). This focus on the sensitivity of the market value of the bank's assets and liabilities is the heart of the economic model of interest-rate risk. The economic model is important because it emphasizes market values, which serve as signals about current interest-rate risk and future earnings. Because both the accounting model and the economic model provide important insights about the management of interest-rate risk, they should be viewed as complements and not substitutes.

The critical element of the economic model of interest-rate risk is the determination of the market value of the bank's equity, both booked and unbooked. Conceptually, we can view the total market value of a bank's equity as the sum of

---

[8] The time horizon can be measured using either maturity or duration. Duration, which is a more direct but more complicated measure, is discussed later in the chapter. For now, GAP is assumed to be measured based on maturity. McNulty [1986] treats gap and duration analyses as complements.

these booked and unbooked components. The market value of booked equity is simply the difference between the market value of booked assets and the market value of booked liabilities—the accounting identity stated in market values rather than book values. The market value of unbooked equity is simply the difference between the market value of unbooked assets and the market value of unbooked liabilities. (Recall our discussion of the statistical market value accounting model (SMVAM) from chapter 3.) Unbooked assets and liabilities arise from bank off-balance-sheet activities such as lines of credit, loan commitments, futures, options, and swaps. These activities need to be valued.

Whether items are on or off a bank's balance sheet, the economic model says to value them by discounting their future cash flows with interest rates that reflect the riskiness of the future cash flows. From an ALM perspective, the emphasis of the economic model is the sensitivity of the market value of bank equity to changes in interest rates across the full maturity spectrum of the bank. Because the economic model has a time horizon beyond the short-term focus of the accounting model, and because it considers off-balance-sheet activities, it is a more comprehensive measure of interest-rate risk. Nevertheless, because the economic model is more difficult to apply, it is less widely used than the accounting model. In either case, however, the focus is on the sensitivity of a particular variable (NII or reported earnings versus market value of equity) to unexpected changes in interest rates.

Illustrating the Accounting and Economic Models

Table 5-3 presents a numerical example to illustrate the accounting and economic approaches to measuring interest-rate risk. Consider a five-year, fixed-rate asset earning 10 percent funded with a one-year liability at 9 percent. Imagine the situation as a simple bank with a 1 percent spread ($= 10\% - 9\%$), an equity or capital value of 10 ($= 100 - 90$), and an equity multiplier of 10 ($= 100/10$). The bank has interest income of 10 (cash inflow), interest expense of 8.1 (cash outflow), and net interest income of 1.9 (net cash flow). As long as interest rates do not increase, the bank's net income and its equity value are protected. However, because the bank is funding a long-term, fixed-rate asset with a short-term liability, it is vulnerable to an increase in interest rates. A bank with this kind of gap can be labeled a **LRBA** bank, where LRBA = **Liabilities Reprice Before Assets.** The bank's dollar gap in the one-to-five-year range is -90 ($= 0 - 90$), and it is described as a "negative dollar gap" or "negative gap."[9]

Suppose that interest rates increase by 300 basis points immediately after the asset is funded and remain at that level through the life of the asset. The shock means that comparable financial instruments now yield 13 percent (asset) and 12 percent (liability). After the shock, because the liability reprices at 12 percent in the second and subsequent years, interest expense increases to 10.8 and net interest income drops to -0.8. The change in net interest income equals -2.7 (the drop from 1.9 to -0.8), or by formula (5-3), $0.03 \times -90 = -2.7$. This change captures the essence of the accounting model with its focus on net interest income.

The economic model highlights the change in the market value of the bank's capital. Before the shock, the market value was 10; after the shock, it is 1.8, a decline of 8.2. The new market value of equity equals the market value of the asset, 89.4, less the market value of the liability, 87.6. Table 5-3 provides details of the

---

[9] When $RSA > RSL$, $GAP > 0$ (described as a positive gap, or ARBL = Assets reprice before liabilities); when $RSA = RSL$, $GAP = 0$ (described as a zero gap); and when $RSA < RSL$, $GAP < 0$ (described as a negative gap, or LRBA = Liabilities Reprice Before Assets).

TABLE 5-3 ALM and Interest-Rate Risk: The Accounting and Economic Models

Premise: Five-year, fixed-rate asset at 10 percent funded with a one-year liability at 9 percent.

Shock: Interest rates increase by 300 basis points immediately after the asset is funded.

BEFORE THE SHOCK

	Market Value	Book Value	Gross and Net Cash Flows (CF)				
			CF1	CF2	CF3	CF4	CF5
Asset	100	100	10.0	10.0	10.0	10.0	10.0
Liability	90	90	−8.1	−8.1	−8.1	−8.1	−8.1
Capital	10	10	1.9	1.9	1.9	1.9	1.9

AFTER THE SHOCK

	Market Value	Book Value	Gross and Net Cash Flows (CF)				
			CF1	CF2	CF3	CF4	CF5
Asset	89.4	100	10.0	10.0	10.0	10.0	10.0
Liability	87.6	90	−8.1	−10.8	−10.8	−10.8	−10.8
Capital	1.8	10	1.9	−0.8	−0.8	−0.8	−0.8

Valuation note: After the shock, an asset that promises annual cash flows of 10 and lump-sum payment of 100 at the end of the fifth year, when comparable assets yield 13 percent, has a market value of 89.4. The liability, which is an asset to a counterparty, promises an annual payment of 10.8 in years two through five (assuming it is rolled over) but only 8.1 in year one and a lump-sum payment of 90 at maturity. Discounting the cash flows at 12 percent, its value is $90 - 2.4 (= 2.7/1.12) = 87.6$.

Source: Adapted from the example in "Overview of Interest-Rate Risk: An OCC Staff Paper" [December 1989], pp. 3–4.

valuation. The economic model discloses the future losses over the full maturity of the loan, including years two through five, which the accounting perspective does not consider. The change in the market value of equity serves as a signal of future net interest income and future *book* value of equity. If interest rates remain at the new level, the book value of equity also will decline as future income losses deplete equity (i.e., the negative net interest income in years two through five).

Duration and the Change in Market Value of Equity

Duration can be viewed as the "effective time to repricing" (Hilliard and Sinkey [1989]).[10] We can construct a formula similar to equation (5-3) for the change in market value of bank equity. The essence of this approach is to take the difference between the market value of assets and the market value of liabilities with each component weighted by its respective duration, and with the difference multiplied by the change in interest rate, that is,

$$\Delta V \approx \{[PV_A \times (-D_A)] - [PV_L \times (-D_L)]\}\Delta r \tag{5-4}$$

---

[10] Technically, duration is calculated as the ratio of an asset's (or liability's) weighted present value of future cash flows divided by its price (unweighted present value of future cash flows), where the weights are the time period in which the cash flows are received. For example, the loan shown in Table 5-3 is similar to a five-year, 10 percent coupon bond with a face or par value of $100. This loan (bond) has a maturity of five years but a duration (at the time of issue when $r = 0.10$) of only 4.17 years, which is calculated as [9.091 × 1 + 8.264 × 2 + 7.513 × 3 + 6.83 × 4 + 68.301 × 5]/100 = 416.983/100 = 4.17.

where the new terms are PV_A = present value of assets, PV_L = present value of liability, D_A = duration of the asset, and D_L = duration of the liability.[11] As with formula (5-3), it is assumed that the interest rates on assets and liabilities change by the same amount. If they do not, then equation (5-4) must be modified as follows:

$$\Delta V \approx [PV_A \times (-D_A)]\Delta r_A - [PV_L \times (-D_L)]\Delta r_L \qquad \textbf{(5-4a)}$$

For the simple bank shown in Table 5-3, PV_A = 89.4, PV_L = 87.6, D_A = 4.17 (see footnote 11), and D_L = 1 (an asset with no interim cash flows has a duration equal to its maturity). Using these inputs, the *approximate change* in the bank's market value of equity using equation (5-3) is as follows:[12]

$$\Delta V \approx [89.4(-4.17) - 87.6(-1)].03 = -8.5$$

Because the bank shown in Table 5-3 is in a LRBA position, the increase in rates decreases the bank's market value of equity by 8.2 (−8.5 is the approximation of the change) and decreases its net interest income by 2.7.

This example and formulas (5-3) and (5-4) prescribe different methods for reducing the variability of a bank's net interest income and its market value of equity to changes in interest rates. The accounting or gap-management approach suggests that if *RSA* = *RSL*, and if the interest rates on assets and liabilities change by the same amount, then the bank's net interest income will not change. In contrast, the economic or duration model suggests that if $D_A = D_L$ and if $PV_A = PV_L$, then the bank's market value of equity will be immunized. Because viable banks do not have net asset or equity values equal to zero, the second condition is not a realistic one. Thus, to immunize their net asset values, most banks must be asset sensitive or ARBL, that is, assets repricing before liabilities.

Variable-Rate Pricing as an ALM Tool

Let's change the asset sensitivity of the bank in Table 5-3 by making the five-year loan reprice annually, all other things being equal, and work through the numbers in this case. The results for the first year are the same as those shown in Table 5-3. In years two through five, however, the net interest income is 100(0.3) − 90(0.12) = 13 − 10.8 = 2.2. The bank's dollar spread actually increases, because its dollar maturity gap beyond one year is positive or ARBL, that is, 100 − 90 = 10. The change in net interest income is 2.2 − 1.9 = 0.3. We get the same result using equation (5-3), that is, 10(0.03) = 0.3. What happens to the bank's market value of equity? The asset has a present value of 97.3 = 110/1.13, whereas the liability has a present value of 87.6 = 98.1/1.12, which means that the present value of the bank's equity is 97.3 − 87.6 = 9.7, a decline of 0.3 = 10 − 9.7. Using formula (5-4), we get

$$\Delta V \approx [97.3(-1) - 87.6(-1)].03 = -0.291$$

Because a five-year loan that reprices every year has an effective time to repricing, or duration, of one year, D_A = 1. Thus, even though the bank has duration matching its assets and liabilities, its market value of equity is not immunized. To do this,

---

[11] The duration terms have negative signs because duration is a measure of price sensitivity or elasticity, which for fixed-rate financial assets is always negative due to the negative price-yield relation. Duration can be expressed approximately as $D \approx -[\Delta V/V]/[\Delta r/1 + r]$. Rearranging $\Delta V \approx -D[V/(1 + r)]\Delta r$ and letting $V = A - L$, you can see the origins of equation (5-4). Appendix B of this chapter explains why duration only approximates the change in value.

[12] Duration analysis holds most precisely for small changes in interest rates. In this example, a change of 300 basis points does not meet that qualification.

as we know from above, the bank must be asset sensitive or ARBL as long as it is solvent, that is, $PV_A > PV_L$. With $D_A < D_L$, the bank is asset sensitive.

Using the numbers for the floating-rate loan and setting $\Delta V = 0$, let's solve for the asset duration that will immunize the bank's market value of equity. In this case, $D_A = 87.6/97.3 = 0.9003$. Or using formula (5-4) and setting $D_L = 1$, $D_A = PV(L)/PV(A)$.

The Tactical and Strategic Banks

In general, the requirement for immunizing a solvent bank's market value of equity is to have the duration of assets slightly less than the duration of liabilities, $D_A < D_L$. Let's define, as Rose [1989] does, the tactical bank as "the under-one-year part of the institution"; the strategic bank is the "over-one-year" part. Furthermore, let's consider the most common shape of yield curve—an upward-sloping one. Because the yield curve gets flatter as maturity increases, the short end of the curve has the largest liquidity premiums. Thus, it is most advantageous for bankers to borrow short and lend long over this segment of the yield curve. However, borrowing short and lending long (the LRBA bank's negative gap or liability-sensitive position) makes a bank vulnerable to a rise in interest rates, meaning that the value of its tactical assets will fall by more than the value of its tactical liabilities. As a result, the bank's tactical equity (the difference between the value of tactical assets and tactical liabilities) will decline. Figure 5-1 summarizes these relationships in several pictures and a numerical example.

Because ALM involves the coordinated management of a bank's assets and liabilities, the strategic bank can be used to offset the interest-rate risk in the tactical bank. To do this, the strategic or over-one-year part of the bank must generate a positive gap or asset-sensitive position. Rather than borrow short and lend long, the strategic bank must borrow long and lend short (i.e., have shorter-term assets than liabilities, the ARBL bank). Although Rose cautions bankers that achieving this tactical and strategic balance is difficult, he also contends that they misunderstand how to achieve it. Assuming that a bank has positive net worth, his key message is that a (duration) matched portfolio, as shown above, should not be the desired objective because "the absolute dollar value of assets will still change by more than the absolute dollar of the liabilities for any given change in interest rates" (p. 9). As a result, the bank's equity value will not be immunized. To achieve the desired balance, the *overall* bank must be asset sensitive, that is, duration of assets must be less than the duration of liabilities. However, to reap the liquidity premium available in the short end of the yield curve, the tactical bank must be liability sensitive. Accordingly, the strategic bank must be asset sensitive such that it more than offsets the liability sensitivity of the tactical bank.

Recapitulation

Table 5-4 presents a catalog of ALM terminology used to describe a bank's interest-rate sensitivity. In a comprehensive assessment of interest-rate risk, the accounting and economic models are complementary. The economic model focuses on the present value of the bank's equity at current interest rates and its sensitivity to changes in interest rates. The idea is to evaluate the effects of unexpected changes in interest rates on the market values of all assets, liabilities, and contingent claims (OBSAs). Potential problems arising from future balance-sheet mismatches are immediately captured by the present-value analysis of the economic approach. The

FIGURE 5-1 ALM in a Bank with Tactical and Strategic Portfolios

Panel A. Playing the normal yield curve

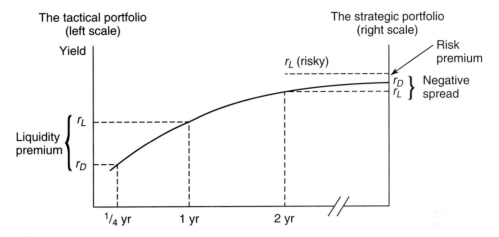

Panel B. The overall bank: An ARBL portfolio (Assets reprice before liabilities)

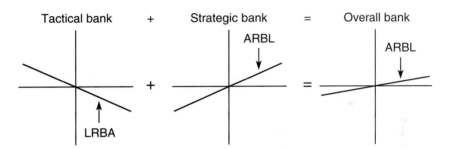

Panel C. A Numerical Example

Overall Bank	*Tactical Bank (LRBA)*	*Strategic Bank (ARBL)*
A = 100	A = 40 @ 8%/1 year	A = 60 @ 10%/2 years
D = 90	D = 36 @ 6%/3 mos.	D = 54 @ 9%/20 years
E = 10	E = 4	E = 6

(Note: A = assets, D = deposits, and E = equity with A = D + E)

NII = 40(.08) + 60(.10) − 36(.06) − 54(.09) = 2.18

MVE = BVE = 10 = 100 − 90

Interest-Rate Shock: All rates rise by 100 basis points (1%)

$$MVE = PV_A - PV_L{}^*$$
$$= (40 \text{ @ } 8\%, 1 \text{ yr. valued @ } 9\%) + (60 \text{ @ } 10\%, 2 \text{ yrs. valued @ } 11\%)$$
$$- (36 \text{ @ } 6\%, 3 \text{ mos. valued @ } 7\%) - (54 \text{ @ } 9\%, 20 \text{ yrs. valued @ } 10\%)$$
$$= 39.63 + 58.97 - 35.91 - 49.4 = 13.29 > 10 = BVE$$

(continued)

FIGURE 5-1 **Panel C** *(continued)*

Analysis of changes in NII using Equation (5–3) where GAP = RSA − RSL:

Tactical Bank:

(0 < GAP ≤ 91 days):	(0 − 36).01 = −0.36
(91 days < GAP ≤ 1 year):	(40 − 0).01 = 0.40
Net	0.04

Strategic Bank:

(0 < GAP ≤ 2 years):	(60 − 0).01 = 0.60
(2 years, < GAP ≤ 20 years):	(0 − 54).01 = −0.54
Net	0.06

Overall Bank:

(0 < GAP ≤ 1 year):	(40 − 36).01 = 0.04
(1 year < GAP ≤ 5 years):	(60 − 0).01 = 0.60
(5 years < GAP ≤ 20 years):	(0 − 54).01 = −0.54
(0 < Gap ≤ 20 years):	(100 − 90).01 = 0.10 = 0.04 + 0.60 − 0.54

*Note on calculation of PVs: The PV_A for the tactical bank is 39.63 = 40(1.08)/1.09 while the PV_A for the strategic bank is 58.97 = 6/1.11 + 66/(1.11)^2. The PV_L for the tactical bank is 35.91 = 36(1.06)$^{0.25}$/(1.07)$^{0.25}$ while the PV_L for the strategic bank is 49.4 = the value of a 9% coupon bond (payment = 54 × 0.09 = 4.86 per year) with a face value of 54, a maturity of 20 years, and a required return of 10%.

TABLE 5-4   A Catalog of ALM Terminology

Panel A. The ARBL Bank: Assets Reprice before Liabilities (borrows long, lends short)
Maturity gap: $RSA > RSL$ → Positive dollar or maturity gap
Duration gap: $D_A < D_L$ → Negative duration gap
Sensitivity: Asset sensitive
Funding: Long funded
Book: Long book

Panel B. The LRBA Bank: Liabilities Reprice before Assets (borrows short, lends long)
Maturity gap: $RSA < RSL$ → Negative dollar or maturity gap
Duration gap: $D_A > D_L$ → Positive duration gap
Sensitivity: Liability sensitive
Funding: Short funded
Book: Short book

Panel C. The Matched or Balanced Bank: Assets and Liabilities Reprice at the Same Time before Assets (borrows short, lends short, or borrows long, lends long)
Maturity gap: $RSA = RSL$ → Zero dollar or maturity gap
Duration gap: $D_A = D_L$ → Zero duration gap
Sensitivity: Nonsensitive
Funding: Balanced funded
Book: Matched book

Panel D. The Immunized (Solvent) Bank
Duration gap: $D_A < D_L$ → Asset sensitive
  Tactical bank in a LRBA position
  Strategic bank in an ARBL position } → Overall bank is ARBL

accounting model identifies when the interest-rate risk will hit the bank's books. In terms of tactical and strategic components, ALM managers can attempt to exploit liquidity premiums contained in the short end of the yield curve. To achieve this objective, the bank's overall balance sheet must be asset sensitive, a liability-sensitive tactical bank more than offset by an asset-sensitive strategic bank.

INTEREST-RATE RISK, BANK RISK PROFILES, AND EMBEDDED OPTIONS IN FINANCIAL CONTRACTS

Banks face four major portfolio risks: credit risk, interest-rate risk, liquidity risk, and prepayment risk. In ALM, the focal variable is interest-rate risk. In addition, because the options embedded in loan contracts and deposit contracts give rise to **prepayment risk** and liquidity risk, respectively, ALM can be viewed as the coordinated management of these three risks. These risks are important because unexpected changes in interest rates can adversely affect bank cash flows (reinvestment risk) and equity values (price risk). Managing assets and liabilities to minimize the adverse effects of interest-rate risk is an alternative statement of the objective of ALM. Also, bank managers must be concerned about the interaction between interest-rate risk and credit risk.

Interest-Rate Risk: Price Risk and Reinvestment Risk

When interest rates change, the values of contracts with fixed interest rates (loans or deposits) change. For example, when interest rates rise, the values of fixed-rate mortgages and other fixed-income securities decline. The adverse price effect is bad for lenders. The good news for lenders (not borrowers) is that new mortgages can be made at the new higher mortgage rate—the favorable reinvestment effect. In contrast, when interest rates decline, the values of fixed-rate mortgages and other fixed-income securities rise. The favorable price effect is good news for lenders. The bad news for lenders (not borrowers) is that new mortgages can be made only at the new lower mortgage rate—the unfavorable reinvestment effect.

Additional Bad News for Lenders: Embedded Options

Because most borrowers have the option of prepaying loans and because most depositors have the option of withdrawing deposits before their maturity, lenders face additional risks associated with changes in interest rates. Table 5-5 summarizes the effects of interest-rate risk with respect to a bank's loans and deposits. Consider the case of rising interest rates. Under these conditions, borrowers don't want to refinance, but depositors might be willing (even if a substantial penalty for early withdrawal exists) to withdraw their funds to invest in higher-yielding assets. If funds are withdrawn from the bank, the bank faces a liquidity problem, which has a quantity effect and a price or cost effect. The bank must replace the funds or shrink its balance sheet. If the bank can replace the funds (the quantity effect), the funds will cost more because rates have risen (the price effect). If the bank can't replace the funds, it must shrink its balance sheet at a time when prices of fixed-rate assets are down because interest rates have risen. Thus, contracting the balance sheet can result in capital losses to generate liquidity.

Now consider the case of falling interest rates. Under these conditions, depositors don't want to withdraw funds but borrowers might want to refinance their

TABLE 5-5   The Effects of Interest-Rate Risk on Loans and Deposits

Panel A. Effects on the Loan Portfolio

↑ *Interest Rates (up)*	*Result*
• Adverse Price Effect	Old Loans Worth Less
• Favorable Reinvestment Effect	New Loans Worth More

↓ *Interest Rates (down)*	*Result*
• Favorable Price Effect	Old Loans Worth More
• Adverse Reinvestment Effect	New Loans Worth Less

Panel B. Effects on Deposits

↑ *Interest Rates (up)*

• Early Withdrawal (Depositors Seek Higher Rates)
• Banks Must Attract New Depositors at Higher Rate or Face Liquidity Problems (Quantity and Price Effects)

↓ *Interest Rates (down)*

• Loan Prepayments Due to Refinancing
• Banks Must Issue New Loans at Lower Rate or Face Shrinking Balance Sheet (Quantity and Price Effects)

loans (even if a prepayment penalty exists) to benefit from the lower interest rates. If loans are refinanced, the bank faces prepayment risk, which has a quantity effect and a price or revenue effect. The bank must replace the loans or see its balance sheet shrink (there is no guarantee that the refinancing will be with the original lender). If the bank can replace the loans with other loans of similar risk (quantity and quality effects), the loans will definitely yield less because rates have declined (the price effect). If the bank can't replace the loans (with loans of any risk, say, because of slack loan demand) and it wants to maintain the size of its balance sheet, it will have to acquire other safer and more liquid assets (e.g., Treasury bills, notes, bonds) at a time when their yields are down (prices up). The price of greater liquidity is lower return. The alternative to replacing the assets is to let deposits run off or to reduce nondeposit sources of funds or both.

To summarize, contracts with **embedded options** complicate the task of ALM. Loan contracts with prepayment options expose lenders to prepayment risk whereas deposit contracts with early-withdrawal options create liquidity risk.

Techniques for Managing the Risks of ALM

Banks have three general techniques for managing interest-rate risk:

1. On-balance-sheet methods such as maturity matching or duration matching of assets and liabilities

2. **Off-balance-sheet** methods for *hedging* interest-rate risk, such as interest-rate futures, options, swaps, caps, collars, and floors

3. **Securitization,** which manages interest-rate risk, assuming no recourse, by removing it from the balance sheet

The first two methods do not control for embedded options in financial contracts, whereas securitization succeeds in removing all portfolio risks from a bank's balance sheet. One qualification, however, is in order. If a bank securitizes assets without recourse and maintains the servicing rights (i.e., it collects interest and principal for a servicing fee and then passes the payments through to investors), then it still faces prepayment risk with respect to its servicing income.

A Picture Is Worth a Thousand Words: Risk Profiles

To visualize the three approaches to ALM and to conceptualize the effects of interest-rate risk on bank value, it is useful to introduce the notion of a risk profile. Consider a bank that borrows short and lends long at fixed rates of interest. Because liabilities reprice before assets (LRBA),[13] the bank is vulnerable to an unexpected increase in interest rates. The LRBA bank also can be described as having a negative maturity gap (a positive duration gap). Panel A of Figure 5-2 depicts

FIGURE 5-2 **Bank Risk Profiles**

Panel A. The LRBA bank (liabilities repricing before assets, or borrowing short and lending long)

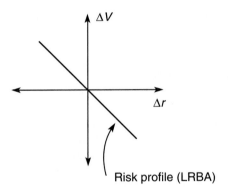

Risk profile (LRBA)

Panel B. The ARBL bank (assets repricing before liabilities, or borrowing long and lending short)

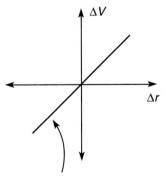

Risk profile (ARBL)

Note: Flatter risk profile → less risk; steeper risk profile → more risk.
ΔV = Change in market value of bank; Δr = unexpected change in interest rate.

---

[13] The terms LRBA and ARBL were first used by Stigum and Branch [1983].

this bank's risk profile as a negatively sloped line in the defined space of unexpected change in rate (Δr) and change in value of the bank (ΔV). If interest rates rise, the value of the LRBA bank declines; if interest rates decline, the value of the bank rises. Thus, managers of LRBA banks are primarily concerned about unexpected increases in interest rates. If they expect rates to rise, this information is incorporated into their ALM decisions.

Now consider a bank that borrows long at fixed rates and lends short. Because assets reprice before liabilities (ARBL), the bank is vulnerable to an unexpected decrease in interest rates. The ARBL bank can be described as having a positive maturity gap or a negative duration gap. Panel B of Figure 5-2 depicts this bank's risk profile as a positively sloped line, defined in the same space as Panel A. If interest rates fall, the value of the ARBL bank declines; if interest rates rise, the value of the bank rises. Thus, managers of ARBL banks are primarily concerned about unexpected decreases in interest rates. If they expect rates to decline, this information is incorporated into their ALM decisions.

A bank that has successfully used on-balance-sheet methods to hedge its interest-rate risk will have a risk profile that corresponds with the horizontal axis in Figure 5-2. The steeper a bank's risk profile is, the greater is its sensitivity to unexpected changes in interest rates.

The Effects of Embedded Options on Risk Profiles

For convenience, the risk profiles shown in Figure 5-2 are linear. As such, they are easy to draw but are not quite real because they ignore embedded interest-rate options arising from prepayment risk and liquidity risk. Pictures of options are nonlinear. Before going on, can you visualize how the risk profiles in Figure 5-2 would change to account for the embedded options of prepayment risk and liquidity risk?[14]

What we want to do is to adjust the risk profiles for the LRBA and ARBL banks to reflect the prepayment risk associated with loan contracts and the liquidity risk associated with deposit contracts—the embedded interest-rate options. A loan that can be prepaid is identical to a callable bond, and we can treat its prepayment risk as call risk; a deposit that can be withdrawn prior to maturity is identical to a putable bond, and we can treat its liquidity risk as the risk associated with a putable bond (the term "put risk" is not as commonly used as "call risk").

Panel A of Figure 5-3 shows the linear and nonlinear risk profiles for the LRBA bank exposed to both prepayment risk and liquidity risk. The underlying logic of the nonlinear picture should not escape you. As interest rates decline, the value of the LRBA bank increases because it is liability sensitive, that is, its liabilities reprice before its assets, which is why it is deemed a LRBA bank. Because of prepayment risk, however, the increase in the value of the bank is retarded. Prepayment penalties serve as disincentives to potential loan refinancings and they generate fees from actual refinancings. As interest rates rise, the value of the LRBA bank declines, but because of liquidity risk associated with deposit withdrawals, the decline in value is exacerbated beyond the simple linear case. Penalties for early withdrawal serve to restrict potential deposit outflows, and they generate fees from actual early withdrawals.

Panel B of Figure 5-3 shows the nonlinear risk profile for the ARBL bank exposed to both prepayment risk and liquidity risk. Again, the underlying logic of this

---

[14] Appendix B of this chapter, which describes bond pricing and "negative convexity," provides some hints on what the nonlinear profiles will look like.

Panel A. The LRBA bank (liabilities repricing before assets)

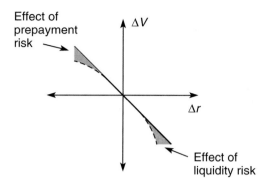

Panel B. The ARBL bank (asset repricing before liabilities)

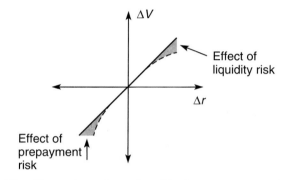

ΔV = Change in market value of bank; Δr = unexpected change in interest rate.

FIGURE 5-3 Bank Risk Profiles

nonlinear picture should not escape you. As interest rates decline, the value of the ARBL bank decreases because it is asset sensitive, that is, its assets reprice before its liabilities, which is why it is deemed an ARBL bank. Because of prepayment risk, however, the decrease in the value of the bank is exacerbated. As interest rates rise, the value of the ARBL bank increases, but because of liquidity risk associated with deposit withdrawals, the increase in value is retarded beyond the simple linear case. Again, penalties for early withdrawal serve to retard deposit outflows and generate fees from premature withdrawals.

In a world with embedded options in loan and deposit contracts, nonlinear risk profiles cannot coincide with a linear horizontal axis. What's a banker to do? The techniques of financial engineering, the next topic, provide potential remedies.

OFF-BALANCE-SHEET TECHNIQUES FOR HEDGING INTEREST-RATE RISK

In addition to maturity or duration methods for managing interest-rate risk, ALM managers also may use off-balance-sheet techniques in the form of **interest-rate contracts** (IRCs). IRCs include such instruments as interest-rate **forwards, futures,**

options, and **swaps.** These off-balance-sheet activities (OBSAs) are also referred to as **derivatives** contracts and as instruments of financial engineering. Although the United States has thousands of commercial banks, only about 600 or so of them use IRCs for hedging, dealing, or selling risk-management services.[15]

Payoff Profiles for Interest-Rate Contracts (IRCs)

The idea behind hedging interest-rate risk with IRCs is to offset or reduce losses in cash or spot markets with gains in derivatives markets. Two key aspects of specific derivatives are (1) different cash-flow requirements for different instruments (e.g., exchange-traded futures must be marked to market, whereas over-the-counter [OTC] contracts, such as forwards and swaps, have no such requirements), and (2) the nature of the **payoff** or profit **profiles** of the derivatives contracts. Futures, forwards, and swaps are "linear" contracts that have symmetrical payoff patterns (see Panel A of Figure 5-4), whereas options are "nonlinear" contracts that have asymmetrical profit profiles[16] (see Panel B of Figure 5-4).

The Linear Contracts: Futures, Forwards, and Swaps

The values of contracts based on futures, forwards, or swaps move proportionally to the value of the underlying asset. Although futures and forwards contracts differ in terms of credit risk, margin requirements, delivery, standardization, and other characteristics, the fundamental nature of the two contracts is the same. Specifically, they are legal agreements today to deliver something ("the underlying") at a specified price at the end of a designated period of time. Two kinds of (linear) contracts ALM managers use are interest-rate futures and forwards in which the underlying asset is some financial instrument (e.g., Treasury bill futures). The kind of swap agreements used in ALM usually are tied to interest rates. In these arrangements, called interest-rate swaps,[17] only interest payments are exchanged, not the underlying principal or notional amounts. The index or reference rate (e.g., LIBOR) times the notional amount determines the interest payment. An example of an interest-rate swap is a bank making payment on the basis of a fixed rate and receiving payment on the basis of a floating rate.

Panel A of Figure 5-5 combines Panel A of Figure 5-3 with Panel A of Figure 5-4 to show how a LRBA bank can hedge its interest-rate risk. The LRBA bank is vulnerable to an unexpected increase in interest rates. If rates rise, the LRBA bank loses money in the cash market. By selling interest-rate futures or forwards or engaging in an interest-rate swap in which the LRBA bank pays fixed and receives floating, the bank generates positive cash flows through the particular IRCs, if rates rise. If the hedge is perfect, then the losses on assets in place will be offset exactly by the positive cash flows in the derivatives markets. In this case, the bank's

---

[15] Sinkey and Carter [1996] report on the derivatives activities of U.S. banks whereas Carter and Sinkey [1996] analyze the use of IRCs by medium-sized U.S. banks. In the United States dealer activities are mainly the domain of the 10 to 20 largest banks.

[16] Because the profit profiles for the option contracts in this chapter assume zero premiums, they go through the origin of the diagrams. Relaxing the assumption simply results in a horizontal displacement of the profile along the vertical axis.

[17] Esty, Tufano, and Headley [1994] present an interesting case regarding Banc One's ALM and its extensive use of amortizing interest-rate swaps (AIRS) or AIR swaps. Also don't miss the commentaries on the case by Albertson [1994], Heisler [1994], James and Smith [1994], and Kane [1994], and the case postscript by Esty and Tufano [1994].

Panel A. Forwards, futures, and swaps

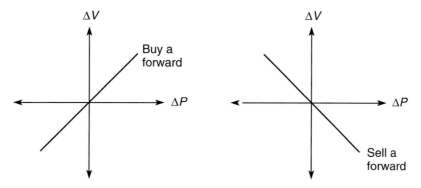

Panel B. Options and put-call parity

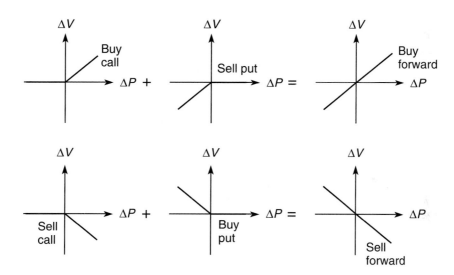

ΔV = Change in value of derivative; Δr = change in price of underlying asset.

FIGURE 5-4 **Payoff Profiles of Forwards, Futures, Swaps, and Options**

net exposure would coincide with the horizontal axis. If the hedge is less than perfect, then losses are not offset completely, and the LRBA bank's net exposure still reflects a vulnerability to unexpected increases in interest rates.

For the LRBA bank, the undesirable part of hedging with symmetrical or linear contracts such as futures, forwards, or swaps is that the bank is not vulnerable to a decline in interest rates. Thus, if rates do decline the bank incurs gains on assets in place but sustains losses on its IRCs. With linear contracts, one cannot have one's cake and eat it too!

Panel B of Figure 5-5 combines Panel B of Figure 5-3 with Panel B of Figure 5-4 to show how an ARBL bank can hedge its interest-rate risk. The ARBL bank is vulnerable to an unexpected decrease in interest rates. If rates decline, the ARBL bank loses money in the cash market. By buying interest-rate futures or forwards or engaging in an interest-rate swap in which the ARBL bank pays

Panel A. How a LRBA bank can hedge interest-rate risk

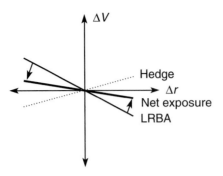

Panel B. How an ARBL bank can hedge interest-rate risk

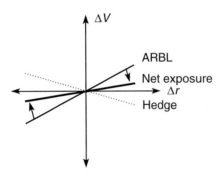

ΔV = Change in market value; Δr = change in interest rate.

FIGURE 5-5 Hedging Interest-Rate Risk with Interest-Rate Contracts

floating and receives fixed, the bank generates positive cash flows through the particular IRCs, if rates fall. If the hedge is perfect, then the losses on assets in place will be offset exactly by the positive cash flows in the derivatives markets. In this case, the bank's net exposure would coincide with the horizontal axis. If the hedge is less than perfect, then losses are not offset completely and the ARBL bank's net exposure still reflects a vulnerability to unexpected decreases in interest rates.

For the ARBL bank, the undesirable part of hedging with symmetrical or linear contracts such as futures, forwards, or swaps is that the bank is not vulnerable to an increase in interest rates. Thus, if rates do rise, the bank incurs gains on assets in place but sustains losses on its IRCs.

Whether a bank is ARBL or LRBA, linear contracts such as interest-rate futures, forwards, or swaps provide protection if rates move one way but extract extra payments (besides transactions costs) if rates move the other way. Given the downside, why would bankers ever use such linear contracts? Several reasons exist. ALM managers might prefer the reduced credit risk provided by exchange-guaranteed contracts such as interest-rate futures. They might prefer the tailor-made specifications provided by OTC forwards or swaps. Or transactions costs may be lower for linear contracts. On the other hand, ALM managers might prefer to hedge interest-rate risk with nonlinear contracts in the form of options (including options on futures), the topics considered next.

The Nonlinear Contracts: Options, Caps, Floors, and Collars

Panel B of Figure 5-4 shows the payoff profiles for option contracts, assuming zero premiums. The profiles generated by option contracts, which are not linear, are associated with such names as caps, floors, and collars. Thus, ALM managers can use option-based IRCs to put a cap on interest expenses without forgoing the potential benefit of declining rates, to put a floor under interest revenues without forgoing the upside potential of rising rates, or to lock in (hedge) a bank's spread, a collar.

Figure 5-6 shows how options on financial instruments (e.g., financial futures)[18] can be used to create caps, floors, and collars. Panel A presents the cash flows from purchasing an interest-rate cap (drawn with a zero premium). An ALM manager would want to purchase such a contract to protect (hedge) against the rising cost of funds. The seller of the cap receives a premium for bearing the risk of rising interest rates. If rates rise, the seller pays the buyer the *difference* between the cap rate and the actual market rate (times the notional value of the contract). For example, assuming a notional contract value of $1 million and a rise in the reference rate of 100 basis points above the cap level, the seller would pay the buyer $10,000 (= 0.01 × 1,000,000). If rates stay below the ceiling rate over the life of the contract, the seller pays nothing and the buyer is out the cost of the "insurance."

Panel B of Figure 5-6 shows the profit profile from selling an interest-rate floor (drawn with a zero premium). The seller of the floor receives a premium for bearing the risk of declining interest rates. If rates fall, the seller pays the buyer the *difference* between the floor rate and the actual market rate (times the notional value of the contract). For example, assuming a notional contract value of $1 million and a drop in the reference rate of 100 basis points below the floor, the seller would pay the buyer $10,000. If rates stay above the floor rate over the life of the contract, the seller pays nothing and the buyer is out the cost of the "insurance."

Although it is clear why an ALM manager would want to buy a floor (i.e., to protect against falling interest revenues), why would anyone want to sell a floor? Sellers of risk-management services, such as large banks that deal in derivatives contracts, undertake these transactions to generate noninterest (premium) income. In addition, by simultaneously buying a cap and selling a floor, an ALM manager can create an interest-rate collar (see Panel C). As long as rates stay within the collar, no cash flows occur. If rates rise above the collar, the holder of the collar receives cash payments; whereas if rates fall below the collar, the holder must make cash payments.

How Banks Can Use Interest-Rate Collars to Manage Interest-Rate Risk

Figures 5-7 and 5-8 illustrate how a LRBA bank and an ARBL bank, respectively, can use interest-rate collars to manage interest-rate risk. Panel A of Figure 5-7 shows the familiar profit profile for the LRBA bank—a negative slope with a vulnerability to increasing rates. Panel B presents the cash flows from simultaneously buying an interest-rate cap and selling an interest-rate floor. The combination of

---

[18] Futures contracts in which the underlying is a financial instrument (such as Treasury bills or bonds) or a financial index are known as "financial futures."

Panel A. Profit profile from purchasing an interest-rate cap

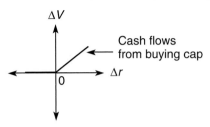

Panel B. Profit profile from selling an interest-rate floor

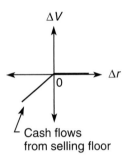

Panel C. Profit profile for an interest-rate collar
(simultaneously buying a cap and selling a floor)

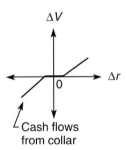

ΔV = Change in value of interest-rate contract; Δr = change in interest rate.

FIGURE 5-6 Profit Profiles for Options on Interest-Rate Contracts: Creating Caps, Floors, and Collars

the economic effects of Panels A and B generates Panel C, which shows the cash flows for a LRBA bank with an interest-rate collar. The important economic effect is the reduction in the variability of firm value arising from the hedge provided by the collar.

If managers are concerned about reducing the probability of financial distress, it is easy to understand why they want a floor on firm value. It is less obvious why they tolerate a cap on firm value, because they certainly do not want to cap it. The logic goes something like this. Since managers consider the chances of a large decrease in rates to be quite small, they are willing to sell an option (the floor shown in Figure 5-6) to generate premium income. The seller's net gain or loss depends on the relation between the premium income received and the interest payments made, if any. Thus, selling the floor results in a cap on firm value for a LRBA bank. A further consideration is that if large decreases in rates do occur, the bank will encounter substantial refinancing by existing borrowers (realized prepayment risk).

Panel A. The profit profile for a LRBA bank

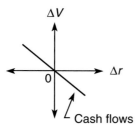

Panel B. Profit profile for an interest-rate collar
(simultaneously buying a cap and selling a floor)

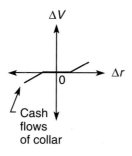

Panel C. The profit profile (net exposure)
for a LRBA bank with an interest-rate collar

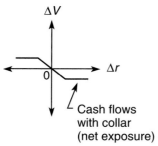

ΔV = Change in value of contract or bank;
Δr = change in interest rate.

**FIGURE 5-7 Illustration of
Using an Interest-Rate Collar
for a LRBA Bank**

Panel A of Figure 5-8 shows the familiar profit profile for the ARBL bank—a positive slope with a vulnerability to decreasing rates. Panel B presents the cash flows from simultaneously selling an interest-rate cap and buying an interest-rate floor (assuming offsetting premiums or costs). The combination of the economic effects of Panels A and B generates Panel C, which shows the cash flows for an ARBL bank with an interest-rate collar. The important economic effect is the reduction in the variability of firm value arising from the hedge provided by the collar.

Again it is easy to understand why the managers of an ARBL bank would want a floor on firm value. Regarding the cap on firm value, they are willing to forgo the opportunity of a large increase in firm value because they view the chances of a large increase in rates to be small. Accordingly, they sell an interest-rate cap, for which they receive premium income. If rates rise above the reference rate, they will have to make interest payments to the buyer of the cap. The seller's net gain or loss depends on the relation between the premium income received and

Panel A. The profit profile for an ARBL bank

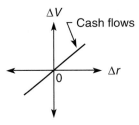

Panel B. Profit profile for an interest-rate collar
(simultaneously selling a cap and buying a floor)

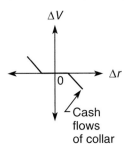

Panel C. The profit profile (net exposure)
for an ARBL bank with an interest-rate collar

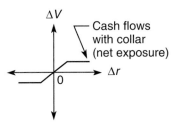

ΔV = Change in value of contract or bank;
Δr = change in interest rate.

**FIGURE 5-8 Illustration of
Using an Interest-Rate Collar
for an ARBL Bank**

the interest payments made, if any. Thus, selling the cap results in a cap on firm value for an ARBL bank. A further consideration is that if large increases in rates do occur, the bank may encounter substantial disintermediation (liquidity risk).

Futures Options

ALM managers can obtain options on interest-rate futures contracts as another means of managing interest-rate risk. Such an instrument is called a **futures option.** It almost permits ALM managers to have their cake and eat it too! The catch is the premium paid for the option to exercise the futures contract. If ALM managers buy call options on an interest-rate contract, they have the right (but not the obligation) to purchase the designated contract at the exercise price (i.e., acquire a "long position") at any time during the exercise period. The seller (writer) of the call receives the call premium and must deliver the designated futures contract if the option is exercised. In contrast, if ALM managers buy put options on an interest-rate contract, they have the right (but not the obligation) to sell the designated contract at the exercise price (i.e., to acquire a "short position") at any time during the exercise period. The seller (writer) of the option receives the put premium and must receive the designated futures contract if the option is exercised.

Recapitulation

Off-balance-sheet activities (OBSAs) offer another way for banks to manage interest-rate risk. Interest-rate contracts (IRCs), which are distinguished by the linearity or nonlinearity of their profit profiles, can be used to hedge or to speculate on the expected movements of interest rates. Interest-rate futures, forwards, and swaps are linear contracts, whereas interest-rate options (caps, floors, and collars) are nonlinear contracts. The objective of hedging is to reduce the probability of financial distress and thereby increase firm value. Banks that use interest-rate collars protect against reductions in firm value, but they also forgo the potential for large increases in firm value. Premium income from selling options compensates for the sacrifice of a small chance for a large gain. Of the thousands of commercial banks in the United States, only about 600 banks actually use IRCs to manage interest-rate risk, and even fewer banks, mainly large dealers, sell risk-management services to their clients.

SECURITIZATION REMOVES INTEREST-RATE RISK
FROM THE BALANCE SHEET

A third technique for managing interest-rate risk is simply to remove risky assets from the balance sheet by selling them. Although banks have sold loans to other banks for years, the market was not well developed. Also, as a means of risk sharing, banks have engaged in loan participations for years. A major financial innovation of the 1980s, **asset securitization,** has fundamentally changed the process of financial intermediation.[19] It involves pooling loans and repackaging them as securities backed by the cash flows of the underlying loans. Residential mortgages were the first asset to be securitized, and they are the major asset subject to such processing. Today, however, just about any loan that a bank makes has the potential to be securitized. Besides mortgages, the other most popular loans for banks to securitize are automobile loans and credit-card receivables. As a technique of ALM, securitization does its job by removing risk from the balance sheet. Moreover, assuming no recourse (i.e, the right to put securitized assets back to the originator), it removes all the risks associated with the loan.

The key to understanding securitization as a major financial innovation is to distinguish between indirect finance and pass-through finance. The traditional intermediation function of a bank is to originate and fund loans. Securitization has led to pass-through finance in which a bank either (1) originates and sells loans or (2) originates, sells, and services loans. "Servicing" means collecting payments of interest and principal and passing them through to investors, hence the term "pass-through finance." Servicers earn fees, of course, for performing this function. Securitization has permitted banks to sell or service large volumes of loans. For example, Fleet Mortgage Group (SC), a subsidiary of Fleet Financial Group (RI), originated $23 billion in residential mortgages in 1993 and serviced over one million

---

[19] Asset securitization is also covered in chapters 9–11.

residential mortgages worth $68 billion in 1993. Of the $68 billion in loans serviced, $64 billion were serviced for investors.[20]

On balance, asset securitization is a major financial innovation that offers banks (and other players) opportunities to remove risk from their balance sheets and to generate fee or servicing income.

BANK ALM IN PRACTICE

This chapter ends with a look at some practical aspects of ALM. Although derivatives, duration, and securitization represent innovative or more sophisticated approaches to managing interest-rate risk, many banks manage their assets and liabilities without such techniques, and as the net margins indicate (Table 5-2), they do ALM quite successfully. Whether they can continue their ALM successfully without these modern methods remains to be seen.

The Building Blocks of ALM

Four key building blocks of ALM are the following:[21]

- Measurement of dollar gaps on the basis of maturity buckets (0–90 days, 91–180 days, etc.) to determine the amount of assets and liabilities being repriced
- Estimating the interest rate at which these funds will be repriced
- Projecting future interest income and interest expense (rate × volume)
- Exploring alternative interest-rate scenarios to estimate the bank's downside vulnerability

Gap Measurement

The measurement of a bank's gap position depends critically on the time horizon over which the gap is measured. A range of three-to-six months or less probably captures the relevant time frame for ALM. In terms of coordination with a bank's annual budget, a one-year horizon is appropriate. To illustrate both of these planning horizons, consider the hypothetical balance sheet presented in Table 5-6. Within the one-year horizon, a maturity composition of both assets and liabilities is determined, and the gap and the cumulative-gap positions are measured at each maturity. If we use a one-year horizon, the bank appears to be relatively balanced, with a negative gap of $10 million. However, over the 30- to 182-day horizon, the bank's cumulative gap ranges from $35 million to $55 million. The one-day gap of $35 million is a money-desk or reserve-position problem. The ALM committee should focus its immediate attention on the $55 million negative gap that occurs within the next 30 days. This gap represents the potential cumulative net outflow or liquidity risk that the bank is subject to within the next month, because the maturing liabilities may be withdrawn even if they are variable-rate instruments.

---

[20] Other subsidiaries of BHCs that are major servicers of residential mortgages include Norwest Mortgage (IA), BankAmerica Mortgage (CA), Chase Manhattan Mortgage (FL), Chemical Residential Mortgage (NJ), and Citicorp Mortgage (CT). Two major thrift servicers of mortgages are Home Savings of America and Great Western Bank, both of California. Four major nonbank servicers of residential mortgages are Countrywide Credit Industries (CA), G. E. Capital Mortgage Services (NC), Prudential Home Mortgage (MO), and GMAC Mortgage (PA). Countrywide was the largest servicer in both 1993 and 1994, whereas G. E. was second in 1994, and Prudential was second in 1993. The data here and in the text are from "Top Mortgage Servicers: An American Banker Special Report," *American Banker* (May 11, 1995), p. 2A.

[21] These building blocks and the subsequent discussions draw on Houghton [1983].

TABLE 5-6 The Time Horizon of Gap Management

Maturity[a]	Assets ($ Millions)	Liabilities ($ Millions)	Gap Position ($ Millions)	Cumulative-Gap Position ($ Millions)
1 day	5	40	−35	−35
30 days	10	30	−20	−55
60 days	15	20	− 5	−60
91 days	20	10	10	−50
182 days	25	10	15	−35
365 days	30	5	25	−10
TOTAL SHORT TERM	105	115	−10	−10
Over one year	95	70	+25	+15
Capital	—	15	−15	0
TOTAL	200	200	0	0

[a]The dollar amounts (in millions) can be viewed as being spread out within the various maturities rather than the total amount maturing on a particular day.

Interest-Rate Forecasting by Time Frame

The interest rates at which dollar flows will be repriced must be estimated. Since spread management is an integral part of ALM, this step permits banks to monitor their spreads by time frame. The idea is to spot potential margin problems early so that knee-jerk ALM reactions can be avoided. Long-term rewards (versus short-term results) require that assets and liabilities be matched profitably.

Projection of Future Income

The quantities (i.e., dollar volumes) and prices (i.e., interest rates) generated by the previous two blocks provide the foundation for the third building block—the projection of future income. This step allows ALM managers to look into the future. Since the idea is to measure the bank's vulnerability to alternative interest-rate scenarios, simulation models are useful in this step. At the minimum, a best case, worst case, and most likely case should be generated.

Testing Different Strategies

This block is where the "art" of ALM is practiced. The previous three blocks are more scientific or mechanical in nature (i.e., grab the data and run them through the simulator). Of course, without the science of ALM, there would be no ALM art to practice. Thus, the previous blocks must be constructed, and constructed solidly. From this foundation, alternative ALM strategies are reviewed and checked for consistency with the bank's strategic plans. Recall that ALM is the first step in implementing the bank's strategic plan. Different ALM strategies must be analyzed with respect to their effects on the bank's bottom line. Unlike decomposition analysis, which works from symptoms to causes, ALM strategy sessions focus on how the arrangement of the basic building blocks affects the performance symptoms (e.g., NIM, ROA, and ROE). The critical decision variables in the arrangement process are pricing strategies; product mix; the size, growth, and composition of the balance sheet; and the extent of off-balance-sheet activities. To be effective management tools, ALM models should generate two products: (1) the optimum short-run portfolio of assets and liabilities in terms of the risk-return parameters of NIM and (2) information for top management to evaluate the short-run direction of its strategic plan so that any necessary adjustments can be made.

Cyclical Management of Interest-Rate Risk

The key to gap management is to maintain balance-sheet flexibility. However, because banks do not have complete discretionary control over all their assets and liabilities, this flexibility is not easily obtained. It would be ideal if a bank could simply switch from a positive gap to a negative one when required by changes in interest rates. This would, however, require a very flexible balance sheet indeed. More realistically, a bank should be flexible enough to take advantage of interest-rate changes. David Cates [1978], a bank consultant, puts it this way:

> To be potentially imbalanced but deliberately and significantly off-balance according to interest-rate trends is an ideal posture. But it is one which (1) is probably available only to larger banks, and (2) depends on proper forecasting and intelligent implementation, with corresponding penalties for poor planning and execution. (p. 25)

Paul Nadler [1990], another noted bank analyst, uses the following analogy to stress the importance of flexibility and a balanced position, especially for small banks: "When I cross the ocean, I don't care how deep it is as long as I am on the top" (p. 16). The point is that banks shouldn't care what happens to rates as long as both their assets and their liabilities have floating rates that move together. This is especially true for small banks with limited resources to play the gap-management game. Thus, for small banks, a low-risk strategy of attempting to maintain a zero gap by maturity-matching their balance sheets is a reasonable second-best approach.

The relationship between a bank's NIM and movements in short-term interest rates depends on its gap position or sensitivity ratio. The three general situations that banks may face are depicted in Figure 5-9. (The federal-funds rate is used to capture the movement of short-term rates.) In (a), the sensitivity ratio is 1 (i.e., a zero-gap position) and thus the bank's NIM remains constant (i.e., it is invariant to changes in the federal-funds rate). In (b), the sensitivity ratio is greater than 1 (i.e., a positive-gap position) and NIM varies directly with the level of short-term rates. In (c), the sensitivity ratio is less than 1 (i.e., a negative-gap position) and NIM varies inversely with the level of short-term rates.

ALM Simulation Models

Testing alternative ALM strategies and different interest-rate scenarios is accomplished most efficiently using ALM simulation models, which can be developed internally or purchased from consulting firms. Grunewald [1990] recommends that banks with assets greater than $500 million consider buying their own ALM models. Community bankers might look to their correspondent banks for assistance or consider developing ALM networks for model sharing. The primary advantage of ALM models is their ability to do simulation analysis. In the process, they generate pro forma or forecasted balance sheets and income-expense statements that permit ALM managers to monitor both accounting and economic measures of interest-rate risk across different economic environments. At the minimum, the scenario analysis or game playing focuses on best-case, most-likely, and worst-case situations. In terms of risk management, the key strategy is to estimate the bank's

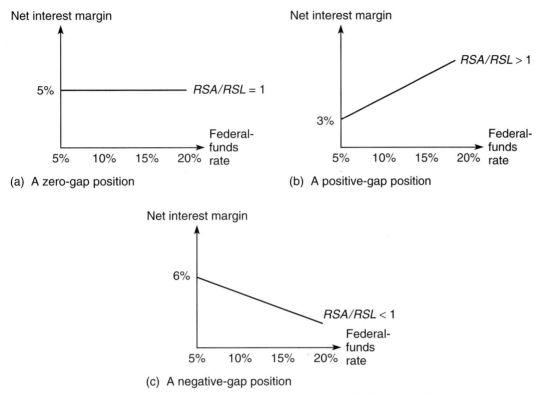

FIGURE 5-9 **NIM, Movements in Short-Term Interest Rates, and the Sensitivity Ratio**

downside vulnerability to avoid betting the bank.

As in strategic planning, ALM model building can be viewed in terms of three questions: Where is the bank today? Where is the bank going? And how is the bank going to get there? Because the data requirements are quite large, a computer model is the most efficient method of analysis. Because projections of rates, volumes, and mixes are involved, the quality of output critically depends on the quality of the inputs—garbage in, garbage out. In addition, ALM managers must understand the intricacies of the model and know how to interpret the results.

ALM and the Effects of Interest-Rate Sensitivity on Bank Performance: A Comparative-Statics Experiment

To demonstrate the effects of interest-rate sensitivity on bank performance, consider the situation depicted in Table 5-7. Given the initial conditions for the bank, we trace through a 200-basis-point, or 2 percent, increase in short-term interest rates, which affects only RSA and RSL. Since the bank has a negative GAP of -100, the increase in rates will worsen bank performance. However, we can expect rational ALM managers to attempt to offset these adverse effects. Nevertheless, market forces may prevent a complete adjustment.

This comparative-statics experiment consists of four stages of analysis: (1) initial conditions, (2) interest-rate shock, (3) portfolio readjustment, and (4) counterbalancing market forces. The bank performance measures analyzed are the dollar or funding gap, net interest income (NII), net interest margin (NIM), net income,

TABLE 5-7 The Effects of Interest-Rate Sensitivity on Bank Performance

Initial Conditions for Balance-Sheet Items

Item	Volume	Rate	Mix (% of Assets)
Rate-sensitive assets	$ 600	11%	.60
Fixed-rate assets	300	14	.30
Nonearning assets	100	0	.10
Totals or averages	$1,000	10.8%[a]	1.00
Rate-sensitive liabilities	$ 700	8%	.70
Fixed-rate liabilities	120	9	.12
Non-interest-bearing liabilities	100	0	.10
Equity capital	80	15[b]	.08
Totals or averages	$1,000	7.88%[a]	1.00

Initial Performance Measures

$$NII = .11(600) + .14(300) - .08(700) - .09(120)$$
$$= 66 + 42 - 56 - 10.8 = 41.2$$
$$NIM = 41.2/900 = 4.58\%$$
$$GAP = RSA - RSL = 600 - 700 = -100$$

Assuming provision for loan losses, burden, securities gains/losses, and taxes total 31.2. Net income is $10 = 41.2 - 31.2$. If the bank's payout ratio is .4, the addition to retained earnings is 6. Thus, $ROE = ROA \times EM = .01 \times 12.5 = .125$ or 12.5%

Comparative-Statics Experiment

System shock: Interest rates on rate-sensitive assets and liabilities increase by 200 basis points or 2 percent.

Balance-sheet adjustments: None; volumes and mix remain constant.

New Performance Measures

$$NII = .13(600) + .14(300) - .10(700) - .09(120)$$
$$= 78 + 42 - 70 - 10.8 = 39.2$$
$$NIM = 39.2/900 = 4.36\%$$

Net income $= 39.2 - 31.2 = 8$ and addition to retained earnings $= 4.8$
$ROE = .008 \times 12.5 = .10$ or 10%

Portfolio Adjustments to Rate Changes

RSA increases to 700 as nonearning assets decline to 50 and fixed-rate assets decline to 250. New $GAP = 700 - 700 = 0$.

Performance Measures after Portfolio Rebalancing

$$NII = .13(700) + .14(250) - .10(700) - .09(120)$$
$$= 91 + 35 - 70 - 10.8 = 45.2$$
$$NIM = 45.2/950 = 4.76\%$$

Net income $= 45.2 - 31.2 = 14$ and addition to retained earnings $= 8.4$
$ROE = .014 \times 12.5 = .175$ or 17.5%

Market Forces Counterbalance

Market forces drive RSL to 770 as non-interest-bearing liabilities decline to 50 and fixed-rate liabilities decline to 100. $GAP = -70$.

Counterbalanced Portfolio Measures

$$NII = .13(700) + .14(250) - .10(770) - .09(100)$$
$$= 91 + 35 - 77 - 9 = 40$$
$$NIM = 40/950 = .042 \text{ or } 4.2\%$$

Net income $= 40 - 31.2 = 8.8$ and addition to retained earnings $= 5.28$
$ROE = .0088 \times 12.5 = .11$ or 11%

[a]Weighted average cost or return.

[b]Shareholders' required return.

addition to retained earnings, and return on equity ($ROE = ROA \times EM$). The experiment can be summarized as follows:

| Performance Measure | *Stages of Analysis* | | | |
	Initial Position	*Interest-Rate Shock*	*Portfolio Adjustment*	*Counterbalancing Market Forces*
Dollar gap	–100	–100	0	–70
Net interest income	41.2	39.2	45.2	40
Net interest margin	4.58%	4.36%	4.76%	4.2%
Net income	10	8	14	8.8
Addition to retained earnings	6	4.8	8.4	5.28
Return on equity	12.5%	10%	17.5%	11%
Return on assets	1%	8%	1.4%	.88%
Equity multiplier	12.5	12.5	12.5	12.5

The analysis presented in Table 5-7 contains several important points. First, when interest rates rise, the existence of a negative gap worsens bank performance. Second, if the change in rates had been anticipated and if the bank had the portfolio flexibility to adjust, the rate increase could have been used to the bank's advantage, as shown in the portfolio-adjustment stage. Third, market forces (e.g., customers' quests for interest-bearing balances and market rates of return) serve to restrict bank profits as they benefit bank customers. And fourth, although the immediate focus of ALM is NIM (and its variability), ALM has a much broader reach because it affects a bank's bottom line, its capital adequacy, and the market value of its equity.

YIELD-CURVE SHAPES, THE EXPECTATIONS THEORY, AND ALM CAVEATS

The expectations theory of the term structure implies that a positively sloped yield curve embodies expectations of higher future short-term interest rates. In contrast, a negatively sloped yield curve embodies expectations of lower short-term interest rates. Thus, if the yield curve is positively sloped and a bank maintains a negative gap to reap funding profits from the difference between long- and short-term rates, it exposes itself to a rise in rates. Figure 5-10 depicts a bank facing this dilemma. If it adopts a positive gap position in anticipation of the rise in rates, it forgoes funding profits; if it goes after funding profits, it's vulnerable to a rise in rates. Two critical elements in the analysis are the extent of the maturity (duration) mismatch and how quickly the yield curve shifts. When interest rates are volatile (e.g., 1979–1982), severe maturity imbalances are highly risky, as evidenced by the thrift crisis. Accordingly, banks must maintain balance-sheet flexibility in going after funding or yield-curve profits. If interest rates move against a bank's gap position, it must have the flexibility to adjust. Alternatively, as discussed earlier in this chapter, a bank can use off-balance-sheet activities to attempt to hedge interest-rate risk.

Panel A. A positively sloped yield curve (interest rates expected to rise)

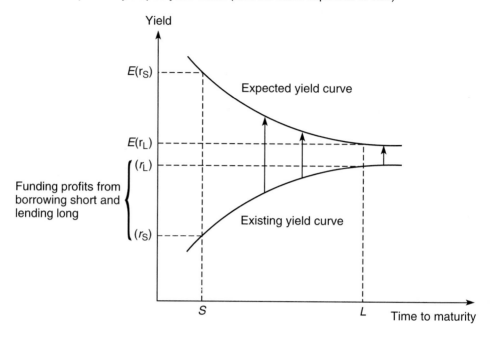

Panel B. A negatively sloped yield curve (interest rates expected to decline)

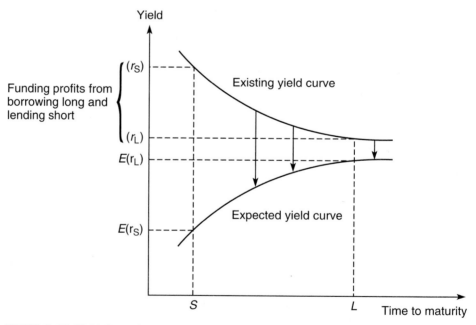

FIGURE 5-10 **Yield-Curve Shapes, the Expectations Theory, and the Dilemmas of Gap Management**

In the case of a negatively sloped yield curve, if the bank borrows long and lends short (a positive gap), it reaps funding profits. In contrast, if it positions itself for a decline in rates by adopting a negative gap, it forgoes the funding profits. The ability of the bank to adjust its gap position combined with its ability to forecast interest rates should govern the size of its interest-rate bet. Although the conventional wisdom about ALM places a heavy burden on superior interest-rate forecasting, any attempt to forecast interest rates beyond three to six months is a tricky business. Keep in mind the quip attributed to Sanford Rose of the *American Banker:* "He who lives by the crystal ball is doomed to eat shattered glass." Because superior forecasting ("beating the market") is a high-risk (speculative) strategy, banks need to consider carefully the cost of being wrong. The key factor here is the size of the bet on interest rates. The nature of banking is such that all banks bet on interest rates to some extent. Win or lose, however, big bets make for unstable earnings.

For some bankers, the cost of being wrong seldom enters their thinking (the hubris or ego hypothesis). First Pennsylvania (bailed out in 1980 by the FDIC and a consortium of big banks) and First Chicago are examples from the 1980s where large interest-rate bets went wrong. In 1994 and early 1995, interest-rate and exchange-rate bets on derivatives products by the largest banks, but especially by Bankers Trust of New York, created financial difficulties and hurt reputational capital.

Chapter Summary

Because the business of banking involves the measuring, managing, and accepting of risk, the heart of bank financial management is risk management. One of the most important risk-management functions in banking is **asset-liability management** (ALM), broadly defined as the coordinated management of a bank's balance sheet to allow for alternative interest-rate, liquidity, and prepayment scenarios. According to Binder and Lindquist [1982], the asset-liability management committee (ALCO) "is the single most important management group and function in the bank."

Three techniques of ALM are: (1) on-balance-sheet maturity or duration matching of the repricing of assets and liabilities, (2) off-balance-sheet **hedging** of on-balance-sheet risks using interest-rate contracts, and (3) securitization, which removes risk from the balance sheet. The key variables of ALM include accounting measures such as net interest income (NII) or its ratio form net interest margin ($NIM = NII$/average assets) and an economic measure: the market value of a bank's equity. Planning and controlling for how a bank's NIM and stock price react to unexpected changes in interest rates is the task of ALM. Risk profiles provide useful pictures for visualizing this sensitivity and for understanding the ALM process. By viewing a bank's ALM in terms of tactical and strategic components, ALM managers can attempt to exploit liquidity premiums contained in the short end of the yield curve without exposing the bank's equity to interest-rate risk. To achieve this objective, the bank's overall balance sheet must be asset sensitive, consisting of a liability-sensitive tactical bank more than offset by an asset-sensitive strategic bank.

Practical aspects of ALM focus on the rates, volumes, and mixes of rate-sensitive assets (RSAs) and rate-sensitive liabilities (RSLs) over the short run. Simulation models permit ALM managers to estimate the effects of different portfolio strategies and different interest-rate scenarios on accounting and economic variables. In addition, strategic choices regarding products, markets, and bank structure need to be linked to ALM.

Key Words, Concepts, and Acronyms

- Accounting model
- Asset-liability management (ALM)
- Asset-liability management committee (ALCO)
- Assets repricing before liabilities (ARBL)

- Asset securitization
- Banks (tactical and strategic for ALM)
- Bond pricing
- Derivatives
- Economic model
- Embedded options
- Financial-services firm (FSF)
- Futures options
- Gap (maturity and duration)
- Hedging
- Interest-rate contracts (IRCs)
- Interest-rate forecasting

- Interest-rate risk
- Liabilities repricing before assets (LRBA)
- Liability management (LM)
- Linear contracts (futures, forwards, swaps)
- Liquidity risk
- Market value of equity (MVE)
- Negativity convexity
- Net interest income (NII)
- Net interest margin (NIM)
- Nonlinear contracts (options, caps, floors, collars)

- Off-balance-sheet activities (OBSAs)
- Payoff (profit) profiles
- Prepayment risk
- Rate-sensitive asset (RSA)
- Rate-sensitive liability (RSL)
- Rate, volume, and mix
- Return on assets (ROA)
- Return on equity ($ROE = ROA \times EM$)
- Risk profiles
- Securitization
- Spread management
- Unexpected changes in interest rates

Review/Discussion Questions

1. Describe the three stages of ALM in the context of coordinated-balance-sheet financial management.
2. Distinguish between the following pairs of terms
   a. Core deposits versus purchased funds
   b. Repurchase agreements versus federal-funds transactions
   c. Reserve-position LM versus loan-position LM
3. What are the objectives and focal variables of ALM?
4. How do NIMs vary with bank size and how have they moved over the past decade?
5. Carefully distinguish between the accounting and economic models of interest-rate risk from an ALM perspective.
6. Draw the risk profiles for a LRBA bank and an ARBL bank with and without embedded options. Describe the nature of the embedded options and the risks they reflect.
7. What are the three general techniques that bankers have for managing interest-rate risk, and what are the two components of interest-rate risk? What is negative convexity?
8. What is the tactical bank? The strategic bank? Explain how a bank must position these banks to take advantage of the liquidity premium in the short end of the yield curve and still protect its equity value from interest-rate risk.
9. Distinguish between the following pairs of terms:
   a. Duration versus maturity
   b. Solvent versus insolvent
   c. Net interest income versus net interest margin
   d. RSA versus RSL
   e. Futures versus futures options
10. Draw the payoff profiles for the linear and nonlinear contracts available for managing interest-rate risk, and describe how they can be used to hedge bank interest-rate risk.
11. Show how to create an interest-rate collar and how a LRBA bank and an ARBL bank would use a collar to hedge its interest-rate risk. Why would anyone sell a cap? Sell a floor?
12. What is securitization? What are the major assets that are securitized? Distinguish between indirect finance (traditional intermediation) and pass-through finance. How is securitization a technique of ALM?
13. What are the building blocks of ALM? Distinguish between the art and science involved in these blocks. What role, if any, do simulation models play in ALM?
14. In the context of ALM, discuss "Those who live by the crystal ball are doomed to eat shattered glass."

15. Give an overview and historical perspective on ALM (appendix A).
16. Banks are the only FSFs that engage in ALM. True or false? See appendix B. If false, explain why and how other FSFs need and use ALM techniques. What risks do NFCs mainly need to hedge? Do NFCs ever use financial futures?
17. What implications, if any, do you draw from the information in footnote 20 about the competition for originating and servicing mortgages?

Problems

1. This problem is a detailed exercise dealing with ALM and asset securitization. At the margin, assume that a bank undertakes the following transactions:
   - It sells $100 million of one-year CDs at a cost of 7 percent.
   - It uses the CD-generated funds to buy $100 million of 30-year government securities yielding 8 percent.
   - It uses the $100 million in securities as collateral to borrow $100 million. In effect, it sells the securities but agrees to repurchase them at the end of the year (a term repo or RP). The RP cost to the bank, stated as an annual rate, is 6 percent.
   - It uses the RP-generated funds to originate $100 million in loans, which it immediately sells at face value to an investment bank that securitizes the loans (i.e., packages them with other loans as securities and sells them to investors). The lending bank will service the loans (i.e., collect interest and principal payments, which marks the beginning of the pass-through process). For originating and servicing the loans for the next year, the bank receives gross fees (fee income) amounting to 2.5 percent of the $100 million in loans originated, consisting of 2 percent for origination and 0.5 percent for servicing.
   - The funds generated by selling the loans are invested overnight in the federal-funds market at an annual rate of 6.25 percent, and rolled over for the year.

   Answer the following analytical and discussion questions on the basis of the information given above:
   a. What does the bank's marginal T-account (balance sheet) look like at the end of the first day?
   b. What are the bank's annual dollar revenues, costs, and profits, and the rate of return associated with these transactions? What, if anything, is missing from the profit calculation?
   c. Define each of the following risks and discuss the degree to which the bank faces any or all of the risks:
      i.   Credit or default risk
      ii. Interest-rate risk
      iii. Liquidity risk
      iv. Prepayment risk
   d. Suppose the bank undertook only the first two transactions described above (a and b).
      i.   What would its marginal T-account (balance sheet) look like? Assume that the market values and book values of the items are equal. What is the bank's expected net interest income for the next year, and for the 29 years after that?
      ii. Suppose that immediately after the bank sells its CDs and buys the government securities, all interest rates double. What will the market values and book values of the CDs and government securities be?
      iii. What kind of risk have you analyzed in the previous question, and what are its two components? How can this type of risk be managed on a bank's balance sheet? What kind of off-balance-sheet activities are available for managing this kind of risk?

2. Complete the following table dealing with the accounting and economic models of interest-rate risk.

   Premise: Five-year, fixed-rate asset at 10 percent funded with a one-year liability at 10 percent.

   Shock: Interest rates increase by 400 basis points immediately after the asset is funded. Assume no basis risk (i.e., both the asset and liability market rates increase by 400 basis points).

BEFORE THE SHOCK:

	Market Value	Book Value	Gross and Net Cash Flows (CF)				
			CF1	CF2	CF3	CF4	CF5
Asset		100					
Liability		90					
Capital		10					

AFTER THE SHOCK:

	Market Value	Book Value	Gross and Net Cash Flows (CF)				
			CF1	CF2	CF3	CF4	CF5
Asset		100					
Liability		90					
Capital		10					

   The accounting perspective focuses on net interest income (NII), for example, $\Delta NII = \Delta r \times GAP$, which in this example for the one-year gap is ____ = .04 × ____.

3. Given the initial conditions in Table 5-3 in the text, assume an interest-rate shock of a 200-basis-point decrease in interest rates and rework the analysis for the comparative-statics experiment. As in the analysis in the text, assume that only rate-sensitive assets and liabilities are affected by the interest-rate shock. Furthermore, assume that the same portfolio adjustments and counterbalancing market forces as described in Table 5-7 exist in this case. Use the appropriate formulas to check your answers for *NII* and *NIM*.

4. Referring to the notes a and b in Table 5-7, define or demonstrate the calculation of (a) the weighted average cost, (b) the weighted average return, and (c) shareholders' required return.

5. The Perpetual Bank has a perpetual asset (A) that returns 10 percent and a perpetual deposit (D) that costs 8 percent. Its balance sheet is

$$A = D + E = 100 = 90 + 10,$$

   where E = equity capital.

   a. If the asset return and deposit cost reflect market rates on obligations of similar risk, what is the bank's balance sheet on a market-value basis?

   b. Find the bank's ROE, ROA, and EM, assuming that the bank has no other revenues or expenses.

   c. If market rates rise to 12 percent for the asset and 10 percent for the liability, what happens to the bank's market value of equity? The return on the perpetual asset (liability) stays at 10 percent (8 percent).

   d. If market rates fall to 8 percent for the asset and 6 percent for the liability, what happens to the bank's market value of equity? The return on the perpetual asset (liability) stays at 10 percent (8 percent).

   e. Based on your answers to c and d, how would you describe this bank's GAP and interest-rate sensitivity?

6. The following equation shows the relationship between the duration of a firm's assets (*A*) and liabilities (*L*) and its net worth (*NW*):

$$\Delta NW = \{ - D_A[\Delta r/(1 + r)]A\} - \{ - D_L[\Delta r/(1 + r)]L\}$$

where *D* = the weighted average duration of the particular balance-sheet category. Note that the equation is just another way of expressing Equation 5-4 in the text. Consider three cases for a firm with the following simple balance: *A* = *L* + *NW* = 100 = 90 + 10. The interest-rate environment is such that *r* = 0.10 and Δr = 0.01.

Case 1: $D_A = D_L = 3$. Has the firm immunized its *NW* against unexpected changes in *r*?

Case 2: $D_A = 3$ and $D_L = 1$. Has the firm immunized its *NW* against unexpected changes in *r*?

Case 3: $D_A = 1$ and $D_L = 1.11$. Has the firm immunized its *NW* against unexpected changes in *r*?

What do you conclude from these three cases?

Case Study

The *Journal of Applied Corporate Finance* (Fall, 1994) contains a very interesting case study of Banc One Corporation's ALM. The case, prepared by Esty, Tufano, and Headley ([1994], pp. 33–51) and the commentaries by Albertson ([1994], pp. 52–54), James and Smith ([1994], pp. 54–59), Heisler ([1984], pp. 59–60), Kane ([1994], pp. 61–63), and Esty and Tufano ([1994], pp. 63–65) provide an excellent discussion and analysis of Banc One's extensive use of interest-rate swaps to hedge its interest-rate risk. Enjoy and learn!

APPENDIX A

ALM HISTORICAL PERSPECTIVE AND ALM FOR OTHER FINANCIAL-SERVICES FIRMS AND NONFINANCIAL CORPORATIONS

Historical Perspective and Overview of ALM

During the 1940s and 1950s, banks had plenty of low-cost funds in the form of demand deposits (checking accounts) and savings deposits. Since the basic financial-management problem was what to do with these funds, the emphasis was on asset management. During the 1960s, funds started to become less plentiful and more costly as corporate treasurers began to economize on cash balances. At the same time, the U.S. guns-and-butter economy was booming because of the Kennedy tax cut and the Johnson administration's attempt to fund both social programs and the war in Vietnam. Loan demand was strong and crowding out existed. In 1966, the prime rate hit 6 percent, a historic high for the post–World War II period. Because the cost of bank funds was correspondingly high, banks turned to managing their liabilities, and the notion of liability management (LM) was born. An important aspect of LM was developing nondeposit sources of funds that were not subject to reserve requirements, Reg Q interest-rate ceilings, or deposit-insurance premiums.

To do this banks had to segment their deposit markets. During the 1960s and early 1970s, LM was the dominant approach to bank balance-sheet management. Its focus was purchasing funds to make use of profitable loan opportunities. Because the way to make money in this game was to mark up loans over the cost of funds (cost-plus pricing), the term spread management became popular during the late 1960s and early 1970s.

Strong loan demand and the higher cost of funds meant that interest rates had only one way to go: up! With rates bumping up against Regulation Q interest-rate ceilings (these restrictions were removed in the early 1980s) and with bankers segmenting deposit markets such that the small saver was getting shafted, consumers became increasingly aware of how inflation was eroding the purchasing power of their savings dollar. By 1974, the prime rate hit double digits, the energy crisis was on, and two billion-dollar banks had failed. All of this turmoil was followed by the stagflation of the mid-to-late 1970s. It was during this period that banks began to concentrate more on both sides of their balance sheets. The technique of managing assets and liabilities together became known as asset-liability management, or ALM. One way to view ALM, which was developed fully in the 1980s, is as the coordination of asset management, liability management, and spread management.

As banking and the FSI approach the year 2000, consolidation, product expansion, globalization of money and capital markets, securitization, financial engineering (derivatives), information technology, and changes in regulation and deposit insurance promise to make ALM even more challenging for managers of FSFs.

ALM for Other Financial-Services Firms and Nonfinancial Corporations

Any firm subject to interest-rate risk, liquidity risk, or prepayment risk needs to engage in a coordinated management of its balance sheet, or ALM. Because of the financial nature of their businesses, nonbank financial-services firms (FSFs) face ALM risks similar to those encountered by banks. Thus, the techniques described in this chapter can be easily applied to other FSFs and even to nonfinancial corporations (NFCs). This section presents some examples of ALM problems faced by these firms and how they can be managed.

Life Insurance Companies

Life insurance companies (LICs) have long-term claims against them (liabilities) that can be estimated quite accurately through the use of mortality tables. The on-balance-sheet ALM of LICs can be accomplished by duration matching, that is, LICs tend to hold long-term assets such as government and corporate bonds (about 55 percent of LIC assets are in these two categories) that match their long-term liabilities. Because LICs do not have the degree of mismatch faced by depository institutions, their traditional ALM problems are more easily managed.

The changing nature of the business of life insurance, however, has complicated ALM for the modern LIC. For example, to remain competitive in the financial-services industry, LICs have developed pure investment-oriented policies to complement their traditional life-insurance products. The guaranteed investment contract, or *GIC,* captures the flavor of this new aspect of the business.[22] Although

---

[22] In the term GIC, "guaranteed" does not mean that an external guarantee exists. The riskiness of a GIC depends on the safety and performance of the LIC that issued it. See Walker [1989] for a complete description of GICs and A. M. Best for ratings of insurance companies.

various types of GICs exist, the most common type is a bullet contract, in which the LIC agrees, for a single premium, to pay a fixed amount at the maturity of the contract. Maturities typically range from one to 20 years. Pension funds or individuals purchase GICs as investments. If an LIC sells a million-dollar GIC at 10 percent for one year, the company knows it owes $1.1 million in one year. In this case, the contract is very similar to a one-year CD issued by a bank but without the risk of early withdrawal. If the LIC can find a one-year investment that returns more than 10 percent, then it can lock in a spread on the claim against it. If the LIC purchases a floating-rate investment, then it might purchase an interest-rate floor to protect against a decline in interest rates.

Pension Funds

Like LICs, pension funds have claims against them (liabilities) that mainly are long term. Thus, like LICs, they can hedge their portfolios by holding long-term assets. Since the end of World War II, pension funds have been one of the fastest-growing segments of the FSI in the United States. To meet the investment needs of pension funds, LICs developed GICs, which permit pension funds to more easily manage their ALM risks. Bullet GICs are especially nice for duration matching, because as zero-coupon securities their maturities and durations are the same.

When managers of pension funds face impending cash inflows (i.e., contributions) or cash outflows (i.e., benefit payments), they can hedge those flows using derivatives or OBSAs. For example, in the case of projected cash inflows and expectations of declining interest rates, the manager of a pension fund could buy an interest-rate floor or buy interest-rate futures. In the case of projected cash outflows (to be met, say, by liquidating bonds) and expectations of rising interest rates, the pension-fund manager could buy an interest-rate cap or sell interest-rate futures.

Investment Banks

Investment banks face underwriting risks and portfolio risks like other FSFs that invest in stocks and bonds. As dealers, investment bankers must hold inventories of securities. Depending on their view of future interest rates, dealers can protect their positions or expected positions in fixed-income securities (bonds) by either buying or selling interest-rate futures. For example, if they expect interest rates to rise (bond prices to fall), dealers can protect inventory positions by selling or "shorting" Treasury bond futures. If the hedge is perfect, then losses in the cash market are offset by gains in the futures market. If the scenario is for rates to fall, existing positions will rise in value but subsequent positions will be more costly (higher bond prices with lower yields). To hedge against falling rates, dealers can buy interest-rate futures. In this case, more costly cash purchases are offset by gains in the futures market.

Nonfinancial Corporations

Debt and equity are the cornerstones of capital markets and the means of financing for all businesses. Unlike financial-services firms (FSFs), nonfinancial corporations (NFCs) hold lots of fixed (plant and equipment) and current physical (e.g., inventories) assets. The assets and liabilities of NFCs tend to be less interest-rate sensitive than those of FSFs. They are, however, more sensitive to changes in commodity prices (inputs and outputs). Thus, commodity-based derivatives are most useful to NFCs for hedging price fluctuations. In addition, multinational NFCs (as well as multinational FSFs) can use foreign-exchange futures, forwards, options, and swaps to hedge currency risks. Financial futures also can be useful to NFCs. For example, consider a major corporation that issues commercial paper (a short-term corporate IOU). If it expects interest rates to rise before it rolls over its next issue of paper, it can hedge the risk of a higher cost of funds by selling Treasury bill or Eurodollar CD futures. At the other end of the maturity spectrum, a corporation can hedge corporate bond issues against rising interest rates by selling Treasury bond futures.

Large dealer banks such as Bankers Trust and J. P. Morgan provide risk-management services to NFCs in the form of derivatives contracts, which have interest rates, exchange rates, or commodity prices as the underlying instrument. Soured derivatives deals in 1994 and early 1995, mainly with Bankers Trust, put a damper on this market as companies such as Procter & Gamble, Gibson Greetings Inc., and Mead Corporation incurred losses associated with exotic or complex derivatives. The buyers of the contracts retaliated through the courts claiming fraud, misleading selling practices, or lack of full disclosure. As damage control, some cases were settled out of court whereas others were contested.

APPENDIX B

BOND PRICING, CONVEXITY, DURATION, AND "NEGATIVITY CONVEXITY"

In bond pricing, there is a technical term "negative convexity" (i.e., concavity). Panel A of Figure B5-1 shows the relationship between the going, or market, rate of interest and the price of a fixed-rate, noncallable, coupon bond. The graph is convex to the origin, depicting the inverse nonlinear relation between interest rates and bond prices. Because the price-yield relationship is not linear, and because the "normal" relationship is convex to the origin, the relationship is also described as bond convexity. A tangent to the price-yield relationship approximates in effect what duration does to approximate the price-yield relationship.

What happens to the price-yield relationship if the bond is callable? If interest rates decline, the borrower (the issuer of the bond) will want to call the bond and refinance. The cost of this option to the issuer is the call premium (usually one year's coupon interest), which is the reward to the lender (bondholder) for giving up the bond. In the case of a callable bond, negative convexity enters the pricing picture as shown in Panel B of Figure B5-1. As interest rates decline, the price of a callable bond drops more than the price of a noncallable bond, resulting in a transformation of the curve from convexity to negative convexity, making the relevant portion of the curve now concave to the origin. The difference in price between a callable bond and a noncallable bond grows as interest rates decline below the coupon rate.

Now consider a bond that gives the holder (lender) an option to put the bond back to the borrower. Because this is a benefit to the holder, the lender will have to pay a premium for this put option. The cost typically comes in the form of forfeiture of coupon interest, a benefit to the borrower (the issuer of the bond). A bondholder, like a bank depositor, would want to get out of a debt contract when

Panel A. Plain-vanilla coupon bond

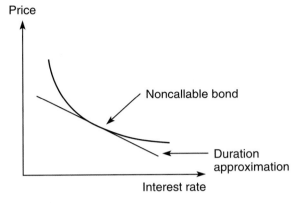

Panel B. Callable bond and "negative convexity"

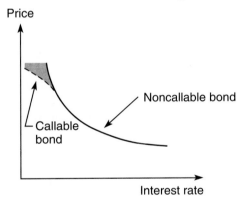

Panel C. Putable bond

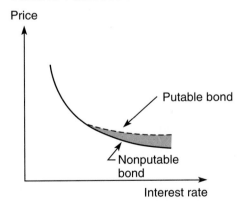

FIGURE B5-1 Price-Yield Relationships for Alternative Kinds of Bonds

interest rates are rising. The idea is to forfeit the coupon interest (penalty for early withdrawal for the bank depositor) in order to roll over into a higher-yielding asset. Thus, as interest rates increase, the price of a putable bond will drop less than the price of a similar but nonputable bond because of the existence of the valuable put option. Panel C of Figure B5-1 shows how changes in interest rates affect the value of a putable bond in comparison to that of a nonputable bond.

Selected References

Albertson, Robert. [1994]. "Derivatives in Banks: The Six Ironies." *Journal of Applied Corporate Finance* (Fall), pp. 52–54.

Binder, Barrett F., and Thomas Lindquist. [1982]. *Asset-Liability Handbook.* Rolling Meadows, IL: Bank Administration Institute.

Carter, David A., and Joseph F. Sinkey, Jr. [1996]. "An Empirical Examination of the Use of Interest-Rate Derivatives by U.S. Commercial Banks." Working Paper, University of Georgia.

Cates, David C. [1978]. "Interest Sensitivity in Banking." *The Bankers Magazine* (January), pp. 23–27.

Esty, Ben, Peter Tufano, and Jonathan Headley. [1994]. "Banc One Corporation: Asset and Liability Management." *Journal of Applied Corporate Finance* (Fall), pp. 33–51, and "Commentaries on Banc One's Hedging Strategy," pp. 52–65.

Esty, Ben, and Peter Tufano. [1994]. "Postscript" (Banc One Case). *Journal of Applied Corporate Finance* (Fall), pp. 63–65.

Grunewald, Alan E. [1990]. "Financial Models Work Well at Heart of A/L Programs." *Bank Management* (October), pp. 75–77.

Hayes, Douglas A. [1980]. *Bank Funds Management.* Ann Arbor: University of Michigan.

Heisler, Ethan. [1994]. "Comments on Banc One." *Journal of Applied Corporate Finance* (Fall), pp. 59–60.

Hilliard, Jimmy E., and Joseph F. Sinkey, Jr. [1989]. "Duration as the Effective Time to Repricing." *Journal of Financial Education* (Fall), pp. 1–7.

Houghton, Kenneth R. [1983]. "Asset & Liability Management: A Practical Approach." Atlanta: Trust Company of Georgia.

James, Christopher, and Clifford Smith. [1994]. "The Use of Index Amortizing Swaps by Banc One." *Journal of Applied Corporate Finance* (Fall), pp. 54–59.

Kane, Edward J. [1994]. "What Can Bankers Learn about Hedging Strategy from the Banc One Case?" *Journal of Applied Corporate Finance* (Fall), pp. 61–63.

———. [1979]. "The Three Faces of Commercial Bank Liability Management." In M. P. Dooley et al., eds., *The Political Economy of Policy-Making.* Beverly Hills: Sage Publications, pp. 149–174.

McNulty, James E. [1986]. "Measuring Interest-Rate Risk: What Do We Really Know?" *Journal of Retail Banking* (Spring/Summer), pp. 49–58.

Nadler, Paul S. [1990]. "Managing the Spread." *Bankers Monthly Magazine* (June 15), p. 13 and passim.

"Overview of Interest-Rate Risk: An OCC Staff Paper." [1989]. Multinational Banking Department, Office of the Comptroller of the Currency (December).

Rose, Sanford. [1982]. "Gleanings from a Major Study." *American Banker* (January 5), pp. 1 and 4.

Rose, Sanford. [1989]. "The Two Faces of A-L Management." *American Banker* (June 5), pp. 1 and 9.

Sinkey, Joseph F., Jr., and David A. Carter. [1996]. "The Derivatives Activities of U.S. Commercial Banks: Why Big Banks Do and Small Banks Don't." Working Paper, University of Georgia.

Smith, Clifford W., Jr. [1993]. "Risk Management in Banking." In Robert J. Schwartz and Clifford W. Smith, Jr., eds., *Advanced Strategies in Financial Risk Management.* Englewood Cliffs, NJ: New York Institute of Finance.

Stigum, Marcia L., and Rene O. Branch. [1983]. *Managing Bank Assets and Liabilities.* Homewood, IL: Dow Jones-Irwin.

Walker, Kenneth L. [1989]. *Guaranteed Investment Contracts: Risk Analysis and Portfolio Strategies.* Homewood Hills, IL: Dow Jones-Irwin.

PART

III

THE PORTFOLIO RISKS OF BANKING AND THEIR MANAGEMENT: THEORY AND PRACTICE

The process of measuring, managing, and accepting risk captures the heart of bank financial management; it is the business of banking. The portfolio risks of banking lead to uncertainty about future net returns (e.g., expected return on assets, $E[ROA]$) and the variability of those returns (e.g., σ_{ROA}). In addition, these risks affect a bank's capital adequacy (CAP). A bank's overall risk exposure can be summarized by the risk index (RI) as follows:

$$RI = [E(ROA) + CAP]/\sigma_{ROA}$$

Banks that do a good job of managing risk will have high RI scores, whereas banks that mismanage risk will have low scores.

It is common to classify risks according to the source of the underlying uncertainty. Banks face three major sources of uncertainty:

1. Credit risk
2. Interest-rate risk (including prepayment risk)
3. Liquidity risk

In addition, the increased globalization of financial and commodity markets and the increased volatility of the underlying prices in these markets have made all banks, not just multinational organizations, more vulnerable to uncertainty about foreign-exchange rates. Thus, an additional source of uncertainty for banks is

4. Foreign-exchange risk

This part of the book focuses on the portfolio risks of banking and how to manage them. Because the major uncertainty lenders accept is whether or not borrowers will repay loans, we begin with an analysis of credit or default risk (chapter 6). The nature of deposit contracts, most of which are payable on demand, requires banks to be liquid. In addition, banks need liquidity to meet the loan demands of new and existing customers, especially preferred clients who use a multitude of bank products and services. Chapter 7 focuses on liquidity risk and its management. Chapter 8 analyzes the risks associated with a bank's securities portfolio and its investment-banking function, if any. Finally, because banks have developed risk-management products (called "derivatives") for hedging, speculating, or dealing, chapter 9 focuses on the risks associated with these activities, which are mainly the province of large banks.

6

CREDIT RISK AND THE LENDING FUNCTION: THEORY AND PRACTICE

Contents

LEARNING OBJECTIVES

■ To understand credit risk as the major uncertainty of commercial banking

■ To understand the methodology and estimation of a bank's allowance for loan losses

■ To understand the agency and incentive problems of the lender-borrower relationship

■ To understand managing credit risk as managing a guarantee business

■ To understand how to measure and manage credit risk

■ To understand the five Cs of creditworthiness

■ To understand how bank loans are priced and the measurement of risk-adjusted returns

■ To understand the importance of a bank's credit culture and loan policies

CHAPTER THEME

Because the business of banking is measuring, managing, and accepting risk and because the major risk banks face is credit risk, it follows that the major risk banks must measure, manage, and accept is **credit** or **default risk.** It is the uncertainty associated with borrowers' loan repayments. In general, when borrowers' asset values exceed their indebtedness, they repay their loans; when borrowers' asset values are less than loan values, they do not repay—they exercise their option to default. Thus, it is imperative that lenders be able to value borrowers' assets and to estimate a borrower's probability of default. In practice, most lenders, except for the largest banks, do not estimate this probability very scientifically. Instead, they rely on proxies that focus on a borrower's creditworthiness as captured, for example, by the five Cs of creditworthiness:

Character, Capacity, Capital, Collateral, and Conditions (economic).

The fundamental dilemma in managing credit risk is overcoming the agency or incentive problems between lenders, as outsiders, and borrowers, as insiders. Incentive problems arise from moral hazard, adverse selection, and asymmetric information. The traditional bank lending function has four components:

Originating, Funding, Servicing, and Monitoring.

The innovation of securitization has changed traditional lending to either a three- or two-step process:

Originate, sell, and service, or originate and sell without servicing.

Although securitization permits banks to remove loans and the accompanying risks from their balance sheets, it comes at the expense of traditional intermediation profits. The majority of a bank's assets (55–60 percent), however, are still held in the form of loans, originated either by the bank itself or by other lenders. Banks establish reserves or an **allowance for loan and lease losses** (ALLL) based on expected loan losses. Methods and estimates for determining a bank's ALLL are an important component of the management of bank credit risk.

KEY CONCEPTS, IDEAS, AND TERMS

- Agency (incentive) problems
- Allowance for loan and lease losses (ALLL)
- Bank-customer relationship
- Contract frictions
  - Adverse selection
  - Asymmetric information
  - Moral hazard
- Credit (default) risk
- Five Cs of creditworthiness
  - Character

- Capacity (cash flow)
- Capital
- Collateral
- Conditions (economic)
- Forbearance
- Lending function
  - Originating
  - Funding
  - Servicing
  - Monitoring

- Loan-loss reserve (LLR)
- Loss-control mechanisms
  - Risk-based pricing
  - Asset restrictions
  - Monitoring
- Managing a guarantee business
- Portfolio risk
- Risk-adjusted return on capital (RAROC)
- Securitization

INTRODUCTION[1]

This chapter focuses on **credit risk** and the **lending function** from both theoretical and practical perspectives, and attempts to blend the two together. The traditional bank lending function has four components:

- Originating
- Funding
- Servicing

---

[1] This chapter draws, in part, on my paper "Credit Risk in Commercial Banks: A Survey of Theory, Practice, and Empirical Evidence," Bank of Israel *Banking Review* (December 1989), pp. 12–35.

- Monitoring

Securitized lending eliminates the need for funding and monitoring and makes servicing optional.[2] For loans that are kept on the balance sheet, funding must be coordinated with loan pricing to avoid interest-rate risk (ALM, discussed in the previous chapter). Servicing involves simply collecting interest and principal payments and retaining them or passing them through in the case of securitized loans. Originating and monitoring, the focus of this chapter, may involve **agency problems.** An important part of monitoring is estimating a bank's expected loan losses and establishing a reasonable and adequate allowance for loan and lease losses (ALLL). The originating and monitoring functions require practical knowledge about borrowers as captured by the **five Cs of creditworthiness:**[3]

- Character (honesty, ethical reputation)
- Capacity (cash flow)
- Capital (real net worth)
- Collateral (security)
- Conditions (vulnerability to economic fluctuations)

This chapter presents the five Cs in terms of a model of default risk.

The gathering, processing, and analyzing of quality information provides the vehicle for developing a profile of a borrower's creditworthiness, whereas financial contracting attempts to reduce the incentive problems between lenders, as principals, and borrowers, as agents. **Bank-customer relationships** and external factors such as economic and competitive business conditions play important roles in the lending function, especially for business borrowers. Unlike direct finance, bank credit (indirect finance) has a relationship aspect that permits lender **forbearance** (i.e., the opportunity to work out problem situations) if the borrower experiences repayment difficulties. Relationships and forbearance are implicit aspects of bank loan agreements.

Because portfolio theory preaches its gospel to lenders as well as investors, lenders must be aware of **portfolio risk** and how to price it, and of the tradeoffs between diversification and specialization. The **loss-control mechanisms** available to banks to manage credit risk include **risk-based pricing, assets restrictions,** and **monitoring.** A method of risk-based pricing known as **risk-adjusted return on capital** (RAROC) is introduced and related to the notion of economic value added (EVA).

PROPER AND PRUDENT MANAGEMENT CREATES VALUE FOR BANKS

Credit or **default risk** is uncertainty about loan repayment. When borrowers do not repay their loans, banks encounter financial difficulties. For example, in 1987, when banks, mainly the largest ones, were experiencing problems associated with

---

[2] Assuming no recourse against the lender for loans that it securitizes, the lender does not need to monitor default risk after loans are sold. However, if a lender securitizes (sells) only bad loans, it will, in an efficient market, lose reputational capital. The market for securitized assets developed with residential mortgages, which have strong collateral values and require little monitoring.

[3] As stressed in this chapter, the most common number of Cs seems to be five, although some approaches have as many as 10 or as few as one. For example, Bathory [1987] has only one C in his seven canons of lending: Character, Ability, Margin, Purpose, Amount, Repayment, and Insurance.

loans to less-developed countries (LDCs), loan-loss provisions, an expense item, were 1.29 percent of industry assets, and industry return on assets (*ROA*) was 0.09 percent. In 1990 and 1991, when bad commercial real estate loans plagued the industry, loan-loss provisions were 0.97 percent and 1.02 percent of assets, respectively, with corresponding *ROA*s of 0.47 percent (1990) and 0.53 percent (1991). In contrast, in 1994 and 1995, when loss provisions were only 0.28 percent and 0.30 percent of average assets, *ROA* was 1.15 percent (1994) and 1.18 percent (1995). Although credit risk is not the only risk banks face, it is the risk that has caused the most financial devastation. The lending crises in the energy and farm belts in the 1980s were other examples of major credit-risk problems U.S. banks have faced.

With the majority of a bank's assets in the form of loans,[4] the **lending function** plays a critical role in bank risk management. The objective of the lending function is simple: Create value for the bank. The primary danger in granting credit is the chance that the borrower will not repay the loan on a timely basis, thereby destroying value. Proper and prudent management of credit risk is the way to create value in the lending function. Excessive credit risk manifests itself in the form of excessive nonperforming loans, loan-loss provisions, and loan losses, which destroy bank value.

The majority of U.S. bank failures, including those in the 1980s, can be traced to problems associated with credit risk, and frequently with credit risk linked to fraud and insider abuse (chapter 17, Ethics in Banking). On the other side of the coin, successful banks have been able to avoid serious problems with credit risk, reflecting greater ability to control the lending function in terms of quality growth. Accepting credit risk is a normal part of the business of banking. Proper and prudent actions permit lenders to behave as responsible fiduciaries.

Credit Risk and a Bank's Risk Index

To see the big-picture effect of credit risk on overall bank risk, let's view it in terms of the risk index (*RI*), which you will recall as

$$RI = [E(ROA) + CAP]/\sigma_{ROA} \tag{6-1}$$

where $E(ROA)$ = expected return on assets, CAP = the ratio of equity capital to assets, and σ_{ROA} = the standard deviation of *ROA*. Since credit risk is a primary driver of each of the components of *RI*, we can view it conceptually as

$$RI = f(\text{credit risk, interest-rate risk, liquidity risk, \dots}) \tag{6-2}$$

One proxy for credit risk and a measure of loan quality is a bank's provision for loan loss (PLL). As shown above, a strong correlation exists between PLL and ROA. In addition, PLL drives the variability of ROA and strongly affects CAP. Other proxies for bank credit risk include net loan losses or charge-offs, nonperforming assets, and bank-examiner adversely classified assets, which are described, in order of increasing risk, as "other assets especially mentioned" (OAEM), "substandard," "doubtful," and "loss."

---

[4] The average insured commercial bank holds roughly six dollars in loans (and leases) for every 10 dollars of total funds raised. At year-end 1995, all insured commercial banks had raised $4.149 trillion in total funds, with $2.422 trillion (58%) on loan, mainly to consumers and businesses.

MEASURING CREDIT RISK AND LOAN QUALITY THROUGH LOAN REVIEW

Profitability measures such as ROE and ROA are symptoms of managerial performance and the underlying risks of banking. In most cases a bank's poor performance can be traced to excessive and mismanaged credit risk. Potential shortcomings include, among other things, liberal lending policies, weak underwriting standards, and poorly managed growth (all evident in the failure of Bank of New England Corporation in 1991),[5] which produce loan losses and nonperforming assets. It is prudent and proper banking practice to establish a reserve for expected loan losses by conducting a loan review to establish the bank's **loan-loss reserve** (LLR) or **allowance for loan and lease losses** (ALLL). The LLR is a contra-asset account, which when deducted from gross loans gives net loans.[6] Net loan losses, which equal gross charge-offs minus recoveries, deplete the reserve account, whereas the provision for loan loss, an expense item, augments it.

Prescribing a Methodology and Determining the Adequacy of a Bank's ALLL

Bankers, directors, auditors, regulators, and other interested parties need to know how a bank calculates its ALLL (methodology) and how to determine the reasonable and adequacy of the ALLL, given the bank's risk exposure. Two general approaches exist for estimating a bank's ALLL: The first focuses on a detailed analysis of all individual loans or of a representative sample of the loan portfolio. This detailed loan review is a micro method that focuses on loss exposure at the level of individual loans. It is how banks should conduct internal checks for loan quality, and it is the heart of the on-site bank examination conducted by bank supervisors.[7] The second approach uses tools such as loan losses, nonperforming loans, and examiner-classified loans, which are reliable indicators of risk and loss exposure at the macro level. When the internal micro approach is unacceptable and unreliable, analysts turn to the external macro approach.

The Micro Approach to Credit Review: Analysis of Individual Loans

Because the micro approach relies on data prepared by bank employees, outside analysts must be confident that the information is reliable. To conserve time, external auditors and bank examiners tend to focus on large concentrations of credit and use statistical sampling techniques to assure a representative sample of other loans. In contrast, insiders should have personnel and systems available for generating such information quickly and, if supporting documentation is reliable, accurately.

It is helpful to think of the analysis of individual loans as an application of the five Cs of creditworthiness to existing loans. Assuming willingness to pay (good character), the other four Cs focus on financial characteristics of borrowers and

---

[5] The General Accounting Office [1991] reports on the failure of Bank of New England Corporation (BNEC) and the OCC's supervision of BNEC banks.

[6] Unearned income is also subtracted from gross loans in deriving net loans.

[7] Although bank regulators do not always have the resources to devote to such a detailed effort, lenders are never excused from such fiduciary responsibilities. Clarke [1986] presents a complete guide to loan documentation.

economic conditions that could adversely affect their ability to repay their loans. Lenders get information on these factors by collecting audited financial statements on a regular basis (e.g., monthly); monitoring the market value of collateral (if any); calling on management; visiting or contacting suppliers, distributors, and customers; and studying industry and economic reports, among other things. Loans for which borrowers have adequate cash flow to service their debt and other strong financials, such as a high degree of liquidity and excess debt capacity, are easy to classify because they have a very high probability of being repaid (e.g., AAA rated). Such loans require little or no ALLL because their estimated losses are zero or very close to it.

Collecting, processing, and generating relevant data and information is required for any loan. The artsy part of loan review revolves around input assumptions, interpreting results, and forecasting future economic conditions. To illustrate, consider the hypothetical loan shown in Table 6-1. It has a book value of $500,000 (line 1). The critical ingredient in the analysis is the estimated loss (line 2). Although experience and judgment are the critical skills needed in making this estimate, expert systems or statistical classification models that attempt to mirror such traits or the characteristics of other bad loans can provide valuable tools for screening purposes. Given the estimated loss, line 3 shows the estimated gross market value as book value (line 1) minus the estimated loss before collection and overhead expenses (line 2). If a loan is adversely classified such that its collection of interest and principal is in doubt, then it will have to be worked to ensure payment. This workout can be done internally, or externally by selling the loan to a collection agency. Either way the workout is costly. Internally, estimated overhead and collection expenses must be estimated (shown on line 4 as 10 percent of the estimated gross recovery on line 3). If the loan is worked externally, then a fee is paid to the vendor. The net fair market value on the loan (line 5) equals the estimated gross market value (line 3) minus the estimated overhead and collection expenses.

The next step is to consider the bank's opportunity cost. If the loan is nonperforming, then the bank is not generating any cash flow from the invested funds. The relevant opportunity cost is the discount rate used to determine the present value of the net market value over the relevant time horizon. In this example, because

TABLE 6-1 Loan Review Based on Estimated Loss, Collection and Overhead Expenses, and Opportunity Costs

(1)	Book value	$500,000
(2)	Estimated loss before collection and overhead	130,000
(3) = (1) − (2)	Estimated gross (fair) market value	370,000
(4)	Estimated overhead and collection expenses (10%)	37,000
(5) = (3) − (4)	Net market value	333,000
(6)	Opportunity cost (8.5%)	26,087
(7) = (5) − (6)	Present value of net market value	306,912
(8) = (1) − (7)	Estimated loss	$193,088
(9) = (8)/(1)	Percentage of loss to book value	38.62%
Asset file No.		ID No.

Note: The asset file number provides the location of documentation to support the loan review. Line 4 equals 0.10 of line 3, line 7 equals line 5 divided by 1.085, and line 6 = line 7 minus line 5.

the discount rate is 8.5 percent and a one-year horizon is assumed, the present value of the net recovery is (line 7)[8]

$$\$306,912 = \$333,000/1.085$$

The estimated loss for the loan is its book value (line 1) minus the estimated loss (line 7), or \$193,088 (line 8). Comparing the estimated loss to the book value of the loan generates line 9, the percentage of loss to book value of 38.6 percent. Alternatively, the loan can be viewed as having a market-to-book ratio of 61–62 percent $(1 - 0.386)$, a relatively deep discount.

The last line in Table 6-1 provides the asset file number for the loan. The file contains documentation for the loan. It includes such items as the loan application, the borrower's relationship with the bank, previous loan reviews, financial statements and other information, file memos by the lending officer, auditor comments, bank examiner ratings (if any), and any other relevant documentation. Because all of this information may not be available on the bank's computer or loan officers' PCs, some paper files will exist. Sorting through these paper documents and determining their accuracy and reliability are what makes analysis of a bank's loan quality on a micro level a slow and deliberate process.

The Macro Approach to Credit Review: Indicators of Risk and Loss Exposure

A faster but less accurate way of estimating the ALLL is to use basic macrolevel tools that are reliable indicators of risk and loss exposure. This approach employs the bank's own risk profiles and trends in conjunction with peer or industry data. The level of the ALLL can be set at the peer-group average, or above or below the average, depending on the strengths and weaknesses of the bank's credit and administrative policies and practices, as well as the trends in key variables. Common risk indicators that can be used as macrolevel tools include net loan losses, nonperforming credits, and loss percentages applied to examiner-classified loan categories.

Net Loan Losses[9]   A quarterly average of net loan losses can be a reliable indicator because it is based on actual experience, aberrations are smoothed, and weights can be used to count most recent experiences more heavily. The major shortcoming with this approach is that it is a lagging and not a leading or forecasted indicator. By using pro forma data, however, this shortcoming can be reduced.

The use of net loan losses relative to total loans as a risk indicator for setting a bank's ALLL is illustrated by the following example.

Quarter	*Net Loss/Total Loans*	*Weight*	*Ratio* × *Weight*
First	0.80%	0.10	0.08%
Second	1.05	0.20	0.21
Third	0.90	0.30	0.27
Fourth	2.30	0.40	0.92
	1.26% (average)	1.00	1.48% (weighted average)

---

[8] If the time horizon on the workout is two years, then the present value of the net recovery would be $\$282,869 = \$333,000/(1.085)^2$. For an n-period workout, the discount factor would be $1/(1 + r)^n$, where r is the opportunity cost or discount rate.

[9] Loans that are charged off reduce loan-loss reserves, whereas recoveries provide an add-back to the reserve account and generate the difference between gross and net charge-offs (i.e., net charge-offs = gross charge-offs − recoveries). The terms "net loan losses" and "net charge-offs" are interchangeable.

Suppose that this bank has a $10-billion loan portfolio and a current ALLL of $100 million. Applying the simple average, the ALLL should be $126 million, implying the need for a $26 million loan-loss provision (PLL).[10] Based on the weighted average, the required PLL would be $48 million. If the bank has serious credit and administrative weaknesses, some multiple of the weighted average would be reasonable and objective. Assuming a factor of 2.0, the required PLL would be $96 million, and the bank's ALLL would rise to $196 million with a ratio of ALLL to loans of 1.96 percent ($= 0.196/10$).

Let's use the required PLL of $96 million to restate the bank's ROA and ROE. Assume that the bank had an *ROA* of 0.75 percent, a loan-to-asset ratio of 0.60, and an equity multiplier (EM) of 12, hence an *ROE* of 9 percent ($= 0.75\% \times 12$). The bank's equity capital is $1.39 billion ($= 16.67/12$). Before reading the next paragraph, try these calculations as an exercise.

Because we know the bank has loans of $10 billion, its total assets are $16.67 billion ($= 10/0.6$), and hence net income equals $125 million ($= 0.0075 \times \$16.67$ billion). Since the bank has to increase its PLL by $96 million (an expense item), its net income will drop to $29 million, and *ROA* will fall to 0.17 percent ($= 0.029/16.67$), and its equity capital will drop to $1.29 billion ($= 1.39 - 0.096$). The bank's *ROE* will drop to 2.20 percent ($= 0.17\% \times 12.9$). Note that EM has increased because of the decline in equity capital, assuming total assets do not change. By underestimating its true PLL and required ALLL, the bank's managers have materially misstated the bank's earnings, profitability, and capital adequacy.

ALLL Relative to Nonperforming Loans   Another method of testing the reasonableness of a bank's ALLL is to compare it to the bank's nonperforming loans. This indicator is a form of coverage ratio. Suppose that the required coverage is 0.70 and that it is estimated that the bank has nonperforming loans of $400 million. The required ALLL is $280 million. Continuing with the example used for the net-loss method, the bank needs a PLL of $180 million, which would wipe out its reported earnings of $129 million. The ratio of ALLL to total loans would rise to 2.8 percent ($= 0.28/10$).

Percentage of Classified/Criticized Loans   Banks are examined by their regulators and assigned CAMEL[11] ratings based on their performance. The heart of the bank-examination process is attempting to determine the quality of a bank's loan portfolio (Sinkey, [1978, 1979, 1989]). In this regard, both bankers and bank examiners rate loans as loss, doubtful, substandard, and other loans (assets) especially mentioned (OLEM or OAEM). Loans or assets considered loss, doubtful, or substandard are sometimes described as "classified," whereas "special mention" loans (assets) are labeled "criticized." All other loans (assets) are considered to be "noncriticized" or "pass" loans. Banks with high volumes of loans (assets) in the loss, doubtful, and substandard categories relative to their capital and loan-loss reserves usually are classified as problem banks (composite CAMEL ratings of 3, 4, or 5).

---

[10] Table 2-6 (chapter 2) shows PLLs by bank size for the years 1985 to 1995.

[11] **CAMEL,** which stands for **C**apital adequacy, **A**sset quality, **M**anagement, **E**arnings, and **L**iquidity, is formally known as the Uniform Financial Institutions Rating System. Banks are rated 1 (best) to 5 (worst) and assigned a composite score of 1 (best) to 5 (worst). The OCC uses the term "Report of Supervisory Activity" (ROSA) to describe the findings of its on-site activities at a national bank.

TABLE 6-2 Bank Loan Ratings, Descriptions, and Relationships Based on Loan Review, Ratings, and Bond Ratings

Loan Review Number	Representative Bank Description	Examiner Class	Potential Bond Rating
0	Secured	Not criticized/pass	AAA
1	Best	Not criticized/pass	AA
2	Strong	Not criticized/pass	A
3	Good	Not criticized/pass	BBB
4	Satisfactory	Not criticized/pass	BB
5	Fair	Not criticized/pass	B
6	Special mention	Special mention	CCC
7	Substandard	Substandard	CC
8	Doubtful	Doubtful	C
9	Loss	Loss	Default

Although CAMEL 3 banks can be turned around, 4- and 5-rated banks tend be so weak that they are eventually closed by regulators.[12] Table 6-2 compares the descriptions and relationships based on bank loan review, examiner-estimated loan quality, and bond ratings.

The method of calculating the ALLL based on criticized/classified loans is illustrated by the following data:

Category	Amount	Weight	Required ALLL
Not criticized/pass	$10.0 bil.	0.01	$100.0 million
Special mention	0.75 bil.	0.05	37.5 million
Substandard	1.25 bil.	0.20	250.0 million
Doubtful	0.25 bil.	0.50	62.5 million
Loss	0.12 bil.	1.0	120.0 million
Required ALLL			$570.0 million

If the bank has an existing ALLL of $175 million, then it needs a PLL of $395 million (570 − 175). With total loans of $12.4 billion, the bank would have a ratio of ALLL to total loans of 4.6 percent (0.57/12.4).

The three alternative macro methods can be used as a check on each other in determining a bank's ALLL. To the extent that extenuating circumstances exist, either internal shortcomings within the bank or expected adverse economic conditions, an additional ALLL requirement can be added to the projected ALLL. The important point is that bank managers and directors need to know the various methods for determining a bank's ALLL and whether or not it is reasonable and accurate for the bank's risk exposure.

---

[12] A substantial lag frequently exists between a bank's economic insolvency and its closure by regulators. For example, Bank of New England was closed on January 6, 1991, but its economic failure occurred at least a year before that.

LENDER-BORROWER AGENCY PROBLEMS AND INCENTIVE PROBLEMS IN FINANCIAL CONTRACTING

Lenders are directly concerned about borrowers repaying their loans on a timely basis so that the value of the bank can be maximized, all other things being equal. To protect their own interests and the wealth of bank shareholders, lenders must investigate and monitor the activities of would-be and existing borrowers. In addition, lenders have a fiduciary responsibility to their depositors and their federal deposit insurers to conduct their businesses in a safe-and-sound manner. In this context, banks serve as "delegated monitors" for their creditors (e.g., depositors).[13] Because most suppliers of funds to banks do not have the time or the skill to evaluate the creditworthiness of existing and would-be borrowers, they in effect delegate banks to do this for them with the understanding that bank regulators are in turn watching the banks. Thus, we have the notions of banks as delegated monitors, and bank regulators (e.g., OCC), deposit insurers (e.g., FDIC), and securities regulators (SEC) as watchdogs over banks to protect taxpayers and to provide equity investors with timely and accurate information through disclosure.

Agency theory deals with the contractual relationships between principals and agents. This chapter's analysis of credit risk and the lending function highlights the incentive problems faced by lenders, as principals, and borrowers, as agents. Incentive problems occur between principals and agents because the contracting parties cannot easily observe or control each other and because contracts cannot be enforced without incurring costs. **Contractual frictions** can arise because of **moral hazard, adverse selection,** or **asymmetric information.** Think of moral hazard as a deception by the borrower or a change in behavior by the borrower. Adverse selection refers to the lender making a bad decision (adverse selection) regarding prospective borrowers, in particular, selecting too many high-risk borrowers. Asymmetric information is the disparity in knowledge between outsiders (lenders) and insiders (borrowers). Financial innovation in the form of new contract designs and enforcement mechanisms attempt to reduce the frictions associated with the sources of agency problems.

Because lenders, as outsiders, lack inside information and cannot continuously monitor the actions of borrowers, they are at a disadvantage vis-à-vis insiders. Borrowers' dishonesty, lack of effort, or failure to supply timely and accurate information create advantages for them, putting lenders at a disadvantage. In addition, since lenders seek information from third parties such as suppliers, credit-rating agencies, and other lenders, the information problems may be compounded by lack of accuracy resulting from reporting or judgment errors made by third parties.[14]

It is useful to think of problems with originating (the application process) and monitoring loans in terms of hidden information and hidden action.[15] As originators, bankers frequently have to make lending decisions, including loan commitments, with less than full information. Specifically, borrowers know more about their financial condition than lenders. This problem of asymmetric information is es-

---

[13] The theory of banks as delegated monitors comes from Diamond [1984].

[14] Harding, McDonald, and Strischek [1987] discuss the importance of proper exchange of credit information among banks.

[15] We can think of hidden action arising from moral hazard or adverse selection, and hidden information originating from informational asymmetries. Hidden action is more of a monitoring problem, whereas hidden information can be a problem in either originating or monitoring loans.

pecially critical during the application process, when the decision to lend or not to lend is made. Because borrowers like prompt answers on loan requests and lenders want to provide quick decisions as a sign of good service, pressures for a timely decision can exacerbate the problem. If bankers make lending decisions too quickly, they risk making too many bad decisions, the adverse-selection problem. Think of it this way. Lenders need to sort potential borrowers into an array based on their **probability of default,** or the opposite, the probability of repaying the loan. The sorting process is costly. To the extent that the process can be automated without loss of quality decision making, cost savings (economies of scale) can be obtained.[16]

The loans that banks hold in their portfolios must be monitored to ensure that they are repaid.[17] Borrowers that change their behavior (moral hazard) and do not supply timely and accurate information (asymmetric information) present the most difficult monitoring challenges.

THE EXPECTED PROBABILITY OF DEFAULT

If the expected probability of default is *d,* then the expected probability of receiving payment is $(1 - d)$.[18] Abstracting from a bank's operating expenses, such as salaries for loan officers, processing costs, and other noninterest expenses, a **profitable loan contract rate,** *r**, must compensate the lender for the time value of money as reflected by the **risk-free rate** of interest, *r,* and the risk of default. For a one-period model, the symbols are as follows:

$$r^* = (1 + r)/(1 - d) - 1 \qquad\qquad \textbf{(6-3)}$$

Because equation (6-3) captures the fundamental notion of a risk-return trade-off, the profitable loan contract rate can also be viewed as a risky loan rate.[19] Specifically, the bank's profitable loan contract rate increases with its perception of the borrower's probability of default (risk). As a risky loan rate, *r** must compensate for default risk if the loan is to be profitable.

Case 1: Risk-Free Lending. In the case of no chance of default ($d = 0$), $r^* = r$. Note that $r = r^* - d - dr^*$ (footnote 19). What kind of loan business would a bank have in this instance? What would the expected profits be? And who would want to own such a bank? The lending business would be restricted to loans to the U.S. Treasury, AAA corporations, and individuals with substantial net worth—the last two groups being almost risk-free borrowers. Unless the bank could attract funds at less than the risk-free rate, the profits would be very small, but very safe, and investors presumably would not be rushing to own shares in this bank.

---

[16] The costs of ensuring that lenders have complete, accurate, and timely information on borrowers are called agency costs, either explicit or implicit. Explicit agency costs are in the form of monitoring, bonding, and other arrangements designed to reduce principal-agent conflicts. Implicit agency costs can be viewed as opportunity losses due to contract imperfections. In a less-than-perfect world, lenders attempt to minimize agency costs by equating the marginal cost of any remaining contract imperfections with the marginal cost of further efforts to control them.

[17] When banks sell loans, potential buyers are concerned about the private information bankers have about the quality of the loans being sold. Third-party guarantees, a standard part of the process of securitization, reduce investors' concerns about this lack of transparency. Nevertheless, this form of information asymmetry contributes to the lack of secondary markets for many bank loans, and it helps explain why banks must be liquid.

[18] This material and the subsequent discussion of the portfolio risk premium draw on Flannery [1985].

[19] Equation (6-1) can be rearranged in risk-neutral form as $(1 + r^*)(1 - d) = (1 + r)$. In this case, expected returns per dollar are equal. Rearranging in terms of the risk-free rate, we get $r = r^* - d - dr^*$.

On balance, it is unrealistic to expect a bank to hold a portfolio consisting entirely of risk-free assets.[20] As part of its overall business strategy of developing customer relationships, managing liquidity, and providing risk-management services, however, banks do hold some risk-free and near-risk-free assets.

Case 2: No Chance of Repayment. Consider the trivial, and seemingly absurd, case of a loan with no chance of repayment. When a borrower is certain to default ($d = 1$), the loan contract rate is undefined (i.e., $\infty - 1$). Clearly, the lender cannot be compensated for the risk. No rational lender, of course, would make such a loan. Nevertheless, with the prospect of booking fee income to boost current earnings and with the ability to purchase funds protected by government guarantees, certain lenders might be willing to "bet the bank" by funding projects with potentially high default rates, that is, "d" close to but not equal to 1. Heads they win, tails the deposit insurer (taxpayers) picks up the pieces.

Case 3: Risky Lending. Under normal circumstances, a borrower's probability of default is neither 0 nor 1 but something in between. For a particular borrower, the difference between the profitable loan contract rate (r^*) and the risk-free rate (r) is the default-risk premium required by the lender. Rearranging equation (6-3),

$$\text{Default-risk premium} = r^* - r \qquad \textbf{(6-4)}$$

where the default-risk premium equals the probability of default (d) plus the interaction between d and r^* or $(1 + r^*)d$. In words, the default-risk premium, which compensates the lender for the expected loss on a loan, is the difference between the return on risky lending and the risk-free rate. In theory, the typical credit analysis performed by a bank focuses on determining a borrower's probability of loan repayment ($1 - d$).

Consider the following illustrations of default-risk premiums for an AAA credit, a prime-rate loan, and a junk bond (CCC). Assuming a risk-free rate of 5 percent, we get the following default-risk structure of interest rates:

Credit/Type of Loan	Interest Rate	Default-Risk Premium (r = 5%)	Pr(Default)
AAA	7%	2%	1.87%
Prime-rate loan	8.25%	3.25%	3.00%
Junk bond	12%	5%	6.25%

As credit risk, captured by the credit rating, increases, the default-risk premium and the probability of default (d) rise. The implied probability of default (d) comes from rearranging equation (6-3) as follows:[21]

$$d = 1 - (1 + r)/(1 + r^*)$$

---

[20] This is not to say that a subsidiary of a bank might not be designated, as Irving Fisher suggested years ago, as a safe haven for insured deposits, with assets invested only in short-term Treasury bills or close equivalents. In response to the recent crisis in deposit insurance, the Fisher plan has been resurrected as a way to guarantee the safety of the payments system and avoid future taxpayer bailouts. See Miller [1995].

[21] In this case, since we are applying a single-period model to a multiperiod problem, the probability of default is only an approximation, or an average. A more exact estimate would require the cumulative default probability (equal to the *product* of marginal probabilities of default for each period), which in this example would be the probability that the borrower would default over the 10-year period. Altman [1989] presents estimates of default probabilities and collection percentages for various risk classes of bonds.

For example, for the junk bond,

$$d = 1 - (1.05/1.12) = 1 - 0.9375 = 0.0625 = 6.25\%$$

Also note that if an AAA company wants to borrow from a bank, it does so at a discount from the prime rate.

The problem for lenders is that they cannot directly observe a borrower's probability of default or, the other side of the coin, the probability of loan repayment $(1 - d)$. Nevertheless, banks have developed substantial amounts of reputational and human capital in establishing proxies for borrowers' creditworthiness (i.e., probability of default).

Risky Loans and Loan Guarantees

Let's rearrange equation (6-4) as

$$r^* = r + drp \qquad \textbf{(6-4a)}$$

where *drp* stands for default-risk premium. What can we do to a risky loan to make it free from default? We can add a **loan guarantee.** What must the value of the guarantee be to make the risky loan free of default risk? The value of the guarantee must, by definition, equal the value of *drp*. Let's look at this fundamental relationship more closely, as Merton and Bodie [1992] do, and think about its meaning.

$$\text{Risky loan} + \text{Loan guarantee} = \text{Risk-free loan} \qquad \textbf{(6-5)}$$

or equivalently

$$\text{Risky loan} = \text{Risk-free loan} - \text{Loan guarantee} \qquad \textbf{(6-5a)}$$

Although banks make some risk-free loans (by buying Treasury bills, notes, or bonds), they are mainly in the business of making risky loans. Focusing on (6-5a), consider the following insight: When a bank makes a risky loan, it is making a risk-free loan and selling a loan guarantee. What will be the selling price of the loan guarantee? It must exactly compensate for the default risk such that the risky loan becomes riskless, equation (6-5). Alternatively, take the loan guarantee away from a risk-free loan and you have a risky loan, equation (6-5a).

Because we can observe the prices of risky loans (e.g., bonds) and we know how to price risk-free debt, we can estimate the value of the implicit loan guarantees embedded in debt contracts. Consider a risky bond (or bank loan) with a face value of $1000 that promises semiannual payments of $75 for 10 years. If sold at par, the bond has an annual yield to maturity (*YTM*) of 15 percent.[22] If the risk-free rate on 10-year debt is 8 percent, what is the value of the loan guarantee that would make the risky bond a risk-free instrument? To find the answer takes two steps: First, find the present value (*PV*) of the risky bond's cash flow discounted at the risk-free rate, that is,

$$
\begin{aligned}
\text{Price} = \ &\text{PV(\$75 every six months for 10 years discounted at 4\%)} \\
&+ \text{PV(\$1,000 in 20 periods discounted at 4\%)} \\
&= \$1475.66
\end{aligned}
$$

---

[22] The doubling convention is used to get the annual *YTM*, that is, $7.5\% \times 2 = 15\%$. Based on interest earned on the coupon, the effective *YTM* is $(1.075)^2 - 1 = 15.56\%$.

This price represents the value of the risky bond's cash flows if the cash flows were guaranteed or free of default risk. The second step is to rearrange either (6-5) or (6-5a) as follows:

$$\text{Risk-free loan} - \text{Risky loan} = \text{Loan guarantee} \qquad \textbf{(6-5b)}$$

Entering the relevant values, we solve for the implied value of the loan guarantee as follows:

$$\$1,475.66 - \$1,000 = \$475.66$$

The implied price of the loan guarantee as a percentage of the no-guarantee (risky) price is 47.6% ($= [475.66/1,000] \times 100$).

The point of this exercise is that by estimating the price of the bond as if its cash flows were risk-free and subtracting the actual market price of the bond, we derived the implied market value of the loan guarantee. The ratio of the implied value of the loan guarantee to the price of the bond without the guarantee provides a relative measure of risk. Consider the following estimates of this ratio as calculated by Merton [1990], based on closing bond prices as of May 11, 1990:[23]

		Bond Prices		Loan Guarantee Value	
Company	*Years to Maturity*	*with g*	*without g*	*Implied Price*	*Ratio*
Pan Am	14	147.23	58.63	88.60	151.1%
MGM/UA	6	118.24	63.38	54.86	86.6
Revlon	20	117.25	80.75	36.50	45.2
Union Carbide	9	102.89	92.25	10.64	11.5

Because the companies are listed according to their risk ratio (most risky to least risky in terms of the value of the implied guarantee needed to make the debt risk free), a check on the relevancy of the ratio is how risky we think the cash flows of the underlying companies are. If we analyze the basic businesses and risk exposures of the companies, the results are intuitively appealing because we could probably agree on the following ranking (in order of decreasing risk as of 1990): air transport, entertainment, cosmetics, and carbide products (a carbide is a binary compound of carbon with a more electropositive element, especially calcium carbide). By the way, the value of Pan Am's implied loan guarantee was estimated before its bankruptcy filing. The large magnitude of the implied price and its relative value suggests that the market was pricing Pan Am's debt correctly.

Expected Cash Flow from a Loan, the Probability of Default, and the Loan-Recovery Factor

Suppose we have a one-period loan that promises a payment of L (principal) at interest rate i, that is, the promised payment is $L(1 + i)$. What is the expected cash flow, $E(CF)$, from this loan?

$$E(CF) = L(1 + i)(1 - d) + d(vL) \qquad \textbf{(6-6)}$$

---

[23] Merton's calculations assume a flat U.S. Treasury yield curve at 9 percent with no adjustment for call provisions. Also, bond prices were not adjusted for cumulative interest.

where d = probability of default and v = recovery rate on the defaulted loan. Rearranging (6-6) to emphasize that the difference between the promised and expected cash flows varies directly with the probability of default (d), we have

$$L(1 + i) - E(CF) = L[(1 + i) - v]d \qquad \textbf{(6-6a)}$$

If default does occur ($d = 1$), then the lender still has a chance to recoup some of its investment based on the loan-recovery factor, v, where $1 \geq v \geq 0$.

The relationships in equation (6-6) or (6-6a) can be clarified by three simple cases:

Case 1: Risk-free lending ($d = 0$). $E(CF) = L(1 + i)$ and the bank receives its promised payments of principal (L) plus interest (iL). This case reflects the banker's adage: The only good loan is one that is repaid.

Case 2: No chance of repayment or recovery ($d = 1, v = 0$). $E(CF) = 0$ and the bank receives nothing. This case is the banker's nightmare.

Case 3: Default but with some chance of recovery ($d = 1, v > 0$). $E(CF) = vL$ and the bank receives some fraction, v, of its original investment (L). This case reflects situations in which bankers must engage in workouts to recover some fraction of their loans. Banks can pursue workouts either within the bank or outside it by selling bad loans to collection agencies. In instances where banks have had large volumes of bad loans, "bad banks" have been established as separate subsidiaries to work problem credits.

The Borrower's Option to Default

In the last chapter, we considered the payoff profiles associated with interest-rate futures, forwards, options, and swaps. The values of these contracts depend on the value of the underlying asset. One of the main businesses of banking is lending. What does the payoff profile for a loan look like? Is there an underlying asset on which the value of a loan depends?

Consider a business with the following simple balance sheet:

$$A = L + NW = 100 = 90 + 10$$

where A = assets, L = liabilities (bank loans, say), and NW = net worth (equity). On a market-value basis, suppose the balance sheet is as follows:

$$NW = 40 - 90 = -50$$

Will the firm repay the loan? No! The borrower will exercise the option to default, the bank will lose 50, and the owners are out 10.

Alternatively, suppose the firm has positive net worth such that

$$NW = 150 - 90 = 60$$

and that the owner/borrower has decided to sell or liquidate the business. The bank receives its payoff of 90 (assume it was a "bullet," or zero-coupon loan) and the owner receives a "liquidating dividend" of 60 for a net gain of 50 ($= 60 - 10$).

Let's consider a third case. Suppose the business has

$$NW = 5 = 95 - 90$$

and the owner wants to get out of the business. Because the firm has assets valued at 95, the owner will repay the bank (90) and recoup 5 of the 10 invested. It should be clear that the borrower will default when $NW < 0$. When $NW > 0$, the bank gets paid and the owner recoups at least some of the investment. When $NW = 0$, the bank still gets repaid, but the owner is indifferent about the default option.[24]

Panel A of Figure 6-1 shows the payoff profile to a bank from a loan. As long as an insolvent firm ($NW < 0$) still has positive asset values, the bank will be repaid a portion of the loan. In fact, as a firm becomes less insolvent, the bank shares proportionally in the gains in asset values. However, once the business becomes solvent ($NW > 0$), the additional gains in asset values go solely to the owners as the residual claimants of the firm. Panel B of Figure 6-1 shows the payoff profile to owners as stockholders of the business.

What are the lessons for bankers from this simple presentation of the option model of default risk?[25] Because bankers are never repaid more than the contractual

FIGURE 6-1   Payoff Profiles for Bankers versus Stockholders

Panel A. The payoff profile to a bank from a loan

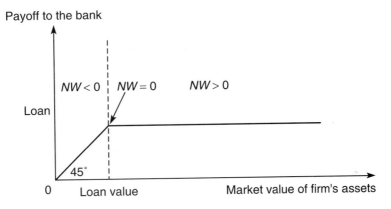

Panel B. The payoff profile to stockholders in a firm with debt

Note: I = equity capital invested by stockholders

---

[24] To preserve reputational capital, a rational borrower, despite being indifferent in a technical sense, would not want a credit-history blemish and would repay the loan rather than default in a legal sense.

[25] Black and Scholes [1973], Merton [1974], and others were pioneers in the development of option-pricing models.

amounts of their loans and because they are always repaid when real $NW > 0$, they have a vested interest in trying to ensure that borrowers remain solvent on a market-value basis. Excessive risk taking that might result in a big payoff to owners will not benefit bankers as creditors. Thus, bankers need to make careful decisions about whom they lend to and they must monitor existing borrowers.

MANAGING CREDIT RISK AS A GUARANTEE BUSINESS

Three techniques of risk management are hedging, diversification, and insurance (Mason [1995]). As equation (6-5) shows, an implicit guarantee (or insurance component) exists in every risky loan. Thus, one way to understand the business of lending and managing credit risk is to understand the techniques for **managing a guarantee business.** Merton and Bodie [1992] describe three techniques for doing this:[26]

- Risk-based pricing
- Asset restrictions
- Monitoring

Risk-Based Pricing and Risk-Adjusted Return on Capital (RAROC)

It has been established that risk-based pricing requires lenders to charge a rate that compensates for the riskiness of the loan. The idea is straightforward: AAA borrowers pay less for credit than BBB borrowers, who in turn pay less than CCC borrowers. Implementation is not so easy, however, because the pricing procedure needs to be forward looking and not based solely on historical loan-loss experience. Therefore, and perhaps not so surprisingly, most banks, except for the largest ones, do not attempt to fine-tune their risk-based pricing, except for broad categories of risk. In practice, **loan pricing** tends to follow the prime-rate convention in which borrowers are priced on a prime-rate-plus (or minus) basis. Because the prime rate is not the lowest rate a bank charges, the most creditworthy customers can negotiate discounts from the prime rate. The discount prime rate is what banks use to attempt to compete with open-market instruments such as commercial paper and corporate bonds.

One way to be more precise about pricing credit risk is to use **risk-adjusted return on capital** (RAROC), a technique pioneered by Bankers Trust of New York. With proprietary variations, large banks in the United States and other developed countries use this approach. The idea behind RAROC is to compare a loan's expected income, including fees, to its risk amount.[27] Risk-adjusted return on capital can be expressed as

$$RAROC = E(Y)/L^* \qquad \textbf{(6-7)}$$

[26] Chapter 1 introduced this approach applied to deposit insurance; chapter 16 expands on the method and presents other techniques for managing deposit insurance, e.g., as a performance or surety bond.

[27] Although risk-based capital requirements (chapter 13) are not a measure of return, the principle of adjusting assets for their default risk is similar. Thus, a risk-based-capital ratio compares a bank's capital to its (credit) risk-weighted assets.

where $E(Y)$ = one-period expected income on a loan and L^* = the amount of the loan at risk. For example, suppose $E(Y) = 10$ and $L^* = 100$. The RAROC on this loan is 10 percent. The decision rule for a RAROC model is to undertake all loans for which

$$RAROC > RAROC^* \tag{6-8}$$

where $RAROC^*$ is the bank's hurdle rate or benchmark weighted average cost of funds, including equity capital. Because banking is a relationship business, if a would-be borrower's $RAROC$ does not exceed the bank's hurdle rate, the loan officer can attempt to work the terms of the loan until it does (i.e., by raising the loan rate, increasing fees, decreasing the loan amount, shortening the duration, etc.).

Using the duration model from the previous chapter, consider the following illustration of RAROC. In this context, duration, D, will be an elasticity measure relating percentage change in loan value ($\Delta L/L$) to percentage change in credit risk or loan quality as captured by the relevant interest rate, r, that is, $[\Delta r/(1 + r)]$. Focusing on the change in loan value, we can write this measure of duration based on credit risk as follows:

$$\Delta L = -D[\Delta r/(1 + r)]L \tag{6-9}$$

Suppose that we have a three-year, zero-coupon loan (its duration is three years) for $1,000,000. If $r = 0.10$ and $\Delta r = 0.01$ (due to a decrease in credit quality), then

$$\Delta L = -3(0.01/1.1)\$1,000,000 = -\$27,273$$

This figure, dropping the negative sign, becomes our estimate of L^* for determining the loan's RAROC. If the spread on the loan is 0.3 percent and the loan generates fee income of 0.06 percent, then the expected annual income on the loan is[28]

Spread:	0.003 × $1,000,000	= $3,000
Fee:	(0.0006 × $1,000,000)/3	= 200
		$3,200

Given these parameters, the loan's estimated RAROC is

$$RAROC = 3,200/27,273 = 0.1173 = 11.7\%$$

If the bank's hurdle rate is 12 percent, this loan would be rejected. Note, however, that if the entire fee was booked upfront, which banks at one time could do, the loan would be accepted as $3,600/27,273 = 13.2$ percent > 12 percent. Because the breakeven point for the loan is expected income of $3,273 ($= 0.12 \times 27,273$), the loan officer can work with the customer to increase the bank's expected income rather than simply decline the loan request.

An alternative way of estimating RAROC is to express it in terms of a risk-adjusted interest rate such as

$$RAROC = \text{loan rate of return}/(\text{unexpected loss rate} \\ \times \text{portion of loan lost on default})$$

Note that the second term in the denominator is $(1 - v)$, where v is the loan-recovery factor from equation (6-6). Using data from the previous example and

---

[28] The fee income is spread evenly over the life of the loan.

assuming that $v = 0.3$, and therefore $1 - v = 0.7$, we can back out the unexpected loss rate (ULR):

$$RAROC = 0.1173 = 0.0032/(0.7ULR) \rightarrow ULR = 0.03897 = 3.9\%$$

Reversing the process, for a loan with an expected spread per dollar of 0.0032, an unexpected loss rate of 0.039, and a proportion of loan lost on default of 0.7, its RAROC would be $0.0032/(0.03897 \times 0.7) = 0.1173 = 11.73$ percent.

To summarize, RAROC models fit nicely with the notion of economic value added (EVA) established in chapter 4. The EVA method says to undertake any project whose return exceeds its cost until $EVA = 0$; the RAROC models says to make any loan whose risk-adjusted return exceeds the bank's weighted average cost of funds. If loans that fail to pass the RAROC hurdle need to be made in order to maintain customer relationships, then they must be repriced to add more interest income or fees or both, or the bank's risk exposure may be reduced by curtailing the size of the loan or shortening its duration or both.

Asset Restrictions

Because assets equal liabilities plus new worth ($A = L + NW$), asset restrictions also can be described in terms of debt (leverage) restrictions or net worth restrictions. Bank lenders and other creditors have a claim on the borrower's assets. As long as the market value of assets exceeds the value of liabilities ($A > L$), creditors are protected because proceeds from the sale of assets cover all the claims (Figure 6-1). Alternatively, as long as positive net worth exists, business firms (or households) are not going to turn over to creditors assets that exceed the value of claims against them. Thus, one way for lenders to protect themselves is to try to ensure that the value of assets always exceeds the value of claims. Restricting the amount of debt a borrower takes on and restricting the variability of the value of assets are basic ways of meeting this objective. **Restrictive covenants** in loan agreements and the strength of **bank-customer relationships** are practical ways that lenders impose asset restrictions or attempt to establish borrower incentives for compliance.

The role of assets restrictions also can be viewed in terms of the option-pricing model of default risk as described earlier and as shown in Figure 6-1.[29] This insightful analogy views a debt contract as the borrower writing a put option on the firm's assets. The owner/borrower has the right (but not the obligation)[30] to sell the firm's assets to the lender for the face value of the debt. The put option is in the money whenever the firm's net worth falls below zero (i.e., $A < L$). When the put is out of the money (i.e., $A > L$ or $NW > 0$), the option is not exercised. Given the volatility of the borrowing firm's cash flows, its net worth or capitalization serves as an inverse proxy for the value of the put option to the owners of the firm. The borrower's degree of leverage,[31] of course, would be a direct proxy for the value of the put.

In this option view of the lending process and management of credit risk, banks want borrowers to have high levels of net worth. In this regard, think of the

---

[29] Merton [1977] drew a similar analogy between deposit insurance and writing a put option on the assets of an insured bank. Kane [1995] claims deposit insurance is better interpreted as a trilateral performance bond that enhances the credit of an insured bank. Chapter 16 discusses deposit insurance and related issues.

[30] The borrower, of course, has the legal and moral obligation to fulfill the terms of the loan agreement. Nevertheless, the right to put the firm's assets to the lender is an option embedded in the loan contract.

[31] The British refer to leverage as "gearing." Thus, a firm that is "geared up" is highly levered.

importance of the capital and collateral components of the five Cs of creditworthiness. The practical ways that lenders attempt to ensure high levels of capitalization are designing loan contracts with provisions that restrict firms from issuing new debt or prohibit them from paying or raising dividends. On balance, imposing capital standards on borrowers is just another loss-control instrument available to lenders to help them control incentive conflicts.[32]

Monitoring

If lenders have a contractual right (covenant) to monitor asset values continuously and to seize assets, then loan losses can be minimized either (1) by auditing asset values and seizing assets before shortfalls exist ($A < L$) or (2) by requiring the posted value of collateral assets to equal or exceed the promised payments ($A > L$). For private (nontraded) loans, for which banks have considerable expertise in origination, monitoring with continuous surveillance is costly. Moreover, even if monitoring were continuous, the problem of transparency would still exist, that is, observing the true or market value of the borrower's assets. Because seizing assets is likely to injure customer relationships and may create problems of lender liability,[33] it is not always an easy or popular choice for lenders. Furthermore, unless the market values of posted collateral are readily observed, the transparency issue surfaces again when banks attempt to value collateral.

According to Merton and Bodie [1992], perhaps the best example of effective monitoring on a continuous basis is the case of broker margin loans. The key ingredients that make this system work are

- Possession of the collateral
- Daily (or more frequent) marking the collateral to market
- The broker's right to instantaneously liquidate the collateral to meet margin calls

Comparing this system to the one used to monitor bank loans reveals the difficulties banks have in monitoring their loan clients. Specifically, banks normally do not have possession of the collateral ("possession is 9/10 of the law"), the collateral is not normally marked to market (lack of transparency), and the collateral normally cannot be liquidated quickly (bad timing). Two kinds of bank loans that come closest to meeting the monitoring standard set by broker margin loans are home-equity loans and loans collateralized by actively traded stocks and bonds.

Lenders, as outsiders, cannot easily monitor or control borrowers, who have inside information and might change their behavior. Designing and enforcing contracts, which are costly endeavors, play a critical role in protecting lenders and ultimately the owners of the bank. Innovations in monitoring technology and financial contracting can reduce transactions and communications costs, but they cannot eliminate the incentive problems (e.g., moral hazard) associated with financial contracts.[34]

---

[32] Banks have to meet capital standards themselves, which are designed to control incentive conflicts associated with the federal safety net of deposit insurance and the discount window. See chapters 15 and 16. Do M&M propositions apply to banks? Merton Miller [1995] says "Yes and no."

[33] "Lender liability" refers to legal action taken against a lender by a borrower who claims to have been injured by the lender's actions. Such claims first appeared in the 1970s. The early 1990s witnessed another claim of client injury against banks in the form of "derivatives liability." See chapter 9.

[34] Froot [1995] discusses incentive problems in financial contracting.

MONITORING TECHNOLOGY AND THE
BORROWER-INFORMATION CONTINUUM

Extending the theory of financial intermediation, Berger and Udell [1993] introduce the idea of a **borrower-information continuum** and a monitoring-technology hypothesis. Three forms of debt exist in their continuum:

- Private or inside debt
- Intermediated debt
- Public or direct-investor-held debt

Figure 6-2 depicts their borrower-information continuum. As advances in monitoring technology occur, information problems are reduced and the boundaries between the forms of debt shift such that banks may lose customers (about whom information is relatively more accurate and more readily available) to instruments of the capital markets (e.g., commercial paper and corporate bonds) but pick up customers that previously were "unbankable." At the high-information end of the spectrum, cross-monitoring exists as borrowers hold direct-investor-held debt and intermediated debt or guarantees. Because financial markets are incomplete, high-information borrowers still need bank services such as payments services (domestic and foreign), syndicated loans, and financial guarantees (e.g., standby or back-up lines of credit for commercial paper).

Berger and Udell call their theory the "monitoring-technology hypothesis" and use it to explain the existence of **securitization.** The idea behind the monitoring-technology theory is that some types of lending are more easily monitored and therefore have lower monitoring-related contract costs; such loans are more likely to be securitized (i.e., packaged and sold as securities). In contrast, loans with high monitoring-related contract costs are less likely to be securitized. Nevertheless, third-party guarantees, operating as performance or surety bonds, permit such loans to be securitized. Improvements in monitoring technology reduce monitoring-related contract costs and thereby stimulate the process, development, and spread

FIGURE 6-2 **The Borrower-Information Continuum**

| Inside debt | Intermediated debt | Public debt (direct-investor-held) |

|← Cross-monitoring range →|

Low information	→	High information
High monitoring costs	→	Low monitoring costs
No cross-monitoring	→	Cross-monitoring
(Conditions found in *developing* countries)		(Conditions found in *developed* countries)

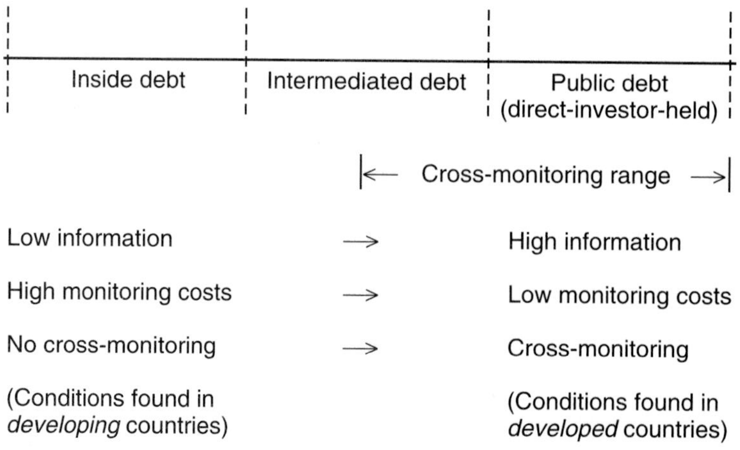

Source: Adapted from Berger and Udell [1993], Figure 4–1, p. 234.

of securitization. This innovation is not without its costs, however, because funding margins, the bread and butter of the business, are lost.

Digression: Monitoring-Related Contract Costs[35]

Booth [1992] tests and accepts two hypotheses dealing with monitoring-related contract costs of large commercial loans: (1) a cross-monitoring hypothesis that suggests less monitoring is required if borrowers bond themselves to generate information that is observable (transparency) and valuable to multiple claimholders, and (2) a financial contract-cost hypothesis that specifies that bank monitoring costs capture the ease or difficulty with which covenants can be written to control borrowers' behavior toward their assets. Booth finds evidence that loans to corporations with actively traded equity and rated debt securities are associated with smaller loan spreads. He also finds that private firms, including private firms going public, pay, on average, 33 basis points more in loan spread (relative to prime, LIBOR, or cost of funds) than public firms.

Banks that fail make too many loans to high-risk borrowers (i.e., ones characterized by hidden actions and hidden information and therefore high monitoring costs). Although the U.S. legal system provides a mechanism for banks to write loan contracts that provide some degree of control over borrowers' behavior toward assets, managers of failed banks frequently do not use this power effectively (e.g., they make loans to insiders such as friends, relatives, and business associates) or engage in criminal misconduct or both.[36] In contrast, loans made to enterprises with investor-held debt benefit from cross-monitoring.

On balance, low-risk borrowers are able to bond themselves to generate information that is observable and valuable to multiple claimholders. Because of structural shifts in the borrower-information continuum over time (e.g., as evidenced by increases in commercial paper and corporate bonds at the expense of bank loans), when banks make important loans that compete with direct-investor-held debt, they signal their ability to compete with the instruments of direct finance.[37]

THE BANK LENDING FUNCTION AND A GENERAL MODEL OF DEFAULT RISK

Recall that the four components of the bank lending function are

- Origination (underwriting)
- Funding
- Servicing
- Monitoring

The credit check a bank performs focuses on determining the underlying relationship between a borrower's characteristics (both financial and nonfinancial) and the

---

[35] This section can be skipped without loss of continuity.

[36] The Committee on Government Operations [1988] found that misconduct was a serious problem resulting in loss of public confidence in thrifts and banks. FDIC and OCC studies suggest that about one out of every three failed banks in the mid- to late-1980s had serious problems with fraud, abuse, or misconduct.

[37] Megginson, Poulsen, and Sinkey [1995] analyze the announcement effects of syndicated loans made by 15 U.S. money-center banks over the years 1966 to 1989.

expected probability of default, *d,* or expected cash flows for loans. This process is an ongoing one that begins when a loan application is made and continues until the loan is repaid—unpaid loans are incomplete transactions for lenders. We can conceptualize the prospects of loan repayment in the following general model of default risk:[38]

$$d = d[I(C), CF, NW, G] \qquad \textbf{(6-10)}$$

where

- *I* stands for **information quality** (i.e., timeliness and accuracy of the information flows)
- *C* for character ("you can't do good business with bad people")
- *I(C)* indicates that information quality, in turn, is a function of the borrower's character
- *CF* for the level and stability of cash flow
- *NW* for real net worth
- *G* for guarantees

As each of these factors deteriorates, a borrower's expected probability of default increases, and as they improve, the probability decreases.

Information Quality and Character

If we ignore the effects of *CF, NW,* and *G,* the expected probability of default reduces to $d = d[I(C)]$, which says that the expected probability of default is a function of information quality, which in turn is a function of the borrower's character—one of the five Cs of creditworthiness. As the accuracy and timeliness of information flows deteriorate, the expected probability of default increases. Since good citizens stand ready to supply reliable and timely information as required by the terms of their explicit lending contracts and by the implicit terms of their relationship with the lender, the accuracy and timeliness of such flows should vary directly with the borrower's strength of character and with the strength of the bank-customer relationship.[39]

The first term in equation (6-10) captures in a meaningful way the relationship between information quality and character. Although slow payers may be honest borrowers who are experiencing cash-flow problems, "slow and inaccurate reporters" of information exhibit character flaws, which should be priced in the form of a higher default-risk premium. Viewed in this context, character becomes potentially more quantifiable. Nevertheless, the banking-and-finance literature is behind other social sciences in the development, testing, and evaluating of social behavior such as borrower character.[40] The application of such methods to borrower (social) behavior could help quantify the character aspect of credit analysis. Bankers appear to operate under the misconception that evaluating character cannot be a scientific process, or they might fear that such methods might be judged discriminatory, or both. In a similar manner, lenders might look at the applicability of expert systems or "artificial intelligence" (chapters 10 and 11) as vehicles for im-

---

[38] The function presented here is similar to Kane's [1986] "confidence" function for a bank. It also is a variation of the probability of default (*d*) expressed as a function of three of the five Cs of creditworthiness.

[39] The notion of the customer relationship can be traced to Hodgeman [1963] and Kane and Malkiel [1965]. Wilke [1991] describes how relationships can deteriorate during a recession.

[40] The evaluation of character by lenders could be linked to human-resource selection. For a description of honesty testing, see chapter 13 of Gatewood and Feild [1990].

proving the credit-decision process. For example, such methods could be used to observe loan officers and their detailed thought processes when they evaluate creditworthiness, with the objective of developing a computer-based program to simulate the credit-decision process.

The Level and Stability of Cash Flow

When commercial banks are described as cash-flow lenders, it simply means they traditionally have relied on cash flow as the primary source of loan repayment, especially for business loans. Other sources of loan repayment include the sale of assets (as in asset-based lending) or alternative sources of financing, either debt or equity or both. These other sources of loan repayment reflect a borrower's ability to generate liquidity and thereby augment cash flow to service outstanding debt. Borrowers with stable cash flows are preferred to those with less stable flows, provided the cash flow can service the debt. On balance, both the level and variability of cash flow are important, and both of these elements are assumed to be captured by the cash-flow variable (CF).[41]

The Signaling Content of Equity[42]

The real economic net worth (or net asset value) of a business is the difference between the market value of its assets and the market value of its liabilities. The relative amount of real (as opposed to book) equity value that a borrower has at risk serves as a signal to the lender. As this equity increases, say as a proportion of total debt or total assets, the probability of default decreases, because the borrower has more to lose by defaulting, all other things being equal. Moreover, as the borrower's equity-to-asset ratio increases, lenders should be willing to trade off other elements of the borrower's profile (e.g., asset-based lending depends more on the ability of borrowers to sell assets than it does on pure cash-flow considerations). Borrowers with stronger net-worth positions (i.e., higher relative net asset values) are generally deemed more creditworthy, all other things being equal.

Like asset-based lending, which focuses on the availability and valuation of such assets as accounts receivable, inventory, and fixed assets, the determination of real economic net worth depends mainly on the market value of the collateral. In addition, however, net asset value takes into account the effects of unbooked assets (such as customer relationships) and unbooked liabilities or contingent claims. On this broader basis, net asset value focuses on the business as a going concern as opposed to its liquidation value.

External Guarantees

In theory, the role of a 100 percent external guarantee (provided the guarantee is credible) reduces to a trivial case of the lender making a risk-free loan (equation 6-5). Since the agent lender faces no default risk, most of the benefits of the

---

[41] In November 1987, following a seven-year study, review, and comment period, the Financial Accounting Standards Board (FASB) released its "statement of cash flows" known formally as Statement of Financial Accounting Standards (SFAS) No. 95. This statement, which went into effect July 15, 1988, is discussed in more detail in chapter 10. Emmanuel [1988] discusses the importance of cash-flow data in credit analysis. Also see O'Leary [1988] and Ginzl [1988].

[42] In the academic literature, the signaling content of equity is discussed by Leland and Pyle [1977], Campbell and Karcaw [1980], and Chan [1983], among others. Also see the discussion earlier in this chapter on "Asset Restrictions" and debt as a put option held by the borrower.

guarantee should be passed on to the borrower, the intended recipient of the guarantee/ subsidy. The generation of origination fees and the potential to establish new customer relationships (with cross-selling opportunities) provide lenders with incentives to enter such contracts. If the lender fails to do the credit analysis (say, for reasons of fraud or insider abuse), then the third-party guarantor has an agency problem.[43]

When guarantees are less than 100 percent (e.g., an SBA 95% guarantee), then both the agent lender and the guarantor share the default risk corresponding to the relative size of the guarantee. In this case, the bank should charge a default-risk premium commensurate with its risk exposure as determined by the borrower's information quality and character (I[C]), cash flow (CF), real net worth (NW), and the size and strength of the external guarantee (G). On balance, as G increases, all other things being equal, lenders should be willing to accept lower quality with respect to a borrower's information flows and financial strength.

Adverse External Conditions, Customer Relationships, and Forbearance

Because each of the arguments of our model of default risk is a function of external conditions or the state of the economy (ECY), we can expand equation (6-10) to

$$d = d\{I[C(ECY)], CF(ECY), NW(ECY), G(ECY)\} \qquad \textbf{(6-11)}$$

Let's define the state of the economy broadly to include technology, competition, and other external factors, in addition to the standard business-cycle components of economic growth, the price level, the employment rate, and the balance of payments. Consider the information component $I[C(ECY)]$ of equation (6-10). This equation says that the default-risk premium depends on information quality, which in turn depends on the character of the borrower, which in turn depends on the state of the economy. The inner function, $C(ECY)$, kicks in only for borrowers with character flaws. Specifically, lenders may find that the willingness of borrowers to repay declines when external conditions affect them adversely. In contrast, good citizens stand ready to pay their debts independent of the state of the economy (i.e., they are willing to pay although they may not be *able* to pay). Moreover, they are willing to inform lenders about adverse economic effects on their ability to pay.

Strong customer relationships are built on trust and the free flow of information between borrowers and lenders. In such relationships, when economic conditions adversely affect borrowers (bad things do happen to good people), lenders are inclined to exercise forbearance (e.g., renewals or workout situations). If lenders exercise too much forbearance, then bank shareholders have an agency problem as their wealth is transferred to borrowers (and perhaps to agent managers if adverse incentives exist).

Although the strength of external guarantees may also depend directly on the state of the economy, we are primarily concerned with the effects of the economy on a borrower's cash flow and real net worth, both of which will vary directly with the state of the economy for procyclical borrowers(i.e., borrowers whose probability of repayment moves directly with the business cycle because their cash flows

---

[43] Third-party guarantors should be viewed as providing trilateral performance bonds. Kane [1995] applies this framework to the analysis of capitalization requirements in insured financial institutions.

move directly with the business cycle). In contrast, borrowers whose cash flow and financial strength vary countercyclically (i.e., the opposite of the business cycle) present lenders with diversification opportunities. The fortunes of most borrowers, of course, tend to move directly with the business cycle (procyclically).

PORTFOLIO CONSIDERATIONS: THE PORTFOLIO RISK PREMIUM AND DIVERSIFICATION BENEFITS

The risk associated with economic conditions leads to the notion of covariation of returns within a loan portfolio. The diversification principle suggests that lenders cannot assess the riskiness of individual loans in isolation; rather, this riskiness must be evaluated with respect to other loans in the portfolio. If the additional or marginal loan added to the portfolio is highly correlated with existing loans (e.g., adding another energy or farm loan to an already concentrated portfolio of energy or farm loans), then the lender is taking on more portfolio risk than if a less-correlated loan (e.g., a securitized loan from a different industry in another part of the country) were added to the portfolio.

To highlight the concept of portfolio risk in bank lending, consider the following example derived from Flannery ([1985], pp. 460–461). A lender has a choice of making two risky loans, A and B. The expected cash flows from the loans are state-dependent, as shown in the following matrix:

Loan	*State* 1	2
A	$4	$2
B	$0	$3

If each of the (economic) states is equally likely to occur, and if the lender holds a portfolio consisting of 60 percent of loan A and 40 percent of loan B, then the expected cash inflow is $2.40 regardless of which state prevails. That is, in state 1, the outcome is

$$0.6\,(\$4) + 0.4\,(\$0) = \$2.40$$

In state 2 it is

$$0.6\,(\$2) + 0.4\,(\$3) = \$2.40$$

The undiversified portfolios have expected outcomes of $3 for loan A and $1.50 for loan B. However, when the loans are combined in the 60/40 portfolio, they generate the same return (i.e., the portfolio return is state independent), resulting in a riskless portfolio. The magic ingredient in this portfolio is the negative correlation between the outcomes for A and B. That is, in state 1, the return on loan A is high, whereas the return on loan B is low; in state 2, the opposite occurs. Negative correlations are desirable because they provide a cushion when earnings (values) turn down. For example, consider a portfolio with two assets: (1) a loan to a manufacturer of swimwear and sunscreen products and (2) a loan to a manufacturer of rainwear and umbrellas. If cool and rainy weather dominate, then the rainwear manufacturer will do well, but the swimwear manufacturer will not. If hot and sunny weather dominates, then the opposite will occur. When one return (loan repayment) is up, the other is down. The important point is that loan pricing and risk management require knowledge of a loan's riskiness in conjunction with the lender's holdings of other loans.

The Portfolio Risk Premium

If loans are to be priced correctly, lenders must be compensated for the portfolio risks they assume. If we let p represent the mark up or down for portfolio risk, the profitable loan contract rate that includes compensation for portfolio risk is

$$r^* = (1 + r)/(1 - d - p) - 1 \qquad \textbf{(6-12)}$$

where r^* is the profitable loan contract rate, r is the risk-free rate, and d is the probability of default. If a loan provides extensive diversification benefits, then conceivably the portfolio risk premium, p, could be less than zero. The important point is that the more highly correlated a new loan is with existing loans, the higher the portfolio risk premium should be to compensate for the lack of diversification. The correlation of each loan's default risk with the business cycle determines its diversification potential. In practice, lenders watch portfolio risk by monitoring industry and geographic concentrations.

To illustrate equation (6-12), if $r = .10$, $d = .01$, and $p = .005$, then $r^* = .1162$, or 11.62 percent. The default-risk premium is 1.62 percent, which is not equal to $d + p$ because of the interaction terms r^*d and r^*p. In words, the default-risk premium consists of compensation for default risk, portfolio risk, and the interaction of these risks with the loan contract rate, that is,

$$r^* - r = d + p + (d + p)r^* \qquad \textbf{(6-12a)}$$

In practice, we can observe only the left-hand side of (6-12a); the components of the right-hand side cannot be observed. On balance, lenders must be compensated for

- The time value of money (r)
- Default risk (d)
- Portfolio risk (p)
- Interaction effects ($[d + p]r^*$)

Another way to see this is to rearrange (6-12a) as

$$r = r^* - d - p - dr^* - pr^* \qquad \textbf{(6-12b)}$$

If the only compensation required is for the time value of money, then we have a risk-free loan, $r = r^*$.

Lack of Diversification, Regulatory Constraints, and Loan Losses

The combination of lack of diversification in banks' loan portfolios and heavy loan losses dot the banking landscape over the quarter century from 1970 to 1994. Examples include the energy-lending Penn Square Bank of Oklahoma City; Continental Illinois National Bank of Chicago, which blindly bought energy loans originated by Penn Square; the LDC-lending, money-center banks; farm-lending banks; and banks with heavy concentrations in commercial real estate, such as

Bank of New England. These lenders failed to diversify their loan portfolios, failed to avoid concentrations of credit, or failed to engage in prudent and proper lending practices.

The problem was that the failed banks described above were not lending to independent borrowers and therefore were not really diversifying. Volatile loan losses mean volatile profits, which mean volatile and reduced equity values. The risk index ($RI = [E(ROA) + CAP]/\sigma_{ROA}$) conveniently captures this aspect of credit risk. The variability of expected loan losses can be reduced by spreading a dollar volume of loans over a large number of borrowers whose return patterns are less than perfectly correlated. The regulatory environment, however, has played an important role in explaining the lack of bank loan diversification. For example, geographic restrictions on branching existed until 1995, examiner criticism of out-of-territory lending has been a long-standing regulatory admonition, and the Community Reinvestment Act (CRA) requires banks to recycle funds into their local markets or service areas. Nevertheless, these constraints do not excuse bankers from practicing sound financial management by diversifying and avoiding concentrations of credit within these boundaries.

Catch-22: Diversification versus Specialized Lending

The gospel of portfolio theory is that portfolios should be diversified. The catch-22 is that institutional lenders develop expertise by specializing in specific industries or sectors of the economy. For example, loan officers may be trained to specialize in such areas as gas and oil, minerals, chemicals, transportation, or services. Banks that develop a reputation and lending skills in a particular area have a vested interest in perpetuating that expertise. The lesson from portfolio theory, however, is that this specialization, with its potential for loan concentration, can mean greater credit risk in the loan portfolio. To compensate for this increased risk exposure, lenders must price loans with portfolio risks in mind. Loan pricing is, of course, only one way of attempting to control risk exposure (e.g., using RAROC). In addition, the nonprice terms of loan agreements should be structured to reflect the borrower's effect on the lender's overall risk exposure.

Recapitulation

The proper pricing of loan contracts requires lenders to make judgments about default and portfolio risks. Default risk depends on the characteristics of the borrowers as reflected by their profiles of [$I(C)$, CF, NW, G]. The elements of this profile are state-dependent variables linked to external conditions. Portfolio risk focuses on each loan's covariation with the state of the economy and thereby highlights its potential diversification benefits to the loan portfolio.

LOAN PRICING, INTERACTION EFFECTS, AND RISK-ADJUSTED RETURNS

Descriptions of bank loan portfolios in terms of commercial and industrial (C&I) loans, consumer loans, real estate loans, or agricultural loans make for convenient cataloging and monitoring of sectoral and industry concentrations, but the terms lack financial content. A more meaningful breakdown of the loan portfolio is in terms of variable-rate loans and fixed-rate loans. In addition to deciding how to price individual loans, depository institutions must decide what ***portion*** of their loan portfolios should be priced on a variable-rate basis. Holding too many fixed-rate assets funded by variable-rate liabilities during a period of rising interest rates is economic suicide (the thrift debacle). The previous chapter described asset-liability management (ALM) as the coordinated management of a bank's balance sheet precisely because it involves more than the management of interest-rate risk. It involves the management of all relevant balance-sheet risks, including the interaction of interest-rate risk and credit risk. The pricing and risk management of the loan portfolio are the two primary determinants of this interaction. Accordingly, the pricing mechanism used in lending agreements should be consistent with the borrower's ability to pay, all other things being equal. To use **variable-rate pricing** in a contract with a borrower who is extremely vulnerable to interest-rate risk increases the chances of default and defeats the fundamental objective of lending (i.e., loan repayment). Banks, of course, face a dilemma in this area because if they do not use variable-rate pricing during periods of volatile interest rates, they are forced to accept both the credit risk and the interest-rate risk in one contract. Under these conditions, it is even more imperative that fixed-rate loans be priced properly.

On balance, the shifting of interest-rate risk from the lender to the borrower cannot be viewed in isolation, because other factors are not likely to stay the same. For example, a borrower's expected cash flows may be sensitive to the pricing mechanism used in the loan contract, and the greater uncertainty associated with variable-rate pricing may destabilize cash flows available for repaying debt. Lenders who make variable-rate loans have an obligation (to their customers and their shareholders) to consider how variable-rate pricing might affect the probability of the borrower's default and the overall risk exposure of the loan portfolio. The bottom line is that loan pricing needs to mesh with the borrower's ability to pay.

The Passive Model of Casualty Insurance, Risk-Adjusted Returns, and Asset Allocations

According to Kane [1995], the passive model of casualty insurance views insurance managers as having three strategic tasks (pp. 435–436):

1. Use actuarial analysis to calculate its expected losses by measuring and pooling the allegedly independent risks of its clients

2. Price each contract to cover the expected losses, to recapture associated expenses, and to generate an appropriate profit

3. Accumulate and manage a reserve fund large enough to cover expected claims and other contingencies

A passive model of credit risk would view bankers as having similar tasks applied to the lending function, where the critical variables would be loan losses, loan pricing, loan-loss reserves, and capital adequacy. Since history may not repeat itself, the passive model has a major drawback. It treats the frequency and severity of loan losses as if they were fixed exogenously. A more meaningful active method is to attempt to forecast future loan-loss rates to estimate expected loan losses.

To make informed asset-allocation decisions, lenders must know their returns adjusted for credit risk. Rose [1990] describes the risk-adjustment process used by IDC Financial Publishing of Hartland, Wisconsin, which attempts to adjust for both expected and unexpected loan losses. Beginning with the gross yield on the loan portfolio (i.e., the profitable loan contract rate), IDC subtracts the five-year average charge-off rate to adjust for expected loan losses. Next, to account for unexpected loan losses, it subtracts the standard deviation of the average charge-off rate. Finally, IDC subtracts the twelve-month average of the 91-day Treasury bill rate to get a risk-adjusted risk premium, or the value added to the bank compared to investing in risk-free Treasury bills.

The risk-adjustment process used by IDC can be viewed as a special case of equation (6-4), in which r^* is the gross loan yield minus the sum of the average charge-off rate and its standard deviation. Netting out the risk-free rate, r, generates a risk-adjusted, default-risk premium. For example, suppose the gross loan yield is 10 percent for a bank with a five-year average charge-off rate of 1 percent and a 0.2 percent standard deviation. Then, if the risk-free rate is 6 percent, the risk-adjusted risk premium is

$$10\% - 1\% - 0.2\% - 6\% = 2.8\%$$

This figure represents the value added to the bank from risky lending using risk-free lending as the benchmark. Note that this is a different standard from the one required by the RAROC model. It is possible that the value added over risk-free lending does not really add value to the bank because $RAROC < RAROC^*$.

To further illustrate, suppose that another bank with the same gross loan rate (10%), but with a more liberal lending policy, had an average charge-off rate of 2 percent with a standard deviation of 2 percent. Then its risk-adjusted risk premium would be

$$10\% - 2\% - 2\% - 6\% = 0\%$$

In this case, risky lending added no value to the bank over the risk-free rate. To achieve the same value added as the first bank, the second bank would need a gross loan yield of 12.8 percent ($12.8\% - 2\% - 2\% - 6\% = 2.8\%$). Thus, historical loss experience with an adjustment for expected losses can be used as part of a bank's loan-pricing process. Again, however, since history may not repeat itself, pro forma or projected loss experience provides a superior method for decision making. The historical approach is fine for determining the effectiveness of past decisions.

Some Empirical Evidence and Words of Caution

Using a sample of 8,300 banks with assets greater than $25 million, IDC estimated the median risk-adjusted loan return (value added over the T-bill rate) to be 2.0 percent in a recent year. This measure, of course, is a crude one, because it lumps all loans together and assumes the same charge-off rate for different types of loans (e.g., commercial real estate vs. residential mortgages). Focusing on the portfolio of real estate loans, IDC estimated the risk-adjusted rate to be 1.9 percent. Rose [1990], however, points out the possibility of a charge-off bias for this estimate (the 1.9%), because the average loan charge-off rate for all loans was 60 basis points (0.6%) compared to 20 basis points (0.2%) for real estate loans. In other words, because of the rapid growth in commercial real estate lending and the downturn in real estate prices that began in 1989, a five-year average of charge-offs on real estate loans might not be a good gauge of future losses. In this situation, charge-off rates present two potential problems: (1) the future may not reflect the past, and (2) historical charge-off rates may not reflect the true quality of the existing loan portfolio.

For 670 domestic banks with assets greater than $300 million, IDC estimated risk-adjusted rates of 2.3 percent (all loans) and 2.2 percent (real estate loans). The corresponding charge-off rates over a five-year period were 40 basis points (0.4%) and 10 basis points (0.1%). Rose [1990] contends that the charge-off figures "create a suspicion of an unwillingness to recognize enough real estate losses, resulting in an inflated risk-adjusted yield" (p. 2). For example, over the preceding year, these 670 large banks expanded real estate loans at 12.7 percent, compared to 8.7 percent for total loans. If the true riskiness of this asset allocation had been known, the growth rates or pricing or both should have been different.

To determine at the margin whether a bank should make loans or buy bonds, risk-adjusted loan and bond returns must be compared. IDC computes a risk-adjusted return on bank investments by subtracting the T-bill yield from the total bond return (i.e., interest plus realized and unrealized gains or losses). For the 8,300 smaller banks described above, the risk-adjusted bond return averaged 3.2 percent over the five-year period. Excluding unrealized gains, the return was 2.9 percent.

Get the picture now: Here's the evidence for the 8,300 banks with assets greater than $25 million for a five-year period:

3.2 percent (bond return including unrealized gains)

2.9 percent (bond return excluding unrealized gains)

2.0 percent (risk-adjusted return on all loans)

1.9 percent (risk-adjusted return on real estate loans)

Even allowing for measurement error, the implications for bank asset allocation (as a Monday morning quarterback) are clear: from 90 to 130 basis points in value added were available from investing in bonds compared to making loans. One important caveat, however, as Rose acknowledges, is interest-rate risk; we have been focusing on credit risk. If the maturity (duration) of the bonds and loans are the same, then the caveat is not necessary. However, if bonds have longer durations than those of bank loans, selecting bonds over loans will involve maturity mismatching because of the lack of long-term liabilities to fund long-term assets. A flat yield curve, of course, would negate the problem.

Another factor that needs to be considered in this comparative analysis of bonds versus bank loans is administrative expenses. Because loans are substantially more expensive to administer than bonds, investing in bonds means lower noninterest operating expenses. Thus, the lower operating expenses may compensate for the greater interest-rate risk of investing in bonds rather than loans.

The data in Table 6-3 provide another view of risk-adjusted returns (RARs) for a broader group of financial assets. The return measure is defined as

$$RAR_i = (R_i - R_f)/\sigma_i \qquad \textbf{(6-13)}$$

where R_i = return on the ith asset (loan), R_f = risk-free rate, and σ_i = standard deviation of the return on the ith asset.

Recapitulation

Lenders need to consider the interaction of credit risk, interest-rate risk, and operating expenses when allocating assets. Moreover, the risk-adjusted rates on asset allocations need to be forward looking and not be based solely on historical experience. Accordingly, IDC's framework for estimating risk-adjusted returns

TABLE 6-3 Risk-Adjusted Returns (RAR) for Financial Assets

$$[RAR_i = (R_i - R_f)/\sigma_i]$$

Financial Asset	RAR
Loan-pricing corporation index	2.80%
High-yield bonds	2.25
S&P 500	1.40
Investment-grade corporation bond index	0.55
Salomon Brothers mortgage bond index	0.50
Lehman Brothers T-bond index	0.45

Note: For the period January 1993 to October 1996, R_f is the 3-month T-bill rate and σ_i is the standard deviation of the return on the *i*th financial asset.

Primary source: CIBC Wood Gundy; secondary source: *The Economist* [November 2, 1996], p. 74.

should be modified for expected developments beyond those extrapolated from the past five years and for any discrepancies between nominal charge-off rates and real ones that reflect the true quality of the bank's loan portfolio. In effect, credit risk is not fixed exogenously, as the passive model of casualty insurance predicts, but is affected by current portfolio allocations and subject to interactions within the portfolio.

THE LENDING FUNCTION AS THE PREVENTION, IDENTIFICATION, AND RESOLUTION OF PROBLEM BORROWERS

In theory, the lending function needs to add value to the bank; in practice, it can achieve this goal by emphasizing the prevention, identification, and resolution of potential borrower problems.

Prevention refers to the decision to grant or not to grant credit—close the barn door before the horse can get out

Identification refers to the monitoring of existing borrowers for signs of weakness

Resolution refers to the working out of problem loans

The gathering, processing, and analyzing of quality (i.e., timely and accurate) information unites the process. With emphasis on the prevention, identification, and resolution of problem borrowers, Table 6-4 summarizes this view of the bank lending process.[44] The common thread in this three-step procedure is the gathering, processing, and analyzing of quality information, binding together the prevention, identification, and disposition of problem loans. Flaws in the gathering, processing, and analyzing of information weaken this common thread, potentially ruining the quality of a bank's loan portfolio.

[44] Altman [1980] reviews various aspects of the process of commercial bank lending. The appendix to this chapter describes problem-loan strategies and the early detection of problem loans.

TABLE 6-4   The Lending Function as the Prevention, Identification, and Disposition of Problem Borrowers

Step 1:   The credit decision: yes or no. The old adage, an ounce of *prevention* is worth a pound of cure, does not ring hollow in the credit-decision process. Achieving the ounce of prevention, however, involves a risk-return tradeoff: If the bank's credit standards are too tight (a pound of prevention rather than an ounce or two), then loan volume, the customer base, opportunities to cross-sell, and loan revenue and fees will be too low. If the bank's credit standards are too lenient, then the advantages of larger loan volume, a larger customer base, and more numerous opportunities to cross-sell will be reduced by nonaccruing loans, lost revenues, and loan losses. The optimal credit standards, all other things being equal, will be those that maximize the equity value of the bank. Given the bank's credit standards, the prevention step focuses on the gathering, processing, and analyzing of *quality* information, where quality refers to the *timeliness* and *accuracy* of the information flows. The four Ps of problem-loan prevention are *philosophy, policy, procedures,* and *people.*

Step 2:   The identification of problem loans: Loan *surveillance,* like the credit decision itself, involves the gathering, processing, and analyzing of quality information. This *monitoring* process has three possible outcomes: (1) classifying a loan as "current" or nonproblem, (2) classifying a loan as "noncurrent" or problem, and (3) needing more information before a decision can be made. The last outcome requires that more information be gathered, processed, and analyzed. In order of increasing risk of default, bank examiners, and many bankers, identify four classes of problem loans: (1) special mention, (2) substandard, (3) doubtful, and (4) loss.

Step 3:   The disposition of problem loans: Once problem loans are identified, they need to be analyzed for possible solutions, which require the gathering, processing, and analyzing of information. Three possible outcomes are (1) workout, (2) collateral liquidation (if any), and (3) legal action (e.g., obtaining a judgment). The bank's objective should be to undertake the *disposition* that promises the highest *net present value* (i.e., one in which the benefit exceeds the cost). Over time a problem loan judged to be a potential workout may deteriorate into a liquidation or legal action.

Synthesis: The *common thread* in these three steps is the *gathering, processing,* and *analyzing* of *quality* information. This thread weaves its way through the texture and fabric of the *lending function,* binding together the prevention, identification, and disposition of problem loans. Flaws in the gathering, processing, and analyzing of information weaken this common thread, potentially ruining the quality of a bank's loan portfolio.

The linkages among the gathering, processing, and analyzing of information and our general model of default risk are as follows:

1. Gathering information and the ability to extract quality information from borrowers provides evidence regarding the information quality and character components of the default-risk model.

2. The processing of information is an intermediate step that leads to analysis of the data.

3. Analyzing the information leads to lender judgments about the financial strength of the borrower in terms of net asset values and the level and stability of cash flow. Combining points 1 and 2 and adding external guarantees, if any, provides the lender with the components of the model of default risk (i.e., with a profile of $[I(C), CF, NW, G]$ for each borrower). Moreover, since each of the components is implicitly a function of the expected state of the economy, the borrower's downside vulnerability is included in the analysis. The outputs of the analysis are judgments about each borrower's default and portfolio risks,

which serve as inputs for determining the profitable loan contract rate. The gathering, processing, and analyzing of information applies to each of the three steps shown in Table 6-3: prevention, identification, and resolution.

Spilled Milk and the Psychology of Workout Situations

The Journal of Commercial Bank Lending has a section called "Spilled Milk," in which lenders share their experiences in dealing with problem loans. The idea is to help other lenders to be aware of past mistakes and alternative methods of damage control. Dying and dead loans (spilled milk) present trying situations for both borrowers and lenders. Application of Elisabeth Kubler-Ross's five stages of death and dying may help lenders to accept problem-loan situations.[45] In Kubler-Ross's framework, the gamut of emotions, which can be generalized to any major human event, runs through five stages:

1. Denial
2. Anger
3. Bargaining
4. Depression
5. Acceptance

Faced with a "terminal situation" (a bad loan, here), the solution is to reach the acceptance stage as quickly as possible. Although some people take a long time to get out of the denial stage, depression usually presents the biggest hurdle. Senior loan officers should be able to recognize and accept (psychologically) some bad loans. Moreover, they can best assist their customers (and junior lenders) by getting them to move to the acceptance stage as quickly as possible. Once that is accomplished, meaningful workout plans can be made.

CREDIT CULTURE AND A BANK'S WRITTEN LOAN POLICY

A bank's credit culture is an integral part of its lending function, either explicitly or implicitly. It includes such factors as organizational design, reporting arrangements, communication practices, and incentive schemes for lending officers. A bank's written loan policy should encompass these elements and other details. Table 6-5 presents the contents of the loan policy of a major regional bank. The loan policy consists of five major components:

1. General policies
2. Specific loan categories
3. Miscellaneous loan policies
4. Quality control
5. Committees

By setting parameters, defining responsibilities, and establishing a system of checks and balances, the loan policy provides a framework for the organization and control

---

[45] See Kubler-Ross [1969]. Because the five stages described above are not necessarily linear, the gamut of emotions frequently bounces from one stage and regresses backward to an earlier one. For example, people frequently regress back to denial or never really get out of it.

TABLE 6-5 Representative Contents of a Bank's Loan Policy

General Policy
  Management
  Trade area
  Balance loan portfolio
  Portfolio administration
  Loan-to-deposit ratio
  Legal loan limit
  Lending authority
  Loan responsibility
  Interest rates
  Loan repayment
  Collateral
  Credit information and documentation
  Delinquency ratios
  Loan-loss reserves
  Charge-offs
  Extensions or renewals of past-due installment loans
  Consumer laws and regulations

Specific Loan Categories
  Business development opportunities
  Desirable loans by loan category:
  1. Commercial loans
  2. Agricultural loans
  3. Mortgage loans
  4. Installment and branch bank loans
  5. VISA and revolving credit
  6. Mortgage-banking subsidiary
  7. Letters of credit
  8. Loan commitments
  9. Undesirable loans

Miscellaneous Loan Policies
  Loans to excutive officers, directors, 10 percent
    shareholders, and companies they control
  Employee loans
  Mortgage-banking subsidiary
  Conflict of interest

Quality Control
  1. Credit department
  2. Loan review
  3. Recovery department

Committees
  Directors Loan Committee of the Board of Directors
  Officers Loan Committee
  Loan Review Committee

of bank lending. It establishes the bank's credit culture. Although the nitty-gritty details of the loan policy shown in Table 6-5 are absent, the skeletal outline captures the basic areas any loan policy needs to address. View it as a summary of some of the terminology and practical aspects of bank lending. In addition, it highlights the importance of the organization, control, and risk management of the lending function.

Chapter Summary

Because the business of banking is the measuring, managing, and accepting of risk and because the major risk banks face is credit risk, it follows that the major risk banks must measure, manage, and accept is credit or default risk. It is the uncertainty associated with borrowers' loan repayments. The effects of credit risk on a bank's overall risk exposure can be summarized by the risk index (RI) as:

$$RI = [E(ROA) + CAP]/\sigma_{ROA}$$

All other things being equal, banks that do a good job of managing credit risk will have high RI scores, whereas banks that mismanage credit risk will have low scores.

When borrowers' asset values exceed their bank indebtedness, they repay their loans; when borrowers' asset values are less than loan values, they do not repay—they exercise their option to default. Thus, it is imperative that lenders be able to value borrowers' assets and to estimate a borrower's probability of default. In practice, most lenders, except for the largest banks, do not estimate this probability very scientifically. Instead, they rely on proxies that focus on a borrower's creditworthiness as captured, for example, by the five Cs of creditworthiness:

Character, Capacity, Capital, Collateral, and Conditions (economic).

The fundamental dilemma in managing credit risk is overcoming the agency or incentive problems between lenders, as outsiders, and borrowers, as insiders. Incentive problems arise from moral hazard, adverse selection, and asymmetric information. The traditional bank lending function has four components:

Originating, Funding, Servicing, and Monitoring.

The innovation of securitization has reduced lending to either a three- or two-step process:

Originate, sell, and service, or originate and sell without servicing.

Securitization permits banks to remove loans and the accompanying risks from their balance sheets at the expense of giving up funding margins, the bread and butter of the business. The majority of a bank's assets (55–60 percent), however, are still held in the form of loans, originated either by the bank itself or by other lenders. The methodology and estimates for determining a bank's loan-loss reserve or its allowance for loan and lease losses (ALLL) is an important part of the management of credit risk.

The bank lending function concentrates on the gathering, processing, and analyzing of timely and accurate information and on establishing customer relationships and incentives to remedy informational asymmetries and hidden actions arising from lender-borrower agency problems. Viewed as managing a guarantee business, credit risk can be managed by risk-based pricing (RAROC), asset restrictions, and monitoring. A borrower's profile of information quality, character, cash flow, real net worth, and guarantees presents, in effect, a model of default risk. Within this framework, the roles of adverse external conditions, customer relationships, and lender forbearance are important. A bank's asset-allocation decisions should be based on risk-adjusted returns. In addition, lenders must consider the interactions among credit risk, interest-rate risk, and operating expenses. More subtly, lenders also must price their portfolio risks (i.e., the covariation among loan returns). A bank's credit culture and its written loan policy capture implicit and explicit aspects of the lending function. Although the evolution of the lending function points to securitization as the innovation shaping the future of bank lending, it comes at the expense of funding margin, the bread and butter of the business.

Key Words, Concepts, and Acronyms

- Adverse selection
- Agency/incentive problems
- Allowance for loan and lease losses (ALLL)
- Asset restrictions
- Asymmetric information
- Bank-customer relationship
- Borrower-information continuum
- Capacity (cash flow)
- Capital (real net worth or net asset value)
- Character (reputation)
- Collateral
- Conditions (economic)
- Credit (default) risk
- Debt (private, intermediated, public)
- Financial contracting
- Five Cs of creditworthiness

- Forbearance
- Information quality
- Insolvency
- Lending function
- Loan charge-offs (gross and net)
- Loan guarantee
- Loan losses (expected and unexpected)
- Loan-loss reserve (LLR)
- Loan policy
- Loan pricing
- Monitoring
- Moral hazard
- Net worth (net asset value)
- Origination
- Portfolio risk premium
- Prevention, identification, and resolution

- Probability of default
- Problem borrowers
- Problem loans (causes and early-warning signals)
- Profitable loan contract rate
- Risk-adjusted return
- Risk-adjusted return on capital (RAROC)
- Risk-based pricing
- Risk-free rate (loan)
- Risky loan (= risk-free loan − loan guarantee)
- Securitization
- Servicing
- Spilled milk
- Transparency
- Variable-rate pricing
- Workout situations

Review/Discussion Questions

1. On average, what portion of a bank's assets are held as loans? What are provisions for loan losses? Loan-loss reserves? Loan charge-offs (gross and net)? What's the relation between loan quality and bank profitability as measured by return on assets (ROA)?

2. Distinguish between the traditional lending function and the securitized lending function. What are the costs to banks of securitization?

3. What is the major risk banks face? What problems do mismanagement of this risk create? Explain in terms of a bank's risk index.

4. What are the lender-borrower-incentive (or agency) problems in financial contracting?

5. What is the option available to borrowers? Describe this option in terms of the balance sheet identify $A = L + NW$, and draw pictures of the payoff profiles for a loan and for the shareholders of a firm with debt.

6. What role does the probability of default (d) play in determining a profitable loan contract rate? What happens when $d = 0$, $d = 1$, and $0 < d < 1$?

7. In modeling the probability of default, what are the key components? What role does the state of the economy play in this function?

8. What can you do to a risky loan to make it risk free? In doing this exercise, how does this change our view of a risky loan?

9. How can we estimate the value of loan guarantees?

10. What are three basic techniques of risk management, and which one of these methods permits a better understanding of the business of lending and managing credit risk?

11. Briefly explain the three techniques for managing the guarantee business.

12. What is RAROC and how does it relate, if at all, to the concept of economic value added (EVA)? A more traditional measure of risk is RAR. How is it defined?

13. Can you think of a good example of effective monitoring on a continuous basis? How does your example compare with the system used by banks? What kinds of loans do banks make that come closest to having this degree of monitoring effectiveness?

14. What three forms of debt exist in the borrower-information continuum? Explain what this continuum is. What do the originators of this approach call it?

15. What are monitoring-related contract costs, and what empirical evidence exists regarding them?

16. With respect to credit risk, what is the typical scenario for a failed bank? Can these failures be traced to shortcomings in contract design? Do banks send any signals when they make loans?

17. What are the basic components of the passive model of casualty insurance? Can it be applied to bank lending? What is the major shortcoming of the model, and how can it be improved?

18. How would you calculate risk-adjusted returns for a bank's assets? What role should these returns play in asset allocation? How important are interest-rate risk and noninterest operating expenses to asset allocation?

19. How does indirect finance with its customer relationships differ from direct finance? Which type of finance practices forbearance?

20. What is the portfolio risk premium and why is it important? How does it enter the formula for a profitable loan contract rate? What components of this formula are observable?

21. What is the common thread in the credit-decision process and what are the three steps in the process?

22. What are the five Cs of creditworthiness and what role do they play in bank lending? Check the Spilled Milk section of recent issues of the *Journal of Commercial Bank Lending* to identify the kinds of problems lenders have been facing recently. When lenders have problem loans, what psychological stages are they likely to go through? What about the borrowers?

23. Bank lenders face at least two dilemmas: (1) They know they should diversify (the basic lesson of portfolio theory), but they have a difficult time estimating the crucial correlations; (2) in pricing loans, if they try to push variable-rate pricing, they have to consider the interaction between interest-rate risk and credit risk. How can these two dilemmas be resolved, if at all, and what role does regulation play in either the problem or the solution or both? Does a lender in west Texas or in Iowa need to know the correlation coefficient among loans to the fourth decimal place?

24. What are the relationships among bank loan review ratings, examiner ratings, and bond ratings?

25. Describe the various methodologies for estimating a bank's loan-loss reserve (LLR) or allowance for loan and lease losses (ALLL). How would you determine if an ALLL was reasonable and accurate for a bank's risk exposure?

Problems

1. Abstracting from real resource costs such as salaries for loan officers, processing costs, and other noninterest expenses, if the risk-free rate of interest is 8 percent and the risk (probability) of default is .05, what is the profitable loan contract rate? What is the default-risk premium in this case? How would your answers change if the portfolio risk premium was .005? What if this premium was −.005?

2. If a loan contract rate is 15 percent and the risk-free rate is 10 percent, what can you say about the components of the RHS of equation 6-12?

3. Although banks can raise some funds at close to the risk-free rate (r), their base cost-of-funds rate typically is the federal-funds rate, a CD rate, or LIBOR. Federal funds

and Eurodollar CDs (at markups over LIBOR) are attractive because they are *not* subject to reserve requirements or deposit-insurance fees. Charging fees and requiring compensating balances are also part of bank business lending. Suppose a bank faces the following situation:

> Base cost of funds (domestic CD rate) = 7.00 percent
> Loan-origination and processing fee = 0.25 percent
> Compensating-balance requirement = 10 percent
> Reserve requirements = 10 percent
> Deposit-insurance fees = 0.125 percent
> Probability of default = 1.00 percent
> Portfolio-risk premium = 0.25 percent

Adjust equation (6-1) to account for all of these factors and calculate the bank's profitable loan rate.

4. Given the following information, calculate risk-adjusted loan and bond returns. Investment in which asset will add the most value to the bank?

> Risk-free rate = 5 percent
> Bond yield (including unrealized gains) = 8.2 percent
> Bond yield (excluding unrealized gains) = 8.0 percent
> Gross loan yield = 10 percent
> Net loan charge-off rates:

Period	Rate
t	1.4 percent
$t - 1$	1.3
$t - 2$	1.2
$t - 3$	1.1
$t - 4$	1.0

If the average duration of the bond portfolio exceeds the average duration of the loan portfolio, how would that affect your decision to allocate assets? What role would non-interest operating expenses play?

5. Consider a risky bond (or bank loan) with a face value of $1,000 that promises semi-annual payments of $100 for five years. If sold at par, the bond has a yield to maturity of 10 percent (doubling convention). If the risk-free rate on five-year debt is 7.5 percent, what is the value of the loan guarantee that would make the risky bond a risk-free instrument?

6. A lender has a choice of two risky loans for each of the following experiments. If the loans are held in 60/40 proportions, what are the expected returns from diversified and undiversified portfolios? Assuming the states are equally likely, explain the results.

	Experiment					
	1		2		3	
	State		*State*		*State*	
Loan	*1*	*2*	*1*	*2*	*1*	*2*
A	$4	$2	$8	$4	$5	$3
B	$2	$1	$0	$6	$2	$6

7. Given the following market-value balance sheets, indicate what the borrower/owner will do if the business is to be terminated. Assume that all debt is in the form of bank loans.
    a. Case 1: $A = L + NW = 150 = 75 + 75$
    b. Case 2: $A = L + NW = 120 = 75 + 75$
    c. Case 2: $A = L + NW = 60 = 75 + 75$
    d. Case 4: $A = L + NW = 0 = 75 + 75$
    e. Case 5: $A = L + NW = 200 = 75 + 125$

8. Trust-Us Bankers (TUB) has a hurdle rate, or weighted average cost of funds, of 10 percent. Given the following components for estimating RAROCs, calculate each loan's RAROC and indicate what the loan officer/relationship manager should do.

Loan Project	Spread Rate	Fee Rate	Nominal Loan	Loan Amount at Risk
Alpha	0.003	0.002	$1,000,000	$30,000
Beta	0.001	0.001	$10,000,000	$100,000
Gamma	0.01	0.005	$5,000,000	$50,000

9. The managers of the Bank of Banks County, a community bank, recently attended a seminar in Atlanta where they learned about RAROC; they have decided to attempt to use it in evaluating the profitability of their loan portfolio. The bank's sources and costs of funding ($ millions) are as follows:

    Core deposits 45 @ cost rate of 3 percent

    Other deposits 45 @ cost rate of 5 percent

    Equity capital 10 @ cost rate of 10 percent

    The balance-sheet constraint ($ millions) is as follows:

    $$100 = 60 \text{ (loans)} + 40 \text{ (other assets)} = 45 + 45 + 10$$

    The management team performs experiments on the following three loans using a *RAROC* based on a rate rather than a dollar approach. Compute each loan's *RAROC* and analyze the findings.

Loan Project	Estimated Annual Income (%)	Unexpected Loss Rate	Default Loss on Loan
Alpha	0.01	0.01	0.10
Delta	0.2	0.04	0.80
Pi	0.3	0.10	0.90

10. Durand Bank of Durango has been using duration to estimate the price sensitivity of particular assets in its portfolio based on unexpected changes in interest rates. A recently hired MBA has told the credit manager that the duration method also can be applied to test the credit-risk sensitivity of loans and other assets, and that the estimated change in the value of the loan can be used as a loan risk amount in a RAROC calculation. The credit manager, David D. Durand, Jr., and his father and the bank president, David D. Durand, Sr., want to see how this can be done. The new MBA, Diane D. Diamond, collects the following information:

    Loan amount = $1,000,000 @10 percent

    Credit-risk change in loan rate = $0.005 = 0.5$ percent

Duration of loan = 2.5 years

Loan spread = 0.0025 = 0.25 percent

Amortized annual loan fee = 0.00075 = 0.075 percent

Prepare Ms. Diamond's calculations and explain the methodology and results to the Durands, known locally as "Daddy" and "Lucky" (to have Daddy as president).

11. The Last National Bank Corporation (LNBC) has the following loan data. Use this information to estimate its required ALLL at the end of year $t - 1$ (beginning of year t) with as many methods as permitted by the data. Assume that LNBC has a current ALLL of $354 million and that it will need an additional ALLL over and above what you estimate by $140 million. The bank's total loan portfolio is $24.5 billion, of which $1.5 billion is nonperforming. The required ratio of ALLL to nonperforming is deemed to be 0.70. At the end of year $t - 1$, LNBC has $20 billion in noncriticized loans, $1.529 billion in special mention loans, $2.472 billion in substandard loans, $519 million in doubtful loans, and $38 million in loss loans.

Year $t - 1$	Net Loan Losses/ Total Loans
Q1	0.80
Q2	1.06
Q3	0.93
Q4	2.29

Assume that the bank needs 2.5 times its historical loss experience to have a reasonable ALLL, based on peer data, the economic outlook, and other factors.

12. Using equation (6-13), calculate RARs (not RAROCs) for the following financial assets. Assume the risk-free rate is 10 percent. Do your results make sense? Explain.

Financial Asset	Return	Standard Deviation
Loan-pricing corporation index	0.28	0.045
High-yield bonds	0.24	0.040
S&P 500	0.20	0.035
Investment-grade corporation bond index	0.16	0.030
Salomon Brothers mortgage bond index	0.14	0.025
Lehman Brothers T-bond index	0.12	0.020

PROBLEM-LOAN STRATEGIES AND EARLY DETECTION OF PROBLEM LOANS[46]

Although an ounce of prevention is worth a pound of cure (see Step 1 in Table 6-4 in the text), lenders need a risk-return balance. Within that framework, a commensurate amount of problem loans is expected. A bank's prevention strategy can be viewed in terms of its specific four Ps of prevention:

1. Philosophy
2. Policy
3. Procedures
4. People

Top management and the Board of Directors establish a bank's prevention strategy. In this framework, early detection of problem loans ranks second to prevention as a means of protecting loan quality. The identification of problem loans (loan surveillance) requires the gathering, processing, and analyzing of information. The swift detection of problem loans requires lenders to have *procedures* and *people* capable of finding early-warning signals in these information flows. The failure of a borrower to supply the lender with timely and accurate information could be an early-warning signal of a potential problem-loan situation.

Causes of Problem Loans

Internal or external factors, or a combination of the two, cause problem loans. Because lending is a two-way street, analysis of the internal factor applies to both the lender and the borrower. Consider the lending institution first and its prevention strategy as captured by its four Ps of prevention. At one extreme, a bank with an aggressive lending philosophy and policy, lax procedures, and bad people (i.e., dishonest or incompetent or both) will find the answers to its loan difficulties inside the bank. Moreover, even if a bank has a sound prevention strategy, it can look for breakdowns in its internal procedures or people.

If we focus on the borrower, external factors that cause loan difficulties are captured by the state of the economy of the default-risk function (i.e., by ECY in equation 6-12). Because these external factors affect the borrower's cash flow and net asset value, they determine the means of loan repayment. The two primary external factors affecting business borrowers are recession and competition. The energy and agricultural downturns of the 1980s and the commercial real estate problems of the early 1990s highlight the effects of sectoral and regional recessions on bank loan quality. For banks with concentrated loan portfolios, these kinds of recessions can be more devastating than nationwide recessions. Other external factors that can cause problem loans include natural disasters (e.g., drought), advances in technology, regulatory changes, industry changes, and demographic and sociological trends.

---

[46] This section draws on McKinley, Johnson, Vollertsen, Batson, and Weitnauer [1985].

The internal factor that determines business success and borrower performance is management. Direct measures of potential managerial success include education, training, motivation, experience, and reputation. How these prerequisites are put together (e.g., in a business plan) and what they generate in terms of product quality and financial performance (e.g., profit margin) are indirect measures or symptoms of the quality of management. Because the bank-customer relationship gives loan officers the opportunity to get to know borrowers/managers both directly and indirectly, bank loan officers should be the primary source of early-warning signals about potential problem borrowers.

Borrower Early-Warning Signals

Early-warning signals can be classified into four categories:[47] (1) financial, (2) operational, (3) banking, and (4) managerial.

> *Financial* early-warning signals focus on performance measures derived from the borrower's balance sheet, income-expense statement, statement of cash flows, and related schedules such as receivables aging

> *Operational* early-warning signals focus on production and inventory management; relationships with suppliers, distributors, customers, and employees; and the appearance of the business

> *Banking* early-warning signals focus on various aspects of the bank-customer relationship ranging from declining deposit balances and check kiting to the frequency of loan requests and the use of loan proceeds

> *Managerial* early-warning signals focus on various aspects of behavior ranging from changes in personal habits and changes in attitudes toward risk-taking to changes in the methods and practices of handling the routine tasks of the day-to-day business

In general, unexpected changes that adversely affect a borrower in these four areas should be treated as early-warning signals. The key relationship for understanding any change is

Actual change = expected change + unexpected change.

The important point is that unexpected change is the source of all uncertainty and risk. An important test of management is its ability to handle change. Good managers are prepared for expected changes and adapt quickly to unanticipated ones. Early detection of problem borrowers requires both art and science. The task is akin to the one performed by bank examiners.[48] The scientific part focuses on detailed knowledge of the borrower's business and industry with respect to finance, production (if any), technology, marketing, accounting, strategic and business planning, and competition. Many of these scientific components can be quantified. Moreover, in today's environment of personal computers and information-retrieval systems, such quantification is becoming easier and more efficient. This information explosion has its downside, however, as loan officers, to keep from being overwhelmed, must be able to separate the relevant information from the less relevant. In contrast, the artsy part of being a loan officer requires more

---

[47] *Ibid.*, pp. 40–41. Also see Benbow [1985], who discusses 25 red flags for preventing problem loans. Herring [1989] analyzes the economics of workout lending.

[48] Hoar [1988] provides an examiner's perspective on loan problems. See Bresler [1988] for the merits of a nonregulatory system for rating loan quality.

judgment, experience, and putting it all together. Much of loan-officer artistry involves dealing with the borrower/manager on a personal level and making qualitative decisions regarding the competency, capacity, depth, and honesty of management.

Analysis and Handling of Problem Loans

If the signals described above indicate a problem situation, the *symptoms* need to be traced to their *causes*. Identification of the causes may indicate whether or not the problem is solvable. Payout, liquidation, or bankruptcy are the options for non-solvable loan problems. If the problem situation appears solvable, the loan officer or workout team need to analyze the benefits and costs to determine if the work-out is a positive net-present-value project for the bank. If it is not, then the fallback position is one of the three options above. If the workout is perceived to be a positive NPV project, then a workout plan must be devised and implemented. If the current management, which has to shoulder some of the blame for the problem, cannot handle the turnaround, then new management will be required.

Workout plans usually involve both short- and longer-run strategies. The immediate concern is to blunt the hemorrhaging of cash flow. The analogous medical solution is pressure. Loan workouts focus on three critical pressure points:

- Cost reductions
- Asset sales
- Revenue generation

Because it is easier to implement cost controls and asset sales than it is to increase revenues, downsizing frequently comes first. Because this strategy may be unpopular, a confrontation may develop between the loan officer or workout team and management. A prerequisite then is to get management to accept that the situation is a crisis calling for swift and effective action. Without such acceptance, the workout is unlikely to get off the ground. To avoid the threat of lender liability, problem situations and workout plans should be handled and developed with the advice of the bank's legal counsel. After the company's cash-flow position has been stabilized, a rehabilitation program needs to be put in place. Five guidelines for assessing the potential success of such an effort are the following:[49]

1. The *common sense* of the plan to both the lender and the borrower
2. The *feasibility* of the plan
3. The *measurability* of the plan in terms of financial performance and benefit to the bank
4. The *ability of management* to handle a *turnaround* situation
5. The *logic* of the plan to outsiders who are familiar with the business and the industry

The last point is critically important if the plan involves specialized or technical aspects that go beyond the bank's areas of expertise.

From Workout to Payout

The lender's objective is simple: recover the bank's money (i.e., achieve payout of the loan). Workouts that go smoothly lead to payout rather quickly. Those that

---

[49] McKinley et al., op. cit., p. 76.

do not go smoothly usually involve one or more of the following actions prior to payout:[50]

- Payout is achieved through *liquidation* of collateral
- Payout is achieved by reducing the debt to *judgment* and then collecting the judgment
- Payout is achieved only after *bankruptcy* proceedings, which may begin at any time during the workout (e.g., when the bank attempts to collect on the collateral or after a judgment is obtained)

Workouts that do not go smoothly usually involve less than full payout to the bank (i.e., loan losses).

Two ways to avoid workout situations are (1) to postpone the day of reckoning by renewing the loan and hope for the best at the next renewal (a rolling loan gathers no loss) or (2) to convince the borrower to move the debt to another lender (one lender's junk is another's treasure). The potential problem with the first approach is that it may only postpone the workout. The upside is that payout occurs or a workout is negotiated under more favorable conditions; the downside may mean default or a workout under less favorable conditions. The second approach achieves payout but at the expense of a severed customer relationship. Premature severing of relationships may give the bank a reputation of not staying with its customers and may injure the bank's prospects for long-run growth.

Selected References

Altman Edward I. [1980]. "Commercial Bank Lending: Process, Credit Scoring, and Costs of Errors in Lending." *Journal of Financial and Quantitative Analysis* Proceedings Issue (November), pp. 813–832.

———. [1989]. "Measuring Corporate Maturity and Performance." *Journal of Finance* (September), pp. 909–922.

Bathory, Alexander. [1987]. *The Analysis of Credit: Foundations and Development of Corporate Credit Assessment.* London: McGraw-Hill.

Benbow, Robert F. [1985]. "Preventing Problem Loans before They Happen: 25 Red Flags." *Journal of Commercial Bank Lending* (April), pp. 18–23.

Berger, Allen N., and Gregory F. Udell. [1993]. "Securitization, Risk, and the Liquidity Problem in Banking." In Michael Klausner and Lawrence J. White, eds., *Structural Change in Banking.* Homewood Hills, IL: Irwin Publishing, pp. 227–294.

Black, Fischer, and Myron Scholes [1973]. "The Pricing of Options and Corporate Liabilities." *Journal of Political Economy* (May/June), pp. 637–654.

Booth, James R. [1992]. "Contract Costs, Bank Loans, and the Cross-Monitoring Hypothesis." *Journal of Financial Economics* 31, pp. 25–41.

Bresler, Paul J. [1988]. "Merits of a Nonregulatory Loan Quality Rating System." *Journal of Commercial Bank Lending* (May), pp. 43–46.

Campbell, T., and W. Kracaw. [1980]. "Information Production, Market Signaling, and the Theory of Intermediation." *Journal of Finance* 35, pp. 863–882.

Chan, Y. [1983]. "On the Positive Role of Financial Intermediation in Allocation of Venture Capital in a Market with Imperfect Information." *Journal of Finance* (December), pp. 1543–1568.

---

[50] *Ibid.,* pp. 95–162.

Clarke, Peter S. [1986]. *Complete Guide to Loan Documentation.* Englewood Cliffs, NJ: Prentice-Hall.

Combating Fraud, Abuse, and Misconduct in the Nation's Financial Institutions. [1988]. Seventy-Second Report by Committee on Government Operations. Washington, D.C.: U.S. Government Printing Office.

Diamond, Douglas. [1984]. "Financial Intermediation and Delegated Monitoring." *Review of Economic Studies* 51, pp. 393–414.

Emmanuel, Christine. [1988]. "Cash Flow Reporting, Part 2: Importance of Cash Flow Data in Credit Analysis." *Journal of Commercial Bank Lending* (June), pp. 16–28.

Federal Reserve Bulletin (various issues). Washington, DC: Board of Governors of the Federal Reserve System.

Flannery, Mark J. [1985]. "A Portfolio View of Loan Selection and Pricing." In R. Aspinwall and R. Eisenbeis, eds., *Handbook for Banking Strategy.* New York: Wiley, pp. 457–472.

Froot, Kenneth A. [1995]. "Incentive Problems in Financial Contracting." In *The Global Financial System.* Boston, MA: Harvard Business School Press, pp. 225–261.

Gatewood, R., and H. Feild. [1990]. *Human Resource Selection.* Hinsdale, IL: Dryden Press.

General Accounting Office. [1991]. "Bank Supervision: OCC's Supervision of the Bank of New England Was Not Timely or Forceful." Report to the Chairman, Committee on Banking, Housing, and Urban Affairs, U.S. Senate, GAO/GGD-91–128 (September).

Ginzl, David J. [1988]. "Cash Flow Reporting, Part 3: Getting—and Using—Quality Financial Information." *Journal of Commercial Bank Lending* (July), pp. 17–21.

Harding, Douglas, Betty McDonald, and Dev Strischek. [1987]. "The Role of Meaningful Credit Information." *Journal of Commercial Bank Lending* (August), pp. 51–61.

Herring, Richard J. [1989]. "The Economics of Workout Lending." *Journal of Money, Credit, and Banking* (February), pp. 1–15.

Hoar, Thomas. [1988]. "An Examiner's Perspective on Loan Problems." *Journal of Commercial Bank Lending* (May), pp. 36–42.

Hodgeman, Donald R. [1963]. *Commercial Bank Loan and Investment Policy.* Champaign, IL: University of Illinois, Bureau of Economic and Business Research.

Kane, Edward J. [1986]. "Competitive Financial Reregulation: An International Perspective." Paper presented at the 1986 Conference of the International Center for Monetary and Banking Studies (August).

———. [1995]. "Three Paradigms for the Role of Capitalization Requirements in Insured Financial Institutions." *Journal of Banking and Finance* 19, pp. 431–459.

Kane, Edward J., and Burton G. Malkiel. [1965]. "Bank Portfolio Allocation, Deposit Variability, and the Availability Doctrine." *Quarterly Journal of Economics* (February), pp. 113–134.

Kubler-Ross, Elisabeth. [1969]. *On Death and Dying.* New York: Macmillan.

Leland, H., and D. Pyle. [1977]. "Information Asymmetries, Financial Structure, and Financial Intermediaries." *Journal of Finance* 32, pp. 371–387.

Mason, Scott P. [1995]. "The Allocation of Risk." In *The Global Financial System.* Boston, MA: Harvard Business School Press, pp. 153–195.

McKinley, J., B. Johnson, E. Vollertsen, R. Neal Batson, and J. Weitnauer. [1985]. *Problem Loan Strategies.* Philadelphia: Robert Morris Associates.

Megginson, William, Annette B. Poulsen, and Joseph F. Sinkey, Jr. [1995]. "Syndicated Loan Announcements and the Market Value of the Banking Firm." *Journal of Money, Credit, and Banking* (May), pp. 457–475.

Merton, Robert C. [1974]. "On the Pricing of Corporate Debt and the Risk Structure of Interest Rates." *Journal of Finance* (May), pp. 449–470.

———. [1977]. "An Analytical Derivation of the Cost of Deposit Insurance Loan Guarantees: An Application of Modern Option Pricing Theory." *Journal of Banking and Finance* 1 (June), pp. 3–11.

———. [1990]. "The Financial System and Economic Performance." *Journal of Financial Services Research* (December), pp. 263-309.

———. [1995]. "Financial Innovation and the Management and Regulation of Financial Institutions." *Journal of Banking and Finance* 19, pp. 461–481.

Merton, Robert C., and Zvi Bodie. [1992]. "On the Management of Financial Guarantees." *Financial Management* (Winter), pp. 87–109.

Miller, Merton H. [1995]. "Do the M&M Propositions Apply to Banks?" *Journal of Banking and Finance* 19, pp. 483–489.

O'Leary, Carolyn D. [1988]. "Cash Flow Reporting, Part 1: An Overview of SFAS 95." *Journal of Commercial Bank Lending* (May), pp. 22–28.

Rose, Sanford. [1990]. "A Case of Mistaken Asset Allocation." *The American Banker* (April 10), p. 4.

Ruth, George E. [1987]. *Commercial Lending.* Washington, DC: American Bankers Association.

Sinkey, Joseph F., Jr. [1978]. "Identifying Problem Banks: How Do the Banking Authorities Measure a Bank's Risk Exposure?" *Journal of Money, Credit, and Banking* (May), pp. 184–193.

———. [1979]. *Problem and Failed Institutions in the Commercial Banking Industry.* Greenwich, CT: JAI Press.

———. [1989]. "Credit Risk in Commercial Banks: A Survey of Theory, Practice, and Empirical Evidence." Bank of Israel *Banking Review* (December), pp. 12–35.

Wilke, John R. [1991]. "New Hampshire Firms Struggle as Bank Crisis Dries Up Their Credit." *The Wall Street Journal* (February 21), pp. A1, A8.

CHAPTER

7

LIQUIDITY RISK AND
LIABILITY MANAGEMENT

Contents

LEARNING OBJECTIVES

- To understand the importance of liquidity to banks and to the economy

- To understand the nature of liquidity risk

- To distinguish between core deposits and volatile liabilities

- To understand the trade-off between liquidity and profitability

- To understand how to measure bank liquidity

- To understand a bank's weighted-average cost of funds

- To understand a bank's reserve-position management

CHAPTER THEME

> *Our whole financial system runs on confidence*
> *and not much else when you get down to it. What we've learned*
> *is that when confidence erodes, it erodes very quickly.*
> —L. WILLIAM SEIDMAN
> *Former Chairman, FDIC*

Banks need **liquidity** to meet **deposit withdrawals** and to satisfy customer **loan demand.** Unexpected changes in the flows of loans and volatile liabilities create liquidity problems for banks. Banks can either store liquidity in their assets or purchase it in money and deposit markets. Because liquid assets have lower returns, **stored liquidity** has an opportunity cost that results in a trade-off between liquidity and profitability. The use of **purchased funds** to meet liquidity needs and to fund assets is known as **liability management.** Multinational banks rely more heavily on purchased funds to finance their balance sheets and generate liquidity, whereas regional and community banks depend more on stored liquidity and **core deposits,** funds gathered in local markets and noted for their greater stability and lower cost compared to purchased funds. Banks with balance sheets heavily funded by volatile liabilities face a greater risk of experiencing "deposit runs," which in today's environment means an **electronic run** (e.g., Continental Illinois in 1984). Money-desk or **reserve-position management** is a daily task for banks. To determine their **weighted-average cost of funds,** banks need to know both the **interest cost** and the **operating cost** of their sources of funds (e.g., checking accounts versus CDs).

KEY CONCEPTS, IDEAS, AND TERMS

- Confidence function
- Core deposits
- Deposit withdrawals
- Electronic (deposit) run
- Federal safety net
- Forecasting techniques

- Interest cost of funds
- Liability management
- Liquid assets
- Liquidity risk
- Loan demand
- Operating cost

- Purchased funds
- Reserve-position management
- Stored liquidity
- Volatile liabilities
- Weighted-average, marginal cost of funds

INTRODUCTION

This chapter focuses on liquidity risk and its management. Because banks can either store liquidity in their assets or purchase it in the marketplace (liability management), we highlight these two aspects of bank liquidity management. Banks need liquidity to meet deposit withdrawals and to fund loan demand. The variability of loan demand and the variability of deposit flows determine a bank's liquidity needs. The more volatile a bank's loan and deposit/liability flows are, the more liquidity it needs. **Confidence** in a bank permits it to avoid deposit runs or liquidity crises. The **federal safety net** of deposit insurance and the discount window provide government guarantees that instill public confidence in the banking system. As the major providers of liquidity to the economy, banks play an important role in stabilizing the overall economy and spreading the confidence effect from the financial sector to the real sector.

The numerous bank failures and a couple of liquidity crises at major banks during the 1980s and early 1990s have made U.S. bankers, regulators, deposit insurers, analysts, and, most importantly, bank creditors, especially uninsured ones, more aware of the need for bank liquidity. Of course, the need for banks to be liquid is not something new. In 1977, a former chief financial officer of Citicorp told a group of analysts that, in terms of priority components, the regulators' CAMEL rating system was reversed—it should be LEMAC.[1] "Liquidity always comes first; without it a bank doesn't open its doors; with it, a bank may have time to solve its basic problems" (as reported by Cates [1990], p. 20).

---

[1] Recall that CAMEL stands for *C*apital adequacy, *A*sset quality, *M*anagement, *E*arnings, and *L*iquidity. It is formally known as the Uniform Financial Institutions Rating System. Banks are rated 1 (best) to 5 (worst) in each category and assigned a composite score of 1 (best) to 5 (worst).

BANK LIQUIDITY AND THE STOCK MARKET CRASH OF 1987[2]

On October 20, 1987, the day after the stock market crash ("Black Monday"), Citibank increased its loans outstanding to 20 securities firms to $1.4 billion from its normal range of $200 to $400 million. E. Gerald Corrigan, then president of the Federal Reserve Bank of New York, had called John Reed, chairman of Citicorp, and asked him to provide liquidity to securities firms. Because the Federal Reserve had announced that the discount window was open, Reed knew the central bank was standing behind Citicorp/Citibank and the banking system. However, Reed did not throw caution to the wind. He summed up the situation this way:[3]

> We were providing as much liquidity as we could. Quite a few of the firms went right up to their loan limits. We didn't take physical possession of securities, but we were damn close to our customers. You have a tremendous conflict there. On one hand, there's a need for liquidity in the system. On the other hand, when you're dealing in $100 million lot sizes, you can't afford to be wrong. We can't take a $100 million write-off to save a broker. The stockholders would lynch me and with good reason.

This event dramatically illustrates the vital role bank liquidity plays in the financial system, and the economy in general, and the potential conflict between meeting that macroeconomic need and the bank's objective of maximizing shareholder wealth. Although the shareholders of Citicorp, or any other FSF, would certainly benefit from a stable financial system, they should not be expected to use their wealth to provide such stability, which explains why Citibank stayed close to its customers in the aftermath of the stock market crash.

The ability of a bank, or any FSF, to provide **liquidity** requires the existence of a highly liquid *and* readily transferable stock of financial assets. Liquidity and transferability are the key ingredients for such transactions. The liquidity requirement means that financial assets must be available to owners on short notice (a day or less) at par. The transferability requirement means that ownership rights in financial assets must be portable, at par, to other economic agents, and in a form acceptable to the other party. Checkable deposits and wire transfers (for large transactions) are the primary instruments of liquidity and transferability. In the case of Citicorp and other large banks supplying liquidity to securities firms following the stock market crash of 1987, electronic payments would have been the preferred means of transfer.

THE ROLE OF CONFIDENCE

Chapter 1 introduced the idea of a **confidence function** for a bank (Kane [1986]), describing it in terms of four factors:

- Net worth ("capital adequacy")
- Stability of earnings

---

[2] K. A. Randall, former chairman of the FDIC in the 1960s and a regular on PBS's *Wall Street Week*, regards the crash of 1987 as a "correction," because the drop in the market, although it was steep, was not long-lasting (PBS program of July 28, 1995).

[3] The information in this paragraph and the quotation are from Guenther [1987]. Also see Ricks [1987].

- Quality of information (transparency)
- Government guarantees

Without government guarantees, what variable would you add to this function? Liquidity seems like a good choice; banks need liquidity to survive and bank regulators consider liquidity important enough to include it in their CAMEL rating system. Adding liquidity to the confidence equation and defining a liquidity function, we get

$$\text{Confidence} = f[NW, \sigma_{ROA}, IQ, L(G, \sigma_L, \sigma_D)] \qquad \text{(7-1)}$$

where NW stands for net worth, σ_{ROA} stands for stability of earnings measured by the standard deviation (σ) of return on assets (ROA), IQ stands for the information quality (transparency) regarding the bank's earnings and asset quality, and $L(G, \sigma_L, \sigma_D)$ stands for liquidity as a function of three variables:

- G for government guarantees (e.g., the **too-big-to-fail doctrine** [TBTF] and the federal safety net of deposit insurance and lender of last resort)
- σ_L for the variability of loan demand
- σ_D for the variability of deposit/liability flows

In a time of crisis (lack of confidence), G is *the* variable of the liquidity function. Under noncrisis conditions, the variability of loan demand and the variability of deposit/liability flows determine a bank's need for liquidity. If these flows were known with certainty, this chapter on liquidity risk and its management would not exist.

A HISTORICAL PERSPECTIVE ON BANK LIQUIDITY MANAGEMENT

The primary assets held by banks are various kinds of loans. From a liquidity perspective, short-term loans are attractive because they are self-liquidating. In fact, the commercial-loan theory or real-bills doctrine, a theory popular prior to the 1930s, argued that this was the sole function of a commercial bank—to make short-term, self-liquidating loans. Because modern banks make various kinds of loans, they generate cash inflows of principal plus interest on a regular nondiscretionary basis, usually monthly. In addition to maturing loans, banks hold investment securities such as government bills, notes, and bonds that pay interest and mature on a regular basis, providing another nondiscretionary source of funds to meet liquidity needs. This aspect of liquidity management is passive in that the bank does not have to take any action to generate the cash inflows.

The liquidity that exists in a bank's assets is stored in its balance sheet, hence the name **stored liquidity.** In contrast to this natural or anticipated inflow of funds, banks can speed up the inflow of funds by selling or lending assets (e.g., repurchase agreements). The primary risk of this form of active liquidity management arises from interest-rate risk (i.e., the possibility of capital losses if assets are converted at prices below their purchased values). An asset-conversion or shiftability approach to liquidity management was popular in the United States following World War II. Today, with the continued development of securitization and secondary markets, it is much easier to sell bank assets to generate liquidity.

When passive asset conversions are used to meet a bank's expected cash outflows, the strategy is known as the anticipated-income theory. It can be viewed as a refinement or extension of the asset-conversion approach with emphasis on expected cash flows of both the bank and the borrower. From the bank's perspective, this approach led to the development in the 1950s of amortized loans and staggered or spaced investment maturities.

In the early 1960s, with the full development of the federal-funds market and the effective introduction of the negotiable certificate of deposit (CD), banks began to focus on liabilities for liquidity and profitable expansion of their balance sheets. Under this approach, known as **liability management** (LM), banks actively acquire deposit and nondeposit debt, called **purchased funds,** in domestic and international money markets. Box 7-1 presents a glossary of the key instruments of liability management. In contrast to stored liquidity, which is generated internally, LM represents an external source of funds that critically depends on a bank's creditworthiness and reputation. When a bank's financial soundness is in question, **volatile liabilities** disappear quickly. The major contribution of liability management has been to give bankers greater flexibility in managing their balance sheets and to force them to think about both sides of the balance sheet as potential instruments of liquidity management. Even more broadly, it has forced bankers to think about the coordinated financial management of their entire balance sheets—asset-liability management (ALM, chapter 5).

To summarize, liquidity management and, in a broader sense, modern bank financial management have evolved to the current state of ALM and securitization by progressing through the following stages:

- Commercial-loan theory or real-bills doctrine (1920s and earlier)
- Asset-conversion or shiftability approach (second half of 1940s)
- Anticipated-income theory (1950s)
- Liability management (late 1960s and early 1970s)
- Asset-liability management and securitization (mid-1970s to present)

LIQUIDITY NEEDS AND RISKS

Banks need liquidity in part to meet their customers' liquidity requirements (e.g., as illustrated by the case of New York securities firms following the stock market crash of 1987). Banks' customers can meet their liquidity needs by

- Withdrawing funds they have on deposit with the bank (i.e., utilizing their existing net cash flows)
- Drawing down established lines of credit
- Establishing new credit facilities
- Selling assets

Only in the case of a severe liquidity crisis or corporate restructuring do businesses want to resort to selling assets.

The operation of the market for commercial paper (CP), which is characterized by orderly exit, is a good example of how major corporations meet their liquidity needs with the help of banks. An important characteristic of the CP market is the use of bank backup or standby lines of credit to support CP issuers. To minimize **liquidity risks** and costs of financial distress, issuers of CP can take several steps. When a firm cannot roll over its commercial paper, which is simply a short-term corporate

BOX 7-1

THE INSTRUMENTS OF LIABILITY MANAGEMENT

Federal funds are excess reserves traded among banks. They are unsecured advances of immediately available funds from excess balances in reserve accounts held at Federal Reserve Banks. A bank that needs liquidity buys Fed funds whereas the counterparty sells Fed funds. The typical maturity is "overnight," or 24 hours.

A *repurchase agreement* (RP or repo) is a (secured) contract to sell and subsequently repurchase securities at a specified price and date (usually overnight). A bank that needs funds does a repo whereas the supplier of funds does a *reverse repo*.

A *negotiable certificate of deposit* (NCD, or simply CD) is a receipt for a time deposit with a face value of $100,000 or more (usually $1 million or more), which can be sold before maturity in the secondary market. Institutional investors dominate the market for these "wholesale" CDs. Although fixed-rate NCDs are the most common, floating-rate and zero-coupon NCDs are available. Typical maturities are in the range of 30–90 days.

A *consumer CD* is a "retail" version of an NCD without the negotiable option, because a secondary market does not exist. These small-denomination instruments impose penalties for early withdrawal.

A *brokered deposit* refers to a CD purchased by a small investor from a broker acting as a two-way agent for (1) depositors seeking high rates of interest and (2) banks and thrifts seeking funds. As long as the original-issue CD is less than $100,000, it is protected by federal deposit insurance, assuming it is issued by an insured bank or thrift. The broker pools the funds of small investors into bundles of less than $100,000 and sells the funds to banks/thrifts for a commission. The investors receive a "safekeeping certificate" from the broker, which usually is a securities broker/dealer such as Merrill Lynch.

A *Eurodollar CD* is a CD issued by a U.S. bank branch located outside the United States. Almost all Euro CDs are issued in London at rates tied to the London Interbank Offered Rate, or LIBOR. An active secondary market for large Eurodollar CDs exists. (A Eurodollar is a dollar deposit in a bank or branch outside the United States.)

A *money-market demand account (MMDA)* is a savings account designed to compete with money-market mutual funds and money-market accounts offered by securities firms. They are classified as savings accounts rather than transaction accounts because of rules that permit no more than six preauthorized, automatic, or other transfers per month, of which no more than three may be checks.

A *global CD* is a foreign CD sold by a domestic bank. The investor earns the foreign CD rate marked up or down depending on the exchange rate at the CD's maturity. For example, you invest $10,000 in a one-year foreign CD at 15 percent when the exchange rate is 4 or 0.25 (40,000 in the foreign currency). If the exchange rate in one year is 3 or 0.33, you earn 53 percent (before taxes and transactions costs); however, if the exchange rate is 5 or 0.20, you actually lose 8 percent or $800 as you recoup only $9,200.

Individual retirement accounts (IRAs) are personal retirement accounts that allow qualifying individuals to set aside a portion of their annual income on a tax-deferred basis. These accounts permit banks to attract longer-term sources of funds from conservative investors.

Commercial paper (bank-related) is a short-term, unsecured debt instrument issued by a bank holding company or a nonbank subsidiary, but not issued by the bank itself. Maturities range from 2–270 days, with under 30 days being the most active maturity segment.

Notes and debentures are unsecured promises to pay issued by banks or bank holding companies. They provide longer-term sources of funds and frequently are issued as a source of Tier-2 or debt capital (see chapters 13–14).

Volatile liabilities are defined by the FDIC as the sum of large-denomination time deposits, foreign-office deposits, federal funds purchased, securities sold under agreements to repurchase, and other borrowings.

IOU, it draws on its lines of credit to pay the maturing debt. If the firm's liquidity crisis continues, then it will resort to selling assets to pay off the holders of its paper. Box 7-2 presents an interesting description of Chrysler's orderly exit from the CP market during the years 1990 to 1993.

Because deposit withdrawals and borrowing activities occur on a regular basis (e.g., daily for funds-using activities such as check writing and wire transfers but usually less frequently for borrowing, except for daily federal-funds sales, overdraft accounts, and active lines of credit), banks must be prepared to meet these needs on a daily, and sometimes hourly, basis (e.g., daylight overdrafts). If the expected inflows from loans and deposits are not adequate to cover expected uses of funds (i.e., new loans, credit draws, and deposit withdrawals), then the bank has a liquidity need. The severity of the problem is defined by the size of the discrepancy between the sources and uses of funds. To repair a shortfall of funds, banks must either draw down their inventories of stored liquidity at a rate faster than they had planned or purchase funds in the marketplace at a greater volume than planned. The Federal Reserve, through its discount window, offers liquidity to member banks for "adjustment," "seasonal," and "extended" credit needs. In the case of the stock market crash of 1987, the Fed was acting in a different capacity, as a lender of last resort, something it did not do after the stock market crash of 1929, resulting in a prolonged economic disaster.

The risks of liquidity management have price, quantity, and reputational effects. Price, or interest-rate risk, focuses on the price at which assets can be sold and the rate at which liabilities can be acquired. For example, as described in the Chrysler case, Chrysler did not want to pay a premium for funds. The quantity factor focuses on whether or not assets exist that can be sold (Chrysler had assets to sell) and whether or not funds can be acquired in the marketplace at any cost. To practice active liability management, a bank must maintain its creditworthiness and its reputation in the money and deposit markets. A bank that doesn't will have to "pay up" for funds (i.e., pay an additional risk premium) or may not even be able

---

BOX 7-2

CHRYSLER CORPORATION'S ORDERLY EXIT FROM THE MARKET FOR COMMERCIAL PAPER[4]

At year-end 1989, Chrysler Financial had $10.1 billion of commercial paper (CP) outstanding, equity of $2.8 billion, and total assets of $30.1 billion, for a capital ratio of 9.3 percent. In 1990, its commercial paper was downgraded from P-2 to P-3 and subsequently to N.P. (Not Prime), and its long-term bond rating was lowered from Baa to Ba. Under these conditions, Chrysler Financial's commercial paper was not attractive. Rather than pay a premium to borrow in the CP market, it sought other sources of financing. By year-end 1990, Chrysler had only $1.1 billion of CP outstanding, a reduction of $9 billion, or nearly one-third the book value of the firm's assets. How did Chrysler handle its liquidity crisis?

Chrysler Financial's first step was to draw on its bank lines of credit. It borrowed $1.1 billion under its parent company's committed bank lines to ease the immediate cash shortfall. Beyond that it engaged in an aggressive program of asset sales and securitization. Proceeds from the sales of receivables in 1990 were $18.3 billion. Total assets shrank by 18 percent to $24.7 billion, and its capital ratio rose to 11.3 percent. The company continued the asset sales strategy to repay maturing debt of $3.6 billion in 1991 and $3 billion in 1992.

[4] This description draws on Schnure [1994].

to obtain funds. Moreover, a bank that is unexpectedly heavy into the "street" for funds will generate suspicion about its unusual need for liquidity and risk tarnishing its reputation. To avoid raising such doubts, some banks maintain a presence in money markets even if they don't need funds.

MODERN LIQUIDITY PROBLEMS: BASKETBALL TO BAILOUT

During the banking collapse of the 1930s, deposit runs were characterized by long lines of bank customers waiting and hoping to recover their funds. Since the advent of federal deposit insurance in the United States (1933), such scenes involving federally insured banks[5] have been virtually nonexistent. In contrast, for large banks, silent or electronic runs, which are invisible, still make news headlines, but without the pictures of long lines of depositors. Although many small commercial banks (and thrift institutions) failed in record numbers during the 1980s, the strength of the federal government's guarantee behind deposit insurance permitted these zombie institutions to avoid deposit runs and to stay in business longer than they should have. These bailouts were not costless, however, because both the FSLIC and the FDIC went bankrupt. The FDIC has since recovered from its de facto insolvency. This section describes how liquidity problems can range from a minor embarrassment resulting from a high school basketball tournament to a crisis so severe that it requires a federal bailout (Continental Illinois in 1984).

Winning Basketball and a Liquidity Crisis for a Community Bank

At the embarrassment end of the spectrum, consider the experience of Robert Bacon, president of the First National Bank of Browning, Montana. On March 5, 1989, his bank virtually ran out of cash. Next to your bank being declared insolvent, can you think of a more embarrassing situation for a banker? According to the OCC and the FDIC, there was no record that this had ever happened to a U.S. bank since the FDIC was established. There was, of course, a federal investigation. It revealed that the cause of the bank's liquidity crisis was the local high school's success in a state basketball tournament. As a result of that victory, weekly paychecks were issued early to government employees on the nearby Blackfoot Indian Reservation and to many of the town's 1,700 residents. Because most of them were planning to watch the basketball team, the Browning Indians, play 200 miles south in Missouri, they wanted to cash their checks. As a result, it did not take long for the only bank and two local check-cashing stores to run out of cash. By 2:10 P.M., First National's tellers were left with only small change in their drawers. Not only was the bank caught out of cash, but the town was without liquidity too. One merchant reported, "Business was way down because nobody in town had money until the bank put out a sign at 11:00 the next morning saying they would cash checks." Another merchant said, "The whole town left for the game and they took the money."

---

[5] It is important to distinguish between federal and state deposit-insurance programs. In the 1980s, the thrift crises associated with state-insured S&Ls in Maryland and Ohio generated deposit runs similar to those of the 1930s. Photographs and videotape of deposit runs made the evening news and the front pages of newspapers and magazines.

President Bacon's reaction to the incident was:

> We can't always plan ahead because the money comes from the Federal Reserve branch office in Helena, and that's 400 miles away. They won't come here more than once a week. We've run low a couple of times before, but never out.[6]

The lesson here is that small banks, especially those in one- or two-bank towns in isolated areas, need to keep in close contact with major employers in their towns so that they can be informed about changes in payroll schedules. Normally, banks can receive funds quickly through the Fed or correspondent banks, but Browning's isolated location prevented such a remedy. First National, a $10 million bank, was able to begin cashing checks at 11:00 the next morning only after Mr. Bacon had driven 130 miles to Great Falls for some cash. As of Friday morning, Mr. Bacon noted that the bank had received a few calls from worried depositors but no accounts had been closed. The OCC's regional administrator in Portland, Oregon, indicated that, "If this happens again, we can conduct an examination to suggest changes in the planning process." Alternatively, since First National is now paying for Fed services, perhaps it can obtain more frequent deliveries of cash to Browning. Although First National's green-out was indeed an isolated incident, it clearly points out the importance of planning for liquidity needs. Thus, the success of the high school basketball team was not the true cause of the liquidity crisis; the real cause was the bank's failure to maintain an information flow with the town's major employer. With such communication, First National could have averted its liquidity crisis.

And Now for the Rest of the Story

In 1983, 48 FDIC-insured banks experienced the ultimate cash-out—insolvency. One of those banks was, you guessed it, First National Bank of Browning. On November 10, 1983, the OCC declared the bank insolvent, and the FDIC arranged a deposit payoff for the bank's 4,000 depositors. Because the FDIC's disbursement of $9,675,000 was about $2,000,000 shy of the bank's total deposits of $11,602,000, some uninsured depositors in this small bank did not get paid in full. A comparison with the treatment of uninsured depositors in Continental Illinois and other big banks points out one of the ugly aspects of the FDIC's handling of smaller failed banks—discrimination against uninsured depositors in those banks.

Because there wasn't a state basketball tournament in Montana on the day First National bit the dust, what could have caused its demise? Perhaps the Browning Indians had an important football game on that Friday in November. The FDIC's news release on the failure did not mention anything about the cause of the bank's demise. However, it did mention that the FDIC did not receive any acceptable bids for a P&A transaction, and therefore the bank had to be handled as a deposit payoff.

Continental's Liquidity Crisis: An Electronic Cash-Out

During the spring and summer of 1984, the liquidity crisis and subsequent bailout of Continental Illinois National Bank and its holding company, Continental Illinois Corporation, dominated the financial news.[7] Continental Illinois had a reputation

---

[6] As reported by *The New York Times,* in *The Atlanta Constitution,* March 21, 1980.

[7] Continental Illinois was bailed out by the FDIC in 1984 and later successfully rejuvenated as Continental Bank. In 1994, Continental was acquired by BankAmerica.

as an aggressive lender. In addition, it (and other large banks) had purchased (what turned out to be) bad energy loans from Penn Square Bank of Oklahoma City, a 1982 failure. As a result, Continental lost both financial and reputational capital,[8] which eventually shook the confidence of large uninsured creditors and precipitated a run on the bank.

The run on Continental was a silent but deadly one—an electronic one in which billions of dollars of hot money "impulsed" out of the bank. For the seven-day period ended May 17, 1984, which was the height of the crisis, Continental required an infusion of $8 billion to stop its electronic hemorrhaging. Continental's liquidity crisis represents, at the extreme, the risks of aggressive liability management. Without a substantial foundation of core deposits (i.e., stable local deposits), Continental was vulnerable to an electronic or silent run. Once the marketplace, in the form of uninsured creditors, lost confidence in Continental's creditworthiness, the stage was set for the electronic run to begin. The liquidity crisis, collapse, and bailout of Continental in 1984 caused liability managers to rethink their assumptions regarding the availability of purchased funds. Prior to Continental's problems, the working assumption was that funds would always be available, especially in the international arena. However, even a guarantee by the FDIC of all of Continental's liabilities could not stop the silent electronic run on the bank.

Bank of New England's Liquidity Crisis

On January 6, 1991, the OCC declared the Bank of New England (and two affiliated banks) insolvent. The story of its failure and liquidity crisis goes like this (Clarke [1991] and Lohr [1991] provide details): Through aggressive lending in the 1980s, Bank of New England developed a large concentration of commercial real estate loans—ventures that seemed like positive net-present-value projects at the time. In 1989, however, as the New England economy turned sour, cash flows from the projects dried up, and the bank's loan quality, earnings, and stock price plunged. Institutional providers of funds such as mutual funds, pension funds, corporations, and other banks began a silent run on the bank. The runoff in liabilities forced Bank of New England into the Fed's discount window. To get out of the Fed's window, the bank had to sell assets, cut employees, and draw on Treasury tax-and-loan accounts. As the economy continued to deteriorate in 1990, the situation worsened. Press coverage of the bank's problems (e.g., the announcement of up to a $450 million loss for the fourth quarter of 1990) and of the insolvency of a private insurance fund in Rhode Island worried small (insured) depositors to the extent they began withdrawing money. In two days (January 4–5), the bank lost almost $1 billion in deposits. On January 6 (Sunday), the bank was closed, opening the next day as a bridge bank under the supervision of the FDIC.

In his statement before the Senate Banking Committee on January 9, 1991, (former) Comptroller Clarke stressed that his office had closely supervised Bank of New England for almost two years before its failure. The supervision included installing new management, asset sales and cost reductions, suspension of dividends, and attempts to recapitalize the bank. He concluded that the salvage attempt had failed because of "the severity of the economic downturn in New England." Nevertheless, the original managers put the bank in a vulnerable position by betting too heavily on commercial real-estate loans. A more diversified

---

[8] Continental's liquidity crisis was a watershed in liability management because it destroyed the notion that large banks could always purchase funds in the marketplace without maintaining reputational capital.

loan portfolio would have given the bank more time; whether it would have saved it can't be answered. A report by the General Accounting Office (GAO [1991]) concluded that Bank of New England failed because of three factors:

1. Liberal lending practices
2. Poorly controlled growth
3. Concentration in commercial real-estate loans in a severely declining regional economy

Should the OCC have stopped the Bank of New England from concentrating its loan portfolio in commercial real estate? No, because in the final analysis, we do not want bank regulators determining how credit is allocated. What we do want is a deposit-insurance system that prevents high-risk banks from being subsidized by low-risk ones and ensures that the costs of bank failures are not foisted on taxpayers.

THE TRADE-OFF BETWEEN LIQUIDITY AND PROFITABILITY

To meet their day-to-day liquidity requirements, banks must hold some non-earning assets in the form of cash or cash equivalents. By their very nature, these assets reduce a bank's profitability (i.e., they are nonearning or low-yielding). Therefore, banks want to hold a minimum amount of such assets and still be able to meet their liquidity requirements. Increased competition and the removal of deposit interest-rate ceilings have reinforced the need for banks to minimize their stocks of nonearning (and low-yielding) assets. Table 7-1 shows the amounts of non-interest-earning assets (as a percentage of average consolidated assets at year-end 1995) held by commercial banks by asset-size class. The large percentage amount of total non-interest-earning assets held by the 10 largest banks can be explained by the revaluation gains associated with their off-balance-sheet activities (OBSAs). Nevertheless, because larger banks play bigger roles in clearing and settling payments, which require substantial amounts of liquidity (e.g., cash and due from banks), an inverse relation still exists between bank size and the relative level of non-interest-earning assets after excluding the OBSA revaluation gains.

TABLE 7-1 Non-Interest-Earning Assets Held by Commercial Banks by Asset-Size Class (as a percentage of average consolidated assets)

	Non-Interest-Earning Assets/Assets		
	OBSAs Gains	*Other*	*Total*
Ten largest banks by assets	10.77%	12.21%	22.98%
Banks ranked 11th to 100th	0.50	11.18	11.69
Banks ranked 101st to 1,000th	0.05	9.83	9.87
Banks not ranked among the 1,000 largest	0.00	8.30	8.30
All reporting banks	2.90	10.26	13.52

Note: The first column refers to revaluation gains on off-balance-sheet activities (OBSAs). Before 1994 the netted value of OBSAs appeared in "trading account securities" if a gain and in "other non-interest-bearing liabilities" if a loss. The second column reflects traditional nonearning assets as cash and due and required reserves.

Source: Federal Reserve Bulletin (June 1996), pp. 495–505.

Liquid Assets and Liquidity Premiums

By their nature, **liquid assets** have minimal amounts of interest-rate risk and credit risk, which limit the reward they generate for risk bearing. Specifically, all other things being equal, short-term assets have less credit risk than long-term assets. Additionally, because market values of short-term assets are less sensitive to changes in interest rates, liquid assets do not embody much interest-rate risk. A further consideration is the normal upward shape (positive slope) of the yield curve with short-term rates lower than with long-term ones. The exception to this situation is when the yield curve is negatively sloped. Under this rate structure, short-term investors get the best of both worlds in the form of low risk and high return. Historically, however, because the normal slope of the yield curve has been positive, this phenomenon has been a short-lived one.

A liquid asset is also characterized by a well-established market in which it can be traded. Given the low risk profile of such assets, their market and book values show little divergence. Accordingly, sellers of liquid assets face little or no capital loss (price depreciation). Three types of liquid assets that banks hold include

- Federal funds sold (including repurchase agreements)
- Interbank deposits (interest-bearing balances only)
- Treasury securities

Table 7-2 shows that these liquid assets vary with bank size. In general, smaller banks hold more liquid assets than larger banks, which is especially true for U.S. Treasury securities. In contrast, interbank, interest-bearing deposits vary inversely with bank size.

Table 7-3 presents one aspect of the trade-off between liquidity and profitability by comparing the effective interest rates on federal funds sold and U.S. government securities. In addition, for comparison, the effective interest rates on loans and leases are included, where gross and net interest rates are shown. The net rate is adjusted for provision for loan losses (PLL). Panel A shows that for 1995 all banks could gain 92 basis points, on average, by holding government securities rather than federal funds, and that they could gain an additional 220 basis points, on average, by making loans and leases rather than buying government securities. For 1985, when the level of interest rates was higher, the corresponding premiums were, on average, 132 basis points and 138 basis points, respectively. In general, liquidity-risk premiums increase with the level of interest rates, as reflected by the premium of 92 basis points for 1995 compared to 132 basis points in 1985. Note, however, that for riskier lending, the spread was actually lower (220 basis points

	Percentage of Assets				
Assets	*10 Largest*	*11–100*	*101–1,000*	*Under Top 1,000*	*All Banks*
Federal funds sold[a]	3.20%	4.52%	3.91%	3.92%	3.93%
Interbank deposits[b]	4.25	2.47	0.94	0.67	2.23
Treasury securities	2.03	4.82	6.47	9.19	5.25
Total	9.48%	11.81%	11.32%	13.78%	11.41%

TABLE 7-2 Liquid Assets Held Vary according to Bank Size, December 31, 1995

[a]Includes repurchase agreements. [b]Interest-bearing balances only.
Source: Federal Reserve Bulletin (June 1996), pp. 495–505.

TABLE 7-3 The Trade-Off between Liquidity and Profitability as Captured by Effective Interest Rates and Bank Size

Panel A. 1995 (the average three-month T-bill rate was 5.49 percent in secondary market)

Assets	10 Largest	11–100	101–1,000	Under Top 1,000	All Banks
Federal funds sold[a]	5.20%	5.91%	5.45%	5.97%	5.63%
Securities	7.54	6.38	6.25	6.11	6.55
Loans & leases, gross	8.84	9.10	9.47	9.82	9.26
Net of PLL	8.62	8.49	8.78	9.41	8.75

Panel B. 1985 (the average three-month T-bill rate was 7.48 percent in secondary market)

Assets	10 Largest	11–100	101–1,000	Under Top 1,000	All Banks
Federal funds sold[a]	7.72%	8.16%	8.22%	8.26%	8.12%
Securities	9.95	9.06	9.15	9.64	9.44
Loans & leases, gross	11.91	11.61	11.89	12.61	11.98
Net of PLL	10.74	10.58	10.89	11.11	10.82

[a]Includes repurchase agreements.

Source: Federal Reserve Bulletin (June 1996), pp. 495–505.

for 1995 versus 138 basis points for 1985), because the PLL adjustment for 1985 was higher (116 basis points) than in 1995 (51 basis points). The important point is that when interest rates are higher, borrowers have greater difficulty making loan and lease payments.

THE FUNCTIONS OF BANK LIQUIDITY

Because a liquid asset is one that is easily converted into cash with little or no capital loss (price depreciation), let's define *bank liquidity management* as the process of generating funds to meet contractual or relationship obligations at reasonable prices at all times. New loan demand, existing loan commitments, and deposit withdrawals are the basic contractual or relationship obligations that banks must meet. Effective liquidity management by a bank serves five important functions:

- It demonstrates to the marketplace that the bank is safe and therefore capable of repaying its borrowings. It provides the confidence factor.
- It enables the bank to meet its prior loan commitments, whether formal (i.e., legally binding) or informal. This function is an integral part of the bank-customer relationship; call it the relationship factor. An important aspect of this is the provision of credit or backup liquidity facilities for customers. The strength of relationships determines, in part, the extent to which banks will go to bat for customers in providing them with liquidity. Because a bank does not want to harm existing strong relationships or inhibit the growth of promising new ones, it wants to provide liquidity for its customers. By the same token, a bank can send a signal to customers with weak relationships by not providing for their liquidity needs, assuming the bank does not have a legally binding commitment. The experience of Citibank following the stock market crash of 1987 illustrates the role of banks in providing relationship liquidity—with the discount window as a safety net.
- It enables the bank to avoid the unprofitable sale of assets. This function permits banks to avoid the sale of assets at fire-sale prices, as opposed to going-concern values, to generate funds.

- It lowers the size of the default-risk premium the bank must pay for funds. This function, like the previous one, focuses on the reasonable-prices aspect of the definition of bank liquidity management. Banks with strong balance sheets will be perceived by the marketplace as being liquid, or safe. Such banks will be able to buy funds at risk premiums reflecting their perceived creditworthiness. For example, think of the market for negotiable CDs as being tiered on the basis of strong, average, or weak balance sheets, with corresponding CD rates below, equal to, or above the going market rate.

- It enables the bank to avoid abusing the privilege of borrowing at the Fed's discount window. This function relates to how frequently and extensively the bank uses the discount window. Because the discount rate is an administered rate set below market rates, banks could arbitrage the discount window without Fed surveillance. Sound liquidity management enables banks to avoid abusing their privilege of borrowing at the discount window. Excessive use of such borrowings could lead to increased Fed surveillance or reduced confidence in the marketplace or both.

LIABILITY MANAGEMENT: THE COMPOSITION AND COST OF BANK LIABILITIES

This section describes the composition and cost of bank liabilities and presents evidence regarding liability management and its counterpart, the availability of core deposits for funding bank assets.

The Composition of Bank Liabilities (Sources of Funds)

Table 7-4 shows the composition of bank liabilities (as a percentage of average consolidated assets for 1985 and 1995) for all insured commercial banks. The appendix to this chapter shows these data for four bank size classes. The data can be summarized by focusing on the two key sources of bank funding:

- **Core deposits** (measured in Table 7-4 and the appendix) as the sum of interest-bearing deposits in domestic offices minus large time deposits in domestic offices plus domestic demand deposits)

TABLE 7-4 The Use of Core Deposits and Managed Liabilities Varies with Bank Size (as a percentage of average consolidated assets for 1995 and 1985)

	1995		1985	
Bank Size Class	*Core*	*MLs*	*Core*	*MLs*
Ten largest banks by assets	25.7%	47.9%	26.0%	59.3%
Banks ranked 11th to 100th	53.0	35.6	46.8	41.8
Banks ranked 101st to 1,000th	64.5	24.7	65.3	25.9
Banks not ranked in top 1,000	76.9	12.0	76.4	13.7
All banks	55.7	32.1	53.3	35.5

Note: Core = core deposits and ML = managed or volatile liabilities. Using the data from the appendix to this chapter, managed liabilities are approximately equal to the sum of deposits in foreign offices, large time deposits, other interest-bearing liabilities, and Fed funds purchased + RPs. Domestic core deposits equal deposits in domestic offices less large time deposits plus domestic demand deposits.

Source: Federal Reserve Bulletin (June 1995), pp. 559–569, and (June 1996), pp.496–505.

- **Managed liabilities** (measured in Table 7-1 and the appendix) as the sum of interest-bearing deposits in foreign offices plus large time deposits in domestic offices plus federal-funds purchases (including RPs plus other interest-bearing liabilities)

Managed liabilities correspond to the definition of volatile liabilities given in Box 7-1. Core deposits are coveted because of their lower cost and greater stability. If a bank lacks core deposits, then it has little choice but to manage its liabilities and purchase funds. Table 7-4 shows that these two sources of funds vary substantially by bank size. The main point to be gleaned from these data is the strong direct relationship between bank size and the use of managed liabilities, or the mirror image of this, the strong inverse relationship between bank size and the availability of core deposits. The most dramatic difference is between the 10 largest banks and the numerous community banks not ranked among the 1,000 largest banks. The largest banks fund only one out of every four dollars in assets with core deposits, compared to three out of every four dollars for community banks.

Sources of Bank Funds: Interest-Bearing and Non-Interest-Bearing Liabilities

Bank liabilities can be classified into two broad categories: **interest-bearing** and **non-interest-bearing** (see the appendix to this chapter for data by bank size class). Interest-bearing liabilities consists of three groups: deposits, federal funds purchased plus RPs, and other liabilities. Table 7-5 shows selected components of bank interest-bearing liabilities for the years 1985 and 1995.

1. Deposits. Although interest-bearing deposits in foreign offices are lumped into a single category, interest-bearing deposits in domestic offices, the major source of funding for all banks except the 10 largest, consist of four kinds:

   a. Interest-bearing checking accounts, consisting of NOW accounts, super-NOW accounts, and other checkable deposits that earn interest. The acronym NOW stands for "negotiable order of withdrawal," a checking account that pays interest. As a source of funds, these accounts are most important to community banks; in 1995, they amounted to 12.4 percent of total assets, up from 8.1 percent in 1985.

   b. Savings accounts, including **money-market demand accounts** (MMDAs). Although MMDAs were designed to compete with money-market accounts such as Merrill Lynch's cash management account (CMA), they are not fully competitive because they are classified as a savings account, with restrictive check-writing privileges (three per month). Below the ten largest banks, savings accounts support one dollar for every five dollars in bank assets, as shown in Table 7-5.

   c. Small time deposits consist of all time deposits under $100,000. Like savings accounts, these funds are an important source of financing for community banks.

   d. Large time deposits, or large denomination CDs, consist of all time accounts with denominations of $100,000 or more. These CDs, which are negotiable instruments, typically trade in blocks of $1 million or more. The interesting thing about these data is the inverse relationship between bank size and the relative decline in the use of large time deposits as a source of funds for all banks. Although the use of interest-bearing deposits in foreign offices increases with bank size, outside of the 100 largest banks, they are not a major source of funding for U.S. commercial banks. Since 1985, however, large banks have substantially reduced their reliance on foreign deposits.

2. Federal funds purchased and repurchase agreements (RPs or repos) are interest-bearing liabilities that are not covered, de jure at least, by federal deposit insurance. Repurchase agreements are secured transactions backed up by the underlying security to be repurchased, whereas federal-funds transactions are unsecured agreements backed only by the reputation and creditworthiness of the borrower. Both types of contracts are typically overnight transactions, although term agreements can be arranged.

TABLE 7-5 Selected Components of Bank Interest-Bearing Liabilities by Bank Size, 1985 and 1995

Panel A. Savings Accounts

Size Class	1995	(1985)
Ten largest banks by assets	10.6%	(8.8%)
Banks ranked 11 to 100	18.8	(14.7)
Banks ranked 101 to 1,000	20.7	(21.5)
Banks not ranked among the largest 1,000	20.4	(21.1)
All banks	17.5	(16.4)

Panel B. Small Time Deposits

Size Class	1995	(1985)
Ten largest banks by assets	4.0%	(4.6%)
Banks ranked 11 to 100	14.2	(11.4)
Banks ranked 101 to 1,000	21.1	(19.9)
Banks not ranked among the largest 1,000	30.1	(32.0)
All banks	16.1	(16.8)

Panel C. Large Time Deposits

Size Class	1995	(1985)
Ten largest banks by assets	2.2%	(8.1%)
Banks ranked 11 to 100	5.5	(12.4)
Banks ranked 101 to 1,000	7.5	(13.6)
Banks not ranked among the largest 1,000	8.9	(11.5)
All banks	5.8	(11.4)

Panel D. Deposits in Foreign Offices

Size Class	1995	(1985)
Ten largest banks by assets	28.4%	(34.6%)
Banks ranked 11 to 100	8.1	(11.8)
Banks ranked 101 to 1,000	1.7	(2.0)
Banks not ranked among the largest 1,000	0.1	(0.1)
All banks	10.3	(12.3)

Panel E. Federal-Funds Purchases and Repos

Size Class	1995	(1985)
Ten largest banks by assets	6.2%	(7.1%)
Banks ranked 11 to 100	11.4	(13.1)
Banks ranked 101 to 1,000	8.3	(7.9)
Banks not ranked among the largest 1,000	1.8	(1.5)
All banks	7.7	(7.7)

Source: Federal Reserve Bulletin (June 1995), pp. 559–569, and (June 1996), pp. 496–505.

3. Other interest-bearing liabilities include, among other items, notes and debentures, which are longer-term sources of funds issued mainly by larger banks. The 100 largest banks fund about 10 percent of their assets with other liabilities, compared to less than 2 percent for community banks.

Non-Interest-Bearing Liabilities

Non-interest-bearing liabilities are the other major component of bank liabilities. They consist of two categories: domestic demand deposits and other non-interest-bearing liabilities. Domestic demand deposits were at one time the major source of bank funding. For example, on December 30, 1950, demand deposits were 70 percent of total bank deposits and 64 percent of total bank assets.[9] By year-end 1995, however, domestic demand deposits supported only 12.7 percent of total assets for all banks, down from 15.5 percent in 1985. Since other non-interest-bearing liabilities include mainly demand deposits in foreign offices, the size of this category varies directly with bank size. For example, the 10 largest banks funded 21.3 percent of their assets from this source in 1995, similar to the figure for 1985 (20.9%).

Combining the interest-bearing (IB) and non-interest-bearing (NIB) liabilities of banks, Table 7-6 shows how total liabilities vary across bank size (as a percentage of average consolidated assets). As bank size increases, the ratio of total debt to total assets increases. Because the balance of bank funding comes from equity capital, this relationship also captures the inverse relation between bank size and capital adequacy, for example, the 10 largest banks had an average capital-to-assets ratio of 6.3 percent (100% − 93.7%) compared to 13.6 percent (100% − 86.4%) for the average community bank. The amount of capital a bank needs depends, of course, on its risk exposure. Bank capital and its management are covered in part 5 of this book (chapters 15 and 16).

The Interest Cost of Bank Liabilities (effective interest rates)

Table A7-2 in the appendix to this chapter shows the effective interest rates paid by banks for interest-bearing liabilities for the years 1985 and 1995. Because these years were relatively high (1985) and low (1995) on the interest-rate cycle, the effective rates are lower in 1995. A fundamental point to keep in mind when analyzing interest rates in financial markets is that competition drives deposit rates up and loan rates down. In a perfectly competitive market, the spread between lending and borrowing rates would be minimized. To the extent that international financial markets are more competitive than domestic markets (e.g., because of less regulation), higher deposit rates and lower loan rates are expected in international markets than in domestic markets, all other things being equal.

TABLE 7-6 Bank Debt-to-Asset Ratios by Asset Size, 1995 (as a percentage of average consolidated assets)

Size Class	Total Liabilities (IB + NIB)	Total Capital
Ten largest banks by assets	93.7% (64.3% + 29.3%)	6.3%
Banks ranked 11 to 100	92.5 (72.9 + 19.6)	7.5
Banks ranked 101 to 1,000	91.6 (74.8 + 16.8)	8.4
Banks not ranked among the largest 1,000	86.4 (76.2 + 14.2)	13.6
All banks	92.2 (71.9 + 20.3)	7.8

Note: IB = interest-bearing liabilities; NIB = non-interest-bearing liabilities; and total capital/assets = 1 − IB/A − NIB/A.

Source: Federal Reserve Bulletin (June 1995), pp. 559–569, and (June 1996), pp. 496–505.

[9] *Annual Report of the Federal Deposit Insurance Corporation* (December 31, 1950), Table 107, pp. 238–239.

1. *Foreign versus domestic cost of funds.* Because only the 100 largest U.S. commercial banks are major players in raising interest-bearing deposits in foreign offices, let's focus on the cost of funds for these banks. In 1995, the spread between interest-bearing deposits in foreign offices and those in domestic offices for the 10 largest U.S. banks was 265 basis points (6.07% − 3.42%), higher than the 206 basis-point spread in 1985 despite the decline in the level of interest rates (Panel B, appendix Table A7-2). In addition to competitive conditions, the greater reduction in inflation in the United States compared to other countries (except in Japan) played a role here. The foreign-domestic spread for banks ranked 11th to 100th was smaller at 229 basis points in 1995, up from 147 basis points in 1985. The higher cost of funds for the 10 largest banks suggests that they might have to pay up to attract a larger volume of funds.

2. *The cost of core deposits versus managed liabilities.* All other things being equal, core deposits should be less expensive than managed liabilities. Less competition, more regulation, and the payment of implicit interest are potential reasons for the lower explicit cost of core deposits. To illustrate the relationship between the interest cost of core deposits and managed liabilities, let's look at the interest rates paid by banks for savings deposits (including MMDAs), large denomination CDs, and federal funds purchased plus RPs. Savings deposits are the basic interest-bearing component of core, whereas large CDs and federal funds purchased plus RPs are the basic domestic components of managed liabilities. The average rates paid for these funds for all banks in 1995 and 1985 were

Type of Liability	1995	1985
Savings deposits (including MMDAs)	3.19%	5.28%
Large denomination CDs	5.47	8.73
Fed funds purchased + RPs	5.65	7.97

The higher interest cost of managed liabilities compared to core deposits holds across the four size classes shown in appendix Table A7-2.

3. *Transactions services as implicit interest.* The effective interest rate on other checkable deposits is substantially lower than the one for savings accounts (including MMDAs); for example, for 1995 the rates for all banks were 2.07 percent versus 3.19 percent. The basic difference between MMDAs, the major component of savings deposits, and other interest-bearing checking accounts is the unlimited check-writing privilege associated with demand deposits. One way to view the total interest paid on interest-bearing checking accounts is as the sum of explicit interest plus implicit interest, where implicit interest exists if the value of the transactions services provided exceeds the explicit fees paid for such services and the opportunity cost of minimum balances. The payment of implicit interest can be viewed as a subsidiary provided by the bank, a practice that was widespread in the past but is less common today as banks try to fully cost the services they provide. It is easy to understand that high-activity checking accounts are more costly to administrate and operate than low-activity accounts. The functional-cost data shown in Table 7-7 illustrate this point. For example, checking accounts had operating expenses (1994) in the range of 3.8 percent to 5.3 percent. In contrast, nonchecking accounts had operating expenses in the range of 0.3 percent to 0.95 percent. Because of the higher operating costs of checking accounts, banks require strong customer relationships before providing free checking (e.g., large minimum balances or greater usage of other bank products and services).

TABLE 7-7 The Interest and Operating Expenses of Bank Deposits, 1994

Panel A. Demand-Deposit Function

Bank Size	Total Operating Expense	Interest Expense	Total Expense
Deposits < $50 million	4.24%	1.13%	5.37%
$50 < D < $200	3.79	1.22	5.01
Deposits > $200	3.95	0.99	4.94

Panel B. Commercial Checking Accounts

Bank Size	Total Operating Expense (no interest expense)
Deposits < $50 million	4.68%
$50 < D < $200	2.70
Deposits > $200	3.86

Panel C. Personal Checking Accounts (including regular, special, and interest-bearing)

Bank Size	Total Operating Expense	Interest Expense	Total Expense
Deposits < $50 million	5.28%	1.45%	6.73%
$50 < D < $200	3.45	1.75	5.20
Deposits > $200	4.62	1.31	5.73

Panel D. Time-Deposit Function

Bank Size	Total Operating Expense	Interest Expense	Total Expense
Deposits < $50 million	0.81%	3.76%	4.57%
$50 < D < $200	0.79	3.75	4.54
Deposits > $200	0.94	3.55	4.49

Panel E. Large Certificates of Deposit ($100,000 or more)

Bank Size	Total Operating Expense	Interest Expense	Total Expense
Deposits < $50 million	0.29%	4.39%	4.68%
$50 < D < $200	0.29	4.32	4.61
Deposits > $200	0.39	4.21	4.60

Panel F. Individual Retirement Accounts (IRAs)

Bank Size	Total Operating Expense	Interest Expense	Total Expense
Deposits < $50 million	0.67%	4.43%	5.10%
$50 < D < $200	0.62	4.76	5.38
Deposits > $200	0.78	4.84	5.62

Note: The number of banks in each size group varies with the type of account analyzed. The maximum numbers are 52 banks (small), 116 banks (medium), and 41 banks (large).

Source: Functional Cost and Profit Analysis, National Average Report, 1994, Commercial Banks, Federal Reserve Bank of Boston, 1995.

A Bank's Weighted-Average, Marginal Cost of Funds

To make profitable asset-allocation decisions, bankers need to know their average cost of funds at the margin. This notion is identical to the weighted-average, marginal cost of capital (WAMCC) for a nonfinancial firm. Consider the simple fund-

TABLE 7-8	Computing a Bank's Weighted-Average, Marginal Cost of Funds				
Source of Funds	*% of Assets*	*Interest Cost +*	*Operating Cost =*	*Total Cost*	*Weighted Cost*
Checking accounts	20%	2%	5%	7%	1.4%
Saving accounts	40	4	1	5	2.0
CDs	30	6	0.5	6.5	1.95
Equity capital[a]	10	12	0.25	12.25	1.225
Weighted average	100	5	1.575	6.575	6.575

[a]Because equity capital is not an interest expense, the cost for this component is the shareholders' required rate of return. Also, the operating cost for equity capital assumes that the bank raises external equity; the expense is the issuing cost paid to investment bankers. Internal equity generated by the bank's retained earnings would not have this additional expense. In this case, the bank's weighted-average, marginal cost of funds would drop to 6.5 percent.

ing and cost structures shown for the hypothetical bank in Table 7-8. The total cost of each source of funding consists of the interest expense plus the operating expense. Each source of funds supports a proportion of the bank's balance sheet. These weights times the total marginal cost of each source of funds gives weighted total cost for each source. The sum of these weighted costs gives the bank's weighted-average, marginal cost of funds, which in this example is 6.575 percent. Suppose that the bank in this example used its interest rate on CDs as its marginal cost of funds. If it wanted a spread of 200 basis points on a loan, the bank would charge 8 percent for the loan. Based on its weighted-average, marginal cost of funds, its effective spread, however, would be only 1.425 percent.

Earning assets represent a bank's output. To price output effectively, businesses, including banks, need to know the effective cost of their inputs. For banks and other financial institutions, this means calculating their weighted-average, marginal cost of funds, and pricing loans accordingly.

Recapitulation

Understanding the interest cost of bank interest-bearing liabilities requires knowing, among other things, how international and domestic deposit markets differ, how core deposits differ from managed liabilities, how banks pay implicit interest, how account activity differs across various types of deposits, and how account activity affects bank operating expenses.

MEASURING BANK LIQUIDITY

Because liquidity can be either stored in a bank's balance sheet or purchased in the marketplace, we need two alternative measures of liquidity. Measuring stored liquidity is a bit easier because it does not involve the confidence factor as much as the ability to purchase funds in money markets does. Recall the words of former FDIC Chairman Seidman: "Our whole financial system runs on confidence and not much else when you get down to it. What we've learned is that when confidence erodes, it erodes very quickly." Banks engaged in liability management must maintain their creditworthiness and reputational capital in order to be able to tap domestic and international money markets. This section presents several ways to measure bank liquidity.

The Cash-Flow Approach: Sources and Uses of Funds

Comparing a bank's sources and uses of funds over the short run, say the next 30 days, provides a cash-flow measure of liquidity. The difference between the uses (liquid assets available over the next 30 days) and sources (short-term liabilities due over the next 30 days) represents a bank's liquidity position in terms of a surplus or a deficit (Darling [1991]). Although a surplus indicates a liquidity cushion, the bank must consider the opportunity cost of such a position. By the same token, the bank must consider the risk of running a liquidity deficit. Darling [1991] regards a surplus (as a percentage of total assets) of less than 3–5 percent as an early-warning signal.

To project a bank's liquidity needs, Darling suggests comparing its liquidity surplus or deficit with funding requirements over various time horizons, say 90 days. The idea is to forecast net new loans (new loans − maturing loans − loan sales), net deposit flows (inflows − outflows), and net flows from other assets and liabilities. The sum of these projected flows, added to the surplus or deficit at the beginning of the period, generates the liquidity position at the end of the horizon.

Large-Liability Dependence

Banks that engage in aggressive liability management can be described as having a "**large-liability dependence**" (LLD).[10] At the extreme, this dependence means a vulnerability to an electronic deposit run like Continental Illinois in 1984. Although various ways exist to measure LLD, Cates Consulting Analysts suggests the following formula:

$$LLD = \frac{\text{Large Liabilities} - \text{Temporary Investments}}{\text{Earning Assets} - \text{Temporary Investments}} \tag{7-2}$$

The ratio is a measure of the extent to which hot money supports the bank's basic earning assets. Because the numerator of equation (7-2) represents short-term, interest-sensitive funds supplied largely by institutions, a positive and high ratio implies some risk of illiquidity. How high is high? Peer-group analysis is used to set some norm or standard on which "high" can be based.[11] For the largest banks, an LLD ratio of 50 percent is not unusual. For the thousands of community banks in the United States that simply do not have many large liabilities, LLD is not a meaningful ratio. Moreover, because community banks frequently carry large amounts of temporary investments, their LLD ratios are negative. Thus, LLD is a relevant measure of liquidity risk only for larger banks.

Core Deposits to Assets

Because core deposits are explicitly insured funds gathered in local markets, they tend to be a stable source of financing for banks. Nevertheless, as the experience of the Bank of New England shows, once confidence in a bank is lost, even core

---

[10] See *Cates* [1984], pp. 80–84.

[11] To determine whether a given LLD ratio is manageable within a particular peer group, Cates [1984] proposes comparing it with the net interest margin (NIM) of the bank or its BHC. The crucial part of the test is the movement of the bank's NIM over the course of the interest-rate cycle. A stable bank with a high and stable NIM is viewed as being better able to handle the level of interest sensitivity implied by LLD.

deposits can run off. The ratio of core deposits to total assets varies inversely with bank size (Table 7-1).

Loans and Leases to Assets

Although the innovation of securitization has made bank loans more liquid, loans and leases have traditionally been viewed as the least liquid of bank earning assets. A bank with a high ratio of loans and leases to assets is viewed as being "loaned up," or relatively illiquid. In contrast, a low ratio indicates a liquid bank with excess lending capacity. How high is high and how low is low depends on peer-group comparisons. The industry average has been in the range of 55–60 over the past decade, with few banks outside the interval of 40–70 percent. In addition, the ratio tends to increase with bank size. Refinements to this traditional ratio would be to weight loans by maturity or by how easily they can be securitized or sold without recourse. Short-term loans, and loans that can be sold, are more liquid, all other things being equal.

Loans and Leases to Core Deposits

The loan-to-deposit ratio is a traditional measure of bank liquidity, indicating the extent to which deposits are used to meet loan requests. A variation on this theme is the ratio of loans and leases to core deposits. It can be obtained by combining the previous two ratios (i.e., by dividing loans and leases to assets by the ratio of core deposits to assets). The lower this ratio is, the more *stored* liquidity a bank has, all other things being equal. Given our analysis of the components of this ratio, we would expect the ratio of loans and leases to core deposits to vary directly with bank size, which it does. Moreover, for the largest banks, the ratio usually is greater than one (1.7 for the 10 largest at year-end 1994). The point at which the ratio of loans and leases to core deposits switches from less than one to greater than one can be regarded as a benchmark separating stored-liquidity banks from liability-management banks. The crossover point tends to occur at an asset size of about $3 billion. Focusing on the components of the ratio of loans and leases to core deposits reveals the reasons for the switching point. First, liability-management banks have fewer core deposits per dollar of assets. Second, they tend to make more loans per dollar of assets. As bank size increases, the interaction of these two components results in a growing relative volume of loans and leases supported by a shrinking relative volume of core deposits.

Temporary Investments to Assets

The ratio of temporary investments to assets measures a bank's most liquid assets as a percentage of total assets. Temporary investments can be defined as the sum of three items: (1) interest-bearing balances due from depository institutions, (2) federal funds sold and securities purchased under agreements to resell (reverse repos), and (3) trading-account assets and investment securities with maturities of one year or less. These items represent funds temporarily stored in the balance sheet, funds that can be easily, quickly, and safely converted into cash. Across these accounts, community banks are more likely to have relatively larger amounts of federal funds sold and investments. In contrast, because of their correspondent activities, larger banks are more likely to have relatively larger amounts of balances due and trading-account assets. On balance, the ratio tends to decline as bank size increases, with the decline cushioned by the effect of greater correspondent activity at larger banks. On average, temporary investments account for 15–20 percent of a bank's total assets.

Brokered Deposits to Total Deposits

A liability-management technique developed in the 1980s permitted aggressive banks and thrifts, of any size, to tap national markets for funds through brokered deposits. Investment bankers, such as Salomon Brothers, Merrill Lynch, and First Boston Corporation, act as money brokers in these transactions and add a third party to the normal two-party deposit transaction. The services of deposit brokers are especially helpful to depository institutions lacking the reputation and size to market their CDs on a national basis. For these banks, the funds are typically parceled out in blocks of $100,000 or less, so they are covered by deposit insurance; however, this size constraint is not binding for creditworthy borrowers. Brokered deposits are another example of financial innovation adapting to market and regulatory forces.[12] In general, a bank needs at least $1 billion in assets before it can tap the market for brokered deposits. However, without the federal deposit insurance guarantee, such contracts would not be viable; with it, even zombie (insolvent) institutions raised brokered deposits in the 1980s. During the mid-1990s, brokered deposits were making a comeback from their sullied and somewhat tainted use during the 1980s.

Investment Securities: Market-to-Book Value

When ratios of market-to-book values of investment securities are less than one, bankers are sometimes described as being locked-in to their investment portfolios because of fears of taking capital losses. Of course, in an efficient market for the bank's equity, discrepancies between market and book values of bank assets will automatically be reflected in the market value of the bank's equity. If market values are substantially below book values and if bankers are reluctant to take capital losses, then a market-to-book ratio of less than one would indicate a lack of liquidity until interest rates drop enough to raise market values. During periods of declining interest rates, bank investment portfolios are most likely to have a market-to-book ratio greater than one.

Pledged Securities to Total Securities

Just as banks require some of their customers to pledge collateral for certain transactions, some bank creditors require banks to supply collateral for certain transactions. Such pledging requirements are typically met by supplying U.S. Treasury securities or municipal obligations as collateral to be held by a third-party trustee. To encourage banks to purchase municipal obligations, such securities frequently

---

[12] In January 1984, the FDIC and the FHLBB attempted a power play that would have stripped deposit insurance protection from brokered deposits. The measure was defeated, however, and several studies have shown that "there is no evidence that brokered deposits are more likely to be misused or to contribute to institutions' losses than other kinds of rate-sensitive purchased liabilities." See Committee on Government Operations [1984], *Federal Regulation of Brokered Deposits in Problem Banks and Savings Institutions,* House Report 98–1112, 98th Congress, 2nd Session, p. 9. On the other side of the coin, Benston [1985] found that 22 failed S&Ls had a mean ratio of brokered deposits to earnings assets of 20 percent, compared to 7 percent for a group of nonfailed S&Ls (Table 1, p. 28). The mean difference of 13 percent had a standard deviation of 5.4 percent.

are valued at 110 percent of par to meet the pledging requirements of state and local governments. Bank investment securities pledged as collateral are not available for liquidity needs until the claims against them have been removed or other collateral is made available. Accordingly, measures of stored liquidity that employ bank debt securities should be net of any pledged securities. Bank liabilities that require collateral are (1) borrowings at the discount window of the various Federal Reserve Banks, (2) securities sold under agreements to repurchase, and (3) the public deposits of various governmental units, including the U.S. Treasury and state and local governments. Pledged securities tend to range between 20 percent and 60 percent of a bank's investment portfolio, with a median of about 25 percent. Because as bank size increases, both the use of repos and the ability to serve larger governmental units increase (i.e., the ability to attract public deposits increases), the ratio of pledged securities to total securities increases with bank size.

THE DYNAMICS OF LIQUIDITY MANAGEMENT

Up to this point, we have viewed the concept of liquidity management in a static framework. Liquidity management, however, is a dynamic problem that depends on the relationship between inflows and outflows of funds. Because the cash flows associated with liquidity management are not completely random, liquidity requirements can be predicted with some degree of accuracy. Thus, the essence of liquidity planning is to be able to forecast a bank's future loan demand, deposit supplies, and shifts in customer preferences in these areas. The formation of expectations and **forecasting techniques** play important roles in liquidity planning.

The Formation of Expectations

Three basic elements that shape the formation of expectations are

- An inertial component
- An extrapolative component
- A regressive component

The first element refers to an expectation of no change—inertia. The second factor extrapolates from past changes to determine future changes in a variable. This component pushes the variable forward or backward on the basis of past changes. The third element can be regarded as a return-to-normality component. It pulls a variable back to its normal or historical level.

Suppose that in the current period t you are attempting to forecast some variable X for the next period $t + 1$. The variable could be a loan demand, a deposit supply, or an interest rate. Combining the three expectational components, a reasonable forecasting equation would be:

$$X_{t+1} = aX_t + b(X_t - X_{t-1}) + c(X_t - X) + e_t \qquad \textbf{(7-3)}$$

where a, b, and c are the parameters or coefficients for the inertial, extrapolative, and regressive elements, respectively; X is the historic norm, approximated perhaps by a moving average; and e represents a random-disturbance term that is supposed to capture the effects of other variables not included in the equation. Equation (7-3) contains the basic ingredients for forecasting a variable on the basis of its past history. Note that if $a = 1$, the equation can be written as an expected change model,[13] that is

$$\Delta X_{t+1} = b\Delta X_t + c(X_t - X) + e_t \qquad \textbf{(7-4)}$$

If $b = c = 0$, the forecasted change is zero and the inertial element dominates. Note, however, that the value of c is expected to be less than zero, because it reflects regressive expectations that are supposed to pull the variable back to normality. On balance, the extrapolative element pushes the variable away from its current level, whereas the regressive element pulls it back to its historic norm. The application of this expectational framework depends upon estimates of the forecast parameters a, b, and c.

The Properties of Time-Series Data

The time-series properties of deposits and loans are the basic determinants of a bank's liquidity needs. A time series can be viewed as consisting of four components: trends, cyclical movements, seasonal fluctuations, and random disturbances. Each of these components has a time dimension associated with it. The trend component captures the long-run part of the time series. The series may be growing, decaying, or flat. Identification and analysis of loan and deposit trends are most important for long-range financial planning and less important for shorter-run liquidity management. The cyclical component has a time dimension associated with interest-rate and business cycles. Typically, these cycles last from one to several years. However, interest-rate cycles over the past quarter century have been shorter and more intense than previous ones. Uncertainty about cyclical movements is a major concern for bank managers.[14] The seasonal component has a time dimension associated with the rhythmic within-year movements common to such industries as agriculture and tourism. Because of the predictable recurrence of these variations, they can be planned for with a fairly high degree of accuracy. The random component has a short-run time dimension. Forecasting errors and random variations creates a need for defensive liquidity.

Seasonal variations have a certain rhythm to them that makes them more predictable than cyclical variations. However, because of such factors as lack of snow, too much rain, drought, or infestation, the seasonal flows of loans and deposits in agricultural and resort areas are not known with certainty; thus, they require some cushion of protective liquidity. For the most part, however, seasonal variations can be anticipated and built into a seasonal liquidity plan. For example, in agricultural areas, production loans are made during the planting season and repaid during the harvest season. In resort areas, loans for capital improvements are made during the off-season and repaid during the season. The primary instruments for meeting seasonal liquidity needs are short-term borrowings and the sale of liquid assets.

---

[13] Kane [1970] and Sinkey [1973] present applications of this model to the term structure of interest rates. In more complex formulations of the expected-change model, the first term on the right-hand side of equation (7-4) frequently is expressed as a distributed lag of past changes (e.g., a polynomial distributed lag, or PDL).

[14] Hayes [1980] stresses this point: "cyclical variations are by far the most important in terms of severity of impact on earnings and possibly on the fundamental soundness of the bank as a going concern" (p. 28).

Forecasting Techniques Used by Commercial Banks[15]

Estimating the parameters of a forecasting or planning model requires the use of a forecasting technique. This section describes the techniques used by commercial banks. Explaining the techniques themselves is beyond the scope of this book. To learn about these methods in detail, you need to take courses in advanced statistics, econometrics, or quantitative business methods.

Panel A of Table 7-9 presents the forecasting techniques used by banks on the basis of four deposit size classes (greater than $1 billion, $400 million to $1 billion, $100 million to $400 million, and less than $100 million) and type of forecasting technique (qualitative, explanatory, time series, and financial planning). Perhaps the most interesting finding is that 120 of the banks (46.3 percent) employ only judgmental forecasts (108 banks, or 42 percent) or no forecasting technique at all. Because Giroux makes no attempt to explain the judgmental technique, let's take a shot at it. My suspicion is that bankers who respond to a survey of forecasting techniques with the reply that they use only a judgmental approach are drawing on their banking experience and are confident of their informal forecasting abilities. Moreover, I conjecture that their judgmental calls informally involve the expectational elements discussed above. For example, if you ask experienced bankers who use the judgmental approach to make a forecast of some variable (such as demand deposits, business loan demand, or the prime rate), they are likely to ask three basic questions:

1. What is the value of the variable today?
2. What has been the change in the variable over the forecast period?
3. How does the variable today compare with what it normally is?

Note that these questions incorporate the three exceptional components of Equation (7-3). The bankers' judgment and experience come in when they informally attach "mental" (as opposed to statistical) values to the parameters a, b, and c. On balance, although the judgmental technique may appear at first glance to be a naive approach, it may be more sophisticated than it looks, especially in local banking markets. Larger banks report the use of more sophisticated forecasting techniques. For example, moving from the largest deposit class to the smallest, the use of the judgmental method drops off dramatically (e.g., 23%, 37%, 66%, and 83%). Simulation models (113 banks, 44% of the sample) were the fourth most commonly used quantitative method.

Panel B of Table 7-9 shows the forecasting techniques and planning variables used by banks with deposits over $400 million. The five planning variables highlighted are (1) deposits, (2) loan demand, (3) interest rates, (4) other economic variables, and (5) financial-statement variables. For the purposes of liquidity planning, forecasting deposits and loan demand are the critical variables. It is interesting to note that of the 157 banks responding, 84 of them indicated the use of a judgmental approach (only) in forecasting loan demand. Because banks are primarily concerned with forecasting business loan demand, this finding would appear to indicate the importance of the customer relationship in such forecasts and hence the use of a judgmental as opposed to a quantitative approach. For example, by maintaining close customer relationships, bankers should be able to judge the extent to which business lines of credit will be drawn down. Thus, close contact with important business

---

[15] This section draws upon the results of a survey by Giroux [1980] of forecasting techniques used by commercial banks.

TABLE 7-9   Forecasting Techniques and Planning Variables Used by Commercial Banks

PANEL A. FORECASTING TECHNIQUES BY BANK SIZE CLASS

Forecasting Technique	Bank Size Class				
	Greater than $1 Billion Number (%)	$400 Million to $1 Billion Number (%)	$100 Million to $400 Million Number (%)	Less than $100 Million Number (%)	Total Sample Number (%)
Quantitative					
Judgmental (only)	18 (23%)	28 (35%)	39 (58%)	23 (66%)	108 (42%)
Delphi method	6 (8)	5 (6)	2 (3)	1 (3)	14 (5)
Market survey	0	1 (1)	1 (1)	0	2 (1)
Explanatory					
Multiple equation	41 (53)	16 (20)	2 (3)	1 (3)	60 (23)
Multiple regression	28 (36)	21 (27)	7 (10)	2 (6)	58 (22)
Input/output	6 (8)	7 (9)	4 (6)	0	17 (7)
Time Series					
Box-Jenkins	2 (3)	4 (5)	0	0	6 (2)
Classical decomposition	4 (5)	6 (8)	2 (3)	1 (3)	13 (5)
Exponential smoothing	13 (17)	10 (13)	8 (12)	0	31 (12)
Trend analysis	3 (4)	4 (5)	4 (6)	1 (3)	12 (5)
Financial Planning					
Optimization	19 (24)	11 (14)	5 (7)	0	31 (12)
Simulation	54 (69)	40 (51)	16 (24)	3 (9)	113 (44)
Other	0	10 (13)	1 (1)	0	11 (4)
None	0	1 (1)	5 (7)	6 (17)	12 (5)
Number of banks responding	78 (100%)[a]	79 (100%)[a]	67 (100%)	35 (100%)	259 (100%)

PANEL B. FORECASTING TECHNIQUES AND PLANNING VARIABLES AT BANKS WITH DEPOSITS
OF $400 MILLION OR MORE

Forecasting Technique	Planning Variable				
	Deposits	Loan Demand	Interest Rates	Other Economic Variables	Financial Statement Variables
Quantitative					
Judgmental (only)	64	84	72	28	76
Delphi method	3	2	8	3	2
Market survey	0	2	0	0	0
Explanatory					
Multiple equation	26	26	39	40	12
Multiple regression	37	33	12	10	12
Input/output	5	4	5	4	8
Time Series					
Box-Jenkins	4	2	3	2	2
Classical decomposition	8	4	2	2	4
Exponential smoothing	15	10	2	0	6
Trend analysis	3	1	1	0	0
Simulation	26	23	16	9	45
No formal forecasts	0	1	2	50	4

[a]Percentages do not add up to 100 percent because some banks use more than one technique.

Source: Giroux [1980], Figures 2 and 3, pp. 52–53. Reprinted by permission.

customers may be more important than some esoteric forecasting technique in determining business loan demand. Although banks use forecasting techniques to project loan demand, the forecasting techniques, according to Giroux's survey, are not linked with particular loan categories. Moreover, from a liquidity perspective, the relationship between inflows and outflows of funds is the crucial one. The most popular quantitative techniques used to forecast loan demand are multiple regression, multiple equation, and simulation. On the deposit side, only 64 banks used the judgmental approach alone. The most common quantitative techniques used to forecast deposits are the same as those used to forecast loan demand.

To summarize, given the large number of community banks in the United States, it is not practical or cost-effective for them to attempt to acquire the expertise and skilled personnel required to develop quantitative forecasting capabilities. Moreover, in the local markets in which these banks operate, a qualitative approach based upon judgment may be just as effective as a quantitative one.

Liquidity Planning at Small Banks

McKinney [1977] contends that the greatest potential for small banks to improve their funds management through quantitative methods is in better planning of their liquidity positions. He claims that the liquidity needs of small banks can be determined accurately enough using worst-case analysis. This technique employs baseline trends to estimate future loan demand and deposit supplies. Given these estimates, the bank's objective is to use stored liquidity or liability-management liquidity or both to meet its funds requirements. The worst-case scenario forecasts the bank's greatest liquidity need by projecting maximum loan demand and minimum deposit supplies. The difference between these projections represents the worst-case liquidity need of the bank. In the worst-case analysis a ceiling trend is employed on variables that use bank funds (e.g., loans) and a floor trend on variables that provide bank funds (e.g., deposits). By reversing this procedure (i.e., by applying a floor trend to uses and a ceiling trend to sources), a bank can project what its most-liquid position is expected to be (i.e., the one resulting from minimum loan demand and maximum deposit supplies). The most-liquid and least-liquid projections represent upper and lower bounds for a bank's liquidity planning. By carrying the analysis one step further, it is easy to construct a most likely situation. This can be accomplished by fitting a trend line to the data using regression analysis or by carefully plotting the data and drawing in the trend line.

The three situations described above are depicted in Figure 7-1 for three types of trends: (1) upward, (2) downward, and (3) level. In each of the situations, the upper and lower bounds represent a range within which future values of the variable are expected to lie. Based upon historical experience or statistical evidence, some degree of confidence will be associated with the upper and lower boundaries (e.g., a 95 percent confidence interval). Of course, this does not mean that some future value cannot punch through the ceiling or floor.

Uncertainties and Expected Values

In a world of perfect certainty, the upper and lower bounds depicted in Figure 7-1 would collapse on the most likely trend line. In this never-never land, bankers would not have to worry about uncertain loan demand and uncertain deposit supplies. The real banking world, however, is an uncertain place. To survive in this world requires

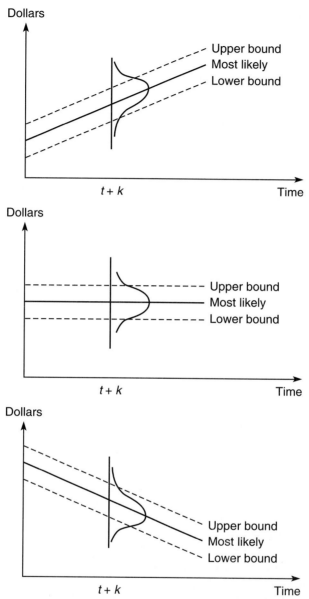

Note: The bell-shaped curves are probability distributions associated with particular dollar values on the vertical axis that relate to the chance of the dollar value occurring as measured by the height of the probability distribution.

FIGURE 7-1 Alternative Trends and Scenarios for Liquidity Planning

good judgment and occasionally some good luck. The uncertainty of the real world is manifested in the fact that the boundary lines and the most likely trends in Figure 7-1 do not coincide. In addition, at any point in the future, a probability distribution can be associated with a particular unknown or random variable such as deposit flows. The extent to which the tails of the distributions extend beyond the upper and lower bounds indicates the chances of punching through the ceiling or the floor. Recall that a flat distribution indicates greater uncertainty or risk than a peaked distribution (see the note to Figure 7-1).

RESERVE-POSITION MANAGEMENT AS A SUBSET OF LIQUIDITY MANAGEMENT

Because of legal reserve requirements imposed by the Federal Reserve,[16] depository institutions in the United States have the problem of **reserve-position management** (RPM), or more generally, **money-desk management.** Because the computation of the legal reserve covers a two-week period (Table 7-10), the planning horizon for RPM spans the same time period. In contrast, money-desk management is a daily

---

TABLE 7-10   Reserve Requirements for U.S. Banks (almost contemporaneous)

Panel A. Maintenance Period Lags Reserve Period by Two Days

Reserve-Computation Period	*$ Res.Com.*	*Reserve-Maintenance Period*
First Tuesday	101 (mil.)	NA
First Wednesday	102	NA
First Thursday	101	First Thursday
First Friday	98	First Friday
First Saturday (first Friday)	98	First Saturday (first Friday)
First Sunday (first Friday)	98	First Sunday (first Friday)
First Monday	102	First Monday
Second Tuesday	100	First Tuesday
Second Wednesday	101	First Wednesday
Second Thursday	100	Second Thursday
Second Friday	99	Second Friday
Second Saturday (second Friday)	99	Second Saturday (second Friday)
Second Sunday (second Friday)	99	Second Sunday (second Friday)
Second Monday	102	Second Monday
NA (but starts next two-week cycle)	1,400 (total)	Second Tuesday
NA	100 (average)	Second Wednesday

Panel B. Computation of the Required Reserve (RR)

$$RR = 0.03(NTA) + 0.10(NTA > \$52 \text{ million})$$

where NTA = daily average net transaction accounts (excluding time and savings deposits) for the two-week computation period shown in Panel A, and NTA is adjusted for an exclusion (zero RR) calculated as 80 percent of the percentage increase (over the preceding calendar year beginning June 30) in accounts subject to reserve requirements at all depository institutions. Effective December 31, 1995, NTA was reduced from $54 million to $52 million.

Example: Bank has $TA = \$100$ million (the average from second column in Panel A)

$$RR = 0.03(52) + 0.10(48) = 1.56 + 4.8 = 6.36$$

The bank must keep $6.36 million in vault cash or as funds on deposit at Federal Reserve Banks.

Note: In Panel A, *NA* means not applicable. Because Friday balances count for weekend balances, the weekend days can be referred to as "first" and "second" Fridays. The figures in the second column are those for computing the daily average for the 14-day period corresponding to column one.

---

[16] Compared to open-market operations, reserve requirements and the discount window are the less frequently used tools of monetary policy. The infrequent use and redundancy of reserve requirements for a bank's safety and soundness suggest two reasons why many analysts have been calling for many years for the elimination of reserve requirements. The United Kingdom no longer imposes minimum reserve requirements on its banks.

task to ensure that a bank has liquidity in the form of cash or cash equivalents to operate on a day-to-day basis. It is helpful to think of this aspect of liquidity management as supplying a bank's working capital.

A bank's reserves can be viewed in terms of the following definitions:

$$\text{Total reserves } (TR) = \text{Required reserves } (RR) + \text{ Excess reserves } (ER) \qquad \textbf{(7-5)}$$

and

$$\text{Required reserves} = \text{Borrowed reserves } (B) \\ + \text{ Nonborrowed or "free" reserves } (FR) \qquad \textbf{(7-6)}$$

From these two statements, "free reserves" can be defined as total reserves that are neither required by law nor borrowed from the Fed, that is,[17]

$$\text{Free reserves } (FR) = \text{Excess reserves } (ER) - \text{Borrowed reserves } (B) \qquad \textbf{(7-7)}$$

When free reserves are aggregated for the banking system, they can be taken as an indicator of monetary policy. For example, when free reserves are negative and decreasing, money and credit are likely to become tighter, because the banking system has more borrowed reserves than excess reserves. In contrast, when free reserves are positive and increasing, money and credit are likely to become easier, because the banking system has more excess reserves than borrowed reserves. Some Fed watchers look for trends and changes in free reserves as signals about the direction of monetary policy.

A bank's required reserves (RR) are defined by law as:

$$RR = 0.03\,(NTA^*) + 0.10\,(NTA > NTA^*) \qquad \textbf{(7-8)}$$

NTA^* is the Fed's cutoff point for distinguishing between the 3 and 10 percent reserve-requirement levels, and NTA stands for net transaction accounts (mainly checking accounts and demand deposits). As of this writing, $NTA^* = \$52$ million. As Table 7-10 shows, a bank's NTA is calculated as a daily average of such balances over a two-week period called the reserve-computation period. Based on this average, banks must keep their average required reserves at that level for the reserve-maintenance period, which is also a two-week period but lagged two days compared to the reserve-computation period.

Box 7-3, which provides a glossary of reserve-requirement terminology, explains what happens if a bank fails to meet its legal reserve requirements. If a bank fails to meet its target for money-desk management, it would be caught cash-out and be in the embarrassing position of not being able to cash checks (e.g., the case of First National Bank of Browning described above), meet loan demand, and pay suppliers and vendors. If a bank is cash-out, it must wait for delivery of currency from the Fed or from a correspondent bank. To generate liquidity or to meet legal reserve requirements, a bank can borrow from the Fed's discount window, borrow from the Fed funds market, borrow from a correspondent bank, or sell short-term assets such as Treasury bills.

Advanced Tennis Registration (ATR)

Bureaucracies have the knack of being able to make anything complicated (e.g., the Fed's reserve accounting). One of the perks at the Fed is its (outdoor) tennis court, which, by the way, is open to the public. The trick is to get a reservation. Here is how

---

[17] Using symbols, this relationship can be seen as: $FR = ER - B$, where $TR = RR + ER$, and $RR = B + NB$. Thus, $FR = TR - RR - B = ER - B$.

BOX 7-3

GLOSSARY OF RESERVE-REQUIREMENT TERMINOLOGY

- *Depository institutions* subject to *reserve requirements* include commercial banks, mutual savings banks, savings and loan associations, credit unions, agencies and branches of foreign banks, and Edge Act Corporations.

- *Transaction accounts* include all deposits against which the account holder is permitted to make withdrawals by negotiable or transferable instruments, payment orders of withdrawal, or telephone or preauthorized transfers for the purpose of making payments to third persons or others. However, money-market deposit accounts (MMDAs) and similar accounts subject to the rules that permit no more than six preauthorized, automatic, or other transfers per month, of which no more than three may be checks, are savings deposits, not transaction accounts.

- *Required reserves* include deposits with Federal Reserve Banks or vault cash at the depository institution.

- *Reserve-computation period* is the two-week period (beginning on a Tuesday and ending 14 days later, on a Monday) over which the daily average of transaction accounts is calculated.

- *Reserve-maintenance period* is the two-week period (lagged two days compared to the reserve-computation period, beginning on the Thursday following the first Tuesday in the reserve-computation period) over which the reserve requirement must be met or exceeded.

- *Contemporaneous reserve accounting* is the system, except for the two-day lag, that the United States almost has. The lag is used to help reduce uncertainty for the reserve-position or "money desk" manager.

- The *Weekend Game* or *Window Dressing* is the term applied to the strategy of attempting to minimize the balances subject to reserve requirements on the Fridays before the two weekends of the reserve-computation period. Because Friday balances are used for the weekend figures, they count three times over a normal weekend and four times over a long holiday weekend.

- *Reserve-requirement penalties* are applied to banks that miss their reserve requirements by more than 4 percent (undershooting the reserve target by 4 percent or less can be made up without penalty). Penalties take the form of explicit interest charges (discount rate plus 2 percent), and implicit charges in the form of more frequent monitoring, examinations, and surveillance.

- *Opportunity cost* of holding excess reserves, which earn nothing, is the difference between the return on the earning asset that would have been held and zero. The relevant net present value or cost-benefit rule is to compare the opportunity cost (as a return) with the sum of the explicit and implicit costs of undershooting the required reserve.

the advanced tennis registration (ATR) system worked when I was with the FDIC (1971–1976). Monday was registration day for court times for the next week, hence the acronym ATR. The registration was a two-part procedure. At noon, the first step was to work your way down into the bowels of the Fed (from outside via a ramp to a parking garage) and pick up a number. The second step was to come back at 1:00 P.M. and sign up for a court time with your priority in the queue determined by the lowness of the number you had picked up an hour earlier. Are you following me? Since ATR was serious business, there was a security guard to oversee the operation. After everyone in the queue had a chance to sign up for one hour, the process was repeated. Tennis-playing members of the Board of Governors, who had more important matters to attend to (like watching the money supply grow), were of course spared this ordeal, because they could register in advance by phone.[18] Because the

---

[18] By the way, anyone could attempt to register at 1:00 P.M. on Monday by phone, but it was virtually impossible to get anything but a busy signal until after the prime court times had been taken.

typical bureaucratic lunch hour runs from about 11:30 A.M. to 1:30 P.M., there is never any problem finding time for ATR or for tennis. Game, set, and match to the Fed.

THE THREE FACES OF LIABILITY MANAGEMENT

The technique of liability management (LM) began in the 1960s with the innovation of the certificate of deposit (CD) and the full development of the market for federal funds. The idea behind LM is to acquire funds and use them profitably, especially to meet loan demand. What was unique about LM at the time it developed was that nontraditional borrowing arrangements were used to acquire funds. This uniqueness was manifested in interest, maturity, and service characteristics that differed in important ways from those of traditional bank sources of funds.

Liability management focuses on a permanent expansion of a bank's asset base as opposed to the compositional change in assets arising from the stored-liquidity approach. The tools of LM include such instruments as federal funds, CDs, Eurodollars, repurchase agreements, brokered deposits, and notes and debentures. Box 7-1 and Tables 7-1 to 7-7 provide descriptions, relative amounts, and effective interest rates for these instruments. By adopting a strategy of LM, a bank does not have to store as much liquidity in its assets, freeing funds for more profitable loan and investment opportunities. Managerial preferences regarding risk-return trade-offs govern the aggressiveness of a bank's LM position and the extent to which a bank stores liquidity or purchases it in the marketplace.

Given the profit motive, Kane [1979] explains the phenomenon of liability management by focusing on three relatively unchanging aspects of the business of U.S. commercial banking:[19]

1. Banks' attempts to minimize deposit interest costs by varying applicable deposit rates with the interest sensitivity of specific pools of customer funds
2. Banks' written and unwritten commitments to meeting spurts in loan demand even when the Federal Reserve is attempting to restrict the supply of money and credit
3. Banks' desire to offset regulatory burdens imposed on them by reserve requirements and deposit-insurance fees[20]

Kane's explanation of liability management hinges on three basic concepts: (1) the minimization of bank interest expenses, (2) the importance of customer relationships, and (3) the circumvention of regulatory restrictions (Figure 7-2). Although we examine the separate role of each of these three ingredients in the creation of LM, keep in mind that it was their interaction that was the driving force behind the development of LM. Moreover, it is this interaction that keeps liability management going as an important component of modern bank financial management.

Minimizing Deposit Interest Costs

The ability to minimize deposit interest costs depends upon the responsiveness of particular deposit groups to changes in deposit rates (i.e., the elasticity of the supply of funds provided by savers). The more interest sensitive specific

---

[19] Kane [1979], pp. 149–150.

[20] Prior to the Depository Institutions Deregulation and Monetary Control Act (DIDMCA) of 1980, deposit-rate ceilings played a major role in the development of liability management.

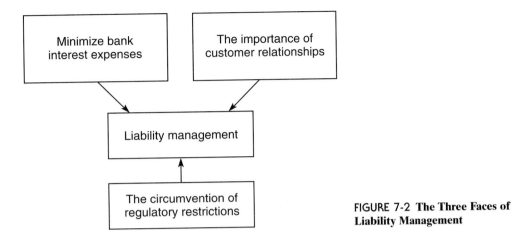

FIGURE 7-2 **The Three Faces of Liability Management**

pools of customer funds are, the more difficult it is to minimize deposit interest expenses.

As illustrated in Figure 7-3, transactions-type balances are less sensitive to rate changes than purchases funds. In Figure 7-3a, the supply curve SS represents a pool of funds that is perfectly inelastic. In this case, no incentive exists for the bank to pay more than some nominal rate of interest. If the supply schedule becomes sensitive to rate changes (as indicated by the clockwise rotation of SS to $S'S'$), a higher rate of interest is needed to generate an equivalent amount of deposits. In addition to transactions-type balances, specific pools of customer funds may be rate insensitive because of ignorance, lack of competition, minimum purchase requirements (e.g., a \$10,000 T-bill investment), transaction costs, or other factors.

Figure 7-3b shows the case of purchased funds that are supplied perfectly elastically. At rate r_0, the prevailing market rate, a bank may obtain all the purchased funds it wants given the supply curve SS. Beyond some level of deposits S_0, however, the supply curve may be less than perfectly elastic (as indicated by the dashed line segment labeled S'), and higher rates may be necessary to generate additional funds.

The important point is the ability of banks to *segment* their deposit customers or markets on the basis of rate sensitivity. By varying deposit rates across these segments (e.g., the rate for savings accounts versus Eurodollar CDs), banks may be able to reduce their deposit costs. Why do banks go after these higher-cost courses of funds? They want such funds primarily to meet the loan demand of their best customers. Of course, if such banks had plentiful supplies of low-cost core deposits, they would prefer them over higher-cost LM funds.

Customer Relationships

The second aspect of liability management explains why banks go after high-cost purchased funds. Bankers enter into formal and informal agreements with their best customers to accommodate requests for credit (e.g., formal and informal loan commitments and lines of credit). Failure to meet these loan demands will not enhance customer relationships and may have an adverse effect upon a bank's long-run profitability. Thus, to ensure that such events do not occur, banks attempt to manage their liabilities even when the Fed is seeking to restrict the growth of the supply of money and credit. The critical point is that customer relationships play

Rate (percent)

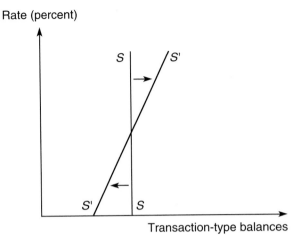

(a) Rate-insensitive funds

Rate (percent)

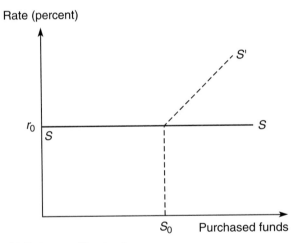

(b) Rate-sensitive funds

FIGURE 7-3 **The Interest-Rate Sensitivity of Alternative Sources of Funds**

an important role in commercial bank loan decisions.[21] Such relationships are valuable because of the broad-based foundation they establish with borrowers, especially corporate ones. Beyond the interest income and loan fees business loans generate, such loans also are important because they are associated with valuable deposit balances and the use of ancillary services that generate noninterest income. Banks' attempts to get existing customers to use more bank services is referred to as *cross-selling,* which is important because it generates noninterest income to offset declining profit margins.

The customer-relationship aspect of liability management involves a combination of deposit balances, customer service, and loans. Historically, corporate deposit balances received implicit interest payments in the form of services provided by the bank at prices below their true costs. As the account size increases relative to account activity, these deposit balances become more valuable to the extent that

---

[21] The notion of the customer relationship was introduced in chapter 6 and is discussed further in chapters 10–12. Hodgman [1963] and Kane and Malkiel [1965] employed the idea of customer relationships in their analyses. Budzeika [1976] has shown that the desire to satisfy loan demand has been the major focus of liability management by New York City banks.

the implicit interest payments result in a declining cost per dollar of deposit balance. As banks have moved to unbundling services and explicit pricing, however, this practice of implicit pricing has declined. In addition, because of the prime rate and compensating-balance conventions, some corporate customers may be given concessions on interest rates charged for credit extensions. The existence of the discount prime rate supports the notion. Moreover, to protect the long-term availability of low-cost corporate balances, the bank even may be willing, during periods of credit restraint, to grant loans at a rate very close to its marginal cost of purchased funds. On balance, banks need to focus on the *net* rate of return on the overall customer relationship with respect to the combination of deposit, loan, and other services used by the client.

Circumventing Regulatory Restrictions

Reserve requirements, deposit-insurance fees, and other regulatory burdens (e.g., Regulation Q prior to DIDMCA) impose costs on firms subject to such restrictions. In the quest for long-run profits, commercial banks have attempted to circumvent these restrictions. Bankers' desires to offset these regulatory burdens constitute the third aspect of liability management.

1. Deposit-Rate Ceilings

Although deposit-rate ceilings no longer exist, they played a major role in the development of liability management. Prior to their removal, Regulation Q ceilings restricted the ability of banks (and thrifts) to attract funds and made them especially vulnerable to disintermediation during periods of high interest rates (e.g., the credit crunches of 1966, 1969, 1974, and the early 1980s). Like other forms of price controls, deposit-rate ceilings cause distortions and inefficiencies. The distinction between explicit and implicit interest is important here. Deposit-rate ceilings restrict the amount of **explicit interest** (i.e., coin of the realm) that banks can pay. However, banks could attempt to make the supply of rate-restricted or small-denomination deposits more interest-rate sensitive by resorting to the payment of **implicit interest** in the form of more branches, longer hours, merchandise premiums, and the like. The effects of deposit-rate ceilings and implicit interest on such deposits are pictured and described in Figure 7-4. In addition to paying implicit interest, banks attempted to develop sources of funds that were not subject to deposit-rate ceilings.

On balance, rate ceilings forced banks to invest time and resources developing and testing implicit-interest and liability-management schemes. Such plans lead to distortions and inefficiencies compared to unrestricted markets. In addition, such arrangements are relatively inflexible, both to put into place and to dismantle (e.g., a branch), compared to explicit payments of interest.

2. Reserve Requirements

Reserve requirements are a form of implicit taxation. Prior to DIDMCA and universal reserve requirements, banks could reduce their reserve-requirements tax by choosing not to be members of the Federal Reserve System.[22] Moreover, because not all bank liabilities are taxed the same way (some liabilities even have a zero reserve requirement), banks are encouraged to develop sources of funds that are less heavily taxed.

---

[22] Membership in the Federal Reserve System is still optional today, but all depository institutions are subject to Federal Reserve requirements based upon the type of deposit and the deposit interval.

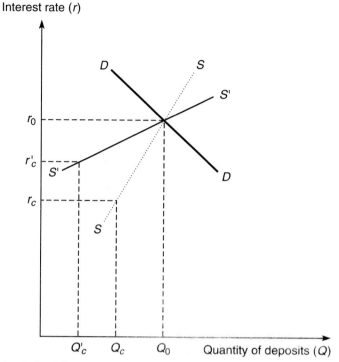

Analysis of Figure 7-4

1. Unconstrained solution: The equilibrium market-clearing solution is (r_0, Q_0).
2. The impact effect of deposit-rate ceilings: The constrained solution is (r_c, Q_c). Disintermediation is equal to the distance Q_0 minus Q_c and the interest loss to savers (or expense saved from the bank's perspective) per dollar of deposits is equal to the distance r_0 minus r_c.
3. The imposition of deposit-rate ceilings leads banks to develop schemes for paying implicit interest, leading to a higher effective ceiling rate at r'_c. With the original supply curve SS, the implicit interest would recoup some of the disintermediated funds. However, becuase of competition from unregulated intermediaries, the supply curve for small-denomination balances becomes more elastic, rotating clockwise to $S'S'$. As a result, disintermediation increases to a total distance of Q_0 minus Q'_0 and the benefits that depository institutions derive from rate ceilings are squeezed.

FIGURE 7-4 A Geometric Analysis of the Effects of Deposit-Rate Ceilings and Implicit Interest on the Market for Small-Denomination Deposits

3. The Pricing and Methods of Deposit Insurance[23]

Prior to 1991, federal deposit insurance was explicitly priced as a fixed-rate premium; one risk was assumed to fit all. To attempt to remedy this shortcoming, implicit pricing in the form of on-site examinations (focused on assessing loan quality), capital-adequacy standards, and other methods was employed, and still is

---

[23] See chapter 16 for full details of the pricing and methods of deposit insurance.

used today. Thus, the effective total deposit-insurance premium consists of an explicit fee *plus* an implicit one, the latter being a unique function of each bank's risk exposure as determined by its annual (or more frequent) on-site examination and other regulatory judgments.

Although the deposit-insurance ceiling was never higher than $100,000, the current level established in 1980, the practice was, and still is, to provide 100 percent insurance coverage in the case of bank failure, especially for large banks. This protection applied to foreign deposits and other liabilities even though they were not subject to assessment for deposit-insurance fees, which apply only to total domestic deposits.

On balance, the mispricing and mishandling of federal deposit insurance created opportunities for banks to exploit deposit-insurance subsidies at taxpayer expense. Banks do this by taking on additional asset risk or by shifting funds from deposit to nondeposit categories or both. The idea in LM is to find sources of funds (such as Eurodollars and federal funds) that are not subject to deposit-insurance fees.

Regulatory Recapitulation

Prior to DIDMCA, the ultimate accomplishment for a bank liability manager was to find a liability instrument that was not subject to deposit-rate ceilings, reserve requirements, or deposit-insurance fees. Such achievements usually were short-lived, however, because the instruments were frequently restricted in some way by the banking authorities. This cat-and-mouse game played in the liability-management arena was another manifestation of the regulatory dialectic. Today, although competitive reregulation has eliminated some restrictions, the game goes on.

THE RISKS OF LIABILITY MANAGEMENT

Kane [1979] contends that the regulation-induced innovations of liability management by large banks built up a panic potential in the U.S. financial system. His argument goes something like this:

> Large U.S. banks have focused on relatively inflexible and cost-increasing ways of paying implicit interest (e.g., branching) and on attracting pools of hot money (e.g., Eurodollars). This strategy increased the volatility of large-bank liabilities. In addition, bank contingent liabilities, such as guarantees of customers' commercial-paper issues, have increased and, to some extent, have become more risky too. In conjunction with their use of costly liability management, large U.S. banks reached out for higher-returning assets. As a result, they tended to accept greater default risk. Whereas bank asset risk has been increasing, the capital cushion held by large banks declined during most of the 1980s.

Kane sees banks that adopt these modern portfolio practices as increasing their exposure to liquidity crises and becoming more dependent upon the Fed and the FDIC to bail them out in the event of adverse market developments. The cases of Bank of New England, Continental Illinois, and First Pennsylvania fit Kane's scenario perfectly. What had the banking authorities worried (and presumably Kane too) was the possibility that a chain of bank failures could trigger a nationwide financial panic. Kane [1979] found an instructive parallel in the TV commercial that encouraged consumers to change their automobile oil filters regularly. His "you-can-pay-me-now-or-pay-me-later" punch line for the financial system was

> Sooner or later, pressures generated by regulatory efforts to plaster over depository institutions' festering solvency problems are going to find release. We can only pray that the valves and rods of our national economic engine are not damaged in the process. (p. 173)

Keep in mind that Kane wrote these words in 1979. The costly thrift and banking crises of the 1980s and early 1990s were on the horizon.

The implementation of risk-based capital requirements and FDICIA's provision for "prompt corrective action" regarding problem banks presumably have helped ease the prospects for further damage to our national economic engine. In the process, large banks have become less aggressive in their practice of LM, although it is still an important part of bank financial management. The next section addresses this rethinking of LM strategies.

Rethinking Liability-Management Strategies: The Roles of Too-Big-to-Fail, Liquidity Crises, Betting the Bank, and FDICIA

Prior to the 1984 bailout of Continental Illinois Corporation (revived as Continental Bank and later acquired by BankAmerica in 1994), the FDIC tried to assure all of Continental's creditors that they were protected—100 percent deposit insurance for everyone, including the creditors of the holding company. It didn't work; Continental experienced an electronic run, a modern-day liquidity crisis. The message was clear: Even government guarantees cannot prevent a liquidity crisis. Afraid of closing a $34 billion BHC known as a money-center bank, the government (read Fed/FDIC/OCC) bailed out Continental Illinois under the de facto too-big-to-fail (TBTF) doctrine. Although the FDIC infused $4.5 billion in cash, the estimated cost to the FDIC was *only* about $1.1 billion.[24] Subsequently, banking problems got so bad that the FDIC itself needed a cash infusion in 1991.

Behind the symptoms of the distressed banks of the 1980s and early 1990s, one sees bad loans, large bets on interest rates, rapid growth, aggressive liability management, lack of controls, inadequate checks and balances, errors in judgment, and (in some cases) dishonesty. Continental's situation, because of Continental's prominence as a money-center bank, was the most intriguing. In testimony before the Senate banking committee, Volcker [1984] described the situation as follows:

> The problems of Continental Bank essentially reflected serious weaknesses in the domestic loan portfolio of a bank that had engaged in aggressive growth and lending practices for some time, including heavy involvement in participations in energy loans of the Penn Square Bank that failed two years ago. As other credit losses surfaced and earnings pressures continued, market sources of funding were reduced and the bank became heavily dependent on discount window borrowings during the spring. As the atmosphere surrounding the bank deteriorated and threatened to disturb markets more generally, the supervisory authorities, together with a group of other major banks, provided a massive financial assistance program pending a more permanent solution. (p. 11)

---

[24] Since Continental's bailout in 1984, seven of the 10 most expensive bank failures to the FDIC have occurred (see chapter 16). The third most expensive ($2.3 billion) and most recent (January 6, 1991) was the Bank of New England.

On the day after Volcker's statement, a more permanent solution, in the form of a $4.5 billion nationalization of Continental, was arranged.

The two major portfolio risks that banks face are credit risk and interest-rate risk. Regarding the interaction of these risks, Volcker went on to say

> In a period of rapid economic and credit expansion, there can be temptations to relax prudent credit standards in an effort to maximize growth. With deposit markets deregulated, there may be a perception by individual banks that added funds can be raised as needed in domestic or foreign markets by bidding rates higher to fund larger and larger loan portfolios—and that loan rates can be raised as fast as deposit rates. But the aggregate supply of funds is ultimately not really inexhaustible; confidence must be maintained, and high and volatile interest rates can undermine the creditworthiness of weaker borrowers. (p. 12)

As a result of Continental's debacle, other big banks began to rethink the aggressiveness of their liability management. In this regard, the chief economist of Republic Bank in Dallas (later NCNB Dallas and now NationsBank Dallas) stated: "We are going back to the drawing board now. Our strategic plans have always assumed that marginal growth could be funded effortlessly abroad. . . . Now we see that money may not always be tappable."[25]

Chapter Summary

The importance and interaction of liquidity and confidence are captured by the following statements:

- "Liquidity always comes first; without it a bank doesn't open its doors; with it, a bank may have time to solve its basic problems" (Donald Howard, Chief Financial Officer, Citicorp).
- "Our whole financial system runs on confidence and not much else when you get down to it. What we've learned is that when confidence erodes, it erodes very quickly" (L. William Seidman, Chairman, FDIC).

Also consider this sentence by David Ruder, former chairman of the Securities and Exchange Commission, before the House Banking Committee's Subcommittee on Financial Institutions Supervision following the stock market crash of October 1987 on the topic of liquidity and the availability of capital:

> I personally regard that question as probably the most important one to come out of the market decline.[26]

As the major supplier of liquidity to the economy and financial markets, commercial banks must have access to liquidity. Bank liquidity can be either stored in a bank's balance-sheet assets or purchased in the marketplace or both. However, since larger banks have greater access to money and capital markets, both international and national, they have greater flexibility than smaller banking organizations to practice liability management, that is, in the sense of purchasing funds to pursue profitable opportunities. In contrast, all banks store a certain degree of liquidity in their balance-sheet assets. The smaller the bank is, the greater is its dependency on stored liquidity. Of course, large banks still need cash balances and other highly liquid assets to conduct their day-to-day operations. Liquidity plan-

---

[25] As quoted in *The Wall Street Journal* [August 7, 1984], p. 35.
[26] Ricks [1987], p. 2.

ning in community banks is marked by a judgmental approach, whereas larger banks use more sophisticated quantitative methods, mainly simulation techniques.

Although all banks have stored liquidity, only the largest banks have the ability to use large amounts of purchased funds to manage their portfolios of earning assets. The greater flexibility enjoyed by large banks is not without its costs, however, as reflected by the need to maintain a trouble-free balance sheet and clean reputation when using volatile liabilities to fund assets. The cases of Continental Illinois and Bank of New England dramatically illustrate the costs of not maintaining such an image.

List of Key Words, Concepts, and Acronyms

- Bank liabilities (interest-bearing, non-interest-bearing)
- Brokered deposits
- Confidence
- Core deposits
- Demand deposits
- Explicit interest
- Federal safety net (government guarantee)
- Forecasting techniques
- Functional cost

- Functions of bank liquidity
- Implicit interest
- Interest-rate risk
- Large-liability dependence (LLD)
- Liability management (LM and three faces of)
- Liquidity
- Liquidity risk
- Managed liabilities
- Money-market demand account (MMDA)

- Pledging requirements
- Purchased funds
- Simulation techniques
- Sources and uses of bank funds
- Stored liquidity
- Too big to fail (TBTF)
- Too big to liquidate (TBTL)
- Trade-off between liquidity and profitability
- Volatile liabilities

Review/Discussion Questions

1. What's the relation between confidence and liquidity? If the CAMEL rating system was prioritized in terms of its components, would it be CAMEL or LEMAC or some other ordering? Distinguish between TBTF and TBTL.

2. Unexpected changes such as the stock market crash of 1987 create liquidity needs for bank customers such as securities firms. Describe the roles played by the Fed and money-center banks in averting a liquidity crisis following the crash.

3. Trace the history of the various approaches to bank liquidity management. What are the basic ideas of each of these techniques and when were they popular? Which methods are used by banks today?

4. Distinguish between internal and external sources of liquidity. How do pledging requirements and predilections against taking capital losses alter a bank's liquidity position?

5. What are the functions of liquidity and the risks of liquidity management? What are some unexpected changes that could affect a bank's liquidity? Can you (or your instructor) explain why Continental's liquidity crisis occurred in May 1984 and not in July 1982? The earlier date is when it was disclosed that Continental had purchased about $1 billion in bad loans from Penn Square Bank.

6. What is the trade-off between liquidity and profitability? How does the shape of the yield curve affect this trade-off?

7. What are the three faces of liability management?

8. Distinguish between core deposits and managed liabilities. How does bank size affect these potential sources of funds? How do managed liabilities and volatile liabilities differ?

9. LM banks must maintain the confidence of the marketplace. What can they do to attempt to assure such confidence? What role do government guarantees play in this process, and how effective are they in stopping a deposit run?

10. Identify who made each of the following statements and discuss the validity of each statement. *(a)* "Liquidity always comes first; without it a bank doesn't open its doors; with it, a bank may have time to solve its basic problems." *(b)* "Our whole financial system runs on confidence and not much else when you get down to it. What we've learned

is that when confidence erodes, it erodes very quickly." *(c)* "I personally regard that question (regarding liquidity) as probably the most important to come out of the market decline (of 1987)."

11. Do you think that the judgmental approach to forecasting has a foundation in the formation of expectations, or is it more akin to flying by the seat of your pants? Explain. Survey some local bankers to discover what forecasting techniques they use.

12. What institutions are subject to reserve requirements? How are required reserves computed? What happens if a bank fails to meet its reserve requirements?

13. How do operating costs vary across different types of bank accounts?

14. How did banks and thrifts segment deposit markets during the late 1960s and the 1970s such that small savers got shafted?

15. Describe the "orderly exit" that exists in the market for commercial paper and the role that banks play in this process.

16. Write an essay about the rethinking of bank liability-management strategies in which you incorporate the roles of too-big-to-fail, liquidity crises, betting the bank, and FDICIA.

Problems

1. Calculate market-to-book ratios for the following bank investments:

Type of Security	Book Value	Market Value
U.S. Treasury and federal agencies	$3,228	$3,415
State and municipal	1,955	1,980
Other (e.g., foreign bonds)	7,697	8,142
Total	$12,880	$13,537

What is likely to have happened to interest rates over the period these securities have been held?

2. Given the following abbreviated balance sheet, calculate as many liquidity ratios as you can and make your best guess regarding the bank's peer size class.

Assets		Liabilities	
Temporary investments	10	Core deposits	25
Loans and leases	65	Volatile liabilities	65
Securities	20	Brokered deposits	3
Other	5	Capital	7
	100		100

Given this bank's liquidity profile, how important is it that this bank maintain the confidence of the marketplace? Contrast and compare this liquidity profile with the one you calculate from the following data:

Assets		Liabilities	
Temporary investments	4	Core deposits	17.0
Loans and leases	10	Volatile liabilities	1.2
Securities	5	Brokered deposits	0.0
Other	1	Capital	1.8
	20		20.0

How important is it that this bank maintain the confidence of the marketplace? Suppose that this bank has 50 percent of both its temporary investments and its securities pledged and that the market-to-book ratio of its securities portfolio is .75. If the bank experiences a run on its volatile liabilities, what will be the size of the bank's liquidity cushion?

3. Calculate the reserve requirement for a bank with the following data:

Reserve-Computation Period	$ Res. Com.	Reserve-Maintenance Period
First Tuesday	201 (mil.)	NA
First Wednesday	202	NA
First Thursday	201	First Thursday
First Friday	198	First Friday
First Saturday (first Friday)	198	First Saturday (first Friday)
First Sunday (first Friday)	198	First Sunday (first Friday)
First Monday	202	First Monday
Second Tuesday	200	First Tuesday
Second Wednesday	201	First Wednesday
Second Thursday	200	Second Thursday
Second Friday	199	Second Friday
Second Saturday (second Friday)	199	Second Saturday (second Friday)
Second Sunday (second Friday)	199	Second Sunday (second Friday)
Second Monday	202	Second Monday
NA (but starts next two-week cycle)	?	Second Tuesday
NA	?	Second Wednesday

4. Find the weighted-average, marginal cost of funds for the following banks and discuss your findings:

Alpha Bank

Source of Funds	% of Assets	Interest Cost	+ Operating Cost
Checking accounts	20	2%	5%
Savings accounts	40	4	1
CDs	30	6	0.5
Equity capital	10	12	0.25

Beta Bank

Source of Funds	% of Assets	Interest Cost	+ Operating Cost
Checking accounts	10	1%	4%
Savings accounts	20	3	1
CDs	60	7	0.5
Equity capital	10	14	0.15

Gamma Bank			
Source of Funds	*% of Assets*	*Interest Cost* +	*Operating Cost*
Checking accounts	30	3%	5%
Savings accounts	40	4	1
CDs	20	5	0.5
Equity capital	10	10	0.35

5. Show how the returns of 53 percent and −8 percent on the "Global CD" described in Box 7-1 are calculated. What theory from the appendix to chapter 20 is linked to this problem?

APPENDIX

THE COMPOSITION OF BANK LIABILITIES AND EFFECTIVE INTEREST RATES PAID BY COMMERCIAL BANKS BY BANK SIZE FOR 1985 AND 1995 (AS A PERCENTAGE OF AVERAGE CONSOLIDATED ASSETS)

TABLE A7-1 The Composition of Bank Liabilities				

Panel A. All Insured Commercial Banks

			Interval Peak	
Source of Funds	*1995*	*1985*	*Amt%*	*Year*
Interest-bearing liabilities	71.9	72.8	76.6	1991
Deposits	56.3	61.5	64.4	1991
In foreign offices	10.3	12.3	11.3	1986
In domestic offices	46.0	49.2	55.9	1991
Other checkable deposits	6.6	4.6	8.2	1993
Savings (including MMDAs)	17.5	16.4	20.9	1993
Small time deposits	16.1	16.8	21.3	1991
Large time deposits	5.8	11.4	12.1	1989
Fed funds purchased & RPs	7.7	7.7	8.2	1989
Other	7.9	3.6	6.2	1993
Non-interest-bearing liabilities	20.1	20.9	20.6	1986
Domestic demand deposits	12.7	15.5	15.9	1986
Other	7.4	5.4	4.7	1986
Memo				
Managed liabilities	32.1	35.5	35.7	1988
Domestic core deposits	55.7	41.9	62.4	1991

(continued)

TABLE A7-1   (Continued)

Panel B. Ten Largest Banks by Assets

			Interval Peak	
Source of Funds	*1995*	*1985*	*Amt%*	*Year*
Interest-bearing liabilities	63.4	72.4	74.6	1991
Deposits	47.5	57.4	57.9	1990
In foreign offices	28.4	34.6	32.6	1987
In domestic offices	19.1	22.8	29.2	1991
Other checkable deposits	2.3	1.3	3.4	1992
Savings (including MMDAs)	10.6	8.8	15.3	1993
Small time deposits	4.0	4.6	6.5	1991
Large time deposits	2.2	8.1	7.8	1989
Fed funds purchased & RPs	6.2	7.1	8.1	1986
Other	9.7	7.1	11.9	1993
Non-interest-bearing liabilities	30.2	22.7	22.5	1986
Domestic demand deposits	8.8	11.3	12.6	1987
Other	21.3	11.4	10.4	1993
Memo				
Managed liabilities	47.9	59.3	57.4	1986
Domestic core deposits	25.7	26.0	35.2	1993

Panel C. Banks Ranked 11 through 100 by Assets

			Interval Peak	
Source of Funds	*1995*	*1985*	*Amt%*	*Year*
Interest-bearing liabilities	74.1	71.3	77.0	1990
Deposits	52.3	54.0	59.2	1991
In foreign offices	8.1	11.8	10.4	1986
In domestic offices	44.2	42.1	52.5	1991
Other checkable deposits	5.6	3.6	7.2	1992
Savings (including MMDAs)	18.8	14.7	20.6	1993
Small time deposits	14.2	11.4	18.0	1991
Large time deposits	5.5	12.4	15.1	1989
Fed funds purchased & RPs	11.4	13.1	14.8	1986
Other	10.4	4.1	7.2	1993
Non-interest-bearing liabilities	18.1	23.2	22.8	1986
Domestic demand deposits	14.3	17.1	17.6	1986
Other	4.9	6.1	5.2	1986
Memo				
Managed liabilities	35.6	41.8	44.3	1988
Domestic core deposits	53.0	46.8	57.4	1993

TABLE A7-1   (Continued)

Panel D. Banks Ranked 101 through 1,000 by Assets

Source of Funds	1995	1985	Interval Peak Amt%	Interval Peak Year
Interest-bearing liabilities	75.0	72.9	77.3	1991
Deposits	59.6	62.6	66.3	1991
In foreign offices	1.7	2.0	2.1	1989
In domestic offices	57.9	60.6	20.3	1986
Other checkable deposits	8.5	5.5	9.2	1989
Savings (including MMDAs)	20.7	21.5	24.0	1993
Small time deposits	21.1	19.9	25.2	1991
Large time deposits	7.5	13.6	13.0	1988
Fed funds purchased & RPs	8.3	7.9	9.2	1986
Other	7.1	2.4	3.9	1993
Non-interest-bearing liabilities	16.3	20.5	20.3	1986
Domestic demand deposits	14.1	18.3	18.2	1986
Other	2.2	2.2	2.1	1992
Memo				
Managed liabilities	24.7	25.9	27.7	1989
Domestic core deposits	64.5	65.3	69.9	1993

Panel E. Banks Not Ranked among the 1,000 Largest by Assets

Source of Funds	1995	1985	Interval Peak Amt%	Interval Peak Year
Interest-bearing liabilities	75.7	74.9	78.4	1991
Deposits	72.7	72.7	76.4	1991
In foreign offices	0.1	0.1	0.1	1993
In domestic offices	72.6	72.7	76.3	1991
Other checkable deposits	12.4	8.1	13.2	1993
Savings (including MMDAs)	20.4	21.1	23.5	1993
Small time deposits	30.1	32.0	35.8	1991
Large time deposits	8.9	11.5	11.5	1986
Fed funds purchased & RPs	1.8	1.5	1.4	1993
Other	1.2	0.7	0.9	1993
Non-interest-bearing liabilities	14.3	16.2	16.2	1986
Domestic demand deposits	13.2	15.2	14.9	1986
Other	1.1	1.6	1.3	1986
Memo				
Managed liabilities	12.0	13.7	13.5	1989
Domestic core deposits	76.9	76.4	79.7	1993

Note: Managed liabilities are *approximately* equal to the sum of deposits in foreign offices, large time deposits, other interest-bearing liabilities, and fed funds purchased & RPs. Domestic core deposits equal deposits in domestic offices less large time deposits plus domestic demand deposits.

Source: Federal Reserve Bulletin (June 1995), pp. 559–569, and (June 1996), pp. 496–505.

TABLE A7-2 Effective Interest Rates Paid, 1985 and 1995

Panel A. All Insured Commercial Banks

Rates Paid for	1995	1985	Change (bp)
Interest-bearing liabilities	5.00%	8.49%	–349
Interest-bearing deposits	4.47	8.18	–371
In foreign offices	6.12	9.48	–336
In domestic offices	4.11	7.87	–376
Other checkable deposits	2.07	4.54*	–247*
Savings (including MMDAs)	3.19	5.28*	–209*
Large denomination CDs	5.47	8.73	–326
Other time deposits	5.45	6.97*	–152*
Federal funds purchased & RPs	5.65	7.97	–232

Panel B. Ten Largest Banks by Assets

Rates Paid for	1995	1985	Change (bp)
Interest-bearing liabilities	5.92%	9.38%	–346
Interest-bearing deposits	4.99	8.68	–369
In foreign offices	6.07	9.58	–351
In domestic offices	3.42	7.52	–410
Other checkable deposits	1.29	3.26*	–197*
Savings (including MMDAs)	3.11	5.13*	–202*
Large denomination CDs	3.73	9.03	–530
Other time deposits	5.08	6.38*	–130*
Federal funds purchased & RPs	5.22	7.99	–277

Panel C. Banks Ranked 11 through 100 by Assets

Rates Paid for	1995	1985	Change (bp)
Interest-bearing liabilities	4.94%	8.45%	–351
Interest-bearing deposits	4.35	8.14	–379
In foreign offices	6.30	9.31	–301
In domestic offices	4.01	7.84	–383
Other checkable deposits	1.89	4.43*	–254*
Savings (including MMDAs)	3.11	5.27*	–516*
Large denomination CDs	5.70	8.74	–304
Other time deposits	5.35	7.06*	–171*
Federal funds purchased & RPs	5.86	8.03	–217

Panel D. Banks Ranked 101 through 1,000 by Assets

Rates Paid for	1995	1985	Change (bp)
Interest-bearing liabilities	4.65%	8.02%	–337
Interest-bearing deposits	4.26	7.85	–359
In foreign offices	5.93	8.65	–272
In domestic offices	4.22	7.82	–360
Other checkable deposits	2.03	4.64*	–261*
Savings (including MMDAs)	3.24	5.28*	–204*
Large denomination CDs	5.62	8.61	–299
Other time deposits	5.54	7.14*	–160*
Federal funds purchased & RPs	5.61	7.87	–216

TABLE A7-2 (continued)

Panel E. Banks not Ranked among the 1,000 Largest by Assets

Rates Paid for	1995	1985	Change (bp)
Interest-bearing liabilities	4.47%	8.09%	−362
Interest-bearing deposits	4.40	8.06	−366
In foreign offices	5.77	8.34	−257
In domestic offices	4.39	8.06	−367
Other checkable deposits	2.50	4.93*	−143*
Savings (including MMDAs)	3.32	5.37*	−205*
Large denomination CDs	5.56	8.69	−313
Other time deposits	5.52	6.96*	−144*
Federal funds purchased & RPs	5.62	7.79	−217

Note: Where possible, the effective interest rates are based on the average of quarterly balance-sheet items on schedule RC-K of the quarterly call report. The starred items are not available for 1985. Data for those years are for 1987 with changes for 1987 to 1995. In the last column, *bp* stands for basis points.

Source: Federal Reserve Bulletin (June 1995), pp. 559–569.

Selected References

Aberth, John. [1988]. "Searching for an Investment Strategy." *ABA Banking Journal* (July), pp. 39–42.

Benston, George J. [1985]. *An Analysis of the Causes of Savings and Loan Failures.* New York: Salomon Brothers Center for the Study of Financial Institutions and Graduate School of Business Administration, New York University, Monograph Series in Finance and Economics, Monograph 1985–4/5.

Budzeika, George. [1976]. "A Study of Liability Management by New York City Banks." Research Paper, Federal Reserve Bank of New York (January).

Carter, David A., and Joseph F. Sinkey, Jr. [1995]. "An Empirical Investigation into the Use of Interest-Rate Derivatives by U.S. Commercial Banks." Working Paper, University of Georgia.

Cates, David C. [1990]. "Liquidity Lessons for the 1990s." *Bank Management* (April), pp. 20–24.

Cates Bank Financial Analysis Course, Book I. [1984]. New York: Cates Consulting Analysts (January).

Clarke, Robert L. [1991]. Statement before the Committee on Banking, Housing, and Urban Affairs of the U.S. Senate (January 9).

Comptroller's Handbook for National Bank Examiners. [1979]. Englewood Cliffs, NJ: Prentice-Hall.

Darling, George K. [1991]. "Liquidity Revisited." *Bank Asset/Liability Management* (February), pp. 1–3.

Federal Reserve Bulletin. Washington, DC: Board of Governors of the Federal Reserve System (various issues).

Garino, David P. [1979]. "Loans Are Hard to Get in Many Small Towns as Banks Lack Funds." *The Wall Street Journal* (April 4), pp. 1, 7.

General Accounting Office. [1991]. "Bank Supervision: OCC's Supervision of the Bank of New England Was Not Timely or Forceful." Report to the Chairman, Committee on Banking, Housing, and Urban Affairs, U.S. Senate, GAO/GGD-91-128 (September), 49 pp.

Giroux, Gary. [1980]. "A Survey of Forecasting Techniques Used by Commercial Banks." *Journal of Bank Research* (Spring), pp. 51–53.

Guenther, Robert. [1987]. "Reed to Tighten Citicorp Investment Bank." *The Wall Street Journal* (December 7), p. 2.

Hayes, Douglas A. [1980]. *Banks Funds Management: Issues and Practices.* Ann Arbor: University of Michigan.

Hodgman, D. R. [1963]. *Commercial Bank Loan and Investment Policy.* Champaign: University of Illinois Press.

Kane, Edward J. [1970]. "The Term Structure of Interest Rates: An Attempt to Reconcile Teaching and Practice." *Journal of Finance* (May), pp. 361–374.

_____. [1979]. "The Three Faces of Commercial Bank Liability Management." In M. P. Dooley et al., eds., *The Political Economy of Policy-Making.* Beverly Hills: Sage Publications, pp. 149–174.

_____. [1980]. "Tax Exemption, Economic Efficiency, and Relative Interest Rates." Prepared for the Conference on Efficiency in the Municipal Bank Market.

_____. [1981]. "Reregulation, Savings-and-Loan Diversification, and the Flow of Housing Finance." Working Paper 81–1, Ohio State University.

_____. [1986]. "Competitive Financial Reregulation: An International Perspective." Paper presented at the 1986 Conference of the International Center for Monetary and Banking Studies (August).

Kane, Edward J., and Burton G. Malkiel. [1965]. "Bank Portfolio Allocation, Deposit Variability, and the Availability Doctrine." *Quarterly Journal of Economics* (February), pp. 113–134.

Kaufman, George G. "The Federal Safety Net: Not for Banks Only." *Economic Perspectives,* Federal Reserve Bank of Chicago (November-December), pp. 19–28.

Lohr, Steve. [1991]. "When a Big Bank Collapsed, U.S. Presence Stemmed Panic." *The New York Times* (February 18), pp. 1, 26.

Manual of Examination Policies. Washington, DC: FDIC (various revision dates).

McKinney, George W., Jr. [1977]. "A Perspective on the Use of Models in the Management of Banks' Funds." *Journal of Bank Research* (Summer), pp. 122–127.

Ricks, Thomas E. [1987]. "Liquidity Seen Main Concern in Market Crash." *The Wall Street Journal* (December 10), p. 2.

Schnure, Calvin D. [1994]. "Debt Maturity Choice and Risk-Free Assets: The 'Clientele Effect' and the Commercial Paper Market." Finance and Economic Discussion Series 94-4, Federal Reserve Board.

Sinkey, Joseph F., Jr. [1973]. "The Term Structure of Interest Rates: A Time-Series Test of the Kane Expected-Change Model of Interest-Rate Forecasting." *Journal of Money, Credit, and Banking* (February), pp. 192–200.

_____. [1979]. *Problem and Failed Institutions in the Commercial Banking Industry.* Greenwich, CT: JAI Press.

Sinkey, Joseph F., Jr., and John S. Jahera, Jr. [1984]. "The Intracyclical Balance-Sheet Behavior of Large Banks, 1972 to 1978." *Journal of Banking and Finance* 8(1), pp. 109–117.

Volcker, Paul A. [1984]. "Statement before the Committee on Banking, Housing, and Urban Affairs." Washington, DC: U.S. Senate (July 25).

"What's Ahead for Cash Management." *ABA Banking Journal* (December 1990), pp. 57–58.

Wilke, John R. [1991]. "New Hampshire Firms Struggle as Bank Crisis Dries Up Their Credit." *The Wall Street Journal* (February 21), pp. A1, A8.

8
BANK INVESTMENT MANAGEMENT AND INVESTMENT BANKING

Contents

LEARNING OBJECTIVES

■ To understand the role of investments in a bank's asset portfolio

■ To distinguish between active and passive investment management

■ To understand alternative strategies for managing investment securities

■ To understand the components of a bank's investment policy

■ To understand the pricing of fixed-income securities

■ To understand yield calculations and the yield curve

■ To distinguish between investment banking and commercial banking

CHAPTER THEME

A bank's investment portfolio, defined as its holdings of investment securities, can be used to generate both income and liquidity. Risk management of the investment portfolio focuses on the trade-off between **liquidity** and **profitability.** The volume of **trading-account securities** a bank holds varies directly with its propensity to engage in **active investment management,** which tends to vary directly with bank size. Financial innovation, in the form of securitization, has led to the development of **mortgage-backed securities** (MBSs). These securities, in the form of **mortgage pass-through securities** and **collateralized mortgage obligations** (CMOs), have become an important part of banks' portfolios of securities. The **Tax Reform Act of 1986** killed the market for **municipal** (tax-free) **securities,** and banks' holdings of these instruments have dropped precipitously since then. As the **Glass-Steagall Act of 1933** has been increasingly eroded, commercial banks have been permitted to increase their activities in investment banking. This development has been uneven, however, as the largest bank holding companies, such as BankAmerica, Bankers Trust, Chase Manhattan, Citicorp, and J. P. Morgan, have become the major players among commercial banks. Effective economic barriers to entry, as opposed to regulatory barriers, bar community banks from playing a major role in most investment banking activities.

KEY CONCEPTS, IDEAS, AND TERMS

- Active (passive) investment management
- Bond valuation
- Collateralized mortgage obligations (CMOs)
- Fixed-income securities
- Investment account
- Investment banking
- Investment-grade securities
- Investment policy and strategies
- Liquidity-profitability trade-off
- Mortgage-backed securities (MBSs)
- Mortgage pass-through securities
- Municipal securities
- Trading-accounting securities
- Yield curve

INTRODUCTION

As of December 31, 1934, there were 14,137 commercial banks in the United States. These banks had more investment securities ($18 billion, 39% of total assets) on their balance sheets than net loans and leases ($14.6 billion, 31% of total assets). As banking approaches the year 2000, the number of banks will be about one-half the number in 1934, and investment securities will be in the range of 15–25 percent of total assets, dwarfed by loans and leases, with 50–60 percent of total assets.[1] Although the role of investment securities in bank portfolios has declined in importance relative to loans and leases, they still play an important part in bank financial management. This chapter explores that role and commercial banking's reentry into **investment banking,** a function which commercial banks enjoyed prior to the passage of the **Glass-Steagall Act of 1933.**

A bank's investment portfolio consists mainly of various investment securities issued by federal, state, and local governments, or securities backed up by mortgages (mortgage-backed securities, or MBSs). An investment security is defined (in 12 Code of Federal Regulations or C.F.R.) as "a *marketable obligation* in the form of a bond, note or debenture which is commonly regarded as an investment security . . . (excluding) investments which are predominantly *speculative* in nature" (emphasis mine). Accordingly, bank investment securities must be marketable but not speculative (i.e., investment quality of at least BBB or Baa). The requirement

---

[1] These data are from the FDIC's *Statistics on Banking, 1934–1994* (volume 1), p. A49, and the *Federal Reserve Bulletin* (June 1996), pp. 495–505.

of investment-grade quality means that credit risk is usually not a major concern in a bank's investment portfolio. Given a bank's loan demand and customer relationships, its investment portfolio serves to balance its structure of earning assets and risk exposure. This purpose is reflected in the results of a 1990 survey by the Bank Administration Institute (Bergquist [1991]) that concluded that the primary objectives of bank investment portfolios are the management of **interest-rate risk** and liquidity. Although the largest banks rely more and more on the use of interest-rate swaps, options, and futures to manage interest-rate risk[2] (chapter 9), the investment portfolios of community banks are still important vehicles for managing interest-rate risk. Prior to the Tax Reform Act of 1986, municipal bonds provided many banks, especially smaller ones, with an important tax shelter from federal income taxes. However, except for special circumstances (described in appendix A of this chapter), this tax shelter has been removed.

The income from a bank's investment portfolio comes in two forms:

- Interest revenue
- Capital gains (losses)

A debt security purchased at par and held to maturity generates only interest income. Securities sold prior to maturity can generate capital gains due to lower interest rates relative to the rates at the time of purchase, or capital losses due to higher interest rates relative to the rates at the time of purchase.

CHAPTER PREREQUISITES

Because the management of interest-rate risk, in the context of asset-liability management (ALM), was covered in chapter 5, and because liquidity management was covered in the previous chapter, this chapter assumes you have a working knowledge of the material from those two chapters. Additional background presented here includes the four credit-extension building blocks, the pricing of fixed income securities, and yield curves.

Credit-Extension Building Blocks and the Valuation of Investment Securities

Credit-extension building blocks come in four basic forms:[3]

- Fixed-rate debt
- Floating- or variable-rate debt
- Zero-coupon debt
- Amortized debt (e.g., a mortgage that pays both principal and interest)

The investment securities that banks hold are of the first three kinds, whereas many bank loans are amortized. As financial markets have become more complete, the supply of instruments to meet banks' demands for investment securities has grown. For example, the development of floating-rate debt and the process of "stripping" bonds into interest-only obligations (IOs) and principal-only obligations (POs) have made bond markets more complete. These innovations, however, have made

---

[2] Only about 600 banks actually use derivatives for managing interest-rate risk (Carter and Sinkey [1997]).

[3] Smith and Smithson [1990] describe bonds, loans, or private placements as "traditional credit extension building blocks."

the study of fixed-income securities a bit more complex. Nevertheless, don't let all of the bells and whistles confuse you, because the most basic valuation principle still holds: The value of a stream of promised payments, including the special case of a zero-coupon bond, equals the present or discounted value of the future cash flows, where the discount rate is the going rate of interest on obligations of similar risk and maturity. Box 8-1 gives a historical perspective on debt-instrument innovations.

Table 8-1 presents the basic **bond-valuation** formula and five cases showing its application to the four credit-extension building blocks. Eight valuation properties of fixed-income securities or assets that are crucial to understanding how changes in interest rates and maturity (duration) affect prices are the following:

Key: i = going rate of interest and c = coupon rate

- If $i = c$, the security sells at par
- If $i > c$, the security sells at a discount
- If $i < c$, the security sells at a premium

BOX 8-1

FINANCIAL INNOVATION IN THE 1860s: A DUAL CURRENCY/COMMODITY BOND

This picture shows a 7 percent cotton loan of the Confederate States of America (stamped in London on June 27, 1863). The debt instrument had a face value of 40,000 pounds of cotton and cost 3 million British pounds sterling, or 75 million French francs. The coupon rate was 7 percent, and the coupon payment was 1,000 pounds sterling, or 25,000 French francs. Since the coupon payments equal .07 × price of cotton × 40,000, the price of cotton per pound was 2.8 pounds sterling (= [.07 × 40,000]/1,000, or .112 French francs. Conspicuous by its absence, however, is the maturity of the obligation. Nevertheless, given the maturity and assuming annual compounding, the future value (FV) of the bond in period t would be $FV_t = (1.07)^t \times$ price of cotton × 40,000, where t = the maturity of the bond. Although it is tempting to call the Confederate debt instrument a dual currency/commodity bond, it is unlikely the Confederacy could have made the principal payment in anything but cotton.

Source: Courtesy of Clifford W. Smith, Jr., University of Rochester.

TABLE 8-1 The Valuation of Bonds and Bond Derivatives

Basic valuation formula: $P_0 = \sum_t [C_t/(1+i)^t] + F/(1+i)^N$

where P_0 = price or present value
C_t = coupon-interest payment in period t
F = face, principal, or maturity value
i = discount rate or going rate of interest
N = maturity
Σ = sigma or summation sign over $t = 1$ to N

Case 1: "Plain Vanilla." A five-year bond with a 10 percent annual coupon and a $1,000 face value. If the going rate of interest on similar obligations is 8 percent, the bond will sell at a *premium* price of $1,080. The cash flows at 10 percent are more valuable because other similar instruments are only paying 8 percent. If the going rate of interest is 12 percent, the bond will sell at a discount price of $927. Its cash flows at 10 percent are less valuable than those at 12 percent.

Case 2: Zero-Coupon Bond. The same bond as above except without any interest payments. As long as the going rate of interest is positive, the instrument must sell at a discount. At $i = 10$ percent, its value is $620.92. By the way, the IRS requires the investor to prorate the discount ($379.08) over the maturity of the obligation and to pay taxes on that portion even though no income is received. The valuation approaches for a PO and a zero-coupon bond are the same.

Case 3: Interest Only. The same bond as in case 1 but stripped of its principal payment. The instrument is simply an annuity. At $i = 10$ percent, the annuity has a present value of $379.08. Note that the addition of the IO and PO values at 10 percent are, of course, equal to the present value of the plain vanilla bond at 10%. The whole is equal to the sum of the parts.

Case 4: Perpetual Bond. The same bond as in case 3, except the interest payments never cease. If the coupon payment is fixed, the valuation is the same as the zero-growth model. Specifically, simply divide the payment by the going rate of interest. For example, at $i = 10$ percent, the value is $100/.10 = $1,000; at 8 percent, it's $1,250; and at 12 percent, it's $833.

Case 5: Floating-Rate Instruments. In this situation, there is uncertainty about the size of the interest payments. For example, if the coupon rate floats at 200 basis points over the prime rate, then coupon payments will vary with the prime rate. Assume the bond in case 1 has its coupon rate so defined and the prime rate (on an annual basis) is 8 percent, 8.5 percent, 9 percent, 9.5 percent, and 10 percent over the maturity of the bond. Given this interest-rate scenario, the coupon payment in each of the five years will be 10 percent, 10.5 percent, 11 percent, 11.5 percent, and 12 percent. If the bond's discount rate moves in proportion to its coupon rate, assuming it sells at par, the present value of the interest-payments stream will not change. Of course, as interest rates rise, the present value of the principal payment will decline. The promised payment of $1,000 at maturity, however, does not vary.

Note: It is assumed that you know how to use a handheld calculator or present-value tables to verify the figures presented in this table.

- Asset prices and yields are inversely related
- The longer an asset's maturity (duration) is, the more sensitive is its price to a change in interest rates
- As the term to maturity (duration) increases, the percentage price changes, described in the previous point, increase but at a diminishing rate for any given change in rate
- For a given maturity and a given change in rate, the capital gain from the decrease in rate exceeds the capital loss from the increase in rate
- Except for one-year and perpetual assets, the higher an asset's coupon rate, the less sensitive is its price to a change in interest rates

Table 8-1 and these eight properties provide a solid foundation for understanding the valuation and price-yield relationships of debt instruments.

Pricing Conventions and the Yields on Treasury Bills

Treasury bills (T-bills) are short-term IOUs of the U.S. Treasury with maturities of 13, 26, and 52 weeks. T-bills are sold at a discount through a competitive-bidding process. The dollar return or discount to the investor is the difference between the face value and the purchase price. Since T-bills do not pay any intermediate cash flows, they are pure-discount or zero-coupon securities.[4]

Three alternative conventions used to express the return or yield on a T-bill are

- Bank-discount method
- Coupon-equivalent or bond-equivalent method
- Effective-yield method

Table 8-2 shows the formula for each of these methods and sample calculations. Viewing the three formulas as a group, it is easy to see the shortcomings of the first two methods. First, because a year has 365 or 366 days rather than the conventional 360 days, and because the investor's cash outflow is not the face value of the bill but its price, the bank-discount method understates the true rate of return. Less obviously, for T-bills that mature in less that one year, reinvestment income or interest on interest for the remainder of the year is ignored. To remedy the first two shortcomings of the bank-discount method, the coupon-equivalent method was developed. It replaces 360 by the number of days in the year (365 or 366) and substitutes P for F. To remedy the interest-on-interest problem requires the use of the

---

TABLE 8-2 Alternative Methods of Calculating Yields and Prices on Treasury Bills

Key: F = face value, P = price, N = maturity of bill in days [(91, 182, or 365 (366)]

Method	*Yield Formula*	*Example for Six-Month Bill*
Bank discount	$[(F - P)/F] \times 360/N$	$[(100 - 96.436]/100 \times 360/182 = 0.0705$ or 7.05%
Coupon Equivalent	$[(F - P)/P] \times 365/N$	$[(100 - 96.436]/96.436 \times 365/182 = 0.0741$ or 7.41%
Effective Yield	$(F/P)^{365/N} - 1$	$100/96.436^{365/182} - 1 = 0.0755$ or 7.55%

Note: Given the yield, one can solve for the corresponding price. The formula for the effective yield can also be written as $[1 + (F - P)/P]365/N - 1]$, which for the six-month bill above gives $[1 + (100 - 96.436)/96.436)^{365/182} - 1] = 0.0755$ or 7.55%. To convert from an effective yield (y_e) to a coupon-equivalent yield (y_{ce}), use the following formula:

$$y_{ce} = 2[(1 + y_e)^{0.5} - 1]$$

For example, $2[(1.0775)^{0.5} - 1] = 0.0741$ or 7.41%.

Going in the opposite direction, the formula is

$$y_e = (1 + y_{ce}/2)^2 - 1$$

For example, $(1 + 0.0741/2)^2 - 1 = 0.0755$ or 7.55%.

---

[4] Other examples of money-market instruments that trade as discount securities are commercial paper and bankers' acceptances (chapter 7). Until the early 1980s, most certificates of deposits (CDs) were issued as interest-bearing securities; although they still dominate the market, zero-coupon CDs have increased in popularity.

effective-yield method as shown in Table 8-2. To compute the effective yield, you need a calculator with a y^x function.

Moving from the bank-discount method to the coupon-equivalent method to the effective-yield method, we get successively higher yields for T-bills with maturities less than one year. This occurs because we remedy the understatement problem with each successive method. Thus, the following relationship exists for bills with maturities of less than one year:

$$y_{bd} < y_{ce} < y_e$$

where y stands for yield and the subscripts *bd, ce,* and *e* stand for bank discount, coupon equivalent, and effective, respectively. The notes to Table 8-2 show how to convert from y_{ce} to y_e or vice versa.

By solving for P (price) in any of the formulas in Table 8-2, one gets the T-bill price corresponding to the method. For example, using the bank-discount method, the corresponding price is

$$P = F - (F \times y_{bd} \times N/360)$$

where F = face value (\$100) and N = 91, 182, or 365 (366 in a leap year). Treating the price as unknown for the 182-day bill shown in Table 8-2, we get

$$P = \$100 - (\$100 \times 0.0705 \times 182/60) = 100 - 3.564 = \$96.436$$

The 13- and 26-week T-bills are auctioned every Monday (or the next business day when Monday is a national holiday); the 52-week bills are also auctioned on Monday but at four-week intervals. Every Tuesday for Monday auctions, *The Wall Street Journal* publishes these results in its financial section. Table 8-3 presents results for a recent T-bill auction.

TABLE 8-3	Results for an Auction of 13-Week and 26-Week U.S. Treasury Bills	
	13-Week[a]	*26-Week[a]*
Applications	\$54,253,706,000	\$48,932,625,000
Accepted bids	\$13,034,551,000	\$13,100,968,000
Accepted at low price	22%	15%
Accepted noncompetitively	\$ 1,404,528,000	\$ 1,131,164,000
Average price (rate)	98.779 (4.83%)	97.478 (4.97%)
High price (rate)	98.782 (4.82%)	97.492 (4.96%)
Low price (rate)	98.779 (4.83%)	97.482 (4.98%)
Coupon equivalent	4.96%	5.17%
Effective yield[b]	5.02%	5.24%

Notes:

[a]Both issues were dated December 12. The 13-week bills matured on March 13, 1997, and the 26-week bills matured June 12, 1997. The average, high, and low prices (rates) are calculated using a 360-day year; the coupon-equivalent yield uses 365 days.

[b]The effective yield was calculated using the conversion formula shown in the notes to Table 8–2.

Source: Adapted from *The Wall Street Journal* (December 10, 1996), p. C24, excluding the effective yield.

Yield Curves and the Term Structure of Interest Rates

A **yield curve** shows the relationship between the yield to maturity (YTM or y) and term to maturity (N) of similar securities (e.g., U.S. Treasury securities or corporate bonds of similar quality). It is a two-dimensional picture of $y = f(N)$, holding all other things constant. In nontechnical language, the yield-curve relationship is a picture of the term structure of interest rates.[5]

Yield curves are described in terms of their shape (slope) and position. As depicted in Figure 8-1, yield curves come in four basic shapes:

1. Positively sloped
2. Negatively sloped ("inverted")
3. Flat (zero slope)
4. Humped

The fact that short-term rates fluctuate more than long-term rates and the fact that yield curves flatten out as term to maturity increases can be linked to the bond valuation properties presented earlier in this chapter.

The position of the yield curve refers to the level of interest rates, which can be described as high, low, or in transition from high to low or vice versa. When rates are at cyclically low levels, the yield curve tends to be positively sloped or ascending. When rates are at cyclically high levels, the yield curve tends to be negatively sloped or humped. When the level of rates is in transition, the yield curve tends to

FIGURE 8-1 Basic Yield-Curve Shapes

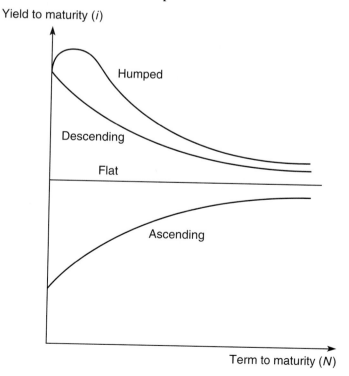

___

[5]The leading explanations of the term structure are expectations-based theories; see appendix A of this chapter.

be flat. If investors demand a liquidity premium for holding longer-term bonds, then the most commonly observed yield curve would be positively sloped, which has been the historical case.

Yield Curves, Interest-Rate Risk, and Duration

If the yield curve is flat and only parallel shifts in it are permitted (the case of simple Macaulay **duration**; Box 8-2 provides a primer on duration), then when the bond's duration equals the holding period, price risk and reinvestment risk are balanced or offsetting (i.e., the bond investment is immunized). Figure 8-2 shows four pictures: Panel A depicts the yield-curve restrictions assumed for Macaulay's duration; Panel B shows that duration is always equal to or less than maturity, depending on the type of bond (e.g., zero-coupon versus coupon); Panel C shows that for a given coupon bond and holding all other things constant, the higher the yield, the shorter Macaulay's duration is; and Panel D shows the duration of bond changes with shifts in interest rates. In particular, Panel D, which presents a yield-duration curve rather than a yield-maturity curve, shows that interest rates and duration are inversely related.

For coupon bonds, interest-rate risk consists of price risk and coupon reinvestment risk. Remove the coupon, as in a zero-coupon bond, and the reinvestment risk disappears. Match the holding period with the maturity of a zero-coupon bond

---

| BOX 8-2

A PRIMER ON DURATION

Definition: Duration is a measure of effective maturity that incorporates the timing and magnitude of a security's cash flows. It captures the combined effects of required yield (discount rate), coupon payments, and maturity on a bond's interest-rate risk.

Intuition: Think of duration as an elasticity measure of the sensitivity of a bond's price to a change in interest rates, that is,

$$\text{DURATION} = D \approx (\Delta P/P)/[\Delta i/(1 + i)]$$

where P = bond price, i = required yield, and Δ = change. Rearranging, we focus on the change in a bond's price as a function of its duration:

$$\Delta P \approx -D[\Delta i(1 + i)]P$$

Calculation: Duration is a weighted average of the number of years until each of a bond's cash flows are received. It can be expressed as a ratio in which the numerator is present value of all cash flows weighted by the time period in which they are received. The denominator is the price of the bond. Thus, assuming annual compounding,

$$D = [\sum_t CF_t(t)/(1 + i)]/[\sum_t CF_t/(1 + i)^t]$$

where CF = cash flow and t = period in which cash flow is received.

Spread-sheet example for a three-year, 9.4 percent coupon bond that pays semiannual interest (par value = $1,000). Assume going rate of interest, i, is 9.4 percent.

Time period	Cash flow	PV of CF	Weighted PV of CF
1	47	47/1.047	44.89
2	47	47/1.047²	85.74
3	47	47/1.047³	122.85
4	47	47/1.047⁴	156.45
5	47	47/1.047⁵	186.78
6	47	47/1.047⁶	214.08
6	1,000	1,000/1.047⁶	4,554.82
Sum	$1,282	$1,000	$5,365.61

$D = 5,365.61/1,000 = 5.4$ half years or 2.7 years < 3 (maturity of the bond); see Panel B of Figure 8–2 for a graphical depiction of $D < N$.

Panel A. Macaulay's assumption
flat yield curve with only parallel shifts

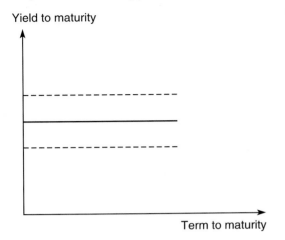

Panel B. Relation between
duration and maturity

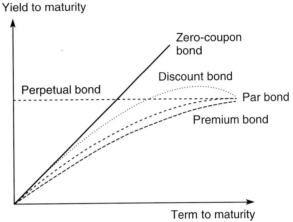

Panel C. Relation between duration and
yield to maturity for a specific bond

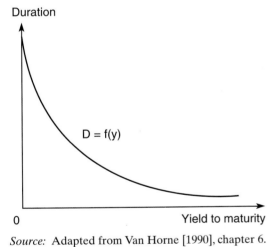

Panel D. Relation between
duration and changes in interest rates

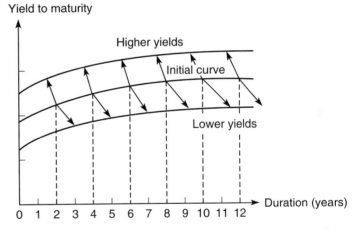

Source: Adapted from Van Horne [1990], chapter 6.

FIGURE 8-2 Yield Curves and Duration

and the price risk also disappears. For coupon bonds, price risk and reinvestment risk can be offset if the bond's duration matches the holding period. The balancing of the components of interest-rate risk is called *immunization.*

ACTIVE INVESTMENT MANAGEMENT, BANKING LAW, AND REGULATORY INTERFERENCE

Symons and White [1991] describe the restrictions placed on bank investment portfolios by banking law (12 C.F.R.). Because investment securities are distinct from loans, they are not subject to the legal lending limit that applies to bank loans. Nevertheless, certain restrictions do apply. To qualify as a bank investment security, the obligation must be both marketable and of investment quality. In general, the bank must exercise "prudent banking judgment" in determining that the issuer of the obligation has the financial resources to service the debt. Also, the statutes define whether a bank may "deal in, underwrite, and purchase and sell for its own account" and the limitation, if any, applied to the particular type of security.[6]

Regulatory Interference

If the managers of bank investment portfolios want to pursue an active investment strategy, regulatory interference in the form of enforcement and interpretation of regulations applying to investment securities may frustrate them. For example, Aberth [1988] tells the following story. In late January and early February 1988, the investment portfolio manager of a major superregional bank (NCNB, now NationsBank) began buying heavily in securities. By the end of February, the bank had a $45 million capital gain that the manager wanted to realize. However, because the bank's examiners required the securities to be held for at least 30 days, the capital gain eventually dropped to $20 million—an opportunity loss to the bank of $25 million. Craig Wardlaw, a senior vice president for NCNB, asked: "I just wonder who at the Office of the Comptroller of the Currency I should send the bill to?" (p. 39).

Bank investment managers have the difficult task of attempting to balance their banks' investment needs and strategies with regulations and examiners' requirements. Wardlaw further describes his frustrations as a bank investment manager:

> Examiners literally walk in and have us prove everything we do. It's as if they don't believe that banks have any integrity. But they're not the ones managing the money. Examiners want us to operate as if it were 1970. Our investment people are inhibited from managing the portfolio based on how they assess interest-rate risk. Of course, there's always the chance that we can lose money. But if you're a good portfolio manager you'll take more gains than losses. I don't think regulators should regulate all banks identically. A $28 billion-asset bank such as ours with an investment staff of 160 people in funds management is going to be more sophisticated than a $90 million-asset bank with a funds management staff of one. (p. 39)

Wardlaw's recommendation is that regulators consider restrictions on bank investment management on a case-by-case basis, as they did with restrictions placed on banks' activities in futures markets in the late 1970s. Specifically, bankers had to document their knowledge and experience of futures trading before they could engage in it. A similar case-by-case approach could be applied to banks that want to engage in active trading of investment securities.[7]

Because of regulatory interference, many managers of bank investment portfolios, especially at smaller institutions, adopt a **passive** approach to portfolio management (e.g., a staggered or laddered approach with spaced maturities, say, every month or quarter, that generate a steady flow of liquidity for the bank and reduce interest-rate risk because some securities are approaching par value as they near maturity). Nevertheless, regulation is not the only constraint faced by banks in this area. Additional factors include the lack of experienced investment personnel in

---

[6] As the wall separating commercial and investment banking continues to crumble, BHCs have gained the power to underwrite corporate debt (1989), and several BHCs (e.g., J. P. Morgan & Co. in 1990) have been authorized to underwrite corporate equities on a limited basis. These powers extend to the securities subsidiary of the BHC.

[7] A more relevant question is whether bank investment managers with the benefit of a *federal guarantee* should be betting on interest rates. You want the guarantee, you play by the guarantor's rules.

many banks and efficient securities markets. As a result, for the thousands of community banks in the United States, passive investment management is the *modus operandi*. In contrast, money-center and regional banks engage in active investment management. However, the increased competition in the financial-services industry has put greater pressure on *all* bank investment managers to attempt to generate more income (per unit of investment risk) from their investment portfolios.

Active versus Passive Investment Management

In distinguishing between active and passive investment policies, Radcliffe ([1982], p. 253) provides some useful insights. He uses the term "passive" simply to distinguish investment policies from the more active trading associated with speculators. Although bank examiners frown on speculative trading, portfolio managers at the larger banks have been known to make an occasional bet or two on the future course of interest rates.

Let's define active investment managers as those who engage jointly in the ongoing practice of betting (speculating) on future interest rates and providing dealer and market-making services. Most of the members of this set will be found in regional, superregional, and money-center banks. Speculating on interest-rate movements is manifested in the active trading of securities (the NCNB story from above), as opposed to a buy-and-hold strategy. Although passive investment management is relatively inactive, it does permit rebalancing to adjust to changing market conditions. Accordingly, if market conditions result in portfolio positions inconsistent with the bank's investment objectives, the portfolio should be realigned whether it is actively or passively managed. On balance, passive investment management can be viewed as active management without speculation and dealer activity. In either case, however, investment portfolios managers focus on yield, maturity, and price volatility.

BANK SECURITIES PORTFOLIOS AND EVIDENCE OF ACTIVE INVESTMENT MANAGEMENT

Under SFAS No. 115,[8] all debt and marketable securities held by banks are classified into one of three categories:

- Held to maturity
- Available for sale
- Held for trading

Securities identified as "held to maturity" are reported at amortized cost, whereas those "available for sale" or "held for trading" must be marked to market (i.e., reported at market value).[9] Securities held to maturity and held for sale

---

[8] SFAS stands for the Statement of Financial Accounting Standards issued by the Financial Accounting Standards Board (FASB). Bank regulators required banks to implement SFAS 115 with the March 1994 call report, although banks were permitted to adopt it for earlier reports.

[9] Prior to SFAS 115, trading-account securities still had to be marked to market, but debt securities held for sale were reported at the lower of amortized cost or market value. Under SFAS 115, changes in the market value of securities held for sale, unlike changes in trading-account securities, do not affect reported income but are reflected (on an after-tax basis) directly in bank equity. Gains (losses) on securities held in the trading account are included as part of noninterest income and therefore affect net operating income or income before securities gains (losses). See *Federal Reserve Bulletin* (June 1995), pp. 548–549.

298 PART III   *The Portfolio Risks of Banking and Their Management: Theory and Practice*

constitute a bank's **investment account,** whereas those held for trading make up the **trading account.**[10] The more securities a bank holds in its trading account and the more securities it makes available for sale, the more active its investment management is.

Table 8-4 shows the securities portfolios of insured commercial banks by bank size for the years 1985 and 1995 (as a percentage of average consolidated assets). The trading accounts shown in Table 8-4 provide some evidence of the existence of active investment management. To illustrate, at year-end 1995 and 1985, trading-account securities (as a percentage of average consolidated assets) across bank size were as follows:

	1995	1985
Ten largest banks ranked by assets	8.9%	3.5%
Banks ranked 11 to 100	0.8	1.0
Banks ranked 101 to 1,000	0.2	0.2
Banks not ranked among the 1,000 largest	0.0	0.0

Although trading activity increases with bank size, the 10 largest banks are the major traders.

The types of debt securities banks hold can be classified into five categories:

- U.S. Treasury

- U.S. agency and corporate

- State and local government

- Mortgage pass-through securities

- Collateralized mortgage obligations (CMOs)

The first three classes are traditional bank investments, and the last two are the result of innovations associated with the development of securitization and pass-through securities. Combining 1995 data for CMOs and government-backed mortgage pools, we get the following profile across bank size:

	1995
Ten largest banks ranked by assets	4.4%
Banks ranked 11 to 100	7.9
Banks ranked 101 to 1,000	8.9
Banks not ranked among the 1,000 largest	6.9
All banks	7.2%

Banks below the 10 largest have been the biggest proportional users of total pass-through securities. Box 8-3 provides a glossary of pass-through finance terms.

---

[10] Insured banks with total assets of $1 billion or more are required to itemize their trading-account assets into eight categories: (1) U.S. Treasury securities, (2) U.S. government agency and corporation obligations, (3) securities issued by states and political subdivisions in the United States, (4) other notes, bonds, and debentures, (5) certificates of deposit, (6) commercial paper, (7) banker's acceptances, and (8) other.

TABLE 8-4	The Securities Portfolios of Insured Commercial Banks by Bank Size for 1985 and 1995 (as a percentage of average consolidated assets)

Panel A. All Insured Commercial Banks

Type or Class of Security	1995	1985
U.S. Treasury	5.3%	6.8%
Other U.S. agency and corporate	2.7	1.8
State and local government	1.8	4.9
Mortgage pass-through securities	4.5	1.0
Collateralized mortgage obligations	2.7	NA
Other debt securities	2.1	1.1
Total debt	19.0	15.6
Equity	0.4	NA
Total investment account	19.4	15.6
Trading account	2.5	1.2
Total securities	21.9%	16.8%

Panel B. Ten Largest Banks by Assets

Type or Class of Security	1995	1985
U.S. Treasury	2.0%	1.9%
Other U.S. agency and corporate	0.1	0.1
State and local government	0.5	1.5
Mortgage pass-through securities	2.9	0.5
Collateralized mortgage obligations	1.5	NA
Other debt securities	3.3	1.8
Total debt	10.3	5.7
Equity	0.4	NA
Total investment account	10.7	5.7
Trading account	8.9	3.5
Total securities	19.5%	9.3%

Panel C. Banks Ranked 11 through 100 by Assets

Type or Class of Security	1995	1985
U.S. Treasury	4.8%	4.5%
Other U.S. agency and corporate	1.5	0.5
State and local government	1.1	3.9
Mortgage pass-through securities	5.1	0.8
Collateralized mortgage obligations	2.8	NA
Other debt securities	2.2	0.7
Total debt	17.5	10.5
Equity	0.4	NA
Total investment account	17.9	10.5
Trading account	0.8	1.0
Total securities	18.6%	11.5%

(continued)

TABLE 8-4 (Continued)

Panel D. Banks Ranked 101 through 1,000 by Assets

Type or Class of Security	1995	1985
U.S. Treasury	6.5%	8.6%
Other U.S. agency and corporate	3.2	2.3
State and local government	2.3	6.2
Mortgage pass-through securities	5.4	1.1
Collateralized mortgage obligations	3.5	NA
Other debt securities	1.6	1.2
Total debt	22.4	19.4
Equity	0.5	NA
Total investment account	22.9	19.4
Trading account	0.2	0.2
Total securities	23.1%	19.6%

Panel E. Banks Not Ranked among the 1,000 Largest by Assets

Type or Class of Security	1995	1985
U.S. Treasury	9.2%	12.6%
Other U.S. agency and corporate	8.2	4.6
State and local government	4.7	8.0
Mortgage pass-through securities	4.2	1.5
Collateralized mortgage obligations	2.7	NA
Other debt securities	1.0	0.7
Total debt	30.0	27.5
Equity	0.5	NA
Total investment account	30.5	27.5
Trading account	0.0	0.0
Total securities	30.5%	27.5%

Source: Federal Reserve Bulletin (June 1996), pp. 495–505, and (June 1995), pp. 559–569.

Focusing on traditional securities, defined as Treasury, agency, and state and local instruments, we get the following profiles for 1985 and 1995 (as a percentage of average consolidated assets):

	1995	1985
Ten largest banks ranked by assets	2.6%	3.5%
Banks ranked 11 to 100	7.9	8.9
Banks ranked 101 to 1,000	12.0	17.1
Banks not ranked among the 1,000 largest	22.1	25.2
All banks	9.8%	13.5%

Two conclusions from these data are as follows: (1) as bank size increases, the relative amount of traditional securities held in bank investment portfolios declines; (2) from 1985 to 1995, the relative amounts of traditional securities held by most banks declined.

BOX 8-3

A GLOSSARY OF PASS-THROUGH FINANCE

Mortgage pool: A group of mortgages (usually residential) classified by original maturity and type (e.g., fixed-rate conventional or adjustable rate) and packaged for sale to investors in the *secondary mortgage market.*

Mortgage pass-through security: A security that passes cash flows through from borrowers to investors as loan payments are collected in the *mortgage pool.* The issuer of the security sells shares or *participation certifications* (PCs) to investors, who receive the passed-through monthly payments of principal and interest. For a *servicing fee,* the seller of the loan usually collects the payments. Loan originators can sell *servicing rights* to third parties.

Agency pass-through securities: Pass-through securities guaranteed by a third party. The three major types of agency pass-throughs are guaranteed by *Ginnie Mae* (a federally related agency) and *Fannie Mae* and *Freddie Mac* (both government-sponsored agencies). Only Ginnie Mae securities are backed by the full faith and credit of the U.S. government.

Conventional or private-label, pass-through securities: Pass-through securities that are not associated with a government agency. To reduce credit risk, these securities, which are evaluated by ratings firms such as Moody's and S & P, are supported by third-party *credit enhancements.*

Prepayment risk: The uncertainty associated with loan payments. As discussed in chapter 5, prepayment risk is an *embedded option* in any loan contract. This option can produce prepayments or *contraction risk* when interest rates are declining, or *extension risk* when interest rates are rising. Contraction risk shortens the life of an asset, whereas extension risk lengthens the life of an asset.

Stripped security: Financial instruments whose cash flows are separated ("stripped") into interest-only (IO) and principal-only (PO) obligations. IOs and POs are highly rate-sensitive assets.

Interest-only obligation: A security whose cash flows consist only of interest payments. The value of an IO strip varies directly with the level of interest rates because of reduced extension risk when interest rates rise.

Principal-only obligation: A security whose cash flows consist only of principal payments. The value of a PO varies inversely with the level of interest rates because of increased prepayment (contraction) risk when interest rates decline.

Collateralized mortgage obligation (CMO): A mortgage-backed security with multiple classes or "tranches" in which cash flows are separated into different payment streams such as fast pay (e.g., of principal only), medium pay (e.g., of interest only), and slow pay (e.g., at a variable rate [LIBOR], even though the underlying mortgages are fixed-rate assets). In addition, the various tranches have pecking orders such that subordinated classes exist. At the bottom of the pecking order, a residual-interests security might be found. CMOs are a good example of financial engineering to suit investors' need for a particular type of cash flow.

Risk-Based capital guidelines: The risk weights assigned to asset-backed securities under risk-based capital requirements for insured commercial banks are as follows:

Type of asset-backed security	Risk weight
GNMA (Ginnie Mae) securities	0%
FHLMC (Freddie Mac) and FNMA (Fannie Mae) securities	20%
Privately issued, mortgage-backed securities collaterized by GNMA, FHLMC, or FNMA, or by FHA- or VA-guaranteed mortgages[a]	20%
Privately issued, mortgage-backed securities collateralized by one-to four-family residential properties[a]	50%
Stripped, mortgage-backed securities, residual interest, and subordinated class securities	100%
Asset-backed securities collateralized by nonmortgage assets	100%

[a]Privately issued, mortgage-backed securities must meet the criteria outlined in the risk-based capital guidelines to be accorded the risk weight of the underlying collateral.

Source: Risk-Based Capital Guidelines, Federal Reserve; also see chapter 13.

Effective Interest Rates on Bank Securities

Table 8-5 shows effective interest rates earned on securities held by insured commercial banks, by bank size, for 1985 and 1995. Interest rates for the investment account, the trading account, all securities, and all securities on a tax-equivalent basis are shown. Because the general level of interest rates was lower in 1995 than 1985, the effective rates earned were lower in 1995 than 1985.

TABLE 8-5 Effective Interest Rates Earned on Securities Held by Insured Commercial Banks by Bank Size for 1985 and 1995

Panel A. All Insured Commercial Banks

Category	1995	1985
Investment account	6.36%	9.39%
Trading account	7.98	10.11
All securities	6.55	9.44
All securities (TE)	6.55	11.04

Panel B. Ten Largest Banks Ranked by Assets

Category	1995	1985
Investment account	7.06%	9.69%
Trading account	8.11	10.35
All securities	7.54	9.95
All securities (TE)	7.54	10.89

Panel C. Banks Ranked 11 through 100 by Assets

Category	1995	1985
Investment account	6.34%	9.01%
Trading account	7.27	9.56
All securities	6.38	10.94
All securities (TE)	6.39	9.06

Panel D. Banks Ranked 101 through 1,000 by Assets

Category	1995	1985
Investment account	6.25%	9.15%
Trading account	5.55	8.88
All securities	6.25	9.15
All securities (TE)	6.26	10.89

Panel E. Banks Not Ranked among the 1,000 Largest by Assets

Category	1995	1985
Investment account	6.11%	9.64%
Trading account	6.09	10.26
All securities	6.11	9.64
All securities (TE)	6.12	11.26

Note: The Fed indicates that, if possible, interest rates were calculated based on "an average of quarterly average balance sheet data reported on schedule RC-K of the quarterly call report."

Source: Federal Reserve Bulletin (June 1995), pp. 559–569.

Regarding tax effects, because the relationship between a tax-equivalent return, $r(TE)$, and a taxable return, r, is

$$r(TE) = r/(1 - t) \qquad \text{(8-1)}$$

where t is the relevant marginal tax rate, the (weighted) tax-equivalent return for a portfolio consisting of taxable and tax-free securities would be

$$r(TE) = [S(t)/S]r + \{[S - S(t)]/S\}[r/(1 - t)] \qquad \text{(8-2)}$$

where $S + S(t) = S =$ total securities, and (t) indicates a taxable yield or taxable security. For example, suppose that a bank has a $100 million investment portfolio consisting of $60 million in taxable securities with an average yield of 8 percent, and $40 in tax-free securities with an average yield of 7 percent. If the bank's marginal tax rate is 0.20, then $r(TE)$ is

$$r(TE) = 0.6(0.08) + .4[0.07/(1 - 0.2)]$$
$$= 0.6(0.08) + 0.4(0.0875)$$
$$= 0.048 + 0.035 = 0.083 = 8.3\%$$

By definition then, the tax-equivalent yields shown in Table 8-5 are all equal to or larger than the unadjusted yields. For example, the interest rate on all securities held by community banks (Panel E in Table 8-5) for 1985 was 9.64 percent, whereas the tax-equivalent yield was 11.26 percent, an adjustment of 162 basis points. Since the Tax Reform Act of 1986 killed the municipal bond market as a tax shelter for banks (see appendix B of this chapter), the difference between taxable and tax-equivalent yields has just about disappeared, as the data for 1995 show.

If active investment management is more efficient than passive investment management, then the yield on the trading account should be higher than the one on the investment account. Measured in basis points (bp) the spreads between the interest rates on these two accounts for 1985 and 1995, by bank size, were as follows:

	1995	1985
Ten largest banks ranked by assets	105(bp)	66(bp)
Banks ranked 11 to 100	93	55
Banks ranked 101 to 1,000	70	–27
Banks not ranked among the 1,000 largest	2	62
All banks	163	72

All other things being equal, and recognizing the crudeness of these data, the 100 largest banks seem to be doing a more efficient job of managing their trading-account securities, especially for 1995.

THE RISK-RETURN CHARACTERISTICS OF INVESTMENT SECURITIES

Returns on a bank's investment portfolio come in the form of interest income, reinvestment income, capital gains, fees generated by providing investment services, and bid-ask spreads on dealer and market-making activities. Net returns depend on the interest cost of funds and the administrative and operating costs of the investment function. Given the quality of bank investment securities (BBB/Baa or better), interest-rate risk and liquidity risk are the primary concerns for government securities. In the case of mortgage-backed securities, prepayment risk must also be considered (Box 8-3).

To understand the risk-return aspects of bank investment securities, we draw on five fundamental principles of financial economics:

1. The Fisher effect, or how inflationary expectations get built into nominal interest rates
2. The term structure of interest rates, or the relationship between yield to maturity and term to maturity of similar securities
3. The default-risk structure of interest rates, or the relationship between return and default risk
4. The notion of liquidity and the tradeoff between it and profitability
5. The treatment of prepayment risk

Unanticipated Inflation and the Interactions among Interest-Rate Risk, Liquidity Risk, and Prepayment Risk

Unanticipated inflation means unexpected changes in interest rates, which produces interest-rate risk (chapter 5). Interest-rate risk has two components: price risk and reinvestment risk. When interest rates rise, prices of fixed-rate instruments fall (bad news), but reinvestment rates rise (good news). When interest rates decline, prices rise (good news), but reinvestment rates fall (bad news).

Suppose that a bank's investment manager anticipates a long-term, risk-free bond rate of 8 percent, consisting of a 4 percent real rate and a 4 percent premium for *expected inflation*. What happens if *unexpected inflation* of 4 percent occurs, so that actual inflation is 8 percent? If the inflation is expected to persist, then the long-term interest rate will move to 12 percent, and the value of fixed-rate debt will decline. The bank now has paper losses in these securities, which represent a liquidity risk, because the market-to-book ratio for the investment is less than 1.[11] Moreover, if the bank is reluctant to take capital losses for fear of reducing reported profits, the bank will be locked in to the investment. On the positive side, the interest payments can be reinvested at the higher rate of interest. However, assuming identical inflationary expectations, the higher cost of bank liabilities will offset this apparent advantage. To avoid such a predicament, the manager could have purchased a variable-rate bond or considered laying off the interest-rate risk of the fixed-rate bond in the futures market (chapter 9).

If actual inflation turned out to be 2 percent instead of the expected 4 percent, and if the 2 percent level became the new expectation, then the long-term rate would drop to 6 percent. In this case, the bank would have a paper gain in the securities.[12] However, the bank has a *reinvestment problem* because the coupon payments cannot be reinvested at the same yield to maturity as the bond originally purchased, because interest rates are lower. To reinvest at the same rate, the manager would have to accept a lower-quality obligation. In addition, if the bond is callable, the bank faces prepayment (contraction) risk.

Note the importance of SFAS No. 115 in these two examples. Specifically, securities identified as "held to maturity" are reported at amortized cost, whereas

---

[11] If the bond has a maturity of 30 years, was purchased at par ($1,000), and the change in inflationary expectations occurred immediately after you purchased the bond, then its present value, assuming annual interest payments, would be $677.79 for a market-to-book ratio of 0.68.

[12] Making the same assumptions as in the previous footnote, the bond's price would be $1,275.30 and its market-to-book ratio would be 1.275.

those "available for sale" or "held for trading" must be marked to market (i.e., reported at market value). The recorded values of a bank's securities, as reported in its *investment account* and *trading account*, capture this distinction between book value and market value. Of course, if a security has to be liquidated, it can be sold only at its market value. How it is classified on an accounting basis does not affect a security's real worth.

Liquidity Risk: Size and Quality Considerations

Because of their reluctance to take capital losses after interest rates have risen, some bank investment managers feel locked in to their portfolios. In other instances, the markets for particular securities may be "thin," which means that the securities cannot be easily traded. When this situation occurs, the security is not very marketable and hence not very liquid. Typically, an illiquid security is a nonrated issue of small size. Accordingly, a security tends to be more liquid the larger its issue size is and the higher its bond rating is.

Regarding trading in thin markets, the old adage about everything (and everyone) having a price applies. It is not that the security cannot be sold, but the discount required can be substantial. If a deep discount must be taken to sell a security, the investment manager may be unwilling to take the hit. The existence of thin markets or rising interest rates may have the effect of eliminating or substantially reducing the liquidity-reserve function of a bank's investment portfolio. However, for banks that do not depend on liquidity stored in their balance sheets (i.e., liability-management banks), such a change is less crucial. Depictions of thin and active markets are captured by the graphical analysis presented in Figure 8-3.[13]

Credit Risk and the Default-Risk Structure of Interest Rates

Credit risk is simply the risk of nonpayment or default (chapter 6). Given the BBB/Baa-or-better regulatory guideline,[14] it is not surprising that credit risk in bank investments has not been a major problem for commercial banks. Because U.S. Treasury securities are considered free of default risk, and because many federal agency securities carry some form of government insurance or guarantee,[15] a large portion of a bank's investment portfolio is free of default risk. In addition, although mortgage-backed securities usually have underlying assets with good quality, they are further supported by guarantees or credit enhancements (Box 8-3). Table 8-6 shows the "acceptable rating classifications" for bank investments used by the Office of the Comptroller of the Currency (OCC, the regulator of national banks). Similar ratings apply to other insured commercial banks. All insured commercial banks must maintain credit files for non-investment-grade securities. Since large banks/BHCs have investment departments or holding-company subsidiaries of considerable size and expertise, they are skilled at analyzing the potential default risk of higher-risk securities, a service available to community banks through their correspondent banks.

---

[13] This paragraph draws on Mason [1979], pp. 42–44.

[14] In the case of debt securities that are not rated, the investment manager has the responsibility to conduct a credit investigation similar to that for a commercial-loan request. The borrower's credit file provides documentation of the credit analysis and enables bank examiners to exercise oversight judgment on the bank's investment decision.

[15] Kaufman [1987] documents the history and scope of federal guarantees and raises the important policy issue of whether the federal government should engage in insurance activities of any kind.

Panel A. Supply curve of U.S. government securities

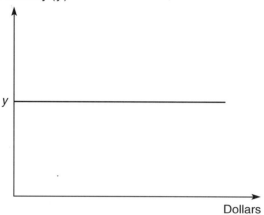

Yield to maturity (y)

Analysis: Because the market for these securities is so extensive, no single buyer (e.g., bank) can influence the yield (price) at which a particular issue trades. This lack of control over price results in a perfectly elastic supply curve.

Panel B. Supply curve for a municipal security

Yield to maturity (y)

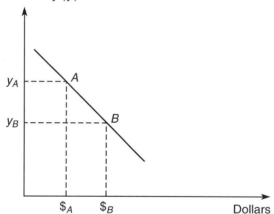

Analysis: Because the market for this issue is thin, if the bank wishes to expand its holdings of the issue (from A to B) it must accept a lower yield by bidding a higher price. In contrast, if it wishes to reduce its holding (from B to A), the bank must discount the price of security. By selling at a lower price, the bank gives the buyer a higher yield. The lower the yield is, the more funds municipalities will demand from banks and other lenders (i.e., the more securities they will supply).

FIGURE 8-3 **Trading Securities in Active versus Inactive Markets**

Another indicator of the credit risk of securities held by commercial banks is suggested by risk-based capital requirements (chapter 13). Box 8-3 shows that capital assessments for asset-backed securities fall into four categories: zero percent (GNMA securities), 20 percent (FHLMC and FNMA securities), 50 percent (mortgage-backed securities), and 100 percent (CMOs).

TABLE 8-6   Acceptable Rating Classifications as Determined by the OCC

Standard & Poor's	Moody's	Description
Bank Quality Investments		
AAA	Aaa	Highest grade obligations
AA	Aa	High grade obligations
A	A-1, A	Upper medium grade
BBB	Baa-1, Baa	Medium grade, on the borderline between definitely sound obligations and those containing predominantly speculative elements. Generally, the lowest quality bond that may qualify for bank investment
Speculative and Defaulted Issues		
BB	Ba	Lower medium grade with only minor investment characteristics
B	B	Low grade, default probable
D	Ca, C	Lowest rated class, defaulted, extremely poor prospects
Provisional or Conditional Rating		
Rating—P	Conditional (rating)	Debt service requirements are largely dependent on reliable estimates as to future events.

Source: Comptroller's Handbook for National Bank Examiners. [1979], Englewood Cliffs, NJ: Prentice-Hall, sec. 203.1,5.

The relationship between bond yields and default risk is referred to as the **default-risk structure of interest rates** (Figure 8-4). As Table 8-6 reflects, insured commercial banks are restricted to the safe end of the default-risk structure (i.e., BBB or better). In addition, if they do hold riskier securities like CMOs, they face the same risk-based capital requirements as commercial and industrial loans.

The spread between a risky bond and a risk-free bond is referred to as a yield spread. It measures the additional return that a risky bond must pay to induce an investor to hold it instead of a riskless bond. Fisher [1959] postulated that the average risk premium on a risky bond was a function of the issuer's probability of default and the marketability of its bonds. He argued further that the risk of default was a function of three variables:

- The variability of the issuer's earnings
- The length of time the firm has been operating without exposing creditors to losses
- The ratio of the market value of the firm's equity to the par value of its debt

To capture the marketability of a firm's debt, Fisher proposed using the market value of the firm's publicly traded debt. Although Fisher applied his model to corporate bonds, it can be generalized to other securities to evaluate credit risk.[16]

---

[16] Jaffee [1975] considered the cyclical variation of risk premiums. Using the term-structure theories presented in appendix A of this chapter, he analyzed three theories of the default-risk structure. Jaffee's empirical work supported a perfect-substitutes explanation in which risk spreads should be constant and independent of the forces of supply and demand.

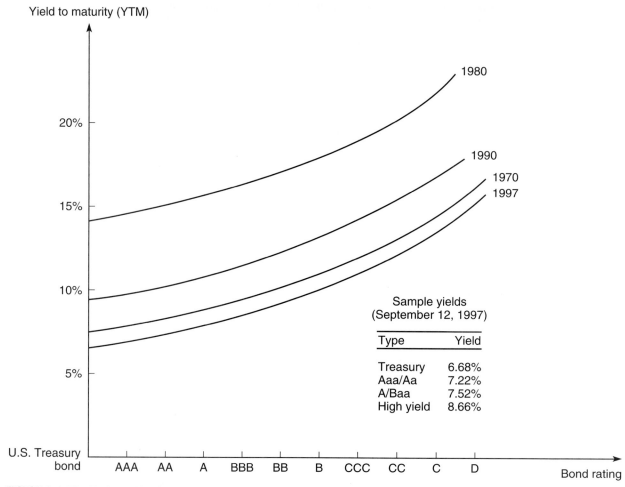

FIGURE 8-4 **The Default-Risk Structure of Interest Rates**

Call Risk

A call feature gives the issuer an option of refunding a debt issue. This feature of a debt contract creates prepayment (contraction) risk for the investor. Chapter 5 and Box 8-3 discuss prepayment risk. Because the exercise of the call eliminates cash inflows beyond the call date, the holder is compensated with a "sweetener" called the *call premium*. As additional reward for bearing uncertainty, callable bonds promise higher yields. Given the bank's investment horizon, callable bonds, with call dates beyond the planned horizon, can be used to increase the return on the portfolio. Bonds are called and mortgages prepaid when interest rates have declined far enough to make refinancings positive-NPV projects. Unlike callable bonds, however, asset-backed securities do not offer call premiums.

THE PORTFOLIO OF MUNICIPAL SECURITIES

The distinguishing feature of municipal securities is that their *coupon interest* is exempt from federal income taxes and most state taxes. Capital gains from municipal securities, however, are fully taxable when realized. (The tax treatment is symmetrical, because realized losses are fully deductible from taxable income.) Regarding tax-exempt securities,[17] it is important to understand the following riddle:

> How are tax-exempt securities like a free lunch?
>
> Answer: When you look closely, there is no such thing.

Although *explicit* taxes are zero, holders of municipal bonds (e.g., banks) pay *implicit* taxes in two ways. First, they accepted, prior to 1987, lower yields than were available on equivalent taxable securities. The difference in interest receivable may be regarded as federal tax payments collected and redirected to the state and local governments that issued the bonds. Second, many holders of municipal bonds give up additional implicit interest by accepting lesser liquidity or greater portfolio risk than they would prefer. Figure 8-1 reflects this situation. These implicit taxes may be called the *costs of tax avoidance*. They include lower yields, illiquidity, and greater risk.

Banks have two basic reasons for acquiring municipal securities, with different policy criteria applicable to each strategy.[18] First, they may acquire *local* obligations through competitive bidding or private negotiation. Bank activity in this area focuses mainly on maintaining or establishing customer relationships with local governments. The idea is to have revenues from other banking services (e.g., data processing) to offset the costs of tax avoidance. The second method involves a strictly investment motive without the customer-relationship linkage. In this situation, securities should be chosen on the basis of an objective evaluation of the risk-return parameters.

Quality Considerations

The financial difficulties of Orange County (California) and cities like New York and Cleveland have caused investors to look more closely at the quality of municipal obligations (i.e., at the creditworthiness of the issuer). These developments suggest that a bank should review its minimum quality standard for such holdings, if it has not done so already. Hayes [1980] found that the larger the bank, the lower the minimum quality standard tends to be (e.g., Baa versus A). In addition, large banks have a greater tendency to accept nonrated obligations; this practice can be traced to their ability to do in-house research on the creditworthiness of municipalities. Hayes recommends that banks adopt a policy requiring at least an A rating on municipal credits (or the equivalent on nonrated obligations). Given the greater perceived risk of municipal bonds, the portfolio should, of course, be well diversified.

The Case for Municipal Bonds

McHugh [1990] makes a case for investing in municipal bonds. A senior vice president for Berks County Bank, an $80 million (1990) community bank in Reading, Pennsylvania, he argues for municipal bonds on five grounds: First, the tax advantage is still available on obligations from those municipalities that do not issue

---

[17] Kane [1980] presents an energetic exposition of some basic tax concepts. Appendix B of this chapter describes the tax treatment of municipal securities.

[18] See Hayes [1980], pp. 85–100.

more than $10 million of bonds or loans in any one year. Second, municipals hedge the bank against an increase in tax rates. Third, fixed-rate, long-term municipals are desirable in a falling-rate environment. Fourth, as interest rates fall, the tax-equivalent yields on municipal bonds rise. And fifth, by holding local municipal issues that benefit the community, the bank demonstrates its support for the Community Reinvestment Act.

Using McHugh's example in equation (8-1) and drawing on appendix B of this chapter, we have

$$r(TE) = [0.06 - (0.2 \times 0.08 \times 0.34)]/(1 - 0.34) = 8.27\%$$

In this case, the coupon rate on the municipal bond is 6 percent, the interest expense disallowance is 0.20, the cost of funds is 8 percent, and the marginal tax rate is 0.34. As a result, the tax-equivalent yield is 8.27 percent. The investment serves as a hedge against a tax increase (the second point), because if $t = .46$, the tax-equivalent yield rises to 9.75 percent. To illustrate the fourth point, if the cost of funds drops to 6 percent, the tax-equivalent yield rises to 8.47 percent.

For community bankers who want to invest in municipal securities, McHugh suggested a program based on ensuring that the bonds are subject to the 20 percent interest-expense disallowance, diversification, and a laddered or staggered maturity structure (discussed below). He sees the benefits of such a program as the ability to reinvest at the highest yield (assuming a positively sloped yield curve), the ability to keep the weighted maturity of the portfolio constant while improving the average weighted yield (again assuming a rising yield curve), a steady flow of liquidity from maturing securities on the ladder, capital gains when rates fall, and rising average yields when rates rise.

McHugh offers three caveats to his program. First, consider the possible adverse effects due to the alternative minimum tax. Second, watch out for callable bonds (prepayment risk) that can disrupt your planned program. And third, avoid zero-coupon issues because you lose the opportunity to reinvest coupon payments. As a benchmark, McHugh suggests a municipal bond portfolio around 3 percent of total assets.[19] His final suggestion is "to weigh the benefits versus the risks and consult your tax experts" (p. 11).

ESTABLISHING A BANK INVESTMENT POLICY

Every business organization should attempt to establish in writing what its various policies are. From an asset-management perspective, commercial banks need to have written loan and investment policies. This section focuses on establishing a bank investment policy.

A Suggested Investment Policy

David Hoffland manages the investment portfolio of the Fifth Third Bank of Cincinnati (no kidding). His views regarding the contents of a written investment policy for a bank[20] are summarized by the 16-point plan in Table 8-7 and the text following it.

---

[19] At year-end 1994, the figure for banks not ranked among the 1,000 largest (community banks) was 5.0 percent, down from 8.0 at year-end 1985; see Table 7–3.
[20] This section draws on Hoffland [1978].

TABLE 8-7	Representative Components of a Bank's Investment Policy

1. Policy objectives: Liquidity versus profitability
2. Responsibility and checks and balances
3. Composition of the portfolio
4. Acceptable Securities
5. Maturities/durations
6. Quality and diversification
7. Portfolio rebalancing
8. Pledging
9. Safekeeping
10. Deliveries
11. Computer hardware/software
12. Gains and losses on securities sales
13. Swapping securities
14. Trading activity and use of derivatives
15. Credit files
16. Exceptions and special circumstances

Source: Adapted from Hoffland [1978].

1. Policy Objectives: Liquidity versus Profitability

One of the best reasons for having a written investment policy is that it forces top management to think about the objectives of the investment portfolio and its integration into the bank's overall asset-liability management scheme. Investment portfolios frequently are designed to provide both liquidity and profitability. Given a positively sloped yield, there is a trade-off between these objectives. In contrast, when the yield curve is negatively sloped, short-term investments provide both liquidity and the highest yield, at least in the short run. Balancing the liquidity and income needs of a bank is perhaps the most important task an investment manager has. Moreover, it is critical that the investment policy be integrated with the bank's overall asset-liability management. For example, a bank that practices liability management can place more emphasis on the earnings objective of the investment portfolio, whereas a bank that does not engage in liability management would emphasize the liquidity objective. Additional investment-portfolio functions are (1) to provide asset diversification and quality, and (2) to provide a countercyclical balance to the interest-rate cycle by generating funds when loan demand is strong and absorbing funds when loan demand is weak, thereby helping to stabilize earnings. What is the appropriate planning horizon for establishing an investment policy? Hoffland suggests a three-to-five-year horizon for both establishing the policy and measuring its performance.

2. Responsibility and Checks and Balances

Another good reason for having a written investment policy is that it establishes responsibility and delegates authority for making investments. In a small bank, the investment task usually is performed by one individual as a secondary responsibility. In a larger bank, the investment function is performed by a department or committee usually headed by a vice president. In general, the larger the bank, the greater the need for a written investment policy. The person in charge of the investment function should make regular reports to top management and the board of directors regarding such factors as alternative strategies, forecasted market conditions, and the condition of the portfolio.

3. Composition of the Portfolio

Hoffland suggests establishing guidelines for the following three areas of a bank's investment portfolio:

1. The federal-funds position
2. The liquidity portfolio
3. The income portfolio

Examples of specific guidelines for each category include the following: under (1) approximate daily sales of federal funds, an acceptable length of indebtedness on fed funds purchases, and a list of banks to which fed funds will be sold; under (2) the dollar amount (as a percentage of total deposits) and number of securities (e.g., 10–20) to be held in the liquidity portfolio; and under (3) a residual account with emphasis on tax-exempt securities, given the bank's level of taxable income (i.e., the objective should be to maximize net income and not to minimize taxes).

4. Acceptable Securities

Hoffland's suggestions for acceptable securities for the liquidity portfolio are as follows:

1. U.S. Treasury obligations
2. U.S. federal agencies, including
   a. Federal National Mortgage Association
   b. Federal Home Loan Bank
   c. Federal Land Bank
   d. Banks for Cooperatives
   e. Federal Intermediate Credit Bank
   f. Export-Import Bank (U.S. guaranteed)
   g. Farmers Home Administration (U.S. guaranteed)
3. Commercial paper of prime-rated corporations with equity capital of at least $250 million
4. Bankers acceptances of major banks with quality ratings
5. Negotiable CDs of major banks with quality ratings
6. Repos using short-term U.S. Treasury or federal agency obligations
7. Tax-exempt, federally guaranteed, project notes

For the income portfolio, Hoffland recommends

1. State and municipal tax-exempt bonds
2. Quality, highly marketable corporate bonds listed on the New York Bond Exchange

Box 8-4 shows three bond innovations of the mid-1990s, two of which did not succeed.

5. Maturities/Durations

Average and maximum maturities should be established for both the liquidity and the income portfolios. Although Hoffland does not recommend a rigid ladder approach to maturity spacing, he expects to have some bonds maturing roughly every year. The average maturity will, of course, be a function of the stage of the interest-rate cycle, lengthening at the peak and shrinking at the trough.

‖ BOX 8-4

‖ THE LAST WORD ON THE BONDS OF 1996

☺ The Dole Bond: No Interest

☺ The Gingrich Bond: No Maturity

☺ The Clinton Bond: No Principles (but rolled over)

Source: Economist Larry Chimerine in a speech at the University of Georgia's annual forecasting luncheon, December 1995. Who says economists are dull? Parentheses mine.

---

6. Quality and Diversification

Hoffland recommends that the quality and diversification of a bank's municipal portfolio be approximated (±5 percent) by the following categories:

Quality	Diversification
Aaa	General obligation
Aa	Revenue
A	Other
Baa	In state
N/R	Out of state

The idea is to specify percentages for each of the quality and diversification subcategories. (See Table 8-6 for a description and listing of bond ratings.) The top four bond ratings or grades are considered to be investment quality. In many cases, the bonds of local municipalities are not rated (N/R). However, as long as these N/R bonds are acceptable credit risks, banks traditionally have supported them as a service to the local community.

7. Portfolio Rebalancing

The focus of portfolio rebalancing is to key portfolio adjustments to the interest-rate cycle (see Figure 8-5). During Stage I of the cycle (maximum cyclical ease), maturities should be kept short (the PET suggests interest rates will rise) and capital gains may be taken (bond prices are high). During Stage II (transition to tightness) funds may be shifted from the liquidity portfolio to the income portfolio and maturities lengthened, or the overall portfolio may be reduced and a waiting-in-the-ways position taken. In Stage III (maximum cyclical tightness), interest rates are high and bond prices are low. This is the time to lengthen maturities and consider tax-loss transactions. In Stage IV (transition to ease), maturities should be shortened somewhat because rates are falling and prices rising.

8. Pledging

Pledging refers to the practice of governmental units requiring banks "to pledge" (i.e., to hold) securities of certain amounts and quality to secure public deposits. These so-called pledging requirements restrict the flexibility of a bank's investment policy. Thus, if a bank plans to attract public deposits, it needs to prepare its investment portfolio for the required pledging. As a general rule, a bank should attempt to pledge securities from its income portfolio and try to keep its liquidity portfolio free from restrictions.

9. Safekeeping

Banks perform a safekeeping function. Bankers' banks, such as the Fed and correspondent banks, provide safekeeping services for banks, for a fee, of course. Except for short-term local municipal notes and corporate bonds registered in the name of the bank, banks do not need to keep securities in their own vaults. However, banks should monitor their safekeeping expenses to avoid unnecessary charges.

10. Deliveries

Like safekeeping services, deliveries of securities and payments can be arranged with the Fed or correspondent banks. Deliveries should be made before payment.

11. Computer Hardware/Software

For a portfolio of 80 or more items, Hoffland recommends that the portfolio be maintained on a computer program with a major correspondent. This approach tends to have substantial accounting, recordkeeping, pricing, and analytical benefits compared to its cost.

12. Gains and Losses on Securities Sales

The minimum benefits of taking tax losses on securities sales can be equated with the earnings on the tax savings. Taking gains and losses should be tied to the interest-rate cycle shown in Figure 8-5. In general, taking gains implies that maturities should be shortened (Stage I), whereas taking losses implies that maturities should be lengthened (Stage III).

13. Swapping Securities

A securities swap involves selling one security and buying another similar one, resulting in a net gain for the bank. If securities markets are efficient, the opportunities for such swaps should be rare. Hoffland approves of a limited number of swaps provided the following conditions are met:

1. The yield differential gained is above normal
2. The transactions are consistent with investment policies and objectives
3. Quality, maturity, and yield considerations are not unduly sacrificed
4. The transactions are reported independently of other investment activity and each swap is reported in detail
5. The transactions accumulate measurable benefits that are reported to the board of directors on at least a quarterly basis

14. Trading Activity and Use of Derivatives

The buying and selling of securities over the short run for profit is speculative trading, an activity that is frowned upon by bank examiners.[21] Because there are occasions when buying new issues of government securities for profits seems justified,

---

[21] The FDIC's Manual of Examination Policies states, "That securities should be purchased and held for income and not in anticipation of speculative profits is axiomatic" (Section H, page 8, revised, December 1, 1962).

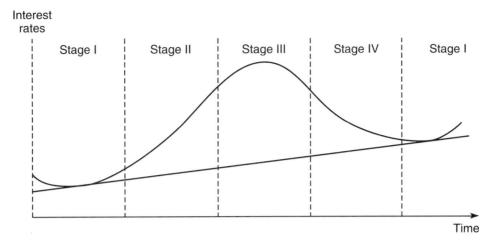

FIGURE 8-5 **Stages and Characteristics of the Interest-Rate Cycle**

Stage	Level of rates	Demand for credit	Bank liquidity
I	Low	Weak	Maximum
II	In transition from low to high	Increasing	Decreasing
III	High	Strong	Minimum
IV	In transition from high to low	Decreasing	Increasing

Characteristics of stages

Hoffland approves of such trades on a limited basis. He recommends that such trading activity be done one transaction at a time and be subject to a ceiling amount.

15. Credit Files

Hoffland suggests that a bank maintain a credit file on every municipal and corporate security in its income portfolio. The minimum information should be a circular or official statement issued at the time of the bond sale. For secondary transactions, a financial statement of the issuer and some analysis should be included. A typical analysis should cover population, gross and net bonded debt, assessed and full market values of taxable property, per capita or per customer debt, relative debt burden, relative tax burden, debt to net plant, and debt-service coverage.

16. Exceptions and Special Circumstances

Significant deviations from a bank's investment policy should require the approval of its board of directors. In contrast, minor deviations are to be expected. On balance, the policy cannot be a straitjacket; it must be a flexible policy tailored to the individual bank's needs, personnel, and anticipated opportunities.

To summarize, Hoffland views his investment policy as a model to be used by other banks in writing their own investment policies. He classifies it as a conservative approach and believes that banks with deposits under $300 million might use the policy as is. Because hundreds of banks exist with deposits of less than $300 million, Hoffland considers his policy to be appropriate for all but the largest banks.

FDIC GUIDELINES

According to the FDIC's Manual of Examination Policies (Section H, page 5), a sound investment policy for a bank should establish standards for the selection of securities with respect to the following:

1. Credit quality (default risk)
2. Maturity
3. Diversification
4. Marketability
5. Income

In evaluating a bank's investment policy, the FDIC's Manual (Section H, page 6) suggests the following factors as a guide for the examiner:

1. The general character of the bank's business as manifested in the characteristics of its loan and deposit accounts and its general economic environment.
2. Analysis of the bank's deposit structure in terms of the number, types, and size of accounts and in terms of deposit trends, composition, and stability.
3. Capital funds. In general, the smaller a bank's capital cushion, the more conservative its investment policy should be because it has fewer funds to absorb potential losses.
4. Economic and monetary factors. It is suggested that intelligent portfolio management should consider basic economic and monetary factors in formulating and executing investment policies. However, the Manual cautions that preoccupation with such analysis may be indicative of "speculative tendencies which are unwholesome in banking."

ALTERNATIVE INVESTMENT STRATEGIES

Like most financial-management problems, the fundamental bank investment quandary is a risk-return dilemma. The investment manager is faced with the task of balancing the conflicting objectives of liquidity and income. One approach to the liquidity-profitability trade-off is to separate the investment portfolio into a liquidity account and an income account, as Hoffland suggested.[22] The liquidity-reserve method, with its primary, secondary, tertiary, and investment reserve accounts is a variation of this approach. An alternative approach to bank investment management is to focus upon a maturity strategy. The basic maturity strategies are the following:

1. A laddered approach (also called a staggered, or spaced-maturity approach)
2. A split-maturity approach consisting of three alternative strategies:[23]
   a. All short-term bonds (a front-end-loaded portfolio),
   b. All long-term bonds, and,
   c. A combination of short- and long-term bonds, called the "barbell" strategy

---

[22] This approach originally was suggested by Woodworth (1967).

[23] Watson [1972] defines the maturity ranges as (1) less than five years for short-term bonds, (2) five-to-ten years for intermediate-term bonds, and (3) ten-to-fifteen years for long-term bonds. Hayes [1980] found that 64 percent of the bankers he surveyed favored the front-end-loaded maturity policy.

The Laddered Approach[24]

Consider a bank that decides that the maximum maturity it will hold in its investment portfolio will be 15 years. If the bank has total assets of $48 million and an investment portfolio of $12 million, what will be the composition of its investment portfolio using the laddered technique? The bank will place $800,000 in each of the 15 years for a total of $12 million, resulting in an evenly distributed portfolio throughout the maturity range. The advantage of this approach is that it does not require any investment management. The bonds can be viewed as riding along a conveyer belt with a simulated length (maturity) of 15 years. As each bond reaches the end of the belt (i.e., matures), its cash proceeds are reinvested in another 15-year obligation. The bank is provided with a steady stream of liquidity. During periods of strong loan demand, the liquidity can be used to meet such demand and a smaller amount would be invested in the longest investment maturity. In contrast, when loan demand is slack, the cash proceeds from both maturing bonds and loans would be placed on the conveyor-belt system. On average, the bank would expect $800,000 in maturing liquidity each year, although the actual stream over a six-year cycle might be $1,200,000, $800,000, $400,000, $400,000, $800,000, and $1,200,000. The advantages of the laddered approach are as follows: (1) It is easy to manage—just place a bucket at the end of the conveyor belt and check its contents regularly for reinvestment; (2) there is no need to attempt to forecast future interest rates or to engage in any trading activity; and (3) the investment portfolio will generate at least an average return while avoiding the risks of potential capital losses.

The disadvantages of the laddered approach (in its rigid form) are as follows: (1) It lacks the flexibility to take advantage of profitable investment opportunities that typically arise over the interest-rate cycle; (2) it is a suboptimal approach because there is no attempt to achieve the highest return for a given level of portfolio risk. By using a modified laddered approach, it is possible to take some advantage of interest-rate movements. For example, when the shape of the yield curve (Figure 8-3) suggests rising interest rates, investment proceeds should be invested in short-term bonds until the term structure is more favorable for long-term investment. This version of the laddered approach requires that a bank attempt to forecast interest rates and avoid blindly placing the contents of the bucket back on the longest part of the conveyor belt. On balance, the modification requires some active investment management, as opposed to the pure version, which is a passive approach. However, even in its modified version, the laddered approach still has limited flexibility because of its basic spaced-maturity structure. The question of suboptimality will be addressed after the split-maturity strategies are discussed.

The Split-Maturity Strategy

This approach consists of three alternative strategies. One version is the all-short-term-bonds strategy. The split in this case is 100 percent in short-term obligations and zero percent in long-term bonds. Such a portfolio would be highly liquid and flexible, with its income-generating ability dependent upon the character of the interest-rate cycle. For example, over an interest-rate cycle dominated by negatively sloped yield curves, the portfolio would be highly profitable. In contrast, if long-term rates are above short-term ones, as they tend to be, there will be a relative shortage of income.

---

[24] Robinson [1962] discusses this approach.

In the all-long-term-bonds strategy, the split is zero percent in short-term obligations and 100 percent in long-term bonds. This approach would be an illiquid and inflexible one (i.e., high risk), but one with the promise of high income because long-term rates tend to be above short-term ones. If a bank engaged in active trading under this strategy, capital gains would have to offset capital losses for the bank to break even.

Consider now the weight lifters' special—the barbell strategy. The idea is to split the investment portfolio between short- and long-term bonds. Moreover, the split does not have to be a 50/50 one. It could be 30/70, 40/60, 70/30, or some other combination. In this approach, bonds in the intermediate-term range, however it is defined, are avoided. Using the 30/70 split as an example, a bank might place 30 percent of its investment portfolio in the zero–two-year maturity range and 70 percent in the 20–30-year range. This split-maturity strategy is designed to provide liquidity, flexibility, and income. More specifically, the approach attempts to achieve the greatest return for a given level of risk, where risk is measured by potential capital losses or the variability of the portfolio's total return (i.e., interest income plus appreciation or depreciation). In portfolio terminology, the approach is designed to determine the bank's efficiency frontier. Some research indicates that barbell portfolios are more likely to lie on a bank's efficiency frontier than alternative strategies.[25] In other words, they tend to produce risk-return combinations that are dominant.

SIX BASIC BANK-INVESTMENT QUESTIONS

Bradley and Crane [1975] suggest that bank investment managers should be concerned with six basic questions. Using laddered and barbell portfolios and statistical models to generate realistic interest-rate scenarios, they attempted to answer their own questions.[26] The questions and their answers are as follows:

1. What basic portfolio structure is likely to provide the best balance between return and risk? Answer: Banks wishing to manage their portfolios more actively probably can obtain better performance with barbell portfolios than laddered ones. The barbell strategy tends to provide the best balance between return and risk.

2. How should the level of risk a bank is willing to tolerate affect the maturity structure of its portfolios? Answer: The greater the level of risk a bank is willing to tolerate, the longer the maturity structure of its portfolios can be, whether barbell or laddered. An important measure of risk is the potential for realized and unrealized losses resulting from a portfolio strategy. Thus, the greater a bank's willingness and ability to absorb such losses, both unrealized and realized, the longer its maturity structure can be.

3. If a portfolio is not to be used for liquidity purposes, so that its size is relatively constant, how does this affect the choice of a maturity structure? Answer: In a barbell

---

[25] See Bradley and Crane [1975] and Watson [1972]. In contrast, Cramer and Seifert [1976] conclude that a laddered strategy and a six-month/10-year barbell strategy both lie on the efficiency frontier, with the laddered portfolio generating both higher return and higher risk.

[26] For a summary of their findings, see Bradley and Crane [1975], pp. 206–211.

portfolio, a decreased use of the portfolio for liquidity purposes allows the maturity of the short-term portion of the portfolio to be lengthened, but the overall proportion of the portfolio (e.g., 30/70) is relatively unaffected.

4. How does the availability of purchased funds affect portfolio strategy? Answer: Purchased funds lessen the need for liquidity from the investment portfolio and offer the possibility of expanding its size. However, the availability and use of purchased funds has little impact on the portfolio's basic maturity structure. The latter is primarily due to the critical role played by constraints on unrealized losses in the portfolio-selection process.

5. How are the maturity structures of U.S. Treasury and tax-exempt securities affected when the total return and risk of the two portfolios are considered jointly? Answer: The recommended barbell structure is one in which short-term securities are a mixture of U.S. Treasury and tax-exempt securities but any longer-term securities are all tax-exempt ones.

6. What is an appropriate planning horizon for a bank to use in selecting a set of portfolio actions? Answer: Because banks are concerned primarily about volatility and unrealized losses that might build up over the next two to three years, the impact longer-term considerations might have on the selection of a portfolio strategy is mitigated. Thus, a two-to-three-year planning horizon is recommended.

Although Bradley and Crane think that their answers might be of significant help to banks and their portfolio managers, the tactical problems of managing a portfolio still remain. They contend that improvements in the tactical area require banks to simplify their descriptions of future environments, including interest rates and funds available for investment, and to study the implications of these future conditions for current portfolio management.

To cope with uncertainty, Bradley and Crane suggest that banks engage in scenario planning. They view this process as consisting of two steps. First, it is necessary to describe and evaluate future economic environments over the relevant planning horizon. The second step is to evaluate the implications of these alternative scenarios for portfolio management, including a set of decisions that will provide a balance between expected return and risk. Although scenario planning increases the amount of analysis that banks must undertake, Bradley and Crane suggest that statistical tools and computer models can be helpful. The types of models they think can be of assistance to portfolio managers in evaluating alternative strategies are based on two dichotomies: certainty versus uncertainty and models that evaluate strategies provided by the portfolio managers and models that are optimized. Bradley and Crane analyzed four different models:[27] (1) deterministic simulations, (2) Monte Carlo simulations, (3) linear programming, and (4) optimization models under uncertainty.

To place Bradley and Crane's empirical results in perspective, consider the following quote from Hayes [1980]:

> In an otherwise excellent book on econometric models and programs useful in managing bank investment portfolios, the policy constraints imposed on linear-programming models designed to optimize portfolio returns do not explicitly include an interest-sensitivity position or exposure constraint. (p. 58, footnote 17)

---

[27] McKinney [1977] opines on the uses of models in the management of bank funds.

What this means in nontechnical terms is that the maturity distribution of the investment portfolio cannot be structured independently of a bank's assets and liabilities. On balance, a bank's investment policy and practices must be an integrated part of its overall asset-liability management (chapter 5).

INVESTMENT BANKING

Rather than buying and selling existing securities, some banks assist issuers in getting their securities to market by advising them and underwriting and distributing the securities. By providing these investment-banking services, banks generate fees. Since most community banks do not engage in investment banking, a dichotomy exists within the banking industry with respect to these sources of revenue. Interest income and capital gains from investment securities represent the traditional sources of revenue for banks, whereas revenues from the provision of investment-banking services are a recent phenomenon associated with the erosion of the Glass-Steagall Act of 1933, which separated commercial and investment banking.

The gradual movement of large commercial banks back into investment banking can be explained by two regulatory factors:

1. Prior to 1991, the Federal Reserve had granted special exemptions to certain large bank holding companies (BHCs) to engage in investment banking on a limited basis

2. The FDIC Improvement Act (FDICIA) of 1991 overrode Glass-Steagall restrictions against commercial banks underwriting corporate securities by granting BHCs the power to engage in these activities through separate subsidiaries, provided the banks were well capitalized and limited their total underwriting.

The overriding reason, however, for the movement back into investment banking can be traced to attempts to increase bank franchise value (chapter 4). Because the largest banks/BHCs have been the hardest hit by the decline of the traditional business of funding loans with deposits, they have searched for opportunities to add value by expanding into investment banking. Although unrestricted entry into investment banking in the United States has yet to be achieved, its time has arrived. Many large U.S. BHCs are engaged in these activities overseas but limited in their home country.[28]

Barriers to Entry and Potential Economies of Scale and Scope

Although the Glass-Steagall Act still represents a hurdle to commercial banks that want to enter investment banking on a full-blown scale, the barriers to entry for community banks are economic in nature. Commercial banking consists of gathering deposits and making loans; this differs from investment banking, which consists of advising and counseling, and the underwriting, distributing, managing, and dealing of securities. Entering investment banking requires a substantial investment beyond that of traditional commercial banking with respect to the additional financial, intellectual, and reputational capital. These considerations represent

---

[28] In Germany and Japan where such artificial barriers between investment and commercial banking do not exist, the activities of commercial and investment banks are commingled and interwoven with the activities of nonfinancial firms; see chapter 1.

the real or economic barriers to entry in investment banking. For example, Tufano [1989], who analyzes financial innovation and first-mover advantages in investment banking, describes the high costs associated with the development of new products. In addition, Hunter and Timme [1986] argue that size and technical efficiencies permit the largest commercial banks to exploit innovations most efficiently. Because only the largest banks/BHCs are able to muster sizable resources, investment banking on a large scale is restricted to such entities. Although all banks have the opportunity to engage in investment banking, the financial, intellectual, and reputational capital needed prohibits many community banks from engaging in such activities.

Once entry has been achieved, investment banking can benefit from substantial informational and scale/scope economies. *Scale economies* (or economies of scale) refer to declining average cost as output increases, whereas *scope economies* (or economies of scope) refer to cost savings generated from joint production. Given the potential for informational scale economies to exist in investment banking, larger banks are more likely to employ the financial engineers needed for modern investment banking and derivatives activities. The existence of significant scale economies in the transactions costs of investment banking means that large banks are also more likely to be dealers in securities and their derivatives. In addition, because large banks are involved in a wider variety of financial activities than community banks, they have greater opportunities to benefit from potential economies of scope.

To summarize, it is easy to see that in investment banking, the economic barriers to entry, mainly in the form of financial, human, and reputational capital, are more important than existing regulatory restrictions.

The Financial Characteristics of Investment Banks/Securities Firms

The financial statements for NYSE member firms presented in Table 8-8 (income-expense statement) and Table 8-9 (balance sheet) permit you to compare the revenues and expenses and sources and uses of funds for investment banks/securities firms with those of commercial banks (chapter 2). Securities firms obtain the bulk (42 percent in 1995) of their revenues from fees and service charges related to securities business. Trading and investments (20 percent) and securities commissions (17 percent) generate the other major sources of revenue. The revenue-generating power of securities commissions for modern investment banks is in sharp contrast to that in the era prior to May 1975, the date when commissions were deregulated. For example, during 1972, NYSE member firms earned 53 percent of their income from securities commissions and only 6 percent from securities-related business. Ten years later (1982) these figures were 26 percent and 19 percent, respectively. For 1995, they were 42 percent and 17 percent, respectively.

Investment banks, like commercial banks, spend most of their revenue on interest on borrowed money (40 percent) and salaries and wages (29 percent). The comparable figures for all commercial banks for 1995 were 38 percent and 17 percent. The smaller figure for salaries and wages reflects how expensive it would be for the average commercial bank to hire the additional skilled personnel to enter investment banking, the major barrier to entry discussed above.

Using data from Tables 8-8 and 8-9, we get the following return on equity (ROE) profile for NYSE member firms:

$$ROE = ROA \times EM = 0.4143\% \times 18.07 = 7.487\%$$

TABLE 8-8   Income-Expense Statement of NYSE Member, Firms, Full Year 1995

Item	Dollars (millions)	Percentage of Gross Income
Securities commissions	$15,999	16.6%
Trading and investments	18,899	19.6
Interest on customers' debt balances	6,238	6.5
Underwriting	7,799	8.1
Mutual-fund sales	3,407	3.5
Commodity-trading revenue	– 448	–0.5
Other income		
Related to securities business[a]	40,857	42.4
Unrelated to securities business	3,529	3.7
Gross income[b]	$96,280	100.0%
Registered representatives' compensation	$12,537	13.0%
Commissions and fees to others	2,727	2.8
Clerical & administrative	15,677	16.3
Communications	2,822	2.9
Occupancy and equipment	3,401	3.5
Promotional	1,244	1.3
Interest	38,157	39.6
Service bureaus and data processing	1,270	1.3
Bad debts, errors, and nonrecurring costs	396	0.4
Other[c]	10,642	11.1
Total expenses[b]	$88,873	92.3%
Net profit before federal taxes[d]	$ 7,407	7.7%
Estimated federal income tax	2,593	2.7
Net profit	$ 4,814	5.0%

Notes:

[a]Fees for investment advice and counsel, service charges and custodian fees, dividends and interest on term investments, miscellaneous other income.

[b]Totals may not add due to rounding.

[c]Licenses, taxes, dues, and assessments paid to exchanges, professional fees, charitable contributions, some officers' and partners' compensation and interest, and other expenses.

[d]Before distributions to partners and federal and state corporate and personal taxes.

Source: Compiled from *NYSE Fact Book 1995 Data*, NYSE, pp. 74–75.

The comparable profile for all insured commercial banks is

$$ROE = 1.18\% \times 12.47 = 14.72\%$$

A better comparison is to use the profile for the 10 largest commercial banks, because they engage in the securities business:

$$ROE = 0.88\% \times 15.66 = 13.78\%$$

These data suggest that the 10 largest commercial banks are more profitable and use less leverage than the average NYSE member firm. This comparison, however, could be improved by focusing on the 10 largest securities firms. For example, Merrill Lynch had the following ROE profile for 1995:

$$ROE = 0.63\% \times 28.79 = 18.14\%$$

TABLE 8-9   Balance Sheet of NYSE Member Firms, December 29, 1995

Assets	Dollars (millions)	Percentage
Bank balances, cash, and other deposits	$ 11,227	1.0%
Receivables from other brokers and lenders	298,374	25.7
Receivables from customers and partners	68,419	5.9
Long positions in securities and commodities	753,773	64.9
Land and other fixed assets	3,575	0.3
Other assets	26,690	2.3
Total assets	$1,162,058	100.0%

Liabilities and Capital		
Money borrowed	$ 657,018	56.5%
Payable to other brokers and dealers	127,472	11.0
Payable to customers and partners	100,567	10.2
Short positions in securities and commodities	135,955	11.7
Other accrued expenses and accounts payable	76,747	6.6
Total liabilities	$1,097,759	94.5%
Total capital	$ 64,299	5.5%
Total liabilities and capital	$1,162,058	100.0%

Note: Totals may not add due to rounding; data are for firms dealing with the public.
Source: Compiled from *NYSE Fact Book 1995 Data,* NYSE, p. 76.

Here we see a company that is more profitable (ROA) than the average securities firm but still not as profitable as the average of the 10 largest commercial banks. However, by using substantially more leverage (EM) than the average large commercial bank, Merrill Lynch generates a higher ROE. As a final comparison, consider the 1995 ROE profile for J. P. Morgan (JPM), a large and prestigious bank holding company headquartered in New York:

$$ROE = 0.70\% \times 17.69 = 12.40\%$$

If we compare JPM with Merrill, they have similar ROAs but their leverages are quite different. All other things being equal, if JPM had Merrill's leverage, its ROE would have been 20.15 percent for 1995.

The Investment Banking Function and Large BHCs

Table 8-10 shows that the typical business sectors of a large bank holding company, for example, JPM, are dominated by investment-banking activities. Notice how these descriptions closely match the sources of "other income: related to securities business" found in Table 8-8. Two traditional functions of investment banking are (1) bringing new securities issues (debt and equity) to market and (2) making secondary markets for these securities. The first activity captures the underwriting function whereas the second reflects the broker/dealer function. As brokers, investment banks bring parties together to trade securities and, as dealers, they trade from their own inventory. As revenue generators (see Table 8-8), however, both of these activities pale in comparison to giving advice and counsel (e.g., on mergers and acquisitions) and providing other financial services.

TABLE 8-10 Representative Business Sectors of a Major Bank Holding Company

Finance and advisory

Advisory
Equities
Debt underwriting
Credit

Sales and trading

Fixed income
Foreign exchange
Commodities
Proprietary

Asset management and servicing

Asset management
Exchange-traded products
Private banking
Operational services

Equity investments

Equity investment portfolio management

Asset-and-liability management

Interest-rate-risk management
Liquidity management

Source: Annual Report [1995], J. P. Morgan, pp. 6–7.

The investment banking industry in the United States has three tiers: large, full-line firms that cater to both retail and corporate clients; national and international firms that concentrate mainly on corporate finance and trading activities; and the rest of the industry (e.g., specialized and regional securities firms and discount brokers). Examples of players in each include Merrill Lynch in the first tier and Goldman Sachs, Salomon Brothers, and Morgan Stanley in the second tier. In the third tier, Robinson Humphrey and Montgomery Securities are regional firms whereas Charles Schwab and Quick and Reilly are discount brokers. In addition, because of the piecemeal dismantling of Glass-Steagall, major U.S. commercial banks such as BankAmerica, Bankers Trust, Chase Manhattan, Chemical, Citicorp, and J. P. Morgan (listed alphabetically) are important global players as investment banks, especially in derivatives activities (see chapter 9).

Financial innovation has been a substantial force in capital markets, and investment banks and large BHCs have played leading roles in this area (e.g., in the development of securitization and in the engineering of risk-management products such as derivatives). First-mover or innovative investment banks tend to be characterized by lower costs of trading, underwriting, and marketing. Tufano's [1989] evidence suggests that compensation for developing new products centers on gaining market share and maintaining reputational capital as opposed to monopoly pricing. The strategy has been to capture the market before imitative products appear rather than attempt to gouge it.

Although the primary regulator of the securities industry in the United States is the Securities and Exchange Commission (SEC, established in 1934), the New York Stock Exchange (NYSE) and National Association of Securities Dealers (NASD) provide self-regulation and monitoring of day-to-day trading practices and activities. The Federal Reserve regulates the permissible activities of BHCs. Market forces have made the separation of investment and commercial banking obsolete. As Germany and Japan have shown, modern developed financial systems can survive and prosper without the compartmentalization of the two. The penetrations made by BHCs into investment banking are an example of the regulatory dialectic (struggle model, chapter 15) at work.

The Market Structures of Investment Management

The three market structures or trading systems used for securities transactions are as follows:[29]

- Brokered trading
- Dealer trading
- Market making

The trading activities of commercial banks focus on dealer trading and market making.[30] Commercial banks are prohibited from trading equity securities (for income purposes as opposed to providing discount-brokerage services to bank customers). Although banks are permitted to make loans with equity securities taken as collateral, they must liquidate the securities within a reasonable time if they are acquired through borrower default. On balance, banks may hold and trade certain debt securities but not equities (e.g., common stock).

Commercial banks are active in dealer trading and market making for the debt securities of federal, state, and local governments and certain foreign issues. They engage in these trading activities for several reasons: (1) to generate income, (2) to provide investment services to their customers (e.g., respondent banks, which are the counterparties of correspondent banks), (3) to maintain a flow of information for pricing securities, and (4) to establish trading relationships in institutional markets, both domestic and foreign. In general, only 300 or so banks engage in trading-account activities. According to Bloch [1986], the trading of debt securities implies "over-the-counter market making on a large scale with large amounts of risky inventories being positioned by dealers such as investment bankers and commercial banks" (p. 54).

Regarding dealer trading, a dozen or so of the largest U.S. banks (plus nonbank dealers) operate with the Federal Reserve Bank of New York as primary

---

[29] See Bloch ([1986], pp. 50–55) for a complete description of these market structures. This section draws in part on his work.

[30] Brokered trading involves agents (the brokers) acting for buyers and sellers by bringing them together for transactions, with the commission paid by the initiator of the transaction or shared by both parties. Because brokered trading usually takes place on an organized exchange, it is supported by the operations, bureaucracy, and regulations of the exchange. Brokers do not bear any of the risk associated with carrying securities because they do not hold inventories of securities. Brokers operate in financial markets as price takers.

TABLE 8-11   List of Primary Government Securities Dealers Reporting to the Market Reports Division of the Federal Reserve Bank of New York (as of July 27, 1995)

BA Securities, Inc.	HSBC Securities, Inc.
Barclays de Zoete Wedd Securities Inc.	Aubrey G. Lanston & Co., Inc.
Bear, Stearns & Co., Inc.	Lehman Government Securities, Inc.
BT Securities Corporation	Merrill Lynch Government Securities Inc.
Chase Securities Inc.	J. P. Morgan Securities, Inc.
Chemical Securities Inc.	Morgan Stanley & Co. Incorporated
Citicorp Securities, Inc.	NationsBanc Capital Markets, Inc.
CS First Boston Corporation	Nesbitt Burns Securities Inc.
Daiwa Securities American Inc.	The Nikko Securities Co. International, Inc.
Dean Witter Reynolds Inc.	Nomura Securities International, Inc.
Deutsche Bank Securities Corporation	Paine Webber Incorporated
Dillon, Read & Co., Inc.	Prudential Securities Incorporated
Donaldson, Lufkin & Jenrette Securities Corporation	Salomon Brothers Inc.
	Sanwa Securities (USA) Co., L. P.
Eastbridge Capital Inc.	Smith Barney Inc.
First Chicago Capital Markets, Inc.	SBC Capital Markets Inc.
Fuji Securities Inc.	UBS Securities Inc.
Goldman, Sachs & Co.	Yamaichi International (America), Inc.
Greenwich Capital Markets, Inc.	Zions First National Bank

Note: This list has been compiled and made available for statistical purposes only and has no significance with respect to other relationships between dealers and the Federal Reserve Bank of New York. Qualification for the reporting list is based on the achievement and maintenance of the standards outlined in the Federal Reserve Bank of New York's memorandum of January 22, 1992.

dealers in government securities; see Table 8-11. When the Federal Reserve is conducting open market operations, it deals only with these primary dealers. By trading with other financial institutions, the primary dealers transmit the effects of monetary policy throughout the financial system.[31] Compared to brokers, who are price takers, dealers are market makers; hence, unlike brokers, dealers hold inventories of securities. To reduce or move their inventories, dealers reduce both bid and ask prices. Inventory reductions serve to lower both carrying costs and exposures to interest-rate and credit risks. However, if inventories become too thin, dealers run the risk of being unable to meet customers' needs at reasonable prices. The problem of maintaining an adequate inventory and managing portfolio risks can be balanced through the use of synthetic contracts such as financial futures and options. For example, the risks of a larger securities inventory can be hedged with interest-rate futures. In this case, the risk is laid off, for a fee, in another market. The dealer's higher cost of a larger and safer inventory may be reflected in a higher

---

[31] Under an expansionary monetary policy, the central bank buys securities and bank dealers become more liquid (i.e., securities decrease, reserves increase). Because bank reserves are nonearning assets, banks seek earning assets, which under this scenario the Fed ultimately hopes will be in the form of loans to stimulate the economy. Under a contractionary policy, the central bank sells securities and bank dealers become less liquid (i.e., securities increase, reserves decrease). To meet reserve requirements, bank dealers sell securities to other banks, who in turn sell securities, and so forth. Because selling securities drives prices down and interest rates up, the Fed hopes that ultimately higher interest rates will restrict the creation of money and credit, and thereby slow down the growth of the economy.

bid-ask price structure. The dealer's ability to trade in volume is one of the major distinctions between dealers and brokers.

As of this writing, the securities eligible for underwriting and dealing by commercial banks fall under five broad categories:[32]

- U.S. Treasury obligations
- Obligations of U.S. government agencies such as Federal Farm Credit Banks, Federal Home Loan Banks, the Student Loan Marketing Association, the Tennessee Valley Authority, and the U.S. Postal Service
- Obligations of states and political subdivisions, including general obligations, revenue obligations, and agencies for housing, university, or dormitory purposes
- Corporate debt (including junk bonds) but limited to 5 percent of gross revenue
- Corporate equity on a limited basis with approval by the Fed on a case-by-case basis (e.g., J. P. Morgan in 1990)

An underwriter is a dealer who purchases securities from an issuer and distributes them to investors. Since it is common for the underwriter to make a market for the issue after the underwriting is closed, the dealer is said to be engaged in **market making.** Market making, however, is not restricted to the underwriting firms, because other dealers may be willing to engage in such activity. As market makers, commercial banks trade primarily U.S. government securities, selected state and local obligations, and selected foreign issues.

Chapter Summary

Risk management of a bank's investment portfolio focuses on the trade-off between **liquidity** and **profitability.** Getting the most of both requires a negatively sloped or humped yield curve. Because a positively sloped yield curve is the norm, banks, like other investors, must sacrifice liquidity for higher returns. The income from a bank's investment portfolio comes in three forms:

- Interest revenue
- Reinvestment income
- Capital gains (losses)

The volume of **trading-account securities** a bank holds varies directly with its propensity to engage in **active investment management,** which tends to vary directly with bank size. Trading-accounting securities must be **marked-to-market,** whereas those in the (passive) investment account can be carried at **historical cost** or book value. Financial innovation, in the form of **securitization,** has led to the development of mortgage-backed securities (MBSs). These securities, in the form of mortgage pass-through securities and collateralized mortgage obligations (CMOs), have become an important part of banks' portfolios of securities. **Stripped securities** are financial instruments whose cash flows are separated ("stripped") into interest-only (IO) and principal-only (PO) obligations. IOs and POs are highly rate-sensitive assets. Because of the nature of the underlying assets, pass-through securities possess **prepayment risk,** which is an embedded option in any loan contract. This option can produce prepayments, or **contraction risk,** when interest rates are

---

[32] The securities activities of commercial banks are described in Kaufman [1985].

declining, or **extension risk,** when interest rates are rising. Contraction risk shortens the life of an asset whereas extension risk lengthens the life of an asset. Because the securities that banks hold are subject to risk-based capital requirements, riskier investments, like IOs and POs, have the same minimum capital standards as risky loans.

As the Glass-Steagall Act of 1933 has been increasingly eroded, commercial banks have been permitted to increase their activities in **investment banking.** This development has been uneven, however, because the largest bank holding companies, such as BankAmerica, Bankers Trust, Chase Manhattan, Citicorp, and J. P. Morgan, have become the major players among commercial banks. Effective economic barriers to entry, as opposed to regulatory barriers, bar community banks from playing a major role in most investment banking activities.

As banking approaches the year 2000, the number of banks will be about one-half the number in 1934 and investment securities will be in the range of 15–25 percent of total assets, dwarfed by loan and leases with 50–60 percent of total assets. Although the role of investment securities in bank portfolios has declined in relative importance (they accounted for $4 out of every $10 in bank assets in 1934), they still play an important part in bank financial management. The Tax Reform Act of 1986 killed the market for municipal (tax-free) securities, and bank's holding of these instruments have dropped precipitously since then.

Bank investment securities must be marketable but not speculative (i.e., investment quality of at least BBB or Baa). The requirement of investment-grade quality means that credit risk usually is not a major concern in a bank's investment portfolio. Given a bank's loan demand and customer relationships, its investment portfolio serves to balance its structure of earning assets and risk exposure. This purpose is reflected by the results of a 1990 survey by the Bank Administration Institute (Bergquist [1991]) that concluded that the primary objectives of bank investment portfolios are the management of interest-rate risk and liquidity. Although the largest banks rely more and more on the use of interest-rate swaps, options, and futures to manage interest-rate risk, the investment portfolios of community banks are still important vehicles for managing interest-rate risk. Duration matching permits a bank to hedge its interest-rate risk by offsetting price risk with reinvestment risk or vice versa.

Key Words, Concepts, and Acronyms

- Active (passive) investment management
- Bond valuation
- Collateralized mortgage obligations (CMOs)
- Contraction risk
- Credit-extension building blocks
- Default-risk structure of interest rates
- Duration
- Extension risk
- Fisher effect
- Fixed-income securities
- Glass-Steagall Act of 1933
- Historical cost

- Interest-only (IO) obligations
- Interest-rate risk
- Investment account
- Investment banking
- Investment function
- Investment-grade securities
- Liquidity
- Liquidity risk
- Market making
- Marked-to-market
- Mortgage-backed securities (MBSs)
- Mortgage pass-through securities
- Municipal securities
- Passive investment management
- Pass-through securities

- Pledging requirements
- Prepayment risk
- Principal-only (PO) obligations
- ROE Model (for securities firms)
- Securitization
- Stripped securities
- Taxable securities
- Tax-equivalent yield
- Tax-exempt securities
- Tax Reform Act of 1986
- Term structure of interest rates
- Trade-off between liquidity and profitability
- Trading-account securities
- Yield curve

Review/Discussion Questions

1. How has the role of investment securities in bank portfolios changed from the 1930s to the 1990s? What are the forms of revenue that banks derive from their securities portfolios?

2. Credit-extension building blocks come in four basic forms. What are they? The bells and whistles of securitization and financial engineering make investment securities more complex. However, what basic principle still holds in valuing these more complex securities? What eight properties make understanding the valuation of fixed-income securities easier?

3. What is duration and how can it be used to manage interest-rate risk?

4. What are the three alternative methods for calculating the yield on a Treasury bill? Explain the shortcomings and remedies, if any, associated with each method.

5. What are the four basic shapes of yield curves, and when during the interest-rate cycle are they most likely to occur? What linkages, if any, exist between yield curves and interest-rate risk?

6. What does 12 C. F. R. have to say about bank investment securities? What role do bank examiners play in restricting bank investment activities?

7. Distinguish between "active" and "passive" bank investment management. Why is this distinction essentially along the lines of big banks versus little ones?

8. What are trading account securities and how are they an indicator of active investment management? What has FASF 115 had to say about how banks report their securities holdings?

9. Describe the investment portfolio of the typical insured commercial bank. How does bank size affect this portfolio? How have taxes and financial innovation affected it?

10. Credit risk, interest-rate risk, liquidity risk, and prepayment risk are the key portfolio risks of banking. How prevalent are each of these risks in bank investment portfolios?

11. Using the terms of liquidity and elasticity, distinguish between "thin" and "active" markets for the securities that banks hold.

12. How have securitization and financial engineering affected the securities that banks hold? Do you understand the terms in the glossary for pass-through finance (Box 8-3)?

13. What five fundamental principles of financial economics permit us to better understand the risk-return aspect of bank investment securities? Carefully explain your understanding of each concept.

14. Do risk-based capital requirements apply to the securities that banks hold? If so, how and why?

15. Prior to the Tax Reform Act of 1986, how real was the "free lunch" aspect of tax-exempt securities? Describe the tax changes that have been responsible for restructuring the municipal bond market. How have some market participants, such as investment banks, commercial banks, and insurance companies, reacted? Can a case still be made for municipal bonds? You need to read appendix B to answer parts of this question.

16. Discuss and evaluate the following quote:

> Examiners literally walk in and have us prove everything we do. It's as if they don't believe that banks have any integrity. But they're not the ones managing the money. Examiners want us to operate as if it were 1970. Our investment people are inhibited from managing the portfolio based on how they assess interest-rate risk. Of course, there's always the chance that we can lose money. But if you're a good portfolio manager you'll take more gains than losses. I don't think regulators should regulate all banks identically. A $28 billion-asset bank such as ours with an investment staff of 160 people in funds management is going to be more sophisticated than a $90 million-asset bank with a funds management staff of one. (p. 39)

17. Was Glass-Steagall a good idea or a bad one? Can investment banking and commercial banking coexist under the same roof? Which U.S. banks are already into investment banking?

18. Describe the various market structures for trading securities. Which ones are commercial banks active in? Why aren't they active in all three? Distinguish between a price taker and a price maker.

19. Summarize as succinctly as possible Hoffland's views on the ingredients needed for a bank's investment policy. For what kind of bank is his plan most applicable?

20. Distinguish between the laddered and split-maturity investment strategies. What evidence exists regarding the effectiveness of these approaches?

21. What are the six questions and answers that Bradley and Crane suggest that bank investment managers must address?

22. What are the economic and regulatory barriers to entering investment banking? What are the business sectors of a major bank holding company compared to those of a community bank?

23. Can the ROE model be applied to investment banks/securities firms? If so, how do investment banks compare to commercial banks in terms of the first stage of ROE decomposition analysis?

24. Describe the financial characteristics of securities firms in terms of the income-expense statements and balance sheets, and compare them to commercial banks.

25. What are the alternative explanations of the term structure of interest rates (appendix A)?

26. Distinguish among the Dole Bond, the Gingrich Bond, and the Clinton Bond.

Problems

1. An investor purchases a bond with a coupon rate of 6 percent for $800 (par = $1,000). If the bond has 20 years to maturity, find the bond's promised yield
   a. assuming annual interest payments.
   b. assuming semiannual interest payments.

2. A bond is currently quoted at $1,100 and has a current yield of 6.36 percent. The remaining life of the bond is 15 years, but it has three years remaining on a deferred call feature.
   a. Calculate the promised yield assuming annual payments.
   b. Calculate yield-to-call, assuming a call premium equal to one year's interest.

3. An investor purchases a bond during a period of high yields, paying $800 for a 7.75 percent bond. Over the next three years rates are expected to drop to a level at which the value of the bond would increase to $1,050. However, interest rates edge slightly upward, so that when the bond is sold three years later, the price received is only $750. Calculate the actual yield realized, assuming semiannual coupon payments.

4. A bond with a 7 percent annual coupon and 10 years to maturity is selling to yield 9 percent. What is its price?

5. A speculator has decided that because of anticipated declines in interest rates, a given bond should be selling for $950 two years from now. It carries a 10 percent coupon, but because of capital gains, he could make 15 percent if he could buy it at a certain price. What is the price, assuming semiannual payments?

6. A 20-year bond with an 8 percent annual coupon is priced to yield 10 percent. An investor purchasing the bond expects that two years from now, yields on comparable bonds will have declined to 9 percent. Calculate the realized yield if the investor expects to sell the bond in two years.

7. A bond carrying a 6 percent coupon has eight years to maturity. What would its price be if similar bonds yield 8 percent? Assume semiannual coupon payments.

8. If a zero-coupon bond with a par value of $1,838 and nine years to maturity is selling for $1,000 today, what rate of interest is the bond paying? What is the bond's duration? What will an investor's return be if the bond prepays in five years?

9. You can buy a note for $13,420. If you buy it, you will receive 10 annual payments of $2,000, the first payment to be made one year from today. What rate of return, or yield, does the note offer?

10. A corporation is offering to sell its new issue of bonds for a price of $895. The bonds have a maturity of 12 years and have a coupon rate of 6%. What yield is the corporation promising on these bonds?

11. You buy an interest-only strip that has a planned payment schedule of $100 per year for three years. If the going rate of interest is 10%, what is the price of the strip? Immediately after you buy the strip, interest rates double and the expected payment schedule extends to four years. What is the new price of the strip? What has happened and why?

12. The formula for calculating tax-equivalent yields is (see appendix B)

$$r(te) = [r - (d \times c \times t)]/[1 - t]$$

Explain each of the components of the formula. Given the various tax regimes described in appendix B, how has this formula changed over time?

13. Given the various tax regimes from the previous problem, compare a five-year, 5 percent municipal bond with a five-year treasury note yielding 6.60 percent. Assume a cost of bank funds of 4.5 percent and use the d and c parameters that apply to the corresponding tax regimes. Explain why the spread, if any, between the tax-equivalent yield for the tax-exempt security and the taxable yield may not be large enough to convince some institutional investors to buy the tax-exempt issue. Are the calculated yields merely representative, or can they be applied to any bank? Discuss.

14. The investment manager of the Kountry Bank of Kennesaw has the opportunity to buy a municipal bond from an issuer that will not be doing more than $10 million dollars in bonds or tax-free loans this year. The coupon rate on the bond is 5 percent, the bank's cost of funds is 7 percent, and the bank's marginal tax rate is 34 percent. What is the tax-equivalent yield on the bond? If the bank's tax rate increases to 46 percent, what will the yield be? What will the yield be if the bank's cost of funds drops to 6 percent? If the TEFRA disallowance on issuers under $10 million per year is removed, what will the yield be? Check appendix B to do this problem.

15. Given a 182-day T-bill price of 97, the bank-discount yield, what are the coupon-equivalent yield and the effective yield? Assume the price is observed in 1996, a leap year.

16. If the average bank-discount yield on the 91-day T-bill is 5 percent, what is the average price of the bill?

17. If the 91-day T-bill rate is 5.00 percent and the 182-day T-bill rate is 4.91 percent, then in equilibrium, what must the expected 91-day T-bill rate be? Use compound interest to find your answer. How can the abbreviated yield curve in this problem be described? You need appendix A to do this problem.

18. Given the following financial information ($ billions) for The Commercial Bank of Youngstown (TCBY) and The Investment Bank of Youngwood (TIBY), do the first stage of ROE decomposition analysis and discuss your findings in terms of profitability and leverage.

Item	TCBY	TIBY
Net income	1	0.5
Average assets	100	100
Average equity	8	4

19. Given: $R_1 = 5$ percent and $R_2 = 6$ percent, what is the equilibrium forward rate using arithmetic averaging? Using geometric averaging? What is the difference between the two methods, and when is it important? If interest rates triple, what will the difference be?

20. If the Fed is able to maintain a "disciplined" monetary policy over the next quarter century, the annual inflation rate is expected to be about 2.0 percent. If this expectation is realized, then what will the purchasing power of $1,000 be in 25 years? Round your answer to the nearest dollar.

21. Given the inflationary expectations expressed in the previous question, what will the nominal rate of interest be if the real rate is 4 percent? Use both the approximate and exact Fisher equations to get your answer.

22. Given the following abbreviated term structure for one-year, two-year, and three-year bonds: (8 percent, 9 percent, 10 percent)
    a. Today, what is the implied one-year forward rate next year expected to be?
    b. Today, what is the implied one-year forward rate in two years expected to be?
    You need appendix A to do this problem and the next one.

23. Suppose you observe the following abbreviated yield curve of one-year, two-year, and three-year bonds: (9 percent, 8 percent, 7 percent) with embodied compensating premiums of 0.5 percent and 0.75 percent. What are the forward rates and pure expected rates that can be derived from these structures? Use arithmetic averaging.

24. Extra Credit: What is the required risk-based capital (Tier 1, Tier 2, and total; see chapter 13 for additional details beyond Box 8-3 to do this problem) needed for the following portfolio of asset-backed securities?

Type of asset	Amount ($ millions)
GNMAs	20
FHLMCs/FNMAs	20
MBSs (1–4 family)	50
CMOs (IOs and POs)	100
Securitized credit-card receivables	100
Total	290

APPENDIX A

ALTERNATIVE THEORIES OF THE TERM STRUCTURE OF INTEREST RATES

Term-structure theories explain the shape (slope) and position of the yield curve. The three basic theories of the term structure of interest rates are

1. The pure-expectations theory
2. The liquidity-preference theory
3. The market-segmentation theory

For expositional purposes, let us refer to those explanations adopting an expectations approach, but stopping short of the pure-expectations approach, as *modified-*

expectations theories. In this framework, the liquidity-preference theory is a modified-expectations approach; its modifier is the notion of a liquidity premium. The pure-expectations theory and the market-segmentation theory represent diametrically opposed explanations of the term structure; the modified theories stand between these two extremes. The major theories of the term structure are summarized in Table A8-1 and explained in the following sections.

The Pure-Expectations Theory (PET)

The PET approach contends that investors' expectations of future short-term interest rates determine the slope of the yield curve. Since expectations and expectations alone are said to explain the term structure, the theory is referred to as the *pure-expectations theory.* PET makes a number of simplifying assumptions, the most important of which are these:

1. Investors are profit maximizers whose expectations are firm, uniform, and endless
2. There is perfect certainty, including accurate forecasts
3. Transaction costs are zero

TABLE A8-1   Alternative Explanations of the Term Structure of Interest Rates

| | *Theory* | | |
Descriptive Category	*Pure Expectations*	*Modified Expectations*	*Market Segmentation*
Key determinant	Expectations	Modified expectations	Institutional behavior
Conceptualization of the key determinant	Forecasts of short-term interest rates	Forecasts of short-term interest rates plus compensating premiums (e.g., liquidity premiums)	Demand and supply curves for securities
Equilibrating mechanism	Profit-maximizing behavior over the investor's holding period	Profit-maximizing behavior plus some nonexpectational element (such as maturity preferences) induced by uncertainty	Forces of supply and demand in segmented markets (i.e., hedging pressure)
Relationship between long- and short-term interest rates	Linkage by formula using expected rates	Linkage by formula using forward rates (i.e., expected rates plus compensating premiums)	No linkage by formula; markets are segmented
Description of forward rates	Pure expected rates	Expected rates plus compensating premiums	None given
Restrictiveness of assumptions	Very restrictive	Less restrictive than PET (e.g., admits uncertainty)	Not restrictive
Intuitive appeal	Expectations are important, although difficult to measure	Nonexpectational elements such as maturity preferences, uncertainty, or transactions costs	Institutional structures and behavior; supply-and-demand forces
Importance of relative supplies of securities	Unimportant unless they affect expectations	Relatively important because they determine the size of compensating premiums	Critically important
Important contributors	Lutz, Meiselman	Hicks, Kessel, Modigliani and Sutch, Kane and Malkiel, Kane, Malkiel	Culbertson, Homer and Johannesen

Given these assumptions and the investor's holding period, each investor selects the portfolio that maximizes the holding-period return. The PET equilibrium condition is

$$(1 + {}_tR_N) = [(1 + {}_tR_1)(1 + {}_{t+1}r_1)\dots(1 + {}_{t+N-1}r_1)]^{1/N} \qquad \textbf{(A8-1)}$$

where R indicates an observed rate and r an expected rate. The presubscript indicates *time* and the postsubscript *maturity*.

Equation A8-1 describes the PET linkage by formula between long-term rates and short-term ones. It specifically states that in equilibrium the actual long-term yield equals the compound yields based on a series of short-term investments. Consider the case for $N = 2$. The equilibrium condition is

$$(1 + {}_tR_2) = [(1 + {}_tR_1)(1 + {}_{t+1}r_1)]^{1/2}$$

or

$$(1 + {}_tR_2)^2 = (1 + {}_tR_1)(1 + {}_{t+1}r_1)$$

A numerical example will help to clarify the equilibrium process. To simplify the calculations, arithmetic averaging is employed. Suppose that the current yield on a one-year security $({}_tR_1)$ is 14 percent, the current yield on a two-year security $({}_tR_2)$ is 12 percent, and the yield anticipated next year for reinvestment in a one-year security $({}_{t+1}r_1)$ is 10 percent. This configuration of rates is an equilibrium one, since $.12 = (.14 + 10)/2$. Thus, an investor with a two-year holding period would find no difference between holding a two-year bond at 12 percent and holding a series of one-year bonds at successive yields of 14 percent and 10 percent. Suppose, however, that a two-year obligation paying 14 percent existed when the equilibrium two-year rate was 12 percent. Profit-maximizing investors would want the 14 percent security and would immediately bid up its price to 103.38, the present value of a two-year, 14 percent coupon bond when the going rate of interest is 12 percent. Alternatively, what's the return on a two-year, 14 percent coupon bond with a price of 103.38? It's 12 percent, the equilibrium rate. At the end of the first year, the price of the 14 percent bond, now with one year until maturity, is $114/1.1 = 103.64$. A one-year holding period return (*HPR*) is defined as

$$HPR = \frac{C + P}{P_0} \qquad \textbf{(A8-2)}$$

where $C =$ the coupon payment, $P =$ the change in price, and $P_0 =$ the purchase price. The *HPR* for the 14 percent bond in year 2 is

$$HPR = \frac{14 - 3.64}{103.64} = \frac{10.36}{103.64} = .10$$

which is the PET equilibrium one-year rate in year 2. Given the assumptions of PET, no matter what investors do, they can't beat the equilibrium rates, which in the previous example can be summarized as going long for $(1.12)^2$ versus rolling over the investment for $(1.14)(1.10)$.

Consider now a positively sloped yield curve with ${}_tR_1 = 12$ percent, ${}_tR_2 = 12.5$ percent, and ${}_{t+1}r_1 = 13$ percent, and an investor with a one-year holding period. Will the investor find no difference between the one-year bond and the two-year bond held for one year? The answer is yes, because the term structure is an equilibrium one $[.125 = (.12 + .13)/2]$. The one-year bond will return 12 percent. At the end of the first year the price of the two-year bond will be

$$P = \frac{12.5 + 100}{1.13} = 99.557 \approx 99.5$$

and its *HPR* will be

$$HPR = \frac{12.5 - .5}{100} = .12$$

Thus, the two-year bond held for one year also will return 12 percent.

To emphasize how future short-term interest rates determine the term structure, consider the following schematic:

$$\begin{bmatrix} {}_tR_1 \\ {}_{t+1}r_1 \\ {}_{t+2}r_1 \\ \cdots \\ {}_{t+N-1}r_1 \end{bmatrix} \xrightarrow{\text{determines}} \begin{bmatrix} {}_tR_2 \\ {}_tR_3 \\ \cdots \\ \cdots \\ {}_tR_N \end{bmatrix}$$

Given the one-year rate $({}_tR_1)$, it is the vector of future short-term rates that determines the term-structure vector.

It is important to note that the PET linkage-by-formula mechanism involves a simple average variable–marginal variable relationship. Because long-term rates are an average of future short-term rates, the following relationships hold:

1. If $_{t+N}r_1 > {}_tR_N$, $N \geq 2$, the yield curve will be positively sloped (i.e., as long as the marginal contribution is greater than the average, the average will rise).
2. If $_{t+N}r_1 < {}_tR_N$, $N \geq 2$, the yield curve will be negatively sloped (i.e., as long as the marginal contribution is less than the average, the average will fall).
3. If $_{t+N}r_1 = {}_tR_N$, $N \geq 2$, the yield curve will be flat (i.e., as long as the marginal contribution equals the average, the average will remain constant).

Given these basic relationships, PET can explain a yield curve of any shape. When these relationships are turned around, they indicate that (1) a positively sloped yield curve implies that investors expect short-term rates to rise, (2) a negatively sloped yield curve implies that investors expect short-term rates to fall, and (3) a flat yield curve implies that investors expect short-term rates to remain unchanged.

Although expected rates cannot be observed directly, the PET equilibrium condition can be used to generate such rates, which are called forward rates and denoted by *F*. According to PET, there is a one-to-one correspondence between forward rates and expected rates. Schematically, the process is as follows:

$$\begin{bmatrix} R_1 \\ R_2 \\ \cdots \\ R_N \end{bmatrix} \xrightarrow{\text{generates}} \begin{bmatrix} {}_{t+1}F_1 \\ {}_{t+2}F_2 \\ \cdots \\ {}_{t+N-1}F_1 \end{bmatrix} = \begin{bmatrix} {}_{t+1}r_1 \\ {}_{t+2}r_1 \\ \cdots \\ {}_{t+N-1}r_1 \end{bmatrix}$$

To illustrate, consider the following T-bill term structure with ${}_tR_1 = 16$ percent, ${}_tR_2 = 17$ percent, ${}_tR_3 = 15.5$ percent, and ${}_tR_4 = 15$ percent, where the maturity postsubscript is a quarterly one. Thus, $_tR_1$ represents the coupon-equivalent yield on three-month T-bills, $_tR_2$ the yield on six-month T-bills, and so on. What forward (expected) rates are implied by this bill-rate structure? According to PET, the expected three-month bill rates, using arithmetic averaging, are

$$_{t+1}r_1 = 2(.17) - .16 = .18$$

$$_{t+2}r_1 = 3(.155) - .16 - .18 = .125$$

$$_{t+3}r_1 = 4(15) - .16 - .18 - .125 = .135$$

In other words, to generate the observed hump in the yield curve, the expected three-month bill rates three, six, and nine months in the future must be 18 percent, 12.5 percent, and 13.5 percent, respectively. That is, the three-month bill rates must be expected to rise, fall, and then rise to generate the hump.

Modified-Expectations Theories

The most famous expositor of the modified-expectations approach is J. R. Hicks [1946], the father of the Hicksian liquidity-premium theory (LPT). Hicks argued that because of uncertainty about future interest rates and bond prices, investors have to be paid a liquidity premium for bearing the interest-rate or maturity risk of going long. This "constitutional weakness" in the bond market is why, even if future short-term rates are expected to remain unchanged, the normal yield-curve relationship is a positive one. Hicks was searching for an explanation of why, on average, long term rates were greater than short-term ones. His theory focused on the notion of liquidity premiums (L) as compensation for bearing interest-rate risk. The equilibrium condition for the Hicksian LPT is

$$(1 + {}_tR_N) = [(1 + {}_tR_1)(1 + {}_{t+1}r_1 + L_2)\ldots(1 + {}_{t+n-1}r_1 + L_N)]^{1/N} \qquad \textbf{(A8-3)}$$

where $L_N > L_{N-1} > 0$, $N \geq 2$ (i.e., the liquidity premiums are strictly positive and increase monotonically). Under this approach, the one-to-one correspondence between forward rates and expected rates disappears, that is,

$$_{t+N-1}F + 1 = {}_{t+N-1}r_1 + L_N \qquad \textbf{(A8-4)}$$

To illustrate, suppose that $_tR_1 = 10$ percent and that expected one-year rates for the next three years are 9.5 percent, 9.25 percent, and 9.00 percent. Furthermore, assume that the following liquidity premiums exist: $L_2 = 75$ percent, $L_3 = 1.20$ percent, and $L_4 = 1.40$ percent. Using arithmetic averaging, the equilibrium term structure implied by these conditions is

$$R_2 = \frac{.10 + (.095 + .0075)}{2} = .1012$$

$$R_3 = \frac{.10 + (.095 + .0075) + (.0925 + .012)}{3} = .1022$$

$$R_4 = \frac{.10 + (.095 + .0075) + (.0925 + .012) + (.09 + .014)}{4} = .1027$$

The existence of the liquidity premiums results in a positively sloped yield curve. If $L_N = 0$, the implied term structure is a negatively sloped one (i.e., .10, .0975, .0958, .0944). In the Hicksian view of the term structure, the shape of the yield curve is explained by expectations of future short-term interest rates *plus* liquidity premiums.

A more general modified-expectations approach is the preferred-habitat theory associated with Modigliani and Sutch [1966].[33] According to this approach, either policy-determined or regulatory-imposed risk aversion leads investors to *hedge* their balance sheets by staying in their preferred (maturity) habitat. Unless the rates on other maturities offer an expected premium sufficient to compensate for the risk and cost of moving out of one's habitat, investors are content to stay with their preferred maturities. The concepts of segmented markets and hedging behavior, which the preferred-habitat theory builds upon, are explained more fully in the next section.

The equilibrium condition for the preferred-habitat theory is similar to Equation A8-3, except that no restrictions are placed on the compensating premiums, a_N (i.e., $a_N \gtreqless 0$). In other words, in Equations A8-3 and A8-4, replace L_N with a_N and note that a_N is unconstrained. Along each segment of the yield curve, the compensating premiums are pegged by the forces of demand and supply. Through the forces of speculation or arbitrage, it is possible that such premiums (or discounts, i.e., $a_N < 0$) could bring about shifts in the flows of funds among different maturity segments. Thus, it is possible for nonexpectational elements to affect the term structure of interest rates.

The Market-Segmentation Theory

The market-segmentation theory adopts an institutional approach focusing on the hedging behavior of market participants. According to this explanation, the forces of supply and demand in *segmented* markets determine the yields in those markets. Since markets are segmented on the basis of maturity preferences tied to hedging behavior, there is no linkage by formula between short- and long-term interest rates as in expectations-based theories. Using the traditional trichotomy of short-, intermediate-, and long-term markets, the concepts of segmented markets is illustrated in Figure A8-1. In each of these segments, the rates are determined by the forces of supply and demand, as manifested by hedging-pressure behavior. The short-term segment is dominated by companies that require liquidity, such as commercial banks, nonfinancial corporations, and money-market funds. Their maturity needs (or habitat preferences) lead them to attempt to hedge their balance sheets by investing in short-term assets. For example, at the beginning of the interest-rate cycle, when loan and product demand is slack, these institutions bid the prices of short-term securities up; hence low yields are observed. At the peak of the cycle, when liquidity is scarce, the opposite occurs. In general, investors in the short-term

FIGURE A8-1 **The Market-Segmentation Theory**

Yield to Maturity

Short-Term Segment	*Intermediate-Term Segment*	*Long-Term Segment*
Forces of supply and demand determine rates based upon the hedging behavior of participants with short-term maturity preferences	Forces of supply and demand determine rates based upon the hedging behavior of particpants with intermediate-term maturity preferences	Forces of supply and demand determine rates based upon the hedging behavior of participants with long-term maturity preferences.

Terms to Maturity

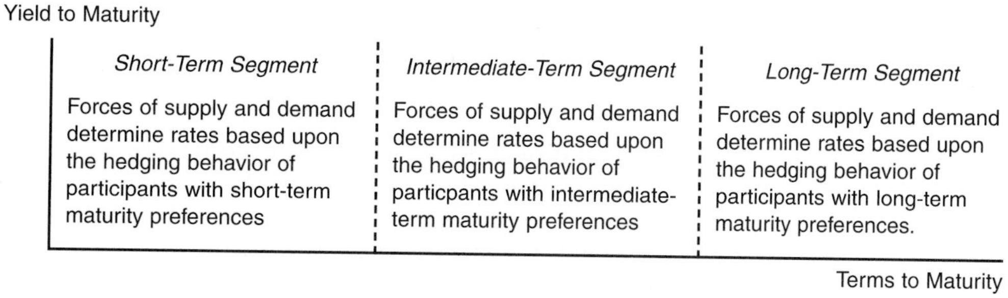

[33] The preferred-habitat theory also could be viewed as a modified market-segmentation theory.

segment of the market are more concerned about certainty of principal than certainty of income.

The long-term segment of the market is dominated by institutions with long-term liabilities, such as life insurance companies and pension funds. Hedging behavior leads these institutions to prefer to operate in the long-term segment of the market, where they tend to generate a fairly uniform demand for long-term assets such as bonds, stocks, and mortgages. (In this segment of the market, investors are more concerned about certainty of income than certainty of principal.) Thus, over the long run, risk-averse behavior prompts them to prefer long-term securities over short-term ones.

The intuitive appeal of market segmentation is diminished somewhat when analyzing the intermediate-term segment of the market. Unlike in the short- and long-term markets, there are no easily identified institutions that prefer to operate solely in the intermediate-term maturity range. This absence of a dominating participant explains why the intermediate-term market is frequently described as thin and inactive compared to the short- and long-term segments. Some of the institutions that overlap into the intermediate-term range are commercial banks, property and casualty insurance companies, life insurance companies, and pension funds. Commercial banks also operate to a limited degree in the long-term U.S. government bond market, whereas property and casualty insurance companies store their "hurricane money" in the short-term segment of the market. These overlapping markets argue against the polar version of market segmentation, which calls for completely segmented markets and no substitutability across maturities.

The concept of market segmentation has intuitive appeal because of the observed preference of certain institutions to operate in particular maturity segments. It is diametrically opposed to PET and argues that, within a particular maturity segment, rates are determined by the forces of supply and demand, to the exclusion of future expected rates and alternative current yields. The preferred-habitat theory of Modigliani and Sutch, which adopts an eclectic approach, uses three building blocks: (1) maturity preferences, (2) expectations of future short-term rates, and (3) the notion of compensating premiums. Under this approach, investors can be coaxed out of their preferred habitats (think of the combined effect of small shifts by many transactors) if the compensating premiums are attractive. In contrast, the market segmentation theory denies such substitutability.

APPENDIX
B

THE TAX REFORM ACT OF 1986

Although investment banks have been the leading underwriters of municipal securities, commercial banks have been the leading institutional holders of these obligations. The Tax Reform Act of 1986, however, caused a major shakeout in the municipal bond market. The biggest shock to the market occurred on October 12, 1987 when Salomon Brothers announced it was withdrawing from the slumping municipal bond business. As the leading underwriter of municipal obligations, Salomon Brothers had such valued clients as New York's Municipal Assistance

Corporation, the state of Massachusetts, and the New York State Transit Authority. The firm also played a crucial role in providing liquidity to the municipal bond market.

Although many observers regarded Salomon's decision to withdraw from the market as "proof" that the municipal bond business would not rebound from its tax-reform slump, at least one analyst saw the move as shortsighted. He stated: "There is between $2 trillion and $3 trillion of municipal financing that will inevitably be financed with some form of municipal securities over the next 20 years. For Salomon Brothers to abandon the field leads me to believe they haven't thought through the long-term strategy for the firm as a whole."[34]

The slump in the municipal bond market was directly attributed to tax-reform-induced changes in both the supply of and demand for municipal securities. On the supply side, the law imposes a state-by-state volume cap on municipal bond issuance, thereby reducing new business. To illustrate the effect, during the first nine months of 1987 Salomon was the lead manager on 77 issues totaling $7.5 billion, compared to 97 issues totaling $9.9 million for the comparable 1986 period. This reduction in longer-term decline (since 1981) in underwriting fees (e.g., from 2.9% in 1982 to 1.9% in the first quarter of 1987) made the municipal bond business less profitable.

On the demand side, the Tax Reform Act of 1986 reduced the tax advantage of purchasing municipal obligations. On the institutional side of the market, commercial banks and insurance companies have been the largest holders of municipal bonds. (As a group, individual investors are the largest holders of municipal bonds.) To illustrate the cutback in institutional demand, MONY Financial Services Inc., the parent company of Mutual Life Insurance Company of New York and a former municipal client of Salomon Brothers, held about $330 million in municipal obligations in its $11 billion portfolio of 1984 compared to only a few issues in its $20 billion portfolio of 1987.

The reduced demand for municipal securities by institutional investors is due to the denial under the 1986 tax law of any deduction for interest expense to purchase or carry tax-exempt securities. The one exception to the repeal of carrying costs applies to small municipalities (but not states) with annual sales of tax-exempt obligations to financial institutions of $10 million or less. In this case, the financial institution can deduct 80 percent of the interest expense associated with the purchase of these "small" issues.

Calculating Tax-Equivalent Yields

The easier way to see how changes in the tax codes have affected the demand for municipal securities is to employ the formula for calculating tax-equivalent yields. Letting $r(te)$ represent the tax-equivalent yield on a tax-exempt security, the relevant formula is

$$r(te) = [r - (d \times c \times t)]/[1 - t] \qquad \textbf{(B8-1)}$$

where r is the nominal yield on the tax-exempt security, d is the percentage disallowance on the interest carrying cost due to TEFRA, c is the average interest cost of funds for carrying the security, and t is the institution's marginal tax rate.[35] Four

---

[34] The quotation and other details in this section (e.g., Salomon Brothers' decision) are from Peers [1987], p. 3.

[35] TEFRA stands for the Tax Equity and Fiscal Reform Act of 1982. Equation A8-1 is from the *ABA Banking Journal* (February 1987), p. 35.

regimes are used to demonstrate how changes in the tax laws have affected the calculation of $r(te)$, which, because it is the effective rate of return on tax-exempt securities, will govern the demand for the securities.

1. The Pre-1983 Era

In the pre-1983 era, financial institutions could deduct the full cost of purchasing and carrying municipal and state obligations. In terms of equation B8-1, the disallowance, d, was zero, which simplified the formula to $r(te) = r/(1 - t)$. Using a marginal tax rate of 0.46, the benchmark rule was to double the tax-exempt yield to get an approximation of the tax-equivalent yield. The exact multiplier was $1.85185... = 1/(1 - .46)$.

Let's consider the following example, which will be carried through into the other three regimes. Suppose we want to compare a tax-exempt security with a 5.75 percent yield to a taxable one with a 7 percent yield. Our first approximation of doubling the yield gives a tax-equivalent return of 11.5 percent. More exactly, we get 10.65 percent ($= 5.75/[1 - .46]$), assuming a marginal tax rate of 46 percent. If the spread of 365 basis points ($= 10.65\% - 7\%$) over the taxable security is enough to offset nonrate factors such as greater credit risk and lack of liquidity, the tax-exempt security is the preferred investment.

2. The 1983–1986 Era

During the 1983–1986 era, TEFRA specified the disallowance to be 20 percent, which means we must use equation B8-1 to calculate the tax-equivalent yield. Continuing with the previous example and assuming an average cost of funds of 4.5 percent, we get $r(te) = 9.88$ percent ($= [5.75 - (.2 \times 4.5 \times .46)/[1 - .46]$). In this case, the tax-equivalent yield has fallen 77 basis points from what it was under the earlier tax regime, resulting in a lower spread over the taxable security (i.e., $2.88\% = 9.88\% - 7\%$ versus $3.65\% = 10.65\% - 7\%$).

3. The Transition Year: 1987

In the 1987 regime, the disallowance rose to 100 percent ($d = 1$) and the marginal tax rate (in transition between 46% and 34%) was approximated by 40 percent. With $d = 1$, the municipal bond market (from an institutional perspective) was devastated because $r(te) = 6.58$ percent ($= [5.75 - (1 \times 4.5 \times .40]/[1 - .4]$). With the taxable yield equal to 7 percent, there was no reason to hold a riskier security that had a lower yield, and more than likely was less liquid.

4. The Post-1987 Era

The only change after 1987 is the lower marginal tax rate of 34 percent, which serves only to push the tax-equivalent yield even lower relative to the taxable one. Specifically, $r(te) = 6.39$ percent ($= [5.75 - (1 \times 4.5 \times .34)/[1 - .34]$). In this case, the tax-exempt security has a 61 basis point disadvantage compared to the taxable yield of 7 percent.

Tax-Reform Recap and Implications for Bank Investment Portfolios

The previous four examples clearly illustrate why the demand for municipal securities has decreased. Formula B8-1 represents an easy method for calculating the tax-equivalent yields associated with the various tax regimes. The reduced demand for municipal securities combined with the supply restrictions on new issues explains the slump in the municipal bond market.

What are the implications of tax reform for bank investment portfolios? One thing is clear: Commercial banks will be holding fewer tax-exempt securities in their portfolios, all other things being equal (Table 8-4). The *ABA Banking Journal* summarized the municipal bond situation this way: "Banks' municipal bond portfolios will in time be just a memory under tax reform. Other instruments may come into their own." As one banker put it, "It's a whole new ball game."[36] Financial innovation and securitization came to the rescue: The instruments that have come into their own have been mortgage-backed securities. They are the new game in town and, as Table 8-4 shows, banks have increased their holdings of pass-through securities and CMOs.

Selected References

Aberth, John. [1988]. "Searching for an Investment Strategy." *ABA Banking Journal* (July), pp. 39–42.

Bergquist, Lizbeth S. [1991]. "Trends in Investment Portfolio Management." *Bank Management* (January), pp. 64–67.

Bloch, Ernest. [1986]. *Inside Investment Banking.* Homewood Hills, IL: Dow Jones-Irwin.

Bradley, Stephen P., and Dwight B. Crane. [1975]. *Management of Bank Portfolio.* New York: Wiley.

Carter, David A., and Joseph F. Sinkey, Jr. [1997]. "An Empirical Investigation of End-Use of Interest-Rate Derivatives by Nondealer U.S. Commercial Banks." Working Paper, University of Georgia.

Comptroller's Handbook for National Bank Examiners. [1979]. Englewood Cliffs, NJ: Prentice-Hall.

Cramer, Robert H., and James A. Seifert. [1976]. "Measuring the Impact of Maturity on Expected Return and Risk." *Journal of Bank Research* (Fall), pp. 229–235.

"Farewell to Municipals and Other Tax Effects" [1987]. *ABA Banking Journal* (February), pp. 35–36.

Federal Reserve Bulletin. Washington, DC: Board of Governors of the Federal Reserve System (various issues).

Fisher, Lawrence. [1959]. "Determinants of Risk Premiums on Corporate Bonds." *Journal of Political Economy* (June), pp. 217–237.

Garbade, Kenneth D. [1982]. *Securities Markets.* New York: McGraw-Hill.

Granito, Michael R. [1984]. *Bond Portfolio Immunization.* Lexington, MA: Lexington Books.

Hayes, Douglas A. [1980]. *Bank Funds Management: Issues and Practices.* Ann Arbor: University of Michigan.

Hicks, J. R. [1946]. *Value and Capital.* London: Oxford University Press.

Hilliard, Jimmy E., and Joseph F. Sinkey, Jr. [1989]. "Duration Analysis as a Tool for Predicting Interest-Sensitive Cash Flows." *Journal of Financial Education* (Fall), pp. 1–7.

Hodgman, D. R. [1963]. *Commercial Bank Loan and Investment Policy.* Champaign: University of Illinois Press.

---

[36] *Ibid.*

Hoffland, David L. [1978]. "A Model Bank Investment Policy." *Financial Analysts Journal* (May-June), pp. 64–67.

Hunter, William C., and Stephen G. Timme. [1986]. "Technical Change, Organizational Form, and the Structure of Bank Production," *Journal of Money, Credit and Banking* (May), pp. 152–166.

Jaffee, Dwight M. [1975]. "Cyclical Variation in the Risk Structure of Interest Rates." *Journal of Monetary Economics* (July), pp. 309–325.

Kane, Edward J. [1980]. "Tax Exemption, Economic Efficiency, and Relative Interest Rates." Prepared for the Conference on Efficiency in the Municipal Bank Market.

Kaufman, George G. [1985]. "The Securities Activities of Commercial Banks." In Richard C. Aspinwall and Robert A. Eisenbeis, eds., *Handbook for Banking Strategy*. New York: Wiley, pp. 661–702.

———. [1987]. "The Federal Safety Net: Not for Banks Only." *Economic Perspectives,* Federal Reserve Bank of Chicago (November-December), pp. 19–28.

Manual of Examination Policies. Washington, DC: FDIC (various revision dates).

Mason, John M. [1979]. *Financial Management of Commercial Banks.* Boston: Warren, Gorham, and Lamont.

McHugh, Robert D., Jr. [1990]. "The Case for Municipal Bonds," *ABA Banking Journal* (August), pp. 10, 14.

McKinney, George W., Jr. [1977]. "A Perspective on the Use of Models in the Management of Banks' Funds." *Journal of Bank Research* (Summer), pp. 122–127.

Modigliani, Franco, and Richard Sutch. [1966]. "Innovations in Interest-Rate Policy," *American Economic Review:* Papers and Proceedings (May), pp. 178–197.

Peers, Alexandra. [1987]. "Public Finance Shakeout Is Signaled by Salomon's Municipal Bond Decision." *The Wall Street Journal* (October 13), p. 3.

Radcliffe, Robert C. [1982]. *Investment: Concepts, Analysis, and Strategy.* Glenview, IL: Scott, Foresman.

Robinson, Roland I. [1962]. *The Management of Bank Funds.* New York: McGraw-Hill.

Sinkey, Joseph F., Jr., and David A. Carter. [1997]. "The Derivatives Activities of U.S. Commercial Banks: Why Big Banks Do and Small Banks Don't." Working Paper, The University of Georgia.

Smith, Clifford W., Jr., and Charles W. Smithson. [1990]. *The Handbook of Financial Engineering: New Financial Product Innovations, Applications, and Analyses.* New York: Harper Business.

Symons, Edward L., Jr., and James J. White. [1991]. *Banking Law: Teaching Materials*, 3rd ed. St. Paul, MN: West Publishing.

Symons, Edward L., Jr., and James J. White, editors. [1991]. *Banking Law: Selected Statutes and Regulations.* St. Paul, MN: West Publishing.

Tufano, Peter. [1989]. "Financial Innovation and First-Mover Advantages." *Journal of Financial Economics* 25, pp. 213–240.

Van Horne, James C. [1990]. *Financial Market Rates & Flows.* Englewood Cliffs, NJ: Prentice Hall.

Watson, Ronald D. [1972]. "Bank Bond Management: The Maturity Dilemma." *Business Review,* Federal Reserve Bank of Philadelphia (March), pp. 23–29.

Woodworth, G. Walter. [1967]. *The Management of Cyclical Liquidity of Commercial Banks.* Boston: The Bankers Publishing Company.

CHAPTER

9

NONINTEREST INCOME, SECURITIZATION, AND DERIVATIVES ACTIVITIES

Contents

LEARNING OBJECTIVES

- ■ To understand bankers' motives for engaging in off-balance-sheet activities (OBSAs) and securitization
- ■ To understand noninterest income as a symptom of OBSAs
- ■ To understand the process of securitization and its net benefits
- ■ To understand why big banks do and little banks don't engage in derivatives
- ■ To understand the risks of derivatives

CHAPTER THEME

This chapter explores two of the most exciting and innovative developments in banking: securitization and derivatives activities. Although the emergence of these two innovations captures two important aspects of modern banking, banks have been doing traditional **off-balance-sheet activities** (OBSAs) such as **loan commitments** and **lines of credit** for years. Combined, the traditional and nontraditional activities are known as off-balance-sheet or **contingent-commitment banking.** Advances in "financial engineering" and pressure on all banks, but especially the largest ones, to generate **fee** or **noninterest income** and to improve **capital adequacy** explain the explosion of nontraditional banking activities. In the context of the return-on-equity model ($ROE = ROA \times EM$), the competitive and regulatory pressures on both ROA and EM reflect, in part, these forces of change. These pressures get bankers' attention because they affect two pillars of bank performance: profitability (ROA) and capital adequacy (EM). Accordingly, bankers, mainly those at the 100 largest banks, are at the margin adding more assets off their balance sheets than on them. Bankers' motives for engaging in derivatives include hedging, speculating, and selling risk-management services. On balance, OBSAs (including the selling of risk-management services) present banks with opportunities to strengthen customer relationships and to reduce the probability of financial distress for client firms, thereby reducing the bank's risk exposure to these customers.

KEY CONCEPTS, IDEAS, AND TERMS

- Asset securitization
- Capital adequacy
- Derivatives contracts
- Derivatives securities
- Financial engineering
- Financial innovation
- Hedging

- Lines of credit
- Noninterest (fee) income
- Off-balance-sheet activities (OBSAs)
- Recourse (loan)
- Return-on-equity model
  ($ROE = ROA \times EM$)
- Risk-management services

- Securitized lending (originating, selling, servicing)
- Speculating
- Traditional lending function (originating, funding, monitoring, servicing)

INTRODUCTION

The phenomena of global*ization,* institutional*ization,* privat*ization,* and securit*ization* suggest the idea of the *ization* of the financial-services industry. **Securitization** is one of the major forms of off-balance-sheet or contingent-commitment banking;

others include loans commitments, standby letters of credit, and **derivatives contracts** (that is, futures, options, swaps, and forward contracts applied to interest rates, exchange rates, and commodity prices). The movement of activities off banks' balance sheets has been one of the major developments of modern commercial banking. As a result, in the aggregate, banks have more assets off their balance sheets than on them. This chapter shows, however, that off-balance-sheet activities (OBSAs), especially derivatives, are concentrated in the largest banks. A bank's noninterest income, which varies directly with bank size (as a percentage of assets), is a symptom of off-balance-sheet banking.

If we view OBSAs and securitization as innovations, they fit neatly into a model of **financial innovation** driven by competitive, technological, and regulatory forces. The regulatory reaction to OBSAs and securitization fit nicely into Kane's model of the struggle between bankers and regulators (that is, the regulatory dialectic; chapters 1 and 15). For example, the regulatory reaction to the surge in OBSAs was to impose **risk-based capital requirements** (chapter 13) on such activities and to make loan sales with **recourse** subject to capital requirements.

MOTIVES FOR MOVING ASSETS OFF THE BALANCE SHEET

Bankers' concerns about profitability and capital adequacy drive them to engage in off-balance-sheet activities, asset securitization, and loan sales. These concerns are captured and illustrated by the first stage of the return-on-equity model, that is,

$$ROE = ROA \times EM \qquad \text{(9-1)}$$

where ROE = return on equity, ROA = return on assets, and EM = equity multiplier. Recall that ROA equals net income divided by total (or average) assets and that EM equals total assets divided by total equity capital (the inverse of EM is the ratio of equity capital to assets). Thus, at the margin, when banks engage in OBSAs, asset securitization, or loan sales,[1] they restrain asset growth and increase fee income. These effects increase ROA and lower EM, all other things being equal.[2] Given that the marketplace and regulators want improved profitability and stronger capital positions, OBSAs and asset securitization can serve both of these ends.

In the ongoing struggle between regulators and banks, the regulatory reaction to these banking innovations has been to impose risk-based capital requirements on OBSAs and recourse restrictions on securitized assets and loan sales. Specifically, because transactions that are not booked on the balance sheet, such as OBSAs, increase risk but do not lower (nominal) bank capital ratios, risk-based capital requirements were introduced. Similarly, because the sale of assets with recourse does not effectively remove risk from the balance sheet, banking regulations require that such assets be supported by bank capital.

---

[1] An important distinction exists between assets that are sold without recourse and those that are sold with recourse (i.e., the ability of a person or entity owning a negotiable instrument to compel payment). With securitized assets usually no recourse exists, whereas in the case of certain loan sales, recourse may exist. In the case of transactions with recourse clauses, the risks of the underlying asset have not been removed from the balance sheet.

[2] At the margin, it is assumed that the transaction does not otherwise affect net income except for the increase in fee income net of any operating and servicing costs. Also, in terms of the balance-sheet constraint ($A = L + NW$), when A declines, L declines (reduced funding), and A/NW (the capital ratio) increases.

In a nutshell, the squeeze on bank earnings and market and regulatory demands for increased capital have been the driving forces behind the surge in OBSAs, asset securitization, and loan sales. Computer technology and financial engineering have provided the data processing and financial instruments to facilitate these developments.

Illustration Using the ROE Model

The effects of OBSAs and securitization can be illustrated using the ROE model. This example assumes three states of nature: (1) an initial position (say, pre-1980), (2) a transition period (the 1980s), in which a competitive-regulatory shock leads to a lower ROA and a maximum EM of 12, or a minimum capital ratio of 0.083, and (3) a rebalancing period (the 1990s) designed to cope with the shock to the banking system. Although hypothetical, the realistic descriptive components of ROE across the three states are as follows:

	Initial Position	*Transition*	*Rebalancing*
Return on assets (ROA)	0.01	0.0075	0.0125
Equity multiplier (EM)	15.00	12.00	11.00
Return on equity ($ROA \times EM$)	0.15	0.09	0.1375

In the rebalanced state, the bank uses higher fee income and cost-cutting measures to improve ROA, and reduced asset growth or increased capital to generate an EM below the maximum allowed (i.e., excess capital, which explains why some large banks began buying back common stock during the mid-to-late 1990s). To return to its initial *ROE* of 15 percent with an *EM* of 11, the bank would have to increase its *ROA* to 0.0136 (= 0.15/11), which would entail a substantial increase in income or improvement in cost efficiency or both. For the years 1993 to 1995, all banks approached this level of profitability, with an average *ROA* of 1.18 percent. Banks ranked 11 to 100 in asset size did even better, with an average *ROA* of 1.25 percent, whereas the 10 largest banks had an average *ROA* of only 0.97 percent.

NONINTEREST INCOME AS A SYMPTOM OF OFF-BALANCE-SHEET BANKING

Banks engage in nontraditional activities for two main reasons: (1) to generate noninterest income, and (2) to get assets off the balance sheet. This section looks at the revenue-generating power of OBSAs by focusing on noninterest income, which has the following five components (revenue flows for 1995 for all banks):

1. Service charges on deposits ($16.1 billion)
2. Income from trust activities ($12.9 billion)
3. Foreign-exchange gains and fees ($2.7 billion)
4. Trading income ($3.6 billion)
5. Other ($48.6 billion)

For the year 1995, all banks generated $84 billion in noninterest income compared to $303 billion in gross interest income for total gross "sales" of $387 billion on total assets of $4,149 billion, and an asset utilization (AU = revenue/assets) of 9.33 percent (= 387/4,149). The interest and noninterest income components of AU were 7.31 percent and 2.02 percent, respectively. Recall that

$$ROA = PM \times AU$$

where PM = profit margin (net income/total revenue). This second stage of the ROE model for all banks for 1995 was

$$ROA = 0.1265 \times 0.0933 = 0.0118$$

For 1985, it was

$$ROA = 0.0640 \times 0.1084 = 0.0069$$

The resulting increase in ROA was due to an improved PM with a deteriorating AU. The two flow variables (net income and total revenue), the one stock variable (total assets), and their annual growth rates for 1985 and 1995 were as follows ($ billions):

Year	Net Income	Interest	Noninterest	Total Assets
1985	17.844	247.848	31.265	2,573
1995	48.935	303.054	83.890	4,149
Annual Growth	10.35%	2.03%	10.37%	4.89%

Several factors resulted in the banking industry's substantial improvement in *ROA* from 0.69 percent in 1985 to 1.18 percent in 1995.[3] Here we focus only on noninterest income. Its growth rate matched the one for net income, which was more than twice the growth rate for industry assets. Hence, *ROA* increased. The decomposition analysis here shows that noninterest income played a major role in that improvement.

Because aggregate data mask the performance of the different groups that make up the banking industry, consider the data in Table 9-1. Panel A shows noninterest income as a percentage of average net consolidated assets by bank size class for 1985 and 1995. Over this period, the 100 largest banks increased this ratio by an average of 90 basis points compared to an average 55 basic points for the numerous community banks below the 100 largest.

To fully understand a ratio, one must examine its components. Panels B and C of Table 9-1 analyze the components of the ratio of noninterest income to total assets. Panel B focuses on the denominator of the ratio, total assets, whereas Panel C highlights the numerator of the ratio, noninterest income. For example, the highest ratio of noninterest income to total assets (2.38% for the banks ranked 11 to 100 in 1995) reflects the faster growth of noninterest income (14 percent) compared to the slower growth of total assets (7.2 percent) over the ten years from 1985 to 1995. Panel D in Table 9-1 shows that the major component of noninterest income is "other" noninterest income. From the list above, we know that "other" does *not* include service charges on deposits, income from trust (fiduciary) activities,

---

[3] Two of those factors were (1) the decline in interest expense from $157 billion in 1985 to $148 billion in 1995 ($111 billion in 1994) and (2) the improvement in loan quality as reflected by the lower loan-loss provision in 1995 ($12.6 billion) compared to 1985 ($17.8 billion). Combining interest income and interest expense into net interest income, we see that it grew by only 5.3 percent from 1985 to 1995, compared to 10.4 percent for noninterest income.

TABLE 9-1   Noninterest Income as a Symptom of Off-Balance-Sheet Banking

Panel A. Noninterest income as a percentage of average net consolidated assets by bank size class for 1985 and 1995

Size Class	1985	1995	Change (bp)
Ten largest banks	1.33%	2.16%	83
Banks ranked 11 to 100	1.40	2.38	98
Banks ranked 101 to 1,000	1.28	1.84	56
Banks below the 1,000 largest	0.84	1.38	54
All banks	1.22	2.02	80

Panel B. Total assets by bank size class for 1985 and 1995 ($ billions)

Size Class	1985	1995	Annual Growth Rate
Ten largest banks	$646	$1,051	4.99%
Banks ranked 11 to 100	668	1,338	7.19
Banks ranked 101 to 1,000	638	1,094	5.54
Banks below the 1,000 largest	621	666	0.70
All banks	$2,573	$4,149	4.89%

Panel C. Total noninterest income by bank size class for 1985 and 1995

Size Class	1985	1995	Annual Growth Rate
Ten largest banks	$ 8.6	$22.7	10.19%
Banks ranked 11 to 100	9.3	31.8	13.99
Banks ranked 101 to 1,000	8.2	20.1	9.40
Banks below the 1,000 largest	5.2	8.7	5.86
All banks	$31.3	$83.8	10.35%

Panel D. Other income as a percentage of total noninterest income by bank size class for 1985 and 1995

Size Class	1985	1995
Ten Largest Banks	60.1%	53.2%
Banks ranked 11 to 100	52.9	60.9
Banks ranked 101 to 1,000	49.2	60.9
Banks below the 1,000 largest	35.7	51.4
All banks	50.8%	57.9%

Panel E. Trading income and foreign-exchange gains and fees as a percentage of average net consolidated assets for the 100 largest banks for 1985 and 1995

Size Class	Trading Income		FX Gains and Fees	
	1985	1995	1985	1995
Ten largest banks	0.05%	0.28%	0.19%	0.18%
Banks ranked 11 to 100	0.05%	0.05%	0.04%	0.04%

Source: Federal Reserve Bulletin (June 1995), pp. 559–569, and (June 1996), pp. 495–505.

foreign-exchange gains and fees, and trading income. It can include revenues from such areas as data processing, rental of safety deposit boxes, stripping securities, consulting and advising, acceptances and letters of credit, and net gains on futures contracts.

Panel E of Table 9-1 reveals that trading income and foreign-exchange (FX) gains and fees are generated mainly by the 10 largest banks. Moreover, below the 100 largest banks, the underlying OBSAs are limited and the corresponding revenues quite small, and not shown in Panel E.

To summarize, the data in Table 9-1 are symptomatic of the fees generated from OBSAs and asset securitization. Over this period, banks also were generating fees and service charges from traditional on-balance-sheet activities. During the 1980s banks learned they could not give away services and still be competitive in the financial-services industry (i.e., they had to fully cost most products and services).

ASSET SECURITIZATION AND LOAN PARTICIPATIONS

The pressures for generating fee income and meeting capital requirements have led all banks, but especially the large ones, to *securitize assets* (i.e., to sell loans that are packaged and resold as securities) and to participate in or share loans with other banks. Although the two activities are quite similar in terms of their fee and capital implications, banks have been doing participations for years, whereas securitization is a more recent phenomenon. **Securitization,** however, is seen by some analysts and regulators as the banking innovation for the 1990s (Rehm [1988]). Nevertheless, when banks have easier access to alternative markets (e.g., bank equity markets), they feel less pressure to get assets off their balance sheets (Holland [1991]). It is helpful to think of these two points in terms of the equity multiplier (EM = assets/equity), that is, securitization restricts asset growth whereas easier access to equity markets provides external sources of capital. Specifically, securitized assets and participated loans are attractive because they remove assets from a bank's balance sheet or at the margin do not add assets to it, thereby improving a bank's capital ratio or preventing it from declining, all other things being equal.

Under current banking laws, assets sold with recourse are treated for the purpose of capital requirements as if they had not been sold. In addition, in the case of loan participations, buybacks are not permitted by banking laws. Thus, they are without recourse to the originator (seller). However, through standby letters of credit or other guarantees, the buyer may attempt to arrange legally to have indirect recourse to the originator.[4] Through the same process, securitized assets may establish contingent claims on the originating bank. To dramatize the substantial changes occurring in commercial banking, Kareken [1987] notes that the business of banking is "very much the business of making contingent promises or commitments; and even just a decade ago it was not" (p. 359).

---

[4] James [1989] shows that loan sales and loans backed by standby letters of credit have payoff characteristics similar to secured debt. As a result, banks can sell a portion of their cash flows associated with future growth options. James concludes that OBSAs permit banks to invest in positive NPV projects that they would have to forego if restricted to deposit financing, which thereby reduces the underinvestment problem in banking. Greenbaum and Thakor [1987] also discuss securitization as an alternative funding mode to deposits.

The Traditional Approach for Removing Risk: Loan Participations

A **loan participation** is an arrangement by a group or syndicate of banks to share a loan that is too large for one bank to make. The constraint can be the bank's legal lending limit (10% of equity capital) or a limit imposed by its prudent risk-management policy. Loan participations, also known as participation financing, are arranged through correspondent-banking networks in which smaller banks buy part of an overall financing package. Thus, another reason for the existence of participations is relationship banking whereby correspondent banks (larger banks) sell or downstream portions of loans to respondent banks (smaller banks). Participations also permit smaller banks to make loans that they could not otherwise make because of their legal lending limits. By upstreaming loans to correspondents, community bankers earn fee income by servicing loans and are better able to serve their loan customers and maintain relationships.

Large syndications may involve more than 100 banks sharing millions of dollars of loans. Credits of $50 million or more are regarded as syndicated loans.[5] During 1996, these loans totaled more than $1 trillion, with corporate mergers driving the volume. The LDC crisis of the 1980s and the commercial real-estate crisis of the late 1980s and early 1990s prompted many large banks to avoid concentrations of credit greater than $20 million. As a result, since 1990, syndicated lending has grown more than 300 percent. According to the Comptroller of the Currency, this growth was fueled by underwriting standards that "continue to erode and have eroded to the point where there is not much farther they can go and remain prudent." The Comptroller was particularly concerned about "downstream participants" who were buying these "thin" loans. Regarding the risks, his view was: "There's lots of money chasing deals, and people who are making decisions are running the risk of making bad decisions."

In a survey of syndicated lending by 82 national banks that covered the 12 months ending May 1996, the OCC found that 30 percent of the largest institutions had eased their lending standards. And since then, examiners uncovered further reductions in underwriting standards. However, according to the OCC, because of its risk-based exams, the agency was on top of the potential problem before any serious losses resulted.

The Comptroller recommended several steps that bankers should take to avoid unnecessary risks posed by syndicated loans:

- Senior management should ensure that systems are in place to monitor exceptions to the bank's underwriting standards
- Downstream participants (buyers) should conduct independent credit analysis of the deals, and these judgments should dictate whether the bank participates in the loan
- Banks should have strategies for backing out of participations
- Buyers should not be pressured into participating so that they have enough time to do due-diligence analysis
- Banks should stress-test their portfolios against alternative economic scenarios to gauge their downside vulnerability ("conditions" (economic), the fifth C of the five Cs of credit-worthiness; see chapters 6 and 10)

---

[5] Data and quotes in this paragraph are from a 1996 speech by the Comptroller of the Currency as reported in the *American Banker* (December 11, 1996), pp. 1–2.

The Modern Approach to Risk Removal: Asset Securitization

John Reed, chairman of Citicorp, says, "Securitization is the substitution of more efficient public capital markets for less efficient, higher cost financial intermediaries in the funding of debt instruments."[6] This statement highlights the major benefit, greater efficiency (lower cost), of securitization and, less obviously, the major threat to banks from securitization. Specifically, **asset securitization** is a double-edged sword for banks. Four important benefits that accrue to banks from securitization affect their liquidity, profitability, and capital adequacy. The specific benefits, which increase ROA and decrease EM, all other things being equal, are the following:

- Increased liquidity from the ability to sell assets
- Enhanced revenue/profits from asset sales
- Increased servicing income
- Conservation of capital

The words "less efficient, higher cost financial intermediaries" capture the major threat to banks, namely, their survival. In a world of securitized assets, banks have diminished roles. The analysis that follows will make this clear, but first let's begin with the distinction between traditional bank lending and securitized lending and then describe the process of securitization.

The Traditional Bank Lending Function versus Securitized Lending

Traditional bank lending has four functions: **originating, funding, servicing,** and **monitoring.** Securitized lending introduces the possibility of selling assets on a bigger scale and eliminating the need for funding and monitoring. The **securitized lending** function has only three steps: **originate, sell,** and **service.** This change from a four-step process to a three-step function has been described as the **fragmentation** or **separation** of traditional lending. Before the 1980s, banks were fairly content with the traditional lending function, including loan participations. Today, however, banks, especially the larger ones, are increasingly originating loans with the idea of selling them or arranging loan syndications.

A bank with the expertise and reputation as an originator, but lacking the liquidity, capital, or cost structures to fund loans,[7] can specialize as a **securitized lender.** In the case of large banks, the effective constraints tend to be equity capital, especially before the mid-1990s, and cost considerations. Because large banks can usually buy all the liquidity they need in the marketplace, provided they maintain their creditworthiness (chapter 7), liquidity is less of a constraint. In contrast, smaller banks with higher capital ratios, less recognition, and slack loan demand usually have the capacity to provide funding. In addition, securitization offers small banks something they cannot buy in their local loan markets: the chance to diversify their loan portfolios.

Although the possibility of engaging in securitization and participations as originators is open to all banks, in reality small banks lack the size and reputational capital to be effective players in these activities. Moreover, since the failure of Penn Square Bank (Oklahoma City) in 1982, bankers (and regulators) are much more

---

[6] In a speech at the Kellogg Graduate School of Management, as reported by Kendall [1996] in Kendall and Fishman [1996], p. 2.
[7] Rose [1986] and [1987] discusses these cost structures.

cautious about who originates loan participations. Accordingly, the separation of the traditional lending function is occurring along the lines of big banks as originators and little banks, but mainly securities investors, as suppliers of funds. In addition, foreign banks have been purchasing loans from large U.S. banks.

Understanding the Process of Securitization[8]

The process of securitization involves five basic parties:

1. The loan originator (bank or financial intermediary)
2. The loan purchaser (an affiliated trust)
3. The loan packager (underwriter of the securities)
4. A guarantor (insurance company)
5. Investors (e.g., individuals or other banks) who buy the securities

Figure 9-1 summarizes the functions and cash flows/claims and provides examples for each of the parties.

The threat to banks from securitization comes from the fact that they are not major players outside of being originators of the underlying assets that are securitized. For this reason, large banks want to make further inroads into underwriting securities and providing insurance. The benefits to investment bankers from securitization include new product lines, increased flows of originations and fees, increased trading volume and profits, and the potential for innovation and market expansion.[9] Since commercial bankers want some of these benefits, they are pushing to get further into investment banking.

Figure 9-2 presents an alternative view of the process of securitization, one that emphasizes the structure and cash flows of pass-through, asset-backed securities. The solid line in the figure represents the structure of the process, whereas the dashed line represents cash flows. Starting with cash flows generated by the sale of the loans or receivables, the process begins when investors agree to buy the **asset-backed securities.** The investors exchange cash for the securities with the underwriter, who received the securities from the trust issuer of the securities. The trust passes the initial cash proceeds to the originator/sponsor/servicer, who is responsible for the transfer of the receivables. Before the receivables are converted to securities, the asset pool receives credit enhancement from a third party (called the "credit enhancer"). The enhancement frequently takes the form of a government guarantee or a **letter of credit** from a private organization such as a commercial bank. Turning to the cash flows to the investors, they begin when the borrowers make principal and interest payments to the originator/sponsor/servicer, who forwards the principal and interest payments to the trustee. The trustee then "passes through" the principal and interest payments to the investors.

The Concept of Pass-Throughs Extended to Nonmortgage Loans

The primary motivation for the development of mortgage-backed securities was avoidance of interest-rate risk by lenders. Neither thrifts nor their customers wanted to bear that risk. In contrast, banks have been motivated to securitize assets by explicit and implicit taxes on bank capital, by competitive pressures on bank profits, and by the desire to exploit their comparative advantage as originators of credit. Although the concept of pass-throughs has been extended to various kinds

---

[8] This section draws on Johnson and Murphy [1987], pp. 30–33.
[9] Kendall [1996], p. 13.

Step 1
Party: The originating bank
Function: Originator and servicer
Cash flows/claims: Loans (downstream)
                                Loan principal + premiums if any (inflow)
                                Interest + principal (passed through over time)
Example: Marine Midland, automobile receivables (CARs)

Step 2
Party: Subsidiary or separate trust
Function: Buys the loans from the bank and issues the securities
Cash flows/claims: Loans (inflow)
                                Loan principal + premiums (upstream outflow)
                                Interest plus principal (passed through)
Example: Salomon Brothers affiliate and a separate trust

Step 3
Party: Investment bankers
Function: Underwrites and packages the securities and advises the
                                trust
Cash flows/claims: Collects fees and sells securities issued by the trust
Example: Salomon Brothers

Step 4
Party: Guarantor
Function: Wholly or partially insures securities
Cash flows/claims: Insurance fees (in) and services (out)
Example: Companies specializing in financial guarantee insurance
                                (e.g., Travelers Insurance Company)

Step 5
Party: Investors
Function: Buys securities
Cash flows/claims: Cash outflow (principal) to buy securities
                                Hold securities (claims)
                                Interest + principal (cash inflow over time)
Example: Certificates for Automobile Receivables (CARs) purchased
                                by individuals, small banks, thrifts, and institutional investors

Note: CARs = certificates for automobile receivables.
Source: The examples shown here are from Johnson and Murphy [1987], p. 31.

FIGURE 9-1 **The Process of Securitization**

of bank loans, automobile loans and credit-card receivables have been the most popular. Nevertheless, the modern banker's calling card reads:

HAVE LOAN, WILL SECURITIZE.

Panel A of Table 9-2 shows the kinds of loans and other financial assets that have been securitized, and Panel B shows the basic requirements needed to securitize loans and other financial assets. Although almost any financial asset can be securitized, loans that have standardized underlying assets, such as mortgages and automobile and credit-card receivables, have been the most successful and have the most developed secondary markets. This fact explains why the establishment of markets for mortgage-backed securities, such as collateralized mortgage obligations (CMOs), have flourished.

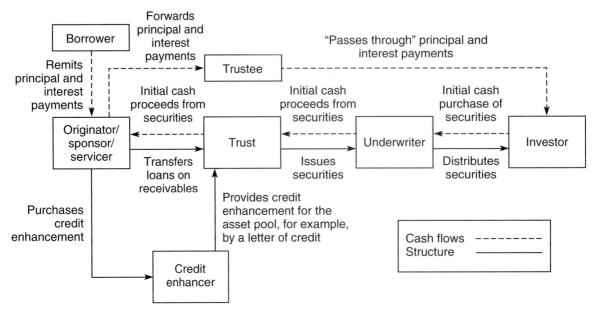

Source: Adapted from Boemio and Edwards [1989], p. 661.

FIGURE 9-2 **Pass-Through, Asset-Backed Securities: Structure and Cash Flows**

Pass-through securities that are not collateralized or secured by hard assets are simply unsecured assets, because the underlying loans are unsecured credits (e.g., credit-card receivables). In contrast, CARs (Figure 9-1) are collateralized by hard (but mobile) assets, namely, automobiles. Both secured and unsecured pass-throughs are enhanced or upgraded through the use of letters of credit, which provide guarantees.[10] However, depending on the structure of the guarantee, bank regulators may not permit the underlying asset to be removed from the bank's books, which of course defeats the purpose of securitizing the asset in the first place.

The process of securitization for bank nonmortgage loans closely follows the one for mortgages (Figures 9-1 and 9-2). Specifically, the loan originator (or sponsor/ servicer) usually handles the task of servicing the loan by collecting the principal and interest payments and passing them through to the ultimate investor. Given the resources for originating loans (e.g., loans officers, customer relationships, computer facilities, capital [dollar and reputational], etc.), the marginal cost of producing additional loans for sale becomes quite low (i.e., economies of scale).

What Drives Securitization?

Two views (not necessarily mutually exclusive) dominate explanations about why securitization exists. One theory emphasizes the process as being driven by changes in and the interaction between taxes and regulation (implicit taxation). These explicit and implicit taxes raise banks' cost of funds relative to those of their competitors—Reed's statement. The other view emphasizes the importance of technological change (chapter 18) in reducing the costs of processing information associated with selling assets and informational asymmetries between borrowers

---

[10] Merton and Bodie [1992] discuss techniques for managing the guarantee business (lending and deposit insurance).

TABLE 9-2 Examples of Loans and Other Financial Assets That Have Been Securitized, and Basic Requirements for Securitization

Panel A. Have Loan, Will Securitize

- Mortgages (fixed-rate, variable-rate, and second mortgages)
- Home-equity lines of credit
- Credit-card receivables
- Certificates of automobile receivables (CARs)
- Third-world or LDC debt
- Commercial real-estate loans
- Junk bonds
- SBA Loans
- Equipment leases
- Mobile-home loans
- Marine loans
- Recreational-vehicle loans

Panel B. Requirements for Securitized Assets to Be Widely Accepted

- Standardized assets (e.g., 8%, fixed-rate mortgages) generate standardized contracts
- Rating of risk through underwriting
- Reliable and reputable credit enhancers
- Standardized framework of applicable laws
- Standardized servicing quality
- Technical capability for handling complex securities analysis
- Database of historical statistics

Note: Although almost any financial asset can be securitized, loans that have standardized underlying assets, such as mortgages and automobile and credit-card receivables, have been the most successful and have the most developed secondary markets.

Source: Both panels have been adapted and expanded from Kendall [1996], Tables 1.2 and 1.3, p. 7 in Kendall and Fishman [1996].

and lenders (chapters 6 and 10). An eclectic approach includes the roles of taxes, regulation, and technology as driving the process of securitization.

Barriers to Securitization

Three barriers that can restrict banks from securitizing assets are size, recourse, and risk.

Size Considerations   Arnold [1986] estimates that it takes a minimum pool of assets of $50 million to cost-justify a private placement of securitized assets, and a pool of $100 million for a public offering. Legal and investment banking fees are the major issuance costs. Since the U.S. banking system has thousands of banks whose total assets do not exceed $250 million, these banks are not capable, on an individual basis, of delivering such large pools of assets for sale. However, on a collective basis, by means of syndication or some other pooling method, community banks can combine resources to enter the business of securitization.

Recourse   A second barrier to securitization focuses on the issue of recourse, which means that if any of the securitized assets default, then the buyer has a claim on the originator. Even if recourse is provided, an asset's risk is not effectively removed from a bank's balance sheet (i.e., it must still be backed by bank capital). Thus, when recourse is available, bank regulators have ruled that securitized assets must remain on a bank's books. As described in Box 9-1, innovative banks can be expected to attempt to circumvent recourse restrictions.

Risk Exposure   Finally, let's consider the riskiness of securitized assets. As pools of loans, securitized assets, from the investor's perspective (e.g., a community bank) are safer than traditional loan sales or participations because they are *diversified*. Specifically, the pooled assets represent a number of borrowers rather than the one (or perhaps the two) found in traditional loan sales. Statistically, pooling results in both the overall risk being lower and the default rate of the pool being more predictable relative to individual loans.

The adverse side of pooling is the inability of the buyer to assess the quality of the underlying credits. Rather than one borrower to analyze, there may be hundreds of credits in the package. Moreover, if the buyer does not have the time and expertise to analyze the credits, providing the documentation would be costly and

---

BOX 9-1

BANK INNOVATIONS DESIGNED TO CIRCUMVENT RESTRICTIONS ON RECOURSE

Innovative banks can be expected to attempt to circumvent recourse restrictions. Johnson and Murphy [1987] describe two examples of such attempts. The first one, which the regulators did not allow, involved an attempt by Citibank in 1984 to arrange a "sale-and-guarantee agreement" whereby loan participations sold by Citibank were effectively issued with recourse. The deal involved the issuance of commercial paper (based on the participated loans) by the buyer of the loans (Chatsworth) with a third-party guarantor (Travelers Insurance Company). The regulators were not sympathetic to this arrangement because they saw it as simply another form of bank borrowing such as a repurchase agreement.

Another example of a recourse innovation, one that the regulators reluctantly approved, involved recourse to the holding company rather than to the bank. In 1985, Marine Midland and Valley National (Arizona) securitized some car loans that granted the guarantor recourse, not to the respective banks, but to the bank holding companies. Of course, unless one believes in corporate separateness, the banks were still to some degree at risk.

A more recent innovation in the area of recourse focuses on something called a "spread account," or "overcollateralization." In this kind of arrangement, the difference between the interest rate on the securitized assets and the return on the underlying assets is placed in an escrow, or spread account, as a reserve against potential loan losses on the underlying assets. The account's size is dictated by the originator's historical loan-loss rate on the underlying assets. In this type of arrangement, the spread or reserve account represents the only recourse open to investors. If actual losses exceed those in the account, then the investors "eat" the excess as a loss. In contrast, if losses are less than those in the account, the originating bank receives the difference as a windfall gain. Although both the OCC and the FDIC have supported the concept of a spread account (i.e., they permit assets securitized with spread-account arrangements to be removed from the bank's balance sheet), the Federal Reserve Board has balked at the idea. On balance, the Fed regards the process of securitization as a financing vehicle and not as a sale of assets. Accordingly, even with a spread account, the Fed considers the bank's future earnings as potentially at risk.

would defeat the purpose of engaging in securitization in the first place. Nevertheless, the buyer must watch out for lemons. In this regard, market discipline is probably the buyer's best defense. Specifically, if an originator or packager of securitized assets gets a reputation for selling lemons (i.e., bad credits), its credibility in the marketplace will be tarnished. In the credit game, being a scorned player can be fatal, because a bank's lifeblood, its liquidity, can dry up.

On the other side of the reputational coin, an originator's quest for maintaining its own quality standing in credit markets may lead it to drain the best credits from its portfolio, leaving only trash behind. Thus, originators face a dilemma: Do they sell the (low-yielding) good credits and keep the (higher-yielding) trash, or do they sell the trash and keep the good stuff? If they choose the former, buyers do not have to worry about lemons; however, if they choose the latter, buyers must beware. Obviously, neither of these extremes would prevail in an efficient market. Specifically, a bank that sells lemons will be discovered and not be able to market its securitized assets. Of course, if the lemons are marketed as "junk securities," then no deception is involved. In this case, however, regulators probably would not permit community banks and thrifts to buy such high-risk securities. In contrast, a bank that keeps too many lemons will find the relative quality of its loan portfolio souring and its credit rating declining.

The solution to the originator's dilemma is to maintain a balance between the quality of its securitized assets and the quality of its own loan portfolio. In an efficient market, extreme behavior in either direction is likely to prove costly and to bring on greater regulatory intervention.

The Bottom Line: Value Added through Securitization

To see the value added through securitization and who receives that value, we need to consider the characteristics of the underlying assets before and after they are securitized. Table 9-3 summarizes this information. In a nutshell, the process of securitization takes loans that are essentially illiquid and lacking transparency and makes them marketable securities that provide benefits to various parties. To echo the words of John Reed: "Securitization is the substitution of more efficient public capital markets for less efficient, higher cost financial intermediaries in the funding of debt instruments." The fly in the ointment is that securitization threatens the

TABLE 9-3   The Bottom Line: Value Added through Securitization

Characteristic of

Underlying Asset (loan)	*Securitized Asset*	*Benefit to*
Illiquid	Liquid	Banks, investors, borrowers
Valuation lacks continuity and precision	Market values more efficient	Investors, banks
Credit analysis and monitoring by lender	Third parties assess risk	Banks, investors, third parties
High operating expenses	Lower operating costs	Banks, borrowers
Limited rates and terms offered to borrowers	Wider range of rates and terms	Borrowers, banks
Local market for investors	National and global investor markets	Investors, banks, third parties

Source: Adapted and expanded from Kendall [1996], Table 1.1, p. 5 in Kendall and Fishman [1996].

survival of traditional banking, the funding of loans with deposits, and the traditional lending function of originating, funding, servicing, and monitoring.

THE RISKS AND RISK MANAGEMENT OF ASSET-BACKED SECURITIES[11]

Although most securitized assets are sold to nonbank investors, an increasing number of depository institutions buy asset-backed securities for their own investment portfolios (chapter 8). As the process of securitization has developed over the past 20 years, the deals have become more numerous and more complex. As a result, all of the parties involved in the securitization process must be aware of the risks and how to evaluate and manage them. The OCC's recommendation for analyzing syndicated loans, discussed above, can be applied here also.

Credit risk, interest-rate risk, and liquidity risk, which are the basic risks of lending, also apply to asset-backed securities. However, with credit enhancements and well-developed secondary markets for securitized assets, credit and liquidity risks are reduced. The credit risk in asset-backed securities is distributed across three parties: the originator, the credit enhancer, and the investor. If the credit enhancer provides a 100 percent guarantee, then no remaining credit risk exists for the investor to bear. The credit enhancer's risk depends on its agreement with the originator (e.g., limited to losses that exceed the originator's cap up to a predetermined limit).

Depending on how deals are structured, the credit risk borne by investors can be divided into various classes, or "tranches," which represent the division of cash flows and maturities of the underlying securities. For example, in pass-through arrangements all interest and principal payments are passed through to all investors at once. However, in "pay-through contracts," the interest and principal payments are split into payment tranches (e.g., IO and PO agreements). In addition, the payments may be structured according to maturity over the life of each tranche. Investors in the last, or Z tranche bear more risk than those in the first, or A tranche.

For the investor, whether individual or institutional, the specific investment risks inherent in the securitization process, as cataloged by Hayes [1990], include fraud, erroneous legal or financial representations, poor performance, credit downgrades, prepayment, and concentration (i.e., lack of diversification). These specific risks, which are beyond the three basic risks discussed above, are more difficult to evaluate. Because fraud risk can occur anywhere in the securitization process, investors must be aware of the reputational capital of the participants and look for hidden action or hidden information or both. Before investors take possession of asset-backed securities, they need their legal counsels to review all agreements, contracts, and legal opinions, especially in cases where the reputational capital of a participant is suspect. Investors also need to judge the representations of accountants, appraisers, investment bankers, and other parties who provide information used to establish the credit rating of the asset-backed security.

Performance risk refers to the possibility of a third-party (e.g., servicers or trustees) not meeting its contractual obligation. Because asset-backed securities, like any other traded security, are subject to downgrading by credit agencies, investors face the risk of such adverse action. For example, in a recession, securities

---

[11] This section draws on Hayes [1990].

backed by unsecured assets such as credit-card receivables would be more vulnerable to a downrating than those backed by hard assets. Risk of prepayment is greatest for mortgage-backed securities with long durations. Finally, although securitization offers banks the opportunity to diversity their portfolios across different products and geographic areas, they must be careful not to concentrate in a particular issue or type of investment.

According to Hayes [1990], the risk-management skills needed by investment officers to handle the increasingly complex task of evaluating asset-backed securities include the following (pp. 40–41):

1. Review of general documentation by investment analysts and legal counsel

2. Identification of specific items to be reviewed (e.g., originator, trustee, underlying collateral, cash-flow schedules, and tranches, etc.)

3. Continuous monitoring of the asset-backed securities and the participants in the securitization process

4. Establishment of a policy that specifies the acceptability of asset-backed securities as investments

To summarize, investors in asset-backed securities primarily face interest-rate risk, and for securities with long durations, prepayment risk. However, numerous specific investment risks exist that must be evaluated and monitored. Moreover, as the complexity of the process of securitization increases, the effort and skills needed for successful risk management of asset-backed securities increase.

DERIVATIVES ACTIVITIES: HEDGING, SPECULATING, AND SELLING RISK-MANAGEMENT SERVICES

Consider the following statements:

- "Like alligators in a swamp, derivatives lurk in the global economy. Even the CEO's of companies that use them don't understand them" [*Fortune* (March 7, 1994)].

- Derivatives "are the basic banking business of the 1990s" [a Citicorp executive (1994)].

- Derivatives have "fundamentally changed financial management" [Group of Thirty (1993)].

Before we get to "the alligators in the swamp," what are derivatives? If those from calculus come to mind, then thinking about derivatives may not bring back pleasant memories.

Webster's second definition of derivative (as a noun) is simply "something derived" (from a specified source). In finance, derivatives are contracts whose value (the "something") is *derived* from some underlying asset such as a commodity, an interest rate, a stock, or a bond. As explained in chapter 5 (do you need a review?), two basic kinds of derivatives exist:[12]

- Forwards and futures (exchange-traded forwards), which are linear contracts

- Options, which are nonlinear contracts

Derivatives contracts include such agreements as interest-rate, foreign-exchange, and commodity forwards, futures, options, and swaps.

---

[12] The terms "linear" and "nonlinear" contracts refer to the payoff profiles drawn in chapter 5.

Table 9-4 shows the major kinds of derivatives contracts and derivatives securities. In addition to the linear (futures/forwards) and nonlinear (options) categories, derivatives contracts are classified as either

- Privately negotiated or over-the-counter (OTC)
- Exchange traded

Derivatives securities also can be grouped into three classes:

- Structured securities and deposits
- Stripped securities
- Securities with option characteristics

Banks use derivatives for hedging, speculating, or selling risk-management or transaction services to clients. In addition, derivatives activities provide banks with opportunities to strengthen customer relationships (Smith [1993] and King and Lipin [1994]). Smith [1993] emphasizes that bankers must recognize the potential benefits of selling risk-management services. The obvious benefits come from the generation of fee income and opportunities for bankers to create value through cross-selling and enhanced customer relationships.[13] Less obviously, since derivatives reduce the probability of financial distress for client firms, banks also benefit by reducing their risk exposure to these customers. Ironically, however, as the cases

TABLE 9-4 Major Kinds of Derivatives Contracts and Derivatives Securities

Derivatives Contracts

Privately Negotiated (OTC) Forwards	*Privately Negotiated (OTC) Options*	*Exchange-Traded Futures*	*Exchange-Traded Options*
Forward commodity contracts	Commodity options	Eurodollar (CME)	S&P futures options (Merc)
Forward foreign-exchange contracts	Currency options	US Treasury Bond (CBT)	Bond futures options (LIFFE)
Forward rate agreements (FRAs)	Equity options	9% British Gilt (LIFFE)	Corn futures options (CBT)
Currency swaps	FRA options	CAC-40 (MATIF)	Yen/$ futures options (IMM)
Interest-rate swaps	Caps, floors, collars	DM/$ (IMM)	
Commodity swaps	Swap options	German Bund (DTB)	
Equity swaps	Bond options	Gold (COMEX)	

Derivative Securities

Structured Securities and Deposits	*Stripped Securities*	*Securities with Option Characteristics*
Dual-currency bonds	Treasury strips	Callable bonds
Commodity-linked bonds	IOs and POs	Putable bonds
Yield-curve notes		Convertible securities
Equity-linked bank deposits		Warrants

Source: Adapted from Group of Thirty [1993a], Table 1, p. 29.

---

[13] Kane and Malkiel [1967] were among the first to emphasize the importance of "other services" (beyond loans and deposits) to the bank-customer relationship. Wigler [1991] describes how to use derivatives to increase customer profitability for the bank.

discussed later in this chapter demonstrate (e.g., Gibson Greetings, Inc., Procter & Gamble, and Mead Corp.), placing clients in speculative contracts may harm customer relationships, and raises the specter of "derivatives liability."

The three statements at the beginning of this section suggest that derivatives connote different things to different folks. We continue by looking at the implications of these three views for the derivatives activities of banks and their customers.

ALLIGATORS IN A SWAMP?

Because magazines, even good ones like *Fortune,* want headlines that sell more copies, let's not judge the book on derivatives by this cover. To understand the bad press about derivatives, we need to know what happened in 1994 and early 1995. The story goes like this.[14]

Background and Summary of the Derivatives Debacles of 1994–1995[15]

Derivatives are tools for managing risk. When used properly, derivatives are essentially benign because they allow organizations or individuals to modify or eliminate exposure to risks from *unexpected* changes in interest rates, exchange rates, or commodity prices. As with any tool, when derivatives are used improperly or without adequate controls and accountability, financial disasters may occur. Examples include the bankruptcies of Orange County, California, and Barings PLC, a British investment bank; and buyers and sellers, such as Bankers Trust (seller) and Gibson Greetings (buyer), may haggle over what was said or not said (disclosure) and when it was said (timing).[16]

Box 9-2 describes how derivatives can be used for hedging. The descriptions are routine and the basic transactions have been going on not only for years but for centuries with little attention or concern. During 1994 and the first part of 1995, however, derivatives made headlines, most of them adversely associated with bankruptcy, earnings losses, or litigation. The bankruptcies of Orange County and Barings and the derivatives losses of Escambia County in Florida's panhandle made news in 1995. Before these messes, major corporations such as Metallgesellschaft AG, Procter & Gamble, Gibson Greetings, and Mead incurred financial losses associated with derivatives.

"*Caveat emptor*" means "let the buyer beware." Because they deal in million-dollar transactions, the managers of banks, pension funds, mutual funds, and government agencies, and the treasurers of major corporations should fully understand any contracts they enter. Moreover, stockholders, directors, and taxpayers

---

[14] Jorion [1995], Corrigan and Hargreaves [1994], Culp and Miller [1994], Lipin, Bleakley, and Granito [1994], Stern and Lipin [1994], and *The Economist* (April 16, September 21, and October 1, 1994) report stories related to those in the following section.

[15] This section draws on Sinkey [1995] and Sinkey and Carter [1997].

[16] On September 12, 1994, Gibson Greetings filed a swaps suit against Bankers Trust of New York, claiming that the bank and its broker unit (BT Securities Corp.) failed to disclose risks in the swap contracts between the parties (Thomas [1994]). On October 13, 1994, Bankers Trust asked the U.S. District Court in Cincinnati to throw out Gibson's suit and for Gibson to pay Bankers Trust's legal fees (Lipin [1994a]). Bankers Trust claimed that Gibson was fully aware of the risk of such investments and that senior officials approved the transactions. P&G filed suit against Bankers Trust on October 28, 1994, claiming fraud and deception in its sales practices and seeking $130 million plus punitive damages.

BOX 9-2

DERIVATIVES AS A TOOL FOR HEDGING RISK

Let's consider some examples of using derivatives as a tool for hedging. A bank that finances fixed-rate mortgages with short-term deposits (the LRBA bank with a negative gap, chapter 5) can hedge its interest-rate risk by using a variety of derivatives, such as interest-rate swaps, futures, or options. A U.S. importer of foreign goods can protect against depreciation of the dollar by buying currency forwards or futures contracts. A soybean farmer can hedge against lower crop prices at harvest by selling soybean futures or forwards at planting time.

Derivatives transactions are zero-sum games between buyers and sellers called "counterparties." Although hedgers and speculators are the usual players, a hedger may contract with another hedger with the opposite risk exposure. Or a spec-ulator may strike a deal with another speculator with an opposite view on the future course of the price of the underlying asset, commodity, or currency. When one counterparty gains, the other loses.

Derivatives transactions span two markets: the cash market and the derivatives market. Soybean farmers bring their harvests to the cash market. To protect against declining (cash) prices for soybeans, they can sell soybean contracts in the futures market. Selling or "shorting" futures means that the investor gains when the price of the underlying asset/commodity declines; the zero-sum constraint means that the buyer of the futures contract loses. If the hedge is perfect (rare in the real world), the gain in one market exactly offsets the loss in the other market.

should demand accountability and control mechanisms from their agent-managers. In the derivatives fiascos of 1994 and early 1995, the traders/managers responsible for the losses did not necessarily act with criminal intent; instead they may be the modern equivalent of riverboat gamblers who simply bet and lost.

Another explanation focuses on the complexity of derivatives contracts. Today's derivatives come in more flavors than those found at many popular ice-cream parlors. The menu ranges from plain vanilla (the simple, traditional contract) to the exotic (complex, financially engineered contract). Complexity, however, does not excuse neglect. Although many managers who enter into complex contracts without complete understanding are undoubtedly guilty of neglect, some are simply responding to incentives without proper internal controls in place—neglect at a higher level.

Some buyers of derivatives claimed fraudulent and deceptive practices by the sellers of derivatives products. For example, Bankers Trust of New York has recently settled out of court with Gibson Greetings, agreeing to accept only $6 million for a $20-million debt, and with P&G, agreeing to accept roughly $30 million for a $180-million debt. Despite denying any guilt or wrongdoing in this and other cases, Bankers Trust

- Was fined $10 million by the Securities and Exchange Commission
- Signed an "unusual enforcement agreement" with the Federal Reserve Bank of New York to improve its supervision of the sale of risky derivatives to corporate clients
- On the basis of its own internal probe, reassigned five executives involved in soured derivatives deals

Both buyers and sellers of derivatives must have adequate internal controls and oversight. The Orange County and Barings cases appear to be the most blatant examples of these shortcomings. In the Barings fiasco, the fact that a 28-year-old trader could bet $30 billion on the future course of interest rates and stock prices without top managers knowing about it strains credulity. The financial-engineering gap separating young traders from older managers is no excuse for an absence of managerial controls and oversight. Also, underestimating the cleverness of the criminal mind with access to computer stealth is understandable but not excusable.

Because most derivatives deals are zero-sum games, the derivatives fiascos of 1994 and 1995 do not require any overreaction by government regulators or politicians. Except for mandating adequate disclosure and attempting to assure transparency, the government should not interfere with private business decisions. Did the government prohibit Coca Cola from gambling when it changed its formula for Coke? Internal business controls and external market mechanisms to monitor and discipline corporate actions are preferable to government interference. Existing regulatory weapons of fines, consent decrees, and enforcement actions are adequate for policing derivatives abusers. Moreover, market forces, aided by ex-post settling up either in or out of the courts, will redistribute contested gains and losses. On balance, let both buyers and sellers beware, and let the government refrain from interfering with private business decisions.

Bankers Trust and Derivatives Liability

The derivatives fiascos of 1994 and 1995 have made bankers more aware of the specter of derivatives liability. On January 20, 1995, Bankers Trust reported that it was reclassifying $423 million payable to it under derivatives contracts as "receivables." The economic meaning of this accounting maneuver was to recognize the probability of default associated with the contracts (Knecht [1995]). The default in these circumstances does *not* arise from the counterparty's inability to pay but from unwillingness to pay because of alleged fraud by the seller. The derivatives problems of 1994 and 1995 are examples of using the courts for ex-post settling up when disputes arise (e.g., misunderstanding by the buyer or deceptive selling practices by the seller).

ARE DERIVATIVES THE BASIC BUSINESS OF BANKING?

Derivatives contracts, defined to include interest-rate and foreign-exchange forwards, futures, options, and swaps, represent an area where banking has *not* been declining. The notional[17] value of these contracts, especially interest-rate derivatives, has grown rapidly during the past decade and total contracts were $17.3 *trillion* by the mid-1990s. Because these contracts are classified as OBSAs, the explosive growth of derivatives activities has not been registered on banks' balance sheets.[18] Moreover, these contracts are almost six times larger than the on-balance-sheet assets of commercial banks. For most of the banking industry, however, the growth has been nonexistent, because only 600 or so commercial banks use derivatives. Within the users' group, derivatives activities are highly concentrated in the 15 "primary members" of the International Swaps and Derivatives Association (ISDA),[19] which account for over 90 percent of the derivatives contracts held by

---

[17] *Notional value* refers to the underlying value upon which cash flows are based. For example, in a fixed-for-floating, interest-rate swap with a notional value of $100 million, the payments would be the respective rates times $100 million.

[18] Beginning with the first quarter of 1994, a new Financial Accounting Standards Board (FASB) rule requires that the unrealized gains on swaps, options, and other derivatives be recorded as assets; unrealized loses must be recorded as liabilities. Layne [1993a, 1993b, 1993c] and Stern [1994] describe the growth and profitability of derivatives activities.

[19] Prior to August 13, 1993, ISDA was known as the International Swap Dealers Association.

U.S. commercial banks. With respect to these 15 ISDA-member banks, Bennett [1993] described six of them as "ruling the world of derivatives," which following the merger of Chase Manhattan and Chemical is down to five banks:[20]

- Bankers Trust (New York)
- BankAmerica (San Francisco)
- Chase Manhattan (New York)
- Chemical Banking (New York, acquired by Chase in 1996)
- Citicorp (New York)
- J. P. Morgan (New York)

These six banks account for about 90 percent of the derivatives held by the 15 U.S. dealers and about 84 percent of the derivatives held by all user banks. The other nine U.S. banks listed as primary members of ISDA are FNB Chicago, Nations-Bank (Charlotte), Continental Bank (Chicago, since acquired by BOA), Republic Bank (New York), First Union (Charlotte), FNB Boston, Bank of New York, Mellon Bank (Pittsburgh), and Maryland National Bank (Baltimore).

The data discussed above do not permit us to conclude that derivatives are the basic banking business of the 1990s. Certainly not for all banks and not even for the Big Five. The fact is that thousands of community banks in the United States do not even use derivatives. Moreover, although derivatives are a basic component of the banking business for large banks, only Bankers Trust has adopted a strategy of concentrating and specializing in "global wholesale finance" (e.g., derivatives). The other banks in the Big Six have a more balanced strategy of wholesale and retail banking, although J. P. Morgan is more wholesale than retail.

Bankers Trust Rethinks Its Derivatives Strategy and Focus

The Economist referred to Bankers Trust's corporate strategy as: "Blurred vision." Reporting for *The Wall Street Journal,* Knecht [1995] quoted one former executive as saying

> Charlie (Sanford, former Chairman of Bankers Trust) caused a mass hypnosis that led everyone to believe that derivatives were the new paradigm of the financial world. Some of us thought that derivatives were a good business, but that we could not rely on them forever. Charlie thought they were the be-all and end-all.

Critics contend that the focus on derivatives led Bankers Trust to neglect developing long-term customer relationships. Since then, Mr. Sanford (who retired in 1996) began talking about rebuilding relationships, and he even appointed a high-level committee to focus on increasing such relationships.

What does the future hold for Bankers Trust? Knecht reports that Mr. Sanford understood that "radical changes" were needed. Will the company downsize its derivatives business and risk a takeover? Will it shift gears and attempt to become a financial conglomerate? Will it attempt to maintain its derivatives vision but without the problems that plagued it in 1994 and early 1995? Whatever course the bank follows, we can expect it still to reflect Mr. Sanford's philosophy, as expressed in a commencement address at The University of Georgia in 1989:

---

[20] Evans [1994] provides a broader survey of "derivatives superstars" by focusing on 115 of the world's top players. McDonough [1993] describes the global derivatives market. Also see appendices B and C at the end of the this chapter.

The real risk in life turns out to be the refusal to take a risk. Risk properly conceived, is often highly productive rather than something to avoid.

It is this view that led Mr. Sanford to say that senior management needs to be "the risk manager of risk managers." This means that risk-management strategies and the selection of specific derivatives should *not* be delegated to financial specialists in the bank. Because the educational gap between younger, hotshot financial engineers and older senior managers can be great, it is even more imperative that Sanford's advice be heeded.

HAVE DERIVATIVES FUNDAMENTALLY CHANGED FINANCIAL MANAGEMENT?

In *Derivatives: Practice and Principles,* the Group of Thirty [1993a] states

> What makes derivatives so important is not so much the size of the activity, as the role it plays in fostering new ways to understand, measure, and manage financial risk. Through derivatives, the complex risks that are bound together in traditional instruments can be teased apart and managed independently, and often more efficiently. (p. 2)

It is in this regard that derivatives have fundamentally changed financial management and in the process made risk management and the selling of risk-management services prominent fixtures of corporate banking and finance.

The importance of risk management to banks, which Merton [1995] claims is "perhaps the central topic for the management of financial institutions in the 1990s" (p. 12), is further illustrated by *The Economist*'s 1993 (April 10) survey of international banking. In it, Freeman [1993] writes: "To survive in a consolidating industry, banks must become better at defining, managing and pricing risk. The best are already trying" (p. 2). Derivatives permit banks to better define, manage, and price risk.

Finance theory suggests that hedging increases firm value by reducing expected costs associated with (1) taxes, (2) financial distress, and (3) other agency problems.[21] The second point means that firms can increase value by decreasing the probability that they will encounter financial distress. Figure 9-3 depicts this situation. This theory, of course, applies to banking firms as well as nonfinancial corporations. If hedging increases the value of the *banking firm*, it does so by reducing expected costs associated with taxes, financial distress, or other agency problems. Moreover, if banks can increase the net asset values of client firms by selling them risk-management services, client firms will be able to reduce their chances of encountering financial distress. If banks (e.g., Bankers Trust) place client firms in speculative contracts, however, the costs and probabilities of financial distress might increase (e.g., Metallgesellschaft) or customer relationships might be injured (e.g., Gibson Greetings and P&G) or both.

---

[21] Nance, Smith, and Smithson [1993] provide evidence that 104 nonfinancial firms, which used hedging instruments in 1986, faced more convex tax functions, had less coverage of fixed claims, were larger, had more growth options in their investment opportunity sets, and employed fewer hedging substitutes. Sinkey and Carter [1997] extend their analysis by applying these principles to hedging by the banking firm and by incorporating banking theory and the determinants of bank dealer activities.

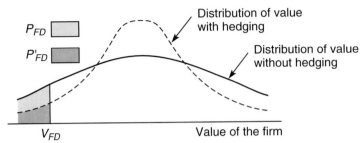

Note: V_{FD} and values below it indicate values of the firm at which it encounters financial distress. Without hedging (or risk management in general), P_{FD} indicates the probability of V_{FD}; with hedging, the probability drops to P'_{FD}.

Source: Adapted from Smith, Smithson, and Wilford [1990], Figure 5.1, p. 127, and Figure 5.7, p. 133.

FIGURE 9-3 How Hedging Can Be Used to Reduce the Volatility of Firm Value

A Framework for Risk Management

The risk-management approach of Froot, Scharfstein, and Stein (FSS, [1993, 1994]), presented in chapter 4, rests on three pillars:

- Making good investment decisions creates corporate value.
- Generating enough cash flow internally is the key to making good investments. Companies that do not generate enough cash flow internally tend to cut investment more substantially than their competitors do.
- Since cash flow can be disrupted by adverse movements in external factors such as interest rates, exchange rates, and commodity prices, a company's ability to invest can be jeopardized.

The first two points have been pillars of modern financial management for years, whereas the third point recognized the importance of derivatives as tools for hedging adverse movements in interest rates, exchange rates, and commodity prices. It is in this regard that derivatives have fundamentally changed financial management.

One view of risk management, similar to the treatment of a company's financial policy, is that it is critical in terms of "*enabling* companies to make valuable investments" (FSS [1994], p. 93). This enabling process of risk management guarantees that a company's supply of funds will equal its demand for funds and thereby permit the company to make value-enhancing investments. By selling risk-management services to clients, banks help them meet this cash-flow objective and in the process help ensure that these borrowers repay their loans and continue to use other bank services.

Regarding the use of specific derivatives instruments, both buyers and sellers need to understand two key aspects of their use:

- Different cash-flow requirements exist for different instruments (e.g., exchange-traded futures that must be marked-to-market)
- The nature of the payoff or profit profiles of the derivatives contracts must be considered.[22]

---

[22] Recall that futures and forwards are linear contracts that have symmetrical payoff patterns whereas options are nonlinear contracts that have asymmetrical profit profiles. The values of linear contracts move proportionally to the value of the underlying asset, whereas the values of nonlinear contracts do not move

To summarize, since the basic business of banking is the measuring, managing, and accepting of risk, it is imperative that bankers have a framework for risk management. Such a program offer two avenues for enhancing the value of the bank: First, by hedging their own risk exposures, banks can reduce the variability of firm value and enhance the value of the bank. And second, by selling risk-management services to client borrowers, banks generate fees and help ensure that borrowers will have funds to repay loans and will take advantage of growth opportunities. To do a good job of selling risk-management services to their corporate clients, bankers must understand the risks, cash flows, and investment opportunities these customers face. On balance, a bank's framework for risk management should be part of its overall corporate strategy for enhancing the value of the bank.

THE RISK OF DERIVATIVES ACTIVITIES

It has been argued (by the Group of Thirty and others) that the risks of derivatives activities are not much different from the risks that bankers have been dealing with for years. Consider the risk of derivatives activities as captured by the mnemonic interrogatory: IS MORC ILL? Table 9-5 summarizes the mnemonic and each of the components. These nine risks can be condensed into four broad risk categories:

- Market risk
- Credit risk
- Liquidity risk
- Operational and legal risk

Because banks have been dealing with these kinds of risks for years, one can argue that the risks of derivatives are not new and therefore should not be a major concern to managers, owners, regulators, or lawmakers. The complexity of certain contracts notwithstanding, derivatives activities, as tools of risk management, present opportunities for risk managers to better become "the risk managers of risk managers."

TABLE 9-5   The Risk of Derivatives Activities: IS MORC ILL?

I = Interaction (Covariance) Risk: Also known as *basis* or *correlation risk*, this uncertainty results from changes in the market value of the combined position when a derivatives transaction is used to hedge another position. This risk is part of the broad category of market risk.

S = Systemic Risk: This uncertainty focuses on the collapse of the financial system. If derivatives make the world a riskier place, then systemic risk would increase, all other things being equal. However, as tools of risk management, they should make the financial world a safer place. Nevertheless, since any tools can be misused, market developments and institutional changes must be reflected in regulatory policies and procedures to help prevent systemic risk to the financial system.

(continued)

---

proportionally. Therefore, a floor can be put under revenues without forgoing the upside potential, a cap can be put on expenses without forgoing the potential benefit of declining costs, and a collar can be used to lock in a bank's spread.

TABLE 9-5   *Continued*

M = Market Risk: This uncertainty arises from changes in market conditions that affect the price behavior of derivatives. The components of market risk and their interactions focus on the net or residual exposure of the overall portfolio.[a] Figure 9–4 captures this view of risk in terms of three portfolios:

- Credit portfolios
- Investment portfolios
- Trading portfolios

O = Operational Risk: This uncertainty arises from inadequate systems and controls, human error, or management failure.

R = Regulatory Risk: This uncertainty arises from regulatory actions or inactions that restrict profitable investment opportunities. Bankers have been dealing with this risk for decades in their ongoing struggle with regulators (Kane's regulatory dialectic).

C = Credit Risk: This uncertainty arises from the possibility of counterparties defaulting. The replacement cost of a contract, which equals the present value of expected future cash flows at the time of default, captures the credit or default risk. Analysis of the credit risk of derivatives transactions focuses on the current and potential exposures for individual derivatives and portfolios.

I = Intellectual Risk: Although derivatives have fundamental building blocks as their foundation, some contracts can be extremely complex. Smart people do not buy or sell contracts that they do not understand, and ethical people practice active ethics by telling the truth, the whole truth, and nothing but the truth (chapter 17).

L = Liquidity Risk: This uncertainty arises from the inability to buy or sell particular contracts. It is more costly to transact in illiquid markets than in liquid ones. Sudden movements in prices or the volatility of prices may cause an erosion of liquidity.

L = Legal Risk: This uncertainty arises from being unable to enforce a contract. Legal risk includes, among other things, problems associated with documentation, capacity or authority of a counterparty, and bankruptcy.

---

[a]Market risk, which is complex, includes absolute price or rate risk (called "delta risk" or "delta"), convexity risk ("gamma"), volatility risk ("vega"), time-decay risk ("theta"), basis or correlation risk, and discount-rate risk ("rho").

Source: Adapted from The Group of Thirty Report [1993a]. The mnemonic is from Richard Miller.

COLLECTING INFORMATION AND MEASURING THE RISK EXPOSURE OF DERIVATIVES ACTIVITIES

Beginning in 1995, bank regulators began to collect better measures of the market size, credit-risk exposure, and revenue from the derivatives activities of commercial banks and their holding companies. This information can be found in the new call-report data supplied by banks to their federal regulators. The glossary in appendix B of this chapter provides a catalog of terms needed to understand these data.

Notional Amounts and Credit-Risk Exposure of Derivatives Contracts

The *notional value* of a derivatives transaction refers to the principal or face value of the underlying contract or obligation. It is simply the value or amount upon which the cash flows of the derivatives contract are based. For example, if the notional value of an interest-rate swap is $1 million and the fixed-rate payer signs on

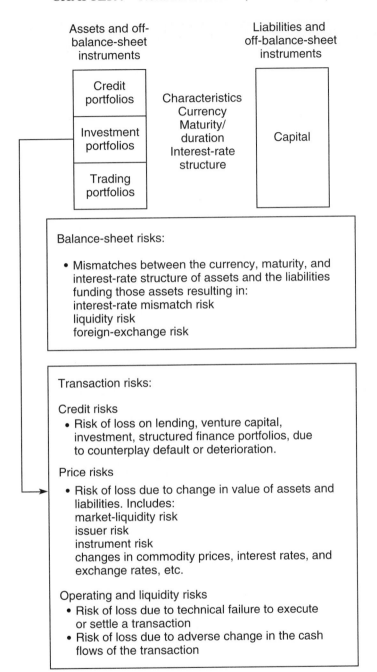

Assets and off-
balance-sheet
instruments

Liabilities and
off-balance-sheet
instruments

Credit
portfolios

Characteristics
Currency
Maturity/
duration
Interest-rate
structure

Capital

Investment
portfolios

Trading
portfolios

Balance-sheet risks:

• Mismatches between the currency, maturity, and
  interest-rate structure of assets and the liabilities
  funding those assets resulting in:
  interest-rate mismatch risk
  liquidity risk
  foreign-exchange risk

Transaction risks:

Credit risks
• Risk of loss on lending, venture capital,
  investment, structured finance portfolios, due
  to counterplay default or deterioration.

Price risks
• Risk of loss due to change in value of assets and
  liabilities. Includes:
  market-liquidity risk
  issuer risk
  instrument risk
  changes in commodity prices, interest rates, and
  exchange rates, etc.

Operating and liquidity risks
• Risk of loss due to technical failure to execute
  or settle a transaction
• Risk of loss due to adverse change in the cash
  flows of the transaction

Source: Price-Waterhouse [1994].

FIGURE 9-4 Bank On- and Off-Balance-Sheet Risks

at 10 percent per year with quarterly payments, then the corresponding quarterly
gross interest payment is $25,000. If the fixed-rate payer receives a floating-rate
payment of less (greater) than $25,000, then it is a net payer (receiver) of funds.
The notional amount simply sets the base to which the rate is applied. Thus, although notional amounts are an indicator of the volume of contracts outstanding,
they are not a measure of risk exposure per se.

TABLE 9-6	Ten U.S. Bank Holding Companies with the Greatest Exposure to Credit Risk from Derivatives on December 31, 1995 (billions of dollars)	
Institution	*Credit Risk Exposure*[a]	*Total Notional Amount of Derivatives Outstanding*
J. P. Morgan & Company	33.6	3,403
Chase Manhattan Corporation[b]	28.0	4,728
Citicorp	19.4	2,301
Bankers Trust New York Corporation	12.1	1,742
BankAmerica Corporation	8.3	1,515
First Chicago NBD Corporation	7.3	801
NationsBank Corporation	3.3	1,006
Republic New York Corporation	3.0	268
State Street Boston Corporation	0.6	58
Bank of New York	0.6	56

[a]Exposure taking into account the effects of legally enforceable bilateral netting agreements.
[b]Pro forma combination for Chemical Banking Corporation and Chase Manhattan Corporation.
Source: Federal Reserve Bulletin (September 1996), Table 1, p. 794.

Table 9-6 shows the credit-risk exposure and total notional amount of derivatives outstanding for the 10 largest U.S. bank holding companies (BHCs) as of December 31, 1995. These 10 BHCs held $13.7 trillion (96%) of the $16.5 trillion in outstanding derivatives contracts. The other 600 or so banks holding derivatives contracts accounted for the remaining $2.8 trillion. Several thousand commercial banks hold no derivatives contracts at all. In terms of credit-risk exposure, measured to take account of legally enforceable bilateral netting agreements, the top five BHCs had a total exposure of $101 billion whereas the next five largest had only $14.8 billion in exposure.

Table 9-7 shows the composition of Citibank's derivatives portfolio. Like other banks' derivatives, Citibank's derivatives are concentrated in OTC contracts (85%), compared to exchange-trades ones (15%). Interest-rate agreements are the predominant type of forwards and swaps held by banks. Within a bank holding

TABLE 9-7	Citibank's Derivatives Portfolio ($ millions, March 31, 1995)
Total forwards (OTC)	$1,656,793 (57.6%)
Total swaps (OTC)	471,503 (16.4%)
Options (OTC)	336,952 (11.7%)
Total futures (exchange traded)	296,845 (10.3%)
Options (exchange traded)	110,850 (3.9%)
Total derivatives	$2,872,943 (100.0%)
Total on-balance-sheet assets	$ 228,000
Ratio of derivatives to assets	12.6

Note: Citibank also had $164 billion in "spot foreign exchange" (see last column of Table B9–1 in appendix B), which is not included in total derivatives.

Source: Comptroller of the Currency, Administrator of National Bank, *News Release* 95–62 (June 14, 1995), preliminary data.

company, most derivatives contracts are held by the lead bank in the organization, for example, Citibank in Table 9-7. Compared to Citicorp, Citibank held 103.6 percent of the company's outstanding derivatives, where a ratio greater than one reflects intracompany transactions.

Viewing bank capital as the ultimate backstop for absorbing losses, whether they arise from activities on or off the balance sheet, bank risk exposures are usually compared to bank capital. Using data from appendix B, twelve banks had credit-equivalent exposures greater than their risk-based capital (the sum of tier 1 plus tier 2 capital; see Table B9-1 or chapter 13). The dirty dozen were

1.	Bankers Trust	588.7%
2.	Morgan Guaranty	570.5
3.	Chemical	375.0
4.	FNB Chicago	295.0
5.	Chase Manhattan	230.3
6.	Citibank	222.9
7.	Harris Trust	214.3
8.	Republic NY	195.7
9.	NationsBank	175.2
10.	BankAmerica	152.2
11.	State Street	136.2
12.	Boston Safe Deposit	106.6
	Average dirty dozen	271.9%
	Average remaining 13	19.9%
	Average top 25	140.9%

The dirty dozen had, on average, almost 14 times the exposure of the other 13 banks in the top 25. Nevertheless, how real are these exposures? Assuming that OBSAs have similar loss rates to on-balance-sheet assets, we would expect an average derivatives loss rate of about 1 percent. Applying this loss rate to the average exposure of 271.9 percent would impair only 2.7 percent of risk-based capital. Moreover, a worst-case scenario of a 10 percent loss rate would deplete capital by only 27.2 percent.

Evidence on Trading of Derivatives Contracts

The term "end user" describes a bank that employs derivatives to hedge on-balance-sheet risk as opposed to dealing, trading, or selling risk-management services. For compactness, let's refer to the non–end users as "traders." Table 9-8 compares the top ten banks to all banks with respect to three factors:

- Type of derivative instrument
- Positions in their trading portfolios
- Type of risk assumed to earn trading profit

Although interest-rate contracts are the volume leaders in both notional amount and source of trading profit, foreign-exchange contracts are more profitable per dollar of notional value. That is, IRCs account for about two out of every three dollars of total notional value of outstanding derivatives but only 51 percent of trading profit, compared to one out of every three dollars and 35 percent for foreign-exchange contracts. Banks make money from foreign-exchange trading based on the spread between the currencies they buy and sell, either for their own account

TABLE 9-8	Derivatives Positions and Trading Activity of the Top Ten Banks and All U.S. Banks (billions of dollars, 1995)

Item	*Top Ten Banks*	*All Banks*
Type of Derivative Instrument	*Notional Amount of Derivatives Outstanding as of Year-End*	
Interest-rate contracts	10,231	10,800
Foreign-exchange contracts	5,286	5,366
Equity, commodity, or other contracts	361	361
Total	15,878	16,527
Positions in Trading Portfolio	*Fair Value as of Year-End*	
Trading assets	255	275
Derivatives	95	100
Trading liabilities	159	169
Derivatives	97	102
Total trading positions (absolute value)	414	444
Derivatives	191	202
Type of Risk Assumed to Earn Profit	*Trading Profit from All Sources for Year*	
Interest rate	2.9	3.3
Foreign exchange	2.0	2.4
Equity, commodity, or other	.3	.3
Total	5.7	6.5

Source: Federal Reserve Bulletin (September 1996), Table 2, p. 794.

or for their customers. Although the spreads tend to be thin (e.g., a fraction of a cent), volume trading and volatility can generate the kinds of revenues shown in Table 9-9. Traders who spot the trends first make the most money. Although some traders make their business sound like a money machine, it of course isn't. Nevertheless, Françoise Soares-Kemp of Credit Suisse says, "It doesn't matter which way it's going as long as you are positioned right" (*American Banker*, April 1, 1991, p. 7).

Volatility is what currency traders want, because of the profit potential.[23] Kraus [1991] contends that when banks guess wrong, "most can quickly adjust their position and profit from any swings in currency values." A downside risk does exist, however, and banks can lose money as quickly as they can earn it; see Bankers Trust in appendix B. A spokesperson for Bankers Trust, when asked about the downside risk (prior to the debacles of 1994 and early 1995), would not elaborate except to say that extraordinary profits were achieved while "staying within . . . traditional risk policies."

---

[23] Charles Sanford, the chairman of Bankers Trust at the time, was the commencement speaker at the 1989 graduation of the University of Georgia. The day before at a luncheon with business school faculty and local bankers, he remarked: "Since Bankers Trust's main business is global wholesale finance, it requires volatility (of exchange and interest rates) to make money; without volatility it makes substantially less money." Although paraphrased, my recollection captures the thrust of one of Bankers Trust's business strategies. Regarding the trading revenues generated by money-center banks in 1990, Françoise Soares-Kemp said: "Banks made it when they rode the dollar down, and they're enjoying the ride back up" (*American Banker*, April 1, 1991, p. 1).

TABLE 9-9 Number of Top Ten Banks Discussing Their Management Objectives and Risks of Derivatives in Their Annual Reports, 1993–1995

TYPE OF QUALITATIVE DISCLOSURE	NUMBER OF BANKS DISCLOSING		
	1993	*1994*	*1995*
Discussion of Management Objectives and Strategies			
For trading activities	4	9	10
For nontrading activities	4	10	10
Discussion of Risks and Management Techniques			
Placed in context with balance sheet risks	7	10	10
Credit risk	6	9	10
Market risk	6	9	10
Liquidity risk	4	6	9
Operating and legal risks	1	3	3

Source: Federal Reserve Bulletin (September 1996), Table 3, p. 795.

The Issues of Transparency and Disclosure

Bank loans and OTC derivatives have three things in common:

- They are customized
- They are privately negotiated
- They often lack liquidity and transparency despite increases in the availability of price information (e.g., from securitization)

Because of these common characteristics, many bank loans and OTC derivatives lack **transparency,** which means they can be rather difficult to quantify and manage.

Transparency can be viewed as the degree of certainty with which one can determine "fair value." The Financial Accounting Standards Board (FASB) defines fair value as "the amount at which an instrument could be exchanged in a current transaction between willing parties, other than in a forced or liquidation sale." Fair values are not "matters of fact"; they are estimates. FASB notes that, when available, quoted market prices are the best indicators of fair values. If quoted prices are not available, the use of quoted prices for related instruments ("comparables") can be employed.

Liquidity is the percentage of a financial instrument's fair value that could be realized in a forced or liquidation sale. Perfect liquidity results in an instantaneous realization of fair value, which is a tough standard. In more realistic cases, sellers encounter search costs with respect to time, counterparty, and size of transaction. Under a very short time constraint, you might not be able to find a counterparty; with unlimited time, your chances would be much better. On balance, realization of fair value is a function of time and size. By these definitions, many OTC derivatives are neither highly transparent nor highly liquid; and in this regard, they are a lot like some bank loans. Opaqueness and illiquidity stem from both the customization of contract terms and differences in creditworthiness across counterparties.[24]

Table 9-9 shows how the top 10 banks have increased their qualitative disclosure of their management objectives and the risk of derivatives in their annual reports over the years 1993 to 1995. These increased disclosures make trading activities, risks, and management techniques more transparent. If this kind of transparency had existed in 1993, Banc One (see appendix A) might have been able to avoid the debate about its extensive use of interest-rate swaps.

REGULATION OF OBSAs AND SECURITIZED ASSETS

Kane's regulatory dialectic or struggle model suggests a regulatory reaction to the development of OBSAs and securitization by regulated firms. This reaction has taken the form of risk-based capital requirements for OBSAs and securitized assets. Although the topics of risk-based capital and capital adequacy are covered in chapters 15–16, Table 9-10 presents the guidelines applied to off-balance-sheet items and asset-backed securities. Panel A of Table 9-10 shows the credit conversion factors for OBSAs, and Panel B presents capital requirements for asset-backed securities. The four weights or conversion factors are 0, 20, 50, or 100 percent, depending on the degree of risk perceived by bank regulators. For example, asset-backed securities collateralized by nonmortgage assets (e.g., credit-card receivables) and standby letters of credit that serve as financial guarantees have a 100 percent capital requirement (i.e., $4 of tier 1 capital for every $100 of the item and $8 of total capital [tier 1 + tier 2] for every $100 of the item). James [1989] argues that regulation designed to restrict OBSAs (e.g., risk-based capital requirements applied to OBSAs) can have the unintended effect of actually increasing the risk borne by the FDIC because it encourages bank underinvestment.

Regarding the regulation of securitization, Owen J. Carney, director of the division of investment securities for the OCC, stated: "The regulators are somewhat anxious about the whole process. Our policy is still evolving . . . it's too complicated for a two-page banking circular."[25] The regulators are "anxious" about the possibility of "imprudent practices," which would bring closer supervision and more regulation.

Kareken [1987] draws two conclusions about the regulation of what he calls contingent-commitment banking (i.e., OBSAs and securitization).[26] First, he argues that even if the last vestiges of traditional banking are removed, "the Federal Reserve need not in the end be less effective as the U.S. monetary authority than it is at present" (p. 359). And second, he contends that neither higher capital standards nor risk-based capital requirements "will make bank failures rarer than they otherwise would be" (p. 359).

---

[24] Two innovations to remedy these shortcomings are (1) "flex" products that allow for greater tailoring of terms than traditional exchange offerings, and (2) bilateral margining agreements for OTC derivatives (e.g., through an OTC clearinghouse).

[25] As quoted in the *American Banker* (February 8, 1988), p. 6.

[26] See the *Journal of Banking and Finance* (September 1987) for selected papers from the conference, "Securitization and Off-Balance-Sheet Risks of Depository Institutions," held at Northwestern University in 1987. Three focal points of the conference were (1) the loss of market share by banking firms, especially money-center banks, to the capital markets; (2) the rapid growth of off-balance-sheet activities and securitization; and (3) the relatively embryonic stage of bank asset securitization compared to housing-finance securitization in the thrift industry. Also see Ronen et al. [1990].

TABLE 9-10   Risk-Based Capital Requirements for OBSAs and Asset-Backed Securities

Panel A. Credit Conversion Factors for Off-Balance-Sheet Items

100 Percent Conversion Factor

1. Direct credit substitutes. (These include general guarantees of indebtedness and all guarantee-type instruments, including SLCs backing the financial obligations of other parties.)
2. Risk participations in bankers acceptances and direct credit substitutes, such as SLCs.
3. Sale and repurchase agreements and assets sold with recourse that are not included on the balance sheet.
4. Forward agreements to purchase assets, including financing facilities on which drawdown is certain.
5. Securities lent for which the banking organization is at risk.

50 Percent Conversion Factor

1. Transaction-related contingencies. (These include bid bonds, performance bonds, warranties, and SLCs backing the nonfinancial performance of other parties.)
2. Unused portions of commitments with an original maturity[a] exceeding one year, including underwriting commitments and commercial credit lines.
3. Revolving underwriting facilities (RUFs), note issuance facilities (NIFs), and similar arrangements.

20 Percent Conversion Factor

1. Short-term, self-liquidating, trade-related contingencies, including commercial letters of credit.

Zero Percent Conversion Factor

1. Unused portions of commitments with an original maturity[a] of one year or less, or that are unconditionally cancellable at any time, provided a separate credit decision is made before each drawing.

Credit Conversion for Interest-Rate and Foreign Exchange Contracts

The total replacement cost of contracts (obtained by summing the positive marked-to-market values of contracts) is added to a measure of future potential increases in credit exposure. This future potential exposure measure is calculated by multiplying the total notional value of contracts by one of the following credit conversion factors, as appropriate:

Remaining Maturity	Interest-Rate Contracts	Exchange-Rate Contracts
One year or less	0	1.0%
Over one year	0.5%	5.0%

No potential exposure is calculated for single-company interest rate swaps in which payments are made based upon two floating rate indices, that is, so-called floating/floating or basis swaps. The credit exposure on these contracts is evaluated solely on the basis of their marked-to-market value. Exchange-rate contracts with an original maturity of 14 days or less are excluded. Instruments traded on exchanges that require daily payment of variation margin are also excluded. The only form of netting recognized is netting by novation.

(continued)

TABLE 9-10 *Continued*

Panel B. Risk Weights Accorded to Asset-Backed Securities under the Risk-Based Capital Guidelines

Type of Asset-Backed Securities	Risk Weight (%)
GNMAs	0
FHLMC and FNMA securities	20
Privately issued, mortgage-backed securities collateralized by GNMA, FHLMC, or FNMA securities, or by FHA- or VA-guaranteed mortgages[b]	20
Privately issued, mortgage-backed securities collateralized by one- to four-family residential properties[b]	50
Stripped, mortgage-backed securities, residual interests, and subordinated class securities	100
Asset-backed securities collateralized by nonmortgage assets	100

[a]Remaining maturity may be used until year-end 1992.

[b]Privately issued, mortgage-backed securities must meet the criteria outlined in the risk-based capital guidelines to be accorded the risk weight of the underlying collateral.

Source: Board of Governors of the Federal Reserve System.

Chapter Summary

Commercial banking can be viewed as undergoing a metamorphosis much like that of a caterpillar into a butterfly. The slow-moving caterpillar reflects traditional banking. The dramatic and dynamic changes taking place in modern banking are the forces pushing the butterfly out of its (protective) cocoon. Although the butterfly of modern banking is not completely free yet (e.g., Glass-Steagall constraints), it is too late to attempt to reverse the process and return to the caterpillar days of traditional banking.

The emergence of off-balance-sheet activities (OBSAs) and securitization captures two of the traits of modern banking. The forces of change associated with technology, taxes, regulation, and competition explain why banks are undertaking these nontraditional activities. Moreover, within the context of the return-on-equity model ($ROE = ROA \times EM$), the downward pressures on both ROA and EM reflect these forces of change in ways that get bankers' attention and explain why they are moving assets off their balance sheets. The second stage of the ROE model ($ROA = PM \times AU$) reflects the important role that noninterest income has played in improving bank profitability and is symptomatic of the shift to OBSAs and securitization, especially by the largest banks. The shift to contingent-commitment banking permits banks, all other things being equal, to increase ROA through the generation of fee income and, by removing assets from their balance sheets, to ease the increasing pressure imposed by higher capital requirements. The imposition of capital requirements on OBSAs may force banks to seek riskier ways for circumventing risk-based capital requirements. In this regard, derivatives are not alligators in the swamp. Although some CEOs let their companies swim in dangerous waters, they discovered in some cases, not wolves in sheep's clothing, but untrustworthy bankers in alligator skins. Finally, derivatives certainly are not the basic business of the thousands of community banks in the United States, but they are an important part of the business of the largest banks. Within this group, however, only Bankers Trust staked its livelihood on derivatives, a plan which it had to rethink in 1995.

List of Key Words, Concepts, and Acronyms

- Asset-backed security
- Collateralized mortgage obligations (CMOs)
- Contingent-commitment banking
- Credit enhancer
- Equity multiplier (EM)
- Exchange-traded contracts
- Fee income (originating and servicing)
- Financial engineering
- Forwards (linear contracts)
- Fragmentation or separation of the traditional lending function
- Funding (warehousing) loans
- Guarantor (e.g., GNMA)
- Interest-rate swap

- IS MORC ILL?
- Letter of credit
- Loan commitments (used versus unused)
- Loan packager (underwriter)
- Loan participation
- Loan purchaser (investor)
- Mortgage-backed security
- Mortgage pool or trust
- Noninterest income
- Notional value (volume indicator)
- Off-balance-sheet activity (OBSA)
- Option (nonlinear contract)
- Originator
- Over-the-counter (OTC) contracts

- Pass-through security
- Profit margin (PM)
- Recourse
- Return on assets ($ROA = PM \times AU$)
- Return on equity ($ROE = ROA \times EM$)
- Risk-based capital requirements
- Risk management
- Securitization
- Servicer/Sponsor
- Speculating
- Standby letter of credit (SLC)
- Traditional lending function
- Transparency
- Trustee

Review/Discussion Questions

1. Use the ROE model and structural changes in banking to explain the existence of OBSAs and securitization (contingent-commitment banking).
2. What are the major kinds of derivatives contracts and derivatives securities? How are these contracts typically classified?
3. True or false? Explain why.
   a. Like alligators in a swamp, derivatives lurk in the global economy. Even the CEOs of companies that use them don't understand them.
   b. Derivatives are the basic business of banking in the 1990s.
   c. Derivatives have fundamentally changed financial management.
4. Is Charles Sanford a CEO who understood derivatives? What was his strategy for managing Bankers Trust? How successful was his approach and what happened to the company in 1994 and 1995?
5. In terms of dollar volumes, growth, and risk considerations, what are the major bank off-balance-sheet activities, and where are they concentrated? Who were the Big Six and why were they dubbed that? How many of these "big ones" are there today?
6. What's a pretty good framework for risk management? Are risk-management strategies irrelevant?
7. IS MORC ILL? What it does mean?[27]
8. What is the notional value of a derivatives contract? Is it a meaningful measure of risk? If not, what's a better measure?
9. What kind of evidence exists about the trading of derivatives contracts by banks? Why isn't this the business of banking?
10. The traditional bank lending function has four components. What are they and what has happened to the function?
11. What are the various steps in securitizing bank assets? Who are the major players in this process? What are the barriers to securitization?
12. What are the problems faced by both buyers and sellers of assets used for securitization? What role, if any, does "market discipline" play in this process? Regarding these problems, how do loan participations differ from securitizations?

---

[27] In my freshman math class at St. Vincent College (Latrobe, PA), Professor Stanley Dudzinski was fond of asking us, in a charming accent: "What it does mean?"

13. What role does "recourse" play in loan participations and securitization? Explain what a "spread account" is and its role in the process of securitization. How have bank regulators reacted to this recourse technique?

14. What are loan syndications? What has happened to them recently and why? What has been the OCC's reaction to this?

15. Has securitization been a value-adding function? Who has benefited? Borrowers? Lenders? Investors? Investment Bankers? Third parties?

16. Consider the following question (by Sanford Rose of the *American Banker*) and answer (by Lowell Bryan, a director of McKinsey & Company). For this and other interesting exchanges, see "The Future of Commercial Banking: A Roundtable Discussion," *Midland Corporate Finance Journal* (Fall 1987), pp. 22–49.

    Question: Would you say that the principal reason why the banks should separate funding from origination is the excess capital tax?

    Answer: Well I think you get different value-added for different functions. If you look at where banks add value to the economy, their major contribution is in origination, the assessment and underwriting of credit. Commercial banks are the best credit risk underwriters in the financial-services industry (though you also have some horrible credit risk underwriters among the banks). Those are the unique, or proprietary, skills that banks have evolved; that is their fundamental comparative advantage.

    Evaluate and discuss the issues related to this exchange.

17. What are the capital requirements for OBSAs and for asset-backed securities? How can the risk of these activities be measured?

18. Are the Big Six simply rolling the dice when they engage in foreign-exchange transactions? How important are these revenues to them? Discuss the following quotes related to this issue: Françoise Soares-Kemp of Credit Suisse says, "It doesn't matter which way it's (the dollar) going as long as you are positioned right." When banks guess wrong "most can quickly adjust their position and profit from any swings in currency values." A spokesperson for Bankers Trust, when asked about the downside risk, would not elaborate except to say that extraordinary profits were achieved while "staying within . . . traditional risk policies."

19. Recently BankAmerica, acting as trustee for some mortgage-backed securities, posted a $95 million loss because it felt compelled to purchase securities backed by worthless loans. Why did it do this? What are the risks that investors must be aware of when they purchase asset-backed securities? What skills are needed to successfully manage the risk of a portfolio of asset-backed securities?

20. To what extent is bank noninterest income a symptom of OBSAs? What are the major components of this source of revenue?

21. "Financial engineering" has played a major role in the development of derivatives activities, especially with respect to the underlying mathematical models. Evaluate and discuss the following statement by Merton [1995]:

    Any virtue can become a vice if taken to an extreme—and just so with the application of mathematical models in finance practice. I therefore close with an added word of caution about their use. At times, the mathematics of the models becomes too interesting, and we lose sight of the model's ultimate purpose. The mathematics of the models are precise, but the models are not, being only approximations to the complex, real world. Their accuracy as a useful approximation to that world varies considerably across time and place. The practitioner should therefore apply the models only tentatively, assessing their limitations carefully in each application. (p. 14)

22. What do bank loans and OTC derivatives have in common? How does disclosure affect transparency? How can fair value be determined? Are banks disclosing more or less about their derivatives activities and management strategies?

Problems

1. For a number of years now, the OBSA Bank has been feeling the squeeze on its earnings because of removal of interest-rate ceilings on deposits and competition from other financial-services firms. In addition, because of higher capital requirements, the bank has had to slow down the growth of its assets. A consulting firm employed by OBSA has suggested a strategic plan based on a reduction in the bank's "burden." On the cost side, certain branches will be closed and early retirements encouraged. In addition, the latest technological developments will be employed as devices for cutting both managerial and staff labor costs. On the revenue side, the consultant has recommended an aggressive expansion into off-balance-sheet activities and asset sales via securitization to generate fee income and move assets off the balance sheet. The consultant's fee is a performance-based one equal to 0.1 percent of the *improvement* in the bank's net income over the next year. Abbreviated financial statements for the beginning and the end of the relevant year are shown below. Use this information to determine the increase, if any, in OBSA's net income and the fee paid to the consultant.

Item	*Period*	
(millions of dollars)	*t*	*t* + 1
Interest income	834	917
Interest expense	559	615
Noninterest income	153	184
Noninterest expense	318	334
Taxes	22	30
Extraordinary items	0	0

Also attempt the following questions:
   a. How much (in dollar terms) did the bank's burden improve over the year? What were the growth rates for the components of burden?
   b. At the beginning of the period (assumed to be one year) OBSA had total assets of $11.7 billion dollars. If assets grew at a 10 percent rate during the year, what was the bank's return on average assets?
   c. Given a dividend payout ratio of 35 percent and an equity multiplier of 14.75 at the beginning of the year, determine the bank's return on average equity and its year-end EM. If OBSA's regulator demands a ratio of equity capital to assets of 6.5 percent, does the bank pass the test?
   d. Was OBSA able to increase its ROA and ROE without taking on any additional risk? What potential risks are behind off-balance-sheet activities and the securitization of assets? Discuss and debate: Should bank regulators slap capital requirements on these activities?

2. Use the following data to find ROA, PM, and AU, if you can.

Interest income	260
Noninterest income	40
Total assets	4,000

If you can't find all three ratios, what other variables do you need?

3. You are the proud owner of a 30-year mortgage-backed security that has been stripped into interest-only (IO) and principal-only (PO) components. Originally issued in a fixed-rate market, rates suddenly and unexpectedly jump by 200 basis points. What would you expect the price movements on each component to be and why? (Hint: Think about what is likely to happen to prepayments under this scenario.)

**APPENDIX
A**

BANC ONE'S USE OF INTEREST-RATE SWAPS

Introduction

If you could report to your bank's shareholders a return on assets of 1.53 percent versus 0.63 percent, which one would you select? It looks like a no-brainer. You would, however, want to know the risk-return trade-offs. Suppose that the only difference between the two ROAs was the use of interest-rate swaps. If you had just read in *Fortune* that, "Like alligators in a swamp, derivatives lurk in the global economy. Even the CEO's of companies that use them don't understand them," you might have second thoughts about the use of the swaps, especially if you didn't understand them and you felt accountable to your shareholders. In contrast, if you viewed derivatives as "the basic banking business of the 1990s" and thought that they had "fundamentally changed financial management," your attitude would be, "This is where it's at, go for it!" Banc One of Columbus, Ohio went for it. This is its story.

Attempting to Calm Jittery Investors[28]

On December 1, 1993, John B. McCoy, chairman of Banc One, met with bank stock analysts to explain his bank's use of interest-rate swaps. Even for a superregional bank, its portfolio of derivatives was unusually large. For example, as of September 30, 1993, Banc One had swap contracts (notional values) amounting to almost 40 percent of its assets. This figure was roughly 25 times larger than that of its nearest swap competitor, First Union, and about five times larger than that of the tenth-ranked player, Wachovia. Nevertheless, compared to the Big Six of BankAmerica, Bankers Trust, Chase, Chemical, Citicorp, and J. P. Morgan, with more assets off their balance sheets than on them, Banc One was not a big player.

McCoy called the off-balance-sheet portfolio an integral part of Banc One's asset and liability management (ALM). McCoy added, "We do not have to take risks or go into derivatives we don't understand."

Why was all of this explanation and hand-holding necessary? Consider what happened to Banc One's stock price. On April 13, 1993, it closed at $48.75. On November 15, 1993, it closed at $36.75, down 24.6 percent. (As of August 25, 1995, Banc One's 52-week trading range was $35.5 to $24.125, closing at $32.375.) According to the financial press, investors/analysts were worried that Banc One was betting primarily on the direction of interest rates rather than managing its

---
[28] This section draws on Layne [1993a].

own interest-rate risk and were concerned about the lack of transparency in the accounting of off-balance-sheet activities such as derivatives. Accepting these hypotheses, Banc One's management responded by organizing a dog-and-pony show to explain to the market its ALM/hedging strategy and its use of derivatives. The show opened off Broadway—on Wall Street. Critics were not raving, and the more management explained, the more the market punished the stock.

Banc One's Corporate Vision and ALM Strategy[29]

When John G. McCoy took control of Banc One in 1959, he envisioned building a high-quality Tiffany bank, not a merely big Woolworth bank, out of an also-ran with $140 million in assets (Wysocki [1984]). McCoy's approach to planning was to thrust "zealots" together with "implementers" and "controllers" and let them engage in "gentle confrontation" to establish Banc One's corporate vision. John F. Fisher, one of the leading zealots at Banc One, led the bank's push into consumer banking and helped the bank gain its reputation as a pioneer in consumer banking. As an innovator, Banc One was not afraid to break with tradition, as it played a major role in launching Merrill Lynch's cash-management account.

John G. McCoy, who retired as CEO in 1984, was succeeded by his son John B. McCoy, who expanded the bank's vision beyond the Midwest. His rules for expansion by acquisition are simple (Hirsch [1990]):

- Keep existing management in place
- Consolidate back-office operations
- Build up the retail business
- Never buy a bank more than one-third the parent company's size

In 1989, Banc One acquired 20 failed banks of the defunct MCorp in Texas. The deal was an FDIC-assisted transaction that cost Banc One only $500 million. At the beginning of 1991, Banc One was the fifth-largest bank in Texas and the 15th-largest in the United States, with total assets of $40 billion. Without its Texas operations, Banc One ranked as the 24th-largest U.S. bank. By the end of the first quarter of 1995, Banc One was the eighth-largest BHC in the United States, with total assets of $87.8 billion, $18 billion of which came from its Texas operations, which had jumped from fifth-largest to third.

Size is not Banc One's only strength, however, because it has consistently been one of the most profitable banks in the United States. Cost efficiency is one of the characteristics of high-performance banks and one of the two cornerstones of Banc One's corporate culture. The other is discipline.

Regarding ALM, Banc One has been an aggressive and innovative user of interest-rate swaps to lower its exposure to unexpected changes in interest rates. The advantages Banc One saw in using swaps compared to more traditional ways of hedging interest-rate risk included greater liquidity, off-balance-sheet reporting of the transactions, and reduced capital requirements. Along with its counterparties, Banc One developed a product called "amortising interest-rate swaps" (AIRS).

Excluding balancing assets, Banc One's basic portfolio was asset sensitive or assets repricing before liabilities (ARBL). By entering a swap in which it paid a floating rate and received a fixed rate, it incurred a floating-rate liability while in-

---

[29] For more information about Banc One's strategic plan, see chapter 4. Esty, Tufano, and Headley [1994] provide a detailed case study of Banc One's ALM. In addition, Albertson [1994], James and Smith [1994], Heisler [1994], Kane [1994], and Esty and Tufano [1994] comment on the case.

vesting in a fixed-rate asset. More specifically, because floating-rate loans usually price off prime and because most conventional swaps (including AIRS) price off three-month LIBOR to set floating-rate payments, Banc One's basis spread was prime minus LIBOR. When rates are rising, this spread will decline, because LIBOR changes more than prime. When rates are falling, however, the spread widens. With interest rates declining in 1993, Banc One's strategy was paying off handsomely in terms of accounting returns, but the stock market wasn't buying the tactic.

What Went Wrong and Why?[30]

Banc One's management expressed surprise that its stock price was getting hammered in 1993. After explaining its strategy to the market, and when the market did not respond favorably, it was dismayed. Clearly, Banc One had protected its accounting earnings, but it had not immunized its market value of equity to interest-rate risk (chapter 5).

Let's look at this apparent dilemma in terms of the accounting and economic models of the firm (chapter 3) and duration (chapters 6 and 8). The accounting model says

$$\text{Stock price} = EPS \times P/E \qquad \textbf{(A9-1)}$$

where *P/E,* the industry price-earnings ratio, is a relatively fixed multiple, and *EPS* presents accounting earnings per share. In this view, if you increase reported *EPS*, which Banc One had done, your stock price is supposed to go up, all other things being equal. In contrast, the economic model says that the discounted value of rationally anticipated future earnings determines stock price, and that both future earnings and the discount rate are assessed on the basis of opportunity cost and not accounting data. Although Banc One's current and perhaps future accounting earnings may have been up, the market's choice of discount rate resulted in its stock price getting hammered. The important point is that although accounting earnings may have been stabilized, economic earnings and the bank's stock price were not.[31]

Duration analysis (chapters 6 and 8) leads us to a potential source of this economic instability. Specifically, it shows that the market value of equity varies inversely with the duration of net worth $\{D(E) = PVA[D(A)] - PVL[D(L)]\}$. Banc One estimated the duration of its net worth at $+4.0$ years, consisting of $D(A) = 1.73$ and $D(L) = 1.51$. Thus, a 1 percent increase in interest rates would decrease bank equity by 4 percent and vice versa. Kane ([1994], p. 62) contends that Banc One's management had not sized the problem accurately for three reasons:

1. The formula for net-worth duration appears to have been wrong. Because bank leverage tends to be high, a small mismatch between asset and liability durations can be magnified into a duration of ten or more years for stockholder capital.

2. Management's justification for hedging with swaps rather than with long-term investment is incomplete. Consider how unbooked losses are factored into a firm's economic value. The market's estimates of unbooked gains and losses on derivatives positions should be treated similarly.

---

[30] This section draws on Kane [1994].

[31] We can also view Banc One's valuation in terms of equation 2 from chapter 3, that is, $P_0 = EPS^* \times P/E \times K$, where EPS^* equals real earnings and K is an adjustment factor that marks the industry *P/E* up or down to reflect Banc One's unique risk profile. Thus, the market may have considered Banc One's earnings not to be real or sustainable, and therefore it discounted them below its reported *EPS;* and it may have viewed Banc One's derivatives activities as increasing its risk exposure and therefore discounted its earnings multiple below the industry average.

3. Back-of-the-envelope calculations of the duration of net worth or earnings produce at best a rough approximation of the target variable's true sensitivity to interest rates. The economic realism of the model and its assumptions must be considered.

Lessons

Kane ([1994], pp. 62–63) suggests that Banc One's experience with hedging offers two important lessons: First, managers must specify what measures of earnings and net worth their hedging strategies intend to stabilize and commit themselves to a theory of why and how these strategies ought to work. Second, managers must realize that it is not easy to isolate the effects of changing interest rates on bank values. It's often what one thinks one knows that does the most damage!

Discussion Questions[32]

1. How should banks manage interest-rate risk? Under what conditions should banks be repricing assets before liabilities (ARBL or a positive gap), repricing liabilities before assets (LRBA or a negative gap), or not sensitive to changes in interest rates (zero gap)?
2. What should be the focal variable of ALM? Accounting earnings? Market values? Cash flow available for investment?
3. What roles should derivatives play in risk management compared to other techniques? What has been the driving force in the surge of derivatives use by banks?
4. Because banks make interest-rate bets on their balance sheets to increase earnings, why shouldn't they do the same thing with off-balance-sheet activities? What role does transparency play in this regard?
5. Under what conditions will risk management, and in particular management of interest-rate risk, increase shareholder value?
6. Do you think that Wall Street analysts might have had a money-center bias against a Midwest bank trying to play the derivatives game? What kind of game was Banc One trying to play? Was it an end user or a speculator? What did analysts and the market believe it was doing?

APPENDIX B

THE DERIVATIVES ACTIVITIES OF U.S. COMMERCIAL BANKS

Beginning in 1995, bank regulators began to collect better measures of the market size, credit-risk exposure, and revenue from the derivatives activities of commercial banks and their holding companies. This information can be found in the new call-report data supplied by banks. Table B9-1 provides a glossary of terms needed to understand these data.

---

[32] These discussion questions parallel those in Esty and Tufano ([1994], p. 63), and they align with many of the issues the commentators identified as important in the case.

TABLE B9-1 Glossary of Derivatives

Bilateral Netting: A legally enforceable arrangement between a bank and a counter-party that creates a single legal obligation covering all included individual contracts, representing that a bank's obligation, in the event of the default or insolvency of one of the parties, would be the net sum of all positive and negative fair values of contracts included in the bilateral netting arrangement.

Derivative: A financial contract whose value is derived from the performance of assets, interest rates, currency exchange rates, or indexes. Derivative transactions include a wide assortment of financial contracts, including structured debt obligations and deposits, swaps, futures, options, caps, floors, collars, forwards, and various combinations thereof.

Exchange-Traded Derivative Contracts: Standardized derivative contracts transacted on an organization exchange, which usually have margin requirements.

Gross Negative Fair Value: The sum total of the fair values of contracts where the bank owes money to its counterparties, without taking into account netting. This represents the maximum losses the bank's counterparties would incur if the bank defaulted and there was no netting of contracts, and no bank collateral was held by the counterparties.

Gross Positive Fair Value: The sum total of the fair values of contracts where the bank is owed money by its counterparties, without taking netting into account. This represents the maximum losses a bank could incur if all its counterparties defaulted and there was no netting of contracts, and the bank held no counterparty collateral.

High-Risk Mortgage Securities: Securities where the price or expected average life is highly sensitive to interest-rate changes, as determined by the FFIEC policy statement on high-risk mortgage securities. See also OCC Banking Circular 228 (rev.).

Off-Balance-Sheet Derivative Contracts: Derivative contracts that generally do not involve booking assets or liabilities (i.e., swaps, futures, forwards, and options).

Over-the-Counter Derivative Contracts: Privately negotiated derivative contracts that are transacted off organized exchanges.

Structured Notes: Non-mortgage-backed debt securities, whose cash flow characteristics depend on one or more indices or have embedded forwards or options.

Total Risk-Based Capital: The sum of tier 1 plus tier 2 capital. Tier 1 capital consists of common shareholders' equity, perpetual preferred shareholders' equity with noncumulative dividends, retained earnings, and minority interests in the equity accounts of consolidated subsidiaries. Tier 2 capital consists of subordinated debt, intermediate-term preferred stock, cumulative and long-term preferred stock, and a portion of a bank's allowance for loan and lease losses.

Source: Comptroller of the Currency, Administrator of National Bank, *News Release* 95–62 (June 14, 1995), p. 3.

Table B9-2 shows the notional amount of off-balance-sheet derivatives held by the 25 commercial banks and trust companies with the most derivatives contracts as of March 31, 1995. These 25 banks held $16.8 trillion (97.1%) of the $17.3 trillion in outstanding derivatives contracts. The other 596 banks holding derivatives contracts accounted for only 515 billion (2.9%) of the total notional value of $17.3 trillion. Several thousand commercial banks hold no derivatives contracts.

Within a bank holding company, which is the dominant organizational structure in U.S. banking, most derivatives contracts are held by the lead bank in the

TABLE B9-2   Notional Amount of Off-Balance-Sheet Derivatives Contracts of the 25 Commercial Banks and Trust Companies with the Most Off-Balance-Sheet Derivatives Contracts March 31, 1995 ($ millions, note: data are preliminary)

Rank	Bank Name	State	Total Assets	Total Derivatives	Total Futures (EXCH TR)	Options (EXCH TR)	Total Forwards (OTC)	Total Swaps (OTC)	Options (OTC)	Spot FX
1	Chemical BK	NY	$149,034	$3,633,994	$494,498	$93,479	$1,377,950	$1,439,228	$228,839	$127,840
2	Citibank NA	NY	228,437	2,872,943	296,845	110,850	1,656,793	471,503	336,952	163,984
3	Morgan Guaranty TC	NY	143,348	2,833,956	177,093	338,868	619,207	1,191,684	507,104	67,555
4	Bankers TC	NY	82,119	2,082,579	287,452	265,470	611,424	654,966	263,267	84,905
5	Bank of Amer NT & SA	CA	159,010	1,603,803	110,059	22,457	893,963	440,360	136,964	55,372
6	Chase Manhattan BK NA	NY	99,349	1,547,905	78,764	23,282	811,525	388,662	245,672	70,950
7	First NB of Chicago	IL	47,679	677,786	27,459	21,806	337,441	174,873	116,206	40,741
8	Nationsbank NA Carolinas	NC	51,144	627,018	160,925	141,867	72,537	101,609	150,081	10,352
9	Republic NB of NY	NY	33,461	284,236	29,657	23,308	75,536	89,253	66,483	16,316
10	First NB of Boston	MA	36,872	88,831	28,072	2,585	33,019	14,272	10,884	2,552
11	Bank of NY	NY	41,703	77,673	6,548	10,410	44,135	13,626	2,954	5,204
12	Natwest BK NA	NJ	29,131	73,148	12,232	10,838	6,738	13,016	324	1,377
13	First Union NB NC	NC	24,190	54,951	7,936	18,623	8,508	14,102	5,783	0
14	State Street B & TC	MA	22,778	52,164	858	920	48,135	2,144	107	5,409
15	Bank of Amer IL	IL	16,902	44,331	7,097	130	839	28,986	7,279	0
16	Mellon BK NA	PA	33,399	39,275	1,398	840	11,714	19,207	6,115	1,052
17	Seattle-First NB	WA	15,775	33,876	14,762	0	4,252	14,671	191	25
18	PNC BK NA	PA	43,817	31,513	3,369	300	63	18,434	9,347	82
19	Wells Fargo BK NA	CA	51,175	29,125	6,017	3	716	3,434	18,956	165
20	Banc One Columbus NA	OH	6,467	27,476	0	0	113	21,739	5,624	24
21	Boston Safe Deposit & TC	MA	6,188	20,688	0	0	18,636	1,950	103	0
22	Harris T & SB	IL	11,690	19,186	476	1,050	12,102	1,484	4,074	1,958
23	Marine Midland BK	NY	18,558	18,680	670	0	3,839	13,709	463	5
24	National City BK	OH	9,628	16,947	933	1,600	368	9,639	4,406	122
25	Corestates BK NA	PA	21,067	16,191	1,068	30	1,611	11,274	2,209	176
	Top 25 commercial banks & TCs with derivatives		$1,382,923	$16,808,276	$1,754,188	$1,118,715	$6,651,162	$5,153,825	$2,130,386	$656,165
	Other 596 commercial banks & TCs with derivatives		$1,727,718	$515,211	$43,835	$20,975	$51,758	$291,301	$107,343	$11,866
	Total amounts for all BKs & TCs with derivatives		$3,110,640	$17,323,486	$1,798,023	$1,139,690	$6,702,919	$5,445,125	$2,237,729	$668,032

Note: In previous quarters, total derivatives included spot foreign exchange. The first quarter 1995 reports spot foreign exchange separately.
Source: Call Report, schedule RC-L

organization, that is, by the banks shown in Table B9-2. Focusing on the six banks that rule world derivatives, their ratios of derivatives held by the lead bank to those held by the total bank holding company (without netting of intracompany transactions) were (as of March 31, 1995) as follows[33]

Chemical Banking Corp.	99.3%
Citicorp	103.6
J. P. Morgan & Co. Inc.	99.0
Bankers Trust NY Corp.	102.7
BankAmerica Corp.	98.9
Chase Manhattan Corp.	101.8

The ratios of greater than one reflect intracompany transactions.

Types of Derivatives Contracts Held by Banks[34]

OTC contracts and interest-rate contracts are the kinds of derivatives mostly held by banks engaged in off-balance-sheet derivatives. Of the 25 banks with the most derivatives contracts, only Natwest Bank NA of New Jersey held more exchange-traded contracts (72.6%) than OTC contracts (27.4%). In this group of the top 25, only five banks (State Street Bank & Trust [95.9%], Boston Safe Deposit & Trust Company [84.8%], Harris Trust & Savings Bank [69.7%], Bank of New York [57.5%], and Republic National Bank of New York [55.9%]) held more foreign-exchange contracts than interest-rate contracts. Citibank at 54/45 (%IRC to %FXC), BankAmerica at 51\49, Chase at 53/46, and First National Bank of Chicago at 49/50 held roughly the same amount of interest-rate contracts (IRCs) and foreign-exchange contracts (FXCs). In addition to IRCs and FXCs, a few banks hold "other" contracts (e.g., commodity contracts). From the top 25, only six banks held more than 1 percent of their derivatives portfolios in other contracts. NationsBank (6.5%), Republic (5.6%), Morgan Guaranty (4.7%), and Bankers Trust (4.4%) were the leaders, followed by FNB Chicago (1.8%) and Chase (1.3%).

Credit-Equivalent Exposure

Because the notional values shown in Table B9-2 do not reflect true risk exposure, let's consider the figures measuring credit-equivalent exposure presented in Table B9-3.[35] Credit-equivalent exposure is the sum of

- *Bilaterally netted current credit exposure* defined as current credit exposure across all off-balance-sheet derivatives contracts, after considering bilateral netting arrangements.

---

[33] These ratios were calculated from (preliminary) data supplied by the Comptroller of the Currency, Administrator of National Bank, *News Release* 95–62 (June 14, 1995), Tables 1 and 2.

[34] Footnote 1 gives the source for the data described in this section.

[35] In its *1990 Annual Report,* Citicorp describes notional values and the calculation of its risk exposure as follows: "Notional principal amounts are often used to express the volume of these transactions and do not reflect the extent to which positions may offset one another. The amounts do not represent the much smaller amounts potentially subject to risk. Citicorp's market exposure related to interest-rate and foreign-exchange products can be estimated by calculating the present value of replacing at current market rates all outstanding contracts; this estimate does not consider the impact that future changes in interest and foreign-exchange rates would have on such costs" (p. 70).

- *Future exposure,* calculated as .01(notional amounts of short-term [i.e., less than one year] contracts from foreign exchange, gold, other precious metals, other commodities, and equity derivative contracts) + .05(notional amount of long-term [i.e., one year through five years] contracts from above) + .005(notional amount of long-term, interest-rate contracts). Because short-term, interest-rate contracts are assigned a risk weight of zero, they do not enter the calculation.[36]

Viewing bank capital as the ultimate backstop for absorbing losses, whether they arise from activities on or off the balance sheet, bank risk exposures usually are compared to bank capital. Focusing on the last column in Table B9-3, 12 banks had credit-equivalent exposures greater than their risk-based capital (the sum of tier 1 plus tier 2 capital; see Table B9-1 or chapter 13).

Evidence on Trading of Derivatives Contracts

The term "end user" describes a bank that employs derivatives to hedge on-balance-sheet risk as opposed to dealing, trading, or selling risk-management services. For compactness, let's refer to the non–end users as "traders." Panels A, B, and C of Table B9-4 present evidence of derivatives contracts held for trading by the nine commercial banks holding the most off-balance-sheet contracts. On average, these nine banks (Panel A) hold 95 percent of their derivatives for trading and mark them to market (MTM). Note also how the top six banks, described as the Big Six that rule world derivatives, are *the* volume traders.

Panel B of Table B9-4 focuses on the gross fair values of the derivatives contracts held by the nine largest traders. Gross fair values can be either positive or negative (see the glossary in Table B9-1). Positive values are owed to the bank by its counterparties, without taking netting into account, whereas negative values are owed by the bank to its counterparties, without taking netting into account. Except for Chemical Bank, with a $1 billion negative net value, the other eight banks have gross positive fair values exceeding gross negative fair values. For the other 612 banks holding derivatives, the positive and negative values were almost identical.

Panel C of Table B9-4 shows the trading revenue from cash instruments and off-balance-sheet derivatives of the nine leading trader banks. Since the transactions underlying these figures are essentially bets on the future courses of interest rates, exchange rates, equity prices, or commodity prices, the trading revenues can be either positive or negative. Except for Bankers Trust, with a loss of $132 million for the first quarter of 1995, all of the other traders had positive revenues totaling $897 billion, or 0.09 percent of total on-balance-sheet assets (36 basis points in terms of annualized ROA). Since these data are for one quarter only, they should be interpreted with caution. Nevertheless, they do capture the importance of trading as a revenue generator for large banks.[37] The bulk (51.5%) of trading revenues of the nine top banks came from trading foreign-exchange contracts.

---

[36] Reducing the verbiage to *W, X, Y,* and *Z,* we can see the formula more compactly as .01[*W*] + .05[*X*] + .005[*Y*] + 0.0[*Z*].

[37] To illustrate how volatile trading revenues can be, in its 1993 *Annual Report,* Bankers Trust reported trading revenues of $2.2 billion for 1993, consisting of market-risk components of $1.7 billion related to interest-rate risk ($642 million of which was trading related to net interest revenue), $191 million related to foreign-exchange risk, and $374 million related to equity and commodity risk.

TABLE B9-3 Credit Equivalent Exposure of the 25 Commercial Banks and Trust Companies with the Most Off-Balance-Sheet Derivatives Contracts, March 31, 1995 ($ Millions, Ratios in percentages; note: data are preliminary)

Rank	Bank Name	State	Total Assets	Total Derivatives	Bilaterally Netted Current Exposure	Future Exposure (RBC Add On)	Credit Exposure from All Contracts	Credit Exposure to Capital Ratio (%)
1	Chemical BK	NY	$149,034	$3,633,994	$30,100	$14,455	$44,555	375.0
2	Citibank NA	NY	228,437	2,872,943	33,838	16,030	49,868	222.9
3	Morgan Guaranty TC	NY	143,348	2,833,956	37,096	16,484	53,580	570.5
4	Bankers TC	NY	82,119	2,082,579	20,287	11,994	32,281	588.7
5	Bank of Amer NT & SA	CA	159,010	1,603,803	13,479	9,442	22,921	152.2
6	Chase Manhattan BK NA	NY	99,349	1,547,905	13,859	9,484	23,343	230.3
7	First NB of Chicago	IL	47,679	677,786	8,808	4,041	12,849	295.0
8	Nationsbank NA Carolinas	NC	51,144	627,018	3,813	1,565	5,378	175.2
9	Republic NB of NY	NY	33,461	284,236	4,509	1,684	6,193	195.7
10	First NB of Boston	MA	36,872	88,831	771	229	1,000	27.2
11	Bank of NY	NY	41,703	77,673	1,697	488	2,185	46.8
12	Natwest BK NA	NJ	29,131	73,148	183	92	275	10.9
13	First Union NB NC	NC	24,190	54,951	145	120	265	12.5
14	State Street B & TC	MA	22,778	52,164	1,306	516	1,821	136.2
15	Bank of Amer IL	IL	16,902	44,331	840	128	968	35.1
16	Mellon BK NA	PA	33,399	39,275	487	167	654	18.0
17	Seattle-First NB	WA	15,775	33,876	87	53	140	8.0
18	PNC BK NA	PA	43,817	31,513	94	102	196	5.6
19	Wells Fargo BK NA	CA	51,175	29,125	122	101	224	4.6
20	Banc One Columbus NA	OH	6,467	27,476	264	59	323	39.2
21	Boston Safe Deposit & TC	MA	6,188	20,688	451	105	556	106.6
22	Harris T & SB	IL	11,690	19,186	2,337	15	2,352	214.3
23	Marine Midland BK	NY	18,558	18,680	136	43	179	9.4
24	National City BK	OH	9,628	16,947	218	68	288	33.3
25	Corestates BK NA	PA	21,067	16,191	106	51	148	8.2
								Average%
Top 25 commercial banks & TCs with derivatives			$1,382,923	$16,808,276	$175,034	$87,516	$282,550	140.9
Other 596 commercial banks & TCs with derivatives			$1,727,718	$515,211	$4,231	$1,647	$5,878	N/A
Total amounts for all BKs and TCs with derivatives			$3,110,640	$17,323,486	$179,265	$89,163	$268,428	8.5

Note: The bilaterally netted current credit exposure is the current credit exposure across all off-balance-sheet derivative contracts, after considering bilateral netting arrangements.

Future exposure is calculated in the following manner: [Notional amounts of short term (i.e., less than one year) contracts from foreign exchange, gold, other precious metals, other commodity, and equity derivative contracts * 01] + [Notional amounts of long term (i.e., one year through five years) of the above contracts) * .05] + [Notional amount of long-term interest rate contracts * .005]. Short-term interest rate contracts get a "0" risk weight, and therefore do not factor into the summation.

Credit exposure is the sum of the bilaterally netted current credit exposure and future exposure.

The credit exposure to capital ratio is calculated using risk-based capital (tier 1 plus tier 2 capital).

Commercial banks also hold on-balance-sheet assets in volumes that are multiples of bank capital. For example:

Exposures from Other Assets; All Commercial Banks	Exposure to Risk-Based Capital: All Banks	Average % of the Top 25 Credit Exposure Ratios in Each Category
1-4 Family mortgages	153%	1,342%
C&I loans	163%	862%
Securities not in trading account	213%	1,291%

Note: In previous quarters, total derivatives included spot foreign exchange. The first quarter 1995 reports spot foreign exchange separately.

Source: Call Report, schedule RC-R

TABLE B9-4   National Amounts, Gross Fair Values, and Trading Revenue of Derivatives Contracts

Panel A. National Amounts of Off-Balance-Sheet Derivatives Contracts Held for Trading of the Nine Commercial Banks and Trust Companies with the Most Off-Balance-Sheet Derivatives Contracts, March 31, 1995 ($ millions, ratios in percentages; note: data are preliminary)

Rank	Bank Name	State	Total Assets	Total Derivatives	Total Held for Trading & MTM	$ Held for Trading & MTM
1	Chemical BK	NY	$149,034	$3,633,994	$3,510,758	96.60
2	Citibank NA	NY	228,437	2,872,943	2,742,873	95.50
3	Morgan Guaranty TC	NY	143,348	2,833,956	2,528,343	89.20
4	Bankers TC	NY	82,119	2,082,579	2,046,815	98.30
5	Bank of Amer NT & SA	CA	159,010	1,603,803	1,538,812	95.90
6	Chase Manhattan BK NA	NY	99,349	1,547,905	1,485,071	95.90
7	First NB of Chicago	IL	47,679	677,786	671,539	99.10
8	Nationsbank NA Carolinas	NC	51,144	627,018	600,673	95.80
9	Republic NB of NY	NY	33,461	284,236	276,523	97.30
Top nine commercial banks & TCs with derivatives			$993,581	$16,164,221	$15,401,407	95.28
Other 612 commercial banks & TCs with derivatives			$2,117,059	$1,159,265	$485,831	41.91
Total amounts for all BKs and TCs with derivatives			$3,110,640	$17,323,486	$15,887,238	91.71

Panel B. Gross Fair Values of Off-Balance-Sheet Derivatives Contracts of the nine Commercial Banks and Trust Companies with the Most Off-Balance-Sheet Derivatives Contracts, March 31, 1995 ($ millions; note: data are preliminary)

Rank	Bank Name	State	Total Assets	Total Derivatives	Traded: (MTM) Gross Positive Fair Value[a]	Traded: (MTM) Gross Negative Fair Value[b]
1	Chemical BK	NY	$149,034	$3,633,994	$54,523	$55,544
2	Citibank NA	NY	228,437	2,872,943	53,420	51,951
3	Morgan Guaranty TC	NY	143,348	2,833,956	47,425	45,547
4	Bankers TC	NY	82,119	2,082,579	45,974	44,407
5	Bank of Amer NT & SA	CA	159,010	1,603,803	27,975	28,397
6	Chase Manhattan BK NA	NY	99,349	1,547,905	28,837	28,551
7	First NB of Chicago	IL	47,679	677,786	13,387	12,984
8	Nationsbank NA Carolinas	NC	51,144	627,018	4,471	4,391
9	Republic NB of NY	NY	33,461	284,236	4,524	4,499
Top nine commercial banks & TCs with derivatives			$993,581	$16,164,221	$280,537	$276,271
Other 612 commercial banks & TCs with derivatives			$2,117,059	$1,159,265	$13,634	$12,263
Total amounts for all BKs and TCs with derivatives			$3,110,640	$17,323,486	$293,171	$288,534

[a]Market value of contracts that have a positive fair value as of the end of the first quarter 1995.

[b]Market value of contracts that have a negative fair value as of the end of the first quarter 1995.

(continued)

TABLE B9-4 (*Continued*)

Panel C. Trading Revenue from Cash Instruments and Off-Balance-Sheet Derivatives of the Nine Commercial Banks and Trust Companies with the Most Off-Balance-Sheet Derivatives Contracts, March 31, 1995 ($ millions; note: data are preliminary)

Rank	Bank Name	State	Total Assets	Total Derivatives	Total Trading Rev from Cash & Off Bal Sheet Activities	Trading Rev from Int Rate Contracts	Trading Rev from Foreign Exch Contracts	Trading Rev from Equity Contracts	Trading Rev from Commod & Oth Contracts
1	Chemical BK	NY	$149,034	$3,633,994	$39	($45.0)	$76.0	$4.0	$4.0
2	Citibank NA	NY	228,437	2,872,943	340	65.0	242.0	33.0	0.0
3	Morgan Guaranty TC	NY	143,348	2,833,956	263	147.3	70.4	25.7	20.0
4	Bankers TC	NY	82,119	2,082,579	(132)	(99.0)	(44.0)	10.0	1.0
5	Bank of Amer NT & SA	CA	159,010	1,603,803	116	148.0	(32.0)	0.0	0.0
6	Chase Manhattan BK NA	NY	99,349	1,547,905	142	51.0	91.0	0.0	0.0
7	First NB of Chicago	IL	47,679	677,786	37	(5.9)	29.6	13.7	0.0
8	Nationsbank NA Carolinas	NC	51,144	627,018	45	24.1	7.9	11.7	1.1
9	Republic NB of NY	NY	33,461	284,236	46	12.2	21.3	(2.0)	14.8
	Top nine commercial banks & TCs with derivatives		$993,581	$16,164,221	$897	$297.7	$462.2	$96.1	$40.9
	Other 612 commercial banks & TCs with derivatives		$2,117,059	$1,159,265	$198	$45.3	$153.7	($0.9)	($0.2)
	Total amounts for all BKs and TCs with derivatives		$3,110,640	$17,323,486	$1,095	$343.0	$615.9	$95.2	$40.7

Notes: Trading revenue is defined here as "trading revenue from cash instruments and off-balance-sheet derivatives instruments."

In previous quarters, total derivatives included spot foreign exchange. The first quarter 1995 reports spot foreign exchange separately.

Trading revenue from interest rate contracts reflects a revision to Chemical Bank's filings after the FDIC released its Quarterly Banking Profile on 6-14-95.

Source: Call Report, schedule RC-I.

**APPENDIX
C**

HIGH-RISK MORTGAGE SECURITIES AND STRUCTURED NOTES: DEFINITION, MEASUREMENT, AND EXPOSURE

Mortgage-backed securities (chapter 8) have led to the development of various derivative securities such as collateralized mortgage obligations (CMOs that permit securities with different interest rates and maturities) and interest-only (IO) and principal-only (PO) obligations. These instruments present alternative ways of dealing with prepayment uncertainty. The complexities of administrating these innovative securities have made the development of markets for these instruments highly dependent on advances in computer and information technology and, to some extent, on research dealing with the pricing of complex options.[38]

A high-risk mortgage security is one in which the price or expected average life is highly sensitive to interest-rate changes. A structured note is a non-mortgage-backed security whose cash-flow characteristics depend on one or more indices or have embedded forwards or options. Panels A and B of Table C9-1 provide information on these two instruments with respect to number of banks holding the securities (693 banks vs. 3,958 banks, respectively), values, and risk exposure. Because the derivatives activities and the securities described here require an investment in intellectual capital in terms of understanding even the plain vanilla transactions, many banks may be reluctant to participate, and wisely so. The more complex transactions can be challenging even to veterans of capital markets.

Panel A of Table C9-1 shows that as of March 31, 1995, only 693 banks (out of 10,241 reporting banks) held any high-risk mortgage securities. These assets had a total book value of $3.6 billion and amounted to only 0.5 percent of total assets, on average. With a market value of $3.4 billion, the average market-to-book ratio was 0.94, a depreciation of $225 million, and average exposure to risk-based capital of 0.38 percent.

Panel B shows that more banks hold structured notes than high-risk mortgage securities. As of March 31, 1995, 3,958 banks held $21.3 billion (book value) in structured notes, 1.8 percent of total assets on average. These notes had a market value of $20.6 billion for an average market-to-book ratio of 0.96 and an average depreciation of $731 million. Average exposure relative to risk-based capital was 0.69 percent.

In measuring, managing, and accepting risk, bankers are expected to exercise prudence. This dictum applies to both on- and off-balance-sheet activities. In this regard, Eugene A. Ludwig, the Comptroller of the Currency (OCC Guidelines, 1993), has warned bankers, "In derivatives, the slicing, dicing, and recombining of risk elements of products makes it harder to see the risk. Banks need to be prepared

---

[38] Smith [1991] presents an option-adjusted spread method for analyzing the risk and return for mortgage-backed securities. Unlike more conventional calculations (e.g., yield to maturity), the option approach adjusts for both the timing and the level of potential prepayment.

TABLE C9-1   High-Risk Mortgage Securities and Structured Notes

Panel A. High-Risk Mortgage Securities for All Commercial Banks Reporting High-Risk Mortgage Securities, March 31, 1995 ($ millions)

Asset Size	Total # of Bks	# Bks with High-Risk Mortgage Securities	Total Assets	Total Risk-Based Capital	High-Risk Mortgage Securities Market Value	High-Risk Mortgage Securities Book Value
$ LT 250 MM	9,021	539	$44,576	$4,590	$670	$737
$250MM–$500 MM	561	60	20,489	1,948	241	260
$500MM–$1B	264	28	19,229	1,742	145	158
$1B–$10B	332	50	176,288	14,704	1,299	1,390
GT $10B	63	16	464,205	35,663	1,081	1,111
Total	10,241	693	$724,787	$58,646	$3,435	$3,657

Asset Size	Total # of Bks	Book Value Concentration (% of Total Assets)	Depreciation (Market–Book)	Depreciation to Book Value	Depreciation to Risk-Based Capital
$ LT 250 MM	9,021	1.65	($68)	–9.16%	–1.47%
$250MM–$500 MM	561	1.27	(20)	–7.83	–1.05
$500MM–$1B	264	0.82	(13)	–8.53	–0.77
$1B–$10B	332	0.79	(93)	–6.72	–0.64
GT $10B	63	0.24	(30)	–2.71	–0.08
Total	10,241		($224.97)		

Panel B. Structured Notes for All Commercial Banks Reporting Structured Notes March 31, 1995 ($ millions)

For Universe of Banks with Structured Notes

Asset Size	Total # of Bks	# Bks with Structured Notes	Total Assets	Total Risk-Based Capital	Structured Notes Dollar Amount Market Value	Structured Notes Dollar Amount Book Value
$ LT 250 MM	9,021	3,487	$258,622	$26,779	$8,171	$8,508
$250MM–$500 MM	561	226	76,813	7,139	1,767	1,863
$500MM–$1B	264	108	74,558	6,801	1,466	1,521
$1B–$10B	332	116	333,358	29,013	5,189	5,362
GT $10B	63	21	422,174	35,590	3,984	4,073
Total	10,241	3,958	$1,165,525	$105,321	$20,577	$21,326

Asset Size	Total # of Bks	Book Value Concentration (% of Total Assets)	Depreciation (Market–Book)	Depreciation to Book Value	Depreciation to Risk-Based Capital
$ LT 250 MM	9,021	3.28	($340)	–3.99%	–1.27%
$250MM–$500 MM	561	2.42	(74)	–3.96	–1.03
$500MM–$1B	264	2.04	(54)	–3.56	–0.80
$1B–$10B	332	1.61	(175)	–3.26	–0.60
GT $10B	63	0.96	(89)	–2.18	–0.25
Total	10,241		($731)		

Notes: High-risk mortgage securities include held-to-maturity and available-for-sale accounts.

Structured notes include held-to-maturity and available-for-sale accounts.

to expect the unexpected. . . ." To illustrate, the Comptroller describes the kind of derivatives situation (structured note) that concerns him:

> A bank with less than $200 million in assets that has a structured note in its investment portfolio whose interest rate is tied to the performance of the deutschemark and the Spanish peseta vs. the dollar.

The Comptroller said, "We are not convinced that they have this instrument for legitimate hedging purposes or that they understand it." Fact: the initial rate on the note was 9 percent, but at one point it was paying no interest—and had lost 20 percent of its market value.

Selected References

Albert, Andrew. [1988]. "Chemical Raids Wall Street to Beef Up Unit That Securitizes and Sells Loans." *American Banker* (February 8), pp. 1, 14.

Albertson, Robert. [1994]. "Derivatives in Banks: The Six Ironies." *Journal of Applied Corporate Finance* (Fall), pp. 52–54.

Arnold, Bruce R. [1986]. "Securitization of Loans." Speech presented at the Securitization of Loans Seminar, Federal Reserve Bank of New York (October 23).

Bacon, Kenneth H. [1993a]. "U.S. Issues Guidelines on 'Derivatives' Obliging Banks to Mull Customer Needs." *The Wall Street Journal* (October 28).

———. [1993b]. "Lawmakers Question Agencies' Ability to Regulate the Derivatives Market." *The Wall Street Journal* (October 29).

Baldwin, Earl, and Saundra Stotts. [1990]. *Mortgage-Backed Securities: A Reference Guide for Lenders and Users.* Chicago: Probus Publishing.

Bennett, Rosemary. [1993]. "The Six Men Who Rule World Derivatives." *Euromoney* (August), pp. 45–49.

Bessembinder, Hendrik. [1991]. "Forward Contracts and Firm Value: Investment Incentives and Contracting Effects." *Journal of Financial and Quantitative Analysis* 26, pp. 519–532.

Bhattacharya, Sudipto, and Anjan Thakor. [1993]. "Contemporary Banking Theory." *Journal of Financial Intermediation* 3, pp. 2–50.

Bierwag, G. O., and George G. Kaufman. [1985]. "Duration Gap for Financial Institutions." *Financial Analysts Journal* (March/April), pp. 69–71.

Binder, J. J. [1989]. "Asset Risk, Bankruptcy, and Equity Risk." Paper No. 18. University of Illinois at Chicago.

Block, S. B., and T. J. Gallagher. [1986]. "The Use of Interest-Rate Futures and Options by Corporate Financial Managers." *Financial Management* 15, pp. 73–78.

Boemio, Thomas R., and Gerald A. Edwards, Jr. [1989]. "Asset Securitization: A Supervisory Perspective." *Federal Reserve Bulletin* (October), pp. 659–669.

Booth, James R., Richard L. Smith, and Richard W. Stolz. [1984]."Use of Interest-Rate Futures by Financial Institutions." *Journal of Bank Research* (Spring), pp. 15–20.

Bowen, John E. [1989]. *Investing in Mortgage Securities: Risks and Rewards for Banks.* Rolling Meadows, IL: Bank Administration Institute.

Burger, Allen N., and Gregory F. Udell. [1993]. "Securitization, Risk, and the Liquidity Problem in Banking." In Michael Klausner and Lawrence J. White, eds., *Structural Change in Banking. Homewood Hills:* Irwin.

Buser, Stephen, Andrew Chen, and Edward Kane. [1981]. "Federal Deposit Insurance, Regulatory Policy, and Optimal Bank Capital." *Journal of Finance* (March), pp. 51–60.

Chessen, James. [1987]. "Third-Quarter Update: Bank Off-Balance-Sheet Activity." *Regulatory Review* (November/December), pp. 1–8, FDIC.

Corrigan, Tracy, and Deborah Hargreaves. [1994]. "Eyeballing the Finance Director." *Financial Times* (January 26), p. 9.

Culp, Christopher L., and Merton H. Miller. [1994]. "Hedging a Flow of Commodity Deliveries with Futures: Lessons from Metallgesellschaft." *Derivatives Quarterly* (Fall), pp. 7–15.

The Economist. [1994]. "Corporate Hedging: Hard Soap." (April 16), p. 82 (and various other issues; see footnote 14).

Edwards, Gerald A., Jr., and Gregory E. Eller. [1996]. "Derivatives Disclosures by Major U.S. Banks, 1995." *Federal Reserve Bulletin* (September), pp.791–801.

Eisenbeis, Robert A., and Myron Kwast. [1991]. "Are Real Estate Depositories Viable?" *Journal of Financial Services Research* (March), pp. 5–24.

Esty, Ben, and Peter Tufano. [1994]. "Postscript" (Banc One Case). *Journal of Applied Corporate Finance* (Fall), pp. 63–65.

Esty, Ben, Peter Tufano, and Jonathan Headley. [1994]. "Banc One Corporation: Asset and Liability Management." *Journal of Applied Corporate Finance* (Fall), pp. 33–51, and "Commentaries on Banc One's Hedging Strategy," pp. 52–65.

Euromoney. [1992]. (September).

Evans, Richard. [1994]. "Derivatives Superstars: Anonymous No Longer." *Global Finance* (February), pp. 39–74.

FDIC Quarterly Banking Profile (Second Quarter). [1994]. Washington, DC: FDIC.

Federal Reserve Bulletin (various issues). Washington, D.C.: Board of Governors of the Federal Reserve System.

Freeman, Andrew. [1993]. "A Survey of International Banking." *The Economist* (April 10), insert, pp. 1–38.

Froot, Kenneth A., David S. Scharfstein, and Jeremy C. Stein. [1993]. "Risk Management: Coordinating Corporate Investment and Financing Policies." *Journal of Finance* (December), pp. 1629–1658.

———. [1994]. "A Framework for Risk Management," *Harvard Business Review* (November/December), pp. 91–102.

"(The) Future of Commercial Banking: A Roundtable Discussion." [1987]. *Midland Corporate Finance Journal* (Fall), pp. 22–49.

Greenbaum, S., and A. Thakor. [1987]. "Bank Funding Modes: Securitization versus Deposits." *Journal of Banking and Finance* (September), pp. 379–401.

Group of Thirty. [1993a]. "Derivatives: Practices and Principles." Global Derivatives Study Group, Washington, DC (July).

———. [1993b]. "Derivatives: Practices and Principles, Appendix I: Working Papers." Global Derivatives Study Group, Washington, DC (July).

———. [1994]. "Derivatives: Practices and Principles, Appendix III: Survey of Industry Practice." Global Derivatives Study Group, Washington, DC (March).

Hayes, William A. [1990]. "The Risks of Investing in Asset-Backed Securities." *The Bankers Magazine* (November/December), pp. 34–41.

Heisler, Ethan. [1994]. "Comments on Banc One," *Journal of Applied Corporate Finance* (Fall), pp. 59–60.

Hill, G. Christian, and Robert Guenther. [1988]. "Major Banks Found Post-Crash Turmoil to Yield Bonanza in Foreign Exchange." *The Wall Street Journal* (January 25), p. 2.

Hirsch, James S. [1990]. "Growing Ambition: Fast-Rising Banc One." *The Wall Street Journal* (December 26), pp. 1–2.

Holland, Kelley. [1991]. "Securitization, after Fast Growth 29 Percent below Last Year's First Quarter." *American Banker* (April 1), pp. 1 and 16.

Hu, Henry T. C. [1993]. "Misunderstood Derivatives: The Causes of Informational Failure and the Promise of Regulatory Incrementalism." *Yale Law Journal* (April), pp. 1457–1513.

Hunter, William, and Stephen Timme. [1986]. "Technical Change, Organization Form, and the Structure of Bank Production." *Journal of Money, Credit, and Banking* (May), pp. 152–166.

James, Christopher. [1989]. "Off-Balance-Sheet Activities and the Underinvestment Problem in Banking." *Journal of Accounting, Auditing, and Finance* (Spring), pp. 111–124.

James, Christopher, and Clifford Smith. [1994]. "The Use of Index Amortizing Swaps by Banc One." *Journal of Applied Corporate Finance* (Fall), pp. 54–59.

Johnson, Sylvester, and Amelia A. Murphy. [1987]. "Going Off the Balance Sheet." *Economic Review,* Federal Reserve Bank of Atlanta (September-October), pp. 23–25.

Jorion, Philippe. [1995]. *Derivatives and Bankruptcy in Orange County: Big Bets Gone Bad.* San Diego: Academic Press.

Journal of Banking and Finance. [1987]. Selected Papers from the Conference on Asset Securitization and Off-Balance-Sheet Risk of Depository Institutions (September), pp. 355–546.

Kane, Edward J. [1985]. *The Gathering Crisis in Deposit Insurance.* Cambridge, MA: MIT Press.

———. [1989]. *The S&L Insurance Mess: How Did It Happen?* Washington DC: Urban Institute Press.

———. [1994]. "What Can Bankers Learn about Hedging Strategy from the Banc One Case?" *Journal of Applied Corporate Finance* (Fall), pp. 61–63.

Kane, Edward J., and Burton G. Malkiel. [1967]. "Bank Portfolio Allocation, Deposit Variability, and the Availability Doctrine." *Quarterly Journal of Economics* (February), pp. 113–134.

Kane, Edward J., and Haluk Unal. [1990]. "Modeling Structural and Temporal Variation in the Market's Valuation of the Banking Firm." *Journal of Finance* 45 (March), pp. 113–136.

Kareken, John H. [1987]. "The Emergence and Regulation of Contingent Commitment Banking." *Journal of Banking and Finance* (September), pp. 359–377.

Kendall, Leon T. [1996]. "Securitization: A New Era in American Finance." In Leon T. Kendall and Michael J. Fishman, eds., *A Primer on Securitization.* Cambridge, MA: MIT Press, pp. 1–16.

Kendall, Leon T., and Michael J. Fishman, eds. [1996]. *A Primer on Securitization.* Cambridge, MA: MIT Press.

Kim, Sung-Hwa, and G. D. Koppenhaver. [1993]. "An Empirical Analysis of Bank Interest-Rate Swaps." *Journal of Financial Services Research* (February), pp. 57–72.

King, Ralph T., Jr., and Steven Lipin. [1994]. "New Profit Center: Corporate Banking, Given Up for Dead, Is Reinventing Itself." *The Wall Street Journal* (January 31), pp. 1ff.

Kmenta, Jan. [1986]. *Elements of Econometrics.* New York: Macmillan.

Knecht, G. Bruce. [1995]. "Bankers Trust Fourth-Period Net Fell 64 Percent as Many Derivatives Pacts May Default." *The Wall Street Journal* (January 20), p. A3.

Kraus, James R. [1991]. "Banks Riding a New Wave of Currency-Trading Profits." *American Banker* (April 1), pp. 1 and 7.

Kuprianov, Anatoli. [1993]. "Over-the-Counter Interest Rate Derivatives." *Federal Reserve Bank of Richmond Quarterly Review* (Summer), pp. 65–94.

Layne, Richard. [1993a]. "Banc One Discloses Details of Giant Swaps Portfolio." *American Banker* (December 2), pp. 1, 22.

———. [1993b]. "BT's Bet on Derivatives Business Paying Off." *American Banker* (August 10), p. 20.

———. [1993c]. "Newcomers Pile into Booming Swaps Field." *American Banker* (June 9), pp. 1ff.

Lipin, Steven. [1990a]. "Banks Fear Corporations Will Tap Lines of Credit." *American Banker* (November 7), pp. 1 and 22.

———. [1990b]. "Loan Sales Growth Heightens Legal Risks." *American Banker* (November 14), pp. 1 and 22.

———. [1994a]. "Bankers Trust Says Gibson Greetings Was Fully Aware of Derivatives Risk." *The Wall Street Journal* (October 13), p. A4.

———. [1994b]. "Bankers Trust Reassigns Executives in Midst of Internal Sales-Practice Probe." *The Wall Street Journal* (November 14), p. A3.

Lipin, Steven, Fred R. Bleakley, and Barbara Donnelly Granito. [1994]. "Portfolio Poker: Just What Firms Do with 'Derivatives' Is Suddenly a Hot Issue." *The Wall Street Journal* (April 14), pp. 1ff.

Loomis, Carol J. [1994]. "The Risk That Won't Go Away." *Fortune* (March 7), pp. 40–57.

Maddala, G. S. [1983]. *Limited-Dependent and Qualitative Variables in Econometrics.* Cambridge: Cambridge University Press.

Mayers, David, and Clifford W. Smith, Jr. [1982]. "On the Corporate Demand for Insurance." *Journal of Business* 55(2), pp. 281–296.

McDonough, William J. [1993]. "The Global Derivatives Market." *Federal Reserve Bank of New York Quarterly Review* (Autumn), pp. 1–5.

Merton, Robert C. [1995]. "Influence of Mathematical Models in Finance Practice: Past, Present, and Future," *Financial Practice and Education* (Spring/Summer), pp. 7–15.

Merton, Robert, and Zvi Bodie. [1992]. "On the Management of Financial Guarantees." *Financial Management* (Winter), pp. 87–109.

Myers, Stewart. [1977]. "Determinants of Corporate Borrowing." *Journal of Financial Economics* 5(2), pp. 147–175.

Nance, Deana R., Clifford W. Smith, Jr., and Charles W. Smithson. [1993]. "On the Determinants of Corporate Hedging." *Journal of Finance* (March), pp. 267–284.

"OCC Issues Guidelines on Bank Derivatives Activities." [1993]. *News Release,* Comptroller of the Currency Administrator of National Banks (October 27), NR 93–116.

Pavel, Christine A. [1989]. *Securitization: The Analysis and Development of the Loan-Based/Asset-Backed Securities Markets.* Chicago: Probus Publishing.

Price-Waterhouse. [1994]. "Bank On- and Off-Balance-Sheet Risks." London: PriceWaterhouse

Rehm, Barbara. [1988]. "Regulator Sees Pluses, Minuses in Asset Securitization Trend." *American Banker,* (February 8), pp. 1, 6.

Report of Condition and Income for Commercial Banks and Selected Other Financial Institutions, Computer Tapes 1989–1993. National Technical Information Service, U.S. Department of Commerce, Springfield, VA.

Ronen, Joshua, Anthony Saunders, and Ashwinpaul C. Sondhi, eds. [1990]. *Off-Balance-Sheet Activities.* New York: Quorum Books.

Rose, Sanford. [1986]. "Rethinking Securitization." *American Banker* (November 4), pp. 1, 6.

———. [1987]. "Extending the Loan-Sales Revolution." *American Banker* (February 18), pp. 1, 6.

Sanford, Charles S., Jr. [1994]. "Financial Markets in 2020." *Economic Review* (First Quarter), Federal Reserve Bank of Kansas City, pp. 19–28.

Schrand, Catherine M., and Haluk Unal. [1995]. "Joint Risk Management at Thrift Institutions: Evidence from Mutual-to-Stock Conversions." Working Paper, Wharton School, University of Pennsylvania.

Senerpont Domis, Olaf de. [1996]. "Syndication Risk Getting Worrisome, Ludwig Warns." *American Banker* (December 11), pp. 1–2.

Simpson, Thomas D. [1988]. "Developments in the U.S. Financial System since the Mid-1970s." *Federal Reserve Bulletin* (January), pp. 1–13.

Sinkey, Joseph F., Jr. [1989]. "Credit Risk in Commercial Banks: A Survey of Theory, Practice, and Empirical Evidence." *Bank of Israel Banking Review* 2, pp. 12–35.

———. [1995]. "Let Derivatives Buyers Beware and Government Keep Hands Off." *The Atlanta Journal/Constitution* (April 2), p. R6.

Sinkey, Joseph F., Jr., and David A Carter. [1997]. "The Derivatives Activities of U.S. Commercial Banks: Why Big Banks Do and Small Banks Don't." Working Paper, University of Georgia.

Smith, Clifford W., Jr. [1993]. "Risk Management in Banking." In Robert J. Schwartz and Clifford W. Smith, Jr., eds., *Advanced Strategies in Financial Risk Management.* Englewood Cliffs, NJ: New York Institute of Finance, pp. 147–162.

Smith, Clifford W., Jr., and Charles W. Smithson, eds. [1990]. *The Handbook of Financial Engineering.* New York: Harper Business.

Smith, Clifford W., Jr., Charles W. Smithson, and Sykes D. Wilford. [1990]. *Financial Risk Management.* New York: Ballinger/Institutional Investor.

Smith, Clifford W., Jr., and Rene Stulz. [1985]. "The Determinants of Firms' Hedging Policies." *Journal of Financial and Quantitative Analysis* 20(4), pp. 391–405.

Smith, Clifford W., Jr., and J. B. Warner. [1979]. "On Financial Contracting: An Analysis of Bond Contracts." *Journal of Financial Economics* 7, pp. 117–161.

Smith, Stephen D. [1991]. "Analyzing Risk and Return for Mortgage-Backed Securities." *Economic Review,* Federal Reserve Bank of Atlanta (January/February), pp. 2–11.

Stern, Gabriella. [1994]. "Banc One's Sliding Stock Price Scuttles Accord to Acquire Nebraska's FirsTier." *The Wall Street Journal* (February 15), p. A5.

Stern, Gabriella, and Steven Lipin. [1994]. "Procter & Gamble to Take a Charge to Close Out Two Interest-Rate Swaps." *The Wall Street Journal* (April 13), p. A3

Thomas, Paulette. [1994]. "Procter & Gamble Sues Bankers Trust Because of Huge Losses on Derivatives." *The Wall Street Journal* (October 28).

Tobin, James. [1958]. "Estimation of Relationships for Limited Dependent Variables." *Econometrica* 26 (January), pp. 24–36.

Tufano, Peter. [1989]. "Financial Innovation and First-Mover Advantages." *Journal of Financial Economics* 25, pp. 213–240.

Whittaker, J. Gregg. [1987]. "Interest-Rate Swaps: Risk and Regulation." *Economic Review* (March), Federal Reserve Bank of Kansas City, pp. 3–13.

Wigler, Lester. [1991]. "Using Financial Derivatives: Customer Profitability Can Be Increased." *American Banker* (December 26), p. 4.

Wysocki, Bernard J. [1984]. "Executive Style." *The Wall Street Journal* (September 11), pp. 1, 12 (first of a five-part series).

PART

IV

MANAGING THE BANK LENDING FUNCTION

The traditional business of banking is the funding of loans with deposits. A modern, financial-management approach defines the business of banking as the measuring, managing, and accepting of risk. In either case, the major uncertainty banks face is credit risk. The bank lending function can be viewed in terms of three broad categories of lending:

- Business or commercial and industrial (C&I) loans
- Consumer loans, including residential mortgages
- Commercial real-estate loans

The originating and monitoring of bank loans in any of these areas require practical knowledge about borrowers as captured by the "five Cs of creditworthiness":[1]

- Character (honesty, ethical reputation)
- Capacity (cash flow)
- Capital (real net worth)
- Collateral (security)
- Conditions (economic, for example, vulnerability to business and interest-rate cycles)

This part of the book applies this basic framework to the credit analysis, pricing, and monitoring of business loans (chapter 10), consumer loans (chapter 11), and commercial real-estate loans (chapter 12).

The gathering, processing, and analyzing of quality information provides the vehicle for developing a profile of a borrower's creditworthiness, while loan contracts attempt to reduce the incentive problems between lenders, as principals, and borrowers, as agents. Bank-customer relationships and external factors such as economic and competitive business conditions play important roles in

---

[1] As presented in chapter 6, the most common number of Cs seems to be five, although some approaches have as many as 10 or as few as one. For example, Bathory [1987] has only one C in his seven canons of lending: Character, Ability, Margin, Purpose, Amount, Repayment, and Insurance, or CAMPARI.

the lending function, especially for business borrowers. Unlike direct finance, bank credit (indirect finance) has a relationship aspect that permits lender forbearance (i.e., the opportunity to work out problem situations) if the borrower experiences repayment difficulties. Relationships and forbearance are implicit aspects of bank loan agreements.

Contents

LEARNING OBJECTIVES

- To understand the market for commercial and industrial (C&I) loans

- To understand the kinds of business loans banks make

- To understand the borrower-information continuum and the role of monitoring technology

- To understand the credit analysis, pricing, and risks of business lending

- To understand the conventions of business lending

- To understand the importance of customer relationships and cross-selling

CHAPTER THEME

Bank business loans are described as "commercial and industrial," or C&I loans. Industry classifications such as manufacturing (durable and nondurable), mining, trade, transportation, communication, and other public utilities, construction, and services further describe the nature of C&I lending. Borrowers included in these classifications include both Fortune 500 companies and small businesses. Because the instruments of direct finance, commercial paper and corporate bonds, compete directly with bank business loans, banks have difficulty keeping Fortune 500 and 1,000 companies as borrowers. When bankers lose corporate customers as borrowers, they attempt to maintain profitable relationships by cross-selling other products and services such as backup lines of credit, cash management, or risk management. Structural changes with respect to monitoring technology permit borrowers to move along a continuum that, at one end, has high-cost, low-information borrowers who are "unbankable," and at the other end, has low-cost, high-information borrowers with access to direct finance. Commercial banks have expertise and reputational capital in gathering, processing, analyzing, and monitoring information flows along this continuum. Credit analysis (the five Cs) and pricing risk are integral parts of this process.

KEY CONCEPTS, IDEAS, AND TERMS

- Borrower-information continuum
- Cash flow
- Classification models
- Commercial and industrial (C&I) loans
- Commercial paper
- Credit analysis

- Cross-selling
- Customer relationship
- Five Cs (character, capacity, collateral, capital, conditions)
- Hunters vs. skinners
- Lines of credit
- Loan commitment

- Loan surveillance (monitoring)
- Pricing business loans
- Prime rate
- Reputational capital
- Sources of loan repayment

Why Merchants Are Liable to Fail in Business

Few things are so precarious as commercial credit. . . . Almost all merchants and bankers who fail know beforehand that their business is very unsafe. Most of them foresee that failure is inevitable; but, instead of bowing at once, they continue to borrow money, try to make a show of wealth by increasing their business, stake the money of others on a desperate cast where success would simply postpone the ruin, miserably fail, and, in their fall, drag down hundreds of honest men who place implicit confidence in their honor and business capacity.

. . . Gamblers can borrow money only from gamblers or from fools. And if borrowing money to speculate . . . is not gambling, by what name shall we call it?

—THE PRAIRIE FARMER
As reprinted in The Weekly Press
*(vol. 2, no. 1, p. 1)February 6, 1858
Philadelphia, Pennsylvania*

INTRODUCTION[2]

As the prologue suggests, commercial credit has long been regarded as "precarious," or, drawing on *Webster's Seventh,* "characterized by a lack of security or stability that threatens with danger." The major danger in granting credit is the risk of default by the borrower (i.e., credit or default risk; chapter 6). The notion of "knowing beforehand" captures one of the fundamental problems of risk management of business credit: asymmetric information. Borrowers, as insiders, know more about their businesses than lenders, as outsiders, can possibly know. The banker's job in the lending area is to bridge this information gap such that any borrowers that do default do not jeopardize the bank's solvency. Portfolio theory preaches *the* lesson for insolvency protection: *diversification.* Banking law prohibits concentration with a single borrower, and prudent banking practice, supplemented by sound regulatory monitoring, avoids industry concentration. In the past, geographic restrictions have limited bank diversification opportunities, whereas product restrictions are still binding constraints (chapter 15).

---

[2] Parts of this chapter draw on my paper, "Credit Risk in Commercial Banks: A Survey of Theory, Practice, and Empirical Evidence," presented at the conference "Risks in Banking" sponsored by the Bank of Israel, March 27–28, 1989, and reprinted in its *Banking Review* (December 1989), pp. 12–35.

To generate business loans and bridge the gap of asymmetric information, banks need both "hunters" and "skinners." Hunters are bank calling officers who sell financial products and services, including traditional extensions of credit (loans), to businesses. Skinners are financial analysts who determine the quality of the credit by investigating the sources and probabilities of loan repayment; they are the stereotypical green eyeshades of yesterday, replaced by the "spreadsheet jockeys" of today. In contrast, the role of the hunter, born of competitive necessity, captures the importance of selling products and services in a dynamic financial-services industry. Nowhere is this competition more evident and fierce than in commercial lending to major corporations where direct finance, in the form of commercial paper and corporate bonds, has supplanted indirect finance. In this segment of the borrower-information continuum, bankers look to sell backup lines of credit, risk-management services, and any other financial services businesses might need (for example, cash management, payroll, pension, trust, and so forth). Moreover, when extensions of credit are made in this market, discounts from the prime rate are not unusual. Advances in monitoring technology have shifted the market for business lending downward to borrowers that do not have alternative sources of financing, which means that middle-market companies and small businesses are the target customers.

Because the bulk of bank business lending is concentrated in **commercial and industrial (C&I) loans,** this chapter focuses on that component. We begin by looking at some characteristics of bank C&I loans and the intense competition large banks have received from **commercial paper** and corporate bonds as alternative sources of business borrowing. If bank business loans are special, the existence of **customer relationships** might be the unique feature that distinguishes them from other forms of corporate debt. **Competition** and customer relationships can be viewed as two additional Cs (White, 1990) to be added to the five Cs of credit analysis or creditworthiness, which you will recall as

- Character (honesty, willingness to pay)
- Capacity (cash flow)
- Capital (real net worth)
- Collateral (security)
- Conditions (vulnerability to economic fluctuations)

Quantifying the five Cs for business borrowers represents one way of viewing the task of credit analysis. This chapter focuses on the tools and techniques used to analyze the creditworthiness of bank business borrowers, and it attempts to reconcile the teaching and practice of commercial lending.

BANK COMMERCIAL AND INDUSTRIAL (C&I) LOANS: PORTFOLIO CHARACTERISTICS AND TRENDS

Table 10-1 presents some characteristics and trends of bank commercial and industrial (C&I) loans. Panel A shows C&I loans as a percentage of average net consolidated assets for four bank size groups for 1985 and 1995. In addition, the data are split according to U.S. and foreign addresses (i.e., domestic and foreign borrowers). For both 1985 and 1995, we observe three phenomena: (1) lending to foreign borrowers for C&I purposes clearly is the domain of the 10 largest banks;

TABLE 10-1   Characteristics of Bank Commercial and Industrial (C&I) Loans

PANEL A. THE C&I LOAN PORTFOLIO, 1985 AND 1995 (AS A PERCENTAGE OF AVERAGE ASSETS)

	1985			*1995*		
Asset size	*Total*	*U.S.*	*Foreign*	*Total*	*U.S.*	*Foreign*
Small	14.33	14.3	0.03	9.66	9.60	0.06
Medium	19.02	18.7	0.32	12.68	12.52	0.16
Large	24.20	21.1	3.10	19.26	18.10	1.16
10 largest	30.68	15.3	15.40	16.16	8.67	7.50
All banks	22.16	17.4	4.8	15.20	12.87	2.33

Memo: Average net consolidated assets for all banks of $2,573 billion (1985) and $4,149 billion (1995) and C&I loans for all banks of $570 billion (1985) and $631 billion (1995). As of year-end 1989, all banks held $616 billion in C&I loans on assets of $2,862 billion.

PANEL B. THE RELATIVE QUALITY OF C&I LOANS COMPARED TO CONSUMER AND REAL-ESTATE LOANS, 1987–1995 (DELINQUENCY AND CHARGE-OFF RATES BY TYPE OF LOAN)

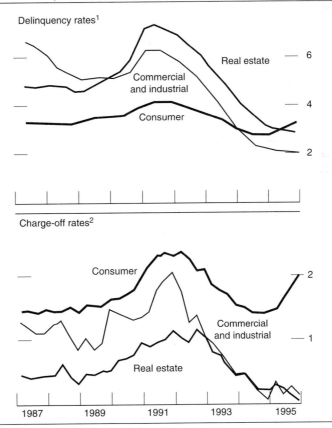

Note: The data are quarterly and seasonally adjusted. Delinquent loans are loans that are not accruing interest and those that are accruing interest but are more than 30 days past due.

1. The delinquency rate for a category of loans is the category's average level of delinquent loans for the period divided by the category's average level of outstanding loans for the period. The first period plotted is 1987:Q2.

2. The charge-off rate for a category of loans is the category's annualized charge-offs for the period, net of recoveries, divided by the category's average level of outstanding loans for the period.

Source: Federal Reserve Bulletin (June 1995), pp. 553 and 559–569.

(2) as bank size increases, the relative amount of C&I lending to *foreign* borrowers increases; and (3) as bank size increases, the relative amount of *domestic* C&I lending increases for the first three size classes and then declines for the 10 largest banks.

Regarding the dollar amount of C&I lending, at year-end 1995, the 10 largest banks held $1,051 billion in aggregate assets, $170 billion in the form of total C&I loans ($91 billion to domestic borrowers and $79 billion to foreign borrowers). In contrast, the next largest 90 banks (the "large" size class in Panel A) held aggregate assets of $1,338 billion, $258 billion in the form of total C&I loans ($242 billion to domestic borrowers and $16 billion to foreign borrowers). For the other two groups, which together included over 9,000 banks at year-end 1995, almost all of their C&I lending was to domestic borrowers. The volume and market share of domestic C&I loans across the four size classes at year-end 1995 were as follows:[3]

Bank Size Class	Domestic C&I Loans, $Billions (% Market Share)
Ten largest banks	$ 91 (17.0%)
Large banks	242 (45.3%)
Medium banks	137 (25.7%)
Small banks	64 (12.0%)
Total	$534 (100%)

The domestic C&I loan portfolio for all banks was up only slightly from the year-end 1985 figure of $447.7 billion. The compound annual growth of 1.8 percent for domestic C&I loans can be compared with the 4.9 percent growth rate of total assets over the same period. Because aggregate data may mask the performance of subgroups, it is interesting to look at the annual growth rates of domestic C&I loans across the size groups shown in Table 10-1:

Size class	Annual Growth Rate of Domestic C&I Loans, 1985–1995
Top ten	−0.8% (5.0%)
Large	5.5% (7.2%)
Medium	1.4% (5.5%)
Small	−3.2% (0.4%)
All banks	1.8% (4.9%)

Figures in parentheses are growth rates for the groups' total assets. The implications from these data are clear and important. C&I lending has not been a growth area for commercial banks, especially for the 10 largest banks and the thousands of community banks. The bigger banks have a strategic plan: Move into investment banking, risk management, and insurance. It is not clear that community banks have a plan, but they continue to look more and more like S&Ls and consumer banks rather than commercial banks.

Regarding total C&I lending (domestic plus foreign), the 100 largest banks are the major players, with volumes at year-end 1995 of $170 billion for the 10

---

[3] These data are derived from the figures presented in Table 10-1 and from the *Federal Reserve Bulletin* (June 1996).

largest banks and $258 billion for the 90 banks ranked 11 to 100. These banks made eight out of every 10 dollars of total C&I loans outstanding at year-end 1995. In contrast, medium and small banks had volumes of $139 billion and $64 billion, respectively.

Delinquency and Charge-Off Rates

Panel B of Table 10-1 shows delinquency and charge-off rates (quarterly and seasonally adjusted) by type of loan for the years 1987(2Q) to 1995($Q). Delinquent loans are defined by the Federal Reserve as nonaccrual loans and those accruing interest but more than 30 days past due. Nonaccrual loans are ones switched to a cash basis, which means that unless payments are actually received, they are not recorded (as they would be on an accrual basis). The delinquency rate for each loan category is the average level of delinquent loans for the period divided by the average level of outstanding loans for the period.

The charge-off rate for a category of loans is its annualized charge-offs for the period, net of recoveries, divided by the category's average level of outstanding loans for the period. Bankers charge off loans at their own discretion or at the urging of bank examiners. Because loans that are charged off are not forgotten, net loan losses are defined as gross charge-offs minus recoveries.

Delinquency and charge-off rates are cyclical, with delinquencies peaking first. An analysis of risk rankings based on these rates, derived from Panel B in Table 10-1, provides the following picture:

	Second quarter 1987		*Year-end 1994*	
Loan category	*Delinquent*	*Charged*	*Delinquent*	*Charged*
C&I	Highest	Middle	Lowest	Middle
Consumer	Lowest	Highest	Highest	Highest
Real estate	Middle	Lowest	Middle	Lowest

The cyclical movements of delinquency and charge-off rates for C&I and real-estate loans reflect two phenomena: (1) the effects of the third-world or LDC debt crisis on the C&I rates during the late 1980s, and (2) the effects of problems in commercial real estate lending during the early 1990s. The high charge-off rate for consumer loans comes mainly from the riskiness of credit-card lending, which is highly profitable but also highly risky (see chapter 11).[4] Because credit-card loans are unsecured, bankers are quicker to charge them off compared to secured credits. However, it is easier for borrowers to keep credit-card loans current by making minimum monthly payments and thereby avoiding delinquency.

The Diversity of C&I Loans at Large Banks

The 100 largest U.S. commercial banks have roughly one dollar out of every three in their loan portfolios in the form of C&I loans. Community banks have a lower C&I concentration, with medium-sized banks at around 20 percent and the smallest banks at 17 percent. Within the C&I category, however, diversity across industries varies directly with bank size. To illustrate, the structure of the C&I portfolios

---

[4] Sinkey and Nash [1993] and Nash and Sinkey [1997] present investigations of the profitability and riskiness of credit-card banks.

of large weekly-reporting banks (assets greater than $3 billion) has the following industry classification:

1. Manufacturing (durable and nondurable)

2. Mining

3. Trade

4. Transportation, communication, and other public utilities

5. Construction

6. Services

Recent data (not shown) indicate that the C&I portfolios of large weekly-reporting banks are well diversified across these three categories.[5] Except for the construction category, at less than 5 percent of the portfolio, the other classifications typically contain between 10 and 20 percent of the loan portfolio. One of the reasons large banks are less risky than small banks is their ability to diversify their loan portfolios on an industry and geographic basis. A *small* bank in a one-industry town has limited opportunities to diversify its loan portfolio. For example, Penn Square Bank of Oklahoma City suffered from a lack of diversification. It was a spectacular failure (July 5, 1982) that led to the collapse and bailout of Continental Illinois (1984) and to losses at other major banks because of upstreamed bad energy loans. Penn Square's loan portfolio had a heavy concentration of C&I loans (e.g., 72 percent on December 31, 1980), mainly in energy-related areas. In contrast, roughly one-half of a *large* bank's loan portfolio tends to be in a diversified C&I portfolio, with about one-half of the portfolio in the form of term loans (i.e., original maturity more than one year).

FUNCTIONAL COST ANALYSIS OF THE COMMERCIAL LOAN FUNCTION

The Federal Reserve's functional cost analysis (FCA) attempts to estimate individual bank incomes and costs across various bank product and service lines. It is designed to assist banks in increasing overall bank efficiency and improving the operating efficiency of each bank function. Bank managers can use it as a tool in evaluating performance. An important caveat is, "Bank cost accounting is not an exact science."[6]

The Fed's FCA classifies commercial loans into three categories:

- Commercial—Time and Demand Loans: This category includes all commercial and industrial (C&I) loans made to proprietorships, partnerships, corporations, and other business enterprises not serviced by the installment loan department

- Agricultural Loans: This category includes all agricultural loans except those carried in the real estate mortgage loan department and the installment loan department

- Other Commercial Loans: This category includes commercial and all other loans (including overdrafts) not recorded in the previous two categories

Table 10-2 shows recent data for the C&I loan function from the FCA *National Average Report*. The number of banks and the deposit size classes in which they

---

[5] Of course, because diversification can be evaluated only at the micro level, this statement says nothing about the diversification within each category.

[6] From the Federal Reserve's *FCA National Average Report* [1994], p. 1.

TABLE 10-2 Functional Cost Analysis of the C&I Loan Function, 1994 National Average Report

	51 Banks Deposits up to $50M		116 Banks Deposits $50–$200M		41 Banks Deposits over $200M	
Composition						
1. Commercial—time & demand	$3,915,423	46.70%	$12,276,834	58.48%	$60,486,990	78.67%
2. Agricultural loans	3,389,026	40.42	4,322,411	20.59	4,737,960	6.16
3. Other commercial loans	1,079,133	12.87	4,394,343	20.93	11,663,582	15.17
4. Total commercial & other loan volume	8,383,582	100.00%	20,993,588	100.00%	76,888,532	100.00%
Income		*Percent of Commercial Loan Volume*				
5. Commercial—time & demand	336,662	8.60%	1,057,299	8.61%	5,079,314	8.40%
6. Agricultural loans	303,029	8.94	371,103	8.59	396,100	8.36
7. Other commercial loans	103,992	9.64	355,536	8.09	848,415	7.27
8. Other income	29,949	.36	46,971	.22	272,504	.35
9. Total income	773,631	9.23%	1,830,910	8.72%	6,596,332	8.58%
Expense						
10. Officer salaries	89,090	1.06%	186,699	.89%	673,550	.88%
11. Employee salaries	19,234	.23	52,715	.25	230,111	.30
12. Fringe benefits	23,916	.29	62,561	.30	234,891	.31
13. Salaries and fringe, subtotal	132,240	1.58%	301,975	1.44%	1,138,551	1.48%
14. Data services	16,859	.20	32,217	.15	138,639	.18
15. Occupancy	15,392	.18	39,727	.19	171,328	.22
16. Fees—legal & other	10,996	.13	26,771	.13	88,609	.12
17. Other operating expense	44,707	.53	113,182	.54	397,118	.52
18. Total operating expense	220,194	2.63%	513,871	2.34%	1,934,246	2.52%
Earnings						
19. Net earnings before losses	553,437	6.60%	1,317,039	6.27%	4,662,087	6.06%
20. Net losses	31,550	.38	86,467	.41	165,458	.22
21. Net earnings	521,887	6.23%	1,230,572	5.86%	4,496,629	5.85%
22. Cost of money	357,154	4.26	866,616	4.13	2,950,081	3.84
23. Net earnings after cost of money	164,734	1.96%	363,956	1.73%	1,546,548	2.01%
Number of Commercial & Other Loan Personnel		*Miscellanous Data*				
24. Officers		1.82		3.65		13.33
25. Employees		1.14		2.93		12.29
26. Total personnel		2.96		6.58		25.62
27. Number of full-service offices		1.45		2.85		11.15
Number of Commercial & Other Loans						
28. Commercial—time & demand		131		365		752
29. Agricultural loans		125		163		139
30. Other commercial loans		53		306		1,007
31. Total commercial & other loans		310		835		1,897
Average Size						
32. Commercial—time & demand		$29,831		$33,608		$80,456
33. Agricultural loans		27,015		26,505		34,176
34. Other commercial loans		20,578		14,341		11,585
35. Number of loans per person		105		127		74
36. 3-Year average loan losses	$53,166	.63%	$125,520	.60%	$413,817	.54%

Source: Federal Reserve, *FCA National Average Report* [1994], p. 39. © Federal Reserve Bank, San Francisco. Used by permission.

fall are as follows: 51 banks with deposits less than $50 million, 116 banks with deposits greater than $50 million but less than $200 million, and 41 banks with deposits greater than $200 million. Since the very largest banks, which dominate C&I lending, are conspicuous by their absence, FCA data are more reflective of an industry without these banks.

The Composition and Net Earnings of C&I Loans

Based on FCA data, Table 10-2 shows that both the proportion and the average dollar volume of commercial (C&I) loans varies directly with bank size (47 percent to 58 percent to 79 percent, and $3.9 million to $12.3 million to $60.5 million). In contrast, the proportion of agricultural loans decreases substantially as bank size increases (40 percent to 21 percent to 6 percent), whereas the average dollar amount of loans increases slightly ($3.4 million to $4.7 million). The earnings profile, as a percentage of commercial loan volume across the three size classes for 1994 was as follows

	FCA Bank Size Class		
	Small	*Medium*	*Large*
Total income	9.23%	8.72%	8.58%
Total operating expense	2.63	2.45	2.52
Net earnings before losses	6.60	6.27	6.06
Net losses	0.38	0.41	0.22
Net earnings	6.23	5.86	5.85
Cost of money	4.26	4.13	3.84
Net earnings after cost of money (before taxes)	1.96%	1.73%	2.01%

On average, for 1994, small and large FCA banks earned about 200 basis points before taxes on the C&I loan function, whereas medium-sized banks were a bit less profitable at 173 basis points. The average loan-loss rate on C&I loans for 1992 to 1994 for all FCA banks was about 0.60 percent compared to the 1994 average rate of 0.34 percent, revealing the trend of improved C&I loan quality during the early 1990s. The average dollar amounts of three-year loan losses were $53,166 (small banks), $125,520 (medium banks), and $413,817 (large banks).

COMMERCIAL PAPER AND THE SHIFT FROM INDIRECT FINANCE TO DIRECT FINANCE

Indirect finance uses financial intermediaries such as commercial banks; direct finance does not.[7] Disintermediation can occur on either side of a bank's balance sheet. When bank borrowers shift from indirect finance to direct finance, the disintermediation occurs on the asset, or lefthand, side of the balance sheet. As large corporations have resorted more and more to issuing debt rather than borrowing from banks, commercial bank C&I lending has suffered. The primary culprit in this

---

[7] Because direct finance still uses investment bankers for advice, underwriting, and distribution of securities, "direct" is a relative term. It is direct in the sense that an additional claim is not created, as in indirect finance (i.e., a bank accepts a deposit, one claim, and turns it into a loan, another claim).

phenomenon has been commercial paper, which is a short-term corporate IOU (chapter 7, boxes 1 and 2).

Table 10-3 shows the volume and annual growth of commercial paper for all issuers for the period 1985 to 1996. Over these eleven years, commercial paper grew at a compound annual rate of 9.0 percent, compared to only 1.8 percent growth for bank C&I loans.

Because corporations with access to the commercial-paper market borrow mainly from the largest banks, those banks have been hit the hardest by the shift to direct finance. However, because most commercial paper is backed by bank standby lines of credit (an OBSA, chapter 9), the increased competition also has generated off-balance-sheet business for large banks, enabling them to increase fee income and reduce risk-based capital requirements compared to that for actual lending. At the same time, however, bank C&I interest revenue has been hurt by the ability of large corporate borrowers to bargain for discounts from the prime rate. Thus, increased competition from commercial paper has had both a quantity and a price (rate) effect on bank C&I interest income. In addition, the trickle-down effect of the competition has forced larger banks to go after the so-called middle-market companies, thereby intensifying competition among banks for business borrowers.

As financial markets become more and more complete, banks and other intermediaries will find it more and more difficult to survive by simply doing what they have done in the past. Accordingly, financial institutions must look for new products and markets to tap. The development of off-balance-sheet activities such as standby lines of credit, financial guarantees to support commercial paper, and derivatives products, as tools for risk management, are good examples of such innovations (chapter 9).

TABLE 10-3	Commercial Paper as a Substitute for Bank Business Loans 1985–1996	
Year-end	*Commercial Paper*	*Annual Growth Rate*
1985	$299 billion	NA
1986	$330 billion	10.4%
1987	$358 billion	8.5
1988	$457 billion	27.6
1989	$529 billion	15.8
1990	$563 billion	6.4
1991	$529 billion	–6.0
1992	$546 billion	9.7
1993	$555 billion	1.0
1994	$595 billion	9.3
1995	$675 billion	13.4
1996	$775 billion	14.8

Memo: From 1985 to 1996, commercial paper grew at a compound annual rate of 9.0 percent, whereas bank C&I loans grew at only 1.8 percent. As of April 30, 1997, CP outstanding was $838.4 billion annualized growth of 24.4 percent.

Source: Federal Reserve Bulletin (various issues), Table 1.32, p. A22 (August 1997).

THE BORROWER-INFORMATION CONTINUUM
AND MONITORING-TECHNOLOGY HYPOTHESIS[8]

Berger and Udell [1993] posit a **borrower-information continuum** and a **monitoring-technology hypothesis** as extensions to the theory of financial intermediation. Three forms of debt exist in their continuum:

- Private or inside debt (i.e., funds supplied by owners or other insiders)
- Intermediated debt (e.g., bank loans)
- Public or direct-investor-held debt (e.g., commercial paper)

Figure 10-1 depicts Berger and Udell's borrower-information continuum. Think of this continuum in terms of direct finance on the right-hand side and indirect finance or intermediation in the middle of the diagram. As advances occur in monitoring technology, information problems are reduced and the boundaries between the forms of debt shift such that banks may lose customers (about whom information is relatively more accurate and more readily available) but pick up customers that previously were unbankable. At the high-information end of the spectrum, cross-monitoring exists because borrowers hold direct-investor-held debt and intermediated debt or guarantees. Because financial markets are incomplete, borrowers characterized by readily available, low-cost information still need bank services such as syndicated loans and financial guarantees (e.g., standby or backup lines of credit for commercial paper).[9]

Berger and Udell call their theory the monitoring-technology hypothesis and use it to explain the existence of securitization (chapter 9). The idea behind the monitoring-technology theory is that some types of lending are more easily moni-

FIGURE 10-1 **The Borrower-Information Continuum**

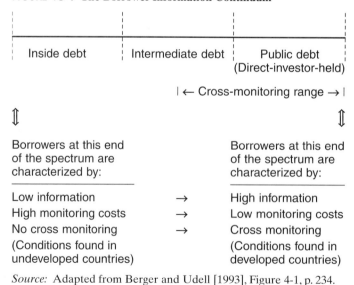

Source: Adapted from Berger and Udell [1993], Figure 4-1, p. 234.

---

[8] This material was introduced in chapter 1.

[9] Megginson, Poulsen, and Sinkey [1995] analyze the effects of announcements of syndicated loans made by 15 U.S. money-center banks on their stock prices for the years 1966 to 1989.

tored and therefore have lower monitoring-related contract costs; such loans are more likely to be securitized (that is, packaged and sold as securities). In contrast, loans with high monitoring-related contract costs are less likely to be securitized. Improvements in monitoring technology reduce monitoring-related contract costs and thereby stimulate the process, development, and spread of securitization.

Monitoring-Related Contract Costs of Large C&I Loans

Booth [1992] tests and accepts two hypotheses dealing with monitoring-related contract costs of large commercial loans: (1) a cross-monitoring hypothesis that suggests that less monitoring is required if borrowers bond themselves to generate information that is observable and valuable to multiple claimholders, and (2) a financial contract-cost hypothesis that specifies that bank monitoring costs capture the ease or difficulty with which covenants can be written to control borrowers' behavior toward their assets. Booth finds evidence that loans to corporations with actively traded equity and rated debt securities are associated with smaller loan spreads, as would be expected, because these markets are much more competitive. He also finds that private firms, including private firms going public, pay, on average, 33 basis points more in loan spread (relative to prime, LIBOR, or cost of funds) than public firms.

On balance, low-risk borrowers are able to bond themselves to generate information that is observable and valuable to multiple claim holders. Because of structural shifts in the borrower-information continuum over time (e.g., as evidenced by increases in commercial paper and corporate bonds at the expense of bank loans), when banks make important loans that compete with direct-investor-held debt, they signal their ability to compete with the instruments of direct finance.

SOURCES OF LOAN REPAYMENT: CASH FLOW IS THE NAME OF THE GAME

Borrowers have three sources of loan repayment:

1. Cash flow
2. Liquidate (sell) an asset
3. Another source of financing

Commercial bankers traditionally have been cash-flow lenders, which explains the banker's penchant for watching cash flow. Over the long haul, accrued profits, adjusted for dividends and capital investments, tend to equal net cash flow. However, over the short run, say, one year, accounting profits and cash flow are rarely equal. Accordingly, bankers, as cash-flow lenders, need to know something about the concept and measurement of cash flow, especially because cash-flow problems are the most common cause of business failures. Beaver [1967], in his classic study of bankruptcy, found the ratio of cash flow to total debt was his best predictor of impending failure.

The Concept of Cash Flow

Because of accounting conventions, the concept of cash flow can become obscured. It shouldn't. Cash flow (net) is simply the difference between cash inflow, or dollars received, and cash outflow, or dollars paid out. This flow process forms the heart of the valuation process because the net-present-value rule is stated in terms of cash flow (chapter 3). In particular, we are interested in incremental (after-tax) cash flows and economic value added.[10] Although profits are a company's major source of cash flow, cash flow, of course, is not equal to accounting profits.

Most introductory finance textbooks define cash flow in an add-back fashion as profits plus noncash outlays, with depreciation as the major noncash outlay or item to be added back. However, because there is no uniformly accepted way of calculating cash flow, the methods used by lenders do vary. According to Kelly [1986], some analysts define cash flow as follows:

$$
\begin{aligned}
&\text{Net profit} \\
&+ \text{Depreciation} \\
&- \text{Increase in accounts receivable} \\
&- \text{Increase in inventories} \\
&+ \text{Increase in accounts payable} \\
&= \text{Cash flow}
\end{aligned}
\tag{10-1}
$$

Because many analysts (e.g., O'Glove [1987]) regard management of accounts receivable and inventories as critical to a firm's success, this definition of cash flow has some merit. Clearly, large increases in these accounts reduce a firm's cash flow. Accordingly, the composition of a firm's cash flow is important. To illustrate further, a cash flow dominated by an increase in accounts payable (say, because of slow bill paying) is not a desirable situation.

When equation (10-1) is expanded to cover all the items on a firm's balance sheet, the familiar sources-and-uses-of-funds statement is generated. On a cash basis, the *uses* of cash are

1. Increases (or investments) in noncash assets (e.g., the accounts receivable and inventories of equation [10-1])
2. Decreases in liabilities or equities

The *sources* of cash are:

1. Decreases in noncash assets
2. Increases in liabilities or equities (e.g., the accounts payable of equation [10-1])

These changes combined with the cash flow from a firm's operations (derived from the profit-loss or income-expense statement) permit analysts to see where a firm's cash comes from and where it goes.

In the commercial lending or credit schools of bank training programs, accounting and analysis of financial statements are emphasized, including the particular methods, techniques, and software packages employed by the bank. In this regard, courses in accounting and working-capital management provide desirable backgrounds for would-be commercial lenders.

Potential Warning Signals about Cash-Flow Problems

As in any other endeavor, experience plays an important role in the credit decision-making and monitoring process. Bennett [1987] discusses some warning signals he looks for as an experienced lender. These factors, which sometimes go beyond financial statements, are described by Bennett from the borrower's perspective.

---

[10] Modern corporate finance also focuses on the notion of "free cash flow," defined as the amount of cash that the firm can distribute to security holders; see Benninga and Sarig [1997].

1. *You Show up on the Wrong Lists.* The lists a borrower does not want to show up on include checks drawn on uncollected funds, overdraft accounts, large transactions, past-due loans, loans with incomplete collateral, and late financial statements.
2. *You Act as if You are Hungry for Cash.* Bennett regards frequent requests for small loans as a potential indicator that your company is not generating enough cash. By the same token, if your company maintains high credit-card balances when interest rates are low, he wonders why you are not paying off the balance.[11] In addition, debt servicing may be a problem for companies with large net-worth positions but small cash flows.
3. *You Make One Change Too Many.* Bennett applies this adage to both personnel and loan requests. Because frequent changes can suggest underlying problems, too many changes are unsettling to most bankers. Frequent changes in loan requests suggest the company can be out of control or not know what it is doing.
4. *You Look a Little Rough Around the Edges.* Because the character factor is difficult to monitor, changes in physical appearance may indicate changes in behavior related to alcoholism, drug abuse, gambling, abrupt changes in marital status, or problems with the business. In addition, if the company and its surroundings are not adequately maintained, this may signal lack of concern for details or inadequate cash for basic maintenance.

From the borrower's perspective, if you see any of these things happening to your company, Bennett suggests it is time to call or see your banker and explain what is going on.

Estimating and monitoring future cash flows is a critical part of credit analysis and risk evaluation. In addition to the cash flows derived from financial statements, ratio analysis offers another tool for use by loan officers. These inputs (ratios and cash flows) provide the nuts and bolts of credit analysis and potential variables for classification models designed to identify risky borrowers.

The Usefulness of Accounting Ratios to Loan Officers

Libby [1975] designed an experiment to determine whether accounting ratios provide useful information to loan officers trying to predict business failures.[12] Commercial bank loan officers were asked to use a set of five variables and analyze the ratios and then to predict either failure or nonfailure. Libby judged the usefulness of the accounting information on the basis of the accuracy of the loan officers' predictions.

Libby's sample consisted of 60 firms, divided equally between failed and nonfailed ones. He began the experiment with 14 ratios computed for *one* of the three years prior to failure (chosen at random), resulting in an equal number of firms for each of the three years before failure (10 failed and 10 nonfailed). Using a statistical technique called *principal components,* Libby identified five independent sources of variation from a 14-variable set. Box 10-1 presents the five dimensions and the five ratios and describes Libby's experiment.

Libby found that the loan officers' predictive accuracy was superior to random assignment (i.e., fail/nonfail) and concluded that they used the ratio information correctly. On the basis of other tests, Libby concluded that (1) no significant difference

---

[11] As explained in the next chapter, interest rates on credit cards have been sticky downward and notoriously high compared to other rates of interest. Thus, one has to question the financial soundness and judgment of borrowers who maintain high balances when the level of interest rates is low.

[12] Although Libby's [1975] experiment might be regarded as dated, the point here is to illustrate the application of financial data in the form of ratios.

BOX 10-1

THE USEFULNESS OF ACCOUNTING RATIOS TO LOAN OFFICERS

Dimension	Ratio
1. Profitability	Net income/total assets
2. Activity	Current assets/sales
3. Liquidity	Current assets/current liabilities
4. Asset balance	Current assets/total assets
5. Cash position	Cash/total assets

Libby's Experiment: Forty-three commercial loan officers participated in the experiment. Sixteen of the officers were from seven small banks located in Champaign-Urbana (CU), Illinois, with each bank providing one to four participants. Twenty-seven of the officers were from five large banks located in Philadelphia, with each bank providing two to eight participants. The typical loan officer was 39 years old, with 16.2 years of formal education and nine years of experience as a loan officer, processing between 51 and more than 250 loan applications annually. For the CU bankers, the average client's total assets were $127,000, whereas for the Philadelphia bankers they were $146,198,000. Libby reported that the CU bankers thought the Philadelphia bankers would win because they had greater experience in analyzing audited financial statements resulting from the larger client size of the Philadelphia market.

Each loan officer was given 70 data sets of five ratios each (60 firms and 10 repeat firms to check for consistency). To set the prior probabilities, the bankers were told that one-half of the firms experienced failure within three years of the statement date. The loan officers were instructed to work independently and to complete the cases within one week. They were told that a correct prediction was worth one point and an incorrect prediction cost one point. The loan officers were given the definition of failure and told that the sample firms were large industrial ones with independently audited financial statements.

existed between the mean predictive accuracy of the CU bankers and the Philadelphia bankers, in spite of the CU bankers' inferiority complex; (2) no significant correlations existed between predictive accuracy and loan officers' characteristics such as age, experience, and the like; (3) no differences existed in short-term, test-retest reliability between user subgroups; and (4) there was a relatively uniform interpretation of the accounting data across bankers.

On balance, he concluded that the set of five accounting ratios permitted bankers with diverse backgrounds to make accurate predictions of business failures. One important caveat, however, focuses on the prior probabilities given to the loan officers (i.e., one-half of the firms failed within three years). In the real world, lenders have to set their own prior probabilities. Without the preinformation, the loan officers' accuracy rates may not have been as high.

PRICING BUSINESS LOANS AND THE ROLE OF THE PRIME RATE: MYTH AND REALITY[13]

Using *Webster's* (seventh), the most appropriate definition of *prime* in terms of an adjective modifying rate is "first in excellence, quality, or value." Because a bank's

---

[13] This section bears a title similar to that of Fischer's [1982] study of the prime rate.

"prime-rate customers" are its most creditworthy, they are the ones who are first in excellence, quality, or value. In a risk-based pricing scheme, with other relevant factors held constant, such customers, as borrowers, deserve the lowest rate of interest. This explanation represents what the prime rate should be. What should be, however, is a myth when it comes to the actual practice of prime-rate pricing. The reality is that the prime rate is simply a benchmark off which rates for other borrowers can be set. The actual rate for an individual borrower could be *above* or *below* the prime rate depending on the borrower's overall creditworthiness. On balance, a lender's loan-pricing decision is not driven solely by the prime rate; it is a complex decision that depends on a number of factors. The *myth* of the prime rate has come from its *misinterpretation* as the *lowest* rate of interest available to a bank's best corporate customers. Some banks made the mistake of perpetuating this myth and, as a result, became involved in costly litigation in the early 1980s. The pathbreaking case was a class-action suit brought against the former First National Bank of Atlanta (now part of Wachovia Corporation). The foundation for the case was the contention that the bank overcharged prime-based borrowers by pegging their interest rate to the bank's *announced* prime rate rather than to the discount prime rate that was the *overall best* rate that corporate customers received. First Atlanta compounded its error when it permitted bank officers to engage in an abusive telephone campaign to attempt to coerce class members to drop out of the case.[14] In March 1984, First Atlanta agreed to an out-of-court settlement amounting to as much as $13.5 million. As a result, any lender who values his or her job today *never* refers to the prime rate as the *lowest* rate of interest charged by the bank. It is a benchmark rate. Depending on the borrower's overall relationship with the bank, the actual rate charged may be above or below the stated or announced prime rate.

Below-Prime Lending Is Not a New Phenomenon

Bankers have been lending at rates below the level of the accounted prime for a number of decades. In contrast, the discovery and publicity of the discount prime has been a more recent phenomenon. For example, consider the results of a Federal Reserve survey of the discount prime rate. The survey, taken during the week of May 5–10, 1980, revealed the posted prime rate to be in the range of 17.5 and 18.5 percent.[15] During this week, however, 53.0 percent of the short-term business loans made at 48 large banks were below the prime rate. The average discount was 413 basis points. In other words, the (unposted) discount prime rate was roughly 14 percent, compared to the posted prime rate of 18 percent. At other banks during this same week, the average discount was 26.8 percent, an average discount of 247 basis points. In contrast, for the week ending May 10, 1980, the three-month commercial paper rate was roughly 10 percent. Thus, a corporation with access to the commercial-paper market would have had bargaining power to get a discount from the posted prime rate.[16]

---

[14] The 11th Circuit Court of Appeals ruled in January 1985 to uphold a lower court's ruling that the bank's law firm and general counsel had committed an "ethical violation" in approving the phone campaign.

[15] Yes, the prime rate was that high in 1980. On February 1, 1996, the prime rate posted by at least 75 percent of the 30 largest U.S. banks was 8.25 percent. In contrast, rates on commercial paper ranged from 4.75 percent to 5.25 percent, which explains why the most creditworthy corporate borrowers will not borrow at the posted prime; they want and get discounts.

[16] During the week of November 5–9, 1990, the discounts had increased to 71.8 percent (large banks) and 51.5 percent (other banks). During November 1990, the three-month commercial paper rate was 7.91 percent, whereas the posted prime rate was 10 percent, a much narrower spread (209 bp) compared to the one (800 bp) in May of 1980.

The strategy of undercutting the prime rate has both advantages and disadvantages. On the plus side, the bank can keep its prime-rate customers happy by giving them discounts and still make a profit. For example, during the week that ended May 10, 1980, the three-month CD rate in the secondary market was 10.26 percent. With the discount prime rate at 14 percent, there was a 374-point spread to cover noninterest expenses and profit, assuming that the CD rate is the appropriate marginal cost of funds. On the minus side, the strategy runs the risk of alienating nonprime customers whose loans are tied to the *posted* prime rate and of incurring greater scrutiny about pricing practices from the banking authorities and the U.S. Congress. In addition, the practice of undercutting the prime rate can erode the effectiveness of the competitive restraints imposed by the coordinated use of the prime-rate and compensating-balance conventions. On balance, it is in the bank's interest to move the posted prime rate up quickly and down slowly. Moreover, if nonprime customers do not have alternative sources of funds and if the political risks are not costly, it makes economic sense to establish a discounted prime rate for good customers. Preferential treatment of good customers is a common practice in any business, and banking is no exception.

Customer Relationships, Compensating Balances, and the Prime Rate

The customer-relationship, compensation-balance, and prime-rate conventions are integral parts of the bank loan-pricing function.[17] The fact that bank loan (and investment) policies have been strategically subordinated to the customer-service aspects of banking has been stressed by Hodgman [1963]. Hodgman contends that these practices have evolved for the purpose of restricting interbank competition for prime depositor-borrower customers. Because banks like customers who have large deposit balances, borrow regularly, and have been with the bank for a long time, these customers receive preferential treatment, especially when credit is tight. Such characteristics usually are associated with commercial or corporate customers; they are the bank's prime depositor-borrower customers. Kane and Malkiel [1965] refer to these customers as a bank's L* (read L-star) customers. They are depositors-borrowers whose relationships play an important and favorable role in calculations of the bank's expected profits and aggregate risk exposure, which explains why they receive preferential treatment.

According to Hodgman, the coordinated use of the compensating-balance and prime-rate conventions may serve as an effective device to restrain interbank competition for L* customers. With a national prime rate and generally accepted minimum compensating-balance requirements, the extension of credit, especially when money is tight, and the provision of customer service are the key instruments in interbank competition for L* customers. Kane and Malkiel stress that to turn down L* requests for loan accommodation is to introduce explicit and ascertainable risks of customer alienation that could endanger deposit relationships. On balance, the concept of the *customer relationship* represents the strategic combination of customer service, loans, and deposits that gives commercial banking its unique institutional character.

---

[17] A *compensating balance* is the percentage of the borrower's loan that must be kept on deposit with the bank as additional compensation for the loan. If the balance requirement is effective, then it increases the effective cost of the loan because the borrower does not have use of the entire amount borrowed.

The Options Available to Lenders and Borrowers

Let's look, in a nontechnical way, at the options available to lenders and borrowers.[18] Lenders have the option to

1. Lend or not to lend
2. Price on a fixed- or variable-rate basis
3. Tailor the nonrate provisions of the loan agreement to suit the needs of the borrower and to protect the interests of the bank
4. Call the loan

In contrast, borrowers have the option to

1. Take their business elsewhere
2. Default
3. Pay slowly
4. Prepay with or without refinancing

Recognition of these options serves to highlight the importance of the overall customer relationship to the lending process. For example, consider the potential ramifications for the customer relationship of the lender's decision to refuse a loan request, to price a loan too high, to make nonrate provisions too restrictive, or to call a loan at an inopportune time for the borrower. Moreover, because the customer relationship is a two-way street, the borrower must be aware of the consequences of defaulting, paying slowly, or prepaying loans without refinancing.[19]

Prime-Plus versus Prime-Time Pricing

A common banking practice is to price credit on the basis of markups on the **prime rate.** The standard procedure is an additive one such that borrowers are quoted something like "prime + 2," which means the prime plus 200 basis points, or 2 percent. Given the existence of the discount prime rate, certain L* customers might be quoted "prime − 2."

An alternative to prime-plus pricing is prime-times pricing, which is a multiplicative formula rather than an additive one. In general, this pricing procedure can be expressed as

$$\text{Quoted rate} = \text{Multiplicative Adjustment Factor} \times \text{Prime Rate}$$

where the adjustment factor can be greater (premium) or less than (discount) 1. To illustrate, if the prime rate is 10 percent and the adjustment factor is 1.1, then the borrower is quoted a rate of 11 percent = 1.1 × 10 percent. Suppose that the spread between the quoted rate and the prime rate accurately compensates the bank for the borrower's greater default risk relative to that of a prime borrower. In this case, the prime-plus formula would be prime + 1. However, notice what happens if rates change. Suppose that the prime increases by 100 basis points to 11 percent. If the borrower has a variable-rate loan outstanding, it would reprice to 12 percent under the additive rule. However, under the multiplicative formula, the loan would reprice

---

[18] Option-pricing theory (OPT) focuses upon the analysis of the determinants of the prices of contingent claims or options. One of the interesting areas of OPT research has been its application to the valuation of the complex options involved in loan agreements (e.g., the default and prepayment options). Lenders need to understand when and how borrowers will be tempted to trade against them in loan agreements.

[19] To discourage prepayments, lenders can build prepayment penalties into loan agreements.

to 12.1 percent (1.1 × 11 percent). In contrast, if the prime rate falls by 100 basis points (from 10 percent to 9 percent), the loan would reprice at 10 percent under the plus scheme and at 9.9 percent under the multiplicative approach.

Assuming that the loan is priced correctly when the multiplicative factor is set, and assuming that the prime rate is at some historic norm (i.e., it is neither too high nor too low), the prime-times approach has an adjustment procedure implying that as interest rates increase, the borrower is more likely to default. Accordingly, the bank is entitled to greater compensation because it is bearing more risk. Moreover, the prime-times approach is symmetrical because it implies that when rates are declining, borrowers are more likely to be able to repay their loans. Accordingly, it permits them to share this reduced risk with lenders by receiving a lower loan rate.

A RISK-MANAGEMENT APPROACH TO COMMERCIAL LOAN PRICING

Once the decision to grant credit has been made, the **terms of the loan** must be set, including the price of the loan or its rate of interest. Nonprice terms include such items as compensating-balance requirements, size of the loan, maturity, and collateral requirements. The concept of loan pricing within a risk-return framework is presented in Figure 10-2. Using the credit-scoring concept to capture the risk element in lending, both the decision to grant credit and a risk-based pricing scheme are illustrated.

FIGURE 10-2 **Loan Pricing**

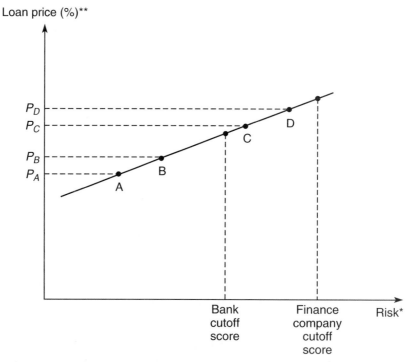

*Risk can be viewed as measured by a credit score, where a low score is "good" and a high score is "bad."
**Loan price is the interest rate required by the bank to provide the loan.

Credit scoring refers to predicting the creditworthiness of would-be borrowers using a statistical model. Although the approach has been used mainly in consumer lending, it can also be applied to business lending. Given the bank's cutoff score as shown in Figure 10-2, all customers with scores below it are eligible for credit. Within this group, the less risky a customer is, the lower the loan price will be, other things being equal. For example, as depicted in Figure 10-2, customer *A* has a better credit score than customer *B*, and therefore *A* is charged a lower price than *B*. Customers *C* and *D*, who are denied credit by the bank, are not excluded from the credit market; they are acceptable risks for the finance company. Because customer *C* is more creditworthy than customer *D*, *C* is charged a lower price than *D* by the finance company. In practice, bank loan losses are relatively low compared to those at finance companies. As a result, finance companies have to charge higher rates of interest.

Loan pricing usually involves some combination of target ROE and markup pricing. Buck [1979] has suggested a risk-management approach to pricing loans that employs these concepts. The basic idea in his framework is to develop a unique target price for each loan, including adjustments for identifiable risks and costs. He defines the profit element as a margin over the cost and risk factors. Thus, the target price equals the cost factor plus the risk factor plus the profit margin. To illustrate, consider the following example:[20]

Profit margin	1.34%
Costs:	
Funds	8.00%
Overhead	0.75%
Risks:	
Credit	1.25%
Maturity	0.75%
Collateral value	0.25%
Target price	12.34%

Let's consider the components of the target price. To calculate the target profit margin, the bank is required to establish a desired ROE. Given the bank's leverage (L) and its tax rate (t), Buck shows that the margin (M) is

$$M = \frac{ROE \times L}{1-t} - (L \times C)$$

where C is the bank's cost of funds and L its ratio of capital to assets, the inverse of the equity multiplier. Note that the term $(ROE \times L)/(1-t)$ is pretax ROA. Given target $ROE = 15$ percent, $L = 10$ percent, $t = 30$ percent, and $C = 8$ percent, the value of M is 1.34 percent, that is,

$$M = \frac{0.15 \times 0.10}{0.7} - 0.10 \times .08 = 0.0134$$

Pretax ROA in this case is 2.14 percent ($= (0.15 \times 0.1)/0.7$).

To determine the costs associated with a loan, the bank needs to know its cost of funds and its overhead or administrative expenses for the loan function. The cost

---

[20] The cost of funds in this example can be viewed as the weighted-average marginal cost of capital. The target price, then, is a risk-adjusted discount rate if the profit margin is excluded.

of funds should reflect the marginal cost of all funds used to support the loan. The administrative costs of the loan function usually are based on functional-cost data, cost-accounting figures allocated to average assets, or the bank's best estimates of the costs. According to Buck, the particular method is not important as long as management is satisfied that the costs of the loan function are covered. Total costs (8.75 percent), which are the sum of the money (8 percent) and overhead expenses (0.75 percent), enter the target-price calculation.

Regarding the risk components, credit, maturity, and collateral-value risks are considered in the example. The credit-risk premium could be provided by a credit-scoring model or by a markup scheme based upon Moody's ratings. For example, the latter might be expressed as follows:

Rating	Credit-Risk Premium
Aaa	0.25%
Aa	0.50%
A	0.75%
Baa	1.25%
Ba	2.00%
B or below	No credit granted

The borrower in this example is assumed to have a Baa rating, and therefore a risk premium of 1.25 percent is assigned. The longer the maturity of a loan, the greater is the interest-rate risk and the risk that the borrower's creditworthiness might deteriorate. As a result, the longer the maturity of a loan, the larger the maturity-risk premium should be. Variable-rate loans can be used to offset interest-rate risk. However, a maturity-risk premium still might be required to compensate for potential deterioration in the borrower's credit strength. *Collateral-value risk* refers to potential decreases in collateral value relative to the loan balance for a secured loan. Collateral that is expected to hold its value over the term of the loan (e.g., corporate aircraft) will have little collateral-value risk, whereas collateral that depreciates more rapidly (e.g., restaurant equipment) has greater collateral-value risk. A simple way to classify collateral-value risk is to use *good, average,* and *poor* categories. In the preceding example, the maturity-risk factor is 0.75 percent (indicating an intermediate-term loan), and the collateral-value factor is 0.25 percent (indicating average risk). The sum of these components equals the target price of 12.34 percent.

The target price of 12.34 percent can be translated into our prime-plus or price-times formulas as follows. Let's assume that the prime rate is 9 percent (= 8 percent cost of money, 0.75 percent overhead, and 0.25 percent credit risk). The target price of 12 percent translates into a prime-plus formula of prime + 3.34%, and a prime-times formula of 1.37 × prime.

The loan-pricing framework discussed in this section is a practical one that builds on the fundamental concepts of a risk-return trade-off and a target ROE. Although the determination and implementation of the loan-pricing mechanism requires some subjective judgments about the cost and risk components of the target price, the establishment of such a framework provides a foundation for consistent decision making by loan officers. Another factor that could be incorporated into the analysis is the portfolio-risk premium discussed in chapter 6. A loan that promises diversification benefits is more valuable to the bank's loan portfolio than one that lacks this potential. The former deserves a discount, whereas the latter might even be assessed a surcharge.

LOAN PRICING AND TERMS OF LENDING FOR C&I LOANS[21]

Large business loans, which account for the bulk of all business loans, are made under two types of credit facilities: (1) lines of credit, or *lines,* and (2) loan commitments, or *commitments.* Lines, which are relatively informal arrangements, oblige banks, on the borrower's request (option), to quote a price on a fixed-rate loan for a particular amount and maturity (usually under one year) within the limits specified by the arrangement. Typically, lines are priced by marking up a reference or base rate, traditionally the prime rate, for the same maturity as the loan. For example, a 30-day loan would be priced off the rate on a 30-day CD. Such arrangements provide banks with full pricing flexibility. The size of the markup is used to regulate the dollar amount of loans outstanding, because the borrower is offered an all-in rate (i.e., the base rate plus the markup) on a take-it-or-leave-it basis.

In contrast, loan commitments, unlike lines, require banks to lend up to the committed amount as long as the borrower meets the restrictions (loan covenants) specified by the contract. The unused credit available under a commitment is subject to a fee. The most common type of loan commitment is a revolving one, or revolver. Under this form of committed facility, the borrower draws funds up to a specified credit limit at a preestablished spread over the base rate. The loan can be repaid in part or in full at any time during the term of the commitment. From the borrower's perspective, revolvers are attractive because they reduce uncertainty about the price and availability of credit over the life of the agreement. From the bank's perspective, revolvers expose banks to interest-rate risks, liquidity risk, capital-adequacy risk, and credit risk. On the plus side, the bank receives a commitment fee from the borrower that secures the revolver.

Loans available under revolving arrangements typically are priced in one of two ways: (1) at a rate tied to the bank's prime rate with no set maturity, or (2) at a rate linked to a money-market rate, such as LIBOR or a CD rate, with a fixed maturity (e.g., 30, 90, or 180 days) selected by the borrower. Regarding the money-market pricing scheme, some customers enter into agreements with banks that permit them to borrow domestic dollars from the bank's head office or Eurodollars from one of its foreign branches. This arrangement is called an either/or facility. According to Stigum and Branch ([1983], p. 285), since the early 1980s, every large-term loan negotiated by a major corporation with a money-market bank has contained an either/or option. In addition, many line and loan agreements for major loans have been written without compensating-balance requirements. These deviations from the prime-rate and compensating-balance conventions are a reflection of the metamorphosis taking place in bank business lending.

The overwhelming majority of C&I loans tend to be short-term ones. The general terms of lending for short-term C&I loans made by large commercial banks can be described as follows. Large banks, relative to other (smaller) banks, tend to make larger short-term C&I loans; at lower, and primarily fixed, rates with the Fed funds rate (as opposed to the prime rate) as the most common base pricing rate; and for shorter maturities. These results, which are not unexpected, are interesting for the insights they give us about the competitiveness of the C&I loan market faced by large banks and their borrowers. Specifically, C&I borrowers from large banks obtain more financing at lower and fixed rates, but for shorter periods, than customers with other banks. Of course, the underlying causes of these

---

[21] This section draws on a Federal Reserve study by Brady [1985].

differences can most likely be traced to the size, creditworthiness, and greater number of alternatives (e.g., commercial paper) open to borrowers who take down loans that average over $1 million. As L* customers, these borrowers are the ones most likely to receive concessions from their banks (e.g., discounts from the prime rate).

For the typical long-term C&I loan, the general description of the terms of lending is similar to that for a short-term C&I loan. One basic difference, however, is the tendency of large banks to shift the base rate from the federal funds rate to a domestic rate, where *domestic* refers to a money-market rate (e.g., the negotiable CD rate) other than the federal-funds rate.

Terms of Lending for Loans to Farmers

Energy, agricultural, developing-country, and commercial real-estate loans were trouble spots in the U.S. banking system during the 1980s and the early 1990s. At the beginning of 1988, analysts and bank regulators were predicting that the farm lending crisis had bottomed out. The terms of lending for loans to farmers made by large banks and other banks provide some evidence about the nature of the farm lending crisis and why it started to bottom out in 1988.

Focusing on the purpose of the loan, large banks make farm loans for two basic purposes: feeder livestock and other current operating expenses. Other (smaller) banks make loans to farmers for the same purposes, but the proportions differ, because they make more loans for current operating expenses and fewer loans for feeder livestock. For large farm loans (i.e., those for $250,000 or more), slightly more than one-half of the dollar volume is made for feeder livestock. Obviously, only urban bankers take seriously the adage: "Don't take anything as collateral that eats." In general, most small loans to farmers are made to cover current operating expenses such as seed, fertilizer, fuel, labor, and the like.

Comparing the typical farm loan made by a large bank with the one made by a smaller bank, we find that community banks make many small loans to farmers for longer terms and at higher rates than large banks. Both groups of banks make primarily floating-rate loans. In contrast, large banks make most of their loans on a commitment basis, whereas other banks are less inclined to do so.

"HUNTERS" VERSUS "SKINNERS": THE PROBLEMS OF INCENTIVES, DISCIPLINE, MONITORING, AND CONCENTRATIONS OF CREDITS

Bankers who work as calling officers today will tell you they are salespersons. They sell banking products and services. The basic product they sell is credit. However, since the credit end of the business has become so competitive, bankers who cannot cross-sell are finding their bottom lines (and their bonuses) shrinking. Nevertheless, selling credit and credit-related products is the name of the game. Bankers who specialize in selling can be viewed as "hunters." Their job is to go out and "hunt down" customers, bringing the "carcasses" (i.e., financial statements and other customer information) back to the bank for "skinning." The job of the "skinner" (sometimes referred to as credit gurus or green eyeshades) is to spread the financials and determine the creditworthiness of the customers. If the hunters are paid up-front fees for bringing in new business, then it is imperative that a system of checks and balances be in place to ensure that they do not give away the shop. One can also see the potential for conflict when the hunters and skinners are at odds regarding a customer's creditworthiness. However, consider the incentive problems that could arise if the hunter also did the skinning. One way to avoid this potential problem when the hunter and skinner roles are combined is to make the hunter/skinner responsible for the ultimate outcome of the credit (e.g., up-front fees may be reduced by back-end penalties). Economic incentives and disincentives in the form of bonuses, fees, penalties, and accountability (i.e., responsibility for one's actions) are the keys to motivating and disciplining people.

Monitoring by Loan Classifications

A well-diversified loan portfolio offers protection against various kinds of risk, and provides an internal safety net for bank shareholders and uninsured creditors. To achieve this diversification, especially for small banks in restricted geographic markets, is not an easy task. Even if a bank can diversify, it requires internal controls in the form of monitoring mechanisms to ensure that diversification is maintained. In this regard, banks have numerous internal codes or methods for classifying loans designed to monitor concentrations of credits. Some common ways that bankers classify loans are the following:

> *Purpose (type) of loan:* seasonal, working capital, mortgage, construction, development, small business, personal, education, home improvement, mobile home, auto, RV, boat, credit card, refinancing, lease, and so on.
>
> *Collateral type:* land, buildings, equipment, manufactured goods, assignments (e.g., government contracts), receivables, investment securities and savings, livestock (Lenders quip: "Don't take anything as collateral that eats"), farm crops, and so on.
>
> *Rate:* floating versus fixed.
>
> *SIC code:* The Standard Industrial Classification (SIC) System provides a numerical scheme, developed by the U.S. Bureau of the Budget, to classify businesses by type of activity. Since loans to businesses engaged in the same activity present a concentration of risk, monitoring by SIC code provides valuable information.
>
> *Credit rating:* AAA, AA, A, and so on (if available).
>
> *Domestic versus foreign:* To monitor country risk exposure,[22] foreign loans are classified by country. "MBA loans" (i.e., to Mexico, Brazil, and Argentina) were a problem for the money-center banks during the 1980s.

To summarize, bankers have various ways of classifying credits. These schemes are valuable because they give lenders a systematic way of monitoring concentrations of credits. Avoiding such concentrations provides a bank with an internal safety net based on the principle of portfolio diversification.

CREDIT ANALYSIS AND THE JOB OF A CREDIT ANALYST

Commercial bankers have considerable reputations as credit analysts. The job of a credit analyst is to assess the **financial performance** (past, current, and projected or pro forma) of credit applicants to determine their creditworthiness. The farther to the right a credit applicant is on the borrower-information continuum in Figure 10-1, the easier the task is, because of access to high-quality, low-cost information. A

---

[22] Regarding country risk, the Coca-Cola Company (still a nonbanking company as of 1997) has an interesting philosophy: Its top management does not worry about, nor does it attempt to measure or monitor, country risk. Why? Whatever happens in a country, they firmly believe that people will always drink their products. Therefore, why worry about country risk and spend resources trying to monitor it? Could a money-center bank adopt the same philosophical approach?

truer test of a credit analyst's ability comes from evaluating borrowers with low-quality information that is costly to obtain. After credit evaluations are completed, credit analysts need to communicate their decisions within the bank.

The Tools Commercial Lenders Need and Use

A good exercise to demonstrate one of the most important tasks that commercial lenders have to do, and one that pulls together the various tools they need, is to practice writing a credit memo.[23] Seven keys in preparing such memoranda are:

- Brevity (your boss does not have time to read a tome, as Bill Tome would say)
- Interpret the information
- Concentrate on facts
- Put yourself in the role of the user
- Maintain a "big-picture perspective"
- Understand the risk (business and banking)
- Understand how the business functions

Given these points, credit memos need to focus on four key areas:

- *Management (Who are we lending to?):* Important areas to analyze here include stability, past performance, depth, reputation, planning (e.g., projected performance of the company), and strengths and weaknesses

- *Company Operations (What do they do and how do they do it?):* Important areas to analyze here include definition of market (product and geographic), structure of the industry, the four Ps of marketing (price, product, promotion, and place),and how they relate to the market and industry degree of competition and substitutes, and basic operations of the business

- *Industry (What does the company face?):* Important areas to analyze here include structure (e.g., cyclical, seasonal, ease of entry/exit, regulated, unionized, etc.), description of the industry, company's position within the industry, position on the product life cycle, industry trends, future concerns, and external concerns

- *Financial Performance (What is quantitative ability to repay?):* Important areas to analyze here include interpretation of the numbers, analysis and reflection of financial statements (balance sheet, income-expense, and cash flow), understanding trends and changes, and how change in financial performance affects business risk

Successful commercial lenders need good communication skills (verbal and written) and, as evidenced by the above list, knowledge of finance, accounting, economics, management, and marketing—the core of the business-school curriculum. Throw in some computer-science skills and you have the complete package. Nevertheless, given our distinction between hunters and skinners, if marketing, management, and an outgoing personality are your strengths, you could be a hunter (e.g., a salesperson whose task is to cross-sell bank credit *and* noncredit products); in contrast, if your strengths are number crunching and spreading financial statements on a PC, you could be a skinner. In some banks, especially small ones, you might have to be both a hunter and a skinner.

Panels A, B, and C of Table 10-4 show sample forms that might be used to summarize the information needed to write a credit memo. Panel A summarizes the company's background, Panel B presents a market/industry/economic summary,

---

[23] Bill Tome, formerly with C&S (later C&S/Sovran and now NationsBank), was the catalyst in helping me develop this exercise.

TABLE 10-4   Information Used in Writing Bank Credit Memos

Panel A. Company Background

Customer:	Analyst:
	Statements received:
	Memo distributed:
Address:	
	Relationship manager:
	Location:
Business:	Division:
Form of organization:	Total exposure:
Established:	Last credit committee review:
Customer since:	(date/committee/statement)
SIC:	
Current FY sales: $	Present rating:
Change from last yr. %:	Recommended rating:

Last agency report: ( ) D&B   ( ) TRW

Bond rating:	Date: ( ) Other:
Commercial paper rating:	
Commercial paper O/S:	Trade experience: ( ) Favorable
	( ) Unfavorable; see report
Total bank lines: $	attached
Lead bank:	
Other lenders:	

Management summary
Principal/officers

name	position	yr. of birth	% ownership	date employed	total compensation

Company/management background and changes:

(Continued)

TABLE 10-4 *Continued*

Panel B. Market/Industry/Economic Summary

Company:

Date:

Section I: market

  Geographic market area:

  Market strategy/niche:

  Assessment of principal customers, suppliers, and product lines:

  Competition:

Section II: industry and economic

  Impact of significant industry and economic factors that affect this company

Panel C. Financial Analysis

Company:

Date:

Section I: financial statements

Statements

Company Name	type F, I	date	prepared by	scope	opinion

Accounting changes or qualifications

Guarantors

Name	amount of guaranty	net worth	statement date	signed?	joint statement

Valuation of guarantees:

Section II: strengths and weaknesses

Strengths: **Weaknesses:**

Problems to which this company is most vulnerable:

and Panel C highlights the financial analysis. If you like what you see in Table 10-4 (as a job description), you might have the potential to be a hunter or a skinner or both.

CLASSIFICATION MODELS AND EMPIRICAL EVIDENCE

Classification models (also called "artificial intelligence") are statistical devices that can be used as tools to complement decision making. For example, credit-scoring models attempt to distinguish between good borrowers and bad ones, bankruptcy-prediction models attempt to differentiate between bankrupt firms and nonbankrupt firms, and problem-bank models attempt to separate problem banks from nonproblem institutions. As devices conceived as artificial intelligence, these models are designed to replicate the decisions of an expert in the field. Although these kinds of models can be used for making final decisions, they are best viewed as tools or aids to decision making. In the areas of consumer lending, especially with respect to credit cards, however, some banks and other businesses use them for making final decisions (chapter 11). In this section, we look at some of these models and their potential application to the decision making related to the granting and monitoring of business loans.

Decision Trees Applied to Loan Classification and Financial Distress

Decision trees can be used to develop binary classification rules to assign observations to a priori groups (e.g., bankrupt vs. nonbankrupt or good loan vs. bad loan). A technique that lends itself to a decision-tree framework is classification and regression trees (CART). It differs from the more widely used classification models (such as discriminant, logit, or probit analyses) because it is a nonparametric or distribution-free technique.[24] Because nonparametric techniques are not specifically related to the parameters of a given population, they are called distribution-free tests. The main advantages of these tests are (1) possibility of use under very general conditions, (2) ease of understanding, and, in some cases, (3) ease of computation.

Marais, Pattell, and Wolfson [1984] and Frydman, Altman, and Kao [1985] have applied CART, under the name of "recursive partitioning," to the problems of classifying commercial bank loans according to default risk and predicting financial distress (corporate bankruptcy), respectively. For the case of bankruptcy prediction, the construction of a classification tree is illustrated in Figure 10-3. Although the statistics behind the tree are quite complex, they need not concern us here. The classification tree, however, is easy to understand. Let's walk through it.

We begin with 200 firms, 58 bankrupt ones and 142 nonbankrupt ones. The first variable to enter the tree is the ratio of cash flow to total debt. This variable enters because it is an important one for distinguishing between the sample firms,

---

[24] Altman, Avery, Eisenbeis, and Sinkey [1981] summarize the application of parametric classification techniques in business, banking, and finance. See Breiman, Friedman, Olshen, and Stone [1984] for a description of RPA or CART. For comparisons of applications of parametric and nonparametric classification techniques, see Holt, Scarpello, and Carroll [1983], Marais, Patell, and Wolfson [1984], Frydman, Altman, and Kao [1985], and Srinivasan and Kim [1987]. Appendix C of this chapter presents a model of credit granting for a nonfinancial corporation.

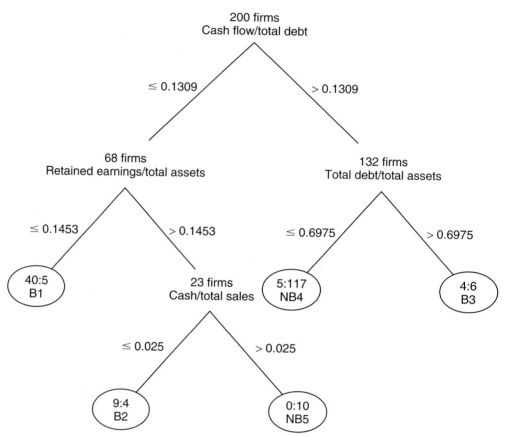

Source: Frydman, Altman, and Kao [1985], Figure 1, p. 272. Used by permission

FIGURE 10-3 **Example of a Classification Tree Applied to the Identification of Bankrupt Firms**

which is not surprising given the importance finance attaches to cash flow. Firms with a ratio greater than 0.1309 go to the right branch of the tree, others to the left. We now have 68 firms on the left and 132 on the right. Focusing on the right branch, the first variable to enter on this side of the tree is the ratio of total debt to total assets, a measure of leverage. Firms with values greater than 0.6975 go to the right and others to the left. In this case, the right branch produces two terminal nodes (indicated by ovals). We will discuss their meaning in a moment. Focusing on the left branch with its 68 firms, the ratio of retained earnings to total assets, a measure of long-term profitability, splits these firms into groups of 45 and 23 firms, with 0.1453 as the critical value. Since the left branch of this split is terminal, the right branch splits again on the basis of the ratio of cash to total sales, a measure of liquidity, with 0.025 as the splitting value. When each branch of the tree ends with a terminal node, the construction of the tree is complete.

To assess the classification accuracy of the tree, we focus on the terminal nodes. The ovals with a *B* in them are bankruptcy nodes; those with *NB* are nonbankruptcy nodes. We have three bankruptcy nodes, labeled *B*1, *B*2, and *B*3, and two nonbankruptcy nodes, labeled *NB*4 and *NB*5. In each node for each group, we count the numbers to the right and the left of the colon. In the *B* nodes, we get 53 (= 40 + 9 + 4) to the left of the colon. These are the bankrupt firms identified as bankrupt firms. The numbers to the right of the colon are the nonbankrupt firms identified as bankrupt ones (i.e., $15 = 5 + 4 + 6$). The classification accuracy rate for the bankrupt firms is $53/58 = 91.4$ percent; for the nonbankrupt firms, it is $127/142 = 89.4$ percent. We get the same results if we look at the two *NB* nodes. Try it. The overall accuracy rate is $180/200$, or 90 percent, which is quite good.

What makes CART, or recursive partitioning, attractive is its combination of multivariate analysis in conjunction with simple splits based on a single variable. Although the statistics behind the tree are quite complex, but no more complex than those behind parametric techniques, the use of the tree procedure has great intuitive appeal.

The application of CART by Marais, Patell, and Wolfson focused on a loan-classification model. Bank examiners and most bank internal review committees classify loans into one of five categories based on the degree of *perceived* default risk, a subjective procedure that is difficult to quantify. The usual risk categories are as follows:

1. *Current.*   If a loan is current, it is being paid back on schedule and is perceived to be an acceptable banking risk. The opposite is a noncurrent loan or one that is delinquent or nonperforming.

2. *Especially Mentioned.*   A loan in this category usually has some minor problem (e.g., incomplete documentation) requiring it to be "criticized." However, the problem is not severe enough to warrant the loan being "adversely classified."

3. *Substandard.*   A loan in this category has weaknesses presenting some chance of default. The weaknesses, however, are usually correctable. The bank regulatory weight attached to the category implies a 20 percent chance of default.

4. *Doubtful.*   A loan in this category has considerable weakness and the bank most likely has a 50 percent chance of sustaining a loss.

5. *Loss.*   A loan in this category is deemed to be uncollectible. Such loans are usually written or charged off.

Most bankers and their examiners regard the last three classes, the substandard, doubtful, and loss categories, as "adversely classified assets."

Marais, Patell, and Wolfson analyzed 921 loans consisting of 839 current loans, 37 especially mentioned loans, 32 substandard loans, and 13 doubtful loans. They had no loss loans in their sample, which consisted of 716 loans to private firms and 205 loans to public firms. Marais, Patell, and Wolfson used 13 standard financial ratios and 13 other variables to construct their models. Although they used the CART methodology, they did not present a tree diagram of their results. Accordingly, it is difficult to summarize their findings compactly. From the perspective of bank loan officers and the credit decision-making process, their most important finding is in line with Libby's conclusion, namely, financial statements provide useful information for credit decisions, although the statements of private firms are not quite as accurate for classification purposes as those of public firms.

Zeta Analysis

Zeta analysis is a term coined by Altman, Haldeman, and Narayanan [1977] to describe their model for identifying the bankruptcy risk of corporations. They found the following seven variables to be good discriminators between failed and non-failed business firms:

1. *Return on assets,* measured by EBIT/total assets

2. *Stability of earnings,* measured by the inverse of the standard error of estimate around a 10-year trend in return on assets

3. *Debt service,* measured by *EBIT*/total interest payments

4. *Cumulative profitability,* measured by retained earnings (BS)/total assets

5. *Liquidity,* measured by current assets/current liabilities

6. *Capitalization,* measured by a five-year average market value of the firm's common stock/total long-term capital

7. *Size,* measured by the firm's total assets

EBIT stands for earnings before interest and taxes, and retained earnings (BS) means that the retained earnings are taken from the firm's balance sheet. These seven variables are designed to measure the following dimensions: (1) current profitability, (2) risk or variability of return, (3) interest coverage, (4) long-run profitability, (5) liquidity, (6) leverage, and (7) size. Because the coefficients of the Zeta model are not publicly available, we use Altman's [1968] model to illustrate the use of this kind of bankruptcy-prediction model. Altman's model has five variables:

$$X_1 = \frac{\text{Working Capital}}{\text{Total Assets}}$$

$$X_2 = \frac{\text{Retained Earnings}}{\text{Total Assets}}$$

$$X_3 = \frac{\text{EBIT}}{\text{Total Assets}} \tag{10-2}$$

$$X_4 = \frac{\text{Market Value of Equity}}{\text{Book Value of Total Debt}}$$

$$X_5 = \frac{\text{Sales}}{\text{Total Assets}}$$

By the way, both the 1968 model and the Zeta model employ a statistical technique called multiple discriminant analysis (MDA). The objective of MDA is to find the set of variables that best discriminates between the two groups, in Altman's case failed and nonfailed firms. Altman's linear MDA or Z-score equation is

$$Z = 1.2X_1 + 1.4X_2 + 3.3X_3 + 0.6X_4 + 1.0X_5 \tag{10-3}$$

The classification rule for Equation (10-3) is

1. If $Z < 2.675$, assign to the bankrupt group

2. If $Z \geq 2.675$, assign to the nonbankrupt group

Because Altman found that misclassifications occurred in the Z-score range of 1.81 to 2.99, he referred to this overlap area as the "zone of ignorance."

Application of Altman's Z-Score Model[25]

Altman [1968] contends that his model could be used to complement (1) business-loan evaluations, (2) accounts-receivable management, (3) internal-control procedures, and (4) investment strategies. Regarding business-loan evaluations, Altman suggests using his "quantitative" model to complement the "more qualitative and

---

[25] This section draws on chapter 7 of my 1981 book (with Altman, Avery, and Eisenbeis) entitled *Application of Classification Techniques in Business, Banking, and Finance.*

intuitive" approach of loan officers. However, he is careful to point out that the model is not a credit-scoring mechanism or a substitute for the evaluations of loan officers. He argues that the model and its generated Z-scores could be a valuable tool for determining the overall creditworthiness of business customers.

One of the most important tasks that a bank loan officer performs is the evaluation of a firm's policies and managerial skills, factors that ultimately determine how well a company performs. Direct measurement of the effectiveness of managerial skills and policies is a difficult task. Consequently, indirect measurement frequently is employed using comparative ratio analysis. Ratios, of course, reflect symptoms, not causes. However, by identifying atypical or abnormal ratios, one can identify problem areas and investigate the cause(s) of the difficulty. Altman's model can be used to rate a company's overall performance (by means of its Z-score) and to pinpoint problem areas (by means of individual ratios). To illustrate this type of application, consider the following example derived from "How to Figure Who's Going Bankrupt," *Dun's Review* [October 1975]. In this article, Z-scores for some 1,200 publicly owned companies were computed. The companies with the 14 highest and 14 lowest Z-scores were listed. In this example, we analyze four companies with the following Z-scores: (1) highest, (2) lowest, (3) highest of the 14 lowest, and (4) lowest of the 14 highest. The Z-scores and ratios for these four companies (Taylor Wine, Memorex, Telex, and Data General) are presented in Table 10-5.

According to Altman's classification rule, Memorex and Telex were headed for bankruptcy, whereas Data General and especially Taylor Wine were performing very well. The managers of Memorex and Telex should have been concerned about their low Z-scores—and their jobs. Moreover, bank managers should have been concerned about making loans to these companies. Looking at Memorex's profile of five variables, it is clear that as of year-end 1974, the company had serious profitability (both current and cumulative), liquidity, and solvency problems. Because the Z-score to Telex (1.78) is quite close to Altman's "zone of ignorance" (i.e., $1.81 - 2.99$), one has less confidence in its prediction of insolvency. However, relative to Memorex's ratios, Telex's five-variable profile is superior. In terms of contribution to Z-score, the cumulative-profitability variable (X_2) accounts for the greatest difference in the Memorex-Telex Z-score spread. For example, if Memorex had Telex's X_2 ratio and vice versa, the Z-score would be Memorex 1.16 and Telex 1.36. As indicated in Table 10-6, Memorex and Telex did *not* go bankrupt. In fact both companies turned their operations around. It is interesting to note that

TABLE 10-5   Z-Scores: Best and Worst Performers

Company[a]	Z-score[b]	Ratios				
		X_1	X_2	X_3	X_4	X_5
Taylor Wine (6/74)	304.09	0.52	0.61	0.24	501.45	0.97
Data General (9/74)	36.32	0.47	0.31	0.27	55.45	1.17
Telex (3/75)	1.78	0.22	−0.19	0.13	0.35	1.12
Memorex (12/74)	0.74	0.19	−0.49	0.04	0.25	0.92

[a]The figures in parentheses beside the company name indicate the date of the data, except for the X_4 data, which are as of year-end 1974.

[b]The Z-scores are calculated using Equation (10-3). Going across the table, the discriminant coefficients are 1.2, 1.4, 3.3, 0.6, and 1.0, respectively.

Source: Dun's Review (October 1975), p. 65. Copyright 1975. Dun & Bradstreet, a company of The Dun & Bradstreet Corporation. Reprinted by permission.

TABLE 10-6 Stock Prices: Best and Worst Z-Scores				
	Closing Prices			
Company (Exchange)	*12/31/74*	*10/12/76*	*4/7/81*	*1/28/88*
Taylor Wine (OTC)	$10^3/_8$	$17^3/_8$	a	a
Data General (NYSE)	$12^7/_8$	$44^1/_8$	$55^3/_4$	$26^1/_2$
Telex (NYSE)	$2^1/_4$	$2^1/_2$	$8^1/_8$	48
Memorex (OTC/PSE/NYSE)	3^b	$21^1/_4$	12	NA

[a]In July 1977, Taylor Wine was acquired by the Coca-Cola Company.
[b]Indicates average of high ($4^3/_4$) and low ($1^1/_4$) prices for the year 1974. Telex's 1975 high was $^3/_4$; its low was $^1/_4$.
Source: Data from *The Wall Street Journal* and *Moody's Industrial Manual.*

Telex received substantial financial assistance from Bank of America in its recovery. One of the problems with statistical models is their inability to take into account the customer relationship that is so important in commercial banking.

It is important to understand in what sense Altman's Z-scores (or the scores from any classification model) are predictions or forecasts. A prediction or forecast usually involves a statement at time t about some future event, at time $t + k$ (e.g., predictions about tomorrow's weather, future interest rates, or next year's GNP). Such forecasts usually incorporate expectational variables, such as anticipated movements of weather systems, expected rates of inflation, and anticipated consumer and investment expenditures. Because Z-scores are not calculated using expectational variables, in what sense are they predictive? They are predictive because the coefficients of the discriminant function are estimated *prior* to actual past bankruptcies. In effect, the coefficients provide the expectational content, *provided that they are stable.* For example, Memorex's Z-score of 0.74 (see Table 10-5) indicated that as of December 31, 1974, Memorex's five-variable profile was more similar to Altman's average bankrupt firm one year before failure than to his average nonbankrupt firm. The predictive implication was that if Memorex's financial condition *continued* to deteriorate, in the manner of the average bankrupt firm, then one year hence, Memorex would probably be bankrupt. It is obvious (after the fact) that Memorex's managers and their bankers were aware of their financial difficulties and took the necessary steps to prevent the company's further deterioration. In the final analysis, a Z-score is simply an early-warning signal.

Classification experiments indicate the usefulness of accounting data and show how to package such information for analytical purposes. From the loan officer's perspective, classification models can be used to complement the loan-evaluation process. They provide a technique for quantifying the capacity and capital components of the five Cs of creditworthiness.

A Loan-Surveillance Model

The objective of the typical credit-or loan-review classification model is to replicate judgments made by loan officers, credit managers, or bank examiners. If an accurate model could be developed, then it could be used as a tool for reviewing and classifying future credit risk. In this context, however, an inaccurate model could be due to misjudgments made by the expert (e.g., the loan officer) or to shortcomings in the classification model or both. Chesser [1974] developed a model to predict noncompliance with the customer's original loan agreement, where *noncompliance* is defined to include not only default but any workout that may have been arranged resulting in a settlement of the loan less favorable to the lender than the original agreement (e.g., the REIT workouts of the 1970s). Chesser used data from four commercial banks in three states over the years 1962 to 1971. His observations consisted of a paired sample of 37 satisfactory loans and 37 unsatisfactory (noncomplicance) loans one year before noncompliance. Two years before noncompliance, he had only 21 pairs.

Chesser's model, which was based on a technique called logit analysis (a method similar to MDA), consisted of the following six variables:

$$X_1 = (\text{Cash} + \text{Marketable Securities})/\text{Total Assets}$$
$$X_2 = \text{Net Sales}/(\text{Cash} + \text{Marketable Securities})$$
$$X_3 = \text{EBIT}/\text{Total Assets}$$
$$X_4 = \text{Total Debt}/\text{Total Assets}$$
$$X_5 = \text{Total Assets}/\text{Net Worth}$$
$$X_6 = \text{Working Capital}/\text{Net Sales}$$

The estimated coefficients, including an intercept term, are

$$y = -2.0434 - 5.24X_1 + 0.0053X_2 - 6.6507X_3 \\ + 4.4009X_4 - 0.0791X_5 - 0.1020X_6 \tag{10-4}$$

The variable *y*, which is a linear combination of the independent variables, is used in the following formula to determine the probability of noncompliance, *P.*

$$P = \frac{1}{1 + e^{-y}} \tag{10-5}$$

where $e = 2.71828$. The estimated *y* value can be viewed as an index of a borrower's propensity for noncompliance; the higher the value of *y*, the higher the probability of noncompliance for a particular borrower. Chesser's classification rule for Equation (10-5) is

1. If $P > .50$, assign to the noncompliance group

2. If $P \le .50$, assign to the compliance group

Using both original and holdout samples, Chesser's model was able to classify correctly roughly three out of every four loans one year before noncompliance. Two years before, the accuracy rate was only 57 percent.

To illustrate the use of Equations (10-4) and (10-5), consider the following ratios calculated from the 1980 Annual Report of General Motors.

$$X_1 = 0.1074$$
$$X_2 = 15.5400$$
$$X_3 = -0.0343$$
$$X_4 = 0.4094$$
$$X_5 = 0.8412$$
$$X_6 = 0.0545$$

Plugging these values into Equation (10-4), $y = -0.5661$. Plugging this value into Equation (10-5), the probability figure is 0.3621, indicating membership in the compliance group. Even though 1980 was not a good year for General Motors, which is reflected by its X_3 value of -0.0343, GM still was predicted to be a member of the compliance group on the strength of its balance sheet. If GM's 1978 EBIT figure of $6.485 billion had been earned in 1980, the value of X_3 would have been 0.1875. In this counterfactual situation, the new y and P values would have been -1.585 and 0.1701, respectively. This example illustrates the importance of looking at more than one ratio to judge performance, and the sensitivity of the logit function to a change in a particular variable.

Chesser's "credit-scoring" model, which is typical of the framework used to build either credit-scoring or loan-review models, can be used to monitor loan compliance.

RECONCILING RESEARCH AND PRACTICE IN COMMERCIAL LENDING

A decision tree is valuable because it enables practitioners to visualize the decision process. Because certain classification procedure can be presented as decision trees and because they have been shown to be at least as accurate as other statistical techniques, they could be the vehicle to help bridge the gap between academic research and the practice of credit management. Nevertheless, four major drawbacks to closing the gap between research (defined as theory and empirical models) and practice remain:

1. The inability to quantify the customer-relationship aspect of the lending process
2. The reluctance of lenders to share information with researchers (under the guise of protecting customer confidentiality)
3. Even if such information sharing did occur, the lack of data on rejected borrowers
4. The backward looking nature of classification studies

Regarding the last point, since loans are repaid in the future, lenders (ideally) need a mechanism that is more forward looking. Timely and accurate pro forma information on the decision inputs required by lenders combined with similar forecasts of competitive and economic conditions would be ideal for the prevention, identification, and resolution of borrowing problems in commercial banks. Absent this ideal, and lacking detailed data on borrower characteristics, the contributions of academics to the bank credit-decision process will be limited. More fundamentally, however, as Ruth [1987] notes: "commercial lending is more than a technical exercise. It is, instead, an interactive process that demands human relations skills as well as the comprehension of technical material" (p. v). Unless researchers can capture the interactive nature of the bank-customer relationship in their theoretical and empirical models, the gap between research and practice will be difficult to bridge.

LOAN QUALITY IS THE NAME OF THE GAME

On February 12, 1988, J. Richard Fredericks, a bank security analyst for Montgomery Securities in San Francisco, appeared on *Wall Street Week* (with Louis Rukeyser on PBS). The scriptwriter's hook for the show was the "number one threat to the U.S. and international banking system: third world debt, or bank loans to less-developed countries (LDCs)."[26] After Fredericks said he thought the banking system was "safe" in 1988, the Q&A discussion turned to the criteria he used to pick bank stocks. What does a bank stock analyst, like Fredericks, look at to separate the winners from the losers? His two main criteria were capital and earnings, or what he calls "fortressed balance sheets." Beyond earnings and capital, he looks for "discipline" with respect to costs, loan losses, and loan growth.

Let's consider the importance of the loan portfolio in Fredericks's analytical framework. Bank capital is an important buffer or cushion for absorbing losses (e.g., loan losses arising from energy loans, LDC debt, or commercial real estate). A bank's main source of capital is its earnings. Its main source of earnings is revenue from loans. "Discipline" of the loan portfolio means controlling its operating costs, losses, and growth. Next to its cost of money, a bank's major operating cost is the one associated with the administration of its loan portfolio (e.g., salaries and other overhead expenses). Banks whose earnings and capital become impaired typically have lost control (discipline) over the growth and quality of their loan portfolios. When this occurs in conjunction with adverse external conditions (i.e., the fifth C of creditworthiness), banks experience financial problems. On balance, loan quality problems in the banking and thrift industries can be traced to overaggressive lending practices and disregard for the principles of sound credit analysis and diversification, in conjunction with mispriced deposit insurance.

If the inability of a bank to monitor and control (discipline) the costs, loan losses, and growth of its loan portfolio is the source of downfall for a bank, then the flip side of the record provides the keys to successful bank lending. Cocheo [1990] asks: "Does anybody out there know how to make a good commercial loan?" (p. 59). As executive editor of the *ABA Banking Journal,* he asked several bank stock analysts to identify some commercial lenders with a reputation for maintaining credit quality. They came up with the list shown in Table 10-7. Panel A lists the banks and some measures of their credit quality (ratios are annualized data as of the first quarter 1990). Panel B presents statements made by officers of the bank about credit quality. To highlight these ideas, Cocheo chose such headings as

- Matter of attitude
- Setting the tone
- Personal connections
- No 90-day wonders
- Limits, committees, and reviews
- Early group action, ongoing monitoring
- Internal examiners
- Thanks, but no thanks

The last item reflects the attitude of City National to four types of credit: foreign loans, agricultural loans, energy loans, and leveraged buyouts (LBOs).

---

[26] The third world debt crisis began to go away when Citicorp in May 1987, explicitly recognized the severity of the problem with a $3 billion provision for loan loss, a move which forced other banks with LDC exposure to follow suit. Large banks faced another lending crisis in the late 1980s and early 1990s because of problems with commercial real-estate loans.

TABLE 10-7   Loan Quality Is the Name of the Game: Giving Credit Where Credit Is Due

PANEL A. THE BANKS AND THEIR LOAN QUALITY

Banking Company	Loan quality performance ratios		
	Nonperforming	Net charge-offs	Loan-loss reserve
Central Fidelity (VA)	0.34%	0.41%	1.00%
City National (CA)	0.61	0.71	1.40
First Alabama Bancshares	0.82	0.24	1.06
First Wachovia (NC)	0.58	0.33	1.11
NBD Bancorp (MI)	0.86	0.25	1.56
Republic New York	0.40	0.11	NA

PANEL B. WHAT BANKERS HAD TO SAY ABOUT CREDIT QUALITY

"We're not adventuresome. We stick to very basic principles. Common sense never changes. And one of the basic things you learn is to know your customer. Acts of God and fraud will take care of giving you some level of bad debt. You shouldn't go out of your way to find bad risks. At our bank, having a problem credit does not get you into trouble. *Hiding* a problem credit gets you fired." (Alexander L. Kyman, president, City National)

Sound credit " . . . comes ahead of profits, growth, and keeping ahead of other banks. We beat that drum continuously." The bank's "credit culture" starts at the very top of the organization. (Chris Stone, executive vice president, First Alabama)

Lending is a team effort at First Wachovia as each loan starts as a joint project of the lending area that originated it and Loan Administration. " . . . if our roles were reversed, we would probably be saying the same things to each other." Since First Wachovia has no workout unit, lenders "own" the loans they make—for good. Lenders know upfront they are responsible for their loans. It's not, "well, if I have a problem I'll just pass it along." Regarding risky credits, "We try to maintain flexibility and not stereotype anything." (Mickey W. Dry, executive vice president, First Wachovia. FW is Wachovia today.)

We are "liability driven." "Profitability is fundamental to our basic mission—the protection of depositors' funds. I have always believed that an institution that can be more selective can be more supportive. Loan limits are more ego driven than practicality driven. We want people to be able to reflect on the situation being presented to them." (George Wendler, executive vice president, Republic National New York)

"Many banks don't use the committee system as consistently as we do. But this practice allows our most senior officers to be aware of the major credit extensions in the portfolio." (Noel Peterson, senior vice president, NBD. Today NBD is First Chicago NBD.)

Written credit policies describe management's attitudes on lending and how loans should be made. "Because everybody buys into it, it works." (Charles H. Rotert, executive vice president, Central Fidelity)

Source: Data from company reports with quotes from source. Cocheo [1990], pp. 59–63.

SMALL-BUSINESS LENDING AND BANK CONSOLIDATION: IS THERE CAUSE FOR CONCERN?[27]

Some opponents of interstate banking and consolidation of the banking industry argue that it will lead to a decline in the availability of credit to small businesses. Given the borrower-information continuum and competition from instruments of direct finance, this argument does not seem tenable. Strahan and Weston [1996]

[27] This section, which has the same title as an article by Strahan and Weston [1996], draws on their findings. In June 1993, the federal banking agencies began collecting data on small business loans.

present evidence that small businesses receive loans from banks of all sizes. Although small banks devote almost all of their C&I lending to small businesses, Panel A of Table 10-8 reveals that large banks make a substantial contribution (35% market share) to financing small businesses. In contrast, small banks cannot possibly generate much volume in large C&I loans ($1 million or more) because of market and capital constraints. In fact, banks with assets greater than $5 billion have an 82 percent share of the market for large C&I loans.

Strahan and Weston [1996] conclude that their research does not support the notion that consolidation from bank mergers reduces the portfolio shares of a bank's small business loans. Moreover, they expect that at least some small banking companies, because of cost advantages in providing credit to small borrowers, will survive the wave of consolidations and continue to serve the financing needs of small businesses.

TABLE 10-8   Profile of Small Business Lending by Bank Size

Panel A: Market Shares of C&I Loans[a]

Banks by Asset Size	Small C&I Loans	Large C&I Loans
Less than $100 million	16.3	0.3
$100 million–$300 million	18.3	1.5
$300 million–$1 billion	13.4	3.7
$1 billion–$5 billion	16.5	12.7
Greater than $5 billion	35.4	81.9
Totals	100.0	100.0

Panel B: Portfolio Shares of Small C&I Loans[b]

Banks by Asset Size	Small C&I Loans/Total C&I Loans	Small C&I Loans/Total Assets
Less than $100 million	96.7	8.9
$100 million–$300 million	85.2	8.8
$300 million–$1 billion	63.2	6.9
$1 billion–$5 billion	37.8	4.9
Greater than $5 billion	16.9	2.9

Data from June 1995 *Report of Condition and Income.*

Note: All figures are in percentages. Data for small C&I loans (those under $1 million) are based on the original amounts. For large C&I loans, the figures are computed by subtracting the original amount for small C&I loans from the book value of all C&I loans.

[a] Market shares equal the sum of all small (large) C&I loans held by banks in that size category divided by the sum of all small (large) C&I loans made by all banks.

[b] Portfolio shares equal the sum of all small C&I loans held by banks in that size category divided by all C&I loans (assets) held by banks in that size category. These figures are equivalent to weighted averages of the small C&I loans to total C&I loans (assets) ratio, weighted by total C&I loans (assets).

Source: Strahan and Weston [1996], Table 1, p. 2.

Chapter Summary

Although commercial credit is precarious, some banks manage it better than others. This chapter has examined some of the tools, techniques, and methods used by commercial lenders. Since the bulk of bank business lending is concentrated in **commercial and industrial** (C&I) **loans,** this component was emphasized. We began by looking at some of the characteristics of bank C&I loans and the intense competition banks have received from **commercial paper.** If bank business loans are special, **customer relationships** could be the unique factor. Competition and customer relationships can be viewed as two additional Cs added to the **five Cs** of credit analysis—character, capacity (cash flow), collateral, capital, and conditions (economic). The **sources of loan repayment** include **cash flow,** liquidation of an asset, or another source of financing. **Loan pricing** and the terms of C&I lending also were presented. The characterizations of commercial lenders as **hunters** and **skinners** were introduced to highlight the problems of incentives, discipline, monitoring, and concentration of credit. Following a look at **classification models,** an attempt to reconcile the research and practice of commercial lending was presented. The chapter concluded by highlighting some of the methods and practices used by successful commercial lenders (loan quality is the name of the game) and by focusing on the effects of bank consolidation on the availability of credit to small businesses.

Key Words, Concepts, and Acronyms

- Accounting ratios
- Borrower-information continuum
- Business lending
- Cash flow
- Commercial and industrial (C&I) loans
- Commercial paper
- Company operations (credit memo)
- Compensating balance
- Competition (credit memo)
- Credit quality
- Customer relationship
- Delegated monitoring
- Direct finance
- Financial performance
- Functional cost analysis (FCA)
- Hunters
- Indirect finance
- Industry (credit memo)
- Loan portfolio
- Loan pricing
- Management (credit memo)
- Prime rate
- Skinners
- Small business lending
- Sources of loan repayment
- Statement of cash flows (appendix)
- Terms of lending
- Writing a credit memo

Review/Discussion Questions

1. How has commercial paper affected bank C&I lending? What are some of the characteristics and trends in bank C&I lending? How does indirect finance with its customer relationships differ from direct finance? Which type of finance practices *forbearance* and why?

2. Describe the diversity of banks' C&I loans at large banks. Explain what FCA is and how it is applied to the commercial loan function.

3. Explain fully what the borrower-information continuum is and how monitoring technology affects it. Given this framework, how much sense does it make that small businesses would have to worry about the availability of credit from large banks? What does the available evidence suggest?

4. What are the five *C*s of creditworthiness and how can they be quantified? What two *C*s could we add to this set?

5. What are the sources of loan repayment? What is cash flow, how important is it to bank lenders, and how can cash flow be measured? What roles do accounts receivable, in-

ventories, and accounts payable play in cash-flow analysis? What are some potential early-warning signals of impending cash-flow problems?

6. Describe the experiment Libby conducted to determine the usefulness of accounting ratios to loan officers? What did he prove, if anything?

7. To what extent are the conventions of the prime rate, compensating balance, and customer relationships integral parts of the bank loan-pricing function. Distinguish between the myth and realities of the prime rate. Why would a bank be willing to lend at below the prime rate? What is the bank-customer relationship of a borrower who receives discounts from the prime rate likely to be like?

8. What are the basic ingredients in a risk-management approach to loan pricing?

9. Classification models such as credit-scoring and bankruptcy-prediction models (and IRS audit models) are designed to look for statistical outliers. In other words, if you are in the middle of the pack, you are not likely to get flagged. Describe what these basic models look like and how they can be useful to bank lenders. How can they be abused? Also distinguish between parametric and nonparametric techniques. In what sense are these models artificial intelligence?

10. How would you develop a loan-classification model for a lender and where would you use it? Origination? Surveillance? Are such models more applicable to retail or wholesale lending?

11. What role has academic research played in the practice of lending? What role can it play? Can the research on and practice of lending be reconciled?

12. Who is J. Richard Fredericks, what does he do, and how does he attempt to do it? Be sure to talk about "fortressed" balance sheets, "discipline," and the role of a bank's loan portfolio.

13. What are the keys to successful management of a bank loan portfolio? Where have the problem areas of bank lending been over the past two decades?

14. What are the various measures of bank loan quality and how do they differ from examiner judgments of loan quality?

15. What is the job of a hunter? A skinner? What problems can arise if the hunter is also the skinner? How would you structure these tasks if you were in charge?

To answer the next three questions, read appendix C.

16. On whom does the incidence of the reserve-requirements tax fall? Does the finding make sense?

17. What evidence exists to suggest bank loans are unique or special? What roles do the notions of delegated monitoring and bank-customer relationships play in explaining this uniqueness? Discuss fully.

18. How do bank business loans, private placements, and straight debt compare with respect to flexibility and in terms of a strategic combination of financial services?

Project

1. Using the forms in Table 10-4 and the text discussion of how to write a credit memo, select a company (assuming it has a credit relation with your bank), collect the relevant data, and write a one-page (250 words) credit memo for your boss.

Problems

1. Given a prime rate of 8.5 percent and a perceived default-risk premium of 200 basis points for Peachtree Manufacturing Company (PMC), determine the interest rate on its variable-rate, three-year term loan under the following interest-rate and pricing scenarios.

Year	Prime rate	Prime-plus	Prime-times
1	8.5%		
2	10.0%		
3	9.5%		

If the bank had perfect information regarding the future course of interest rates and complete flexibility in structuring the loan pricing scheme for PMC, what should the bank do if (*a*) it wants to cultivate the customer relationship versus (*b*) it wants to maximize interest revenue?

2. JFS and Company has the following simplified balance sheet:

JFS

A = 200	D = 50
	E = 150

If an LBO is arranged such that the firm's debt-to-asset ratio triples, without changing the firm's total assets, what will the post-LBO balance sheet look like? If your bank were asked to finance the deal, what would be your primary areas of concern?

3. The CPA Bank has a target ROE for each of its business customers of 15 percent and a target equity multiplier of 12 for the bank. Its marginal tax rate is 0.28 and its weighted average cost of funds is 0.075.
   a. What is the bank's pretax ROA for each of its business customers?
   b. What is the bank's target profit margin for each customer?

4. Czinki State Bank prices its commercial loans on a cost (of funds) plus basis. Without reserve requirements, its cost of funds is 10 percent. What will the bank's cost of funds be if reserve requirements of 3 percent, 5 percent, and 10 percent are imposed on the bank? What happens to the bank's effective lending and borrowing rates if the incidence of the tax is borne fully by depositors? By borrowers? Shared equally? Why would either group willingly accept the incidence of the tax? (see appendix C.)

5. Using Equation (10-1), calculate and analyze the cash flows of JFS Corporation for the years $t, t-1, t-2$, and $t-3$, given the following information (millions of dollars).

	t	$t-1$	$t-2$	$t-3$
Net profit	(370)	369	420	475
Depreciation	130	127	124	121
Accounts receivable (change)	(169)	114	110	100
Inventories (change)	(11)	450	400	375
Accounts payable (change)	(41)	(334)	250	150

6. Using the classification tree in Figure 10-3, indicate whether the following firms would be classified as bankrupt or nonbankrupt.

	Firm A	Firm B	Firm C	Firm D	Firm E
Cash flow/total debt	.10	.13	.15	.16	.12
Total debt/total assets	.60	.75	.80	.55	.70
Retained earnings/total assets	.12	.15	.14	.17	.16
Cash/total assets	.01	.03	.02	.04	.00

7. Given the following financial profiles, describe what each of the variables measures. Then use Equation (10-3) to determine if the companies are more like bankrupt or nonbankrupt firms.

Variable	Corp. ABC	Corp. JFS	Corp. XYZ
NITA	0.03	0.04	0.01
NWTD	0.48	0.55	0.16
CR	1.26	2.00	0.69
PAY	1.00	2.00	1.00
LOGTA	2.23	4.00	1.50

APPENDIX A

CASH-FLOW REPORTING AND SFAS NO. 95

In November 1987, following a seven-year study, review, and comment period, the Financial Accounting Standards Board (FASB) released its "statement of cash flows," known formally as Statement of Financial Accounting Standards (SFAS) No. 95. For lenders, the major benefit of such standards as SFAS No. 95 is the assurance that financial statements are prepared in an "objective, consistent, and reliable fashion."[28] The statement of cash flows, which replaces the traditional sources-and-uses or changes-in-financial-position statement, reports cash receipts and cash payments for a period and classifies them into operating, investing, and financing activities. The statement also calls for a reconciliation to cash and cash equivalents, with the latter defined as investments with original maturities of three months or less. SFAS No. 95 went into effect July 15, 1988.

Table A10-1 shows statements of cash flows for Citicorp (Panel A) and the Coca Cola Company (Panel B) for 1995 and the previous two years. Citicorp's cash flows for 1995 were $11,154 million from operating activities, −$17,527 million used for investing activities, and $5,688 million from financing activities. Adjusting for the effects of changes in exchange rates on cash (−$62 million), Citicorp's net decrease in cash (and due from banks) was $747 million, resulting in a year-end level of cash and due of $5,723 million. The supplemental disclosure of cash-flow information reveals that Citicorp paid $12,037 million in interest and $1,723 million in income taxes in 1995.

Coca Cola's cash flows for 1995 were $3,115 million from operating activities, −$1,013 million from investing activities, and −$2,278 million used in financing activities. Adjusting for the effects of changes in exchange rates on cash ($43 million), Coca Cola's net decrease in cash and cash equivalents was $219 million, resulting in a year-end cash balance of $1,167 million.

---

[28] See Emmanuel [1988], which is the second part of a three-part series on cash-flow reporting. The first part is by O'Leary [1988] and the third part is by Ginzl [1988].

TABLE A10-1 Cash-Flow Reporting and SFAS No. 95

PANEL A. CONSOLIDATED STATEMENT OF CASH FLOWS, CITICORP AND SUBSIDIARIES ($ MILLIONS)

	1995	*1994*	*1993*
Cash Flows from Operating Activities			
Net income	$3,464	$3,366	$2,219
Adjustments to reconcile net income to net cash provided by operating activities:			
Provision for credit losses	1,991	1,881	2,600
Depreciation and amortization of premises and equipment	636	571	568
Amortization of goodwill	49	47	55
Restructuring charge	—	—	425
Business writedowns	—	—	179
Provision for deferred taxes	(70)	(299)	(612)
Cumulative effects of accounting changes	—	56	(300)
Venture capital activity	155	(520)	(161)
Net gain on sale of securities	(132)	(200)	(94)
Net loss (gain) on the sale of subsidiaries and affiliates	6	(12)	(77)
Changes in accruals and other, net	2,381	(3,159)	996
Net decrease (increase) in trading account assets	6,782	(15,092)	(3,449)
Net (decrease) increase in trading account liabilities	(4,108)	16,904	638
Total adjustments	7,690	177	768
Net cash provided by operating activities	11,154	3,543	2,987
Cash Flows from Investing Activities			
Net increase in deposits at interest with banks	(2,166)	(113)	(199)
Securities—available for sale			
Purchases	(21,198)	(20,422)	(15,636)
Proceeds from sales	9,495	10,928	7,886
Maturities	11,853	7,185	5,202
Securities—held to maturity			
Purchases	(6,852)	(9,645)	(15,381)
Maturities	7,149	11,722	16,397
Net (increase) decrease in federal funds sold and securities purchased under resale agreements	(1,118)	344	(958)
Net increase in loans	(107,853)	(108,473)	(86,698)
Proceeds from sales of loans and credit-card receivables	92,884	90,184	82,961
Capital expenditures on premises and equipment	(1,189)	(941)	(829)
Proceeds from sales of premises and equipment	170	155	175
Proceeds from sales of subsidiaries and affiliates	57	25	230
Proceeds from sales of other real estate owned (OREO)	1,241	2,213	1,740
Net cash used in investing activities	(17,527)	(16,838)	(5,110)

(continued)

TABLE A10-1 *Continued*

PANEL A. CONSOLIDATED STATEMENT OF CASH FLOWS, CITICORP AND SUBSIDIARIES ($ MILLIONS) *(Continued)*

	1995	1994	1993
Cash Flows from Financing Activities			
Net increase in deposits	$11,405	$10,637	$2,816
Net (decrease) increase in federal funds purchased and securities sold under repurchase agreements	(4,193)	2,448	(1,336)
Proceeds from issuance of commercial paper and funds borrowed with original maturities of less than one year	514,298	402,773	335,235
Repayment of commercial paper and funds borrowed with original maturities of less than one year	(514,656)	(400,471)	(333,417)
Proceeds from issuance of long-term debt	4,669	4,576	4,682
Repayment of long-term debt and subordinated capital notes	(4,150)	(5,039)	(6,444)
Proceeds from issuance of preferred stock	390	388	654
Redemption of preferred stock	(125)	(100)	—
Proceeds from issuance of common stock	416	226	302
Purchase of treasury stock	(1,531)	(5)	(3)
Dividends paid	(835)	(533)	(313)
Net cash provided by financing activities	5,688	14,900	2,176
Effect of Exchange Rate Changes on Cash and Due from Banks	*(62)*	*29*	*(355)*
Net (decrease) increase in cash and due from banks	(747)	1,634	(302)
Cash and due from banks at beginning of year	6,470	4,836	5,138
Cash and due from banks at end of year	$5,723	$6,470	$4,836
Supplemental Disclosure of Cash Flow Information			
Cash paid during the year for			
Interest	$12,037	$12,977	$14,481
Income taxes	1,723	1,522	1,197
Noncash Investing Activities			
Transfers from loans to OREO and assets pending disposition	730	1,152	1,644

Accounting policies and explanatory notes not shown here form an integral part of the financial statements.

(continued)

TABLE A10-1 *Continued*

PANEL B. CONSOLIDATED STATEMENT OF CASH FLOWS, THE COCA-COLA COMPANY
AND SUBSIDIARIES ($ MILLIONS)

Year Ended December 31	*1995*	*1994*	*1993*
Operating Activities			
Net income	$2,986	$2,554	$2,176
Transition effect of change in accounting principle	—	—	12
Depreciation and amortization	454	411	360
Deferred income taxes	157	58	(62)
Equity income, net of dividends	(25)	(4)	(35)
Foreign currency adjustments	(23)	(6)	9
Gains on sales of assets	—	—	(84)
Other noncash items	(29)	41	78
Net change in operating assets and liabilities	(405)	129	54
Net cash provided by operating activities	3,115	3,183	2,508
Investing Activities			
Additions to finance subsidiary receivables	(144)	(94)	(177)
Collections of finance subsidiary receivables	46	50	44
Acquisitions and investments, principally bottling companies	(338)	(311)	(611)
Purchases of securities	(190)	(201)	(245)
Proceeds from disposals of investments and other assets	580	299	690
Purchases of property, plant, and equipment	(937)	(878)	(800)
Proceeds from disposals of property, plant, and equipment	44	109	312
Other investing activities	(74)	(11)	(98)
Net cash used in investing activities	(1,013)	(1,037)	(885)
Net cash provided by operations after reinvestment	2,102	2,146	1,623
Financing Activities			
Issuances of debt	754	491	445
Payments of debt	(212)	(154)	(567)
Issuances of stock	86	69	145
Purchases of stock for treasury	(1,796)	(1,192)	(680)
Dividends	(1,110)	(1,006)	(883)
Net cash used in financing activities	(2,278)	(1,792)	(1,540)
Effect of Exchange Rate Changes on Cash and Cash Equivalents	(43)	34	(41)
Cash and cash equivalents			
Net increase (decrease) during the year	(219)	388	42
Balance at beginning of year	1,386	988	956
Balance at end of year	$1,167	$1,386	$998

Source: Coca-Cola Company Annual Report [1995], p. 53.

Although Panel A of Table A10-1 provides important insights regarding the cash flows of a large bank holding company, from the bank's perspective as a lender, the statement of cash flows in Panel B provides a basis for analyzing the cash flows of existing or would-be borrowers' business operations. Because cash-flow reporting focuses on the nature of transactions (e.g., operating versus investing) as opposed to the nature of the cash receipt or payment, it was developed for two basic reasons:

1. To assist users in understanding the differences between net income and cash receipts and payments

2. To separate noncash investing and financing transactions (e.g., debt-equity conversions) from operating transactions

Highlighting noncash transactions in a separate schedule maintains the cash-flow focus of SFAS No. 95 and improves on the 17-year-old statement of changes in financial position.

Although two methods of preparing the statement of cash flows are permitted, FASB recommends the direct method as opposed to the indirect method. The latter more closely resembles the old statement of changes in financial position. The direct method differs from the indirect one only in the reporting of cash flows from operations. A minimum of seven separate operating classifications are required by the direct method:[29]

1. Cash received from customers

2. Cash paid to suppliers and employers

3. Interest and dividends received

4. Interest paid

5. Income taxes paid

6. Other operating cash receipts, if any

7. Other operating cash expenditures, if any

The direct method also requires, in a separate schedule, the reconciliation of net income to net cash flow from operations.

Because bankers commonly convert accrual statements to a cash basis, cash-flow reporting should make this transformation more efficient and help bridge the information gap between borrowers and lenders. In conjunction with income-expense and balance-sheet data, the statement of cash flows offers lenders a better opportunity to assess the creditworthiness of borrowers. Finally, because SFAS No. 95 combines the notions of liquidity and profitability, it provides a synthesis and overview of managerial expertise and the financial flexibility of the business.

---

[29] Emmanuel [1988], p. 19.

A MODEL OF CREDIT GRANTING FOR A NONFINANCIAL CORPORATION

Introduction

Using four statistical models (MDA, logit, goal programming, and RPA) and a judgmental model (Analytical Hierarchy Process, AHP), Srinivasan and Kim ([1987], hereafter S&K) analyzed the relative performance of classification procedures for credit granting by a Fortune 500 nonfinancial corporation. They wanted to find the classification procedure that would best replicate the expert judgment of the corporation, where a senior level credit manager was the expert. Because **credit analysis,** whether conducted by a financial institution or, as demonstrated by this appendix, by a nonfinancial corporation, should have the same underlying structure, the methods presented here can be applied to banks and other lenders.

Extent and Scope of Analysis

Although the degree of credit investigation varies with the size of the credit request, credit granting by this corporation has four stages: Stage I (less than $5,000) has little or no investigation, whereas Stage IV (greater than $50,000) has extensive investigation. Stages II ($5,001 to $20,000) and III ($20,001 to $50,000) have *intermediate* credit investigations. S&K had 215 customer files to analyze consisting of 39 *high-risk* (HR) customers and 176 *non-high-risk* (NHR) customers. The files, as of July 1986, were for customers with credit lines in excess of $50,000 who had data available for at least seven months prior to July 1986. Thirty-four of the high-risk customers had restrictive actions on their credit lines.

Data

For each customer, the following information profile was available: current ratio (CR), quick ratio (QR), net worth to total debt (NWTD), logarithm of total assets (LOGTA), net income to sales (NIS), net income to total assets (NITA or ROA), payment record (PAY defined as "good," "fair," or "poor" and measured categorically as 2, 1, or 0), and number of years the customer has been in business (YRS defined as less than two years, two to five years, and more than five years and measured categorically as 0, 1, or 2).

Decision Tree and Findings

S&K concluded that RPA was "slightly superior" as a classification model in replicating the judgments of the senior credit manager. Their optimal RPA tree is shown in Figure B10-1. The first split in the tree is on net income to total assets (NITA) with 39 customers going to the left ($NITA \leq 0.03$) and 176 to the right ($NITA > 0.03$). Continuing down the left side, the next split is on net worth to total

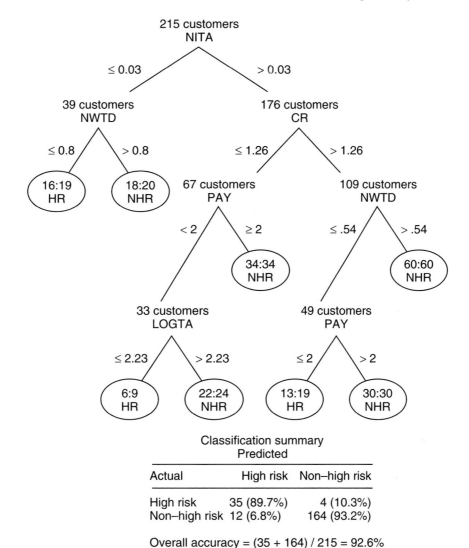

Source: Srinivasan and Kim [1987], Exhibit 2, p. 677. Reprinted by permission.

FIGURE B10-1 Srinivasan and Kim's Optimal RPA Tree for Replicating the Credit-Granting Process of a Fortune 500 Corporation, July 1986

debt (NWTD) with 19 customers going to the left ($NWTD \leq 0.8$) and 20 going to the right ($NWTD > 0.8$). The left side split is a terminal node for high-risk customers and correctly identifies 16 out of 19 as such. The right side also is a terminal node but for non-high-risk customers, with 18 out of 20 correctly replicated. Coming back to the 176 customers on the right, the next split is on the current ratio (CR) with 67 customers going to the left ($CR \leq 1.26$) and 109 going to the right ($CR > 1.26$). Because this split does not lead to any terminal nodes, further pruning of the tree is required. On the left, the next split is on payment record (PAY), with 33 customers going to the left ($PAY < 2$) and 34 going to right ($PAY = 2$). The right split is an NHR terminal node with 34 non-high-risk customers. Continuing on the left, the next split is on the logarithm of total assets (LOGTA), with nine customers going to the left ($LOGTA \leq 2.23$) and 24 to the right. These two branches are terminal nodes with six out of nine and 22 out of 24 customers correctly classified. Coming back to the right, NWTD splits 60 customers to the right with $NWTD > 0.54$, resulting in an NHR terminal node with 100 percent accuracy. On the left, the 49 customers with $NWTD \leq 0.54$ split on PAY with 19 going to the left and 30 to the right. Both nodes are terminal, with accuracy rates of 13 out of 16 on the left, and 30 out of 30 on the right.

Focusing on the overall classification accuracy of the tree, the three HR terminal nodes have an aggregate accuracy rate of 35 out of 39 (89.7 percent). In these three nodes, however, 12 non-high-risk customers are identified as high-risk ($12/176 = 6.8$ percent). This inaccuracy rate is called a "type-II error" and is considered to be less costly than the opposite misclassification, or "type-I error." Focusing on the five NHR nodes, 164 of the 176 non-high-risk customers are correctly classified (93.2 percent $= 1 -$ type-II error of 6.8 percent). Four high-risk customers (out of 39) are found in the five NHR nodes, for a type-I error of 10.2 percent. On balance, the tree has an overall reclassification accuracy rate of 199 out of 215 (92.6 percent); or alternatively, an overall misclassification rate of 16 out of 215 (7.4 percent).

APPENDIX C

ARE BANK BUSINESS LOANS SPECIAL?

Introduction

Are banks special? Regulators tend to think they are, because banks administer the payments system, grant credit, and serve as conduits for monetary policy. Perhaps a more interesting question is, are bank loans special? More specifically, *are bank business loans special*? One way to attempt to answer this question, which may seem to be a roundabout method, is to focus on bank reserve requirements.

The Incidence of the Reserve-Requirement Tax

One of the things that makes banks different (special) is reserve requirements (along with deposit insurance, access to the discount window, bank examination, etc.). Reserve requirements are, of course, an implicit tax imposed on banks. An important question is, who pays this tax? Is it depositors or borrowers or a combination of the two? This issue is known as the incidence of the reserve-requirement tax.

Empirical Evidence

Fama [1985] and James [1987] present evidence that bank borrowers (and not CD holders) bear the burden of the reserve-requirement tax. Unless bank loans are special (unique), why would bank borrowers bear this burden? Suppose the use of bank loans by nonfinancial corporations increases shareholder wealth. This proposition is exactly the one tested by James. Moreover, he accepted it. His tests and findings can be summarized briefly as follows. James looked at public announcements of three classes of debt:

1. New bank credit agreements
2. Privately placed debt agreements (mainly with insurance companies)
3. Public straight debt offerings for cash (i.e., bonds)

His sample consisted of 207 financing announcements, including 80 bank loan agreements, 37 private placements, and 90 straight debt offerings covering the period 1974 through 1983.

Using the market model,[30] James tested for the announcement effects of the alternative debt instruments. Such tests are designed to determine the "wealth effects" or "excess returns" associated with particular events, and are commonly known in finance as "event studies." James measured the "average prediction error" (APE) across the three types of debt to look for abnormal stock returns. His findings were as follows:

1. Positive (and statistically significant) stock price responses to the announcement of new bank credit agreements
2. Negative abnormal returns accruing to stockholders of firms announcing private placements
3. Negative abnormal returns associated with the announcement of private placements and straight debt issues used to retire bank debt

James performed a series of additional tests to determine if the differences in abnormal performance were due to differences in the characteristics of the loan (e.g., maturity) or the characteristics of the borrower (e.g., size and default risk). Controlling for these factors did *not* explain the abnormal returns.

To summarize, James's results suggest the following: (1) The incidence of the reserve-requirements tax falls on borrowers; (2) the announcement of new bank loan agreements generates positive abnormal returns; (3) controlling for other factors does not explain the abnormal returns. On the basis of these findings, James concludes, " . . . banks provide some special service not available from other lenders. Further research is needed to identify that unique service or unique attribute of bank loans and to explain its relation to the market value of the firm" (p. 234).

Delegated Monitoring and the Bank-Customer Relationship as Explanations for Why Bank Business Loans Might Be Special

In chapter 1, the notion of banks as delegated monitors was presented. To review, this idea simply says that not all savers (bank depositors and other creditors) have the time, inclination, or expertise to monitor institutional borrowers for default risk. Therefore, they engage in indirect finance rather than direct finance. Bank depositors believe in a Greyhound bus–type motto: "Save in the bank and leave the monitoring to us." Commercial banks have developed substantial amounts of reputational capital as monitors of credit risk. If the marketplace values such monitoring highly, this phenomenon could explain the excess returns found by James. Without any hard evidence on this matter, this is simply a conjecture. Moreover, although James references the key article on the theory of delegated monitoring, Diamond [1984], he never explicitly claims delegated monitoring as a potential explanation.

---

[30] The market model adjusts stock returns for market risk to determine if announcements of particular events generate excess or abnormal returns or what James calls "average prediction errors."

When it comes to monitoring, are all financial firms equal? In particular, do insurance companies have the same reputational capital, as monitors, as commercial banks?[31] Consider the following statement by Lowell Bryan, a director of McKinsey & Company:[32]

> Well I think you get different value-added for different functions. If you look at where banks add value to the economy, their major contribution is in origination, the assessment and underwriting of credit. Commercial banks are the best credit-risk underwriters in the financial-services industry (though you also have some horrible credit-risk underwriters among the banks). Those are the unique, or proprietary, skills that banks have evolved; that is their fundamental comparative advantage.

Accordingly, when a borrowing firm switches from *the* monitor in the system to another (second-rate?) monitor, the marketplace may view this negatively and penalize shareholder returns. This explanation raises a question, which James calls a "curious" one: Why do managers switch from bank financing to private placements or straight debt, given the adverse price reaction? James finds that differences in maturity between bank loans and either private placements or public debt offerings do not explain this curiosity.

If banks are special, deposit insurance, access to the discount window, and regulation are the stuff of this specialness. In addition, the largest banks have a safety net in the form of the too-big-to-fail doctrine. Finance theory and empirical evidence suggest that these trappings enhance the wealth of bank shareholders (e.g., Buser, Chen, and Kane [1981] and Harris, Scott, and Sinkey [1986]). In a similar fashion, the deposit insurance and regulatory trappings of banks should enhance their reputational capital as delegated monitors. Confidence in the banking system is closely and explicitly (since 1989) tied to the "full faith and credit of the U.S. government." Because insurance companies do not have this explicit government guarantee nor the same extent and degree of regulation and supervision as commercial banks, the marketplace may look at insurance companies as second-rate monitors. To satisfy policyholders' concerns about safety, most insurance companies locate in states, like New York, that have stringent insurance regulations and supervision.

On balance, bank creditors and equity investors may have more confidence in banks, as delegated monitors, because of two phenomena: (1) the reputational capital of banks, and (2) the reputational capital of the systems of deposit insurance and bank regulation. The latter serves as a delegated monitor for taxpayers of the safety and soundness of the banking system. Moreover, the interaction between these two phenomena may create a synergy that makes the whole greater than the sum of its parts.

One important caveat, however, is that the reputational capital of both banks and the deposit-insurance system were severely damaged by the S&L crisis; the insolvency of the FSLIC; the banking problems due to energy, farm, LDC, and commercial real-estate loans; and the need to recapitalize the FDIC in 1991 (see Kane [1991]). Nevertheless, because the entire financial system, including insurance com-

---

[31] Because insurance companies are not depository institutions protected by the explicit federal safety net, they may have less reputational capital (from a safety-net perspective) than the kingpins of the financial system—commercial banks.

[32] For this and other interesting exchanges, see "The Future of Commercial Banking: A Roundtable Discussion," *Midland Corporate Finance Journal* (Fall 1987), pp. 22–49.

panies, has been under stress, relative losses of reputational capital may have left institutional rankings unchanged. On these grounds, it seems reasonable for the marketplace to penalize firms for shifting from bank debt to debt placed with insurance companies. It is more difficult to explain why the market penalizes borrowers who shift from bank debt to public debt. If the lead steers (chapter 3) are doing their job, why should their monitoring differ from bank monitoring or be perceived by the marketplace as different?

Relationship Banking

As a line from an old-time song goes, "Is that all there is?" Does delegated monitoring tell it all? An alternative explanation focuses on the notion of the bank-customer relationship (Hodgman [1961, 1963] and Kane and Malkiel [1965]). Although James refers to Kane and Malkiel, he is reluctant to attach much weight to the bank-customer relationship as an explanation for his findings. What is the bank-customer relationship? It is a concept (and a recognized practice) representing a strategic combination of deposits, loans, and other financial services that gives commercial banking its unique institutional character. Under current laws, such combinations or bundles are not available to insurance companies or investment banks. The bank-customer relationship is that "special service not available from other lenders" that James needs to enrich the interpretation of his results. In this context, it makes sense that bank borrowers might accept the incidence of reserve-requirements taxation in exchange for a bundle of services not available from any other player in the financial-services industry.

Is there a hook in this strategic combination of financial services that draws business firms into the bank? The logical choice is transaction accounts and access to the large dollar payments system. Perhaps this is the "unique service" to complete James's puzzle. To test this conjecture, however, would require the transaction-account balances of individual firms, which are not publicly available.

To summarize, although the bank-customer relationship offers a reasonable explanation for why bank borrowers would submit to the reserve-requirements tax, it does not add any insight into the abnormal returns uncovered by James. However, as explained above, the notion of banks as delegated monitors seems to complete that part of James's puzzle.

Loan Revisions versus New Loans

Lummer and McConnell [1989] have added an important piece to James's puzzle. They compared capital-market responses to the announcement of new bank loans versus the announcement of bank loan revisions, both favorable and unfavorable. If banks are to be effective delegated monitors, they need time to get to know the strengths and weaknesses of their customers. This basic idea suggests that when banks make new loans, the market may wait for a second signal from lenders before it responds favorably. In contrast, *favorable* loan revisions would signal an ongoing confidence on the part of the lender. Lummer and McConnell found evidence to support these notions. Specifically, they found that (1) the market did not react to the announcement of new loans, (2) the market reacted positively to the announcement of favorable loan revisions, and (3) the market reacted negatively to the announcement of unfavorable loan revisions. They concluded that "banks play an important role as transmitters of information in capital markets, but new bank loans per se do not communicate information" (p. 99).

Selected References

Allen, Randy. [1990]. "The Rule Ag Bank in a New Environment." *ABA Banking Journal* (August), p. 75.

Altman, Edward I. [1968]. "Financial Ratios, Discriminant Analysis, and the Prediction of Corporate Bankruptcy." *Journal of Finance* (September), pp. 589–609.

———. [1980]. "Commercial Bank Lending: Process, Credit Scoring, and Costs of Errors in Lending." *Journal of Financial and Quantitative Analysis* Proceedings Issue (November), pp. 813–832.

Altman, Edward I., Robert B. Avery, Robert A. Eisenbeis, and Joseph F. Sinkey, Jr. [1981]. *Application of Classification Techniques in Business, Banking, and Finance.* Greenwich, CT: JAI Press.

Altman, Edward I., R. G. Haldeman, and P. Narayanan. [1977]. "ZETA Analysis: A New Model to Identify the Bankruptcy Risk of Corporations." *Journal of Banking and Finance* 1, pp. 29–54.

Azhar, Shariq. [1990]. "Expert Lenders' Insights: Evaluating Private Company Credit." *Commercial Lending Review,* pp. 38–43.

Barrickman, John R. [1990]. "Successful Commercial Lending from the Ground Up." *Bottomline* (February), pp. 12–14.

Bathory, Alexander. [1987]. *The Analysis of Credit: Foundations and Development of Corporate Credit Assessment.* London: McGraw-Hill.

Beaver, William H. [1967]. "Financial Ratios as Predictors of Failure." *Empirical Research in Accounting: Selected Studies 1966, Journal of Accounting Research* (Supplement to Volume 4), pp. 71–111.

Benbow, Robert F. [1985]. "Preventing Problem Loans, before They Happen: 25 Red Flags." *Journal of Commercial Bank Lending* (April), pp. 18–23.

Bennett, Thomas E., Jr. [1987]. "Mixed Signals." *INC.* (October), p. 153.

Benninga, Simon Z., and Oded H. Sarig. [1997]. *Corporate Finance: A Valuation Approach.* New York: McGraw-Hill.

Berger, Allen N., and Gregory F. Udell. [1993]. "Securitization, Risk, and the Liquidity Problem in Banking." In Michael Klausner and Lawrence J. White, eds., *Structural Change in Banking.* Homewood Hills, IL: Irwin, 227–294.

Bird, Anat, and Richard Israel. [1990]. "Cut the Fat from Lending." *ABA Banking Journal* (October), pp. 137–142.

Booth, James R. [1992]. "Contract Costs, Bank Loans, and the Cross-Monitoring Hypothesis." *Journal of Financial Economics* 31, pp. 25–41.

Brady, Thomas F. [1985]. "Changes in Loan Pricing and Business Lending at Commercial Banks." *Federal Reserve Bulletin* (January), pp. 1–13.

Breiman, Leo, Jerome H. Freidman, Richard A. Olshen, and Charles J. Stone. [1984]. *Classification and Regression Trees.* Belmont, CA: Wadsworth International Group.

Buck, Walter H. [1979]. "Risk-Management Approach to Pricing Loans and Leases." *Journal of Commercial Bank Lending* (April), pp. 2–15.

Buser, Stephen A., Andrew H. Chen, and Edward J. Kane. [1981]. "Federal Deposit Insurance, Regulatory Policy, and Optimal Bank Capital." *Journal of Finance* 36, pp. 51–60.

Capon, Noel. [1982]. "Credit Scoring Systems: A Critical Analysis." *Journal of Marketing* (Spring), pp. 82–91.

Chesser, Delton L. [1974]. "Predicting Loan Noncompliance." *Journal of Commercial Bank Lending* (August), pp. 2–15.

Clarke, Donald F. [1990]. "The Evolution of Asset-Based Lending." *The Secured Lender,* pp. 40–42.

Cocheo, Steve. [1990]. "Giving Credit Where Credit Is Due." *ABA Banking Journal* (July), pp. 59–63.

Diamond, Douglas. [1984]. "Financial Intermediation and Delegated Monitoring." *Review of Economic Studies* 51, pp. 393–414.

Durand, David. [1941]. *Risk Elements in Consumer Installment Lending.* New York: National Bureau of Economic Research.

Emmanuel, Christine. [1988]. "Cash Flow Reporting, Part 2: Importance of Cash Flow Data in Credit Analysis." *Journal of Commercial Bank Lending* (June), pp. 16–28.

Fama, Eugene F. [1985]. "What's Different about Banks?" *Journal of Monetary Economics* 15, pp. 29–36.

Federal Reserve Bulletin (various issues). Washington, D.C.: Board of Governors of the Federal Reserve System.

Fischer, Gerald C. [1982]. *The Prime: Myth and Reality.* Philadelphia: Temple University.

Flannery, Mark J. [1985]. "A Portfolio View of Loan Selection and Pricing." In R. Aspinwall and R. Eisenbeis, eds., *Handbook for Banking Strategy.* New York: Wiley, pp. 457–472.

Fox, Lawrence E. [1987]. "Banks Are Not Too Eager." *Journal of Commercial Bank Lending* (February), pp. 24–26.

Frydman, Halina, Edward Altman, and Duen-Li Kao. [1985]. "Introducing Recursive Partitioning for Financial Classification: The Case of Financial Distress." *Journal of Finance* (March), pp. 269–291.

Functional Cost and Profit Analysis (FCA). [1994]. "National Average Report: Commercial Banks," Federal Reserve Bank of Boston.

Ginzl, David J. [1988]. "Cash Flow Reporting, Part 3: Getting—and Using—Quality Financial Information." *Journal of Commercial Bank Lending* (July), pp. 17–21.

Harding, Douglas, Betty McDonald, and Dev Strischeck. [1987]. "The Role of Meaningful Credit Information." *Journal of Commercial Bank Lending* (August), pp. 51–61.

Harris, John M., Jr., James R. Scott, and Joseph F. Sinkey, Jr. [1986]. "The Wealth Effects of Regulatory Intervention Surrounding the Bailout of Continental Illinois." *Proceedings of a Conference on Bank Structure and Competition,* Federal Reserve Bank of Chicago, pp. 104–126.

Herring, Richard J. [1989]. "The Economics of Workout Lending." *Journal of Money, Credit and Banking* (February), pp. 1–15.

Hodgman, Donald R. [1961]. "The Deposit Relationship and Commercial Bank Investment Behavior." *Review of Economics and Statistics* 42, pp. 257–268.

———. [1963]. *Commercial Bank Loan and Investment Policy.* Champaign, IL: University of Illinois, Bureau of Economic and Business Research.

Holt, Robert N., Vida Scarpello, and Raymond J. Carroll. [1983]. "Toward Understanding the Contents of the 'Black Box' for Predicting Complex Decision-Making Outcomes." *Decisions Sciences,* pp. 253–267.

James, Christopher. [1987]. "Some Evidence on the Uniqueness of Bank Loans." *Journal of Financial Economics* (December), pp. 217–235.

Kane, Edward J. [1991]. "Banks Are Looking a Lot Like S&Ls." *The New York Times* (January 28), op. ed. page.

Kane, Edward J., and Burton G. Malkiel. [1965]. "Bank Portfolio Allocation, Deposit Variability, and the Availability Doctrine." *Quarterly Journal of Economics* (February), pp. 113–134.

Kelly, John M. [1986]. *Managing Cash Flow.* New York: Franklin Watts.

Knight, Robert E. [1975]. "Customer Profitability Analysis." Federal Reserve Bank of Philadelphia *Monthly Review* (April), pp. 11–20.

Libby, Robert E. [1975]. "Accounting Ratios and the Prediction of Failure: Some Behavioral Evidence." *Journal of Accounting Research* (Spring), pp. 150–161.

Lummer, Scott L., and John J. McConnell. [1989]. "Further Evidence on the Bank Lending Process and the Capital-Market Response to Bank Loan Agreements." *Journal of Financial Economics* (November), pp. 99–122.

Marais, M. Laurentius, James M. Patell, and Mark A. Wolfson. [1984]. "The Experimental Design of Classification Models: An Application of Recursive Partitioning and Bootstrapping to Commercial Bank Loan Classifications." *Journal of Accounting Research* 22 Supplement, pp. 87–118.

Megginson, William L., Annette B. Poulsen, and Joseph F. Sinkey, Jr. [1995]. "Syndicated Loan Announcements and the Market Value of the Banking Firm." *Journal of Money, Credit and Banking* (May), pp. 457–475.

Miller, Robert A. [1987]. "Banks Are Too Eager." *Journal of Commercial Bank Lending* (February), pp. 20–24.

Nash, Robert C., and Joseph F. Sinkey, Jr. [1997]. "On Competition, Risk, and Hidden Assets in the Market for Bank Credit Cards." *Journal of Banking and Finance* (January), pp. 89–112.

O'Glove, Thorton L. [1987]. *Quality of Earnings.* New York: Free Press.

O'Leary, Carolyn D. [1988]. "Cash Flow Reporting, Part I: An Overview of SFAS 95." *Journal of Commercial Bank Lending* (May), pp. 22–28.

Ruth, George E. [1987]. *Commercial Lending.* Washington, DC: American Bankers Association.

Sinkey, Joseph F., Jr. [1979]. *Problem and Failed Institutions in the Commercial Banking Industry.* Greenwich, CT: JAI Press.

———. [1985]. "Regulatory Attitudes toward Risk." In R. Aspinwall and R. Eisenbeis, eds., *Handbook for Banking Strategy.* New York: John Wiley & Sons, pp. 347–380.

———. [1989]. "Credit Risk in Commercial Banks: A Survey of Theory, Practice, and Empirical Evidence." Bank of Israel *Banking Review* (December), pp. 12–35.

Sinkey, Joseph F., Jr., and Robert C. Nash, [1993]. "Assessing the Riskiness and Profitability of Credit-Card Banks." *Journal of Financial Services Research* 2, pp. 127–150.

Squires, Jan R. [1990]. "Strengthening Credit Analysis by Determining Shareholder Value." *Bankers Magazine* (July/August), pp. 73–77.

Srinivasan, Venkat, and Yong H. Kim. [1987]. "Credit Granting: A Comparative Analysis of Classification Procedures." *Journal of Finance* (July), pp. 665–683.

Stigum, Marcia L., and Rene O. Branch. [1983]. *Managing Bank Assets and Liabilities.* Homewood Hills, IL: Dow Jones-Irwin.

Strahan, Philip E., and James Weston. [1996]. "Small Business Lending and Bank Consolidation: Is There Cause for Concern?" *Current Issues in Economics and Finance,* Federal Reserve Bank of New York (March), pp. 1–6.

White, Larry R. [1990]. "Credit Analysis: Two More 'C's' of Credit." *Journal of Commercial Bank Lending* (October), pp. 11–15.

CHAPTER
11 | CONSUMER LENDING

Contents

LEARNING OBJECTIVES

■ To understand the market for consumer installment credit

■ To understand the kinds of consumer loans banks make and their terms

■ To understand why banks favor credit-card loans and home-equity loans

■ To understand the credit analysis, pricing, and risks of consumer lending

■ To understand the regulation of consumer lending

CHAPTER THEME

Commercial banks dominate the market for **consumer installment credit.** Consumer loans made by commercial banks grew at 5.9 percent per year for the ten-year period 1985 to 1995. **Credit-card loans,** the fastest growing component of bank consumer lending, grew at an annual rate of 11.2 percent over the same period. The consumers of the United States, like no other citizens in the world, know how to charge—plastic is their preferred deferred means of payment. Charge now, pay later. Banks love those credit-card customers who do not pay their balances on time. Credit cards generate both interest and noninterest revenues for banks. **Competition, securitization, automation,** and **regulation** are major forces shaping consumer lending. With the decline of the S&L industry, many commercial banks have increased their holdings of residential mortgages and expanded their **home-equity lines of credit.**

KEY CONCEPTS, IDEAS, AND TERMS

- Adjustable-rate mortgages (ARMs)
- Amount financed
- Consumer installment credit
- Credit-card loans
- Credit (default) risk
- Credit-scoring model (system)
- Delinquent loans (delinquency rates)
- Fees and service charges (credit cards)
- Home-equity lines of credit
- Interest rate
- Interest-rate risk
- Loan losses
- Loan-to-value ratio
- Maturity
- Nonperforming loans
- Regulation
- Residential mortgage
- Securitization

OVERVIEW OF CONSUMER LENDING AND TRENDS

Banks sell financial services and products to businesses, households, and governments. As financial markets become more complete, direct finance supplants indirect finance. This move toward more complete markets occurs in wholesale markets first and only later trickles down to retail markets (i.e., to the small businesses and consumers served by retail banking). With banks being squeezed in wholesale markets, they have devoted increasing attention to tapping retail markets. At year-end 1985, commercial banks held total consumer loans of $284 billion; by year-end 1995, the figure was $502 billion, a compound annual growth of 5.9 percent.[1] Over this same period, the total assets held by all commercial banks grew by an only slightly lower figure of 4.9 percent. Averages, of course, mask the performance of the components of consumer lending. Credit-card loans, the fastest growing component of bank consumer lending, grew from $67.7 billion at year-end 1985 to $196.2 billion at year-end 1995, a compound annual growth of 11.2 percent. In addition, commercial banks have made substantial inroads into the market for **home-equity loans,** which can be considered a hybrid between a consumer loan and a mortgage loan. Since year-end 1988 (previous data are not available), home-equity loans held by all commercial banks, and secured by one–four family residential properties, have grown from $34.7 billion to $78 billion at year-end 1995, a compound annual growth of 12.3 percent.[2]

By far, however, the biggest change in bank consumer lending, broadly defined, has resulted from the restructuring of the savings-and-loan industry. Banks have charged into the market for loans secured by **one–four family residential properties.** At year-end 1985, all commercial banks held $188 billion in first mortgages backed by residential properties; by year-end 1995, these loans totaled $520 billion, a compound annual growth of 10.7 percent. Because residential mortgages have substantially less credit risk than credit-card loans or real-estate construction and development loans, the financial-management challenge for banks is how well they handle the **interest-rate risk** (chapter 5) associated with fixed-rate mortgages. The mishandling of this risk led to the downfall of many S&Ls. Banks and surviving S&Ls, however, have better tools and markets for managing interest-rate risk as reflected by adjustable-rate mortgages (ARMs), well-developed markets for selling/securitizing mortgages, and the availability of derivatives for hedging interest-rate risk (chapter 9).

The major trends in bank consumer lending are captured by Figure 11-1. Panel A shows the composition and growth of consumer lending from 1984 to 1996. Panel B shows how commercial banks have become more consumer-loan oriented over this time period. Panels C and D reveal the quality of consumer credit, showing the greater **credit risk** of credit-card loans compared to installment and residential real-estate loans, observations that hold for both **loan-loss rates** and **delinquency rates.**

Although this chapter includes residential mortgages under the category of consumer loans (because they are extensions of credit to households or consumers), it begins with an analysis of the traditional (narrow) definition of consumer credit as short-term installment loans. The chapter then looks at the market for residential mortgages and the growing role commercial banks are playing in

---

[1] At year-end 1942, commercial banks held only $2.3 billion in loans to individuals out of total loans of $18.9 billion and total assets of $95.5 billion. Over the next 52 years, consumer loans grew at an annual rate of 10.6 percent, total loans at 14.2 percent, and total assets at 15.4 percent. To finance World War II, U.S. banks held $47.3 billion in government securities at year-end 1942, a figure that rose to $96.1 billion (61.4%) by year-end 1945. These data can be found in *Statistics on Banking: A Statistical History of the United States Banking Industry, Volume I,* August 1995, Washington, DC: FDIC.

[2] The data in this paragraph are from the *Federal Reserve Bulletin* (June 1996), p. 496. Growth rates were calculated from dollar data derived from the reported data.

FIGURE 11-1 **Trends in Consumer Loans Made by Commercial Banks**

Panel A. Growth and composition of consumer loans, 1984–1996

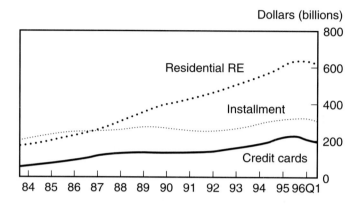

Panel B. The relationship between consumer loans and commercial loans, 1984–1996

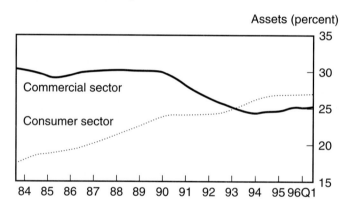

Panel C. Consumer loan loss rates for commercial banks, 1984–1996

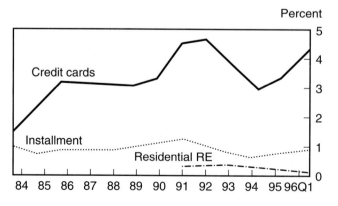

(continued)

Panel D. Loans past due 30 days or more
and nonaccrual loans, 1991–1996

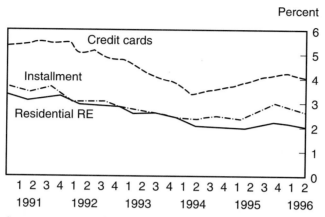

Source: Bank Call Reports from Ludwig [1996].

FIGURE 11-1 *Continued*

that market. The combination of consumer loans, as reflected by the following data, dominate bank lending to households:

Loan Category	Volume at Year-end 1995	Annual Growth since 1985
Residential mortgages	$ 520 billion	10.7%
Installment loans	$ 306 billion	3.5%
Credit-card loans	$ 196 billion	11.2%
Home-equity loans	$ 78 billion	12.3% (since 1988)
Total	$1,100 billion	8.8%

At year-end 1995, all commercial banks held $4.149 trillion in total assets. As shown above, more than one out of every four of these dollars can be described as consumer loans. In terms of the total loan portfolio held by banks ($2.326 trillion at year-end 1995), these loans play an even larger role, at almost 47.3 percent of total loans. At year-end 1985, consumer loans as broadly defined here were only 18.3 percent of banks' total assets and 30.8 percent of total loans. Consumer lending is an important part of retail banking. Citicorp, a major player in global consumer lending, describes its consumers' businesses as including retail banking, mortgages, credit cards, and private banking (i.e., banking for wealthy individuals).

   This chapter concludes with a look at consumer lending in the future and the forces likely to shape it.

CONSUMER INSTALLMENT CREDIT:
MARKET SHARE, TYPES OF LOANS, AND TERMS

For transactions that cannot be paid for by cash, check, or debit card, or delayed by using a credit card, consumers need credit. Generally, these purchases are for big-ticket items such as automobiles, home improvements, college tuition, boats, and airplanes. Another reason for consumer borrowing is a direct result of the growth of the use of credit cards in the United States. Specifically, consumers who turn out to be "credit junkies" need installment loans to consolidate their credit-card debts and to help them break the habit of spending compulsively beyond their means.

Table 11-1 presents a snapshot of the market for **consumer installment credit.**[3] Commercial banks, with a market share of 44 percent, are the major player in this $1.1 trillion market. In addition, because commercial banks originate a substantial portion of the pools of securitized assets (which have a 21% market share), they clearly dominate the market for consumer installment credit. Because these pools of securitized installment credits represent loans that have been sold, they are no longer carried on the balance sheets of the loan originators (chapter 9). The pools are financial claims upon which securities have been issued. Banking's closest competitor in the extension of consumer installment credit, finance companies, had a market share of only 13.5 percent, less than one-third of banks' share. Credit unions ranked third in market share of consumer installment credit with 11.7 percent.

Panel B of Table 11-1 shows three categories of bank installment loans:

- Automobile loans
- Revolving loans (mainly credit-card loans)
- Other loans

In general, a revolving loan is a line of credit that may be used repeatedly up to a specified limit like a credit card. The "other" category includes mobile-home loans and all other installment loans not included in automobile and revolving credit.

Panels C, D, and E of Table 11-1 show the market share of automobile credit, revolving credit, and other installment credit, respectively. Commercial banks are the dominant players in each of these market segments, with $154 billion in outstanding auto loans (42.1% market share), $205 billion in revolving credit (46.3% market share), and $146 billion in other installment credit (43.1% market share). The pools of securitized assets (described in chapter 9) across these three categories were as follows:

$45 billion (12.2% market share of auto loans)

$170 billion (38.4% market share of revolving credit)

$25 billion (7.3% market share of other installment credit)

Of the total pool of securitized installment credit ($240 billion), revolving credit (mainly credit-card loans) accounted for 71 percent of the outstanding volume. In the markets for automobile and other installment loans, banking's major competition comes from finance companies. In the market for revolving credit, the major competition comes from nonfinancial businesses, including retailers and gasoline companies.

The basic **terms of consumer installment credit** include

- **Interest rate**
- **Maturity**
- **Amount financed**
- **Loan-to-value ratio** (new car, used car)

---

[3] This data series of consumer installment credit, reported by the Board of Governors of the Federal Reserve System, "covers most short- and intermediate-term credit extended to individuals that is scheduled to be repaid (or has the option of repayment) in two or more installments" (see note 1, Table 1.55, p. A36, *Federal Reserve Bulletin* (October 1996).

TABLE 11-1   Consumer Installment Credit: Market Share and Types of Loans June 30, 1996 (not seasonally adjusted)

Panel A. Market Share of Total Consumer Installment Credit

By Major Holder	$ Millions	Market Share
Commercial banks	$504.9	44.0%
Finance companies	154.6	13.5
Credit unions	134.7	11.7
Savings institutions	40.3	3.5
Nonfinancial business	72.5	6.3
Pools of securitized assets	239.5	20.9
Total	$1,146.5	100.0%

Panel B. Commercial Bank Composition by Major Type of Credit

By Major Type of Credit	$ Millions	Market Share
Automobile	$ 153.8	30.5%
Revolving	204.6	40.5
Other	146.4	29.0
Total	$504.8	100.0%

Panel C. Market Share of Automobile Credit

By Major Holder	$ Millions	Market Share
Commercial banks	$153.8	42.1%
Finance companies	74.3	20.3
Pools of securitized assets	44.8	12.2
Other	92.5	25.3
Total	$365.4	100.0%

Panel D. Market Share of Revolving Credit

By Major Holder	$ Millions	Market Share
Commercial banks	$204.6	46.3%
Nonfinancial business	43.1	9.7
Pools of securitized assets	169.9	38.4
Other	24.2	5.5
Total	$441.8	100.0%

Panel E. Market Share of Other Installment Credit

By Major Holder	$ Millions	Market Share
Commercial banks	$146.4	43.1%
Finance companies	80.3	23.7
Nonfinancial business	29.4	8.7
Pools of securitized assets	24.8	7.3
Other	58.4	17.2
Total	$339.3	100.0%

Note: The data for nonfinancial businesses include retailers and gasoline companies. Due to rounding, the figures for totals may not add up.

Source: Federal Reserve Bulletin (October 1996), Table 1.55, p. A36.

In making decisions about the terms of consumer installment loans, lenders offer borrowers trade-offs with respect to these four basic terms. Treating interest rate as the key variable, lenders generally offer lower rates for loans with shorter maturities and higher loan-to-value ratios, all other things being equal.

Let's illustrate the use of the terms of consumer installment lending by considering some examples. During May 1996, a 48-month new-car loan from a commercial bank had an average interest rate of 8.93 percent. In contrast, a 24-month personal loan had an average interest rate of 13.52 percent, whereas credit-card plans had an average interest rate of 15.44 percent. All other things being equal, secured credit is less expensive than unsecured credit. Interest rates, of course, vary with the interest-rate cycle. For example, during February of 1994, a 48-month new-car loan had an average interest rate of 7.54 percent. However, due to the downward stickiness of interest rates on credit cards (discussed later in this chapter; see Figure 11-2), the average rate on credit cards, at 16.04 percent, was not lower than it was in May 1996.

As automobiles have become more expensive, lenders have increased their loan-to-value ratio and the amount they are willing to finance. For example, during 1991, the average loan-to-value ratio for new-car loans was 88 percent, with $12,494 the average amount financed. In contrast, during May 1996, the comparable figures were 91 percent and $16,686. A similar trend has occurred with used-car loans. For example, during 1991 the average nonrate terms were 96 percent and $8,884, compared to 99 percent and $12,233 during May 1996. Two other characteristics common to loans for used cars are higher interest rates (e.g., 9.37% vs. 13.49% during May 1996 on loans made by auto finance companies) and shorter maturities.[4]

INSTALLMENT LOANS AND CREDIT-CARD LOANS BY BANK SIZE

Traditionally consumer loans made by commercial banks have been classified as installment loans and credit-card loans. Using this designation, Panel A of Table A11-1 in appendix A of this chapter shows these loans (as a percentage of total bank assets) for four bank size classes for the years 1985 to 1995. At year-end 1985, installment and credit-card loans accounted for 11 percent of the total assets held by commercial banks. By year-end 1995, the figure had risen slightly, to 12.1 percent of total assets with a volume of $502 billion. Across the four size classes shown in Table A11-1 (appendix A), the dollar rankings of consumer loans at year-end 1995 were as follows:

Bank Size Class (# Banks)	Consumer Loans ($ Billions, % of Assets)	Loans per Bank ($ millions)
Large (90)	$190.4 (14.2%)	$2,115.5
Medium (900)	$179.3 (16.4%)	$ 199.2
Ten largest	$ 69.4 (6.6%)	$6,936.6
Small (9,000)	$ 63.5 (9.5%)	$ 7.1

Consumer loans (narrowly defined as installment plus credit-card loans) have been made mainly by the 990 banks that make up the medium- and large-sized groups,

---

[4] These data, which are for auto finance companies, are from the *Federal Reserve Bulletin* (October 1996), p. A36, and (September 1994), A38. Data in the previous paragraph are also from these sources.

$370 billion, or 74 percent of the $502 billion. However, on a per bank basis, the 10 largest banks, which include wholesale banks such as J. P. Morgan and Bankers Trust, dominate, with average consumer loans of $6.9 billion. The leading players in this market include such names as Citibank, BankAmerica, Chase Manhattan, NationsBank, and BancOne.

The trends in installment loans and credit-card loans over the years 1985 to 1995 reveal the decline of installment loans and the rise of credit-card loans (see Panels B and C of Table A11-1 in the appendix). Nevertheless, as of year-end 1995, only one of the four bank size classes (the group of 90 large banks) had more credit-card loans than installment loans, $98 billion (7.3%) in credit-card loans compared to $92 billion (6.9%) in installment loans. The greatest disparity is for the thousands of community banks that had $57 billion (9.5%) in installment loans but only $6.7 billion (1%) in credit-card loans.

The pattern of consumer lending across the bank size classes suggests a pattern of risk taking across these banks. Gorton and Rosen [1995] describe consumer loans as the "safest" that banks make.[5] Credit-card loans as unsecured debt, however, are much riskier than ordinary installment loans, which are secured by such things as automobiles, residential property, personal property, or financial assets. What we observe (in appendix Table A11-1) is that, above the group of smallest banks, the relative proportion of safer installment loans declines as bank size increases. And as described above, the bulk of riskier credit-card loans are made by the 1,000 largest banks. These patterns suggest that, all other things being equal, risk taking tends to increase with bank size. An alternative and equally plausible hypothesis is that economies of scale exist in the marketing, making, processing, and monitoring of credit-card loans.

Table 11-2 presents credit-card loans as a percentage of total consumer loans by bank size. For all banks, the relative proportion of credit-card loans has in-

TABLE 11-2	Bank Credit-Card Loans as a Percentage of Total Consumer Loans by Bank Size, 1985–1995				
Year	*All Banks*	*Small*	*Medium*	*Large*	*Ten Largest*
1985	23.82%	4.69%	24.20%	37.18%	38.08%
1986	26.19	5.48	27.30	38.14	37.85
1987	27.76	6.81	30.31	37.51	36.51
1988	29.63	7.49	32.75	39.75	33.60
1989	31.03	8.12	31.14	44.87	32.05
1990	32.12	8.94	33.74	44.82	32.02
1991	33.89	10.30	37.81	43.22	35.14
1992	34.66	10.33	38.12	44.03	35.70
1993	35.36	9.92	38.06	45.60	34.11
1994	36.83	10.23	38.23	47.46	34.60
1995	39.06%	10.59%	39.35%	51.58%	29.70%

Source: Calculated from Panels A and B of Table A11–1 in appendix A of this chapter. Data are from the *Federal Reserve Bulletin* (June 1995), pp. 559–569, and (June 1996), pp. 495–505.

---

[5] Gorton and Rosen [1995] attempt to link bank portfolio choice to bank ownership structure for 458 BHCs with adequately capitalized banks over the years 1985 to 1990. Their focus is on "the decline of banking" narrowly defined as "financing loans by issuing deposits" (p. 1410). They conclude that corporate-control (or agency) problems were more important than moral-hazard problems over their test period.

creased steadily from 23.8 percent at year-end 1985 to 39.1 percent at year-end 1995. Except for 1985, an inverted U-shaped pattern holds across the four size classes for each of the years.

CITICORP'S "GLOBAL CONSUMER" BUSINESS

Citicorp views its core business franchises as "consumer" (average assets of $120 billion at year-end 1995) and "commercial banking" (average assets of $136 billion at year-end 1995). These two core businesses accounted for 99 percent of Citicorp's total on-balance-sheet assets of $257 billion. Citicorp's *Annual Report* (1995, p. 24) defines its global consumer business as "a uniquely global, full-service consumer franchise encompassing branch banking, credit and charge cards, and private banking." Table 11-3 provides a financial summary of Citicorp's global consumer business in terms of revenues, expenses, profitability, and loan quality. The ratio section of Panel A presents the return on asset (ROA) components of Citicorp's consumer business. Recall that $ROA = PM \times AU$, where PM = profit margin = net income/revenue, and AU = asset utilization = revenue/assets. For 1995, this financial profile for Citicorp was

$$ROA = 0.1614 \times 0.1022 = 0.0165 = 1.65\%$$

For comparison, Citicorp's ROA profile for its global-finance business, with average assets of $136 billion in 1995, was

$$ROA = 0.2583 \times 0.0457 = 0.0118 = 1.18\%$$

Although commercial banking had a higher profit margin in 1995 (25.8%), it had a substantially lower revenue generation per dollar of assets (4.57%), resulting in a much lower *ROA*. In 1992, however, when the global consumer business was doing only 0.77 percent return on assets, commercial banking had an *ROA* of 1.1 percent. Each core business has its own unique ups and downs.

Net credit losses (net write-offs) and *delinquency rates* reflect *loan quality*. Panels B and C of Table 11-3 capture the quality of Citicorp's consumer loan portfolio for the years 1993 to 1995. From Panel B, we observe three phenomena: (1) the net credit loss ratio for U.S. mortgages, which are secured loans, was 1.0 percent compared to 3.7 percent for U.S. bankcards, which are unsecured loans; (2) net credit loss ratios are lower in developed markets outside the United States; and (3) loan quality improved over the years 1993 to 1995.

Panel C presents delinquency ratios for Citicorp's consumer loan portfolio for the years 1993 to 1995. Delinquent loans are defined as 90 days or more past due. Compared to the actual charge-offs shown in Panel B, delinquency ratios can be misleading. For example, we know a priori (before the fact) that credit-card loans, as unsecured credits, tend to be riskier than residential mortgages and other installment loans, all other things being equal. In addition, with credit-card loans, consumers can keep these loans current by making the minimum payment—a practice that banks love because the unpaid balance earns interest at a relatively high rate. On balance, it is easier to keep credit-card loans current than mortgage loans, and actual charge-offs provide a better indication of true loan quality. Nevertheless, although not revealed by Citicorp's experience as shown in Table 11-3, high delinquency rates can be a precursor of impending future loan losses.

TABLE 11-3 Citicorp's Global Consumer Business, 1995

PANEL A. REVENUE, EXPENSES, PROFITS, AND PERFORMANCE RATIOS

Dollars in millions	1995
Total revenue	$11,343
Effect of credit-card securitization	917
Net cost of carry	12
Adjusted revenue	12,272
Adjusted operating expenses	6,700
Operating margin	5,572
Net write-offs	1,554
Effect of credit-card securitization	917
Net cost to carry and net OREO costs	12
Credit costs	2,473
Operating margin less credit costs	3,099
Additional provision	200
Income before taxes	2,899
Income taxes	918
Net income	$1,981
Average assets (in billions)	$ 120
Return on assets (net income/assets)	1.65%
Loan quality (write-offs/assets)	1.29%
Asset utilization (adjusted revenue/assets)	10.23%
Profit margin (net income/revenue)	16.14%
Operating efficiency (adj. oper. expense/assets)	5.58%

PANEL B. LOAN-LOSS RATIOS, 1995 AND 1993

Product	Average Loans $ Bils	Net Credit Losses $ Mils	1995 Loss Ratio	1993 Loss Ratio
U. S. mortgages	$18.8	$176	0.99%	1.40%
U.S. bankcards	44.2	1,476	3.70	5.26
Developed markets—other	39.4	512	1.33	1.59
Total developed markets	102.4	2,164	2.25	2.92
Emerging markets	28.7	297	1.09	0.82
Total managed	$131.1	$2,461	1.99	2.54
Effect of credit-card securitization	(25.5)	(917)	na	na
Total on-balance-sheet	$105.6	$1,544	1.55%	1.73%

PANEL C. CONSUMER DELINQUENCY RATES (90 DAYS OR MORE PAST DUE), 1993–1995

Product	**Delinquency Ratios** 1995	1994	1993
U.S. mortgages	5.2%	5.8%	6.6%
U.S. bankcards	1.6	1.6	2.4
Other developed markets	4.9	5.2	5.4
Total developed markets	3.6	3.8	4.5
Emerging markets	1.0	0.7	0.8
Total managed	3.0	3.1	3.8
Total on-balance-sheet	3.3	3.4	4.2

Source: Citicorp Annual Report 1995, pp. 25–28.

The data in Panel C reveal the same trend and pattern observed in Panel B, namely, improved credit quality as delinquency rates declined from 1993 to 1995, and greater risk taking in Citicorp's U.S. consumer loan portfolio compared to other developed markets.

THE COST OF MAKING BANK INSTALLMENT LOANS

What does it cost a bank to make a consumer loan and to collect a payment? To answer these questions, we turn to the Federal Reserve's **functional cost analysis** (FCA).[6] The FCA program started in 1957 is a joint venture between the Fed and participating banks. It is designed as a tool for bank management in evaluating performance and is specifically aimed at increasing overall bank earnings as well as improving the operational efficiency of each bank function. The FCA program attempts to provide bank managers with three things:

1. Reasonable approximations of functional costs
2. Year-to-year cost comparisons within the bank
3. Reliable interbank comparisons with group averages for similar banks

Regarding the reliability of FCA data, keep in mind the Fed's caveat: "Bank cost accounting is not an exact science" (p. 1).

Banks participating in the FCA program are separated into groups by deposit size: banks with deposits less than $50 million, banks with deposits from $50 million to $200 million, and banks with deposits over $200 million. Table 11-4 presents some interesting institutional characteristics of the banks participating in the 1994 FCA survey. Note that these data are averages for the banks in each deposit size class. For example, for the 41 banks with deposits over $200 million, the average bank had 11 full-service offices, 13.5 ATMs, and 252 total personnel, 70 of whom were officers.

Table 11-5 shows the average cost of making bank installment loans in 1994 for the three bank size classes. Since the data are averages, they do not reflect the

	TABLE 11-4 Institutional Characteristics of Commercial Banks Participating in the Federal Reserve's Survey of Functional Cost Analysis, 1994		
Characteristics	*49 Banks Deposits up to $50M*	*115 Banks Deposits $50–$200M*	*41 Banks Deposits over $200M*
1. Number of full service offices	1.39	2.82	11.15
2. Number of ATMs	1.62	3.37	13.49
3. Total personnel	20.73	59.50	252.53
4. Officers (included in personnel)	7.06	17.59	70.44
5. Personnel/$millions in assets	.60	.49	.48

Note: Data are averages per bank for each deposit size class.

Source: "Executive Summary," *FCA 1994 National Report.* © Federal Reserve Bank, San Francisco. Used by permission.

---

[6] Background information in this paragraph is from the Introduction of the 1994 FCA National Average Report for commercial banks (p. 1).

TABLE 11-5   The Cost of Making Bank Installment Loans, 1994

Bank Deposit Size ($ millions)

Cost category	Up to $50	$50–$200	Over $200
Making a loan	$123.76	$117.63	$145.48
Collecting a payment	$13.29	$12.06	$10.19
Loan-loss rate (three-year average)	0.40%	0.41%	0.27%
Cost of money rate	4.33%	4.05%	3.86%
Number of banks	52	116	41

Note: Data are averages for the banks within each deposit size class.

Source: FCA: Functional Cost and Profit Analysis, National Average Report, 1994 Commercial Banks, pp. 30–35. © Federal Reserve Bank, San Francisco. Used by permission.

marginal cost of making an additional installment loan. In 1994, the average cost of making an installment loan ranged from $118 to $145. In contrast, Hall and Cloonen [1984] claim that "for a simple consumer loan" an average cost of "$25 to $35 . . . seems to be typical" (p. 140). As you can see, bank cost accounting is not an exact science. However, since the Fed's survey covers all installment loans, and Hall and Cloonen are referring to "simple loans," we are mixing apples and oranges. In illustrating the cost of making a simple consumer loan, Hall and Cloonen allocate cost across four categories:

- Office space (including depreciation on furniture, fixtures, and equipment)
- Supplies (e.g., various kinds of applications, forms, envelopes, etc.)
- Services (e.g., telephone, utilities, computer, insurance, and advertising)
- Labor (defined to include loan officers, collectors, and clerks)

Obviously, more complex loans are more costly to make than simple ones. The important point, however, is that no matter how inexact bank cost accounting is, lenders must attempt to determine the cost of making loans.

Table 11-5 suggests some economies of scale (i.e., costs decrease as bank size increases) with respect to the cost of collecting a loan payment, loan-loss experience, and the cost of money. For example, the cost of collecting a loan payment decreased from $13.29 for the first size group, to $12.06 for the second size group, to $10.19 for the largest size group, all other things being equal.

The Installment Loan Function and Installment Loan Data

Table 11-6 shows the installment loan function and installment loan data for 1994. The FCA data for the installment loan function includes four kinds of loans:

1. Consumer installment loans (82–90% of the loans in the function)
2. Check-credit loans (only 1–2% of the loans)
3. Commercial, equipment, and other loans (4–16% of the loans)
4. Floor-plan loans (1–5% of the loans)

The third category includes all loans carried in the installment loan department, except those normally considered consumer installment loans or floor-plan loans (categories 1 and 4). Examples of commercial, equipment, and other loans include single-payment loans, trailer loans, commercial installment loans, and farm and heavy equipment loans. *Floor-plan loans* are advances made for financing

TABLE 11-6 Installment Loan Function

	52 BANKS, DEPOSITS UP TO $50M		116 BANKS, DEPOSITS $50–$200M		41 BANKS, DEPOSITS OVER $200M	
1. ***Number of Loans Outstanding***	570		1,980		8,318	
Composition	Percentage of Installment Loan Volume					
2. Consumer installment loans	$2,486,669	82.48%	$7,870,756	88.56%	$53,378,046	89.98%
3. Check credit loans	22,143	.73	152,759	1.72	674,254	1.14
4. Commercial and other installment loans	483,387	16.03	729,326	8.21	2,134,784	3.60
5. Floor plan loans	22,588	.75	135,084	1.52	3,134,146	5.28
6. Total installment loans	$3,014,787	100.00%	$8,887,925	100.00%	$59,321,230	100.00%
Income						
7. Consumer installment loans—gross yield	$241,337	9.71%	$715,316	9.09%	$4,255,431	7.92%
8. Check credit loans—gross yield	3,752	16.95	21,132	13.83	89,967	13.34
9. Commercial and other instal. loans—gross yield	46,388	9.60	62,694	8.60	188,895	8.85
10. Floor plan loans	2,095	9.28	7,897	5.85	233,782	7.46
11. Interest and discount subtotal	$293,573	9.74	$807,039	9.08	$4,738,075	7.99%
12. Other income	19,455	.65	47,011	.53	227,156	.38
13. Total income	$313,028	10.38%	$854,050	9.61%	$4,965,230	8.37%
Expense						
14. Officer salaries	$37,897	1.26%	$105,233	1.18%	$399,122	.67%
15. Employee salaries	16,816	.56	53,258	.60	271,836	.46
16. Fringe benefits	12,410	.41	41,267	.47	176,705	.30
17. Salaries and fringe, subtotal	$67,123	2.23%	$200,058	2.25%	$847,663	1.43%
18. Data services	17,859	.59	37,934	.43	178,053	.30
19. Furniture and equipment	4,388	.15	16,547	.19	56,384	.10
20. Occupancy	8,402	.28	25,415	.29	131,455	.22
21. Publicity and advertising	4,972	.16	13,005	.15	55,404	.09
22. Other operating expense	29,306	.97	72,379	.81	347,195	.59
23. Total operating expense	$132,049	4.38%	$365,338	4.11%	$1,616,155	2.72%
Earnings						
24. Net earnings before losses	$180,979	6.00%	$488,713	5.50%	$3,349,076	5.65%
25. Net losses	10,531	.35	26,118	.29	121,566	.20
26. Net earnings	$170,448	5.65%	$462,595	5.20%	$3,227,510	5.44%
27. Cost of money	130,665	4.33	360,073	4.05	2,289,908	3.86
28. Net earnings after cost of money	$39,783	1.32%	$102,522	1.15%	$937,602	1.58%
Number of Installment Loan Personnel	Miscellanous Data					
29. Officers	96		2.58		9.52	
30. Employees	1.04		3.12		14.74	
31. Total personnel	2.00		5.70		24.26	
32. Number of full service offices	1.44		2.85		11.15	
33. 3-year average loan losses	$12,105	.40%	$36,587	.41%	$157,874	.27%

Source: FCA: Functional Cost and Profit Analysis, National Average Report, 1994 Commercial Banks, p. 31.
© Federal Reserve Bank, San Francisco. Used by permission.

inventories of durable goods such as automobiles, equipment, and appliances. Because the sale of these "floor" items usually generates installment paper for the bank, most banks with floor-plan loans carry them in their installment loan department. (Floor-plan loans not included in the installment-loan function are included in the commercial and other loan function.)

Line 28 of Table 11-6 shows the bottom line of the installment-loan function, net earnings after the cost of money (including net loan losses). The figures reveal a U-shaped pattern across the three size classes as the earnings rate first declines from 1.32 percent to 1.15 percent, then rises to 1.58 percent. The corresponding net earnings before loan losses and cost of money were 6.00 percent, 5.50 percent, and 5.65 percent. Across the three size classes, the income and expense functions that determine net earnings are interesting because they move in the same direction. Specifically, total income (line 13) divided by total installment loans (line 6) declines as bank size increases—10.38 percent, 9.61 percent, and 8.37 percent. In addition, total operating expense (line 23) divided by total installment loans (line 6) decreases as bank size increases—4.38 percent, 4.11 percent, and 2.72 percent. As bank size increases, the picture is one of revenue generation declining while operating efficiency improves. The former suggests that the smallest FCA banks rely more on monopoly power than operating efficiency to generate their net installment loan earnings.

Consider, however, the following data drawn from lines 7 and 25 of Table 11-6:

Deposit Size Class	Gross Yield	Loss Rate	Net Yield
Under $50 million	9.71%	0.35%	9.36%
$50 to $200 million	9.09%	0.29%	8.80%
Over $200 million	7.92%	0.20%	7.72%

Note that the net yield as calculated here is simply net of ex post credit risk as captured by net loan losses; it is not adjusted for any operating expenses. Thus, although the conjecture that greater monopoly power is held by the smallest FCA banks could be true, they also have higher loss rates. Thus, part of their higher gross yields reflect greater risk taking. The higher net yields suggest that they have monopoly power, or that they need these higher yields to compensate for their inferior operating performance, or both.

Table 11-7 shows seven interesting aspects of the installment-loan function:

1. Number of loans outstanding by category (lines 1–5)
2. Average size loan (lines 6–10)
3. Number of applications processed (lines 10–11)
4. Number of loans made (lines 12–15)
5. Loans made as a percentage of applicants (lines 16–17)
6. Number of loan payments collected (lines 18–19)
7. Productivity data (lines 20–25)

Let's link the risk-adjusted net yields described above with the loan-acceptance rates shown in lines 16 and 17. For consumer installment loans, the largest component of the installment loan function, the acceptance rate decreases as bank size increases: 86 percent, 72 percent, 61 percent. By accepting relatively more installment loan applications, the smallest banks provide more service (credit) to their

TABLE 11-7 Functional Cost Analysis of Installment Loan Data, Loan Characteristics			
	52 Banks Deposits up to $50M	**116 Banks Deposits $50–$200M**	**41 Banks Deposits over $200M**
Number of Loans Outstanding			
1. Consumer installment	488	1,519	6,657
2. Check credit	40	279	1,256
3. Commercial & other installment loans	41	169	323
4. Floor plan	1	12	83
5. Total	570	1,980	8,318
Average Size Loan			
6. Consumer installment	$5,097	$5,180	$8,019
7. Check credit	556	547	537
8. Commercial & other installment loans	11,879	4,305	6,619
9. Floor plan	$16,090	$11,746	$37,839
Number of Applications Processed			
10. Consumer installment	463	1,546	6,273
11. Commercial & other installment loans	24	83	169
Number of Loans Made			
12. Consumer installment	399	1,113	3,812
13. Check credit	9	41	134
14. Commercial & other installment loans	17	66	151
15. Floor plan	3	22	346
Loans Made as Percentage of Applicants			
16. Consumer installment	86.10%	71.99%	60.78%
17. Commercial & other installment loans	70.24%	79.79%	89.66%
Number of Loan Payments Collected			
18. Consumer installment	5,569	16,995	91,761
19. Commercial & other installment loans	393	1,186	3,376
Productivity Data			
20. Volume of loans per officer ($000)	$3,147	$3,444	$6,230
21. Loans made per officer	445	481	467
22. Loans outstanding per person	285	347	343
23. Applications processed per person	244	286	265
24. Loans made per person	214	218	183
25. Payments collected per employee	5,735	5,823	6,454

Source: FCA: Functional Cost and Profit Analysis, National Average Report, 1994 Commercial Banks, p. 32.
© Federal Reserve Bank, Boston. Used by permission.

communities, but they also take on more risk. Alternatively, if the larger banks accepted the same relative number of loan applications, they would be serving their markets better but at the expense of higher loan-loss rates.

BANK CREDIT CARDS: ORIGINS, COMPETITION, PROFITABILITY, AND SECURITIZATION

In 1949, the credit-card industry began with the development of the first modern credit card called Diners Club.[7] It was the first modern credit card, because its designers, Alfred Bloomingdale, Frank McNamara, and Ralph Snyder, conceived of it as a "universal" card that would reach beyond retailers and gas stations and be accepted everywhere. Today, with well over a billion credit cards in existence worldwide, plastic is a way of life around the world, but especially in the United States, where an estimated 111 million Americans have at least one credit card, and roughly one out of four retail purchases are made with credit or charge cards. Table 11-8 presents a profile of the role of credit cards in the United States by highlighting the number and kinds of cards in force and their dollar volumes and the dollar amount of receivables outstanding. Mandell [1990] claims that "the primary reason for the success of the credit card (in the United States) has been its *credit* feature rather than its *convenience*" (p. 11, emphasis mine).

Because Diners Club was first used most extensively by salespersons to entertain clients or while traveling, it and its followers (e.g., American Express and Carte Blanche) became known as travel and entertainment (T&E) cards. In 1958, bank credit cards began when Bank of America and Chase Manhattan, then the largest and second-largest banks in the United States, launched credit-card operations. In 1962, Chase, unable to make its card operation profitable, sold it. Many other banks had the same experience. In 1966, however, Bank of America, recognizing that a national network was the key to success, licensed its new BankAmericard across the United States. In 1976, to enhance its international appeal, BankAmericard's name was changed to Visa. Although Visa is the leading bank card today, in 1970, it was second to Master Charge in both domestic and international markets. In 1980, Master Charge's name was changed to MasterCard. At the end of the 1970s, 50 banks issued over one-half of all bank credit cards in the United States. In 1987, 20 banks controlled almost 40 percent of the combined Visa and MasterCard accounts and 53 percent of outstanding balances; Citibank was the industry leader, with 10 million accounts (8.4% of market share) and outstanding balances of $15.3 billion (16.3% of market share). At the beginning of 1991, the number of credit cards issued by banks was over 218 million, up from 161 million in 1985. In addition, approximately 28 million in T&E cards were in circulation. Sears's Discover card, introduced in 1985, has since grown to almost 50 million cards in force. Table 11-8 presents a profile of the U.S. card industry as of the second quarter of 1996.

At year-end 1967, commercial banks in the United States held only $1.35 billion in credit-card loans (and related plans). By year-end 1995, credit-card loans had grown to $196.2 billion, an annual growth rate of 19.5 percent over this 28-year period.

---

[7] Information in this section draws in part on Ausubel [1991] and Mandell [1990].

TABLE 11-8 A Profile of the Credit-Card Industry in the United States: Cards in Force, Volume, and Receivables (second quarter 1996)

Panel A. U.S. Cards in Force (in millions)

Card	Number	Percent
Visa[a]	263.1	52.4%
MasterCard[a]	162.3	32.3
Discover	48.9	9.7
American Express	27.5	5.5
Total	501.8	100.0%

Panel B. U.S. Gross Volume ($ billions for second quarter 1996)

Card	Number	Percent
Visa[a]	103.7	50.5%
MasterCard[a]	54.2	26.4
American Express	32.6	15.9
Discover	14.9	7.3
Total	205.4	100.0%

Panel C. U.S. Receivables ($ billions for second quarter 1996)

Card	Number	Percent
Visa[a]	204.9	54.9%
MasterCard[a]	129.3	34.6
Discover	28.8	7.7
American Express	10.5	2.8
Total	373.5	100.0%

Note: [a]Estimate based on issuer reported data.

Source: Data compiled from Bankcard Barometer/Bankcard Update at ramresearch.com/carddata

Citicorp's Global Card Products[8]

At year-end 1995, Citicorp was the world's largest issuer of bankcards and charge cards, with 58 million cards in force worldwide (including affiliates). Citibank, the heart of Citicorp, had 38 million cards in force in the United States at year-end 1995. In addition to bankcards, Citicorp had seven million Diners Club cards outstanding, and it issues and services about five million private-label cards to department stores. Citicorp reports that its card products in force have grown almost 50 percent since 1990. Citibank's pricing strategy in the 1990s has been to eliminate the annual fee for Citibank Classic, Preferred Visa, and MasterCard customers with good credit histories and to move to variable-rate charges on outstanding balances. These tactics were seen as necessary to "reinforce its dominance by building customer loyalty in this highly competitive market" (*1994 Annual Report,* p. 7).

---

[8] Unless otherwise indicated, information in this section is from Citicorp's 1995 *Annual Report,* p. 26, and from "CardFlash" on-line at ramresearch.com.crdflash.

Nonprice competition by Citibank mainly takes the form of attempts at product differentiation as it offers an array of cards targeted at specific customers. For example, Citibank Classic claims to offer security, quality, and value; Citibank Preferred offers a higher credit line; Choice is for price-sensitive customers; and a range of cobranded cards (e.g., with American Airlines, Apple, and Ford) provide credits for purchasing the cobranded product. Another differentiating and security feature pioneered by Citibank has been the Photocard, which bears the cardholder's photo digitally imprinted on the card. Since Citibank introduced its Photocard in the United States in 1992, it has been acclaimed as an important factor in the 62 percent reduction in fraud expenses for Citibank's U.S. bankcard operations.[9]

Citicorp contends that its historical strength in the credit-card business results from years of investing in technology, funding, treasury management (including asset sales), credit scoring, collections, and marketing. During 1995, Citicorp sold $8.9 billion of credit-card receivables compared to $3.5 billion in 1994 and $6.8 billion in 1992. Since 1982, Citicorp's card processing costs per transaction have dropped 30 percent because of economies of scale. Moreover, Citicorp's management thinks the potential for growth in its card business still exists.

The Credit and Convenience Segments of the Credit-Card Market

Two kinds of credit-card users exist: **credit users** and **convenience users.**[10] Bankers love credit users and tolerate convenience users. Bankers love credit users because they generate the major source of credit-card revenues: interest income. Credit users take the name credit card literally, because they actually draw down their lines of credit and do not pay off their outstanding balances on the due date. MBNA, a leading player in the card industry says, "The right Customer is someone who will borrow from us and, of course, someone who will pay us back on time" (*1994 Annual Report,* p. 5). Of course, if it was completely candid, MBNA would add that it wants its customers to make only the *minimum* payment on time. This kind of customer always has an outstanding balance that generates interest income. Fees and service charges, including annual, late, overlimit, returned check, and cash-advance fees, are the other sources of revenues produced by credit cards.

Cardholders who pay off their entire balances each billing cycle use credit cards as pure convenience devices; they are dubbed *convenience users.* They generate fewer revenues for banks than credit users because their outstanding balances are zero; they pay no interest charges. Nevertheless, convenience users generate revenues directly through annual fees (if any) and indirectly through interchange fees (i.e., the portion of the merchant discount paid to the customer's bank).

Bank credit-card services, of course, are not costless to produce because bankers incur costs associated with operating (including fraud), processing, funding, and loan losses.

---

[9] When *60 Minutes* tested a photo credit card, it found (in New York City at least) that most store clerks did not compare the photo with the customer.

[10] Another group of users is the criminal one, whose members make counterfeit cards for use or sale, or steal legitimate cards. Banks incur substantial operating costs due to fraud, which tend to run at 0.15 to 0.19 of the dollar value of total tickets (sales). MBNA, an industry leader, has a ratio of 0.12, which it claims is due to its use of superior fraud-detection practices and technology, and a more thorough screening of applications.

The Stickiness of Interest Rates on Bank Credit Cards

Figure 11-2 shows the stickiness of interest rates on bank credit cards for the years 1982 to 1996. The cost-of-funds line is measured as the quarterly one-year Treasury bill yield plus 75 basis points, or 0.75 percent. Ausubel [1991] estimated this risk premium based on the fact that over the period 1987 to 1989, securitized credit-card receivables averaged about 75 basis points over Treasury securities with comparable maturities. Although some banks have attempted to compete in the credit-card business on the basis of lower interest rates, most banks have kept their rates substantially above their cost of funds. Compared to the average credit-card interest rate of 18–19 percent for the 1980s, the average rate has declined in the early 1990s, but not as much as the general decline in interest rates.

FIGURE 11-2 The Interest Rate on Commercial Bank Credit Cards and Cost of Funds, 1982–1996

Estimating the Stickiness of Credit-Card Interest Rates

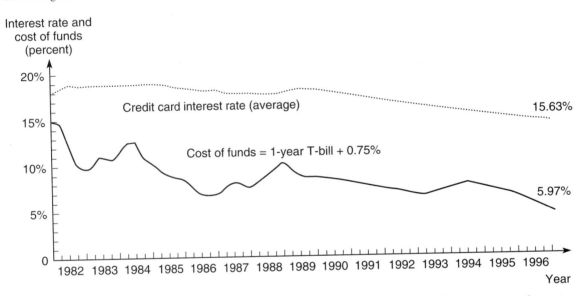

Using quarterly data for the years 1982 to 1989, Ausubel [1991] regressed the credit-card interest rate on the cost of funds and the credit-card rate both lagged one-period. He got the following result:

$$r_{cc} = 2.06 + 0.0439r_{tb,t-1} + 0.864r_{cc,t-1} \qquad N = 32, R^2 = 0.96,$$

where r_{cc} is the credit-card rate and r_{tb} is the Treasury bill as defined in the text and $t - 1$ indicates a one-period lag. The estimated standard errors were such that both regression coefficients were significantly different from both zero *and* one. How do we interpret this equation? If we write the equation as

$$r_{cc} = a + br_{tb,t-1} + cr_{cc,t-1},$$

then, in a competitive market, the joint hypothesis is [$b = 1, c = 0$] and the intercept, a, estimates all other costs over the adjusted T-bill rate. In a market with a sticky credit-card rate that does not respond to the cost of funds, we would observe [$b = 0, c = 1$]. Since the estimated coefficients are close to these, they support the stickiness hypothesis rather than the competitive one. Moreover, the estimated coefficient on the adjusted T-bill rate (0.0439) suggests that the credit-card rate adjusts less than five percent per quarter to the previous quarter's cost of funds and takes on 86 percent of the value of the previous quarter's credit-card rate. As Ausubel [1991] concludes, this finding suggests that " . . . credit cards must become extraordinarily profitable when the cost of funds drops" (p. 56).

Source: Adapted and expanded from *Federal Reserve Bulletin* (various issues). The cost of funds is the quarterly one-year Treasury bill rate (Table 1.35) plus 0.75 percent. The credit-card rate is from Table 1.56, Terms of Consumer Installment Credit. Ausubel [1991], Figure 1, p. 54 shows these data for the years 1981–1989.

For example, during 1995, the unweighted average rate on standard bank credit cards was 17.1 percent (18.15% based on a weighted average of receivables). From July 1995 until December 1995, the unweighted average rate declined from 17.25 percent to 16.96 percent (the weighted average declined from 18.3% to 18.0% over the same period).[11] All other things being equal, this continued stickiness suggests the major reason why credit cards generate such extraordinary accounting profits.

The Accounting Profitability of Bank Credit Cards

The accounting components of credit-card revenue consist of interest charges, annual fees, other customer charges (e.g., fees for late payments, exceeding credit limits, and returned checks), and interchange fees. The cost of credit-card operations include interest expenses, noninterest or operating expenses, and **loan losses** or net charge-offs. The difference between these items as a percentage of outstanding credit-card balances generates pretax ROA for the bank credit-card function. A typical revenue-expense profile for a bank specializing in credit cards looks as follows:[12]

Interest revenue	15.18%
Interest expense	6.59
Net interest margin	8.59
Net loan losses	3.30
NIM after NLL	5.29
Noninterest revenue	5.25
Noninterest expense	7.20
Pre-tax ROA	3.36%

Compared to banks that do not specialize in credit-card operation, pre-tax ROAs are two-to-three times more profitable from an accounting perspective. For example, high-performing banks without a specialization in credit cards generated about 1.5 percent on assets.

Product Differentiation and Card Profitability

If you have seen one piece of plastic, you have not seen them all. Card issuers want consumers to believe this statement. In addition to affinity cards, a more basic marketing strategy is to attempt to segment markets on a prestige factor: regular cards versus gold cards. However, as Table 11-9 shows, the differences in profitability between these two cards is not great: 3.6 percent pretax ROA for gold cards in 1995

[11] The rates presented in this paragraph are averages for standard cards. Lower rates, either fixed or floating, exist. For example, many banks now offer floating-rate cards at 300–400 basis points above the prime rate, which on February 1, 1996, would have meant a rate in the range of 11.25 percent to 12.25 percent. "Teaser rates" are also common, e.g., 185 basis points *below* prime for the first six months. The smart cardholder shops around for the best deal.

[12] These data, for the years 1984 to 1991, are from Sinkey and Nash [1993]. Also see Ausubel [1991] and Nash and Sinkey [1997]. Using alternative data sources, Ausubel estimates that for the years 1983 to 1988 bank credit-card businesses earned annual returns on investment of 60 to 100 percent or more. Using a benchmark ROE of 20 percent, bank credit cards were three-to-five times more profitable. He estimates credit-card ROAs in the range of 4-to-6 percent; in contrast, a 1-to-1.5 percent pre-tax ROA on bank total assets is considered good.

TABLE 11-9 1995 Comparative Card Industry Profit Estimates

P/L Yield Categories	National Brand ROA Estimate	National Brand ROA Range	Private Label Retail Credit ROA Estimate	Private Label Retail Credit ROA Range	Regular Cards ROA Estimate	Gold Cards ROA Estimate
Total income	18.0%	14–20%	16.0%	13–18%	18.0%	17.9%
Operating expense	4.2%	3–6%	5.5%	5–9%	4.3%	4.2%
Charge-offs (net)	4.1%	1–7%	6.5%	5–10%	4.2%	4.0%
Cost of funds	6.1%	4–7%	6.0%	4–8%	6.1%	6.1%
Pretax net income	3.6%	1–6%	0.5%	N/A–2.5%	3.4%	3.6%

Note: The pretax ROA estimates reflect an overall industry perspective and are not meant to be indicative of any one issuer or region. *Profit yields* vary widely between individual card issuers, based upon credit quality, credit and collection practices, maturity of the portfolios, source of the accounts, and the percentage of cardholders who revolve their balances. Compared to 1994, the 1995 yields reflect declining income due to severe price competition and attrition, due to balance transfer "cannibalism"; operating expense and charge-off improvements due to prior investment in technology and scoring techniques; and a boost in "blended" cost of funds; all leading to a 30 basis point softening of pretax profit.

Source: Data courtesy of R. K. Hammer Investment Bankers.

compared to 3.4 percent for regular cards. Regular cards are generally characterized by higher interest rates, delinquency rates, and charge-off rates compared to gold cards; gold cards tend to have higher start-up/marketing expenses and higher usage to go with lower interest rates and better credit quality.

Compared to private-label cards (e.g., those issued by department stores and other businesses to provide retail credit), bank cards are, on average, about seven times more profitable, that is, 0.5 percent compared to 3.5 percent, based on pretax ROA. Private-label accounts generally are characterized by limited utility value (e.g., no cash-advance capability), higher interest rates than national brands, lower annual fee (if any), higher delinquency and charge-offs (driven by instant credit at point of sale, POS), and higher operating expense due to customization of the product line.

Focusing on the ROA ranges presented in Table 11-9, it is easy to see how some card businesses can be losing propositions. For example, the highest estimate for each of the income-expense categories produces a zero yield ($0.20 - 0.06 - 0.07 - 0.07$) or in a worst-case situation a negative yield of -0.06 ($0.14 - 0.06 - 0.07 - 0.07$). On balance, profit yields vary widely across individual card issuers based on credit quality, credit and collection practices, maturity of the portfolios, source of the accounts, and the percentage of cardholders who revolve their balances.

The outlook for credit-card profitability[13] depends on several factors: the degree of rate and fee competition; account attrition due to balance transfer "cannibalism"; operating expense and charge-off improvements due to prior investment in technology and credit-scoring techniques; and a bank's "blended" cost of funds. From 1994 to 1995, these factors led to a 30 basis-point softening of pretax ROA for the average credit-card bank.

---

[13] Appendix B presents an alternative measure of profitability by focusing on the premium paid for credit-card receivables.

Credit-Card Portfolios: Sales versus Securitization

A history of the sale of credit-card portfolios over the years 1985 to 1995 (see Panel A of Table B11-1 in appendix B of this chapter) reveals that although the average premium[14] has declined slightly, the biggest change has been the decline in the dollar amount of assets sold. With the number of transactions also declining, the average size deal has declined from $264 million (1989) to $48 million (1995). The large growth in securitization of credit-card receivables has increased in direct proportion (and far greater) to the decline in card assets sold during the same period.

Regarding expected developments, Hammer [1996], the leading investment banker in the sale of card portfolios, contends,

> Look for a few surprise sellers, including larger deals, portfolio prices rising (in some cases to near historic high levels) depending upon credit quality, source or origin of accounts, maturity or seasoning of accounts, and portfolio size. Major players managing their balance sheets through asset sales/purchases will continue to bring larger (partial sale) deals to market.

In contrast to the sale of credit-card receivables, major credit-card players also engage in the **securitization** of their receivables. In securitized transactions, it is typical for the issuer to retain the servicing and the customer relationships of the credit-card accounts. Deals typically range in size from $200 million to $1 billion. These transactions are debt securities that carry either fixed or floating rates of interest rates with maturities usually in the range of three–six years. Box 11-1 presents an example of a credit-card securitization.

Credit-card securitizations are highly profitable, especially when they are set as floating-rate contracts in a declining-rate environment. For example, consider

BOX 11-1

AN EXAMPLE OF A CREDIT-CARD SECURITIZATION

On August 23, 1995, AT&T Universal Card Services Corporation (UCS) announced that it had priced a $1 billion credit-card securitization transaction. The securitization, Series 1995-1, consisted of two classes of publicly traded, floating-rate certificates issued by AT&T Universal Card Master Trust: Class A Certificates (a senior class) representing $870 million in receivables with a three-year life and an interest rate of eight basis points over three-month LIBOR, priced at par; and $60 million in subordinated three-year Class B Certificates priced at par and accruing interest at 20 basis points over three-month LIBOR.[a] Both of the certificates reprice quarterly. The Class A certificates were rated "AAA," whereas the Class B Certificates were rated "A." At the time of this securitization, AT&T UCS had 16.4 million accounts, 23 million cards issued, and $12.5 billion in outstanding receivables.

Note: [a]The Series 1995-1 also included a privately-funded $70 million collateral invested amount, subordinated to the Class A and Class B certificates, that provides credit enhancement for the benefit of certificate holders.

---

[14] The reported sales are *gross* premiums for good, open-to-buy accounts and balances, prior to any deduction or discounting for credit quality. The transactions are for *unsecured national brand* portfolios only; they do not include private label, retail, or secured accounts collateralized by consumer deposits. The figures do not include numerous small transactions, typically less than $15,000,000, which are often unknown to anyone other than the parties in the transactions.

the following excess-spread analysis for a $1-billion, floating-rate deal done by MBNA in 1993 with an expected maturity of January 15, 1997:[15]

Cash yield	18.37%
Less: Coupon (floating)	6.15
Servicing fees	2.50
Charge-offs	3.35
Excess spread: Dec-95	5.96
Nov-95	6.81
Oct-95	6.75
Three month average excess spread	6.51%

This illustration, which is not atypical for MBNA, clearly demonstrates how profitable the securitization of credit-card receivables can be. By securitizing its receivables but retaining servicing and customer relationships, MBNA generates liquidity, continues to generate servicing fees, and maintains customer relationships. Because the certificates are credit enhanced, investors face minimal credit risk. MBNA must continue to monitor credit quality, however, because if charge-offs increase, its excess spread is reduced. In addition, if interest rates increase, MBNA is exposed to interest-rate risk to the extent that the underlying receivables are based on fixed rates.

Has Competition Failed in the Credit-Card Market?

Ausubel [1991] argues that the large premiums paid in 1989 and 1990 for credit-card businesses (appendix B) are difficult to justify unless the buyers expected future returns at least three times the ordinary returns in banking. Part of the premiums, however, may be due to expected profits in other businesses that the buyers hope to develop by cross-selling additional products and services to the newly acquired account holders. Although premiums for "good deals" have dropped only slightly, the volume of new sales has dropped substantially as securitization of card receivables has soared. Investment banker Robert K. Hammer claims, "The days of mid-twenties and higher premiums may not be gone forever, but prices on portfolios have fallen. It's not the best time for a card portfolio to go to market" (*American Banker,* January 24, 1991, p. 5).

Ausubel also presents evidence that the market for bank credit cards does not conform "with the predictions of a competitive model in continuous spot-market equilibrium" (p. 75). Sticky interest rates on credit cards (Figure 11-2) and high profit rates on card businesses (Table 11-9) present telling evidence. He was concerned about "a breakdown of the optimizing consumer behavior so basic to the model of perfect competition" (p. 75). According to Ausubel, his findings are "roughly consistent with a model of adverse selection in which many consumers are insensitive to interest-rate differentials because they believe they will pay within the grace period (although they repeatedly fail to do so)" (pp. 75–76).

An alternative story is that the market has not failed and that risk-adjusted profit rates have been overestimated. For example, focusing on Citicorp's loan-loss ratio for its card businesses, it averaged 4.4 percent over the years 1988 to 1990, finishing at 4.7 percent for 1990. The loss rates presented by Ausubel were 2.6 percent

---

[15] The maturity is described as "expected" because prepayment of the receivables could shorten the life of the certificates. I thank Jeff Unkle of MBNA for supplying these data, which were compiled by Bloomberg.

for fewer than nine banks in his 1987 survey, 1.8 percent for Maryland Bank, N.A. (which, as described in appendix B, was spun off by its parent, MNC, in 1991 at a premium of only 13.7 percent compared to Ausubel's average premium of 20 percent). In addition, during 1995, bankcard delinquency rates increased by 25 percent. Although these differences in loss rates would not account for all of the excess profits estimated by Ausubel, they would reduce them. In this regard, Mandell [1990] contends that "increased competition will probably prevent companies from reaping profits similar to those of the boom years of the 1980s" (p. 156). Moreover, at the end of 1990, both Fitch Investor Service (in November) and Moody's (in December) warned that rising personal bankruptcies and consumer loan defaults would hurt the quality of credit-card securities.

More recently, MBNA, in its *1994 Annual Report,* notes, "It is not surprising that ours is a very competitive business" (p. 5). In this environment, MBNA goes on to say, analysts and investors ask, "How will MBNA continue to be successful in such a competitive environment?" MBNA's answer is that it thinks it can distinguish itself from the competition (i.e., "the recognized industry leader in affinity marketing with 3,700 endorsements") and by providing "excellent service delivered consistently." MBNA claims that its business has four key strengths:

- Widespread demand
- Long (product) life cycle
- Low-risk assets[16]
- Being distinguishable from the competition

MBNA summarizes its strategic plan in nine words: "Success is getting the right customers and keeping them."

On balance, the reported demise of competition in the market for credit cards, like Mark Twain's death, appears to have been exaggerated.

CONSUMER CREDIT ANALYSIS

As a banker, Hamlet would say: "To lend or not to lend, that is the question." Given a lending philosophy, bankers need a methodical approach to granting credit (e.g., the five Cs of credit analysis, chapter 10). Rouse [1989] identifies five stages in the analysis of new customers:

1. Initial contact or introduction
2. Credit application
3. Review of the application
4. Credit analysis or evaluation
5. Monitoring and control

The fourth step is the crucial one in terms of deciding whether or not to grant credit. Because of potential hidden action or hidden information on the part of the

---

[16] By low-risk assets, it means a lack of "concentration risk" with respect to industry, geography, and individual accounts; for example, at year-end 1994, it held a well-diversified portfolio of $18.7 billion in loans spread across seven million active accounts. Like other card specialists, however, it had a high overall credit risk compared to nonspecialized bank lenders. For example, for 1994, MBNA, with its top-of-the-line credit quality, had a delinquency ratio of 2.6 percent and a loan-loss ratio of 1.96 percent. Table 11-9 shows that industry credit risk is even higher.

borrower, lenders face principal-agent problems. The costs of monitoring and controlling borrowers generate costs for lenders. By varying the terms of lending (rate, maturity, amount financed, and loan-to-value ratio), lenders attempt to control their risk exposures.

As an alternative to the five Cs of **credit analysis,** Rouse [1989] suggests a decision framework based on the acronym **CAMPARI,** which stands for

*C*haracter (the first of the five Cs)

*A*bility (in managing financial affairs)

*M*argin (interest rate, commissions, and fees)

*P*urpose (of the loan)

*A*mount (of the loan)

*R*epayment (probability of)

*I*nsurance (the collateral component of the five Cs)

In contrast to the five Cs (character, capacity, capital, collateral, and conditions), the CAMPARI framework is more specific with respect to the purpose and terms (e.g., amount, rate, and fees) of the loan.

A Systems Approach versus Individual Appraisal

Rouse ([1989], p. 11) contends that for consumer lending a **systems approach,** as opposed to dealing with each customer individually, is the most cost effective for most personal lending. By a *systems approach,* he means:

- Credit-scoring techniques
- Artificial intelligence
- The widespread use of unadvised overdraft limits

Because of the time it takes to develop the expertise and generate the experience to judge borrowers' creditworthiness, "expert systems" offer a viable alternative to the traditional loan officer's appraisal of individual applicants. According to Hall and Cloonen [1984],

> . . . credit scoring has become a sophisticated tool used by many of the nation's leading consumer lenders. Judgmental processing of consumer credit applications is rapidly being assisted and in some cases replaced entirely by computerized scoring systems. This is becoming even more the case since the ECOA [Equal Credit Opportunity Act as amended in 1976] permits the use of a credit-scoring system if it is "demonstrably and statistically sound and empirically derived" (p. 85).
>
> The Equal Credit Opportunity Act (ECOA, as amended in 1976) permits lenders to use two types of credit evaluation: (1) credit scoring (if it meets the requirements described above), and (2) judgmental credit evaluation, defined as anything other than credit scoring. For routine credit decisions, credit scoring has substantial cost advantages.[17]

Consumer Credit Scoring

Banks and large retailers such as J. C. Penney and Sears, Roebuck, make extensive use of **credit-scoring models.** However, because of the proprietary nature of these systems, information about their specific content and structure is relatively scarce.

---

[17] Durand [1941] produced the seminal work on consumer credit scoring. He analyzed "good" and "bad" loans made by commercial banks.

Sexton [1977] reports that the following variables have been common to the credit-scoring system of large retailers.

1. Good credit record
2. Married
3. Single
4. Divorced or separated
5. Number of dependents
6. Age
7. Primary monthly income
8. Presence of extra income
9. Home owner
10. Home renter
11. Home telephone
12. Credit investigation made

An additional 24 variables were used by various retailers for credit scoring. Five of the more important ones were gender, number of months at present job, presence of savings account, number of derogatory comments related to credit inquiries, and occupation. The passage of the ECOA in 1974, its amendments in 1976, and its implementation through the Fed's Regulation B have placed the burden of proof on any institution using credit-score mechanisms to ensure that their models are methodologically and statistically sound.[18]

Wills [1983] presents another example of credit scoring based on eight variables: seven supplied by the applicant and another based on credit-bureau information. The seven variables are as follows:

1. Years on the job (e.g., 20 points for 2.5 to 6.49 years)
2. Home phone (yes = 35, no = 0, close by = 30)
3. Years at address (e.g., 19 points for 2.5 to 6.49 years)
4. Department store/major CC (none = 0, dept. = 11, both = 27)
5. Age of auto (e.g., 22 points for 1–2 years)
6. Finance company references (yes = 5, no = 11)
7. Source (new or present customer = 5, former customer = 18)

The score for the eighth variable, which is based on a credit bureau's report, has five categories:

8. Credit bureau report:
   a. Derogatory ratings only = −15
   b. no record = −4
   c. one, two, or three excellent or satisfactory ratings = 0, 8, or 18

To illustrate this credit-scoring model, an applicant with a phone (35), both credit cards (27), no finance company references (11), two excellent or satisfactory credit bureau ratings (8), who is a present customer (5), and who has 61 points for

---

[18] The 1974 act prohibited discrimination in the granting of credit on the basis of sex or marital status. The 1976 amendment added the following factors: race, color, religion, national origin, age, receipt of public assistance benefits, and good-faith exercise of rights under the Consumer Credit Protection Act. Regulation B describes the statistical criteria that credit-scoring models must satisfy before they can qualify legally to use the prohibited age variable.

the other three factors as given in the previous example has a total score of 147. Because Wills's model has a cutoff score of 120, the applicant with a score of 147 passes the credit-scoring test.

Credit-scoring systems have been used by financial institutions and retailers for many years. According to Maland [1991], over 50 percent of commercial banks with one billion dollars or more in assets used some type of credit-scoring system to evaluate applicants for their credit cards.[19] Credit-scoring models must to be able to distinguish statistically between good and bad credit risks. The primary value of a statistical credit-scoring system is to reduce a multidimensional problem to a single dimension—the credit score (e.g., 147 as shown in the example above). Figure 11-3 illustrates graphically the statistical methodology behind a credit-scoring problem.

FIGURE 11-3 Reduced-Space Transformation: A Credit-Scoring Example

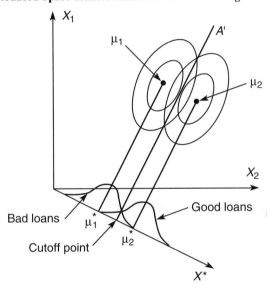

Analysis: This figure illustrates a reduced-space transformation for the two-dimensional case. It shows a mapping from the two-dimensional space given by the X_1 and X_2 axes into the reduced space represented by the line X*. The ellipses indicate the locus of points of equal likelihood within each group in the space $[X_1, X_2]$, and the distributions along X* indicate density in reduced space. If we think of X_1 as monthly income and X_2 as stability of employment measured by number of years on the job, we can illustrate a simple two-variable credit-scoring model. On the reduced-space line, X*, we get the distributions of good and bad credit risks and the cutoff score, which bisects the area of overlap. The area of group overlap represents observations with the greatest amount of uncertainty regarding their actual riskiness or probability of repayment. A conservative lender would move the cutoff score to the right while an aggressive one would move it to the left. All observations along any ray perpendicular to X* (such as *A*ı) will have the same reduced-space value or credit score.

Note: μ_1 and μ_2 are group means and μ_1^* and μ_2^*, are the transformed-space group means or *centroids*.

Source: Adapted from Altman, Avery, Eisenbeis, and Sinkey [1981], Figure I.10, p. 51.

---

[19] A credit-scoring system uses a statistical model (such as the MDA, logit, or CART models described in chapter 10) to assign values (scores) to the characteristics (e.g., monthly income) of existing or would-be borrowers.

Predicting Personal Bankruptcy

In 1990, an estimated 735,000 debtors filed for personal bankruptcy, more than double the number of filings in 1984; see Palmieri [1991]. If lenders can identify potential personal (and corporate, chapter 10) bankrupts, they can avoid making loans to those borrowers; for existing borrowers, they can close or reduce the credit limit on the account. Palmieri contends that with present-day technology the task is a manageable one. Moreover, he argues that because bankruptcy and default (i.e., the prediction given by a credit-scoring model) are different events that are not perfectly correlated, they require different predictive models. Accordingly, he advocates that lenders use scores from personal-bankruptcy prediction models to supplement their credit evaluations.

Personal-bankruptcy prediction scores are available from three national credit bureaus: Equifax Inc., Trans Union, and TRW Credit Data Division. Lenders that already have a terminal link with one of these companies can get personal bankruptcy scores as part of the basic credit report for only a few cents more additional cost. In addition to bankruptcy prediction, these three companies also predict good/bad credit risks. Both kinds of models can be used to assist in making credit decisions and in monitoring and reviewing existing loans. Palmieri [1991] reports that one of the sellers of scoring models claims, "The only time a human evaluator can beat the automated scoring systems is when the person is a highly experienced lender with personal knowledge of the borrower. There are not enough of those people to go around" (p. 31). Another argument in favor of classification models is that a bank's rules and guidelines are applied uniformly without subjectivity.

Rather than obtaining credit scores externally (called "outsourcing"), banks may elect to develop their own models for predicting personal (or corporate) bankruptcy. Such decisions must be evaluated using cost-benefit analysis. One argument in favor of outsourcing is that scoring models need to be updated to keep them current. Thus, model development and refinement is an ongoing task requiring a long-term commitment.

Maland [1991] reports how a large bank used its credit-scoring system as a surveillance mechanism for its credit-card accounts. Her story goes like this. In early 1990, the bank noticed a substantial increase in bankruptcy filings among its credit-card holders in several northeastern and mid-Atlantic States. In August 1990, the bank analyzed the financial characteristics of its card customers in a nine-state area to review their creditworthiness. In particular, the bank wanted to identify its high-risk cardholders, in this case, those most likely to file bankruptcy. Customers who had been delinquent in making payments to the bank over the previous 14 months, or who were over their credit limit when the analysis was undertaken, were evaluated using scoring models. As permitted by the credit-card contract with the customer, the bank closed or reduced the credit limit on accounts that were identified as posing a risk of loss. Prior to terminating a cardholder's account or reducing its credit line, the bank sent each customer a notice of the action.

Maland's story was the first reported case of a bank using credit scoring on a regional basis to evaluate cardholders in reaction to increased bankruptcy filings in the region. If other banks are not doing the same thing, they should be. On balance, such surveillance models can be a routine part of the credit-review process for both retail and wholesale customers.

A Credit-Scoring Faux Pas

A credit-scoring model, or any type of model, should not be used without human judgment. Consider the case of Lawrence B. Lindsey, a member of the Federal Reserve Board in Washington, DC.[20] He applied for a credit card (private label, see Table 11-9) from Toys R Us. Why he would want such a card we won't consider here. The Bank of New York issues credit cards for Toys R Us. In 1995, Mr. Lindsey received a computer-generated letter from the bank. It read: "We have received your new account application. We regret that we are not able to approve it at this time." His application was rejected because he scored too low on the bank's computerized scoring system. The reason given: "Multiple companies requested your credit report in the past six months." Commenting on the reason for rejection, a spokesperson for a major credit-scoring business said that a large number of credit inquiries by would-be lenders "is a sign that people are searching for a lot of credit and that's not necessarily a good thing." Five of the eight inquiries in Mr. Lindsey's case were the result of his refinancing his mortgage last spring and transferring his home-equity line to another bank. The other inquiries resulted from a routine annual review by one of his card issuers whereas the other two came from his application for a new credit card and an overdraft line. Prodded by inquiries from *The Wall Street Journal,* Bank of New York told Mr. Lindsey that another contributing factor to his low score was lack of a savings account, which was not mentioned in his rejection letter.

The issue here is not that a member of the Board of Governors of the Federal Reserve should automatically receive credit but that a scoring system without any human touch will occasionally generate a bad decision, in this case a very embarrassing one. Prior to his rejection, Mr. Lindsey said in a speech before the Boston Bar Association: "We will obtain the fairness of the machine (referring to credit scoring by computer), but lose the judgment, talents, and sense of justice that only humans can bring to decision making."

How can such faux pas be avoided? At some point a human touch needs to be involved. Lenders use computers for credit scoring because they cut costs and permit decisions to be made quickly, and usually accurately. Smart lenders use credit scoring as a tool. A spokesperson for MBNA contends that it uses "judgmental lending," with credit scoring as a tool. The credit scoring is done first, but no credit decision is rendered until the application has been reviewed by a human being. Because everyone in the card industry has heard of Bank of New York's faux pas, other lenders that could have been caught in the same trap will perhaps add the human touch. Or at the minimum, add a mechanical screen to flag absurd decisions. Mr. Lindsey adds a more important concern, however. He contends that using computer models to obey antidiscrimination laws may actually injure the intended beneficiaries. Until computers can measure subjective traits such as character, integrity, and hard work, they will not be able to capture the richness of human decision making.

Now for the rest of the story: In an attempt to save face, Bank of New York offered Mr. Lindsey a card with a $15,000 credit limit. He could charge lots of toys and games with that line of credit but Mr. Lindsey refused the card. Of course, with annual earnings of $123,000 (for 1995), he still has the economic power to buy all the toys he wants.

---

[20] Facts, figures, and quotations reported in this section are from Wessel [1995].

RESIDENTIAL REAL-ESTATE LENDING: FIRST LIENS AND HOME-EQUITY LOANS

One of the biggest changes in bank consumer lending, broadly defined, has resulted from the restructuring of the savings-and-loan industry. Because residential mortgages have substantially less credit risk than credit-card loans or real-estate construction and development loans, the financial-management challenge for banks is to handle well the interest-rate risk associated with fixed-rate mortgages (see chapter 5). The mishandling of this risk led to the downfall of many S&Ls. Banks and surviving S&Ls, however, have better tools and markets for managing interest-rate risk, as reflected in adjustable-rate mortgages (ARMs), well-developed markets for selling/securitizing mortgages, and the availability of derivatives for hedging interest-rate risk.

At the end of 1985, all commercial banks held $188 billion in loans backed by one–four family residential property; ten years later (1995), the stock was $598 billion, an annual growth of 12 percent. The 1995 stock consisted of $520 in first liens and $78 billion in home-equity loans (second liens, assuming a first exists). At year-end 1988, the first year for which data are available, the stock of home-equity loans held by commercial banks was $35 billion, an annual growth of 12 percent through 1995.[21]

Residential Mortgage Lending by Bank Size

Table 11-10 shows lending by bank size for loans secured by one–four family residential property. Panel A presents data for one–four family residential property (excluding home-equity loans) as a percentage of average consolidated assets. Two clear patterns emerge from these data: (1) the relative proportion of residential mortgages held by banks has increased across all four bank size classes from 1985 to 1995, and (2) as bank size increases, the relative proportion of these "safe" loans (safe from default risk but not from interest-rate risk) decreases.

In terms of the dollar amount of residential mortgage credit extended at year-end 1995, the following data (ranked by dollar volume for bank size class) are instructive:

Bank Size Class	Volume at Year-end 1995	Growth since 1985
Medium (900 banks)	$165.3 billion	11.9%
Large (90 banks)	$160.1 billion	15.4%
Small (9,000 banks)	$108.2 billion	4.5%
Ten largest	$ 86.4 billion	12.5%
Total	$520.3 billion	10.7%

The low growth rate for small banks is a bit misleading because at year-end 1985, this group had the largest stock of residential mortgages at $70 billion (37% of the total amount lent by all banks). The other amounts in 1985, which declined with the bank size group, were $54 billion (medium), $38 billion (large), and $26 billion (ten largest).

---

[21] Timmons [1996] reports concerns expressed by analysts and regulators that the home-equity market could be headed for a fall because of overextension and weakened credit standards.

> **TABLE 11-10** One–Four Family Residential Real-Estate Loans (first liens) and Home-Equity Loans (second liens) Made by Commercial Banks by Size Class, 1985–1995

Panel A. One–Four Family Residential Real Estate Loans as a Percentage of Average Consolidated Assets (excluding home equity loans except for 1985 to 1987)

Year	All Banks	Small	Medium	Large	Ten Largest
1985	7.31	11.23	8.42	5.71	4.10
1986	7.45	11.62	8.49	5.27	4.76
1987	8.22	12.80	9.48	5.88	5.17
1988	8.07	13.32	8.91	5.68	5.07
1989	8.73	13.62	9.47	6.13	6.41
1990	9.54	14.21	10.18	6.86	8.00
1991	10.32	14.70	10.68	8.10	8.71
1992	10.82	15.10	11.69	8.85	8.46
1993	11.42	15.55	12.66	9.76	8.68
1994	11.84	15.74	13.92	10.64	8.29
1995	12.54	16.25	15.11	11.97	8.22

Panel B. Home-Equity Loans (second liens, secured by one–four family residential property) as a Percentage of Average Consolidated Assets, 1988–1995

Year	All Banks	Small	Medium	Large	Ten Largest
1988	1.14	0.73	1.73	1.17	0.76
1989	1.42	0.95	2.08	1.41	1.04
1990	1.67	1.16	2.31	1.66	1.31
1991	1.95	1.29	2.53	2.07	1.63
1992	2.09	1.34	2.56	2.50	1.63
1993	2.07	1.27	2.50	2.54	1.60
1994	1.91	1.21	2.33	2.33	1.40
1995	1.88	1.20	2.36	2.19	1.40

Note: Small banks are those not ranked among the 1,000 largest by assets, medium banks are those ranked 101–1,000 by assets, large banks are those ranked 11–100 by assets, and the 10 largest are the 10 largest banks by assets. In Panel A, the years 1985 to 1987 may include home-equity loans; in Panel B, data prior to 1985 are not available.

Source: Federal Reserve Bulletin (June 1996), pp. 496–505, and (June 1995), pp. 559–569.

The data for home-equity loans paint a slightly different picture, as revealed by the following data for year-end 1995:

Bank Size Class	Volume at Year-end 1995	Growth since 1988
Large (90 banks)	$29.3 billion	16.3%
Medium (990 banks)	$25.8 billion	8.6%
Ten largest banks	$14.7 billion	16.0%
Small (9,000 banks)	$ 8.0 billion	7.6%
Total	$78.0 billion	12.2%

Here the banks in the large and medium groups with $55 billion (71%) generate the bulk of home-equity loans. At year-end 1988, these 990 banks held $25 billion in home-equity loans. Over the next seven years, their home-equity loans grew at an annual rate of 13.2 percent.

The Restructuring of Residential Real-Estate Lending[22]

With the advent of securitization in the 1970s, the option to sell and service mortgage loans became available to traditional mortgage lenders such as S&Ls, mortgage bankers, and commercial banks. The result was a restructuring of the mortgage-lending process with an eye toward specialization or fragmentation (chapter 9). The traditional mortgage-lending process has four parts: originate, fund, service, and monitor. Assuming credible guarantees, a securitized lender engages in only three steps: originate, sell, and service. Participants in securitized lending can elect to perform one or more of the functions. Garrett [1989] argues that "this restructuring . . . will so radically change the traditional ways we finance the American homebuyer that those who do not recognize these changes will be the dinosaurs of tomorrow" (p. 30).

Although the securitization of residential mortgages began in the 1970s, it was the interest-rate crunch of 1979–1982 that gave restructuring its real momentum. The interest-rate crisis also led to the ravaging of the thrift industry and the demise of its federal deposit insurer, the FSLIC. As documented in Table 11-10, many commercial banks have jumped at the chance to replace thrifts as residential mortgage lenders. Commercial banks, however, must recognize the structural changes in the business to avoid being the dinosaurs of tomorrow. Eisenbeis and Kwast [1991] present evidence for the years 1978 to 1988 that commercial banks specializing in real estate (they call them "REBs" for real-estate-lending banks) were viable.[23] Specifically, they found REBs had similar earnings to non–real-estate banks, and that REBs that specialized for a longer period of time had higher returns and less risk than more diversified banks. In addition, real-estate banks showed considerable flexibility in adjusting their portfolios of specialized loans.

The Fragmentation of the Mortgage-Lending Process

Garrett [1989] describes the restructuring of the mortgage-lending process as a new paradigm (a fancy word for model) for mortgage lenders, one marked by the "unraveling and unbundling of the housing-finance delivery system" (p. 31). The first step in the mortgage-lending process is origination. Primarily, it is a marketing or sales effort, followed by the processing of the application, which includes appraisal of the property, credit investigation, preparing the loan contract, and other work for which the originator receives an origination fee. Prior to the restructuring, mortgage loan brokering was almost a dirty word; today, it is legitimized. A loan broker works with realtors to originate loans as an independent contractor for

---

[22] This section draws on Garrett [1989]. Also see chapter 9. Appendix C of this chapter describes the characteristics of home mortgage debt, with emphasis on the growth of adjustable-rate mortgages (ARMs).

[23] They defined a real-estate bank (REB) as any commercial bank that held 40 percent or more of its assets in loans secured by real estate in any one of their sample years. In addition, they studied a subset of these banks that were in the sample for five or more years (5REBs). The REB sample ranged from a low of 207 banks (1983) to a high of 1,328 banks (1988). The 5REB subsample ranged from a low of 140 banks (1983) to a high 275 banks (1978). In 1988, there were 221 5REBs. The majority of REBs and 5REBs had total assets of less than $100 million and had the majority of their real-estate loans secured by one–four family residential properties.

a financial institution such as a thrift or bank. The broker, also known as a wholesaler, splits the origination fee with the financial institution. In some cases, financial institutions set up departments, not to originate loans, but to acquire them from originating brokers. In fact, Garrett contends that if mortgage lenders substitute the word "acquire" for "originate," they will have the components of the new paradigm for survival in the mortgage-lending business, that is, acquire, fund, sell, and service.

The second step is the funding process. Traditional depository mortgage lenders have done both origination and funding. The funding step is critical because funders (assuming they hold the loans) bear the liquidity, credit, and interest-rate risks associated with the loan. To perform the funding function, the lender must have access to either debt (e.g., deposit) or equity markets or both. During the credit crunch of the early 1980s, depository institutions, especially thrift institutions, were squeezed for funds due to disintermediation, and squeezed for profits because of higher interest costs to support fixed-rate assets. Garrett makes an important point when he says, "There is nothing about the skills needed for originations and funding that tie them together . . . no logic (suggests that) competence in one area implies competence in the other" (p. 31). This idea represents the fundamental reason for the fragmentation or restructuring of the business, which has led to the third and fourth steps in the mortgage-lending process.

In securitized lending, the funding step is replaced by selling the loan. In this case, the various risk-management functions previously performed by the funder and holder are now done in the secondary market. Specifically, the selling function involves, among other things:

- Managing the "pipeline" or flow of mortgages
- Knowing how and when to hedge interest-rate risk
- Finding investors to purchase loans
- Knowing when loans should be securitized or sold for cash

Again, the selling or secondary-market function and skills are distinct from the origination function, and competence in one does not imply competence in the other.

Whether a loan is held in a bank's portfolio or sold (assuming servicing rights are not sold), it must be serviced, which entails collecting payments and, if the loans have been securitized, then passing through the proceeds for distribution in the form of interest (IO = interest-only obligation) or principal (PO = principal-only obligation) or both, reporting to investors, meeting legal requirements for different political jurisdictions, and other activities. Since servicing requires extensive data-processing capabilities, they are a prerequisite for this function. Again, servicing skills are distinct from originating, funding, and selling skills, and competence in one does not imply competence in any of the others.

Table 11-11 presents a summary of the fragmentation of the residential mortgage-lending process. It adds a fifth step or participant to the process, the ultimate investor or holder of the mortgage or a particular piece of it (e.g., an IO or PO). As a participant in the secondary market, the investor needs to make risk-return judgments about the asset (security). As is the case with other financial assets, the holder bears the liquidity, interest-rate, and credit risks associated with the product. However, to the extent that the asset (mortgage) has been enhanced or guaranteed against default, credit risk has been reduced and ultimately depends on the credibility of the enhancement or guarantee.

Garrett argues that the restructuring of the mortgage-lending process means that mortgage banking will no longer be a full-service industry in terms of origination

TABLE 11-11 Fragmentation of the Residential Mortgage-Lending Process

Function	Expertise/Skills Required	Rewards	Risks
Origination	Marketing, sales, processing, appraising, documenting, brokering	Fees	Default and pipeline
Funding/underwriting	Funds acquisition and risk assessment and management in the primary market	Spread	Liquidity, interest rate, and credit
Selling	Risk assessment and management in the secondary market	Fees & commissions	Liquidity, interest rate, and credit
Servicing	Collection, disbursement, reporting, legal, data processing	Fees	Operating and legal
Investor	Judgment of risk-return trade-offs	Interest or principal or both	Liquidity, interest rate

(acquisition), funding, selling, and servicing. According to his view, survival will depend on recognizing one's strengths and specializing in that part of the housing-finance delivery system. This view is consistent with the one for the banking industry as a whole that argues for specialization or the development of "boutiques" based on the strengths of individual institutions. It is, of course, at odds with the view that banks should become department stores of finance or full-service firms.

The Market for Mortgage-Backed Securities (MBSs)

Although the markets for nonmortgage securitized assets (e.g., credit-card receivables) are relatively new, the market for mortgage-backed or mortgage pass-through securities is well developed. At year-end 1995, total mortgage debt outstanding totaled $4.7 trillion with $1.8 trillion (38%) in the form of mortgage pools or trusts. Commercial banks held $1 trillion or 21 percent of the mortgage debt outstanding. Borrowers' preferences for fixed-rate mortgages have played an important role in the phenomenal growth of mortgage-backed securities (MBSs). First, since many borrowers want the certainty of a fixed mortgage payment, they do not want to bear the interest-rate risk of a variable-rate mortgage. And second, from 1966 through 1983, but especially from 1979 to 1982, thrift institutions were burned (many beyond recognition) by interest-rate risk; accordingly, many thrifts did not want to bear interest-rate risk either. The solution: Make fixed-rate loans, but get them off the balance sheet and into the hands of investors who are willing (and presumably more able) to bear interest-rate risk. This task, of course, is accomplished through securitization, which permits originators to shift interest-rate, credit, and prepayment risks to investors.

Most mortgage pass-throughs are federally related in that they are guaranteed or issued by GNMA, FNMA, or FHLMC (chapter 9). These agencies account for all but a small portion of mortgage-backed securities. For example, at the end of 1995, "private mortgage conduits" totaled only $283 billion or 15 percent of total mortgage pools or trusts. The dominance of GNMA, FNMA, and FHLMC can be attributed to three factors: (1) the standardization requirement for the underlying mortgages, (2) the size and hence the liquidity of the market, and (3) the federal safety net (guarantee) backing the mortgage pools. Given the guarantee feature of mortgage-backed securities, GNMA securities ($472 billion outstanding as of December 31, 1995) commanded an average risk premium of about 140 basis points over the 10-year Treasury note from 1984 to 1989. The risk premium over this period ranged from 65 basis points to 245 basis points.

Because investors in mortgage-backed securities are willing to bear interest-rate risk, the primary risk they face is **prepayment uncertainty** (risk). Specifically, debt holders (borrowers) will refinance when interest rates fall far enough below the rates on outstanding debt to offset transaction costs. Accordingly, prepayments tend to rise as interest rates decline, reflecting the refinancing of existing mortgages and the greater activity in residential construction and trading of existing residences. Conversely, when interest rates are rising, prepayments tend to drop off. Nevertheless, because these relationships are not exact (i.e., completely predictable), mortgage-backed securities command an uncertainty premium relative to Treasury and U.S. government securities. The more unpredictable (volatile) interest rates are, the larger is the prepayment or call premium.

CONSUMER LENDING IN THE FUTURE

Price [1989] argues that consumer lending in the future will be shaped by

- Regulation
- New sources of fee income
- Automation

In addition, securitization has and will continue to shape consumer lending. Let's analyze the importance of each of these factors by recalling that competition for financial products and services exists in three dimensions:

- Price (interest rates and fees)
- Convenience
- Confidence or safety

The convenience function for a financial-services firm is driven by the organization's geographic reach, menu of products, product cost, and quality of service. Many consumers select a bank for its convenience.

Regulation of Consumer Lending

Because regulations can affect a bank's pricing, geographic reach (e.g., branching restrictions), menu of products (e.g, separation of commercial and investment banking), product cost (e.g., various forms of regulation act as implicit taxes), and quality of service (e.g., through improved disclosure), **regulation** plays a crucial role in shaping a bank's pricing and convenience functions. Of course when it comes to confidence, the federal safety net of deposit insurance and the discount window is the ultimate guarantee of safety.

Should Credit-Card Interest Rates Be Subject to Interest-Rate Ceilings?

In 1987 and 1988, the U.S. Congress conducted extensive (and sometimes heated) debates about disclosure requirements for credit cards and the ("high") level of interest rates on credit cards. One lawmaker even proposed imposing an interest-rate ceiling on credit cards. Fortunately, rational minds prevailed and no ceiling was imposed. Figure 11-4 shows how price controls can distort resource allocation.

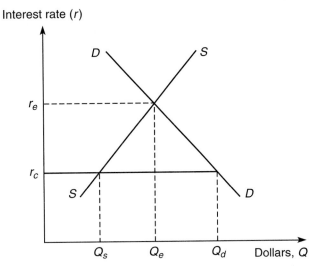

Analysis: Without any rate ceiling the forces of supply and demand would clear the market at the equilibrium rate and quantity indicated by the coordinates $[r_e, Q_e]$. However, if an effective ceiling (r_c) is imposed (i.e., one below the equilibrium rate), then a distortion between supply and demand is created such that the quantity of credit demanded is greater than the quantity supplied. Thus, a ceiling would be self-defeating as it would hurt the groups it was designed to help because the least creditworthy consumers, those who can least afford to pay high interest rates, would presumably be rationed out of the market. Alternatively, suppliers could meet the demand (Q_d) by changing other terms of the credit-card agreement to offset the lower rates of interest (e.g., by increasing the annual fee or reducing/eliminating the grace period). Changing these other terms, however, would serve to increase the effective rate of interest, which again would not be the result Congress intended. Good intentions frequently have unintended evils. Market forces work best when they are unrestricted.

FIGURE 11-4 The Effects of an Interest-Rate Ceiling

Federal Statutes Affecting Consumer Lending

Table 11-12 shows the major pieces of federal legislation relating to consumer credit in the United States over the years 1968 to 1996. Because some of the legislation created compliance burdens for banks (e.g., Truth in Lending, TIL, in 1968), later legislation sometimes attempted to reduce the burdens (e.g., TIL Simplification and Reform Act in 1980). Because bank regulations, whether in the form of reserve requirements or consumer protection, act as a tax, banks try to pass on as much of the tax as they can to the customer. As a result, the intended benefits of the laws may come at a higher price to consumers, depending on the elasticity of demand for the taxed products and services. Moreover, if bankers do not accurately measure the burden of such taxes, they do not know the true profitability or value added of their output.

The Supervisory Approach to Consumer Credit

In line with the OCC's Supervision by Risk, near the end of 1996 the OCC released new guidelines for consumer credit that focus on installment lending, credit cards, residential and home-equity lending, and merchant processing. It is also working on developing examiner guidelines to focus on risk management of retail securitizations. The new guidelines, as summarized in Figure 11-5, concentrate on the effectiveness of a bank's lending process rather than focusing on loan outcomes.

TABLE 11-12 Federal Statutes Relating to Consumer Credit

Law/Year	Purpose
Truth-in-Lending (TIL), 1968	Through disclosure of credit terms, to facilitate comparison of credit terms by consumers.
Fair Housing Act (FHA), 1968	To prohibit discrimination in housing and housing credit on the basis of race, color, religion, national origin, or sex. It prohibits redlining of housing credit.
Fair Credit Reporting Act, 1971	To give consumers access to credit bureau reports to check sources and accuracy. Denials of credit by banks on the basis of information supplied by credit bureaus must be reported to consumers.
Fair Credit Billing Act, 1974	To give consumers the opportunity to question errors in billing statements.
Equal Credit Opportunity Act (ECOA), 1976	To prohibit discrimination against a credit applicant on the basis of race, color, religion, national origin, sex, marital status, age, or receipt of public assistance in any credit transaction.
Uniform Commercial Code "Holder-in-Due-Course Rule," 1976	To require all consumer credit contracts to state specifically the liability of all holders of the contract for all claims against the seller.
Community Reinvestment Act (CRA), 1977	To require disclosure of an institution's involvement in the local community and to give consumers access to such information.
Bankruptcy Reform Act, 1978	To establish procedures for the discharge of debts of insolvent debtors.
Electronic Funds Transfer (EFT) Act, 1978	To limit consumer liability for unauthorized use of lost or stolen credit or debit cards and to require disclosure of information related to consumer use of EFT devices.
Right to Privacy Act, 1979	To prohibit federal government investigation of consumer financial information without proper documentation.
Truth-in-Lending Simplification and Reform Act, 1980	To simplify disclosure requirements under the TIL of 1968.
Depository Institutions Deregulation and Monetary Control Act (DIDMCA), 1980	To expand consumer lending authority for federally chartered thrifts.
Garn-St Germain Depository Institutions Act, 1982	To expand further the asset powers of federally chartered institutions.
Consumer Protection: Unfair or Deceptive Credit Practices, 1985	To protect borrowers against unfair or deceptive credit practices such as pyramiding late charges and lack of full disclosure to potential cosigners.

New Sources of Fee Income and Consumer Choice

Loan origination fees are a traditional source of bank fee income. In an environment in which traditional banking is declining (i.e., financing loans by issuing deposits), banks are continually looking for new sources of **fee income.** The development of new products and services and the repricing of old products and services offer opportunities for banks to increase their fee income.

In 1995, the U.S. Public Interest Research Group (PIRG) reported that bank customers were being nickeled-and-dimed by banks' fees to the tune of hundreds

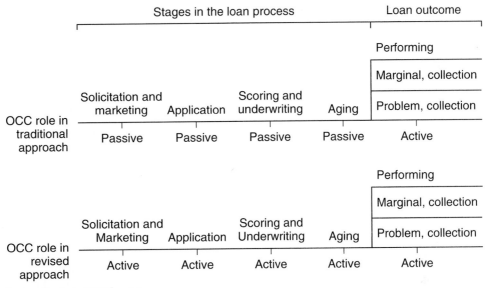

	Stages in the loan process				Loan outcome
					Performing
					Marginal, collection
OCC role in traditional approach	Solicitation and marketing	Application	Scoring and underwriting	Aging	Problem, collection
	Passive	Passive	Passive	Passive	Active
					Performing
					Marginal, collection
OCC role in revised approach	Solicitation and Marketing	Application	Scoring and Underwriting	Aging	Problem, collection
	Active	Active	Active	Active	Active

Source: Ludwig [1996], p. 10.

FIGURE 11-5 Consumer Credit Supervisory Approach

of dollars a year per customer. Consumers make choices for products and services, including those offered by financial institutions, based on their perceptions of value received. The PIRG survey of 271 banks focused on only one aspect of bank competition: *explicit* fees. It ignores *implicit* pricing, convenience, and safety. To understand how banks make money and what it costs them to produce financial services, you need to look at all aspects of the *business* of banking.

Banks have two sources of revenue or income ("sales" for nonfinancial businesses): interest income and noninterest income. Over the past 15 years, banks' net interest income (interest income minus interest expense) has been squeezed by removal of Reg Q interest-rate ceilings and intense competition from nonbank financial institutions such as mutual funds and from capital-market instruments such as commercial paper and corporate bonds. To maintain their earnings, banks have had to price products and services to cover costs. Bank fees and service charges have risen accordingly.

Bank noninterest income consists of explicit fees and service charges and implicit fees. For example, suppose a consumer has a so-called free checking account that requires a minimum balance of $500 to get the "free" service. The implicit cost to the consumer is not an out-of-pocket expense but what financial economists call an opportunity cost. That is, if the consumer could earn 5 percent on the $500 for a year, then the opportunity cost is $25. If the bank also promises to pay interest on the balance in the checking account, then the consumer's opportunity cost is reduced by the interest earned.

From the bank's point of view, it has the $500 to lend to someone and earn interest income, and can make a profit after adjusting for the costs of bank regulation (reserve requirements and deposit-insurance fees), the direct and indirect costs of processing the checking account, the direct and indirect cost of processing the loan, and interest expense if the checking account is interest bearing.

Many consumers choose their financial institution on the basis of convenience. If an office or branch is close to home or work or if the institution has easily accessible ATMs, these consumers chant the old real-estate adage: Location, location, location. Although bank fees (consumers' explicit costs) are secondary to them, they do not ignore total costs, which are the sum of explicit costs and implicit (opportunity) costs. In this case, the opportunity costs are the time, energy, and expense (e.g., gas for the car) of going to a financial institution with a less convenient location. Of course, we all know someone who would drive across town and spend an hour to save a dime. Different strokes for different folks.

To make it convenient for retail customers (individuals and small businesses), banks have invested substantial amounts of money in brick-and-mortar branches, ATMs, ATM networks, check-processing facilities, and credit-card systems.[24] Banks and their investors are entitled to a return on these capital investments. Part of this return comes in the form of fees and service charges, which also have to be used to maintain and support the various systems.

To summarize, the dimensions of price, convenience, and safety represent three basic ways banks compete for business. Consumers weigh these factors and pick the institutions, products, and services they want. Fees and service charges are a critical and growing part of the business of banking.[25]

Automation and Securitization

Automation presents a way for banks to reduce expenses, whereas **securitization** presents banks with ways to remove risk from their balance sheets and to generate fee income. Because borrowers should not be concerned about what lenders do with their loans after they are made (i.e., whether they are securitized or not), securitization does not directly affect customer convenience. However, to the extent that it removes portfolio risk from the bank's balance sheet, securitization may permit banks to offer additional products and services over wider areas and at lower costs, regulation permitting.

As we have seen, the most cost-effective method of consumer lending involves a systems approach based on credit scoring and unadvised overdrafts (Rouse [1989]). Such automation, however, can be a double-edged sword with respect to the cost and quality of financial services. On the one hand, it may make bank operations more efficient by decreasing the time and expense it takes to make a consumer loan decision (e.g., using artificial intelligence to make routine loan decisions or to evaluate requests for increases in credit-card limits). Customers who want quick answers will view speedy decisions as an increase in the quality of service. On the other hand, some consumers may view such automation as being impersonal and consider it a decrease in the quality of service. And as the Bank of New York's credit-scoring faux pas shows, automation without a human touch can produce embarrassing results.

---

[24] Citicorp calls its approach "Citibanking" and describes it as using "technology to deliver faster, more flexible service . . . through 24-hour Citicard Banking Centers, Citiphone or personal computers (to) deliver a unique customer experience in 39 countries" (*Annual Report* 1995, p. 7).

[25] Because bank fees and services charges are here to stay, learn to live with them. You don't have to like or tolerate them, however. My mother always told me: "It doesn't hurt to ask." Accordingly, when I don't like a certain bank fee or charge, I ask for it to be reversed or lowered. Sometimes it works, sometimes it doesn't, and sometimes I change institutions. There's lots of competition in the financial-services industry just looking for new (profitable) customers.

Financial innovation will play a crucial role in the future of consumer lending. Past innovations include credit and debit cards, ATMs that permit cash advances (loans), systems approaches to lending, and home-equity loans. The combination of a systems approach and home-equity lending permits banks to generate secured loans relatively quickly. Moreover, when home-equity borrowers need additional credit (within their credit limits), they don't have to reapply for a loan. As with any kind of credit, home-equity borrowers must be disciplined enough to avoid overextending themselves.

Chapter Summary

Although commercial banks have been losing market share, they still dominate the market for consumer installment credit, which includes installment loans and credit-card loans. Credit-card loans have been the fastest-growing component of traditionally defined bank consumer lending. Although credit-card loans have higher loss rates than installment loans, bank credit-card operations have been highly profitable in the 1980s and the 1990s. Taking a broader view of consumer lending, commercial banks, spurred by the S&L crisis, have made major inroads into **residential mortgage** lending. An important aspect of this business has been establishing home-equity lines of credit. Banks favor making credit-card and home-equity loans for different reasons. The administering and processing of credit-card loans has been highly profitable and easily automated. Home-equity loans, unlike unsecured credit-card loans, are secured and a natural extension of banks' move into residential lending. Home-equity loans require less monitoring but have higher origination costs. These costs, however, can be circumvented by buying mortgage-backed securities in the secondary market. Customers with home-equity lines of credit do not have to apply for additional loans because they can simply write checks on the lines.

An alternative to the five C's of credit analysis is captured by CAMPARI, which stands for character, ability, margin, purpose, amount, repayment, and insurance (security). The basic terms of consumer installment lending are interest rate, maturity, amount financed, and loan-to-value ratio. Lenders offer borrowers various combinations of these terms as a means of controlling and monitoring credit risk. A systems approach such as **credit scoring** (based on statistical analysis of good and bad borrowers) is widely used to decide who gets consumer credit and is increasingly used to monitor outstanding loans, especially those based on credit cards.

The modern mortgage-lending process has four parts: origination or acquisition, funding, selling, and servicing. The high interest rates of the early 1980s were a catalyst in hastening the unraveling and unbundling of the housing-finance delivery system. As a result, many analysts foresee specialization as the way to survive as a participant in the mortgage-lending process. Regulation, new sources of fee income, securitization, and automation are the major forces that will shape the future of consumer lending. The securitization of credit-card receivables, automobile loans, and residential mortgages offers banks the opportunity to reduce assets and generate fee income. Consumer lending in the United States is heavily regulated to ensure that borrowers and neighborhoods are not discriminated against and to ensure that the terms of lending (e.g., APR and finance charges) are properly disclosed and easy to understand. Such regulation, however, acts as a tax, some or all of which bankers attempt to pass on to bank customers.

Key Words, Concepts, and Acronyms

- Adjustable rate mortgage
- Amount financed
- Automation
- Bankruptcy prediction (personal)
- Consumer installment credit (types, major holders, and terms)
- Convenience users (of credit cards)
- Credit analysis (CAMPARI)
- Credit-card loans
- Credit (default) risk
- Credit-scoring model (system)
- Credit users (of credit cards)
- Delinquent loans/rates
- Fees and service charges (credit cards)

- Functional cost analysis (FCA)
- Home-equity lines of credit/loans
- Individual appraisal
- Installment loan
- Interchange fees
- Interest rate
- Interest-rate risk
- Loan losses
- Loan-to-value ratio
- Maturity
- Merchant discount
- Nonperforming loans
- One–four-family residential mortgages

- Premiums paid for resale of credit-card accounts (appendix B)
- Prepayment uncertainty (risk)
- Profitability of credit cards
- Regulation of consumer lending
- Residential mortgage
- Securitization
- Stickiness of credit-card interest rates
- Systems approach
- Terms of consumer installment credit
- Travel and entertainment (T&E) card
- Truth-in-lending disclosure

Review Questions

1. Describe the market for consumer installment credit. Who are the major players? What kinds of loans fall into this category? What are the basic terms of these loans?

2. What kinds of consumer loans are made by commercial banks, how risky are they, and how do the loans vary with bank size?

3. How has the S&L crisis affected the composition of bank loans?

4. What are Citicorp's core businesses and how profitable are they?

5. How much does it cost a bank to make a consumer loan and to collect a loan payment? What is "functional cost analysis"?

6. When and how did the credit-card industry begin? What does a typical revenue-expense profile for a credit card look like? What's an alternative way of measuring the profitability of the credit-card business and what do market data indicate (see appendix B)?

7. What are lenders doing with their credit-card receivables? Why are they making these transactions?

8. Distinguish between credit users and convenience users of credit cards. Which ones do bankers prefer and why?

9. What forms of nonprice competition exist in the market for credit cards?

10. What are the characteristics of a market that is perfectly competitive? What evidence suggests that the market for credit cards does not conform to this model? Describe the regression experiment run by Ausubel [1991] to test for the stickiness of credit-card interest rates.

11. Has competition failed in the market for credit cards? If so, for whom has it failed? Has it failed for "disciplined convenience users"? Who subsidizes this kind of user?

12. Describe what effects an interest-rate ceiling would have on the market for bank credit cards.

13. Contrast and compare the CAMPARI framework for credit analysis with the five Cs of credit analysis.

14. Discuss the credit-scoring faux pas made by Bank of New York in 1995. What are the pros and cons of credit scoring versus individual appraisal?

15. Distinguish between a first (mortgage) lien and a home-equity loan. Why have banks come to like both of these forms of lending?

16. How does bank residential lending vary by bank size?
17. Describe the restructuring and fragmentation of residential real-estate lending.
18. Should consumer lending be as heavily regulated as it is? Who pays for the costs of such regulation?
19. What forces will shape consumer lending in the 1990s? How, if at all, will these forces affect the price, confidence, and convenience functions?
20. How do VISA, MasterCard, Discover, and American Express compare in the battle for control of the market for credit cards in the United States?
21. Describe the components of a systems approach to consumer lending. Does this approach have to be done in-house?

Problems/Analysis/Projects

1. Get some credit-card applications from banks and major retailers and try to figure out what information they are using in their credit-scoring models. Why and how does the fact that a credit-card applicant does or does not have a telephone enter such a model?
2. If you regressed over time on a quarterly basis the credit-card interest rate (dependent variable) on an adjusted T-bill rate of comparable maturity and on the previous period's credit-card rate (independent variables), how would you interpret the following estimated slope coefficients?

Estimated Regression Coefficients

Equation	Adjusted T-bill	Lagged CC Rate
1	1.0	0.0
2	0.0	1.0
3	0.0439	0.864

Assume that all nonzero coefficients are significantly different from zero. Regarding the coefficient on the adjusted T-bill rate in equation 3, Ausubel [1991] says " . . . while statistically significant . . . [it] . . . is economically insignificant" (p. 55). What does he mean?

3. The Credit-Card Bank has average outstanding balances of $2,000 per month on all of its credit-card accounts. However, 25 percent of its one million cardholders pay their balances within 30 days to avoid finance charges. If the remaining account holders pay finance charges at a rate of 1.583 percent per month (19% APR), how much revenue does the bank generate in finance charges per month and per year? The bank charges an annual fee of $50 per account, generates other customer fees at a rate of 1 percent of total outstanding balances for the year, and receives interchange fees of $5 million per year. What is the bank's total revenue from credit-card operations for the year? If the bank's cost of funds is 10 percent, noninterest expenses 4 percent of total outstanding balances, and net charge-offs 2 percent of credit card users' total outstanding balances, what are the bank's total costs and pretax profits for the year? What is the *ROA* for the credit-card function and how does it compare with the bank's overall *ROA* of, say, 1 percent?

4. Determine the excess spread on the following securitization done by MBNA America Bank during 1995. The deal was for $500 million at a fixed rate of 6.20 percent with a maturity of September 15, 2000. The cash yield on the receivables was estimated at 17.14 percent. MBNA was to receive servicing fees at the rate of 2.5 percent. It expected charge-offs at the rate of 3.51 percent.

5. Auto Finance Corp. (AFC) offers the following terms on new-car loans: prime + 2 (fixed or floating), 48-month, loan-to-value ratio of 0.95, and maximum amount financed of $50,000. If the prime rate is 7% and if you will need the maximum amount to purchase your dream luxury car, what will be your monthly amortized payment to AFC if you select the fixed-rate option for 48 months?

APPENDIX A

CONSUMER LOANS BY BANK SIZE, 1985–1995 (AS A PERCENTAGE OF AVERAGE NET CONSOLIDATED ASSETS)

TABLE A11-1 Consumer Loans by Bank Size, 1985–1995 (as a percentage of average net consolidated assets)

Panel A. Total Consumer Loans

Year	All Banks	Small	Medium	Large	Ten Largest
1985	11.04	13.01	14.46	11.19	5.62
1986	11.38	12.41	14.69	11.80	6.50
1987	11.42	11.74	15.34	11.73	6.41
1988	11.71	11.48	15.91	12.20	6.19
1989	11.89	11.46	15.48	12.97	6.21
1990	11.77	11.19	15.47	12.25	6.87
1991	11.45	10.49	15.10	11.66	7.20
1992	11.02	9.68	14.22	11.72	7.31
1993	11.00	9.17	14.82	11.47	7.33
1994	11.43	9.38	15.85	12.62	6.59
1995	11.38	9.54	16.39	14.23	6.60

Panel B. Installment and Other Consumer Loans (excluding credit-card loans)

Year	All Banks	Small	Medium	Large	Ten Largest
1985	8.41	12.40	10.96	7.04	3.49
1986	8.40	11.74	10.68	7.30	4.03
1987	8.26	10.94	10.69	7.33	4.07
1988	8.25	10.62	10.70	7.35	4.10
1989	8.20	10.53	10.65	7.16	4.22
1990	7.99	10.19	10.25	6.76	4.67
1991	7.57	9.41	9.39	6.62	4.67
1992	7.20	8.68	8.80	6.56	4.70
1993	7.11	8.26	9.18	6.24	4.83
1994	7.22	8.41	9.79	6.63	4.31
1995	7.39	8.53	9.93	6.89	4.65

TABLE A11-1 *Continued*

Panel C. Credit-Card Loans

Year	All Banks	Small	Medium	Large	Ten Largest
1985	2.63	0.61	3.50	4.16	2.14
1986	2.98	0.68	4.01	4.50	2.46
1987	3.17	0.80	4.65	4.40	2.34
1988	3.47	0.86	5.21	4.85	2.08
1989	3.69	0.93	4.82	5.82	1.99
1990	3.78	1.00	5.22	5.49	2.20
1991	3.88	1.08	5.71	5.04	2.53
1992	3.82	1.00	5.42	5.16	2.61
1993	3.89	0.91	5.64	5.23	2.50
1994	4.21	0.96	6.06	5.99	2.28
1995	4.73	1.01	6.45	7.34	1.96

Note: Small banks are those not ranked among the 1,000 largest by assets, medium banks are those ranked 101 to 1,000 by assets, large banks are those ranked 11 to 100 by assets, and the ten largest are the ten largest banks by assets.

Source: Federal Reserve Bulletin (June 1995), pp. 559–569.

APPENDIX B

AN ALTERNATIVE MEASURE OF CREDIT-CARD PROFITABILITY: THE PREMIUMS PAID FOR CREDIT-CARD RECEIVABLES[26]

Ausubel [1991] was the first researcher to present an alternative measure of the profitability of bank credit cards by focusing on the premium paid on the resale of credit-card accounts. His findings through April 1990 revealed an average premium of 20 percent, with a range of 3 percent to 27 percent. The highest premium (27 percent) was paid by Citicorp to Bank of New England in January 1990 (one year before Bank of New England failed) for $625 million of outstanding credit-card balances. In contrast, Citicorp paid only a 3 percent premium for $650 million in balances from Empire of America in May 1989.

Panel A of Table B11-1 presents a ten-year history of card portfolio sales.[27] Although the average premium has declined slightly from Asubel's estimate of 20 percent in the mid-to-late 1980s to 17.7 percent for the 1990s, the biggest change

---

[26] This appendix draws on Ausubel [1991], Sinkey and Nash [1993], and Nash and Sinkey [1997].

[27] The reported sales are *gross* premiums for good, open-to-buy accounts and balances, before any deduction or discounting for credit quality. The transactions are for *unsecured national brand* portfolios only; they do not include private label, retail, or secured accounts collateralized by consumer deposits. The figures do not include numerous small transactions, typically less than $15,000,000, which are often unknown to anyone other than the parties in the transactions.

TABLE B11-1 Credit-Card Portfolio Sales and Initial-Public Offerings, 1985–1995

Panel A. Card Portfolio Sales, 1985–1995[a]

	Range of Estimated Gross Premiums	Avg. Wtd. Gross Premiums[b]	# Transactions[c]	Assets Sold[d] ($ Billions)
1995	5.0–27.5%	20.7%	19	$0.91
1994	7.0–21.0%	18.0%	18	$0.75
1993	7.1–23.0%	18.1%	14	$0.82
1992	16.8–25.0%	16.8%	17	$0.88
1991	7.0–24.0%	14.0%	32	$3.80
1990	7.0–27.0%	18.7%	26	$5.40
1989	3.0–25.0%	18.9%	25	$6.60
1988	7.8–25.5%	20.3%	15	$1.60
1987	10.5–16.0%	20.3%	6	$0.86
1986	14.3–29.0%	20.4%	3	$1.60

Notes:

[a]National Brand deals only (MC-VISA); not private label or retail transactions.

[b]"Gross" premiums, prior to discounting for delinquent accounts. Average weighted premiums calculated show strong correlation to supply and demand: the fewer deals done, the higher prices tend to be.

[c]Does not include numerous smaller deals, typically < $15MM.

[d]Does not include 18 "mergers of equals" or total organization purchases in 1995.

Source: Data courtesy of R. K. Hammer Investment Bankers.

Panel B. Initial Public Offerings (IPOs) of Credit Cards[e]

Issuer (exchange, date)	Shares Issued		Issue Price	Ratios(2/1/96)	
	Mils.	%Public		Mkt to Issue	Price to EPS
VeriFone (NYSE, 3/90)	2.5	12	$16	2.38	28
MBNA Corp. (NYSE, 1/91)	49.5	100	22.5[e]	1.78	17
Envoy Corp. (OTC, 5/91)	2.0	20	10	2.07	nm
Sears Pmt. (NYSE, 2/92)	3.0	25	16	1.91	19
First Data (NYSE, 4/92)	50.0	46	22	3.30	nm
First USA (NYSE, 5/92)	4.5	89	9.5	5.34	16
Capital One (NYSE, 11/94)	7.1	94	16	1.67	14
Averages	16.9	55	16	2.64	19

[e]John Stewart [1991] reported in *Credit Card Management* that "when underwriting fees and other obligations were subtracted, MBNA was left with a disappointing 7% premium" (p. 54). However, because MNC's sale of MBNA was made under distressed conditions, its premium may be atypical. Sears Payment is listed on the NYSE as SPS Transaction Service (PAY). On February 28, 1995, Capital One was spun off by Signet Banking Corp. to its shareholders as a dividend. The ratios of market price to issue price and the P/E ratio are based on the closing prices as of February 1, 1996, as reported in *The Wall Street Journal* (2-2-96). The P/E ratios marked *nm* are meaningful because of very low or negative earnings in the previous year. Verifone's IPO was an OTC issue; in 1995, the company began trading on the NYSE.

Sources: Nash and Sinkey [1997]. WS = *Wall Street Journal*, NY = *New York Times*, and AB = *American Banker*. Summary data for Ausubel [1991] calculated from his Table 9, p. 66. Information in Panel B is from Stewart [1992], p. 29 and *The Wall Street Journal* (2-2-96).

has been the decline in the dollar amount of assets sold. With the number of transactions also declining, the average size deal has declined from $264 billion (1989) to $48 million (1995). The large growth in securitization of credit-card receivables has increased in direct proportion (and far greater) to the decline in card assets sold during the same period.

Panel B of Table B11-1 presents credit-card IPOs for the period March 1990 to July 1995. Unfortunately, only one of these IPOs—MNC Financial's offering—has a reported premium. Moreover, Stewart ([1991]; see notes to Table B11-1) regards MNC's reported premium of 14 percent as overstated by 100 percent. Because MNC's IPO of MBNA was made under distressed conditions, a 7 percent premium may not be unusual. Nevertheless, as analyzed below, MBNA's subsequent performance suggests substantial PVGO arising from the hidden assets embodied in its IPO.

Although the IPO data in Panel B lack reported premiums (except for MNC), other aspects of the transactions and the market's subsequent reaction to the offerings provide interesting insights concerning the riskiness of credit-card assets. Consider MBNA's stock market performance after the IPO. (MBNA, which is traded on the NYSE, is the name of MNC's IPO spinoff.) For the first 14 months of MBNA's trading, Sullivan [1992] reports an equity beta of 1.6, which means that, on average, MBNA's stock return moves 1.6 percent for a 1.0 percent change in the market portfolio (as captured by a market index).[28] Over this same period, the NYSE's Financial Index (a composite of the stocks of financial-services firms) had a beta of 1.18. Betas for (nondistressed) bank holding companies with actively traded equities tend to range between 0.65 and 1.2 over this period.[29] MBNA's higher beta provides a market-determined case of the greater relative riskiness of credit-card banks.

These market measures of relative risk, which complement and confirm accounting measures of the greater riskiness of credit-card activities, suggest that credit-card receivables should be priced to yield a higher rate of return than other banking products. For example, assuming a risk-free rate of 5 percent and a market risk premium of 8 percent, the required return on the NYSE Financial Index would be 14.4 percent ($= 5\% + 1.18 \times 8\%$), whereas the required return on MBNA's stock would be 17.8 percent ($= 5\% + 1.6 \times 8\%$).

The last two columns of Panel B show the ratio of market price (as of 2-1-96) of each credit-card IPO to its issue price and its most recent price-earnings (P/E) multiple. Both of these variables embody investors' return *and* risk expectations.[30] The average market-to-issue ratio of 2.64 suggests growth (or wealth-creation) opportunities in credit-card assets or enhanced value due to a more favorable interest-rate environment or both. For comparative purposes, however, P/E ratios are easier to use because the data are reported daily. The credit-card IPOs in Panel C

---

[28] The only other "pure play" in credit cards is Advanta Corp., which trades on the OTC and has about one-fourth the amount of credit-card loans as MBNA but a similar volatility of returns. Advanta is not included in Panel C of Table 11-8 because it has been a stand-alone company since 1974 and does not qualify as a recent IPO. See Stewart [1992] and Sullivan [1992].

[29] Distressed BHCs such as the failed Bank of New England and the once-troubled Bank of Boston have higher betas, 1.3 and 1.4, respectively. In contrast, as of December 14, 1990, *Value Line* reported betas of 1.05 for J. P. Morgan, BankAmerica, Chemical Bank, Wells Fargo, and Security Pacific. Musumeci [1996] provides additional evidence of the above-average market sensitivity of banks with heavy concentrations in credit-card receivables. For 84 bank holding companies (BHCs), he reports an average beta of 1.41 for the second half of 1991. The most exposed BHCs, as captured by the top quartile, had an average beta of 1.58.

[30] Both of these variables are widely accepted as proxies for a firm's investment opportunity set. For example, see Booth [1992], Gaver and Gaver [1993], and Smith and Watts [1993].

have an average *P/E* of 19, compared to 10.1 for the top 14 bank holding companies (ranked in terms of total loans outstanding).[31] The higher average *P/E* for the specialized credit-card firms could reflect either higher growth prospects (e.g., PVGO associated with hidden assets embedded in a portfolio concentrated in credit-card receivables) or the higher expected earnings and the greater risk associated with an undiversified portfolio of unsecured assets.

IPO Insights and Anecdotal Evidence

The literature on IPOs offers further insight into proxies for the economic value of a portfolio of credit-card receivables. Ritter [1991] reports that "many firms go public near the peak of industry-specific fads" (p. 23), and that "issuers successfully time offers to lower their cost of capital" (p. 24). Credit cards, of course, cannot be regarded as a "fad." Nevertheless, like other products, credit cards can be expected to have a life cycle—one that industry analysts agree is in its "maturity stage" (Mandell [1990]). If sales of credit-card receivables occur as the bank-credit industry matures, and if sellers successfully time offers to lower their cost of capital, the values of hidden assets are further enhanced.

In the future, convenience users of credit cards (those paying off their outstanding balances each billing cycle and not incurring any interest charges) could be priced into becoming debit-card users if banks would simply eliminate the interest-free grace period. By spinning off credit-card receivables before such changes occur, sellers of credit-card receivables enhance the value of the hidden assets embedded in credit-card receivables. The behavior of the resale market during the 1990s provides some support for this timing phenomenon as reflected by the drop in resale premiums (Table B11-1), which could result from the credit card's transition into the maturity stage of its life cycle. Although the timing aspect is important, the underlying economic value derives from the potential customer relationships (list)— the intangible or hidden asset—attached to the tangible cash flows associated with the credit-card receivable. Accordingly, credit-card receivables should continue to sell at a premium to reflect the value of the hidden assets.[32]

The Case of MBNA

The largest sale reported by Ausubel was made by a distressed bank holding company, MNC Financial, as it spun off its $7.4 billion credit-card subsidiary, MBNA Corp., as an initial public offering (IPO) sold on the NYSE. The stock issue, which sold at $22.5 a share on January 22, 1991, generated $1.012 billion for MNC for a premium of 13.7 percent. According to the *American Banker,* the sale of the 45 million shares took only a few hours and was oversubscribed. MNC chairman Alfred Lerner and the insurance company he chairs together bought 14.9 percent of the issue. The sale, however, was not an easy one. MNC began testing the market in the fourth quarter of 1990, hoping to unload its card subsidiary before the end of the year.

Kantrow [1990] reported that MNC's credit-card portfolio had some good and bad selling points. On the positive side, the portfolio had excellent credit quality,

---

[31] The *P/E* ratios are as of February 1, 1996. See Stewart ([1992], p. 28) for the list of companies, which was led by Citicorp with total loans of $150.9 billion including $34 billion in credit-card loans (22.5%) as of year-end 1991. He listed 15 BHCs, but since then Security Pacific was acquired by BOA.

[32] "Card Flash" of Ram Research reported that sales of "good accounts" of credit-card receivables during 1995 continued to command premiums of 20 percent over face value, "substantiating the financial stability of the business."

a high-income customer base likely to use cards even in a recession, high average loan balances, and strong profitability. On the negative side, the timing of the sale was poor (i.e., a market flooded with other sellers and a recession were sure to depress the selling price), the large size of the portfolio limited the number of potential buyers, the high percentage of securitized assets complicated the acquisition, and affinity contracts made the portfolio difficult to service. On balance, bidders, if any, were not expected to offer the 20–25 percent premiums paid over the past two years, which was bad news for MNC because the $27 billion BHC had reported a $173 million loss for the third quarter of 1990. Like other BHCs along the East Coast, MNC was suffering because of problems with its commercial real-estate loans. In 1989, MNC's credit-card subsidiary, based in Newark, Delaware, generated 40 percent of the holding company's net income. MNC was between a rock and a hard place. If it was to survive, it had to sell its most profitable business. Moreover, MNC was seeking to sell its entire credit-card subsidiary, the fourth-largest credit-card portfolio in the United States. In a typical credit-card sale, only the receivables and accounts are sold and the transaction is made by simply transferring the operation's computer tapes to the buyer. MNC, however, wanted to unload its entire card subsidiary, including the physical plant with computers and employees.

APPENDIX C

CHARACTERISTICS OF HOME MORTGAGE DEBT: TRENDS AND IMPLICATIONS

Goodman [1991] conducted an extensive analysis of the characteristics of home mortgage debt over the years 1970 to 1989. With the stock of home loans close to $2.5 trillion, it is a market whose size alone merits close scrutiny. One of the objectives of the study was to track home loans after their origination. In addition, Goodman wanted to develop a comprehensive data base of improved estimates of the average level of interest rates on the entire stock of home mortgage debt over the years 1970 to 1989.

Figure C11-1 shows the contract interest rates on fixed mortgages for the years 1970 through 1989. The current market rate reflects the marginal rate at which new fixed-rate mortgages were made whereas the average rate reflects the overall rate for the outstanding stock of home mortgages. The spread between the two rates reflects the drag on earnings due to the historical stock of fixed-rate mortgages made during a period of rising interest rates. The huge spreads (marginal or market above average) from 1979 to 1982 sounded the death knell for many thrift institutions.

Panel A of Table C11-1 shows how **adjustable-rate mortgages** (ARMs) grew in the 1980s. At midyear 1981, the stock of ARMs was only $12.4 billion; by midyear 1989, it stood at $635 billion, a compound annual growth rate of 63.5 percent. Adjustable-rate mortgages represent a financial innovation that permits lenders to

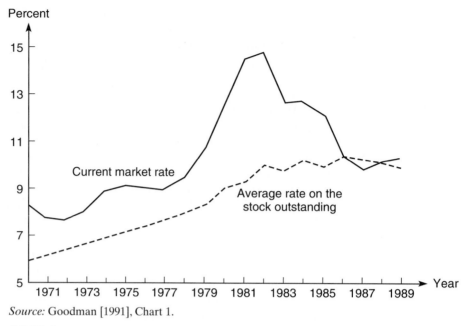

Percent

Source: Goodman [1991], Chart 1.

FIGURE C11-1 **Contract Interest Rates on Fixed-Rate Mortgages, 1970–1989**

share interest-rate risk and benefits with borrowers. When rates rise, the lender receives some protection against erosion of earnings and capital not provided by fixed-rate mortgages. Of course, if interest rates fall, then the lender loses and the borrower benefits. Nevertheless, even with fixed-rate mortgages, the borrower always has the option to refinance if rates decline. Panel B of Table 11-13 shows mortgage credit flows for the years 1970 to 1988. The difference between home mortgage originations (Y1) and the net change in mortgage debt (Y2) measures refinancing ($Y3 = Y1 - Y2$). Following the period from 1979 to 1985, when the current mortgage rate was above 11 percent (Figure C11-1), home-mortgage refinancings skyrocketed during the next three years (Panel B of Table C11-1). In 1986 alone, $236.8 billion of refinancings occurred, up from $85.7 billion in the previous year.

TABLE C11-1 The Stock of ARMs and Mortgage Credit Flows

Panel A. Stock of ARMs, 1981–1989 (midyear estimates, $ Millions)

Current Year	1981	1982	1983	1984	1985	1986	1987	1988	1989	Total
1981	12,414									12,414
1982	24,369	15,425								39,794
1983	22,645	30,280	28,251							81,175
1984	20,767	28,137	55,457	46,842						151,204
1985	18,888	25,804	51,533	91,953	45,066					233,244
1986	17,497	23,470	47,261	85,445	88,467	41,592				303,731
1987	16,296	21,741	42,985	78,362	82,206	81,646	63,893			387,129
1988	15,200	20,249	39,818	71,272	75,391	75,868	125,425	95,796		519,020
1989	14,195	18,887	37,085	66,022	68,570	69,579	116,549	188,051	56,113	635,051

(continued)

TABLE C11-1   *Continued*

Panel B. Mortgage Credit Flows, 1970–1988 ($ Billions)

Year	Y1 Home Mortgage Originations	Y2 Net Change in Mortgage Debt	Y3 Refinancing (Y3 = Y1 − Y2)
1970	35.6	14.3	21.3
1971	57.8	28.5	29.3
1972	75.9	40.6	35.3
1973	79.1	41.4	37.7
1974	67.5	32.8	34.7
1975	77.9	41.4	36.5
1976	112.8	64.3	48.5
1977	162.0	96.3	65.6
1978	185.0	110.9	74.1
1979	186.6	117.0	69.6
1980	133.8	94.5	39.2
1981	98.2	74.7	23.5
1982	97.0	40.3	56.7
1983	201.9	125.5	76.4
1984	203.7	138.5	65.2
1985	243.1	157.4	85.7
1986	455.1	218.3	236.8
1987	450.3	239.9	209.1
1988	386.1	216.8	157.6

Correlation Matrix

	Y1	Y2	Y3
Y1	1		
Y2	.978	1	
Y3	.972	.903	1

Source: Goodman [1991], Tables 2 and 6.

Selected References

Altman, Edward I., Robert B. Avery, Robert A. Eisenbeis, and Joseph F. Sinkey, Jr. [1981]. *Application of Classification Techniques in Business, Banking, and Finance.* Greenwich, CT: JAI Press.

Ausubel, Lawrence. [1991]. "The Failure of Competition in the Credit Card Market." *American Economic Review* (March), pp. 50–81.

Booth, James R. [1992]. "Contract Costs, Bank Loans, and the Cross-Monitoring Hypothesis," *Journal of Financial Economics* 31, pp. 25–41.

"Capital Treatment of Intangible Assets." [1993]. *Federal Register,* Vol. 58, No. 58, March 29, pp. 16481–16486.

Comptroller of the Currency. [1993]. *News Release 93-22.* Washington, DC, April 1.

Consolidated Reports of Condition and Income. [1984–1991]. Springfield, VA, National Technical Information Service, U.S. Department of Commerce.

Consumer Lending. [1987]. Chicago: Institute of Financial Education.

Durand, David. [1941]. *Risk Elements in Consumer Installment Lending.* New York: National Bureau of Economic Research.

Eisenbeis, Robert A., and Myron L. Kwast. [1991]. "Are Real Estate Depositories Viable? Evidence from Commercial Banks." *Journal of Financial Services Research* (March), pp. 5–24.

Garrett, Joseph. [1989]. "A New Paradigm for Lenders." *Mortgage Banking* (April), pp. 30–38.

Gaver, Jennifer, and Kenneth Gaver. [1993]. "Additional Evidence on the Association between the Investment Opportunity Set and Corporate Financing, Dividend, and Compensation Policies." *Journal of Accounting and Economics* 16, pp. 125–160.

General Accounting Office. [1994]. "U.S. Credit Card Industry: Competitive Developments Need to Be Closely Monitored." Washington, DC: United States GAO, April.

Goodman, Jack L., Jr., with Yana Hudson and Scott Yermish. [1991]. "The Characteristics of the Home Mortgage Debt, 1970–89: Trends and Implications." Board of Governors of the Federal Reserve System, Finance and Economics and Discussion Series 149 (January).

Gorton, Gary, and Richard Rosen. [1995]. "Corporate Control, Portfolio Choice, and the Decline of Banking." *Journal of Finance* (December), pp. 1377–1420.

Hall, Robert D., Jr., and F. Blake Cloonen. [1984]. *Profitable Consumer Lending.* Boston: Bankers Publishing.

Hammer, Robert K. [1996]. "Credit-Card Portfolio Transactions." R. K. Hammer Investment Bankers, Thousand Oaks, California.

Harris, Jack C. [1995]. "The Real Cost of the Savings and Loan Crisis." *Real Estate Finance* (Summer), pp. 46–53.

Kantrow, Yvette D. [1990]. "MNC May Run into Snags Selling Its Card Business." *American Banker* (November 5), pp. 1 and 6.

Ludwig, Eugene A. [1996]. "Testimony before the Subcommittee on Financial Institutions and Regulatory Relief of the Committee on Banking, Housing, and Urban Affairs of the United States Senate." (July 24), Comptroller of the Currency, NR 96–80.

Maland, Ellen. [1991]. Statement before the Subcommittee on General Oversight and Investigations of the Committee on Banking, Finance, and Urban Affairs, United States House of Representatives, Boston, MA (April 8). Released by Division of Consumer and Community Affairs, Board of Governors of the Federal Reserve System.

Mandell, Lewis. [1990]. *The Credit Card Industry: A History.* Boston: Twayne Publishers.

Musumeci, James J. [1996]. "Credit-Card Cap Legislation and Bank Stock Prices." Working Paper, Southern Illinois University.

Nash, Robert C., and Joseph F. Sinkey, Jr. [1997]. "On Competition, Risk, and Hidden Assets in the Market for Bank Credit Cards." *Journal of Banking and Finance* (January), pp. 89–112.

Palmieri, Mario. [1991]. "Lending Systems: Know the Score." *Bankers Monthly* (February), pp. 30–31.

Price, Joan. [1989]. "Consumer Lending in the 1990s Faces Pluses and Pitfalls." *Savings Institutions* (July/August), pp. 36–39.

Ritter, Jay R. [1991]. "The Long-Run Performance of Initial Public Offerings." *Journal of Finance* 1 (March), pp. 3–27.

Rose, Sanford. [1990]. "The Coming Revolution in Credit Cards." *American Banker* (April 4), pp. 4, 15.

Rouse, Nicholas. [1989]. *Bankers' Lending Techniques.* London: Bankers Books.

Sexton, Donald E., Jr. [1977]. "Determining Good and Bad Credit Risk among High and Low Income Families." *Journal of Business* (April), pp. 236–239.

Sinkey, Joseph F., Jr., and Robert C. Nash. [1993]. "Assessing the Riskiness and Profitability of Credit-Card Banks." *Journal of Financial Services Research* 2, pp. 127–150.

Smith, Clifford W., Jr., and Ross Watts. [1993]. "The Investment Opportunity Set and Corporate Financing, Dividend, and Compensation Policies." *Journal of Financial Economics* 32, pp. 263–292.

Stewart, John. [1991]. "The Gravy Train Loses Steam." *Credit Card Management* (May), pp. 60–61.

———. [1992]. "Is Wall Street around the Corner?" *Credit Card Management* (June), pp. 26–31.

Sullivan, A. Charlene. [1992]. "What the MBNA Stock Price is Telling Us." *Credit Card Management* (June), pp. 32–35.

Timmons, Heather. [1996]. "Home Equity Market Could Be Headed for a Fall." *American Banker* (August 7), pp. 1, 12.

Wessel, David. [1995]. "A Man Who Governs Credit Is Denied a Toys 'R' Us Card." *The Wall Street Journal* (December 14), p. B1.

Wills, Ronald Kent. [1983]. *Consumer Credit Analysis.* Washington, DC: American Bankers Association.

12 COMMERCIAL REAL-ESTATE LENDING

Contents

LEARNING OBJECTIVES

■ To understand the market for commercial real-estate lending

■ To understand the kinds of commercial real-estate loans banks make

■ To understand the credit analysis, loan documentation, pricing, and risks of commercial real-estate lending

■ To understand how securitization affects the market for commercial real-estate lending

■ To understand the linkages between commercial real-estate lending and the failure of Bank of New England (appendix case study)

CHAPTER THEME

In the good old days before globalization, securitization, and financial engineering, the three principles of real-estate finance were simple: location, location, and location. Banks make both commercial and residential real-estate loans. Because of their speculative nature, commercial real-estate ventures are riskier investments (e.g., **acquisition, development, and construction (ADC) loans).** ADC loans and completed projects such as commercial buildings (viewed as a portfolio of leases) should be evaluated using discounted-cash-flow (DCF) analysis. The portfolio approach has three diversification principles: location, type of property, and type of lease structure. The four components of the new residential-lending paradigm (originating, funding, selling, and servicing), as covered in the previous chapter, are working their way into the market and process of commercial real-estate lending. The credit analysis and loan documentation for commercial real-estate lending is more complex and requires greater attention to detail than other forms of bank lending. Careful analysis of regional economic conditions is a must. The case study of the Bank of New England (appendix A) shows how both internal and external factors contributed to one of the largest and most costly bank failures in U.S. history.

KEY CONCEPTS, IDEAS, AND TERMS

- Acquisition, development, and construction (ADC) loan
- Bank of New England (appendix A, case study)
- Cash-basis loan
- Collateral
- Commercial real-estate lending
- Component DCF analysis
- Construction and land development
- Credit analysis (the importance of regional economic conditions)

- Debt-equity model
- Differential-income model
- Discounted-cash-flow (DCF) analysis
- Diversification
- Foreign investment in real estate
- Functional cost analysis (FCA)
- Globalization
- Institutionalization of real estate
- Lending fads or bubbles

- Loan documentation
- Net loan losses or charge-offs
- Noncurrent loans
- Other real estate owned (OREO)
- Portfolio of leases
- Real-estate investment trust (REIT)
- Securitization
- Tenant credit quality and risk premiums

*The unfavorable conditions were greatly aggravated by the collapse of
unwise speculation in real estate, especially in city and suburban property.*

—THE COMPTROLLER OF THE CURRENCY
1890—Report to Congress

INTRODUCTION

The date on the epigram is *not* an oversight or typesetter's error.[1] Moreover, the same remarks by the Comptroller of the Currency in 1990, a century later, would have been correct. Reflecting on his 50 years in the business of banking, Dennis Weatherstone, retired chairman of J. P. Morgan & Company, stated on October 8, 1995, that one of three important ways to avoid problems in banking is to "beware the generation or corporate memory gap," especially with respect to credit experiences.[2] Bankers just don't get it, do they? Part of this chapter looks at why bankers have not gotten it when it comes to **commercial real-estate lending.**

Three out of every four dollars of mortgage debt is secured by one–four family residences (chapter 11). The remaining 25 percent is backed by multifamily residences, commercial property, or farmland. This chapter focuses on the role of commercial banks in this smaller commercial segment of the mortgage market. It describes the market for commercial real-estate lending, highlights the kinds of commercial real-estate loans banks make, and explains the credit analysis, loan documentation, pricing, and risks of commercial real-estate lending. The recurring theme of **securitization** is also stressed because it reshapes credit markets and the roles of traditional lenders in these markets. This process, which began in the market for residential mortgages, is filtering down into the commercial mortgage market.

Excluding mortgages backed by one–four family residences and home-equity loans, the four categories of commercial bank real-estate lending include the following:

- Construction and land development
- Multifamily residential
- Farmland
- Commercial or nonfarm nonresidential

WHO ARE THE PLAYERS?

During most of the 1980s, the market for commercial real-estate lending flourished. For example, in 1986, the commercial and multifamily mortgage flow was $112 billion. The leading providers were commercial banks with $48.7 billion (43.5%), life insurance companies with $22.5 billion (20.1%), and savings institutions with $12.6 billion (11.3%).[3] Together these lenders generated three out of every four dollars

---

[1] The source for the epigram is Pollack [1993].

[2] Weatherstone's [1995] other two lessons are the need for a bank to have a strategic focus and for a bank to have accountability, both internal and external.

[3] These data are from the Federal Reserve Board. Savings institutions include S&Ls, mutual savings banks, and federal savings banks.

of the 1986 flow. Other suppliers of funds to this market include households, mortgage pools, private pension funds, mortgage companies, real estate investment trusts (REITs), state and local retirement funds, other insurance companies, sponsored credit agencies, and federal, state, and local governments.

The crisis in this market during the late 1980s and early 1990s is captured by the outflow of funds, which in 1992 totaled almost $57 billion—more than one-half of the 1986 inflow. Savings institutions accounted for the bulk of the outflow (61%). Since 1992, the market has been recovering slowly. However, until 1995 most of the recovery was simply a reduced outflow of funds. During the first quarter of 1995 the recovery became real, because $28.6 billion flowed into commercial mortgages and $3.6 billion into multifamily mortgages. Neverloff [1996] reports that two things are clear for the remainder of the 1990s: real-estate lending is back, and banks and other institutions such as insurance companies and pension funds will be competing more directly with private money, as well as with each other, for market share. The key to success, according to Neverloff, is the ability of lending officers to focus on specialized market niches (e.g., the hotel industry) so they can evaluate projects and react quickly to loan proposals. Among other things, this chapter presents financial-management techniques that lending officers need to evaluate projects and avoid the costly mistakes of the past.

Table 12-1 presents a snapshot of the mortgage market and its major players. It provides data on mortgage debt outstanding as of March 31, 1996, by holder and type of property. The stock of total mortgage debt outstanding at this time was $4.8 trillion. With $3.7 trillion backed by one–four family properties, the remainder, or $1.1 trillion (25% of the market), is backed by commercial property ($714 billion), multifamily residences ($292 billion), and farmland ($85 billion). Commercial banks' share of these components was $666 billion, backed by one–four family residences (18%), $352 billion secured by commercial property (49%), $45 billion backed by multifamily residences (15%), and $24 billion secured by farmland (28%). This chapter focuses on bank lending secured by the last three types of property, a market with $421 billion in assets, or roughly 10 percent of total bank assets.

Table 12-2 shows the top 10 bank holding companies (BHCs) in **commercial real-estate lending** as of December 31, 1994. These ten banks held $100 billion in commercial real-estate loans, about 25 percent of the $400 billion held by all commercial banks. The average BHC in the top 10 had $10 billion in commercial real-estate loans outstanding. On average, $443,400 of the loans were noncurrent, amounting to 4.3 percent of the loan volume and 5.2 percent of equity capital. In terms of lack of loan quality, Citicorp had at that time almost 11 percent of its portfolio noncurrent (see appendix B for details of Citicorp's portfolio of commercial real estate), whereas Wells Fargo had almost 12 percent of equity capital exposed to noncurrent commercial real-estate loans. Although NationsBank had the most commercial real-estate loans outstanding ($17.5 billion), it was able to maintain its loan quality with noncurrent ratios of 2.15 percent relative to loan volume, and 3.42 percent relative to equity capital.

The top 50 BHCs in commercial real-estate (CRE) lending had total loans of $214.6 billion at year-end 1994, up 6.4 percent from the previous year, over one-half of the CRE loans made by the banking industry. Of this total, $7.6 billion were noncurrent, down from $12.2 billion at year-end 1993. The ratios of noncurrent to CRE loans was 3.54 percent, and noncurrent to equity capital was 4.29 percent, compared to 6.07 percent and 7.56 percent for 1993. The top 50 BHCs charged off

TABLE 12-1 Mortgage Debt Outstanding by Type of Holder and Property, March 31, 1996

Panel A. By Type of Holder

Holder	$ Billions	Market Share (%)
Commercial banks	$1,087	22.7%
Savings institutions	596	12.5
Life insurance companies	213	4.5
Federal and related agencies	322	6.7
Individuals and others[a]	661	13.8
Mortgage pools and trusts[b]	1,895	39.7
Total	$4,774	100.0%

Panel B. By Type of Property

Secured by	$ Billions	Composition (%)
One–four family residences	$3,683	77.1%
Commercial	714	15.0
Multifamily residences	292	6.1
Farm	85	1.8
Total	$4,774	100.0%

Panel C. By Property Held by Commercial Banks

Secured by	$ Billions	Composition (%)
One–four family residences	$ 666	61.3%
Commercial	352	32.4
Multifamily residences	45	3.9
Farm	24	2.2
Total	$1,087	100.0%

Notes:

[a] Outstanding principal balances of mortgage-backed securities insured or guaranteed by government or private agencies.

[b] Other holders include mortgage companies, REITs, state and local credit agencies, state and local retirement funds, noninsured pension funds, credit unions, and finance companies.

Source: Federal Reserve Bulletin (October 1996), Table 1.54, p. A35.

$1.6 billion in 1994 compared to $3.5 billion in 1993. On balance, by restricting the volume of commercial real-estate lending, the 40 BHCs under the top 10 lenders have been able to maintain better loan quality, all other things being equal.

COMMERCIAL REAL-ESTATE LENDING BY BANK SIZE

Table 12-3 shows commercial real-estate lending as a percentage of average consolidated assets by bank size for the years 1985, 1990, and 1995. Panel A presents information for all banks. The cyclical nature of this lending is most evident in **con-**

TABLE 12-2 The Top 10 BHCs in Commercial Real-Estate Lending, December 31, 1994

		Noncurrent Loans		
BHC	*Commercial Real-Estate Loans (bils.)*	*$ Volume*	*% of CRE Loans*	*% of Equity Cap.*
1. NationsBank	$17.542	$0.377	2.15%	3.42%
2. BankAmerica	16.325	1.092	6.69	5.78
3. First Union	10.318	0.305	2.96	5.66
4. Citicorp	10.298	1.106	10.74	6.22
5. Banc One	9.282	0.177	1.91	2.38
6. Wells Fargo	9.219	0.459	4.97	11.73
7. KeyCorp	7.985	0.113	1.42	2.41
8. Chemical	7.124	0.481	6.75	4.49
9. Fleet Financial	6.287	0.226	3.59	6.68
10. First Interstate	5.750	0.098	1.70	2.85
Average	$10.013	$0.443	4.29%	5.21%

Note: The top 50 BHCs in commercial real-estate lending had total loans of $214.6 billion at year-end 1994, up 6.4 percent from the previous year. Of this total, $7.6 billion were noncurrent, down from $12.2 billion at year-end 1993. The ratios of noncurrent to CRE loans was 3.54 percent, and noncurrent to equity capital was 4.29 percent, compared to 6.07 percent and 7.56 percent for 1993. The top 50 BHCs charged off $1.6 billion in 1994, compared to $3.5 billion in 1993. Chemical was acquired by Chase Manhattan in 1996.

Source: Data adapted from compilations in *The American Banker* (June 21, 1995), p. 28, from federal regulatory report of condition.

struction and land development, because it primarily drives the swings in total domestic lending, from 8 percent of total assets in 1985 to almost 12 percent in 1990 and back to 10 percent in 1994. In terms of relative volume, the rankings for 1995 were as follows:

1. Nonfarm nonresidential, or commercial (7 percent)
2. Construction and land development (1.6 percent)
3. Multifamily residential (0.8 percent)
4. Farmland (0.6 percent)

Figures in parentheses are the loan category as a percentage of average assets. Except for construction and land development, the other three categories showed upward trends for the selected years.

Panel B presents data for the 10 largest banks. Their commercial real-estate business differs in two important ways from the rest of the banking industry. First, they make relatively fewer loans secured by farmland. And second, they account for the bulk of the real-estate lending conducted in foreign offices—92 percent of the $27 billion held in foreign offices.[4] Of the total volume of domestic commercial real estate, the top 10 banks accounted for about 10 percent of the $412 billion total.

Panel C shows data for the 90 banks ranked 11–100 by assets. Similar to the 10 largest banks, these superregionals make relatively fewer loans secured by

---

[4] Data for foreign offices include loans secured by one–four family residential property. Most foreign-real-estate lending, however, is commercial in nature.

TABLE 12-3 Bank Commercial Real-Estate Lending as a Percentage of Average Consolidated Assets, Selected Years by Bank Size

Panel A. All Commercial Banks

Type of Loan (Domestic)	1985	1990	1995
Construction and land development	3.22%	4.00%	1.59%
Farmland	0.41	0.51	0.56
Multifamily residential	0.45	0.51	0.81
Nonfarm nonresidential	4.03	6.76	6.97
Total domestic	8.11	11.78	9.93
In foreign offices	0.46	0.76	0.65
Memo: Domestic volume ($ billions)	209	393	412
Total assets ($ billions)	2,573	3,338	4,149

Panel B. Ten Largest Banks

Type of Loan (Domestic)	1985	1990	1995
Construction and land development	2.24%	3.79%	0.58%
Farmland	0.07	0.08	0.06
Multifamily residential	0.41	0.68	0.38
Nonfarm nonresidential	1.85	3.51	2.83
Total domestic	4.57	8.06	3.85
In foreign offices	1.71	3.20	2.35
Memo: Domestic volume ($ billions)	29	58	40
Total assets ($ billions)	646	725	1,051

Panel C. Banks Ranked 11–100 by Assets

Type of Loan (Domestic)	1985	1990	1995
Construction and land development	4.46%	4.91%	1.50%
Farmland	0.08	0.12	0.13
Multifamily residential	0.31	0.46	0.77
Nonfarm nonresidential	3.09	6.01	6.54
Total domestic	7.94	11.50	8.94
In foreign offices	0.12	0.18	0.15
Memo: Domestic volume ($ billions)	53	114	120
Total assets ($ billions)	668	995	1,338

Panel D. Banks Ranked 101–1,000 by Assets

Type of Loan (Domestic)	1985	1990	1995
Construction and land development	3.94%	4.37%	2.21%
Farmland	0.23	0.28	0.40
Multifamily residential	0.59	0.74	1.21
Nonfarm nonresidential	5.68	9.12	9.47
Total domestic	10.44	14.51	13.29
In foreign offices	*	0.03	0.02
Memo: Domestic volume ($ billions)	67	136	145
Total assets ($ billions)	638	937	1,094

(continued)

TABLE 12-3 *Continued*

Panel E. Banks Not Ranked among the 1,000 Largest

Type of Loan (Domestic)	1985	1990	1995
Construction and land development	2.16%	2.37%	2.38%
Farmland	1.32	1.86	2.48
Multifamily residential	0.50	0.66	0.95
Nonfarm nonresidential	5.62	8.09	10.27
Total domestic	9.60	12.28	16.08
In foreign offices	*	*	*
Memo: Domestic volume ($ billions)	60	84	107
Total assets ($ billions)	621	681	666

Note: Loans in foreign offices may include those secured by one–four family residential properties. * indicates that the amount is less than 0.005 percent. Dollar figures for domestic volume may not add to total due to rounding. The growth rates (1985 to 1995) for the domestic volumes are 7.0 percent (all banks), 3.3 percent (top ten), 8.5 percent (next 90), 8.0 percent (next 900), and 5.9 percent (community banks).

Source: Federal Reserve Bulletin (June 1995), pp. 559–569, and (June 1996), pp. 495–504.

farmland. They also account for most of the remaining portion of real-estate lending done offshore.

Panel D presents data for the 900 banks ranked 101 to 1,000 by assets. This group provides the largest amount of total bank real-estate financing with $67 billion (32%) in 1985, $136 billion (35%) in 1990, and $145 billion (35.2%) in 1995.

Panel E provides data for the numerous community banks not ranked among the 1,000 largest by assets. As a group, these banks finance more commercial real-estate loans ($107 billion) than the 10 largest banks ($40 billion). On a relative basis, they are the leading financiers of farmland and for the most part have no real-estate loans generated in foreign offices.

It is interesting to look at the real-estate loans secured by farmland across the size classes shown in Table 12-3. The total loans outstanding in this category at year-end 1995 were $23.2 billion. With $16.5 billion of the total, community banks accounted for 71 percent of this type of lending. The other percentages were 19 percent ($4.4 billion) for banks ranked 101 to 1,000, 7.3 percent ($1.7 billion) for banks ranked 11 to 100, and 2.6 percent ($0.6 billion) for the 10 largest banks. Clearly, as bank size decreases, real-estate loans secured by farmland increase.

> **Exercise:** Using the dollar data in Panel A of Table 12-3, practice your interest rate mathematics by calculating the annual growth rates between 1985 and 1990, and between 1990 and 1995. The data are year-end figures. A discussion of these growth rates follows.

From year-end 1985 to year-end 1990, commercial real-estate lending by all commercial banks expanded at an annual rate of 13.2 percent. In contrast, from year-end 1990 to year-end 1995, the rate of growth was only 0.9 percent per year, and through 1994 these loans contracted at a rate of 0.25 percent per annum. To put these figures in perspective, bank total assets grew at an annual rate of 5.4 percent from 1985 to 1990, whereas from 1990 to 1995 they grew at 4.2 percent per annum. Across the four bank size classes, we observe the following annual growth rates for real-estate lending:

	Annual Growth Rates of Commercial Real-Estate Lending	
Size Class	*1985–1990*	*1990–1995*
Ten largest	14.9%	−7.2%
11 to 100	16.5%	1.0%
101 to 1,000	16.8%	1.3%
Under 1,000 largest	5.6%	4.9%

To put the 1985–1990 growth rates in perspective, expansion rates for total assets across the four size classes were 2.3 percent for the 10 largest banks, 8.3 percent for banks ranked 11 to 100, 8.0 percent for banks ranked 101 to 1,000, and 1.9 percent for banks not ranked among the 1,000 largest. Although the fever for real-estate lending was epidemic throughout the industry, the financial damage caused by the excitement was confined mainly to the 100 largest banks, especially the 10 largest. However, the contraction for the years 1990 to 1994 was not all damage control, because securitization played a major role in removing real-estate assets from large banks' balance sheets.

BUBBLES, FADS, AND STRUCTURAL CHANGES IN BANK LENDING

In the early 1970s, large commercial banks lent heavily to **real-estate investment trusts,** or **REIT**s. In the mid-1970s, they faced the REIT debt crisis. In the late 1970s and the early 1980s, large banks lent heavily to less developed countries, or LDCs. From 1982 forward, they faced the LDC debt crisis. As the thrift industry collapsed in the 1980s, commercial banks took up the slack by becoming heavily involved in real-estate lending. In particular, large banks got heavily involved in commercial real estate. In addition, they helped finance the takeover boom of the 1980s, especially in the form of highly levered transactions (HLTs), such as leveraged buyouts (LBOs). In the late 1980s and the early 1990s, large commercial banks faced a crisis in commercial real estate and problems with some HLTs.

What was behind the crisis in bank commercial real-estate lending? According to Zisler [1988], it was a "misallocation of analytical resources." Specifically, he argues that the problem can be attributed to

> an inability or a lack of incentive for industry analysts to underwrite risk properly. A great deal of resources are typically invested in activities—such as forecasting interest rates—that are largely a function of capital-market forces beyond anyone's control. In contrast, not enough resources are invested in factors over which financiers would have some control. (p. 2)

Zisler argues that the most significant change in real-estate finance has been the **globalization** of markets in the United States. This change, in conjunction with **financial engineering,** frequently makes the typical real-estate deal a complex package involving LIBOR, put and call options, and foreign-bank guarantees. The financial engineering or new technologies of real-estate finance include the layering of risk, the segmentation of debt and equity sources, and the emergence of foreign banks as both guarantors and sources of funding. Zisler predicts that securitization, which has transformed residential real estate, will have a similar effect on commercial real estate, especially with respect to high-yield loans.

Zisler contends that the changes in real-estate finance have made it too easy to ignore fundamentals, which is why banks got into trouble. In particular, he argues that a commercial building should be viewed as a **portfolio of leases.** Because certain types of commercial real estate, such as those with higher-risk lease rolls, trade as bonds do, the portfolio idea has intuitive appeal. In this context, when lease prices are above market prices, an increase in long-term interest rates will have a negative effect on building values similar to the adverse effect on any other long-term, fixed-rate asset. High vacancy rates signal that tenants will not pay higher rates to bail out owners. Although viewing a commercial building as a portfolio of leases is complex (because of the embedded options), the task must be done to estimate real values and risk-adjusted returns. To put the risk-return characteristics of a building on common ground, lease-turnover percentages can highlight risk exposures. Without attention to these analytics, how can portfolio managers justify increasing their holdings of commercial real estate?

Zisler's portfolio framework has three tenets of diversification for commercial real-estate lending:

- Location
- Type of property
- Type of lease structure

In the good old days before globalization, securitization, and financial engineering, the three principles of real estate finance were simpler: location, location, and location.

THE COMMERCIAL REAL-ESTATE CRISIS OF THE EARLY 1990s[5]

One of the mantras value-minded business people should chant is: Profitable growth adds value! Growth for growth's sake may look good in the short run but not over the long haul. During the 1980s, the managers of commercial real-estate portfolios at large U.S. banks got their mantras mixed up. The case study of Bank of New England (appendix A of this chapter) presents a classic example of mismanagement of commercial real-estate lending.

The above-average growth rates for commercial real-estate lending during the 1980s came home to roost during the early 1990s, mainly for the largest banks/BHCs (appendix B). The problems were driven, in part, by adverse conditions in U.S. real-estate markets. Specifically, with high vacancy rates in commercial office space in many metropolitan areas, rents and asset values plunged. In addition, although the cyclical downturn also affected retail and residential real estate adversely, price declines varied by region. New England was the hardest hit. The excessive commercial real-estate lending by the Bank of New England during the 1980s led to its demise on January 6, 1991. Many other banks in New England, big and small, were plagued by serious financial difficulties. Moreover, from Boston to Washington, DC, large BHCs such as Maryland National

---

[5] Appendix B presents data showing that this crisis was confined mainly to the largest banks.

Corporation (MNC)[6] and C&S/Sovran (now part of NationsBank) were hit by the real-estate crisis. In addition, banks in Arizona and California suffered with overextended commercial real-estate lending.

The epigram at the beginning of this chapter dates to 1890. Perhaps asking bankers to remember century-old mistakes is too tough a standard. Let's try a quarter of a century. Going back to the REIT crisis of the mid-1970s, C&S (Citizens and Southern, Atlanta) almost failed because of its excessive real-estate lending, and many other banks, especially the largest ones, experienced financial difficulties.[7] When C&S merged with Sovran in 1990, in response to a hostile takeover attempt by NCNB (now NationsBank), its loan portfolio was relatively clean. However, as a result of the merger C&S had to share in Sovran's portfolio of bad real-estate loans, mainly in the Washington, DC area. The Chairman of C&S, Bennett A. Brown, told shareholders at the 1990 annual meeting that if C&S had known about Sovran's real-estate problems: "We would have gone back to the table."[8] Aren't buyers supposed to check such things out before they buy?

The crisis in real-estate lending of the late 1980s and the early 1990s primarily was a problem for money-center and regional banks located in the Northeast but extended along the east coast from New York City to Washington, DC to Miami. (Appendices A and B present a case study and data, respectively). Mainly because of bad commercial real-estate loans, the banking industry earned only $16.6 billion in 1990 for a return on assets of 0.49 percent based on total assets of $3.4 trillion. For the 100 largest BHCs, where the bulk of the real-estate problems were, the average ROA was only 0.34 percent. With an equity multiplier, or leverage factor, of 19.2, the 100 largest BHCs had an average return on equity of only 6.5 percent. By 1993, however, the 100 largest banks had recovered, with average ROAs of 1.13 percent (top 10) and 1.26 percent (next 90), and ROEs of 16.7 percent and 16.9 percent, respectively. Since then, the accounting profitability at the 10 largest banks has declined (e.g., ROA of 0.88 percent in 1995), whereas the next 90 have held their own (e.g., ROA of 1.31 percent for 1995).

TERMS OF LENDING FOR CONSTRUCTION AND LAND DEVELOPMENT LOANS

Because construction and land development loans, as defined in the Fed's survey of the terms of lending, include both unsecured loans and loans secured by real estate, some of the construction and land development loans are reported as real-estate loans and the remainder as business loans. As classified by type of construction, the loans are made for three purposes: (1) single family, (2) multifamily, and (3) nonresidential. For large banks, about 90 percent of their construction and land development loans are for nonresidential purposes. In contrast, other (smaller)

---

[6] Recall from the previous chapter (appendix B) that MNC was forced to sell its profitable credit-card subsidiary because of its sour real-estate loans.

[7] Sinkey [1975, 1979] and Sinkey and Gerdnic [1975] document the problems experienced by banks during the REIT crisis of the 1970s. More recent studies include Corgel and Gay [1987], Corcoran [1987], Corgel and Clauretie [1990], Moscovitch [1990], and McNulty [1995].

[8] See King [1991]. In the "merger of equals," since C&S shareholders received one share of C&S/Sovran for one share of C&S while Sovran shareholders received 1.23 shares of C&S/Sovaran for one share of Sovran, the old Sovran shareholders received a greater share of post-merger gains and losses (see chapter 19 for more on bank mergers and acquisitions).

banks lend about one-half of their construction and land development loans for single-family purposes.

Further insight into the typical construction and land development loan is provided by the following data:[9]

	Large Banks	Other Banks
Average size	$1,019,000	$48,000
Weighted average maturity	5 months	14 months
Weighted average effective loan rate	12.35%	13.32%
Interquartile range	11.51–12.68%	12.96–13.80%
Loans made under commitment	96.6%	83.3%
Participation loans	41.5%	5.2%
Percent floating rate	57.8%	83.0%

To summarize, large banks tend to make larger construction and land development loans at shorter maturities and lower rates relative to other (smaller) banks. For both groups, the majority of construction and land development loans are made under commitments and priced on a floating-rate basis. Large banks, however, make more fixed-rate loans than smaller banks and make more loans under commitments.

FCA Evidence on the Commercial Real-Estate Loan Function

Table 12-4 presents data for the commercial real-estate loan function based on the Federal Reserve's *Functional Cost Analysis* (FCA). These data, which are more

TABLE 12-4 The Commercial Real-Estate Loan Function, 1994

Category	Deposit Size Class ($ millions)		
	Small (< $50)	Medium ($50–$200)	Large (>$200)
Number of loans outstanding			
Commercial	32	83	209
Construction/land development	5	18	46
Average size loan			
Commercial	$67,553	$89,087	$240,457
Construction/land development	$52,627	$67,062	$247,416
Applications processed			
Commercial	24	81	84
Construction/land development	6	23	52
Number of loans made			
Commercial	17	49	65
Construction/land development	6	20	44
Loan acceptance rate (%)			
Commercial	71%	60%	77%
Construction/land development	87%	84%	84%
Number of payments collected			
Commercial	322	982	2,482
Construction/land development	36	154	488
Number of banks	52	116	41

Source: FCA National Average Report [1994], p. 29. © Federal Reserve Bank, San Francisco. Used by permission.

[9] These data are for the survey week of May 1–5, 1989.

reflective of the activities of smaller banks, provide information for three size classes: small (deposits less than $50 million), medium ($50-to-$200 million), and large (over $200 million). Except for loan-acceptance rates, the data show that the number of loans outstanding, the average size loan, the number of applications processed, the number of loans made, and the number of payments collected increase as bank size increases.

CREDIT ANALYSIS: THE IMPORTANCE OF REGIONAL ECONOMIC CONDITIONS

In making commercial real-estate loans, the "C" that lenders must get right is Conditions (economics). Recall the five Cs as:

- *Character* (honesty, ethical reputation)
- *Capacity* (cash flow)
- *Capital* (real net worth)
- *Collateral* (security)
- *Conditions* (economic, e.g., vulnerability to business and interest-rate cycles)

As reported above, overbuilding of commercial real estate presented problems for the banking industry in the 1970s and the 1980s. Presumably, if lenders get the conditions factor correct, they would restrain their lending. McNulty ([1995], p. 37) reports the following anecdote about the importance of correctly analyzing regional economic conditions:

> When the Orlando, Florida real estate market crashed in 1974–1975 because of a massive wave of speculative overbuilding, one real estate consultant made the following comment: "We were running close to 100% occupancy, so we continued to build more and more apartments. What we failed to realize was that most of the apartments were being rented to construction workers."

A decade later, many commercial real-estate lenders made the same mistake. Appendix A describes the mistakes made by Bank of New England, one of the largest and most costly bank failures in U.S. history.

Another view on the problems in commercial real-estate lending is captured by the words of Samuel Lefrak, at the time (1975) the largest builder and owner of apartments in the United States:[10]

> Why didn't those usurers (i.e., the bankers) call me before? Now they're asking me questions about the guys that they lent money to two years ago. Their properties are in trouble, so now they beg, "Sam, bail me out."

There is no substitute for sound credit analysis and due diligence by lenders. A growing body of evidence points to the importance of the proper evaluation of regional economic conditions in making prudent decisions regarding commercial real-estate lending.[11] These studies suggest a number of conclusions.

---

[10] As reported in *The Bankers Magazine* (Spring 1975), p. 30.
[11] See Corgel and Gay [1987], Corgel and Clauretie [1990], Moscovitch [1990], and McNulty [1995].

First, it is imperative that lenders analyze the strength of their region's economic base. This means concentrating on basic economic variables such as levels and changes in property income, sectoral payrolls (e.g., manufacturing), and construction income. McNulty [1995] suggests that because "overbuilding may actually be inherent in real estate markets," it suggests "the need for much more caution in real-estate construction lending" (p. 49).

Second, lenders must consider the lags in economic activity between basic and nonbasic sectors and the lag between approval and completion of construction projects. The latter takes on added importance because construction plays a special role in transmitting economic changes from basic to nonbasic sectors.

Third, to effectively monitor the viability of existing projects, lenders need to track the performance of their region's economic base. Moscovitch [1990] contends that such an analysis would have revealed that the New England economy showed signs of deterioration as early as 1985. The important point is that construction growth must be transmitted to other sectors if economic growth is to be sustained. Otherwise, as McNulty's story reveals, when the construction workers leave, the local economy collapses.

To summarize, conventional wisdom frequently attributes waves of speculative overbuilding to "greedy lenders." Recent evidence suggests, however, that the causes of overbuilding may be more complex, involving economic lags and feedback effects. Needless to say, unless bankers use due diligence and conduct proper credit analysis, something that the Bank of New England did not do, they need to distinguish between lenders that are greedy and those that are just plain incompetent or dishonest or both.

LOAN DOCUMENTATION FOR COMMERCIAL REAL-ESTATE LENDING

Table 12-5 presents a list of the key documents needed for the proper recording of commercial real-estate loans. This section describes the importance and function of these documents.[12]

- *Deed of trust:* This document is used to convey, transfer, assign, and grant a collateral interest in real property. If the borrower defaults, then the trustee (lender) named in the document has the right to sell the property to repay the principal and interest on the note (loan).

- *Promissory note:* Legal evidence of a debt (written promise to pay) used for all commercial lending purposes regardless of the amount. A promissory note may be transferred to a third party as a negotiable instrument. The holder who in due course wants payment before maturity can negotiate the note by endorsing it and presenting it to the payer for payment.

- *Real-estate appraisal certificate:* This document certifies that the property has been appraised by a qualified real-estate officer of the bank, or by an outside agent if required by law. One of the problems in the Texas real-estate crisis of the 1980s was that S&Ls and banks made "flip loans" that were passed from one institution to another on the basis of higher and higher real-estate appraisals. The result was a house of cards that soon came crashing to the ground.

- *Extension of real-estate note and lien:* This form extends the maturity of a real-estate construction loan and the underlying lien on the property. Extensions of construction loans are normally for six months.

---

[12] This section draws on Clarke [1986], pp. 254–294.

TABLE 12-5 Loan Documents Needed for Commercial Real-Estate Lending

- Deed of trust
- Promissory note
- Real-estate appraisal certificate
- Extension of real-estate note and lien
- Transfer of lien
- Partial release of lien
- Release of lien
- Request for an advance
- Contractor's lien waivers
- Subcontractor's and material supplier's release of lien and affidavit
- Contractor's affidavit of substantial completion
- Insurance and taxes:
  Hazard insurance expiration notice
  Increase in monthly escrow payments
  Delinquency tax notice

Note: The information common to most of these documents includes county, grantors, trustee, bank, addresses, date, property (including description), promissory note, insurance, signatures, prior liens, principal, rate, repayment schedule, and acknowledgements. When the proceeds of a loan are to be used "primarily" for business, commercial, or agricultural credit, truth-in-lending disclosures are not required.
Source: Clarke [1986], pp. 254–294.

- *Transfer of lien:* This document is used when a promissory note, secured by a lien on real property, is assigned to the bank by a party other than the payee of the note. For the bank to be a holder in due course, the note must be endorsed over to the bank.

- *Partial release of lien:* A standard legal form used when a bank wants to release its lien on only a portion of real estate being held as collateral for a loan.

- *Release of lien:* A standard legal form used when a bank wants to release its entire lien on real estate being held as collateral for a loan. Because a debtor's attorney or title company normally handles this matter, it is done by the bank only to accommodate a good customer's request.

- *Request for an advance:* This form permit draws on construction loans to be made by the contractor as work proceeds.

- *Contractor's lien waivers:* When advances are made directly to the owner/borrower, this document assures the lender that the contractor, subcontractors, and suppliers have been paid to date and at the completion of the project. If the bank cuts checks and distributes funds directly to these parties, then it has even greater assurance that no liens will be filed against a project after it is completed.

- *Subcontractor's and material supplier's release of lien and affidavit:* See previous description. An affidavit of receipt of payment signed by a notary public should be included.

- *Contractor's affidavit of substantial completion:* See previous description. An affidavit of substantial completion signed by a notary public should be included.

- *Insurance and taxes:**
  Hazard insurance expiration notice
  Increase in monthly escrow payments
  Delinquency tax notice

---

*These three notices are self-explanatory. When insurance and taxes are escrowed by the bank, the borrower makes payments to the bank and the bank pays the insurance and tax bills.

The documentation of commercial real-estate loans requires careful attention to detail. In the waves of speculative overbuilding that occurred in the 1970s and 1980s, many lenders failed to pay attention to these details.

THE FUNDAMENTALS OF FINANCING COMMERCIAL REAL ESTATE[13]

Figure 12-1 depicts Bacow's [1990] view of value creation in real estate. Except for the last stage (called investment asset), lenders and financing are needed in each of the other five stages, which are:

- Land assemblage
- Horizontal development
- Vertical development
- Leasing/sales
- Asset management

Land assemblage is the collecting of adjoining locations to allow the development of larger projects. **Horizontal development** involves the preparation of the infrastructure (roads, utilities, permits, approvals, etc.) needed to support the building phase. **Vertical development** is the construction of buildings for occupancy. **Leasing/sales, asset management,** and **investment asset** are postconstruction stages needed to generate occupants, income, and property management and investment.

Financial intermediaries such as banks and thrifts sometimes make loans for the **acquisition, development, and construction** of real estate, called **ADC loans.** Such loans involve vertical integration in terms of the acquisition of land, its development, and the construction of buildings. Because ADC loans frequently involve equity participations on the part of lenders, they can be quite risky. Commercial banks, however, are restricted by law regarding the extent of such

FIGURE 12-1 The Creation of Value in Real Estate

Activity	Market Participant	Services Needed
Land assemblage ↓	Land speculators, land brokers	Brokerage, financing lenders
Horizontal development ↓	Land developers, lenders	Legal, planning, construction, financing
Vertical development ↓	Architects, builders, lenders	Design, construction, financing
Leasing/sales ↓	Lessors, brokers, marketing and sales personnel, lenders	Brokerage, marketing, financing
Asset management ↓	Property managers, lenders	Property management, permanent financing
Investment asset	Brokers, portfolio managers	Investment brokerage and management

Source: Adapted from Bacow [1990], Figure 1, p. 6.

---

[13] This section draws on Bacow [1990], Brady [1990], Chesler [1990], Ebbert [1991], and Greig and Young [1991].

involvement. In contrast, thrifts are less confined. In fact, many thrifts in the Southwest were heavily involved in ADC lending (including equity participations) in the 1980s. The deals became known as "flip loans" because one lender would obtain a higher appraisal on a project and flip it to another lender. Such transactions are built on foundations of cards, which collapse when deflation or realistic appraisals or both burst the speculative bubble. The downturn in energy prices corrected the problem in the Southwest in the 1980s, whereas recession brought the excesses of commercial real-estate lending to its knees in the late 1980s and the early 1990s.

Vertical Integration and the Structure of the Real-Estate Industry in the United States

When the activities shown in Figure 12-1 are combined in one business, the firm is described as completely vertically integrated. Such a firm is involved in all of the stages and methods of adding value to real estate. Although Japan and some European countries have such integration, its existence in the United States is rare. Bacow [1990] attributes the lack of vertical integration in the real-estate industry in the United States to three factors:

1. The local nature of such services as the knowledge of local buying opportunities, local planning laws, local politics, and local building trades and contractors

2. The compensation problem associated with the different pay arrangements for real-estate developers (salary plus equity interest), brokers (commissions), and managers (salary plus bonus or share of the profits based on performance of the company)

3. Greater exposure to macroeconomic risk because of the increasing length of time to complete value creation in real estate

Despite their renowned managerial expertise, Bacow [1990] argues that not even the Japanese have discovered a way to overcome the structural obstacles to vertical integration in U.S. real estate.[14] Accordingly, foreign firms face the same structural problems as domestic operators.

The Consequences of Foreign Investment

Bacow [1990] sees two important consequences of large-scale ownership of U.S. buildings. First, more foreign buyers means more foreign competition in related businesses, because some foreign buyers will prefer service providers with a common language and culture. Thus, just as we have seen foreign ownership of U.S. banks, we will see foreign ownership of other companies that provide services to the real-estate industry. Moreover, because domestic firms will be seeking to serve the same clientele, competition for both domestic and foreign business will increase. Bacow, however, does not see the development of huge integrated real-estate firms in the United States.

The second and more important consequence that Bacow sees is the institutionalization of the real-estate industry. The institutionalization of savings has been reflected in the increased savings held by institutional investors such as pension funds, insurance companies, and nonfinancial corporations, both domestic and

---

[14] Bacow ([1990], p. 6) gives a counterexample based on the experience of Hasegawa Komuten, Japan's largest developer of condominiums. In Honolulu, where it caters mainly to Japanese buyers, the firm develops, constructs, markets, and manages its properties. In narrow markets such as the one for Japanese buyers in Honolulu, vertical integration should be successful; however, in more diverse markets, such as the mainland of the United States, the structural problems described in the text may prohibit successful vertical integration.

foreign. Not surprisingly, this influx of foreign capital, along with domestic institutional money, has resulted in institutional ownership of U.S. real estate. As a result, the yields on investment-grade assets have been bid down below the long-term cost of debt. Because of recession-related high vacancy rates and declining real-estate prices, the investment return for new buildings in many markets does not cover the long-term cost of capital. Under these conditions, because many developers cannot afford to own the buildings they develop, they sell them or develop buildings for institutional buyers at discount or capitalization rates below investment returns. Bacow [1990] concludes that "This process reinforces the institutionalization of the real-estate market, and at the same time, forces developers to pursue a fee-based, merchant-build strategy" (p. 8).

Institutionalization of Real Estate: A Numerical Example

To illustrate the institutionalization of the real-estate industry in the United States, Bacow [1990] presents the following numerical example.

Project cost	$10 million
Project net operating income (NOI)	$950,000 per year
Cost of long-term debt	10 percent
Debt-service coverage ratio required by lender	1.2

In this example, net operating income (NOI) refers to income after expenses but before debt service (i.e., usually principal plus interest). Because the lender requires a debt-service coverage ratio of 1.2, the maximum debt service the lender will provide is $791,667 (= $950,000/1.2). On an interest-only obligation, the maximum amount the developer can borrow from the lender is $7,916,667 (= $791,667/0.10). If the lender requires the principal to be amortized, then the developer can borrow only a smaller amount. Thus, the developer must generate a minimum equity investment of almost $2.1 million to fund the project. In contrast, an institutional investor with a required return of 8.5 percent would be willing to spend $11,176,471 (= $950,000/0.085) to buy the project. Under these circumstances, most developers sell to the institutional investor and look for another project to start.

The major factors responsible for these conditions have been (1) declining profit margins to developers due to declining real rents and the lengthening of the value-creation or development process (greater risk exposure), (2) the bidding up of prices (yields down) by institutional buyers even in the face of decreasing cash flows from properties, and (3) the cost of debt relative to the return on investment.

Underwriting Income-Property Investment

Brady [1990] contends that lenders need three sets of data to determine whether they should finance an income property. First, given the characteristics of the property to be financed, the lender needs to answer three questions:

1. What is the lowest interest rate the lender will offer?
2. What is the longest maturity the lender will offer?
3. What is the highest loan-to-value ratio the lender will accept?

The answers to these rate, maturity, and amount questions serve to define the lender's risk-return requirements. The lender also must evaluate the borrower's risk-return requirements with respect to minimum return on equity and maximum relative equity contribution. The third data set focuses on evaluating the expected net operating income (NOI discussed above) for the project. In real-estate jargon, NOI is frequently referred to as "stabilized NOI," or SNOI. Because the borrower's forecasted cash flows may be inflated, Brady cautions lenders to analyze projected income and operating expenses carefully.

Given these data, Brady claims that the calculation of five fundamental ratios provides a framework for sound underwriting of income property. He uses the following example to illustrate the approach. The project is an office building that requires a $22 million mortgage loan. The lender's parameters are an interest rate of 10.5 percent for 360 months with 80 percent financing (i.e., a maximum loan-to-value ratio of 80%). Based on an expected SNOI of $2.59 million per year and a capitalization rate of 10.36 percent, the borrower's appraisal reports an economic value of $25 million for the building (= $2.59 million/0.1036). Although the lender's maximum loan-to-value ratio is 80 percent, implying a maximum loan of $20 million ($2 million less than the $22 million requested), the developer would be willing to accept the lower amount because it is persuaded that it will receive a 15 percent ROE on its 20 percent equity contribution. However, because the lender's underwriting staff concludes that the expected NOI is overstated by $200,000, it uses a stabilized NOI figure of $2,390,625 for its loan underwriting.

According to Brady, the five ratios the underwriting staff should calculate are

1. Composite debt factor = the annual mortgage constant times
   loan-to-value ratio
   $$= 0.1098 \times 0.80 = 0.0878$$

The annual mortgage constant is simply the annual loan repayment factor. Under the terms of a $20 million loan at 10.5 percent for 360 months, the monthly payment is $182,947.86, or $2,195,537.30 per year. Dividing the annual payment by the loan amount gives the annual mortgage constant, or 0.1098 = $2,195,537.3/$20,000,000.

2. Composite equity factor = borrower's ROE × equity contribution
   $$= 0.15 \times 0.20 = 0.03$$

3. Composite financing factor = composite debt factor
   + composite equity factor
   $$= 0.0878 + 0.03 = 0.1178$$

The fourth and fifth ratios are simply the first and second ratios each divided by the third one, or the debt and equity factors relative to the financing factor. Thus, the composite debt factor relative to the composite financing factor is 0.0878/0.1178 = 0.7453, and the composite equity factor relative to the composite financing factor is 0.03/0.1178 = 0.2547. And of course, 0.7453 + 0.2547 = 1.0. Given the lender's revised SNOI of $2,390,625, the underwriting staff's analysis implies that 74.5 percent of SNOI ($1,781,733) will be used for debt service and 25.5 percent for ROE ($608,892).

With roughly $1.8 million available for annual debt service, the lender recalculates the maximum loan amount by dividing the amount available for debt servicing by the annual mortgage constant, that is, maximum loan amount = $1,781,733/0.1098 = $16,227,077. The developer's equity contribution equals its dollar ROE divided by its required return, that is, $608,892/0.15 = $4,059,280. Thus, the underwriting staff has estimated the economic value of the project as $20,286,357, roughly $4.3 million less than the developer's estimate. As a result, the lender is willing to lend only $16.2 million rather than the requested $22 million.

Because the lender's underwriting approach does not require it to justify the borrower's capitalization rate (10.36%), it simply combines the lender's desired mortgage rate (10.5%) and the borrower's required ROE to determine the property's lendable value of $20.2 million. The critical input in the analysis is the lender's estimate of stabilized net operating income. Given an accurate SNOI, Brady claims that his approach provides the lender with "the exact allocations of debt and equity that the property can economically support" (p. 60).

Discounted-Cash-Flow Analysis

Although some analysts (e.g., Brady [1990]) still emphasize traditional underwriting based on stabilized net operating income, Chesler [1990] and Ebbert [1991] focus on discounted-cash-flow (DCF) analysis. Chesler claims that "valuation techniques predicated on stabilized NOI estimates came to be viewed as artificial" (p. 64) after the economic instability of the early 1980s. Two other factors that increased the popularity of DCF analysis in real estate finance have been competition from institutional investors and the spread of computerization. Although DCF analysis is generally accepted as the industry standard today, it was not broadly adopted until the early 1980s. Ebbert argues that "Using traditional underwriting to finance property . . . , the lender may find itself without a takeout at maturity" (p. 73). "Takeout" refers to permanent financing following the acquisition, development, and construction (ADC) of a project. Insurance companies and pension funds, seeking to hedge their long-term liabilities, typically provide such financing. The problem, according to Ebbert, is that many banks continue to use traditional underwriting methods for ADC loans. If DCF analysis is more accurate than traditional underwriting, then short-term lenders (using SNOI) can provide more funding than takeout lenders (using DCF) are willing to supply.

As a refinement of DCF analysis, Chesler suggests segmenting a property's projected net cash flow to more accurately reflect its risk-return profile. He argues that because each rentable unit within a given property is unique, it should be valued separately to highlight its risk and return characteristics. To keep the task manageable, Chesler suggests grouping leases according to use (office or retail) or by industry (Standard Industrial Classification [SIC] Code). In addition, speculative spaces can be grouped according to perceived marketability. For example, he mentions the substantially different risks and rewards associated with the marketability of mezzanine retail space in an office building versus office space in the same building. Because Chesler proposes grouping spaces to generate component cash flows, he calls his framework "component discounted-cash-flow analysis."

Table 12-6 presents a **component discounted-cash-flow (DCF) analysis** applied to a multitenant office building. To illustrate the technique, only one year (the eighth year) of a 16-year projection used by Chesler [1990] is shown. According to Chesler, the example reflects space groupings and risk assessments likely to be used by a passive investor. The office building is segmented into two cash-flow components:

- **Leases in place,** which account for 497,072 square feet of the building's net rentable space (92.6%)
- **Speculative space,** which accounts for 39,770 square feet (7.4%)

TABLE 12-6 Component Discounted-Cash-Flow Analysis Applied to a Multi-Tenant Office Building

Cash-flow Components	Year Eight of a 16-Year Projection	
	Leases in Place	Speculative Space
Income		
Base rent	$ 9,762,848	$859,865
Parking rent	32,571	2,606
Total rent	$ 9,795,419	$862,571
Operating recovery	852,493	$ 30,239
Total gross income	$10,647,912	$892,810
Less: Vacancy allowance	(530,767)	(44,510)
Effective gross income	$10,117,145	$848,300
Expenses		
Utilities	$954,115	$78,408
Insurance	139,886	11,192
Real-estate taxes	839,316	67,152
Operating expenses	1,643,660	131,507
Management fee	349,715	27,980
Total expenses	$3,926,692	$316,239
Net operating income	$6,190,453	$532,061
Capital items		
Alterations	$1,084,064	$131,507
Commissions	295,842	11,192
Replacement reserve	49,707	67,152
Total capital items	$1,429,613	$209,851
Net cash flow	$4,760,840	$322,210
Ratios/measures/returns		
Cash on cash	8.90%	21.48%
Cumulative cash on cash	68.25%	66.71%
Average cash on cash	8.53%	8.34%
Residual capitalization rate	8.70%	9.70%
Sale price per foot	$137.06	$ 2.81
Base rents	$ 19.64	$21.62
Market rents	$ 24.00	$24.00
Spread to market	81.84%	90.10%
Average compound increase in base rents	3.93%	19.94%
Average compound increase in market rents	6.20%	6.20%
Internal rate	10.77%	14.07%
Component values (full 16 years)		
Total	$53,500,000	$1,500,000
Per square foot of net rentable area	$107.63	$37.72

Aggregate property value = $55,000,000 = $53,500,000 + $1,500,000
Per square foot value = $102.45 = .926 ($107.63) + .074 ($37.72)

Source: Chesler [1990], appendix A, p. 68, and appendix B, p. 69. Used by permission.

Because the building's major tenant was a Fortune 100 company with a nine-year lease (accounting for 45% of leases in place), the cash flow from base rent was relatively secure and predictable, resulting in a low discount rate or internal rate of return (IRR) requirement. If the property is sold in the tenth year after the Fortune 100 company renews its lease, Chesler posits, for a risk-averse investor, an 11 percent IRR over years 12 to 16 of the projection. In conjunction with this target IRR, Chesler applies an initial capitalization rate of 8 percent in year one but has it increase by ten basis points each year to account for depreciation and uncertainty. Hence, as shown in Table 12-6, the residual cap rate is 8.70 percent in year eight. Under these assumptions, the component value of leases in place is $53.5, or $107.63 per square foot.

Regarding the speculative space in the office building, which of course has a higher perceived market risk, Chesler applies a 12 percent IRR hurdle rate over the last five years of the projection and assumes an initial capitalization rate of 9 percent with an increase of 10 basis points each year (e.g., the 9.70% in year eight). On this basis, the speculative component has an estimated price of $1.5 million, or $37.72 per square foot. Overall, the building has an aggregate value of $55 million, or $102.45 per square foot (calculated as a weighted average, i.e., 0.926[$107.63] + 0.074[$37.72]).[15]

Using DCF analysis without segmenting the components of the property's cash flow, Chesler estimates a value of $56 million, or $104.31 per square foot. The difference of $1 million (1.79%) equals the risk premium the investor attributes to the project's speculative component. "More importantly," Chesler argues, "it represents the investor's acknowledgment of the property's unique risks and rewards relative to its own risk profile. If acted on, this pricing should produce an investment decision that more accurately reflects the buyer's investment philosophy" (p. 67).

The Debt-Equity Model of Commercial Real Estate

Greig and Young [1991] propose a methodology for performance expectations for multitenant commercial properties based on the character of existing leases and the credit quality of the tenants. Their starting point is the **debt-equity model** developed by Real Asset Management, Inc. (RAM). According to RAM, the present value of a property equals the sum of the present value of existing leases (debt) and the present value of future leases (equity), that is,

$$PV \text{ of property} = PV \text{ of existing leases} + PV \text{ of future leases} \qquad \textbf{(12-1)}$$

This view postulates that existing leases are analogous to corporate debt and that ownership of property capable of producing future leases is analogous to equity. Thus, the approach views commercial real estate as a combination of debt and equity. Treating existing leases as bonds means that bond-valuation techniques can be used to value them. Accordingly, only three variables are needed to value leases as bonds: (1) net rents or cash flows over time, (2) the credit quality of the tenant, and (3) the risk premium corresponding to the credit quality. Table 12-7 presents Greig and Young's approach for quantifying the second and third variables. The analysis assumes that the asset manager measures **tenant credit quality** as the risk of default

---

[15] According to Chesler ([1990], p. 67), the component DCF analysis presented here and partially illustrated in Table 12-6 was based on a 75-tenant office building and took only about four hours to complete. Ebbert [1991] presents a similar analysis, including a direct comparison between DCF analysis and traditional underwriting.

TABLE 12-7   Tenant Credit Quality and Risk Premiums

Credit Rating	Description	Risk Premium over Treasuries	Default Risk
A	Highest possible rating; better than commercial credit (e.g., tenant is a government office). Virtually no default risk.	0.75%	1%
B	Best commercial credit. Very low probability of default.	0.95%	4%
C	Good commercial credit. Small probability of default.	1.40%	8%
D	Average commercial credit. Real potential for default.	1.90%	14%
E	No credit or little business experience. New "mom and pop" or undercapitalized start-up.	2.30%	22%

Note: The analysis assumes that the asset manager measures credit quality as the risk of default on lease obligations and expresses the risk in percentage terms. The risk premium over Treasuries is based on matching the duration of the lease with the yield on a Treasury of the same duration. The Treasury yield plus the tenant's risk premium represents the discount rate for determining the value of the tenant's lease. Using the principle of value additivity, the present value of the property equals the present value of existing leases plus the present value of future leases.
Source: Greig and Young [1991], Exhibit 2, p. 19. Used by permission.

on lease obligations and expresses the risk in percentage terms. The risk premium over Treasuries is based on matching the duration of the lease with the yield on a Treasury of the same duration.[16] The Treasury yield plus the tenant's **risk premium** represents the discount rate for determining the value of the tenant's lease. Using the principle of value additivity, the present value of the property equals the present value of existing leases plus the present value of future leases. Given the current market value of the property, the present value of future leases or the equity value of the property equals the difference between the market value of the property and the estimated value of existing leases.

The Differential-Income Model of Commercial Real Estate

Although the **differential-income model** was developed by Sykes and Young [1981], this section draws on the version of it presented in Greig and Young [1991]. The approach builds on the valuation of a perpetual annuity, $V = I/r$, where V = value, I = income or cash flow, and r = discount rate. To enhance this simple framework, a second term, representing the difference between existing net rents, or current income I_c, and market net rents, or net income at market rents I_m, is added. The complete model, also known as the United Kingdom or U. K. valuation model, is

$$V = I_c/r + (I_m - I_c)/[r(1 + r)^n]   \qquad (12\text{-}2)$$

where n = the time until lease rollover. Panel A of Figure 12-2 presents a picture of the differential-income model. Both equation (12-2) and Panel A of Figure 12-2 say that a property's present value equals the value of existing leases assuming a perpetual term with current rents of I_c discounted at r plus the present value of

---

[16] Greig and Young ([1991], p. 19) suggest the following rule of thumb for approximating the duration of a lease in years: divide the lease term in months by 25. Thus, a 60-month lease has a duration of approximately 2.4 years.

Panel A. The differential-income model

Dollars

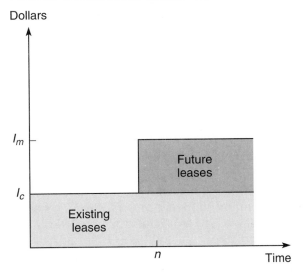

Panel B. The debt-equity model

Dollars

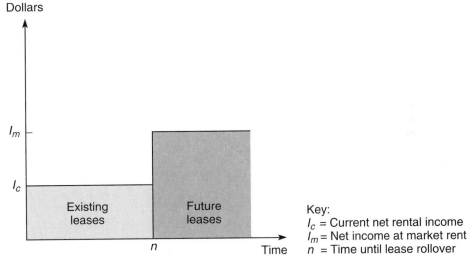

Key:
I_c = Current net rental income
I_m = Net income at market rent
n = Time until lease rollover

Source: Greig and Young [1991], Exhibit 1 and 4, pp. 19 and 21. Used by permission.

FIGURE 12-2 **Alternative Views of the Valuation of Commercial Real Estate**

future leases at some market rental increment over current rents, $(I_m - I_c)$ deferred n years but also extended into perpetuity. The second term in equation (12-2) can be rearranged as

$$[1/(1 + r)^n][(I_m - I_c)/r] \qquad\qquad \textbf{(12-3)}$$

where the second term in (12-3) is the present value of a perpetual annuity starting in year n, and the first term is the discount factor that values it at time zero. Focusing on Panel B of Figure (12-2), the debt-equity model and the differential-income model are simply different ways of slicing property value.

Sykes and Young's major contribution to the valuation of income property is their sensitivity analysis, which focused on changes in the value of a property relative to changes in market rental value or to changes in the capitalization rate or both. Ignoring the mathematics (which is based on partial differentiation of equation 12-2) and focusing on the intuitive appeal of the sensitivity analysis, the total change in a property's value consists of three components:

1. The rate of change in rental value
2. The rate of change in the capitalization rate
3. The rate of change or intrinsic growth due to the approach of the lease rollover date

Empirical Tests

Using detailed data on properties and tenants from a portfolio of eight properties (including four community shopping centers with 95 tenants and aggregate market value of about $51 million, and four industrial properties with 105 tenants and an aggregate market value of about $54 million), Greig and Young [1991] tested the debt-equity and the differential-income models. The properties were managed by a major institutional real-estate advisor for a group of domestic pension funds. For each tenant, its credit quality and default risk, described earlier, were estimated. Along with the estimated values of the properties, four measures of risk were computed:

1. An implicit (letter) credit rating derived as a weighted average of each tenant's credit rating
2. An estimate of default risk calculated as a weighted average of each tenant's default risk
3. The actual risk-adjusted lease yield computed as a weighted average of each tenant's risk-adjusted lease rate weighted by the value of the lease
4. The market lease yield based on what the risk-adjusted discount rate for the property would be if all tenants had lease terms typical of the market

Based on their experiments, Greig and Young drew a number of conclusions. Both the debt-equity model and the income-differential model provided useful insights regarding the risk characteristics inherent in a commercial property's underlying lease structure. Because both models estimate each tenant's credit quality and risk premium over Treasuries, either one permits quantification of a property's risk exposure. Because properties differ in their debt-equity compositions, their sensitivities with respect to interest rates or market rents or both differ, characteristics that can be more important than conventional measures such as location or type of property. Finally, lease duration best measures a property's lease rollover risk because, like bond duration, it incorporates the time value of lease payments into its calculation. In this case, the nominal number of years to lease rollover, like a bond's maturity, does not measure the effective time until repricing as duration does.

Recapitulation

Zisler [1988] contends that the changes in real-estate finance have made it too easy for lenders to ignore fundamentals, which is why banks got into trouble. Specifically, he argues that a commercial building should be viewed as a *portfolio of leases*. Because certain types of commercial real estate, such as those with higher-risk lease rolls, trade as bonds do, the portfolio idea has intuitive appeal. Although viewing a commercial building as a portfolio of leases is complex (because of the embedded options), the task must be done to estimate real values and risk-adjusted returns. This section has demonstrated how some of these tasks can be tackled using the fundamental tools of financial management (e.g., DCF analysis, risk-adjusted returns, duration, value additivity, portfolio theory, etc.). Without attention to these analytics, how can portfolio managers justify increasing their holdings of commercial real estate?

Zisler's portfolio framework has three tenets of diversification: location, type of property, and type of lease structure. Moreover, since properties differ in their debt-equity compositions, their lease sensitivities with respect to interest rates or market rents or both may be more important than conventional measures such as location or type of property. As this section has shown, the good old days of location, location, and location as the three principles of real estate finance have given way to a more complex era.

SECURITIZATION OF COMMERCIAL REAL-ESTATE LOANS

Because one–four family residential mortgages were relatively easy to homogenize in terms of a uniform asset, securitization of the residential real-estate market was accomplished quickly and efficiently in the 1970s and was followed by various innovations related to mortgage-backed securities (MBSs) in the 1980s. In contrast, securitization of commercial real-estate (CRE) loans (also called realty assets) did not begin until the early 1990s. For example, according to Commercial Mortgage Alert, the volume of publicly and privately issued securities collateralized by commercial and multifamily real-estate assets was only $14.6 billion (representing 55 issues) at year-end 1992. Gullo [1993] reported, however, that the market was "about to take off, and many bankers can't wait." And Robert A. McCormack, an executive vice president and head of the real-estate group of Citicorp, sees securitization of CRE loans as the "future of the business, fundamentally."[17]

What is it that bankers are anticipating? The proponents of securitization of CRE loans have pushed the process as an important way to prevent another boom-bust situation like that of the late 1980s and early 1990s. The benefits of securitization of CRE loans include

- The provision of liquidity to the market and more funds for developers
- The creation of more reliable prices than appraised values
- The generation of underwriting fees as an additional revenue source for banks
- The opportunity to purge lenders' balance sheets of excess CRE loans
- A mechanism for smoothing the peaks and valleys of the CRE market

The downside of securitization is that CRE lenders run the risk of losing their importance as dedicated CRE financiers—the same problem faced by S&Ls in the residential real-estate market during the 1970s and 1980s.

Two benefits of securitization of CRE loans that are particularly attractive to commercial banks are the opportunity to shed realty assets and to provide investment-banking services that generate fee income. Although traditional investment

---

[17] The data in this paragraph and the quotes are from Gullo [1993]. Most of the volume of securitized CRE loans in 1992 came from Resolution Trust Corporation (RTC) deals. As these deals have tapered off, however, the market has become dominated by securities backed by assets from banks, insurance companies, and other lenders. For example, during the first nine months of 1993, 66 transactions worth $6.8 billion were completed. RTC deals are referred to as government transactions whereas nongovernment deals are called private transactions and are described as taking place in the private marketplace as opposed to the government marketplace.

banks such as Bear Stearns, Goldman Sachs, and CS First Boston have dominated the market for securitized CRE loans, commercial banks such as Citicorp, Bankers Trust, Chemical (now part of Chase), and J. P. Morgan are anxious to tap the market for structuring, underwriting, and servicing CRE issues.

The process of securitizing CRE loans works similarly to the one for residential mortgage loans. The bank (investment or commercial) buys pools of real-estate loans backed by such assets as office buildings, shopping centers, or hotels and packages them as securities that are assigned credit ratings (i.e., investment grade or noninvestment grade depending on the quality of the underlying assets).[18] The securities, which carry yields commensurate with their risks, are then sold to investors. In the early stages of the development of this market, most of the deals were private placements, but more and more the securities are publicly registered. It is these traded issues that generate important pricing information regarding the values of underlying assets that individually are highly illiquid.

The stumbling block to securitization of the CRE market has been the uniqueness of CRE loans; they come in too many shapes and sizes to make the market as liquid as the residential real-estate market.[19] However, by employing the idea of the underlying realty assets as a portfolio of leases, as discussed in this chapter, financial markets have become more willing to accept the packaging of these diverse assets. In this regard, it is interesting to compare, as Greenspan [1996b] does, bank loans to OTC derivatives contracts. In this context, the loans are backed by realty assets. Both CRE loans and OTC derivatives share the following characteristics:

- They are customized
- They are privately negotiated
- They often lack liquidity and transparency

Customization and private negotiations are characteristics of funding (and building) commercial real estate that are unlikely to change. But notice what securitization does. It provides liquidity and transparency (i.e., the degree of certainty with which one can determine fair value).

To facilitate the securitization of CRE (and small-business loans), Congress passed the Small Business Loan Securitization and Secondary Market Enhancement Act of 1994. The law eased regulatory and capital rules that previously had inhibited the development of a secondary market.

Chapter Summary

In 1890, the Comptroller of the Currency reported to Congress that "The unfavorable conditions were greatly aggravated by the collapse of unwise speculation in real estate, especially in city and suburban property." When the Orlando, Florida, real estate market crashed in 1974–1975 because of a massive wave of speculative overbuilding, a real-estate consultant said: "We were running close to 100 percent occupancy, so we continued to build more and more apartments. What we failed to realize was that most of the apartments were being rented to construction work-

---

[18] In addition, new originations are being securitized. Risk-based capital requirements for banks and new accounting rules that require insurance companies to set aside more capital for realty assets encourage lenders to securitize new originations.

[19] Small-business loans have the same shortcoming, which is why they also are difficult to package and securitize.

ers." Reflecting on his 50 years in the business of banking, Dennis Weatherstone, retired chairman of J. P. Morgan & Company, contends that one of three important ways to avoid problems in banking is to "beware of the generation or corporate memory gap," especially with respect to credit experiences. Bankers seems to have short memories when it comes to commercial real-estate lending.

Maintaining loan quality is critical to the success of a commercial bank. Over the past two decades, U.S. commercial banks, especially the largest ones, have been caught in lending fads or bubbles associated with loans to REITs in the mid-1970s, LDC loans in the late 1970s and early 1980s, and loans for HLTs (e.g., LBOs) and commercial real estate in the 1980s. The combination of excessive growth and sloppy credit analysis, followed by regional economic downturns, is the stuff of credit crises and costly bank failures such as that of the Bank of New England.

This chapter has focused on commercial real-estate lending, the latest area of financial difficulty for large banks. Excluding loans secured by one–four family residential properties, commercial banks make real-estate loans secured by construction and land development, multifamily (five or more) residential properties, farmland, and nonfarm nonresidential properties, that is, **commercial real estate.** The **credit analysis** and **loan documentation** for commercial real-estate lending is more complex and requires greater attention to detail than other forms of bank lending. Careful analysis of **regional economic conditions** is a must. The case study of the Bank of New England (appendix A) shows how both internal and external factors contributed to one of the largest and most costly bank failures in U.S. history.

The fundamentals of financing commercial real estate should focus on **value creation.** Basic finance tools such as **DCF analysis, risk-adjusted returns, duration,** value additivity, and portfolio theory provide the building blocks of valuation. The creation of value in real estate has five stages: land assemblage, horizontal development (e.g., building the infrastructure), vertical development (construction of buildings), leasing/sales, and asset management. **Discounted-cash-flow analysis** represents the industry standard for evaluating income property. In addition, commercial real-estate holdings such as a commercial building should be viewed as a portfolio of leases with individual risk-return profiles analyzed separately (e.g., leases in place versus speculative leases). Because this portfolio concept is applied to the packaging of CRE loans, the process of securitization has filtered down from the market for residential mortgages to the market for CRE loans. Although securitization has not changed the fact that CRE loans are customized and privately negotiated, it has increased the liquidity and the transparency of the underlying assets.

Key Words, Concepts, and Acronyms

- Accrual basis
- Acquisition, development, and construction (ADC) loans
- Allocation of analytical resources
- Asset management
- Base lending rates (prime, Fed funds, domestic, foreign)
- Cash-basis loan
- Collateral
- Commercial real-estate (CRE) lending
- Component DCF analysis

- Composite debt, equity, and financing factors
- Construction and land development
- Credit analysis (the conditions factor)
- Debt-equity model
- Differential-income model
- Discounted-cash-flow (DCF) analysis
- Diversification
- Duration (of a lease)
- Fee income
- Financial engineering

- Foreign investment in real estate
- Fragmentation (specialization) of mortgage-lending process
- Functional cost analysis (FCA)
- Funding
- Globalization
- Horizontal development
- Institutionalization of real estate
- Investment asset
- Land assemblage
- Leases (in place vs. speculative)
- Leasing/sales

- Lending fads or bubbles
- Loan brokering
- Loan documentation
- Loans secured by real estate (one–four family, multifamily, nonfarm nonresidential)
- Net loan losses or charge-offs
- Noncurrent loans
- Origination (and acquisition)

- Other real estate owned (OREO)
- Portfolio of leases
- Real-estate investment trust (REIT)
- Risk-adjusted return
- Securitization
- Selling
- Servicing
- Tenant credit quality and risk premiums

- Terms of lending
- Underwriting income-property investment
- Value creation
- Vertical development
- Vertical integration and structure of real estate industry

Review/Discussion Questions

1. What does the epigram at the beginning of this chapter suggest about the error-learning mechanism of bankers when it comes to commercial real-estate lending?

2. Who are the major suppliers of mortgage debt in the United States? What types of properties provide security and what is the composition of this collateral for commercial banks?

3. How does commercial real-estate lending vary by bank size? Based on the data in appendix B, what appears to be the correlation between CRE loan volume and loan quality?

4. Describe the bubbles, fads, and structural changes in bank lending that occurred during the 1970s and the 1980s. What segment of the banking industry has been most affected by these events? Compare the growth of CRE loans in the 1980s to that in the 1990s.

5. What is Zisler's view of the crisis in commercial real-estate lending and what are his three components of diversification?

6. What kinds of real-estate loans do commercial banks make? How have these loans varied over time, and how do they vary with bank asset size?

7. Describe the Federal Reserve's survey of the terms of bank lending. How do the terms for construction and land development loans vary between large and small banks?

8. Describe the activities, participants, and services needed for the creation of value in real estate.

9. Does vertical integration of the real-estate industry exist in the United States? Why or why not? Does such integration exist anywhere? What are the consequences of foreign investment in the United States with respect to the structure of the real estate industry?

10. Brady's approach to underwriting income property requires lenders to ask three questions and calculate five ratios. What are the questions and the ratios? What is the focal variable of the analysis?

11. What is the industry standard for valuing real-estate property and when and why was it adopted? Explain Chesler's refinement of this approach.

12. Distinguish between the debt-equity model and the differential-income model of commercial real estate.

13. Evaluate and discuss the following statement:

> Real estate is a different matter. You can use a two-pronged test for commercial real estate. . . . First, look at local vacancy rates. . . . Are they rising or falling? If they're falling, then the local real-estate scene might be a good idea. If they're rising, take a drive around town. How many new office buildings are under construction? If office buildings are beginning to sprout like dandelions on a spring lawn and vacancy rates are rising, it's probably wise to abandon the idea of investing in yet another one.

14. Congress and bank regulators tend to react rather than act. On April 12, 1991, the *American Banker* reported that L. William Seidman, then chairman of the FDIC, urged Congress to put a lid on banks' real-estate loans and prohibit them from financing any

raw land deals or lending to construction projects lacking a 25 percent down payment by the builder. He said, "Excessive concentration has been one of the principal causes of bank failures. The supervisors, and the insurer in its backup role, should have clearer authority to limit undue concentrations in banks' portfolios." Is his idea a good one? Because he did not define "undue concentration," how would you define it?

15. Explain fully why securitization developed so quickly and efficiently in the market for residential mortgages and why the opposite occurred in the market for CRE loans. What are the benefits of securitization for CRE loans and how are these loans similar to OTC derivatives?

16. Describe the kinds of documents that commercial real-estate lenders need. Do these kinds of loans require truth-in-lending disclosures?

17. Discuss the importance of the conditions "C" to the credit analysis of commercial real-estate lending. What kinds of lags exist in regional economies that might make the analysis of commercial real-estate lending more complicated? What does McNulty [1995] argue is the case?

Problems

1. Given: Project cost: $12 million

   Project net operating income (NOI): $1 million per year

   Cost of long-term debt: 11 percent

   Debt-service coverage ratio required by the lender: 1.25

   What is the maximum debt service the lender will provide? On an interest-only obligation, what is the maximum amount the developer can borrow from the lender? What will happen to the loan amount if the lender requires the loan to be amortized? What is the minimum equity the developer must invest in the project?

2. A project for an office building requires a $25 million mortgage loan. The lender's parameters include a 12 percent interest rate for 360 months with 75 percent financing. What are the annual mortgage constant and the annual loan payment for the loan? If the developer reports a "stabilized NOI" of $3.583 million per year and a capitalization rate of 10.75 percent, what is the building's estimated value? Assuming the lender's underwriting staff agrees with the estimated value of the building, calculate the composite debt, equity, and financing factors for the loan. The borrower's ROE is 20 percent. What are the relative debt and equity factors, and how much of SNOI is available for debt service and for ROE?

3. The headquarters building for the Last National Bank has 500,000 square feet. Leases in place account for 90 percent of the building's net rentable space, and the remainder is speculative space. Treating the building as a perpetual investment, what are the values of the component parts of the lease if the annual cash flows are $5 million for leases in place and $500,000 for speculative space? Assume that the risk premium over the appropriate risk-free rate for the speculative space is twice that for the cash flows from leases in place and that the risk-free rate is 7 percent and the discount rate for the speculative space is 17 percent. What is the square-foot value of the property and its components?

4. Using the differential-income model (equation [20-2]), find the value of the following property:

   Current income $=$ $7.5 million per year

   Time until lease rollover $=$ 10 years

   Net income at market rents $=$ current income growing at a compound rate
   of 5 percent per year for 10 years

   Capitalization or discount rate $=$ 0.15

CASE STUDY: THE BANK OF NEW ENGLAND AND MISMANAGEMENT OF COMMERCIAL REAL-ESTATE LENDING

Introduction

This case addresses several important economic issues related to the failure of Bank of New England Corporation (BNEC) and the failure of its lead bank, Bank of New England, N.A. (BNENA). It is presented as an appendix to this chapter because mismanagement of BNENA's portfolio of commercial real-estate loans caused BNEC and BNENA to fail. In telling the story of the failure of BNEC/BNENA, this case provides information for understanding, among other things, the risks of banking, the causes of bank failure, the measurement of bank performance, the ways bank regulators and deposit insurers handle problem banks and resolve failing banks, the important distinction between economic failure and regulatory closure, and last but not least, ways to judge the adequacy of a bank's allowance for loan and lease losses (ALLL).

The Risks of Banking and Causes of Bank Failures

Banks face three major risks: credit risk, interest-rate risk, and liquidity risk. Credit or default risk, which is the uncertainty that borrowers will repay their loans, has been the major cause of financial difficulties and failures among commercial banks in the United States.[20] For example, over the past 20 years, but especially in the 1980s, mismanaged credit risk associated with energy loans, farm loans, loans to less developed countries, and as in the case of BNEC, commercial real-estate loans has been the culprit.[21]

 The typical failure scenario for a troubled bank, whether big or small, goes like this: Mismanagement of credit risk, as reflected by poor loan quality, followed by a liquidity crisis in which the bank, if it is considered too big to fail (TBTF), is supplied emergency funding by the Federal Reserve's (the Fed's) discount window. While the Fed's lifeline keeps the bank alive, the FDIC works to arrange a permanent solution, which usually takes the form of a government-assisted merger called a purchase-and-assumption (P&A) transaction. For a nationally chartered bank like BNENA and its parent company BNEC, the failure-resolution process is a concerted action of the Fed, the FDIC, and the OCC. It is during this workout or forbearance period, the time between economic failure and regulatory

---

[20] Check the references in chapters 3 and 6 for evidence on this subject.

[21] In contrast to the credit risk or loan quality problems of commercial banks, the savings-and-loan (S&L) crisis in the United States is mainly attributed to the mismanagement of interest-rate risk and the failure of S&L regulators and deposit insurers to properly price interest-rate risk; see the references to Kane in chapters 15 and 16.

closure, that bank asset values can dissipate, to the detriment of the FDIC and taxpayers.

In general, the failure scenario described above reflects the actual decline and collapse of BNEC and its lead bank, BNENA. Although some particulars are presented here, *The Bank of New England Failure and Resolution* [1991], a Congressional staff report, provides what Chairman Gonzalez describes as the "most thorough autopsy of a major bank collapse ever undertaken by the Committee" (transmittal letter, "Gonzalez report").

Management Policies and Practices at BNEC and Its Banks

The General Accounting Office (GAO, 1991) concluded that BNEC banks failed because of three factors:

- Liberal lending practices
- Poorly controlled growth
- Concentration in commercial real-estate loans in a severely declining regional economy

The next three sections consider how each of these factors contributed to BNEC's economic insolvency.[22]

Liberal Lending Practices

BNEC's lending policies were more than just liberal; they appeared to be improper and imprudent. Bank managers and directors have fiduciary responsibilities to act properly and prudently. Various regulatory sanctions, such as cease-and-desist orders and memoranda of understanding, were imposed on BNENA and Connecticut Bank and Trust (CBT). The OCC's News Release 91-3 provides a chronolgy of major events in the case. In general, the overall supervision and administration of the BNENA's and CBT's operations and policies appeared to be seriously deficient. Management failed, among other things, to exercise reasonable diligence and due care to see that their banks' financial conditions remained sound, especially regarding the portfolio of commercial real-estate loans. Moreover, as early as 1987, managers and directors were aware of and failed to respond adequately to bank internal reports and regulatory criticisms that pointed out problems in loan underwriting and credit-administration practices at BNENA. Had these warnings been heeded, BNEC might not have become one of the largest and most costly bank failures in U.S. history.

Poorly Controlled Growth

According to a study by Salomon Brothers, "the best single predictor of future asset quality is the rate of loan growth."[23] The managerial principle is simple: It is easier to maintain asset quality when growth is controlled; excessive growth results

---

[22] Economic insolvency can be defined in terms of cash flow or net worth (NW). The cash-flow test is whether or not the business can meet its obligations as they come due; the net-worth test is whether or not the fair market value of assets exceeded the fair market value of liabilities. Thomson ([1992], footnote 2) reports that since 1933 the OCC has tended to use only a maturing-obligations test rather than a balance-sheet test for determining the insolvency of national banks. The OCC's balance-sheet test is seriously flawed because it relies on book value or historical cost to measure a bank's net worth. Compare 12 U.S.C. Section 191 (balance sheet or maturing obligations) with Section 91 (usually interpreted as maturing obligations only).

[23] *The Economist* (May 2, 1992), p. 3. This finding is, of course, not new, because Sinkey [1978, 1979, 1989] and others have noted the existence of such a relationship.

in poor loan quality, because to achieve the growth usually requires liberal lending policies. Such policies, as documented by the GAO's report on BNEC, were rampant at BNEC.

From March 31, 1985, to December 31, 1988, a period of only 3.75 years, total assets at BNEC grew at the phenomenal rate of 48 percent per year.[24] In contrast, a national peer group of 90 similarly sized banks had average asset growth of only 8.9 percent from year-end 1985 to year-end 1989. An aggressive strategy of mergers and acquisitions and the liberal lending practices of BNEC explain this extremely high asset growth rate, one that would have challenged even an exceptional team of bank managers and directors. Under a management team that appeared to be negligent, reckless, and lacking in accountability, this excessive growth was a recipe for disaster.

Concentration in Commercial Real-Estate Loans in a Severely Declining Regional Economy

A fundamental tenet of sound risk management is not to put all your eggs in one basket. Financial economists calls this *diversification*. BNEC did not have a diversified loan portfolio. Its loans were concentrated in commercial real estate, and, mirroring the rapid growth of BNEC's assets, these loans grew at an annual rate of 42 percent from year-end 1985 to year-end 1988. At year-end 1985, BNEC had commercial real-estate loans totaling $2.4 billion, 16.9 percent of its total loans; by year-end 1988, this figure had grown to $6.9 billion, or 27.9 percent of total loans.[25] Compared to banks of similar size, BNEC's 1988 concentration was almost double that of more prudent lenders.[26] This rapid growth and excessive concentration came at the expense of sound underwriting standards.

Controlled expansion in a growing market would be good business judgment; in a declining market, it is imprudent decision making. This statement is more than just Monday-morning quarterbacking because the signals of a declining real-estate market in New England were evident in late 1987 and early 1988.[27]

Recapitulation

Internal and external factors determine whether businesses, including banks, succeed or fail. The quality of management is the key internal factor. Weak managers are the most vulnerable to adverse external conditions. The management at BNEC and its lead bank, BNENA, was extremely weak as reflected by liberal lending policies, lax underwriting standards, and poorly controlled growth. This reckless disregard for prudent banking practices made the bank extremely vulnerable to an economic downturn. Chairman Gonzalez described the failure as closing "the book on a half decade of rampant commercial real-estate lending activities and growth accompanied by failed and ineffectual controls and deficient oversight by the institution's Board of Directors and management" (p. vi).

---

[24] This growth rate is calculated from data in the GAO's report on BNEC, Table 1, p. 8. In the next sentence, peer-group data for banks ranked 11th to 100th in total assets are calculated from the *Federal Reserve Bulletin* (June 1995, and June 1996), pp. 564 and 500, respectively.

[25] GAO report [1991], Table 2, p. 9.

[26] The figure (16.5%) was calculated for banks ranked in size from 11th to 100th in total assets based on data reported in *Federal Reserve Bulletin* (June 1996), Table A.2, p. 500.

[27] For example, Moscovitch [1990] argues that as early as 1985 a careful analysis of the New England economy indicated that its economic base was deteriorating and that the economic boom was unsustainable.

The Linkages from Mismanagement to Insolvency

Banks, like other profit-making enterprises, are in business to make money for their owners. Owners judge performance on the basis of return on investment, or ROI. This return has two components: dividend yield and capital-gains yield. The cash flows generated by a bank provide the funds for paying dividends, whereas the size, timing, and riskiness of the cash flows are critical ingredients for the marketplace's determination of value, and hence the potential for stock-price appreciation. The theory of finance treats the objective of the firm as the maximization of shareholder value.[28] Operationally, this means that bank managers should make decisions that add value to the bank. Their role is to create value. An important corollary to this axiom is to eliminate value destroyers (i.e., to get out of businesses that are not adding value to the bank).[29]

Because bank managers act as agents for owners, managers who do not maximize shareholder value can expect to be removed by owners. As outsiders, however, owners are at a disadvantage compared to managers, as insiders. In addition, if a bank's board of directors does not conduct proper oversight of management, as BNEC's board failed to do, owners' control over management is further reduced. The executives of bank holding companies and insured depositories also face the threat of being removed from office by their regulators or deposit insurers.

When the reckless and dismal performance of BNEC's management became public knowledge near the end of 1989, three things happened (regulators, as quasi-insiders, had known about the problems for months):

- BNEC's common-stock cash dividend had to be eliminated, because its cash flow was insufficient to maintain it
- BNEC's stock price plunged by 65 percent, from $21 per share to $7.25 per share, because earnings were expected to be negative (on 15 December 1989, BNEC announced a projected loss of more than $1 billion)
- BNEC's top management was forced to resign and was replaced by caretaker managers who would cooperate with the FDIC/OCC/FED[30]

The essence of effective bank management is to know how to take and manage risk for profit. The management of BNEC had demonstrated that it knew how to take on excessive risk, that it could not manage the risk it had assumed, and that its risk-taking was not economically profitable although it reported accounting profits.

---

[28] Both bank managers and bank regulators seem to agree about this objective. To illustrate, the American Bankers Association (ABA) is the major trade organization for commercial banks. At the ABA's 1996 Annual Convention in Honolulu, Hawaii, Alan Greenspan, chairman of the Federal Reserve, was the leadoff speaker. His opening remarks were as follows:

> You may well wonder why a regulator is the first speaker at a conference in which a major theme is *maximizing shareholder value.* I hope that by the end of my remarks this morning it will be clear that we, the regulators, share with you ultimately the same objective of a *strong and profitable banking system.* Such a banking system knows *how to take and manage risk for profit.* The problem is what, if anything, regulators should do to constrain the amount of risk bankers take in trying to meet their *corporate objectives.* I have given considerable thought to this issue over the years, and today I would like to address this theme once again (Greenspan [1996a], p. 1; emphasis mine).

[29] Chapter 3 presents a discussion and references for *economic value added* (*EVA*™).

[30] On January 26, 1990, an interim CEO (Bullock) was appointed; a permanent CEO (Fish) was named on March 5, 1990.

Accounting and Fair-Value Measures of Bank Performance

Although dividend yields, price-earnings ratios, and market-to-book ratios provide market measures of bank performance, accountants and regulators focus on alternative yardsticks for judging bank performance.

1. Return on Assets (ROA)

The most comprehensive *accounting* measure of a bank's overall performance is its return on assets (ROA), defined as net income or profits over average total assets. The banking industry's benchmark in the 1980s was an ROA of 1.0 percent; today it is about 1.25 percent. The variability of an ROA captures the riskiness of a bank's overall operations.[31] Table A12-1 shows BNEC's ROA compared to that of a peer group of banks ranked 11th through 100th by assets for the years 1986 to 1989.[32] BNEC's average ROA performance was a dismal −0.28 percent compared to 0.40 percent for its peer group. Because the peer group had a standard deviation of ROA of 0.30 percent, BNEC's ROA was more than two standard deviations away from the peer group's mean, that is, 0.40 percent − 0.30 percent − 0.30 percent = −0.20 percent > −0.28 percent. Comparing the standard deviations, BNEC,

TABLE A12-1   BNEC's Profitability and Risk Relative to Its Peer Banks, 1986–1989

	Return on Assets (ROA)	
Year	*BNEC*	*Peer Group*
1986	0.93%	0.72%
1987	0.51	−0.09
1988	0.94	0.51
1989	−3.48	0.47
Average	−0.28%	0.40%
Standard deviation	1.86%	0.30%
Coefficient of variation	−6.76	0.74

Note: The peer group consists of the 90 U.S. banks ranked 11th through 100th by assets for the years 1986 to 1989. The negative ROA for the peer group in 1987 was due to above-average provisions for loan losses (PLL) on LDC debt taken by the largest banks in the peer group. In contrast, BNEC's loan concentration was in commercial real estate, which in 1989 required a PLL of $1.6 billion. The standard deviation is a measure of dispersion and a common measure of risk in finance. The higher the standard deviation is, the greater is the variability of ROA and hence risk. The coefficient of variation is a relative measure of risk defined as the standard deviation divided by the average. The higher its absolute value is, the greater the risk is.

Sources: BNEC data are from its 1989 10-K report filed with the Securities and Exchange Commission, p. 10; peer-group data are from the *Federal Reserve Bulletin* (June 1996), p. 501.

---

[31] The *standard deviation* of *ROA* about its average is the statistical measure of this variability. In finance, the standard deviation of returns is a common measure of a portfolio's or a firm's overall riskiness.

[32] See the notes and sources to Table A12-1 for details about these data and the calculations.

with a standard deviation of 1.86 percent, was much riskier compared to the standard deviation for the peer group of 0.30 percent. These data indicate that BNEC was an outlier compared to a national peer group of similarly sized banks.

The economic implications of the data in Table A12-1 are clear: BNEC was a highly unprofitable, high-risk bank that was significantly and adversely different from its peers. If BNEC's ROA for 1989 was an aberration, this interpretation might be misleading. However, given the qualitative information from the GAO and Gonzalez reports, BNEC's accounting earnings for prior years were misstated.

2. Capital Adequacy and Return on Equity (ROE)

Bank capital is regarded as a buffer or cushion for absorbing losses arising from the risks of banking. Banks with strong capital positions are said to have "adequate capital"—hence the term "capital adequacy." Numerous measures of a bank's capital adequacy exist. One measure is the ratio of total shareholders' equity to total assets (CAP). This measure is useful because it provides a link with a bank's return on equity (ROE) such that

$$ROE = ROA/CAP = ROA \times EM$$

where $EM = 1/CAP$ is called the equity multiplier. This multiplier (EM or $1/CAP$) is what makes $ROE > ROA$. For example, at year-end 1989, BNEC had a CAP ratio of 1.54 percent, or an equity multiplier of 64.9 ($= 1/0.0154$) compared to the average CAP of its peer group of 5.55 percent, or an equity multiplier of 18.0. Based on average equity for the year, BNEC's ROE profile for 1989 was[33]

$$ROE = -0.0348 \times 19.56 = -0.6808 \text{ or } -68.1\%$$

In contrast, BNEC's average peer bank had the following ROE profile for 1989:

$$ROE = 0.0047 \times 17.89 = 0.0841 \text{ or } 8.4\%$$

Whereas peer banks were returning 8.4 percent on their book equity for 1989, BNEC's loss ate up almost 70 percent of its book equity. For the four years 1986 to 1989, BNEC had an average ROE of −5.76 percent compared to 7.30 percent for its peer group. Because the peer group had a standard deviation of ROE of 5.43 percent, BNEC's ROE, like its ROA, was more than two standard deviations away from the peer group's mean, that is,

$$7.30\% - 5.430\% - 5.43\% = -3.56\% > -5.76\%[34]$$

To summarize, whereas ROA measures profitability from the point of view of the overall efficiency of a bank's use of its total assets, ROE captures profitability from the shareholders' perspective. As noted above, however, shareholders are more concerned about cash dividends and stock-price appreciation. Nevertheless, return on book equity is a useful and common proxy for measuring shareholders'

---

[33] These data are from the same sources listed in Table A12-1. The use of average equity, as opposed to year-end equity, paints a rosier picture of a bank experiencing a decline in its equity capital, such as BNEC was undergoing. That is, BNEC had an ROE and EM based on year-end equity of −226 percent and 64.9, respectively. Using average equity for the year, the corresponding figures are −68 percent and 19.6.

[34] The standard deviations of ROE for BNEC and its peer group mirror those for ROA in terms of revealing greater variability, that is, BNEC's standard deviation of ROE was 36.13 percent compared to 5.43 percent for the peer group. The substantially and significantly higher standard deviation of ROE for BNEC indicated that it was much riskier compared to its average peer bank.

returns. In addition, ROE can be decomposed into ROA and EM, which show how a bank's profitability and leverage combine to generate ROE. This evidence suggests that BNEC was not a going concern that would-be investors would want to support financially.

3. Credit Risk, Loan Quality, Provision for Loan Loss, and Loan-Loss Reserves

Profitability measures such as ROE and ROA are symptoms of managerial performance and the underlying risks of banking. In BNEC's case, the negative ROE and negative ROA were a reflection of the excessive credit risk inherent in its loan portfolio and a direct result of BNEC's liberal lending policies, weak underwriting standards, and poorly managed growth. Given these critical shortcomings, BNEC's $1.6 billion provision for loan loss taken in 1989 should have been spread over earlier years. If it had been, then BNEC's ROA would have averaged −0.28 percent over the years 1986 to 1989 (Table A12-1) whereas its ROE would have averaged −5.76 percent. As a result, the accounting earnings reported by BNEC for the years 1986 to 1988 were not a true measure of its economic earnings; they did not capture the true quality of BNEC's loan portfolio as driven by an extremely weak and highly concentrated subportfolio of commercial real-estate loans.

It is prudent and proper banking practice to establish a reserve for expected loan losses. The loan-loss reserve, or allowance for loan and lease loss (ALLL), is a contra-asset account, which when deducted from gross loans gives net loans.[35] Net loan losses deplete the reserve account, whereas the provision for loan loss, an expense item, augments it. For the years 1986 to 1989, BNEC's peer banks had ratios of loan-loss reserves to average assets of 1.03 percent (1986), 1.51 percent (1987), 1.80 percent (1988), and 1.48 percent (1989), respectively. In contrast, BNEC's ratios were 1.17 percent (1986), 1.61 percent (1987), 1.01 percent (1988), and 5.11 percent (1989).[36] Because BNEC held a much riskier loan portfolio than its peers, it should have had a substantially higher ratio of loan-loss reserves to assets before 1989. To achieve this, BNEC would have needed substantially higher loan-loss provisions for the years 1986 to 1988, which would have reduced its overstated accounting earnings and made them more reflective of its true economic or risk-adjusted earnings.

4. Fair Value: Computing BNEC's Allowance for Loan and Lease Losses (ALLL)

Bankers, directors, auditors, regulators, would-be investors, and other interested parties need to know how a bank calculates its allowance for loan and lease losses (ALLL) and how to determine if the ALLL, or loan-loss reserve (LLR), is reasonable and adequate for the bank's risk exposure. As described in chapter 6, two general approaches exist for estimating a bank's ALLL: The first method involves a detailed analysis of all individual loans, or of a representative sample of the loan portfolio. This internal approach, which focuses on loss exposure at the micro level, is the heart of the regulators' on-site bank examination, although the regulators

---

[35] Unearned income is also subtracted from gross loans in deriving net loans.
[36] See Table A12-1 for data sources.

don't always have the resources to devote to such a detailed effort.[37] The second method uses tools that are reliable indicators of risk and loss exposure at the macro level. This external approach employs peer groups, industry standards, and economic trends to estimate a required ALLL.

Common risk indicators that can be used as macrolevel tools include net loan losses, nonperforming credits, and loss percentages applied to criticized/classified loan categories.[38] To estimate BNEC's required ALLL, these indicators are applied to BNEC as of third quarter 1989.

The use of actual net loan losses relative to total loans as a risk indicator for BNEC is demonstrated by the following data:[39]

Year/Quarter	Net Loss/Total Loans	Weight	Ratio × Weight
1988, 2nd	0.26%	0.05	0.0130%
1988, 3rd	3.51	0.10	0.3510
1988, 4th	0.47	0.15	0.0705
1989, 1st	0.80	0.15	0.1200
1989, 2nd	1.05	0.15	0.1575
1989, 3rd	0.98	0.40	0.3920
	1.18% (average)	1.00	1.105% (weighted average)

With a loan portfolio of $25.3 billion, BNEC would need an ALLL of $279 to $298 million based on the two averages. Because BNEC had an ALLL of $342 million, no PLL would be required using this rear-view-mirror approach. Given BNEC's abysmal financial condition, this method's major weakness is clearly evident. Using the weighted average marked up by a factor of 2.5, the approach gives a loss rate of 2.76 percent, which implies a required ALLL of $698 million.

The critical assumption in the previous analysis is that history repeats itself. Given how badly BNEC was mismanaged, the only historical charge-off rate that looks realistic is the 3.51 percent for the third quarter of 1988. From the end of the third quarter of 1988 to the end of the third quarter of 1989, BNEC's total loans grew at 7.6 percent, whereas real-estate construction loans grew at 12.9 percent. Applying the latter to the third quarter charge-off rate gives 3.96 percent as an expected charge-off rate. This rate times the loan volume of $25.3 billion suggests a required ALLL of $1 billion, which takes a $646-million bite out of BNEC's book equity capital of $1.691 billion.[40] Alternatively and more realistically, applying an adjustment factor of 3.0 (explained below) to the 3.96 percent loss rate, we find that BNEC would be insolvent by $961 million.

Another method of testing the reasonableness of a bank's ALLL is to compare it to the bank's nonperforming loans. This indicator is a form of coverage ratio. On September 30, 1989, BNEC had an ALLL of $354 million and nonperforming loans of $900 million, coverage of 39.3 percent. A year earlier, this ratio

---

[37] Prior to September 30, 1989, the OCC did not have the resources to conduct such an inspection of BNEC's banks presumably because of the banking crisis in Texas. See the Gonzalez report, Table 7, page 97.

[38] Lacking the data to conduct an analysis at the micro level, this case focuses on macro estimates of BNEC's loan quality.

[39] Bank of New England Corporation, Financial Review Second Quarter 1989 and Third Quarter 1989.

[40] Data in this paragraph are from Bank of New England Corporation, Financial Review Second Quarter 1989 and Third Quarter 1989.

was 57 percent. Simply maintaining this coverage would have meant a required ALLL of $513 million and a PLL of $159 million. Using the OCC's 70-percent standard, the estimated ALLL and PLL would be $630 million and $276 million, respectively. The shortcoming in both of these analyses is taking the reported $900 million in nonperforming assets as realistic.

Examiner-classified assets of substandard, doubtful, and loss are considered a good estimate of a bank's nonperforming loans. Unfortunately, these data are not publicly available. Given the weakened condition of BNEC, we use an adjustment factor of 3.0 to estimate BNEC's true nonperforming loans, which gives $2.7 billion.[41] Applying this standard and netting out the existing *ALLL* of $354 million, we find the required PLL is $1.536, which reduces the bank's book equity capital from $1.691 billion to a mere $155 million.

From the end of the third quarter of 1988 to the end of the third quarter of 1989, BNEC's ratio of ALLL to total loans increased from 1.3 percent to 1.4 percent. With BNEC's higher-risk loans growing at almost double that rate, and with the New England economy deteriorating rapidly, this ratio of ALLL to total loans was clearly inadequate. For example, a national peer group of banks ranked 11th to 100th by assets had a ratio of 2.9 percent at the end of 1988; by the end of 1989, however, the ratio had dropped to 2.4 percent. Taking an average of these two figures (2.65%), applying the 3.0 factor and netting out the existing ALLL of $354 million, we find that BNEC should have had a PLL for the third quarter of 1989 of $1.657 billion, which would have left BNEC with equity capital of only $33 million. If we use the peer group's ratio at the end of 1988 (2.9% instead of 2.65%) and apply the 3.0 adjustment factor, BNEC would need a PLL of $1.847, leaving the bank insolvent million by $156 million.

BNEC's Insolvency Was Driven by NBENA's Insolvency

The preceding analysis has focused on determination of BNEC's ALLL and its accompanying insolvency after incorporating appropriate and realistic internal and external circumstances relevant to the situation. As a holding company, BNEC is simply an accounting aggregation of its component subsidiaries (e.g., BNENA and other subsidiaries) after adjusting for intercompany relationships. BNENA, the holding company's lead bank, was its weakest subsidiary. At year-end 1989, its ratio of shareholders' equity to assets was only 1.42 percent on a pro forma basis adjusted for the February 9, 1990, mergers with BNE-North, BNE-South, and BNE-Worcester.[42]

ALLL Recapitulation

As of September 29, 1989, no doubt existed that BNEC's ALLL of $354 million was not appropriate for its level of risk exposure. What should the ALLL have been, and would the required amount have rendered BNEC insolvent? The various ALLL methodologies and scenarios presented above show BNEC to be insolvent or close to it. Table A12-2 summarizes the methods and results. Based on an average of the three methods, BNEC's required PLL for September 30, 1989 is $2.129 billion and it is insolvent by $321 million.

---

[41] Judgment, experience and knowledge about a bank's internal and external conditions play important roles in determining adjustment factors.

[42] BNEC Form 10-K, 1989, p. 26.

TABLE A12-2 ALLL Methodologies and Estimates of BNEC's ALLL, September 29, 1989	

Method 1. Net Loan Losses as a Percentage of Total Loans

Third quarter 1989 loan-loss rate =	3.51%
Times 1.129 (1 + growth rate of real estate construction loans) =	3.96%
Apply factor of 3.0 =	11.88%
Required ALLL (total loans of $25.3 billion)	$3.0 billion
Less existing ALLL of $354 million =	$2.65 billion
ALLL to total loans =	10.5%

Result: BNEC is insolvent by $961 million

Method 2. ALLL as a Percentage of Nonperforming Loans ("Coverage")

Estimate nonperforming loans as 3.0 × $900 million =	$2.7 billion
Required ALLL applying a 70% rule =	$1.89 billion
Less existing ALLL of $354 million =	$1.536 billion
ALLL to total loans =	6.1%

Result: BNEC is solvent by $155 million

Method 3. ALLL as a Percentage of Total Loans

Third-quarter 1989 ratio of ALLL to total loans =	1.4%
National peer group average =	2.9%
Apply factor of 3.0 =	8.7%
Required ALLL for loans of $25.3 billion =	$2.2 billion
Less existing ALLL of $354 million =	$1.847 billion

Result: BNEC is insolvent by $156 million

Recap: Required PLL for September 30, 1989, based on average of three methods = $2.129 billion, and BNEC is insolvent by $321 million.

A Bank's Risk Index and Probability of Book-Value Insolvency

The performance measures ROA, CAP, and the standard deviation of ROA can be combined in a risk index (RI) for banks. The empirical form of this risk index is[43]

$$RI = [E(ROA) + CAP]/\sigma_{ROA}$$

where

$$E(ROA) = \text{expected return on assets}$$
$$CAP = \text{the bank's ratio of equity capital to total assets}$$
$$\sigma_{ROA} = \text{the standard deviation of } ROA$$

From an accounting perspective, this risk index is intuitively appealing because it includes ROA (the most widely accepted accounting measure of overall bank performance), the variability of ROA (a standard measure of risk in financial economics),

---

[43] Chapter 3 describes this risk index and presents relevant references. Using the symbols from this equation, Hannan and Hanweck ([1988], pp. 204–205) derive the probability of book-value insolvency, p, as $p \leq .5\sigma^2/[E(ROA) + CAP]^2$. The p expresses the (upper bound) probability of book-value insolvency $[Pr(BVE < 0)]$ which can differ significantly from market-value insolvency. In terms of *RI,* the probability of book-value insolvency can be expressed as $1/[2(RI)^2]$. For values of $RI \leq 0.7071$, $Pr(BVE < 0) = 1.0$ or 100 percent (as an upper bound).

and book capital adequacy (an industry standard for bank safety and soundness). One can think of RI as the thickness of the book-value cushion a bank has available to absorb accounting losses.[44] Therefore, a lower RI implies a riskier bank; a higher RI implies a safer bank.

To illustrate the use of RI, consider a couple of extreme cases. First, consider a bank with a high expected ROA, a strong capital position, and low variability of ROA. Its RI will be a relatively high value. In contrast, a bank with negative expected earnings, minimum capital, and highly variable earnings will have a low RI. The second case fits the description of BNEC during the late 1980s. Using BNEC's December 31, 1989, data to reflect a truer picture of its financial condition as of September 29, 1989, we get the following components for BNEC's risk index at the end of the third quarter of 1989:

Component	BNEC	Peer Group
$E(ROA)$	−0.0348	0.0023
CAP	0.0154	0.0550
σ_{ROA}	0.0186	0.0030
Risk index	−1.04	19.1
$Pr(BVE < 0)$	1.0	0.0014

The last line above captures the probability of book-value insolvency, or $Pr(BVE < 0)$, which equals $1/[2(RI)^2]$ (see footnote 44). Because BNEC's risk index (RI) is less than 0.7, it had an upper bound probability of insolvency of 100 percent. In contrast, the average peer-group bank had a probability of insolvency of less than 1 percent (0.0065).[45]

To summarize, the bank risk index (RI) is useful because it collapses three pieces of information into a single number. In this regard, an index is similar to a ratio that collapses two pieces of information into one. In either case, we gain some informational economies but we also lose some detail. The bank index presented here is interesting because it employs two key measures of banking performance, ROA and CAP, and a common measure of risk in finance, the standard deviation of a return distribution. This framework reveals BNEC to be a very high risk bank with a high probability of book-value insolvency as early as September 30, 1989. Thus, this bank was in sharp contrast to BNEC's peer group, where the average bank had a probability of book-value insolvency of less than 1 percent.

---

[44] Technically, the risk index is a measure, expressed in units of standard deviations of *ROA,* of how much a bank's accounting earnings can decline before it has a negative book value.

[45] Risk indices tend to decrease with bank size. For example, using Federal Reserve data for the 11-year period 1985 through 1995, the risk indices are as follows:

	Risk Index	$Pr(BVE < 0)$
Top 10	13.2	0.29%
Banks ranked 11–100	20.4	0.12%
Banks ranked 101–1,000	36.6	0.04%
Banks not ranked among the 1,000 largest	48.6	0.02%

If it seems strange that this framework suggests that the nation's largest banks, on average, are more vulnerable to failure than the average community bank, keep two points in mind: (1) the probability of book-value insolvency for the average bank in each size class is very low—less than .5 percent, and (2) we are dealing with book values and not market values.

The Role of Bank Regulators

The GAO [1991] concluded that the OCC's supervision of the Bank of New England was not timely or forceful. In a declining New England economy, BNEC's weak management and the OCC's lax supervision[46] resulted in a banking company headed for economic failure by September 29, 1989.

Similarities to the Case of Franklin National Bank of New York (1974)

Following the collapse of Franklin National Bank (FNB) of New York and its parent company, Franklin New York Corporation (FNYC), in 1974,[47] when no buyers could be found to purchase FNB, it was concluded that, on a going-concern basis, FNB had virtually no "present fair salable value" (¶79, p. 701). Although BNEC might have had some suitors before its massive ALLL adjustment, it appears reasonable to assume that BNEC, like FNB, was not a going concern.[48] Under these circumstances, no one would risk recapitalizing BNENA or BNEC. For example, in 1988, BNEC reported net income of $282 million; in 1989, it reported a loss of $1.1 billion. To recapitalize BNEC at its 1988 level would have required an investment of $1.6 billion. With BNEC's future net income expected to be negative, the return on capital would be negative. No rational investor would undertake such a transaction. Like FNB, BNEC apparently never received an offer for an unassisted takeover or merger. As with FNB, the risks to a prospective buyer were too great to pursue a merger.

On balance, BNEC, like FNYC, was not salable as an entity. Both BNENA and FNB were kept from immediate collapse by massive loans from their Federal Reserve Banks acting as lenders of last resort. Unlike FNB, BNENA was able to repay the Fed through the transfer of Treasury tax-and-loan accounts (TT&Ls) to BNENA and through the transfer of BNEC assets to BNENA. The fact that BNENA was able to repay its indebtedness to the Fed's discount window should not be taken as an indicator that it was a going concern. This balance sheet maneuver was simply a ploy to create the appearance that BNENA was a viable entity and to permit the Fed to say it was not subsidizing an insolvent bank. Without the asset transfers and influx of TT&L funds, the Fed's discount-window loan to BNENA could not have been repaid.

Recapitulation

BNENA's problems, like those of FNB, were so pervasive and hopeless that only a massive injection of new capital could have saved the bank. The signals from the marketplace were that no investors would accept such a transaction without FDIC financial assistance and indemnities against future losses.

---

[46] At the 1984 ABA National Convention in New York City, C. T. Conover, then comptroller of the currency, proposed the following strength-in-banking equation:

$$\text{New powers} + \text{Firm Supervision} = \text{Strength in Banking.}$$

Clearly, as the GAO [1991] found, the lax supervision applied to BNEC before September 30, 1989 did not meet the OCC's standard of "firm supervision."

[47] *Bankruptcy Reporter*, 2 B.R. 687 (1979).

[48] On a liquidating basis, it was established that FNB would have been worth even less. Similarly, under fire-sale conditions, BNEC would have been worth less than the estimates presented in Table A12-2.

Case Summary and Conclusions

This case has focused on several important economic issues related to the failure of Bank of New England Corporation (BNEC) and the failure of its lead bank, Bank of New England, N. A. (BNENA). On a fair-value basis BNENA was most likely economically insolvent no later than the third quarter of 1989 and remained insolvent until its regulatory closure on January 6, 1991. Specifically, a due-diligence analysis of BNEC's loan portfolio, based on a macro approach employing three alternative methods, suggests that BNEC was insolvent, on average, by roughly $300 million by September 30, 1989.

This case has provided information for understanding, among other things, the risks of banking, the causes of bank failure, the measurement of bank performance (including the critical calculation of a bank's allowance for loan and lease losses, ALLL), the way bank regulators and deposit insurers handle problem banks and resolve failing banks, and the important distinction between economic failure and regulatory closure. These concepts and models permit the following additional conclusions. The actions of federal bank regulators in keeping BNEC banks open conformed to their established practices and policies even though there was no realistic chance of saving the entities.[49] The lag between economic failure and regulatory closure provided the opportunity for regulators to protect their positions. The FDIC had the strongest motive to encourage asset transfers that would benefit its insurance fund (through lower failure-resolution costs associated with BNEC banks) because of three factors:

- The FDIC was itself on the brink of insolvency
- It was under pressure from Congress to reform deposit insurance
- It would have to put its financial capital (insurance fund) on the line

The causes of BNEC's failure can be directly attributed to mismanagement; the high cost ($733 million to the FDIC) of resolving its failure can be attributed, in part, to the OCC's lax supervision, which was not timely or forceful (GAO Report, 1991).

Case Review/Discussion Questions

1. What factors led to the failure of Bank of New England? Were internal or external (economic) considerations more important?
2. What were the management policies and practices at BNEC and its banks?
3. Standard measures of bank performance include ROE, ROA, and capital adequacy. How did BNEC perform in this regard? What did BNEC's risk index tell about the bank's performance?
4. Describe how you would measure the adequacy of a bank's ALLL. How adequate was BNEC's ALLL?
5. Should the OCC have prevented BNENA from failing? How could it have prevented it from failing? What role did the Fed and FDIC play in monitoring or assisting BNEC/BNENA?
6. Carefully distinguish between economic insolvency and regulatory closure. When did these events occur for BNEC/BNENA?
7. In mid-September 1989, BNEC successfully issued $250 million of 9.875 percent subordinated notes payable on September 15, 1999. The Securities and Exchange Com-

---

[49] Since the passage of the FDIC Improvement Act of 1991, regulators are required by law to take "prompt corrective action" in supervising problem banks.

mission (SEC) subsequently ruled that the financial information disclosed in BNEC's registration statement was materially inaccurate. The bulk of the note issue, $150 million, was transferred to BNENA as a subordinated loan from BNEC. In addition, $1.5 million of the note issue was used for an equity infusion to BNENA.

a. Had the true financial condition of BNEC been known at the time of issue, would-be investors would have demanded a much higher interest rate or been unwilling to supply funds at the stated rate. If investors would have required a junk-bond rate of 20 percent, how much money would BNEC have been able to raise at the stated rate of 9.875 percent? Assume semiannual interest payments and a 10-year maturity.

b. What were the prospects that BNENA would be able to service its debt to the parent company?

c. When parent-company debt is downstreamed to a subsidiary bank as equity, the transaction is referred to as "double leverage." The idea is to attempt to make a subsidiary bank, in this case the lead bank, look stronger by increasing its equity capital ratio. However, if the bank cannot upstream dividends to help service the debt, then the parent company will not be able to service its debt. What were the prospects that BNENA would be able to pay any dividends to the parent company?

d. If you were a BNEC bondholder, would you have preferred that BNENA be shut down at the exact time of its economic insolvency (NW = 0) or when the regulators declared it book-value insolvent? Whose responsibility is it to determine that a bank's ALLL is adequate? See Securities and Exchange Commission [1996] for the SEC's answer to the latter.

APPENDIX B

DATA ON THE CRISIS IN COMMERCIAL REAL-ESTATE LENDING AND CITICORP'S PORTFOLIO OF COMMERCIAL REAL-ESTATE LOANS

Concentration of the Crisis in Large Banks

The trend in the deterioration of loan quality at the 48 banks with total assets greater than $10 billion is revealed by the following FDIC data (annualized through the first three quarters of each year):

Year	Net Charge-Offs	Noncurrent Assets + OREO	Return on Assets
1985	0.71%	2.55	0.52%
1987	0.79	3.53	−1.04
1989	1.08	3.24	0.08
1990	1.83	3.38	0.50

The acronym OREO stands for "other real estate owned." Because these data mix LDC loans, HLT loans, and real-estate loans, we can't attribute all of the deterioration in loan quality to real-estate loans. In fact, the bulk of the net charge-offs in 1987 and 1989 were LDC-related; however, in 1990, bad commercial real-estate loans were the culprit.

Focusing on aggregate performance data for national banks, we get a better picture of the deterioration of real-estate loans:

Year	*Noncurrent RE Loans to RE Loans*	*(Noncurrent* RE + OREO) *to* (RE + OREO)
1985	2.34%	3.77%
1986	2.76	4.31
1987	3.14	4.79
1988	2.60	4.19
1989	3.40	5.28
1990	5.04	7.69

These OCC data cover the full year. At year-end 1990, the 3,965 reporting national banks held noncurrent real-estate loans of $25.2 billion, up from $15.9 billion a year earlier. OREO for these banks totaled $14.4 billion, up from $9.2 billion in 1989. The 445 national banks located in the Northeast (11.2% of all national banks) accounted for 35.1 percent ($8.86 billion) of noncurrent real estate loans and 26.4 percent ($3.81 billion) of OREO.

The 36 national banks with assets greater than $10 billion (less than 1 percent of all national banks) accounted for $15.9 billion (62.8%) of noncurrent real-estate loans at year-end 1990, up from $7.9 billion in 1989, and $9.2 billion (63.8%) of OREO at year-end 1990, up from $6.8 billion in 1989. The performance ratios for noncurrent real-estate loans and for OREO for the 36 largest national banks in 1990 were 6.3 percent and 8.9 percent, compared to 5.0 percent and 7.7 percent for all national banks. In contrast, the 3,450 national banks (96.1% of all national banks) with assets under $300 million had ratios of 1.86 percent (noncurrent real estate loans to real estate loans) and 4.0 percent (noncurrent *RE + OREO* to *RE + OREO*).

Focusing on the 10 largest banking companies as of December 31, 1990, we get the following picture of loan quality:[50]

Rank/BHC	*Net Charge-Offs as a % of Loans*	*Nonperforming Assets (including OREO) as % of Assets*
1. Citicorp	1.8%	6.0%
2. BankAmerica	1.0	3.2
3. Chase Manhattan	2.4	5.4
4. Morgan (J. P.)	2.9	1.1
5. Security Pacific	1.4	3.3
6. Chemical Bank	1.5	4.5
7. NCNB	0.9	1.5
8. Bankers Trust NY	2.3	3.0
9. Manufacturers Hanover	3.1	5.5
10. Wells Fargo	0.3	2.5
Averages: Top 10	1.8%	3.6%
Top 100	1.5%	3.1%

[50] Since 1990, Chase has acquired Chemical and Manufacturers, and NCNB is now NationsBank.

To summarize, the crisis in real-estate lending of the late 1980s and the early 1990s primarily was a problem for money-center and regional banks located in the Northeast, but extended along the east coast from New York City to Washington, DC, to Miami. Mainly because of bad commercial real-estate loans, the banking industry earned only $16.6 billion in 1990 for a return on assets of 0.49 percent, based on total assets of $3.4 trillion. For the 100 largest BHCs, where the bulk of the real-estate problems are, the average ROA was only 0.34 percent. With an equity multiplier, or leverage factor, of 19.2, the 100 largest BHCs had an average return on equity of only 6.5 percent.

Citicorp's Portfolio of Commercial Real-Estate Loans

Table B12-1 shows Citicorp's portfolio of commercial real estate by project and region of the United States as of December 31, 1990. These data from 1990 are instructive for several reasons. First, they illustrate how large banks diversify their real-estate loans by type of property and geographic regions. Second, they provide important details on the quality of real-estate loans following the rapid expansion of the 1980s. Let's examine some of the details. The portfolio consisted of $13.5 billion, only 6.2

TABLE B12-1 Citicorp's Portfolio of Commercial Real Estate by Project and by Region, December 31, 1990 (millions of dollars)

	Office	Retail	Res'l.	Hotel	Mixed	Wrkg. Cap.	Ind'l.	Land	Multi-Proj.	Other	Total
Mid-Atlantic											
Loans	$ 932	$ 448	$ 623	$ 337	$ 436	$238	$ 53	$158	$ 12	$101	$ 3,338
Cash-basis loans	121	16	235	40	54	54	13	24	4	74	635
Midwest											
Loans	1,183	294	133	133	12	75	59	14	5	—	1,908
Cash-basis loans	258	96	14	25	6	3	—	3	—	—	405
New England											
Loans	73	14	18	26	57	1	7	16	—	—	212
Cash-basis loans	19	—	5	—	—	—	3	12	—	—	39
Southeast											
Loans	419	304	487	127	34	23	26	72	99	1	1,592
Cash-basis loans	216	49	155	21	—	8	5	26	36	1	517
Southwest											
Loans	163	211	30	89	241	79	15	34	13	1	876
Cash-basis loans	53	61	20	37	—	—	15	19	—	—	205
West											
Loans	1,117	924	684	510	324	145	309	166	48	122	4,349
Cash-basis loans	218	43	96	21	71	8	80	13	—	4	554
Other											
Loans	—	300	—	9	59	204	57	20	155	440	1,244
Cash-basis loans	—	—	—	—	—	124	—	20	54	10	208
Total											
Loans[a,b]	$3,887	$2,495	$1,975	$1,231	$1,163	$765	$526	$480	$332	$665	$13,519
Cash-basis loans[b,c]	$ 885	$ 265	$ 525	$ 144	$ 131	$197	$116	$117	$ 94	$ 89	$ 2,563

[a]Cash-basis loans are included in loans.

[b]Includes $0.4 billion of real-estate related loans of which $51 million were on a cash basis.

[c]Includes $26 million of renegotiated loans.

Source: Citicorp 1990 Annual Report, p. 35.

percent of Citicorp's total assets of $217 billion at year-end 1990. However, almost $2.6 billion (19%) of the portfolio was listed as nonperforming and classified as "cash-basis loans." Normally, banks use accrual accounting. When loans are nonperforming, they may be placed on a cash basis, which means that loan payments are credited only when they are actually received rather than when they are due (accrual basis).

Citicorp's portfolio of commercial real estate was diversified by both region and type of project. Geographically, the bank focuses on seven regions of the United States: West (32%), Mid-Atlantic (primarily New York and New Jersey, 25%), Midwest (14%), Southeast (12%), Southwest (6%), New England (2%), and other (9%). By project type, Citicorp employs 10 classifications based on use or purpose of the loan: office (28.7%), retail (18.4%), residential (14.6%), hotel (9.1%), mixed use (8.6%), working capital (5.6%), industrial (3.9%), land (3.5%), multiproject (2.4%), and other (4.9%). The ratio of cash-basis loans to loans (including cash-basis loans) provides a measure of risk exposure or loan quality. Calculating these ratios from Table B12-1 and ranking them from highest to lowest, we get the following risk profile of Citicorp's portfolio of commercial real-estate loans:

Project Type	Risk Ratio	Portfolio Weight	Ratio × Weight
Multiproject	28.3%	2.4%	0.7%
Residential	26.6	14.6	3.9
Working capital	25.7	5.6	1.4
Land	24.4	3.5	0.8
Office	22.8	28.7	6.5
Industrial	22.0	3.9	0.9
Other	13.4	4.9	0.7
Hotel	11.7	9.1	1.1
Mixed	11.3	8.6	1.0
Retail	10.6	18.4	1.9
Weighted risk			18.9%

The portfolio-weighted risk ratio (18.9%) equals the ratio of cash-basis loans to loans, that is, $2,563/$13,519 = 18.9 percent. If we focus on the last column above, the portfolio-weighted projects contributing the most risk exposure to Citicorp were office (6.5%), residential (3.9%), and retail (1.9%). Although land loans are considered the riskiest form of real-estate lending, they rank fourth in Citicorp's risk profile. Moreover, with a portfolio weight of only 3.5 percent, Citicorp does not have a heavy concentration in this area.

Calculating the risk ratio by region (again from Table 12-3) and ranking them from highest to lowest, we get the following regional risk profile:

Region	Risk Ratio	Regional Weight	Ratio × Weight
Southeast	32.5%	11.8%	3.8%
Southwest	23.4	6.5	1.5
Midwest	21.2	14.1	3.0
Mid-Atlantic	19.0	24.7	4.7
New England	18.4	1.6	0.3
Other	16.7	9.2	1.5
West	12.7	32.2	4.1
Weighted risk			18.9%

As with the portfolio-weighted risk ratio, the regional-weighted risk ratio (18.9%) equals the ratio of cash-basis loans to loans, that is, $2,563/$13,519 = 18.9 percent. If we focus on the last column above, the risk-weighted regions contributing the most risk exposure to Citicorp were Mid-Atlantic (4.7%), West (4.1%), Southeast (3.8%), and Midwest (3.0%).

In addition to cash-basis loans, two other symptoms of problems in bank real-estate loan portfolios are write-offs and OREO (Other Real Estate Owned—there's no cream in the center of this bank cookie). Continuing with the Citicorp example, in 1990 net write-offs for its real-estate loan portfolio rose to $228 million from $39 million in 1989. Citicorp's OREO jumped from $247 million at year-end 1989 to $1,165 million at year-end 1990. Cash-basis loans increased to $2.5 billion at the end of 1990 from $887 million a year earlier. Citicorp, of course, did not stand alone with these problems; many other large banks face similar situations.

The Rest of the Story

By year-end 1995, the Citicorp portfolio of commercial real-estate loans (in North America) had shrunk to $6,918 million, down from $13,519 million at year-end 1990, an annual contraction of 12.5 percent.[51] Cash-basis loans were down to $862 million, a decline of $1,701 million from year-end 1990. This shrinkage was costly. For example, net write-offs from 1990 to 1995 were $244 million (1990), $559 million (1991), $1,146 million (1992), $431 million (1993), $244 million (1994), and $102 million (1995). On balance, for Citicorp and other real-estate lenders, the adverse effects of the rapid growth of the 1980s finally seemed to have worked their way out of the banking system.

Selected References

Bacow, Lawrence S. [1990]. "Foreign Investment, Vertical Integration, and the Structure of the U.S. Real Estate Industry." *Real Estate Issues* (Fall/Winter), pp. 1–8.

Badger, Peter W. [1990]. "Seasoned Single-Family Mortgages: A Lot of Bang for Your Bucks." *Bank Management* (October), pp. 84–85.

Bank of New England Failure and Resolution. [1991]. Staff Report to the Committee on Banking, Finance, and Urban Affairs, House of Representatives. Washington, D.C.: U.S. Government Printing Office.

Brady, Paul M. [1990]. "A Methodology for Underwriting Commercial Real Estate." *Real Estate Review* (Winter), pp. 58–60.

Chesler, Alan. [1990]. "Component Discounted Cash-Flow Analysis." *Real Estate Finance Journal* (Summer), pp. 64–69.

Clarke, Peter S. [1986]. *Complete Guide to Loan Documentation.* Englewood Cliffs, NJ: Prentice-Hall.

"Commercial Banks Become Dominant Force in Mortgage Business." [1991]. *Commercial Lender's Alert* (January), pp. 2–4.

Conover, C. T. [1984]. "Strength in Banking." Speech before the 1984 American Bankers Association, National Convention, OCC News Release.

Corcoran, Patrick J. [1987]. "Explaining the Commercial Real Estate Market." *Journal of Portfolio Management* 13 (Spring), pp. 15–21.

---

[51] The data in this section are from Citicorp's 1995 *Annual Report,* p. 31.

Corgel, John B., and Terrance M. Clauretie. [1990]. "Diversification Strategies for Mortgage Default Risk Management." *Real Estate Finance Journal* (Spring), pp. 94–96.

Corgel, John B., and Gerald D. Gay. [1987]. "Local Economic Base, Geographic Diversification, and Risk Management of Mortgage Portfolios." *Journal of the American Real Estate and Urban Economics Association* 15 (Fall), pp. 256–267.

Cranmer, Charles N. [1990]. "Commercial Banks: Real Estate—Real Trouble." *Issues in Bank Regulation* (Summer), pp. 26–32.

Ebbert, James C. [1991]. "What Banking Institutions Must Know about DCF Valuation Analysis." *Real Estate Finance* (Winter), pp. 67–73.

Federal Reserve Bulletin (various issues). Washington, DC: Board of Governors of the Federal Reserve System.

General Accounting Office. [1991]. "Bank Supervision: OCC's Supervision of the Bank of New England Was Not Timely or Forceful." Report to the Chairman, Committee on Banking, Housing and Urban Affairs, U.S. Senate, GAO/GGD-91-128 (September).

Goodman, Jack L., Jr. (with Yana Hudson and Scott Yermish). [1991]. "The Characteristics of the Home Mortgage Debt, 1970–89: Trends and Implications." Board of Governors of the Federal Reserve System, Finance and Economics and Discussion Series 149 (January).

Greenspan, Alan. [1996a]. Speech before the Annual Convention of the American Bankers Association, Honolulu, Hawaii (October 5). Board of Governors of the Federal Reserve System, Washington, DC.

————. [1996b]. "Remarks at the Financial Markets Conference of the Federal Reserve Bank of Atlanta," Coral Gables, FL (February 23). Board of Governors of the Federal Reserve System, Washington, DC.

Greig, D. Wylie, and Michael S. Young. [1991]. "New Measures of Future Property Performance and Risk." *Real Estate Review* (Spring), pp. 17–25.

Gullo, Karen. [1993]. "Banks Seek Tickets on Realty-Backed Express." *American Banker* (October 19), p. 5.

Hannan, Timothy H., and Gerald A. Hanweck. [1988]. "Bank Insolvency Risk and the Market for Large Certificates of Deposit." *Journal of Money, Credit, and Banking* (May), pp. 203–211.

King, Jim. [1991]. "Earnings Anger C&S Chairman, Stockholders." *Atlanta Constitution* (April 17), pp. B1 and B8.

Marsh, John D. [1990]. "Tough Times Ahead for Mortgage Lending." *Southern Banker* (October), pp. 14–16.

McNulty, James E. [1995]. "Overbuilding, Real Estate Lending Decisions, and the Regional Economic Base." *Journal of Real Estate Finance and Economics* 11, pp. 37–53.

Moscovitch, Edward. [1990]. "The Downturn in the New England Economy: What Lies Behind It?" *New England Economic Review* (July/August), pp. 53–65.

Neverloff, Jay A. [1996]. "Institutional Lenders Must Speed Up to Profit on Return of Realty Market." *American Banker* (January 26), p. 26.

OCC. [1991]. *News Release,* NR 91-3, (January 6). OCC, Washington, D.C.

"Office and Industrial Vacancy Rates." [1991]. *Mortgage and Real Estate Executives Report* (April 1), pp. 5–6.

Pacelle, Mitchell, and Steven Lipin. [1993]. "Real-Estate Swaps Could Become Hot Property." *Wall Street Journal* (December 21), pp. C1 and C18.

Pollack, Alex J. [1993]. "A Century of Lending Laws That Didn't Work," *American Banker* (February 5), p. 4.

"Prime Real Estate Performance Report." [1990]. *Mortgage and Real Estate Executives Report* (May 1), pp. 1–2.

"Real Estate Performance Remains Stable." [1990]. *Mortgage and Real Estate Executives Report* (July 1), pp. 2–3.

Roulac, Stephen E., Lloyd Lynford, and Gilbert H. Castle III. [1990]. "Real Estate Decision Making in an Information Era." *Real Estate Finance Journal* (Summer), pp. 8–15.

Roulac Real Estate Consulting Group of Deloitte & Touche. [1990]. "A Quarterly Survey of Trends in Commercial Lending." *Real Estate Finance* (Summer), pp. 7–11.

Schneider, Howard. [1990]. "Building Construction Loans on Solid Ground." *Bankers Monthly* (June), pp. 60–61.

Schultz, Vernon F. [1990]. "Auctions Spur Sales Success." *Commercial Investment Real Estate Journal* (Summer), pp. 15–17.

Securities and Exchange Commission. [1996]. "In the Matter of Bank of Boston Corp.," Proceeding File No. 3-8270, Commerce Clearing House, Inc., ¶85,719.

Sinkey, Joseph F., Jr. [1975]. "REITs and Commercial Banks: An Update." Executive Summary 75–9, FDIC.

———. [1978]. "Identifying Problem Banks: How Do the Banking Authorities Measure a Bank's Risk Exposure?" *Journal of Money, Credit, and Banking* (May), pp. 184–193.

———. [1979]. *Problem and Failed Institutions in the Commercial Banking Industry.* Greenwich, CT: JAI Press.

———. [1989]. "Credit Risk in Commercial Banks: A Survey of Theory, Practice, and Empirical Evidence." Bank of Israel Conference on "Risks in Banking" March 26, 1989. *Banking Review* (December), pp. 12–35.

Sinkey, Joseph F., Jr., and Julia P. Gerdnic. [1975]. "A Look at the REIT Industry and Its Relationship with Commercial Banks." Executive Summary 75-4, FDIC.

Smith, David A. [1990]. "Working Out Troubled Real Estate Properties: Making Stone Soup." *Real Estate Review* (Spring), pp. 20–25.

Solomon, Kenneth I. [1990]. "Judging Success in Real Estate." *Commercial Investment Real Estate Journal* (Summer), pp. 11–14.

Sykes, Stephen G., and Michael S. Young. [1981]. "A Different Approach to Income Property Valuation: A New Measurement Technique." *Appraisal Journal* 49 (April), pp. 214–233.

Thomson, James B. [1992]. "Modeling the Bank Regulator's Closure Option: A Two-Step Logit Regression Approach." *Journal of Financial Services Research* 6, pp. 5–23.

Weatherstone, Dennis. [1995]. "Reflections on the Business of Banking." Remarks at the Institute of International Finance, Washington, DC, October 8.

Zisler, Randall C. [1988]. "Trends in Real Estate Finance." *Bank Director's Report* (October), pp. 2, 5.

V
BANK CAPITAL: THEORY, MANAGEMENT, AND REGULATION

To complete our balance-sheet framework for commercial bank financial management, this part of the book focuses on the theory, management, and regulation of bank capital. In a frictionless world of full information and complete markets, finance theory suggests that capital structure does not matter (i.e., it does not affect firm value or cost of capital). Of course in this kind of world, financial intermediaries do not exist. In the real world of agency problems, taxes, costs of financial distress, transactions costs, asymmetric information, and regulation, which is especially important for banks, capital structure matters.

Risk exposure in any industry arises from unpredictable fluctuations in exchange rates, interest rates, and commodity prices. Four key risks in banking are credit risk, interest-rate risk, liquidity risk, and foreign-exchange risk. A bank's capital serves, among other things, as a buffer or cushion to absorb potential losses arising from these key risks and any other risks the bank faces. In practice, managing a bank's capital focuses on assuring investors, creditors, and regulators that a bank's capital is adequate for absorbing normal operating losses. Only a bank with all-equity financing would have enough capital to absorb abnormal or catastrophic losses.

In the absence of a regulatory capital requirement, the capital standard set by the marketplace would be the capital ratio (e.g., equity to assets) that maximizes the value of the bank. For years both the marketplace and regulators perceived that large banks, because they had greater access to money and capital markets and a greater ability to attract more highly skilled and trained personnel, could operate with less capital than community banks. Today, the market and regulatory standard around the world is that capital requirements should be the same for all banks after adjustment for relevant risk exposures.

During July 1988, the Basle Accord on International Convergence of Capital Measurement and Capital Standards was finalized in Basle, Switzerland, a renowned international bank center. This agreement mandated risk-based capital requirements for all banks regardless of their size. The original

Basle Accord, however, was narrowly focused solely on credit risk. Its basic premise is that riskier assets (in terms of probability of default or credit risk), whether on or off a bank's balance sheet, require more capital to support them, hence the term risk-based capital requirements. By December 31, 1992, all U.S. commercial banks and larger bank holding companies had to meet minimum risk-based capital requirements established jointly by the Federal Reserve, the Office of the Comptroller of the Currency (OCC), and the Federal Deposit Insurance Corporation (FDIC). Although risk-based capital requirements are a step in the right direction, a comprehensive measure of capital adequacy must account for all the major risks banks face. This task, however, is easier said than done. For example, after years of attempting to devise a capital standard for interest-rate risk, U.S. banking agencies abandoned such efforts in 1996. Since 1988, the Basle Committee has been struggling with incorporating a complete array of risks, beyond credit risk, into risk-based capital requirements.

For banks with actively traded securities in efficient markets, the values of their securities are adjusted for all relevant risk exposures, whether on or off the balance sheet. Two problems with a market approach to capital adequacy are that most banks do not have actively traded securities, and those that do may not be measuring their risk exposures accurately and may be imperfectly gauging how much capital to set aside for fluctuations in the values of their securities and derivatives. Starting in 1998, the 25 or so largest U.S. banks will have to meet a standardized market-risk capital formula. The objective of this standard is to translate the estimated change in the value of a bank's trading portfolio (i.e., market risk) into a fair capital standard. In January 1996, the Basle Committee formalized its 1998 capital agreement by letting banks choose between a regulatory formula and their own computer models to determine how much capital to set aside for market risk.

This part of the book consists of two chapters on bank capital. Chapter 13 deals with the theory and regulation of bank capital. The notions of capital adequacy, risk-based capital requirements, optimal capital structure, cost of equity capital, and the determinants of the value of the banking firm are the theoretical and regulatory cornerstones of the chapter. In chapter 14, we turn to some practical aspects of bank capital and dividend management by focusing on the market valuation of bank stock, as well as dividend and financing issues. Such topics as the internal capital generation rate, dividend policy and payout, instruments for raising capital, long-term debt management, double leverage, and capital planning are analyzed.

Contents

LEARNING OBJECTIVES

■ To understand the optimal capital structure of a regulated firm

■ To understand the importance and role of bank capital

■ To understand how government guarantees substitute for bank capital

■ To understand capital-adequacy standards as implicit pricing of risk

■ To understand and calculate risk-based capital requirements

CHAPTER THEME

In theory, under a set of restrictive assumptions, capital structure does not matter (i.e., does not affect the value of the firm or its cost of capital). In practice, and especially in banking, capital structure does matter.

The term "capital adequacy" captures the overall soundness or risk exposure of an individual bank or the banking system; it reflects the idea of bank capital as a cushion or buffer to absorb losses. Because bank losses arise from unexpected changes associated with, among other things, fluctuations in interest rates, exchange rates, and commodity prices, a true measure of capital adequacy must be adjusted for each bank's unique risk exposure. In this context, capital-adequacy standards implicitly price risk.

Although risk-based capital requirements established by regulators in 1992 represent a step in the direction of a comprehensive capital-adequacy standard, they recognize only one source of exposure—credit risk. The inclusion of off-balance-sheet activities (OBSAs) in the risk-based capital formulas reflects regulatory concern about the risks associated with contingent claims and derivatives activities. Under risk-based capital guidelines, total bank capital for regulatory purposes equals Tier 1, or core capital, plus Tier 2, or supplementary capital. Starting in 1998, the 25 or so largest U.S. banks will have to meet a standardized market-risk capital formula. The objective of this requirement is to translate the estimated change in the value of a bank's portfolio (i.e., market risk) into a fair capital standard. In January 1996, the Basle Committee formalized its 1998 capital agreement by allowing banks to choose between a regulatory formula and their own computer models to determine how much capital to set aside for market risk.

KEY CONCEPTS, IDEAS, AND TERMS

- Agency conflicts/costs
- Capital adequacy/regulation
- Confidence function
- Cost of equity capital
- Credit risk
- Government guarantees (federal safety net)

- Deposit insurance
- Implicit pricing of deposit insurance
- Lender of last resort (discount window)
- Market value of equity
- Modigliani-and-Miller (M&M) propositions

- Off-balance-sheet activities (OBSAs)
- Regulatory interference (monitoring and bonding)
- Risk-based capital requirements
- Tier 1 (core) capital
- Tier 2 (supplementary) capital

DO MODIGLIANI-AND-MILLER (M&M) PROPOSITIONS APPLY TO BANKS?[1]

When asked whether **M&M propositions** apply to banks, Miller [1995], one-half of the M&M team, replied, "Yes and no." The old joke about economists never being able to reach a conclusion seems appropriate here. In fairness, however, difficult questions do not lend themselves to simple yes or no answers. Nevertheless, if you ask bankers if capital matters (they will of course be thinking in terms of "capital adequacy" and not M&M propositions), they will respond with a resounding, "Yes, bank capital does matter!" Although this chapter builds on this answer, it begins with a look at the applicability of M&M propositions to banks.

OPTIMAL BANK CAPITAL AND THE VALUE OF THE BANKING FIRM

Modigliani and Miller [1958] have shown that in a perfect capital market without bankruptcy costs and taxes, the value of the firm is independent of its financial structure. Relaxing one or more of the simplifying assumptions leads to an optimal capital structure. Consider first the situation in which interest on debt is tax deductible but there are no bankruptcy costs. In this case, an incentive exists to substitute debt for equity in the firm's financial structure. In the absence of bankruptcy costs, the positive incentive for debt (in the form of tax savings) leads to a corner solution with all debt and no equity. In the case of no taxes but positive bankruptcy costs, the value of the firm is maximized when it is unlevered (that is, when it is a pure equity firm without any debt). Combining costly bankruptcy with the tax deductibility of interest produces a situation in which bankruptcy costs provide a disincentive that offsets the tax-shield incentive to expand debt. Under these dual conditions, an optimal capital structure exists in which the value of the firm is maximized.[2] These theorems of Modigliani and Miller (the so-called M&M propositions) are illustrated in the four panels of Figure 13-1. Figure 13-1(a) shows the capital-structure-doesn't-matter case; Figure 13-1(b) depicts the corner solution with all debt; Figure 13-1(c) shows the unlevered firm with all equity and no debt; and Figure 13-1(d) depicts the existence of an optimal capital structure $(D/A)^*$ that maximizes the value of the firm (V^*).

---

[1] M&M refers to Modigliani and Miller [1958].
[2] Agency costs offer an alternative rationale for an optimal capital structure.

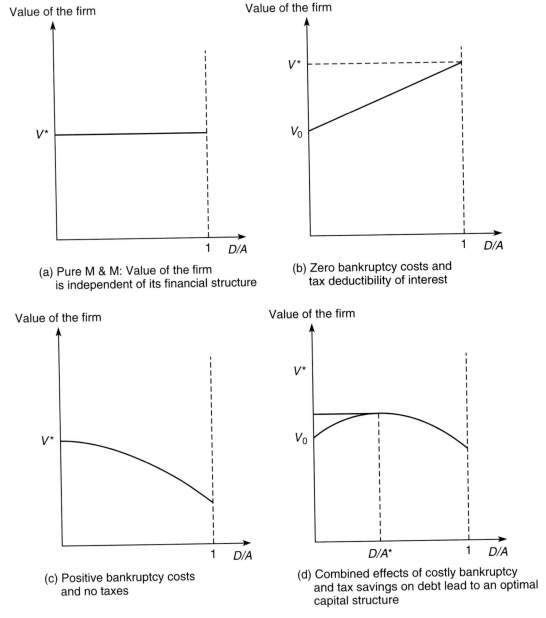

Note: D/A = debt-to-asset ratio.

FIGURE 13-1 **Financial Structure and the Value of the Firm**

Market Imperfections: Taxes and Bankruptcy Costs

To understand how financial structure affects the value of the firm, the concepts of **tax shield** and **bankruptcy costs** are critical. First, consider the concept of the tax shield. The important point is that the tax deductibility of interest expense increases the total income that a levered firm (relative to an unlevered or pure-equity firm) can pay out to both its stockholders and its bondholders. In this case, the value of the firm is equal to its value as a purely equity-financed firm plus the present value of the tax shield.

If this proposition is true, however, what stops firms from becoming purely debt-financed entities? Enter bankruptcy costs or, in general, the potential costs of financial distress. The standard argument is as follows: As a firm increases its use of debt, its risk of not being able to cover its fixed interest expenses increases. Thus, the highly levered firm may incur a cash-flow or debt-service problem that could eventually lead to bankruptcy. This greater leverage and greater potential for bankruptcy are not costless. The costs reflect the higher ex ante interest rates that creditors demand for holding the debt of highly levered firms as compensation for the potential ex post bankruptcy costs (e.g., legal fees) they might have to pay if the firm fails. The costs of bankruptcy depend on the probability of the event occurring and the size of the associated costs if it does occur. Of course, the costs of financial distress need to be evaluated in present-value terms. Thus, the value of a levered firm can be expressed as its value as a pure-equity firm *plus* the present value of its tax shield *minus* the present value of the cost of bankruptcy. In symbols, this important proposition is,

$$PV \text{ Firm} = [PV \text{ Pure-Equity Firm}] + [PV \text{ Tax Shield}] \\ - [PV \text{ Bankruptcy Costs}] \tag{13-1}$$

Another way to view M&M's theory of capital structure is to employ the following logic:[3] The statement "if A then B" (or A → B) is equivalent to "if not B then not A" (not B → not A). Given a firm's investment policy and assuming no taxes and contracting (e.g., bankruptcy) costs, M&M say that the firm's choice of capital structure does not affect the current value of the firm, which is the if-A-then-B statement. If the choice of capital structure does affect firm value, then the choice is driven by (1) changing tax liabilities, (2) changing contracting costs, or (3) changing investment incentives, which is the if-not-B-then-not-A statement.

Deposit Insurance and the Value of the Banking Firm[4]

Panel (*d*) of Figure 13-1 shows the optimal capital structure for an uninsured bank. This section focuses on the effects of having a government agency (the FDIC) guarantee a bank's debt. In general, the government guarantee ("G") is the **federal safety net** for banks. It consists of deposit insurance, the Fed's discount window, which functions as a lender of last resort, and the too-big-to-fail (TBTF) doctrine.

Following Buser, Chen, and Kane [1981a], we assume that the deposit-insurance coverage applies to all deposit balances and that no doubts exist about the ability or willingness of the FDIC to meet its insurance obligations. In other words, the federal safety net is credible. Widespread use of the deposit-assumption technique for handling failed banks, Treasury backing of the insurance fund, and the existence of TBTF attest to the credibility of the government guarantee.

To illustrate the insight that M&M's framework provides for analyzing the effects of deposit insurance on the value of the banking firm, we begin with the case where FDIC insurance is provided free of charge. This means that no deposit-insurance fees exist, either explicitly in the form of dollar premiums or implicitly in the form of regulatory interference (e.g., capital regulation). In this case, the FDIC simply pays off all depositors in full in the event of bank failure without imposing any restraints on the bank. Panel (*a*) of Figure 13-2 depicts this situation. Free

---

[3] Smith [1991].

[4] This section draws on Buser, Chen, and Kane [1981a].

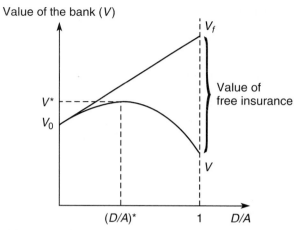

Value of the bank (V)

V_f

Value of free insurance

V^*
V_0

V

$(D/A)^*$ 1 D/A

(a) Impact of "free" insurance on the value of the bank

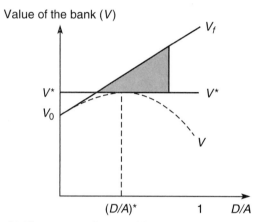

Value of the bank (V)

V_f

V^*
V_0

V^*

V

$(D/A)^*$ 1 D/A

(b) The opportunity set of "acceptable" insurance contracts

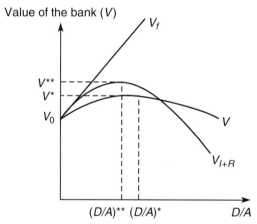

Value of the bank (V)

V_f

V^{**}
V^*
V_0

V

V_{I+R}

$(D/A)^{**}$ $(D/A)^*$ D/A

(c) The impact of costly insurance and regulatory interference on the value of an insured bank

Adapted from Buser, Chen, and Kane [1981a], Figures 2, 3, and 5, pp. 55 and 58.

FIGURE 13-2 **Deposit Insurance and the Value of the Banking Firm**

insurance, like zero bankruptcy costs, leads to the zero-equity corner solution. The preliminary conclusion suggested by this simple case is that perhaps deposit insurance is responsible for the decline in bank capital ratios. Further analysis is required, however.

By adding panel (*d*) of Figure 13-1 to panel (*a*) of Figure 13-2, we can compare the value of the bank with free insurance (V_f) to its value without insurance (*V*). At any financial structure (as measured by the bank's deposit-to-asset ratio), the vertical distance between the two curves (V_f and *V*) reflects the value of free insurance to the bank. Merton [1977], Sharpe [1978], and others contend that the FDIC should charge an explicit insurance fee sufficient to exhaust this increase in value. If this "fair-value" pricing scheme were enforced, the V_f curve would collapse on the *V* curve, because the value of the free insurance would be wiped out by the fair insurance premium. In this situation, with or without deposit insurance, managers who attempted to maximize the value of the bank would operate at (*D/A*)* and the bank would be worth *V**.

If the FDIC's only business were insurance,[5] then, in a competitive market for deposit insurance, the neutral insurance contract described above would exist. However, a major part of the FDIC's business is bank regulation. To avoid going out of business, the FDIC must price and administer its insurance contract so that it presents an insured bank with the opportunity to increase its value above the market-determined value, *V**, that it would obtain as an uninsured bank. The shaded triangle in panel (*b*) of Figure 13-2 shows the opportunity set of acceptable deposit-insurance contracts. The boundaries of the set are defined by V_f, *V**, and *D/A* = 1. The latter assumes that the FDIC requires an insured bank to have some positive amount of equity capital.[6] Excluding the three boundary lines, the area inside the shaded triangle represents the set of *mutually acceptable* contracting opportunities.

To understand deposit insurance and its effects on a bank's capital structure and behavior, you must understand and distinguish between implicit and explicit deposit-insurance premiums. The original explicit deposit-insurance premium (chapter 16) was fixed by law at 1/12th of 1 percent (of domestic deposits). The effective rate, until the 1980s, was about one-half of the nominal rate, because of an annual rebate based on the FDIC's loss experience during the year. This explicit pricing structure encourages moral-hazard behavior because no *explicit* penalty (in the form of higher insurance premiums) exists for excessive risk taking.[7] Under this scheme, high-risk banks are subsidized by low-risk banks. To discourage moral-hazard behavior (i.e., excessive risk taking) and to price its insurance more fairly, the FDIC uses regulatory interference to extract *implicit* insurance premiums from all banks, but especially from the highest-risk or "problem" banks. Although this regulatory interference (monitoring) can take many forms, it is manifested mainly in the form of capital regulation, which typically is administered by calling for an infusion of capital or by restricting growth opportunities or both.[8] The ultimate

---

[5] Chapter 16 shows that we shouldn't judge a book or a government agency by its cover initials.

[6] In practice, this minimum amount of capital is prescribed by risk-based capital requirements, which are discussed later in this chapter.

[7] On September 15, 1992, the FDIC announced that it would charge higher insurance rates to banks and savings associations that pose greater risks to the deposit-insurance funds. This variable-rate pricing scheme went into effect on January 1, 1993. Chapter 16 provides detailed information about the FDIC and its operations and practices.

[8] Capital regulation for national banks and state-member banks is enforced by the OCC and the Fed, respectively. Thus, these banks pay their implicit insurance premiums indirectly. OCC and Fed bank-examination reports are passed on to the FDIC for further analysis. By law, the FDIC has the right to examine any insured bank.

objective of capital regulation can be viewed as an attempt to improve the bank's capital-to-asset ratio or, in terms of Figure 13-2, its debt-to-asset ratio.

The effects of costly insurance and regulatory interference (i.e., explicit and implicit pricing of deposit insurance) on the value of an insured bank is depicted in panel (*c*) of Figure 13-2. The curve V_{I+R} ($I + R$ stands for *insurance* plus *regulation*) lies between the curves for free insurance (V_f) and no insurance (V) at safe levels of deposit debt (i.e., when capital is adequate). However, when deposit debt becomes excessive (i.e., when capital is inadequate), V_{I+R} falls below V. The vertical distance between V_f and V_{I+R} measures the varying value of implicit insurance premiums plus the fixed implicit premium. As a part of the insurance contract, an insured bank agrees to pay explicit premiums by subjecting itself to contingent regulatory interference. The vertical distance between V_{I+R} and V measures the net benefit to the bank of the insurance contracts or, more generally, the net benefit of the government guarantee. The net benefit is positive when capital is perceived by examiners to be adequate but negative when capital is perceived to be inadequate. The net benefit involves a trade-off between potential losses from costly bankruptcy without insurance and regulatory interference.

The optimal capital structure with implicit and explicit insurance premiums occurs at $(D/A)^{**}$ as shown in panel (*c*) of Figure 13-2. The corresponding value of the insured bank is V^{**}, which is greater than V^*. Because V^{**} is greater than V^*, a value-maximizing bank is willing to contract for deposit insurance.

Regulatory Interference and Capital Regulation as Attempts to Solve Agency Conflicts

Bank regulators face **agency conflicts** regarding the firms they supervise. Agency problems can arise because of different goals and objectives (e.g., profits versus safety and soundness), asymmetric information, or dishonesty. **Regulatory interference** (what finance theory calls monitoring ["stick"] and bonding ["carrot"] through incentive compatible contracts) is the process through which the banking authorities attempt to correct a perceived unsafe or unsound banking practice or to coerce bankers to behave in a certain way (e.g., community reinvestment). The major instrument in this process is **capital regulation.** Other instruments include cease-and-desist orders, removal of bank officers and directors, the threat of termination of deposit insurance, and denial of requests for expansion into new products or markets. The concept and process of capital regulation are manifested in policy statements on capital by the banking authorities. For example, FDIC capital regulation requires banks to submit a "comprehensive capital plan" or a "specific program for remedying the equity capital deficiency promptly." These plans or programs are costly for banks to prepare and implement. In addition, capital regulation takes the form of withholding approval on various types of applications (e.g., branching or holding-company expansion). These denials are costly because bank resources have been spent on the projects.

Capital regulation requires banks to divert resources to combat regulatory interference. The opportunity costs to banks of this diversion of resources represents one form of the implicit cost of deposit insurance. In the case of denials, both out-of-pocket and opportunity costs are incurred. Only in cases where the regulatory interference has become public knowledge or the market has diagnosed the bank's financial difficulties itself (e.g., Bank of New England, Continental Illinois, and First Pennsylvania) is it likely to result in higher risk premiums demanded by uninsured creditors or in deposit runs or both.

Implicit Variable-Rate Pricing of Deposit Insurance

In analyzing the pricing of deposit insurance, both the explicit and implicit components must be considered. On the surface, FDIC pricing *appears* to be a fixed-rate scheme. However, on closer scrutiny, the total insurance premium has always been a variable-rate one with adjustment for bank risk based on examiners' ratings and judgments (e.g., CAMEL ratings). Consequently, until January 1, 1993, the FDIC's total *effective* premium consisted of the explicit, flat-rate premium plus the implicit, variable-rate one. We can think of implicit pricing in a general sense as regulatory interference and in particular as capital regulation. As of this writing, the explicit deposit-insurance premium charged by the FDIC was 23 cents per $100 dollars of domestic deposits, up substantially from the original effective premium of about four cents. And since the beginning of 1993, the explicit premium has been variable, ranging from a 23-cent rate for "safe-and-sound" banks to a 31-cent rate for undercapitalized, high-risk banks. The major merit of a risk-based pricing structure is its fairness (i.e., low-risk banks provide smaller subsidies to high-risk banks). Until 1993, the FDIC claimed that it agreed in principle with the concept of variable-rate deposit insurance but always rejected it as too difficult to implement.

THE COST OF EQUITY CAPITAL

Banks pay interest on most of their deposits and on their debt capital (i.e., notes and debentures). What do they have to pay for equity capital? The return that shareholders expect to earn on their investment represents the implicit **cost of equity capital**. This **expected total return** $[E(r)]$ can be viewed in terms of a **dividend yield** (D/P) and a **price-appreciation** or **capital-gains yield** ($\Delta P/P$). In symbols, we have:

$$E(r) = D/P + \Delta P/P \tag{13-2}$$

where D = dividend per share, P = price per share, and ΔP = change in price per share. The change in price, of course, can be positive, negative, or zero; but unless the investor is selling the stock short (expecting a decline in the value of the stock), the expectation is for the stock to appreciate in value. For example, suppose that investors expect a bank whose stock has a market value of $80 per share to generate a dividend yield of 3 percent and a price appreciation of 12 percent over the next year. The expected annual return then is 15 percent = 3 percent + 12 percent, or, in terms of equation (13-2), $E(r) = 2.4/80 + 9.6/80$. Because almost all bank stocks pay dividends and because banks are not considered growth stocks, bank stocks tend to trade on a combination of relatively attractive dividend yield and modest potential for price appreciation.[9]

Important insights about the cost of equity capital and the valuation of bank equity can be gained by solving equation (13-2) for price or value. Letting $g = \Delta P/P$ and assuming g to be constant, we get

$$P = D_1 / [E(r) - g] \tag{13-3}$$

---

[9] Another way to look at this situation is to say that banks (with actively traded shares) tend to have betas close to 1.0, which means that they tend to move with the market portfolio. Recall that beta is a measure of systematic risk.

which you will recognize as the **constant-growth model** with $D_1 = D_0(1 + g)$. This simple model, which holds only as long as $E(r) > g$, has great intuitive appeal because it says that, all other things being equal, value is positively affected by higher dividends and more rapid growth and negatively affected by greater risk in the form of a higher expected or required rate of return.

Treating equation (13-3) as an earnings-growth model in perpetuity, we get

$$P = EPS/E(r) \qquad \qquad \textbf{(13-4)}$$

where EPS = earnings per share. Solving for the price-earnings, or P/E ratio, we get $P/EPS = 1/E(r)$. When analyzing any ratio, it is critical not to ignore the component parts. In the case of a P/E ratio, it can be high because the market values the bank's earnings highly, or simply because the bank has very low earnings. For example, consider a P/E ratio of 11 with component parts of 80/7.27, versus another one with component parts of 0.11/0.01. Assuming the latter is not a penny stock, it could be a firm on its way to failure. Careful analysts always check the components of any ratio.

Taking the reciprocal of both sides of equation (13-4), we have, $E(r) = EPS/P$. If we know a bank's P/E ratio, its reciprocal gives us a benchmark estimate of its cost of equity capital in a zero-growth situation. For example, on May 15, 1996, Citicorp's P/E was 11.0. Therefore, $E(r)_{g=0} = 1/11 = 0.0909 = 9.09$ percent. More realistically, let's assume $g = 12.5$ percent, and use the May 15 closing price ($80) and dividend ($1.80) in equation (13-3). This growth scenario produces a benchmark cost of equity capital for Citicorp of $(1.8 \times 1.125)/80 + 12.5$ percent = 2.53 percent + 12.5 percent = 15.03 percent.

THE ROLE OF CAPITAL IN A BANK'S CONFIDENCE FUNCTION

Chapter 1 introduced the idea of a **confidence function** for modeling the public's trust in an individual bank or the banking system. In symbols, the confidence function is

$$\text{Confidence} = f(NW^*, SOE, IQ, G) \qquad \qquad \textbf{(13-5)}$$

where NW* represents the **market value** of net worth, or the bank's real equity capital, SOE stands for stability of economic or real earnings, IQ indicates information quality, and G represents the credibility or market value of **government guarantees.**[10] Each of these factors has a positive and direct effect on confidence (or perceived safety) for individual banks and the banking system. Holding all other things constant (*ceteris paribus*), we can evaluate these factors as follows:

- The more economic (not book) net worth a bank has, the safer it is perceived to be.
- The more stable a bank's (real) earnings are, the safer it is perceived to be.
- The better the quality of information available about a bank's financial condition, the more confidence interested parties have in the bank. For example, as information quality increases (e.g., regarding the market value of bank loans or the risks of derivatives activities), interested parties will have greater confidence in their estimates of the bank's true value.
- As the credibility (market value) of government guarantees increases, confidence should increase, all other things being equal. Given the too-big-to-fail (TBTF) doctrine, the perceived market value of the government guarantees may vary with the size of the bank.

---

[10] The confidence function is from Kane [1986].

From a finance perspective, banks hold capital to resolve agency conflicts between shareholders and depositors, creditors, and guarantors. In this view, equity capital provides assurances to these parties that banks won't take on excessive risk. On balance, the confidence of depositors and other creditors plays a critical role in determining the stability of individual banks and of the financial system.

Excluding the government guarantee, which is not subject to direct managerial control, and assuming uniform disclosure of quality information, net worth and stability of earnings are the determinants of confidence subject to some degree of managerial discretion. Moreover, because it is common to view bank capital or net worth as a buffer or cushion to absorb unexpected losses arising from credit, interest-rate, and operating risks (the major sources of instability in bank earnings), bank capital can be viewed as *the* critical element in generating confidence about a bank's ability to handle uncertainty, and as the frontline defense for the government guarantee (i.e., federal deposit insurance and the Fed's discount window or lender-of-last-resort function).

Figure 13-3 illustrates three critical components of a bank's confidence function. The data are for national banks for the years 1984 to 1994. Panel A shows return on equity (*ROE*), which captures the volatility of bank earnings. The sharp

Panel A. Return on equity (ROE), national banks

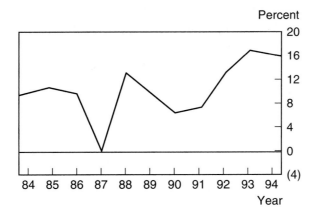

Panel B. Noncurrent loans to loans, national banks

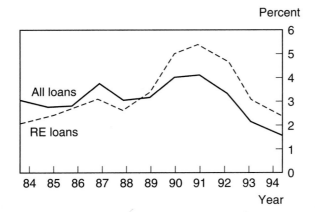

FIGURE 13-3 **Critical Components of a Bank's Confidence Function: Data for All National Banks, 1984–1994**

(continued)

Panel C. Equity capital, national banks

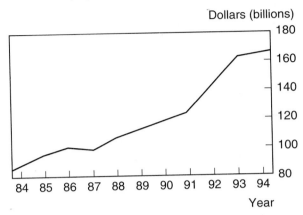

Note: *RE loans* refers to *real-estate loans,* and the corresponding ratio is noncurrent *RE* loans to total *RE* loans. See chapter 12 and the appendix case study of Bank of New England.
Source: Call Reports, Office of the Comptroller of the Currency.

FIGURE 13-3 *Continued*

decline in *ROE* for 1987 was due to the massive provision for loan losses taken by large national banks for loans made to less developed countries (the LDC debt crisis). These banks took another LDC hit in 1989, followed by provisions for bad commercial-real-estate loans. Panel B reflects loan quality, the underlying cause of earnings volatility, as captured by the ratio of noncurrent loans to loans. The upswings in noncurrent loans coincide with the downswings in ROE shown in panel A. Panel C shows that national banks almost doubled their equity capital (book value) to offset greater risk taking, from 1984 to 1994.[11] The greatest growth in equity capital (indicated by the steepness of the line in panel C) occurred from 1991 to 1993, which includes the year (1992) when commercial banks had to meet the new minimum risk-based capital requirements. This equity capital serves as the buffer or cushion for absorbing bank losses and for protecting the federal deposit insurance fund from loss.

THE ISSUE OF CAPITAL ADEQUACY

How much capital does a bank need to ensure the confidence of depositors, creditors, investors, and regulators? In the banking-and-finance literature, this question is known as the issue of bank **capital adequacy.** Anyone who knows the answer to this question can gain instant notoriety in the banking, financial, and regulatory communities. Because this chapter does not contain *the* answer, your opportunity for fame (but not much fortune) still exists. However, a word of caution: Some of the best minds in banking and finance have been struggling with this issue for years, but without much success. Of course, we should not expect an easy answer

---

[11] Over the latter part of this 10-year period, total assets grew at a slower rate such that the ratio of equity capital to total assets rose. In addition, the number of national banks declined by about one-half over this period to 3,075 (1994) and 2,858 (1995). As of December 31, 1995, there were 9,941 insured commercial banks.

to a complex problem. Nevertheless, the financial-management approach of this book suggests a reasonable answer: "The adequacy of a bank's capital depends on its risk exposure. More risk requires more capital." This proposition is nothing more than the basic risk-return trade-off expressed in terms of bank capital as a cushion or buffer for absorbing unexpected losses.

Risk Management and Regulatory Capital Standards

A financial-management standard mandates that a bank's capital adequacy reflects its risk exposure. In this context, the issue of capital adequacy ties directly to risk management, which is as much art as science. In July 1988, the Basle Accord on International Convergence of Capital Measurement and Capital Standards was established. By mandating risk-based capital requirements for all banks regardless of their size, this agreement marked a formal linkage between bank capital and risk management. The original Basle agreement, however, was narrowly focused solely on **credit risk.** Its basic premise is that the riskier a bank's assets, whether on or off the balance sheet, the more capital is required to support them, hence the term **risk-based capital requirements.** By December 31, 1992, all U.S. commercial banks and bank holding companies had to meet the minimum risk-based capital requirements established jointly by the Federal Reserve, the Office of the Comptroller of the Currency (OCC), and the Federal Deposit Insurance Corporation (FDIC).[12] Although risk-based capital requirements are a step in the right direction, a comprehensive measure of capital adequacy must account for all the major risks banks face—the financial-management standard. This task, however, is easier said than done. For example, after years of attempting to devise a capital standard for interest-rate risk, U.S. banking agencies abandoned such efforts in 1996 (Fox [1996c]). For banks with actively traded securities in efficient markets, the values of their assets and liabilities are adjusted for all available information flows. Two problems exist, however, with a market-valuation approach to capital adequacy: (1) Most banks do not have actively traded equity; (2) those that do may not be accurately measuring their risk exposures and may be imperfectly gauging how much capital to set aside for future fluctuations in the values of their assets and liabilities, whether on or off their balance sheets. Consolidation and the further development of tools for risk management will mitigate these problems. For example, if the Fed's prediction of 2,000 bank holding companies by the year 2016 holds true, more of these organizations will have actively traded common stock and be subject to market discipline. However, because the artsy, or judgment, part of risk management cannot be eliminated, determining the adequacy of bank capital will continue to be a financial-management challenge.

Since 1988, the Basle Committee has been struggling to incorporate an array of risks, beyond credit risk, into risk-based capital requirements. Starting in 1998, the 25 or so largest U.S. banks will have to meet a standardized market-risk capital formula. The objective of this standard is to translate the estimated change in the value of a bank's portfolio (i.e., market risk) into a fair capital standard. In January 1996, the Basle Committee formalized its 1998 capital agreement by letting banks choose between a regulatory formula and their own computer models to determine how much capital to set aside for market risk.[13] The notion of a market-risk

---

[12] These standards, which are discussed later in this chapter, are summarized in Table 13-1.

[13] Appendix B of this chapter focuses on market risk and on bank computer models for measuring market risk, e.g., J. P. Morgan's RiskMetrics™.

capital formula comes closest to a comprehensive measure of capital adequacy that accounts for all the major risks banks face.

We can use the **confidence function** (equation [13-5]) to illustrate how a comprehensive measure of capital adequacy would incorporate all the relevant risk exposures a bank faces. Taking the government guarantee and quality of information as given, confidence becomes a function of earnings volatility and the **market value of bank equity** (NW*). Earnings volatility arises from unexpected changes in commodity prices, interest rates, and exchange rates, as well as the interaction among these underlying variables. In a static framework, as each of these underlying variables deteriorates, real or economic bank capital should increase to attempt to offset the increased risk exposure. In a dynamic situation with all factors changing simultaneously, the net effect on confidence would depend on the various interaction effects. On balance, as overall risk increases, bank capital, which is the cushion or buffer available to absorb losses, should increase. The idea behind a market-risk formula is to measure a bank's future risk exposure from all sources and to require the bank to set aside enough (or adequate) capital to cover the exposures or loss potential. The questions of adequacy and measurement represent the heart of the dilemma of bank capital management.

Look Ma, No Risk!

At one time or another in our earliest bicycle-riding days, we might have yelled to our mothers: "Look Ma, no hands!" What if a financial institution could yell to the marketplace (like its mother): "Look Ma, no risk!" In this situation, how much leverage (the finance term for capital adequacy) would the marketplace allow? Again, we are not concerned with the absolute or dollar amount of capital (or leverage) but with the relative amount. We can answer unambiguously that relative to a financial institution with risk exposure (say, credit and interest rate), the firm without risk would be permitted a higher degree of financial leverage (i.e., a lower level of relative capital adequacy).

To illustrate such a trade-off, let me introduce you to **Sallie Mae** and tell you about her leverage. You may have heard about her three mortgage cousins: Ginnie Mae, Fannie Mae, and Freddy Mac.[14] Sallie Mae is the nickname for the Student Loan Marketing Association, which was created by the U.S. Congress in 1972. Sallie Mae, now a stockholder-owned corporation, is the leading provider of financial services for postsecondary education needs. It primarily provides funding and servicing support for education loans to students and their parents. In a nutshell, Sallie Mae operates a secondary market for qualifying student loans. In addition, it provides financing to colleges and universities for facilities and equipment.

With a portfolio of about $35.3 billion in student loans (as of year-end 1995), Sallie Mae is the major player in the market for guaranteed student loans. What

---

[14] In general, these organizations are referred to as government-sponsored enterprises (GSEs). They are financial intermediaries chartered by the federal government to increase the flow of credit to designated uses such as housing, agriculture, or education. GSEs borrow funds in public markets and lend to private parties. They differ from government agencies because they are owned by private stockholders. Like federally insured intermediaries, however, they benefit from an implicit federal guarantee (G). As of this writing, the latest proposed GSEs (H. R. 3167, the "Baker Bill") are Enterprise Resource Banks (ERBs), which are designed to permit member banks to borrow from them on collateral in the form of loans to rural areas or inner cities or any loans to any small businesses. According to the Shadow Financial Regulatory Committee (Statement No. 133, May 6, 1996), ERBs, which are existing Federal Home Loan Banks, are "likely to become the Godzilla of GSEs." Needless to say, the Shadow Financial Regulatory Committee strongly opposes the proposed legislation.

makes Sallie Mae unique is that she can say with a straight face, "Look Ma, no risk!" Sallie Mae can speak with such verisimilitude because she has a portfolio that is free of both credit risk and interest-rate risk. (She is, however, still subject to operating risks, but we will ignore that little white lie—for the moment.) Sallie Mae's credit risk is absorbed by her uncle, Sam (the sugar daddy and creator of huge deficits), in the form of the federal guarantee that stands behind student loans. All federal guarantees, of course, are financed by U.S. taxpayers. (By the way, student loan defaults cost U.S. taxpayers millions of dollars each year, e.g., about $1.6 billion in 1987.)

Regarding interest-rate risk, Sallie Mae runs, for the most part, an immunized or hedged portfolio because she borrows funds at the 91-day T-bill rate plus 30 or 40 basis points, and lends funds at the same T-bill rate plus 325 basis points (350 basis points for loans made prior to November 16, 1986). Sallie Mae lends by buying loans from originators of student loans (e.g., banks and thrifts). In the process, of course, she provides liquidity to the originators.[15]

Now that we know what Sallie Mae does, let's look at her leverage. At year-end 1990, she had an equity multiplier of 37.6, which means $37.6 in assets for every one dollar of equity capital. With an *ROA* of about 0.75 percent, Sallie Mae's 1990 *ROE* was slightly over 28 percent (i.e., $0.0075 \times 37.6 = 0.282$). Before the 1980s, when the credit and interest-rate risks of banking were not so obvious, some money-center banks had similarly sized equity multipliers and returns. If we focus on Sallie Mae's "capital adequacy," she had a capital-to-asset ratio of 2.66 percent. In contrast, as of 1992, commercial banks had to maintain an equity capital ratio of 4 percent and a total capital ratio of 8 percent (against risk-adjusted assets). By year-end 1995, Sallie Mae's equity multiplier was 46.2, consisting of total assets of $50 billion and shareholders' equity of $1.081 billion. Because commercial banks cannot say, "Look Ma, no risk," they should be expected to have less leverage, or higher capital ratios than an almost risk-free intermediary. Compared to Sallie Mae, the average commercial bank has a portfolio exposed to unexpected changes in commodity prices, interest rates, and exchange rates. In the final analysis, the amount of capital a bank should have depends on its risk profile.

Oops, What about Sallie Mae's Operating Risks?

During the summer of 1990, Sallie Mae was hit by credit problems and allegations of fraud (Matthews [1990]). The troubles stemmed from the disclosure that the Higher Education Assistance Foundation (HEAF), a major client located in Overland, Kansas, was near insolvency. On the heels of this disclosure came news in October 1990 that two former employees of the Foundation had allegedly overbilled Sallie Mae (a moral-hazard problem). The adverse information sent Sallie Mae's stock price plummeting from the mid-$50s to an all-time low of $33.50 on October 31, 1990. During May of 1991, however, the stock rebounded to the mid-$50s.[16] Matthews [1990] attributed Sallie Mae's quick rebound to four factors: (1) addressing its problems quickly and efficiently, (2) the sale of student loans to it by banks

---

[15] Three brief but interesting articles on Sallie Mae can be found in Kantrow [1990], Novack [1988], and Strauss [1987]. The data presented in this paragraph and the next one are from these sources and from the Sallie Mae "home page" on the WWW. Matthews [1990] discusses Sallie Mae's problems in 1990.

[16] Sallie Mae closed at $92.625 (NYSE, December 23, 1996). Its previous 52-week high was $98.25, with a low of $63.25. Its *P/E* was 13, *EPS* of $1.76, and dividend yield of 1.9 percent.

trying to reduce their assets to meet capital requirements,[17] (3) the initiation of an aggressive stock repurchase program that resulted in two million shares taken off the market (as of November 21, 1990), and (4) the Department of Education signing an agreement with HEAF confirming its backing of the suspect student loans and relieving Sallie Mae of liability. Look Ma, no credit risk—with Big Brother's backing!

BANK CAPITAL STRUCTURE AND BOOKKEEPING

A firm's capital structure usually is defined in terms of its debt-to-asset or debt-to-equity ratio. Given the following balance sheet,

$$\text{Assets } (A) = \text{Debt } (D) + \text{Equity } (E) \qquad \qquad \textbf{(13-6)}$$

with $A = 100$, $D = 95$, and $E = 5$, the two ratios are $D/A = 0.95$ and $D/E = 19$. For banks, we can describe leverage in terms of the equity multiplier (EM = assets/equity) and the reciprocal of EM, the ratio of equity to assets. In this example, $EM = 20$ and the equity-to-asset ratio is 0.05. Now if someone were to suggest that we take five of the debt and call it "regulatory capital," we would be justified in questioning the logic of such a move.[18] This revised capital structure would have $D/A = 0.90$ and $D/E = 9$. Using bank measures, EM would equal 10, or a capital-to-asset ratio of 0.10. Our gut reaction is to dismiss the revised capital structure as a figment of someone's imagination. After all, debt is debt and equity is equity. Isn't defining a portion of debt as equity like calling an orange an apple? If this is *Alice in Wonderland*, how can we expect to apply modern financial theory to it?

The Many Veils of Bank Bookkeeping[19]

Most businesses keep at least two sets of books: one for the tax collector and one for the accountant/auditor. Banks keep in addition another set of books for the regulator.[20] In finance and economics, however, the only books that count are those

---

[17] Regarding the sale of student loans by banks to Sallie Mae, Matthews reported (as of November 21, 1990) that commercial banks held an estimated $21 billion, or 40 percent of the $52 billion in outstanding student loans. Citicorp, Chase Manhattan, and Manufacturers Hanover (now part of Chase) were estimated to hold about $5 billion, or almost one-fourth of total bank student loans. With many banks between a rock and a hard place, especially the three mentioned above, Sallie Mae was able to extract favorable premiums on purchased student loans, called a "bluebird sale" because of the favorable terms to the buyer. At that time, analysts expected Sallie Mae's annual market share of student-loan servicing to grow between 2 and 3 percent in the early 1990s, which was expected to support earnings growth of 15 to 20 percent. From a bank financial-management perspective, the important point is that loan sales permit a bank to improve its capital adequacy, all other things being equal.

[18] The issue here is which financial instruments should count as regulatory capital. Berger, Herring, and Szego ([1995], p. 408) state that the components of regulatory capital should have three main characteristics: (1) As claims, they should be junior to those of the deposit insurer (the buffer or cushion function); (2) they should be "patient money" or long-dated instruments that provide a stable source of funds during periods of financial distress; and (3) they should reduce the moral-hazard incentives to exploit the federal safety net.

[19] Think of these bookkeeping veils in terms of the transparency, which was introduced in chapters 1 and 2.

[20] Some bankers have been known to keep another set of more private books (hidden information). For example, C. Arnholt Smith, the head of USNB of San Diego (a 1973 failure), kept some of his bank's records at his personal residence to hide them from bank examiners. The Butcher brothers of Tennessee (Jake and C. H., who ran United American Bank of Knoxville, a 1978 failure) kept "portable books" that they shuttled from one of their banks to another to hide bad loans from the FDIC. More recently, Nicholas Leeson was successful in hiding huge losses on futures trades that led to the collapse of Barings Bank (Great Britain) in 1995. Kuprianov [1995] describes the derivatives debacles of Barings and Metallgesellschaft, while Sinkey [1979] analyzes U.S. bank failures of the 1970s.

kept by the marketplace. Unfortunately, with thousands of closely held community banks in the United States, market values are not readily available. Moreover, even for banks with actively traded shares (the *American Banker* reports share prices for about 225 commercial banks and the top 25 thrift institutions), the lack of active secondary markets for most of the assets held by banks (securitization, of course, is helping to change this) makes it difficult to estimate the market value of bank assets. Nevertheless, capital markets for banks with actively traded equity securities have been found to be at least weak-form efficient.

If we set aside the books kept by banks for the tax collector, banks adhere to three different accounting standards:

1. **Book-value accounting** (GAAP)

2. **Regulatory accounting** (RAP)

3. **Market-value accounting**

The first two standards are referred to as GAAP and RAP, respectively, which stand for generally accepted accounting principles and regulatory accounting procedures. In getting at market values, it is necessary to cut through the veils of GAAP and RAP. Although this double-veiled two-step is not as exciting as the dance of the seven veils, it can be just as revealing once the veils are removed.

The GAAP Veil on Bank Capital

Most bank accounting records are kept on a *book value* or *historical cost* basis. To measure bank capital or accounting net worth, one simply subtracts the book value of liabilities from the book value of assets—nothing more than the accounting identity rearranged as $NW = A - L$. As long as $NW > 0$, the bank is book-value solvent. When $NW < 0$, the bank is book-value insolvent. What counts here, of course, is the market value of equity, or NW^* from our confidence function (13-5). The market value of equity represents the real net worth available for settling claims. It is important to recognize that a bank can be book-value solvent but insolvent on a market-value basis. Such a situation could exist because a bank has not adjusted its loan-loss reserves to accurately reflect the true quality of its loan portfolio, or because assets have not been marked-to-market to reflect changes in interest rates or exchange rates.

When book and market values diverge, one gets a distorted view of bank capital and its adequacy. To illustrate, consider the book value of shareholders' equity for a **money-center bank** compared to the market value of its equity at the height of the international debt crisis or at the height of the crisis in commercial-real-estate lending. Or consider the book value of an S&L's net worth relative to the market value of its equity during the height of the thrift crisis. Expressed in terms of ratios of market values to book values, we would get market-to-book ratios less than one. The important point is that devalued assets, whether in the form of underwater mortgages or questionable loans, must be marked-to-market if the accounting veil of book values is to be pierced.

Regarding book values, Miller ([1995], pp. 483–484) told an interesting story at a conference dealing with capital requirements in banking. The setting is the early 1980s. A banker was lamenting the loss of profitable investment opportunities because banks did not have enough capital. Miller suggested a simple solution: Raise more capital. The banker responded: "They can't. It's too expensive. Their stock is selling for only 50 percent of book value." Miller's counterthrust was, "Book values have nothing to do with the cost of equity capital. That's just the market's way of saying, We gave those guys a dollar and they managed to turn it into 50 cents."[21] Touché! The audience of bankers, many of whom had stocks selling for even less than 50 percent of book value, became uncomfortable. Looking out the window, Miller saw a platoon of Revolutionary War soldiers (the conference was in colonial Williamsburg, Virginia) marching toward the Town Hall where the conference was being held. My God, he thought, the bankers have sent for the firing squad! Needless to say, Miller did not get shot. The moderator, however, did shoot him down by not letting him speak again that day.

The RAP Veil on Bank Capital

One of the worst elements of RAP is its treatment of bank capital. The crazy-quilt regulation of bank capital can be traced to two sources: (1) the notion that bank regulators are captives or pawns of the industry, and (2) the tendency of the regulators to handle problems with stopgap measures and patchwork methods. Both of these points are illustrated by the RAP treatment of bank capital. No rational lender would look at a would-be borrower's reserve for bad debts as part of the firm's capital, or at part of the firm's subordinated debt as the equivalent of equity capital. The banks love this double standard because they would not want to be scrutinized in the same way that they look at their customers' balance sheets. "Do as I say, not as I do" reflects the bankers' higher capital standards for their customers compared to themselves. A dual explanation for this double standard, and the creative accounting associated with it, focuses on two ideas: (1) Regulators are "in the industry's hip pocket" or "pawns of the industry," and (2) regulators tend to protect their own turf and to tell Congress that everything is all right at any cost (e.g., the thrift and bank insurance crises).

RISK-BASED CAPITAL REQUIREMENTS: A STEP IN THE RIGHT DIRECTION

On January 27, 1988, the U.S. federal banking agencies announced their plan for **risk-based capital requirements.**[22] Table 13-1 shows these capital definitions and standards. Because the new RAP veils are a little more transparent than the old ones, some analysts see the plan as a step in the right direction.[23] The requirements are the response by U.S. bank regulators to an agreement for risk-based international

---

[21] Recall the discussion of hidden capital in chapter 3. When hidden capital does not exist, market value and book value are equal. Hidden capital, of course, can be a positive or negative amount. When the ratio of market value to book value is less than one (as described in Miller's story), then hidden capital is negative. In Miller's words, you gave the firm a dollar and its managers turned it into 50 cents for you.

[22] Prior to 1985, RAP capital requirements varied with bank size, with large banks permitted to have lower standards. On March 11, 1986, however, the FDIC and OCC adopted common definitions of capital for commercial banks. Shortly afterwards, the Federal Reserve adopted identical guidelines for member banks and bank holding companies. The rules raised total capital levels to 6 percent of total assets and required that "primary capital" be 5.5 percent of assets. The definitions of capital were, *primary capital* consisted of shareholders' equity (including equity reserves), perpetual preferred stock, reserves for loan and lease losses, some mandatory convertible debt, minority interests in consolidated subsidiaries, and net worth certificates. Total capital consisted of primary capital plus secondary capital, where *secondary capital* was defined to include only limited-life preferred stock and subordinated notes and debentures. Secondary capital was limited to 50 percent of primary capital.

[23] For a contrary view, see "Statement of the Shadow Financial Regulatory Committee on Regulatory Proposal for Risk-Related Capital Standards" [February 8, 1988]. Bhala [1989] presents a detailed analysis of the risk-based capital guidelines established by U.S. bank regulators.

TABLE 13-1	Capital Standards for U.S. Commercial Banks and Bank Holding Companies (established in 1988, fully effective in 1992)

Capital Definitions and Standards

Core Capital (Tier 1) consists of common stockholders' equity plus noncumulative perpetual preferred stock and any related surplus plus minority interest in the equity accounts of consolidated subsidiaries less goodwill and other intangibles with the exception of identified intangibles that satisfy the criteria included in the guidelines (existing goodwill was grandfathered for the transition period 1988 to 1992). By 1992, core capital must equal or exceed 4 percent of weighted-risk assets.

Supplementary Capital (Tier 2) consists of allowance for losses on loans and leases (general reserves only); cumulative perpetual, long-term and convertible preferred stock; perpetual debt and other hybrid debt/equity instruments; intermediate-term preferred stock and term subordinated debt. The total of Tier 2 is limited to 100 percent of Tier 1 (amounts in excess of this limitation are permitted but do not qualify as capital). Within Tier 2, loan-loss reserves are limited by 1992 to 1.25 percent of weighted-risk assets, and subordinated debt and intermediate-term preferred stock (which are amortized for capital purposes as they approach maturity) are limited to 50 percent of Tier 1. The other components of Tier 2 have no limits, and amounts in excess of components with limitations are permitted but do not qualify as capital.

Deductions from total capital (Tier 1 plus Tier 2) consist of investments in unconsolidated banking and finance subsidiaries, reciprocal holdings of capital securities, and other deductions (such as other subsidiaries or joint ventures) as determined by supervisory authority with handling on a case-by-case basis or as a matter of policy after formal rule making.

Total capital (Tier 1 + Tier 2 − Deductions) must equal or exceed 8 percent of weighted-risk assets.

Risk categories and weights
1. Category 1 (e.g., cash and equivalents): Zero percent
2. Category 2 (e.g., short-term claims maturing in one year or less): 20 percent
3. Category 3 (e.g., one–four family residential mortgages): 50 percent
4. Category 4 (e.g., commercial and consumer loans): 100 percent

Note: Some differences exist between the requirements for BHCs and those for banks. For example, BHCs may count cumulative perpetual preferred stock as part of Tier 1 capital, whereas banks may not. See Bhala [1989], p. 57. Preferred stock is stock that pays a fixed dividend and has a claim to assets ahead of common stockholders. Perpetual preferred stock has no stated maturity and cannot be redeemed. Because limited-life preferred stock has a maturity of at least 25 years, intermediate-term preferred has a maturity of less than 25 years. Subordinated debt represents a claim against assets that is lower ranking ("junior to") than other obligations and is paid after holders of "senior" debt. It is frequently listed as "subordinated notes and debentures."

Source: "Rules and Regulation," *Federal Register* Vol. 54, No. 17, (Friday, January 27, 1989, pp. 4183–4184, as filed by Robert L. Clarke, Comptroller of the Currency).

capital standards established by the Bank for International Settlements on December 10, 1987. The accord, which was reached by the Basle Committee on Banking Regulations and Supervisory Practices, called for international convergence of capital measurement and capital standards in 12 developed countries. The Basle Committee comprised representatives of the central banks and supervisory authorities of Belgium, Canada, France, Germany, Italy, Japan, Luxembourg, Netherlands, Sweden, Switzerland, United Kingdom, and the United States. Each country was responsible for constructing its own capital plan within the framework (and spirit) of the international agreement. The purpose of the international plan was to promote more equitable competition as well as increased safety for the international financial system. Both U.S. bank regulators and the Bank of England have adopted conservative interpretations of the international agreement; in contrast, Japanese regulators have been less conservative.

The foundations of the Basle Agreement are two pillars: **capital** and **credit risk.** The capital pillar recognizes bank capital for its ability to absorb losses. Thus, as Bhala [1989] notes, the constituent parts of capital depend on their substance (i.e., ability to absorb loss) rather than their form (i.e., common stock, preferred stock, goodwill, loan-loss reserves, etc.). Although credit risk has been the major risk faced by commercial banks in the past and most likely will be the critical risk for the future, the Basle Agreement ignores other sources of bank risk, for example, interest-rate and foreign-exchange risks, operating risk, and liquidity risk. The link between capital and credit risk is the capital's ability to absorb losses due to default by banks' customers. To the extent that off-balance-sheet activities (OBSAs) involve credit risk, they are subject to capital requirements.[24]

On balance, although the risk-based capital requirements established by the Basle Agreement are a step in the right direction, the requirements suffer from myopia because they explicitly recognize only credit risk and ignore other forms of bank risk. Nevertheless, a journey of a thousand miles starts with the first step.

Tier 1 and Tier 2 Capital for U.S. Banks and BHCs

The definitions of bank capital mandated by U.S. bank regulators recognize two types of capital (Table 13-1): (1) **Tier 1** (core) **capital** defined as common stockholders' equity plus perpetual preferred stock (and any related surplus) plus minority interest in the equity accounts of consolidated subsidiaries minus goodwill and other intangibles (with the exception of identified intangibles that satisfy the criteria in the guidelines), and (2) **Tier 2** (supplemental) **capital** defined as allowance for losses on loans and leases (general reserves only; some countries, but not the United States, permit "undisclosed" reserves); cumulative perpetual, long-term and convertible **preferred stock;** perpetual debt and other hybrid debt-equity instruments; and intermediate-term preferred stock and term subordinated debt. The total of Tier 2 is limited to 100 percent of Tier 1, although amounts in excess of this limitation are permitted but do not qualify as capital. Within Tier 2, loan-loss reserves are limited by 1992 to 1.25 percent of weighted-risk assets, and subordinated debt and intermediate-term preferred stock (which are amortized for capital purposes as they approach maturity) are limited to 50 percent of Tier 1. The other components of Tier 2 have no limits, and amounts in excess of components with limitations are permitted but do not qualify as capital.

Tier 1 plus Tier 2 capital makes up a bank's total capital, which by 1992 had to be a *minimum* of 8 percent of risk-adjusted assets. Moreover, a minimum of one-half of the total capital must be in the form of core or Tier 1 capital (i.e., 4 percent of risk-adjusted assets must be in the form of core capital). A five-year transition period (1987 to 1992) was established for the new capital standards. At year-end 1990 and 1991, U.S. banks had to meet an interim standard of 7.25 percent for total capital with a pure equity standard of approximately 3.625 percent.

To summarize, U.S. banks were on a 6 percent capital standard for 1988 and 1989 (under the old definitions of capital and relative to total assets; see footnote

---

[24] Bhala ([1989], p. 190) notes that it is "curious" that the Basle Agreement uses the concept of replacement cost to measure the credit risk of swaps. This usage puts the nondefaulting party (e.g., the bank) back in the position it was in just before the default. Bhala also finds it "curious" that the Basle Agreement focuses on the distribution of interest- and currency-rate movements in measuring swap-replacement costs. The curiosity is that looking at such movements recognizes the importance of interest-rate and foreign-exchange risks for swaps but ignores these risks for different kinds of swaps (e.g., hedging versus speculative ones) and for items on banks' balance sheets.

22), and on a 7.25 percent standard for 1990–1991 followed by the 8 percent standard for year-end 1992 and beyond (under the new definitions and relative to risk-adjusted assets; see Table 13-1).

Risk Categories and Risk Weights for U.S. Banks and BHCs

Because the Basle Agreement focuses on credit risk and ignores other forms of bank risk, its risk-weighting system is based solely on credit or default risk (i.e., the probability of default). The original Basle Agreement called for five risk classes with weights of 0, .10, .20, .50, and 1.0, as perceived credit risk increases. The highest risk class (1.0) is referred to as the "standard" risk class. U.S. bank regulators subsequently established the following weighted-risk system for on-balance-sheet activities based on only four risk classes:

1. Category 1 (e.g., cash and equivalents): zero percent
2. Category 2 (e.g., short-term claims maturing in one year or less): 20 percent
3. Category 3 (e.g., one–four family residential mortgages): 50 percent
4. Category 4 (e.g., commercial and consumer loans): 100 percent

Given these weights, the corresponding minimum total capital requirement for each risk category is 0 percent, 1.6 percent ($= .2 \times .08$), 4 percent ($= .5 \times .08$), and 8 percent ($= 1.0 \times .08$). The formulas for *minimum* required capital for each on-balance-sheet item are

$$\text{Required core or Tier 1 capital} = \text{risk weight} \times 4 \text{ percent}$$

and

$$\text{Required total capital (Tier 1 + Tier 2)} = \text{risk weight} \times 8 \text{ percent}$$

Additional details of the risk-weighted categories along with sample calculations are presented in appendix A of this chapter.

Neither the concept nor the attempt to implement risk-based capital requirements is new. However, because of the recent surge and concern about off-balance-sheet activities (OBSAs, see chapter 9), the requirement that banks allocate capital for these activities is new. For example, standby letters of credit (SLCs serving as financial guarantees) are assigned a 100 percent conversion factor, which means that for each $100 of SLCs a bank will need $4 of equity plus $4 of supplemental capital for a total capital requirement of $8. The other three conversion factors are 50 percent (e.g., unused lines of credit with an original maturity longer than one year), 20 percent (e.g., commercial letters of credit), and zero percent (e.g., unused commitments with an original maturity of less than one year). The appendix to this chapter presents a complete description of the conversion factors for OBSAs.

Letting A1 through A4 represent the total on- and off-balance-sheet assets in the four risk categories, and letting E and T represent equity (core or Tier 1) capital and total (core + supplemental or Tier 1 + Tier 2) capital, respectively, the *minimum* capital standards that U.S. commercial banks and bank holding companies must meet are as follows:

$$T = .08\,[0\,(A1) + .20\,(A2) + .50\,(A3) + 1.0\,(A4)] \tag{13-7}$$

$$E = .50T = .04\,[0\,(A1) + .20\,(A2) + .50\,(A3) + 1.0\,(A4)] \tag{13-8}$$

How Banks Adjusted to Risk-Based Capital Standards

Capital-deficient banks/BHCs have essentially three ways of meeting risk-based capital standards: (1) Increase their capital, (2) change the composition of their risk-adjusted assets, including their OBSAs, or (3) shrink their assets. In practice, banks under the heaviest pressure to adjust did all three things. First, they increased capital, in the short run, by either cutting dividends or raising external capital or both, and in the long run, they attempted to improve their profitability. Second, they realigned their on- and off-balance-sheet portfolios away from the higher risk asset categories (i.e., A3 and A4 in equations [13-7] and [13-8]) toward the lower risk ones (i.e., A1 and A2). And third, they shrank their asset size by restricting growth or by selling assets or both. Regarding the last point, from December 31, 1989, to December 31, 1990, Citicorp and Chase Manhattan, the first- and third-largest BHCs in the United States at the time, reduced their total assets from $230 billion to $217 billion ($-5.6\%$) and from $107 billion to $98 billion ($-8.4\%$), respectively. In contrast, BankAmerica, on the rebound from its slump during most of the 1980s, moved to second place (at the time) in the size rankings, as its total assets grew from $98.8 billion (1989) to $110.7 billion (1990), a 12 percent increase.

On balance, the fewer riskier assets (loans), off-balance-sheet activities (OBSAs), and intangible assets (e.g., goodwill) a bank had relative to its equity capital, the easier it was for it to adjust to risk-based capital requirements. Since large banks, and especially the money-center institutions, typically did *not* fit this description, they faced the most difficult adjustments over the transition period 1989 to 1992.[25] Table 13-2 shows how large banks and various bank size classes fared under risk-based capital standards.

Panel A of Table 13-2 shows that, as of December 31, 1990, 15 banks (not BHCs) out of the 50 largest U.S. banks were shy of the 8 percent standard for the risk-based total capital ratio. Excluding the failed Bank of New England, which was acquired by Fleet/Norstar in April 1991, Maryland National Bank, Baltimore, had the lowest total capital ratio, at 5.63 percent with a Tier 1 ratio of 3.43 percent. Panel B of Table 13-2 shows that as of December 31, 1989, 642 commercial banks were capital deficient under the 8 percent standard and that they needed $34.6 billion in total capital to remedy the deficiency. Of the 642 banks, 98 banks with assets greater than $1 billion (15%) accounted for $33.1 billion (96%) of the total capital shortfall.

The Important Role of Retained Earnings

The major source of capital for banks, especially smaller ones without access to capital markets, is **retained earnings.** For a particular year, this internally generated capital equals a bank's net income minus its total dividend payment, that is,

Addition to retained earnings (ΔRE) = Net income (NI) $-$ Dividends (D)

When dividend payments exceed net income, then, of course, the addition to retained earnings is negative. When a bank is financially distressed, it usually cuts or eliminates its dividend to mitigate the adverse effect of low or negative net income. In good times when competitive or regulatory pressures exist to bolster capital, a bank attempts to improve its bottom-line earnings so that larger additions to

---

[25] In previous chapters, we have shown that the volumes of loans and OBSAs vary directly with bank size.

TABLE 13-2   How U.S. Commercial Banks Fared under Risk-Based Capital Requirements

Panel A. Commercial Banks Among the 50 Largest Banks Failing to Meet the 1992 8 Percent Capital Standard (as of December 31, 1990)

	Assets ($)	Tier 1 Ratio	Total Cap. Ratio (%)
Citibank, New York	157.8	4.88%	7.76
Chase Manhattan Bank, New York	73.4	4.08	7.44
Security Pacific National Bank, Los Angeles	55.7	5.67	7.44
Wells Fargo Bank, San Francisco	53.8	5.15	7.84
Bank of New York	42.4	5.22	7.42
First National Bank, Chicago	36.0	4.90	7.50
Continental Bank, Chicago	26.7	7.17	7.53
First National Bank, Boston	24.9	4.90	7.40
National Westmister Bank USA, New York	16.2	4.96	7.32
Sovran Bank, Richmond	14.3	6.78	7.53
Maryland National Bank, Baltimore	14.2	3.43	5.63
Bank of New England, Boston[a]	13.4	NA	NA
Commerce Bank—Detroit	10.4	6.61	7.83
Meridian Bank, Reading, Pa.	10.2	5.41	7.42
Harris Trust & Savings Bank, Chicago	10.0	6.71	7.38
Assets of the 15 banks	$559.6		
Assets of the top 50 banks	$1,335.6		

Note: Total assets in billions of dollars.

[a]The FDIC reported that Bank of New England's ratios were below the 1992 minimum levels. NA indicates not available.

Source: Data from call reports in *American Banker* (March 28, 1991), p. 12.

Panel B. Estimated Capital-Deficient and Capital-Surplus Banks Under the 8 Percent Risk-Based Capital Requirement (December 31, 1989)

Asset Size		Capital Deficit		Capital Surplus		
		More Than + 2% of Assets	0% to + 2% of Assets	0% to + 3% of Assets	More Than + 3% of Assets	Totals
Small banks: up to $250 million	Number	188	280	3,068	8,020	11,556
	Assets	$8,172	$17,877	$222,681	$394,805	$643,535
	Surplus/deficit	($564)	($125)	$4,256	$22,676	$26,243
Mid-sized banks: $250 million–$1 billion	Number	15	61	458	239	773
	Assets	$7,720	$31,637	$211,306	$97,247	$347,910
	Surplus/deficit	($573)	($230)	$3,332	$4,615	$7,144
Large banks: greater than $1 billion	Number	26	72	242	37	377
	Assets	$647,689	$525,938	$1,044,076	$89,977	$2,307,679
	Surplus/deficit	($28,852)	($4,284)	$9,411	$4,363	($19,361)
All commercial banks	Number	229	413	3,768	8,296	12,706
	Assets	$663,581	$575,452	$1,478,063	$582,028	$3,299,124
	Surplus/deficit	($29,989)	($4,639)	$17,000	$31,654	$14,026

Source: Adapted from data compiled by Petty [1991], Exhibit 3, p. 54.

retained earnings can be made, while dividend payments are maintained or even increased.

Table 13-3 presents some interesting data in the form of additions to retained earnings by bank size class for the years 1985 to 1995. The column for all banks shows that the years 1987 and 1989 to 1991 were particularly lean for the industry's addition to retained earnings. These data also say something about how unreal the earnings of the industry were in 1985, 1986, and 1988. The underlying causes of the scarce additions to retained earnings were the loan-loss provisions associated with the LDC debt crisis for the years 1987 and 1989 and loan-loss provisions for the crisis in commercial-real-estate lending in 1990 and 1991. Of course, underlying these loan losses were bad loans. As the data for the size classes show, the 100 largest banks were largely responsible for the $8 billion decline in retained earnings in 1987, with the 10 largest banks reducing their retained earnings by $7.5 bil-

TABLE 13-3 Additions to Retained Earnings by Bank Size, 1985–1995

Year	All Banks $mils	All Banks % of Assets	Ten Largest Banks $mils	Ten Largest Banks % of Assets	Ratio of ΔRE Top Ten to ΔRE All Banks
1985	9,321	0.36	1,421	0.22	15.2%
1986	7,994	0.29	1,702	0.25	21.3
1987	−8,332	−0.29	−7,463	−1.08	89.6
1988	8,496	0.28	4,726	0.69	55.6
1989	729	0.02	−3,950	−0.57	−541.8
1990	1,646	0.05	1,522	0.21	92.5
1991	2,292	0.07	36	0.005	1.6
1992	17,050	0.50	3,332	0.43	19.5
1993	20,873	0.59	6,953	0.85	33.4
1994	16,436	0.43	3,132	0.33	19.1
1995	17,814	0.43	3,258	0.31	18.3

Year	Banks Ranked 11–100 $mils	Banks Ranked 11–100 % of Assets	Banks Ranked 101–1,000 $mils	Banks Ranked 101–1,000 % of Assets	All Other Banks $mils	All Other Banks % of Assets
1985	3,206	0.48	2,871	0.45	1,863	0.30
1986	2,867	0.39	2,343	0.33	1,038	0.16
1987	−3,449	−0.43	1,388	0.18	1,186	0.18
1988	783	0.09	1,510	0.18	1,373	0.21
1989	564	0.06	2,052	0.23	1,986	0.30
1990	−1,393	−0.14	−19	−0.02	1,634	0.24
1991	50	0.005	19	0.02	2,085	0.30
1992	5,817	0.58	4,259	0.44	3,694	0.53
1993	5,307	0.49	4,205	0.43	4,334	0.63
1994	4,334	0.36	4,954	0.48	3,938	0.58
1995	6,155	0.46	4,485	0.41	3,929	0.59

Note: Due to rounding the sum of the addition to retained earnings for the four size classes may not equal the figure for all banks.

Source: Figures for the size classes calculated from data presented in the *Federal Reserve Bulletin* (June 1995), pp. 560–569, and (June 1996), pp. 495–505.

lion whereas banks ranked 11–100 had a reduction of almost $3.5 billion. All other banks increased their retained earnings in 1987 by $2.6 billion.[26] In 1989, the 10 largest banks took another LDC hit, which reduced their retained earnings by almost $4 billion, or 542 percent of the industry's addition to retained earnings.

In the early 1990s, bank earnings and loan quality were adversely affected by problems associated with commercial-real-estate loans. As Table 13-3 shows, these financial difficulties were more widespread than the LDC debt crisis because they extend down through the 1,000 largest U.S. commercial banks. For example, for 1990, the banks ranked 11–100 and 101–1,000 had reductions in retained earnings of $1.3 billion and $94 million, respectively. For 1991, the 10 largest banks had an addition to retained earnings of only $72 million. In contrast, the years 1992 to 1994 were a gold mine for bank retained earnings. Over this period, the industry increased its retained earnings by more than $54.4 billion dollars, or 0.5 percent of its assets. Across the four size classes, the additions were $13.4 billion (ten largest banks), $15.5 billion (banks ranked 11–100), $13.5 billion (banks ranked 101–1,000), and $12 billion (banks not ranked among the 1,000 largest). As a percentage of group assets, the average ratios of additions to retained earnings to assets were 0.39 percent, 0.48 percent, 0.45 percent, and 0.58 percent, respectively.

Another interesting aspect of the data in Table 13-3 is the consistent performance of community banks (those not ranked among the 1,000 largest). Additions to retained earnings by these banks as a group have been steady, ranging between a low of 0.16 percent of their assets in 1986 and a high of 0.63 percent in 1993, and averaging 0.365 percent for the eleven-year period. The relatively low dollar figures and rates in 1986 and 1987 were due to the crisis in agricultural lending that hit mainly community banks.

The consistent performance of community banks with respect to additions to retained earnings is in sharp contrast to that of the 1,000 largest banks, and especially to that of the 100 largest banks. Because stability or variability of earnings (SOE in our confidence function) is a standard measure of risk in finance, these data suggest that because variability of (retained) earnings increases with bank size, that risk varied directly with size for U.S. commercial banks over the period 1985 to 1995. Moreover, with an eye toward the future, what happens to the industry tends to be dominated by the 1,000 largest banks and even more so by the 100 largest banks. Furthermore, how the 10 largest banks perform plays an even more critical role.

Recapitulation

During the years 1989 to 1990, when risk-based capital requirements were in the process of being imposed, almost 13,000 insured commercial banks existed. Of this total only about 5 percent of the banks failed to meet the new risk-based capital requirements. Of course, at that time, they did not have to meet the interim (1991) and final (1992) target ratios. On balance, meeting minimum risk-based capital requirements was a nonevent for 95 percent of the banking population. Additions to retained earnings represent a bank's major source of equity capital. Over the years 1992 to 1995, the banking industry generated $72.1 billion in additions to retained earnings, a sum that has substantially bolstered the capital adequacy of the industry and its banks.

---

[26] Due to rounding, the sum of the addition to retained earnings for the four size classes may not equal the figure for all banks. For example, the text figures for 1987 are $-7.5 - 3.4 + 2.6 = -8.3 \approx -8.332$.

The Leverage-Ratio Requirement for U.S. Banks and BHCs

At year-end 1990, banks/BHCs with the strongest regulatory performance ratings[27] had to meet a *minimum* leverage ratio of 3 percent. Other banks/BHCs with weaker ratings were required to have higher ratios. The leverage ratio defined as Tier 1 capital divided by average assets replaces the primary and total capital standards described in footnote 22. It is intended to supplement the risk-based ratios shown in Table 13-1. As with the risk-based capital requirements, most banks did not have problems meeting the 3 percent standard (Bailey and Valenza [1990]).

Market Values Cut the GAAP and RAP Veils

To cut the GAAP and RAP veils, all one has to do is to look at market values, if they are available. Using asterisks to indicate market values, equation (13-6) can be rewritten as

$$A^* = D^* + E^* \qquad \textbf{(13-6)}$$

In the marketplace, only the residual value of the balance-sheet identity is observed, that is, $E^* = A^* - D^*$. The total equity value of the firm is equal to

$$\text{Total market value of equity} = \text{price per share} \times \text{number of shares outstanding} \qquad \textbf{(13-9)}$$

Critics of market-value accounting pooh-pooh it because market values are more volatile than book values. Although this criticism is certainly valid, one has to weigh the trade-off between volatility and removing the GAAP and RAP veils such that true worth or economic value is observed.

Let's illustrate equation (13-9) for Citicorp and look at its market value of equity over time. On December 31, 1986, Citicorp's stock price was $53 per share. With 150,577,830 shares of common stock outstanding, its market value of equity was almost $8 billion. The book value of stockholders' equity was only slightly less, at almost $7.7 billion for a market-to-book ratio of 1.04, or 104 percent. With year-end 1986 total assets of $196 billion, the GAAP, RAP (using the 1985 definitions), and market-value versions of Citicorp's capital ratios were as follows:

Market value of equity/total assets	4.07%
Book value of equity/total assets (GAAP)	3.92%
Primary capital/total assets (RAP)	6.82%
Total capital/total assets (RAP)	10.88%

The important point is that GAAP and RAP measures of capital ratios do not reflect the real value of the relative buffer or cushion available for absorbing the realized risks of banking.

Moving ahead four years to December 31, 1990, the market value of Citicorp's common equity had fallen to $4.6 billion ($12.625 × 363,009,068). The price per share had declined by more than 75 percent, whereas the number of shares outstanding had more than doubled. Its market-to-book ratio had dropped to 0.56, and its ratio of market value of common equity to total assets was 2.1 percent, compared to the book-value ratio of 3.8 percent. Its Tier 1 and total capital ratios were 4.88 percent and 7.76 percent. At this time, some analysts dared to think that Citi-

---

[27] For banks, the regulatory rating is captured by the acronym CAMEL, which stand for capital (C), asset quality (A), management (M), earnings (E), and liquidity (L); for BHCs, BOPEC represents bank subsidiaries (B), other subsidiaries (O), parent company (P), consolidated earnings (E), and consolidated capital (C).

corp might be in danger of failing. A rescue plan, a sort of reverse Desert Storm, had been in the making, however, since 1987.

Not a White Knight But a Prince to the Rescue[28]

This story begins in late 1987, when Prince Alwaleed (bin Talal bin Abdulaziz Al-saud) of Saudi Arabia called one of his Swiss private bankers asking him to collect as much information as possible about U.S. money-center banks. By 1989, Al-waleed had invested close to $250 million in Citicorp, Chase Manhattan, Manufacturers Hanover, and Chemical.[29] He then decided to sell everything and concentrate on Citicorp, amassing 4.9 percent of Citicorp's common stock at an average price of about $12 per share. His thinking, according to Rossant ([1995], p. 94), was that Chase and Chemical were too concentrated in New York and lacked the global perspective and presence of Citicorp. Of the four BHCs, Citicorp was the worst performer, but it was relatively cheap. As noted above, Citicorp's stock price had declined from $53 (1986) to $12.625 (1990).

The prince's big move came during the Gulf War. Negotiations between Al-waleed's lawyers and Citicorp in 1991 were lengthy and were interrupted several times by Iraqi attacks. When the dust settled on both fronts, the prince provided Citicorp with a capital injection of $590 million in return for a special convertible-preferred issue (41.7 million shares that are convertible at $16 per share). The deal gave Alwaleed a 9.9 percent stake in Citicorp. The prince says that the claim that he was contacted by the Federal Reserve Bank of New York to bail out Citicorp is "nonsense." He claims that his only contact with the Fed was getting approval for his more than 9 percent stake in the company.

The Rest of the Story

At year-end 1996, Citicorp's stock price was $103.[30] With 506,298,235 shares outstanding, its market value of equity was $52 billion, a more than ten-fold increase over its market value at year-end 1990.[31] Prince Alwaleed, with 41.7 million shares, had seen his investment of $590 million grow to $4.3 billion. At this point, Citicorp's market-to-book ratio was 2.1 (up from 0.56 at year-end 1990), whereas its Tier 1 and total-capital (Tier 1 + Tier 2) ratios were 8.39 percent and 12.23 percent (up from 4.88% and 7.76%). Citicorp's ratio of market value of common equity to total assets was 18.5 percent, compared to its book-value ratio of 7.4 percent (up from 2.1% and 3.8%).

CITICORP'S CAPITAL STRUCTURE

Table 13-4 shows the capital structures of Citicorp and Citibank as of December 31, 1995. Citicorp/Citibank finances 65–71 percent of its total assets in deposit markets, either domestic or foreign, with the bulk of the funds gathered in offices outside the United States in the form of interest-bearing funds. Nondeposit liabilities account for another 22–27 percent of funded assets, whereas the balance comes

[28] Rossant [1995] reports on "The Prince" in *Business Week* (September 25), pp. 88–99.
[29] In the M&A game in banking, Chemical acquired Manny Hanny and then Chase acquired Chemical.
[30] On September 11, 1997, Citicorp closed at $126.125 and was paying an annual divident of $2.10 per share.
[31] Chapter 4, which deals with managing value and strategic planning in the financial-services industry, explains how Citicorp turned itself around.

TABLE 13-4 Citicorp/Citibank Capital Structure, December 31, 1995

Component	Citicorp $mil	%	Citibank $mil	%	Bank/BHC %
Non-interest-bearing deposits	13,388	5.2	10,959	5.2	81.8
Interest-bearing deposits	36,700	14.3	22,676	10.7	61.8
Total domestic deposits	50,088	19.5	33,635	15.7	67.1
Non-interest-bearing deposits	8,164	3.2	7,955	3.8	97.4
Interest-bearing deposits	108,879	42.4	108,018	51.1	99.2
Total foreign deposits	117,043	45.6	106,973	54.9	98.2
Total deposits	167,131	65.1	149,608	70.7	89.5
Trading-account liabilities	18,274	7.1	17,544	8.3	96.0
Purchased funds & other borrowings	16,334	6.3	10,106	4.8	61.9
Acceptances outstanding	1,559	1.0	1,559	1.0	100.0
Accrued taxes and other expenses	5,719	2.2	3,263	1.5	57.1
Other liabilities	9,767	3.8	5,300	2.5	54.3
Long-term debt	17,151	6.7	4,428	2.1	25.8
Subordinated capital notes	1,337	0.5	4,700	2.2	351.5
Total nondeposit liabilities	70,141	27.3	46,900	22.2	66.9
Preferred stock	3,071	1.2	NA	NA	NA
Common stock ($1 and $20 par)	461	0.0	751	0.4	162.9
Surplus	5,702	2.2	6,744	3.2	118.3
Retained earnings	12,190	4.7	7,972	3.8	65.4
Net unrealized gains/sec. for sale	132	0.0	55	0.0	41.7
Foreign currency translation	(437)	(0.0)	(556)	(0.3)	127.2
Common stock in treasury, at cost	(556)	(0.6)	NA	NA	NA
Total stockholders' equity	19,581	7.6	14,966	7.1	76.4
Total liabilities and equity	$256,853	100%	$211,474	100%	82.3%

Note: On December 31, 1995, Citicorp's market value of common equity (= price per share × number of shares outstanding) was $31 billion (= $67.25 × 461,319,265) for a market-to-book ratio of 1.74, and a ratio of market value of common equity to total assets of 12.1 percent compared to the book-value ratio of 7.6 percent.

Source: Citicorp Annual Report 1995, pp. 47, 50.

from equity capital to the tune of 7.1–7.6 percent. With 82.3 percent of Citicorp's assets held by Citibank, Citicorp, for the most part, is Citibank. This type of relationship, in which the lead bank dominates the holding company, holds for most BHCs. Notable exceptions are BHCs such as NationsBank and First Interstate (acquired by Wells Fargo in 1996).

UNDERSTANDING THE COMPONENTS OF BANK CAPITAL

Because the key component of bank capital is (common) equity capital, let's begin with the items that make up this account. It consists of three components: (1) **common stock,** (2) **surplus,** and (3) **retained earnings** or undivided profits. Common stock, as opposed to preferred stock, is *common* in the sense that it has no special preference with respect to dividends or bankruptcy. The book entry for common stock equals the par value of the stock times the number of shares outstanding. Surplus or capital in excess of par value is the amount of directly contributed equity capital in excess of par value. The book entry is the difference between the price at which the common stock sold and its par value, times the number of shares sold. Surplus also is affected by dividend-reinvestment plans, executive-incentive compensation, and other stock activities. Retained earnings represent that part of after-tax profits that are not paid out as dividends. National banks are required to carry a minimum of 10 percent of each previous six months' earnings to their surplus before the OCC will approve the payment of a dividend. State laws deal with dividend payments and surplus requirements in various ways.

Let's consider the common equity components of Citicorp and Citibank from Table 13-4 (millions of dollars as of December 31, 1995):[32]

	Citicorp	*Citibank*
Common stock ($1 and $20 par values)	$ 461	$ 751
Surplus	5,702	6,744
Retained earnings	12,190	7,972
Common stock in treasury, at cost	(556)	0
Total common equity	$17,797	$15,467

Because Citicorp's common stock has a par value of $1 and because its common stock has an entry of $461 million, the number of shares *issued* must be 461 million. With 34 million shares held as Treasury stock, the number of shares *outstanding* is 427 million (461 − 34). Because Citicorp's *authorized* common stock was 800 million shares (as of December 31, 1995), it had 373 million shares (800 − 461 + 34) authorized but not issued.

Let's compare Citicorp with Citibank; note the differences in par values and the absence of Treasury stock in Citibank. Treasury stock is stock that a corporation has reacquired by purchase, gift, donation, inheritance, or other means. The value of treasury stock is treated as a deduction from equity capital. In addition, Citicorp had $3.1 billion in preferred stock outstanding, $2.1 billion in perpetual preferred and $1 billion in convertible preferred. Preferred stock is simply capital stock to which preferences or special rights are attached, usually with respect to dividends (e.g., cumulative, adjustable rate, or fixed/adjustable) and liquidation.

For comparative purposes, let's consider the components of Citicorp's equity capital as of December 31, 1990, a time at which Citicorp was considered by many to be in financial distress. The data, in millions of dollars, are as follows:

	Citicorp	*Citibank*
Common stock ($1 and $20 par values)	$ 363	$ 751
Surplus	3,187	3,978
Retained earnings	5,045	3,534
Common stock in treasury, at cost	(405)	0
Total common equity	$8,190	$8,263

From 1990 to 1995, Citicorp/Citibank was adjusting to risk-based capital requirements. These data reveal how changes in equity capital were used to meet the requirements. First, Citicorp issued common stock, an increase of 98 million shares ($1 par) resulting

---

[32] Because these data exclude preferred stock, net unrealized gains from securities available for resale, and foreign-currency translation, which are shown in Table 13-4, total stockholders' equity shown above differs from the figure in Table 13-4.

in an increase in surplus of $2.5 billion. Second, due mainly to the increased profitability of Citibank, Citicorp was able to increase its retained earnings by $7.1 billion. The increase in Citibank's capital can be traced to its improved profitability, which resulted in an increase in retained earnings of $4.4 billion. As described above, since Citicorp was meeting its internal capital targets, as determined by its free-capital test, in the mid-1990s it began new programs for repurchasing its common stock.[33] The increase in Treasury stock from 1990 to 1995 of $151 million reflects this strategy. In addition, by year-end 1995 Citicorp almost doubled its preferred stock, which totaled only $1.54 billion at year-end 1990. A big chunk of this issuance was the convertible preferred that went to Prince Alwaleed for his capital injection of $590 million.

Let's also consider the components of equity capital for Citicorp as of December 31, 1986, prior to its $3 billion provision for loan losses on LDC debt. The data, in millions of dollars, are as follows:

	Citicorp	Citibank
Common stock ($1 and $20 par values)	$ 602	$ 751
Surplus	1,421	2,015
Retained earnings	6,059	5,243
Common stock in treasury, at cost	(387)	0
Total common equity	$7,695	$8,009

From 1986 to 1990, Citicorp's total common equity increased by only $495 million whereas Citibank's total common equity increased by only $254 million. Because the retained earnings of both entities decreased from 1986 to 1990, external sources of equity were used to offset the decreases in retained earnings. Citicorp's perpetual preferred stock totaled $1,365 million at the end of 1986.

Core Capital = Equity Capital – Goodwill

By December 31, 1992, banks with the intangible asset **goodwill** were required to deduct the amount of this asset from equity capital in determining their ratios of core or Tier 1 capital to risk-adjusted assets. Goodwill usually is listed as an "other asset," and if it is material, is described in a footnote to the account. For example, in its 1995 annual report, Citicorp reported (Note 3, p. 61) goodwill, defined as "the excess of purchase price over the estimated fair value of net assets acquired, accounted for under the purchase method of accounting," of $267 million, down from $316 million in the previous year. And down substantially from the $972 million reported for 1989. Citicorp amortizes its goodwill using the straight-line method over the periods of expected benefits, which on a weighted-average basis approximates 11 years as of December 31, 1995.

Supplementary Capital

The four components of supplementary or Tier 2 capital are (1) loan-loss reserves, (2) cumulative perpetual, long-term, and convertible preferred stock, (3) perpetual debt and other hybrid capital instruments (e.g., convertible securities), and (4) subordinated debt and limited-life preferred stock (Table 13-1). Because the allowance or reserve for loan losses has been analyzed in previous chapters (recall that

---

[33] This was not the first time that Citicorp initiated a stock-repurchase plan. Such programs tend to be a standard part of capital management for large firms. Like any "long" investment strategy, the idea is buy low and sell high. For regulated firms such as banks, stock repurchases may be encouraged when banks overshoot regulatory capital requirements.

the loan-loss provision is an expense and the loan-loss reserve or allowance is a contra-asset), let's focus on the other three components of supplementary capital. Continuing with our example using Citicorp's capital structure from (Table 13-4), Citicorp had, on December 31, 1995, $3.1 billion in preferred stock outstanding, down from $4.2 billion in the previous year. Citicorp's preferred consisted of two major types: (1) perpetual preferred (issued at fixed, adjustable, or graduated rates) of $2.1 billion spread over 13 series or issues, and (2) convertible preferred of $1 billion. All of Citicorp's preferred series rank prior to common stock with respect to dividends and liquidation, but holders do not have general voting rights.

Regarding debt capital, Citicorp had $18.4 billion in this type of financing outstanding on December 31, 1995, consisting of $17.1 billion in long-term debt and $1.3 billion in subordinated capital notes. Table 13-5 shows the maturity structure and rate composition (fixed vs. floating) of Citicorp's long-term debt and its subordinated capital notes. Most of the long-term debt (70%) was issued by the parent company with a little more than one-half of it issued at a fixed rate of interest. In contrast, two out of every three dollars of subsidiary debt was issued at a fixed rate of interest. The subordinated capital notes shown in Panel B of Table 13-5 are unsecured obligations. The combination of long-term debt (or debentures) and subordinated capital notes is referred to as "subordinated notes and debentures" in banking jargon.

Although Citicorp's capital structure is a complex one, it is representative of the kind of capital structure found in **money-center** or **multinational banks.** Moving down the ladder of complex capital structures, although superregional and regional BHCs/banks certainly use innovative capital instruments, they have, on balance, less complex capital structures. At the bottom of the ladder stand the thousands of U.S. **community banks,** whose capital structures are simpler frameworks driven by retained earnings.

The data in Table 13-6 illustrate how the use of capital instruments such as **subordinated notes and debentures** and **preferred stock** varies with bank size. The dominance of the largest banks (421 banks with assets greater than $1 billion) is clear-cut. Specifically, of the $43.5 billion in subordinated notes and debentures held by all insured commercial banks on December 31, 1995, the largest banks had issued 99.2 percent of the total (almost $43.2 billion, 17% of equity and 1.3% of assets). With respect to the issuance of perpetual preferred stock, the dominance is only slightly less because the largest banks issued almost $8 out of every $10 of the $1.8 billion outstanding. From year-end 1989 to year-end 1995, no doubt in response to risk-based capital requirements, the banking industry's use of notes and debentures (Tier 2 capital) increased by almost $26 billion. In contrast, the industry's use of preferred stock actually declined by $145 million from year-end 1989 to year-end 1994. However, during 1995, the industry raised $331 million in perpetual preferred stock.

HOW MUCH BANK CAPITAL IS ADEQUATE?

Addressing the issue of bank capital adequacy, James G. Ehlen, Jr., formerly with Goldman Sachs & Company, put it this way:[34]

> In both banking and industry, the adequacy of capital is an elusive measure. Perhaps the only real determinant of adequacy is the aggregate consensus of the marketplace—

[34] "Bank-Track: Emerging Trends for Bank Stocks," *Investment Research* (December 1987), Special Third Issue, Goldman Sachs.

TABLE 13-5   Citicorp's Long-Term Debt and Subordinated Capital Notes, December 31, 1995

Panel A. Long-Term Debt[a] *(millions of dollars)*

	Various Fixed-Rate Obligations[b]	Various Floating-Rate Obligations[b]	1995 Total	1994 Total
Parent company				
Due in 1995	$ —	$ —	$ —	$ 1,730
Due in 1996	1,068	593	1,661	1,368
Due in 1997	445	471	916	813
Due in 1998	356	1,352	1,708	1,378
Due in 1999	45	1,073	1,118	1,112
Due in 2000	604	914	1,518	1,253
Due in 2001–2005	2,688	1,113	3,801	3,217
Due in 2006–2010	890	—	890	423
Due after 2010	269	356	625	694
	6,365	5,872	12,237	11,988
Subsidiaries[c]				
Due in 1995	—	—	—	1,035
Due in 1996	969	179	1,148	1,605
Due in 1997	891	384	1,275	655
Due in 1998	722	649	1,371	415
Due in 1999	295	36	331	203
Due in 2000	190	178	368	253
Due in 2001–2005	150	113	263	248
Due in 2006–2010	14	48	62	44
Due after 2010	31	65	96	51
	3,262	1,652	4,914	4,509
Total	$9,627	$7,524	$17,151	$16,497

Panel B. Subordinated Capital Notes *(millions of dollars)*

	Rate	1995	1994
Due 1997	Floating	$ 500	$ 500
Due 1999	9%	300	300
Due 1999	9¾%	300	300
No stated maturity	Floating	237	297
Total		$1,337	$1,397

[a]Original maturities of one year or more. Maturity distribution is based upon contractual maturities or earlier dates at which debt is repayable at the option of the holder, due to required mandatory sinking fund payments or due-to-call notices issued.

[b]Based on contractual terms. Repricing characteristics may be effectively modified from time to time using derivative contracts.

[c]Approximately 4 percent in 1995 and 17 percent in 1994 of subsidiary long-term debt was guaranteed by Citicorp, and of the debt not guaranteed by Citicorp, approximately 38 percent in 1995 and 36 percent in 1994 was secured by the assets of the subsidiary.

Source: Citicorp Annual Report 1995, pp. 56–57.

TABLE 13-6 The Effects of Bank Size on the Use of Debt Capital and Preferred Stock,
December 31, 1995

| | Subordinated Notes and Debentures | | | Perpetual Preferred Stock | | |
| | | Percentage of | | | Percentage of | |
	$millions	Equity	Assets	$millions	Equity	Assets
Banks with assets of						
Less than $100 million	29	0.1	0.00	100	0.32	0.03
$100 mil. to $1 billion	321	0.5	0.05	271	0.41	0.04
$1 billion or more	43,186	17.1	1.30	1,465	0.58	0.04
Total commercial banks	$43,536	12.4	1.01	1,836	0.52	0.04
Large banks/total banks	99.2%			79.8%		

Note: Number of banks in each group is 9,941 (total), 421 (large banks), 2,861 (medium), and 6,659 (small).
Source: Statistics on Banking, FDIC, 1995, Table RC-1, p. C-2.

that is, leverage, or the inverse of the capital ratio, should be extended until the marketplace reacts adversely and reflects concern.

Ehlen's definition sounds like the trade-offs discussed in the capital-structure theory of the firm. If you want something more specific, consider the words of Wayne D. Angell, a member of the Board of Governors of the Federal Reserve System (Angell [1991], pp. 6–7):

> While picking an exact number is difficult, I am thinking of minimum bank capital on the order of ten percent tier one capital to risk-weighted assets. If ten percent seems surprisingly high, recall that prior to the institution of deposit insurance, bank capital ratios were normally above twenty percent. Moreover, median capital ratios in financial-services industries that do not have deposit insurance are today significantly higher than ten percent. Clearly, any move to increase bank capital requirements would need a long transition period, to minimize the problems banks might face raising capital.

Figure 13-4, which puts Angell's recommendation in historical perspective, shows the ratio of equity capital to assets for commercial banks for the period 1910 to 1996. Four important events in bank regulatory history are highlighted in Figure 13-4: (1) the National Banking Act of 1863, (2) the creation of the Federal Reserve in 1913, (3) the creation of the FDIC in 1933, and (4) the implementation of risk-based capital requirements in 1989.

Rather than have federal regulators pick some number as a benchmark for adequate capital, Ehlen's suggestion of letting the marketplace determine the adequacy of bank capital seems much more reasonable. Nevertheless, bank regulators usually pick some number and apply it to all banks. However, with thousands of local or community banks not subject to the discipline of the marketplace, a benchmark capital ratio for them does not seem unreasonable.

Too Much of a Good Thing? Stock Repurchases by Large Banks

Large banks and their holding companies had to make the greatest adjustments in meeting the standards set by risk-based capital requirements. These adjustments,

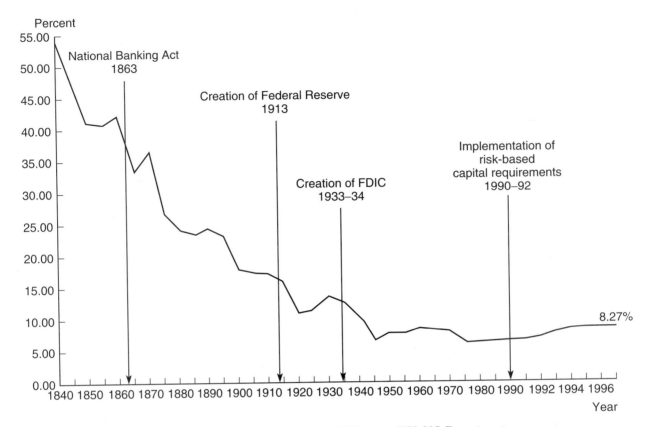

Primary sources: Historical statistics of the United States, colonial times to 1970, U.S. Department of Commerce and the Federal Reserve.

Secondary source: Deposit Insurance: A Strategy for Reform, U.S. General Accounting Office Report to the Chairman, Committee on Banking, Housing and Urban Affairs, U.S. Senate, and the chairman, Committee on Banking, Finance, and Urban Affairs, House of Representatives (March 1991), Figure 4.1, p. 84. Data for 1991 to 1996 from the *Federal Reserve Bulletin.*

FIGURE 13-4 **Ratio of Equity Capital to Total Assets for Commercial Banks, 1840–1996**

coupled with a favorable interest-rate environment, resulted in substantial improvements in the capital positions of large banks. In fact, these banks became flush with capital. Some analysts feared that these banks would engage in another lending frenzy (e.g., syndicated international lending) that would result in the next round of loan losses. As of this writing, banks appear to be learning from past lending mistakes (e.g., LDC loans and commercial-real-estate loans), and they have not engaged in excessive lending. Instead, they have found another way of reducing their capital—stock-repurchase plans. Alternatively, share repurchases are an increasingly popular way for firms to pay cash to their shareholders, as opposed to paying cash dividends.

Share stock repurchases are simple transactions: The company simply uses cash to buy back some of its outstanding shares.[35] The reacquired shares are rarely

---

[35] Three major methods of share repurchase exist: (1) open-market transactions subject to SEC restrictions and guidelines, (2) general tender offers to all shareholders or to small shareholders only, and (3) direct negotiation with a major shareholder. When direct negotiation is aimed at taking out a hostile bidder, the

deregistered and canceled. Instead, they are kept as a negative entry in a capital account called "common stock in treasury," or "treasury stock"; they can be resold when the company needs funds. To illustrate, consider the components of Citicorp's shareholders' equity as of December 31, 1995:[36]

Account	$ millions
Common stock ($1 par, 461,319, 265 shares)	461
Surplus	5,702
Retained earnings	12,190
Preferred stock	3,071
Net unrealized gains—securities available for sale	132
Foreign-currency translation	(437)
Common stock in treasury, at cost (34,030,205 shares)	(1,538)
Total shareholders' equity	$19,581

Because Citicorp had 25.5 million shares of common stock in treasury at year-end 1994, it added about 8.5 million shares ($1.1 billion) of treasury stock in 1995. Citicorp began this latest episode of repurchasing common stock in June 1995, when it achieved its target ratios for risk-based capital (e.g., target range for Tier-1 ratio is 8% to 8.3%). At that time, it announced a two-year $3 billion repurchase program, which was expanded to $4.5 billion through January 31, 1998. To determine the amount of funds available for repurchase of stock, Citicorp calculates what it calls "free capital," which represents Tier 1 capital generated during the period, reduced by capital attributed to funding business expansion during the year and building the Tier 1 ratio to target levels. The components of Citicorp's free capital for 1995 were as follows:[37]

Component	$ millions
Tier 1 capital generated:	
Net income	$3,464
Issuances of common stock/other	893
Cash dividends declared	
Common stock	(492)
Preferred stock	(343)
Total Tier 1 capital generated	3,522
Capital attributed to:	
Growth in risk-adjusted assets	(699)
Build in Tier 1 capital ratio	(1,084)
Free capital	$1,769

---

transaction is called "greenmail" because the company offers to repurchase shares at a price that makes the bidder happy to be taken out. Share-repurchase plans do not require shareholder authorization and do provide preemptive rights to existing shareholders. See Brealey and Myers [1991] and Scholes and Wolford [1989] for more on stock-repurchase plans.

[36] These data and the following information are from Citicorp's 1995 *Annual Report,* pp. 38–39 and 47. Table 13-4 shows both Citicorp's and Citibank's sources of funds.

[37] These data show how stock repurchases and the payment of cash dividends are simply alternative ways of paying cash to shareholders. In this example, either transaction results in a decline in free capital. The major difference between the two methods is that share repurchases reduce the number of shares traded whereas the payment of cash dividends does not.

Citicorp used $1.528 billion of its free capital to repurchase 23.1 million shares of its common stock at an average price of $66.17 per share. Roughly one-third of the repurchased shares were added to treasury stock (8.5 million shares), whereas Citicorp used the remaining 14.6 million shares of common stock mainly for conversions of preferred stock, and to a lesser extent in employee stock ownership plans or ESOPs.

Stock Repurchases and Capital Regulation

Given the banking agencies' penchant for capital regulation, stock repurchases by banks/BHCs are anathema to them. From a financial-management perspective, the effect of stock repurchases on the value of the firm is a bit ambiguous. On the one hand, the repurchase should, all other things being equal, improve the company's EPS and its ROE, because fewer shares are outstanding and because the EM is larger, respectively. On the other hand, the repurchase will change the firm's capital structure and its perceived risk exposure. Thus, like any financial decision, a stock repurchase involves a risk-return trade-off. In terms of the constant-growth model, a stock repurchase would be expected to increase D_1, k, and g, and thus the effect on value $P_0 = D_1/(k - g)$ would depend upon the changes in D_1 and g relative to the change in k. Managers' expectations regarding these changes should determine the appropriate action.[38]

Citicorp has been one of the most active BHCs in the capital markets, both in issuing stock and in repurchasing it. During October 1977, Citicorp announced that it would repurchase on the open market three million shares of its 128 million outstanding common shares, less than 2 percent of its total dollar capital. By January 19, 1978, the repurchase plan was completed. Since Citicorp shares were trading in the low 20s over this period (the 1977 high was 33½), the repurchases cost roughly $65 million, approximately 10 weeks of the company's earnings. Citicorp's rationale for the repurchase scheme was to enhance its "ability to access capital markets in the future." That is, repurchases decrease the number of shares outstanding, thereby increasing EPS and reducing *total* dividend costs. All other things being equal, the lower total cash dividends will over time gradually replenish the reduced common stock through increased transfers to net income to retained earnings. In addition, Citicorp was counting on debt conversion, exercise of stock options, and a projected 10–15 percent annual earnings growth to augment its capital base.

In a letter dated December 16, 1977, the Comptroller of the Currency, John G. Heimann, criticized Citicorp for shrinking its capital base. Heimann wrote, "Since one of the major functions of equity capital is to provide a cushion against unforeseen occurrences, any reduction in equity capital, be it to the bank or its inseparable partner—the holding company—is of concern to me." In addition, Heimann expressed concern about (1) the *timing* of the reduction, (2) the fact that Citicorp "does not appear to be overcapitalized," and (3) Citicorp's earning projection ("it is always possible [that they] will not be realized"). Heimann's letter is an example of the kind of jawboning that goes on in capital regulation. The effectiveness of this weapon on giant banks is indicated by Citicorp's response to it. Chairman Walter B. Wriston wrote in reply, "Your letter of December 16 is duly noted."[39]

---

[38] Schall and Haley ([1977], p. 624) report that managers are often overly optimistic regarding the effect of stock repurchases. Some evidence indicates that the share prices of companies that have repurchased stock do not outperform the market.

[39] Personal communication from the late Robert R. Dince, who was a deputy comptroller at the time. It is not known if Comptroller Ludwig criticized John Reed for Citicorp's stock repurchases during the mid-1990s.

ODE TO BANK CAPITAL

The pecking order of capital regulation goes from senators and congressmen to bank regulators and then to bankers. The Heimann-Wriston exchange is an example of what happens between regulators and bankers.[40] On another level, politicians peck on the regulators. To illustrate, Senator William Proxmire of Wisconsin once charged former Comptroller James Smith with failing to exert pressure on large banks to increase their capital. He told Smith, "I'm not asking you to apply it [capital regulation] ruthlessly. Apply it in a namby-pamby way. Play the violin and sing while you're doing it. Just do it."

On March 11, 1977, I was testifying before the Committee on Banking, Housing, and Urban Affairs of the U.S. Senate, a committee that at the time was chaired by William Proxmire. The hearings focused on the condition of the banking system and how effectively the banking agencies had carried out their statutory responsibility to ensure a safe-and-sound banking system. I concluded my statement on a lighthearted note with my "Ode to Bank Capital" (see Exhibit 13-1):

> Oh bank capital, oh bank capital
> Our regulators' stricken hero,
> Please don't, please don't
> Please don't go to zero.

Senator Proxmire, showing a lack of appreciation for my Ogden Nashism and, more important, an apparent misunderstanding of *how markets work,* responded,

EXHIBIT 13-1 Ode to Bank Capital

Source: Sinkey [1979], p. 43. Courtesy of JAI Press.

---

[40] The Heimann-Wriston exchange and the "Ode to Bank Capital" are from Sinkey [1979].

"If it [bank capital] does [go to zero], that is just something that will happen because of the markets and we can't do anything about it."[41] There is, of course, no need to "do anything about it." In an efficient market, risk-averse investors and creditors would not permit bank capital to go to zero (technically, infinite financial leverage) or even to approach zero, without demanding compensation for the increased riskiness or withdrawing their funds. As a bank's capital decreases below the industry or market norm, the risk premiums demanded by investors increase, forcing the bank to reduce its leverage (i.e., increase its capital) *or* to pay for its increased risk exposure. The market's signal for greater riskiness is a higher required rate of return and reduced value. In the case of Continental Illinois, the market's signal was immediate in the form of a liquidity crisis that eventually led to a bailout and nationalization of the bank. Even in a world with mispriced deposit insurance and other market imperfections, bank capital and money markets have worked quite efficiently.

Chapter Summary

Under a set of restrictive assumptions, finance theory suggests that **capital structure** does not matter. In the real world of taxes, bankruptcy costs, agency problems, asymmetric information, and regulation, capital structure matters. Moreover, in banking it seems that capital structure matters more than in other industries, because of the importance of confidence to banks, and to the financial-services industry in general. Other factors that determine confidence include stability of earnings, quality of information, and the strength of government guarantees. In an unregulated environment without government guarantees, a market measure of **capital adequacy** would be the ultimate determinant of the public's confidence in a bank or the banking system. However, when a federal safety net in the form of **deposit insurance** and a **lender of last resort** exists, these government guarantees affect the optimal capital structure of a regulated firm because they substitute for bank capital. Moreover, unless the government guarantees are priced correctly and managed efficiently and effectively, taxpayer-backed subsidies will be exploited. Although a variable-rate pricing component was added to the explicit deposit-insurance premium in the early 1990s, **regulatory interference,** in the form of capital requirements and the bank-examination process, has been a longstanding form of **implicit pricing,** resulting in an effective deposit-insurance premium that always has been implicitly risk-based. For federally insured banks, the government guarantee represents an unbooked intangible asset whose value varies inversely with the real or market value of bank capital.

The idea of capital adequacy has been used to capture the overall soundness or risk exposure of individual banks. The notion of bank capital as a cushion or buffer (to absorb losses associated with credit risk, interest-rate risk, foreign-exchange risk, etc.) suggests an inverse relationship between the level of bank capital and risk exposure. Although the Basle Agreement on risk-based capital requirements reflects this basic idea, it recognizes only one source of exposure—credit risk. The inclusion of off-balance-sheet activities in the risk-based capital formulas for core and supplementary capital reflects regulatory concern about the risks associated with contingent claims. Under the 1992 risk-based capital guidelines, total bank capital equals **Tier 1** or **core capital** plus **Tier 2** or **supplementary**

---

[41] Unedited transcript, Committee on Banking, Housing and Urban Affairs, March 11, 1977, lines 1–3, p. 150; inserts mine.

capital. Banks that can say, "Look Ma (to the marketplace and to regulators), no risk," are entitled to greater leverage. In contrast, banks with riskier portfolios and lots of OBSAs are forced to hold more capital to support their greater risk exposure. Because money-center and other large banks fit this description, they had the most difficult time adjusting to risk-based capital standards. For these banks, the adjustment process included dividend cuts, employee reductions, new equity issues, and asset sales. Since too much of a good thing is no good, many large banks reinstituted stock repurchase programs during the mid-1990s.

On balance, the theory and regulation of bank capital structure make for interesting, challenging, and thought-provoking study. In the next chapter, we turn to some of the practical aspects of the financial management of bank capital and dividends.

Key Words, Concepts, and Acronyms

- Agency conflicts/costs
- Bankruptcy costs
- Capital adequacy/regulation
- Capital structure (optimal)
- Common stock (authorized, issued, outstanding, treasury)
- Community bank
- Confidence function
    [= f(NW, SOE, IQ, G)]
- Constant-growth model
- Cost of equity capital
- Credit risk
- Debt capital (notes and debentures)
- Deposit insurance
- Dividend yield
- Expected return
- Federal safety net

- Generally accepted accounting principles (GAAP)
- Goodwill
- Government guarantees
- Government-sponsored enterprises (GSEs)
- Implicit pricing
- Leverage
- Loan-loss reserves
- Market value of equity
- Modigliani-and-Miller (M&M) propositions
- Money-center/multinational banks
- Off-balance-sheet activities (OBSAs)
- Preferred stock

- Price-appreciation (capital-gains) yield
- Price-earnings (P/E) ratio
- Regulatory accounting principles (RAP)
- Regulatory interference (monitoring and bonding)
- Retained earnings
- Risk-based capital requirements
- Risk-based (implicit) pricing of deposit insurance
- Sallie Mae (Look Ma, no risk!)
- Share (stock) repurchases
- Tax accounting principles (TAP)
- Tax shield
- Tier 1 (core) capital
- Tier 2 (supplemental) capital

Review/Discussion Questions

1. When asked whether M&M propositions apply to banks, Miller [1995], one-half of the M&M team, replied: "Yes and no." What is your answer and why?
2. In an M&M world, would financial intermediaries exist? Explain and defend your answer.
3. What insights can be gained from the application of M&M propositions to determining the value of the banking firm? How do Buser, Chen, and Kane model the banking firm and what are their conclusions regarding deposit insurance, capital regulation, and optimal bank capital? In developing your answer, be sure to identify and explain the importance of implicit pricing, regulatory interference (monitoring and bonding to solve agency problems), and capital regulation.
4. Why is bank capital important? In an article in the *Journal of Political Economy*, Peltzman [1970] wrote about the substitution of deposit insurance for bank capital. Using the confidence function (equation [13-5]), describe the interaction between NW* and G from the end of World War II until the early 1970s. What has happened since then, and especially in the 1980s? Use Figure 13-4 in your discussion too.
5. By 1992, commercial banks and bank holding companies had to meet new capital standards. What are they and how do they compare with the capital requirements established in 1985? Which banks had the most difficulty adjusting to the new capital

standards, and how did they do it? When, where, and why were the risk-based capital requirements established?

6. Describe the use of preferred stock and capital notes and debentures by U.S. commercial banks.

7. The term *capital adequacy* can be viewed as simply another way of describing leverage. What is the relationship between portfolio risks, such as credit risk and interest-rate risk, and leverage? Use this relationship to explain Sallie Mae's claim of "Look Ma, no risk!" How are capital and risk viewed by the Basle Agreement?

8. What's the logic behind risk-based capital requirements?

9. Distinguish among common stock that is authorized, authorized but not issued, issued, outstanding, and in treasury.

10. How much does equity capital cost a bank? How can you estimate this cost? What's the linkage between an investor's expected return on a stock and the constant-growth model?

11. Distinguish between internal and external equity for a bank. Is there a cost difference between these two sources of capital?

12. What, if anything, does the variability of retained earnings across bank size classes have to say about the riskiness of the banks in those size categories?

13. What are the many veils of bank bookkeeping? How effective is the market-value knife at cutting the GAAP and RAP veils? Can this knife be applied to all banks?

14. How is it possible for a bank to be solvent on a book-value basis but insolvent on a market-value basis? Explain fully.

15. Regarding the definition of adequate bank capital, Maisel [1981], building on an earlier study by Sharpe [1978], wrote,

> *Capital is adequate* either when it reduces the chances of future insolvency of an institution to some predetermined minimum level or, alternatively, when the premium paid by the bank to the insurer is "fair"; that is, when it fully covers the risks borne by the insurer. Such risks, in turn, depend upon the risk in the portfolio selected by the bank, on its capital, and on terms of the insurance with respect to when insolvency will be determined and what losses will be paid. (p. 20)

Discuss and evaluate this statement.

16. Is there a conflict between stock repurchases and capital regulation? Do stock repurchases increase the value of the firm? What is the pecking order in the capital-regulation process?

Problems

1. Determine the equity capital-to-asset ratios for each of the following banks:

Bank	ROE	ROA
Alpha	0.2000	0.0150
Beta	−0.1000	−0.0010
Gamma	0.1500	0.0075
Delta	0.1500	0.0065
Eta	0.2500	0.0150
Phi	0.2080	0.0129

What conclusions do you draw about each bank?

2. The Debt Bank has the following capital structure:

Item	$ millions
Notes and debentures	11.5
Limited-life preferred stock	0.0
Perpetual preferred stock	0.0
Common stock	51.4
Surplus	78.5
Undivided profits	405.2
Loan-loss reserve	66.7

If the bank's common stock is selling for $50 per share and there are 51.4 million shares outstanding, calculate its capital position on the basis of (a) GAAP, (b) RAP using the 1992 capital standards, and (c) market value. What is the bank's market-to-book ratio?

3. If investors expected the Constant-Growth Bank to grow at 10 percent a year, find their expected return and the bank's cost of equity capital given the following initial conditions: current dividend = $1.80 and current price per share = $75.

4. In 1991, Prince Alwaleed provided Citicorp with a $590-million injection of capital. When Rossant wrote his *Business Week* article, the prince's investment was worth $2.8 billion. Assuming a four-year holding period, what was the prince's compound annual rate of return? The prince's investment rule of thumb (as quoted in the *BW* article) is "Anything that's worth $4 billion and costs $1 billion, buy it." How did he do on this deal?

5. Given the following pro forma information for the West Bank and the East Bank, determine their required risk-based capital, both core and supplementary, using the 1992 standards (check the appendix for the appropriate weights and conversion factors). All dollar items are in thousands.

	West Bank	East Bank
Balance-sheet items:		
Risk category 1	$ 5,000	$10,000
Risk category 2	50,000	80,000
Risk category 3	15,000	20,000
Risk category 4	60,000	95,000
OBSAs:		
Standby letters of credit	50,000	100,000
Loan commitments (2-yr. maturity)	25,000	50,000
Commercial letters of credit	5,000	25,000

6. Use the appropriate valuation model to determine the value of each of the following banks:

Bank	Current Dividend	Expected Growth Rate	Required Return
Multinational	$2.00	0.20	0.18
Global	$2.00	0.15	0.18
Regional	$1.00	0.13	0.12
Community	$2.00	0.04	0.10
Zombie	$0.00	0.0	0.40

7. The Last National Bank of Athens had net income of $10 million over the past six months. How much of this amount does the OCC require the bank to allocate to its surplus and how much to its retained earnings?

APPENDIX A

THE 1992 RISK-BASED CAPITAL REQUIREMENTS

Overview

This appendix consists of six tables describing and illustrating the risk-based capital requirements for U.S. banks and BHCs. Table 13-1 in the text shows the capital definitions and standards. Table A13-1 summarizes the risk weights and risk categories. Table A13-2 presents the credit conversion factors for off-balance-sheet activities. Table A13-3 shows the treatment of interest-rate and exchange-rate contracts. Tables A13-4 and A13-5 show some examples of how to compute the risk-based capital requirements. The appendix concludes with Table A13-6, which describes the transitional and final arrangements for the initial, year-end 1990, and year-end 1992 capital standards. Tables A13-1 to A13-3 are from the *Federal Register,* Vol. 54, No. 17 (January 27, 1989), Rules and Regulations. The other three tables are from the Federal Reserve's proposal for risk-based capital requirements dated January 25, 1988.

TABLE A13-1 Summary of Risk Weights and Risk Categories

Category 1: Zero Percent
1. Cash (domestic and foreign)
2. Balances due from, and claims on, Federal Reserve Banks and central banks in other OECD countries
3. Claims on, or unconditionally guaranteed by, the U.S. government or its agencies, or other OECD central governments[a]
4. Local currency claims on non-OECD central governments and central banks, to the extent the bank has local currency liabilities in that country
5. Gold bullion held in the bank's own vaults or in another bank's vaults on an allocated basis, to the extent it is backed by gold bullion liabilities
6. Federal Reserve Bank stock

Category 2: 20 Percent
1. Portions of loans and other assets collateralized by securities issued or guaranteed by the U.S. government or its agencies, or other OECD central governments[b]
2. Portions of loans and other assets conditionally guaranteed by the U.S. government or its agencies, or other OECD central governments
3. Portions of loans and other assets collateralized by cash on deposit in the lending institution
4. All claims (long- and short-term) on, or guaranteed by, OECD depository institutions
5. Claims on, or guaranteed by, non-OECD depository institutions, including central banks, with a residual maturity of one year or less

---

[a] For the purpose of calculating the risk-based capital ratio, a U.S. government agency is defined as an instrumentality of the U.S. government whose obligations are fully and explicitly guaranteed as to the timely repayment of principal and interest by the full faith and credit of the U.S. government.

[b] Degree of collateralization is determined by current market value.

(continued)

TABLE A13-1 *Continued*

6. Cash items in the process of collection
7. Securities and other claims on, or guaranteed by, U.S. government–sponsored agencies[c]
8. Portions of loans and other assets collateralized by securities issued by, or guaranteed by, U.S. government–sponsored agencies[d]
9. Claims that represent general obligations of, and portions of claims guaranteed by, public-sector entities in OECD countries, below the level of central government
10. Claims on or guaranteed by official multilateral lending institutions or regional development institutions in which the U.S. government is a shareholder or a contributing member
11. Portions of loans and other assets collateralized with securities issued by official multilateral lending institutions or regional development institutions in which the U.S. government is a shareholder or a contributing member

Category 3: 50 Percent
1. Revenue bonds or similar obligations, including loans and leases, that are obligations of public sector entities in OECD countries, but for which the government entity is committed to repay the debt only out of revenues from the facilities financed
2. Credit equivalent amounts of interest rate and exchange rate related contracts, except for those assigned to a lower risk category
3. Assets secured by a first mortgage on a one–four family residential property that are not more than 90 days past due, on nonaccrual or restructured

Category 4: 100 Percent
1. All other claims on private obligors
2. Claims on non-OECD financial institutions with a residual maturity exceeding one year. Claims on non-OECD central banks with a residual maturity exceeding one year are included in this category unless they qualify for item 4 of Category 1
3. Claims on non-OECD central governments that are not included in item 4 of Category 1
4. Obligations issued by state or local governments (including industrial development authorities and similar entities) repayable solely by a private party or enterprise
5. Premises, plant, and equipment; other fixed assets; and other real estate owned
6. Investments in unconsolidated subsidiaries, joint ventures, or associated companies (unless deducted from capital)
7. Capital instruments issued by other banking organizations
8. All other assets (including claims on commercial firms owned by the private sector)

---

[c] For the purpose of calculating the risk-based capital ratio, a U.S. government–sponsored agency is defined as an agency originally established or chartered to serve public purposes specified by the U.S. Congress but whose obligations are not explicitly guaranteed by the full faith and credit of the U.S. government.
[d] Degree of collateralization is determined by current market value.

TABLE A13-2 Credit Conversion Factors for Off-Balance-Sheet Items

100 Percent Conversion Factor
1. Direct credit substitutes (general guarantees of indebtedness and guarantee-type instruments, including standby letters of credit serving as financial guarantees for, or supporting, loans and securities)
2. Risk participations in bankers acceptances and participations in direct credit substitutes (e.g., standby letters of credit)
3. Sale and repurchase agreements and asset sales with recourse, if not already included on the balance sheet
4. Forward agreements (i.e., contractual obligations) to purchase assets, including financing facilities with *certain* drawdown

50 Percent Conversion Factor
1. Transaction-related contingencies (e.g., bid bonds, performance bonds, warranties, and standby letters of credit related to particular transactions)
2. Unused commitments with an original maturity exceeding one year
3. Revolving underwriting facilities (RUFs), note issuance facilities (NIFs) and other similar arrangements

20 Percent Conversion Factor
1. Short-term, self-liquidating trade-related contingencies, including commercial letters of credit

Zero Percent Conversion Factor
1. Unused commitments with an original maturity of one year or less
2. Unused commitments which are unconditionally cancellable at any time, regardless of maturity

TABLE A13-3 Treatment of Interest-Rate and Exchange-Rate Contracts

The current exposure method (described below) is utilized to calculate the "credit equivalent amounts" of these instruments. These amounts are assigned a risk weight appropriate to the obligor or any collateral or guarantee. However, the maximum risk weight is limited to 50 percent. Multiple contracts with a single counterparty may be netted if those contracts are subject to innovation.

Residual Maturity	Interest-Rate Contracts	Exchange-Rate Contracts
One year and less	Replacement Cost (RC)	RC+ 1.0% of total notional principal (NP)
Over one year	RC+ 0.5% of NP	RC+ 5.0% of NP

The following instruments will be excluded:
- Exchange rate contracts with an original maturity of 14 calendar days or less
- Instruments traded on exchanges and subject to daily margin requirements

TABLE A13-4 Computing Risk-Based Capital Requirements

The following table illustrates the calculation of risk-based capital ratio, as proposed in the original Basle Agreement. This example assumes a banking organization with $100,000 in total assets, $52,000 in certain off-balance-sheet credit equivalent amounts, and $7,000 in Tier 1 and Tier 2 capital as defined by the proposal.

Risk Category[a]	On-Balance-Sheet and Credit Equivalent Amounts		Risk Weight		Weighted-Risk Assets and Off-Balance-Sheet Items
0 percent	$ 5,000	×	0	=	0
10 percent	10,000	×	0.10	=	$ 1,000
20 percent	30,000	×	0.20	=	6,000
50 percent	20,000	×	0.50	=	10,000
100 percent	87,000	×	1.00	=	87,000
Total	$152,000				$104,000

(including $100,000 in total assets and $52,000 in credit equivalent off-balance-sheet items, as derived in the example below)

Total Tier 1 and Tier 2 capital $7,000

Risk-based capital ratio (as proposed) $\frac{7,000}{\$104,000} = 6.7\%$

The following table illustrates the calculation of the "credit equivalent" value of selected off-balance-sheet items by multiplying the principal amount by the appropriate "credit conversion factor." Each credit equivalent value would subsequently be assigned to one of the five risk categories (in the table above) depending on the identity of the obligor.

Off-Balance-Sheet Item	Principal Amount	Credit Conversion Factor	On-Balance-Sheet Credit Equivalent Amount[b]
Standby letter of credit (financial guarantee)	$40,000	× 1.00	= $40,000
Commitment with original maturity of 3 years	20,000	× 0.50	= 10,000
Commercial letter of credit	10,000	× 0.20	= 2,000
Total	$70,000		$52,000

[a]The original Basle Agreement had five risk categories. Table 13-A1 shows the *four* risk categories used by U.S. bank regulators.
[b]Assumes the item is assigned to Category 5 (100 percent risk weight) on the basis of the obligor.

TABLE A13-5 Calculation of Credit Equivalent Amounts: Interest-Rate- and Foreign-Rate-Related Transactions

Type of Contract (remaining maturity)	Potential Exposure — Notional Primary (dollars) (1)	×	Potential Exposure Conversion Factor (2)	=	Potential Exposure (dollars) (3)	Current Exposure — Replacement Cost[a] (4)	Current Exposure (dollars)[b] (5)	Credit Equivalent Amount (dollars)
(1) 120-day forward foreign exchange	5,000,000		.01		50,000	100,000	100,000	150,000
(2) 120-day forward foreign exchange	6,000,000		.01		60,000	−120,000	0	60,000
(3) 3-year single-currency fixed/floating interest-rate swap	10,000,000		.005		50,000	200,000	200,000	250,000
(4) 3-year single-currency fixed/floating interest-rate swap	10,000,000		.005		50,000	−250,000	0	50,000
(5) 7-year cross-currency floating/floating interest-rate swap	20,000,000		.05		1,000,000	−1,300,000	0	1,000,000
Total	$51,000,000							$1,510,000

[a]These numbers are purely for illustration.
[b]The larger of zero or a positive marked-to-market value.

TABLE A13-6 The Scheduled Phase-In of Risk-Based Capital Requirements

	Transitional Arrangements — Initial	Transitional Arrangements — Year-end 1990	Final Arrangement — Year-end 1992
1. Minimum standard of total capital to weighted-risk assets	None	7.25%	8.0%
2. Definition of Tier 1 capital	Common equity *plus* supplementary elements *less* goodwill[a] (For bank holding companies, goodwill acquired before—will be grandfathered for transition period)	Common equity *plus* supplementary elements *less* goodwill[b] (For bank holding companies, goodwill acquired before—will be grandfathered for transition period)	Common equity *less* all goodwill
3. Minimum standard of Tier 1 capital to weighted-risk assets	None	3.625%	4.0%
4. Minimum standard of common stockholders' equity to weighted-risk assets	None	3.25%	4.0%
5. Limitations on supplementary capital elements			
a. General reserves	No limit within supplementary capital	1.5% of weighted risk assets	1.25% of weighted-risk assets
b. Subordinated debt and intermediate-term preferred stock	Combined maximum of 50% of Tier 1	Combined maximum of 50% of Tier 1	Combined maximum of 50% of Tier 1

[a]Up to 25% of Tier 1 (before deduction of goodwill) may include supplementary elements.
[b]Up to 10% of Tier 1 (before deduction of goodwill) may include supplementary elements.
BHCs may count preferred stock as part of Tier 1 but it cannot count for more than 25% of Tier 1 total capital.

MARKET RISK, MARKET-RISK CAPITAL FORMULAS, AND J. P. MORGAN'S RISKMETRICS™

Introduction

Starting in 1998, the 25 or so largest U.S. banks will have to meet a standardized market-risk capital formula. The objective of this standard is to translate the estimated change in the value of a bank's portfolio (i.e., market risk) into a fair capital standard. In January 1996, the Basle Committee formalized its 1998 capital agreement by letting banks choose between a regulatory formula and their own computer models to determine how much capital to set aside for market risk. This appendix does three things: (1) defines and explains market risk, (2) explains the why, what, and how of the regulators' (Basle Accord) market-risk capital formula, and (3) presents a brief introduction to J. P. Morgan's RiskMetrics™.

Market Risk

Finance equates risk with the degree of uncertainty about future returns. Because a traditional bank's returns come mainly from loans, its two major sources of uncertainty are credit risk and interest-rate risk (i.e., the quality of loans and how the loans are priced). Modern banks, especially the largest ones, have more numerous sources of returns and hence more sources of uncertainty, especially those arising from trading and derivatives activities, where the risks arise from unexpected changes with respect to interest rates, exchange rates, equity prices, and commodity prices. Of course, all banks, big and small, also face uncertainty with respect to liquidity and operational risks.

 Market risk, as defined by J. P. Morgan (JPM) in its "Introduction to Risk-Metrics" (p. 2), is the uncertainty of earnings arising from changes in market conditions associated with asset prices, interest rates, volatility, and market liquidity. In portfolio theory, *market risk* refers to systematic risk that cannot be diversified away and is captured by *beta* or the volatility of a stock or portfolio's return relative to the return on the market portfolio. To the extent that a bank can hedge its portfolio risk through geographic and product diversification, duration matching its assets and liabilities, or entering derivatives contracts, market risk is reduced. The remaining or unhedged market risk becomes the relevant risk. However, if derivatives contracts are used for speculative purposes, then market risk is increased.

 Now that we know what market risk is, how can we measure it? JPM focuses on measuring it in absolute and relative terms. The former attempts to measure a potential loss exposure in currency terms such as dollars, yen, or Swiss francs. JPM's concept is DEaR for "Daily Earnings at Risk." Because the *D* stands for daily, the time horizon is one day. When the investment horizon is longer, a month, for example, JPM employs the concept of VaR, or "Value at Risk." Regarding relative market risk, JPM measures the potential for underperformance against a benchmark index (estimated tracking error).

Overview of the Basle Committee's Capital Accord to Incorporate Market Risk[42]

On July 31, 1995, the FDIC, Federal Reserve, and OCC issued for public comment a proposed rule that would establish a risk-based capital requirement for market risk in foreign exchange, commodity activities, and the trading of debt and equity instruments. The proposed rule would affect institutions with large trading portfolios and activities. All national banks, state member banks, and BHCs that meet the following criteria would be affected:

1. Total assets exceed $5 billion, and
   a. The gross sum of trading assets and liabilities on a daily average basis for the quarter account for 3.0 percent or more of total assets, or
   b. The sum of the notional amount of interest-rate, exchange-rate, equity, and commodity off-balance-sheet derivatives contracts relating to trading activities exceeds $5 billion, or
2. The institution has total assets of $5 billion or less and trading assets and liabilities exceed 10 percent of total assets.

The banking agencies may apply the capital requirement to other institutions for safety-and-soundness purposes in limited circumstances and on a case-by-case basis. The agencies expect about 25 relatively large institutions and a few other smaller institutions to be affected by the rule.

To meet capital requirements for market risk, institutions can use Tier 1 and Tier 2 capital (as defined in the text and in appendix A) plus a third tier of capital (Tier 3) consisting of short-term subordinated debt. However, to meet capital requirements for market risk, Tier 3 capital must have an ordinal maturity of at least two years, be unsecured and fully paid up, and be subject to a lock-on provision that prevents the issuer from repaying the debt even at maturity if the issuer's capital ratios are, or with repayment would become, less than the minimum 8.0 percent risk-based capital requirement. To calculate capital charges for market risk, institutions can use either their own internal value-at-risk model or risk-measurement techniques developed by the banking agencies. In effect, this rule expands risk-based capital requirements beyond credit risk to include market risk for the institutions meeting the criteria defined above.

On March 7, 1996, the banking agencies further proposed that banks with large trading portfolios be required to "backtest" their internal models for predicting market risk. The proposal stipulates that banks would compare past estimates of market risk with actual results—hence the term *backtesting*. Banks using models that generate poor backtesting results may be required to increase their capital for market risk.

J. P. Morgan's RiskMetrics™

JPM's RiskMetrics is a methodology for estimating market risk based on what JPM uses for its own risk management. The model attempts to generate a set of consistently calculated volatilities and correlation forecasts as inputs to estimate

---

[42] For details on the capital requirements for market risk, see *Federal Register* Vol. 60, No. 142 (July 25, 1995) and Vol. 61, No. 46 (March 7, 1996).

market risks. Third parties have used JPM's approach and data to develop their own risk-management systems. JPM published and promotes RiskMetrics [1996] for three reasons:

1. To promote greater *transparency* of market risks

2. To establish a *benchmark* for measuring market risk that will permit comparisons of risks

3. To provide JPM's clients with *sound advice,* including advice on managing their market risks (i.e., selling risk-management services)

Regarding practical uses of market-risk information, JPM sees it as serving a number of purposes: keeping management informed (counterexamples of managers not being informed include Barings, Orange County, P&G, Bankers Trust, and Metallgesellschaft), setting exposure limits especially with respect to value at risk, allocating resources across trading portfolios and businesses, evaluating performance, and reporting to regulators. To obtain the details of JPM's RiskMetrics, interested readers can check jpmorgan.com on the WWW.

Selected References

Angell, Wayne D. [1991]. "Rules, Risk, and Reform: A Proposal for the Next Decade." Board of Governors of the Federal Reserve System, Address at the Banking Conference of the Federal Reserve Bank of Atlanta (March 19).

Bailey, John M., and Charlene G. Valenza. [1990]. "Regulating Capital Adequacy." *Bank Management* (February), pp. 30–33.

"Bank-Track: Emerging Trends for Bank Stocks." [1987]. *Investment Research,* Special Third Issue, Goldman Sachs, December.

Barth, M. E., W. R. Landsman, and J. M. Wahlen. [1995]. "Fair Value Accounting: Effects on Banks' Earnings Volatility, Regulatory Capital, and Value of Contractual Cash Flows." *Journal of Banking and Finance* 19 (June), pp. 577–606.

"Basle on Market Risk." [1996]. *U.S. Banker* 146 (January), p. 6.

Berger, Allen N., Richard J. Herring, and Giorgio P. Szego. [1995]. "The Role of Capital in Financial Institutions." *Journal of Banking and Finance* 19 (June), pp. 393–742.

Bhala, Raj. [1989]. *Risk-Based Capital: A Guide to the New Risk-Based Capital Adequacy Rules.* Rolling Meadows, IL: Bank Administration Institute.

Brealey, Richard A., and Stewart C. Myers. [1991]. *Principles of Corporate Finance.* New York: McGraw-Hill.

Buser, Stephen A., Andrew H. Chen, and Edward J. Kane. [1981a]. "Federal Deposit Insurance, Regulatory Policy, and Optimal Bank Capital." *Journal of Finance* 35 (March), pp. 51–60.

———. [1981b]. "Federal Deposit Insurance and Its Implications for the Management of Commercial Banks." Paper presented at the 1981 Eastern Finance Association Meetings, Ohio State University.

"Capital: Risk-Based Capital Guidelines." [1988]. *News Release* 88-14, Comptroller of the Currency Administrator of National Banks, March 1.

Carlstrom, C. T., and K. A. Samolyk. [1995]. "Loan Sales as a Response to Market-Based Capital Constraints." *Journal of Banking and Finance* 19 (June), pp. 627–646.

Citicorp Annual Report. [various years]. New York: Citicorp.

Cordell, L. R., and K. K. King. [1995]. "A Market Evaluation of the Risk-Based Capital Standards for the U.S. Financial System." *Journal of Banking and Finance* 19 (June), pp. 531–562.

Ehlen, James G., Jr. [1983]. "A Review of Bank Capital and Its Adequacy." Federal Reserve Bank of Atlanta *Economic Review* (November), pp. 54–60.

Estrella, Arturo. [1995]. "A Prolegomenon to Future Capital Requirements." *Economic Policy Review* 1 (July), pp. 1–12.

Fairlamb, David. [1994]. "Beyond Capital." *Institutional Investor* (August), p. 40.

"Final Market Risk Capital Standards Published." [1996]. *Financial Regulation Report* (January).

"Financial Services Capital Adequacy Directive: 'Implementation before Any Change.'" [1995]. *Multinational Service* (April 4), No. 353.

Fox, Justin. [1996a]. "Agencies Say Loans, Capital Will Remain Vital in Exams." *American Banker* (March 14), pp. 1–2.

———. [1996b]. "Debate: Risk Standards Based on Computer Models." *American Banker* (February 22), pp. 1, 4.

———. [1996c]. "Regulators Dropping Idea of Rate-Risk Capital Rule." *American Banker* (February 14), pp. 1–2.

Guttentag, Jack, and Richard Herring. [1981]. "The Insolvency of Financial Institutions: Assessment and Regulatory Disposition." University of Pennsylvania, Wharton School, Working Paper No. 17-81.

Huertas, Thomas F. [1988]. "Risk-Based Capital Requirements: Should They Apply to Bank Holding Companies?" *Issues in Bank Regulation* (Summer), pp. 8–12.

Ingersall, Bruce. [1988]. "Fed Clears Minimum Capital Standards, Forcing Some Banks to Raise $15 Billion." *The Wall Street Journal* (August 4), p. 6.

Introduction to RiskMetrics. [1994]. New York: J. P. Morgan.

Kane, Edward J. [1986]. "Competitive Financial Reregulation: An International Perspective." Paper presented at the 1986 Conference of the International Center for Monetary and Banking Studies (August), WPS 86-15, Ohio State University.

———. [1995]. "Three Paradigms for the Role of Capitalization Requirements in Insured Financial Institutions." *Journal of Banking and Finance* 19 (June), pp. 431–460.

Kantrow, Yvette D. [1990]. "Banks, Sallie Mae Battle on Writing Student Loans." *American Banker* (May 7), pp. 1 and 8.

Kleege, Stephen. [1996]. "Banks' High Level of Excess Capital Is Seen Putting Profitability at Risk." *American Banker* (March 12), pp. 1, 18.

Kraus, James R. [1996]. "Top U.S. Banks Set Records in Profitability Last Year." *American Banker* (March 12), pp. 9–12.

Kuprianov, Anatoli. [1995]. "Derivatives Debacles: Case Studies of Large Losses in Derivatives Markets." *Economic Quarterly* 81 (Fall), pp. 1–40.

Maisel, Sherman J. [1981]. *Risk and Capital Adequacy in Commercial Banks.* National Bureau of Economic Research Monograph. Chicago: University of Chicago Press.

Matthews, Gordon. [1990]. "Anticipated Loan Sales by Banks Put Bloom Back on Sallie Mae." *American Banker* (November 21), pp. 1 and 20.

Merton, Robert C. [1977]. "An Analytical Derivation of the Cost of Deposit Insurance Loan Guarantees: An Application of Modern Option Pricing Theory." *Journal of Banking and Finance* 1 (June), pp. 3–11.

———. [1978]. "On the Cost of Deposit Insurance When There Are Surveillance Costs." *Journal of Business* 51 (July), pp. 439–452.

———. [1995]. "Financial Innovation and the Management and Regulation of Financial Institutions." *Journal of Banking and Finance* 19 (June), pp. 461–482.

Miller, M. H. [1995]. "Do the M&M Propositions Apply to Banks?" *Journal of Banking and Finance* 19 (June), pp. 483–490.

Modigliani, Franco, and Merton Miller. [1958]. "The Cost of Capital, Corporation Finance, and the Theory of Investment." *American Economic Review* 48 (June), pp. 261–297.

Novack, Janet. [1988]. "Look Ma, No Risk." *Forbes* (January 25), pp. 52, 54.

Osterberg, William P. [1990]. "Bank Capital Requirements and Leverage: A Review of the Literature." *Economic Review* (Quarter 4), Federal Reserve Bank of Cleveland, pp. 2–12.

Peltzman, Sam. [1970]. "Capital Investment in Commercial Banking and Its Relationship to Portfolio Regulation." *Journal of Political Economy* 78(1), pp. 1–26.

Petty, Phillip N. [1991]. "The Impact of Complying with Risk-Based Capital." *Bankers Magazine* (January/February), pp. 49–54.

Pickering, C. J. [1990]. "Examining Risk-Based Capital Guidelines." *Independent Banker* (October), pp. 4–5.

Price Waterhouse. [1991]. *Bank Capital Adequacy and Capital Convergence.* London: Price Waterhouse (July).

Rehm, Barbara A. [1988]. "Fed Announces Plan to Enforce Risk-Based Capital Requirements." *American Banker* (January 28), pp. 1, 12.

"Risk-Based Capital." Office Correspondence, Division of Banking Supervision and Regulation, Board of Governors of the Federal Reserve System, January 25, 1988.

"Risk-Based Capital Standards: Market Risk." [1995]. *Federal Register* 60 (July 25).

"Risk-Based Capital Standards; Market Risk; Internal Models Backtesting." [1996]. *Federal Register* 61 (March 7).

RiskMetrics™—Technical Document. [1966]. Fourth edition, New York: J. P. Morgan/Reuters.

Rossant, John. [1995]. "The Prince: Inside the $10 Billion Empire of Power Player Alwaleed." *BusinessWeek* (September 25), pp. 88–99.

"Rules and Regulation." *Federal Register* 54 (Friday, January 27, 1989), pp. 4183–4184, as filed by Robert L. Clarke, Comptroller of the Currency.

"Scaling Factor Unchanged: Basle Takes Strict Line on Market Risk Standard." [1995]. *Thomson's International Banking Regulator* (December) 7(48), p. 1.

Schall, Lawrence, and Charles W. Haley. [1977]. *Introduction to Financial Management.* New York: McGraw-Hill.

Scholes, M. A., and M. A. Wolford. [1989]. "Decentralized Investment Banking: The Case of Dividend Reinvestment and Stock-Repurchase Plans." *Journal of Financial Economics* (September), pp. 7–36.

Sharpe, William F. [1978]. "Bank Capital Adequacy, Deposit Insurance, and Security Values." *Journal of Financial and Quantitative Analysis* 13 (November), pp. 701–718.

Shirreff, David. [1995]. "Regulatory Overload." *Euromoney* (June), pp. 115–117.

Sinkey, Joseph F., Jr. [1979]. *Problem and Failed Institutions in the Commercial Banking Industry.* Greenwich, CT.: JAI Press, Inc., 287 pp.

Smith, Clifford W., Jr. [1991]. Finance Ph.D. Seminar Notes, Visiting Professor, University of Georgia.

Sollenberger, Harold M., and Kurt Schneckenburger. [1994]. "Risk-Based Capital: How Would Credit Unions Look?" *Credit Union Executive* 34 (September), p. 18.

"Statement of the Shadow Financial Regulatory Committee on Regulatory Proposal for Risk-Related Capital Standards." [1988]. Shadow Financial Regulatory Committee, Chicago, February 8.

Statistics on Banking. Washington, DC: FDIC (various issues).

Strauss, Michael. [1987]. "Maximizing Returns on Student Loans with Secondary Market Assistance." *Bank Administration* (November), pp. 44, 46, 50.

"The Top 100 Banking Companies in Market Capitalization." [1996]. *American Banker* (January), p. 5.

"Tripartite Group Report on the Supervision of Financial Conglomerates." [1995]. *Financial Regulation Report* (July).

14

CAPITAL AND DIVIDEND MANAGEMENT

Contents

Chapter Summary
Key Words, Concepts, and Acronyms
Review/Discussion Questions
Problems/Projects
Selected References

LEARNING OBJECTIVES

■ To understand how the market values bank equity

■ To understand market measures of bank performance

■ To understand the sources of bank capital and to distinguish between internal and external sources of bank capital

■ To understand the connection between bank internal capital generation and the ROE model

■ To understand bank capital-formation strategies

CHAPTER THEME

What happened to the valuation of bank equity from the mid-1970s to the mid-1990s? The financial difficulties of the 1980s and early 1990s and the imposition of risk-based capital requirements in 1987–1988 (mandated by 1992) forced many banks to engage in corporate restructuring and to rethink their capital-formation strategies. Dividend cuts, new equity issues, assets sales, and cost cutting were signals banks sent to the marketplace. This chapter focuses on the signals emitted by a bank's capital-formation strategy and how the market values bank equity. To maintain its capital adequacy without tapping external sources of equity, a bank's asset growth is constrained to its internal capital generation rate ($g \approx ROE \times RR$). Retained earnings are a bank's major source of capital and a bank's retention ratio (RR) measures that portion of net income allocated to undivided profits.

KEY WORDS, CONCEPTS, AND TERMS

- Access to capital markets
- Dividend-payout ratio
- Dividend yield
- Double leverage
- Earnings per share (EPS)
- Equity multiplier (EM)
- External equity
- Internal capital generation rate ($g \approx ROE \times RR$)
- Market-to-book ratio
- Preferred stock
- Price-earnings ratio (P/E)
- Retained earnings
- Retention ratio (RR)
- Return on equity (ROE)
- Stock repurchases
- Subordinated notes and debentures
- Supremacy of equity

INTRODUCTION

A good story is worth repeating (Miller [1995], pp. 483–484). A banker was lamenting the loss of profitable investment opportunities because banks did not have enough capital. Miller suggested a simple solution: Raise more capital. The banker responded, "They can't. It's too expensive. Their stock is selling for only 50 percent of book value." Miller's counterthrust was, "Book values have nothing to do with the cost of equity capital. That's just the market's way of saying: We gave those guys a dollar and they managed to turn it into 50 cents."[1] Touché!

That was then (the early 1980s), what about now? Are bankers still turning a dollar of equity into 50 cents? At year-end 1995, if you gave the manager of a mega bank a dollar, it was turned into $1.56, on average. The manager of a superregional bank turned a dollar into $2.02, on average, whereas the manager of a large regional bank turned it into $1.83, on average. A year earlier (1994), the average figures were $1.20 (mega), $1.50 (superregional), and $1.38 (regional).[2] On balance, 1995 and 1996 were good years to give bankers, protected by a federal safety net, a dollar of equity. Although this chapter describes what happened to the valuation of bank equity between the mid-1970s and the mid-1990s, the important idea is how the market values bank stocks.

MARKET VALUATION OF BANK STOCKS

During the 1980s, a bank's capital adequacy, as reflected by its ratio of common equity to total assets, was "discovered" as the "dominant tool" for the valuation of bank stocks. Specifically, the new rule in banking was,

> Core or equity capital has become one of the major determinants of the valuation of bank stocks.

Investment analysts at **Goldman Sachs,** who claim to have discovered the rule, put it this way:[3]

> While the bank stock market always cared about equity ratios, today it has become the supreme ratio. For once the regulatory view and the market are undeniably in sync. (p. 1)

Glory be, the FDIC (*Forever Demanding Increased Capital*) was right all along! Let's take a look at this new rule for the market valuation of bank stocks.

How Can This Be New?

Now wait a minute, isn't capital adequacy just another way of measuring leverage and risk? Yes, it is. Then how can the market for valuing bank stocks have discovered such a fundamental financial relationship only in the 1980s? To echo the words from a Bob Dylan song of the 1960s: "The times, they are a changin'." Before we look at how the times have changed, let's focus on how the people at Goldman Sachs came up with this new valuation relationship for banks (actually bank holding companies).

---

[1] When the ratio of market value to book value is less than one (as described in Miller's story), then "hidden capital" (chapter 3) is negative. When hidden capital does not exist, market value and book value are equal. Hidden capital, of course, can be a positive or negative amount.

[2] The data are from Kraus [1996].

[3] This section draws on Albertson *et al.* [1988].

Two Pictures Worth 1,000 Words Each

Figures 14-1 and 14-2 capture the essence of the new valuation rule. In both figures, three fundamental variables are emphasized. The two primary ones are

1. The ratio of common equity to total assets (the inverse of the equity multiplier, *EM*)
2. The **price-earnings (P/E) multiple,** or the ratio of market value or price per share to earnings per share (EPS)

In both figures, the equity ratio is measured on the horizontal axis and the P/E ratio on the vertical axis.[4] In this two-dimensional space, what would we expect the relationship between P/E and the capital ratio to be? Because we are dealing with a risk-value relationship (risk is captured by the capital ratio, and value by the P/E ratio), we would expect low values of the equity ratio to be associated with low values of the P/E ratio, and high values of the equity ratio to be associated with high P/E multiples, all other things being equal.[5] If the expected relationship is a linear one, a line fitted to the points will have a constant positive slope. Moreover, if the relationship is a strong one, the scatter of points (each point representing a pair of equity ratios and P/E ratios) will be tightly bunched around the fitted (regression) line.

FIGURE 14-1 The Relationship between BHC P/E Ratios and Equity Ratios, December 31, 1977

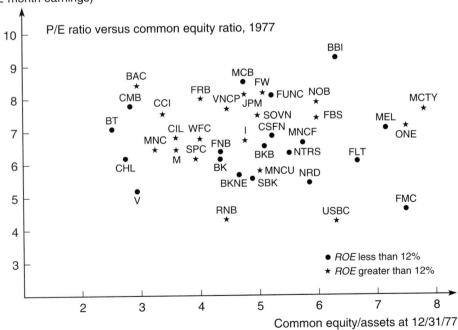

Source: Albertson *et al.* [1988]. Used by permission.

---

[4] Note that the equity ratio (horizontal axis) is measured in percent whereas the P/E ratio (vertical axis) is not.

[5] Of course, trying to capture a complexity like valuation by a simple one-variable model is a deliberate oversimplification. The assumption of "all other things being equal" (*ceteris paribus*) permits this narrow focus.

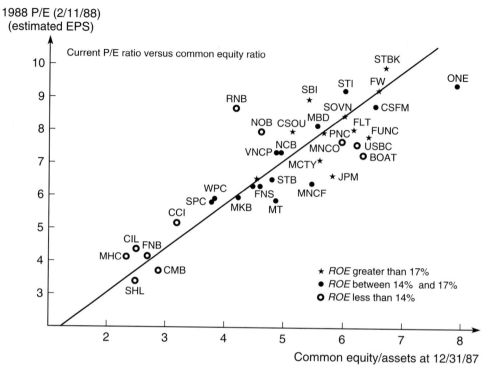

1988 P/E (2/11/88)
(estimated EPS)

Source: Albertson *et al.* [1988]. Used by permission.

FIGURE 14-2 The Relationship between BHC P/E Ratios and Equity Ratios, February 11, 1988

Suppose now that we add a third dimension to our analysis, **return on equity** (ROE), and consider the following two ROE profiles of the familiar form $ROE = ROA \times EM$:

The Leverage Bank: $0.20 = 0.005 \times 40$
The Equity Bank: $0.20 = 0.010 \times 20$

As an investor, which bank would you (and the marketplace) value more highly? Being rational, you would select the earnings stream associated with the Equity Bank because its profitability comes with less financial risk, as reflected by its lower equity multiplier (20 versus 40), or higher ratio of equity capital to total assets (0.05 versus 0.025). Suppose now that we want to incorporate ROE into our two-dimensional picture of the equity ratio and the P/E ratio. How can we do it without resorting to one of those (confusing) three-dimensional diagrams? By being innovative, as the Goldman Sachs researchers were, we can have each pair of [P/E, CAP] points also represent a particular range of ROE and identify banks within a particular range by a different symbol. On this basis, we would expect BHCs with high ROEs to be in the northeast portion of the diagram, and those with low ROEs to be in the southwest portion.

To recap, we are going to look at a scatter diagram in two-dimensional space with the coordinates of each point mapped with a symbol representing a particular range of ROE. Moreover, we should be comfortable with the expectation of a positive relationship between the two main variables, and with how and where we expect ROE to fit into the picture. Are you ready?

The Relationship for 1977

Figure 14-1 shows the scatter diagram for December 31, 1977. For this picture, the profitability ranges are ROE less than 12 percent, represented by the dots, and ROE greater than 12 percent, represented by the stars. Each star or dot is also labeled with letters identifying a particular bank holding company (BHC), 39 in all. Let's first focus on the overall picture. Clearly, our expectations are dashed. The 39 stars and dots (20 and 19, respectively) appear to be randomly distributed. Based on these data for large BHCs, capital structure, as measured by the ratio of equity to assets, does not seem to matter, because high P/E ratios are associated with both high leverage and low leverage. In addition, high P/E multiples are associated with both high and low ROE firms. Focusing on a P/E ratio of 7 as a cutoff, we have 13 BHCs with ROE less than 12 percent below the cutoff, and only 6 BHCs above it. In contrast, the 20 BHCs with ROE above 12 percent are more equally distributed with respect to the P/E cutoff, with 11 above it and 9 below it. Nevertheless, nothing systematic emerges regarding the relationship between P/E and ROE. On balance, Figure 14-1 does not generate any rule for valuing BHC stocks.

The Relationship for 1988

Figure 14-2 is in stark contrast to Figure 14-1. Our expectations are not dashed in Figure 14-2; in fact, they are fulfilled because a strong positive relationship exists between the P/E ratios for large BHCs and their ratios of common equity to total assets. Moreover (but not as strongly as the value-risk relationship), direct relationships between ROE and P/E value and between ROE and capital adequacy are observed. Specifically, BHCs with low ROEs tend to have low P/E ratios and low equity ratios; in contrast, BHCs with higher ROEs tend to have more adequate capital and higher P/E ratios. Because Figure 14-2 is constructed slightly differently from Figure 14-1, let's consider the differences. First, Figure 14-2 uses a mixture of data from the period 1986 to 1988. Specifically, the equity ratio is measured as of December 31, 1987, ROE is measured for 1986 (to escape the distortions caused by the massive provision for LDC loan losses taken by most of the sample BHCs in 1987), and the P/E ratio is measured as of February 11, 1988, using projected EPS figures for 1988. In estimating 1988 earnings, the Goldman Sachs analysts excluded nonrecurring items and tax benefits that might distort core earnings, especially among the multinational BHCs. Regarding the breakdown of 1986 ROE figures, three ranges were used: (1) ROE less than 14 percent indicated by rings, (2) ROE between 14 percent and 17 percent indicated by dots, and (3) ROE greater than 17 percent indicated by stars. Because of mergers and acquisitions, three fewer observations exist in Figure 14-2 than in Figure 14-1. Except for these details in construction, the figures attempt to measure the same relationships at two different points in time. The findings, however, are dramatically different.

The regression line fitted to the data in Figure 14-2 reveals the expected positive relationship between risk and value. Although the estimated regression equation was not reported by Goldman Sachs, it was described as "almost exactly one-for-one." For our purposes, the exact relationship is not critical; the important point is the positive relationship and the relatively tight fit around the regression line. In other words, the message for the managers of large BHCs in the late 1980s was clear: An increase in your ratio of common equity to total assets is most likely to lead to an increase in the firm's P/E ratio, all other things being equal. Moreover, based on the estimated relationship for 1977, such a prescription could not have been made back then.

Regarding the role of ROE, although some exceptions exist, as we move up the regression line from the southwest to the northeast, we tend to see rings, dots, and then stars. These symbols, of course, correspond to the ROE ranges described above. Let's focus on a few of the BHCs plotted in Figure 14-2. Specifically, let's look at Continental Illinois (CIL, bailed out by the FDIC in 1984, later restructured as Continental Bank, and acquired by BankAmerica in 1995), Bankers Trust (BT), J. P. Morgan (JPM), First Wachovia (FW, now Wachovia), and Banc One (One). Their profiles of *P/E, EM*$^{-1}$, and *ROE* are as follows:[6]

Bank holding company	P/E	EM^{-1}	ROE
Continental Illinois (CIL)	4.3	2.9%	8.5%
Bankers Trust (BT)	5.8	5.1%	16.3%
J. P. Morgan (JPM)	6.8	5.9%	19.9%
First Wachovia (FW)	9.1	6.7%	17.6%
Banc One (One)	9.3	7.9%	16.3%

The first three firms were, prior to Continental's bailout in 1984 and its subsequent restructuring into a smaller merchant/wholesale entity, considered as money-center BHCs. Given their equity ratios and ROEs, we would expect the monotonic increase in the P/E ratios as observed. The interesting point, and the point the Goldman Sachs's rule is making, comes from observing the profiles for the two superregional BHCs and comparing them to the money-center BHCs. First, consider the two superregionals. They illustrate a fundamental risk-return trade-off. Assuming no knowledge of the P/E ratios, we can ask whether investors will value Wachovia's higher risk-return profile more highly than Banc One's lower risk-return profile, or vice versa. The market's answer on February 11, 1988, was to value Banc One slightly higher at 9.3, versus Wachovia's 9.1.[7]

Next, let's compare Bankers Trust and Banc One. They both had an *ROE* of 16.3 percent in 1986. However, their year-end 1987 equity ratios were substantially different, at 5.1 percent and 7.9 percent. Other things equal, the higher equity ratio translated into a *P/E* ratio 60 percent higher for Banc One compared to that of Bankers Trust (i.e., 9.3 versus 5.8). As of May 15, 1991, the *P/E* ratios were 7 (Bankers Trust) and 13 (Banc One). As of May 2, 1996, they were 12 (Bankers Trust) and 11 (Banc One); on this date, however, Bankers Trust's earnings were substantially below what they had been in the past because of various derivatives debacles (chapter 9).

In a nutshell, these examples represent the Goldman Sachs rule for valuing bank stock: More equity is better than less, all other things being equal and at this point in time.

Why Now and Not Earlier?

In answering the question "Why Now and Not Earlier?" the Goldman Sachs report focused on a section entitled "Simply a Sign of the Times." In retrospect, the

---

[6] The P/E ratios are read from Figure 14-2, whereas the ROEs and equity ratios are from Albertson, *et al.* [1987], "Bank Ratios and Rankings," Investment Research, Goldman Sachs (Fourth Quarter), p. 3 and p. 11, respectively.

[7] As of May 15, 1991, the *P/E* ratios were 13 (Banc One) and 12 (Wachovia); as of September 11, 1997, they were 2 (Banc One) and 17 (Wachovia). During 1993–1995, Banc One encountered adverse publicity associated with its large volume of interest-rate swaps (chapter 9, appendix A).

analysts suggested three reasons (signs) for the clustering of the P/E and equity ratios in 1988 but not in 1977:

1. The focus on the "integrity" of a bank's balance sheet, which has been assaulted by LDC, energy, farm, and real estate lending problems[8]

2. The importance of tangible equity capital for BHC expansion and the regulatory refocusing on equity, or core capital, as the key element in international capital guidelines

3. Investor suspicion about ROA and ROE as performance measures because of adjustments being made to either the numerators (e.g., nonrecurring items) or the denominators of the ratios

Regarding the second point, since 1991, federal bank regulators have been required to take "prompt corrective action" with respect to problem banks.[9] In addition, they have been strongly criticized for their too-big-to-fail policies and practices. As evidenced by the OCC's closing of the Bank of New England in 1991, regulators may be sensitive to such criticism and more willing to pull the plug on large banks/BHCs. Accordingly, a lower equity-to-asset ratio may imply a greater probability of such regulatory action.

The Supremacy of Equity: A Recapitulation

The Goldman Sachs Bank-Track investment report of March 1988 was titled: "The Supremacy of Equity." The focus of the investment research was the recognition of a new relationship in which common equity was viewed as the dominant determinant of bank stock values. Given the random dispersion (lack of clustering) in Figure 14-1, the critical evidence for the new relationship was the clustering of bank stock *P/E* ratios around equity values as shown in Figure 14-2. The investment report concluded (p. 5),

> The most provocative conclusion might simply be to expect banks to issue new equity more readily than in the past! If bank managements accept the foregoing analysis and believe these two diagrams, the risk of dilution (of EPS) now appears secondary to the benefits of higher capital.

OPTIMAL CAPITAL STRUCTURE AND THE VALUATION OF BANK STOCKS IN THE TWENTY-FIRST CENTURY

When asked whether M&M propositions apply to banks, Miller [1995], one-half of the M&M team, replied: "Yes and no." According to Goldman Sachs, the answer, in practice not theory, was no in 1977 but yes in 1988. What about the upcoming twenty-first century? If an optimal capital structure for banks does exist, having too much or too little capital will reduce the value of the banking firm. Bankers need to find the amount that is just right. The fact that some banks, especially the largest ones, renewed stock-repurchase programs in the mid-1990s suggests that these managers may think that they have excess equity capital (e.g., Citicorp as described in the previous chapter).

---

[8] A bank stock analyst with Montgomery Securities in San Francisco describes "integrity" in terms of a "fortressed balance sheet," or one supported by strong earnings and capital.

[9] This charge comes from the Federal Deposit Insurance Corporation Improvement Act of 1991, known as FDICIA.

The Relationship for 1995: The Supremacy of Equity Is Tarnished a Bit

Figure 14-3 shows an updated supremacy-of-equity test for 1995. The relationship, or lack of it, is clear.[10] Although the scatter diagram is not as dispersed as for 1977, it is not as tight as it was in 1988. On balance, only a weak positive relationship is detected. Since the sample BHCs are different from those used in the Goldman Sachs study, we are, strictly speaking, comparing apples and oranges. Forty-one of the 50 largest BHCs were used for this updated test. The capital ratios and ROEs were as of year-end 1995, whereas the P/E multiples were as of March 29, 1996.[11] Splitting the 41 BHCs into groups of mega, superregional, large regional, and other regional BHCs, the relevant data, ranked by P/E multiple within groups, are shown in Table 14-1.[12]

What do we conclude from the 1995–1996 supremacy-of-equity test? Perhaps Miller is right after all that the answer to the question of the relevancy of capital

FIGURE 14-3 **The Supremacy of Equity, 1995–1996**

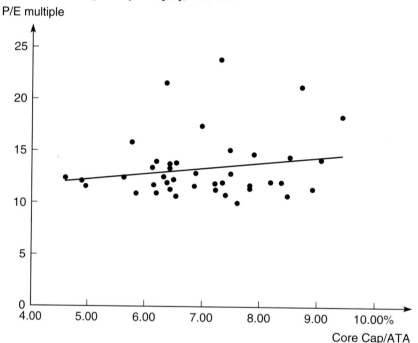

Note: Core capital and average total assets (*ATA*) are expressed as percentages for data as of December 31, 1995. The *P/E* multiples are as of 29 March 1996. The regression of *P/E* on the capital ratio is not statistically significant at the standard 5 percent level of significance. The t-statistic on the capital ratio is 1.25 percent ($= [0.5358/0.4268] \times 100$), which is significantly different from zero at the 22 percent level. The R-square is 0.0388, whereas the simple correlation coefficient is 0.1971.

Data Sources: "Bank Search," Sheshunoff Information Services Inc., 1996 for balance-sheet data; American Banker (April 1, 1996) for *P/E* multiples.

---

[10] The regression of *P/E* on the capital ratio is not statistically significant at the standard 5 percent level of significance. The t-statistic on the capital ratio is 1.25 percent, which is significantly different from zero at the 22 percent level.

[11] Using a contemporaneous P/E ratio (12 December 1995) or a P/E ratio as of 2 February 1996 resulted in even weaker positive relationships between the two variables.

[12] The first three size classes are those reported by Kraus [1996].

TABLE 14-1 Price-Earnings Multiples, Capital Ratios, and Return on Equity by BHC Size Groups (ranked by *P/E* as of of 29 March 1996)

Size Class/Bank Holding Company	P/E	Capital Ratio	ROE
Mega (10)			
BankAmerica	10.6	6.53%	13.62%
NationsBank	10.8	5.82	16.64
Banc One	11.3	8.90	16.24
J. P. Morgan	11.4	5.03	13.05
Citicorp	11.6	7.22	18.29
First Chicago NBD Corp	11.9	6.40	25.44
First Union	12.1	4.96	17.80
Bankers Trust	12.2	4.57	4.42
Chase Manhattan	13.7	6.55	13.37
Fleet Banking	23.8	7.30	12.70
Superregional (18)			
CoreStates	9.9	7.59%	19.52%
Bank of Boston	10.7	7.38	15.65
Bank of New York	10.7	8.46	19.09
KeyCorp	10.8	6.20	16.15
Southtrust	11.2	6.42	15.50
Wells Fargo	11.2	7.21	26.40
Mellon Bank	11.2	7.81	16.83
Southern National	11.4	7.81	12.76
Comerica	11.5	6.86	16.48
Barnett Banks	11.6	6.15	16.32
National City	11.9	7.33	16.86
Wachovia	12.0	8.36	17.08
Norwest	12.3	5.61	20.59
Republic NY	12.4	6.32	10.33
First Bank System	13.3	6.13	21.34
State Street Boston	13.5	5.75	17.01
SunTrust	13.5	6.44	14.51
PNC Bank Corp	21.5	6.37	8.69
Large Regional (10)			
AmSouth Bancorp	12.1	6.47%	12.91%
Crestar Financial	12.7	7.48	14.31
Huntington Bancshares	12.8	6.88	16.38
Northern Trust	13.8	6.19	15.98
Marshall & Ilsley	14.1	9.05	16.57
MercantileBancorp	14.3	8.51	16.00
U.S. Bancorp	14.6	7.89	16.33
Firstar Corp	15.0	7.47	15.57
Integra Financial	17.3	6.98	13.01
Fifth Third Bancorp	18.3	9.43	18.48
Other Regional (3)			
Boatmen's Bancshares	12.0	8.17%	15.66%
First Tennessee	13.1	6.43	20.24
Synovus Financial	21.1	8.71	18.35

Source: Bank Call Reports, December 31, 1995 for capital ratios and *ROE,* and *American Banker* (April 1, 1996) for *P/E*s as of March 29, 1996.

structure for banks is yes and no. When banks need capital (as in the 1980s and early 1990s), it is relevant; when they don't need as much of it (as in the mid-1990s), it isn't as relevant. On balance, capital structure matters to managers, regulators, and investors. Perhaps we should think of bank capital as some professors think about tenure in academia: If you don't have it (tenure), it is relevant; if you do have it, it isn't relevant. *C'est la vie—That's life!*

WAS THE VALUE OF BANKS' CAPITAL UNDERESTIMATED IN THE 1980S?

To address the question of whether the value of banks' capital was underestimated in the 1980s, let's consider the words of Martin Feldstein, former chairman of the president's Council of Economic Advisers, in an op-ed piece in *The Wall Street Journal* (February 21, 1991):

> The measurement of a bank's capital is now far more important than when bank failures were very rare and capital requirements were less central to bank regulatory supervision. Banks with less than the prescribed minimum ratios of capital to assets are being forced by the regulators to shrink their size, reduce their dividends, and refrain from new activities.... (However,) ... the current regulatory accounting rules understate the true value of bank assets and therefore of bank capital.... An increased attention to bank capital is very desirable, but only if the full value of a bank's assets is properly recognized (insert mine).

To clarify Feldstein's conjecture of the understatement of a bank's regulatory capital, consider the idea of the value of a bank (or any firm) as consisting of the present value (PV) of assets in place plus the present value of future growth opportunities or options (call the second component PVGO for the *Present Value of Growth Opportunities*). Thus,

$$\text{Market value of bank} = PV \text{ of assets in place} + PVGO \qquad \textbf{(14-1)}$$

Feldstein describes the "true total assets" of a bank as including all the components of the bank as an "operating business that will produce future profits." The inclusion sounds like PVGO, doesn't it? Some of the PVGOs Feldstein has in mind include credit-card businesses that earn high net rates of interest (e.g., recall the discussion of Maryland National's sale of its credit card subsidiary as an IPO in 1991; see chapter 11), the reputational capital associated with loan origination (e.g., single-family mortgages), a branching network that generates stable and low-cost core deposits, and profitable customer relationships with corporate clients.

Feldstein sees two potential ways to remedy the problem of regulators' underestimating the true, or market, value of a bank's capital. First, he suggests adding the future value of a bank's "operating business" (i.e., its PVGO) to the (market) value of its net on-balance-sheet items (i.e., assets in place). Or second, instead of splitting a bank into the two components of value shown in equation (14-1), he suggests finding value on an aggregate basis by estimating the present value of the bank's future cash flows from all activities. The critical problem with the second approach is the uncertainty of the future cash flows and the difficulty of choosing the appropriate discount rate to determine the present values. Because some people might have seen the first approach as similar to the solution to the thrift problem of letting them grow their way out of difficulty, Feldstein says that bank regulators should be "conservative and look only at earnings that would be achieved without expanding the bank's size or range of activities." Feldstein contends that, in retrospect, the regulators' handling of the bank LDC crisis recognized, implicitly at least, the operating-business approach to judging bank solvency.

THE MARKET CAPITALIZATION OF LARGE BANKS AND HOW THE MARKET LOOKS AT BANKS

A bank's market capitalization is calculated by multiplying the price of its common stock by the number of shares outstanding. Table 14-2 shows the 10 largest banking companies ranked by total market capitalization as of year-end 1995 and the percentage change in market value for 1995. These firms, led by Citicorp, with $28.5 billion in market value of common equity, had total market capitalization of $160.6 billion, which accounted for 40 percent of the total market capitalization of the 100 top banking companies ($400 billion). The merger of Chase and Chemical in 1996 moved the resulting bank (Chase) into second on the list on a pro forma basis; Wells Fargo's 1996 acquisition of First Interstate moved it into the number three spot, with $19.1 billion in market capitalization. Prior to the acquisition, Wells Fargo ranked 11th.

Although dollar data on market capitalization are interesting, the market value of equity needs to be judged relative to something. As described in the previous

TABLE 14-2   The Top 10 Banking Companies in Market Capitalization ($ billions as of December 29, 1995)

	Market Capitalization	
Rank/Company	*1995[a]*	*Annual % change*
1. Citicorp, New York	$28.5B	74.9%
2. BankAmerica Corp., San Francisco	23.9	63.4
3. NationsBank, Charlotte, NC	18.9	51.2
4. J. P. Morgan & Co., New York	15.1	43.0
5. Banc One, Columbus, OH	14.7	46.1
6. Chemical Banking Corp., New York	14.7	67.5
7. First Chicago NBD Corp.	12.6	195.0
8. Norwest Corp., Minneapolis	11.1	54.3
9. Chase Manhattan Corp., New York	10.8	78.1
10. First Interstate Bancorp, Los Angeles	10.3	106.0
Total Top 10/Average %Δ	$160.6B	60.4%
Memo:		
Pro formas for mergers, entry in top 10		
2. Chase + Chemical	25.5	72.0[b]
3. Wells Fargo + First Interstate	19.1	74.0[b]
10. Bank of New York Co. Inc.	9.0	75.0

[a]1996 was another banner year for bank stocks—e.g., Citicorp's market capitalization rose to $52B (82%).

[b]Weighted average growth based on proportion of equity.

Source: Adapted from data reported in the *American Banker* (January 12, 1996), p. 5.

chapter, we might judge it relative to risk-weighted assets, based on all relevant risk exposures. Because such a comprehensive measure does not exist, we take a second-best approach and compare market value of equity to book value of equity—the market-to-book ratio. Two other commonly used measures of market performance are the price-earnings (P/E) ratio, or multiple, and dividend yield. These three measures of market performance are defined as

Market-to-book ratio = market price per share divided by book value per share

P/E ratio = market price per share divided by earnings per share

Dividend yield = annual dividend divided by year-end price per share

Again, keep in mind the important caveat that any ratio or multiple has two component parts which cannot be ignored when analyzing the ratio. We illustrate this important point below.

Table 14-3 presents market-to-book ratios for three bank size classes: mega (assets of $75 billion or more as of December 31, 1995), superregional (assets between $25 billion and $75 billion), and large regional banks (assets between $10 billion and $25 billion). The number of banks in each group for which data are available is 11 (mega), 19 (of 20 superregional), and 17 (of 20 large regional). The banks are ranked within the groups by their market-to-book ratios, with *P/E* multiples and dividend yields also provided. For comparison, data for 1994 are also provided. As of December 31, 1995, the largest banks in each group were Citicorp, with total assets of $257 billion, PNC Bank Corp, with $73 billion in assets, and First of American Bank Corp, with $24 billion.[13] Within their respective groups, however, size is not the key to the relative market-to-book rankings. For example, the ranks for these three banks are 4th, 10th, and 15th.

The following profiles reveal how the market looked at the average bank in each of the three groups at year-end 1995:

	Market/book	*P/E*	*Dividend yield*
Average megabank	1.56	14.2	3.47%
Average superregional	2.02	13.1	3.03%
Average large regional	1.83	13.3	3.00%
All 47 banks	1.85	13.4	3.12%

How the Market Looks at Mega Banks

Panel A of Table 14-3 presents measures of market performance for the 11 banking companies in the megabank group. Because the BHCs in this group ranged in total assets from Citicorp, with $257 billion, to Fleet Financial Group, with $84 billion, a wide size gap exists. Market-to-book ratios for the group ranged from 1.84 (Banc One) to 1.31 (Bankers Trust), *P/E* ratios ranged from 32.9 (Bankers Trust) to 9.1 (Chemical), and dividend yields ranged from 6.02 percent (Bankers Trust) to 1.78 percent (Citicorp). Bankers Trust, which did not have a good year in 1995, had the lowest market-to-book ratio, because its market value was low, but had the highest P/E ratio, because its earnings per share were low. Its dividend yield was the highest, because its dividend remained high while its price was low. Bankers

---

[13] If we do a forma on the merger between Chase and Chemical, the resulting bank with total assets of $304 billion would be the largest U.S. megabank.

TABLE 14-3   How the Market Looks at Banks: Market-to-Book Ratios, *P/E* Multiples, and Dividend Yields

PANEL A. MEGABANKS

Market-to-Book Rank			Ratio of Market-to-Book Value		Price-Earnings Multiple		Dividend Yield (%)	
1995	*1994*	*Megabanks*	*1995*	*1994*	*1995*	*1994*	*1995*	*1994*
1	3	Banc One Corp.	184.10	137.72	11.75	10.49	3.61	4.89
2	1	Fleet Financial Group Inc.*	179.44	156.55	25.96	10.48	4.00	4.32
3	2	First Union Corp.*	174.43	146.77	11.04	8.77	3.52	4.16
4	5	Citicorp	174.04	120.35	10.38	6.58	1.78	1.09
5	6	J. P. Morgan & Co. Inc.	158.25	120.10	12.62	9.32	3.81	4.97
6	4	First Chicago NBD Corp.*	156.44	121.13	11.58	7.65	3.42	4.49
7	7	NationsBank Corp.	149.67	113.66	9.89	7.45	2.99	4.17
8	11	Chase Manhattan Corp.	139.05	87.51	10.60	5.89	2.89	4.25
9	9	Chemical Banking Corp.	138.04	94.71	9.08	7.73	3.30	4.57
10	10	BankAmerica Corp.	135.18	92.66	10.04	7.41	2.84	4.05
11	8	Bankers Trust New York Corp.	131.47	103.18	32.92	7.72	6.02	6.68
		Mean value for the group	156.37	117.67	14.17	8.14	3.47	4.33
		Median value for the group	156.44	120.10	11.04	7.72	3.42	4.32

PANEL B. SUPERREGIONAL BANKS

Market-to-Book Rank			Ratio of Market-to-Book Value		Price-Earnings Multiple		Dividend Yield (%)	
		Superregional Banks						
1	1	Wells Fargo & Co.	284.47	217.16	10.60	10.06	2.13	2.76
2	6	First Interstate Bancorp	272.46	162.60	12.39	7.76	2.27	4.07
3	3	First Bank System Inc.*	241.02	178.48	12.07	15.54	2.92	3.49
4	4	State Street Boston Corp.*	233.52	176.48	15.25	10.84	1.51	2.10
5	2	Norwest Corp.	232.39	216.64	12.09	9.70	2.73	3.27
6	7	CoreStates Financial Corp.	219.69	160.30	11.91	15.03	3.80	4.77
7	5	Wachovia Corp.	206.55	167.71	13.11	10.34	3.02	3.81
8	16	Mellon Bank Corp.	205.39	122.21	12.05	12.65	3.72	5.13
9	10	U.S. Bancorp*	205.28	146.92	16.09	14.14	3.15	4.15
10	14	PNC Bank Corp.*	191.17	127.34	27.10	8.38	4.34	6.20
11	11	Bank of New York Co. Inc.	188.52	133.30	11.34	8.04	2.79	3.68
12	8	SunTrust Banks Inc.	181.60	159.97	13.87	10.93	2.16	2.76
13	13	Boatmen's Bancshares Inc.	180.70	128.55	12.58	7.98	3.47	4.79
14	9	National City Corp.	176.20	158.16	11.23	9.80	3.92	4.56
15	18	Comerica Inc.	175.98	119.37	11.30	7.43	3.43	5.09
16	15	Barnett Banks Inc.	172.26	123.83	11.50	8.26	3.08	4.13
17	12	KeyCorp	169.71	132.42	10.51	7.25	3.97	5.12
18	19	Bank of Boston Corp.	159.87	104.67	10.44	7.17	2.77	3.59
19	17	Republic New York Corp.	143.67	121.05	13.53	8.07	2.32	2.92
		Mean value for the group	202.13	150.38	13.10	9.97	3.03	4.02
		Median value for the group	191.17	146.92	12.07	9.70	3.02	4.07

(Continued)

TABLE 14-3 *Continued*

PANEL C. LARGE REGIONAL BANKS

Market-to-Book Rank		Large Regional Banks: the 20 Largest	Ratio of Market-to-Book Value		Price Earnings Multiple		Dividend Yield (%)	
1995	*1994*		*1995*	*1994*	*1995*	*1994*	*1995*	*1994*
1	1	Fifth Third Bancorp	284.41	222.07	17.26	12.90	1.97	2.50
2	3	Northern Trust Corp.	243.06	170.40	15.14	11.08	1.95	2.63
3	4	Huntington Bancshares Inc.	210.16	159.20	13.48	9.28	3.25	4.17
4	2	Marshall & Ilsley Corp.	201.24	172.57	13.68	18.27	2.48	3.11
5	11	Meridian Bancorp, Inc.	200.09	123.84	15.60	9.68	3.12	5.03
6	6	Firstar Corp.*	192.26	138.17	13.21	9.02	3.33	4.32
7	5	Integra Financial Corp.	182.02	157.21	16.27	8.21	3.09	4.13
8	9	Mercantile Bancorp. Inc.*	174.71	133.15	11.50	9.70	2.87	3.58
9	13	Crestar Financial Corp.*	174.41	123.48	14.39	8.87	2.96	4.07
10	7	Regions Financial Corp.	173.74	137.59	11.47	9.12	3.07	3.87
11	8	Southern National Corp.*	169.14	137.39	16.01	8.65	3.28	3.87
12	15	AmSouth Bancorp.	167.12	114.09	13.46	11.44	3.81	5.55
13	12	Summit Bancorp.	162.52	123.53	11.91	10.27	3.34	3.90
14	10	SouthTrust Corp.	157.40	129.12	10.86	8.37	3.12	3.78
15	14	First of America Bank Corp.	153.60	119.43	11.90	8.13	3.88	5.47
16	17	Union Bank	141.72	79.54	10.08	14.86	2.58	5.23
17	16	BanPonce Corp.	122.55	102.35	9.25	7.66	2.97	3.56
		HSBC Americas, Inc.	NA	NA	NA	NA	NA	NA
		Harris Bank	NA	NA	NA	NA	NA	NA
		LaSalle National Corp.	NA	NA	NA	NA	NA	NA
		Mean value for the group	182.95	137.83	13.26	10.32	3.00	4.05
		Median value for the group	174.41	133.15	13.46	9.28	3.09	3.90
		Summary Totals for All 47 Publicly Held Banks in Survey						
		Mean values for all 47 banks	184.48	138.18	13.41	9.67	3.12	4.10
		Median values for all 47 banks	175.98	132.42	12.05	9.02	3.09	4.13

*The 1994 data have been restated for subsequent mergers or changes in accounting principles.

Source: Adapted from data reported in the *American Banker* (March 18, 1996), p. 10.

Trust's dismal market performance in 1995 reflected its weak accounting performance as captured by the following ROE decomposition analysis:[14]

$$ROE = ROA \times EM = 0.0398 = 0.0020 \times 19.9$$

The *ROE* and *ROA* were the lowest among the 11 mega BHCs, whereas the *EM* was the highest (i.e., lowest ratio of average common equity to average assets at 0.0502). In contrast, Citicorp's 1995 ROE profile was

---

[14] The accounting data presented in this section are from the *American Banker* (March 18, 1996), p. 8. The EMs were calculated by dividing *ROE* by *ROA*. The ROEs in this section differ slightly from those reported in Table 14-1 because in Table 14-1 total equity capital is used in the denominator of *ROE*, whereas the figures here use common equity in the denominator. Because common equity is less than total equity capital, the ROEs here are larger, for example, Citicorp here is 20.74 percent versus 18.29 in Table 14-1.

$$ROE = 0.2074 = 0.0137 \times 15.14$$

Citicorp's almost 21 percent (accounting) return on common equity in 1995 was the highest in the megabank group. Banc One, the mega BHC with the highest ROA for 1995, had the following ROE profile:

$$ROE = 0.1677 = 0.0147 \times 11.41$$

Banc One, however, had about 25 percent less leverage (lower EM) than Citicorp.[15] If Banc One had Citicorp's EM, all other things being equal, its *ROE* would have been 29.25 percent (0.0147×19.9). If Citicorp had Banc One's EM, its *ROE* would have been 15.63 percent (0.0137×11.41). Recall that leverage is the yeast that raises ROE to a multiple of ROA.

The market valuations of Banc One and Citicorp as shown in Panel A of Table 14-3 and the components of *ROE* shown above suggest that, all other things being equal, the market values higher ROA and lower EM (Banc One's lower-accounting ROE) more than lower ROA and higher EM (Citicorp's higher-accounting ROE). The evidence is Banc One's market-to-book ratio of 1.84 and its *P/E* of 11.75 versus Citicorp's 1.74 and 10.38. The market likes both higher profitability (ROA) and greater safety (stronger capital adequacy).

How the Market Looks at Superregional Banks

Panel B of Table 14-3 presents our three measures of market performance for 19 superregional banks. Size differences within this group are of the same magnitude (about 3-to-1) as they were for the 11 mega BHCs. For example, PNC had total assets of $73 billion whereas State Street Bank had $26 billion. Wells Fargo, famous for its cost-efficient operating performance, led this group with a market-to-book ratio of 2.84; at the bottom end, Republic New York's ratio was about 50 percent lower, at 1.44. Focusing on P/E ratios, however, paints a completely different picture and illustrates the need to look carefully at the component parts of any ratio. Wells Fargo's *P/E* ratio (10.6) was the lowest among the 20 superregional banks, whereas Republic's was the highest (13.5). Why? Wells Fargo had very strong EPS for 1995, especially compared to Republic's EPS. All other things being equal, high EPS makes for low P/E and vice versa. Regarding dividend yield, Wells Fargo (2.13%) and Republic (2.32%) were more similar.

Wells Fargo's strong ROE profile provides a good indication of why the market values it so highly, that is,

$$ROE = 0.2969 = 0.0203 \times 14.62$$

An *ROA* of 2 percent represents an exceptional performance for a large bank. Although Wells is noted for its cost-efficient operations, the bank does not skimp on its lending activities. In fact, it is an aggressive lender as indicated by its high ratio of nonperforming assets to total assets of 1.49 percent, highest among the group of 20 superregional banks, which had a group mean of 0.57 percent. In contrast, Republic New York, which prefers investing in securities to making loans, had a lower ratio of nonperforming assets to assets, of 0.23 percent. Republic's ROE profile at year-end 1995 was

$$ROE = 0.1146 = 0.0068 \times 16.85$$

---

[15] As of year-end 1990, the *ROE* profiles for these two BHCs were Citicorp: $0.0210 = 0.0008 \times 26.25$, and Banc One: $0.1620 = 0.0152 \times 10.66$.

Because Republic's balance-sheet composition is the exception rather than the rule, it appears that the market values a combination of cost efficiency and aggressive lending more than passive banking.

How the Market Looks at Large Regional Banks

Panel C of Table 14-3 presents our three measures of market performance for 17 large regional banks. Size differences within this group are less dramatic than those in the mega and superregional groups. For example, First of America Bank Corp. (Kalamazoo, Michigan), the largest of the large regional banks, had total assets of $23.6 billion compared to $13.3 billion for Marshall & Ilsley Corp. of Milwaukee, the smallest bank in the group. Fifth Third Bank of Cincinnati led this group with a market-to-book ratio of 2.84 (second only to Wells Fargo's 2.845); at the bottom end, Union Bank of San Francisco had a market-to-book ratio of 1.42.[16] Unlike the two previous groups, Fifth Third had the highest P/E ratio (17.3) in its group. Its dividend yield (1.97%), however, was the second-lowest in its group. Fifth Third's ROE profile reveals a strong accounting performance to match its market valuation, that is,

$$ROE = 0.1813 = 0.0178 \times 10.18$$

Its *ROA* of 1.78 percent is second only to Wells Fargo's among the banks in these three groups. If Fifth Third had Wells Fargo's equity multiplier (EM), its *ROE* would be $0.0178 \times 14.62 = 26$ percent instead of 18 percent. In addition to being conservative with its leverage, Fifth Third maintains a very high quality loan portfolio as reflected by its nonperforming-assets ratio of 0.24 percent, well below the group mean of 0.62 percent and second only to Northern Trust's 0.17 percent.

Recapitulation

Across all three size groups, ROA appears to be the key accounting ratio that drives higher market valuation. Moreover, the market does not seem to care how that higher ROA is achieved. For example, Wells Fargo achieves its high ROA through more aggressive lending but offsets higher loan losses with greater operating efficiency; in contrast, Fifth Third relies on a high-quality loan portfolio (lower loan losses).

THE INTERNAL CAPITAL GENERATION RATE (g)

A bank's or BHC's major source of equity capital is its flow of net income after dividends. Over time, this flow, if positive, builds up a bank's major component of shareholders' equity, namely, **retained earnings,** or undivided profits. Community banks without easy **access to capital markets** especially depend on internal equity to build their capital bases. Retained earnings for any company are a function of its investment, financing, and dividend policies. For banks/BHCs, these policy decisions are reflected in such income-expense symptoms as net interest income, provision for loan losses (loan quality), burden (i.e., the difference between noninterest income and noninterest expense), nonrecurring items, taxes, and dividends. The importance of equity capital to the market valuation of bank stocks has been

---

[16] We exclude BanPonce Corp. of San Juan, PR, which had a lower market-to-book ratio, at 1.22.

established. This section focuses on how lack of capital can limit a bank's growth opportunities.

Consider the following situation. Suppose a bank has the following simple balance sheet: $100 = 90 + 10$ of the form $A = D + E$. If assets (A) and deposits (D) grow at 10 percent per period, then the bank's capital base (E) also must grow at 10 percent for its relative capital position not to deteriorate. That is, at 10 percent growth, the next period's balance sheet would be $110 = 99 + 11$. However, the bank's capital-to-asset and capital-to-deposit ratios would be unchanged from the previous period, at 10 percent and 11.1 percent, respectively. If the bank does *not* pay out any of its earnings in the form of dividends, the bank's *ROE* must be 10 percent to maintain its relative capital position. If regulatory and market pressures restrict asset and deposit growth to the same growth rate as the capital base, then a positive payout ratio means that the bank must generate a higher ROE or seek external sources of capital or both. For example, with an *ROE* of 10 percent and a payout ratio of 30 percent, the capital base expands by only 7 percent (i.e., $0.07 = 0.10[1 - 0.3]$) and growth would be restricted to 7 percent. Balance-sheet expansion at a 10 percent rate would require an *ROE* of 14.28 percent, or a smaller ROE plus external capital.

An important concept and tool for the financial management of bank equity capital is the **internal capital generation rate** (g), which is approximately equal to the product of a bank's ROE and its retention ratio (RR), that is,[17]

$$g \approx ROE \times RR \qquad \text{(14-2)}$$

The retention ratio is simply 1 minus the payout ratio (i.e., $RR = 1 - PR$). From the ROE model, we know that $ROE = ROA \times EM$, and that $ROA = PM \times AU$, where PM = profit margin and AU = asset utilization. Thus, the capital generation rate can be expressed as

$$g \approx PM \times AU \times EM \times RR \qquad \text{(14-3)}$$

In words, a bank's internal capital generation rate depends upon its profitability (PM), asset utilization (AU), equity multiplier (EM), and retention ratio (RR). By increasing any one of these factors, all other things being equal, internal capital generation will improve. From an internal perspective, the key to a bank's capital generation, and hence its capital adequacy, rests with the four components of equation (14-3). Thus, if a bank wants to improve its capital position through internal capital generation, it needs to get down to such basics as effective spread management, cost control, operating efficiency, and optimal financial and dividend policies.

If we focus on equation (14-2), the interaction between selected ROEs and RRs is summarized in the internal-capital-generation matrix presented in Table 14-4. Each cell in the matrix represents a particular internal capital generation rate determined by the product of the corresponding row and column elements. For example, if a BHC generates an *ROE* of 15 percent and pays out 40 percent of its earnings in dividends (i.e., $RR = 1 - PR = 0.60$), it will have a capital generation rate of 9 percent.

The capital-generation matrix is a useful tool for capital planning. For example, suppose that a bank anticipates (1) growth opportunities of 12 percent, (2) *ROE*

---

[17] Equation (14-2) is an approximation of the internal capital generation rate that understates the true rate. To be more accurate, g is equal to $(ROE \times RR)/(1 - ROE \times RR)$. The difference between the two formulas is the adjustment factor in the denominator. The approximation of g is accurate enough for our purposes, and it is used in the examples in the text.

TABLE 14-4	The Internal-Capital-Generation Matrix[a]						
	Retention Ratio (RR)						
Return on Equity (ROE)	*0.00*	*0.20*	*0.40*	*0.50*	*0.60*	*0.80*	*1.00*
0.00	0.00	0.00	0.00	0.000	0.00	0.00	0.00
0.05	0.00	0.01	0.02	0.025	0.03	0.04	0.05
0.10	0.00	0.02	0.04	0.050	0.06	0.08	0.10
0.15	0.00	0.03	0.06	0.075	0.09	0.12	0.15
0.20	0.00	0.04	0.08	0.100	0.12	0.16	0.20
0.25	0.00	0.05	0.10	0.125	0.15	0.20	0.25
0.30	0.00	0.06	0.12	0.150	0.18	0.24	0.30

[a]Each cell in the matrix represents an internal capital generation rate (g), which is equal to $ROE \times RR$. See footnote 17 for the exact specification of g; the product of ROE and RR is only an approximation of g.

of 15 percent, and (3) *RR* of 60 percent. The bank's internal capital generation rate is 9 percent, whereas its expected growth in assets and deposits is 12 percent. To prevent its capital ratios from deteriorating, the bank needs to plan for capital growth of 12 percent. Of course, if a bank wants its capital ratio to decline (because it has too much capital), the bank does not have to worry about raising external capital. Various combinations of ROE and RR exist that will generate an internal capital generation rate of 12 percent. As shown in Table 14-4, three such pairs are (0.15 and 0.80), (0.20 and 0.60), and (0.30 and 0.40).

If a combination of ROE and RR that generates a target internal capital generation cannot be obtained, the bank/BHC has three choices: (1) restrict asset

FIGURE 14-4 Market Value Capital-to-Asset Ratios

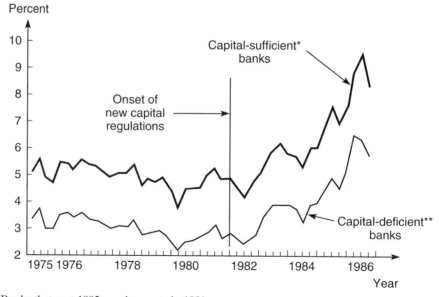

*Banks that met 1985 requirements in 1981.
**Banks that did not meet 1985 requirements in 1981.
Source: Keeley [1988], Chart 4, p. 15.

growth, (2) raise external equity, or (3) let its capital ratio deteriorate, or some combination of the three. Until the early 1980s, many large banks/BHCs simply let their capital positions deteriorate. Since then, however, as Figure 14-4 shows, market and regulatory pressures have jointly forced a reversal of this trend. By the mid-1990s, however, some large banking companies began to buy back their common stock to reduce excess capital.

THE DIVIDEND-PAYOUT RATIO

Because $g \approx ROE \times RR$, and because $RR = 1 - PR$, where PR is the **dividend-payout ratio,** we can approximate g as $ROE \times [1 - PR]$. For firms that pay dividends, the rule is, don't cut the dividend. Even in the face of declining earnings, dividend-paying firms attempt to maintain dollar dividends to shareholders. Consider the banking industry. From 1940 until 1986, the aggregate payout ratio has been about 44 percent. However, in 1987, when net income declined by almost $14 billion to $3.2 billion, commercial banks paid cash dividends of $10.5 billion, for a payout ratio of 330 percent. In 1988, the bank payout ratio declined to 53 percent (the same as it was in 1986) but rose again in 1989 to 87 percent. In 1990, it dropped only slightly, to 83 percent. By 1995, it was 64 percent. Within the industry, the payout ratio varies considerably between the 1000 largest banks and the rest of the industry. For example, for 1995, the ten largest banks had an average payout ratio of 65 percent, whereas community banks paid out only 51 percent of their earnings. Banks ranked 11th to 100th, and 101st to 1000th, have payouts similar to those of the 10 largest, at 65 percent and 68 percent, respectively. Because community banks depend more heavily on retained earnings to generate capital, they tend to pay out a smaller portion of their earnings.[18]

The culprit in the fluctuating payout ratio over time has been the variability of the industry's net income, which over the years 1985 to 1995 has bounced around from $17.8 billion in 1985, down to $3.2 billion in 1987, up to $24.8 billion in 1988, and down again to $15.7 billion in 1989. Since 1989, net income has grown steadily, reaching almost $53 billion by year-end 1996. The primary source of the variation in net income in 1987 and 1989 was the provision for loan losses against loans to less developed countries (LDCs) taken by money-center banks in those years.

Because the dividend-payout ratio can be unstable as a result of the variability in bank earnings, an alternative measure of payout is to compare cash dividends to total assets. Table 14-5 shows this measure of payout for four size classes of banks plus all insured commercial banks for the years 1985, 1989, and 1995. In addition, the table shows ratios of net income to total assets (ROA) and the addition to retained earnings to total assets. Except for rounding error,

$$\text{Return on assets } (ROA) = \text{payout/assets} + \text{retention/assets} \qquad \textbf{(14-4)}$$

We observe three phenomena in these data. First, among the 1,000 largest banks, as asset size increased, average ROA declined steadily, except for 1995. Second, as bank size increased, dividend payout (relative to total assets) declined, except for

---

[18] Cross-sectional payout ratios also vary over time. For example, the mean payout ratio in 1990 was 36.4 percent (median = 35.4%). From the first to the 20th percentile, the payout ratio was zero in 1990. Thereafter, the payout ratios were 67 percent (75th percentile), 100 percent (90th percentile), 141 percent (95th percentile), and 382 percent (100th percentile). These data are from the Uniform Bank Performance Report for December 31, 1990, for all insured commercial banks as reported in the March 15, 1991, *Press Release* by the Federal Financial Institutions Examination Council.

TABLE 14-5	Net Income, Dividend Payout, and Earnings Retention as a Percentage of Total Assets for Various Bank Size Classes, 1985, 1989, and 1995		

Bank Size Class by Total Assets	1985	1989	1995
Ten largest banks			
Net income/assets	0.46%	−0.19%	0.88%
Payout/assets	0.24%	0.26%	0.57%
Retention/assets	0.22%	−0.57%	0.31%
Banks ranked 11 to 100			
Net income/assets	0.74%	0.49%	1.31%
Payout/assets	0.26%	0.40%	0.85%
Retention/assets	0.48%	0.09%	0.46%
Banks ranked 101 to 1,000			
Net income/assets	0.85%	0.73%	1.28%
Payout/assets	0.40%	0.48%	0.87%
Retention/assets	0.45%	0.25%	0.41%
Banks not ranked among the 1,000 largest			
Net income/assets	0.72%	0.83%	1.21%
Payout/assets	0.43%	0.53%	0.62%
Retention/assets	0.30%	0.30%	0.59%
All insured commercial banks			
Net income/assets	0.69%	0.48%	1.18%
Payout/assets	0.33%	0.44%	0.75%
Retention/assets	0.36%	0.04%	0.43%
Number of banks	13,898	12,323	9,941

Note: Due to rounding, the sum of the payout and retention ratios may not add to the ratio of net income to assets (*ROA*).

Source: Federal Reserve Bulletin (June 1996), pp. 495–505.

1995. And third, as bank size increased, retention (relative to total assets) declined, except for 1985. Competition and access to capital markets offer potential explanations for these phenomena. Specifically, the greater competitiveness of loan and deposit markets for larger banks means fewer dollars of profit relative to total assets (lower ROA), hence less net income for distribution between payout and retention (relative to total assets). However, because of their greater access to capital markets, larger banks are able to reduce their profitability/retention disadvantage by raising external capital, if needed. To illustrate, for the 10 largest banks, the negative average retention in 1989 (and in 1987, of −1.08%, not shown in Table 14-5) indicated a strong need for external equity.

BANK DIVIDEND YIELDS AND DIVIDEND CUTS

During 1990 and 1991, many large BHCs were forced to cut or eliminate their dividends as part of corporate restructurings designed to improve their capital adequacy. Because the stock prices of many BHCs had been depressed in 1989 and 1990, and because they attempted to maintain their dividends, their **dividend yields** soared into double-digit returns. Panel A of Table 14-6, which presents dividend

TABLE 14-6 BHC Dividend Yields and Cuts

PANEL A. SELECTED BHC DIVIDEND YIELDS, 1990, 1991, 1996
(RANKED BY YIELD)

	Dividend Yield		
Bank Holding Company	*(12/18/90)*	*(1/28/91)*	*5/23/96*
Shawmut National	17.02%	0.00%	NA
Midlantic	16.67	0.00	NA
Signet Banking	16.21	10.95	3.00%
Manufacturers Hanover	15.71	7.34	NA
UJB Financial	14.28	5.39	NA
First Interstate	11.88	8.99	NA
Bank of New York	11.54	7.25	3.10
Security Pacific	11.45	10.23	NA
Meridian Bancorp	11.43	7.80	NA
Michigan National	11.19	9.20	NA
Continental Bank	10.96	8.60	NA
First Chicago	10.96	9.09	3.20
Chase Manhattan	10.43	7.74	3.10
Average	14.15%	8.40%	3.10%

PANEL B. ANNOUNCEMENTS OF QUARTERLY DIVIDEND CUTS
(LISTED IN ALPHABETICAL ORDER)

Bank Holding Company	Quarterly Dividend		Dividend Cut	
	3/31/90	*12/18/90*	*Cents*	*Percent*
Ameritrust	32	16	16	50
BayBanks	45	30	15	33
Bank of Boston	31	10	21	68
Chemical Bank	68	25	43	63
Chase Manhattan	62	30	32	52
Citicorp	44.5	25	19.5	44
First City Bancorp	43.5	5	38.5	88
First Fidelity	50	30	20	40
Fleet/Norstar	35	20	15	43
Midlantic	47	25	22	47
Southeast Banking	28	0	28	100
Average	44	20	24	57

Sources: Data adapted and compiled from *The Wall Street Journal* for 1991 and 1996 and the *American Banker,* December 20, 1990, p. 24.

yields for selected BHCs on selected days in 1990, 1991, and 1996, shows how high some BHC dividend yields soared, and how they subsequently plummeted. Nine of the 13 BHCs, however, did not survive to restore their dividends, because they were acquired by other BHCs (e.g., Chase Manhattan acquired Manufacturers Hanover).

Of course, because any ratio has a numerator and a denominator, the decline in dividend yields could be due to the rise in bank stock prices experienced in the first quarter of 1991. For example, during the first quarter of 1991, the *American Banker* ([2 April 1991], p. 1) reported that its index of the nation's 225 largest publicly traded bank stocks rose 25 percent, compared to 13.6 percent growth for the S&P 500 and 10.6 percent for the Dow Jones industrial average. Matthews [1991] contends that the "bank stock rally was built chiefly on expectations of an imminent turnaround [while ignoring] weak fundamentals such as fourth-quarter earnings and a stubborn real estate market" (p. 1, insert mine). The cases of Shawmut National and Midlantic are unambiguous, however, as they both eliminated their dividends. Although Bank of New York's dividend yield declined from 11.54 percent (1990) to 7.25 percent (1991) because of the rise in its stock price, it announced on April 9, 1991, a 28 percent reduction in its dividend, from 53 cents per share to 38 cents per share. When Bank of New York announced its dividend cut, its stock price fell $2.125 to $27.125. However, the announcement of the dividend cut was confounded by the simultaneous announcement by the bank of a $343 million provision for possible loan losses that resulted in a $63 million loss for the first quarter of 1991. On 23 May 1996, Bank of New York was paying an annual dividend of $1.60 for a yield of 3.1 percent.

Panel B of Table 14-6 presents a sample of BHCs that had announced quarterly dividend cuts before 18 December 1990 but after 1 April 1990. The companies are listed alphabetically. Banks with the greatest shortages of capital were under pressure from both financial markets and their regulators to cut their dividends as a means of bolstering bank capital. With the bank insurance fund (BIF) close to insolvency at this time, the FDIC was especially concerned about banks paying dividends out of retained earnings when current earnings were negative (see Table 14-4).

EXTERNAL SOURCES OF CAPITAL

When regulatory or market forces or both require a bank/BHC to increase its capital beyond its internal capital generation rate, the organization must turn to **external sources of capital.** Although both equity and debt capital are available for such purposes, under the new capital guidelines established for 1992, common equity has been assigned a more critical role. Accordingly, nonperpetual preferred stock and subordinated notes and debentures will count less in the eyes of the regulators in terms of meeting capital standards. Healthy banks that are not under pressure to increase capital need external equity to permit them to pursue profitable growth opportunities beyond their capacities to generate capital internally. In contrast, banks with financial difficulties need external equity to replenish their depleted capital positions.

If a bank has a choice between equity or debt capital, the advantages and disadvantages must be weighed carefully. Debt capital, for example, **subordinated notes and debentures,** is desirable because the interest payments are a tax-deductible expense. In addition, debt capital does not dilute EPS or control, all other things being equal, as an equity issue does. The three disadvantages of a debt issue are (1) the interest expense, which can be either fixed or variable depending on the instrument (unlike common stock dividends, interest payments must be made to avoid default); (2) because debt capital (at maturity) must be rolled over, it is not a "permanent" source of funding; (3) only a portion of debt may actually count in meeting a bank's regulatory capital requirements.

Equity capital is attractive because all of it counts in meeting risk-based capital requirements, because it is permanent, and because dividend payments are not a fixed expense. The disadvantages of equity are its higher issue cost relative to debt and its potential dilutive effects.

Preferred stock, as a hybrid instrument, has some of the advantages and disadvantages of equity capital and some of the advantages and disadvantages of debt capital. Under the 1992 risk-based capital guidelines, only noncumulative perpetual preferred stock can be included in Tier 1, or core capital.[19] The exclusion of perpetual preferred stock from core capital would have been a severe blow to the largest banks/BHCs, because they have been heavy issuers of this source of capital. To illustrate, in 1978, all insured commercial banks had only $114 million in perpetual preferred stock outstanding; by year-end 1989, this figure had risen to $1.6 billion, a compound annual growth rate of 27 percent. More importantly, 66 percent of the preferred stock was issued by 247 of the nation's largest banks. By year-end 1994, the amount of preferred stock outstanding had declined slightly, to $1.5 billion. Industry figures on limited-life preferred stock, which were not available until 1984, show less extensive use. For example, the amount outstanding for all insured commercial banks in 1984 was $122 million, but by 1989 it had declined to $86 million.[20]

Other sources of external capital for banks/BHCs include debt/equity swaps and mandatory convertible securities. Debt/equity swaps for banks were devised in 1982 by Salomon Brothers. These transactions involve the swapping of new shares of common stock (equity) for outstanding discounted bonds (debt). However, since the amount of debt outstanding is limited, these swaps cannot generate much equity. Another instrument developed in 1982 was mandatory convertibles. Typically, this instrument is a 12-year floating-rate note pegged to LIBOR, which, at the option of the issuer, is convertible into equity at or before maturity. In addition, the investor has the option of receiving cash if the issuer can sell the issue. The beauty of these transactions, as described by an official of Chase Manhattan Bank, is, "Because we're issuing common stock as a payment of interest, we get a tax deduction, there's no dilution, and it's counted as primary (core) capital."[21]

Access to Capital Markets and Capital Financing

In finance theory, the assumption of equal access to capital markets is frequently invoked. For commercial banks and BHCs, however, equal access is a fiction, because numerous community banks have greater difficulty tapping domestic capital markets, and certainly do not have access to foreign capital markets. The $1.5 billion (1994) in perpetual preferred stock (two-thirds of which was issued by large banks) illustrates this point. Regarding subordinated notes and debentures, a similar but more concentrated tale can be told because the 1,000 largest banks held about 85 percent of the $40.7 billion outstanding at year-end 1994.

Consider the major components of bank external capital. From 1986 to 1995, bank common stock plus surplus increased more than three times as much as subordinated notes and debentures. Notes and debentures, however, grew at a higher annual rate of 11.1 percent compared to 7.7 percent for common stock plus surplus.

---

[19] Under 1985 guidelines, permanent or perpetual preferred stock counted as primary capital, whereas limited-life or sinking-fund preferred was part of secondary or other capital. Other forms of preferred stock include convertible preferred, adjustable-rate preferred, and convertible-exchangeable preferred. The latter can be converted into subordinated debt after a period of years. See Nagle and Petersen [1985].

[20] These data are from the FDIC's *Statistics on Banking* (various years).

[21] As reported by Miller [1986], p. 18.

Who are the investment bankers that commercial banks (and thrift institutions) seek out when they want to raise capital? During 1985, the leading underwriters of capital for banks and S&Ls were as follows:[22]

Manager	$ millions	% total	Issues
Salomon Brothers	5,580	27.1	72
First Boston	3,302	16.0	59
Shearson Lehman Brothers	2,925	14.2	43
Merrill Lynch Capital Markets	2,660	12.9	39
Goldman Sachs	2,109	10.2	22
Drexel Burnham Lambert	1,274	6.2	25
Six-firm totals	17,850	86.6	260
Industry totals	20,597	100.0	369

Of the 369 issues brought to market in 1985, the six leading firms accounted for 70 percent of the activity. Moreover, these 260 issues accounted for almost 87 percent of the dollar volume of capital raised. Accordingly, the remaining 109 issues totaled only $2.7 billion for an average issue size of roughly $25 million.

Regarding initial public offerings (IPOs) by banks and S&Ls in 1985, the leading managers were the following:

Manager	$ millions	% total	Issues
Merrill Lynch Capital Markets	193	22.4	7
Salomon Brothers	179	20.8	3
First Boston	144	16.6	2
Drexel Burnham Lambert	135	15.7	4
Four-firm totals	651	75.5	16
Industry totals	862	100.0	46

With 16 IPOs accounting for 75 percent of new issue volume in 1985, the remaining 30 IPOs totaled only $211 million, for an average issue size of only $7 million.

The Announcement Effects of New Securities Issued by BHCs

Smith [1986] summarizes the findings of the market's reaction to announcements of public issues of debt and equity securities. His synthesis concludes that the average abnormal returns (i.e., price movements after adjustment for movements in some index of market prices) are "consistently either negative or not significantly different from zero; in no case is there evidence of a significant positive reaction" (p. 4). Until a study by Horvitz, Lee, and Robertson [1991], similar results were found for securities issued by banks/BHCs. However, Horvitz et al. found no statistically significant negative announcement effect associated with 14 issues of BHC common stock covering the years 1970 to 1986. They concluded that an increase in a bank's/BHC's capital ratio, "under certain circumstances," may have a positive effect on its stock price. Their findings and conclusion are consistent with Goldman Sachs's conjecture (reported at the beginning of this chapter) that "the risk of dilution (of EPS) now appears secondary to the benefits of higher capital."

---

[22] These data, and those in the next paragraph, are from Miller [1986], pp. 19–20.

Inadequate Capital and Ability to Obtain Equity Financing

When a bank's capital adequacy is deteriorating, is it still able to tap capital market to improve its capital position? Yes and no is the answer Dahl and Spivey [1996] provide. Specifically, the answer depends, according to their tests, on a "threshold level of capital" below which banks are perceived as "unworthy of investment by current or prospective shareholders" (p. 901). The important conclusion Dahl and Spivey derive from their work is that the inability to access capital markets can be taken as an indicator of a distressed bank's lack of viability or going-concern value. The policy conclusion they draw is that such information "could be useful to regulators in their evaluation of capital-restoration plans and in their decisions on early closure under FDICIA" (p. 914).

Dahl and Spivey present some interesting data for their sample banks, which are classified over time as "before undercapitalization" and "during undercapitalization." They define *undercapitalization* as the ratio of equity capital to total assets being less than 3 percent. Their test period runs from 1982 to 1991, and they have 3,931 bank years for the before period and 1,584 bank years for the during period. The bank years equal the sum of the number of years a bank was classified as before or during undercapitalization. The number of banks they analyzed as being undercapitalized during their test period was 1,289. Before being undercapitalized, 11–32 percent of the banks were able to issue equity during a particular year. During the period of undercapitalization, in eight of the 10 years (1982 to 1991) a higher percentage of banks was able to issue equity capital. In the before period, the average bank was able to raise equity capital equal to 0.312 percent of its total assets; in the during period, the figure was 0.574 percent.

It is interesting to look at the ROE profiles for the average bank in Dahl and Spivey's sample before and during the periods of undercapitalization:[23]

$$\text{Before: } ROE = -0.0495 = -0.00361 \times 13.72 \ (= ROA \times EM)$$

$$\text{During: } ROE = -11.85 = -0.0539 \times 219.78$$

Taking the reciprocals of the EMs, the average bank had ratios of equity capital to total assets of 7.29 percent (before) and 0.455 percent (during), showing a substantial deterioration in its capital adequacy. Other characteristics for the average bank across the two periods were as follows:

	Before	*During*
Asset growth (annual)	20.1%	5.9%
Dividends/total assets	0.3%	0.04%
Nonperforming loans/assets	6.4%	16.9%

These profiles paint a familiar picture for banks that encounter financial difficulties: rapid asset growth (20.1%) followed by lack of loan quality (16.9% nonperforming loans).[24] Because distressed banks are strapped for equity capital, they seek both internal (dividend cuts) and external (issuance of equity) sources of capital.

---

[23] The ROE profiles are derived from Dahl and Spivey's Table 2, p. 906.

[24] The case of Bank of New England (appendix A, chapter 12), one of the largest and most costly U.S. bank failures, is a good example of this phenomenon.

HOW CITICORP REVITALIZED ITS CAPITAL BASE

On March 28, 1991, although Citicorp had almost $5 billion in market value of equity, its ratio of market value of equity to book value of assets was only 2.27 percent, an equity multiplier of 44. Because Citicorp's management explicitly recognized that it had too much leverage, it decided to raise $4–$5 billion in cash. Part of its plan to revitalize its capital base was its 44 percent dividend cut (announced December 18, 1990). In addition to the dividend cut, the other major components of Citicorp's plan included

1. Reducing operating expenses by $1.5 billion by 1993, including a cut of 8,000 in the number of employees
2. Issuing equity capital in the form of either convertible preferred stock or common stock or both to the tune of $1.5 billion (including Prince Alwaleed's capital injection [February 24, 1991] of $590 million in a private issue of Citicorp convertible preferred stock carrying a dividend of 11 percent)
3. Loan and assets sales to raise cash and reduce its asset base

Regarding the last point, Citicorp had been looking to sell its municipal bond insurance company, called AMBAC; to sell part of its credit-card portfolio (about 20%); and to sell part of its $7.5 billion portfolio of highly leveraged transactions.

Citicorp's plan was not unique, of course, because several distressed money-center or mega banks embarked on similar plans of action. In a nutshell, the building blocks of the plans included dividend and staff cuts and asset sales and raising external equity. For example, in May 1991, Manufacturers Hanover (since acquired by Chase Manhattan) made a private placement of about $250 million in convertible preferred stock. The reported terms of the deal, at a dividend rate of 9.25 percent, were more favorable than the 11-percent issue placed by Citicorp in February 1991.

RAISING EQUITY THROUGH A DIRECT PUBLIC OFFERING

Field [1991] reports that General Motors and IBM have successfully raised billions of dollars by offering money-market accounts to their employees and shareholders. Based on this success, Field argues, "If industrial corporations can do so well with direct marketing deposit-like instruments to shareowners, banks should be able to perform the mirror image of that activity and market shares directly to their depositors and other customers" (p. 39). He proposes that banks attempt to raise equity capital by direct public offering or share marketing to individuals. The advantages of a direct-marketing approach include better prices for shares at lower transaction costs and a wider distribution of shares over potentially long-term investors. Moreover, banks already have in place marketing and distribution systems to deliver equity products along with deposit, loan, and other financial services. If banks are successful in direct marketing their own equities, they can do it for other businesses as another source of fee income. The Glass-Steagall Act does not prohibit commercial banks from providing advisory services in direct-share marketing.

Field suggests the direct-marketing method because he contends that Wall Street does not have the capacity to meet the needs for bank capital. The reason Wall Street lacks the capacity can be traced to consolidation of the investment-banking industry. With regional and midsized firms hit the hardest, the distribution system for issues of regional and community bank securities have been decimated.

Although investment bankers are available to do private placements (e.g., the Citicorp placement described above) and to assist in the sale of bank assets, Field claims that "private placements are not a viable option for most banks, and the terms can be painful to the present shareholders and management" (p. 40).

Nevertheless, Field sees three potential obstacles to direct-share marketing by banks. First, the market tends to dictate access. For example, the market for bank equities was bad in the early 1990s but much improved by the mid-1990s. The second potential obstacle is the fear of alienating underwriters. Because direct-share marketing would take business away from underwriters, the competition could jeopardize relationships and the delivery of services related to liquidity and market making. The last obstacle deals with developing a different perspective on the process of equity capital formation for banks. A direct-marketing effort means that the bank's top management and board of directors must have confidence in the bank as a good investment—good enough that they can recommend it to friends, neighbors, and bank customers. Without this confidence (as a signal to potential investors), direct-share marketing is unlikely to succeed. Unlike securities issued through an investment banker in a lump sum, direct-share marketing can be viewed as a continuous process and a way of developing core equity to go with core deposits.

Another potential obstacle to direct-share marketing could come from bank regulators who will be concerned about investors who might think their shares are backed by the full faith and credit of the U.S. government. Regulators have expressed similar concern with respect to bank marketing of mutual funds. However, as long as proper disclosure procedures are followed, bank regulators should welcome any method that enables banks to raise capital. On balance, regulators cannot object too strongly to innovative methods for raising bank capital.

CAPITAL-FORMATION STRATEGIES

In addition to raising capital in debt and equity markets, banks have three additional internal methods, besides retained earnings, for generating capital. Sellers [1990] describes three methods for banks to build capital: (1) dividend-reinvestment plans, (2) employee stock ownership plans (ESOPs), and (3) stock dividends.

Dividend-Reinvestment Plans

Because these plans substitute stock dividends for cash dividends, they permit banks to conserve retained earnings that would otherwise be paid out in the form of cash dividends. Sellers recommends that banks offer a 5 percent discount from fair market value to encourage participation in dividend-reinvestment plans. The 5 percent discount permits existing shareholders to acquire stock at 95 percent of the stock price (or fair market value) on the dividend payment date. The time line in Figure 14-5 depicts the dividend-payment process. Under a dividend-reinvestment plan with a 5 percent discount, rather than pay a cash dividend at time T, the bank would retain the cash and issue new shares to the owner in place of the cash dividend. For example, if the shareholder was entitled to a cash dividend of $285 and the stock had a price of $100, then with the 5 percent discount, the shareholders would receive three shares of the stock (285/95 = 3) instead of the $285. The incentive for the shareholder to participate in a plan with a discount is the instant paper capital gain equal to the amount of the discount (e.g., $5 per share in the example, or $15 total).

```
    ────────►  T-4 ──────► T-3 ──────► T-2 ──────► T-1 ──────► T  ──────►
                                       Time
```

(T-4) On the *adoption date,* the Board of Directors votes to declare a dividend to shareholders of record on a specified date (T-1) on a specified payment date (T).

(T-3) On the *announcement date,* the Board's dividend decision is announced to the public.

(T-2) Given the record date (T-1) decided by the Board of Directors, the exchange on which the stock is traded sets the *ex-dividend date,* which usually is five business days before the record date. The exchange processes the paperwork such that all shareholders who purchase stock before the ex-dividend date are on the list to receive the dividend payment.

(T-1) The *record date* established by the Board for dividend payments to stockholders of record.

(T) The *payment date* is the day on which stockholders' accounts should be credited or they should receive their dividend check.

Source: Adapted from Smith [1991].

FIGURE 14-5 **The Dividend-Payment Process**

Employee Stock Ownership Plans (ESOPs)

Sellers [1990] claims that ESOPs are one of the most innovative ways for banks to obtain additional capital. An **ESOP** is an arrangement or program through which employees are encouraged to purchase stock of the company. The device may serve as a bonding mechanism between management and employees by giving employees a sense of participation in the management and direction of the company (bank). Under an ESOP, a trust is created for the benefit of the employees. Newly issued shares contributed to the trust create a broader market for the bank's stock. In addition, because ESOPs fall under unique tax legislation (defined in the Tax Reform Act of 1976), they are the only tax-deductible employee benefit plan that can be used as a direct source of capital for a bank. As a result, ESOPs can be financed largely with pretax dollars. For example, if a bank makes a $100,000 annual contribution to an ESOP, and assuming a 30 percent marginal tax rate, the after-tax cost of the contribution to the plan is only $70,000. Moreover, it is possible to borrow funds from a third party to finance an ESOP. Under risk-based capital guidelines, however, while the ESOP loan is outstanding, the proceeds from the sale of the bank's stock can be counted only as Tier 2 capital. As the ESOP loan is repaid, the funds shift to Tier 1 capital.

Stock Dividends in Conjunction with ESOPs

Because ESOPs can be used in conjunction with stock dividends, they offer a dual way for banks to raise capital. A stock dividend is simply a payment to shareholders in the form of stock rather than cash. Sellers ([1990], Figure 1, p. 55) provides the following example of this dual usage. Suppose that a bank with only two shareholders issues an $800,000 stock dividend to each of them. Stock dividends can be held for potential appreciation or sold for cash. Suppose one of the shareholders keeps the stock dividend whereas the other sells $250,000 of stock to the ESOP. To complete the transaction, the bank makes a $250,000 contribution to the ESOP to purchase the stock. Because the ESOP purchase is financed with pretax dollars, and assuming no reallocation of pension or profit-sharing contributions to ESOP, the bank retains net capital of $635,000 (= $800,000 − $250,000 × [1 − t], where t = 0.34).

ESOPs Are Not a Panacea

Sellers [1990] cautions that ESOPs are not for all banks. Like other bank investments, they should be undertaken only if they can be shown to be positive net-present-value projects. The critical factors in an ESOP decision include the economic outlook for the bank such that employee benefits have a good chance of increasing in value, management's commitment to sharing ownership with employees, management's commitment to proper design and administration of the plan, employees' understanding of what an ESOP is and their commitment to improving the bank's productivity, and management's understanding of their liability and responsibility under the Employee Retirement Income Security Act (ERISA) of an ESOP.

BANK HOLDING COMPANY CAPITAL AND LEVERAGE

One of the major functions of a BHC is to generate external capital for its rapidly growing affiliates, either bank or nonbank subsidiaries. A common practice is for the parent company to issue long-term debt and to channel it to subsidiaries as either equity or debt capital. When parent debt is downstreamed as equity, the transaction is referred to as **double leverage.**[25] The fact that the subsidiary uses the equity to boost its assets explains this term. The parent company uses the dividends paid by the equity investment in its subsidiaries to service its debt. If these subsidiaries encounter financial difficulties, then the ability of the parent to service the debt could be in danger. Moreover, if the subsidiary is a bank, regulatory pressure to maintain adequate bank capital may impede the flow of dividends to the parent. In contrast, because the nonbank subsidiaries of BHCs are less heavily regulated, they are less likely to encounter this kind of regulatory interference.

BHC Financial Statements and Double Leverage

To illustrate the concept of double leverage, we need to look at the relationships among parent, subsidiary, and consolidated financial statements, as depicted in Table 14-7. In this illustration, the parent company is assumed to have two wholly owned subsidiaries: a bank subsidiary and a nonbank subsidiary. The balance sheet for the consolidated holding company is obtained by summing up each of the accounts (i.e., assets, liabilities, and equity) across the parent *and* all of the subsidiaries and then eliminating all intercompany relationships. The only intercompany relationships in this example are the parent's investments in the wholly owned subsidiaries. If these relationships were ignored, the consolidated balance sheet would be 120 = 111 + 9 instead of 114 = 111 + 3.

After the double-leverage transaction, in which parent debt is downstreamed as equity in the bank subsidiary, the consolidated balance sheet reads 115 = 112 + 3.

---

[25] Boczar and Talley [1981] and Harris [1987] analyze BHC double leverage.

TABLE 14-7 An Illustration of Double Leverage and the Relationships among BHC Financial Statements ($ billions)

Before

Parent Company

Investment in subsidiaries	6	Liabilities	10
Other assets	7	Equity	3
	13		13

Nonbank Subsidiary

Assets	7	Liabilities	6
		Equity	1
	7		7

Bank Subsidiary

Assets	100	Liabilities	95
		Equity	5
	100		100

Consolidated Holding Company

Assets		Liabilities	
Parent	7	Parent	10
Nonbank subsidiary	7	Nonbank subsidiary	6
Bank subsidiary	100	Bank subsidiary	95
			111
		Equity	
		Parent	3
	114		114

After

Parent Company

Investment in subsidiaries	7	Liabilities	11
Other assets	7	Equity	3
	14		14

Nonbank Subsidiary

Assets	7	Liabilities	6
		Equity	1
	7		7

Bank Subsidiary

Assets	101	Liabilities	95
		Equity	6
	101		101

Consolidated Holding Company

Assets		Liabilities	
Parent	7	Parent	11
Nonbank subsidiary	7	Nonbank subsidiary	6
Bank subsidiary	101	Bank subsidiary	95
			112
		Equity	
		Parent	3
	115		115

Using the debt-to-equity ratio to measure leverage, the double-leverage operation has the following effects:

	Debt/Equity	
	Before	*After*
Parent	10/3 = 3.3	11/3 = 3.6
Bank	95/5 = 19.0	95/6 = 15.8
Consolidated holding company	111/3 = 37.0	112/3 = 37.3

As a result of the transaction, the leverage of the bank has been reduced, whereas the leverage of the parent and the consolidated holding company have increased.

The Significance and Measurement of Double Leverage

Prior to the establishment of uniform capital guidelines for both banks and BHCs (effective in 1992), BHCs could attempt to have their cake and eat it too by using double leverage. Specifically, they could attempt to leverage holding-company ROE by issuing debt capital and simultaneously using the funds to meet regulatory requirements for adequate bank capital in their bank subsidiaries. The regulatory penchant for focusing on the adequacy of bank capital, but not to the total exclusion of BHC capital adequacy, encouraged such behavior. After having induced such behavior by BHCs, bank regulators became concerned that many banks had too much double leverage.

There are two primary measure of double leverage.[26] The first one is an absolute measure defined as the parent's investments in subsidiaries minus the parent's equity. Given the example in Table 14-7, the measures of double leverage are $3 billion (before) and $4 billion (after). This measure represents the dollar amount of the parent company's investments in subsidiaries that have been debt financed. The second measure is a relative one called the *double leverage ratio* (DLR). It is constructed as the ratio of the parent's investments in subsidiaries to the parent's equity. In Table 14-7, the DLRs are 2.0 (before) and 2.3 (after). As a relative measure, DLRs are useful in making comparisons across BHCs.

Double-Leverage Activity by Large BHCs

During the 1970s, the 50 largest BHCs increased their absolute double leverage on an aggregate basis almost tenfold, from $572 million in 1970 to $5,087 million in 1979. The DLR for these 50 companies increased from 104.86 to 114.37 percent over the same period. Table 14-8 shows DLRs for the 50-firm sample described previously and for selected companies in the sample. The selected BHCs include Citicorp, BankAmerica, J. P. Morgan, First Pennsylvania, and Wachovia. The aggregate data in Table 14-8 reveal that extensive use of double leverage occurred from 1972 to 1974. This leverage was used primarily to accommodate the growth of lead banks and to finance the acquisition of both bank and nonbank subsidiaries. The aggregate data, of course, masked the diversity of individual companies' approaches to double leverage. The data for the five selected companies reveal this diversity. For example, Citicorp made extensive use of double leverage to finance its aggressive worldwide expansion. In contrast, J. P. Morgan and Wachovia adopted

---

[26] See Boczar and Talley [1981], p. 53.

| | 50 Large | | | | First | |
Year	BHCs[a]	Citicorp	BankAmerica	J. P. Morgan	Pennsylvania	Wachovia
TABLE 14-8 Double-Leverage Ratios for Selected BHCs, 1970–1979						
1970	104.86	115.63	98.74	99.53	99.68	100.02
1971	104.91	107.70	98.08	99.16	101.59	99.97
1972	106.83	115.66	97.38	98.33	100.66	99.48
1973	110.07	115.64	103.76	107.83	116.51	99.07
1974	112.95	121.35	109.57	106.21	118.53	98.87
1975	113.72	131.94	111.70	102.89	119.27	98.59
1976	113.89	129.27	116.96	100.58	119.06	97.26
1977	114.23	139.27	117.96	99.85	119.31	97.11
1978	113.55	142.77	117.86	106.76	107.07	98.33
1979	114.37	152.13	114.60	105.87	113.92	97.92
Average	110.94	127.14	108.66	102.70	111.56	98.66

[a]Based upon aggregate data. From 1970 through 1974, the number of BHCs in the sample was not 50 but 31, 36, 41, 45, and 49, respectively. All figures are expressed as percentages.

Source: Boczar and Talley [1981], Figure 1, p. 54, and Figure 2, p. 56. Figures given in the text are from this source. Reprinted by permission.

conservative strategies, whereas BankAmerica and First Pennsylvania were more reflective of the typical large BHC's use of double leverage. On balance, substantial variation exists in the use of double leverage by large BHCs.

The following data from 1986 provide another view of double-leverage activity by money-center BHCs:[27]

Bank Holding Company	Equity Invested in Subsidiaries ($ millions)	Total Equity ($ millions)	DLR (%)
Citicorp	16,648	9,060	184
Manufacturers Hanover	5,416	3,776	144
Bankers Trust	3,544	2,721	130
Chase Manhattan	6,245	4,883	128
Chemical	3,544	3,120	114
J. P. Morgan	4,724	5,130	92

Compared to what they did in the decade of the 1970s, Citicorp continued its aggressive use of double leverage, whereas J. P. Morgan showed a posture even more conservative than in the 1970s. In contrast, by year-end 1995, Citicorp had $31.8 billion invested in subsidiaries (including advances) for a DLR of 162 percent, whereas J. P. Morgan had $19.5 billion invested in subsidiaries (including advances) for a DLR of 187 percent. NationsBank, an aggressive newcomer to the 10 largest banks, had $25.6 billion invested in its subsidiaries (including "receivables"), for a DLR of 200 percent.[28]

---

[27] These data are from Harris [1987], p. 50. The figure for equity invested in subsidiaries includes intangibles to reflect the price paid in excess of book value for holding company subsidiaries.

[28] These data are from 1995 annual reports. Because Citicorp (p. 71) did not separate its advances to subsidiaries from investments in subsidiaries, the combined figures for both BHCs are reported here. For NationsBank (p. 66), "receivables from" subsidiaries are counted as "advances" to subsidiaries.

The Major Risk of Double Leverage

Is double leverage all return and no risk? Can it keep stockholders and regulators satisfied without affecting a BHC's risk exposure? Of course it can't! Leverage is a double-edged sword that works for the BHC when times are good but cuts against the company when times are bad. The primary risk of double leverage focuses on *interest coverage* of the parent company's debt. Interest coverage is concerned with the funds (usually earnings before interest and taxes) that are available to meet interest payments. The major cash flow to the parent is created by dividends from its subsidiaries, especially those from the lead bank. If the lead bank experiences a cash-flow problem, the parent company might have difficulty servicing its debt. Furthermore, bank dividends are subject to statutory limitations and regulatory control. For example, without prior approval of the OCC, the maximum dividend that a national bank can pay in a given year is equal to its current year's earnings plus the additions to retained earnings for the two previous years.

To measure the risk inherent in double leverage, analysts focus on a number of factors. In general, the parent's liquidity and cash-flow position are the main concerns. More specifically, such factors as the parent's dependence on bank dividends, the probability that bank dividends might be reduced, the DLR, and the payback period associated with double leverage are considered.[29] In recent years, the potential risk of some double leverage has been realized to the extent that several holding companies have had trouble servicing their debt.

BANKING, INVESTMENT BANKING, AND CAPITAL PLANNING

One of the most important steps in the life cycle of a bank or BHC is the formation of an effective investment-banking relationship.[30] Community banks frequently do not have such relationships. The value of an investment-banking relationship to the community bank is that it eases some of the burden of raising capital and of worrying about the appeal of the bank's stock. Because it is difficult for a bank's CEO to be both the market maker and the manager of the bank, Nadler [1980] strongly recommends that an outside investment firm be found to be the market maker for the community bank's stock. Given the limited access that small banks have to capital markets, strong investment-banking relationships are all the more important for such institutions.

For banks that are looking to establish investment-banking relationships or that are reviewing existing relationships, Cates [1974] has suggested two basic guidelines. First, consider the range and content of investment-banking services that are needed. And second, follow a formal selection procedure in selecting an investment-banking firm (or firms) so as to establish a presence as a client. Cates, who has had experience on both sides of the bargaining table, regards the selection process as one of overriding importance. He recommends a team approach in terms of the bank's screening, selecting, and doing business with an investment firm.

---

[29] The double-leverage payback period is defined as the dollar amount of double leverage divided by the holding company's annual consolidated earnings. It measures the time it would take to pay off the double-leveraged debt using after-tax earnings. See Boczar and Talley [1981], p. 57. The consolidated income-expense statement for a holding company is calculated in a manner similar to the derivation of the consolidated balance sheet, that is, we add up each income or expense item and then adjust for any within-company flows. The idea is to eliminate all inside income and expenses and consider only the outside flows.

[30] Both Cates [1974] and Nadler [1980] stress the importance of this relationship.

Once an investment-banking relationship has been established, the bank team has professionals available who can help them with the capital-planning process. Developing or improving a bank's stock appeal is an important step in long-range capital planning. Because capital regulation is a fact of banking life, it is important that bankers develop capital-planning programs and tap the resources of investment bankers in their endeavors.

Nevertheless, if community bankers follow Field's [1991] suggestion of direct public stock offerings, they may jeopardize their investment banking relations. Other avenues open to community banks for conserving or generating capital include the dividend investment plans, ESOPs, and stock dividends discussed earlier.

Chapter Summary

During the 1980s, a bank's "capital adequacy," as reflected by its ratio of common equity to total assets, was "discovered" as the "dominant tool" for the valuation of bank stocks. Core, or equity, capital become one of the major determinants of the valuation of bank stocks. Investment analysts at Goldman Sachs, who claim to have discovered this rule, put it this way:

> While the bank stock market always cared about equity ratios, today it has become the supreme ratio. For once the regulatory view and the market are undeniably in sync.

The FDIC (*Forever Demanding Increased Capital*) was right all along. By the mid-1990s, however, only a weak positive relation existed. In addition, some big banks began buying back their common stock, suggesting that they had raised/generated too much capital. Thus, perhaps Merton Miller's answer has more substance than cuteness: "Yes and no!" The question is, is capital structure relevant for banks? After the fact, it's easy: Bank capital was very relevant in the 1980s and early 1990s; by the mid-1990s, it was less relevant but certainly not irrelevant.

Market measures of bank performance include price-earnings (P/E) multiples, market-to-book ratios, and dividend yields. To accurately measure a bank's total value requires estimating the value of assets in place and the present value of future growth opportunities (PVGO). Alternatively, finding the present value of all future net cash flows, discounted at the appropriate required rate of return, would measure the value of the bank.

To maintain its capital adequacy without tapping external sources of equity, a bank needs to constrain asset growth to its internal capital generation rate ($g \approx ROE \times RR$). Retained earnings are a bank's major source of capital, and a bank's retention ratio (RR) measures that portion of net income allocated to undivided profits. Because ROE can be decomposed into $PM \times AU \times EM$, the ability of banks to generate capital internally is a complex function of revenue generation, cost efficiency, leverage, and dividend payout. External sources of bank capital include issues of common stock, preferred stock, and capital notes and debentures.

The financial difficulties of the 1980s and the early 1990s forced the managers and directors of many banks, both large and small, to rethink their capital plans and strategies. To meet the stringent market and regulatory demands for bank capital in the 1990s, many institutions, but especially the largest ones, undertook major corporate restructurings including dividend cuts, employee reductions, asset sales, and new equity issues. Other means for raising or conserving bank capital include direct public offerings of common stock, dividend investment plans, ESOPs, and stock dividends. By the mid-1990s, the banking industry had successfully replenished its capital position. The ability of banks to deliver cost-effective capital will be the standard by which they are judged in the 21st century.

Key Words, Concepts, and Acronyms

- Access to capital markets
- Common stock
- Direct public offering or share marketing
- Dividend reinvestment plan
- Dividend-payout ratio
- Dividend yield
- Double leverage
- Earnings per share (EPS)
- Employee stock ownership plan (ESOP)
- Equity multiplier (EM)

- External equity (sources)
- Financial statements (parent, subsidiary, consolidated)
- Goldman Sachs
- Initial public offering (IPO)
- Internal capital generation rate $(g \approx ROE \times RR = RM \times AU \times EM \times RR)$
- Internal equity
- Investment bankers
- Market measures of bank performance

- Market-to-book ratio
- Preferred stock
- Price-earnings multiple (P/E)
- Retained earnings
- Retention ratio (RR)
- Return on equity $(ROE = ROA \times EM = PM \times AU \times EM)$
- Stock repurchase
- Subordinated notes and debentures
- Supremacy of equity (1970s, 1980s, 1990s)

Review/Discussion Questions

1. Investment researchers at Goldman Sachs claim to have found a rule for valuing bank stocks. What is the rule? Explain in detail how they found it. Why wasn't this relationship found in earlier data? Does this rule still hold in the mid-1990s?

2. Regarding the relevancy of capital structure for banks, Merton Miller says the answer is yes and no. How does your answer to the previous question affect your answer to this question?

3. Which view(s) of the value of the firm can be used to help explain Feldstein's conjecture that bank capital might have been underestimated during the 1980s?

4. Define, distinguish among, and evaluate the following market measures of bank performance:
   a. Total market capitalization
   b. P/E multiple
   c. Market-to-book ratio
   d. Dividend yield

5. Do financial markets look at mega, superregional, large regional, regional, and community banks differently?

6. What is the internal capital generation rate and what are its determinants? How do these factors relate to the capital problem faced by banks?

7. What is the potential problem in measuring dividend payout as the ratio of dividends per share (DPS) to earnings per share (EPS)? How can this problem be remedied? Using this alternative measurement, how do net income, payout, and retention ratios vary with bank size?

8. What are the external sources of capital available to banks? Do all banks have equal access to these sources? Which firms are the heaviest users of external capital? Who assists bankers in tapping capital markets? Can distressed banks still tap financial markets for equity capital? How should regulators interpret this ability?

9. Describe and explain four ways for community bankers to tap capital markets or to conserve on their capital or both.

10. What is double leverage, who uses it, and what are the risks involved?

11. How are the consolidated financial statements for a bank holding company constructed?

12. What are the relationships between (*a*) a bank's liquidity, profitability, and quality of management and (*b*) its capital adequacy? Would your answer differ based on the size of the bank? If so, how?

13. According to bank stock analysts at Goldman Sachs, bank balance sheets are more "believable" than bank income-expense statements. In contrast, consider what another analyst has to say (as reported by Kreuzer [1987], p. 46):

    > Balance sheets reflect less and less the true condition of a bank today, but nonetheless net interest income is still a major contributor to profitability. Understanding the quality that underlies that stream of income is of paramount importance to an analyst. Difficult to get at—but of paramount importance.

    Evaluate and discuss both positions. Fredericks likes to use the notion of a "fortressed balance sheet." What do you think he means?

14. Discuss and evaluate the following statement by Sellers [1991]:

    > . . . the ultimate success of any financial institution will be determined by management's ability to forecast capital needs accurately and to have an ongoing capital formation program to meet those needs. (p. 56)

15. How have financial markets reacted to the issuance of new securities? Is the evidence the same for banks and BHCs? In view of Goldman Sachs's claim of the supremacy of equity, what would you expect the market's reaction to be?

Problems/Projects

1. Using the procedures to produce Figures 14-1, 14-2, and 14-3, collect the relevant data, plot the data, and estimate the appropriate regression equation. Write a one–two page summary of your procedures and findings.

2. Using the most recently available data, find the 10 most valued bank holding companies (either overall or within a particular group, e.g., mega or superregional) and rank them on the basis of their ratios of market value of equity to book value of equity. Write a brief (250 words) report on your findings. Could you do this project for community banks? Suppose your boss told you to do it!

3. The Leverage Bank currently has an *EM* of 44; in contrast, the Equity Bank has an *EM* of 6. Using Figure 14-3, determine the *P/E* ratios for each bank. If the Leverage Bank is able to reduce its *EM* to 20, what will the change in its *P/E* ratio be, assuming the relationship in Figure 14-3 holds? If the Equity Bank falls on hard times and its *EM* soars to 30, what will its *P/E* multiple be? Explain how your analysis would change if you used Figure 14-1 or 14-2 instead of Figure 14-3?

5. If the Togetherness Bank, which has a marginal tax rate of 30 percent, adopts an ESOP that calls for a $1 million annual contribution by the bank, what is the after-tax annual cost to the bank? If the bank borrows the money from a third party to finance the ESOP, how will the capital be classified under the 1992 risk-based capital guidelines?

6. Calculate the internal capital generation rate for each of the following banks and describe each bank's situation.

Bank	PM	AU	EM	Payout Ratio
A	.07	.10	15	.30
B	.00	.11	25	.40
C	.10	.10	20	.45
D	.08	.12	16	.35
E	.05	.10	30	.50

7. Determine the present value of the bank that has the following characteristics:

$$k = 0.20, \quad g = 0.12, \quad EPS_0 = \$5, \text{ and } \quad RR = 0.6$$

8. Determine the dollar amount of double leverage, *DLR*, for the following BHC on a before and after basis.

Parent Company (before)			
Investment in subsidiaries	7	Liabilities	11
Other assets	8	Equity	4
	15		15

Parent Company (after)			
Investment in subsidiaries	9	Liabilities	13
Other assets	8	Equity	4
	17		17

Selected References

Albertson, Robert, Charles Cranmer, Richard Goleniewski, and Janice Meehan. [1987]. "Bank Ratios and Rankings." *Investment Research* (Fourth Quarter), Goldman Sachs.

———. [1988]. "Bank-Track Emerging Trends for Bank Stocks: The Supremacy of Equity." *Investment Research* (March), Goldman Sachs.

American Banker (various issues).

Boczar, Gregory E. [1981]. "External Sources of Bank Holding Company Equity." *Magazine of Bank Administration* (February), pp. 41–44.

Boczar, Gregory E., and Samuel H. Talley. [1981]. "Bank Holding Company Leverage." *Magazine of Bank Administration* (May), pp. 53–57.

Brealey, Richard, and Stewart Myers. [1981]. *Principles of Corporate Finance.* New York: McGraw-Hill.

Cates, David C. [1974]. "Bank Capital Management." *Bankers Magazine* (Winter), pp. 11–12.

Dahl, Drew, and Michael F. Spivey. [1996]. "The Effects of Declining Capitalization on Equity Acquisition by Commercial Banks." *Journal of Banking and Finance* (June), pp. 901–915.

Feldstein, Martin. [1991]. "Don't Underestimate Banks' Capital Value." *The Wall Street Journal* (February 21), op-ed page.

Field, Drew. [1991]. "Raising Equity through a Direct Public Offering." *Bankers Magazine* (March/April), pp. 39–43.

Harris, Timothy J. [1987]. "Bank Double Leverage." *Bankers Monthly* (November), pp. 49–52.

Horvitz, Paul M., Insup Lee, and Kerry L. Robertson. [1991]. "Valuation Effects of New Securities Issuance by Bank Holding Companies: New Evidence." *Financial Review* (February), pp. 91–104.

Howard, Donald S., and Gail M. Hoffman. [1980]. *Evolving Concepts of Bank Capital Management.* New York: Citicorp.

Keeley, Michael C. [1988]. "Bank Capital Regulation in the 1980s: Effective or Ineffective?" *Economic Review* (Winter), Federal Reserve Bank of San Francisco, pp. 3–20.

Keen, Howard, Jr. [1978]. "Bank Dividend Cuts: Recent Experience and the Traditional View." *Business Review* (November-December), Federal Reserve Bank of Philadelphia, pp. 5–13.

Kelly, Charles W. [1974]. *Valuing Your Money Inventory.* New York: Citicorp.

Kennedy, William F. [1980]. *Determinants of Large Bank Dividend Policy.* Ann Arbor, MI: UMI Research Press.

Kraus, James R. [1996]. "Top U.S. Banks Set Records in Profitability Last Year." *American Banker* (March 18), pp. 9–13.

Kreuzer, Terese. [1987]. "Who Owns the Big Banks?" *Bankers Monthly Magazine* (August), pp. 43–46.

Matthews, Gordon. [1991]. "Analysts Say Fundamentals Will Reverse Bank Stock Rally." *American Banker* (April 2), pp. 1 and 16.

Meehan, John, and Leah Nathans Spiro. [1991]. "Wanted: $5 Billion, Contact Citicorp." *Business Week* (February 11), pp. 64–65.

Miller, M. H. [1995]. "Do the M&M Propositions Apply to Banks?" *Journal of Banking and Finance* 19 (June), pp. 483–490.

Miller, Merton H., and Franco Modigliani. [1961]. "Wanted: $5 Billion, Contact Citicorp." *Business Week* (February 11), pp. 64–65.

Miller, Richard B. [1986]. "Raising Bank Capital." *Bankers Monthly Magazine* (January 15), pp. 17–21.

Modigliani, Franco, and Merton H. Miller. [1958]. "The Cost of Capital, Corporate Finance, and the Theory of Investment." *American Economic Review* (June), pp. 261–297.

———. [1981a]. "Managing the Bank Capital Position." *Bankers Monthly Magazine* (April 15), pp. 6–10.

———. [1981b]. "How Attractive Is Your Stock?" *Bankers Monthly Magazine* (May 15), pp. 10–12.

Nadler, Paul S. [1980]. "Community Banks in Capital Squeezes." *Bankers Monthly Magazine* (March 15), pp. 5–9.

Nagle, Reid, and Bruce Petersen. [1985]. "Capitalization Problems in Perspective." In R. C. Aspinwall and R. A. Eisenbeis, eds., *Handbook for Banking Strategy.* New York: Wiley, pp. 293–316.

Nelson, William R., and Brian K. Reid. [1996]. "Profits and Balance-Sheet Developments at U.S. Commercial Banks in 1995." *Federal Reserve Bulletin* (June), pp. 483–505.

Ogden, William S. [1981]. "Debt Management: A Key to Capital Planning." *Magazine of Bank Administration* (March), pp. 24–31.

Schall, Lawrence, and Charles W. Haley. [1977]. *Introduction to Financial Management.* New York: McGraw-Hill.

Sellers, Bob L. [1990]. "Capital Formation Strategies." *Independent Banker* (March), pp. 50–56.

Sinkey, Joseph F., Jr. [1979]. *Problem and Failed Institutions in the Commercial Banking Industry.* Greenwich, CT: JAI Press.

Smith, Clifford W., Jr. [1986]. "Investment Banking and the Capital Acquisition Process." *Journal of Financial Economics* (January-February), pp. 3–29.

———. [1991]. Finance Ph.D. Seminar Notes, Visiting Professor, University of Georgia. *Statistics on Banking,* FDIC, Washington, DC (various issues).

VI

THE ROLES OF REGULATION, DEPOSIT INSURANCE, AND ETHICS IN SHAPING BANKING AND THE FINANCIAL-SERVICES INDUSTRY

Regulation and federal deposit insurance are hallmarks of the U.S. banking system that affect how managers of financial-services firms make strategic and financial decisions. The combination of a lender-of-last-resort function, administered through the Federal Reserve's discount window, and a guarantee function, administered by the FDIC, provides a federal safety net for insured depositories. Although bank managers like the safety net, they are less fond of regulations that restrict profitable investment opportunities. Accordingly, they seek to circumvent restrictions that limit their permissible product lines and geographic reach. This regulatory dialectic, or struggle model, results in an ongoing battle between regulators and regulatees. Agency theory, or a principal-agent model, which provides a framework for analyzing these issues, spotlights the importance of moral hazard and ethics in understanding and shaping the behavior of bankers, regulators, deposit insurers, and politicians.

This part of the book focuses on the why, what, how, and for whom of bank regulation and deposit insurance, and on the role of ethics in banking and the financial-services industry. It consists of three chapters: chapter 15 focuses on the theories, objectives, and agencies of *bank regulation.* Chapter 16 shows that you can't judge the FDIC by its initials, because its functions and tasks extend beyond mere *deposit insurance,* which is best viewed as a surety or trilateral performance bond. Chapter 17 analyzes how *ethics,* viewed as conflict resolution, affects bank managers, regulators, deposit insurers, and politicians.

THE THEORY, OBJECTIVES, AND AGENCIES OF BANK REGULATION

Contents

LEARNING OBJECTIVES

- To understand the why, what, how, and for whom of bank regulation

- To understand bank regulation in the context of agency theory (principal-agent model)

- To understand the layers of competition for regulatory services

- To understand regulation as a tax and an ongoing struggle between regulators and regulatees

- To distinguish between the good intentions and the unintended evils of regulation

- To understand the purpose, structure, and regulation of bank holding companies

CHAPTER THEME

Bank regulators try to serve the conflicting objectives of safety and stability on the one hand and efficient banking structure (competition) on the other hand. The U.S. Congress, acting as agent for taxpayer principals, monitors bank regulators (including deposit insurers), who in turn monitor insured depositories. Monitoring and bonding are costly activities. Because regulation acts as a tax, bankers attempt to pass the incidence of it onto their customers. The struggle between regulators and regulatees, which can be described as the "regulatory dialectic," serves to stimulate financial innovation but at the expense of wasting costly resources to circumvent regulations. Bank regulators, like bankers, compete on the basis of price, confidence, and convenience. Bank holding companies, the dominant form of banking structure in the United States, are heavily regulated by the Federal Reserve.

KEY CONCEPTS, IDEAS, AND TERMS

- Agency costs/problems/theory
- Bank holding companies (BHCs)
- Competition for regulatory services
- Domino (contagion) theory of bank failures
- Federal Deposit Insurance Corporation (FDIC)

- Federal Reserve System (Fed)
- Federal safety net
- Good intentions/unintended evils
- Office of the Comptroller of the Currency (OCC)
- Principal-agent model/relations

- Regulation (as a tax)
- Regulatory dialectic (struggle model)
- Safety, stability, and structure (regulatory objectives)
- Systemic risk

INTRODUCTION

We believe financial institutions should be operated as if there were no regulators for supervision, no discount window for liquidity, and no deposit insurance for bailouts.

—JOHN G. MEDLIN, JR.
Chief Executive Officer
Wachovia Corporation

The epigram tells us three things that bank regulators and deposit insurers do: they supervise, they provide liquidity, and they bail out distressed banks. The second and third functions form the **federal safety net** for banks, which has two key institutional arrangements: the Federal Reserve's discount window and the FDIC's failure-resolution methods. The discount window provides liquidity to stem deposit runs or cash-flow insolvency, whereas a "too-big-to-fail" policy, under the guise of deposit insurance as a **government guarantee,** provides cash infusions for economic insolvencies such as the bailout of Continental Illinois in 1984, and the "bridge bank" for Bank of New England in 1991. The bailouts of Lockheed and Chrysler demonstrate that the U.S. policy of protecting big business has not been applied only to banks. Nevertheless, assuming a **domino,** or **contagion theory of bank failures,** fear of collapse of the financial system (**systemic risk**) leads bank regulators to a national policy of treating banks as special and overprotecting them. The economic distortions and costs of such a policy over the past decade and a half cry out for banking reform.

In conjunction with banking laws, regulations, and supervision, the federal safety net places commercial banking under the microscope of federal investigation, jurisdiction, and protection. Although bankers like the protection, they are less fond of regulations that restrict profitable investment opportunities. Because regulation acts as a tax, bankers seek ways to circumvent regulatory restrictions or to pass the incidence of regulatory taxes onto their customers. This **regulatory** dialectic, or struggle model, results in an ongoing battle between regulators and regulatees. The benefits and costs of this struggle are not always obvious.

This chapter employs several important concepts to explain the theories, objectives, and agencies of bank regulation. First, **agency theory** highlights the principal-agent relations, problems, and costs of bank regulation. Second, the notions of regulators as producers of regulatory services and the three layers of financial-services competition—price, confidence, and convenience—explain the role of regulation in shaping such competition. And third, the regulatory dialectic or struggle model explains the ongoing battle between regulators and regulatees and regulation-induced innovation.

Because **bank holding companies** (BHCs) are the dominant organizational form in U.S. banking, their regulation and supervision (by the Federal Reserve) are highlighted. Important banking acts of the 1980s and 1990s were designed, in part, to reverse the unintended evils of prior legislation and to make the regulatory and deposit-insurance systems more compatible with a modern financial-services industry. Nevertheless, as analysts at CS First Boston [1994] state: "The United States has by far the most fragmented banking system in the world, and its structure is out of sync with banking systems in the rest of the industrialized world" (p. 4). The jurisdictional tangle of the U.S. system of bank regulation and deposit insurance has played a major role in this fragmentation and lack of synchronization. To help prevent systemic risk to the banking system, market developments and institutional changes must be reflected in modern regulatory policies and procedures. Unfortunately, as *The Economist* (May 4, 1996) notes: "For the time being, however, America seems incapable of enacting sensible and long overdue banking reforms" (p. 74).

PRINCIPAL-AGENT RELATIONS: SOME PRELIMINARIES

An **agent** is someone (or an institution) acting on behalf of a **principal.** Because principals are responsible for looking out for their own self-interest, they must monitor the actions of agents with whom they contract. When we visit a doctor, lawyer, or mechanic, we contract either explicitly or implicitly for their services or expertise. Because agents depend on their reputations for a major part of their business, it is in their own self-interest to do a good job. However, because of differences among agents with respect to effort, ethics, and competency, the quality of work/service done by agents varies. Principals behave naively if they assume that all agents are faithful in this respect. When principals (customers) canvas markets for credible agents, they incur search costs.

Principal-agent conflicts can be described as problems related to hidden action, (e.g., moral hazard; see Box 15-1) or hidden information (e.g., adverse selection).[1] The most common hidden action is the effort of the agent. Monitoring, bonding, and incentive pricing by the principal may elicit the desired effort or action by the agent. On balance, principals must attempt to establish a common *bond* with their counterparties. Hidden-information problems arise from asymmetric infor-

---

[1] The problem of adverse selection in insurance occurs when a population is heterogeneous with respect to risk and the same premium is charged to all customers. The insurer that selects the high-risk client has made an "adverse selection." In deposit insurance (see the next chapter for details), because high-risk banks cannot explicitly buy more insurance coverage, they buy it implicitly by taking on more risk at the expense (subsidy) of low-risk banks, resulting in an inefficient allocation of risk bearing.

BOX 15-1

MORAL-HAZARD BEHAVIOR IN THE EXTREME:
MY LEFT FOOT (CUT OFF)

This story should not be confused with the 1990 Academy Award–winning movie *My Left Foot*. This story makes your skin crawl. Nevertheless, it illustrates in the extreme the moral-hazard behavior associated with insurance. In 1979, Robert Yarrington of San Francisco recruited two friends, Bruce Wayne Krafft, 29, and Connie Martinez, 47, to chop off his foot with a hatchet to perpetrate a $210,000 insurance scam. The Associated Press reported that even hardened accident investigators were shocked at the scheme. Yarrington allegedly offered his friends $5,000 each for the hatchet job. According to Ms. Martinez, after a meeting, the three drove to an isolated spot in the Santa Cruz mountains, where they staged an accident in which Yarrington's motorcycle would be sideswiped by a truck. Yarrington, loaded with tranquilizers to kill the pain, lay on the road so his friends could hack at his foot. (With friends like these, who needs enemies?) Although they chopped and they chopped, Yarrington's left foot was not completely severed. After doctors amputated his foot, Yarrington was paid $100,000 by Farmers Insurance and $110,000 by another insurance company. Two years later, with Ms. Martinez's cooperation, insurance investigators uncovered the scam and police charged the two men with insurance fraud, grand theft, and conspiracy.

mation. When an agent has information unknown to the principal, the principal has no way of knowing whether or not the agent has used the information, or even if the agent has the information. Hidden action or hidden information may derive from (1) different goals and objectives between principals and agents, (2) dishonesty by agents (e.g., embezzlement, fraud, etc.), or (3) differential or asymmetric information between principals and agents.

These preliminaries provide the essentials for understanding the principal-agent relations, problems, and costs involved in bank regulation and supervision and for understanding the next chapter's discussion of managing the guarantee business (e.g., federal deposit insurance as a surety or trilateral performance bond).

A PRINCIPAL-AGENT MODEL OF REGULATORY DISCIPLINE IN THE FINANCIAL-SERVICES INDUSTRY (FSI)

Given the objectives of regulation (e.g., safe-and-sound banking), regulatory discipline attempts to provide the means (through carrot or stick) for meeting the ends. This section presents a principal-agent model of regulatory discipline for the FSI. In this model, the players, their objective functions, and the sectors they represent are the following:

Taxpayers represent society. In a representative democracy, their role is to elect government officials. Maximization of net social benefits is their objective.

Lawmakers represent taxpayers. Through their lawmaking, they set the regulatory regime for the FSI, which at present, according to bankers, is an unlevel playing field tilted in favor of less-regulated nonbanks. Lawmakers collect explicit and implicit wages, which influence their behavior and affect their objective functions.

Regulators/deposit insurers enforce the regulatory regime, and, like the lawmakers, they receive explicit and implicit wages, which influence their behavior and objective functions.

Big banks (commercial and investment) represent the institutions that control the majority of assets and deposits in the financial system. They favor deregulation and a willingness to compete in the FSI, especially with a federal safety net and too-big-to-fail to support them. They are, however, subject to market discipline. Although they attempt to maximize shareholders' wealth, they may engage in expense-preference behavior, size/sales maximization, or other forms of suboptimal behavior.

Small banks represent local communities. They tend to favor protected markets and the status quo. Nonpecuniary benefits derived from prestigious positions in communities may shape managerial behavior.[2]

Nonbanks (e.g., insurance companies, mutual funds, pension funds, and nonfinancial corporations) represent nonbank interests. They (e.g., mutual funds) have made substantial inroads into banking markets. Nonbanks are subject to fewer restrictions than banks. Some sectors (e.g., insurance (Kane [1996b])), oppose bank intrusions into their markets. Objective functions vary by sector and type of organizational structure (i.e., stock versus mutual company).

The basic principal-agent relations in bank regulation and supervision (including deposit insurance) can be viewed in terms of the following flow of "regulatory discipline":[3]

Principal	*(Monitor)*	*Agent*
Taxpayers	→	Congress
Congress	→	Regulators/deposit insurers
Regulators/deposit insurers	→	Managers of insured depositories

Voters or taxpayer citizens elect Congress, which makes banking laws, confirms regulatory appointees, and oversees the operations of regulators and deposit insurers. Regulators and deposit insurers, in turn, regulate, supervise, insure, and examine depository institutions. As the savings-and-loan (S&L) mess has shown, the buck, $160 billion excluding interest, stops at the taxpayer's desk. In the case of Congress, special interest groups, through financial contributions or (im)moral suasion, may attempt to influence banking laws, regulations, and supervisory actions to the detriment of the common good.[4]

---

[2] In previous editions of this book, the distinction between big and small banks has been referred to as "real dual banking," as opposed to de jure dual banking based on federal and state chartering and regulation of banks. Real dual banking builds on the economic and political realities of the banking environment, which in the past had the economic power with the big banks but the political power (one bank one vote) with the small banks. Today, both the economic and political power resides with the big banks. As a result, geographic and product restrictions, opposed by the big banks, have been relaxed.

[3] Two other important principal-agent relations, covered in the next chapter's analysis of the federal deposit insurance contract (as a nexus of principal-agent relations), are (1) the relation between stockholders (as principals) and managers (as agents), and (2) the relation between other stakeholders in the bank (e.g., customers and employees) and managers. Although these relations may reinforce regulatory discipline, they are not part of it per se in terms of the flow that runs from taxpayers to elected and appointed government officials to managers of insured depositories. In this context, regulatory discipline is distinct from market discipline (e.g., threat of takeover and cost of capital).

[4] Kane [1996a, 1996b] describes a formal rent-seeking model of selecting and revising a regulatory regime. The idea is to look at the rents accruing to lawmakers, regulators, and deposit insurers if we want to understand their behavior. An economic rent refers to a payment to a factor of production in excess of what is necessary to keep it presently employed. It can be measured relative to a factor's next best alternative (Pareto) or relative to unemployment (Ricardo, Mill, and Marshall). For example, assume a person's reservation wage for working is $10,000, with present employment at $15,000 and the next best alternative at $14,000. Pareto measures the rent as $1,000 (= $15,000 − $14,000) while Ricardo et al. measure it as $5,000 (= $15,000 − $10,000). See the *MIT Dictionary of Modern Economics* [1986], pp. 120–121.

Faithful versus Unfaithful Agents

Let's define a *faithful agent* as one who is firm in adherence to promises or in observance of duty. An important trait of a faithful agent is not to engage in the dissemination of disinformation, which Kane [1996a] defines as descriptive of "regulators' efforts to use their 'bully pulpits' to distort the flow of information taxpayers receive about the potential and actual effects of alternative regulatory schemes" (p. 155). An *unfaithful agent* is one who, for whatever reasons, fails at these tasks. In our principal-agent model of regulatory discipline, should we assume that the agents (Congress and regulators) are faithful or unfaithful? In a faithful-agent model, Kane [1996a] notes that shortfalls in maximizing net social benefits arise from "innocent errors rooted in the inherent difficulty of observing and controlling circumventive behavior by regulatees" (p. 154). In contrast, the unfaithful-agent (or agency-cost) model, as developed by Kane, attributes the breakdown in regulatory discipline, as captured by inefficiency and inequity, to "hard-to-resolve principal-agent conflict between venal government officials and poorly informed taxpayers" (ibid.).

Incentive Pricing for Regulators and Deposit Insurers

What incentives do our political and regulatory agents have to be faithful? Kane [1989] suggests viewing incentive pricing for regulators and deposit insurers as a two-part compensation package consisting of explicit and implicit wages. High-ranking government officials such as bank regulators make an explicit salary while in office; one that is low, however, relative to what they could earn in the private sector. In addition, they earn implicit wages in two forms: (1) the perks and prestige of their high offices, and (2) deferred compensation from the private sector after they leave office. To enhance their opportunities for receiving the deferred, post-government compensation from the private sector, regulators must attempt to minimize crises while in office. To achieve this objective, they may be inclined to take "tribute" from interested parties such as lobbyists and to practice disinformation.

Because hiding the true risk of depository institutions and the solvency of deposit-insurance funds is a potential way for regulators and deposit insurers to attempt to maximize their deferred compensation, regulators and deposit insurers face a potential conflict of interest between long-term career interests and their responsibilities to taxpayers. The dilemma is further captured by the view that regulators are pawns, or captives, of the industry they attempt to regulate. If they give the industry what it wants, they can expect preferential treatment in their post-government careers.

Examples of hidden action and hidden information by agents in the flow of regulatory discipline include the following:

Agent	Hidden Action/Hidden Information
Congress	Denying that problems exist, off-budget spending, secret campaign contributions, being unduly influenced by the lobbying of special-interest groups, and so on.
Regulators/deposit insurers	Capital forbearance, overstating the solvency of insurance funds, conflicts of interest, denying that problems exist, and so on.
Managers of depository	Excessive risk-taking behavior, inadequate disclosure, denying bank insolvency, dishonesty, denying that problems exist, and so on.

Recapitulation

On balance, the principal-agent model of regulatory discipline, which follows Kane [1996a, 1996b], depicts lawmakers as imperfectly faithful agents for taxpayers, and regulators and deposit insurers as less-than-perfect agents for taxpayers and their agent lawmakers. In addition, to the extent that regulators and deposit insurers are pawns of the banking industry, they simultaneously attempt to serve three masters, only one of which—the industry—offers postemployment rewards.

Solving principal-agent problems requires costly monitoring and incentive-compatible contracts. Because bank regulation and deposit insurance play important roles in providing confidence in the financial system, reform in these areas must weigh the agency costs of monitoring and contracting against the benefits to society. We next discuss the objectives of bank regulation and clarify the potential benefits to society of regulation and deposit insurance.

THE OBJECTIVES OF BANK REGULATION AND THE OPTIMAL DEGREE OF REGULATION

Bank regulators have traditionally attempted to serve three masters: (1) **safety,** (2) **stability,** and (3) **structure.** Think of *safety* in terms of protecting depositors and the deposit-insurance funds. *Stability* is protecting the economy from the vicissitudes of the financial system (e.g., financial panic or contagion in the form of deposit runs). This objective focuses on systemic risk, or fear of collapse of the financial system. In contrast, *structure* focuses on promoting competition (protecting bank customers from the monopoly power of banks) and achieving efficiency.

Because it is unlikely that the financial-services industry (FSI) will ever be totally unregulated, what should taxpayers expect optimally from FSI regulators? Kane [1996b] suggests a reasonable expectation: improving outcomes for taxpayers. Specifically, he defines regulation as optimal "when officials minimize the net costs (or equivalently, maximize the net benefits) that operative regulatory schemes impose on society. Absent agency costs, optimality can be assumed to be the goal of career bureaucrats" (p. 352). Maximizing the net benefits of safety, stability, and competition poses a major hurdle for bank regulators.

Safety and Stability

Prior to the introduction of deposit insurance in 1933, the safety objective was to reduce the risk associated with bank liabilities (i.e., protecting banks from deposit runs and liquidity crises). Today, the safety objective is under the guise (and subsidy) of deposit insurance. The bank stability objective is closely linked with the goal of macroeconomic stabilization of the economy. The *domino theory* of bank failure dominates regulatory thinking in this area.[5] According to it, bank failures are contagious and therefore must be contained to prevent the system from col-

---

[5] In addition to falling dominos, other metaphors focus on failing power grids and stationary elephant parts. Kane [1995] analyzes systemic risk in terms of the two ways in which a system can break down: (1) contagious conflagration, or what he calls conflagration risk, and (2) disintegration of linkages among vital parts or what he calls deterioration risk. Kane's metaphors for these two risks are a power surge in a component stereo system, say from a lightning strike, that blows out the entire system, versus a gradual decay or sudden breach in the electrical connections of the system. In terms of the large dollar payments system, systemic risk focuses on the potential for contagion or a chain reaction that would cause the system to collapse; see Angelini, Maresca, and Russo [1996].

lapsing. A modern example of this kind of regulatory thinking was the handling of the collapse of Continental Illinois National Bank in 1984. Rather than close the bank and give *de jure* recognition to its *de facto* failure, the regulators argued that "hundreds" of banks would have been adversely affected if Continental was closed, and therefore it had to be bailed out. The FDIC's cash infusion was $5.4 billion, with an estimated cost to the FDIC of $1.1 billion.[6]

The stability and safety objectives build on some fundamental microeconomic and macroeconomic ideas. First, on the macroeconomic level, the money supply is an important determinant of total economic activity—monetarists would say *the* most important. Alternative views of the macroeconomic transmission mechanism focus on interest rates (the Keynesian approach) or the supply of bank credit as the critical linkage. Although in today's economy, commercial banks are only one of the creators of money, they still are the most important component of the money-supply process. Thus, to protect the money supply and give the central bank some leverage to attempt to control bank reserves, interest rates, or credit, banks are regulated. The MC component (MC = Monetary Control) of the Depository Institutions Deregulation and Monetary Control Act of 1980 (DIDMCA) is an example of this kind of *control* regulation.

One of the tasks of macroeconomic stabilization policy is to protect the money supply from rapid shrinkage through open-market operations and access to the discount window, a task that was not accomplished in the 1930s. Because the Fed failed to prevent the financial crisis of the early 1930s, the U.S. Congress established the Federal Deposit Insurance Corporation in 1933–1934 and imposed various restrictions on commercial banks (e.g., prohibition of interest payments on demand deposits and rate ceilings on savings and time deposits) to attempt to control "ruinous competition." Deposit insurance was perceived as having made the banking system "panic-proof." By 1980, however, after a decade and a half of increasingly severe disintermediation, savers were saying that deposit-rate ceilings had to go, and the thrifts were dying because of the ceilings *and* product restrictions. As a result, the banking acts of 1980 and 1982 aimed directly at dismantling the interest-rate and product restrictions imposed by the legislation of the 1930s and subsequent amendments.[7]

The overall goal of bank regulation and deposit insurance is to maintain public confidence in the banking system. Building confidence at the microeconomic level focuses on limiting the risk exposure of individual banks (unsystemic risk) and, at the macroeconomic level, isolating bank failures to avoid a domino effect within the system (systemic risk). Regarding the unsystemic risk of individual bank failures, the banking authorities try to see that each bank is operated in a safe-and-sound manner. Historically, the main tool for the prompt detection of problem and failing banks has been the on-site bank examination. Today, however, off-site examination and analysis using computer technology and requirements for bank managers to have risk-management policies in place complement the traditional on-site examination. As such, failure-prevention regulation is manifested in such factors as capital and liquidity requirements, asset-quality standards, risk-management policies, and compliance with laws and regulations. The banking authorities use regulatory

---

[6] The $1.1 billion cost is still an estimate, because, as of June 14, 1996 (the bailout was in 1984), the case had not been closed because some assets were still in disposition.

[7] Geographic restrictions, the other major class of bank regulation, are due to the McFadden Act of 1927, and the Douglas amendment (1970) to the 1956 BHC Act. Thanks to the Reigle-Neal Interstate Banking and Branching Efficiency Act (IBBEA) of 1994, geographic restrictions on banks were removed on July 1, 1997.

interference (e.g., cease-and-desist orders, removal of officers, required capital injections) to channel bank behavior in the desired direction. By pursuing the microeconomic goal of (limited) failure prevention, the banking authorities expect to maintain public confidence in the banking system.

The Federal Safety Net and the Too-Big-To-Fail Doctrine

The **federal safety net** applied to depository institutions reflects a dual mixture of banking legislation and regulatory practice: (1) the discount window and (2) the too-big-to-fail (TBTF) doctrine as a manifestation of the government guarantee behind deposit insurance. When a bank, especially a large one, has serious financial difficulties, the scenario goes like this. The discount window provides the funds to keep the bank afloat. Because the Fed's liquidity cannot be used indefinitely, however, a permanent solution must be arranged within a few weeks.[8] At this stage three options exist: (1) recovery without government assistance, (2) closure, and (3) bailout. If the bank is declared insolvent (i.e., closed), the FDIC, as receiver, has basically two options: (1) pay off the insured depositors or (2) arrange for another bank to assume the insured deposits.[9] When the latter, called a "purchase-and-assumption transaction," or P&A, is used, the buyer usually assumes all of the failed bank's liabilities. This practice, routine in the case of large banks/BHCs, results in 100 percent insurance protection for all creditors. In the case of troubled banks that federal regulators refuse to close, a bailout through the FDIC has been the modus operandi (e.g., First Pennsylvania Bank of Philadelphia in 1980 and Continental Illinois of Chicago in 1984). This practice of protecting large banks/BHCs has established a public perception and expectation that big banks are too important to be liquidated (TBTL = too big to liquidate, which is more precise than TBTF = too big to fail).

The combined use of the discount window and the handling of large failed banks with a too-big-to-fail policy under the guise of deposit insurance constitutes the federal safety net that protects commercial banks and their holding companies. The federal safety net is a joint product of the three federal banking agencies: the Fed, the FDIC, and the Office of the Comptroller of the Currency (OCC).

Exhibit 15-1 shows that until 1989, the deposit-insurance component of the federal safety net was not backed *explicitly* by the full faith and credit of the U.S. government. Before that, participants in financial markets assumed that an *implicit* guarantee existed. When President Bush signed the Financial Institutions Reform, Recovery, and Enforcement Act (FIRREA) on August 9, 1989, any uncertainty about the government's credibility in standing behind federal deposit insurance should have been eliminated.

Does the Federal Safety Net Curtail or Promote Systemic Risk?

The federal safety net, which consists of the Fed as lender of last resort and the FDIC as deposit guarantor, attempts to contain **systemic risk** in the United States. The mismanagement of this safety net, however, raises questions about its costs and effectiveness and its role in promoting rather than curtailing individual bank failures.

---

[8] Franklin National Bank of New York, a 1974 failure, was into the discount window daily from May 8 until October 7, with borrowing averaging slightly over $1 billion a day; see Sinkey [1977a,1979]. Also see appendix A in chapter 12 for Bank of New England's discount-window borrowing prior to its failure in early 1991.

[9] The FDIC's methods for handling failed and failing banks are discussed in detail in the next chapter.

EXHIBIT 15-1

THE NEW DEPOSIT-INSURANCE LOGO

The Financial Institutions Reform, Recovery, and Enforcement Act (FIRREA) of 1989 placed the full faith and credit of the United States Government behind federal deposit insurance.

Anna Schwartz [1995], a noted monetary historian, contends that in a drama about systemic risk (farce seems more appropriate), omitting the government as a cause of instability in banking is like omitting the Prince of Denmark from the first act of *Hamlet*. Although it is important to avoid the fallacy of *post hoc ergo propter hoc* (after this, therefore on account of this), let's look at the two most important periods of banking instability in the United States: 1929–1933 and 1980–1993. Before these two crises, the "this" that occurred was (1) the establishment of the Federal Reserve System in 1913 and (2) the establishment of the FDIC in 1933–1934. Time lags were of course involved (e.g., deposit insurance worked well for almost 50 years). On balance, however, both of these systems failed when they were needed to stem systemic risk and promote safety and stability. The costs of the Great Depression were enormous in terms of human suffering and hardship, not to mention dollars. The costs of the savings-and-loan mess were more concrete and measurable: $160 billion excluding interest. Previous banking problems and their financial aftermaths were minor scratches compared to the Great Depression and the S&L hemorrhages.

Through reform and better management, the Fed and the FDIC are becoming better organizations than they were in the past. Nevertheless, taxpayers need to be concerned about how they will perform in the future and the costs of such performance. Black [1995] has an outlook that fits his name:

> When you hear the government talking about systemic risk, hold on to your wallets! It means they want you to pay more taxes to pay for more regulations, which are likely to create systemic risk by interfering with private contracting. Or it means they want you

to pay for more regulations to offset the incentives created to add to the risk of government-guaranteed debt.

In sum, when you think about systemic risks, you'll be closer to the truth if you think of the government as causing them rather than protecting us from them. (p. 8)

Promoting Competition and Efficiency through Banking Structure

The structure objective is best viewed in terms of the degree of competitiveness and efficiency in the banking industry. The linkage between structure and competition is provided by the **IO model,** where IO stands for **industrial organization.** Because this model links structure with conduct and then with performance, it is also referred to as the **structure-conduct-performance model.** Given the basic conditions of supply and demand, the IO model postulates the following linkages:

$$\text{Structure} \rightarrow \text{Conduct} \rightarrow \text{Performance}$$

where *structure* refers to the number of firms in the market, *conduct* to the behavior of the firms in the market, and *performance* to the quantity and quality of products and services produced by firms in the market. The fundamental conclusion of the model is: The more firms that exist in the market, the smaller the chances of anticompetitive behavior and the greater the chances of high-quality products and services being provided at competitive prices. In traditional banking, defined as the business of gathering deposits and making loans, competitive prices for customers mean low loan rates and high deposit rates, the exact opposite of the rate configuration bankers want for maximizing their interest-rate spreads.

If monopoly profits exist in an industry, firms are encouraged to enter and compete away the excess profits. The historical tradition in banking has been restricted entry. The relaxation of geographic and product restrictions, driven by advances in technology and nonbank competition, have made it easier for banks to enter new markets.

Table 15-1 shows how the aggregate structure of **depository institutions** (DIs) has changed from 1984 to 1994. DIs are banks, thrifts, and credit unions. At year-end 1984, there were 29,882 DIs in the United States; by year-end 1994, the number was 21,883. This trend in consolidation is expected to continue into the 21st century. Banking organizations, including independent banks, one-bank holding companies (OBHCs), and multibank holding companies (MBHCs), controlled 71.7 percent ($2.4 trillion) of the total deposits held by DIs at year-end 1994, up from 61.4 percent ($1.6 trillion) at year-end 1984. MBHCs made the biggest surge as the deposits they control rose from $936 billion (35.6%) in 1984 to almost $1.7 trillion (50.9%) in 1994. Because MBHCs control 70.9 percent of bank deposits and 50.9 percent of DI deposits, they are considered the dominant organizational form of bank and DI. The fierce competition that DIs face in gathering deposits is reflected by the fact that all DIs held $3.3 trillion in deposits at year-end 1994, up only 2.2 percent per annum from the $2.6 trillion at year-end 1984. The major competitors DIs encounter in deposits markets are mutual funds, pension funds, insurance companies, and the stock and bond markets.

Conflicting Regulatory Objectives

Because the structure (competition) objective conflicts with the safety and stability objectives, regulators and legislators must weight the trade-offs between them. Both banks and nonbanks, and their taxpaying customers, have a vested interest in

TABLE 15-1 The Structure of Depository Institutions: Number of Firms and Deposits, 1984 and 1994

	1984					1994				
Type of Institution	*Number of Firms*	*Per- centage of Total*	*Deposits (billions of dollars)*	*Per- centage of Deposits*	*Mean Deposits per Firm (millions of dollars)*	*Number of Firms*	*Per- centage of Total*	*Deposits (billions of dollars)*	*Per- centage of Deposits*	*Mean Deposits per Firm (millions of dollars)*
Banking organizations	11,342	38.0	1,613.7	61.4	142.3	7,898	36.1	2,382.7	71.7	301.7
Independent banks	5,698	19.1	209.9	8.0	36.8	2,634	12.0	170.0	5.1	64.5
One-bank holding companies	4,926	16.5	467.7	17.8	94.9	4,464	20.4	523.0	15.7	117.2
Multibank holding companies	718	2.4	936.1	35.6	1,303.7	800	3.7	1,689.6	50.9	2,112.1
Thrift institutions	3,414	11.4	929.8	35.4	272.3	2,058	9.4	684.5	20.6	332.6
Savings-and-loan associations	2,882	9.6	697.5	26.5	242.0	776	3.5	147.2	4.4	189.7
Federal savings banks	264	.9	121.6	4.6	460.6	756	3.5	357.5	10.8	472.9
State savings banks	268	.9	110.7	4.2	413.0	526	2.4	179.8	5.4	341.8
Credit unions	15,126	50.6	84.1	3.2	5.6	11,927	54.5	254.0	7.6	21.3
Total	29,882	100.0	2,627.6	100.0	87.9	21,883	100.0	3,321.2	100.0	151.8

Note: Data are as of the end of the year. Figures may not add up due to rounding.
Source: Amel [1996], Table 1, p. 5.

the outcome of this struggle. Banks, nonbanks, and customers make their wishes known to Congress and the regulators through lobbying efforts. Because the regulatory environment is not a static one, various regimes, as summarized in Table 15-2, have existed in U.S. banking over the past 200 years.[10]

The attempt to strike a better balance among the conflicting objectives of safety, stability, and structure began on a Saturday night, October 6, 1979, when a dramatic event, sometimes called the "Saturday night special," took place. Paul Volcker, then chairman of the Fed, initiated a shift in monetary policy from an interest-rate target to a monetary-aggregates target. The shift, which would permit greater interest-rate volatility, marked a willingness on the part of the Fed to accept

TABLE 15-2 Regulatory Regimes Experienced by the United States, 1776–Present

Regime Description	*Period*	*Dominant Objective*
Chartered banking	1776–1837	Anticompetitive structure (as manifested by the prohibition against nationwide banking)
Free banking	1838–1932	Competitive structure and efficiency
Cartel banking	1933–1978	Safety and stability
Competitive/reregulated banking	1979–1989	A better balance between competition and efficiency versus safety and stability
Competitive/reregulated banking with attempts at reform and better enforcement	1989–	Balance still important but deposit-insurance reform and prompt corrective action needed to remedy the deficiencies of the 1980s and early 1990s

---

[10] The first three regimes are described by Huertas [1983].

greater instability in the financial system. If regulated firms were to survive in such an environment, some of the shackles of cartel banking would have to be removed. The banking acts of 1980, 1982, and 1987 were reactions to the economic and technological changes operating in the financial system. As a result of these legislative actions (and other inactions), interest-rate and product controls were relaxed and windows to greater geographic freedom were opened. This regime also promoted competition and stressed the importance of the efficiency of the financial marketplace. This focus, in turn, created concern about the ability of the deposit-insurance and regulatory structures to function in the new environment. Bailouts (e.g., Continental Illinois in 1984) and other stopgap measures (especially for thrifts) were used to camouflage the structural weaknesses in the system during the 1980s.[11]

Many observers described the 1979–1989 regime with the term *deregulation*, although *reregulation* is more appropriate. And, more importantly, but incorrectly, some of them even attributed the thrift and banking crises of the 1980s and early 1990s to deregulation—a good example of the *post-hoc-ergo-propter-hoc fallacy*. What reregulation did was permit banks and thrifts to compete more fully in the FSI. Without reregulation (e.g., the removal of interest-rate ceilings), the financial devastation would have been even worse. Moreover, in terms of a causal linkage, it is better to think of reregulation as the escape valve for the systemic buildup of pressure in the financial system caused by the restrictive and ineffectual banking legislation enacted in 1933 and 1934.

The current regulatory regime began in 1989 with the **Financial Institutions Reform, Recovery, and Enforcement Act** (FIRREA) and continued with the **FDIC Improvement Act** (FDICIA) of 1991 and its call for prompt corrective action (PCA). The theme of reregulation continued in this regime with the passage of the **Reigle-Neal Interstate Banking and Branching Efficiency Act** (IBBEA) of 1994, which removed geographic restrictions on banks as of July 1, 1997. The current regime focuses on competitive-but-safer banking in a stable, low-inflation environment augmented by deposit-insurance reform and PCA.

The SEC Effect, Disclosure, and Market Discipline

Because the banking authorities are concerned with promoting the safety and soundness of the banking system, they have a tendency to paint a rosier picture of a troubled bank's financial condition than reality dictates. In contrast, the **Securities and Exchange Commission** (SEC) is concerned that stockholders and would-be investors have full information through disclosure for making investment decisions. The failure of several large banks, the international debt crisis, and the derivatives debacle of 1994–1995 promote an ongoing call for greater bank disclosure. The clash between secrecy and disclosure was inevitable. The fact that something called the "SEC effect" exists indicates who is winning some of the battles. At present, the banking agencies must adopt disclosure requirements "substantially similar" to the corresponding SEC regulations or publish reasons for the differences.[12] Moreover, the Fed, FDIC, and OCC have established Securities-Disclosure Units (in effect, mini-SECs) within their own agencies. A bank or BHC with 500 or more shareholders is subject to SEC disclosure standards.

---

[11] Kane [1995] views these stopgap measures as lack of attention to deterioration risk, which he considers the more important form of systemic risk. See footnote 5.

[12] See Dince [1979].

The basic bank-disclosure issue relates to the amount of detail that should be supplied, for example, with respect to loan-loss reserves, nonearning or nonperforming assets, and more recently, with respect to derivatives activities. More effective disclosure means greater transparency. In cases involving litigation, shareholders frequently claim that they do not have enough information to judge a bank's risk exposure.

The fact that bank regulators have become more user oriented in terms of financial disclosure is a manifestation of the SEC effect and of the recognition that market discipline has an important role to play in constraining bank risk exposure. If the marketplace is to perform this function effectively, it must have adequate and reliable information through disclosure. Two principal-agent relations are involved here: (1) owners and managers and (2) uninsured creditors and managers. Owners are represented by their boards of directors, who are responsible for monitoring and providing incentive contracts. In contrast, uninsured creditors discipline bank managers by moving or threatening to move funds away from situations where risk-return parameters are misaligned. Market discipline also arises from the threat of takeover by outsiders through merger or acquisition.

THREE LAYERS OF FINANCIAL-SERVICES COMPETITION[13]

Models of the banking firm have emphasized two primary dimensions of competition: *explicit price* and *user convenience*. Prior to the deregulation of the 1980s, the post-Depression era of banking was characterized by lack of explicit pricing and reliance on implicit pricing through convenience devices such as more branches and longer banking hours. In 1973, the U.S. banking system experienced its first billion-dollar bank failure in FDIC history when the United States National Bank of San Diego was closed. Since then, numerous banks and thrift institutions have failed at a cost second only to the banking crisis of the Great Depression. The burden of the thrift failures was so great that its federal insurance agency, the Federal Savings and Loan Insurance Corporation (FSLIC), went belly-up and had to be bailed out by FIRREA (1989). In addition, several state or private deposit-insurance agencies were forced to close, most notably in Ohio, Maryland, and Rhode Island.

Because volatile interest rates and numerous failures of financial institutions erode the public's confidence in the FSI in the United States, it is appropriate, as Kane [1984, 1986] has suggested, to introduce a third dimension of financial-services competition: *public confidence.* Accordingly, let's think of three layers of financial-services competition: (1) explicit price, (2) user convenience, and (3) public confidence. Because these three dimensions have important effects on the demand for borrowing and lending arrangements, they can be regarded as intermediate services produced jointly by banks and their regulators. Because various aspects of pricing behavior are discussed elsewhere in this book, our focus here is on modeling the convenience and confidence elements, with emphasis on the regulatory effects.

---

[13] This section, including the various subsections, relies heavily on the work of Kane [1986]. Regarding the importance of public confidence to the financial system, see Apcar [1987]. His article "Frightened Money" deals with depositor worries over troubled banks and S&Ls in Texas.

Modeling the Confidence Function[14]

Without a government guarantee, the public's confidence in the banking system can be expressed as

$$\text{Confidence} = f(\text{Net Worth, Stability of Earnings, Information Quality})$$

Deposit insurance in the United States is not insurance per se, but a government or external guarantee.[15] It is the most visible, and arguably the most vital, component of the federal safety net. Our concern is with the market value of the guarantee to insured institutions. Using G to represent the market value of the government guarantee and obvious mnemonics for the arguments in the previous function, we have,

$$\text{Confidence} = f(NW, SOE, IQ, G)$$

As with the other three independent variables, as G increases, confidence increases. The market value of G depends, among other things, on the explicit and implicit promises made by the government and its willingness to back them up. In the United States, the explicit promise by the government is deposit insurance up to a maximum of $100,000 per account. In practice, the implicit promise is one of 100 percent deposit insurance, especially for large banks such as Continental Illinois in 1984 and First Pennsylvania in 1980, which were bailed out—the too-big-to-fail (TBTF) doctrine. As Lockheed and Chrysler bear witness, however, the government's bailout policy does not apply only to financial institutions.

The role and importance of government guarantees are most easily demonstrated in the case of distressed institutions. Let's define a distressed institution as one with low or negative net worth, unstable earnings, and unreliable and costly information (i.e., low-quality information). In an environment without a government guarantee, such an institution would be dead or close to it. With a government guarantee, it survives as a *zombie* (Kane [1986]) in the land of the living dead. Examples of zombies include the numerous thrift institutions kept alive by government guarantees during the 1980s. Because the FSLIC was *de facto* bankrupt by the mid-1980s, it was the government's promise to make good on the FSLIC's liabilities that created value in the form of G as an unbooked intangible asset to offset NW < 0.

Modeling the Convenience Function

When you shop for anything, what attracts you? Most of us look for some combination of price, convenience, service, or quality. Given the G component of the confidence function, shopping for financial services is no different from shopping for nonfinancial services. Regulations in the form of geographic and product restrictions make it less convenient for customers to use institutions subject to such constraints. Absent such restrictions, the firm's capital base is the primary determinant of the breadth and depth of its product and geographic markets. For example, a community bank does not have the resources to be a multinational organization. Given these parameters, the cost of services and the quality of prod-

---

[14] Because the idea of a confidence function for banks was introduced in chapter 1 and covered in detail in chapter 13, a brief review of it suffices here.

[15] In the next chapter, this deposit-insurance guarantee is analyzed as a surety or trilateral performance bond.

ucts and services can be viewed as important arguments of the convenience function. Quality can be measured by the speed and reliability of the services the institution provides.

This discussion suggests the following model of the convenience function for a financial-services firm:

$$\text{Convenience} = f(\text{Geog, Prod, Cost, Qual})$$

where *Geog* stands for the firm's geographic reach in terms of owned and shared facilities (e.g., ATM networks), *Prod* stands for the vector of products and services supplied by the firm, *Cost* stands for the average cost of accessing the firm's facilities, and *Qual* stands for the quality, speed, and reliability of the services generated by the firm. Except for the cost factor, user convenience is positively related to the arguments of this function. Specifically, as a firm's geographic reach, products, and quality of service expand, user convenience is enhanced. Conversely, as the average cost of using a firm's facilities increases, user convenience is reduced.

The Role of Regulation in Shaping the Confidence and Convenience Functions

Let's think of regulators as producing regulatory services. As such, they should have profit, revenue, and cost functions. Why would regulatees (e.g., insured banks) pay for regulatory services? The answers are found in the expressions for confidence and convenience. Regulatees pay for such services because by doing so they expect to improve their confidence and convenience functions vis-à-vis their competitors.[16] With respect to confidence, regulatory services can help improve the quality of information and the market value of government guarantees. Regarding convenience, regulatory services (think of the absence of restrictions on valuable services) can have a direct effect on all of the arguments of the convenience function.

To understand the notion of regulatory services, recall the three objectives of bank regulation: safety, stability, and structure. To achieve these objectives, bank regulation attempts to monitor, correct, and coordinate the behavior of supervised firms. The benefits of regulatory services may accrue directly to the firm in the form of greater safety, to the customers in the form of a more favorable financial structure (i.e., the benefits of a more competitive environment), or to society as a whole in the form of a more stable financial system (lower systemic risk).

Because the production of regulatory services entails costs, a regulator's profit (or loss) is simply the difference between its regulatory revenues and its costs. As government or quasi-government entities, regulatory agencies may be required, perhaps under political duress, to transfer their profits to the national Treasury. Obviously, the inability to transfer funds may be a source of political discontent. Even more disquieting to politicians would be to force them to live up to their deposit-insurance guarantees, as in the case of the $160 billion cost (excluding interest) of the S&L mess.

---

[16] Until DIDMCA (1980) required the Fed to start charging full cost for the services it provided, banks also had a price incentive to buy regulatory services. Prior to this structural change, banks were prone to give away certain services or charge fees that did not fully cover the costs of producing the service. "Giveaways" are more difficult to maintain in the competitive FSI. The transition to full-cost pricing is a double-edged sword, however, because some consumers and their lobbyists complain about being nickeled-and-dimed to death by bank fees and service charges.

The Competition for Regulatory Services

Competition for customers among financial-services firms (FSFs) is a fundamental determinant of the structure of the FSI. Kane [1986] argues that "running parallel to this competition . . . is a less-visible layer of competition for rights to produce and deliver regulatory services to these institutions" (p. 10). To model this behavior, Kane proposes a **contestable-markets** view of regulation. According to Baumol [1982], the contestable-markets model is a generalization of the concept of a perfectly competitive market. Although both frameworks imply optimal behavior, the contestable-markets version is more general because it applies to the full range of market structures, including monopoly and oligopoly. Baumol, Panzar, and Willig [1983] define a contestable market as one in which entry and exit costs are zero such that the possibility of hit-and-run entry by outside competitors serves to constrain industry profits (i.e., the threat of potential competition).

Because regulators cannot exist without client firms to buy their regulatory services, it makes sense to talk about market share for regulators. Like other participants in contestable markets, regulators want to protect their market shares, which generate regulatory revenues and profits. Regulatory quests for market share are sometimes referred to as "turf battles." In terms of numbers of depository institutions, Table 15-1 shows the shrinking turf covered by banks, thrifts, and credit unions. Given these conditions, reregulation (i.e., the relaxing of a regulatory restriction) can be seen as complex behavior driven by the desire to increase or maintain market share and preserve regulatory revenues and profits. The multidimensional nature of this rational behavior requires regulators to keep their clients satisfied and the financial system safe and sound while regulators maintain market share. Like other forms of competition, competition for regulatory services should be healthy. However, Kane [1986] warns that "many of the benefits of regulatory competition can be undone by explicit and implicit government subsidies to risk-bearing" (p. 2).

THE REGULATORY DIALECTIC OR STRUGGLE MODEL[17]

The battle between regulators and regulatees can be viewed as a struggle model. The foundation of the theory is based on the philosopher Hegel's concept of the dialectic. Hegelian change consists of three stages: (1) thesis, (2) antithesis, and (3) synthesis. In this process, the thesis and antithesis clash and through an ongoing struggle evolve into a synthesis. The synthesis then becomes a new thesis, and the process of change or struggle goes on and on. Cast in a regulatory framework, the **regulatory dialectic** pits the regulators against the regulatees in an ongoing struggle. The regulators attempt to impose constraints on the financial system (e.g., interest-rate, product, or geographic controls). The regulatees, who are assumed to be driven by profit- or wealth-maximization motives, attempt to circumvent the restrictions because they implicitly tax their profits. Because profit-motivated individuals tend to move faster and more efficiently than bureaucrats, circumvention usually is successful, which leads regulators to attempt to close the window or loop-

---

[17] Kane's [1977, 1981, 1984] notion of the "regulatory dialectic" is fashioned after Hegel's model of change. Georg Wilhelm Friedrich Hegel (1770–1831) was a German philosopher.

hole, and the struggle becomes an ongoing one. One positive aspect of the regulatory dialectic is that it tends to spur financial innovation by regulated firms and to encourage less-regulated firms to infringe on more-regulated ones.[18]

Two important innovations in commercial banking, the negotiable CD and the holding-company movement, were developed (in part at least) to circumvent interest-rate and geographic restrictions, respectively. Another example is Citicorp's decision to move its credit-card operations to South Dakota, a state without usury laws. Citicorp found a provision in the pre-1994 federal law that prohibited interstate branching that allowed banks to set up brand-new banks in other states if they are invited to do so by the state's legislature. Hans Angermueller, Citicorp's regulatory expert at the time, captures the spirit of the regulatory dialectic with these words: "We're willing to go to bat either by pushing forward with innovation until stopped or by trying to persuade legislators to drop restrictions or modify them." In this view of the regulatory world, innovations are seen as being induced by regulation.

Regulation as a Tax

Tax avoidance is legal, whereas tax evasion is illegal. Because bank regulation is an implicit form of taxation, banks attempt to avoid such restrictions. Reserve requirements, deposit-insurance fees, and other regulatory burdens (e.g., Regulation Q prior to DIDMCA) impose costs on firms subject to such restrictions. In their quest for long-run profits, bankers have attempted to circumvent burdensome regulations. Bankers' desires to offset these regulatory burdens and regulators' attempts to frustrate such efforts represent a tax-avoidance view of the regulatory dialectic. For example, reserve requirements are a form of implicit taxation. Before DIDMCA (1980) and universal reserve requirements, banks could reduce their reserve-requirements tax by choosing not to be members of the Federal Reserve System.[19] Moreover, because not all bank liabilities are taxed the same way (some liabilities have no reserve requirements), banks are encouraged to develop sources of funds that are less heavily taxed. In financing their portfolios, the ultimate accomplishment for a tax-avoidance banker is to find a liability/deposit instrument that is not subject to reserve requirements or deposit-insurance fees.

THE EFFECTS OF BANK REGULATION: GOOD INTENTIONS AND UNINTENDED EVILS

Following the Great Depression and the banking crisis of the early 1930s, the good intentions of bank legislation and regulation focused on creating safety and stability through an overprotected environment that Huertas [1983] described as "cartel banking." For almost 50 years, this regime worked fairly well. Underneath the surface, however, unintended evils were brewing, which when combined with interest-rate volatility, advances in technology, and heightened competition made the 1980s and the early 1990s highly volatile. Since 1989 legislation has been directed at

---

[18] The regulatory dialectic also can be viewed as a theory of financial innovation. Part 7 of this book, in particular chapter 18, deals with financial innovation.

[19] Membership in the Federal Reserve System still is optional today, but all depository institutions are subject to Federal Reserve requirements based upon the type of deposit and the deposit interval.

correcting the unintended evils of the past and making the regulatory and deposit-insurance structures more compatible with a modern financial-services industry.

Appendix A of this chapter presents a history of the good intentions and unintended evils of major pieces of bank legislation since 1863. To avoid breaking the continuity of the chapter, this material is placed in an appendix. Its location should not lead you to think that the information is unimportant. It is especially relevant if you want to understand the current state of the jurisdictional tangle of bank regulation and how it evolved. To provide a chronological perspective, Table 15-3 lists the major U.S. banking laws and when they were enacted. For additional insight, the laws are grouped by decade. The amount of legislation enacted in the 1960s, 1970s, 1980s, and 1990s reveals an increase in government interference in banking and financial markets. In general, the legislative/regulatory themes for these decades focused on bank mergers and holding-company activities (1960s), consumer protection (1970s), expanded banking services and reform (the reregulation of the 1980s), and banking efficiency and continued reform (1990s). In many cases, subsequent legislation was needed to undo the unintended evils of previous good intentions.

TABLE 15-3	A Chronological List of Selected U.S. Banking Legislation, 1863–1996 (grouped by selected decades)
Year	*Legislation Enacted*
1863–64	National Bank Act
1913	Federal Reserve Act
1927	McFadden-Pepper Act
1933	Glass-Steagall Act (Banking Act of 1933)
1935	Banking Act of 1935
1956	Bank Holding Company Act
1960	Bank Merger Act
1966	Amendment to the BHC Act of 1956
1966	Amendment to the Bank Merger Act of 1960
1968	Consumer Credit Protection Act
1970	Amendment to the BHC Act of 1956
1974	Equal Credit Opportunity Act
1974	Fair Credit Reporting Act
1977	Community Reinvestment Act (CRA)
1978	International Banking Act (IBA)
1980	Depository Institutions Deregulation and Monetary Control Act (DIDMCA)
1982	Garn-St Germain Depository Institutions Act
1987	Competitive Equality Banking Act (CEBA)
1989	Financial Institutions Reform, Recovery, and Enforcement Act (FIRREA)
1991	Federal Deposit Insurance Corporation Improvement Act (FDICIA)
1991	Truth in Savings Act
1993	Resolution Trust Corporation Completion Act
1993	National Depositor Preference Act
1994	Reigle-Neil Interstate Banking and Branching Efficiency Act
1994	Reigle Community Development and Regulatory Improvement Act

Note: Appendix A provides a description of the good intentions and unintended evils of most of these acts.

GEOGRAPHIC AND PRODUCT RESTRICTIONS: THE GRADUAL MOVEMENT TOWARD INTERSTATE BANKING AND PIECEMEAL DISMANTLING OF THE GLASS-STEAGALL ACT

For over one-half of a century beginning in 1933, federal banking laws have constrained profitable investment opportunities for commercial banks by restricting their geographic and product reach. The passage of the **Reigle-Neal Interstate Banking and Branching Efficiency Act of 1994** marked the end of the battle over geographic expansion (effective July 1, 1997). The conflict over product expansion continues. This section focuses on how these two battles evolved.

Branching Restrictions and Interstate Banking

Banks/BHCs can expand geographically by de novo entry or by acquiring existing businesses. Until 1927 national banks were not permitted to branch. The precedence for this was an interpretation of the failure of the National Bank Act of 1864 to mention branching rights for federally chartered banks to mean that de novo branching for national banks was not permitted. The McFadden Act of 1927 (12 U.S.C.A. 36), which prohibited interstate banking, amended the National Bank Act to permit national banks to branch only within the cities or towns in which they were located, provided state-chartered banks had the same authority. Because the Banking Act of 1933 gave national banks the same branching authority as the state banks in the state in which they were located, it effectively ceded branching authority to individual states. On a state-by-state basis, the McFadden Act and its 1933 amendment produced fairly uniform criteria for branching by both national and state banks. However, because no statutory uniformity existed across states with respect to branching, three broad categories of geographic restrictions developed: (1) unit-banking states (U), (2) limited-branching states (L), and (3) statewide-branching states (S).

A loophole in the McFadden Act, which would have permitted the interstate acquisition of banks, was closed by the Douglas Amendment to the BHC Act of 1956. The amendment prohibited the interstate acquisition of banks by BHCs unless specifically allowed by the laws of the state in which the bank is located. Because in 1956 no states had such laws, the act restricted BHCs to operating banks only in the state in which the holding company was headquartered. Holding companies that already had acquired banks across state lines were permitted to keep them as "grandfathered banks." BHCs are permitted to have *nonbank* subsidiaries located in states outside the states in which they are headquartered. In 1987, state legislatures were given the authority to invite out-of-state banks into their markets. By the time the Reigle-Neal Interstate Banking and Branching Efficiency Act was passed in 1994, 242 interstate multibank holding companies (MBHCs) existed.

The BHC as a Vehicle for Circumventing Geographic Restrictions

If branching restrictions encouraged the development of bank holding companies, BHCs would be more prevalent in unit-banking and limited-branching states. The data in Table 15-4 support this claim. For example, on December 31, 1985, there were 5,522 BHCs (83%) located in the 26 jurisdictions with restricted branching.

TABLE 15-4 · BHCs and Branching Restrictions, December 31, 1985

Branching Restrictions[a]	Number of States + DC	BHCs Number	BHCs Percentage	State Deposits $ Billions	State Deposits Percentage
U	8	2,338	35	308.7	19
L	18	3,184	48	491.6	31
S	25	1,140	17	800.7	50
Total	51	6,662	100	1,601.0	100

[a]Code   U = Unit banking
       L = Limited branching
       S = Statewide branching

Source: Annual Statistical Digest [1986], Table 80, p. 199.

The following data from the Conference of State Bank Supervisors (CSBS) reveal the shifting composition of branching restrictions across states (excluding the District of Columbia):

	Type of State Restriction		
Year	Unit Banking	Limited Branching	Statewide Branching
1960	18	16	16
1977	12	16	22
1985	8	18	24
1990	3	14	33
1994	Interstate banking permitted (effective July 1, 1997)		

At year-end 1990, the three unit-banking states were Colorado, North Dakota, and Wyoming; the 14 states that permitted limited branching were Alabama, Arkansas, Georgia, Illinois, Indiana, Iowa, Kentucky, Minnesota, Missouri, Montana, Nebraska, New Mexico, New York, and Oklahoma. All other states as well as the District of Columbia and Puerto Rico permitted statewide branching at year-end 1990.[20] When nationwide interstate banking was established in 1994 (effective in 1997), it was already a done deal to the extent that most states and groups of states (e.g., regional interstate banking; Table 15-5) had accepted some form of branching.[21] Accordingly, permitting branching across the nation was not much of a legal change. From the perspectives of economic efficiency and convenience, however, proponents of interstate banking argued that an interstate branching network would be more cost-efficient because it would eliminate the need for establishing separate BHC bank subsidiaries and would provide greater convenience for customers with respect to certain transactions previously prohibited across state lines (e.g., making a deposit).

[20] Guam permitted only limited branching at year-end 1990.

[21] In the early 1980s, states began to pass laws that would permit regional or interstate banking. Table 15-5 shows that as of January 1, 1991, 32 states permitted nationwide banking (13 without reciprocity and 18 with reciprocity). Fourteen states plus the District of Columbia permitted only some form of regional banking, and four states prohibited interstate entry.

TABLE 15-5 Types of Interstate Banking Allowed by State Law (as of January 1, 1991)			
Nationwide Entry without Reciprocity	*Nationwide Entry with Reciprocity*	*Regional or Contiguous State Entry with Reciprocity*	*Entry Not Allowed*
Alaska	California	Alabama	Hawaii
Arizona	Connecticut	Arkansas[b]	Kansas
Colorado	Delaware	District of Columbia	Montana
Idaho	Illinois	Florida	North Dakota
Maine	Kentucky	Georgia	
Nevada	Louisiana	Indiana[c]	
New Hampshire	Massachusetts	Iowa	
New Mexico	Michigan	Maryland	
Oklahoma[a]	Nebraska	Minnesota	
Oregon	New Jersey	Mississippi	
Texas	New York	Missouri	
Utah	Ohio	North Carolina	
Wyoming	Pennsylvania	South Carolina	
	Rhode Island	Virginia	
	South Dakota	Wisconsin	
	Tennessee		
	Vermont		
	Washington		
	West Virginia		

[a]Bank holding companies from states not granting reciprocal entry to Oklahoma banking organizations must wait four years before making additional acquisitions.

[b]Entry into Arkansas is contingent on submission, approval, and compliance with an extensive plan guaranteeing certain levels of community service and investment.

[c]Indiana ... [permitted] nationwide entry with reciprocity on January 1, 1992.

Source: Spong [1990], Table 6, p. 127.

Product Restrictions and the Futility of Compartmentalizing the FSI: The Separation of Commercial and Investment Banking and Other Artificial Barriers

Americans' experiences with compartments in trains would for the most part be nil without movies (e.g., *The Orient Express*). Train compartments provide separation and privacy. In the FSI, legal compartmentalization has been the exception rather than the rule. These exclusionary rules, however, have become increasingly difficult to enforce in the face of innovations in financial contracting, organizational form, and electronic delivery systems. This section explains why financial compartmentalization will not work in the 21st century. The principal-agent model of regulatory discipline (or what Kane [1996b] calls the working of "money politics") provides the analytical foundation.

Background

The Glass-Steagall Act of 1933 is, among other things, notorious for its separation of commercial and investment banking. The separation of securities underwriting (investment banking) from gathering deposits and making loans (commercial banking) in 1933 was motivated by concerns about excessive risk taking and the potential for conflict of interest if both activities were conducted under the same roof (e.g., requiring loan customers to buy stock the bank was underwriting as a condition for receiving loans). From a business perspective, the debate has been confined to big commercial banks battling the investment-banking industry: the big banks wanting to be in the business and securities firms not wanting them as competitors. Because the wholesale securities business is so volatile and capital intensive, only big banks have the capacity to be major players. The retail side is a different story because all banks seem capable of at least offering mutual funds to their customers.[22]

The Section-20 Loophole

In today's financial-services industry, the issue of permissible product lines for banks extends beyond the separation of commercial and investment banking. Moreover, the erosion of this particular artificial barrier through a loophole found in Section 20 of the Banking Act of 1933 (the regulatory dialectic at work) has made this issue somewhat less controversial today. Under the loophole, the Federal Reserve allows certain commercial banks to underwrite corporate debt and equity securities in separately capitalized subsidiaries, provided the revenue generated does not exceed 10 percent of the affiliates' total revenue. Underwriting general obligation (GO) municipal bonds, selling Treasury notes, and other activities can be used to generate the remaining 90 percent of revenues for these affiliates.[23]

Insurance Activities

The controversy surrounding the separation of commercial and investment banking has become intertwined with banks' quest to get into the insurance business.[24] At present, most commercial banks can sell insurance in most parts of the United States, although underwriting is restricted. Because some bankers fear that reform of Glass-Steagall will have strings attached that will limit their insurance sales, they are not keen about lobbying for such reform. Banks that are involved in both the securities and insurance businesses would like to have their cake and eat it too. This best of both worlds would be one with a cap higher than 10 percent on debt and equity underwritings without any restrictions on insurance sales.

Table 15-6, which summarizes the ways in which banking organizations can link up with insurance companies to share risk and returns, shows that substantial legal variation exists across organizational form, defined as national banks, the nonbanking subsidiaries of BHCs, and state banks that are independent or owned by a BHC. There are two simple ways that banking organizations can establish cross-industry cash flows arising from insurance production and distribution: (1) form an insurance agency at a bank or BHC or (2) negotiate a participating lease agreement, a joint employee or marketing program, or a joint-venture contract with an insurance agency or underwriter. From an insurance perspective, a third way would be to establish a bank subsidiary at an insurance company or agency.

The *Association of Banks-In-Insurance* ([1994], p. 6) reports that U.S. banks have made substantial inroads in marketing insurance to households. It estimates that one-third of U.S. banks (mainly large ones because they hold almost 70 percent of industry deposits) have found ways to market insurance to their customers. The

---

[22] The different views of big banks versus little banks on reform of Glass-Steagall is another reflection of the real dual-banking system. See footnote 2.

[23] Frank [1996] reported that as of midyear 1996, 38 BHCs (less than 1 percent of all BHCs in the United States) had Section-20 affiliates. The affiliates bumping up against the 10 percent ceiling at this time (e.g., J. P. Morgan, Bankers Trust, and NationsBank) strongly favor Glass-Steagall reform.

[24] Kane [1996b] analyzes the increasing futility of restricting bank participation in insurance activities.

TABLE 15-6	State-Authorized Insurance Activities of Banks and Bank Holding Companies

National Banks	*BHCs (nonbanking subsidies)*	*State Banks (independent or owned by a BHC)*
A. Sales	*A. Sales*	*A. Credit Life Brokerage*
• Sales of general insurance from offices in towns of 5,000 • Sales of involuntary unemployment insurance • Sales of vendor's single-interest insurance • Sales of fixed and variable rate annuities	• Sales of limited property and casualty insurance • Sales of general insurance from offices located in towns of 5,000 • Sales of general insurance by subsidiaries of small BHCs ($50 million or less in assets) • Sales of general insurance by grandfathered BHCs	Alabama, Alaska, Arizona, Arkansas, California, Colorado, Connecticut, Delaware, DC, Florida, Georgia, Hawaii, Idaho, Illinois, Indiana, Iowa, Kansas, Kentucky, Louisiana, Maine, Maryland, Massachusetts, Michigan, Minnesota, Mississippi, Missouri, Montana, Nebraska, Nevada, New Hampshire, New Jersey, New Mexico, New York, North Carolina, North Dakota, Ohio, Oklahoma, Oregon, Pennsylvania, Rhode Island, South Carolina, South Dakota, Tennessee, Texas, Utah, Vermont, Virginia, Washington, West Virginia, Wisconsin, Wyoming
B. Underwriting	*B. Underwriting*	*B. General Insurance Brokerage*
• Underwriting and sales of credit life, health, accident, and disability insurance • Underwriting and sales of mortgage life and disability insurance • Underwriting and sales of title insurance • Underwriting and sales of financial guarantees	• Underwriting and sales of credit insurance	Alabama, California, Delaware, Idaho, Iowa, Massachusetts, Minnesota, Nebraska, New Jersey, North Carolina, Ohio, Oregon, South Dakota, Virginia, Washington, Wisconsin, Wyoming
C. Other	*C. Other*	*C. Insurance Underwriting*
• Debt cancellation contracts • Percentage leases with insurance agents • Joint marketing programs with licensed agents	• Supervising of retail agents • Service corporations • Joint marketing programs	Delaware, New Jersey, North Carolina, South Dakota

Source: Sivon (April 1992). The list of state-authorized insurance activities is based on an FDIC survey dated January 1991, as updated by the American Bankers Association, and is intended for illustrative purposes only—not to reflect current laws. © 1992 American Bankers Association. Reprinted with permission. All rights reserved.

Association also reported that in 1993 alone, 1,000 banks became involved in insurance activities. Four traditional insurance products marketed by banks are annuities, life insurance, property-casualty insurance, and health insurance.

THE JURISDICTIONAL TANGLE OF FEDERAL REGULATION OF DEPOSITORY INSTITUTIONS

Arthur Burns, a former chairman of the Board of Governors of the Federal Reserve, once described bank regulation as a "jurisdictional tangle that boggles the mind" and a system that encourages "competition in laxity." Figure 15-1 depicts the

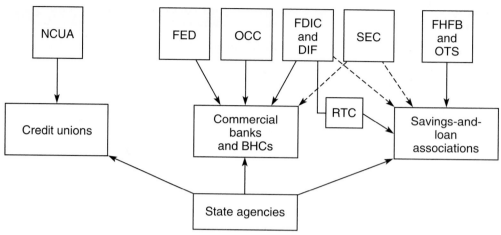

Glossary

For commercial banks:
   FDIC = Federal Deposit Insurance Corporation
   BIF = Bank Insurance Fund
   FED = Federal Reserve System
   OCC = Office of the Comptroller of the Currency
   State agencies (51 including the District of Columbia)

For savings-and-loan associations or thrift institutions:
   OTS = Office of Thrift Supervision (formerly FHLBB)
   RTC = Resolution Trust Corporation (formerly FSLIC)
   SAIF = Savings Association Insurance Fund (formerly FSLIC)
   FHFB = Federal Housing Finance Board (formerly FHLBB)
   State agencies (51 including the District of Columbia)

For credit unions:
   NCUA = National Credit Union Association
   State agencies (51 including the District of Columbia)

For banks and thrifts:
   SEC = Securities and Exchange Commission
   DIF = Deposit Insurance Fund (DIF = BIF + SAIF, where BIF = Bank Insurance Fund and
   SAIF = Savings Association Insurance Fund)

For mergers and acquisitions:
   Justice Department may challenge mergers and acquisitions judged as anticompetitive or in
   restraint of trade.

FIGURE 15-1 The Regulation of Depository Institutions

current regulatory system for depository institutions. Although the Fed, the FDIC, and the Office of the Comptroller of the Currency (OCC) are the regulatory king-pins for commercial banks, let's first consider the regulatory system for thrift institutions and credit unions.

The thrift regulatory structure was substantially rearranged by FIRREA in 1989. The Federal Home Loan Bank Board (FHLBB) was replaced by the **Federal Housing Finance Board** (FHFB) as the agency to oversee housing lending by the regional Federal Home Loan Banks. In addition, the regulatory and supervisory activities of the FHLBB were moved to the newly created **Office of Thrift Supervision** (OTS),[25] a new arm of the Treasury Department equivalent to the

---

[25] It is expected that OTS will be merged into the OCC in the near future. Speculation on this consolidation was heightened when the acting OTS chief announced his resignation on June 21, 1996.

OCC for commercial banks. The deposit-insurance business of the Federal Savings and Loan Corporation (FSLIC) was taken over by the Savings Association Insurance Fund (SAIF). The FDIC's insurance fund was renamed the **Bank Insurance Fund** (BIF), and together SAIF and BIF make up the **Deposit Insurance Fund** (DIF). The rescue and liquidation functions of the FSLIC were moved to the **Resolution Trust Corporation** (RTC), which was responsible for managing bankrupt S&Ls.[26] With a portfolio of roughly $350 billion in real estate obtained from failed S&Ls, RTC became overnight the world's largest bank. Both SAIF and RTC were placed under operation of the FDIC—an attempt to rebuild on the FDIC's reputational capital. To fund RTC operations, the Resolution Funding Corporation (RFC) was created. It is only a shell corporation, however, because it is staffed by the Treasury and its operating expenses are the responsibility of the regional Federal Home Loan Banks. To the extent that the Treasury could borrow more cheaply than RFC, the creation of this shell corporation simply raises the cost to taxpayers of the S&L mess.

The **National Credit Union Administration** (NCUA) handles the regulation, supervision, liquidity needs, and share insurance for credit unions. Its discount window is called the NCUA Central Liquidity Facility, and its insurance fund is the NCU Share Insurance Fund. Three other dimensions of the regulation of depository institutions include the dual system of federal and state chartering and supervision, SEC monitoring of banks and thrifts with actively traded shares of equity, and regulation of bank and thrift holding companies by the Fed and OTC.

To summarize, the federal and state agencies depicted in Figure 15-2 have the same "stockholder principals": federal or state taxpayers or both. To maximize returns (minimize costs), federal taxpayers through Congress must monitor agency operations and provide incentive-compatible contracts. Without such devices, the chances of costly messes like the S&L debacle are greatly enhanced.

FDIC: DON'T JUDGE A BOOK BY ITS COVER

The words behind the FDIC's initials describe only part of its formal operations. In addition to selling deposit insurance (prior to 1991 at bargain *explicit* rates), the FDIC performs three regulatory functions: (1) entry regulation, (2) examination, and (3) disposition of failed and failing banks. Before the phaseout of Regulation Q in the early 1980s, the FDIC performed a fourth regulatory function: regulation of deposit rates for state nonmember banks. In addition, as noted above and as a result of FIRREA (1989), the operations of RTC and SAIF come under the jurisdiction of the FDIC.

Entry Regulation

Because it is almost impossible to get a bank charter without federal deposit insurance, the entry of new firms into the industry is in effect controlled at the federal level by the FDIC/Fed/OCC. Recall that national banks must join the Federal Reserve and that all Fed member banks must be insured. This power enables the

---

[26] To oversee the management of RTC and create the appearance of improved accountability to taxpayers, the RTC Oversight Board was created. It had five members and was chaired by the secretary of the Treasury; other members include the secretary of housing and urban development, the chairman of the Fed, and two independent members appointed by the president and confirmed by the Senate.

federal regulators to attempt to protect the value of existing bank charters, which is the first line of defense for the deposit-insurance fund. The FDIC also rules on merger and branch proposals for insured nonmember banks.

Examination

Two-thirds of the FDIC's employees are associated with the **bank-examination process.** By inspecting and monitoring a bank's records, operations, policies, and management, the FDIC is able to extract *implicit* fees for deposit insurance. Prior to 1991, the combination of explicit and implicit fees gave the FDIC, in effect, a variable-rate deposit-insurance scheme. Today, banks pay variable-rate premiums based on risk (see chapter 16 for details) and they are still subject to implicit pricing based on their risk exposures. Since high-risk banks pay higher explicit premiums and encounter regulatory interference, they have incentives to change their behavior. The overall purpose of the bank-examination process is to preserve a bank's capital so that its franchise value is maintained and the insurance fund protected. Both on-site and off-site examinations are part of the inspection package designed to ensure the safety and soundness of individual banks and the banking system.

Disposition of Failed and Failing Banks

When an insured bank fails, the FDIC is responsible for disposing of the bank's assets and liabilities (and net worth, if any). Prior to failure, the FDIC has the power, under special circumstances, to provide financial assistance to *failing* banks. The techniques used in handling failed and failing banks are discussed in detail in chapter 16.

Regulation of Deposit Rates

Before DIDMCA (1980), the FDIC set deposit-rate ceilings for insured nonmember banks and insured mutual savings banks (MSBs). These policies were coordinated with the Federal Reserve so that all commercial banks faced the same rate constraints. The phaseout of interest-rate ceilings, as required by DIDMCA, was completed in 1986.

Recapitulation

Congress created the FDIC in 1933 to restore public confidence in the U.S. banking system. The FDIC insures deposits at banks and savings associations and promotes the safety and soundness of these institutions by identifying, monitoring, and addressing the risks they face. Although the system of deposit insurance worked well for about 50 years, by 1989 Congress had to pledge the "full faith and credit of the U.S. government" behind the FDIC. The next chapter deals with deposit insurance, bank failures, and the S&L mess.

THE OFFICE OF THE COMPTROLLER OF THE CURRENCY

If we can't judge the FDIC by its initials, what can we say about the OCC? Not much. The name of the agency is a historical relic dating back to the Civil War years when the agency's function was to provide the nation with a safe and uniform currency system. Today, the OCC is simply the chartering and regulatory agency for national banks. The agency performs two regulatory functions: (1) entry-and-exit regulation and (2) examination. The head of the OCC, who is appointed by the president for a five-year (renewable) term, is called the Comptroller of the Currency. The following six divisions report to the Comptroller:

1. Corporate and Economic Programs
2. Administration
3. Bank Supervision Policy (sets exam policies and schedules)
4. Bank Supervision Operations (conducts exams)
5. Legislative and Public Affairs
6. Legal

The OCC's mission is to ensure the safety and soundness of the national banking system, which at midyear 1996 consisted of approximately 2,800 national banks and 70 federal branches and agencies of foreign banks in the United States.

A Strength-in-Banking Equation

At the 1984 American Bankers Association National Convention in New York City, C. T. Conover, then comptroller of the currency, proposed the following strength-in-banking equation:

$$\text{Strength} = \text{New Powers} + \text{Firm Supervision}$$

New powers refers to reregulation on the geographic and product frontiers, with the latter focused on insurance, securities, and real estate. Firm supervision is likely to be manifested in the form of (1) a modernized legal structure to accompany the new regulatory and competitive environment, (2) tougher enforcement for either violations of the law or imprudent banking practices, and (3) higher capital standards. Since 1984, the second and third points have been addressed but not completely. Regarding modernization, as *The Economist* (May 4, 1996) noted: "For the time being, however, America seems incapable of enacting sensible and long overdue banking reforms" (p. 74).

To encourage the process of change, Comptroller Conover urged bankers to do three things: (1) send a consistent message regarding legislative changes through a united front, with consideration given to other segments of the marketplace; (2) garner the support of consumers and small businesses; and (3) continue to be prudent bankers and honest custodians of depositors' money so that the public trust is maintained. His message of 1984 is still relevant as bankers move into the 21st century.

Bank Examinations as a Tool of Firm Supervision

The major focus of the traditional bank examination (Sinkey [1978]), whether it be an exam conducted by the OCC, the FDIC, or the Fed, is an assessment of loan quality (credit or default risk) relative to a bank's capital (capital adequacy). In late 1989 and throughout 1990, the OCC conducted a series of tough real-estate exams that forced many banks to increase their loan-loss provisions for real-estate loans. (The lead banks in most major BHCs are nationally chartered organizations.) This get-tough policy illustrates the firm-supervision aspect of the Comptroller's strength-in-banking equation.

The bank-examination process, which traditionally has been an on-site inspection, is relying more and more on off-premises computer analyses. For example, the

OCC has an expert computer program called "BERT," which is short for "bank expert" (*American Banker,* 6-14-90, p. 3). BERT is called an expert system because it incorporates the financial experience and knowledge of seasoned examiners regarding how they analyze a bank. In the past, when *Jaws* was a popular movie, the FDIC had a similar program called JAWS—Just A Warning System! Because BERT can be used to analyze a bank's financial condition and draw conclusions about its performance, the OCC's 1,800 field examiners use it as a safety net on their analysis of the 12-page Uniform Bank Performance Report. Although a 90-day lag exists between the date a quarterly call report (i.e., balance sheet and income-expense statement) is filed and when it is available on BERT, an unedited version of the program is available within 30 days. The 30-day version of BERT uses peer-group averages from the previous quarter rather than the current one. According to the OCC, BERT can analyze a bank's financials in 10 minutes and it can be programmed to review up to 100 banks a night without monitoring by an outside agent.

In addition to focusing on off-site examination techniques, the OCC has been concentrating more of its examination force on the nation's largest banks. At the beginning of the 1990s, the OCC had one full-time examiner in each of the 17 biggest banks and nearly the equivalent of a full-time examiner in the next 43 largest ones. For the 10 or so biggest banks, the OCC was planning to increase its full-time presence from one to as many as 10 examiners.

The Fed/OCC/FDIC have also considered placing resident examiners in the 400 banks with more than $1 billion in deposits (*The Wall Street Journal,* October 2, 1990, pp. A3, A19). The issue has been a controversial one, however. As one Fed spokesman noted, "I'd hate to think we had a situation where Big Brother had to be there all the time" (p. A3). More importantly, what can one examiner, or 10 for that matter, do in a multibillion-dollar bank?

The OCC's Supervision-by-Risk Program[27]

On September 26, 1995, the OCC announced that it was expanding, enhancing, and standardizing the way its examiners evaluate risk in national banks. This **supervision-by-risk program,** which defines specific categories of risk for use in assessing risks in banking activities, serves as the basis for OCC supervision and examination. It focuses on evaluating the quantity of risk exposure in an institution and determining the quality of the risk-management systems in place to control risk. The program attempts to blend art with science by building on examiners' experience in risk assessment and thereby adding quality to quantitative methods.

To achieve more comprehensive and efficient examinations of national banks, the OCC defined nine categories of risk that will be evaluated by OCC examiners. The intention is to treat the same risks consistently in all banks and across various products and activities. The definitions also clarify for bankers the kinds of risk the OCC will be assessing in their institutions. The nine categories of risk are the following:

> *Credit risk* arising from a debtor's failure to meet the terms of any contract with the bank or otherwise fail to perform as agreed
>
> *Interest-rate risk* arising from unexpected movements in interest rates
>
> *Liquidity risk* arising from a bank's inability to meet its obligations when they come due, without incurring unacceptable losses

---

[27] "OCC Launches 'Supervision-by-Risk' Program," *News Release* NR 95–101, Comptroller of the Currency, Administrator of National Banks.

Price risk (also called "market risk") arising from changes in the value of portfolios of financial instruments

Foreign-exchange risk arising from unexpected movements in exchange rates

Transaction risk arising from problems with service or product delivery

Compliance risk arising from violations or nonconformance with laws, rules, regulations, prescribed practices, or ethical standards

Strategic risk arising from adverse business decisions or improper implementation of those decisions

Reputation risk arising from negative public opinion

It is helpful to think of these risks in terms of changes in earnings and capital arising from changes in the underlying variables. From a finance perspective, changes in these underlying risks also lead to variability of earnings—the standard finance measure of risk.

The supervision-by-risk program generates risk profiles for each bank designed to focus examiner attention on the most serious concerns within a bank. In addition, the program concentrates OCC resources on banks where the need is the greatest. Examiners are to determine whether a bank has identified the risks associated with particular activities and whether it has the systems and control to mange the risks. If risk is not properly managed, the OCC intends to work with managers to ensure (prompt) corrective action (PCA) to return the bank to safe-and-sound status.

The OCC's supervision-by-risk program captures the thrust of the federal banking agencies movement into the 21st century. The theme of that movement is emphasis on the supervision of risk management in banks.

The Role of Market Discipline in Firm Supervision

One approach to monitoring banks (Sinkey [1977a,b]) is to let financial markets (i.e., equity, debt, and money markets) discipline banks active in those markets. The only relevant variable to monitor is a bank's real or economic net worth. If it approaches zero, the bank should be closed regardless of its size—no more too-big-to-fail! To monitor the economic net worth of the largest banks, federal bank regulators should focus resources on developing a system of market-value accounting and direct every large bank to do the same. Examination resources should be focused on institutions that financial markets do not have a chance to discipline. Moreover, even for the smaller banks only one rule is needed: If economic net worth approaches zero, the bank is closed. Banks headed toward zero economic net worth should be reminded of the closure rule and supervised with traditional methods such as moral suasion (to raise equity capital or reduce risk exposure or both), cease-and-desist orders, removal of officers, and removal of deposit-insurance protection. The prompt-corrective-action (PCA) provision of FDICIA (1991) requires regulators to do some of these things; whether they do them or not remains to be seen.

THE FEDERAL RESERVE SYSTEM

The **Federal Reserve System** was created in 1913 as the nation's central bank. Although the Fed's heart is in Washington, DC, in the form of the **Board of Governors** and its chairman, the Federal Reserve System is spread throughout the United States and consists of (1) 12 district Federal Reserve Banks, located in Boston, New

York, Philadelphia, Cleveland, Richmond, Atlanta, Chicago, St. Louis, Minneapolis, Kansas City, Dallas, and San Francisco; (2) branches of the district banks; (3) regional check-processing centers;[28] and (4) a communications center called the Network Management Center located in Culpeper, Virginia.

As the central bank of the United States, the Fed is concerned mainly with the formulation and implementation of monetary policy. As a bank regulator, the Fed has the main responsibility of the regulation and supervision of BHCs. In addition, the Fed is charged with examining the 1,000 or so state member banks, a task that could easily be handled by the FDIC and state banking agencies. Until 1986, deposit-rate ceilings for all member banks were set by the Fed.

The extent of the Fed's involvement in the regulation of the banking system is captured by its list of regulations, shown in Table 15-7. As you can see, the Fed is on its second pass through the alphabet. Of course, without an expansive and elaborate turf to regulate, the Fed's role would be diminished vis-à-vis other regulatory agencies. The Fed, as central bank, provides the lender-of-last-resort function to the economy. This function is an important one to bank managers because it means that when an emergency arises, liquidity usually will be available from the discount window. The Fed, however, regards such borrowing as a privilege and conducts surveillance of the discount window to guard against abuses. For seasonal liquidity needs that can be anticipated, the Fed is sympathetic and permits banks to arrange for such borrowing in advance. Attempts to arbitrage the discount window are considered an abuse of the borrowing privilege.

The BHC Act of 1956 and Fed Supervision of BHC Activities

Because the BHC Act of 1956 applied only to BHCs that controlled two or more banks, it was custom-made for Kane's regulatory dialectic. The act gave primary authority and responsibility for the administration of the law to the Board of Governors of the Federal Reserve System. Granting the Fed substantial control over the activities of BHCs was a significant break away from the regulatory trinity of OCC-Fed-FDIC. Under the BHC Act and its amendments, the board has responsibility for the following:[29]

1. Granting prior approval for BHC formations
2. Granting prior approval for bank acquisitions by BHCs
3. Determination of permissible nonbanking activities for BHCs
4. Granting prior approval for nonbank acquisitions by BHCs
5. Granting prior approval and regulation of foreign bank and nonbank affiliates of BHCs, as well as joint ventures (minority interests) abroad
6. General supervision of holding companies and their subsidiaries, including the power to examine each affiliate and to obtain examination reports from the OCC, the FDIC, and state bank supervisors
7. Restricting unlawful tie-ins between banking and nonbanking affiliates; in addition, the board exercises authority with respect to interaffililates' financial transactions under Section 23A of the Federal Reserve Act

From 1956 to 1965, the number of registered BHCs remained fairly constant, although there was some growth in the number of subsidiary banks and the deposits

---

[28] The subject of competition between the Fed and private suppliers to provide correspondent services to depository institutions is discussed in chapter 5.

[29] See Shull [1980], p. 28.

TABLE 15-7	The Alphabet Soup of Federal Reserve Regulations

Regulation	Subject Matter
A	Loans by the Fed to depository institutions
B	Equal credit opportunity
C	Home mortgage disclosure
D	Reserve requirements
E	Electronic funds transfers
F	Registration and filing of securities statements by state-chartered member banks
G	Extensions of credit to finance securities transactions
H	Membership requirements
I	Member stock in federal reserve banks
J	Check collection and funds transfer
K	International banking operations
L	Interlocking bank relationships
M	Consumer leasing
N	Relationships with foreign banks
O	Loans to executive officers of member banks
P	Member bank protection standards
Q[a]	Interest on deposits
R	Interlocking relationships between securities dealers and member banks
S	Reimbursement for providing financial records
T	Margin credit extended by brokers and dealers
U	Margin credit extended by banks
V	Guarantee of loans for national defense work
X[b]	Borrowers who obtain margin credit
Y	Bank holding companies
Z	Truth in lending
AA	Consumer complaint procedures
BB	Community reinvestment
CC	Availability of funds and collection of checks
DD	Truth in savings
EE	Netting eligibility for financial institutions

[a]As of 1986, the only remaining restriction was on the payment of interest on commercial demand deposits.
[b]Regulation *W*, which was revoked in 1952, pertained to extensions of consumer credit.
Source: "A Guide to Federal Reserve Regulations," Board of Governors of the Federal Reserve System (September 1981), plus updates.

they controlled. Over the same time period, the number of OBHCs was increasing, but by 1965 they still controlled less than 5 percent of total bank deposits. However, from 1965 to 1970, OBHC activities exploded. In particular, large banks became interested in forming OBHCs. This is illustrated by the fact that the average OBHC increased in size from roughly $25 million in 1965 to approximately $125 million in 1970.

Because OBHCs do not circumvent branching restrictions, how does the OBHC movement fit into the regulatory dialectic? Four important developments in other banking areas were occurring that fit nicely into the regulatory-dialectic model of the OBHC movement. First, the Bank Merger Act was passed in 1960, and the first important antimerger decision under the act came down in 1963, in the Philadelphia National Bank case. As a result, big banks became cautious about expanding via the merger route. Second, the Fed was applying the BHC Act fairly strictly, making it difficult to expand via the MBHC avenue.

Third, the OCC's "Saxon era" was coming to an end. This period, from November 16, 1961, to November 16, 1966, marked the reign of James J. Saxon as comptroller of the currency. He was a firm believer in competition. His philosophy involved relaxing chartering and branching restrictions for *national* banks and permitting them to engage in other related activities (e.g., data processing) on the grounds that a macroeconomic stabilization policy was effective enough to permit freer competition in banking. Unfortunately, the bank competition was not welcomed in some nonbanking circles, and some banks became involved in costly litigations. As a result, banks were reluctant to expand along the Saxon nonbank route.

Fourth, the negotiable CD, which had been introduced in the early 1960s as a tool of liability management, had its effectiveness as an expansionary device reduced by Regulation Q interest-rate ceilings. Thus, in our continuing saga of the regulatory dialectic, these four factors pushed the OBHC as the means of expansion, especially for large banks. Because the OBHC was exempt from the BHC Act of 1956, it became the vehicle for expansion into nonbanking activities and for circumventing Regulation Q (e.g., by parent company issues of commercial paper, notes, and debentures). And fifth, OBHCs were a vehicle for tax avoidance.

Closing the OBHC Loophole

The 1970 amendment to the BHC Act of 1956, which was the result of a two-year legislative battle, was signed into law by President Nixon on December 31, 1970.[30] The main provisions of the 1970 amendment are: (1) The OBHC loophole is closed by adopting a broader definition of a BHC; (2) permissible BHC nonbanking activities have to be "closely related to banking," with specific permissions or denials to be determined by the Board of Governors; and (3) the board has the power to determine by means of a grandfather clause whether a BHC with subsidiaries engaged in subsequently denied activities.[31] A summary of Fed rulings on activities that have been permitted to BHCs is presented in Table 15-8.

The Nonbank-Bank Loophole

The 1970 amendment to the BHC Act of 1956 defines a commercial bank as an institution that both accepts demand deposits and makes commercial loans. If it engages in only one of these activities, an institution is not legally a commercial bank. It is easy to see how innovative firms would exploit this loophole by engaging in one of the activities but not both. It is important to understand that once the particular activity is selected, the organization is not limited to that activity. For example, if an institution wants to be a consumer bank, it accepts demand deposits and offers a host of other financial services and products, except for commercial loans. In 1987, the U.S. Congress closed the nonbank-bank loophole, although it grandfathered some 160 or so existing nonbank banks.

---

[30] See Jessee and Seelig [1977], pp. 19–32, for a summary of the amendments and their legislative history.

[31] A 10-year divestiture period was allowed for any activity that the Board decided was not in the public interest.

TABLE 15-8   List of Permissible Nonbanking Activities for Bank Holding Companies

Closely related nonbanking activities. The activities listed below are so closely related to banking or managing or controlling banks as to be a proper incident thereto and may be engaged in by a bank holding company or a subsidiary thereof in accordance with and subject to the requirements of this regulation.

1. Making and servicing loans (such as would be made, for example, by the following types of companies: consumer finance, credit card, mortgage, commercial finance, and factoring)
2. Industrial banking (Morris Plan bank or industrial loan company as authorized under state law, so long as the institution is not a bank)
3. Trust company functions
4. Investment or financial advice
5. Leasing personal or real property
6. Community development
7. Data processing
8. Insurance agency and underwriting
9. Operating savings association
10. Courier services
11. Management consulting to depository institutions
12. Money orders, savings bonds, and traveler's checks
13. Real-estate and personal property appraisal
14. Arranging commercial real-estate equity financing
15. Securities brokerage
16. Underwriting and dealing in government obligations and money market instruments
17. Foreign-exchange advisory and transactional services
18. Futures commission merchant
19. Investment advice on financial futures and options on futures
20. Consumer financial counseling
21. Tax planning and preparation
22. Check-guaranty services
23. Operating collection agency
24. Operating credit bureau

Note: Most of the activities listed are also permissible to national banks. Some permissible activities are determined on a case-by-case basis (e.g., granting permission in 1990 to Morgan Guaranty to engage in limited underwriting of equity securities).

Source: Regulation Y Bank Holding Companies and Change in Bank Control, 12 CFR 225; as revised effective March 15, 1989, and amendments, April 1990, Board of Governors of the Federal Reserve System.

Ten Cs of Holding-Company Regulation

In a 1976 speech before the Association of BHCs, Philip E. Coldwell, then a member of the Fed's Board of Governors, spelled out a framework for analyzing the regulation of BHCs. He called his framework the "Ten Cs of Holding-Company Regulation" and regarded BHC regulatory concerns as reflective of broader financial concerns for the entire United States. Coldwell's ten Cs, which are still relevant today, are as follows:

1. Convenience and needs
2. Competition
3. Compromise of small banks

4. Concentration
5. Conflicts of ownership and control
6. Concerns of classified assets, capital adequacy, and management
7. Compliance with prior agreements, conditions of acquisition, and divestiture
8. Capacity to handle and control impact of nonbank activities
9. Contributions of MBHCs
10. Congressional limitations

Of these 10 factors, the four most important are convenience and needs (or service); competition; concerns of classified assets, capital adequacy, and management; and capacity to handle and control the impact of nonbank activities. Because the last two items reflect concerns about safety and soundness, the priority areas of BHC regulation are service, competition, and safety. Like the three objectives of overall bank regulation (i.e., safety, stability and structure), the objectives of service, competition, and safety are conflicting ones. In the structure-conduct-performance model, competitive structure produces high-performance service.

Convenience and Needs

In all BHC applications, the Fed is charged with looking out for the public interest—the so-called public-benefits test. Public benefits are associated with such factors as increased competition, improved services, lower prices, greater efficiency, or rescue of a failing institution. Most proposed BHC applications are likely to result in at least some public benefits. However, only when this convenience-and-need factor substantially outweighs the competitive and banking factors will the acquisition be approved. Thus, convenience and needs seldom carry enough weight to overcome significantly adverse findings with respect to competitive, financial, and managerial considerations.

Competition

The Fed must investigate the competitive implications of the proposed acquisition by determining the relevant market and the applicant's position in the market. In horizontal acquisitions, three important factors are considered: (1) the resulting change in market share; (2) the extent of overlap of the deposit or loan patterns between the parties in the proposed acquisition; and (3) analysis of the potential loss of a means of market entry for another BHC. If the firms are in different markets, the key elements in the analysis are (1) the market share of the firm to be acquired; (2) the likelihood that the acquiring organization will be a future *de novo* entrant into the market if the acquisition is denied; (3) the number of other potential entrants; and (4) the existing level of concentration in the market.

The importance of a structure-conduct-performance model in Fed analysis of proposed acquisitions is highlighted by the following quote from Coldwell [1976]:

> The Board has traditionally taken a rather "hard" stand on competitive issues. The position is based on the view that the bank market *structure* importantly affects bank *conduct,* which in turn affects market *performance.* (p. 4, italics mine)

To further illustrate the Fed's "hard" stand on the competitive factor, consider the following order disapproving the acquisition of a BHC. On April 3, 1987, the Board of Governors of the Federal Reserve System (see *Federal Reserve Bulletin,* June 1987, pp. 463–469) did not approve the application of Sunwest Financial Services,

Inc., of Albuquerque, New Mexico, to acquire Rio Grande Bancshares, Inc., of Las Cruces, New Mexico. Chairman Volcker and Governor Angell stated that "consummation of the proposed acquisition . . . would substantially lessen competition in two of the three relevant banking markets." In contrast, Governors Johnson and Heller, who did not object to the approval, stated,

> We believe that consummation of the proposal would not substantially reduce competition in any market. We believe that the concentration ratio and other statistics set out in the statement of the other Board members do not reflect the true state of competition in the Las Cruces and Silver City markets. While these statistics give consideration to the competition afforded by savings-and-loan institutions, they ignore the substantial competition banks face from a broad array of products and services provided by other financial institutions in these markets.

Although the analysis of competitive factors at the Fed includes some softer views, the majority opinion still favors a relatively narrow definition of product markets.

Concerns of Classified Assets, Capital Adequacy, and Management

Concerns of classified assets, capital adequacy, and management reflect the traditional bank regulatory concern about safety and soundness as manifested in asset quality, leverage, and managerial ratings. This regulatory concern was illustrated dramatically during the 1974 interest-rate crunch and recession, when the Fed issued its famous "go-slow policy." The purpose of the directive was to encourage BHCs to get their own financial houses in order, especially their banking operations, before they considered any additional acquisitions.

In 1987, an interesting series of events took place regarding concerns about the asset quality and capital adequacy of major banks/BHCs. The interesting twist is that the concern came from the BHCs, and not from the Fed or other banking agencies. During May 1987, Citicorp announced that it was adding $3 billion to its loan-loss reserve to cover potential loan defaults by third world countries (e.g., Brazil, Mexico). This dramatic move forced other BHCs with similar (relative) exposures to follow Citicorp's reserve leadership, which resulted in a massive second-quarter loss for the industry (see Musumeci and Sinkey [1990]). Citicorp continued its leadership role by announcing in August 1987 its intention to raise slightly over $1 billion in equity to bolster its capital position. From a financial-management perspective, the decision to raise equity seemed to be a wise one. Although some shortsighted analysts talked about earnings dilution, the insightful ones saw the move as strengthening Citicorp's balance sheet. Following Citicorp's lead, Manufacturers Hanover and several other BHCs adopted similar plans to raise equity capital.

Capacity to Handle and Control Impact of Nonbank Activities

The Fed wants to know whether BHCs have the capacity to handle and control the impact of permissible nonbank activities. Nonbank subsidiaries may create financial problems for a BHC because of either internal (e.g., poor judgment on the part of management) or external (e.g., recession) factors. The financial difficulties that REITs and mortgage-banking subsidiaries created for certain BHCs during the mid-1970s are good examples of such difficulties.[32] The Fed is concerned about protecting subsidiary banks from potential problems that might be

---

[32] For a description and analysis of the commercial bank-REIT crisis, see Sinkey [1979], chapter 8; for an abbreviated version, see chapter 12 of this book.

created by nonbank subsidiaries or the parent company (i.e., the issue of corporate separateness). Three subsidiary banks that got into financial trouble in the 1970s because of BHC-related difficulties included Beverly Hills National Bank (California, 1974), Hamilton National Bank (Tennessee, 1976), and Palmer National Bank (Florida, 1976). By monitoring BHC financial statements and using on-site examination of subsidiary banks, the Fed hopes to be able to identify future BHC problems before they become serious.

The Ten Cs: A Recapitulation

Coldwell's 10 Cs of BHC regulation provide a convenient framework for analyzing Fed and congressional concerns about the regulation of BHCs. The key concepts of the approach are (1) service, (2) competition, and (3) safety and control. Increased service is important in meeting the convenience and needs of the public; greater competition promotes economic efficiency; and safety and control help ensure against excessive concentration, potential abuses, and unsound banking practices. Although emphasis on the safety-and-control factor tends to restrict the service and competition elements, the Fed needs to balance these risk-return trade-offs to achieve the greatest degree of public benefit.

CONFERENCE OF STATE BANK SUPERVISORS (CSBS)

Just as the Fed, OCC, and FDIC attempt to cooperate on matters of bank regulation and supervision (through an interagency task force), the 50 state banking departments (plus three territorial departments) have a central organization called the **Conference of State Bank Supervisors** (CSBS).[33] Although each state agency concentrates on regulatory matters in its own state, the CSBS provides a vehicle for cooperation among the various states. State banking departments perform two main functions (identical to the OCC): (1) entry-and-exit regulation and (2) examination. Regarding on-site examinations, state departments are handicapped by a lack of resources. Greater cooperation between the state agencies and the FDIC has resulted in a more efficient allocation of both federal and state resources. Regarding entry regulation, the FDIC plays an important de facto role at the state level because it would be highly unusual for a state charter to be granted without deposit insurance.

Regarding the failure of state banks, only the chartering agency can declare a state bank insolvent. Then the FDIC usually is appointed the receiver or liquidator of the closed bank. Of the 2,000 or so commercial banks that have failed from 1934 to 1994, roughly three out of four have been state banks. In addition, the average failed state bank has been about one-fourth the size of the average failed national bank.[34]

According to Kreider [1978], the CSBS has two major objectives: (1) to achieve and maintain strong and effective state banking departments nationwide and (2) to

---

[33] See Kreider [1978] for a detailed description of the CSBS.

[34] Prior to 1986, the FDIC disposed of more small failed banks as deposit payoffs rather than purchase-and-assumption (P&A) transactions. Because more small state banks were located in unit-banking states, more failed state banks had been handled by the FDIC as deposit payoffs than failed national banks. Since 1986, however, when the FDIC became more sensitive to criticism about potential discrimination against uninsured depositors in small banks, the FDIC's use of deposit payoffs has dropped substantially. Chapter 16 describes the FDIC's methods for handling failed banks.

achieve and maintain a banking and bank regulatory structure with adequate state/federal checks and balances so as to minimize government monopoly in bank regulation. The latter can be interpreted as a mandate to preserve the dual-system state and federal bank regulation. Given this stance, it is not surprising that many members of the CSBS viewed the universal reserve requirements imposed by DIDMCA (1980) as an attempt by the Fed to undermine state banking authority. To counteract this federal power play and to avoid a potential state membership problem, some banking commissioners (e.g., in California, Delaware, Georgia, Missouri, New York, and Pennsylvania) eliminated or reduced reserve requirements for nonmember banks in their states.

State legislatures (e.g., in Delaware and South Dakota) have also attempted to lure out-of-state affiliates of BHCs to their states. The demand for such opportunities can be traced to banks' efforts to reduce the burden of state tax and usury laws. Although DIDMCA succeeded in diffusing the Fed's membership problem, it did not succeed in diffusing the competition between federal and state regulators, which now has shifted to the issue of what banking services may be provided legally by nonbanking companies.

With the large number of small independent state banks, the CSBS can be viewed as having a large secondary constituency. In the past, the political clout of these banks far exceeded their economic power. As the banking industry is consolidated over the next decade, this political power will decline. On balance, the reregulation of the industry is viewed more kindly by larger banks.

DERIVATIVES SUPERVISION AND REGULATION IN PERSPECTIVE

Because the derivatives activities of banks are concentrated in the largest banking organizations and because the Fed and the OCC supervise the largest BHCs and banks, the Fed and the OCC have the most direct interest in derivatives supervision. In a speech at the Federal Reserve Bank of Chicago, Phillips [1996] focused on the lessons for prudential supervision to be learned from derivatives and how those lessons can be applied more generally to banking activities.

The most basic lesson stressed by Phillips is that what is important for prudential supervision (and for bank risk management) is the underlying risk characteristics of a financial instrument or banking activity. Although derivatives activities do not involve any new types of risk, some complex derivatives do combine or separate out different types of risk in ways that require sophisticated risk-management capabilities.

The second lesson is that risk must be measured on a portfolio basis rather than instrument by instrument. The portfolio approach is a basic tenet of modern finance. A third lesson from derivatives' experience is the vital importance of internal risk controls. Such controls are critical for all of a bank's major activities. The final lesson focuses on the need to align financial incentives with managers' objectives. Phillips highlights this lesson with two applications: The first one relates to tying compensation to both the returns and the risks of a particular activity. The linkage to risk provides discipline, a facet that was absent from some derivatives trading of the early and mid-1990s. The second application is the linkage of an activity's risk exposure to bank capital. In this regard, the last word on a comprehensive risk-based-capital system has yet to be written.

FINANCIAL REFORM

We close this chapter on bank regulation with an open letter (dated December 9, 1996) to President Clinton on financial reform by the Shadow Financial Regulatory Committee.[35] The letter, shown in Box 15-2, highlights eight interlocking principles that the members of the committee submit as fundamental to their thinking about the role of government in financial markets. You will recognize in the committee's letter many of the ideas, concepts, and terms presented in this book (e.g., market segmentation, regulatory restrictions, competition, government subsidies, transparency, disclosure, etc.). As a taxpayer principal, you should be informed about these issues and express your concerns to your lawmaking agents.

Chapter Summary

Regulation and federal deposit insurance are hallmarks of the U.S. banking system that affect how managers of financial-services firms make strategic and financial decisions. The combination of a lender-of-last-resort function, administered through the Federal Reserve's discount window, and a guarantee function, administered by the FDIC, provide a federal safety net for insured depositories. Although bank managers like the safety net, they are less fond of regulations that restrict profitable investment opportunities. Accordingly, they seek to circumvent restrictions that limit their permissible product lines and geographic reach. This regulatory dialectic or struggle model results in an ongoing battle between regulators and regulatees. Agency theory or a principal-agent model, which provides a framework for analyzing these issues, spotlights the importance of moral hazard and ethics in understanding and shaping the behavior of bankers, regulators, deposit insurers, and politicians.

As the CEO of a major superregional bank has suggested, banks should be operated as if there were no regulators for supervision, no discount window for liquidity, and no deposit insurance for bailouts. Under these counterfactual circumstances, the need for a federal safety net for banks would be greatly reduced. In conjunction with banking laws, regulations, and supervision, the federal safety net places commercial banking under the microscope of federal investigation, jurisdiction, and protection.

Bank regulators try to serve the conflicting objectives of safety and stability on the one hand and efficient banking structure (competition) on the other hand. The flow of regulatory discipline runs from the U.S. Congress, acting as agent for taxpayer principals, to bank regulators (including deposit insurers) to insured depositories. Monitoring and bonding are costly activities. Because regulation acts as a tax, bankers attempt to pass its incidence onto their customers. The struggle between regulators and regulatees, which can be described as the "regulatory dialectic," serves to stimulate financial innovation but at the expense of wasting costly resources to circumvent regulations. Bank regulators, like bankers, compete on the basis of price, confidence, and convenience. Bank holding companies, the dominant form of banking structure in the United States, are heavily regulated by the Federal Reserve.

---

[35] For information about this committee, contact Professor George Kaufman at Loyola University of Chicago, TEL (312) 915–7075 or FAX (312) 915–6118. Or by mail at Administrative Office, c/o Professor Kaufman, Loyola University, 820 North Michigan Avenue, Chicago, IL 60611.

BOX 15-2

STATEMENT OF SHADOW FINANCIAL REGULATORY COMMITTEE (STATEMENT NO. 135)

AN OPEN LETTER TO PRESIDENT CLINTON ON FINANCIAL REFORM

December 9, 1996

Dear Mr. President:

Financial innovations, technological changes, and an enhanced competitive environment have profoundly changed what financial institutions do and how they do it. Government regulation, however, has not kept pace with developments in the private sector. Changes in regulation have been piecemeal and have lacked both coherent objectives and clear public policy principles. You have the opportunity to introduce and support legislation that establishes a clear vision of the role that government should play in regulating financial institutions and markets in the future.

As economists and lawyers who have devoted much of their professional lives to the study of financial markets and institutions, we would like to submit eight interlocking principles that have proven fundamental to our thinking about the role of government in financial markets.

(1) It is folly to continue to try to segment financial markets and institutions by imposing government or charter restrictions on the activities that different financial institutions can engage in. A fundamental objective should be to permit financial institutions to compete across the full spectrum of financial services, without limitations by the government.

(2) Government subsidies to participants in the payments system should be eliminated so that participants compete on equal terms without prospect of taxpayer liability.

(3) Participation in the Fedwire system should be open to nonbank institutions.

(4) Residual government subsidies associated with deposit insurance should be eliminated.

(5) Government subsidies associated with government-sponsored financial entities should be eliminated.

(6) There should be incentives for financial institutions to provide public disclosure that is sufficient to make their activities transparent to depositors, investors, and creditors, so that private markets can effectively discipline poorly-managed and inefficient institutions.

(7) The objectives and decision criteria employed by regulators should be disclosed in a way that makes their activities transparent and permits an objective evaluation of their performance by taxpayers and Congress.

(8) Finally, the thrust of government prudential regulation should be to insure the efficiency and stability of the payments system, and not to maintain the solvency of individual financial institutions or to protect uninsured depositors, non-deposit creditors, or the stockholders of individual institutions.

We recognize that there are alternative legislative approaches to regulating financial institutions and strong opinions about which approach is preferable. Any approach that satisfies the foregoing principles will be a vast improvement over the financial and regulatory system that we have now.

We would be pleased to discuss our views with members of your administration as they begin the process of formulating an approach to restructuring the financial system. Thank you for the opportunity to be heard on this issue.

Several key ideas explain the theories, objectives, and agencies of bank regulation. Agency theory highlights the principal-agent relations and problems of bank regulation. The notions of regulators as producers of regulatory services and the three layers of financial-services competition (price, confidence, and convenience) explain the role of regulation in shaping competition. The U.S. system for regulating depository institutions fits Arthur Burns's description as a "jurisdictional tangle that boggles the mind." At the federal level, the Fed, FDIC, OCC, and

SEC are the dominant players in the regulation of commercial banks and their holding companies. In the throes of the S&L mess, the system of thrift regulation, supervision, and insurance was substantially revised by FIRREA in 1989 and FDICIA in 1991. Because BHCs are the dominant organizational form in U.S. banking, their regulation and supervision by the Fed is pivotal. The major banking acts of the 1980s and 1990s were designed, in part, to reverse the unintended evils of prior legislation and make the deposit-insurance and regulatory systems more compatible with a modern financial-services industry.

Key Words, Concepts, and Acronyms

- Agency costs/problems/theory
- Bank-examination process
- Bank holding company (BHC)
- Bank Insurance Fund (BIF)
- BHC rating system (BOPEC, see appendix B)
- Board of Governors of the Federal Reserve System
- Competition for regulatory services
- Conference of State Bank Supervisors (CABS)
- Confidence and convenience functions
- Contestable markets
- Deposit Insurance Fund ($DIF = SAIF + BIF$)
- Depository institutions
- Domino (contagion) theory
- Federal Deposit Insurance Corporation (FDIC)
- FDIC Improvement Act (1991)
- Federal Housing Finance Board (formerly part of FHLBB)
- Federal Reserve System ("the Fed")
- Federal safety net
- Financial Institutions Reform, Recovery, and Enforcement Act (FIRREA) of 1989
- Good intentions and unintended evils (of regulation)
- Government guarantee
- Industrial-organization (IO) model (structure-conduct-performance model)
- Jurisdictional tangle
- Multibank holding company (MBHC)
- National Credit Union Administration (NCUA)
- Objectives of bank regulation (safety, stability, and structure)
- Office of the Comptroller of the Currency (OCC)
- Office of Thrift Supervision (OTS, formerly part of FSLIC)
- One-bank holding company (OBHC)
- Principal-agent model/relations
- Regulatory dialectic (struggle model)
- Reigle-Neal Interstate Banking and Branching Efficiency Act of 1994 (IBBEA)
- Resolution Trust Corporation (RTC)
- Savings Association Insurance Fund (SAIF)
- Securities and Exchange Commission (SEC)
- Supervision-by-risk program
- Systemic risk

Review/Discussion Questions

1. Discuss and evaluate the following statement: "We believe financial institutions should be operated as if there were no regulators for supervision, no discount window for liquidity, and no deposit insurance for bailouts." Who would make such a statement? A banker? A regulator?
2. Define each of the following terms and explain how they are related: the federal safety net, TBTF, and the confidence function.
3. Explain the principal-agent model of regulatory discipline in the financial-services industry. What evidence exists, if any, to suggest that regulators are faithful agents?
4. The objectives of bank regulation can be described as safety, stability, and structure. In what sense are they conflicting and how have these objectives changed over time? Describe the banking eras of the 1980s and 1990s.
5. Distinguish between the domino theory and systemic risk. Does the federal safety net curtail or promote systemic risk?
6. Fed economists tend to like the IO model. What is it and how does it relate to competition with economic efficiency? What is a "contestable market"?
7. What is the philosophical foundation of the regulatory dialectic? How well does the theory serve as an explanation of the regulatory process? Can the regulatory dialectic be viewed as a theory of financial innovation?

8. What is the contestability theory of multimarket competition? How well does it explain (*a*) the process of change in the FSI and (*b*) regulatory behavior? Regarding the latter, explain the role of the confidence and convenience functions in the FSI. What are the three layers of financial-services competition?

9. Explain why you can't judge the FDIC by its cover (i.e., acronym). What about the OCC?

10. What role, if any, does the FDIC play in entry regulation?

11. During 1984, some bankers described OCC examiners as behaving in a "redneck fashion" with respect to problem loans. How do these stories jibe with the comptroller's strength-in-banking equation? How did OCC examiners behave in 1990? Contrast these actions and reports with the following quote by the comptroller in 1995:

    > Rather than seeing regulation as a ball and chain weighing them down, or supervision as a shackle holding them back, I want the industry to view OCC examiners as adding value to their business without needless burden.

12. Federal Reserve Regulations *A, D, Q, Y,* and *Z* are more commonly known than the other members of the alphabet-soup gang. What are these five regulations?

13. Why are state banking agencies at a disadvantage vis-à-vis federal ones? What are the chances that there will always be a (*de jure*) dual-banking system? Will there always be a *real* dual-banking system?

14. Do you agree with Arthur Burns that the U.S. system of bank regulation is a "jurisdictional tangle that boggles the mind" and that it "promotes competition in laxity?" Explain and discuss.

15. Describe the OCC's supervision-by-risk program and the nine categories of risk that comprise it. What are the lessons from derivatives activities for prudential supervision and for bank risk management? Which of the OCC's nine risks were most affected by the derivatives debacles of 1994?

16. What can the bank examination process hope to accomplish? What role, if any, should financial markets play in this process? What role should market-value accounting play? If you were Banking Czar, how would you allocate scarce examination and supervision resources? Would you place 10 full-time examiners in a huge organization like Citibank?

17. Discuss the good intentions and unintended evils, if any, of the banking laws in appendix A.

18. Although Coldwell recommends 10 Cs for analyzing the regulation of bank holding companies, four of them capture the thrust of the Fed's concerns. List and explain what these four factors are.

19. What are BOPEC and CAMEL and how are they related, if at all? To answer this question, you need to have read appendix B to this chapter.

20. Discuss and evaluate the following statement made by former Federal Reserve Governor Jackson in 1978:

    > I think the industry as a whole has become overregulated by the way its supervisors set standards for a bank's capital and assets. We need to stop treating banks like public utilities and allow the marketplace by its own risk analysis to make a determination between the successful and the unsuccessful bank. No government official, regardless of how competent or well intentioned, can manage an individual bank or the industry as a whole as well as the collective effort of bank stockholders, directors and officers.

21. Since the Great Depression of the early 1930s, the modus operandi of U.S. banking regulation has focused on geographic and product restrictions. What kind of restrictions exist today, how have they changed, and what role have the restrictions played in the development of bank holding companies?

22. Should commercial banks be allowed to offer investment-banking and insurance services? Discuss this.

23. Given the open letter to President Clinton by the Shadow Financial Regulatory Committee, do you agree or disagree with the eight principles expressed in the letter?

APPENDIX A

A BRIEF HISTORY OF THE GOOD INTENTIONS AND UNINTENDED EVILS OF MAJOR PIECES OF BANK LEGISLATION, 1863–1996

THE NATIONAL BANK ACT (1863)

Known as the National Currency Act from 1863 to 1874. Created the Office of the Comptroller of the Currency.

Good intentions: To ensure a workable and safe national banking system and, primarily, to finance the Union's war effort.

Unintended evils: Created a dual-banking system and planted the seeds for the jurisdictional tangle of federal and state bank regulation.

FEDERAL RESERVE ACT (1913)

Created the Federal Reserve System (central bank).

Good intentions: To establish an elastic currency and a more effective means for bank supervision.

Unintended evils: A sad day for monetarists such as Milton Friedman who abhor discretionary monetary policy in favor of a fixed monetary rule for growth of the money supply. Added to the tangled web of bank regulation.

MCFADDEN-PEPPER ACT (1927)

Placed geographic restrictions on national banks such that they are subject to the branching restrictions of the state in which they are headquartered.

Good intention: Give national banks the same branching powers as state banks in which the national banks are located.

Unintended evil: Limited the ability of banks to diversify geographically. (In the 1980s, regional banking agreements among states permitted mergers and acquisitions across state lines, and federal deregulation permitted bank acquisition of distressed banks and of distressed and healthy thrifts across state lines.)

BANKING ACT OF 1933, OR GLASS-STEAGALL ACT

Separated commercial and investment banking.

Prohibited payment of interest on demand deposits and imposed interest-rate ceilings on other deposits.

Created federal deposit insurance.

Good intentions: To promote safe-and-sound banking practices and to protect small depositors.

Unintended evils: Limited product diversification, restricted pricing flexibility, created an overly protected banking environment, and left banks, especially thrifts, unprepared for the interest-rate volatility of 1966 to 1983.

BANKING ACT OF 1935

Fine-tuned certain aspects of the 1933 Banking Act.

BANK HOLDING COMPANY ACT OF 1956 AND 1970 AMENDMENT

Gave the Federal Reserve primary control over BHCs that controlled two or more banks. Among other things, the Fed could determine permissible nonbanking activities for BHCs, effectively separating banking and commerce.

Made any foreign bank that *owns* a U.S. bank subject to the BHC Act.

OBHC loophole was closed by the 1970 amendment.

Good intentions: To keep banking and commerce separate and to promote safe-and-sound banking.

Unintended evils: Limited product diversification and reinforced the separation of banking and commerce.

BANK MERGER ACT OF 1960

Made bank mergers subject to the approval of the federal banking agencies (OCC for national banks, Fed for state member banks, and FDIC for insured nonmember banks).

Merger guidelines established, with competition as one of the criteria.

Good intention: To prevent anticompetitive mergers and acquisitions.

Unintended evils: Subsequent court decisions treated banking as a narrow line of commerce, with loans and deposits as the relevant products in narrowly defined geographic markets such as metropolitan areas or rural counties. Product and market definitions were too narrow for the FSI.

INTERNATIONAL BANKING ACT OF 1978 (IBA)

Established an overall framework for regulating the full range of activities of foreign banks in the United States and provided for a federal role in the supervision of branches and agencies of foreign banks.

Central concept involved "national treatment" for all banks, whether domestic or foreign (e.g., loopholes available to foreign banks in the McFadden Act, the Glass-Steagall Act, and the BHC Act were closed). Prior to the IBA, the operations of U.S. branches and agencies of foreign banks were licensed and supervised solely by state banking authorities.

DEPOSITORY INSTITUTIONS DEREGULATION AND MONETARY CONTROL ACT OF 1980 (DIDMCA)

Imposed reserve requirements on all depository institutions.

Called for phasing out (by 1986) of Regulation Q interest-rate ceilings.

Increased the ceiling on deposit insurance to $100,000.

Good intentions: Remove interest-rate ceilings and raise deposit-insurance ceiling.

Unintended evils: Raising the insurance ceiling permitted high-risk institutions determined to "bet the bank" to aggressively seek funds. The *timing* of the removal of Reg Q was horrible, especially for thrifts, as interest rates spiked in the early 1980s.

GARN-ST GERMAIN ACT OF 1982

Granted S&Ls new investment powers.

Permitted banks to offer money market demand accounts (MMDAs).

Federal preemption extended to state laws restricting due-on-sale and alternative mortgage instruments.

FDIC and FSLIC granted broader authority to aid troubled institutions.

Good intentions: To permit insured depositories to compete with money-market mutual funds, to expand thrift investment powers, and to give federal regulators more power to deal with troubled depositories.

Unintended evil: Encouraged capital forbearance and lax supervision of banks and thrifts.

COMPETITIVE EQUALITY BANKING ACT OF 1987 (CEBA)

Designed to rescue the FSLIC and provide for supervisory forbearance for troubled thrifts and farm banks.

Nonbank-bank loophole closed and existing ones grandfathered.

FDIC permitted to arrange interstate mergers for failing institutions with assets over $500 million.

Check-clearing rules established.

Fed given authority to regulate new nonbanking activities.

Good intention: To save the FSLIC and the thrift industry.

Unintended evils: Failed to recognize the seriousness of the S&L mess and the crisis in deposit insurance. Capital forbearance still encouraged. Restricted bank/BHC investment opportunities in new nonbanking activities.

FINANCIAL INSTITUTIONS REFORM, RECOVERY, AND ENFORCEMENT ACT OF 1989 (FIRREA)

The S&L bailout bill (recovery) aimed at promoting a safe and stable system of affordable housing finance.

Reorganization of thrift regulation, supervision, and deposit insurance (reform and enforcement).

Permitted commercial banks to buy healthy thrifts.

Strengthened enforcement powers of federal regulators of depository institutions and attempted to provide additional funding to deal expeditiously with failed depositories.

Attempted to put federal deposit insurance on a sound footing and to place the full faith and credit of the United States government behind federal deposit insurance (see Exhibit 15-1).

Good intentions: To reform deposit insurance, to provide for the recovery of the thrift industry, and to enhance regulatory enforcement.

Unintended evils: The Resolution Trust Corporation (RTC), charged with the orderly disposal of the assets of failed thrifts, was not given enough flexibility or financing to do an effective job. Effective deposit-insurance reform still not addressed.

FEDERAL DEPOSIT INSURANCE CORPORATION IMPROVEMENT ACT OF 1991 (FDICIA)

Provided liquidity to the FDIC by permitting it to borrow $30 billion from the U.S. Treasury and authorized it to borrow $45 billion using its assets as collateral, with the loans to be repaid from the sale of failed banks' assets.

Required bank regulators to develop measurements describing the capitalization of banks and thrifts and to take "prompt corrective action" (PCA) when an insured depository becomes undercapitalized. When PCA fails to solve a problem situation and the institution's ratio of capital to total risk-adjusted assets is 2 percent or less, regulators may seize the bank and sell it to a viable institution.

Required regulators to set and monitor standards for sound bank management relating to such areas as internal controls, credit underwriting, management information systems, exposure to interest-rate risk, asset growth, and compensation for officers. With certain expectations, federally insured depositories must undergo an on-site, safety-and-soundness examination at least once a year.

FDIC must choose the least-cost alternative in resolving failing institutions, although an escape valve exists for situations involving "systemic risk."

FDIC required to develop risk-related premiums to make the deposit-insurance system fairer to well-run institutions and encourage weak institutions to improve their condition.

Foreign banks must seek approval of the Federal Reserve before opening or closing any U.S. offices, they must apply for FDIC insurance if they wish to accept deposits of under $100,000, and they can be closed if they are not adequately supervised by their home-country regulators.

Additional consumer protection with respect to affordable housing, truth in savings, incentives for banks to provide "lifeline accounts" for low-income persons, and provision for 90-day notice on branch closings.

Good Intentions: To strengthen the deposit-insurance funds, to encourage supervisory reform, to reduce the costs of resolving failing banks, to reform the management of deposit insurance, and to provide additional consumer protection.

Unintended Evils: Short sighted strengthening of insurance funds does not prepare for the next banking crisis whereas "escape valve" permits regulators to practice forbearance in the name of protecting the economy from systemic risk.

RESOLUTION TRUST CORPORATION COMPLETION ACT OF 1993

Provided $18 billion in funding for the RTC.

Restructured the funding of the Savings Association Insurance Fund (SAIF).

Accelerated by one year (from December 31, 1996, to December 31, 1995) the termination of the RTC and the transfer of its operations to the FDIC.

NATIONAL DEPOSITOR PREFERENCE ACT (1993)

By giving priority to the claims of the FDIC and to depositors, the costs of resolving failed institutions are expected to be reduced.

REIGLE COMMUNITY DEVELOPMENT AND REGULATORY IMPROVEMENT ACT OF 1994

Authorizes funding for community-development financial institutions, provides regulatory and paperwork relief for financial institutions, encourages development of secondary loans for small businesses, and makes changes to reporting requirements for money laundering.

REIGLE-NEIL INTERSTATE BANKING AND BRANCHING EFFICIENCY ACT (1994)

Authorizes interstate banking and branching to U.S. and foreign banks over a three-year period.

Note: No major acts in 1995, 1996, and the first half of 1997. For laws in which no good intentions–unintended evils are listed, no discernible unintended evils are present.

APPENDIX B

THE FEDERAL RESERVE'S BHC RATING SYSTEM[36]

To evaluate the safety and soundness of BHCs, the Fed employs a rating system grounded in the on-site bank examination process. The system is a management information and supervisory tool designed to assess the condition of BHCs in a systematic way. It uses a "component approach" consisting of (1) evaluating the financial condition and risk characteristics of each major component of the BHC, (2) assessing the important interrelationships among the components, and (3) analyzing the strength and significance of key consolidated financial and operating performance characteristics. This approach is particularly appropriate because holding companies are supposed to be a source of financial and managerial strength to their bank subsidiaries.

To arrive at an overall assessment of financial condition, the following elements of a BHC are evaluated and rated

1. Bank subsidiaries (B)
2. Other (nonbank) subsidiaries (O)
3. Parent company (P)
4. Earnings—consolidated (E)
5. Capital adequacy—consolidated (C)

The acronym for the rating system is BOPEC; scores are assigned on a scale of 1 (excellent) to 5 (terrible) in descending order of performance quality. The ideal rating is the golfer's fantasy of five aces (i.e., B = 1, O = 1, P = 1, E = 1, C = 1). BHCs that are out of bounds score 5s on the BOPEC course.

The first three elements of the BOPEC rating (bank subsidiaries, other subsidiaries, and parent company) reflect the contribution of each component to the fundamental financial soundness of the holding company. The ratings of consolidated earnings and consolidated capital recognize the importance that regulators place on these factors and their crucial roles in maintaining the financial strength and supporting the risk characteristics of the entire organization. Because the ability and competence of holding-company management bear importantly on every aspect of holding-company operations, the quality of management is a major factor in the evaluation of each of the five principal elements of the rating, as well as in the assignment of an overall holding-company rating.

In addition to the individual elements described earlier, each company is assigned an overall or composite rating in both the financial and managerial areas. The financial composite score is based on an overall evaluation of the ratings of each of the five principal elements of BOPEC. The financial composite rating is also based on a scale of 1 to 5 in descending order of performance quality. The managerial composite is predicted on a comprehensive evaluation of holding-company manage-

---

[36] Condensed from "BHC Rating System," Federal Reserve Press Release (February 7, 1979).

ment, as reflected in the conduct of the affairs of the bank and nonbank subsidiaries and the parent company. The managerial composite is indicated by the assignment of S, F, or U for management that is found to be satisfactory, fair, or unsatisfactory.

The complete rating represents a summary evaluation of the BHC in the form of a rating "fraction." The numerator reflects the condition of the major components of the holding company, as well as assessments of certain key consolidated financial and operating factors. The denominator represents the composite rating, including both its financial and managerial components. Although the elements in the numerator represent the essential foundation on which the composite rating is based, the Fed insists that the composite need not reflect a simple arithmetic mean of the individual performance dimensions. Because any kind of formula could be misleading and inappropriate, the composite should reflect the rater's judgment of the overall condition of the BHC based upon his/her knowledge and experience with the company. The complete BHC rating is displayed as follows:

$$\frac{[B, O, P, E, C]}{[F, M]}$$

The BHC rating system, to some degree, parallels the Uniform Interagency Bank Rating System by utilizing similar rating scales and performance definitions to evaluate both the individual elements and the summary or overall condition of the holding company. The bank rating system is based upon a financial profile called CAMEL, which stands for *C*apital, *A*sset quality, *M*anagement, *E*arnings, and *L*iquidity. Because the bank-condition component of the BHC rating system is a CAMEL-driven rating and since banks account for most of BHC revenues and assets, BOPEC is driven by CAMEL, which in turn is driven by bank examiners' perceptions of asset quality and bank capital adequacy (Sinkey [1978]). The Fed's BHC rating system is summarized in Figure B15-1.

Both BOPEC and CAMEL scores are treated as confidential information by the banking agencies. Attempts by the author, under the Freedom of Information

FIGURE B15-1 The Fed's BHC Rating System

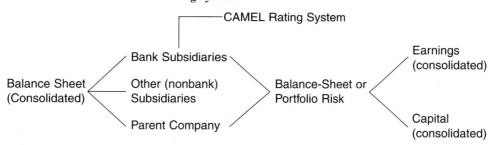

The overall BHC rating is summarized as [B,O,P,E,C]/[F,M] where *F* and *M* are financial and managerial composite ratings. The financial composite is some examiner-determined weighted average of the elements of BOPEC whereas the managerial composite is a comprehensive evaluation of overall holding-company management (i.e., banks, nonbank subsidiaries, and parent companies). The bank-condition component (B) of BOPEC is a CAMEL-driven rating derived as a weighted average (based upon asset size) of the subsidiary banks' composite CAMEL scores. Two sample ratings are

Best Possible Rating	*Worst Possible Rating*
CAMEL = [1,1,1,1,1]	CAMEL = [5,5,5,5,5]
BOPEC = [1,1,1,1,1]	BOPEC = [5,5,5,5,5]
FM = [1,S]	FM = [5,U]

Act, to obtain such ratings for troubled BHCs/banks of the 1980s were denied. However, based on my research at the FDIC from 1971 to 1976 and on information disclosed at congressional hearings since then, it is clear that the banking agencies have been highly successful over the past 15 years in *identifying* almost all problem situations at least one year prior to failure. Thus, the regulatory problem appears to be one of *enforcement* rather than *identification*. For example, in the congressional hearings regarding the collapse of Continental Illinois, the OCC was charged by the chairman of the House Banking Committee with "timid regulation." The apparent regulatory policy of "benign neglect" is desirable, however, because high-risk institutions *should* fail. Unfortunately, the regulators, in the name of financial stability, have bailed out, at taxpayers' expense, some of the nation's largest high-risk banks/BHCs (e.g., Continental Illinois, First Pennsylvania, and Bank of the Commonwealth). As a result the marketplace has come to expect a 100 percent government guarantee behind the debt of large banks/BHCs. To illustrate, regarding the bank-LDC problems, Moody's Investor Service stated, "Major banks are too important to the economy, too interconnected, and too confidence-sensitive to run the risk of permitting default" (*Wall Street Journal,* September 7, 1984, p. 7).

To summarize, although bank (and therefore BHC) examination data are available only every year or two and involve some subjective judgments by examiners, the data have been successful in providing early-warning signals of most problem situations at least one full year in advance of failure. Of course, about 90 percent of the BHCs/banks with problems don't fail, but those seldom make the financial news. Regarding the ones that do fail, the objective of bank regulation and examination is not, and should not be, a zero failure rate. The ultimate goal is to preserve *confidence* in the supply of money and credit and to provide a stable or safe-and-sound financial system for the U.S. and world economies.

Selected References

Amel, Dean F. [1996]. "Trends in the Structure of Federally Insured Depository Institutions, 1984–94." *Federal Reserve Bulletin* (January), pp. 1–15.

Angelini, P., G. Maresca, and D. Russo. [1996]. "Systemic Risk in the Netting System." *Journal of Banking and Finance* (June), pp. 853–868.

Annual Statistical Digest. [1986]. Washington, D.C.: Board of Governors of the Federal Reserve System.

Apcar, Leonard. [1987]. "Frightened Money." *The Wall Street Journal* (September 1), pp. 1 and 14.

Association of Banks-In-Insurance. *1994 Banks in Insurance Fact Book.* Washington, DC.

Baumol, William J. [1982]. "Contestable Markets: An Uprising in the Theory of Industry Structure." *American Economic Review* (March), pp. 1–15.

Baumol, W. J., J. C. Panzar, and R. D. Willig. [1983]. "On the Theory of Perfectly Contestable Markets." Bell Laboratories, Economic Discussion Paper no. 268 (June).

Black, Fischer. [1995]. "Hedging, Speculation, and Systemic Risk." *Journal of Derivatives* (Summer), pp. 6–8.

Bremer, C. D. [1935]. *American Bank Failures.* New York: Columbia University Press.

Burns, A. F. [1974]. "Maintaining the Soundness of Our Banking System." Federal Reserve Bank of New York, *Monthly Review* (November), pp. 263–267.

Buser, Stephen A., Andrew H. Chen, and Edward J. Kane. [1981]. "Federal Deposit Insurance, Regulatory Policy, and Optimal Bank Capital." *Journal of Finance* (March), pp. 51–60.

Coldwell, Philip E. [1976]. "Ten Cs of Holding Company Regulation." Speech before the Association of BHCs, Board of Governors of the Federal Reserve System, Washington, DC.

Conover, C. T. [1984]. "Strength in Banking." Speech before the 1984 American Bankers Association, National Convention, OCC news release.

CS First Boston. [1994]. *U.S. Bank Regulation.* New York: CS First Boston.

Dince, R. R. [1979]. "The Bank Regulators Have a New Point of View." *Fortune* (October 8), pp. 166–168.

Frank, Stephen E. [1996]. "Not All Banks Want to Kill Glass-Steagall." *The Wall Street Journal* (May 21), pp. C1 and C21.

"Guide to Federal Reserve Regulations." [1981]. Board of Governors of the Federal Reserve System (September).

Hammond, B. [1957]. *Banks and Politics in America.* Princeton: Princeton University Press.

Horvitz, P. M. [1980]. "A Reconsideration of the Role of Bank Examination." *Journal of Money, Credit, and Banking* (November), pp. 654–659.

Huertas, Thomas F. [1983]. "The Regulation of Financial Institutions: A Historical Perspective on Current Issues." In George Benston, ed., *Financial Services.* Englewood Cliffs, NJ: Prentice-Hall, pp. 6–27.

Jackson, P. C. [1978]. Address before the Alabama Bankers Association, Mobile, Alabama, May 11, 1978. Board of Governors of the Federal Reserve System, Washington, DC.

Jessee, Michael A., and Steven A. Seelig. [1977]. *Bank Holding Companies and the Public Interest.* Lexington, MA: Lexington Books, D.C. Heath.

Johnson, Shane A., and Salil K. Sarkar. [1996]. "The Valuation Effects of the 1977 Community Reinvestment Act and Its Enforcement." *Journal of Banking and Finance* (June), pp. 783–803.

Kane, Edward J. [1977]. "Good Intentions and Unintended Evil . . ." *Journal of Money, Credit, and Banking* (February), pp. 55–69.

———. [1978]. "Getting Along without Regulation Z . . ." *Journal of Finance* (June), pp. 921–932.

———. [1981]. "Accelerating Inflation, Technological Innovation, and the Decreasing Effectiveness of Banking Regulation." *Journal of Finance* (May), pp. 355–367.

———. [1983]. "Metamorphosis in Financial-Services Delivery and Production." In *Strategic Planning for Economics and Technological Change in the FSI.* San Francisco: FHLBB, pp. 49–64.

———. [1984]. "Technological and Regulatory Forces in the Developing Fusion of Financial-Services Competition." Columbus: Ohio State University, WPS 84–4.

———. [1986]. "Competitive Financial Reregulation: An International Perspective." Paper presented at the 1986 Conference of the International Center for Monetary and Banking Studies (August).

———. [1989]. *The S&L Insurance Mess: How Did It Happen?* Washington, DC: Urban Institute.

———. [1990]. "Principal-Agent Relations in S&L Salvage." *Journal of Finance* (July), pp. 755–764.

———. [1995]. "Missing Entailments of Public-Policy Definitions of Systemic Risk." In *Research in Financial Services Private and Public Policy,* vol. 7. Greenwich, CT: JAI Press, pp. 337–346.

———. [1996a]. "De Jure Interstate Banking: Why Only Now?" *Journal of Money, Credit, and Banking* (May), pp. 141–161.

————. [1996b]. "The Increasing Futility of Restricting Bank Participation in Insurance Activities." In Anthony Saunders and Ingo Walter, eds., *Universal Banking.* Homewood Hills, IL: Irwin Professional Publishers, pp. 338–354.

Kreider, Laurence E. [1978]. "Regulations on Bank Soundness, Competition, and Structure—State Banking Departments." In W. H. Gaughn and E. C. Walker, eds., *The Banker's Handbook.* Homewood Hills, IL: Dow Jones-Irwin, pp. 1060–1066.

Leveling the Playing Field. [1983]. Readings in Economics and Finance from the Federal Reserve Bank of Chicago (December).

McCord, Thom. [1980]. "The Depository Institutions Deregulation and Monetary Control Act of 1980." *Issues in Bank Regulation* (Spring), pp. 3–7.

Medlin, John G., Jr. [1989]. "The True Measure of Bank Quality." *First Wachovia Magazine* (Summer), pp. 2–5.

Musumeci, James J., and Joseph F. Sinkey, Jr. [1990]. "The International Debt Crisis and Bank Loan-Loss Reserve Decisions: The Signalling Content of Partially Anticipated Events." *Journal of Money, Credit, and Banking* (August), pp. 370–387.

Partee, J. C. [1980]. Address before the American Institute of Certified Public Accountants Annual National Conference on Banking, Capital Hilton, Washington, DC, December 4, 1980. Washington, DC: Board of Governors of the Federal Reserve System.

Phillips, Susan M. [1996]. "Derivatives Supervision and Regulation in Perspective." Remarks at a Conference on Derivatives and Public Policy, Federal Reserve Bank of Chicago (June 6).

Rose, S. [1977]. "Bank Regulation: The Reforms We Really Need." *Fortune* (December), pp. 123–134.

Schwartz, Anna. [1995]. "Systemic Risk and the Macroeconomy." In George G. Kaufman, ed., *Research in Financial Services,* vol. 7. Greenwich, CT: JAI Press.

Shull, Bernard. [1980]. "Federal and State Supervision of Bank Holding Companies." In *State and Federal Regulation of Commercial Banks.* Washington, DC: FDIC, pp. 271–374.

Sinkey, Joseph F., Jr. [1977a]. "Problem and Failed Banks, Bank Examinations, and Early-Warning Systems: A Summary." In E. Altman and A. Sametz, eds., *Financial-Crises.* New York: Wiley-Interscience, pp. 24–47.

————. [1977b]. "Identifying Large Problem/Failed Banks: The Case of Franklin National Bank of New York." *Journal of Financial and Quantitative Analysis,* (December) pp. 779–800.

————. [1978]. "Identifying Problem Banks: How Do the Banking Authorities Measure a Bank's Risk Exposure?" *Journal of Money, Credit, and Banking* (May), pp. 184–193.

————. [1979]. *Problem and Failed Institutions in the Commercial Banking Industry.* Greenwich, CT: JAI Press.

Sivon, James C. [1992]. "Insurance Activities Permissible for Banks and Bank Holding Companies." Washington, DC: American Bankers Association.

Smith, James E., and Robert R. Dince. [1978]. "The Office of the Comptroller of the Currency and the Structure of American Banking." In W. H. Baughn and C. E. Walker, eds., *The Banker's Handbook.* Homewood Hills, IL: Dow Jones-Irwin, pp. 1049–1059.

Spong, Kenneth. [1990]. *Banking Regulation: Its Purposes, Implementation, and Effects.* 3rd ed. Federal Reserve Bank of Kansas City.

Thakor, Anjan V. [1996]. "The Design of Financial Systems: An Overview." *Journal of Banking and Finance* (June), pp. 917–948.

Volcker, P. A. [1980a]. "The Burden of Banking Regulation." Remarks at the American Bankers Association Annual Convention, Chicago, October 14. Washington, DC: Board of Governors of the Federal Reserve System.

————. [1980b]. Statement before the Committee on Banking, Housing, and Urban Affairs. Washington, DC: U.S. Senate, August 5.

CHAPTER

16

DEPOSIT INSURANCE, BANK FAILURES, AND THE SAVINGS-AND-LOAN MESS

Contents

Chapter Summary
Key Words, Concepts, and Acronyms
Review/Discussion Questions
Problems
Selected References

LEARNING OBJECTIVES

- To understand the moral hazard and cost of government guarantees

- To understand three alternative models of deposit insurance

- To understand how the FDIC resolves and handles failed banks

- To understand the causes of bank failure

- To distinguish between economic insolvency and bank closure

- To understand the causes and costs of the S&L mess

CHAPTER THEME

For almost 50 years, federal deposit insurance worked too well in the United States. The financial devastation of the 1980s, however, wrecked it. Whereas the FDIC was able to survive, the Federal Savings and Loan Insurance Corporation (FSLIC) went bankrupt. Although the Financial Institutions Reform, Recovery, and Enforcement Act (FIRREA) of 1989 and the FDIC Improvement Act (FDICIA) of 1991 revamped federal deposit insurance, a lot of unfinished work remains (e.g., pricing deposit insurance, failure-resolution policies and procedures, and resolving incentive conflicts). FIRREA, which placed the "full faith and credit of the U.S. government" behind federal deposit insurance, created the Deposit Insurance Fund (DIF), consisting of the Bank Insurance Fund (BIF) and the Savings Association Insurance Fund (SAIF), established the Resolution Trust Corporation (RTC) to dispose of the assets of zombie S&Ls, and stuck U.S. taxpayers with a $160-billion tab (excluding interest) for the S&L mess. FDICIA requires bank supervisors to take "prompt corrective action" in dealing with problem banks. When economically insolvent banks (zombies) are kept open, they drain taxpayer-backed deposit-insurance funds. Viewing deposit insurance as a surety or trilateral performance bond endogenizes risk, highlights incentive conflict, and focuses on optimal loss-control activity.

KEY CONCEPTS, IDEAS, AND TERMS

- Cash-flow model (of FDIC)
- Casualty-insurance model
- Closure rule
- Economic failure/insolvency
- Failure-resolution methods
- FDIC Improvement Act (FDICIA)

- Financial Institutions Reform, Recovery, and Enforcement Act (FIRREA)
- Forbearance
- Government guarantee
- Incentive conflict
- Loss-control instruments

- Moral hazard
- Option-pricing model
- Passive casualty-insurance model
- Prompt corrective action (PCA)
- Savings-and-loan (S&L) mess
- Surety (trilateral performance bond)

INTRODUCTION: YOU CAN PAY ME NOW OR YOU CAN PAY ME LATER; U.S. TAXPAYERS PAID LATER

Several years ago, a clever television commercial tried to convince the American public that replacing an oil filter was cheaper than getting a valve job. Although the punch line, "You can pay me now or you can pay me later," reflects sound auto-maintenance advice, its message was even more appropriate for the **savings-and-loan (S&L) mess.** If only a commercial had advised the American public of the consequences of not changing the oil filter in the federal deposit-insurance system, we might have been able to reduce the $150-billion (excluding interest) "S&L valve job."

Unlike the **Federal Savings and Loan Insurance Corporation** (FSLIC), the **Federal Deposit Insurance Corporation** (FDIC) did not go belly up. The Sword of Damocles,[1] however, did hang over the FDIC because its reserves were seriously drained by the bank failures of the 1980s and the rash of commercial-real-estate problems in the early 1990s.[2] The FDIC was able to rebuild its reserves by charging higher deposit-insurance premiums during the early 1990s. Although bankers complained about the higher fees, they could afford them, because as interest rates declined and remained relatively low, banks earned record profits. By mid-1995, when the FDIC reached its mandated reserve level of $1.25 per $100 of deposits, it announced a reduction in deposit-insurance fees, which bankers applauded because it saved them about $4.4 billion in annual operating expenses. Some critics, however, did not applaud because they saw the move as myopic, especially since bankers and regulators do not seem to learn from past mistakes.

This chapter, which includes an analysis of the S&L mess and its implications for deposit insurance, explains FDIC insurance as a **government guarantee.** Kane [1995] refers to this guarantee as a **surety** or **trilateral performance bond.** This approach incorporates agency costs into the nexus of contracts that makes up deposit insurance. Kane's model is insightful because it **views risk as endogenous,** highlights **incentive conflict,** and focuses on **optimal loss-control activity.** Alternative models of deposit insurance focus on the **passive casualty-insurance model,** which views bank capital as a deductible, or on the **option-pricing model,** which treats bank capital as an inverse proxy for insurer loss exposure. Because the FDIC resolves and handles failed banks and regulates and examines insured nonmember banks, one can't judge the FDIC by its initials. The chapter also explains the causes of bank failure and distinguishes between **economic insolvency** and **bank closure.**

RESPONSIBILITY FOR THE DEPOSIT-INSURANCE MESS

Who is responsible for the deposit-insurance mess? **Principal-agent relations** suggest four potential culprits: (1) voting taxpayers for not electing more responsible government officials; (2) Congress for not doing a better job of monitoring federal

---

[1] According to Greek history, Damocles, a courtier of ancient Syracuse, was seated at a banquet beneath a sword held by a single hair. Denys the Ancient, less famous than his colleagues Aristotle and Socrates, cooked up this scheme to teach Damocles a lesson that life hung by a thread.

[2] From 1988 through 1991, the FDIC had a cumulative loss of $25.3 billion. The $11.1 billion loss in 1991 dropped its reserve fund to −$7 billion at year-end 1991. By year-end 1994, however, the fund was up to $21.8 billion, an all-time high.

deposit insurers; (3) deposit insurers for not doing a better job of monitoring insured depositories—savings-and-loans associations, savings banks, and commercial banks; (4) the managers of insured depositories for not doing a better job of monitoring their employees and their borrowers; and (5) the owners of insured depositories for not doing a better job of monitoring the managers. Inadequate and suspect monitoring suggest a lack of discipline and lack of incentive compatible contracts. Although taxpayers have been stuck with the bill for the savings-and-loan bailout, they had the least amount of control over the messy outcome. More direct blame lies with Congress, deposit insurers (including thrift and bank regulators), and managers/owners of insured depositories. Understanding who was asleep at a particular switch is important. Because there's plenty of blame to go around, assign your own weights for blame after you hear the rest of the story.

First, Congress was asleep for not recognizing the underlying structural weaknesses in the system of deposit insurance and regulation and for not passing appropriate legislation to correct the problems. Moreover, some of the legislation that Congress did pass (e.g., raising the insurance ceiling to $100,000 in 1980) made it too easy for high-flying depositories to obtain insured funds and too easy for thrifts with expanded asset powers and tax incentives to speculate with depositors' money. Congress also was asleep for not monitoring regulators and deposit insurers more closely. Finally, some members of Congress (e.g., the Keating Five) allegedly sacrificed the public interest in favor of special interest groups or individuals.

Second, deposit insurers and regulators were asleep for not monitoring more effectively the risk exposure of insured depositories and closing them when their economic or real new worths were exhausted. **Book values,** which are based on **historical cost** and not market values, are pretty much a charade. Richard C. Breeden, former chairman of the Securities and Exchange Commission (SEC), says, "Financial institution balance sheets should have the words 'once upon a time' on top of them. They are a statement of history" (*The Wall Street Journal,* September 27, 1990, p. A1). If a failing institution is closed when its market value of equity is zero, then just enough market value exists in its remaining assets to pay all its depositors and other creditors, which means no loss to the deposit insurer. The implementation of such a closure rule in the early 1980s would have prevented the deposit-insurance mess of the 1980s and early 1990s. Instead, by not closing economically bankrupt institutions soon enough, capital **forbearance** was practiced, with taxpayers bearing the cost.

Third, the managers of insured depositories were asleep for not monitoring more closely their employees for fraud and incompetence and for not exercising better fiduciary judgment on how depositors' funds were invested. For thrift institutions, the long-term problem has been the mismanagement of interest-rate risk—borrowing short and lending long—topped off with a heavy dose of real-estate speculation, especially in the Southwest. For banks, the credit risks associated with energy loans, farm loans, loans to less developed countries, loans for leveraged buyouts, and most recently, commercial real-estate loans resulted in 1,311 failed commercial banks from 1985 through 1992.[3]

Fourth, the stockholders of insolvent or near-insolvent banks have little incentive to discourage their agent managers from betting the bank: Heads they win;

---

[3] This period covers the eight years (1985–1992) in which the FDIC handled triple-digit bank closures per year, with a maximum number of 221 cases in 1988 and a minimum of 120 in 1985.

tails taxpayers get stuck with the tab. Moreover, in the absence of agency conflicts and in the presence of 100 percent deposit insurance, Buser, Chen, and Kane [1981a] show (chapter 13 here) that bank stockholders should rely completely on government-contributed capital. Ethical bank managers, however, serve to constrain bank risk-taking, and regulatory interference reinforces such risk-averse behavior by imposing penalties on unsafe and unsound banking practices. In nonproblem banks, owners want managers to undertake optimal risk-return decisions to maximize their wealth (or utility of wealth). When these strategies do not mesh with those of regulators and deposit insurers, conflicts arise. To align managerial and shareholder interests, optimally designed contracts for executive compensation typically provide rewards that depend on stock performance and opportunities for stock options. In addition, the threat of takeover by another bank keeps managers on their toes.

Because the deposit-insurance problem festered for over a decade, it didn't go away quickly. Thanks to risk-based capital requirements (effective as of 1992) and to the **prompt-corrective-action** provision of **FDICIA** (1991), bankers and their regulators may be better prepared for the next round of financial difficulties. These reforms, however, do not get at what Kane [1995] sees as the fundamental problem with government deposit insurance: "the shortcircuiting of customer, creditor, managerial, and stockholder discipline" (p. 449). Although **FIRREA** (1989) explicitly placed the "full faith and credit of the United States Government" (read American taxpayers) behind federal deposit insurance, an implicit guarantee was assumed to exist prior to FIRREA. Thus, the incentive for interested parties to provide discipline has been lacking since 1933 when deposit insurance was instituted.

MODELS OF DEPOSIT INSURANCE[4]

Three alternative frameworks exist for understanding the management of deposit insurance:

- The **passive model of casualty insurance,** which treats bank capital as a deductible
- The **option-pricing model,** which treats bank capital as an inverse proxy for insurer loss exposure
- A **trilateral performance bond** (surety or guarantee), which incorporates agency costs into the bundle of contracts that makes up deposit insurance

Kane [1995] described the first two approaches as bilateral models that conceive of risk as exogenous. More importantly, he argues that "delays in acknowledging the wreck of the S&L industry and its federal insurer (FSLIC) discredit these models as guides to managing a deposit-insurance fund" (p. 431). Kane claims that deposit insurance is better interpreted as a trilateral performance bond that enhances the credit of an insured institution. His interpretation views risk as endogenous, stresses incentive conflict, and highlights the need to optimize loss-control activity. His "bonding model" shows that some of the FDIC's monitoring and policing activities can be usefully privatized. Because all three models provide insights regarding the management or mismanagement of deposit insurance, we examine each beginning with the two discredited models.

---

[4] This section draws extensively on Kane [1995].

The Passive Casualty-Insurance Model of Deposit Insurance[5]

The passive casualty-insurance model, which can be regarded as the traditional approach to analyzing deposit insurance, treats the FDIC's function as similar to the passive business of underwriting casualty insurance. The FDIC's 1994 *Annual Report* reflects this theme: "As the deposit *underwriter* for banks and savings associations, the FDIC must be able to make *underwriting* decisions independently" (p. 3, emphasis mine). Because the passive-insurance model treats client claims as exogenously determined, insurance managers perform three main functions: they use actuarial analysis to estimate expected losses, depending on the law of large numbers to diffuse bunching of losses; (2) they charge premiums to cover the sum of each client's expected loss, operating expenses, and a normal profit; and (3) they accumulate and manage reserves large enough to cover expected losses and other contingencies.

The key implication of the passive-insurance model is that deposit-insurance managers, through pricing, can overcome the lack of independence in bank risks and the lack of transparency in observing bank behavior. Until 1991, the only variable component of FDIC pricing was implicit through examination, supervision, and regulation (recall Buser, Chen, and Kane's model and discussion of "regulatory interference" from chapter 13). In this framework, bank capital (tangible only) serves as a deductible to attempt to control moral hazard. Intangible capital, however, cannot be ignored (as noted in chapter 14; e.g., Feldstein's [1991] argument that banks' capital is underestimated).[6]

For almost 50 years from its inception in 1933–1934, the FDIC's scheme of implicit pricing to extract risk-sensitive premiums worked well. The true test of a system's effectiveness, however, is how well it functions under stress. Under the stresses of the 1980s and early 1990s, deposit insurance collapsed. In the process, as Kane ([1995], p. 436) argues, two major flaws were revealed: (1) implicit pricing did not minimize the social costs of the S&L and banking crises, and (2) the assumption of regulators and deposit insurers as "faithful agents" led analysts to focus on pricing and regulatory structure rather than on the real issues of incentive abuse, deceptive reporting, and managerial incompetence.

The Option-Pricing Model of Deposit Insurance[7]

The option-pricing model of deposit insurance, like the casualty-insurance model, assumes a bilateral relationship, exogenous risk, and the possibility of accurate risk measurement and ex ante pricing. How to price and model risk are the theoretical cornerstones of this approach. According to Kane [1995], the critical challenge is to price the incentive conflict that deposit insurers face in pricing and managing their risk exposure.

Merton [1977] was the first to describe deposit insurance as a put option written on bank assets. The idea is straightforward: the owners of the bank have the right to sell ("put back") the bank's assets to the insurer for the face value of the bank's insured deposits. When a bank's net worth (stockholders' equity) falls below

---

[5] In addition to Kane [1995], Barth [1991]; Black, Miller, and Posner [1978]; Schlesinger and Venezian [1986]; Scott and Mayer [1971]; and Williams and Heins [1985] discuss this model and its implications.

[6] James [1991] and Keeley [1990] present empirical evidence on the importance of intangible capital (think of it in terms of the present value of growth opportunities, PVGO).

[7] In addition to Kane [1995], this section draws on Black and Scholes [1973], Kane [1985, 1986], Kareken [1983], Marcus and Shaked [1984], Merton [1977, 1978], Pennachi [1987], and Sharpe [1978].

zero, this put option is "in the money." Risk-based capital requirements and the prompt-corrective-action provision of FDICIA attempt to force a more optimal exercise of the deposit-insurance put option in the FDIC's favor. However, stockholders of zombie institutions have no incentive to give up this valuable option on the bank's future cash flows. For a solvent bank, the put option is "out of the money," and it approaches zero for an all-equity bank. Clearly, in the option-pricing model, bank capital serves as an inverse proxy for the value of the put option to the owners of the bank. Moreover, when a bank is insolvent, a deposit insurer is likely to incur losses. Thus, bank capital also serves as an inverse proxy for the deposit insurer's loss exposure.

The first empirical tests of the option model applied to deposit insurance (Marcus and Shaked [1984] and Ronn and Verma [1986]) attempted to estimate fair premiums for different banks and to determine if the deposit insurance was fairly priced. The fair-premium estimates suggested that FDIC insurance was overpriced, which was puzzling because common sense indicated dangerous FDIC/FSLIC loss exposures due to the underlying interest-rate and credit risks faced by insured depositories. The overpriced story was good news and bad news: The bad news was that it provided deposit insurers and bank and S&L regulators with ammunition to say that everything was okay—nothing's wrong with deposit insurance. The good news was that it led academic researchers to question the application of the option-pricing model to deposit insurance.

Deposit Insurance as a Government Guarantee (Trilateral Performance Bond or Surety)[8]

In financial contracts, *surety* refers to a bond, guaranty, or other security that protects a party in case of another party's (the counterparty's) default, lack of performance, or malfeasance. In construction contracts, such a guarantee is called a *performance bond*. For example, such a bond simply guarantees that a party will perform a certain function or duty. When two bonds (guarantees) are required in a construction contract, one covers faithful performance of the actual construction whereas the other covers payment of labor and material. The former is called a *performance bond* and the latter is a *payment bond*.

In guaranteed or surety arrangements (i.e., a bonding contract), three parties, rather than two parties, are involved: the obliged party (insured bank, which receives the immediate benefit of lower financing cost), the obligee (depositor, who receives contingent protection), and a third party, the guarantor or surety (deposit, insurer/government). Three other differences exist between a surety bond and the casualty-insurance and option contracts:

1. Nonperformance by an insured bank (the obliged party) is the loss-causing event for the FDIC (the surety). Because it is assumed that nonperformance generally occurs with intent, or at least control, the perils faced by the FDIC are a function of the character, capital, and strategies of the managers of the insured bank. Past experience and monitoring of insured banks become loss-control instruments for the FDIC. In this view, risk is endogenous because some losses result from the choices made by managers of insured depositories, which is in sharp contrast to the treatment of risk in the passive-insurance and option models as an exogenous, stochastic event.

---

[8] This subsection also mirrors Kane [1995].

2. Claims against the FDIC must be honored even when managers of insured banks do not adopt the appropriate safeguards. Moreover, with taxpayers' backing, the FDIC has deep pockets. In passive-casualty and option contracts, claims can be voided if the counterparty fails to adopt promised safeguards. Claimants must prove that they have legitimate claims. In this case, demands for safeguards (e.g., smoke detectors, alarm systems, etc.) can be described as self-enforcing. In contrast, in a surety contract, the FDIC (in conjunction with the OCC/Fed/SEC), is responsible for bankers engaging in safe-and-sound banking practices, providing proper disclosure, and maintaining adequate capital.

3. If FDIC monitoring of banks were perfect and if its recovery efforts were complete and costless, then it would never incur any losses. Because perfection and completeness are not in the FDIC's arsenal, losses arise from shortcomings in monitoring, policing, and enforcing its rights.

These differences should make it clearer why Kane [1995] describes deposit insurance as a trilateral performance bond or surety.[9] His interpretation incorporates explicit and implicit agency costs into the nexus of the deposit-insurance contract. These costs are opportunity losses arising from conflicts or incentive incompatibilities that poison a principal-agent relationship. (The various principal-agent relations that make up regulatory discipline/deposit insurance were described above and in chapters 1 and 15.) The benefits of the deposit-insurance guarantee are split between depositors who receive protection and the guaranteed institution (bank) that receives a credit enhancement (guarantee) that lowers its funding costs.

Moral Hazard, Agency Costs, and the Marginal Net Benefit or Burden of Deposit Insurance.[10]

If you take a position in a risk-sharing instrument such as a stock, bond, or certificate of deposit, your risk (through the instrument) that the counterparty's action may harm your financial position is called **moral hazard.** In deposit insurance, moral hazard passes through federal insurance funds to taxpayers. The insurer's dilemma is to prevent losses arising from bank insolvencies from draining insurance reserves.[11] The bank's buffer or cushion for absorbing losses is funds provided by stockholders and uninsured creditors, who have contracted to bear the bank's failure risk. Because the owners of economically insolvent, or zombie, institutions may want managers to bet the bank, moral hazard is exacerbated in these situations. Ethical managers, however, would be inclined to refrain from such behavior, whereas unethical managers (or owner/managers) would have no qualms about sticking taxpayers with negative returns from ex ante distributions of high-risk projects.

Does deposit insurance provide a net benefit or a burden to bank shareholders? The gross benefit is the lower cost of funding achieved by the bank. The costs of the benefit are the explicit deposit-insurance premium and the implicit or opportunity cost of regulatory interference (Buser, Chen, and Kane [1981a]). The sum of these three components, each of which depends on the bank's portfolio of on- and off-balance-sheet items and the degree of regulatory interference, determine

---

[9] The Financial Institutions Reform, Recovery, and Enforcement Act (FIRREA) of 1991 placed the "full faith and credit of the U.S. government" behind federal deposit insurance. We understand this promise by the government as an explicit and credible third-party guarantee. Prior to FIRREA, most people assumed that the U.S. government implicitly stood behind federal deposit insurance.

[10] This section also draws on Kane [1995].

[11] From 1988 through 1991, the FDIC could not stop the bleeding because it lost $25.4 billion of its lifeblood.

the net benefit or burden of deposit insurance. Ideally, a problem or high-risk bank encounters a net burden because it pays a higher explicit premium, faces more extensive and intensive supervision, and derives a smaller reduction in its cost of funding. Without risk-based pricing of funds and insurance, and with lax supervision, high-risk banks extract a subsidy from low-risk banks.

Let's consider the nexus of contracts or principal-agent relationships[12] important to the management of deposit insurance. Conflicts among these parties generate layers of agency costs that affect the net benefit or burden of deposit insurance. Four principal-agent relations are critical for understanding the management of deposit insurance as a surety or guarantee:

- Stockholders' conflict with and monitoring of managers of insured depositories
- Taxpayers' conflict with and monitoring of elected and appointed government officials
- Bank regulators' and deposit insurers' conflict with and monitoring of managers of insured depositories
- Stakeholders' (in deposit institutions) conflict with and monitoring of bank regulators and deposit insurers

In the last relationship, stakeholders include bank stockholders and all others with a claim or stake in the bank, specifically customers, managers, employees, and creditors.[13] The various stakeholders, as principals, want managers, as their agents, to act in their behalf. Kane argues that deposit insurance distorts these relationships and removes discipline from the system. Costly monitoring (think about monitoring in terms of loss-control mechanisms) attempts to resolve the incentive conflicts among the principal-agent relationships, and efficiency demands that these costs be minimized by equating marginal costs of each monitoring device with the marginal benefit of conflict resolution.[14]

1. Conflict between Stockholders and Managers

The federal safety net (narrowly the deposit-insurance subsidy) that supports insured depositories might encourage managers of these institutions to bet the bank. Such gambles can take the form of extreme duration mismatches as in the case of S&Ls, high concentrations of credit risk in the loan portfolio as the case of commercial banks (e.g., energy-related loans, LDC loans, and commercial-real-estate loans), or aggressive trading of financial instruments and underlying derivatives by large banks.[15] Such high-risk strategies increase the probability that the bank will become economically insolvent and lose its charter value. The owners of insolvent or near-insolvent banks have little incentive to discourage their agent managers from betting the bank: Heads they win; tails taxpayers get stuck with the tab. Moreover, in the absence of agency conflicts and in the presence of 100 percent deposit insurance, Buser, Chen, and Kane [1981a] show that bank stockholders should rely completely on government-contributed capital.

Unlike the other three categories of agency costs, ethical bank managers or managers with nonpecuniary concerns such as reputation, preserving human capital,

---

[12] Jensen and Meckling [1975] and Smith and Warner [1979] develop these concepts.

[13] Jensen and Meckling's [1975] idea of the firm as a nexus of contracts provides the impetus for considering the role of various stakeholders in shaping managerial behavior.

[14] Risk-based capital requirements and prompt corrective action attempt to set bank capital requirements high enough to minimize risk to the deposit-insurance fund and taxpayers. In this context, bank capital is just another loss-control instrument for controlling incentive conflict.

[15] Sinkey and Carter [1997] show that when it comes to derivatives, big banks do and small banks don't.

and health factors may be reluctant to bet the bank. Such managers serve to constrain bank risk taking. Regulatory interference reinforces such conservative behavior because it frequently imposes penalties (such as cease-and-desist orders, banishment from banking, or civil and criminal damages) on the managers and directors of problem banks.[16] However, as Kane [1985] notes, when banks become undercapitalized (problem institutions), managerial and stockholder interest converges. Ethical managers of problem banks may think that because their reputations may already be tarnished, they should go for broke.

In nonproblem banks, owners do not want their agent managers to go for broke. Instead, they want them to undertake optimal risk-return decisions that will maximize their wealth (or utility of wealth). Because these strategies may not be conservative enough for regulators and deposit insurers, conflicts arise with such managers. To align managerial and shareholder interests, optimally designed contracts for executive compensation typically provide incentives for good stock performance and opportunities for stock options. In addition, the threat of takeover by another bank keeps managers on their toes.[17]

2. Conflicts between Taxpayers and Stakeholders in Insured Banks   Although limited liability is a *de jure* right for bank stockholders and for other stakeholders in an insured bank, their upside potential, as a group, is unconstrained. In contrast, taxpayers have little to gain at the margin when banks are successful.[18] When banks fail, however, taxpayers are indirectly liable through the deposit-insurance fund for covering losses on at least the full amount of insured deposits. This asymmetry presents an incentive conflict, which the FDIC is responsible for controlling. The FDIC's risk-management arsenal consists of two weapons: explicit pricing (p_e) of risk by charging high deposit-insurance assessments, and implicit pricing (p_i) through regulatory interference. Examples of implicit pricing include the frequency and intensity of bank examinations, various reporting requirements, the denial of requests for expansion, and the threat of removal of deposit insurance. The FDIC depends on the Fed, the OCC, the SEC, and various state banking agencies to provide regulatory interference across all insured banks.

What are the chances that deposit insurers/regulators will employ these risk-control tools in taxpayers' interests? Discipline in the private sector is achieved through incentive contracting, making managers accountable for their actions, and the threat of outside takeover. Because these devices are conspicuous by their absence in the government sector, we should not expect deposit insurance (or any government-run business, e.g., social security) to run as efficiently as it would in the private sector. One common factor, however, may be the propensity to employ a go-for-broke strategy when bankruptcy approaches. Consider the case of the FSLIC. Once it became insolvent and was not shut down immediately, its managers had nothing to lose by permitting its clients (insured S&Ls) either to also go for

---

[16] The vigor with which the FDIC has pursued to punish bank managers and directors is good news and bad news: The good news is that such actions may increase communication and information flows within the bank, but the bad news is that it may be difficult for banks to recruit competent managers and directors.

[17] With the elimination of geographic restrictions on banking (1995) and the gradual reduction of product restrictions, the threat of an outside takeover has increased in banking. In the past, the threat was relatively weak. Gorton and Rosen [1995], who analyze the market for corporate control in banking, claim that managerial entrenchment played a more important role than moral hazard in explaining the decline of traditional banking (i.e., gathering deposits and making loans). Saunders, Strock, and Tavlos [1990] report that for the years 1978 to 1985, bank managers with large stockholdings imposed more risk on the FDIC than other bank managers.

[18] When banks are successful, taxpayers benefit indirectly because of higher taxes paid by banks.

broke or simply to continue to exist as zombie institutions (forbearance).[19] These joint gambles came, of course, at the expense of taxpayers as the ultimate guarantors of federal deposit insurance.[20]

During the S&L and banking crises of the 1980s and early 1990s, the regulators' lament was that forbearance (i.e., recapitalization with dividend-free funds provided by taxpayers) was their only option. Moreover, they hoped to gain public sympathy by pretending that the only alternative was massive liquidations of zombie S&Ls and banks. According to Kane [1995], the efficient way to resolve the insolvency of any institution with substantial going-concern value is explicit recapitalization. Private parties would be willing to pay premiums over liquidation values to obtain these franchise values.

Modeling the FDIC's Cash Flows

The components of Kane's [1995] stationary-state model of the FDIC's annual cash flows are summarized in Table 16-1. Panel A shows that the FDIC has four major cash flows, two inflows and two outflows. Revenues are generated by the premiums or assessments paid by insured banks and from interest income earned on the portfolio of insurance-fund reserves (think of the fund as taxpayers' equity, but unlike common equity, the contract does not specify limited liability). During 1995, the Bank Insurance Fund (BIF) assessments totaled $2.9 billion (down from $5.6 billion in 1994), whereas interest earned on U.S. Treasury obligations was $1.1 billion (up from $521 million in 1994). With an average investment of $16.8 billion, the implied risk-free return is 6.55 percent (= 1.1/16.8).[21] The FDIC incurs two major expenses: monitoring costs associated with bank examinations and supervision and the costs of resolving problem and failed banks. During 1995, FDIC operating expenses were $471 million, whereas provision for insurance losses was −$33 million (up from −$2.9 billion in 1994). When the provision is a negative number, as it also was for 1993, it represents a recovery of previous disbursements in resolving problem and failed banks.[22] For example, during 1991 the FDIC set aside $15.5 billion for insurance losses. Over the next two years, provisions were −$2.3 billion (1992) and −$7.7 billion (1993). Combined with 1994, the three-year total was −$12.9 billion. For the years 1984 to 1990, FDIC provisions for insurance losses were $1.6 billion (1984), $1.6 billion (1985), $2.8 billion (1986), $3.0 billion (1987), $6.3 billion (1988), $3.8 billion (1989), and $4.4 billion (1990). Including 1991, provisions for the years 1984 through 1991 totaled $39 billion, a clear indicator of the financial difficulties of the banking system over this period and a proxy for the amount of dividend-free equity provided by taxpayers to the banking system. With recoveries of almost $13 billion for the years 1991 through 1994, the ex post net provision for the years 1984 through 1994 was about $26 billion.

---

[19] Kane [1989a] analyzes the changing incentives facing financial-services regulators.

[20] Kane [1995] sees the costs of FDIC forbearance as more subtle than taxpayers' losses from FSLIC forbearance. He contends that "the cost to taxpayers from FDIC gambling lies in offering the equivalent of dividend-free equity capital to undercapitalized banks," and that FDIC accountants' failure "to run this opportunity-cost test supports the incentive-conflict hypothesis" (p. 444).

[21] These data and other figures reported in this section are from the FDIC's 1995 Annual Report, pp. 45–47. The Savings Association Insurance Fund (SAIF) is separate from BIF. During 1995, SAIF collected $970 million in assessments and earned $169 million in interest on U.S. Treasury obligations. With average Treasury holdings of $2.6 billion, SAIF's implied risk-free return was 6.5 percent. The SAIF data are from pp. 63–65 of the FDIC's 1995 Annual Report.

[22] The FDIC's provision for insurance losses includes a component for allowance for losses and a component for estimated liabilities; see footnote 10 (p. 69) of the FDIC's 1994 Annual Report.

TABLE 16-1 Kane's [1995] Stationary-State Model of the FDIC's Annual Cash Flow

Panel A. Four Components of Annual Cash Flow ($F = P + r_pR - C_M - C_L$) (1)

P = Premium income paid by insured banks

r_pR = Interest income earned at the rate r_p on the portfolio of reserves (R)

C_M = Monitoring costs equal to the product of resources devoted to monitoring (M) times the unit price (m) of monitoring resources

C_L = Losses due to resolving problem and failed banks, viewed as function of volatility of the economy (V) and of the expected ability of insured banks to shift losses to the insurance fund (E_R)

Panel B. Loss-Control Instruments Available to the FDIC/OCC/Fed/SEC

M = Quantity of resources committed to monitoring

T = Transparency of the information system (e.g., book-value vs. market-value accounting) imposed on banks by FDIC/OCC/Fed/SEC

$P(O_R)$ = Function that relates explicit premium income to the observed aggregate loss exposure of insured banks ($O_R = TE_R$)

K = Capital standards imposed by regulators

L = Potential liability faced by bank directors and officers arising from the severity of standards for civil and criminal penalties against them, designed to create agency costs (A_M) to prevent bank managers from maximizing value

$s(TE_R)$ = Regulatory sanctions imposed on problem banks, which may include restrictions on the bank's combined rate of dividend payout and stock buyback, r_k

R = Level of prepaid premiums held in the insurance fund's reserve account[a]

Panel C. Equations That Link Loss-Control Instruments to FDIC Cash Flow

$$C_M = mM \quad (2)$$
$$C_L = C_L(V, E_R) \quad (3)$$
$$P = P(O_R) = P(T_E) \quad (4)$$
$$E_R = [r_f, p_e, p_i, r_k, T, M, A_M(L)], \quad (5)$$

where

r_f = the proportional reduction in the bank's annual cost of funds due to the credit enhancement associated with deposit insurance

p_e = the explicit deposit-insurance premium

p_i = the implicit cost of deposit insurance arising from regulatory interference

$$p_i = u[K, s(TE_R), M, L, T, R] \quad (6)$$

Panel D. FDIC's Goal Function

$$\text{Maximize } W = W(F, D, J, B) \quad (7)$$

where

W = Multidimensional goal function (e.g., minimize costs to the insurance fund)

F = Annual cash flow

D = Distortions caused by macroeconomic policy variables (e.g., credit allocation)

J = Perception of regulators' job performance

B = Bribes or tribute (explicit or implicit) to politicians and top regulators

[a]An instrument available only to the FDIC.

Source: Adapted from Kane [1995], pp. 443–447.

Except for the year 1945, the FDIC's insurance fund increased every year from 1934 to 1988, which means that its net cash flow was positive in those years. In fact for the years 1950 to 1983, the effective explicit premium was about one-half of the nominal rate of 8.3 cents per $100 of deposits. The accounting practice was for insured banks to pay the nominal rate and then to receive a rebate, or what the FDIC calls an assessment credit. The 1980s and early 1990s were a different story, however: No rebates and increases in the explicit premium. In 1991, the FDIC's net cash flow reached an all-time low of −$11 billion, resulting in a decline in its insurance fund from $4 billion to −$7 billion. The components of the 1991 loss and the components for the only other years (1988–1990) in which the FDIC experienced book-value losses were as follows:[23]

Cash-flow component ($ billions)	1991	1990	1989	1988
Assessment income (P)	5.160	2.855	1.885	1.773
Investment income ($r_p P$)	0.629	0.983	1.610	1.547
Administrative and operating expenses (C_M)	0.284	0.220	0.214	0.224
Deposit insurance losses and expenses (C_L)	16.578	12.784	4.132	7.365
Net cash flow (F)	−11.072	−9.165	−0.852	−4.241

The reason for the negative net cash flow is clear: Losses due to resolving problem and failed banks, or what the FDIC calls deposit-insurance losses and expenses. Recall from Table 16-1 that underlying these losses is a cost function that depends on the volatility of the economy (V) and the expected ability of insured banks to shift losses to the FDIC (E_R). The volatility of the U.S. economy in the 1980s and early 1990s can be traced to unstable interest rates and commodity prices; especially troublesome were deflations in energy, agricultural, and real-estate (both farm and commercial) prices and problems with LDC debt. These economic difficulties were compounded by regulatory forbearance and the various incentive conflicts discussed above, which permitted banks to shift losses to the FDIC (taxpayers).

Table 16-2 shows how FDIC cash flow, driven by losses associated with resolving problem and failed banks, affects the deposit-insurance fund and FDIC coverage ratios. The critical piece of information in these data, which are for the years 1980 through 1995, is the FDIC's estimated losses. These estimated figures are lower than the deposit-insurance losses and expenses reported above, because they include estimated recoveries. Several big jumps occurred in these estimated losses over the period. For example, the estimated losses more than doubled, from $3.1 billion in 1987 to $7.4 billion in 1988. For the first time in FDIC history, this decline resulted in the ratio of the insurance fund to insured deposits dropping below 1 percent to 0.80 percent. In 1989, the coverage ratio dropped to its nadir at −0.36 percent, as estimated losses were $6.3 billion. By 1995, however, the coverage ratio had rebounded to 1.30 percent, slightly above the 1.25 required by FIRREA for 1995. The large number of failures and the high costs of resolving them drive the estimated losses shown in Table 16-2 (e.g., the FDIC estimates a $3.6 billion loss for the resolution of First Republic of Texas).

---

[23] The components are from equation (1) in Table 16-1. The data are from the FDIC's 1994 *Annual Report*, Table D, p. 128. Figures may not add up due to rounding.

TABLE 16-2 Bank Failures and the FDIC's Losses, Insurance Fund, and Coverage Ratios, 1980–1995

Year	Economic Failures	Estimated Losses	Insurance Fund	Ratio of Insurance Fund to Total Dep.	Insured Deposits
1980	10	30	11.0	0.83%	1.16%
1981	10	721	12.2	0.87	1.24
1982	42	867	13.8	0.89	1.21
1983	48	834	15.4	0.91	1.22
1984	80	1,848	16.5	0.92	1.19
1985	120	1,779	17.9	0.91	1.19
1986	145	2,783	18.2	0.84	1.12
1987	203	3,066	18.3	0.83	1.10
1988	221	7,365	14.1	0.60	0.80
1989	207	1,100	13.0	0.53	0.70
1990	169	4,000	9.0	0.45	0.60
1991	127	6,269	(7.0)	(0.28)	(0.36)
1992	122	3,960	(0.1)	(0.00)	(0.01)
1993	41	584	13.1	0.53	0.69
1994	13	139	21.8	0.89	1.15
1995	6	194	25.4	0.99	1.30

Note: Economic failures are defined as closed banks plus assistance transactions. Losses stated in millions of dollars, fund in billions, and ratios in percentages.
Source: Annual Report, FDIC, 1989, Tables 128–129; 1994, Table C, p. 127; and 1995, Tables 108, 110.

Loss-Control Instruments Available to the FDIC/OCC/Fed/SEC

Given that the system of U.S. bank regulation is a "jurisdictional tangle that boggles the mind," the job of attempting to control losses to the FDIC's insurance fund involves more agencies than just the FDIC. At the federal level, the OCC/Fed/SEC conduct monitoring activities whereas various state banking agencies (with limited resources) attempt to do the job at the state level. Panel B of Table 16-1 presents the **loss-control instruments** available to these agencies. Although the FDIC controls the explicit deposit-insurance premium, its sister agencies extract implicit premiums through regulatory interference from the banks/BHCs they supervise and monitor. Outside of explicit pricing of the deposit-insurance guarantee, the loss-control instruments available to bank supervisors include the following:

1. The quantity and quality of resources available for monitoring (e.g., for on- and off-site examinations)
2. The transparency of collected information
3. Capital requirements
4. Threat of liability (civil and criminal) against bank officers and directors
5. Sanctions imposed on problem banks

Another way of looking at the process of loss control is to consider the techniques for managing the guarantee business (first introduced in chapter 1). Merton and Bodie [1992] describe three interrelated methods available to a guarantor (or *surety,* Kane's term) to manage its business:

- Monitoring the value of the collateral (e.g., bank assets)
- Restricting the kinds of assets acceptable as collateral (e.g., the kinds of assets banks can hold)
- Charging risk-based premiums (e.g., explicit risk-based premiums and risk-based capital requirements as implicit pricing)

In general, the loss-control instruments described in Panel B of Table 16-1 fall under one of these categories.

1. Monitoring Bank Asset Values   Available resources and transparency of information are critical to effective monitoring. It is helpful to think of monitoring as funneling into an effective or market-value closure rule that would eliminate forbearance for zombie depositories. Such a rule, however, critically depends on the ability of regulators (or market participants) to measure bank asset values accurately (transparency). For monitoring to work, regulators must have the right to seize a bank as its economic net worth approaches zero. In this case, the real value of the assets will fully protect all of the bank's debtholders. If the FDIC guarantee is credible, then depositors and other bank creditors will have confidence in the banking system. Because monitoring bank asset values is difficult at best (e.g., continuous monitoring is costly and the available resources are limited), there are likely to be some shortfalls in value when banks' assets are seized.

2. Asset Restrictions   A second technique for managing guarantees centers on asset restrictions, which limit the amount of risk an insured bank may incur. Product restrictions and the definition of what a bank is impose direct asset constraints on banks. Risk-based capital requirements, bank-examiner portfolio criticisms, and sanctions against individual banks act indirectly to restrict particular bank assets. This approach can be viewed as requiring an insured bank to attempt to hedge its government-guaranteed (credit-enhanced) liabilities. The hedge limits the volatility of the bank's net worth. Because reduced risk means reduced return, this approach limits the rate of interest banks can pay their depositors and thereby restricts their ability to compete with unregulated financial institutions. Asset restrictions attempt to reduce the credit, interest-rate, foreign-exchange, and liquidity risks banks have in their portfolios of assets and liabilities.

3. Risk-Based Pricing   A third technique for managing guarantees is risk-based pricing. The idea is a straightforward one: The more risk an institution has, the higher its guarantee/surety/insurance premium. Until 1993, the FDIC relied strictly on implicit risk-based pricing through risk-based capital requirements and other forms of regulatory tax.[24] Unlike the Basle Agreement (1987) on international risk-based capital requirements, which focuses only on credit risk, a comprehensive risk-based pricing system should be based on all the major portfolio risks of banking (e.g., credit risk, interest-rate risk, foreign-exchange risk, and liq-

---

[24] Avery and Belton [1987] provide a comparison of risk-based capital and risk-based deposit insurance. The objectives of both systems are the same: Price risk and make banks pay for greater risk taking, either with higher premium or with more capital.

uidity risk). Although risk-based capital requirements also are straightforward (i.e., more risk, more capital—as a cushion or buffer to absorb potential losses), measuring (pricing) the relevant risks is the major operational stumbling block in any kind of risk-based scheme.

The FDIC's Goal Function and Linking Loss-Control Instruments to FDIC Cash Flow

Panel C of Table 16-1 shows how Kane [1995] links the loss-control instruments available to bank regulators to FDIC cash flow. The relevant equations describe and highlight three important linkages:

- The cost of monitoring
- A loss function for resolving problem and failed banks
- Explicit premium income as a function of bank risk exposure, transparency of information, and implicit pricing of bank risk exposure

Kane portrays the FDIC goal function, $W = W(F, D, J, B)$, as multidimensional, depending on four factors:[25]

- Annual cash flow (F)
- Potential distortions from macroeconomic goals such as credit allocation (D)
- Public perception of regulators' job performance (J)
- Flow of bribes and tributes (explicit and implicit) to politicians and top regulators (B)

If deposit insurance were privatized, stockholders would demand that managers focus on cash flow (F) as the key variable and would provide discipline to reduce the importance of D, J, and B. However, because deposit insurance is housed in the public sector, the FDIC's goal function is more complex and less efficient. Taxpayers should demand a simpler and more efficient goal function from deposit insurers and bank regulators.

DON'T JUDGE THE FDIC BY ITS INITIALS

An old adage says: Don't judge a book by its cover. A new adage says: Don't judge a government agency by its initials. In addition to insuring deposits, the FDIC performs three regulatory functions:[26]

- *Entry regulation:* Because it would be very difficult, if not impossible, for a state bank to be chartered without federal deposit insurance (banks with national charters must join the Fed and be insured), the FDIC has effective control over bank entry. By restricting bank entry, the FDIC, the OCC, and the Fed attempt to preserve the value of existing bank charters, which serves as a front-line defense for the deposit-insurance fund. The FDIC also rules on mergers and branch proposals for state nonmember banks.
- *On- and off-site bank examination and supervision:* By inspecting and monitoring a state nonmember bank's financial information (e.g., capital adequacy), recordkeeping practices

---

[25] Chapter 17, which deals with ethics in banking, will deal with the third and fourth factors (J and B) in more detail.

[26] Prior to DIDMCA (1980), the FDIC was also in the business of setting deposit-rate ceilings (Reg Q) for insured nonmember banks and insured mutual savings banks. Its policies were coordinated with those of the Fed such that all insured commercial banks faced the same rate constraints. As required by DIDMCA, deposit-rate ceilings were eliminated in 1986.

and procedures (e.g., loan documentation), strategic and financial policies (e.g., business plan, risk management, lending, etc.), and compliance (e.g., with the Community Reinvestment Act, CRA), the FDIC engages in implicit pricing of deposit insurance.[27] High-risk or so-called problem banks encounter more intense regulatory scrutiny and restrictions than safe-and-sound banks. With advances in information technologies, the potential for off-site examinations and supervision has reduced, but not eliminated, the need for the traditional on-site visit by the stereotyped blue suits with green eyeshades. Assuming that a bank complies with various nonfinancial rules and regulations, the purpose of examination and supervision is to preserve a bank's capital and its franchise value as shock absorbers for the deposit-insurance fund.

- *Disposition of failed and failing banks:* The FDIC's Division of Depositor and Asset Services (euphemism for the old Division of Liquidation) is responsible for the disposition of a failed bank's assets and liabilities (and net worth if any). Prior to failure, the FDIC has the power to provide financial assistance to failing banks. The techniques for handling failing and failed banks (i.e., providing depositor and asset services) are described in detail later in this chapter.

Origins and Operations of the FDIC

The Banking Act of 1933 provided for the establishment of a federal deposit insurance corporation. Although deposit-insurance coverage started on January 1, 1934, the Federal Deposit Insurance (FDI) Act was not passed until June 16, 1934, and was amended the next year by the Banking Act of 1935. The purpose of the Federal Deposit Insurance Corporation (FDIC) was to provide for the speedy liquidation of failed banks and to protect the deposits of small savers against losses due to bank failures.

The bulk of FDIC employees have always clustered around two functions: supervision and liquidation. For example, at year-end 1995, the FDIC's Division of Supervision had 3,055 employees whereas the Division of Depositor and Asset Services (liquidation) had 2,623 (down from 3,796 for 1994). Together these two divisions accounted for 58 percent of the FDIC's 9,789 employees. Corporate downsizing, a major phenomenon outside the government, affected the FDIC in both 1994 and 1995, as reflected by decreases in the number of employees of 2,592 (1994) and 1,838 (1995). Counting employees of the Resolution Trust Corporation (RTC), which is managed by the FDIC, the combined employment for the FDIC and the RTC was 11,856 (1995), compared to 20,994 (1993) and 17,526 (1994), a two-year decrease of 9,138 employees. FDIC downsizing relates directly to three factors: (1) improvement in the condition of the banking industry, (2) consolidation of the industry (fewer but bigger banks monitored by better information technologies), and (3) the light at the end of the S&L tunnel—the mess is just about cleaned up.

FDIC Failure-Resolution Policies and Procedures[28]

After a national bank is closed by the OCC, the FDIC becomes by law the "receiver," or liquidator. After a state bank is closed by its state banking authority, it is not required by law that the FDIC be appointed receiver by the state. The FDIC

---

[27] Recall that the OCC monitors national banks, the Fed monitors state member banks and BHCs, and the various state banking agencies, either concurrently or independently with the FDIC and the Fed, monitor state banks.

[28] Bovenzi and Murton [1988] provide additional detail on these policies and procedures and an analysis of FDIC resolution costs.

does, however, routinely handle the liquidation of failed state banks. Contrary to popular opinion, the FDIC does not have the de jure power to close either a state or national bank. It does, however, have substantial de facto power to influence a bank's closure.

By law, the FDIC must select the least costly failure-resolution method. In addition to cost considerations, the FDIC also analyzes how the resolution method will affect

- Public confidence and stability in the banking system
- The fairness of treatment with respect to uninsured depositors and creditors across different bank sizes
- Market discipline

Given the too-big-to-fail doctrine, the last point appears moot. As secondary objectives, the FDIC wants to minimize disruption to the markets the failed bank services and to try to keep as much of the ownership, management, and financing of failed-bank transactions in the private sector. By closing a bank on Friday and opening it the next business day (Monday, or Tuesday in the case of a holiday weekend) or by being ready to pay off insured depositors by then, the FDIC attempts to minimize disruption to the customers served by the failed bank.

Today, as in 1934, the FDIC has two basic failure-resolution methods:

- A deposit payoff
- A purchase-and-assumption (P&A) transaction

Although variations in these two methods have evolved, especially in the 1980s, they still represent the basic ways the FDIC handles failed commercial banks. Given the costs of the two methods, payoffs should be good for market discipline but bad for confidence, stability, and fairness. In contrast, P&As should be good for confidence, stability, and fairness but bad for market discipline.

Deposit Payoff

In this method of handling a failed bank, the FDIC, as receiver of the failed bank, pays off the insured depositors and proceeds to liquidate the assets of the failed bank. Because uninsured depositors, other general creditors, and equity owners are at risk, this method has the potential for market discipline. Equityholders, of course, are at the bottom of the liquidation pecking order. After the FDIC covers its expenses, all uninsured creditors and nonsubordinated debtholders get first crack, on a pro rata basis, at liquidated assets or collections. Shortly after the bank is closed, uninsured creditors get documents called "receivers' certificates" that entitle them to their proportionate share of the failed bank's liquidated assets. In cases where the FDIC pays uninsured creditors a portion of their claims upfront, the transaction is called a "modified payoff" (e.g., in the case of Penn Square Bank of Oklahoma City in 1982, receivers' certificates were valued at 80 percent of claims).

Purchase-and-Assumption Transaction

In a **purchase-and-assumption transaction,** the FDIC contracts with a healthy bank to purchase specified assets of the failed bank and assume all its liabilities—insured and uninsured. Because this practice provides 100 percent insurance protection to all creditors and continuity of banking services to customers, it promotes confidence and stability and minimizes disruption to the community, but at the expense of market discipline. A sealed-bid auction determines the winning bidder.

Unfortunately, the auctions are not always competitive because of scarcity of bidders. Nevertheless, even with few bidders, P&As tend to be cheaper to arrange than deposit payoffs. When no bidders exist, the FDIC must resort to a deposit payoff or some other temporary arrangement such as a bridge bank. In a P&A transaction, the FDIC makes up the difference between the liabilities assumed and the assets purchased by infusing cash minus the amount of the winning bid. The assets of the failed bank that are not purchased by the assuming bank are placed in FDIC receivership for liquidation. Collections on these "bad" assets are used to offset the FDIC's cash infusion. In a P&A, the assuming bank usually has the option over an agreed short-term period to return some of the purchased assets to the FDIC.

To meet its goal of trying to keep the ownership of failed bank assets in the private sector, the FDIC has attempted to arrange "whole-bank transactions," or whole-bank P&As. The arrangement is similar to a P&A except that the winning bidder buys all or most of the failed bank's assets at a discount from their book value. The technique keeps the FDIC out of the liquidation business and permits continued banking contact with the borrowers of the failed bank. The first whole-bank transaction was completed by the FDIC in April 1987, with 17 completed in 1987. In 1989 the FDIC arranged 36 whole-bank transactions, down from 69 in 1988.

Payoffs versus Assumptions

Table 16-3 shows that, from 1934 through 1995, the FDIC arranged 472 deposit payoffs and 1,427 P&As, a ratio of deposit payoffs to P&A transactions (including whole-bank P&As) of one to three. During the first five years of the FDIC's existence the ratio of payoffs to P&As was two to one. During the 1940s and 1950s, the FDIC arranged more P&As (77) than deposit payoffs (50). In the 1960s, however, deposit payoffs (27) exceeded P&As (16). Since then, 1,229 P&As have been arranged, compared to only 192 deposit payoffs. Two main reasons account for the increased use of P&As. First, because deposit payoffs were used mainly in the case of small failed banks,[29] the FDIC was made more aware that this method discriminated against uninsured deposits in such banks. In fact, since 1986, when the FDIC became more sensitive to criticism about potential discrimination against uninsured depositors in small banks, its use of deposit payoffs has dropped substantially. Second, as the bank failure rate increased, especially during the 1980s, bankers were more willing to bid on franchises as a means of expansion, frequently at very attractive acquisition prices.

Insured Deposit Transfers

In 1984 the FDIC began using a new resolution technique called an *insured deposit transfer;* from 1984 through 1989, the FDIC arranged 149 of them. An insured deposit transfer is a form of deposit payoff in which only the insured deposits and secured liabilities are transferred to another bank. The FDIC injects cash equal to the transferred funds. The acquiring bank may use some of the cash to buy certain assets of the failed bank. The receivership holds the remaining assets, the uninsured deposits, and the unsecured liabilities. FDIC experience suggests that "when

---

[29] Of the 2,000 or so commercial banks that have failed from 1934 through 1994, roughly three out of four have been state banks. In addition, the average failed state bank has been about one-fourth the size of the average failed national bank. Prior to 1986, the FDIC was more prone to handle small failed banks in unit-banking states as deposit payoffs rather than as P&As. Since more small state banks were located in unit-banking states, more failed state banks have been handled by the FDIC as deposit payoffs than failed national banks.

TABLE 16-3	The Number of Deposit Payoffs and Purchase-and-Assumption (P&A) Transactions Used by the FDIC, 1934–1994		
Years	*Deposit Payoff*	*P&A*	*Ratio Payoff/P&A*
1934–1939	207	105	1.98
1940–1949	38	61	0.62
1950–1959	12	16	0.75
1960–1969	27	16	1.69
1970–1979	23	53	0.43
1980–1983	21	75	0.28
1984–1989	74	699	0.11
1990–1995	70	402	0.17
Total	472	1,427	0.33

Note: From 1984 through 1989, the FDIC arranged 149 insured deposit transfers; see Table 16–4.

Source: 1995 Annual Report, FDIC and "Closed Banks and Assistance Transactions for 1989" (mimeographed), FDIC.

a bank has high-cost volatile funds, bidders will opt for an insured-deposit transfer because, unlike in a P&A, they have the ability to renegotiate the terms on debt instruments" (Bovenzi and Murton [1988], p. 3). In other words, the bidders go after the low-cost, core deposits, leaving the purchased funds behind.

Open-Bank Assistance

Open-bank assistance represents the FDIC's euphemism for bailout. Because the assisted bank is economically insolvent, it is *open* only because of the strength of government guarantees behind deposit insurance (e.g., Continental Illinois prior to its bailout in 1984). The failing bank actually is dead, but the federal banking authorities (Fed/FDIC/OCC) won't sign the death certificate, that is, declare it insolvent. This forbearance creates a gap between economic failure and closure. In this land of the living dead, Kane [1989b] calls such institutions "zombies."

The FDI Act, Section 13(c), authorizes the FDIC to provide financial assistance to prevent the closing of an insured bank. The assistance may take the form of a cash infusion, facilitation of a merger, or facilitation of an acquisition by a bank holding company. The amount of FDIC assistance usually equals the difference between the market value of the bank's assets and its liabilities, or the bank's negative net worth. If a deposit runoff has occurred, as it did with Continental Illinois, the cash contribution can be substantial. To determine if open-bank assistance is warranted, the FDIC applies a joint test based on costs, needs, and the likelihood of contagion. Although the cost of assisting the open bank must be less than liquidating it, the needs of the community or concerns about confidence and stability (contagion) may outweigh the cost differential. The needs test suggests that an institution in a one-bank town or in an isolated metropolitan area might be bailed out; the contagion test suggests the too-big-to-fail doctrine. The FDIC arranged 21 assistance transactions in 1988 and 19 in 1987 but only one in 1989. The 21 assistance transactions in 1988 were expensive because they required FDIC disbursements of $1.75 billion (estimated loss of $1.6 billion) compared to only $161 million for the 19 deals in 1987. For the 1980s, 68 assistance transactions were arranged, with disbursements of $10.8 billion and estimated losses of $5.0 billion. From 1990 to 1994, the FDIC undertook only six assistance transactions, with none in 1993 and 1994.[30]

Although the largest bank/BHC bailed out by the FDIC has been Continental Illinois, it was not the most costly FDIC bailout. The FDIC dumped $4.5 billion on Continental in 1984 but lost only about one-third of the amount. In contrast, the FDIC expected to lose $3 billion on an outlay of $3.8 billion for the bailout of First RepublicBank of Dallas in 1988 (*1988 Annual Report,* FDIC, p. 8).

Bridge Bank and DINB

A **bridge bank,** like a bridge loan, represents a temporary transaction until a permanent solution can be arranged. It permits existing or newly appointed management to run the bank under federal supervision while the FDIC attempts to arrange a sale. The idea is that assets of a failed bank have more value in a going concern than they do in liquidation. The bridge device is designed to give potential bidders time to assess the condition and value of the failing bank so that they may enter the bidding process. Although the FDIC received the authority to operate bridge banks only in 1987, it always could set up a Deposit Insurance National Bank, or DINB, which is simply a limited bridge bank run by the FDIC for no more than two years. When a buyer is found, the acquiring bank usually buys a part of the bridge bank and agrees to buy the FDIC's interest over time. Bridge-bank transactions have been used in the three most costly bank failures. In 1988 NCNB (now NationsBank) acquired First Republic Bancorp (Texas), and in 1989 Banc One acquired MCorp (Texas). After the Bank of New England was declared insolvent in 1991, the FDIC established a bridge bank. The FDIC estimates the costs of these three bridge-bank transactions to be $2.9 billion (First Republic), $2.7 billion (MCorp), and $2.3 billion (Bank of New England).

Mix-and-Match Deals

Creative financing, a buzzword of the 1980s, applies to FDIC deal making in the 1980s. A large bank/BHC with financial difficulties is a prerequisite for such creativity. First RepublicBank Corporation, Dallas, presented the opportunity for such creative financing.[31] On March 17, 1988, the FDIC provided First Republic with an open-bank-assistance package consisting of a $1 billion loan to First Republic's two largest banks. The loan was guaranteed by all the bank's subsidiaries and collateralized by the stock of 30 bank subsidiaries. On July 29, the FDIC called its loan and forced 41 of First Republic's subsidiaries into insolvency, 40 banks in Texas and a credit-card subsidiary in Delaware. Two bridge banks were arranged. The first one, a controversial deal between the FDIC and NCNB Corporation (now NationsBank, Charlotte, NC), called for NCNB Texas National Bank, a bridge bank, to manage under an interim contract the 40 failed banks in Texas. In November the deal was made permanent with a $1.05 billion infusion of new equity into the bridge bank, based on a 20/80 NCNB-FDIC split. NCNB had the option over the next five years of purchasing at increasing premiums the FDIC's 80 percent interest.

The second bridge bank was created to assume the assets and liabilities of First Republic's credit-card subsidiary in Delaware. The bridge bank, which opened on August 2, was sold on September 9 to Citibank Delaware, New Castle, Delaware. To summarize, the FDIC's failure resolution for First Republic involved open-bank

---

[30] Data in this paragraph are from the FDIC's 1994 *Annual Report,* Table C, p. 127.

[31] The FDIC's *1988 Annual Report,* pp. 8–10, provides the details.

assistance and two bridge banks, and an expected loss to the FDIC of $3 billion on an outlay of $3.8 billion.

Recapitulation

Table 16-4 summarizes the five failure-resolution techniques available to the FDIC. Its most frequently used methods, however, are variations of deposit pay-offs or purchase-and-assumption (P&A) transactions. In addition, as First Republic's resolution demonstrates, the techniques can be combined for handling complex situations.

Resolving Bank Failures in the 1980s.

Table 16-5 shows how the FDIC used its **failure-resolution methods** during the 1980s. Over one-half of 2,127 economic failures (through 1995) handled by the FDIC during its existence occurred during this ten-year period. Of the 1,086 economic failures during the 1980s, 93.7 percent of the banks were closed, whereas the remaining 6.3 percent were given FDIC financial assistance. Of the 1,018 closed banks, 774 (76 percent) of them were resolved with some form of P&A transaction. The FDIC first used insured deposit transfers in 1984, and they were the second most popular method of failure resolution during the 1980s.

TABLE 16-4 Failure-Resolution Methods Used by the FDIC

1. *Deposit payoff:* Insured depositors paid by the FDIC. All other creditors are at risk; they get receiver's certificates from the FDIC. The FDIC, as receiver, liquidates all of the failed bank's assets. The FDIC arranged 207 deposit payoffs during the first five years of its existence (1934–1939), but since then (55 years) has arranged only 265 payoffs (see Table 16–3).

2. *Purchase-and-assumption (P&A) transaction:* Insured deposits and usually all other liabilities assumed by the acquiring bank, which purchases only some of the failed banks assets, leaving the "junk" for the FDIC to liquidate. The winning bidder is determined by a competitive sealed-bid auction. In a whole-bank P&A, the acquiring bank purchases almost all the assets of the failed bank at a discount from book value. The FDIC arranged 1,421 P&As (including whole-bank transactions) over the 60 years 1934 to 1994 (see Table 16–3).

3. *Insured deposit transfer:* Only insured deposits and secured liabilities are transferred to the acquiring banks, with FDIC cash as the offsetting entry. The acquiring bank uses the cash to buy some of the failed bank's assets. The FDIC arranged 149 insured deposit transfers in the 1980s, 14 percent of total failures, including assistance transactions.

4. *Open-bank assistance:* Technique used to bail out failing banks. The FDIC infuses cash equal to the difference between the distressed bank's assets and liabilities. The assisted bank may continue to exist, as in the case of Continental Illinois (now Continental Bank after its name change), or the FDIC might pull the plug on the financial assistance and force the bank into insolvency, as in the case of First Republic of Dallas (NCNB Texas National Bank at the time of its acquisition by NCNB, now NationsBank of Texas and NationsBank). The FDIC arranged 68 assistance transactions in the 1980s, 6 percent of total failures, including assistance transactions. The FDIC has arranged only 80 assistance transactions from 1934 through 1994.

5. *Bridge bank and DINB:* Interim arrangements until permanent solutions can be found. A bridge bank stays in the private sector, whereas a Deposit Insurance National Bank (DINB) is a limited-service operation run by the FDIC for a maximum of two years. DINBs are not widely used by the FDIC. The idea with a bridge bank is to try to preserve asset values through continuity of operation and to give potential bidders a chance to analyze the situation. The FDIC was given the power to establish bridge banks in 1987, and since then it has arranged only a handful of them.

TABLE 16-5 Failure-Resolution Methods Used by the FDIC during the 1980s

| Year | Economic Failures | | Resolution of Closed Banks | | |
	Closed	Assistance Transaction	Purchase and Assumption (P&A)	Insured Deposit Transfer	Insured Deposit Payoff
1980	10	0	7	0	3
1981	7	3	5	0	2
1982	34	8	27	0	7
1983	45	3	36	0	9
1984	78	2	62	12	4
1985	116	4	87	7	22
1986	138	7	98	19	21
1987	184	19	133	40	11
1988	200	21	164	30	6
1989	206	1	155	41	10
Total	1,018	68	774	149	95
Percentage of 1,018	100	NA	76.1	14.6	9.3
Percentage of 1,086	93.7	6.3	71.3	13.7	8.7

Note: The sum of closed banks and assistance transactions equals the number of economic failures, 1,086 for the 1980s. The sum of P&As, insured deposit transfers, and insured deposit payoffs equals the number of closed banks. From 1934 to 1994, the FDIC has handled 2,121 bank failures.

Source: "Closed Banks and Assistance Transactions," 1988 and 1989 (mimeographed), Federal Deposit Insurance Corporation.

Although the number of closed banks increased by only 16, from 184 in 1987 to 200 in 1988, the total assets of closed banks jumped almost fivefold, from $6.9 billion in 1987 to $35.7 billion in 1988. Alternatively, the average closed bank had total assets of $37.5 million in 1987 compared to $178.5 million in 1988. The skyrocketing volume of assets to be liquidated resulted in a sixfold increase in the number of FDIC's division of liquidation, from 500 in 1980 to 3,386 in 1988.[32]

Asset Liquidation: Function, Operations, and Performance

Kane [1990] likens the **asset-liquidation** process to the salvage or value-recovery operation of an automobile junkyard. Efficient management of a junkyard or a scrap heap of failed-bank assets requires "aggressive operating flexibility" (p. 755). A General Accounting Office [GAO, 1988] study of the FDIC's asset liquidation operations made "no recommendations," implying a vote of confidence in the FDIC's operations.

Although the GAO was not investigating the FDIC's "closure policy," if the FDIC saw the failures on the horizon, why didn't it try to get the banks closed

---

[32] To prepare for the anticipated increase in its workload, the FDIC's Division of Liquidation moved to a decentralized structure with delegation of authority and reliance on a large number of temporary employees—a move suggesting aggressive operating flexibility. Oversight of the decentralized operation was provided by internal management reviews, an approval process for liquidation decisions, audits, and information decisions (GAO [1988], p. 2). As the RTC Oversight Board has demonstrated, however, oversight has the potential to stifle the efficiency of an operation.

sooner—before their economic net worths became so negative? Remember, however, that the FDIC does not have the de jure authority to close a bank. The GAO's findings suggest that the bank regulation-and-supervision problem is not one of identification of problem situations but one of enforcement and timely closure.

Building on Thomas and Reed [1977], Kane [1990] describes the four essential functions of a salvage operation (p. 757):

- Rescue or peril reduction
- Appraisal or damage evaluation: documenting and valuing inventories of damaged goods (e.g., loans of failed banks)
- Efficient asset or property management such that values are protected or enhanced
- Sales: searching for potential buyers, communicating appraisal information, running auctions, and bargaining for the best price

Because the assets of failed banks run from the exotic (a brothel in Nevada or bull semen in Texas) to the mundane (plant and equipment, inventory, office buildings, apartment complexes, hotels, houses, and automobiles), an efficient liquidator needs the assistance of outside experts or specialists in each of the four functional areas. By moving to a large temporary work force, the FDIC created the opportunity and flexibility to use outside experts. The combination of proper incentives and specialists provides an environment conducive to the swift and efficient valuation, management, and movement of the assets of failed banks.

Although the FDIC acts quickly to reopen a closed bank or pay off depositors, the asset liquidation (mainly loans) is not as swift. For example, the GAO (1988, p. 57) reported that the average life of a bank liquidation was almost 12 years, with a range of 4.3 years to 23 years. Litigation and complex assets and contracts suggest why liquidations can take so long and they also suggest why the FDIC likes, if possible, to keep assets in the private sector. The FDIC calls the end of liquidation "termination of receivership." As of March 15, 1988, none of the 516 receiverships set up as a result of the banks closed in the previous four years (1983–1987) had been terminated (GAO, p. 58). Only after a court agrees with the FDIC's request for termination are any claimants paid their share of any collections from the liquidation.

Figure 16-1 shows the estimated cost to the FDIC of the banks that failed in 1985 and 1986. Resolution costs were, on average, roughly 30 percent of total failed-bank assets (see Bovenzi and Murton [1988]). Although the FDIC's high resolution costs suggest that distressed banks may not be closed soon enough, Bovenzi and Murton (p. 13) argue otherwise. They claim that one must distinguish between the assets of failed banks in terms of going-concern value versus liquidation value. Going-concern value should always be higher than liquidation value. When Bovenzi and Murton compare open-bank-assistance transactions and whole-bank P&As with other resolution methods, they find the average resolution cost to be only 20 percent of total failed-bank assets. They conclude that much of the 10 percent difference is likely due to the possibility that assets are worth more in a going concern than in a liquidation.

Bovenzi and Murton define "loss on assets," which is part of the FDIC's cost of any failure resolution, as the difference between the book value of the bank's assets and the value of the assets to the FDIC. When the assets are held by the FDIC, the value is the difference between the present value of collections and the present value of liquidation expenses. For assets retained by the private sector, the value is the price paid for the assets by the acquiring bank. Bovenzi and Murton

Number of banks

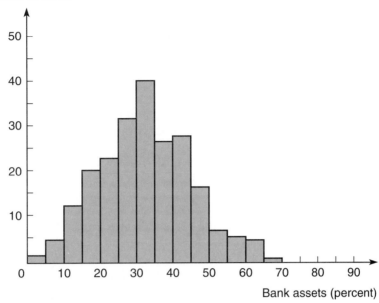

Source: Bovenzi and Murton [1988], Figure 1, p. 6.

FIGURE 16-1 **Estimated Cost to the FDIC of Individual Bank Failures (as a percentage of bank assets)**

estimate the FDIC's loss on assets for the average failed bank at 33 percent, with a range of 3 percent to 64 percent. Using the loss on assets as the dependent variable, they developed the following regression model to explain the loss on assets (pp. 6–7):

$$\text{Loss on assets} = 0.198(N) + 0.609(S) + 0.918(DL) + 1.980(I)$$

where the letters in parentheses stand for nonclassified risk assets (N), substandard assets (S), doubtful and loss assets (DL), and income earned but not collected (I). These variables are the independent variables of the model, and the numbers are the estimated regression coefficients.[33] The sample consisted of 218 failed banks. From an economic perspective, the model says that for a dollar increase in one of the independent variables, the loss on assets increases by the size of the corresponding regression coefficient. For example, a dollar increase in nonclassified risk assets raises the loss on assets by 19.8 cents, all other things being equal. For the other three variables, the increases in loss on assets are 60.9 cents (substandard), 91.8 cents (doubtful and loss), and $1.98 (income earned but not collected). On balance, the riskier a bank's portfolio of assets is, the higher the loss on assets. Income earned but not collected could reflect nonperforming assets that have not been adversely classified (i.e., loss, doubtful, or substandard) or different accounting practices regarding the treatment of interest payments or both.

---

[33] With significant *t*-statistics of 7.4, 9.8, 10.1, and 4.2, an *R*-squared statistic of .54 (i.e., the proportion of the variation in loss on assets explained by the regression), and a standard error for the regression of 8.3 percent, the model is statistically significant.

Deposit-Insurance Assessments and Explicit Risk-Based Pricing

The problem of adverse selection in insurance occurs when a population is heterogeneous with respect to risk and the same premium is charged to everyone. In deposit insurance, because high-risk banks cannot explicitly buy more insurance coverage, they buy it implicitly by taking on more risk at the expense (subsidy) of low-risk banks, resulting in an inefficient allocation of risk-bearing.

From 1934 until 1988, the explicit assessment or premium for deposit insurance was fixed at 1/12 of one percent of a bank's average domestic deposits, or 8.3 cents per $100 of these deposits. Although the premium was raised to 12 cents in mid-1989 and to a minimum of 15 cents in 1991,[34] it was still not explicitly related to a bank's risk exposure. Recall, however, that through examination and supervision, the federal troika of FDIC/OCC/Fed imposes implicit fees on all insured banks, and especially on high-risk institutions. Beginning in 1991, the FDIC exercised its new authority to increase assessments above the statutory rate when needed, for example, the effective rates were 21.25 cents in 1991 and 23 cents in 1992. Beginning in 1993, the FDIC moved to an effective rate based on a risk-related system under which banks pay premiums in the range of 23 cents to 31 cents. The effective rates were 24.4 cents in 1993 and 23.6 cents in 1994. The FDIC's total assessment income (for BIF) in 1994 was $5.6 billion, down slightly from the all-time high of $5.8 billion in 1993. However, in 1995, the assessment rate was reduced to 4.4 cents per $100 of insured deposits, and assessment premiums of $1.5 billion were refunded in September. For 1995, FDIC assessment income was $2.9 billion.

The FDIC Improvement Act of 1991 mandated that the FDIC develop a risk-related premium system and implement it no later than January 1, 1994. On September 15, 1992, the FDIC Board of Directors agreed on an assessment schedule that charges higher insurance rates to those banks and savings associations that pose greater risks to BIF and SAIF. The system went into effect January 1, 1993, almost 60 years after the FDIC was established. Here's how the system works. Nine risk categories exist, as defined by the following matrix (premiums in cents per $100 of domestic deposits):[35]

| | Supervisory Group | | |
Meets numerical standards for:	A	B	C
Well capitalized	23	26	29
Adequately capitalized	26	29	30
Undercapitalized	29	30	31

Banks and thrifts are assigned to one of the nine risk categories based on a two-step process: Capital adequacy comes first. What else from FDIC = *F*orever *De*manding *I*ncreased *C*apital? A well-capitalized institution must jump three hurdles: a total risk-based capital ratio of 10 percent or more, a 6 percent Tier 1

---

[34] In this section, assessment figures given in cents are always per $100 of domestic deposits.

[35] When the system was announced, the FDIC Board expected to meet at least every six months to review the premium rates. Information on the risk-based system can be found in summary form in FIL-71–92 (FDIC memo to CEOs, October 7, 1992) and in detail in "Rules and Regulation," *Federal Register,* vol. 57, no. 191 (October 1, 1992), pp. 45263–45287.

capital ratio, and a 5 percent ratio of Tier 1 capital to total assets. Recall that the first ratio is total capital divided by risk-weighted assets, where total capital is the sum of the Tier 1 and Tier 2 capital (see chapter 13). The three lower hurdles for an adequately capitalized institution are: 8 percent, 4 percent, and 4 percent. An undercapitalized institution is one that does not meet either of the above definitions.[36]

Given an institution's capital-adequacy rating, it is assigned to one of three supervisory subgroups (*A, B, C*) based on an evaluation of the risk the institution poses to BIF or SAIF. Group *A* is for institutions that are financially sound and with only a few minor weaknesses. Group *B* is for institutions with weakness which, if not corrected, could result in substantial deterioration of the institution and increased risk to the insurance fund. Group *C* is for institutions that pose a high probability of loss to the insurance fund unless effective corrective action is taken. The FDIC evaluates each institution on the basis of three information sets:

- Reviews supplied by the institution's primary federal or state supervisor
- Statistical analyses of financial statements
- Other information relevant to gauging the risk posed by the institution

The FDIC Board gave several reasons for its two-part method of risk evaluation. First, it viewed the capital component as giving an institution a financial reward, in the form of a lower premium, for having relatively more capital in a clearly defined manner. Second, bank capital protects the FDIC against loss and gives the institution's owners a greater stake in a safe-and-sound operation. However, because numerical capital ratios alone may not capture an institution's riskiness, other factors, such as asset quality, loan underwriting standards, and other operating systems, need to be evaluated. Thus, the system includes a component based on the ongoing process of supervisory monitoring. By including the supervisory component, the FDIC hoped to reduce potential inequities in the pricing of risk that a system based solely on financial data might generate. The FDIC pricing scheme includes an appeals process for institutions that wish to challenge their risk classification.

The Deposit-Insurance Ceiling

From January 1 to June 30, 1934, the deposit-insurance ceiling or maximum protection for a small saver was $2,500; on July 1, 1934, it jumped to $5,000. In 1980 the ceiling was raised from $40,000 to $100,000. Prior to 1980 the ceiling was raised to $10,000 in 1950, $15,000 in 1966, $20,000 in 1969, and $40,000 in 1974. Assuming a 5 percent rate of inflation for 61 years, the deposit-insurance ceiling in 1994 would have grown to $49,033 based on the $2,500 ceiling, or $98,066 based on the $5,000 ceiling. Some analysts have suggested that one way to put more discipline in the system would be to reduce the deposit-insurance ceiling. However, like social-security reform, no politician wants to touch this hot potato. Moreover, because this might have an adverse effect on confidence and stability, it might be a dubious trade-off. An alternative plan with more appeal is to leave the ceiling at $100,000 but restrict the ability of depositors to manipulate accounts to obtain more than the $100,000 coverage.

---

[36] These capital definitions are identical to those developed by federal regulators for use in identifying banks in need of "prompt corrective action" (PCA), another FDICIA stipulation.

STRUCTURAL WEAKNESSES AND REFORM OF DEPOSIT INSURANCE

The failure of deposit insurers to recognize the serious problem facing the deposit-insurance system in the 1980s calls to mind a scene from the movie *Young Frankenstein.* As Dr. Frankenstein arrives at the Transylvania railroad station and hands his baggage to the faithful humpbacked assistant, Igor, he says, "I am a great doctor." Dr. Frankenstein leans forward to peer at the mountainous hump rising from poor Igor's shoulder and adds, "I can fix that hump for you, Igor." From his perpetual crouch, Igor casts a baleful eye up to the doctor and says, "Vot Hoomp?"

The willful suspension of belief in the obvious must have been great comfort to deposit insurers as they inquired, "Vot problem?" There is no disputing that federal deposit insurance in the United States worked well for half a century; even such antagonists as Milton Friedman and John Kenneth Galbraith agree on that point. Moreover, risk-based pricing and prompt corrective action are noteworthy improvements. Nevertheless, structural weaknesses remain, which suggest that further reform is needed. Table 16-6 summarizes these points, which draw on Kane [1985, 1989b]. Although Kane's reforms are in the form of a package, he sees the adoption of any part of the package as an important step in the direction of deposit-insurance reform. Accordingly, the adoption of risk-based premiums and the call for prompt corrective action (PCA) are steps in the right direction.

TABLE 16-6   Federal Deposit Insurance: Structural Weaknesses and Potential Reforms

Weakness	Potential Reform	Status
1. Premiums unrelated to risk	Risk-based pricing	Introduced in 1993
2. Hidden information in insuree's financial statements because of historical cost or book-value accounting	Market-value accounting	Little prospect
3. Hidden action through managers' fraud, abuse, and misconduct	Increased supervision of criminal activity (difficult because such conduct is deliberately masked)	Vigorous prosecution of criminal activity
4. Insurance coverage is too broad with ceiling at $100,000 plus multiple-account manipulation	Reduce coverage either by lowering ceiling or reducing number of accounts covered or both	"Too hot to handle"
5. Closure rule and bailout policy too lenient	Play hardball on closure: When economic net worth is exhausted, bank is closed	Will PCA be effective? A step in the right direction
6. Mismanagement of the insurance product and risk exposure	Copy the management, pricing, and product strategies, policies, and practices of private insurers, for example, with respect to cancellation, deductibles, coinsurance, pricing, loss-sharing, and so on	Nothing in the works
7. Lack of competition	Permit private insurers to provide full or supplemental coverage	No interest
8. De facto nationalization and inefficiencies of reprivatization	Avoiding nationalization will eliminate the need for reprivatization. Try to keep the assets of failed firms in the private sector	Whole-bank P&As a good idea

An Effective Closure Rule: A Panacea?

By closing a bank at the moment its economic net worth is exhausted, remaining asset values cover all liabilities and the deposit insurer incurs no losses. In theory, this **closure rule** works very well. Because the prompt-corrective-action (PCA) provision of FDICIA approximates an effective closure rule, the gap between theory and practice may narrow. Measurement and timing are critical practical issues to be tackled. Can economic net worth be measured precisely, and can the information be generated in a timely fashion? Effective measurement requires transparency through market-value accounting, but bankers and regulators show little interest in it. Although finding the present values of fixed-rate assets when interest-rates change is no big deal, the options embedded in such contracts (e.g., prepayment) make the calculations a bit more complicated. Nevertheless, it can be done. Government securities, securitized loans, and loans with secondary markets make valuing the underlying assets of the bank easier today than in the past. Regarding the timing of closure, or PCA, if it is not biased, then, on average, over a large sample of closings, real net worth will be zero. The bottom line is, market-value accounting can be done, although it is not easy.

Will closing financial institutions when their economic net worths are exhausted (i.e., an effective closure rule) cause financial instability and lack of confidence in the banking system? Let's turn this around. Failure to do so resulted in a thrift and banking crisis that we survived but at a high price (e.g., $160 billion, excluding interest, for the S&L mess). As long as an effective closure rule exists in conjunction with the federal safety net, depositors and other bank creditors will be protected. Thus, financial instability should not be a problem. Shareholders and top managers lose as they should when mismanagement and failure occur, but most importantly, taxpayers, as stockholder principals of the federal safety net, are protected.

Private Deposit Insurance: The Credit-Union Model and Experience

By law, federally chartered credit unions must belong to the National Credit Union Share Insurance Fund, and prior to 1992, state-chartered credit unions had the effective option to be privately insured. Rehm [1990] contends that the credit-union industry might serve as a model for reform of federal deposit insurance, for two reasons: (1) the greater safety as reflected by higher coverage ratios, and (2) prior to 1992, private insurance existed for credit unions. Although the private funds have gone out of existence, why did both the federal and private credit union funds appear to be safer in 1990 (i.e., why did they have better coverage)? The reason appears to be that credit unions have better control over credit risk, and therefore they are safer, perhaps because they are specialists in consumer lending. Credit unions, which are not-for-profit, tax-exempt organizations, make loans and provide other financial services to members, who have a common bond, usually through employment.[37]

The nature of the business of credit unions is relatively low risk. Credit unions make basic consumer loans for automobiles, appliances, home improvements, personal expenses, and, since the early 1980s, for residential mortgages. Credit unions

---

[37] I found it a bit ironic that when I worked at the FDIC from 1971 to 1976, even it had a credit union. The Navy Federal Credit Union is the largest in the United States with over $5 billion in assets, $400 million in capital or reserves, and over one million members.

have very few commercial or farm loans and don't make loans to LDCs or loans for leveraged buyouts. By law, credit unions can make loans only to their members, not to corporate or institutional borrowers. Because loan payments usually are made through payroll deductions, credit unions get paid off the top. Borrowers do not have as much opportunity to default. The combination of low-risk loans and payroll deductions means that credit unions have fewer loan defaults and fewer failures, which means lower losses to their insurance funds and therefore better coverage ratios.

The private insurers interviewed by Rehm [1990] claimed that it was the quality of supervision that made their funds safer. The general counsel of the largest private insurer,[38] National Deposit Insurance Corp. in Dublin, Ohio which insured 460 credit unions in 22 states, claimed, "We audit our credit unions monthly. You don't have the poor, dumb taxpayer to pick up your bill in the private world. If you don't do it right, you're out of business" (p. 6). The Rhode Island Share and Deposit Indemnity Corp. also conducted monthly audits of its 46 credit union clients. Its president ironically noted prior to the collapse of the Rhode Island fund: "I think we need a lot of data; we need it frequently; and we need to get it on-site. If you catch something early, it is going to save you a lot of money" (ibid.). Unfortunately, his examiners did not catch the embezzlement by the president of Heritage Loan and Investment Co. As a result, the private insurance fund's reserves were effectively wiped out, which forced Rhode Island Governor Sundlun, on his first day in office (January 1, 1991), to close 45 credit unions and small banks.

The aftermath of the Rhode Island crisis was the demise of private insurance for credit unions in the United States as credit unions across the country lost confidence in their private insurers and applied for conversion to federal insurance under the National Credit Union Association (NCUA). Prior to the Rhode Island crisis, the NCUA chairman claimed that private insurers had to "spread the risk to make it work." From 1985 to 1990, however, the number of private insurers of credit unions had declined from 20 to 10. None of them went bankrupt, however. Rehm [1990] reported that some were legislated out of existence when Utah, Wisconsin, North Carolina, and Virginia required federal insurance. In contrast, in Ohio and Maryland, private thrift insurance funds went bankrupt when crises developed in the late 1980s.

Lessons from Private Insurance

In the case of credit unions, the pricing is different and loss sharing exists between the insurer and the insuree. Credit unions place 1 percent of their deposits with their insurer (whether federal or private). Moreover, the credit unions have the option of carrying the premium on their books as capital. If the insurer takes a hit, however, credit unions share the loss. In effect, the credit-union approach for pricing deposit insurance creates a two-way, principal-agent relation. The insurer monitors the insuree to protect its business interests, and the insurees monitor the insurer to protect their contributions to the credit-union insurance fund. The pricing and loss-sharing aspects of the federal insurance system for credit unions originated in the private sector. This ingenuity is conspicuous by its absence in deposit insurance for banks and thrifts. Callahan's Credit Union Report [1989] claimed that the choice of deposit or share insurance presents "an opportunity to innovate and change ahead of the consensus that sometimes slows a national system of supervision" (p. 2).

---

[38] The second-largest of the 10 private insurers of credit unions, Mutual Guaranty Corporation of Chattanooga, Tennessee, insured 325 credit unions in five states (Rehm [1990]).

The general counsel of the largest private insurer for credit unions claimed, "The federal government has done a pitiful job of insuring deposits. If they want to solve the problem, then they'll privatize the insurance system and operate not on the backs of the taxpayers but on the basis of profit margin" (Rehm [1990], p. 6). He suggested starting with the credit union's pricing structure of 1 percent of deposits and then moving to one based on the insured institution's risk to the insurance fund. With $1.9 trillion of insured deposits in 1994, the bank insurance fund (BIF) would be $190 billion, based on a 1 percent contribution by each bank, quite a jump from the $22 billion in BIF at year-end 1994.[39] With banks sharing in the losses incurred by a credit union–type fund, banks would want to see troubled banks closed when their economic net worths approach zero.

Compared to banks and S&Ls, where the bulk of failures came in the second half of the 1980s, credit unions had a more difficult time in the first half of the 1980s. In 1981, 349 credit unions failed, with the number of failures declining steadily to 85 in fiscal year 1988 before jumping slightly to 114 in 1989. In the last three fiscal years of the 1980s, the number of problem credit unions was 977 in 1987, 1,022 in 1988, and 794 in 1989. The NCUA adopted a hard line with troubled federal credit unions based on a three-pronged approach: (1) forcing distressed institutions to recognize problems early, (2) written recognition of the problems along with a plan to correct them, and (3) a required turnaround period of one to two years. If an ailing credit union doesn't show signs of improvement, then NCUA pulls the plug on it—limited forbearance (Atkinson [1990]).

Recapitulation

The higher insurance-coverage ratios maintained by credit-union insurers compared to bank and thrift insurers result from a combination of three factors: (1) relatively better asset quality, (2) a deposit-insurance contract that is more incentive compatible, and (3) stricter supervision of distressed institutions. As long as credit unions continue specializing in relatively safe lending and as long as their regulators and deposit insurers continue to do their jobs, their record of superior performance should continue.

Reforming Deposit Insurance without Losing Its Benefits

Because we do not want to throw the baby out with the bathwater, deposit insurance needs to be reformed without losing its benefits to society. Kane [1989b] describes the benefits as confidence in the financial system, fair treatment for small depositors, and promoting efficiency in financial intermediation and risk taking. Although incentive-compatible contracts are the means to achieve these benefits, housing finance and deposit insurance have created stubborn subsidies. Incentive incompatibilities exist in the various principal-agent relations associated with the nexus of contracts that make up the deposit-insurance guarantee. Table 16-6 summarizes the weaknesses and potential reforms associated with the pricing and structure of the contract. More generally, voters can cause reform at the ballot box by voting intelligently. We need to elect better people to Congress and to make them and appointed government officials accountable to taxpayers as stockholder principals in the system of deposit insurance and regulation.

---

[39] With $692 billion of insured deposits in 1994, the savings association insurance fund (SAIF) would be $6.9 billion, based on a 1 percent contribution by each bank, quite a jump from the $1.9 billion in SAIF at year-end 1994.

The Prospects for Insurance and Regulatory Reform

To dramatize the prospects for continued insurance and regulatory reform, let's take refuge in a (slightly altered) apocryphal story.[40] In this story, the president of the American Bankers Association, the president of the U.S. League of Savings Associations, and an academic economist are ushered into the presence of God, and each is allowed to ask Him a single question. The ABA president inquires, "Tell me, Father, how long before we can get into the insurance business?" God replies: "Half a decade." The ABA president weeps and leaves. The president of the U.S. League of Savings Associations steps up next and asks, "Tell me, Father, will my membership survive into the 21st century?" "When hell freezes over," answers God. The U.S. League president weeps and leaves. Finally, the academic economist goes to God and asks a deeper question: "How long will it be until federal deposit insurance is completely reformed and bank regulation is no longer a jurisdictional tangle that boggles the mind?" This time, *God* weeps and leaves.

BANK FAILURES: HIDDEN ACTION AND HIDDEN INFORMATION

For the sake of argument, let's refer to fraud, abuse, and misconduct by bankers as **hidden action,** and to misvaluation of on- and off-balance-sheet items as **hidden information.** Although market-value accounting would go a long way in solving the hidden-information problem, the solution to hidden action is a bit more complicated, because fraud, abuse, and misconduct tend to be deliberately masked by the cleverness and cunning of the criminal mind. In terms of identifying potential bank failures and minimizing losses to taxpayers, the main tasks of bank regulators and deposit insurers are to monitor the activities of insured institutions, to attempt to correct weaknesses and deficiencies, and to provide incentive compatible contracts (e.g., the deposit-insurance contract) to achieve these goals. These devices are the regulatory-insurance tools for solving the principal-agent problem involved here.

Economic Insolvency and Bank Closure

Consider a time line with two points: T and $T + K$. The difference between the two points is, of course, K. Under an effective closure rule in which a bank is shut down when its economic net worth is exhausted, $K = 0$. That is, no lag exists between economic insolvency and bank closure. Because such perfect timing and measurement does not exist in the real world of problem and failed banks, $K > 0$. A reasonable second-best objective is to try to minimize K, given relevant constraints and other policy considerations (e.g., avoiding a financial panic). Let's consider two Ks: an optimal one, K^*, and a suboptimal one, K_F, where the subscript indicates forbearance. The important relationship is

$$K_F > K^* > 0 \tag{16-8}$$

During the thrift and banking crises of the 1980s and early 1990s, the amount of **forbearance** was unacceptable.[41] The various incentive incompatibilities associated with the deposit-insurance guarantee explain why such forbearance occurred and

---

[40] This story is adapted from a draft version of Kane [1985].
[41] Thomson [1992] models the bank regulators' closure option using a two-step logit regression.

suggest how to remedy the problem. The good news is that the prompt-corrective-action (PCA) provision of FDICIA (1991) takes a step in the direction of reducing the lag between economic insolvencies and more optimal bank closures.

Financial Early-Warning Signals[42]

Given the absence of market-value accounting, regulators and deposit insurers rely mainly on book values to generate early-warning signals. Without knowledge of a bank's true net worth, however, an effective closure rule or even a PCA rule is difficult to enforce. Early-warning research in banking has been going on for several decades. The idea is to compare failed and nonfailed banks (or problem and non-problem banks) or use peer-group analysis to develop financial profiles or characteristics that distinguish between the groups or that simply flag outliers. Ratios, growth rates, and measures of variability are the kinds of variables analyzed in such studies. The standard categories of variables used in financial-statement analysis are employed, such as profitability (ROA), leverage (capital adequacy), balance-sheet composition, sources and uses of funds, and loan-loss experience. Although different statistical techniques and refinements have been used over the years, the story of bank failure has not changed much. Because credit risk has been the main culprit, symptoms related to the loan portfolio tend to be good early-warning signals. The OCC's 1988 study of bank failures put it this way: "The major cause of decline for problem banks continues to be poor asset quality that eventually erodes a bank's capital" (p. 5). The on-site bank examination is the primary vehicle for identifying poor asset quality. This approach, which describes adversely classified assets as substandard, doubtful, and loss, is also the basis for identifying problem banks; see Sinkey [1978]. Examples of by-products or applications of early-warning research include the FDIC's JAWS (Just A Warning System) and the OCC's BERT (Bank Expert, an expert computer system used in the bank-examination process).

Causes of Bank Failures

A 1988 study of bank failures by the OCC identified several factors that had an important contributing effect on a bank's demise. Poor **asset quality,** a factor in 98 percent of the failed banks studied, was the major symptom of bank failure. This finding was not new, because credit risk has been the major uncertainty and undoing of commercial banks for a long time (Sinkey [1979]). On balance, what causes poor asset quality causes banks to fail. The OCC's study identified eight loan practices as key determinants of poor asset quality: liberal lending practices (85%); excessive financial-statement exceptions (79%); overlending (73%); excessive collateral-documentation exceptions (67%); collateral-based lending (55%); excessive growth relative to management, staff, systems, and funding (52%); unwarranted concentrations of credit (37%); and out-of-area lending (23%). The figures in parentheses are the percentage of failed banks in which the factor was identified. The corresponding figures for healthy banks were 0 percent, 29 percent, 0 percent, 0 percent, 3 percent, 3 percent, 0 percent, and 3 percent.

Ranked in order of importance, other factors commonly found in failed banks include (1) weaknesses in planning, policies, and management (90%); (2,3) insider abuse (35%) and a weak economic environment (35%); (4) lack of proper audits,

---

[42] Sinkey [1975, 1978, 1979] provides examples of the early-warning signals and Altman, Avery, Eisenbeis, and Sinkey [1981] illustrate applications of classification techniques in business, banking, and finance.

controls, and systems (25%); (5) material fraud, meaning an attempt to deceive or conceal or both (11%); and (6) nonfunding expenses (9%). Again, figures in parentheses are the percentage of failed banks in which the factor was identified.

Fraud, Abuse, and Misconduct

In 1988, The Commerce, Consumer, and Monetary Affairs Subcommittee of the House of Representatives conducted an investigation regarding **fraud, abuse,** and **misconduct** in the nation's federally insured financial institutions; they concluded that federal efforts were "inadequate." The committee focused on (1) the nature, extent, and impact of fraud, abuse, and misconduct by senior insiders and outsiders, and (2) the adequacy of efforts by the federal bank regulatory agencies and criminal justice systems to combat such activities. The investigation illustrates Congress's role, as a principal, monitoring the efforts of bank regulators and deposit insurers as agents acting on behalf of Congress and taxpayers.

The committee found that misconduct was a serious problem resulting in the loss of public confidence in thrifts and banks. It concluded that the consequences were "serious" for commercial banks but "disastrous" for the thrift industry. FDIC and OCC studies suggest that about one out of every three failed banks in the mid to late 1980s had serious problems with fraud, abuse, or misconduct; the Federal Home Loan Bank Board (FHLBB) found misconduct in 80 percent of insolvent thrifts over the period January 1984 to June 1987. The committee identified three patterns, trends, and characteristics of abuse and criminal misconduct in banks and thrifts: (1) the predominance of fraudulent real-estate schemes, (2) the increased involvement of insiders and affiliated outsiders with more than one institution, and (3) the impact of participations in fraudulent loans on other institutions and the absence of adequate regulation. Regarding the latter, the committee concluded that examination forces were insufficient, inadequately compensated, and untrained, and that there were problems with interagency exchanges of information, coordination, and consultation. The committee recommended the need for improvement in these areas and for an expanded role of independent audits.

An Insider's Account of Bank Failures and Rescues[43]

According to Sprague [1986], a former director of the FDIC during the turbulent 1980s, "Bailout is a bad word." This word is so bad that he suggests that "It sounds almost un-American." Of course, if the bailout is in your own self-interest, it can be "un-anything" as long as you are protected.

Bailed-out organizations are the offspring of a national policy that does not permit *large* enterprises to fail when market forces have dictated their demise. Capital infusions and loans from the government or its agencies are the financial methods for bailing out troubled firms. Both banks and nonbanks in the United States have been the beneficiaries of such financial assistance.

Four important bailouts crafted by the FDIC were (1) Unity Bank (Roxbury, Mass) in 1971, (2) Bank of the Commonwealth (Detroit) in 1972, (3) First Pennsylvania Bank (Philadelphia) in 1980, and (4) Continental Illinois (Chicago) in 1984. At the time of their bailouts, these institutions had total assets of $11.4 million, $1.26 billion, $8.4 billion, and $41 billion, respectively. As you can see, the bailouts have gotten bigger and bigger with more and more of a drain and contingent claim

---

[43] This section is adapted from my review of Sprague's book: Sinkey [1987].

on the FDIC's insurance fund. However, unless one considers the mutual savings bank crisis and the bailouts in that industry (e.g., Bowery Savings Bank [New York] in 1985, with total assets of $5.3 billion), the total claims on the insurance fund are underestimated. Unless taxpayers consider the phoenix story about the thrift failures and rescues, they will not know the full story and cost of the crises in deposit insurance. Table 16-7 provides some insight into this story and the embedded costs by showing the 10 largest bank resolutions handled by the FDIC (Panel A) and the 10 costliest bank resolutions to the FDIC (Panel B).

Let's step back a minute. What is a bank bailout and what is the legal framework for its implementation? The key concept here is the "essentiality doctrine." It simply means (as interpreted by the FDIC) that if a bank or its holding company can be found to be "essential" to its community, then the FDIC may provide financial assistance to prevent the organization from failing. Because the FDIC insures banks, and not bank holding companies (BHCs), the bailout of BHCs shows the breadth of the FDIC's interpretation. Both social and financial considerations have been important in establishing the essentiality doctrine. The definition of community (market) has been as narrow as ghettos in metropolitan areas and as wide as the international financial market. Sprague [1986] tells us the "real reason"

TABLE 16-7   The Ten Largest and Ten Costliest Bank Resolutions, 1986–1995

Institution	Type	City	State	Fail Date	Total Assets	Estimated Loss
Panel A: Ten Largest Bank Resolutions, 1986–1995 ($ in millions)						
First Republic Bank Corp.	TA	Dallas	TX	07/29/88	33,448	3,857
Bank of New England	PA	Boston	MA	01/06/91	21,804	733
MCorp—Dallas	TA	Dallas	TX	03/29/89	15,749	2,844
First City Bancorporation	AT	Houston	TX	04/20/88	11,200	1,101
Southeast Bank, N. A.	PA	Miami	FL	09/19/91	10,478	0
First City Bancorporation	PA	Houston	TX	10/30/92	8,850	0
Goldome Federal Savings Bank	PA	Buffalo	NY	05/31/91	8,690	848
Crossland Federal Savings	PA	Brooklyn	NY	01/24/92	7,269	548
Texas American Bankcshares	TA	Fort Worth	TX	07/20/89	4,753	1,077
New Hampshire Savings Bank	PA	Concord	NH	10/10/91	4,377	891
Totals					126,619	11,898
Panel B: Ten Costliest Bank Resolutions, 1986–1995 ($ in millions)						
First Republic Bank Corp.	TA	Dallas	TX	07/29/88	33,448	3,857
MCorp—Dallas	TA	Dallas	TX	03/29/89	15,749	2,844
First City Bancorporation	AT	Houston	TX	04/20/88	11,200	1,101
Texas American Bancshares	TA	Fort Worth	TX	07/20/89	4,753	1,077
Goldome Federal Savings Bank	PA	Buffalo	NY	05/31/91	8,690	891
New Hampshire Savings Bank	PA	Concord	NH	10/10/91	4,377	848
Bank of New England	PA	Boston	MA	01/06/91	21,804	733
Crossland Federal Savings	PA	Brooklyn	NY	01/24/92	7,269	548
American Savings Bank	PI	White Plains	NY	06/12/92	1,958	505
CityTrust	PA	Bridgeport	CT	08/09/91	3,198	470
Totals					112,447	12,873

Source: "Failed Bank Cost Analysis, 1986–1995," FDIC, p. 39. Continental Illinois (1984) had total assets of $33.6 billion and an estimated loss of $1.157 billion.

for doing the four bank bailouts: "Simply put, we were afraid not to" (p. 10). Even recognizing that fear is a great motivating factor, should not we expect something more from our highest policymakers? Although Sprague and his colleagues spent hours agonizing about these bailout decisions and additional hours justifying their actions, they appear to have made the "easy" decision. The "hard" decision (and perhaps the wrong one) would have been to apply the Darwinian rule of survival of the fittest. Unlike the physical sciences, however, where controlled experiments can be conducted, "social scientists," such as regulators, do not have the luxury of an experimental laboratory.[44]

What were bank regulators afraid of in these cases? The prospects for social unrest and ghetto violence played a major role in the decisions to bail out Unity and Commonwealth. The bailout of First Pennsylvania is noteworthy because it provided the prototype for bailing out distressed megabanks. Nevertheless, it is not clear why First Pennsylvania should have been bailed out in the first place. Regarding First Pennsy's bailout, Sprague [1986] tells the amusing story of trying to get a check for $325 million from the U.S. Treasury and how he personally carried it to Philadelphia to close the deal. In Continental's case, once the potential for a financial panic had abated and the possibility of limited contagion had been assured, what did the regulators fear?

Sprague [1986] describes two potential bailouts that never occurred: Penn Square and Seafirst. Penn Square was unique because uninsured depositors and other creditors were not protected by the FDIC's safety net of 100 percent insurance, which for a bank with $517 million in assets was unusual FDIC treatment. Presumably, the handling of Penn Square in this way was intended to be a signal to the marketplace that the regulators were serious about market discipline. However, with Continental on the horizon, the signal was short-lived. Seafirst, which was absorbed by BankAmerica Corporation in 1983, was the first major casualty from Penn Square. Sprague suggests that without the appearance of the white knight, Seafirst would have been a serious bailout candidate.

Sprague [1986] sees two major lessons to draw from the public-policy debate regarding bailouts. First, because certain bank managers fail to learn from past mistakes, those mistakes will be committed again in the future. The main culprit here, according to Sprague, is greed in the form of growth at any cost, myopic profit maximization without regard to risk, insider transactions, and betting on interest rates. The second lesson focuses on the jurisdictional tangle of bank regulation. Sprague recommends consolidating the agencies, as former Senator Proxmire (D.-Wis) proposed in the mid-1970s. Sprague's monolithic agency would have responsibility for regulating and supervising all banks and their holding companies, regardless of their chartering authority or Federal Reserve membership. To keep the agency insulated from political influence, it would be headed by a seven-person board whose chairperson would be named by the President, and whose members would be balanced to ensure that all competing interests are represented.[45]

Given Sprague's role as an architect in a national policy of bailing out large banks/BHC's, we would be surprised if his answer to the public policy debate was

---

[44] Sprague [1986] describes the high stress of top management at the FDIC during the 1980s by revealing in his book that on separate occasions he and William Isaac (FDIC chairman when Sprague was Director), both suffering from exhaustion, thought that they were having heart attacks. Only after hospitalization did they learn that it was just stress-related symptoms. It is less stressful for academics to sit in their ivory towers and simply say that no bank is too big *not* to fail.

[45] Because the details of Sprague's restructuring are sketchy, especially with respect to the role of the FDIC, his reform ideas require more thought.

not in favor of such a policy. His answer is: "megabanks must and will continue to be bailed out if they are failing" (p. 262). That is the bad news. The good news is "but they should pay a price for this protection, and they should be handled so that management and stockholders suffer, as nearly as possible, the same fate as an outright failure" (p. 262). To equalize the cost of deposit insurance, Sprague suggests that FDIC assessments be levied on all deposits, foreign and domestic. Because the current assessment applies only to domestic deposits, the megabanks, which have the bulk of foreign deposits, receive a free lunch, ultimately at taxpayers' expense. The megabanks like the too-big-to-fail doctrine as long as they can continue to book it on taxpayers' accounts.

THE SAVINGS-AND-LOAN (S&L) MESS

At year-end 1980, almost 4,000 S&Ls existed, with total assets of $621 billion. By year-end 1995, their numbers had dwindled to 1,727, with total assets of $749 billion. Prior to the industry's bailout in 1989, however, 3,000 S&Ls existed, holding total assets of $1.3 trillion. Table 16-8 shows what happened to the S&L industry from 1980 through 1995. The ability of a dying industry to double its total assets in eight years attests to the strength of the deposit-insurance guarantee. The estimated

TABLE 16-8	Consolidation of the Thrift Industry, 1980–1995		
Year	*Number*	*Total Assets ($billions)*	*Average Size ($millions)*
1980	3,998	621	155
1981	3,757	659	175
1982	3,295	700	212
1983	3,146	819	260
1984	3,136	978	312
1985	3,246	1,070	330
1986	3,220	1,164	361
1987	3,147	1,251	397
1988	3,001	1,334	444
1989	2,684	1,168	435
1990	2,367	1,002	423
1991	2,177	883	406
1992	2,039	824	404
1993	1,929	757	392
1994	1,844	772	419
1995	1,727	749	434
Changes:			
1980–1995	−2,271	+128	+279
1980–1988	−997	+713	+289
1989–1995	−640	−253	−11

Sources: FDIC, *Quarterly Banking Profile* (Fourth Quarter), 1995; Resolution Trust Corporation; and Barth, Bartholomew, and Bradley [1990], Table I, p. 733.

expense of bailing out the S&L industry ($160 billion, excluding interest) reflects the cost of supplying this guarantee.[46]

Understanding the Origins of the Thrift Crisis

The S&L crisis had three underlying causes: (1) economic and financial shortcomings associated with the nature of the S&L balance sheet and the mismanagement of interest-rate risk, then credit risk; (2) deposit insurance and regulatory failings linked with the mispricing of deposit insurance, lax supervision and regulation, and adverse incentives; and (3) legislative and political causes associated with subsidies provided by making housing finance and deposit insurance national goals without concerns for proper pricing and incentives.[47] Although the origins of the S&L financial problems can be traced to the mid-1960s, the crisis was not officially recognized until 1989, when the S&L bailout bill (Financial Institutions Reform, Recovery, and Enforcement Act, FIRREA) was signed by President Bush as one of his first official duties. FIRREA reorganized the thrift regulatory and insurance system (e.g., created SAIF) and created the Resolution Trust Corporation (RTC) to clean up the mess. Table 16-9 shows the condition of the thrift industry at the beginning of the 1990s and Table 16-10 reveals how 1,715 thrifts exited the industry over the years 1980 through 1988.

Poor Asset Quality: Mismanaged Interest-Rate Risk and Credit Risk

S&L interest-rate-risk problems began in 1966, the year marking the first of a series of increasingly severe interest-rate spikes. Additional spikes followed in 1969–1970, 1974, and the killer in 1979–1982. The cumulative effects of the interest-rate crunches were an erosion of S&L net worth. The erosion is what happens

TABLE 16-9 Condition of the Thrift Industry, March 31, 1990

Group	Description	Number of S&Ls	Total Assets ($billions)
1	Well capitalized and profitable	1,175 (47.9%)	363 (34.6%)
2	Meeting, or expected to meet, capital requirements	680 (27.7%)	351 (33.5%)
3	Troubled with poor earnings and low capital	352 (14.3%)	169 (16.1%)
4	Expected to be taken over by the government and sold off or closed	246 (10.0%)	166 (15.8%)
1–4	Total	2,453 (100%)	1,049 (100%)

Note: These data do not include S&Ls already taken over and being run by the government. Based on the above figures, the average S&L had total assets of $427.6 million; the averages for groups 1 to 4 are $308.9 million, $516 million, $480.1 million, and $674.8 million, respectively.

Source: Resolution Trust Corporation.

---

[46] Meredith [1994] reported that the author of a Congressional Budget Office report on the S&L cleanup said: "We won't know the actual cost until all of the receiverships are finally closed, which could be well into the next century." Subsequent estimates have added another $10 billion to the $150 billion reported by Meredith.

[47] Kane [1989b] provides a detailed and complete analysis of these points.

TABLE 16-10   How Thrifts Exited the Industry, 1980–1988

| Year | NUMBER OF FAILED INSTITUTIONS | | | | Voluntary Mergers | Total |
| | **FSLIC Assisted Transactions** | | **No FSLIC Assistance** | | | |
	Liquidations	Assumptions	Consignment	Merger		
1980	0	11	0	21	63	95
1981	1	27	0	54	215	297
1982	1	62	0	184	215	462
1983	5	31	0	34	83	153
1984	9	13	0	14	31	67
1985	9	22	23	10	47	111
1986	10	36	29	5	45	125
1987	17	30	25	5	74	151
1988	26	179	18	6	25	254
Totals	78	411	95	333	798	1,715

Note: "Assumptions" includes mergers and other types of assisted transactions; "Consignment" stands for management consignment cases, which for 1988 represents "stabilizations" at a cost of $7 billion; and "Merger" means supervisory merger. From 1934 through 1979, only 143 thrifts (with total assets of $4,458 million) failed at a cost of $306 million to the FSLIC. In contrast, from 1980 through 1988, 917 thrifts failed (with total assets of $172.8 billion) at a cost of $41.7 billion to the FSLIC, $35 billion attributed to nonliquidations cases. The cost figures include present-value estimates of the costs of resolution.

Source: Adapted from Barth, Bartholomew, and Bradley [1990], Table I, p. 733.

to an intermediary with a negative gap position during a period of rising interest rates (chapter 5). Borrowing short and lending long at fixed rates is a scenario for financial disaster during a period of rising interest rates. S&L managers, deposit insurers, and thrift regulators share the blame for this fiasco because they were mismanaging, mispricing, and misregulating interest-rate risk, respectively.

Until it was too late, S&L managers were myopically focused on protecting their markets and were not focused on strategic issues such as removal of Reg Q interest-rate ceiling and alternative pricing schemes beyond the fixed-rate mortgage. The national goal for S&Ls was to provide housing finance, and they did it without managing interest-rate risk. Because deposit insurers were not pricing interest-rate risk and regulators were not supervising it, why should S&L managers worry about it? Thus, for almost two decades (1966–1982), interest-rate risk eroded S&L real net worth. Thanks to government guarantees, however, numerous zombie S&Ls were able to continue to exist.

Although bank deregulation started with DIDMCA in 1980, it affected thrifts more than banks because thrifts gained additional asset powers at both the federal and state levels. In certain states, such as Texas and California, liberal lending powers were granted; at the federal level, adverse tax incentives fueled speculation in real estate. Mismanagement of credit risk on top of mismanagement of interest-rate risk in an economy with falling energy and farm prices were the ingredients for a disaster. In addition, fraud, abuse, and misconduct were also widespread. The reaction of thrift regulators and deposit insurers was to practice capital forbearance and to understate the seriousness of the problem. Congress also refused to recognize the underlying crisis and did not want to tamper with the subsidies associated with housing finance and deposit insurance. In addition, some lawmakers, such as the "Keating five," violated their duty to taxpayers and worked for special interest groups.

Chapter Summary

"You can pay me now or you can pay me later." The savings-and-loan mess has demonstrated that paying later can be very expensive—$160 billion plus interest. The costs of the numerous bank failures of the 1980s and early 1990s have been more subtle. Understanding the moral-hazard aspect of deposit insurance as a government guarantee captures a major theme of this chapter and provides a framework for analyzing the S&L and banking crises. Viewing deposit insurance as a surety, or trilateral performance bond, makes risk endogenous, highlights incentive conflict, and focuses on optimal loss-control activity. Alternative bilateral, but discredited, views of deposit insurance are the casualty-insurance model and the option-pricing model.

Incorporating explicit and implicit agency costs into the nexus of the deposit-insurance contract highlights the opportunity losses arising from conflicts or incentive incompatibilities in four key principal-agent (monitoring) relationships: (1) taxpayers monitoring elected and appointed government officials, (2) Congress monitoring deposit insurers and regulators, (3) deposit insurers and regulators monitoring managers of insured depositories, and (4) bank shareholders and other stakeholders monitoring managers of insured institutions. Distorted incentives in these relations provide keys to understanding why deposit insurance broke down and what reforms are needed. Deposit-insurance reform needs to be grounded in accountability and incentive-compatible contracts that do not sacrifice the benefits to society of deposit insurance. The benefits include confidence in the financial system, fair treatment of small depositors, and the promotion of efficiency in financial intermediation and risk taking. Elimination of incentive incompatibilities associated with the goals of housing finance and deposit insurance is difficult because of the stubbornness of subsidies and the difficulty of making Congress accountable for backdoor spending.

The FDIC cannot be judged by its initials because its businesses also include bank regulation and supervision and the resolution of problem and failed banks. Although the FDIC has several ways of resolving bank failures, each of the methods is some variation of either a deposit payoff or a purchase-and-assumption (P&A) transaction. The inability or unwillingness of "faithful agents" to close institutions when their economic net worths are exhausted means that taxpayers, as principals, can get stuck with the mismanagement, mistakes, and dishonesty of managers of insured depositories. The prompt-corrective-action provision of FDICIA is a first step toward a more optimal closure rule. An effective closure rule, however, must be based on economic net worth, and that depends on the ability to measure the market value of a bank's equity in a timely and accurate fashion. Until 1993, the explicit pricing of deposit insurance was not risk-based. Nevertheless, the FDIC's total risk premium (explicit fees plus implicit charges) has always been risk-related. This implicit pricing is achieved through the bank-examination process and various supervisory and regulatory constraints that act as taxes. The FDIC depends on its sister agencies, the OCC, the Fed, and various state banking agencies, to police banks that it does not monitor directly.

Key Words, Concepts, and Acronyms

- Asset liquidation
- Asset quality
- Bank examination
- Bank Insurance Fund (BIF)
- Book-value or historical-cost accounting
- Bridge bank
- Cash-flow model of FDIC
- Casualty-insurance model

- Classified assets (substandard, doubtful, loss)
- Closure rule
- Contracts (incentive-compatible)
- Credit union model of deposit insurance
- Deposit-insurance contract (as a nexus of relations)
- Deposit-Insurance Fund (DIF)
- Deposit Insurance National Bank (DINB)
- Deposit payoff
- Deposit transfer
- Economic insolvency/failure
- Economic net worth
- Endogenous risk

- Failure-resolution methods
- Federal Deposit Insurance Corporation (FDIC)
- FDIC Improvement Act (FDICIA, 1991)
- Federal Savings and Loan Insurance Corporation (FSLIC)
- Federal safety net
- Financial Institutions Reform, Recovery, and Enforcement Act (FIRREA, 1989)
- Forbearance
- Fraud, abuse, and misconduct
- Government guarantee
- Hidden action
- Hidden information

- Implicit pricing
- Incentive conflict
- Loss-control instruments
- Loss-sharing
- Market-value accounting
- Moral hazard
- Open-bank assistance
- Option-pricing model
- Principal-agent relations
- Prompt corrective action (PCA)
- Purchase-and-assumption (P&A) transaction
- Savings-and-loan (S&L) mess
- Savings Association Insurance Fund (SAIF)
- Surety (trilateral performance bond)

Review/Discussion Questions

1. Explain how the statement "Pay me now or pay me latter" applies to the crisis in deposit insurance. How much was the payment that U.S. taxpayers had to make for bailing out the S&L industry? Do we know the true costs? Why or why not? If we don't know, when will we know? What can we say about the costs to taxpayers of the commercial bank failures of the 1980s and early 1990s?
2. Carefully distinguish among the following models of deposit insurance: (*a*) casualty-insurance model, (*b*) option-pricing model, and (*c*) surety, or trilateral-performance-bond model.
3. What are the components of the Kane [1995] stationary-state model of the FDIC's cash flow?
   a. What are the four components of the FDIC annual cash flow? What has happened to this cash flow over the FDIC's history?
   b. What loss-control instruments are available to the FDIC? Which ones are also available to the OCC? The Fed? The SEC? State banking agencies?
   c. What are the linkages between the instruments in (*b*) and the cash flow in (*a*)?
   d. Describe the FDIC's goal function. How would it differ if deposit insurance were in the private sector?
4. Why did the chairman of the SEC say that bank financial statements should have at the top of them, "Once upon a time?" What kind of accounting does he say banks need? If we had this kind of accounting, would an effective closure rule be possible?
5. What are the various failure-resolution methods available to the FDIC and which two form the foundation for the others?
6. What are the four basic functions of an asset liquidator? What did the GAO have to say about the FDIC's asset-liquidation performance?
7. Distinguish between the explicit and implicit components of FDIC pricing. When and why was explicit pricing introduced?
8. What has happened to the deposit-insurance ceiling since 1933? What should the ceiling be? Should depositors be permitted to manipulate accounts to exceed the ceiling?
9. What are the hidden actions and hidden information that deposit insurers and bank and thrift regulators need to uncover? Describe the principal-agent relations and problems and how they might be solved.
10. What role have fraud, abuse, and misconduct played in thrift and bank failures? What can be done about this?

11. What is the primary cause of bank failure? What other factors are important, and what weaknesses in loan portfolio management practices contribute to bank failures?

12. Describe the role that private insurance has played in the development of the deposit-insurance system for credit unions. Is it a good model for insurance reform for banks and thrifts? Explain and discuss this.

13. What are the weaknesses in deposit insurance and how can these shortcomings be corrected? What reforms have been implemented during the 1990s?

14. What was the "real reason" Sprague gave for doing the four bailouts described in this chapter and in his book? Discuss and evaluate this reason and the stress that bank regulators were under during the 1980s and early 1990s.

15. In a 1963 speech dedicating the FDIC's headquarters building, Wright Patman, then chairman of the House Banking and Currency Committee said,

> ...I think we should have more bank failures. The record of the last several years of almost no failures and, finally last year, no bank failure, is to me a danger signal that we have gone too far in the direction of bank safety.

Discuss what Patman's reaction might be to the thrift crisis and the bank failures of the 1980s and the early 1990s. Did we go too far in the direction of *lack* of bank safety during this period?

16. Establish and discuss fully the principal-agent relations and problems associated with the following groups: taxpayers, Congress, deposit insurers, bank and thrift regulators, managers of insured depositories, and shareholders and other stakeholders in insured depositories. What is an incentive-compatible contract? What are the subsidies associated with housing finance and deposit insurance?

17. Describe and explain the following aspects of the S&L mess: (*a*) economic/financial, (*b*) deposit insurance/regulatory, and (*c*) legislative/political. Did deregulation cause the S&L crisis? Did the crooks or bad apples cause the S&L crisis? If not, what's the real cause?

18. What are the benefits to society of deposit insurance? How can deposit insurance be reformed without losing the benefits?

19. On January 1, 1991, the governor of Rhode Island ordered 45 credit unions and small banks closed because the private deposit insurance company that insured them had its reserves depleted by the failure of a small Providence bank. Does this experience mean that private deposit insurance cannot work? Discuss this.

Problems

1. If a troubled bank has $90 million in nonclassified risk assets, $10 million in substandard assets, $5 million in doubtful assets, and $3 million in loss assets, what would be the FDIC's estimate of the loss on assets? How confident would you be of this estimate?

2. Using Table 16-1, find the FDIC's annual cash flow given the following information:

Premium income from assessments = $2,851,561,000
U.S. Treasury Obligation = $7,250,000,000
Average yield on investments = 11.8%
Other revenue = $127,796,000
Administrative and operating expense = $219,581,000
Merger assistance losses and expenses = $178,339,000
Provision for insurance losses (actual) = $4,448,055,000
Provision for insurance losses (unresolved) = $7,685,033,000
Nonrecoverable insurance expenses = $472,340,000

3. Given the cash flow from the previous problem, what was the ending balance in the FDIC's insurance fund, if the beginning balance was $13.2 billion? Was this year good or bad for the FDIC?

Selected References

Acharya, S., and J.-F. Dreyfus. [1989]. "Optimal Bank Reorganization Policies and the Pricing of Federal Deposit Insurance." *Journal of Finance* 44 (December), pp. 1313–1333.

Akerlof, G. A., and P. M. Romber. [1993]. "Looting: The Economic Underworld of Bankruptcy for Profit." *Brookings Papers on Economic Activity* 2, pp. 1–60.

Allen, L., and A. Saunders. [1993]. "Forbearance and Valuation of Deposit Insurance as a Callable Put." *Journal of Banking and Finance* 17 (June), pp. 629–643.

Altman, Edward I., Robert B. Avery, Robert A. Eisenbeis, and Joseph F. Sinkey, Jr. [1981]. *Application of Classification Techniques in Business, Banking, and Finance.* Greenwich, CT: JAI Press.

Atkinson, Bill. [1990]. "Credit Unions: The Failure Rate Increases and the Reasons Are Debated." *American Banker* (September 4), p. 6.

Avery, Robert B., and Terrence M. Belton. [1987]. "A Comparison of Risk-Based Capital and Risk-Based Deposit Insurance." *Economic Review* (Quarter 4), Federal Reserve Bank of Cleveland, pp. 20–30.

Bank Failure: An Evaluation of the Factors Contributing to the Failure of National Banks. [1988]. Washington, DC: Office of the Comptroller of the Currency (June).

Barth, James R. [1991]. *The Great Savings and Loan Debacle.* Washington, DC: AEI Press.

Barth, James R., Philip F. Bartholomew, and Michael G. Bradley. [1990]. "Determinants of Thrift Resolution Costs." *Journal of Finance,* pp. 731–754.

Belton, Willie J., Jr., and Richard J. Cebula. [1995]. "A Brief Note on Thrift Failures: A More Rigorous Analysis of Causal Factors." *Southern Economic Journal* 62, p. 247.

Black, F., M. Miller, and R. Posner. [1978]. "An Approach to the Regulation of Bank Holding Companies." *Journal of Business* 51 (July), pp. 379–412.

Black, F., and M. Scholes. [1973]. "The Pricing of Options and Corporate Liabilities." *Journal of Political Economy* (May-June), pp. 637–659.

Boot, A., and A. Thakor. [1993]. "Self-Interested Bank Regulation." *American Economic Review* 83 (May), pp. 206–212.

Bovenzi, John F., and Arthur J. Murton. [1988]. "Resolution Costs of Bank Failures." *FDIC Banking Review* (Fall), pp. 1–13.

Burstein, Melvin L. [1995]. "Is Deposit Insurance the Bankers' Faustian Bargain?" *Fedgazette* 7 (January) pp. 14–15.

Buser, Stephen A., Andrew H. Chen, and Edward J. Kane. [1981a]. "Federal Deposit Insurance, Regulatory Policy, and Optimal Bank Capital." *Journal of Finance* 35 (March), pp. 51–60.

Buser, Stephen A., Andrew H. Chen, and Edward J. Kane. [1981b]. "Federal Deposit Insurance and Its Implications for the Management of Commercial Banks." Paper presented at the 1981 Eastern Finance Association Meetings, Ohio State University.

Callahan's Credit Union Report. [1989]. Washington, DC: Callahan & Associates, Inc.

Cole, Rebel A., and Jeffery W. Gunther. [1994]. "When Are Failing Banks Closed?" *Federal Reserve Bank of Dallas Financial Industry Studies* 45 (December), pp. 1–12.

Combating Fraud, Abuse, and Misconduct in the Nation's Financial Institutions: Current Federal Efforts Are Inadequate. [1988]. Seventy-Second Report by the Committee on Government Operations, Washington, DC: U.S. Government Printing Office.

Edwards, Franklin R., and Frederic S. Michkin. [1995]. "The Decline of Traditional Banking: Implications for Financial Stability and Regulatory Policy." *Economic Policy Review* 1 (July) pp. 27–45.

Feldstein, Martin. [1991]. "Don't Underestimate Banks' Capital Value." *The Wall Street Journal* (February 21), op-ed page.

General Accounting Office. [1988]. *Failed Banks: FDIC's Asset Liquidation Operations.* Report to the Chairman, Committee on Banking, Housing, and Urban Affairs, U.S. Senate (September).

Gorton, Gary, and Richard Rosen. [1995]. "Corporate Control, Portfolio Choice, and the Decline of Banking." *Journal of Finance* (December), pp. 1377–1420.

Harrison, Patricia, and Wade R. Ragas. [1995]. "Financial Variables Contributing to Savings and Loan Failures from 1980–1989." *Review of Financial Economics* 4 (March), p. 197.

Houston, J., and C. James. [1993]. "Management and Organizational Changes in Banking: A Comparison of Regulatory Intervention with Private Creditor Actions in Nonbank Firms." *Carnegie-Rochester Conference Series on Public Policy* 38, pp. 143–178.

James C. [1991]. "The Losses Realized in Bank Failures." *Journal of Finance* 46 (September), pp. 1223–1242.

Jensen, M. C., and W. H. Meckling. [1975]. "Theory of the Firm: Managerial Behavior, Agency Costs, and Ownership Structure." *Journal of Financial Economics* 3 (June), pp. 305–360.

Kane, Edward J. [1981]. "Deregulation, Savings and Loan Diversification, and the Flow of Housing Finance." In Federal Home Loan Bank of San Francisco, Savings and Loan Asset Management under Deregulation (San Francisco), pp. 81–109.

———. [1985]. *The Gathering Crisis in Federal Deposit Insurance: Origins, Evolution, and Possible Reforms.* Cambridge, MA: MIT Press.

———. [1986]. "Appearance and Reality in Deposit Insurance: The Case for Reform." *Journal of Banking and Finance* 10 (June), pp. 175–188.

———. [1989a]. "Changing Incentives Facing Financial-Services Regulators." *Journal of Financial Services Research* (September), pp. 265–274.

———. [1989b]. *The S&L Insurance Mess: How Did It Happen?* Washington, DC: Urban Institute Press.

———. [1990]. "Principal-Agent Problems in S&L Salvage." *Journal of Finance* (July), pp. 755–764.

———. [1991]. "Econometric Estimates of the 1986–1989 Time Profile of Taxpayer Losses in the S&L Insurance Mess." Final project report, Congressional Budget Office, Washington, DC (February 18).

———. [1995]. "Three Paradigms for the Role of Capitalization Requirements in Insured Financial Institutions." *Journal of Banking and Finance* (June), pp. 431–459

Kane, E. J., J. Hickman, and A. Burger. [1993]. "A Plan for Private-Federal Deposit-Insurance Partnership." *Center for Credit Union Research,* University of Wisconsin-Madison.

Kareken, J. [1983]. "Deposit Insurance Reform; or Deregulation is the Cart, not the Horse." *Federal Reserve Bank of Minneapolis Quarterly Review* 7 (Spring), pp. 1–9.

Keeley, M. C. [1990]. "Deposit Insurance, Risk, and Market Power in Banking." *American Economic Review* 80 (December), pp. 1183–1200.

Klinkerman, Steven. "The Thrift Bailout: Five Years Later" (a five-part series). *American Banker* (August 8–12).

Levine, Daniel S. [1995]. "It's Bottom of the Ninth for Savings and Loan Industry." *San Francisco Business Times* 10 (November), p. 21.

Marcus, A., and I. Shaked. [1984]. "The Valuation of FDIC Deposit Insurance Using Option-Pricing Estimates." *Journal of Money, Credit, and Banking* 16 (November), pp. 446–460.

Meredith, Robyn. [1994]. "Ultimate Tab for the S&L Crisis Pegged at $150 Billion, Plus Interest." *American Banker* (August 8).

Merton, R. C. [1977]. "An Analytical Derivation of the Cost of Deposit Insurance Loan Guarantees: An Application of Modern Option Pricing Theory." *Journal of Banking and Finance* 1 (June), pp. 3–11.

Merton, R. C. [1978]. "On the Cost of Deposit Insurance When There Are Surveillance Costs." *Journal of Business* 51 (July), pp. 439–452.

Merton, R. C., and Z. Bodie. [1992]. "On the Management of Financial Guarantees." *Financial Management* 21 (Winter), 87–109.

Office of the Comptroller of the Currency. [1988]. *Bank Failure: An Evaluation of the Factors Contributing to the Failure of National Banks* (June). Washington, DC.

Pennachi, G. C. [1987]. A Re-examination of the Over- (or Under-) Pricing of Deposit Insurance." *Journal of Money, Credit and Banking* 19 (August), pp. 340–360.

Rehm, Barbara A. [1990]. "Credit Unions: Private Insurance a Model for Troubled Bank Fund?" *American Banker* (October), p. 6.

Ronn, E., and A. Verma. [1986]. "Pricing Risk-adjusted Deposit Insurance: An Options-Based Model." *Journal of Finance* 41 (September), pp. 871–895.

Roth, Michael. [1994]. "'Too-big-to-fail' and the Stability of the Banking System: Some Insights from Foreign Countries." *Business Economics* 29 (October), p. 43.

Saltz, Ira S. [1995]. "The Impact of Federal Deposit Insurance on Savings and Loan Failures: A Comment." *Southern Economics Journal* 62, p. 253.

Saunders, Anthony, Elizabeth Strock, and Nicholas Travlos. [1990]. "Ownership Structure, Deregulation, and Bank Risk-Taking," *Journal of Finance* (June), pp. 643–654.

Schlesinger, H., and E. Venezian. [1986]. "Insurance Markets with Loss-Prevention Activity: Profits, Market Structure, and Consumer Welfare." *Rand Journal of Economics* 17 (July), pp. 227–238.

Scott, K. E., and T. Mayer. [1971]. "Risk and Regulation in Banking: Some Proposals for Deposit Insurance Reform." *Stanford Law Review* 23 (May), pp. 857–902.

Sharpe, W. F. [1978]. "Bank Capital Adequacy, Deposit Insurance, and Security Values." *Journal of Financial and Quantitative Analysis* 13 (November), pp. 701–718.

Shiers, Alden F. [1994]. "Deposit Insurance and Banking System Risk: Some Empirical Evidence." *Quarterly Review of Economics and Finance* 34 (December) p. 347.

Sinkey, Joseph F., Jr. [1975]. "A Multivariate Statistical Analysis of the Characteristics of Problem Banks." *Journal of Finance* (March), pp. 21–26.

———. [1978]. "Identifying Problem Banks: How Do the Banking Authorities Measure a Bank's Risk Exposure?" *Journal of Money, Credit, and Banking* (May), pp. 184–193.

———. [1979]. *Problem and Failed Institutions in the Commercial Banking Industry.* Greenwich, CT: JAI Press.

———. [1987]. "Review of *Bailout: An Insider's Account of Bank Failures and Rescues* by Irvine H. Sprague." *Journal of Banking and Finance* (March, 1987), pp. 178–182.

Sinkey, Joseph F., Jr., and David A. Carter. [1997]. "The Derivatives Activities of U.S. Commercial Banks: Why Big Banks Do and Small Banks Don't," Working Paper. The University of Georgia.

Smith, C. W., Jr., and J. Warner. [1979]. "On Financial Contracting: An Analysis of Bond Covenants." *Journal of Financial Economics* 7 (June), pp. 117–161.

Sprague, Irvine H. [1986]. *Bailout: An Insider's Account of Bank Failures and Rescues.* New York: Basic Books.

Thomas, Paul, and Prentiss B. Reed, Sr. [1977]. "Salvaging and Use of Salvors." In *Adjustment of Property Losses.* 4th ed. New York: McGraw-Hill.

Thomson, James. [1992]. "Modeling the Bank Regulators' Closure Option: A Two-Step Logit Regression Approach." *Journal of Financial Services Research* (May), pp. 5–23.

United States General Accounting Office. [1988]. *Failed Banks: FDIC's Asset Liquidation Operations.* Report to the Chairman, Committee on Banking, Housing, and Urban Affairs, U.S. Senate (September).

Wheelock, David C., and Subal C. Kumbhakar. [1995]. "Which Banks Choose Deposit Insurance? Evidence of Adverse Selection and Moral Hazard in a Voluntary Insurance System: Study of Kansas Banking Insurance System." *Journal of Money, Credit and Banking* 27 (February), p. 186.

"Where Is The Safety Net in Japan?" [1995]. *JEI Report* 44 (December).

White, Larry. [1991]. *The S&L Debacle: Public Policy Lessons for Bank and Thrift Regulation.* New York: Oxford University Press.

Williams, C. A., Jr., and R. M. Heins. [1985]. *Risk Management and Insurance.* 5th ed. New York: McGraw Hill.

Zakaria, Tabassum. [1996]. "Thrift Study Shows No Big Failure Threat." *Reuter Business Report* (February 29).

ETHICS IN BANKING AND THE FINANCIAL-SERVICES INDUSTRY (FSI)

Contents

LEARNING OBJECTIVES

■ To understand ethics and how society uses ethics

■ To understand the concern about lack of ethical behavior in banking and the FSI

■ To understand unethical behavior in banking and the FSI as fraud and negligent misrepresentation

■ To understand that value maximization requires ethical behavior

■ To understand markets in terms of efficiency, failure, and information costs

■ To understand the role of ethics in information

■ To distinguish between agency in law and in the theory of the firm

CHAPTER THEME

Ethics is the discipline dealing with what is good and bad and with **moral duty** and obligation. Moral, institutional, and legal guidelines determine how societies use ethics. From a pragmatic view, legal guidelines and the role of government (deposit insurance) are important determinants of how people behave. The concern about lack of ethical behavior in the FSI in the 1980s and the 1990s resulted in a call from both academicians and practitioners for a rededication to ethics. Unethical behavior in banking and the FSI manifests itself mainly as **fraud** and **negligent misrepresentation.** The roles of ethics in information and the **disclosure of private information** play key roles in resolving these problems. If we view ethics as **conflict resolution,** the **principal-agent model** provides a framework for resolving ethical conflicts. The concepts of **free markets, market efficiency, market failure,** and common-law definitions of fraud and negligent misrepresentation provide analytical foundations for this chapter. The analysis addresses and analyzes the ethical dilemmas facing bankers and their competitors in the FSI, with particular emphasis on the role of ethics in bank regulation, deposit insurance, and the S&L mess. Although a good reputation is an important intangible asset to any enterprise, it is paramount for banks and other financial-services firms, which depend more heavily on trust and confidence for their business.

KEY CONCEPTS, IDEAS, AND TERMS

- Character
- Common law
- Conflict resolution
- Disclosure of private information
- Discrimination (ordinary use)
- Disinformation
- Economic discrimination
- Ethics
- Fraud (financial)

• Free markets	• Market failure	• Opportunistic behavior
• Incentives	• Moral behavior	• Opportunity cost
• Information	• Moral duty	• Principal-agent model
• Market efficiency	• Negligent misrepresentation	• Role of government

*The greatest responsibility for our national welfare does not rest with
statutes carved in stone but with the principles, conscience, and morality
of the individuals that constitute this generation.*[1]

INTRODUCTION: WHAT REALLY MATTERS MORE THAN ANYTHING IS CHARACTER

On October 8, 1995, Dennis Weatherstone, retired chairman of J. P. Morgan & Co.,
spoke at the Institute of International Finance in Washington, DC. His topic was
"Reflections on the Business of Banking." His conclusion about the key to success
in the business of banking was,[2]

> What really matters more than anything is **character.** The character of our people de-
> termines the *quality* of our institutions, which means that *trust* and *confidence* in our
> *ethical standard* is paramount. True character is often revealed under pressure. The mo-
> ments when I learned who could be trusted to come through in times of crisis are some
> of the most memorable of my life.
>
> After 49 years I know that talking about character and writing down principles
> is okay, but it's what you do that finally counts. (p. 4; emphasis mine)

On balance, unethical human behavior is the major impediment to the trustworthy, healthy, and efficient functioning of business enterprises.[3] As bankers, regulators, and deposit insurers move into the twenty-first century they need to prove to
the world that all the talk about character and ethics is more than just rhetoric. Actions speak louder than words.

WHAT IS ETHICS?

Webster's (tenth) gives the following definition of ethic or ethics (emphasis mine):

1. The *discipline* dealing with what is *good* or *bad* and with *moral duty* and *obligation*

2a. A set of *moral principles* or values

2b. A theory or system of *moral values*

2c. The principles of *conduct* governing an individual or group

---

[1] The epigram, as reported by McCarthy [1996], is attributed to Sol Wachtler, a former judge who, not by his
own choice, spent some time in a no-frills jail.

[2] Until cash-flow lending and asset-based lending became lenders' *modus operandi,* banks made loans on the
basis of character. Because good citizens stand ready to pay their debts, this technique was, and still is, good
business practice.

[3] Bear and Maldonado-Bear [1994], among others, take this view.

For our purposes, let's focus on ethics as the principles of conduct governing participants in the financial-services industry (FSI), including bankers, customers, regulators, deposit insurers, and any other interested parties.

In *The Economist as Preacher,* Stigler [1982] adds these insights on ethics: The ethical person is "one whose principles of right conduct are adopted independently of [the] consequences" (p. 25, insert mine). In his view, ethics "is a set of rules with respect to dealings with other persons, rules which in general prohibit behavior which is myopically self-serving, or which imposes large costs on others and small gains to oneself" (p. 35).

The Philosophical Roots of Ethics

Religions and cultures of the world provide philosophical foundations for ethical behavior. For example, the golden rule of Christianity is, "Do unto others as you would have them do unto you." One of the 10 perfections of Buddhism is "ethicality" (morality). The Japanese concept of *kyosei* means living and working together for the common good. The notion of human dignity captures the sacredness of each person as an end and not as the means of fulfilling another's objectives.

Ethics as Conflict Resolution

Viewing ethics as conflict resolution, French and Granrose [1995] suggest this practical definition of ethics for the business world: "Ethics consists of a set of normative guidelines directed toward resolving conflicts of interest, so as to enhance societal well-being" (p. 8). Given the importance of the principal-agent model as a theme for this book, the view of ethics as conflict resolution fits nicely in this chapter. In general, principals use social norms as a way of protecting themselves. More specifically, they use incentive contracting and monitoring to protect themselves from the actions (conduct) of agents. Box 17-1 shows some examples of the kinds of unethical behavior that has occurred in the FSI, and that call for conflict resolution.

What Is versus What Ought to Be

Bear and Maldonado-Bear [1994] define ethics or ethical principles to mean "statements that humans make about what their conduct (actions), or the conduct of others, *ought to be,* which is to say, expressions of opinion as to how persons *ought to* behave" (p. 1). Economists (e.g., Friedman [1953]) make the distinction between positive economics (what is) and normative economics (what ought to be). Ethics makes a similar type distinction. Bear and Maldonado-Bear ([1994], pp. 1–2) explain it this way: Conduct refers to what we do whereas ethics refers to an appraisal of that conduct, or what we ought to do. They link conduct (the *is*) and ethics (the *ought*) together to define *morality* as the relation between conduct and ethics. In this context, they see an evaluation of human conduct (an ethical standard) as "good" if it is morally desirable and "bad" if it is morally undesirable.

Regarding good (right) or bad (wrong), Plato argued that an objective basis existed for distinguishing between the two:[4]

> . . . there is a true right and wrong, which is a universal principle for all times. We do not make values or truth; we find them; they do not alter with races, places or fortune. Thus there are two worlds; the world of absolute beauty, and the world of opinion, with its conventions and delusions. This is the root of dualism in Plato's philosophy . . .

---

[4] From Plato (427–347 B.C.), *The Republic* in translations edited by Jowett [1937].

BOX 17-1

EXAMPLES OF UNETHICAL BEHAVIOR IN BANKING AND THE FSI

- ☹ The S&L mess cost U.S. taxpayers $160 billion (excluding interest)
- ☹ Fraud and insider abuse contributed to one-third of bank failures from 1986 to 1988
- ☹ Missing trader at the center of fiasco that tumbled Barings Bank (England)
- ☹ Hubris and ambition in Orange County: Robert Citron's story
- ☹ Prudential Insurance Co. of America pays a record $35 million in fines and sets up $100-million restitution program because it misled customers throughout the United States
- ☹ Bank of Japan admits to false report
- ☹ Senate's reprimand of Cranston climaxes "Keating Five" scandal
- ☹ Bankers Trust now facing RICO charges as P&G ups the ante in its derivatives suit
- ☹ Funny business you know? Lure people into that calm and then just totally f—— 'em
- ☹ Here's the positive side: I've burned my clients so much that it's going to take me four years to trade them out of the loss
- ☹ What Bankers Trust can do for Sony and IBM is get in the middle and rip them off
- ☹ Tricky ledgers: Accounting flimflam and wishful thinking pervade the financial system
- ☹ Good connections put hedge fund in business but a bad bet sank it
- ☹ Jim Guy Tucker, governor of Arkansas, guilty of fraud and conspiracy (Whitewater affair)
- ☹ E. F. Hutton & Company pleads guilty to 2,000 counts of mail and wire fraud
- ☹ Fleet settles loan-bias suit; will pay $4 million, monitor staff
- ☹ Peat Marwick settles with FDIC, RTC, and OTS for $186.5 million
- ☹ New unit of KPMG Peat Marwick offers to audit corporation's ethics (calls its service "ethics vulnerability risk assessment")
- ☹ "Padding" bank loan rates: Some lenders give an extra commission to mortgage-loan officers when they are able to charge a customer an "overage" above the firm's going rate for such a loan (not illegal per se but likely to be discriminatory)

Plato as a modern-day banker would say that it is truly wrong for providers of financial services to discriminate on the basis of race, religion, sex, or age.

Economic Decision Making and Discrimination in Ordinary Usage

Because the kind of discrimination that disturbed Plato and that disturbs ethical human beings today is the way in which most people think about discrimination (i.e., prejudging), we can call it **discrimination in ordinary usage.** It is imperative to distinguish between discrimination in ordinary usage, which is wrong, and certain kinds of economic decision making (e.g., attempts by lenders to distinguish among risky borrowers through credit scoring). Economic decision making is based on **opportunity cost** or the value of an alternative foregone action—the next-best alternative. **Economic discrimination** is, in fact, the heart of financial management. It is not discrimination in the sense of prejudging but in the sense of differentiating, discerning, distinguishing, or separating on the basis of economic and financial characteristics. The key point is that this kind of economic decision making can be justified on the basis of opportunity cost, one of the most fundamental concepts of economics.[5]

---

[5] Economists distinguish between *private* opportunity cost in terms of private benefits of a foregone action and *social* opportunity cost in terms of a much wider range of foregone benefits.

In banking, for example, lenders attempt to separate good borrowers from bad borrowers. Failure to make such distinctions, for whatever reason, can lead to economic ruin. In fact, mismanaged credit risk has been the major cause of bank failure. If a particular class of borrowers cannot obtain credit and that class happens to be of a certain race, religion, sex, or age, then that decision is not discrimination as most people know it in ordinary usage. In contrast, if lenders prejudge borrowers and will not lend to borrowers of a certain race, religion, sex, or age, then that behavior is discrimination in ordinary usage. It is unethical and in the United States a violation of equal-credit-opportunity laws.

WHY STUDY ETHICS IN BANKING AND THE FSI?

The two overriding themes of this book are that banks operate in the financial-services industry (FSI) and that banks are still the kingpins of the FSI. Bear and Maldonado-Bear [1994] expand on these themes and provide the linkage to ethics. They write,

> *Commercial banking* is the cornerstone of America's financial system. How it is set up and how it operates are matters not only of enormous economic significance but also of legal, political, social, and *ethical significance*. How American banking fares determines in some consequential degree how every American citizen fares—as well as a sizable number of people living in other nations. (p. 239, emphasis mine)

Although this chapter focuses on the "ethical significance" of commercial banking for the United States and the world, the analysis cannot ignore the economic, legal, political, and social aspects of banking in the FSI (i.e., the analysis cannot be conducted in an ethical vacuum).

If the shortest book in the world, as some cynics would claim, is *Ethics for Lawyers,* then the second-shortest one might be *Ethics for Bankers and Their Regulators.* Lawyers, bankers, and regulators, who have been known to "sleep together" (not in the biblical sense), are the major characters in this second shortest book. Hyperbole for sure, but it gets your attention. If our national welfare depends on ethics,[6] and if "what really matters more than anything is character," we need to study ethics. This chapter focuses on the role of ethics in shaping behavior in banking and the financial-services industry (FSI).

The Ethical Crisis in Banking and the FSI

Box 17-1 shows that one has to look neither far nor wide to see the need for the rebirth of ethics in banking and the FSI. The image of banking and the FSI around the world, but especially in the United States, has been tarnished in recent years. Clearly, a need for the rebirth of ethics exists. This chapter contributes to filling that void.

Good Deeds, Bad Deeds, and the Effects of Negative Reporting

Do you see the glass with 50 percent of its space occupied with liquid as half-full or half-empty? According to an old adage, the optimist sees the glass as half-full

---

[6] The recent concern about ethics is not confined to the United States. As Carmichael [1995] writes, "Ethics used to be a rare word in British public life" (p. 11).

whereas the pessimist sees it as half-empty. A clever answer to this pseudo-psychological query is: It depends on whether I'm drinking or pouring—wine.

Researchers need to be concerned about how data are distributed. When data are normally distributed, they form a bell-shaped pattern. The symptom of this shape is that one-half of the observations are above the mean and one-half below it. As you get further from the mean in either direction, you get better or worse observations. The direction of better or worse depends on what you are measuring. For example, businesses want higher earnings; golfers strive for lower scores; students and their parents want higher grades and higher SAT/ACT scores; and social workers and concerned citizens want lower teen-pregnancy rates.[7]

Let's consider how measures of ethical behavior (e.g., honesty), kindness, and, in general, good deeds might be distributed. Although I have no hard evidence to back me up, I conjecture that the disposition to perform these acts is distributed normally, like intelligence (for which evidence does exist). On average, most people exhibit these good qualities. Some people qualify as Mother Teresas who love, share, and care more than mere mortals; others are at the other end of the spectrum: They kill, rape, rob, and cheat. When you watch TV, listen to the radio, or read newspapers, what do you get? You get overreporting of negative stories and underreporting of good news.

Is banking, and the FSI in general, getting a bum rap because of negative reporting? That might be part of the answer. Nevertheless, where there's smoke, there's almost sure to be fire. As Box 17-1 shows, enough evidence exists to suggest that the lack of ethical behavior in banking and the FSI is for real. Moreover, the concern about ethics in both the FSI and academia is *prima facie* evidence that something is wrong.[8] Business schools are preaching ethics more strongly and managers of financial-services firms (FSFs) are training their employees to practice it. To illustrate, many business schools, especially in their MBA programs, are beefing up ethics in the curriculum. In the real world, the American Bankers Association has published a how-to booklet entitled "Developing or Revising a Bank Code of Ethics." And Chemical Bank (acquired by Chase Manhattan in 1996) required all employees to read and sign a code of ethics, whereas vice presidents had to complete a two-day seminar on ethical decision making. The lack of ethical behavior in banking and the FSI, however, does not appear to be systemic in the sense of a conspiracy by all segments of the industry and its participants.

AN INTERNATIONAL CODE OF ETHICS FOR BUSINESS: THE CAUX PRINCIPLES

The first international code of ethics for business was established by the Caux Round Table.[9] Its purpose is to set "a world standard against which business behavior can be measured" and in the process to establish a yardstick by which

---

[7] If you are a pregnant teen, you might not want to apply for public assistance in Gem County, Idaho, because you could get arrested and charged with fornication. Hardy [1996] reports that the county's strategy is to haul pregnant girls and their boyfriends into court in an attempt to control welfare costs.

[8] Although there has been a long-standing interest in business ethics (e.g., Cicero, 106–43 BC), the recent surge in interest is captured by the following events of the 1980s: the founding of two journals: *Journal of Business Ethics* and *Business Ethics,* and the establishment of the European Business Ethics Network (EBEN).

[9] For details, see www.bath.ac.uk/Centers/Ethical/Papers/caux.htm. This section draws on information from this website.

individual companies can write their own ethical codes. The basic principles for this foundation are two ethical ideals: *kyosei* and human dignity, both of which were explained above in the section on the philosophical roots of ethics. The preamble of the Caux Principles contends that laws and market forces are necessary but insufficient guides for conduct. In addition, it affirms the necessity for moral values in business decision making, arguing that without such values stable business relationships and a sustainable world community are impossible.

Table 17-1 lists the seven principles established by the Caux Round Table. These principles apply to the following stakeholders of a business:

- Customers
- Employees
- Owners/investors
- Suppliers
- Competitors
- Communities

This stakeholder view of a business parallels Jensen and Meckling's [1976] theory of the firm as a nexus of contracts. This managerial perspective stresses the importance of managers getting incentives "right," meaning "compatible," across the stakeholders of any enterprise. Incentive-compatible contracts accomplish this task. Kane [1996e] says that incentive compatibility exists when a set of contracts (explicit and implicit) designed to promote the common good leaves individual stakeholders unable to gain an advantage from other members of the group, even if they violate the rules of the game.

Maximizing Value and the Role of Ethics

Chapter 4 stressed the importance of managing value and stressed that firms need to add value creators and eliminate value destroyers in order to maximize value. The linkage with ethics is that firms cannot maximize long-run values if they engage in unethical behavior. Although they can earn short-run excess profits by such behavior, market and civil penalties ensure that the profits are not sustained once bad faith is revealed.[10] Chambers and Lacey ([1996], p. 93), for example, conclude that shareholder wealth maximization serves as a conduit of ethics rather than a net determinant of ethical behavior. Markets can price ethics just as they can price anything else. Stakeholders (e.g, owners, customers, employees, etc.) serve as regulators by punishing rogue firms and rewarding ethical firms. Whereas a good reputation is an important intangible asset to any enterprise, it is paramount for banks and other financial-services firms, which depend more heavily on trust and confidence for their business.

Social Responsibility of Business in a Free Economy

Although businesses face ethical decisions in many different areas, Warneryd and Lewis ([1994], p. 6) list eight dimensions as critical:

- Product design, function, and safety (design of financial contracts)
- Pollution of the environment (indirectly through lender liability)

---

[10] Cannella, Fraser, and Lee [1995] provide evidence that markets sanction unethical behavior in banking once it is revealed.

TABLE 17-1   The Caux Principles of General Business Ethics Established by the Caux Round Table

Principle 1. The Responsibilities of Businesses: Beyond Shareholders toward Stakeholders

The value of a business to society is the wealth and employment it creates and the marketable products and practices it provides to consumers at a reasonable price commensurate with quality. To create such value, a business must maintain its own economic health and viability, but survival is not a sufficient goal.

Businesses have a role to play in improving the lives of all their customers, employees, and shareholders by sharing with them the wealth they have created. Suppliers and competitors as well should expect businesses to honor their obligations in a spirit of honesty and fairness. As responsible citizens of the local, national, regional, and global communities in which they operate, businesses share a part in shaping the future of those communities.

Principle 2. The Economic and Social Impact of Businesses:
Toward Innovation, Justice, and World Community

Businesses established in foreign countries to develop, produce, or sell should also contribute to the social advancement of those countries by creating productive employment and helping to raise the purchasing power of their citizens. Businesses also should contribute to human rights, education, welfare, and vitalization of the countries in which they operate. Businesses should contribute to economic and social development not only in the countries in which they operate but also in the world community at large, through effective and prudent use of resources, free and fair competition, and emphasis upon innovation in technology, production methods, marketing, and communications.

Principle 3. Business Behavior: Beyond the Letter of the Law toward a Spirit of Trust

Although accepting the legitimacy of trade secrets, businesses should recognize that sincerity, keeping of promises, and transparency contribute not only to their own credibility and stability but also to the smoothness and efficiency of business transactions, particularly on the international level.

Principle 4. Respect for the Rules

To avoid trade frictions and to promote freer trade, equal conditions for competition, and fair and equitable treatment for all participants, businesses should respect international and domestic rules. In addition, they should recognize that some behavior, although legal, may still have adverse consequences.

Principle 5. Support for Multilateral Trade

Businesses should support the multilateral trade systems of the GATT/World Trade Organization and similar international agreements. They should cooperate in efforts to promote the progressive and judicious liberalization of trade and to relax those domestic measures that unreasonably hinder global commerce, while giving due respect to national policy objectives.

Principle 6. Respect for the Environment

A business should protect and, where possible, improve the environment, promote sustainable development, and prevent the waste of natural resources.

Principle 7. Avoidance of Illicit Operations

A business should not participate in or condone bribery, money laundering, or other corrupt practices; indeed, it should seek cooperation with others to eliminate them. It should not trade in arms or other materials used for terrorist activities, drug traffic, or other organized crime.

Source: The Caux Principles, Section 2, General Principles, which can found at www.bath.ac.uk/Centers/ Ethical/Papers/caux.htm. Used by permission of *Business Ethics,* Minneapolis.

- Employee relations (women in management positions)
- Marketing and distribution policies (equal credit opportunity, redlining)
- Gifts and bribery (the "Keating Five")
- Taxes and charges (loan-loss provisions)
- Accounting practices (disclosure and transparency)
- Financial operations (risk management, fiduciary responsibility)

Except for pollution of the environment,[11] each of these ethical dimensions is important to financial-services firms (FSFs). The words in parentheses serve to clarify the importance of the dimension for FSFs.

Friedman [1962] captures what the "social responsibility" of a business should be in a free economy:

> . . . there is one and only one social responsibility of business—to use its resources and engage in activities designed to increase its profits so long as it stays within the rules of the game, which is to say, engages in open and free competition without deception or fraud. (p. 133)

To Friedman, the rules of the game are clear: economic freedom without deception or fraud. When deception or fraud occur, we have market failure. The question then is, what do we do about market failure?

COMMON LAW AND FINANCIAL FRAUDS

Moral, institutional, and legal guidelines determine how societies use ethics. The guidelines we have considered so far have been moral (derived from various religions/philosophies) and institutional (the Caux Principles). From a pragmatic view, legal guidelines and the role of government (deposit insurance) are important determinants of how people behave. This perspective tends toward efficient outcomes because more incentives exist for plaintiffs to challenge injuries or bad rulings.

Common law is a legal system based upon rules deduced, mainly by judges, from the customs and institutions of the people and related to their sociopolitical/economic conditions. Although the deduced rules of common law do change as society changes, they are treated as precedent, and changes are made only after cautious deliberations. The legal concepts of fraud and fiduciary (trust) relationship bring common law as close as it gets to dealing with the unethically opportunistic behavior found in banking and the FSI. Ethically unacceptable market behavior suggests that fraud and negligent misrepresentation are the major problems. Legal definitions of these terms focus on breaches of duties of trust and managerial stewardship. The law in many cases distinguishes between being negligent, careless, or mistaken from being fraudulent or dishonest.[12] Although violations of these codes can be labeled as morally wrong, common law provides a legal system for prosecuting financial fraud.

---

[11] Because of "lender liability," banks may become indirectly involved in pollution cases by lending to borrowers who pollute the environment.

[12] This paragraph draws on Bear and Maldonado-Bear [1994], pp. 99 and 172. Regarding the term "common law," they say that it is "really quite ambiguous."

Bear and Maldonado-Bear ([1994], pp. 173–174) identify five cumulative common-law tests for fraud:

- A conscious misrepresentation or concealment of the truth
- An intent to benefit by causing another party to rely on the untruth to his or her detriment
- The misrepresentation was *material*
- An *intent* existed to cause the other party to rely on the misrepresentation to his or her detriment
- The other party did *believe, rely,* and *suffer* provable harm

Although common-law fraud deals with unethical behavior, what if the misrepresentation or concealment results from stupidity or negligence by a counterparty? In this case, the violation is known as negligent misrepresentation, and a remedy exists in common law for it, too.

In a negligent misrepresentation (Bear and Maldonado-Bear [1994], p. 174), a party is responsible at law if, in the course of his or her business or profession, the party supplies misinformation to others in their transactions that they rely on to their detriment. A recipient of information is justified in expecting the informing party to exercise "care and competence in obtaining and communicating information."

The S&L mess provides numerous examples of negligence lawsuits filed against directors and consultants of failed S&Ls and accounting firms that audited the zombies. Exhibit 17-1 shows the results of a $186.5 million settlement in favor of the FDIC, RTC, and OTS against a major accounting firm charged with malpractice

EXHIBIT 17-1

Joint Release	Federal Deposit Insurance Corporation
	Resolution Trust Corporation
	Office of Thrift Supervision

For Release at 3:20 P.M. EDT
Thursday, August 9, 1994
(PR-52-94)

Peat Marwick Settles with FDIC, RTC, and OTS for $186.5 Million

Washington, D.C., August 9, 1994—KPMG Peat Marwick (Peat Marwick), one of the nation's largest accounting firms, has agreed to pay $186.5 million to the federal government to settle claims based on alleged accounting and auditing failures at financial institutions it audited.

In a global settlement of all claims and charges brought by federal regulators, the accounting firm has agreed to pay $128 million in cash to the Resolution Trust Corporation (RTC), $58.5 million to the Federal Deposit Insurance Corporation (FDIC), and consented to a cease and desist order

of the Office of Thrift Supervision (OTS). The payment to the FDIC will consist of $23.5 million in cash and $35 million in a two-year note.

The settlement resolves five pending suits brought by the RTC, two suits brought by the FDIC, and settles all claims for professional work Peat Marwick did for financial institutions that failed on or before April 4, 1994.

The OTS cease and desist order requires specific changes in accounting policies for future audits of federally insured depository institutions during the next five years.

The OTS order specifies levels of experience in insured depository audits for partners, engagement partners and managers, and increases the required experience levels for audits of thrifts with assets exceeding $500 million.

on the basis of allegations of negligent misrepresentation. Other Big Six account-ing firms that agreed to similar settlements are Ernst & Young ($400 million), De-loitte & Touche ($312 million), and Arthur Anderson ($82 million). Although these settlements are minuscule compared to the $160 billion cost (excluding interest) of the S&L scandal, pursuit of such violations is an important step in attempting to restore ethical behavior in banking and the FSI.

MARKETS: EFFICIENCY, FAILURE, AND INFORMATION COSTS

A *free market* is one in which the forces of supply and demand operate without outside intervention (e.g., from the government). The concept is, of course, an ab-stract ideal. In the real world, the best we can hope for is some approximation of free markets (e.g., the New York Stock Exchange). Economic systems with free markets tend to generate the most economic prosperity. Taking Ancient Rome and Greece as examples provides a critical linkage between markets and ethics. Specif-ically, corruption in government and society precipitates or at least speeds a na-tion's economic decline.

In Search of Free Markets: An Index of Economic Freedom[13]

How does economic freedom affect economic prosperity? A study by the Heritage Foundation concluded that "the main cause of poverty around the world is not the failure of rich countries to spread wealth through foreign-aid programs, but the misguided economic policies of developing countries themselves" (Holmes [1994]). To arrive at this conclusion, the Heritage Foundation constructed an "Index of Economic Freedom" for 101 countries. Table 17-2 lists the countries ac-cording to their degree of economic freedom: 43 countries were found to have "free" or "mostly free" economies, 50 economies were rated "mostly unfree," and eight economies were classified as "repressed." The striking thing about Table 17-2 is the strong correlation between economic wealth (per capita GDP measured by purchasing power parity) and economic freedom. Specifically, the countries that are most free economically have the highest standards of living.

The Index of Economic Freedom, which claims to be the first comparative analysis of its kind, measures the degree of economic freedom each country allows in 10 key areas:[14]

1. Trade policy
2. Taxation policy
3. Government consumption of economic output $[Y = C + I + G + (X - M)]$[15]
4. Monetary policy
5. Capital flows and foreign investment
6. Banking policy
7. Wage and price controls

---

[13] This section draws on Johnson and Sheehy [1994] and the summary of their work by Holmes [1994].

[14] Each country's performance in these areas was assigned a numerical "score" from 1 = free to 5 = re-pressed. The lower a country's score is, the greater is its degree of economic freedom.

[15] Recall from principles of macroeconomics that Y = gross national product (GNP) or total expenditures in an economy, C = consumption expenditures, I = investment expenditures, G = government expenditures, and $(X - M)$ = exports minus imports, or the net trade balance.

TABLE 17-2 The Heritage Foundation's Index of Economic Freedom

Free	*Mostly Free*		*Mostly Unfree*		*Repressed*
1. Hong Kong	8. Canada	26. Belize	44. South Africa	70. Dominican	94. Moldova
2. Singapore	9. Germany	27. Columbia	45. Turkey	Republic	95. Haiti
3. Bahrain	10. Austria	28. Panama	46. Venezuela	71. Malawi	96. Sudan
4. United	11. Bahamas	29. Paraguay	47. Botswana	72. Peru	97. Angola
States	12. Czech	30. Slovakia	48. Gabon	73. Russia	98. Mozambique
5. Japan	Republic	31. Greece	49. Guatemala	74. Bulgaria	99. Vietnam
6. Taiwan	13. S. Korea	32. Hungary	50. Kenya	75. Cameroon	100. Cuba
7. United	14. Malaysia	33. Jamaica	51. Mexico	76. Egypt	101. North Korea
Kingdom	15. Australia	34. Portugal	52. Zambia	77. Madagascar	
	16. Ireland	35. Sri Lanka	53. Israel	78. Mali	
	17. Estonia	36. Argentina	54. Algeria	79. Tanzania	
	18. France	37. Tunisia	55. Honduras	80. Zimbabwe	
	19. Thailand	38. Costa Rica	56. Nigeria	81. Albania	
	20. Chile	39. Jordan	57. Pakistan	82. Romania	
	21. Italy	40. Morocco	58. Bolivia	83. Belarus	
	22. Spain	41. Swaziland	59. Ecuador	84. Yemen	
	23. El Salvador	42. Uruguay	60. Ivory Coast	85. Guyana	
	24. Oman	43. Uganda	61. Malta	86. India	
	25. Sweden		62. Poland	87. China	
			63. Brazil	88. Ethiopia	
			64. Fiji	89. Bangladesh	
			65. Ghana	90. Congo	
			66. Philippines	91. Nicaragua	
			67. Mongolia	92. Ukraine	
			68. Guinea	93. Sierra	
			69. Indonesia	Leone	

Note: Rankings are for all countries graded in order from most economically free to least economically free. In case of a tie, the countries were listed alphabetically.
Source: Adapted from The Heritage Foundation; see Johnson and Sheehy [1994] and Holmes [1994].

8. Property rights
9. Regulations
10. The black market

For the purposes of this book, items 4 (monetary policy), 5 (capital flows), 6 (banking policy), and 9 (regulation) are the critical factors. Although the United States can be described as having a disciplined monetary policy that creates an environment in which capital flows freely both internally and externally, only since the early 1980s has U.S. banking policy been more conducive to a competitive environment in the financial-services industry.

Economic Efficiency and Market Failure

In addition to generating the greatest amount of economic prosperity, free markets or free-enterprise systems provide for the highest degree of economic efficiency in terms of an optimal allocation of resources. Economists describe this condition as "Pareto optimal" after the Italian economist and sociologist, Wilfred

Pareto (1848–1923). It means that efficient markets allocate resources such that it is not possible to make someone better off without making someone else worse off. Short of Pareto optimality, we have some degree of market failure. Consider the following logical propositions:

Perfect market conditions → Pareto optimality (first welfare theorem)

Failure to achieve Pareto optimality → Less-than-perfect market conditions

The existence of market imperfections such as barriers to trade and externalities explains why markets fail to achieve Pareto optimality. This framework, however, provides no ethical view of the distribution of wealth; it is simply a pure property optimality. Pareto optimality is a necessary but not a sufficient condition for maximizing social welfare. If particular economic societies evolve into an imbalance of haves and have-nots that leads to revolution and the destruction of property, then clearly such a development is not a social-welfare optimum.

"Interventionists" think that "market failure" justifies government interference with market processes. In contrast, free-market thinkers, from Adam Smith [1776] to Milton Friedman [1962] to George Stigler [1982] favor letting markets work because they perceive the alternative, government intervention, as usually worse (e.g., creating bigger externalities). For example, drawing on Smith, Stigler writes,

> . . . the conduct of economic affairs is best left to private citizens . . . the state will be doing remarkably well if it succeeds in its unavoidable tasks of winning wars, *preserving justice,* and maintaining the various highways of commerce. (p. 119, emphasis mine)

By preserving justice, governments can create an environment in which ethical behavior has a greater opportunity to flourish.

Given the view of ethics as conflict resolution and the degree of economic freedom within an economic system, the art of compromise determines the extent of government involvement in a democratic society.

The Causes of Market Failure[16]

Before considering what to do, if anything, about market failure, let's expand on its causes. This approach suggests that eliminating or reducing the cause of market failure may be an appropriate role for government in a quasi-free-market economy. Market failure arises from four imperfections:[17]

1. Monopoly   The imperfection of pure monopoly is the absolute control over price by the monopolist (seller).[18] Free markets assume lots of buyers and sellers without any control over price (participants are price takers not price setters). Because pure monopolies are rare, it is more common to talk about markets in which a degree of control over price (short of absolute control) exists. Thus, the phrase "some degree of monopoly power" (e.g., an oligopoly with cartel pricing) means some degree of control over price. Market failure in this type of situation means

---

[16] This section draws on Friedman [1962], Bear and Maldonando-Bear [1994], and "Schools Brief: State and Market," *The Economist* (February 17th, 1996), pp. 64–65.

[17] Bear and Maldonado-Bear [1994] classify these four types of market failure as "misallocation of resources." In addition to this problem, they identify three other major areas of concern within markets: instability; maldistribution of wealth, income, and power; and moral hazard (insider information).

[18] When only one buyer exists, the situation is called a monopsony.

that consumption and production are less than the efficient amount, resulting in a deadweight loss of welfare, because price is greater than marginal cost. In a free market, entry of new firms would compete away the excess profit, or the difference between price and marginal cost. In a perfectly competitive equilibrium, marginal revenue (price) equals marginal cost.

Although banking markets have become more competitive in recent years, the numerous geographic and product restrictions (chapter 15) served the dual purpose of protecting banks from competition and conferring on them varying degrees of monopoly power with respect to loan and deposit rates. In the long run, however, these restrictions weakened banks rather than strengthened them (i.e., government intervention made matters worse).

2. Information Asymmetry   Banks and communication firms are similar in that they are both entities that establish networking relationships through which they collect, store, process, and transmit **information** for themselves and customers' accounts. Because modern economic and financial theories say that information matters, externalities associated with information may lead to market failure. The classic example of this is the market for lemons (e.g., used cars). If the potential buyer of a used car (the principal) uses price to judge the quality of the used car, the seller (the agent) faces a dilemma: Cutting prices suggests that the agent has only lemons for sale. When information is imperfect or costly, market failure can result. In the used-car market, sellers can attempt to solve their dilemma by protecting their reputational capital or by offering guarantees or both. Buyers can attempt to solve the problem by incurring search costs to find reputable agents or only buying used cars with guarantees or both.

In banking, the federal safety net (deposit insurance and the lender of last resort) can repress the potential benefits of market discipline such that many depositors and other creditors do not incur search costs in seeking information about safe-and-sound banks. On balance, information is a scarce resource, which, in an information society, the institutions of capitalism attempt to use as efficiently as possible.

3. Public Goods   Some goods, like national defense, clean air, and law and order, cannot be supplied by markets. These public goods can be described as nonexcludable or nonexclusionary, which means that consumers cannot refuse them and producers cannot deny consumers the right to consume them. In addition, consumption of national defense or law and order by one person does not affect another person's consumption of it (nonrival consumption). Because free-rider problems exist, private sellers cannot expect to recover the costs of producing public goods because consumers have no incentive to pay. Thus, it is left to the public sector to provide public good, collecting taxes to pay for the services.

Some products, such as a lighthouse and television broadcasting, that once were thought to be public goods have been proven otherwise. For example, private-sector innovations in the form of cable television and pay-per-view have permitted producers to segment markets and collect fees for the services they provide. In the case of federal deposit insurance, private-sector practices and innovations have only recently made their way into this business.

4. Externalities   Two kinds of externalities exist: good and bad. The bad ones, like pollution, are best known. Examples of good externalities include antilock brakes[19] and education, especially about smoking, drug abuse, alcoholism, AIDS, and teen pregnancy. Externalities bring about the divergence between private and societal marginal costs and benefits. To the extent that markets can internalize the costs to society, market solutions to externalities can be generated. On balance, when markets supply too many bad externalities and not enough good externalities, they fail.

Four major policy approaches to addressing negative externalities, such as pollution, include: prevention (by prohibiting particular practices), control (anti-pollution measures or cleaning devices), compensation or redress for harm, and direct consumer action.[20]

Solutions to Market Failure: The Invisible Hand versus the Heavy Hand of Government Intervention

How to handle market failure is a politically and emotionally charged issue. At the extremes, interventionists want the government to protect and provide for us from the womb to the tomb; extreme noninterventionists want the government to stay out of everything. Because politics is the art of compromise, neither of these positions is plausible. This chapter suggests benign or harmless government intervention as the best solution and a reasonable compromise. In this mode, the government creates an environment for ethical behavior and provides procedures for ex post settling up when unethical behavior occurs. What we want to avoid at all costs is government intervention that makes matters worse. Friedman [1962] stresses this point:

> Monetary reforms, intended to promote stability in economic activity and prices, exacerbated inflation during and after World War I and fostered a higher degree of instability thereafter than had ever been experienced before. The monetary authorities they established bear primary responsibility for converting a serious economic contract into the catastrophe of the Great Depression from 1929–33. A system established largely to prevent bank panics produced the most severe banking panic in American history. (p. 198)

The second-worst banking crisis in the United States occurred during the 1980s and early 1990s. Kane [1989, 1990, 1993] extensively documents how the government made this mess worse. He contends that "The root question (of the S&L mess) is to explain the inefficient ways in which authorities have managed the deposit-insurance funds" ([1993], p. 12). He continues,

> That's part of why I call the S&L debacle a mess: because we expect authorities to act as faithful agents for us. We persist in this expectation despite lots of evidence that many of them don't. As institutions, Congress and recent administrations have been full of faithless stewards. Part of the mess we have to clean up is to straighten out incentives to exploit taxpayers in government service. We have to make officials accountable in timely and meaningful fashion for deposit-insurance losses as the losses accrue. (p. 12)

Kane questions the assumption of faithful agents (as discussed in the previous two chapters), which we consider next in the context of ethics as conflict resolution.

---

[19] To the extent that antilock brakes and air bags cause some consumers to drive faster and less carefully, the good aspects of these externalities are reduced by these moral-hazard problems.

[20] Bear and Maldonado-Bear ([1994], chapter 4) provide details.

PUBLIC STEWARDSHIP, FIDUCIARY RELATIONSHIPS, AND THE PRINCIPAL-AGENT MODEL

Bear and Maldonado-Bear ([1994], p. 253) ask, What is the moral link between deposit insurance and banking? Their answer is public stewardship, which they define as the "very high duty and responsibility [of each and every insured and protected bank] to assure the safety and soundness of the system"(p. 254; insert mine). This call for public stewardship, or fiduciary responsibility, also extends, as Kane argues, to deposit insurers and bank regulators to be faithful agents, as in the principal-agent model. It also extends more broadly to our notion of regulatory discipline (chapter 15) and thus includes Congress and the administration as taxpayers' agents. On balance, taxpayers rely on the various agents of regulatory discipline to maintain the integrity of the system and to protect their pocketbooks from $160-billion disasters like the S&L mess.

Faithful versus Unfaithful Agents

What incentives do our political and regulatory agents have to be faithful? Kane [1989] suggests viewing incentive pricing for regulators and deposit insurers as a two-part compensation package consisting of explicit and implicit wages. High-ranking government officials such as bank regulators earn an explicit salary while in office; one that is low, however, relative to what they could make in the private sector. In addition, they receive implicit wages in two forms: (1) the perks and prestige of their high offices and (2) deferred compensation from the private sector after they leave office. To enhance their opportunities for receiving the deferred compensation, regulators must avoid crises or messes while in office. To achieve this objective, they may be inclined to take tribute from interested parties such as lobbyists and to practice disinformation.

Disinformation and the Role of Ethics in Bank Regulation, Deposit Insurance, and the S&L Mess

Kane [1996b] uses the term **disinformation** to describe how regulators use their "bully pulpits" to distort the flow of information taxpayers receive about the banking system and deposit insurance. Lawyers, who tend to dominate the bank regulatory arena, find this distortion of information congenial to their professional ethics. Kane describes it this way:

> It is important to recognize that what an academic economist would characterize as deliberate misrepresentation, a lawyer can define as conscientious professional advocacy. This benign view of disinformation makes trained lawyers ideal heads of regulatory enterprises. The ethics of scientific debate demand that all relevant logical arguments and empirical evidence be examined on their own merits and weighed against one another. But where scientists view debate as a "search for truth," courtroom lawyers learn to view debate as a contest that the cleverest side deserves to win. Unlike witnesses, lawyers are not made to swear to tell the truth. The ethics of legal advocacy expressly authorize disingenuous efforts to inflate the case for one's own policy positions and to exclude or unfairly denigrate the most telling arguments of the other side. (p. 155)

An important trait of a faithful agent is not to engage in the dissemination of disinformation. An unfaithful agent is one who, for whatever reasons, fails at this task. In our principal-agent model of regulatory discipline, should we assume that the agents (Congress and regulators) are faithful or unfaithful? Kane [1996a] notes that in a faithful-agent model, shortfalls in maximizing net social benefits arise from "innocent errors rooted in the inherent difficulty of observing and controlling circumventive behavior by regulatees" (p. 154). In contrast, the unfaithful-agent (or agency-cost) model, as developed by Kane, attributes the breakdown in regulatory discipline, as captured by inefficiency and inequity, to "hard-to-resolve principal-agent conflict between venal government officials and poorly informed taxpayers" (*Ibid.*).

How Agency Differs in Law and in the Theory of the Firm

Modern agency theory in finance and economics traces to Ross [1973] and Jensen and Meckling [1976].[21] Law, like finance, has an agency model but the two are different. Bear and Maldonado-Bear ([1994], p. 202) contend that it is important to understand how they differ.

The financial version of agency theory depicts the firm as a nexus of contracts in which agency costs are the key ingredients for understanding behavior. Agency costs have three components:

1. Monitoring expenditures by the principal
2. Bonding expenditures by the agent
3. Residual loss

Bear and Maldonado-Bear ([1994], pp. 202–203) describe legal agency as control of the agent by the principal. They argue that the managers/directors of a firm are not, legally, agents of stockholders because they do not have legal authority to direct and control the activities of the agent. They describe the "spectacle of many thousands of 'principals' (stockholders) . . . 'delegating' authority 'by contract' to one board of directors and a few executives, . . . [as] a fiction that severely challenges any willing suspension of disbelief" (p. 203; second insert mine).[22]

To bridge the gap between the legal and economic/financial aspects of agency, Bear and Maldonado-Bear [1994] propose the following fiduciary concept:

> . . . while some elements of the fiduciary concept might well be what parties to a corporate endeavor might reduce to a written contract (if they could negotiate without transaction costs) much is not. And what is not is rooted in the law's insistence that very special moral behaviors are expected in particular circumstances that are beyond the scope of all usual specific, contractual terms. (p. 204)

Regarding this fiduciary duty as an ethical construct and appealing to case law (the cases of Unocal and Paramount Communications), they see two major issues related to their concept:

1. To whom, exactly, is a corporate manager's fiduciary duty owed, and why?
2. Why does such a fiduciary duty exist in law at all?

---

[21] Bowie and Freeman [1992] contend that Mitnick [1974] does not receive adequate recognition for his contributions to the development of agency theory. Their bibliography (p. 223) lists 11 works by Mitnick. The "property-rights tradition" of agency theory traces to Coase [1937], a Nobel prize winner, and Alchian and Demsetz [1972]. In addition, Berle and Means [1932] addressed the problem of the separation of ownership and control in the modern corporation. Adam Smith's *Wealth of Nations* [1776] represents the seminal work.

[22] Regarding the role of stockholders in managing and controlling a business, Clark [1985] states: "Stockholders of a large publicly held corporation *do not* do these things; as a matter of efficient operation of a large firm with numerous residual claimants they *should not* do them; and under the typical corporate statute and case law they *cannot* do them" (p. 57).

Their answer to the first question mirrors Friedman's view of the social responsibility of a business, that is, the manager's fiduciary duty is "to the development, enrichment, and continued healthy existence of the corporation *in the society within which it functions*" (p. 205). This view of the corporate agent's fiduciary duty is consistent with the finance objective of wealth maximization.[23]

Bear and Maldonado-Bear see unethical (or opportunistic) human behavior as the major impediment to the trustworthy, healthy, and efficient functioning of business enterprises. Box 17-1 presents a list of unethical conduct in the FSI in the recent past. It serves as a good indication of how tarnished the FSI is in terms of lack of trust, unhealthiness, and inefficiency. Deposit insurers and regulators share in this tarnishment and in many instances bear direct responsibility for making the situations worse rather than better.

Capital Forbearance and Money Politics

For lack of a better term, let's use **capital forbearance** to capture the willingness of deposit insurers/regulators to tolerate weaker and weaker capital positions (greater and greater risk exposure) on the part of banks and S&Ls.[24] Regarding the evolution of S&L losses, Kane [1993] notes,

> If one tracks the pattern of *official* losses, it looks as if the FSLIC lost most of its money in 1988 and 1989. Actually its losses start accumulating about 1965. Although amounts fluctuated, losses were well over $100 billion at the end of 1981. Losses improved a bit in late 1982 and early 1983, but subsequently rose until leveling off in 1988 at around $160 billion. They did not surge in 1988 and 1989 as official figures suggest. (p. 12)

To add insult to financial injury, just when U.S. taxpayers thought the S&L mess was behind them, the U.S. Supreme Court ruled on July 1, 1996 that the government had acted improperly (unethically?) in 1989 when it altered accounting rules dealing with "supervisory goodwill" for S&Ls (Seiberg [1996]). The ruling says that the government can change rules and regulations at whim but if in doing so it violates previous contracts, then it creates a liability. These new liabilities could add another $10 billion or so to the cost of cleaning up the S&L mess.

Vaughan's [1996b] analysis of the *Challenger* disaster of 1986 provides insight into the organizational failings of deposit insurers and bank regulators during the 1980s and early 1990s. She concludes with a lesson that fits the S&L mess as well:

> The story of the *Challenger* is a story of how people developed patterns that blinded them to the consequences of their actions and of how slight deviations from the usual course gradually became the norm, providing a basis for accepting additional deviations. . . . It's a story that illustrates how disastrous consequences can emerge from the banality of organizational life. (p. 36)

---

[23] Regarding the existence of a fiduciary duty in law, Bear and Maldonado-Bear state: ". . . the duty is tied, specifically, to the inability of these enterprises (and, by extension, society) to survive *in a democratic republic* in the absence of a *legally enforceable* duty of all agents charged with serving the enterprise's best interests, to do so *honorably* and with *integrity*" (p. 206).

[24] Vaughan [1996] has shown that the *Challenger* disaster was caused by NASA's willingness to accept greater and greater risks with respect to O-ring damage. She writes [1996a], "Each time that engineers found a little more damage to an O-ring, without a catastrophe, they loosened their definition of what constituted an acceptable risk. What they had first viewed as deviance came to seem normal. They came to expect O-ring damage" (p. 29).

She also notes that "Bad things *do* happen to good organizations" (p. 24). The important point, however, and one emphasized by both Kane and Vaughan, is that government agencies (NASA and FSLIC/FDIC), by engaging in what Vaughan calls "risky business," bear direct responsibility for disasters that occur because of their actions or inactions. In resolving conflicts of O-ring tolerance (NASA) and inadequate capital (FSLIC/FDIC), they compromised their ethical positions.[25]

The Role of Money Politics in Risky Business

It is risky business to mess with O-ring tolerances and capital-adequacy standards. A song from *Cabaret* says: "Money, money, money makes the world go round." Money politics, Kane's term [1996b], can lower financial and engineering tolerances. Think of money politics as a perverted version of the golden rule: Whoever has the gold makes the rules.[26] It is a particular class of corruption in which side payments determine votes.

Banking rules and regulations impose costs on taxpayers in two ways: (1) If they confer monopoly power on banks (one of the causes of market failure), then customers pay more for financial services than they would in a fully competitive system; and (2) taxpayers implicitly finance the federal safety net that provides subsidies to depository risk taking. Taxpayers should expect the costs of regulation to be minimized. Failure to minimize costs constitutes misregulation. Citizens vote for a particular regulatory regime (proposed by lawmakers) based on the perceived net benefits (or costs) of the regime. When money politics distort the information about a regime (the tribute is shared by legislators and regulators), then voters cannot make informed decisions.

PRINCIPAL-AGENT RELATIONS, INFLUENCE PEDDLING, AND DISINFORMATION

The risks to taxpayers from poor regulatory performance arise from three sources:

- Lack of transparency (in the accounts of regulated financial-services firms)
- Opportunities for cover-ups by regulators and lawmakers
- Disinformation transmitted by regulators and lawmakers

Kane [1996c] argues that fair and efficient regulation requires society to demand a chain of incentive-compatible contracts across the principal-agent relations shown by the solid lines in Figure 17-1. The dashed lines in the figure reflect the incentive to engage in taxpayer-exploiting behavior through disinformation and influence peddling. The role of incentive-based contracts for public officials is to

---

[25] For example, Vaughan [1996b] reports that when NASA managers began challenging the 53-degree cutoff temperature for launching, Thiokol managers lowered the cutoff. When *Challenger* was launched at 11:38 A.M. on January 28, 1986, the temperature was 36 degrees. Seventy-three seconds later the O-rings failed and a fireball erupted. The crew compartment plunged nine miles in two-and-one-half minutes, slamming into the ocean at 200 miles per hour.

[26] Kane [1996b] puts it this way: " . . . legislators respond separately to the dollar value of bank and insurance lobbying and to the electoral discipline that they expect taxpayers to exercise at the voting booth. The wrinkle introduced here is that of allowing legislators to enhance the flow of corporate profits, as well as taxpayers' willingness to reelect incumbents by rewarding regulators for generating reports and speeches that, in lawyer-like fashion, credibly overstate the benefits taxpayers should project from regulatory activity" (p. 347).

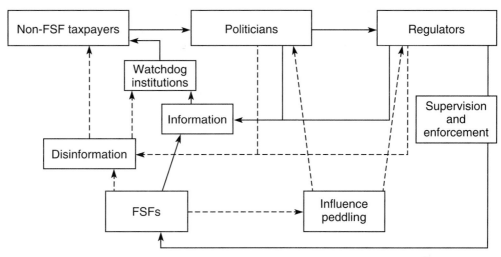

Key: Solid lines → principal-agent relations. Dashed lines → incentives to engage in taxpayer-exploiting behavior.

Source: Kane [1996c], Figure 1, p. 24. Reprinted by permission of the author.

FIGURE 17-1 **Principal-Agent Relations and Influence Peddling in the FSI**

shrink the costs of the interaction captured by the dashed lines in Figure 17-1. Kane [1996d] suggests three specific actions Congress could take to create incentives for fairer and more efficient regulation:

- Defining what information supervisory authorities are to disclose in an operational manner free of obvious loopholes
- Specifying criminal penalties for officials that sign off on willful inaccuracies and nondisclosures
- Establishing a credible enforcement mechanism

CONFLICT RESOLUTION

Because conflict is a natural phenomenon, and because ethics can be viewed as conflict resolution, what does ethics have to say about resolving conflicts? Incentive-compatible contracts, described above, represent one way of attempting to resolve conflicts. Fisher and Ury [1991] suggest a sequential five-step procedure for resolving conflict:

- Separate the precepts behind both parties' views from the positions themselves
- Obtain agreement on mutual goals regarding the precepts
- Understand and support aspects of the other party's reasoning and position
- Calculate consequences of each act versus the precepts
- Accede to precepts but not to pressure

Socrates and Plato observed that an ethical person is a reasoning one and that when conflicts of interest exist, moral issues arise. Table 17-3 shows how the process of resolving conflict varies at different levels of moral reasoning. The six stages of moral reasoning are described as[27] "obedience and punishment" (stage 1), "individualism and reciprocity" (stage 2), "interpersonal communication" (stage 3), "social system" or "law and order" (stage 4), "social contract" (stage 5), and "universal ethical principles" (stage 6). In Table 17-3, these six stages of moral thought are reduced to three levels: preconventional (stages 1 and 2), conventional (stages 3 and 4), and postconventional (stages 5 and 6). French and Granrose [1995] define the conventional level of moral thought as "the type of moral thinking that is characterized by mutual interpersonal expectations, relationships, and interpersonal conformity" (p. 227). They explain the postconventional level as reflecting decisions which keep the interests of both the individual and others in mind, whereas the preconventional level focuses solely on the individual. Across the three levels of moral thinking, the process for resolving conflict focuses on one's personal perspective, the span of concerns, goals, behavioral norms, negative sanctions, and types of communication.

Because lack of communication can create problems, communication can be used to avoid problems and to resolve conflicts. French and Granrose [1995] consider two different methods of communication for resolving conflicts of interest: strategic

TABLE 17-3 The Process of Resolving Conflict at Different Levels of Moral Reasoning

Preconventional Level (Stages 1 and 2)	*Conventional Level (Stages 3 and 4)*	*Postconventional Level (Stages 5 and 6)*
Personal Perspective		
Personal natural identity	Social role identity	Identity of true self
Span of Concern		
Personal natural and social environment	Primary reference group or members of political community	All interacting associates or all humans as private individuals or all people as members of a world society
Goals		
Maximize personal pleasure and avoid pain through obedience or reciprocity	Acquiescence to concrete morality of primary reference group or secondary reference groups	Civil liberties and public welfare or moral freedom or political freedom
Behavioral Norms		
Understand and follow behavior expectations with respect to actions and consequences of actions	Understand roles and follow legal/social norms	Understand and apply universalizable personal principles
Negative Sanctions		
Punishment	Shame	Guilt
Types of Communication		
Incomplete interaction: emphasize subjective instrumental purpose	Complete interaction: emphasize system maintenance or group conformity	Discursive communication: emphasize utility or social contract or universal principles

Note: The six stages of moral reasoning are described as: "obedience and punishment" (Stage One), "individualism and reciprocity" (Stage Two), "interpersonal communication" (Stage Three), "social system" or "law and order" (Stage Four), "social contract" (Stage Five), and "universal ethical principles" (Stage Six).

Source: French and Granrose [1995], Table 7–1, p. 151, who adapted the material from Habermas [1979]. Used by permission.

---

[27] The six stages were developed by Lawrence Kohlberg and are summarized in French and Granrose [1995], pp. 5–7.

TABLE 17-4 Resolving Conflicts: Strategic versus Discursive Communication

Strategic Communication	*Discursive Communication*
Holds personal reason for position (in accord with)	Identifies similarities between positions (in accord with)
Closed-minded conviction while listening to opposition (leads to)	Open-minded approach while listening to opposition (leads to)
Identifying contradictions	Separating principles from positions
Focuses on differences in original positions (then)	Calculates consequences of new position (then)
Takes adversarial stance (then)	Tests against principles (then)
Offers counterevidence based on own interest and custom of habit (relying on)	Seeks mutual integration based on agreement and convention of reason (relying on)
Power or manipulation	Shared analysis

Source: French and Granrose [1995], Table 7–2, p. 153. Used by permission.

communication and discursive communication. Strategic communication is a confrontational approach that bluntly attempts to obtain agreement even if a consensus does not exist. In contrast, discursive communication focuses on an explicit understanding of the facts and principles underlying the conflict and attempts to establish a shared ground of mutually accepted facts and principles. Table 17-4 shows how French and Granrose view these two approaches operating to resolve conflicts. Because strategic communication relies on power or manipulation, it usually can resolve conflicts quickly but not without stepping on someone's toes. Discursive communication, with its shared analysis, evolves more slowly because it attempts to arrive at some consensus without power or manipulation, instead relying on joint problem solving.

Considering the S&L loan mess and the crisis in deposit insurance, regulators, lawmakers, and S&L managers relied on power and manipulation to hide the truth from taxpayers. Lack of transparency, cover-ups, influence peddling, and disinformation provided the means to that end. This unethically opportunistic behavior contributed greatly to the $160-billion cost, excluding interest, of the S&L mess.

Chapter Summary

Ethics is the discipline dealing with what is good and bad and with moral duty and obligation. Moral, institutional, and legal guidelines determine how societies use ethics. From a pragmatic view, legal guidelines and the role of government (deposit insurance) are important determinants of how people behave. The concern about lack of ethical behavior in the FSI in the 1980s and the 1990s resulted in a call from both academicians and practitioners for a rededication to ethics. Unethical behavior in banking and the FSI manifests itself mainly as **fraud** and **negligent misrepresentation**. The roles of **ethics in information** and the **disclosure of private information** play key roles in resolving these problems. If we view ethics as **conflict resolution,** the principal-agent model provides a framework for resolving ethical conflicts. The concepts of **free markets, market efficiency, market failure**

and **common-law definitions** of fraud and negligent misrepresentation provide analytical foundations for this chapter. The analysis addressed and analyzed the ethical dilemmas facing bankers and their competitors in the FSI with particular emphasis on the role of ethics in bank regulation, deposit insurance, and the S&L mess. Money politics plays an important role in shaping regulation and the ethical environment of the FSI.

Firms cannot maximize long-run values if they engage in unethical behavior. Although short-run excess profits can be earned by such behavior, market and civil penalties ensure that they are not sustained once bad faith is revealed. Stakeholders (e.g., owners, customers, employees, etc.) serve as regulators by punishing rogue firms and rewarding ethical firms. Whereas a good reputation is an important intangible asset to any enterprise, it is paramount for banks and other financial-services firms, which depend more heavily on trust and confidence for their business. This notion is captured by Dennis Weatherstone, who says that what matters more than anything is **character,** because it determines the quality of our institutions. In banking and the FSI, trust and confidence are ethical standards that cannot be compromised. As bankers, regulators, and deposit insurers move into the twenty-first century, they need to prove to the world that all this talk about character and ethics is more than just rhetoric.

Key Concepts, Ideas, and Terms

- Capital forbearance
- Character
- Common law
- Conflict resolution
- Disclosure of private information
- Discrimination (in ordinary usage)
- Disinformation

- Economic discrimination
- Ethics
- Free markets
- Information
- Market efficiency
- Market failure
- Moral duty

- Negligent misrepresentation
- Opportunistic behavior
- Opportunity cost
- Pareto optimum
- Principal-agent model
- Role of government
- Unethically opportunistic behavior

Review/Discussion Questions and Ethical Dilemmas

1. What are some examples of why banking's reputation was tarnished during the 1980s and early 1990s? Is banking getting a bum rap because negative stories get the most coverage? Is the FSI the only industry that seemed to lack ethical behavior?
2. How have bankers and academicians responded to the tarnished reputation of the FSI?
3. Why is it important to study ethics in banking and the FSI?
4. What is ethics? Distinguish between what is and what ought to be and between right and wrong.
5. Distinguish between discrimination in ordinary usage and economic decision making.
6. What is common law and what does it have to say about ethically unacceptable market behavior? Can moral duty provide the same standard?
7. What is the difference between fraud and negligent misrepresentation?
8. Distinguish among free markets, efficient markets, and market failure. What are the causes of market failure? Is government intervention the only solution to market failure?
9. What is the relationship between free markets and economic prosperity?
10. What are the major ethical dimensions for a business firm? Do these dimensions differ for financial-services firms (FSF)? How might lenders get involved in pollution cases?
11. What is disinformation? Is the use of disinformation by bank regulators a market failure or an ethical failure? What profession is most prevalent in the federal banking agencies?

12. What similarities and differences exist between the S&L mess and the *Challenger* disaster? In this context, consider the last sentence in Vaughan's [1996] book, *The Challenger Launch Decision:*

> The lingering uncertainty in the social control of risky technology is how to control the institutional forces that generate competition and scarcity and the powerful leaders who, in response, establish goals and allocate resources, using high-risk technical systems. (p. 422)

13. What are the three components of agency cost?

14. Distinguish between agency in law and in the theory of the firm. What concept can bridge the gap between the two?

15. What is money politics? Is it good or bad? Is it risky business?

16. What did Dennis Weatherstone have to say about the importance of character?

17. What's the major impediment to the trustworthy, healthy, and efficient functioning of business enterprises?

18. What should a bank manager do after discovering that an employee eligible for a promotion was hired partly because of falsified educational records?

19. The Roman orator Cicero (106–43 BC) would tell stories to stimulate ethical thinking. Here's one he used:[28]

> Suppose a food shortage and famine exists at Rhodes, and the price of corn is extremely high. An honest person from Alexandria has brought to Rhodes a large harvest of corn. Having seen other ships with substantial cargoes of grain on their way to Rhodes, the seller is aware that other traders are on their way from Alexandria. Should the seller disclose this information to the Rhodians? Or should the seller say nothing and trade at the best possible price? I am assuming the seller is an honest, enlightened person. What I am imagining are the deliberations and self-searchings of a person who would keep the Rhodians in ignorance if the seller thought it dishonest to do so, but who is not certain that it would be dishonest.

Does this story illustrate market failure due to asymmetric information? Discuss.

20. Here's another ethical dilemma from Cicero:[29]

> Suppose that a good person is selling a house that has several faults that would-be buyers do not know exist. No one except the owner/seller knows about the defects. My question is this: If the seller does not tell the potential buyers these things but sells the house at a higher price than that at which the seller thought it could be sold, will the seller not have acted unjustly or dishonestly?

21. During the late 1980s Fleet Financial (aka Fleece Financial) was pushing home-equity loans (second mortgages). When some customers overextended themselves and could not keep their debt payments current, Fleet foreclosed on the properties. Fleet's actions generated a lot of bad press for it and it eventually settled with most of its clients. My wife and I have signed three of these types of contracts. From our perspective, it's no big deal and we don't even read the fine print—a bad move if you don't know what you are signing. The contract is simple: You borrow against the equity (usually up to a max of 80 percent and, depending on the contract, at either a fixed or a variable rate). If you take down too much debt and can't make the payments, the lender can take your house. Construct some scenarios in which the sellers of home-equity contracts might behave unethically.

---

[28] The modern version of this story appeared on the back cover of the *Journal of Political Economy* 96(4) [1988]. I discovered it not on the JPE's back cover but in Warneryd and Lewis [1994], p. 2. My edited version appears here.

[29] This one is from Cicero [updated 1991], p. 120, as found in Warneryd and Lewis [1994], p. 2. Except for content, I have edited the story.

22. Several years ago in New York City, two colleagues and I finished lunch at a deli, and as we exited it started raining. At a nearby street corner an instant market for umbrellas appeared as a store owner brought out a box of compact black umbrellas. The price was $4 or $5 apiece. I said, "three for $10." The auction was over and we went to our hotel drier than we otherwise would have been. If the non-rainy-day price of the umbrella was regularly $3, was it fair for the owner to raise the price because it was raining? If someone else came along and paid the asking price for one umbrella, was it fair for the seller to give us a quantity discount?

23. Mutual funds sold by banks are not protected by deposit insurance. Is it the customers' responsibility to know this? How much disclosure does the bank have to make to behave ethically?

24. On collegiate football weekends in Athens, Georgia, State College, Pennsylvania, South Bend, Indiana, Ann Arbor, Michigan, and other university towns, hotel/motel prices go up either explicitly or implicitly (e.g., minimum-stay requirement). Is this pricing fair? Unethical?

25. *Caveat emptor* means "let the buyer beware." Buddhism teaches responsibility for one's actions. Bleeding hearts can see a victim in just about everyone. Assuming ethical negotiations have occurred, a signed contract is a signed contract. You are responsible for your end of the deal or you pay the consequences. Is this hard-line approach fair? How much government intervention is needed to protect innocent victims and the naive? Would industry or private policing be better than government interference? Is self-policing by an industry like assigning the fox to guard the chicken coop?

26. In *Hamlet* (2.2.319), Hamlet says, "What a piece of work is a man! how noble in reason! how infinite in faculties!" In contrast, in *Midsummer Night's Dream* (3.3.116), Puck says, "Lord, what fools these mortals be." Can markets function in an ethical fashion given this wide range of rationality? Can/should disclosure and transparency vary depending on whether the customer is a fool or infinite in faculties? Discuss.

27. In chapter 11 we reported that Ausubel [1991] concluded that competition had failed in the market for credit cards. Given the four causes of market failure discussed in this chapter, which one (or more of them) might explain his finding?

28. The Massachusetts Executive Office of Consumer Affairs and Business Regulation provides the following information on "12 Credit-Card Secrets Banks Don't Want You to Know":

   • Interest backdating (if you don't pay in full monthly)
   • Two-cycle billing (two-months interest if you don't pay in full the first time)
   • The right to setoff (bank can claim your deposits if you default)
   • Fees are negotiable (it never hurts to ask)
   • Interest-rate hikes are retroactive (watch out for teaser low rates)
   • Shortened due dates (watch the fine print of notices)
   • Eliminating grace periods (watch for strings attached to gold cards)
   • Disappearing benefits (enticements may be only short-term incentives)
   • Double fees on cash advances (finance charges and transaction fee)
   • Fewer rights on debit cards (a different animal from a credit card)
   • Misleading monthly minimums (banks make money from finance charges)
   • Interest from day 1 (no grace period if you carry a monthly balance)

   If customers are informed about these secrets only in fine print or after customers have been sucked in, are credit-card issuers behaving ethically? Would this list of secrets affect your answer to the previous question, and if so, how?

29. Can Bankers Trust really get in the middle and rip off a Sony or an IBM? When does the quest for profits or spread become unethical?

30. To add insult to financial injury, just when U.S. taxpayers thought the S&L mess was behind them, the U.S. Supreme Court ruled on July 1, 1996 that the government had acted improperly in 1989 when it altered accounting rules dealing with "supervisory goodwill" for S&Ls (Seiberg [1996]). The ruling says that the government can change rules and regulations at whim, but if in so doing it violates previous contracts, then it creates a liability. These new liabilities could add another $10 billion or so to the cost of cleaning up the S&L mess, making the new total $160 billion excluding interest. Did the government act unethically when it changed the accounting rules? Is this behavior consistent with the government's handling of the whole S&L mess?

Project

Given the list of unethically opportunistic behavior found in banking and the FSI presented in Box 17-1, research one or two of the cases in detail and discuss the situations in terms of the following questions posed by French and Granrose [1995], p. 155:
a. Are corporate values readily identified by actions of the employees?
b. Does the behavior of those employees generate internal conflict?
c. Would those businesspersons invite others, particularly those with whom they transact, to adopt the same behaviors and values?

Selected References

Albrecht, W. Steve, Gerald W. Wernz, and Timothy L. Williams. [1995]. *Fraud: Bringing Light to the Dark Side of Business*. Burr Ridge, IL: Irwin Professional Publishing.

Alchian, Armen, and Harold Demsetz. [1972]. "Production, Information Costs, and Economic Organization." *American Economic Review* (December), pp. 777–795.

Andrews, Kenneth R., ed. [1989]. *Ethics in Practice: Managing the Moral Corporation*. Boston: Harvard Business School Press.

Ausubel, Lawrence. [1991]. "The Failure of Competition in the Credit Card Market." *American Economic Review* (March), pp. 50–81.

Bear, Larry A., and Rita Maldonado-Bear. [1994]. *Free Markets, Finance, Ethics, and Law*. Englewood Cliffs, NJ: Prentice-Hall.

Beauchamp, Tom L., and Norman E. Bowie, eds. [1988]. *Ethical Theory in Business*. Englewood Cliffs, NJ: Prentice-Hall.

Berle, Adolf A., Jr., and Gardiner C. Means. [1932]. *The Modern Corporation and Private Property*. New York: Macmillan.

Bowie, Norman E., and R. Edward Freeman, eds. [1992]. *Ethics and Agency Theory: An Introduction*. New York: Oxford University Press.

Bradsher, Keith. [1994]. "Fed Tightens Its Policies on Ethics." *The New York Times,* June 9, p. D1.

Braitman, Ellen. [1990]. "Private Banking: Executives Say Ethics Important in Choice of Bank." *American Banker* (October 31).

Burritt, Chris. [1996]. "Survivor Sickness." *Atlanta Journal Constitution,* March 4, p. E1.

Cannella, Albert A., Jr., Donald R. Frazer, and D. Scott Lee. [1995]. "Firm Failure and Managerial Labor Markets: Evidence from Texas Banking." *Journal of Financial Economics,* pp. 185–210.

Carmichael, Shenna. [1995]. *Business Ethics: The New Bottom Line*. London: Demos.

Chambers, Donald R., and Nelson R. Lacey. [1996]. "Corporate Ethics and Shareholder Wealth Maximization." *Financial Practice and Education* (Spring/Summer), pp. 93–96.

Clark, R. C. [1985]. "Agency Costs versus Fiduciary Duties." In Pratt and Zeckhauser, eds., *Principals and Agents: The Structure of Business,* pp. 55–79.

Coase, Ronald. [1937]. "The Nature of the Firm." *Economica* 4, pp. 386–405.

Cummins, Claudia. [1993]. "Fed Watchdog Cites Conflicts of Interest by Examiners." *American Banker* (February 24), p. 1.

Darcy, Keith T. [1993]. "Comment: Strong Ethical Standards Crucial for Banks to Survive." *American Banker* (June 17).

Dickens, Ross N. [1996]. *Contestable Markets Theory, Competition, and the United States Commercial Banking Industry.* New York: Garland.

Donaldson, Thomas, and Patricia H. Werhane, eds. [1988]. *Ethical Issues in Business: A Philosophical Approach.* Englewood Cliffs, NJ: Prentice-Hall.

Fisher, Roger, and William Ury. [1991]. *Getting to Yes: Negotiating Agreement Without Giving In.* New York: Penguin Books.

French, Warren A., and John Granrose. [1995]. *Practical Business Ethics.* Englewood Cliffs, NJ: Prentice-Hall.

Friedman, Milton. [1953]. "The Methodology of Positive Economics." In *Essays in Positive Economics.* Chicago: University of Chicago Press.

———. [1962]. *Capitalism and Freedom.* Chicago: University of Chicago Press.

———. [1970]. "The Social Responsibility of Business Is to Increase Its Profit." *The New York Times Magazine* (September 13). Reprinted in Donaldson and Werhane [1988], pp. 217–223, and in Nelson and Cavey [1991], pp. 245–253.

Geewax, Marilyn. [1996]. "Downsizing Is Undermining Faith in the American System." *Atlanta Journal Constitution,* February 4, p. B5.

Habermas, Jurgen. [1979]. *Communication and the Evolution of Society.* Boston: Beacon Press.

Hardy, Quentin. [1996]. "Idaho County Tests a New Way to Curb Teen Sex: Prosecute." *The Wall Street Journal,* July 8, pp. A1, A4.

Heady, Robert. [1996]. "1995 Was a Record Year for Banks—But Not for Their Customers." *Atlanta Journal Constitution,* March 4, p. E2.

Holmes, Kim R. [1994]. "In Search of Free Markets." *The Wall Street Journal,* December 12, p. A14.

Jensen, Michael C., and William H. Meckling. [1976]. "Theory of the Firm: Managerial Behavior, Agency Costs, and Ownership Structure." *Journal of Financial Economics* (October), pp. 305–360.

Johnson, Bryan, and Thomas Sheehy. [1994]. *Index of Economic Freedom.* Washington, DC: Heritage Foundation.

Jowett, Benjamin. [1937]. *The Dialogues of Plato.* New York: Random House.

Kane, Edward J. [1989]. *The S&L Insurance Mess: How Did It Happen?* Washington, DC: Urban Institute.

———. [1990]. "Principal-Agent Relations in S&L Salvage." *Journal of Finance* (July), pp. 755–764.

———. [1993]. "The S&L Mess, Part One." *The Carrol Research Report Boston College* (Winter), pp. 11–13.

———. [1995]. "Missing Entailments of Public-Policy Definitions of Systemic Risk." In *Research in Financial Services Private and Public Policy,* vol. 7, pp. 337–346. Greenwich, CT: JAI Press.

———. [1996a]. "De Jure Interstate Banking: Why Only Now?" *Journal of Money, Credit and Banking* (May), pp. 141–161.

————. [1996b]. "The Increasing Futility of Restricting Bank Participation in Insurance Activities." In Anthony Saunders and Ingo Walter, eds., *Universal Banking.* Homewood Hills, IL: Irwin Professional Publishers, pp. 338–354.

————. [1996c]. "Foundations of Financial Regulation." Working Paper, Boston College (May 20).

————. [1996d]. "Ethical Conflicts in Managing the S&L Insurance Mess." In Edward J. O'Boyle, ed., *Social Economics: Premises, Findings, and Policies.* London: Routledge, pp. 125–144.

————. [1996e]. "Managing Ethical Conflict and Exposure to Financial Fraud." Boston College, Carroll School of Management, MF820. Class notes, dated week 96-4, p. 1.

Kelly, Edward W., Jr. [1996]. "Statement before the Committee on Banking and Financial Services, U.S. House of Representatives" (February 28).

Leeson, Nick. [1996]. *Rogue Trader: How I Brought Down Barings Bank and Shook the Financial World.* Boston: Little, Brown.

Lewis, Alan, and Karl-Erik Warneryd, eds. [1994]. *Ethics and Economic Affairs.* New York: Routledge.

McCarthy, Colman. [1996]. "Jail's No-Frills Reality Enlightens a Judge." *International Herald Tribune,* April 3, p. 9.

McCarthy, Joseph L. [1992]. "Ethics Training Gains Popularity: Banks Reacting to Turmoil and Tarnished Image." *American Banker* (January 9), p. 7.

Mitchell, William J., Phillip V. Lewis, and N. L. Reinsch, Jr. [1992]. "Bank Ethics: An Exploratory Study of Ethical Behaviors and Perceptions in Small, Local Banks." *Journal of Business Ethics* (March), pp. 197–205.

Mitnick, Barry M. [1974]. "The Theory of Agency: The Concept of Fiduciary Rationality and Some Consequences." Unpublished Ph.D. Dissertation, Department of Political Science, University of Pennsylvania.

Nadler, Paul S. [1991]. "Wanted: More Ethical Management." *American Banker* (November 25), p. 4.

Nelson, Charles A., and Robert D. Cavey, eds. [1991]. *Ethics, Leadership, and the Bottom Line.* Croton-on-Hudson, NY: North River Press.

Plato. *The Republic.* [1937]. In Benjamin Jowett, ed., *The Dialogues of Plato,* vol. 1. New York: Random House.

Pratt, John W., and Richard J. Zeckhauser, eds. [1985]. *Principals and Agents: The Structure of Business.* Boston: Harvard Business School Press.

Putterman, Louis, and Randall S. Kroszner, eds. [1996]. *The Economic Nature of the Firm.* Cambridge: Cambridge University Press.

Quinn, Jane Bryant. [1996]. "They've Got Your Number." *Newsweek,* March 4, p. 44.

Reinhardt, Ken S. [1994]. "Ethics 'R' Us." *Executive Speaker,* pp. 46–48. From speech delivered on May 26, 1989.

Ross, Stephen A. [1973]. "The Economic Theory of Agency: The Principal's Problem." *American Economic Review* (May), pp. 134–139.

Schelling, Thomas. [1978]. *Micromotives and Macrobehavior.* New York: Norton.

"Schools Brief: State and Market." [1996]. *The Economist,* February 17, pp. 64–65.

Seiberg, Jaret. [1996]. "Top Court: U.S. Must Pay for Accounting-Policy Shift." *American Banker* (July 2), pp. 1–2.

Sloan, Allan. [1996]. "Take This Job and Cut It: How Wells Fargo Won the Battle of the Banks." *Newsweek,* February 5, p. 47.

Smith, Adam. [1776]. *The Wealth of Nations.* Oxford: Clarendon Press, 1976.

Stigler, George J. [1982]. *The Economist as Preacher.* Chicago: University of Chicago Press.

Tharpe, Gene. [1996]. "Know Your Rights as a Credit-Card User." *Atlanta Journal Constitution,* March 4, p. E2.

"Twelve Credit-Card Secrets Banks Don't Want You to Know." [1994]. Massachusetts Executive Office of Consumer Affairs and Business Regulation, Boston, MA, (October).

Vaughan, Diane. [1983]. *Controlling Unlawful Organizational Behavior: Social Structure and Corporate Misconduct.* Chicago: University of Chicago Press.

———. [1996a]. *The Challenger Launch Decision.* Chicago: University of Chicago Press.

———. [1996b]. "Risky Business." *Boston College Magazine* (Spring), pp. 24–36.

Warneryd, Karl-Erik, and Alan Lewis. [1994]. "The Longstanding Interest in Business Ethics: An Introduction." In Lewis and Warneryd, eds. [1994]. *Ethics and Economic Affairs.* London: Routledge, pp. 1–14.

Weatherstone, Dennis. [1995]. "Reflections on the Business of Banking." Remarks at the Institute of International Finance, Washington, DC (October 8). Available from J. P. Morgan's Corporate Information/Perspectives.

Whyte, David. [1994]. *The Heart Aroused: Poetry and Preservation of the Soul in Corporate America.* New York: Currency Doubleday.

Williams, Steven P. [1993]. "Comment: Risk Management in Banking: Rationality or Reregulation?" *American Banker* (August 3), p. 14.

APPENDIX

CONTINENTAL ILLINOIS CORPORATION: HOW DID IT BECOME "NOT WORTH A CONTINENTAL"?

Introduction

On October 15, 1981, the front page of *The Wall Street Journal* described the lead bank of Continental Illinois Corporation as "On the Offensive: Behind Homely Image of Continental Illinois Is an Aggressive Bank." The subheadline read: "Its Risks Sometimes Backfire, But Its Cut-Rate Lending Has Yielded Major Gains." The risks that Continental Illinois National Bank & Trust Co. was taking were in lending and on interest rates. Stuart Greenbaum, then of Northwestern University, described the bank's managers as " . . . extraordinarily aggressive. They've sold the hell out of the corporate market by taking more than average risks in well selected areas." Sanford Rose of the *American Banker* said, "Continental has been a bigger dice thrower than most."

Regarding Continental's perceived gambler's posture, Chairman Roger E. Anderson said, "I think we're conservative but aggressive." How does an organization serve both of these masters? One interpretation is low risk and high return. Which, of course, is nonsense because it violates the fundamental principle of a risk–return trade-off. Another interpretation is more basic and focuses upon the possible deception of self-perception or self-evaluation. What we think or perceive about ourselves or our organizations may not be what objective outsiders see. Alternatively, and more plausibly, Continental's managers knew exactly what they were doing; they were not misguided village idiots who thought high return could be generated by a low-risk portfolio. As Paul Gigot, a staff reporter for the WSJ, wrote, "Behind that homely, country-boy self-image stand some of the nation's slickest, most aggressive bankers."

And Now for the Rest of the Story: The Dice Came Up Snake Eyes

Radio and television commentator Paul Harvey is famous for his line, "And now, the rest of the story." In the Continental story, the gambling bank rolled snake eyes at the Penn Square table in, of all places, Oklahoma City. The good old boys from Chicago were roped in by some real country bumpkins at the shopping-center bank.

By December 31, 1981, Continental Illinois appeared to be in sound financial condition and performing well. Its assets totaled $47 billion, with $33 billion in loans, $30 billion in deposits, and $1.7 billion in equity capital. On the earnings side, net interest income (TE) was $910 million, and net income was $255 million. On a per share basis, *EPS* was $6.44, with a *DPS* of $1.90. The Corporation's *ROE* was 15.8 percent, consisting of an *ROA* of 0.58 percent and an *EM* of 27.3, figures which were about average for its peer group of money-center banks. On December 31, 1981, Continental Illinois's common stock closed on the NYSE at $33.125, or 77 percent of its book value of $43.19. (Discounts from book values were not uncommon for the stocks of financial institutions at this time.)

Continental's Achilles' Heel: Penn Square Bank

On July 5, 1982, Penn Square Bank was declared insolvent by the OCC. The FDIC, as receiver, established a Deposit Insurance National Bank (DINB) to pay off the insured deposits of the failed institution. How does the failure of a $465 million bank in Oklahoma City affect a $47 billion, multinational bank headquartered in Chicago? When the Chicago bank has purchased more than $1 billion in loans from the fly-by-night bank, it has a severe effect, especially when substantial amounts of the participations are bad credits. Mainly as a result of the failure of Penn Square, Continental's 1982 net income dropped to $78 million as net credit losses rose to $393 million (from $71 million in 1981), with $191 million of the charge-offs due to participations purchased from Penn Square. In addition, Continental's provision for credit losses increased to $492 million in 1982 from $120 million the year before.

The 1984 Liquidity Crisis and Bailout

On Thursday, May 10, 1984, Continental began experiencing liquidity problems as "rumors" about the bank's financial condition spread throughout both national and international financial markets. The following week, as described in Exhibit A17–1, was one of turmoil at Continental Illinois. The week culminated with the announcement of an unprecedented bailout arranged by the FDIC, the OCC, the Fed, and a group of 24 major banks. The financial-assistance program provided Continental with the liquidity, capital, and time to resolve its problems in an orderly and permanent fashion. However, by July 1, 1984, even the $7.5 billion safety net was proving inadequate, as Continental was forced to sell almost $5 billion of

EXHIBIT A17–1

WEEK OF TURMOIL AT CONTINENTAL ILLINOIS

Thursday, May 10: Continental's stock falls $1\frac{1}{8}$ points in heavy trading on rumors the bank's financial condition has worsened. Continental issues denial.

Friday, May 11: Continental's stock rebounds as rumors of deteriorating financial condition appear to die down. Illinois commissioner of banks and trust companies assures state-chartered banks Continental can meet its obligations.

Monday, May 14: Banking industry, in plan backed by Federal Reserve Board, arranges $4.5 billion safety net for Continental in attempt to halt an outflow of deposits. Fund to be provided by 16-bank group led by Morgan Guaranty Trust Co. of New York. Standard & Poor's lowers the bank's debt ratings.

Tuesday, May 15: Continental draws on safety net. Money markets appear to have been calmed.

Wednesday, May 16: Safety net appears to calm commercial depositors as trading in Continental's certificates of deposit stabilizes some.

Thursday, May 17: Continental says it is seeking a merger as federal regulators arrange $2 billion of financial assistance and group of 24 major United States banks agrees to provide more than $5.3 billion in funding. This package replaces $4.5 billion, 16-bank safety net. Continental also omits common stock dividend and says nonperforming loans in second quarter to be above first-quarter level of $2.3 billion.

Continental's average daily overnight funding needs during the last week: $2.25 billion from the 16-bank group, $4 billion from the Federal Reserve Board, $1.75 billion from other sources. Total: $8 billion.

Source: Bailey and Hill [1984].

---

its assets over the months of May and June. The shrinkage trimmed Continental's asset base to roughly $37 billion, down $10 billion from year-end 1981.

Throughout July, regulatory attempts to find a "private solution" to Continental's problems continued to be futile. Because no investor was willing to come to Continental's rescue without government financial assistance, the regulators did it themselves on July 26, 1984. The rescue package, which nonregulators called a "nationalization" and the regulators denied, was, in effect, a blank check that provided whatever financial aid was needed to ensure Continental's survival. The details of the rescue, which are complex, are summarized in Exhibit A17–2. In a nutshell, the plan gave the FDIC 80 percent ownership of Continental for buying up $4.5 billion of its problem loans. The ownership structures of Continental before and after its nationalization are shown in Figure A17-1.

One of the interesting aspects of Continental's *de facto* failure was that accounting made the early revelation of its problem as a liquidity crisis. At the time, Continental had book net worth, including reserves, of roughly $2.3 billion. However, the market value of its shareholders' equity was dropping rapidly as the stock price fell from $13.125 at the close on May 9 to $10.25 on May 17. The low price on the day of the May bailout was $8.625 and the volume was 2,659,500 shares traded. With about 40 million shares outstanding, Continental's total market value was roughly $400 million. On February 1, 1984, Continental's stock price was $21.25; by March 30, it had dropped to $17.875. During Independence week, the price had plummeted to $4.125, down $1.375. During this same week, Continental's preferred stock (1,788,000 shares outstanding) dropped $1.25 to $13.625. Over the previous 52-week period, its high price was $51.25, with a new low established on July 6, 1984, at $13.50.

EXHIBIT A17–2

	Office of the Comptroller of the Currency
July 26, 1984	Federal Deposit Insurance Corporation
	Federal Reserve Board

For Release
9:00 A.M. e.d.t., 7-26-84

*Permanent Assistance Program
for Continental Illinois National Bank
and Trust Company, Chicago, Illinois*

Summary Statement

A multi-billion-dollar program to rehabilitate the Continental Illinois National Bank and Trust Company and restore it to financial health was announced today by the Federal Deposit Insurance Corporation, the Comptroller of the Currency, and the Federal Reserve Board.

Major components of the plan include installation of a proven, internationally recognized mangement team, the removal from the bank of $4.5 billion in problem loans, the infusion of $1 billion in new capital, and ongoing lines of credit from the Federal Reserve and a group of major U.S. banks. The resulting institution will be smaller, but immeasurably stronger and positioned to profitably serve the full range of banking needs of its customers.

Key management appointments are John E. Swearingen as Chairman of the Board and Chief Executive Officer of Continental Illinois Corporation and William S. Ogden as Chairman of the Board and Chief Executive Officer of Continental Illinois National Bank.

Mr. Swearingen, 65, widely acclaimed throughout international business circles, recently retired as Chief Executive Officer of the Standard Oil Company (Indiana), headquartered in Chicago. In addition to his extensive background in the energy business, where a significant amount of Continental Illinois's loans reside, he is a director of The Chase Manhattan Bank (a position he will resign).

On May 17, 1984, the Federal Deposit Insurance Corporation, the Federal Reserve Board and the Comptroller of the Currency announced an interim financial assistance package for the Continental Illinois National Bank and Trust Company. The program was designed to alleviate the liquidity pressures facing the bank in order to provide the time needed to resolve the bank's problems in an orderly and permanent way and to avoid general instability in the financial system.

Since the announcement the agencies have conducted an examination of the bank and have held extensive discussions with prospective merger partners and potential investors. A number of proposals from various sources have been reviewed.

After careful evaluation of all of the alternatives, the agencies have decided that the best solution is to provide sufficient permanent capital and other direct assistance to enable the bank to restore its position as a viable, self-financing entity. Factors considered in reaching this determination included the cost to the FDIC, competitive consequences and the banking needs of the public.

Financial Information

Tables A17-1 to A17-3 provide financial data on Continental Illinois Corporation for the period 1979 through 1983. In Table A17-1, selected balance-sheet and income-expense figures are presented. Information to conduct an analysis of Continental's interest-rate sensitivity is shown in Table A17-2. In Table A17-3, selected loan data are provided. As of year-end 1983, the assets of Continental Illinois National Bank accounted for 96.54 percent of the assets of Continental Illinois Corporation. Thus, for all practical purposes, the bank is the holding company.

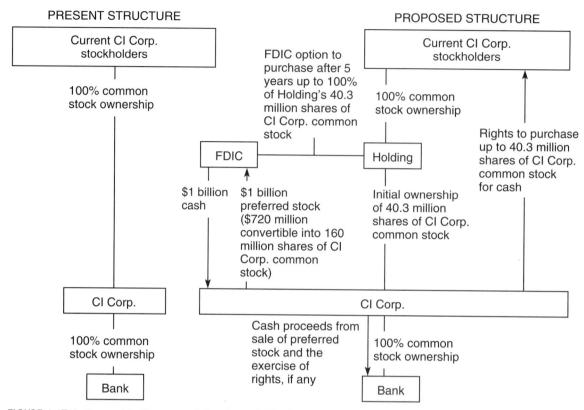

FIGURE A17-1 **Ownership Structure of Continental Illinois**

TABLE A17-1	Continental Illinois Corporation, Selected Financial Data, 1979–1983				
Average Balance Sheet Items	*1983*	*1982*	*1981*	*1980*	*1979*
Earning assets	$36,167[a]	$40,254	$37,113	$32,979	$27,427
Total assets	40,268	45,662	44,004	39,565	33,252
Deposits	26,747	28,225	27,428	24,953	22,370
Long-term debt	1,273	1,088	722	600	521
Common stockholders' equity	1,722	1,721	1,616	1,443	1,294
Income-Expense Items					
Total operating income	$4,381	$5,889	$6,286	$4,715	$3,376
Total interest income	3,977	5,579	5,964	4,472	3,168
Total interest expense	3,146	4,688	5,158	3,742	2,594
Net interest income	831	891	806	730	574
Total other operating exp.	721	673	624	558	464
Net income	108	78	255	226	196
Interest income (TE) adjust.	81	105	105	107	103
Per Share Items					
EPS	$ 2.63	$ 1.95	$ 6.44	$ 5.75	$ 4.99
DPS	2.00	2.00	1.90	1.70	1.52
Book value	43.13	42.80	43.19	38.76	34.75
Market value	21.87	20.37	33.12	31.25	31.12

[a]All figures are millions, except per share data.

Source: Continental Illinois Corporation, Annual Reports and Form 10-K [1979–1983].

TABLE A17-2 Continental Illinois Corporation Interest-Rate Sensitivity, 1980–1983

Earning Assets	1983	1982	1981	1980
0–30 days	$22,099[a]	$21,394	$17,850	$14,073
31–90 days	5,371	5,413	9,568	7,626
91–180 days	2,069	2,442	4,233	3,524
181–365 days	815	1,603	1,148	1,920
Over 1 year	7,072	7,939	7,907	7,832
Total	37,426	38,791	40,706	34,975
Interest-Bearing Liabilities				
0–30 days	$20,908	$21,434	$20,107	$14,770
31–90 days	7,781	7,289	8,085	6,833
91–180 days	1,984	3,448	5,227	5,280
181–365 days	821	825	1,235	2,152
Over 1 year	2,209	1,947	1,447	2,477
Total	33,703	34,943	36,131	31,512
Interest-Sensitive Gap				
0–30 days	$ 1,191	$ (40)	$(2,257)	$ (697)
31–90 days	(2,410)	(1,876)	1,483	793
91–180 days	85	(1,006)	(994)	(1,756)
181–365 days	(6)	778	(87)	(232)
Over 1 year	4,863	5,992	6,430	5,355
Total	3,723	3,848	4,575	3,463

[a]All figures are millions.
Source: Continental Illinois Corporation, Annual Reports and Form 10-K [1980–1983].

TABLE A17-3 Continental Illinois Corporation, Selected Loan Data, 1979–1983

Domestic Loans	1983	1982	1981	1980	1979
Commercial & industrial (C&I)	$12,258[a]	$13,715	$12,862	$ 9,845	$ 8,221
All other loans	7,929	8,338	9,268	8,683	8,145
Total	20,187	22,053	22,130	18,528	16,366
Foreign Loans					
Commercial & industrial (C&I)	7,454	7,979	7,434	6,202	5,180
All other loans	2,749	2,838	2,612	2,180	1,636
Total	10,203	10,817	10,046	8,382	6,816
Total Loans					
Commercial & industrial (C&I)	19,712	21,694	20,296	16,047	13,401
All other loans	10,678	11,176	11,880	10,863	9,781
Total	30,390	32,870	32,176	26,910	23,182
Reserves for credit losses	382	381	289	246	212
Net credit losses	387	393	71	61	49
Nonperforming domestic C&I loans	1,149	1,077	187	134	84
Total nonperforming loans	1,964	1,937	53	444	446

[a]All figures are millions.
Source: Continental Illinois Corporation, Annual Reports and Form 10-K [1979–1983].

Analytical and Discussion Questions

1. Financial-statement analysis
   a. Conduct an *ROE* decomposition analysis of Continental's performance from 1979 through 1983 and compute its risk index. Describe your findings in a brief report.
   b. What happened to Continental's net interest margin and its "burden" over the period 1979 through 1983? What about its operating efficiency as measured by the ratio of total operating expense to total operating income?
   c. How fast was Continental growing over this period? What are the relevant variables to be analyzed in answering this question?
   d. Conduct an analysis of Continental's interest-rate sensitivity over the period 1980 through 1983 and summarize your findings in a brief report.
   e. A bank's loan portfolio is its "heart and soul." How healthy was Continental's loan portfolio? Prior to Penn Square, what characteristics about it, if any, would have concerned you?
   f. This question is for advanced and ambitious students only. Conduct an "event study" to determine what information Continental's investors had about its impending collapse. As critical dates you might look at July 5, 1982, May 14, 1984, and/or May 17, 1984. If you don't have access to the CRSP tapes, you probably should skip this project.

2. When he opened the Congressional hearing into the failure of Penn State bank, Representative Fernand St. Germain was looking for answers to numerous questions, one of which was, "How were some of the nation's most sophisticated financial institutions, with all varieties of expertise at hand, lured like moths to the glow of this go-go bank sitting in a shopping center in Oklahoma City?" What is your answer?

3. To what extent, if any, was regulation or deregulation a cause of Continental's collapse? Explain fully.

4. Prior to Continental's collapse, FDIC chairman William M. Isaac was talking boldly about "market discipline" playing a greater role in regulating bank risk taking. When the financial markets answered by disciplining Continental with a liquidity crisis in May 1984, Isaac (and Volcker and Conover too) reacted by bailing out Continental. Did the regulators have any other choice? What was the message sent to other major banks by the bailout? What was the message to the "other half" of the real dual-banking system? Do you think that the 24 major banks that participated in the bailout did so freely or under regulatory pressure? Wasn't it in their own self-interest to participate?

5. Because most failed banks are identified by the regulators as "problem banks" with substantial lead times before they are closed, isn't the regulatory problem one of enforcement rather than *identification?* Discuss. As a regulator, what would you have done with Continental in the time between the Penn Square fiasco (July, 1983) and its liquidity crisis (May, 1984)?

6. On May 29, 1984, Jeffery E. Garten, a vice president of Shearson Lehman/American Express Inc., stated, "It is tempting to say that the 1930s are no longer relevant. Don't believe it. Modern banking has become riskier than ever. Advances in communication and information gathering have not prevented lending debacles." Discuss the pros and cons of his statement. Also keep in mind where he is coming from and that he is in favor of more bank regulation, or at least a slower pace of deregulation.

7. What similarities, if any, do you see among the collapse of Continental Illinois, the S&L mess, and the *Challenger* disaster?

Appendix References

Bailey, Jeff, John Heylar, and Tim Carrington. [1984]. "Anatomy of Failure." *The Wall Street Journal,* July 30, pp. 1 and 12.

Bailey, Jeff, and G. Christian Hill. [1984]. "Continental Gets Full U.S. Support. . . ." *The Wall Street Journal,* May 18, pp. 3 and 14.

Gigot, Paul A. [1981]. "Behind Image of Continental Illinois Is an Aggressive Bank." *The Wall Street Journal,* October 15, pp. 3 and 14.

Sinkey, Joseph F., Jr. [1984]. "The Characteristics of Large Problem and Failed Banks." For an invited Symposium on Issues and Options in Dealing with Large Banks' Problems and Failures sponsored by the Bank Administration Institute at the Amos Tuck School of Business, Dartmouth College, Hanover, New Hampshire, August 29–30.

Volcker, Paul A. [1984]. Statement before the Committee on Banking, Housing, and Urban Affairs. Washington, DC: U.S. Senate (July 25).

PART

VII

FINANCIAL INNOVATION, INFORMATION TECHNOLOGY, AND CORPORATE RESTRUCTURING IN THE FINANCIAL-SERVICES INDUSTRY

E lectronic and contracting technologies are two stimuli for change in the financial-services industry (FSI). Because financial-services firms (FSFs) transfer funds and process information, they are especially concerned about advances in electronic funds transfer systems (EFTS or EFT systems) and in information technology. The joint development of EFT and information technology has led to the innovations of electronic money, or e-money, and electronic banking or e-banking. Because these technological advances have made geographic and product restrictions obsolete, consolidation and corporate restructuring within and across the various segments of the FSI have occurred and will continue to occur. This final part of the book, which contains three chapters, focuses on the roles of financial innovation, information technology, and corporate restructuring (including mergers and acquisitions) in the FSI.

The FSI can be described as undergoing an *-ization* as captured by such innovations as securitization, globalization, institutionalization, and privatization. In former centrally planned economies (CPEs), privatization has coincided with the collapse of communism and the USSR. From a global perspective, this part of the book focuses on, among other things, the financial aspects of globalization and privatization.

Chapter 18 explains the process of financial innovation by describing innovation as a diffusion process. This framework provides the foundation for analyzing how technology, reregulation, and the economy affect financial innovation. Although home banking was predicted for the twentieth century, it never happened. The development of the Internet presents a better opportunity for home and virtual banking to become realities in the twenty-first century.

Chapter 19 focuses on consolidation in the FSI by analyzing mergers and acquisitions and corporate restructuring. The removal of geographic barriers to domestic expansion and the financial difficulties of commercial banks and thrift institutions have prompted a wave of mergers and acquisitions in banking. For example, during the 1980s, 3,555 bank mergers, absorptions, or consolidations occurred, *excluding* bank failures. This rate of 355 per year was more than double the annual rate for any of the preceding four decades. From 1940 through 1990 (51 years), a total of 8,867 banks merged, 45 percent of them over the last 11 years (1980–1990). The consolidation trend has continued in the 1990s as witnessed by 611 combinations among commercial banks in 1995. The 1980s also witnessed a new phenomenon in banking, the hostile takeover. These activities and other types of corporate restructurings (e.g., bank divestitures), along with market reactions to the announcement of such deals, are covered in chapter 19.

In chapter 20, international banking, with its focus on globalization and the Americanization of finance, is analyzed. The inroads made by foreign banks in the United States and lessons from the international debt crisis also receive special attention. The appendix to chapter 20 deals with the relationships among exchange rates, interest rates, and inflation.

The key word for this part of the book is restructuring. In chapter 18, the focus is on the restructuring arising from technological innovations; in chapter 19, the focus is on the corporate restructuring arising from mergers and acquisitions and internal reorganizations; and in chapter 20, it's restructuring arising from globalization.

CHAPTER

18

INNOVATION AS A DIFFUSION PROCESS, INFORMATION TECHNOLOGY, AND ELECTRONIC BANKING

Contents

LEARNING OBJECTIVES

■ To understand innovation as a diffusion process

■ To understand the importance of information technology to financial-services firms

■ To understand traditional electronic banking as a delivery system based on electronic funds transfer (EFT)

■ To understand the components of EFT as ATMs, POSs, and ACHs

■ To understand that home banking was a bust in the twentieth century but that it has the opportunity to boom on the Internet in the twenty century

■ To understand banks as communications firms

CHAPTER THEME

Microsoft's Bill Gates was misquoted when the statement "banks are dinosaurs" was attributed to him. What he intended to say was that banks' back-office databases belong in Jurassic Park. Because banks have never been accused of being on the cutting edge of technology, his intended remarks ring true. If banks are to survive in the financial-services industry (FSI) of the twenty-first century, they must get on the information highway quickly, because electronic, information-based innovations are adopted quickly. Banks and communications firms are similar in that they both establish networking relationships through which they collect, store, process, and transmit information for themselves and customers' accounts. The potential foundation of the FSI rests on two pillars: home or on-line banking via the Internet and virtual banking on a worldwide basis.

KEY CONCEPTS, IDEAS, AND TERMS

- Automated clearing house (ACH)
- Automated teller machine (ATM)
- Communications firms
- Diffusion process
- Electronic banking (e-banking)
- Electronic data interchange (EDI)
- Electronic funds transfer system (EFTS)
- Electronic money (e-money)
- Home banking
- Information technology
- Innovation
- Internet
- Invention
- Networking
- Payments system
- Point-of-sale (POS)
- TRICK + Rational self-interest → Financial innovation
- Virtual banking

ARE BANKS DINOSAURS?

If you ask three economists, Are banks dinosaurs? their answers might be yes, no, and maybe. Taking an equally weighted average, their consensus answer is maybe—the old joke about economists never being able to reach a conclusion.

In 1994, Bill Gates, chairman of Microsoft, was misquoted as saying that banks had become dinosaurs. The *American Banker* (January 5, 1995) later reported that his remarks set off "technology alarms" for many bankers. What Gates actually intended to say, as clarified in his 1995 book, *The Road Ahead* [1995b], was that he views the back-office databases of banks as dinosaurs. If your bank still returns your checks and has yet to produce a consolidated statement that summarizes all of your accounts, its back-office databases are likely to be on exhibit in the Jurassic Park for banks' backroom operations.

Financial-services firms in the twenty-first century will strive to be "virtual banks," which according to Citicorp/Citibank means ability to serve customers "anywhere, anytime, (in) any way." In addition, they will permit you to bank from your home as with home-shopping networks. Innovations related to **information technology** will pave the way for **electronic banking** (e-banking), and **electronic money** (e-money). These linkages suggest an important similarity between banks and **communications firms:** They both establish **networking** relationships through which they collect, store, process, and transmit information for themselves and customers' accounts.

This chapter deals with the technological side of banking, which has both back-office and front-office aspects. Before technological advances (inventions) can be applied in any business, however, they must pass a value-added, or profitability test. A key learning objective is to view **innovation,** defined as a profitable invention, as a **diffusion process.** Because diffusion does not happen overnight, innovations tend to spread slowly. Moreover, electronic and information-based technological innovations have not diffused as rapidly as some analysts anticipated. Nevertheless, in the competitive environment of the twenty-first century, technological innovation presents banks with an opportunity to gain a competitive advantage through cost-effective delivery systems and to use these systems to generate fee income.

A DYNAMIC MODEL OF CHANGE AND THE PROCESS OF FINANCIAL INNOVATION

Five components of a dynamic model of change are

> *T*ransparency
>
> *R*isk management
>
> *I*nformation technology
>
> *C*ustomers
>
> *K*apital adequacy

This chapter focuses on using information technology to attract and service customers.

As a comprehensive conceptual device, TRICK captures the major forces of change operating in the FSI. For comparison, Van Horne [1985] list six stimuli that prompt financial innovation:

- Volatile inflation rates and interest rates, the *R* component of TRICK in terms of the underlying forces driving risk management
- Regulatory changes and circumvention of regulations, the *K* component of TRICK in terms of capital adequacy capturing the thrust of bank regulation
- Tax changes, the notion of regulation as a tax, also captured by the *K* component
- Technological advances, the *I* component of TRICK
- The level of economic activity, the *R* component (e.g., deflation has been the culprit driving bank loan losses whereas interest-rate volatility has made net interest income volatile)
- Academic work on market efficiency and inefficiencies, much of it directed toward issues of transparency and adequate disclosure

Although commercial bankers might not include academic work on their lists of important stimuli, modern investment bankers would be hard pressed to exclude it. The fact that a number of high-powered finance academics were hired by Wall Street investment bankers (prior to the stock market crash of 1987—no causality implied) gives considerable credence to Van Horne's point. Moreover, by the early 1990s, the largest U.S. commercial banks were dominating the world of derivatives,[1] which they could not have done without research on the pricing and structuring of derivatives contracts.

The combination of TRICK and rational self-interest generates a model of change, or a framework for analyzing the process of financial innovation, that is,

$$\text{TRICK} + \text{Rational self-interest} \rightarrow \text{Financial innovation} \qquad \textbf{(18-1)}$$

To make the notion of rational self-interest more palatable, think of it as profitable opportunities. When such opportunities exist, rational businesspersons go after them. What explains the existence of profitable opportunities? Given the paradigm of perfect competition and efficient markets, we can look for market imperfections and inefficiencies as potential sources of profitable opportunities. Of course, if markets are competitive, then the mere existence of such opportunities would, over time, bring about their demise because other innovators (or followers) would compete away the profits. Assuming efficient, lowest-cost producers, the competitive process works such that the consumers of financial services eventually reap the benefits of the process of financial innovation through lower prices or better-quality products and services or both. These benefits, however, may not be achieved without some costs associated with consolidation, failures, and financial instability.

INNOVATION AS A DIFFUSION PROCESS

Innovation means the introduction of something new, such as a new idea, method, or device. From the end of World War II until the early 1960s, nothing new seemed to happen in banking—no new ideas, methods, or devices. Moreover, except for the Korean War, the economic, political, and social climate of this period was one of

---

[1] Sinkey and Carter [1997], among others, document this dominance.

relative calm and stability; it was the period of the "generals"—General Motors, General Electric, and General Eisenhower. The saving graces of the 1950s were rock-and-roll music and '57 Chevy convertibles.

By February 1961, a key banking innovation occurred—the introduction of the first effective negotiable *certificate of deposit* (CD), an innovation that eventually spread to the retail level such that *CD* had a universal and unambiguous meaning in banking. However, with the innovation of compact disks, also known as CDs, from the recording industry, the meaning of CD has become ambiguous.[2] The (financial) CD, introduced by First National City Bank of New York (now Citibank/ Citicorp), was important because it permitted banks to purchase funds and thereby manage their liabilities, hence the term liability management (chapter 7). Since then, numerous financial and technological innovations have been introduced on an ongoing basis. Relative to the 1960s and the 1970s, however, the greatest rush of innovations and other changes (e.g., mergers, consolidations, and failures) occurred in the 1980s and 1990s, and will continue in the twenty-first century.

The Diffusion of Financial Innovations: Some Preliminary Distinctions

To make the diffusion of financial innovations more intelligible, let's consider three preliminary distinctions made by Kane [1983] with respect to

- Invention versus innovation
- Autonomous innovation versus induced innovation
- Market-induced innovation versus regulation-induced innovation

As shown in Figure 18-1, the first distinction defines an **invention** as an unfolding technological opportunity, and innovation as the profitable application of an invention. The lag between an invention and its embodiment in an innovation is called the innovation lag. For example, although personal computers have been available for years, the profitable application of these devices to home banking has yet to be fully realized. Whether the Internet will bring home banking to fruition in the twenty-first century remains to be seen.

Financial-services technology tends to be downstreamed, after a delay, from wholesale applications to retail ones. The lag reflects the time it takes to reduce the operating costs of the new technology or generate the sales volume to make retail applications profitable. Thus, one way to forecast future products and services at the retail level is to look at the technology on the wholesale level.

The second distinction separates innovations into those induced by market or regulatory forces and autonomous ones (i.e., those not caused by market or regulatory forces). Think of autonomous innovations as just happening. For example, in the birth process, labor can occur naturally (say autonomously), or it can be induced chemically. Regarding autonomous innovation, psychologists might look for the catalyst in the innovator's toilet training or lack of it.[3]

---

[2] In addition to storing music, compact disks are great devices for storing data and other information. For example, a CD ROM can store several years of banking data for all the firms in the industry, which in the past would have required one bulky computer tape for only one year of data.

[3] Or we might look for an explanation from Shakespeare. In *Hamlet* (2.2.319), Hamlet says: "What a piece of work is a man! how noble in reason! how infinite in faculties!" In contrast, in *Midsummer Night's Dream* (3.3.116), Puck says, "Lord, what fools these mortals be." It is interesting to note, however, that some inventors have been looked upon as fools flying kites in thunderstorms. Those with infinite faculties may not accomplish as much because they are too smart (risk averse) to go out in bad weather.

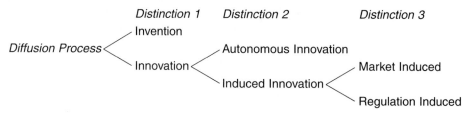

Glossary: Invention is an unfolding technological opportunity

Innovation is a profitable application of an invention

Autonomous innovation is one not induced by outside forces; it just happens. Psychologists might look at toilet training (or the lack of it) as the catalyst.

Induced innovation is one generated by outside forces.

Market-induced innovation is one generated by market forces such as price or interest-rate movements.

Regulation-induced innovation is one stimulated by regulatory constraints such as geographic, price, or product restrictions.

Source: Adapted from Kane [1983].

FIGURE 18-1 The Diffusion of Financial Innovations: Three Important Distinctions

Financial innovations, however, are most easily explained as induced by either market or regulatory factors, Kane's third distinction. Of course, in some instances, market and regulatory forces work jointly to induce financial innovations. For example, in the late 1970s and early 1980s new savings products and institutions (e.g., money-market mutual funds) were induced jointly by Regulation Q (interest-rate ceilings) and inflation-generated high interest rates.

Because few financial institutions, especially commercial banks, operate on the cutting edge of technology, most of their innovations are induced by regulatory or market forces. The major environmental factors driving the process of financial innovation can, of course, be captured by the components of TRICK. Kane argues that during the 1970s and the early 1980s, financial adaptation responded primarily to reregulation, interest-rate volatility, and advances in technology. In the remainder of the 1980s and in the 1990s, financial adaptions were stimulated by disinflation, increased competition, loan-quality problems (e.g., LDC, energy, farm, and real estate), record numbers of bank failures followed by record high bank profits, the S&L mess, reregulation and reform of deposit insurance, and risk-based capital requirements. Perhaps most importantly, computer networking and the Internet came of age, opening possibilities for virtual and home banking.

New Technology, Innovation, and Product Diffusion

To understand the interrelationships among new technology, the process of innovation, and the process of diffusion, we first focus on Exhibit 18-1, which describes how a new technology spreads. Please read it before proceeding.

Now that you have some idea of how technology spreads, let's consider how long it takes for a product to spread throughout society. Figure 18-2, which focuses on the speed of diffusion of major consumer products, shows how long it has taken for various products to increase their penetration from 10 percent of U.S. households to 50 percent. For the products shown in Figure 18-2, black-and-white televisions had the fastest penetration time, at three years whereas freezers were the

EXHIBIT 18-1

HOW A NEW TECHNOLOGY SPREADS

Adoption of check substitutes represents an example of the technological innovation process. We expect that the adoption of check alternatives will follow the same pattern as the adoption of other technologies ranging from hybrid corn to color television.

Consumer acceptance or rejection clearly determines any product's success—or failure. Technology itself is virtually never the primary determinant. We feel that the adoption process of technology, regardless of [the] product, involves a similar set of consumer responses. Collectively, individual consumer decisions produce a diffusion process that research has shown to be consistent.[a]

An *innovation* is an idea perceived as new by an individual.[b] The "newness" of the discovery underlying the innovation is not crucial; its "newness" to the individual is the critical consideration. Thus, when we look at innovations such as electronic payment products, we must look beyond the products themselves to the perceptions that individuals hold about them. The definition suggests that the product alone cannot be the innovation.

According to marketing expert Everett M. Rogers, who took a broad look at the implications of diffusion, "the essence of the diffusion process is the human interaction in which one person communicates a new idea to another person."[c] The product itself is not the critical factor. Communication of the idea is the significant element in analyzing the diffusion of innovations.

The adoption or rejection of electronic payment products probably will begin with individual opinion leaders. Many people will defer their adoption of an electronic product until enough others are also willing to accept it.

Rogers makes an important distinction between adoption and diffusion, saying:

> . . . the adoption process deals with adoption of a new idea by one individual while the diffusion process deals with the spread of new ideas in a social system, or with the spread of innovations between social systems or societies.[d]

. . . We intend to maintain the distinction between the diffusion process and the five classes in the adoption process.

In the adoption process an individual passes through five stages: "awareness, interest, evaluation, trial, and adoption."[e] Many people may hear of an idea at about the same time. However, some will complete the adoption process sooner than others. Five "adopter categories" classify individuals according to the length of time it takes them to adopt an innovation: innovators, early adopters, early majority, late majority, and laggards.[f]

Of course, not everyone who hears of a new idea adopts it. People may reject it at the conceptual level if they never try it, or they may reject it after a trial.[g] Similarly, we can anticipate that some people will reject electronic payment alternatives at various stages within and after the adoption process.

One practical application of the diffusion process, the product life cycle concept, has evolved for use in marketing. Market researchers identify five stages through which a product typically passes: pioneering, market acceptance, turbulence, saturation, and obsolescence.[h] Those five stages in the product life cycle parallel the five classes in the adoption process.

Rogers also emphasizes a distinction between the invention and the innovation, saying that economists have stressed the distinction on the grounds that an invention has little or no economic significance until it is applied.[i] An innovation, then, represents application of an invention.

Usually there is a distinct time lag between invention and innovation. According to Rogers, the lag "seems to vary considerably and is commonly 10 years or more for major inventions."[j]

In reality, a gray area exists between invention and wide-scale innovation because most inventions are very crude and inefficient at the date when they are recognized as constituting a new invention. They are, of necessity, badly adapted to many of the ultimate uses to which they will eventually be put; therefore, they may offer only very

Continued

small advantages, or perhaps none at all, over previously existing techniques.[k]

By trying to identify a specific time lag between a "crude" invention and its diffusion as an innovation, we sometimes engage in a sort of conceptual foreshortening which distorts our view of later events. We are led to treat the period after the conventional dating of an invention as one where a fairly well-established technique is awaiting adoption when, in fact, major adaptations typically are waiting to be made. It is this same foreshortening of perspective that greatly increases our general impression of the slowness of diffusion.[l]

Where, then, do we draw the line between invention and innovation? We will proceed on the assumption that invention status continues beyond the initial "discovery" while a product evolves a marketable configuration. We will start referring to the product as an innovation when it becomes available, beyond test marketing.

Implicit in the distinction is some degree of consumer acceptance, a pivotal concept in our personal check displacement model. An invention does not seek or does not win consumer acceptance. An innovation has some consumer acceptance. We expect that each of our check-displacement phases will be preceded by an extensive period of "tinkering" with the invention leading to the requisite innovation.

---

[a] Everett M. Rogers, *Diffusion of Innovations* (The Free Press, [1962]), pp. 12–13. This discussion relies on Rogers' description of the diffusion of innovations. For a more traditional "economics-based" treatment, see "How the Economic System Generates Evolution," in Joseph Schumpeter's *Business Cycles*, Vol. 1.

[b] Rogers, p. 13.

[c] Rogers, p. 13.

[d] Rogers, pp. 17–18.

[e] Rogers, p. 17.

[f] Rogers, p. 19.

[g] Rogers, pp. 18–19.

[h] Thomas A. Staudt and Donald A. Taylor, *A Managerial Introduction to Marketing* (Prentice-Hall, Inc., 1965), p. 144.

[i] Edwin Mansfield, *Microeconomics Theory and Application* (W. W. Norton and Company, Inc., 1970), pp. 456–457.

[j] Mansfield, p. 457.

[k] Nathan Rosenberg, "Factors Affecting Diffusion of Technology," *Explorations in Economic History* (Academic Press, 1972), p. 10.

[l] Rosenberg, p. 9.

Source: Federal Reserve Bank of Atlanta, *Economic Review* (August 1983), p. 10.

---

slowest, at 30 years. Where do personal computers (PCs), which were not part of the 1979 study, fit in this time frame? Somewhere between black-and-white TVs (three years) and freezers (30 years), depending on when you date the availability of PCs. Gates [1995a] reports that 35 percent of U.S. households used PCs in 1995. If we date availability conservatively in the range of 1980 to 1985, it is at least 10-to-15 years without 50 percent penetration.

The important point is that product diffusion takes time, and if you have seen one product diffusion, you have not seen them all. Moreover, tracing the entire process from technological invention to innovation to marketing to consumer acceptance of the product takes many years. The times are changing, but not as fast as you might think.

The Diffusion of Electronic Banking (e-banking)

Although the diffusion of electronic banking (e-banking) typically starts at the wholesale level before spreading to consumers and small businesses, acceptance at the retail level has been slow, except for **ATMs.** The acceptance of ATMs has been widespread because these devices do not require consumers to change their payment habits, which are notoriously slow to change. Edward W. Kelley, Jr., a

Years

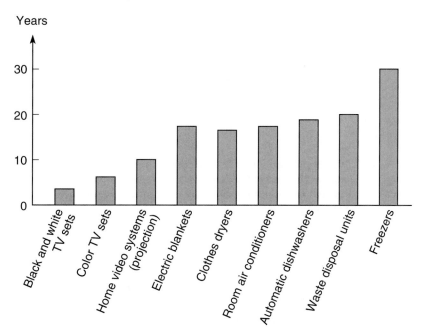

Source: Video: A New Era. Research Report 621 (November 1979), p. 10. Menlo Park, CA: SRI International. Reprinted by permission.

FIGURE 18-2 **Speed of Diffusion of Major Consumer Products**

member of the Board of Governors of the Federal Reserve System, reminds us of this fact:[4]

> Yet today [June 18, 1996], paper currency and checks are still used for the overwhelming majority of consumer payments, while electronic transfer, such as those made over the ACH, account for a very small fraction. In contrast, for the major money and securities markets in this country, electronic payments are the rule rather than the exception. (p. 1, insert mine)

Because wholesale transactions dominate in the "major money and securities markets," we are still waiting for the electronic trickle-down to the consumer level.

For the past three decades, some analysts have predicted that the next decade would witness a cashless society dominated by electronic money (e-money) and e-banking.[5] Although it's unlikely that cash transactions will ever go away completely,[6] further acceptance of the applications of bank technology, for example, home banking via the Internet, seem probable in the twenty-first century. At the very least, electronic bill paying and **point-of-sale (POS) systems** are likely to develop further. ATMs are, of course, an accepted form of financial technology that is

---

[4] Remarks at the CyberPayments 1996 Conference, June 18, 1996.

[5] The latest prediction comes from Marjanovic [1996b]. He writes: "Taking the nation a giant step toward a checkless society, Congress and the Clinton administration have enacted legislation requiring nearly all federal payments to be made electronically by 1999" (p. 1). The measure was a little-noticed provision of the 1996 omnibus budget bill signed by President Clinton on April 26, 1996.

[6] Based on a survey of 1,000 consumers and 79 retailers by Ernst and Young, Jennings [1996] reports, "Cash remains the favored payment method of consumers and retailers" (p. 11). In fact, 58 percent of retailers said they preferred cash sales, and 54 percent of consumers favor paying by cash. Third-party credit cards (38.5 percent) and checks (23.4 percent) were consumers' second and third choices of payment.

available on a worldwide basis, and ACHs have been working behind the scenes for years. On balance, however, as the past three decades have witnessed, rapid technological breakthroughs in the FSI, especially in banking, are not common. As banks lose franchise value in traditional areas (e.g., borrowing and lending), they must gain it in other areas (e.g., information processing, servicing, and cross-selling). Technology as manifested in integrated computer systems at both the wholesale and retail levels offer banks opportunities to create franchise value. As Kelley [1996] notes,

> It is the private sector that must play the pivotal role in identifying which services consumers and businesses want, and are willing to pay for, in areas such as stored-value or "smart" cards and payments over the Internet, and in the development of new home-banking products. (p. 2)

Regarding the Fed's role in this area, Kelley stated that it "has adopted a view toward the development of new electronic money and banking products that emphasizes the need for *innovation,* particularly in the retail sector" (p. 2, emphasis mine). He also stressed that this innovation needs to come from the private sector, and that although the Fed would support and encourage such innovation, it would not subsidize its development as it did with ACHs.

TECHNOLOGY IN BANKING

How important is technology to banking? According to John B. McCoy, the chairman of Banc One of Columbus, Ohio, "With deregulation, technology is how we're going to be able to beat the other guys."[7] Banking, however, has never been on the leading edge of technology. Consider the results of a special report, "Technology in the Workplace," which attempted to grade the technological prowess of nine industries. The grades were based on the following, admittedly subjective, criteria:[8]

- Has the industry made use of technological advances in a timely manner?
- Did it participate in or encourage the development of new technologies?
- Has the industry improved its competitive standing, efficiency, or profitability?

Banking's grade of C– suggests that it is not on the cutting edge of technology.[9] Why? Two reasons: paper and people. Banking has too much of both. Moreover, it has had too much of both for a long time. The paper comes in the form of processed checks, deposit slips, credit-card receipts, multiple customer statements, and so forth. Regarding people, the banking industry came in first across the nine industries surveyed with 1,509,000 employees (1987).[10]

According to the *American Banker*'s 1990 "Technology Survey," U.S. banks have been increasing their expenditures on information technology and the people needed to manage and operate information systems. These expenditures mark an investment in the future of electronic banking. The projects that are profitable

---

[7] Apcar [1987], p. 42D.

[8] This information is from a survey conducted by *The Wall Street Journal* (section 4, June 12, 1987).

[9] For your information, the other industries and their grades were petroleum (A), money management (A–), computers (B+), airlines (B), pharmaceuticals (B), publishing (B–), autos (C), and telecommunications (C–).

[10] Since 1987, all industries, including banking, have downsized.

and add franchise value will separate high-performance banks from the rest of their FSI competitors.

On balance, banking is a labor-intensive industry with paper as a major by-product. Combine these facts with the inertia of an historically conservative industry and you can see why banking has been slow moving into the technological age. In addition, because many retail customers, especially older ones, have grown accustomed to the faces and the paper, they are reluctant to change their banking habits. The future Internet generation of banking customers should be more technologically attuned and willing to accept computer screens instead of faces, and electronic impulses instead of paper. As a result, banks should have greater opportunities in the twenty-first century to reduce both paper and people.

Applications of Technology in Banking

Technological innovations in banking have been manifested primarily in the form of electronic funds transfer systems (EFTS, or EFT systems). The basic components of EFTS are[11]

- Automated teller machines (ATMs)
- Automated clearing houses (ACHs)
- Point-of-sale (POS) terminals

Less visible than EFT but more important to bank operating efficiency is a bank's "backroom technology" (i.e., its computer operating systems). Here is where Bill Gates claims that banks are "dinosaurs." A typical example of backroom inefficiency in banking is the failure to link separate computer systems to provide a complete profile of customers and their needs. A common symptom of this problem is the inability of a bank to provide a single financial statement covering various customer accounts. In contrast, the brokerage industry, a primary bank competitor with its cash-management accounts, had been supplying such statements for years.

The Dinosaurs in Banks' Backrooms

To illustrate the kinds of systems and the problems involved in integrating a bank's computer systems, consider the case of PNC Financial Corporation (*American Banker,* June 6, 1990, p. 8). For years, PNC's policy was to let affiliate banks operate autonomously. In 1983, however, when Pittsburgh National Bank bought Provident National Bank of Philadelphia and PNC was formed, the company began a move toward common computer systems. Between 1983 and 1990, PNC, a Pittsburgh-based company, had acquired 15 banks, and by 1990 it was the 14th-largest BHC, with total assets of $46.6 billion.[12] In 1990, with almost 600 banking offices in four states, PNC had a formidable task of integrating its retail network. To cut costs and add revenue to a retail network, its system experts focused on three areas:

- A deposit system
- Branch automation
- Consolidated data-processing operations

---

[11] The Electronic Fund Transfer Act of 1978 (Regulation E) provides a framework for establishing the rights, liabilities, and responsibilities of participants in EFTS, with the Federal Reserve given the authority to write rules. In addition to ATMs, ACHs, and POS, the EFT Act also covers telephone-bill-paying systems and home-banking programs.

[12] As of March 31, 1996, PNC was the 11th-largest BHC, with total assets of $72.7 billion and an *ROA* of 1.33 percent.

Although PNC moved from eight to three data centers in February 1990, it did not plan to move to one data center because of pressure on *people* from such a consolidation. Nevertheless, by the mid-1990s, PNC had a more fully integrated retail network. A key factor in PNC's acquisition strategy has been its ability to cut technology expenses. Nevertheless, a PNC spokesperson said, "It is a lot easier to negotiate a purchase (of another bank) than get on with what we need to do to make this one company rather than separate ones."

Another example of the difficulties in integrating product lines comes from Mellon Bank Corporation's acquisition of Dreyfus Corporation in 1994. It wasn't until the fall of 1996 that Mellon unveiled the Lion Account, named after the "dignified beast" that served as Dreyfus's signature logo. At the same time, Mellon became the first bank to offer what essentially is a brokerage outlet for nonload mutual funds. Mellon's Lion Account offers a consolidated financial-services package that mixes such traditional banking products as checking and loans with insurance and investment services.[13] Considering that Merrill Lynch began offering its CMA account in the 1970s, you can see how long it takes banks to move on integration and back-office technology. Cope and Kapiloff [1996] reported that Mellon had to overcome both personnel problems and operational difficulties before it was able to integrate its banking, insurance, and investment systems to generate comprehensive customer profiles.

Companies that integrate faster and more efficiently than others will have a better chance of succeeding and surviving in the FSI of the twenty-first century. In describing Microsoft's long-term vision for helping banks deliver their products and services online, Gates [1995a] described four key products:

- Development tools and core technologies for creating a compelling presence on the Internet
- A universal, rich, and secure e-mail platform for interaction with customers
- Microsoft Money, a brandable and extensible personal financial-management software application
- Powerful end-to-end solutions from Microsoft Solutions Providers

THE SUCCESS STORIES OF ELECTRONIC BANKING: ACHs AND ATMs

Because ACHs and ATMs have been the relative success stories of EFTS or electronic banking, let's consider what they are, how they work, and why they took off whereas other EFT devices, such as point-of-sale (POS) and home banking, are still waiting in the wings.

The Evolution of Money from the Concrete to the Ethereal

Money has evolved from the concrete (e.g., animals, hides, and trinkets) to the ethereal (e.g., electronic impulses). Households and businesses in the United States employ three generations of money: coin and paper currency (cash), checks, and electronic funds. Retail transactions are conducted by cash, check, credit card, or debit card. Those made by credit card are either paid off in full by check on the next billing cycle ("convenience users") or paid partially, again by check, with the outstanding

---

[13] As of March 31, 1996, Mellon was the leading bank mutual-fund manager, with $76.8 billion, or 18.3 percent of the almost $420 billion of the total funds managed by banks. PNC was second with $29.9 billion.

balance financed ("credit users").[14] In contrast, many wholesale transactions, especially those in money and securities markets, are made by electronic transfer.

The Automated Clearing House (ACH)

In a traditional (paper-based) clearing house, bankers meet in a central location and exchange or clear checks, hence the term "clearing house." In an **automated clearing house,** or **ACH,** computer images or tapes are exchanged as ACH items are directed to on-line institutions or data processors. Because ACHs are very efficient at handling recurring transactions such as preauthorized deposits or payments, they benefit from economies of scale or **scale economies.** This favorable cost characteristic results from relatively high fixed costs being spread over a large volume of transactions, which at the margin are very inexpensive to process, so that average cost declines.[15]

According to Payment Systems Inc., banks save an average of 12 cents on each bill paid electronically; businesses save an average of seven cents on each transaction, whereas consumers save an average of 35 cents. In electronic bill paying, which is most efficient for recurring transactions such as monthly mortgage, insurance, and utility bills, payees authorize banks to debit their accounts and forward the payments electronically through the ACH system. Knowing exactly when payments will be received makes the task of corporate and household cash management easier. As the opportunity costs of not using electronic bill payments increase, the number of households willing to use such systems should increase. Nevertheless, at the beginning of the 1990s, 52 percent of households expressed no interest in using electronic bill payment (*American Banker,* June 10, 1990, pp. 1, 3).

Figure 18-3 presents a schematic for two common types of ACH activity: direct deposit of payroll and a preauthorized insurance premium.

Funds Transfer and Fedwire

Since 1918, the Federal Reserve System, which was established in 1913, has been moving funds for clearing and settlement. Until the early 1970s, the transfer of funds and securities was conducted mainly through a private telegraph system managed by the 12 Federal Reserve Banks. Since then, the Fed has developed and maintained an electronic transfer system called **Fedwire.**[16] As the linchpin of the U.S. **payments system,** Fedwire is used by Federal Reserve Banks and branches, the Treasury and other government agencies, and over 10,000 depository institutions. The on-line users of the system,[17] which number about 7,000, account for 99 percent of total funds transfers. Fedwire transfers, which are usually completed within a few minutes and which require relatively few bookkeeping entries, are guaranteed by the Fed to be final as soon as the receiving institution is notified of the credit to its account.[18] To upgrade Fedwire and its general electronic capabilities in the 1980s, the Fed undertook a project called **Federal Reserve Communications System for the Eighties**

---

[14] Chapter 11 describes the importance of credit cards to banks and consumers.

[15] Recall that total cost equals total fixed cost plus total variable cost, and that average total cost equals average fixed cost plus average variable or marginal cost.

[16] Information and statistics on Fedwire used in this section are from "Fedpoint 43: Fedwire," which can be found at http://www.ny.frb.org/pihome/fedpoint/fed43.html.

[17] On-line users communicate directly with the Fedwire network through computers or terminals. Off-line customers have access to Fedwire for a limited number of transactions.

[18] Assuming an interdistrict transfer, the parties involved would be the sender, the sender's bank, the Federal Reserve bank in the sender's district, the receiver, the receiver's bank, and the Federal Reserve bank in the receiver's district. An intradistrict transfer would involve only one Federal Reserve bank.

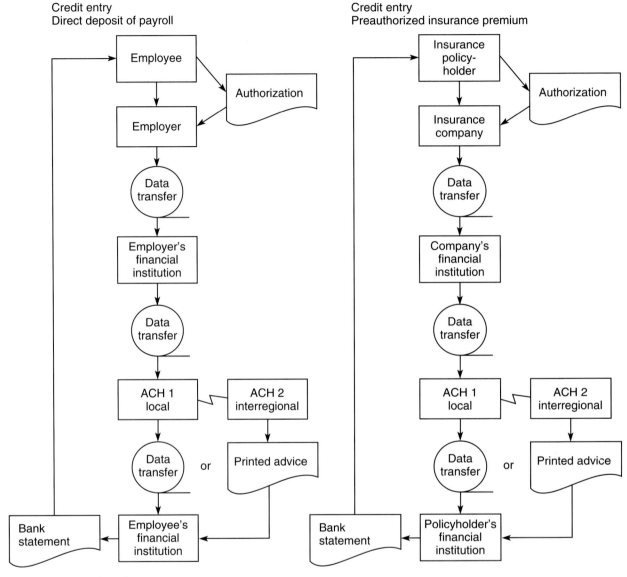

Source: Hamilton [1979], p. 526.

FIGURE 18-3 **The ACH Processing of a Direct Deposit of Payroll and a Preauthorized Insurance Premium**

(FRCS-80). It was designed as a general-purpose data communications network, and the functions of the Fed's existing separate communications network were consolidated into a monolithic system. Panel A of Figure 18-4 shows the FRCS-80, district-office spine network. This system, which has no single central switching site (called the "Culpeper switch" under the old system), distributes the FRCS computer power among the 12 Federal Reserve Banks, the Treasury Department in Washington, DC, and the Culpeper operations center called the Network Management Center (NMC). With FRCS-80, the Fed positioned itself to operate a national ACH network.

Panel A. FRCS district-office spine network

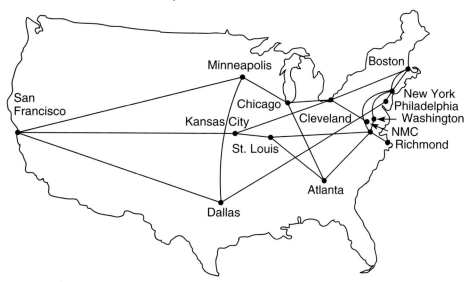

Panel B. The globalization of ATMs: How to get cash from an ATM abroad

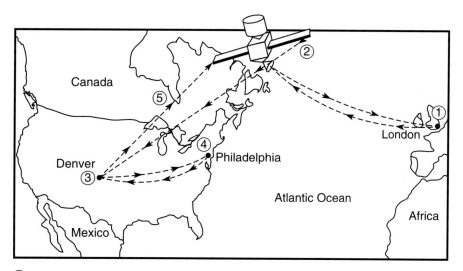

① Traveler inserts card into an ATM in London and requests British pounds, which are converted into dollars at a wholesale rate.

② The bank's computer recognizes the card as American and relays the request by satellite to a central switching computer.

③ The central computer identifies the traveler's hometown bank.

④ The computer relays the transaction request to the local bank, which checks for sufficient funds.

⑤ The approval is relayed through the central computer back to London, where the traveler receives the cash. The entire process takes about 10 seconds.

Sources: Panel A from Mitchell and Hodgdon [1981], pp. 110–111. Panel B from Plus Systems, Inc.

FIGURE 18-4 Illustrations of Electronic Funds Transfer Systems

In 1994, Fedwire handled about 72 million funds transfers valued at $211 trillion. The center of the world of banking and finance, the Second Federal Reserve District, with its heart at the Federal Reserve Bank of New York (FRBNY), accounted for only 36 percent of these transfers (26 million) but 58 percent of the value ($123 trillion). Fedwire also processed 13 million transfers of Treasury and agency securities worth $152 trillion in 1994. The FRBNY, however, had even greater dominance in this activity with nine million transfers (69%) worth $119 trillion (78%). The FRBNY serves as the Wholesale Payments Product Office for the Federal Reserve System. As such, it is responsible for strategic planning and oversight of Fed's large-dollar funds and securities transfer business and net settlement services.

Pricing Fed Services

The Depository Institutions Deregulation and Monetary Control Act (DIDMCA) of 1980 required the Federal Reserve to begin pricing its services such that they are fully costed. Prior to this, Fed services were subsidized (i.e., not fully costed). As the nation's central bank, the Fed is a banker's bank, which means that it supplies services to the FSI but mainly to the banking system. In addition, because the Fed acts as fiscal agent for the government, government agencies, especially the Treasury, are major clients. The major services provided by the Fed include check clearing and processing (e.g., via Fedwire for banks, ACHs, and the government); selling, servicing, redeeming, and safekeeping securities; transferring and noncash collection; and placing coin and paper currency into circulation and withdrawing it from circulation.

Private-Sector Competition for Funds Transfer

The private sector's major answer to Fedwire is the **Clearing House Interbank Payment System,** or **CHIPS.** It was organized, primarily for international payments, in 1970 by the New York Clearing House Association (NYCHA), a group of the largest commercial banks located in New York City. The original members of CHIPS were the eight banks of NYCHA with Federal Reserve System membership. Today, participation in CHIPS has expanded to include other commercial banks, Edge Corporations, United States agencies and branches of foreign banks, investment companies, and private banks. Transactions among CHIPS' participants work similarly to those on Fedwire. A special Fedwire escrow account at the FRBNY facilitates same-day settlement of transfers.[19] The risk-management tools used by CHIPS and its participants include bilateral limits, net debit caps, loss-sharing agreements, and collateral.

CHIPS is the largest private-sector payments network in the world. It is estimated that CHIPS handles about 182,000 interbank transfers a day valued at almost $1.2 trillion. Annualizing these figures (assuming 250 operating days a year) gives 46 million transactions compared to Fedwire's 72 million, but a value of $300 trillion for CHIPS compared to $211 trillion for Fedwire. These figures generate an average size transfer for CHIPS of $6,522 compared to $2,931 for Fedwire.[20] Together, Fedwire and CHIPS handle most large-dollar wire transfers.

ACHs have banned together to form ACH networks. For example, the **National Automated Clearing House Association (NACHA)** had 38 member ACH

---

[19] In CHIPS or any other private ACH transfer, only five parties are involved: the originator, the originating bank, the ACH, the receiver, and the receiving bank. Unlike with Fedwire, a Federal Reserve bank (or two) is not required.

[20] If the Fed becomes the "clearer of last resort" (i.e., stuck with the smallest and least profitable transfers), as some private players would like it to be, then Kane [1981] sees private ACHs and correspondents as playing the role of United Parcel Service whereas Fedwire is relegated to a bit player akin to the U.S. Postal Service.

associations in 1995 representing 13,000 financial institutions, which provided ACH services to 500,000 companies and millions of consumers. For 1995, NACHA reported that 45 percent of nongovernment employees and 91 percent of government employees used direct deposit of payroll whereas 59 percent of Social-Security recipients used direct deposit. In the early development of ACHs, government payments dominated ACH activity (e.g., 40% of the payments in 1988; see Table 18-1). In 1995, however, they accounted for only 21 percent of total payments, excluding on-us volume.

ACH transactions have been widely accepted by households, businesses, and governments because of convenience, low cost, safety, and reliability. The ACH data shown in Table 18-1 capture the extent of this acceptance. For example, from 1988 to 1995, the volume of ACH payments, excluding on-us volume, grew at a compound annual rate of 14.6 percent, from 1.1 billion transactions to 2.9 billion transactions.[21] Over this same period, dollar volume rose from $4.2 trillion (1988) to $11.1 trillion (1995), or 14.9 percent.

Two other players in the ACH game are Bankwire's Cashwire and SWIFT. Bankwire is an electronic communications network owned by an association of

TABLE 18-1 Number of Payments and Dollar Volume of Payments Handled by NACHA Member Associations, 1988–1995

	1988	1989	1990	1991	1992	1993	1994	1995
Total payments								
Volume (million)	1,113	1,331	1,549	1,714	1,955	2,216	2,522	2,885
% increase	19.0	19.6	16.4	10.6	14.1	13.4	13.8	14.4
On-us ACH volume (million)	—	—	—	250	300	402	480	595
Grand total ACH volume (million)	—	—	—	1,964	2,255	2,618	3,002	3,480
% increase	—	—	—	—	14.8	16.1	14.7	15.9
Dollar volume (trillion)	$4.2	$5.1	$6.1	$6.9	$7.8	$8.8	$10.1	$11.1
% increase	16.2	21.4	19.6	13.1	13.0	12.8	14.8	9.9
Commercial credits								
Volume (million)	288	375	477	582	719	859	1,033	1,229
% increase	33.0	30.2	27.2	22.0	23.5	19.5	20.3	19
Commercial debits								
Volume (million)	383	469	553	611	708	803	914	1,055
% increase	22.7	22.5	17.9	10.5	15.9	13.4	13.9	15.4
Government payments								
Volume (million)	442	487	519	521	531	554	574	601
% increase	8.6	10.2	6.6	.4	1.9	4.3	3.6	4.7
Number of companies using the ACH network (thousand)	40	80	100	130	150	300	400	500
% of private sector workforce using direct deposit	8.1	11.9	15.0	19.0	30.0	35.0	42.0	45.2
% government employees using direct deposit	73	75	78	79	82	83	84	91
% Social Security recipients using direct deposit	45.7	47.6	49.6	51.2	52.6	54.2	58	59

Source: Adapted from "ACH Statistics Fact Sheet 1988–1995," NACHA.

---

[21] Since 1991, when on-us data became available, total payments grew from almost 2.0 billion to almost 3.5 billion, 15.4 percent annual growth.

banks and used to transfer messages between subscribing banks. Bankwire's clearing and settlement service is called Cashwire. SWIFT, which stands for the Society of World Interbank Financial Telecommunications, includes both foreign and U.S. banks. Because it is primarily a message-writing system used to communicate payment information, it must be used in conjunction with a payment system, such as CHIPS, to fully implement transactions.

Major ACH Players in the United States

For 1995, the major U.S. players among ACH banks, those that originated 100 million or more in ACH payments, were[22] Chase Manhattan with 300 million originations and 22 percent growth over the year, Norwest with 182 million originations (20% growth), Banc One with 133.6 million originations (18% growth), BankAmerica with 110.6 million originations (9% growth), and Wachovia with 107.7 million originations (30% growth). For comparison with the top five, the 20th, 50th, and 100th largest players in origination of ACH payments were SunTrust (Atlanta) with 24.9 million (14% growth), Comerica Bank (Detroit) with 10.2 million (34% growth), and Hibernia National Bank of New Orleans with 2.4 million (42% growth), respectively. With automatic payroll deposits and bill payments becoming increasingly concentrated among the top 100 ACH banks, Kutler [1996] considers the list as a proxy for banking consolidation and back-office economies of scale (declining costs as the volume of transactions increases).

Payment and Settlement Risks

Globalization and electronic banking mean that the banking, payment systems, and financial markets of the world are closely linked. Although any disruptions to these systems generate concerns, the large-dollar payment mechanisms get special attention. In the United States, Fedwire and CHIPS handle most of the large-dollar transactions. The major AHC players described above are the key components of these systems. Corrigan [1987] says, "Because they are so large, so fast and so interdependent, even temporary computer or mechanical failures can be highly disruptive beyond the institution where the breakdown originates" (p. 10). Uncertainties with respect to operations, liquidity, and credit interdependencies underlie the payment and settlement risks of ACHs. In conjunction with the size and speed of the transactions, the concerns about the potential for ACH disruptions are genuine and focus on the possibility of contagion among the major ACH players. The risk-management tools in this area focus on bilateral limits, net debit caps, loss-sharing agreements, and collateral. On the positive side, financial contagion related to liquidity and credit concerns has not been a problem since the banking crisis of the early 1930s. In contrast, the financial system has little experience with operational crises that could lead to contagion—the focus of Corrigan's concern.[23]

Automated Teller Machines (ATMs)

In contrast to ACHs, which handle both large and small transactions, ATMs are strictly a retail EFT device for handling routine transactions. The first ATMs were simply cash-dispensing machines, and for many customers, especially students, this is all they needed or wanted from ATMs. With 24-hour availability, ATMs were the

---

[22] These data are from Kutler [1996], pp. 8–9.

[23] Roberds [1995] draws lessons for the payments system from financial crises in the era of "National Banking."

first EFT system to provide **virtual banking** on a limited basis. With the globalization of ATMs, they are the ultimate convenience device for travelers. Panel B of Figure 18-4 shows how one gets cash from an ATM abroad.

Banks like ATMs because of their potential for cost reduction, revenue generation, and the gaining of market share. The main cost advantage of ATMs over human tellers is with respect to salaries and benefits. ATMs, however, do have large start-up costs and require maintenance and servicing, and for the most part, they handle only routine transactions. On the other hand, ATMs don't call in sick, but when the computer is down, they don't function. For example, during May of 1996, about 800,000 customers of NationsBank in Georgia lost access to ATMs because of technological glitches. They were without access for a little more than 24 hours. On at least one occasion, an ATM has been stolen by means of a forklift, and on at least one occasion in a movie (e.g., *Dog Day Afternoon*), human tellers have been held hostage. To my knowledge, an ATM has never been held hostage nor has it starred in a film.

All other things being equal, if one bank has an ATM system that is more attractive to potential clients than that of its competitors, then it should be able to increase its market share and enhance revenue generation. The only other way for ATMs to generate revenue is through fees charged for usage. The topic of fees and surcharges for use of ATMs is an emotionally charged subject for many consumer groups. For example, Block [1996b] reports that the Public Interest Research Group (PIRG) accuses the banking industry of "gouging consumers with new and higher fees" (p. 1). Exhibit 18-2 presents an alternative view of bank ATM fees.

The bank service charge that has received the widest publicity has been First Chicago's charge to customers of $3 for visiting a human teller for transactions that could be handled through electronic alternatives. The objective of First Chicago's pricing strategy was to reduce the number of unprofitable customers, which, according to Thomas Tremain, the bank's manager of e-banking, was successful. He said: "Ten months after the announcement, I can report that the accounts we lost were mostly unprofitable, with average balances of half our balance requirement" (Piskora [1996a], p. 8.). The one regret that First Chicago had about its pricing decision was not the decision itself but the way it was announced—at a press conference. If it could do it over, First Chicago would send direct mail to customers announcing the pricing decision.

ATMs: The Numbers Game

According to the *Bank Network News,* the U.S. banking industry had 122,706 ATMs installed at year-end 1995, an increase of 12 percent over the previous year. BankAmerica, with 5,500 ATMs, down 2.7 percent from the previous year, was the industry's leader.[24] A distant second in the ATM race was NationsBank, with 2,200 ATMs, up 5.4 percent from the previous year, followed by First Bank System (Minneapolis) with 2,097 ATMs, Wells Fargo with 2,058, Banc One (Columbus) with 1,927, and Citicorp with 1,800.[25] Although data were not available for Bank-America, NationsBank had 1,792 (81%) of its ATMs inside its bank offices, up 3.6 percent from the previous year. In contrast, however, its off-premises units (ATMs outside bank offices) grew at 14 percent but were still at a relatively low level of 408. First Bank System and Banc One, the only other banks in the top five with

---

[24] The ATM figures for individual banks are as of June 30, 1995, from a survey by the *American Banker;* see Piskora [1995].

[25] Kraus [1996] reports that Citibank, which closed six branches in 1995 and 11 in 1996, has converted 26 full-service offices to automated facilities, much to the chagrin of community activists and some small businesses.

EXHIBIT 18-2

ATM FEES AND CONSUMER CHOICE

In the movie, *The Fugitive,* when Dr. Richard Kimble (played by Harrison Ford) gets caught between a rock and a hard place in an aqueduct, he tells U.S. Marshall Samuel Gerard (played by Tommy Lee Jones), "I didn't kill my wife!" Agent Gerard, who is soaking wet and staring down the barrel of his own pistol, replies, "I don't care!" When it comes to ATM fees, I don't care!

If you have been caught up in all the recent publicity and hand wringing about ATM fees, I suggest that you not jump off a nearby dam as Richard Kimble did. His chances of surviving the fall were one in a million; as the star of the movie, however, it was in the script that he would survive. Your chances of surviving such a leap are not worth a $1 ATM fee.

Suppose you are not as cavalier about ATM fees, what can you do about them? First, let's make sure that you understand how economic, financial, and political factors affect ATM prices.

Banking and the financial-services industry are undergoing substantial structural changes. Banks can no longer afford to give away services and expect to survive in this new competitive environment. Because ATMs provide convenience (a service) to customers, bankers have a right to charge for ATM transactions. If it galls you that you should have to pay a fee to withdraw your own money from your bank's ATM, you should go inside and wait in line for a human teller or find a new bank. By the way, the Federal Reserve's 1995 report to Congress on Retail Fees and Services of Depository Institutions indicated that only 9.6 percent of banks charged their customers fees for cash withdrawals at their banks' own ATMs. Because it is a common and long-standing practice to charge customers for use of other institutions' ATMs, this pricing phenomenon is not new. For 1995, the Fed reported that 83–85 percent of banks and savings institutions

charged about $1 for these so-called nonproprietary transactions. If you cannot find one of your own bank's ATMs, isn't it reasonable that you be charged for the convenience of using another bank's ATM?

What would consumers do without someone, such as the U.S. Public Interest Research Group (PIRG), to tell them that they are being nickeled-and-dimed by banks' fees to the tune of hundreds of dollars a year per customer? Consumers are smart enough to buy what they want and to know what it costs. Consumers make choices for products and services, including those offered by financial institutions, based on their perceptions of value received. Banks compete for business on the basis of price, convenience, and safety. Consumers weigh these factors and pick the institutions, products, and services they want. Fees and services charges are a critical and growing part of the business of banking. Because they are here to stay, learn to live with them. You don't, however, have to like or tolerate them. My mother frequently said, "It never hurts to ask." When I don't like a certain bank fee or charge, I ask for it to be reversed or lowered. Sometimes it works, sometimes it doesn't, and sometimes I change institutions.

At the end of *The Fugitive,* Agent Gerard reveals to Dr. Kimble that he did care about who killed Mrs. Kimble. I must confess that as a financial economist, I do care about prices. However, as a consumer, I don't worry about products or services that I think are fairly priced. Because fairness, like beauty, is in the eye of the beholder, my words will not be the last ones about ATM fees. On balance, however, there's a lot of competition and choices in the financial-services industry. So shop around. But don't expect something for nothing. There's no such thing as a free lunch or a free banking service.

available data, had 15 percent and 64 percent, respectively, of their ATMs inside bank offices. First Bank System is the only bank in the top 50 with more ATMs off premises than inside its offices.

For the 201 banks participating in the *American Banker*'s survey, the growth of ATMs outside bank offices was 39.1 percent compared to 11.3 percent for in-office ATM growth and 13.9 percent for overall growth of ATMs. The 201 banks surveyed had a ratio of ATMs to domestic branches of 56,022/38,713, or 1.45, on average. With aggregate total assets of almost $3.2 trillion, the average survey bank's size was almost $16 billion. The top 50 banks in the survey had 43,537 ATMs, or 78 percent of the total ATMs installed by the 201 banks. These 50 banks accounted for roughly 35 percent of all ATMs in the industry.

Because (as of this writing) POS and home banking have been busts, ATM deployment and usage have been the phenomena of retail electronic banking. A director of marketing for an ATM manufacturer says, "Most of the larger banks have an aggressive stance on ATM deployment. Meanwhile, smaller banks are getting very interested in providing better service and more functionality" (Piskora [1995], p. 10). The marketing director has a solution for the smaller banks: Buy more ATMs. According to him, ATMs will permit smaller banks to meet the goals of being functional and continuing to provide better service. The aggressive stance of big banks is captured by NationsBank's installation of 1,400 new ATMs during 1996, with about one-half of the machines placed in nonbranch locations.

Although bankers describe the ATM market as saturated, deployment of ATMs continues at double-digit growth rates. Moreover, as noted above, the boom has been in off-premises ATMs compared to in-office units. Where are banks putting their off-premises ATMs? If they put them where customers use them or are likely to use them (based on a survey of 452 consumers, see Piskora [1995], p. 11), the top five locations will be shopping centers (42%), supermarkets (38%), hotels (37%), airports (32%), and department stores and theme parks (tied at 29%).[26]

ATM Networks

Networks and networking have become commonplace in the business world and in the FSI. In particular, ATM networks, which are systems of electronic banking connections, have become commonplace. Based on 1995 data, the leading ATM network was the California-based Star System, which connects 20,751 ATMs and which processed 36 million switch transactions per month. A switch transaction is one that goes from one bank's ATM to another bank's ATM. When a customer uses another bank's ATM, a fee is charged, which helps pay for the switch and its maintenance. How can consumer groups complain about banks' charging for such a convenience and service?

The MAC system, which serves the Middle Atlantic region of the United States, has fewer ATMs (19,400) than the Star System, but it processes about 2.4 times as many transactions (85 million per month). The third-largest ATM network is NYCE, with 17,034 ATMs that process 32 million transactions per month. NYCE serves the Northeast. Honor and Pulse ranked fourth and fifth with 10,974 ATMs (34 million transactions per month) and 9,500 ATMs (15 million transactions per month), respectively.

Like the banking industry itself and the FSI in general, ATM networks have been undergoing consolidation. For example, in 1996, Honor and Most (sixth largest) merged. The deal, which was one of the biggest in the world of multibank ATMs and POS networks, is expected to make the resulting network the third largest in the United States, with 17,174 ATMs processing 53 million transactions per month. The president and CEO of Internet Inc., the company that runs Most, said, "We believe bigger will make us more powerful. Scale and scope are going to

---

[26] Figures in parentheses are the sum of "use" or "likely to use" an ATM based on the survey results. Shopping centers and supermarkets tied for greatest usage at 15 percent.

be needed to grow our menu of services and build an infrastructure that can support that growing menu."[27] He added that chip cards (also called smart cards) and home banking were likely to be included on that menu.

POINT-OF-SALE (POS) AND HOME BANKING IN THE TWENTIETH CENTURY: A BUST!

The state of technology in banking was aptly described by Fisher [1979] as, "Right now, EFT is not the grand and glorious future—it's another hole in the wall for the ATM" (p. 22). As banking moves into the twenty-first century, Fisher's statement, made in 1979, is not far from the truth. Nevertheless, bank CEOs recognize the strategic importance of technology and are becoming more involved in automation issues and the Internet. Hugh McColl, chairman of NationsBank, has warned that technology companies, such as Microsoft and Intuit Inc., could gain control of customer relationships and thereby win the battle for delivering financial services. Although the technology companies have the proprietary software, the banks have something better—the customer relationships and linkage with the payments system. Bill Gates, the chairman of Microsoft, says he wants to enter partnerships with banks, not take over their business. Before looking further ahead at bank technology in the twenty-first century, let's see why POS and home banking failed in the twentieth century.

Point-of-sale (POS) Systems and Debit Cards

A POS system is an on-line device that allows customers to transfer funds instantaneously to pay for goods and services. The transaction, which is handled using a debit card, moves funds from the customer's account to the merchant's account on command. A debit card, unlike a credit card, is simply an electronic-check device—the epitome of e-banking. A debit card with a line of credit attached permits customers to access credit when insufficient funds exist in their accounts. Because debit cards do not come with interest-free grace periods, the interest clock starts ticking as soon as the draw on the line of credit is made.

Two reasons explain why POS has not been widely accepted: (1) customers prefer credit cards (with a grace period) to debit cards, and (2) merchants have gone with technologies more focused on electronic cash registers and inventory control rather than EFT. Reversal of these two factors will pave the way for POS to emerge as a relevant EFT system. For that to occur, the interest-free grace period on credit cards would have to be eliminated, which would provide the financial incentive to replace credit cards with debit cards. In addition, merchants would have to be hard-wired for POS systems.

The primary POS function is to move funds electronically. Because this has not happened in a big way, existing POS systems have fallen back on providing secondary POS services. In particular, they have been used for credit-card authorization and check verification. Electronic authorization through POS terminals is designed to reduce the chronic problem of bank-card fraud and credit losses and to eliminate much of the manual paper-based recovery system. Based on loss-control tests, Visa found that electronic authorization reduces its losses by 80 percent. To encourage merchant participation in its program, Visa adopted a two-tier inter-

---

[27] The quote and data in this paragraph are from Piskora [1996b], p. 1.

change rate. Under this pricing scheme, an incentive exists (in the form of a lower discount rate) for a merchant to obtain a "zero-floor limit" authorization (i.e., authorization for every noncash purchase). Visa offers a guaranteed response time with its electronic-authorization program. J. C. Penney was the first major retailer to push for direct interconnection for bank credit-card authorization.

When debit cards are widely held and merchants are hard wired, POS systems will become true EFT devices.

Home Banking and Other On-Line Services

The development of home banking requires that customers be wired, or on-line, through computers in the home, to their bank's computer. Although the technology exists to do this, home banking has yet to hit a home run. In fact, it has struck out several times and is in a race with POS to be the strikeout king of EFT. For example, in 1979, John Fisher of Banc One, a gee-whiz advocate of home banking and videotex (in modern parlance, the Internet), saw these devices taking off by the end of the 1980s.[28] Here we are at the end of the 1990s, and the home-banking plane is still taxiing on the EFT runway.

Home banking has been constrained by two major impediments: (1) the hardware, software, and access costs of home computing, and (2) the failure of home-banking devices to deliver two basic banking services: dispensing cash and accepting deposits. In a society that is far from being cashless, these shortcomings are critical. Moreover, many of the other home-banking services, such as balance inquiry, bill payment, stop payment, funds transfer, loan application, can be conducted by telephone banking. Exhibit 18-3 describes Citicorp's venture into telephone/home banking.

EXHIBIT 18-3

E.T.—PLEASE PHONE THE BANK, FROM HOME!

To circumvent potential customer apprehension about dealing with a personal computer for home-banking transactions, Citicorp made a major investment in E.T.—"Enhanced Telephone" (*The Wall Street Journal*, February 28, 1990, pp. B1, B4). Citicorp's E.T. is a home-banking terminal that looks like an enlarged telephone with a small screen above the standard telephone keypad. (The screen is a cathode ray tube that can display 40 characters and 18 lines. A second-generation E.T. has a liquid-crystal display screen and is trimmer than the original E.T.) Users are able to do home banking on the telephone keypad as if they had a personal computer but at a lower start-up cost. In addition, Citicorp claimed that E.T.'s design flexibility could accommodate innovations in electronic payments like the smart card (a charge card with a computer chip to store data). The smart card will permit customers to get credit at home for spending later by transferring funds from their accounts to the computer chip on the smart card. Unlike home-banking systems based in videotex services (e.g., Prodigy, the videotex system launched by IBM and Sears in 1988), E.T. is a specialist. Citicorp leases E.T.'s to customers for an installation charge and a monthly service fee. Citicorp's previous venture in home banking, called "Direct Access," could generate only 40,000 subscribers from a customer base of 1.5 million in the New York area. Citicorp is optimistic that customers will use E.T. to phone, not home, but the bank!

---

[28] "A Futuristic View of Banking," remarks by John Fisher at the 1981 annual meeting of the Financial Management Association. Banc One conducted a home-banking experiment, called Channel 2000, in 1981. Videotex is a generic term referring to home information retrieval systems.

Speaking to *BusinessWeek* in 1981 (issue of June 29), John Fisher said, "We're absolutely convinced that the technology is sound and the consumer will accept them (home banking and videotex) greedily" (p. 83). Although the technology is still sound, consumer acceptance has been slow. Even "2001: A Home-Banking Odyssey" might seem a bit far-fetched.

THE INTERNET AND HOME BANKING IN THE TWENTY-FIRST CENTURY: A BOOM?

In *Fortune* (July 8, 1996), Andy Grove, the CEO of Intel, had this to say about the **Internet:**

> The Internet is like a 20-foot tidal wave coming, and we are in kayaks. It's been coming across the Pacific for thousands of miles and gaining momentum, and it's going to lift you and drop you. We're just a step away from the point when every computer is connected to every other computer, at least, in the U.S., Japan, and Europe. It affects everybody—the computer industry, telecommunications, the media, chipmakers, and the software world. Some are more aware of this than others. (p. 46)

Is the fact that Grove failed to mention the banking industry another banks-are-dinosaurs dig at bankers?

In the FSI, opinions differ on the potential of the Internet for commercial transactions and therefore on the role banks will play on the Internet. Pessimists focus on problems of lack of security, privacy, and reliability as reasons why commercial transactions will never be widespread on the Internet. In addition, they argue that since no one is in charge, no one is accountable for fixing the problems. In contrast, Elliott C. McEntee, the president of the National Automated Clearing House Association (NACHA), has the opposite view. In fact, he sees the weaknesses as the strengths of the Internet. He argues,[29]

> ...as a result of those characteristics, a powerful force will ensure that the security, privacy, reliability, and capacity problems will be resolved. That powerful force is the force that Adam Smith describes in "The Theory of Moral Sentiments" and "The Nature and Causes of the Wealth of Nations"—it's the "Invisible Hand" that promotes ends which are not part of the original intention.

When will this happen? Not in the next 18 to 24 months (1998 to mid-1999) according to McEntee (1996), but within the next three to five years (mid-1999 to mid-2001).

A modern debit card (i.e., a really smart card) would mesh nicely with home banking via the Internet. Such a card would offer a menu of financial services such as electronic checking (POS), bill payment, money-market funds, and any other retail service offered by the bank. Combined with a home computer, the card's computer chip could be loaded for a particular service or the account accommodation needed.

Using the World Wide Web (WWW) for More Than a Banking Home Page

As more and more banks offer home pages on the World Wide Web (WWW), they are looking to provide more than basic information about themselves and their

---

[29] These pro and con views can be found in McEntee [1996].

products. Two of the first banks to go beyond the simple home page were Wells Fargo and First Interstate, two California-based banks that merged in April 1996 to create a West Coast behemoth. From their home pages, both institutions permitted depositors to check balances, apply for loans, and conduct other transactions on the Internet. Analysts and bankers are curious to see if the combined banks can generate any merger-related synergies from **on-line banking.**

Centura Banks of Rocky Mount, North Carolina, a relatively small bank with assets of $5.5 billion (June 1996), was the first bank in its state to offer PC-based home banking. In doing so, it beat such big players as NationsBank, First Union, and Wachovia to the Internet. Being first, however, was expensive, because Centura spent $14 million in 1995 on new sales systems and other technology. The cost was 24 percent of the bank's $58 million in net income in 1995. Taking a long-run view, Centura's CEO said: "we believe the best way to run a company is as if it's going to be in existence forever" (Cline [1996], p. 5). Assuming unbounded technological advances, Centura's strategy makes sense.

Although the new technology of e-banking and e-money is not cheap, it may be the best way for smaller institutions, like Centura, not only to compete and survive but also to beat the big players. Whether Centura can exist forever remains to be seen. Its as-if-forever strategy, however, is sound financially because it concentrates on maximizing value over the long run without focusing myopically on short-term earnings.

Personal Financial Software and Joint Ventures[30]

The battle for the provision of personal financial software for home banking via the Internet has been shaping up as a three-way struggle among three competitors:

Company	Software	Estimated Number of Users
Intuit Inc.	Quicken	9.0 million
Microsoft	Money	2.0 million
Meca	Managing Your Money	0.6 million

Bloom and Clark [1996] report that Intuit and Microsoft are engaged in a version of "Coke versus Pepsi" in the battle of choice of processors for home-banking transactions. Although Microsoft's "Money" has substantially fewer users, it offers a wider choice of processors that run through its software. Microsoft's goal is simple: Become the leader in providing software tools to financial institutions, including technologies that will facilitate banking over the Internet.

In 1996, Intuit and America On-Line began offering a home-banking service called BankNOW. Combined with America On-Line's more than six million subscribers, BankNOW has the potential to tap over 15 million existing customers between the two companies. By late 1996, BankNOW was made available to Internet surfers who browse using Netscape. BankNOW, which permits bill paying and other EFT transactions using Intuit's Quicken, is "branded" by the bank, priced by the bank, and sold by the bank.

The new kid on the block in the home-banking software race is Meca Software Inc. It was formed when NationsBank and BankAmerica purchased Meca in May of 1995. A year later IBM joined NationsBank and BankAmerica, along with

---

[30] Information in this section is from Bloom [1996a, b] and Bloom and Clark [1996].

several other banks (e.g., Fleet, First Bank System, Royal Bank of Canada, Barnett, KeyCorp, and Banc One), to form a new company but retaining the Meca name. The heart of the new company's personal financial services is Meca's "Managing Your Money." In a throwback to the toaster-giveaway days of nonelectronic banking and as a move to catch up with Intuit's "Quicken" and Microsoft's "Money," in the summer of 1996 Meca began to make it possible for banks to give their customers free copies of "Managing Your Money" (a $30 value).

ELECTRONIC DATA INTERCHANGE (EDI) AND NETTING ARRANGEMENTS

Electronic data interchange, or EDI, is the process of exchanging information electronically. EDI enables companies to transmit routine business data such as invoices, purchase orders, and remittances electronically. The purpose of EDI is simple—speed the flow of dollars and data. At the beginning of the 1990s banks were just getting into EDI but not very eagerly. As one consultant noted: "It is my sense that for most banks, EDI is not a thing they want to do but something they have to do (to keep pace with nonbank competitors)" (*American Banker,* "Focus on EDI," May 21, 1990, p. 1).

By 1996, EDI providers were looking to get banks more involved with EDI through the Internet. A status report for 1996 reveals the following profile of the EDI business:

- Participating businesses: 100,000
- Participating banks: 500+
- Annual transactions: 500 million
- Transaction growth rate: 20 percent
- Annual revenues from EDI services: $1 billion

Because of the high-cost technology involved in getting started in EDI, it has not been profitable for most banks. The possibility of generating EDI volume over the Internet could change that outlook for banks.

Netting arrangements are an example of electronic data interchange. To illustrate, if company *A* buys goods or services from company *B* at a cost of $1 million whereas *B* buys goods or services from *A* that cost $2 million, then the net flow is $1 million from *B* to *A*. In a netting arrangement, the parties involved make net settlements only at the end of the day—credits and debits are summed for the day to generate a single ledger entry. Netting arrangements have been common for airlines, chemical firms, and government securities dealers.

Netting arrangements involve risk-return trade-offs for banks. On the return side, banks lose potential fees and franchise value by being involved in the process only at the end of the day; however, on the risk side, payment-system risks for banks are reduced. From the Fed's perspective, privatization of the payments system shifts control of system risk from the public to the private sector. On balance, whoever runs the system bears the risk and the task of controlling it. Because privatization of payments systems could shift some bank operations to nonbanking firms, banks as traditional administrators of such systems would lose additional franchise value.

TO OUTSOURCE OR NOT TO OUTSOURCE, THAT IS THE QUESTION[31]

An important strategic question for bank managers is, Do we do our processing and other computer operations in-house or contract with a third party to provide the services? The buzz word for this is *outsourcing.* All other things being equal (e.g., revenue generation and customer relationships), the alternative that is least costly determines where to have the function performed. As banks strive to keep costs in line, this economic approach to outsourcing means that everything is on the table, including critical and unconventional operations. One vendor puts it this way: "The way the market is going, people will have to come up with reasons why not to outsource."

Outsourcing is not something that is new as it has been part of the banking industry for decades. Table 18-2 shows examples of areas in which banks have sought third parties for selected applications, including the percentage of banks using the service in 1992 and 1994. What is new is that the largest banks ($10 billion or more in assets) have been looking to "unbundle" their outsourcing contracts, which means they are seeking contracts that focus on specific functions. One consultant refers to outsourcing as "Rent-a-brain time—it's employee leasing." One of the important drivers for increased and more specific outsourcing is that banks cannot afford to retain on a full-time basis the technical expertise needed in today's high-tech, high-cost environment.

TABLE 18-2 Outsourcing: Percentage of Banks Using Third Parties for Selected Applications

	Percentage of Banks Using		
Application	*1994*	*1992*	*Change*
Core banking or data processing	48	51	−3
Commercial-loan processing	36	38	−2
Mortgage processing	36	41	−5
Branch-terminal driving	44	37	+7
ATM transaction processing	46	36	+10
Check processing	49	42	+7
Statement rendering	39	36	+3
Disaster recovery	45	42	+3
POS/merchant services	31	21	+10
Automated-bill-payment processing	9	9	0
Other	2	NA	NA
Memo:			
Banks with no outsourcing contracts	20	33	−13

Source: Adapted from data compiled by Mentis Corp., from *American Banker* (May 22, 1996), p. 3A.

---

[31] This section draws on Barthel [1996] and two inserts from the *American Banker,* "Outsourcing '96: Taking a Hard Look at the Strategic Options," May 22, 1996, and "Management Strategies," July 1, 1996.

An important trend in the FSI that has had a major effect on the demand for outsourcing is the movement by thrift institutions to become full-service retail banks. As a result, thrifts have entered operational areas where they needed help and needed it quickly (e.g., check processing). For example, when Great Western Financial Corporation (Chatsworth, CA) increased the number of its checking accounts from about 0.5 million in 1989 to over 1.5 million by mid-year 1996 (with total balances growing from just under $2 billion [1989] to over $4.5 billion [1996]), it could not have managed the growth without outsourcing. An executive at First Manhattan Consulting Group explains why so many thrifts have chosen outsourcing (and why it can be so beneficial for any new financial-services firm): "You don't have the up-front capital to create your own infrastructure. And two, you can leverage off the scale infrastructure that is in place to support multiple clients." Once scale is achieved, however, a thrift (or bank) has the realistic option of bringing the operation in-house. For example, Charter One Financial Corporation (Cleveland) used outsourcing for its check processing from the early 1980s to the early 1990s, when it brought the operation in-house.

On April 18, 1996, Washington Mutual Inc. (a Seattle-based, thrift holding company) signed a 10-year outsourcing agreement with IBM for a record $533 million. The previous record for a single company had been a $500-million deal in 1991 between Continental Bank (since acquired by BankAmerica) and IBM. IBM's computer-services unit, Integrated Systems Solutions Corp, provided Washington Mutual Bank (WMB, the fifth-largest U.S. thrift institution) with 2,500 desktop workstations in 270 offices and will support them with various new system applications. Barthel [1996] sees the WMB/IBM deal as having two important implications for financial data processing: "the increasing importance of managing networks of personal computers and the reemergence of large-dollar, long-term outsourcing" (p. 1).

In contrast to Washington Mutual's operations, which are mainly on the West Coast, consider Citicorp, which operates on a global basis. With assets of $264 billion at mid-year 1996, Citicorp had 60,000 PCs (compared to WMB's 2,500) and used 2,000 local area networks to link them. On June 27, 1996, Citicorp announced that it had awarded contracts totaling $750 million to Digital Equipment Corporation ($500 million) and Electronic Data Systems Corporation ($250 million) to "accelerate . . . a global technology standardization program" linking thousands of PCs around the world. The task, which will take three years, is called Project Enterprise. The project, which is designed to build a "global infrastructure," is considered so vast and complex that Citicorp needed both Digital and EDS to accomplish the task. Citicorp's technological tradition, which dates back to John Reed's days as a backroom technocrat (Reed is Citicorp's chairman), has been to emphasize aggressive innovation. Because Citicorp intends to "control the architecture and the tools" although relying on Digital and EDS for execution, it prefers to call its approach "insourcing." Moyer [1996] says that on balance, because Citicorp has never favored outsourcing, the project would have been considered a break with tradition except for the insourcing label.

Regarding the significance of Citicorp's Project Enterprise, the general manager of Digital's services division said, "This contract represents a significant change in the way global corporations choose to manage their information systems." By shifting the focus from management of mainframe data centers to desktop computers, Citicorp is focusing on an environment "where worldwide standardization and consistent management can reap the greatest benefits" (Moyer [1996], p. 15).

The Role of Service Subsidiaries in Large Bank Holding Companies (BHCs)

Large bank holding companies (BHCs) that set up separate services subsidiaries to handle information and transactions processing at the wholesale level view them as profit centers rather than cost centers. Services subsidiaries typically supply cash management, securities processing, funds transfer, and other operating services to corporate customers. Moreover, most of these services (e.g., transactions processing) have little capital risk, no funds risk, and little credit risk. In the past, services subsidiaries at large BHCs such as Bankers Trust and Chase Manhattan have generated 10–25 percent of the firms' total profits.

Services subsidiaries also exist at the retail level. For example, Banc One of Columbus, Ohio (one of the biggest credit-card processors in the FSI), has a service subsidiary called Financial Card Services Corporation, the customer-services portion of its card-processing system. The card system, called Triumph, integrates information and stores it in a relational database. Its scope includes, among other services, card issuance, merchant acquiring, and an artificial-intelligence program designed to handle customer requests for higher credit limits. Because card processing is an important source of fee income and offers banks the opportunity to make cardholders multiple users of financial services, it is a potential source of franchise value.

The services-subsidiary approach represents the kind of strategic innovation that large banks can pursue to add franchise value to their companies. In the dynamic technological environment of the FSI, franchise values that have eroded in traditional businesses must be replaced by franchise values in new innovative areas. In 1996, the Federal Reserve ruled that BHCs could establish subsidiaries to provide data-processing services that have nothing to do with banking. This decision was a marked change in Fed policy, which until then had ruled that BHCs could supply only data-processing services that were closely linked to banking. This opportunity was opened when a foreign bank, Compagnie financière de Paribas of Paris, asked the Fed to let it prepare customer bills for a cellular phone company, including several reports that are not closely related to banking.[32] The Fed's reregulation decision recognizes that if banks are to survive, they must be given new opportunities to tap new sources of franchise value to replace declining value in the traditional business of gathering deposits to fund loans.

Outsourcing, Vendor Consolidation, and Community Banks[33]

Because of potential scale economies, small or community banks may be at a disadvantage in supplying some operating services to their customers (e.g., cash management or payroll processing). To reap cost savings, small banks can outsource scale-sensitive products to larger banks or nonbank players. Although the importance of customer relationships is diminishing in banking, the relationships tend to be stronger between small banks and small businesses. To many of these businesses, credit or access to liquidity is the key product; operating services are secondary. Thus, small banks have the opportunity to price operating services more aggressively in

---

[32] Table 15-8 in chapter 15 shows the Fed's list of permissible activities for BHCs, whereas Seiberg [1996] reports on the Fed's decision for expanded data-processing opportunities for BHCs.

[33] This section draws on "Management Strategies." *American Banker* (inserted section), July 1, 1996, and Tracey [1996].

their favor and to seek outsourcing arrangements without risking customer dissatisfaction or loyalty. Together these tactics can increase overall customer profitability.

Consolidation has been affecting all segments of the financial-services industry (FSI), including the vendors that supply outsourcing services. In 1987, for example, 24 processors (with more than 100 customers) controlled 73 percent of the market for core processing provided to banks under outsourcing agreements. By 1995, the figures were 14 firms controlling 93 percent of the business. Of these 14 processors, six were affiliated with banks and seven were national companies.

Vendors are also affected by bank mergers, especially when one merger partner favors outsourcing and the other prefers in-housing processing. For example, when Chase Manhattan and Chemical Bank merged in 1996, Fiserv Inc.'s 12-year, $480-million deal with Chase, which was signed on 1 March 1995, came into jeopardy because Chemical, the bigger bank, did not want to relinquish control of its internal check operations. Fiserv manages four processing centers for Chase with an annual volume of 700 million items.

As outsourcing providers get larger and as deals get larger, such as the WMB/IBM contract, small bankers might be left behind. As one community banker puts it, We "simply don't have any voice" in getting system upgrades and new products from many outsourcing vendors. In addition, outsourcing can present cost problems for smaller banks. One outsourcer says, "The people on my staff are not people [community banks] could afford to hire." Nevertheless, to date, one constant in the outsourcing business has been that community banks have been avid users of third-party services. This fact combined with the consensus among bankers and providers that the outsourcing industry has matured but continues to improve with respect to quality of service suggests that community banks will be able to find quality third-party services.

TECHNOLOGY AND THE FUTURE OF COMMUNITY BANKS[34]

Community banks are broadly defined as those with assets of less than $1 billion. They are locally owned banks that serve consumers and small and medium-sized businesses in local markets. Community banks face fierce competition from larger banks, thrifts, credit unions, finance companies, mutual funds, and brokerage firms. For example, at year-end 1984, community banks had a 6.4 percent share ($723 billion) of the total assets held by households ($11.3 trillion); by year-end 1995, the share was 3.2 percent ($842 billion) of $26.3 trillion. The growth rate of 1.4 percent does not bode well for the future of community banking. Within the banking industry, community banks' share of total assets has fallen from 36 percent in 1984 to 23 percent in 1995. Over this same period, almost 5,400 community banks exited the industry through mergers, and hundreds of others failed. The remaining community banks are described as being at a fork in the road: Make a huge investment in technology and diversify or sell out.

Epstein [1996] attributes the decline of community banks to several key factors:

- Failure to address the financial needs of baby boomers
- Burdensome regulations that create an unlevel playing field favoring nonbank competitors

---

[34] This section draws on Epstein [1996] and Rhoads [1996a, 1996b].

- Inability to afford the high-cost technology necessary to compete
- Financial innovations, such as securitization and the development of secondary markets, that are transforming banking into a "pure commodity business"

Because the first and third points relate directly to bank technology, let's consider them in more detail. What do bank customers want? During 1995, the American Bankers Association commissioned a Gallup Poll to answer this question. The top two motives for picking a bank were convenience (39%) and personal service (19%). Regarding these motives, Harry V. Keefe, chairman of Keefe Managers, a well-known institutional investor in bank stocks, says, "This personal-service stuff is great, but the public wants more than that. My wife is very computer-oriented and she doesn't care about personal service." In contrast, one community banker says that how much a bank spends on technology should be determined by its customers and their needs. He adds, "It's great to have all the latest bells and whistles but what the hell good are they if your customers don't want or don't need them?"[35]

The critical factor, however, is not what customers want now but what they will want in the future. If a bank isn't waiting in the wings with the appropriate technology, it may be too late to retain a viable customer base.

For the baby-boom generation, convenience in delivering financial services means computer technology and e-banking via ATMs, POS, ACHs (wire transfers), and home banking on the Internet, not to mention backroom technologies that provide greater convenience and efficiency. Because many community banks simply cannot afford to invest in these technologies, and because the technologies have the potential for making the concept of "local" (as in community bank) irrelevant, many analysts see community banks as between a rock and a hard place.

According to Rhoads [1996a], the keys to survival for community banks are as follows:

- Exploiting the bank's unique leadership role
- Staying abreast of technology
- Establishing formal systems for evaluating customer needs and wants
- Accepting nontraditional concepts of customer service
- Exploring new sources of funding beyond the core banking business

The middle points dealing with technology, customer wants and needs, and nontraditional customer service fit nicely into a future environment based on e-money and e-banking. An important question is whether community banks will spend enough on technology to be viable in such an environment. A survey of community bankers' plans for spending on technology in 1996 was not encouraging, because 57 percent intended to spend less than $50,000 whereas only 7 percent were looking to spend more than $250,000. The most popular spending range was greater than $10,000 but less than $50,000, indicated by 41 percent of the survey respondents. Consultants at Grant Thornton (Chicago) regarded these "stingy" spending plans for technology as a threat to small banks.

---

[35] Rhoads ([1996], p. 7) reports that this same banker tells the funny story about the "flood" of phone calls his bank received from some of its older customers after the bank had implemented an automated-telephone service. They wanted to know what the pound key is. They were told, "It's the tick-tack-toe sign under the number nine." The next generation of customers is unlikely to have this type of problem and may want to know why they can't do e-banking on the Internet.

THE FINANCIAL-MANAGEMENT IMPLICATIONS OF ELECTRONIC BANKING

Cutting through the electronic wizardry, the acronyms, and the jargon, what are the financial-management implications of electronic banking for financial-services firms? Adapting technological advances for their own sake won't cut it. Nevertheless, because the delivery systems of the future are most likely to be predominately electronic, banks must have them in place or waiting in the wings to be put in place. They should be deployed when managers decide that the investments will add value to the firm. The added value will have to come from enhanced cash flows due to increased fee income or lower costs from greater operating efficiency or both.

Let's consider these effects in terms of the return-on-equity (ROE) model:

$$ROE = PM \times AU \times EM$$

where ROE = return on equity, PM = profit margin, AU = operating efficiency, EM = equity multiplier, and $PM \times AU = ROA$ = return on assets. The key variables are PM = net income/total revenue (profits/"sales") and total revenue/assets. All other things being equal, investments in electronic banking need to increase PM by reducing costs and increase AU through additions to fee income, which will increase ROA and ROE. To the extent that a bank can use these technological advances to expand its market share and its asset base relatively faster than its capital growth, then this additional leverage (higher EM) will further boost ROE. Because many banks appear to have excess capital, at least compared to the minimum regulatory requirements, the time for investing in electronic banking and other technological advances appears to be ripe.

Because the barriers to entry in electronic banking are not that great, banks can be waiting in the wings to enter at the appropriate time. The former manager of strategic planning at Wells Fargo tells the following story: In the mid-1980s, Chemical Bank (since merged with Chase Manhattan) approached Wells Fargo about joining its home banking venture. After studying the offer, Wells Fargo turned it down for two main reasons: First, no business justification for the move existed. And second, no barrier to entry existed if Wells Fargo wanted to get into home banking in the future. In short, little risk existed in waiting, but there was a high probability of loss by going in headfirst. Since then, several of Wells Fargo's competitors (e.g., BankAmerica) that had gone into home banking earlier got out of the field with substantial write-offs. Chemical Bank also abandoned the business a little later. As described earlier in this chapter, Wells later entered home banking and, having also acquired First Interstate (and its home-banking effort), it is regarded by many as the leader in banking on the Internet.

BANKS AS COMMUNICATIONS FIRMS

Banks and communications firms are similar in that they both establish networking relationships through which they collect, store, process, and transmit information for themselves and customers' accounts. In the past, firms in these two industries would have never been confused and in the communication area only one industry and one firm would come to mind: Telecommunications and AT&T. Like the financial-services industry (FSI), however, the telecommunications industry has undergone fusion or decompartmentalization. Today we have numerous players in the communications field, defined to include software/services: AT&T, the various Baby Bells, Microsoft, Intel, Oracle, Cisco Systems, MCI, Sprint, Airtouch, Ascend, Cascade, and Netscape, to mention a few. All of these companies manage information in one way or another. In the process of delivering financial services, financial-services firms (FSFs) also collect, process, store, and transmit information. The well-established networks in banking include ATMs at the retail/consumer level and ACHs at the wholesale/business/government levels. Banking on the Internet and POS systems are fledgling networks likely to come of age in the twenty-first century.

Because of regulations that restrict the activities of BHCs, banks face obstacles if they want to expand in the communications area. In contrast, communications firms encounter fewer roadblocks. Nevertheless, communications firms could not become banks in the narrow sense of making commercial loans financed in part by demand deposits (checking accounts) without being restricted to BHC regulations imposed by the Federal Reserve.

Microsoft's Bill Gates predicts that on-line banking, defined as "virtual branches" on the Internet plus expanded e-mail capabilities, will become the primary vehicles for delivering products and services in the future. Firms that have access to both the payments system (banks) and the technology (communications firms) will dominate this environment. Including communications as a service of the FSI, it is easy to see that in the twenty-first century the collecting, storing, processing, and transmitting of information, including financial transactions and related data, could be in one industry.

Chapter Summary

Jupiter Communications, a New York multimedia research firm, predicts that 13 million customers will be using PC-based **home banking** by the year 2000. From a starting base of 754,000 at year-end 1995, that's an annual growth rate of almost 77 percent. Although other firms project more modest growth rates, all agree that the technology will dramatically alter the way banks deliver financial services. Financial-services firms in the twenty-first century will strive to be virtual banks, which according to Citicorp means ability to serve customers "anywhere, anytime, (in) any way."

Because financial-services firms (FSFs) transfer funds and process information, they are especially concerned about advances in **electronic funds transfer systems** (**EFTS** or EFT systems) and in **information technology.** The joint development of EFT and information technology are driving the innovations of electronic banking, or e-banking, and its counterpart, e-money. These technological advances have made geographic and product restrictions in banking obsolete. As a result, consolidation and corporate restructuring within and across the various segments of the financial-services industry (FSI) have occurred and will continue to occur. Banks and communications firms are similar in that they both establish networking relationships through which they collect, store, process, and transmit information for themselves and customers' accounts.

The technological side of banking has both back-office and front-office aspects. It is in their backroom operations that Bill Gates says, "Banks are dinosaurs." Before technological advances (inventions) can be applied in any business, however, they must pass a value-added or profitability test. A key learning objective is to view **innovation,** defined as a profitable invention, as a **diffusion process.** Because diffusion does not happen overnight, innovations tend to spread slowly. Moreover, electronic and information-based technological innovations have not diffused as rapidly as some analysts anticipated. Nevertheless, in the competitive environment of the twenty-first century, technological innovation presents banks with an opportunity to gain a competitive advantage through cost-effective delivery systems and to use these systems to generate fee income.

Key Concepts, Ideas, and Acronyms

- Automated clearing house (ACH)
- Automated teller machine (ATM, ATM network)
- Clearing House Interbank Payment System (CHIPS)
- Communications firms
- Diffusion process
- Electronic banking (e-banking)
- Electronic data interchange (EDI)
- Electronic funds transfer system (EFTS)
- Electronic money (e-money)
- Fedwire
- Federal Reserve Communications System for the Eighties (FRCS-80)
- Franchise value
- Home banking
- Information technology
- Innovation
- Internet
- Invention
- National Automated Clearing House Association (NACHA)
- Netting arrangements
- Networking
- On-line banking
- Payments system
- Point-of-sale (POS)
- Scale economies
- TRICK + Rational self-interest → Financial innovation
- Virtual banking

Review/Discussion Questions

1. In what ways, if any, are banks and communications firms alike? Who are some of the players in the communications industry?
2. Who said, "Banks are dinosaurs," and what did he really mean?
3. What are the components of TRICK and how does it provide a framework for analyzing the process of financial innovation?
4. In the diffusion of financial innovation, what three preliminary distinctions can be made? Describe the interrelationships among new technology, the process of innovation, and product diffusion. What evidence exists regarding the speed of diffusion of consumer products?
5. How close is the United States to becoming a cashless society? Checkless society? How do your answers mesh with the prediction by Jupiter Communications that 13 million customers will be using PC-based home banking by the year 2000?
6. Who said, "With deregulation, technology is how we're going to beat the other guy"? If you are the "other guy," what are you going to do? Based on past experience, how have banks been graded on their technological prowess?
7. What are the basic components of EFT and which ones have been the most successful to date and why? What do you think are the prospects for home or on-line banking, and how much would you be willing to pay for such a service?
8. What is Fedwire? CHIPS? SWIFT? FRCS-80? Should the Fed own and operate a national ACH? How can payment and settlement risks be managed?
9. What are products and the companies battling for the market for personal financial software to support home banking on the Internet?
10. What is EDI and what are netting arrangements?
11. What is outsourcing and what kinds of activities do banks typically outsource? What is "insourcing"?
12. Describe the when, what, and importance of the Fed's ruling regarding BHCs' provisions of data-processing services?
13. Discuss the dilemma and future for community banks in an era of technology-driven e-banking.

14. What are the financial-management implications of electronic banking for commercial banks? Use the ROE model to illustrate your points.
15. Compare, discuss, and evaluate the following two quotes with the position taken (by me) in Exhibit 18-2:
    a. In a letter to *USA Today,* Srini Anne of Herdon, VA, writes: "It's outrageous that consumers are getting ripped off (by ATM fees) in this fashion. . . . (Banks) have the audacity to actually charge us for using ATMs, saying that it's a convenience to us and hence we should pay for it."
    b. Senator Alfonse D'Amato says that ATM surcharges are an "abusive practice" that can "coerce" customers at small banks to move to larger institutions with more extensive networks of machines. He adds that smaller institutions are at a competitive disadvantage.
16. Walter Wriston, retired chairman of Citicorp, said: "The information standard has replaced the gold standard as the basis for world finance." John Reed, Wriston's protégé and successor, said: "Bricks and mortar didn't interest me, communications did." Explain and discuss these statements. How do they mesh with Citicorp's position in the FSI today and with the similarity between banks and communications firms?

Problems

1. At year-end 1995, it was estimated that 754,000 customers were using PC-based home banking of some form. Calculate how many customers will be using this service at the end of the year 2000, if the growth rate is 10 percent? 25 percent? 50 percent? Or as Jupiter Communications predicts, 77 percent?
2. High-Tech Bank plans some technological-related investments that its consultants predict will increase the bank's profit margin and asset utilization by 10 percent each, all other things being equal. If the bank has the following ROE profile, what will its new one look like if the predictions are realized?

$$ROE = 0.10 \times 0.10 \times 16 = 0.16$$

3. The Last National Bank (LNB) is planning to consolidate its backroom operations at a one-time cost of $500,000. Its existing equipment has no remaining value. If the bank expects to reduce its operating expenses by $75,000 a year and if the project has a useful life of 10 years, should LNB undertake this investment? Its opportunity cost, or required return, on the project is 12 percent.
4. Outback Outsourcers from Downunder has approached Kountry Kommunity Bank (KKB) with a plan for streamlining its check-processing operations. Here's the deal, a five-year contract:

Up-front fee:	$50,000
Annual fee:	25,000
Annual cost saving to bank	35,000

If KKB's required return is 10 percent, should it accept the offer?

Selected References

Apcar, Leonard M. [1987]. "A Special Report: Technology in the Workplace." *The Wall Street Journal* (June 12), Section 4.

Barthel, Matt. [1996]. "Wash. Mutual Signs Record Outsourcing Deal with IBM." *American Banker* (April 19), pp. 1 and 18.

Bedford, N. H. [1995]. "Client/Server Technology Gaining Momentum with Banks." *Business Wire* (October 10).

Block, Valerie. [1996a]. "Amex Accepts Bank Cards' Standard for the Internet." *American Banker* (March 1), pp. 1 and 11.

———. [1996b]. "Consumer Groups Blast Banks on ATM Surcharges." *American Banker* (April 1), pp. 1 and 11.

Bloom, Jennifer K. [1996a]. "America Online, Intuit Team Up to Offer a Home Banking Service." *American Banker* (June 13), pp. 1 and 22.

———. [1996b]. "IBM, 10 Banks Forming Firm to Join Fray in Home Banking." *American Banker* (May 15), pp. 1 and 16.

———. [1996c]. "Wells Looks Like Leader in Internet Banking Race." *American Banker* (March 8), pp. 1 and 12.

Bloom, Jennifer K., and Drew Clark. [1996]. "Intuit, Microsoft Duel for Home Banking Crown." *American Banker* (July 9), pp. 1, 16, 18.

"Chemical to Re-engineer Check Processing with IBM Image Technology." [1995]. *Business Wire* (August 7).

Cline, Kenneth. [1996]. "Centura Makes Hay by Beating the Big Players." *American Banker* (April 18), p. 5.

"Community Banks Need to Assess Business Strategy before Technology Strategy." [1996]. *Business Wire* (March 29).

"Conversation with the Lords of Wintel: Andy Grove and Bill Gates." *Fortune* (July 8), pp. 42–58.

Cope, Debra, and Howard Kapiloff. [1996]. "Mellon Package Would Combine Investment and Bank Accounts." *American Banker* (May 23), pp. 1 and 18.

Corrigan, E. Gerald. [1987]. "Financial Market Structure: A Longer View." *Annual Report* Federal Reserve Bank of New York, pp. 3–54.

Epper, Karen. [1996]. "Visa to Support Banking by Hand-Held Computer." *American Banker* (February 27), pp. 1 and 12.

Epper, Karen, and Jeffrey Kutler. [1995]. "Dinosaur Remark by Gates Sets Off Technology Alarms." *American Banker* (January 4), p. 16.

Epstein, Jonathan E. [1996]. "Do Community Banks Have a Future without Bold Moves Now, Maybe Not." *American Banker* (June 5), pp. 1, 6–7.

Essinger, James. [1996]. "Information Technology: It's All in the Network." *Euromoney* (January) (321), pp. 45–46.

Fisher, John. [1979]. "New Concepts for the World of Banking." *The Bankers Magazine* (March-April), pp. 21–22.

"Focus on EDI." [1990]. Special Report in the *American Banker* (May 21).

Gates, Bill. [1995a]. "Enabling Technology for Expanding Customer Relationships." Speech given at "Retail Delivery '95," sponsored by the Bank Administration Institute.

———. [1995b]. *The Road Ahead.* New York: Viking Press.

Golden, Kathleen. [1996]. "Banks Separate, but Equal in Securities with Technology." *Bank Systems & Technology* (February) 33(2), pp. 16–18.

Hamilton, Earl G. [1979]. "An Update on the Automated Clearing House," *Federal Reserve Bulletin* (July), pp. 525–531.

Jennings, Robert. [1996]. "Survey: Retailers Overestimate Importance of Cards." *American Banker* (February 8), pp. 11–12.

Jenson, Edmund P. [1995]. "The Road Ahead: Banking and Technology." *Credit World* 83 (July/August), pp. 24–27, (January 4), p. 1.

Kane, Edward J. [1981]. "Changes in the Provision of Correspondent-Banking Services and the Role of Federal Reserve Banks under DIDMC Act." Ohio State University College of Administrative Sciences, Working Paper Series 81-55 (July).

———. [1983]. "The Metamorphosis in Financial-Services Delivery and Production." In *Strategic Planning for Economic and Technological Change in the Financial-Services Industry.* San Francisco: Federal Home Loan Bank, pp. 49–64.

Kelley, Edward W., Jr. [1996]. "Remarks" at the CyberPayments '96 Conference (18 June), Dallas, TX.

Kraus, James R. [1996]. "Citibank's Quest Branch Closings and Switch to ATMs Stir Outrage." *American Banker* (February 12), pp. 1 and 6.

Kutler, Jeffrey. [1995]. "Technology Bringing Banks a Revolution, But Not a Panacea." *American Banker* (March 22), p. 2A.

———. [1996]. "Chase Again Clear Leader in Automated Clearing." *American Banker* (April 15), pp. 8–9.

Mankowski, Cal. [1996]. "Banking Sees New Technology as Opportunity." *The Reuter Business Report* (January 1).

Marjanovic, Steven. [1996a]. "EDI Pioneer Beckons Banks to the Internet." *American Banker* (June 20), pp. 18–19.

———. [1996b]. "Electronic Payment Law May Hasten End of Checks." *American Banker* (May 1), pp. 1 and 12.

McEntee, Elliott C. [1996]. "Adam Smith's Dream Has Come True." *President's Column* (June), National Automated Clearing House Association.

Mitchell, George W., and Raymond F. Hodgdon. [1981]. "Federal Reserve and the Payments System: Upgrading Electronic Capabilities for the 1980s." *Federal Reserve Bulletin* (February), pp. 109–116.

Moyer, Liz. [1996]. "Citi Will Pay Digital, EDS $750 Million to Link PCs Worldwide." *American Banker* (June 27), pp. 1 and 15.

Piskora, Beth. [1995]. "Off-Premises Units Dominate ATM Growth." *American Banker* (December 4), pp. 10–19.

———. [1996a]. "Debit Card Takes Center Stage at Industry Conference." *American Banker* (March 4), pp. 8–9.

———. [1996b]. "2 Leading ATM Networks Form Superregional Giant." *American Banker* (March 4), pp. 1 and 10.

Prince, Cheryl J. [1995]. "U.S. Banks Rely on Technology to Increase Profits, Customer Focus." *Bank Systems and Technology* (December).

Rhoads, Christopher. [1996a]. "Small Banks Need to Know Customers and Show Them the Way to the Future." *American Banker* (June 6), pp. 1 and 7.

———. [1996b]. "Stingy Tech Plan Threatens Small Banks, Study Says." *American Banker* (March 5), pp. 1 and 7.

Roberds, William. [1995]. "Financial Crises and the Payments System: Lessons from the National Banking Era." *Economic Review,* Federal Reserve Bank of Atlanta (September/October), pp. 15–31.

Seiberg, Jaret. [1996]. "Fed Expands Data Processing Opportunities for BHCs." *American Banker* (September 6), pp. 1–2.

Sinkey, Joseph F., Jr., and David A. Carter. [1997]. "Why Big Banks Do and Little Banks Don't." Working Paper, University of Georgia.

Taylor, Paul. [1995]. "Evolution of 'the Virtual Bank.' " *Financial Times* (July 5), p. VIII.

"Technology Survey." [1990]. New York: *American Banker.*

Teixeira, Diego. [1996]. "Maximizing the Potential of Technology Support Services." *American Banker* (March 4), p. 13A.

Tracey, Brian. [1996]. "New Chase May End Check Processing Deal with Fiserv." *American Banker* (March 11), pp. 1 and 18.

"Two Hundred Bankers Meet at Microsoft to Discuss Strategy for Embracing the Internet." [1996]. *PR Newswire* (March 18).

Van Horne, James. [1985]. "Of Financial Innovations and Excesses." *Journal of Finance* (July), pp. 621–631.

Vartanian, Thomas P. [1996]. "Technology's Silver Lining and Banking's Dark Clouds." *American Banker* (March 18), p. 14A.

Video: A New Era. [1979]. Research Report 621 (November). Menlo Park, CA: SRI International.

Zakaria, Tabassum. [1996]. "Bankers See Increased Competition, Technology Challenge." *Reuter Business Report* (March 6).

CHAPTER

19

CONSOLIDATION IN THE FINANCIAL-SERVICES INDUSTRY: BANK MERGERS, CORPORATE RESTRUCTURING, AND THE FUTURE STRUCTURE OF BANKING

Contents

831

LEARNING OBJECTIVES

■ To understand the forces driving consolidation in the financial-services industry (FSI)

■ To understand the effects of consolidation

■ To understand the future structure of the banking industry

■ To understand bank mergers and the corporate restructuring of BHCs

■ To understand the costs and benefits of bank mergers

CHAPTER THEME

Banking reregulation and thrift failures initiated a wave of bank mergers during the 1980s and early 1990s. For different reasons, related to revenue growth, cost cutting, and corporate restructuring, the merger wave continues in the 1990s and is expected to persist into the twenty-first century. Megamergers, as illustrated by the combination of Chase Manhattan Corporation and Chemical Banking Corporation (announced in August 1995, completed in April 1996, and resulting in Chase becoming the nation's largest bank), have been an important part of this merger wave. Will the consolidation trend be good or bad for U.S. banking, its customers, and taxpayers? This chapter, which investigates alternative answers to these questions, explores the forces driving consolidation into the twenty-first century. Many analysts see the future structure of banking in terms of a barbell shape, with a few megabanks, such as the new Chase Manhattan with over $300 billion in assets, on one end, and numerous small banks on the other end.

KEY CONCEPTS, IDEAS, AND TERMS

- Bank holding company (BHC)
- Banking companies
- Banking structure
- Consolidation
- Corporate control

- Corporate restructuring
- Financial-services firm (FSF)
- Financial-services industry (FSI)
- Hostile takeover
- Independent bank

- Mergers and acquisitions (M&A)
- Multibank holding company (MBHC)
- Multistate MBHC
- One-state MBHC
- Reasons for mergers

INTRODUCTION

The **financial-services industry** (FSI) in the United States used to be compartmentalized, meaning that commercial banks, savings banks, investment banks/securities firms, insurance companies, and other **financial-services firms** (FSFs) were separated. Although we are unlikely to see, even in the twenty-first century, a completely homogenized FSI consisting only of generic FSFs, **consolidation** is occurring within segments of the FSI and across it. This chapter focuses on consolidation among commercial banks and the main vehicle for this contraction—bank mergers. In addition, bank **corporate restructurings** and the battles for corporate control in banking and in the FSI are covered. We begin by looking at banking consolidation in the United States and then present some theoretical underpinnings to provide a foundation for understanding bank mergers, **corporate control,** and restructuring activity.

BANKING CONSOLIDATION IN THE UNITED STATES[1]

Compared to other developed countries, the United States always has had an overabundance of banks. Edward E. Furash, a noted bank consultant, says, "We have markets in this country that are grossly overbanked. We have an industry with chronic overcapacity."[2] Decades of government overprotection and mispricing of deposit insurance contributed greatly to this condition. The wave of consolidation that began in the 1980s can be viewed as an expected counterbalancing to that overbanked condition.

During the 1980s, as Table 19-1 shows, 3,555 bank mergers occurred. This rate of 355 per year was more than double the annual rate for any of the preceding four decades.[3] The first six years of the 1990s saw the number of bank mergers rise even higher, to an average 485 per year.

Banking reregulation and thrift failures initiated the wave of bank mergers in the 1980s. Although the merger trend is expected to continue into the twenty-first

---

[1] Data in this section are from Ludwig [1995] and the FDIC's *Statistics on Banking.*

[2] As reported by Marshall [1996], p. 2.

[3] On average, the figures are 70 per year during the 1940s, 142 per year during the 1950s, 138 per year during the 1960s, and 140 per year during the 1970s.

TABLE 19-1	Mergers, Absorptions, and Consolidations among Insured Commercial Banks 1940–1995	
Year(s)		Mergers, Absorptions, and Consolidations
1940–49		698 (6.1%)
1950–59		1,416 (12.5%)
1960–69		1,382 (12.2%)
1970–79		1,399 (12.3%)
1980	135	
1981	216	
1982	289	
1983	359	
1984	334	
1985	330	
1986	339	
1987	545	
1988	597	
1989	411	
1980–89		3,555 (31.3%)
1990	393	
1991	447	
1992	428	
1993	481	
1994	549	
1995	612	
1990–95		2,910 (25.6%)
1940–95		11,360 (100%)
Subperiods:		
1940–79		4,895 (43.1%)
1980–95		6,465 (56.9%)

Note: These data exclude banks closed because of financial difficulties (i.e., those explicitly recognized as bank failures), which were 438 from 1990 through 1995, 1,037 in the 1980s, 76 in the 1970s, 44 in the 1960s, 31 in the 1950s, and 100 in the 1940s.

Sources: Statistics on Banking, FDIC, for years 1981 to 1995, and *Annual Report,* FDIC for 1940 to 1980. Table 101 or 102, depending on the year.

century, the forces driving it are different from those of the 1980s and early 1990s. According to "Bank Consolidation," a study by the Bank Administration Institute (BAI, [1996]), the forces driving this phenomenon will be the following:

- Using mergers as an attempt to enhance revenue growth
- Using mergers to attempt to take advantage of economies of scale in specialty businesses (for example, credit cards and mortgage banking)

- Using mergers as a vehicle for restructuring retail banking in terms of what is sold, how it is sold (for example, home banking), and to whom it is sold

The role of economies of scale (or scale economies) is especially important because it is turning many of the businesses of banking into commodity businesses. In a commodity business, product differentiation does not matter because output is homogeneous.

The forces driving bank consolidation can be summarized in terms of the return-on-equity (ROE) model, that is,

$$ROE = ROA \times EM = PM \times AU \times EM \qquad \text{(19-1)}$$

where ROA = return on assets, EM = equity multiplier, PM = profit margin, and AU = asset utilization. All other things being equal, greater revenue growth will increase both PM and AU, and hence it will increase $ROA = PM \times AU$, and $ROE = ROA \times EM$. In contrast, the benefits of cost economies, all other things being equal, work only through PM, by reducing operating costs, to increase ROA and ROE.

The accounting framework of the ROE decomposition model must, however, be used cautiously. Although accounting measures of revenue, cost, and profitability are certainly potential drivers of stock price, higher PM or AU do not necessarily mean that value has been created. According to the discounted-cash-flow (DCF) model, the keys to creating value are the size, timing, and riskiness of cash flows. Because mergers are tricky, it is difficult to determine what future cash flows will be, when they will be received, and how risky they will be. We will return to this issue of value creation from bank mergers later in this chapter.

Bank Mergers and the Decline in the Number of Banks

On December 31, 1934, there were 14,146 insured commercial banks in the United States. Following the banking crisis of the 1930s and the accompanying economic stagnation, the number of banks declined to 13,268 at year-end 1944. Over the next four decades, this number increased almost steadily to 14,496 in 1984. Since then, the number of banks has declined steadily, to 9,941 at year-end 1995, a drop of almost one-third since 1984. If this rate of contraction continues, look for 6,500 or so banks by 2005.

The contraction in the number of banks can be traced mainly to merger activity. Table 19-1 shows that from the beginning of 1940 through 1995, 11,360 banks, excluding bank failures, exited the banking industry through mergers, absorptions, and consolidations. Over this 56-year period, 57 percent of these mergers (6,465) took place in the 16 years from 1980 through 1995. During the 1980s, 3,555 mergers occurred, whereas in the first six years of the 1990s, 2,910 deals were made. Projecting this rate over the remaining four years of the 1990s, the number of mergers during the 1990s could total 4,850.

Banks, Branches, and Offices

It is interesting to compare the number of banks in the United States with the number of banking offices, where the number of offices equals the number of banks plus the number of bank branches. In 1935, the number of offices was 17,237 (14,125 + 3,112).[4] By 1984, 56,295 banking offices existed including 41,799 branches.

---

[4] The number of branches for 1934 is not available.

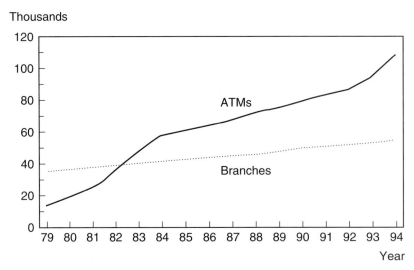

Source: NIC Structure Database, Federal Reserve System, and commercial bank Call Reports.

FIGURE 19-1 **The Number of Branches and ATMs in U.S. Banking, 1979–1994**

By 1995, the number of offices was 66,454, including 56,513 bank branches. From 1935 to 1995, the number of bank branches grew at a compound rate of 4.95 percent. Because of the decline in the number of banks, the number of offices grew at only 2.27 percent.

Another way to look at the tremendous expansion in the number of branches is to consider the number of branches per bank. In 1935, this number was less than one, because only 3,112 branches existed. By 1984, the number of branches per bank was 2.9; by 1995, the number had almost doubled, to 5.7. Since 1984, both numerator and denominator effects have been at work on this ratio, because the number of banks has declined but the number of branches has increased. In addition to brick-and-mortar banking offices, bank customers have thousands of ATMs at which they can do routine banking transactions and increasing opportunities to use personal computers to bank from their homes. On balance, the number of locations and opportunities to deal with banks has increased despite the decline in the number of banks.

Figure 19-1, which compares the growth of ATMs with the growth of bank branches, shows that by year-end 1983, the number of ATMs exceeded the number of branches. Since then, the growth of ATMs has outstripped the growth in number of branches by two to one (10% versus 5%).

Banks and Bank Holding Companies (BHCs)

In U.S. banking, three organizational forms exist: **independent banks** (i.e., banks not affiliated with a holding company), **one-bank holding companies** (OBHCs), and **multibank holding companies** (MBHCs). In addition, since the mid-1980s and the spread of **interstate banking,** MBHCs have been classified as one-state MBHCs (OSMBHCs) and **multistate MBHCs** (MSMBHCs). Together independent banks and BHCs are referred to as **banking companies.** The number of banking companies has mirrored the decline in the number of banks. For example, in 1980 over 12,000 separate banking companies existed; by 1995, fewer than 8,000 existed. The decline in the number of banking companies can be traced to three phenomena:

- Mergers among BHCs, which typically involve a larger BHC acquiring a smaller BHC in a different geographic market
- BHCs acquiring viable independent banks
- The failure of independent banks, most of which were acquired by BHCs in FDIC-assisted deals called purchase-and-assumptions transactions, or P&As (chapter 16)

Regarding the last two points, from 1980 to 1995 the number of independent banks has declined by 70 percent to fewer than 4,000.

The OBHC is the most numerous form of bank organizational structure. By 1995, OBHCs numbered over 4,000, almost doubling since 1980. The growth of OBHCs can be attributed to the popularity of the BHC as a corporate form of organization and to the conversion of holding-company banks to branch banks. Since 1980 the average number of banks per MBHC (both one-state and multistate MBHCs) has declined from 22 to six for multistate MBHCs, and from seven to three for one-state MBHCs.

As the number of banking companies has declined, the economic importance of the different organizational structures has shifted. Although large banking companies have always controlled the bulk of the industry's assets, multistate MBHCs have become the dominant economic form, because they control about three out of every four dollars of assets held by banking companies. Figure 19-2 shows how the economic clout of the various banking companies has shifted over time (1980–1994). One-state MBHCs have been the biggest losers, whereas MSMBHCs have been the biggest winners. The fact that independent banks and OBHCs (think of these two groups as community banks) have been better able to maintain their asset bases in the 1990s lends some credence to the prediction of a barbell shape for the future structure of banking.

Competition and Access to Credit and Other Banking Services

Bank consolidation raises important issues about competition and access to credit and other banking services. Historically, banking markets have been defined narrowly in terms of products and geographic reach. The term "local markets" has been the common description. In a world with, among other things, globalization of ATMs, multistate BHCs, and home banking, the notion of a local market might appear obsolete. However, even if U.S. **banking structure** evolves into a barbell shape, as some are predicting, then the notion of a local market would still be relevant. For example, Furash describes the future structure of banking as follows:

> The whole banking structure is turning into an oligopoly in which four or five institutions dominate any particular geographic-based market—anything from a town to a county to a state or a region, to the whole country. Our projection is that (by 1999) 300 organizations will have about 85% of whatever banks do. Now, banks are doing less and less; they're down to about 25% of financial services as we've been able to measure it. (Marshall [1996], pp. 1–2)

Yellen [1995] reports that although bank mergers have substantially increased the nationwide concentration of assets at the 100 largest banks, from 51.4 percent in 1980 to 71.5 percent in 1995 (June), concentration in local banking markets, which is still relevant for analyzing anticompetitive effects, has remained virtually

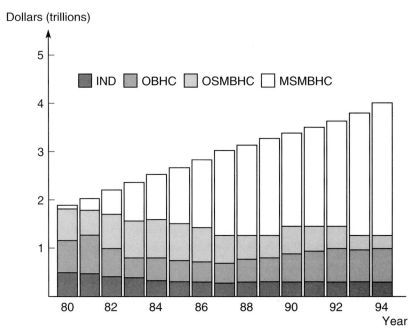

Assets in banking companies by Company Type

Note: IND = independent bank; OBHC = one-bank holding company; OSMBHC = one-state multibank holding company; MSMBHC = multistate multibank holding company.

Source: NIC Structure Database, Federal Reserve System, and commercial bank Call Reports.

FIGURE 19-2 Assets Held by Banking Companies by Organizational Type and Year, 1980–1994

unchanged.[5] This view of bank market structure draws on the Fed's favorite paradigm, the industrial-organization or IO model, which says

$$\text{Market structure} \rightarrow \text{Conduct} \rightarrow \text{Performance}$$

As long as local markets remain relatively unconcentrated, the IO model implies that the desired performance of competitive deposit and loan rates and access to credit will be achieved. Or to use Furash's jargon, the desired performance of whatever banks do will be achieved.

When change occurs, the most challenging times are the transition periods. Consolidation in banking can mean disruption to bank customers and employees as long-standing relationships are severed. These changes, however, can also present opportunities for customers to get more and better services as competition increases. To protect bank customers against any anticompetitive effects of consolidation, fed-

---

[5] The standard measure of concentration in banking markets is the Herfindahl-Hirschman Index (HHI), which equals sum of squared market shares. For example, suppose in a three-bank market, the shares (of deposits, loans, or an index of output) are 0.5, 0.3, and 0.2. These shares, of course, must sum to one. Expressed as percentages and squared, the HHI = 2,500 percent + 900 percent + 400 percent = 3,800 percent. For a monopolist, HHI = 100 percent × 100 percent = 10,000 percent; in a highly competitive market, HHI = 0.0. According to Jayaratne and Hall [1996], the national average HHI for the United States was 1,602 in 1994, up from 1,423 in 1989. For the New York (second) Federal Reserve District, they report, for five MSAs in 1994, HHIs ranging from 536 (Metro NYC/NJ) to 2,003 (Buffalo), up from 459 and 1,565, respectively, in 1989. Reported HHIs ignore the percent sign.

eral antitrust and consumer-protection laws exist. In contrast, although top managers may have golden parachutes, bank employees in middle- and upper-management positions have little protection, and they are the most vulnerable to disruption due to consolidation and downsizing.[6] Early retirement, opportunities in other segments of the FSI, and starting *de novo* banks offer potential solutions to these dilemmas.[7]

MERGERS AND THE CREATION OF VALUE

One of the interesting and controversial questions in corporate finance is, Do takeovers create value? With the proliferation of antitakeover measures, one might assume a takeover was a fate worse than (corporate) death. However, the laissez-faire approach to financial economics contends (and the evidence suggests) that takeovers are good for the economy because they guarantee that a firm's assets are controlled by managers who can use them most productively (i.e., maximize their value). The issue here is one of **corporate control.** The buying and selling of firms is called the market for corporate control. Given the objective of maximization of shareholder wealth, a strong case can be made in favor of takeovers. Those who do not believe in this objective and the accompanying view of a corporation as a bundle of contracts argue against takeovers. These critics favor a more subjective, or soft, view of the corporation based on values like loyalty and commitment rather than the hard values (prices) found in the stock market.[8] These groups also tend to be very sensitive to the downsizing occuring in banking and in corporate America in general.

Takeovers, Corporate Control, and Restructuring Activities[9]

Corporate-control transactions are activities that fundamentally restructure an organization. *Control* and *restructuring* are the key words. Takeovers, mergers, and leveraged buyouts are the transactions that make financial news headlines. Closely associated with these transactions, but less well known, are such activities as divestitures, spinoffs, and stock repurchases. Control transactions affect firms fundamentally in terms of their expansion, contraction, corporate control, and ownership structure. The emotional and colorful terms used in fighting takeovers, and referred to as antitakeover measures, are "shark repellents," "poison pills," "greenmail," and "golden parachutes." In general, these measures are designed to make it harder (more expensive) for a would-be acquirer to hit a target company. With the advent

---

[6] Sloan [1996] discusses the downsizing implications of Wells Fargo's acquisition in 1996 of First Interstate Bank.

[7] Deogun [1996] describes how a former thrift executive, who was displaced by a series of mergers, used the disruption as an opportunity to launch a de novo bank. Other bankers doing the same thing are contributing to the community-bank component of the projected barbell shape of the future structure of banking.

[8] Helm and Dobrzynski [1988] summarize the issues and provide an interesting profile of Professor Mike Jensen, formerly of the University of Rochester and now at the Harvard Business School. Jensen is a leading advocate of the benefits of takeovers. Crovitz [1990], in an op-ed piece for *The Wall Street Journal,* asks: "Can Takeover Targets Just Say No to Stockholders?" Footnote 9 and the references to this chapter provide suggestions for further reading.

[9] Jensen [1986]; Copeland and Weston [1988], chapter 19; Ross and Westerfield [1988], chapter 26; and the four papers in the "Symposium on Takeovers," Varian [1988], provide detailed discussion of these issues. Beatty, Santomero, and Smirlock [1987], Neely [1987], Matthews [1988], and Hawawini and Swary [1990] focus on bank mergers and acquisitions. See also Stern [1987] in "The Future of Commercial Banking: A Roundtable Discussion."

of **hostile takeovers,** discussed next, banks have been trying to protect themselves and adopting poison pills. Typically, a poison pill would work as follows: If an investor buys more than a predetermined share of a company, usually in the range of 10–20 percent, the poison pill kicks in, permitting current shareholders to buy shares at a discount, say 50 percent, from the company. Because other shareholders can now buy the shares at a discount, the task of buying the entire company can become prohibitively expensive. Hostile bidders, however, are not defenseless against poison pills because threats of lawsuits or proxy fights or both provide potential antitoxins.

Hostile Takeovers in Banking

Is nothing sacred? In the club that banking once was, a hostile takeover would have been totally unacceptable behavior. Banking was much too civilized for such activity. However, because the club has fallen by the wayside and because the rule of the FSI merger game is "gobble or be gobbled," hostile takeovers have made their way into banking. Bank of New York's hostile takeover of Irving Trust in 1987, the first deal of its kind for a major U.S. bank and the largest at the time (a $1.4 billion offer of common stock and cash), is regarded as the watershed transaction for such activity.

Table 19-2 provides a list of significant hostile takeover attempts in banking for the period 1981 through 1996. The largest, and also the most recent, hostile takeover on the list is Wells Fargo's successful acquisition of First Interstate Bank in 1996. The battle for First Interstate began in 1995. First Interstate sought refuge in a friendly merger with First Bank System (Minneapolis), and a deal was arranged in November 1995. The arrangement went sour, however, when the Securities and Exchange Commission (SEC) ruled that First Bank would have to suspend a share repurchase for two years if the transaction was completed.

In touting the benefits of the Wells Fargo–First Interstate merger, Wells's chairman, Paul Hazen, told the Federal Reserve that the deal would bring more jobs, more inner-city lending, and more small-business financing to California. Regarding the jobs issue, Sloan [1996] had a decidedly different view. He argued that the battle between Wells and First Bank for First Interstate was "probably the first big takeover battle ever decided by how many people Wall Street thought each bidder could fire" (p. 47). Sloan's argument was based on the fact that First Bank did not have any branches in California, whereas Wells and First Interstate had overlapping offices. Wells Fargo, by the way, is noted for its ability to cut costs and its drive to continue as the most profitable major U.S. bank. Reflecting this efficiency reputation, an analyst for Salomon Brothers said, "Conceptually, this is an extraordinary transaction in the creation of shareholder value. Huge cost savings . . . could create a powerhouse."[10] At the time of the deal, the merger of Wells and First Interstate created the eighth largest BHC in the United States, with total assets of almost $110 billion.

Prior to being gobbled up by Wells Fargo, First Interstate attempted to do some gobbling of its own. In 1986, First Interstate attempted to acquire BankAmerica with a $3.2 billion package of common stock, preferred stock, and convertible notes. First Interstate withdrew its bid when BankAmerica sold strategic assets and proposed to issue new equity capital. BankAmerica's defense against First Interstate was handled by Salomon Brothers and was described as "Defense

---

[10] As reported in *The Wall Street Journal* (October 19, 1995), p. 1.

TABLE 19-2 Significant Hostile Takeover Attempts in Banking, 1981–1996

Date	Bidder[a]	Target[a]	Offer	Outcome
1995–96	Wells Fargo ($51B)	First Interstate ($55B)	$10.8B stock exchange	Deal closed early in 1996.
1995	Banc One ($92B)	Bank of Boston ($47B)	NA	Unsuccessful.
1989	NCNB ($55.2B)	C&S ($23.3B)	NA	NCNB withdrew its offer.
1987	Bank of New York ($22.1B)	Irving Trust ($24.2B)	$1.4B common stock and cash	Deal finally closed in October 1988. First hostile takeover of a major U.S. bank.
1987	Marshall & Illsley ($5.3B)	Marine Corp ($4.3B)	$560MM common stock or cash	M&I intended to eliminate dilution through savings from in-market consolidation. Marine Corp. accepted a lower $525 MM stock-for-stock bid from out-of-state white knight Banc One.
1987	Wilmington Trust ($2.8B)	Delaware Trust ($1.1B)	$190MM common stock	Wilmington intended to eliminate dilution through savings from in-market consolidation. Delaware Trust accepted a comparably priced stock-for-stock bid from out-of-state white knight Meridian Bancorp.
1986	First Interstate ($52.5B)	BankAmerica Corp ($107.2B)	$3.2B common and preferred stock and convertible notes	First Interstate withdrew bid following BankAmerica's sale of strategic assets and proposals to issue new capital.
1986	Fleet Financial Group ($10.0B)	The Conifer Group ($3.9B)	$540MM common stock	Conifer accepted a higher $656 MM stock-for-stock bid from in-state white knight Bank of New England.
1985	Comerica ($9.5B)	Michigan National ($6.8B)	$350MM common stock	Marine Midland, acting as white knight, made a stake-out equity infusion into Michigan National. Additional capital restructuring was undertaken to frustrate the proposed acquisition.
1985	Meridian Bancorp ($5.7B)	Commonwealth ($1.3B)	$113MM common stock	Commonwealth accepted a higher $119-MM bid from Mellon Bank.
1984	Midlantic Banks ($6.4B)	Statewide Bancorp ($0.8B)	$70MM stock or cash	Marine Midland, acting as white knight, made a stake-out equity infusion into Statewide.
1983	Norstar Bancorp ($3.6B)	Security New York ($1.6B)	$95MM common stock and cash	Norstar acquired Security New York.
1983	Barnett Banks ($6.9B)	Florida Coast ($0.6B)	$75MM cash	Barnett acquired Florida Coast.
1982	Huntington Bancshares ($3.6B)	Union Commerce ($1.5B)	$96MM common stock and cash	Huntington Bancshares acquired Union Commerce following a tender offer. Subsequent asset quality and personnel problems made earning out dilution substantially more difficult than Huntington had anticipated.
1981	Southeast Banking Corp ($5.8B)	Florida National Banks ($2.5B)	$240MM cash	Florida National struck a deferred merger agreement with Chemical New York.

[a] Figures in parentheses are total assets.

Sources: Information from O'Rourke [1988], p. 18, for 1981 to 1987; and thereafter from the *American Banker.*

against unsolicited offer (i.e., hostile takeover) by First Interstate Bancorp." It is interesting to note that investment bankers, such as Salomon Brothers, work both sides of the merger street. On the one hand, they put deals together, and on the other hand, they work to stop hostile deals from taking place. Because BankAmerica was a near zombie for most of the 1980s, one has to wonder what its shareholders thought about the transfer of wealth to Salomon Brothers (and other expenses) to prevent the takeover. Recall that takeover evidence suggests takeovers are good for the economy because they entrust a company's assets to those who can manage them most efficiently.

Regarding BankAmerica's shareholders, it is interesting to note that as of March 31, 1987, the third-, fifth-, and sixth-largest shareholders of BankAmerica were Citicorp, with 3,133,495 shares, Wells Fargo Bank, with 2,442,179, and Bankers Trust, with 1,490,683.[11] Although some of these shares are likely to be custodial in nature, others are not. Thus, as one money manager noted, "Banks do, in fact, vote the shares of other banks."[12] Wonder how Citicorp, Wells Fargo, and Bankers Trust voted on First Interstate's hostile takeover attempt of BankAmerica? Suppose Citicorp or Bankers Trust had their eyes on BankAmerica as a future takeover target; would they want First Interstate to be in control of a larger company? What if Wells Fargo wanted to keep First Interstate out of northern California? Intriguing questions. In searching for these and other answers, Kreuzer [1987] found some of the major holders of bank stocks unwilling to be interviewed, even off the record.

Alternative Acquisition Structures

Most **mergers and acquisitions** are made by BHCs, the dominant organizational structure in U.S. commercial banking. Four alternative legal structures exist to put a deal together. First, a banking company (BHC or independent bank) may acquire another banking company, called the *target*. The ruling federal agency in the case of an acquisition by a bank (as opposed to a BHC) is the agency with jurisdiction over the surviving or acquiring bank. The Fed has jurisdiction over all acquisitions made by a holding company. When a bank subsidiary of a holding company acquires a target, it is called a *merger into a subsidiary bank*. If the holding company acquires the target, it is called a *direct acquisition*.

A third structure is one called a *phantom*, or *triangular*, bank merger. In this arrangement, a new phantom bank is chartered solely for the purpose of acquiring the target organization. The description of the deal as triangular comes from the three entities involved: the holding company, the phantom, and the target. In this form, the arrangement is called a *forward* triangular merger because it is possible to do a *reverse* triangular merger. In a reverse, the target bank acquires the phantom organization, which maintains the charter of the target bank.

A fourth major structural form is the merger or acquisition of two holding companies directly, with the target company disappearing and its subsidiaries becoming subsidiaries of the acquiring company. With the advent of regional and then nationwide interstate banking, this type of transaction has become increasingly popular.

---

[11] For these and other interesting facts about "Who Owns the Big Banks?" see Kreuzer [1987].

[12] *Ibid.*, p. 44. A bank holding company is permitted only to own up to 5 percent of the stock of another bank under the Federal Reserve Board's Regulation Y. With the Board's permission, however, a BHC may go over the 5 percent limit.

Megamergers: The Marriage of Chase Manhattan and Chemical Banking

To date, the megamerger of megamergers in U.S. banking has been the marriage of Chase Manhattan and Chemical Banking into Chase Manhattan, a combination resulting in a $300 billion bank—the largest in the United States.[13] In the international arena, the megamerger in banking was the marriage of two giant Japanese banks, Mitsubishi Bank ($474 billion) and Bank of Tokyo ($298 billion), into the world's largest bank ($772 billion). This deal was announced on the day that the Chase–Chemical transaction was consummated (April 1, 1996, no fooling).

Is bigger always better? Based on Japan's experience, the answer seems to be no. Japanese banks, the largest in the world, have not been the most efficient or the most profitable. Regarding the Chase–Chemical deal, Silber and Smith [1995] contend, "After the cost-cutting, the new bank will have to be different to be better. Other than cutting costs, there are very few benefits to be gained." As noted at the beginning of this chapter, potential areas for synergy from mergers, beyond cost cutting, will have to come from greater revenue generation and reconfiguration of a bank's retail business.

An alternative to using the total assets of the resulting bank for ranking mergers is to use the market value of the deal. Table 19-3 shows the top five deals of all time (as of this writing), all of which took place between 1995 and 1997. On this basis, the NationsBank–Barnett valued at $15.5 billion ranks first, with the Wells Fargo–First Interstate deal second at $12.3 billion. The Chase–Chemical was a close third at $11.4 billion. NationsBank also had the fourth largest deal at $9.8 billion while First Bank System's acquisition of U.S. Bancorp was fifth as $9.1 billion.

TABLE 19-3 Top Five Bank Merger Deals in Terms of Market Value of the Transaction (as of September 24, 1997)

Rank/Buyer	Seller	Date Announced	Value of Deal (billions)
1. NationsBank Charlotte, NC	Barnett Banks Jacksonville, FL	August 1997	$15.5
2. Wells Fargo San Francisco	First Interstate Los Angeles	January 1996	$12.4
3. Chase Manhattan New York	Chemical Banking New York	August 1995	$11.4
4. NationsBank Charlotte, NC	Boatmen's Bancshares St. Louis	August 1996	$ 9.8
5. First Bank System Minneapolis	U.S. Bancorp Portland	March 1997	$ 9.1

Notes: The Chase–Chemical deal was a merger of equals. Value represents the price on the announcement date.

Source: The Wall Street Journal (September 2, 1997), p. A3. Data from SNL Securities LC, Charlotte, VA.

---

[13] During the summer of 1995, it was rumored that BankAmerica and NationsBank would merge to form a $420 billion company. The rumor never materialized. A year later, however, on August 30, 1996, NationsBank settled for a smaller fish when it acquired Boatmen's Bancshares Inc. of St. Louis in a transaction valued at $9.5 billion. On the announcement, NationsBank's stock price dropped $7.25, from $92.375 to $85.125. The deal moved NationsBank to third on the U.S. asset-size list, behind Chase and Citicorp.

Investment-banking firms play a major role, as deal makers, in facilitating the consolidation of commercial banking. A perennial leader among deal makers is Salomon Brothers. Other major players in FSI deal-making include Goldman Sachs, CS First Boston, Morgan Stanley, J. P. Morgan Securities, and Merrill Lynch Capital Markets. Montgomery Securities of San Francisco has appeared as a new kid on the deal-making block.

M&A deals have not always been as valuable as those shown in Table 19-3. For example, during 1987 the five leading **investment bankers** serving as advisors to banks in M&A transactions were J. P. Morgan Securities (four deals worth $4.1B), Morgan Stanley (four deals worth $2.7B), Goldman Sachs (three deals worth $2.2B), Salomon Brothers (three deals worth $0.7B), and Merrill Lynch Capital Markets (two deals worth $0.5B). The five-firm total value for the 16 deals was $10.2 billion.[14] Goldman Sachs was involved in the largest banking deal of 1987, the $1.34 billion acquisition of Fidelcor (Philadelphia) by First Fidelity Bancorp (Newark).

The values of bank mergers during the 1980s appear minuscule compared to the megamerger deals of the 1990s (Table 19-3). In either decade, however, the deals capture the importance of the adage: gobble or be gobbled. Moreover, even those that gobble (First Fidelity in 1987) can be gobbled later (First Fidelity in 1996).

Megamergers: California S&Ls[15]

During the last week of July 1996, mergers among major thrifts on the West Coast shook up the S&L market in California. Two deals created the second- and fourth-largest thrifts in the United States. In the first deal, Washington Mutual Bank (Seattle, $21 billion in assets) acquired American Savings (Irvine, $20 billion) for $1.2 billion in stock. The resulting bank will tie Great Western Bank (Chatsworth, CA, $41 billion) as the second-largest thrift. Home Savings of America (Irwindale, CA, $50 billion) was the nation's largest thrift at mid-year 1996.

The second deal saw First Nationwide (San Francisco, $18 billion) buy Cal Fed Bancorp (Los Angeles, $14 billion) for $1.2 billion in cash. The transaction involved a complicated plan to share any proceeds from Cal Fed's lawsuit against the U.S. government (FDIC) in which the government changed the terms of deals made with Cal Fed.

These two megadeals were expected to provide the impetus for additional mergers among other California thrifts and to open the market for purchase of the resulting institutions by out-of-state commercial banks.

Opportunities for Acquisitions of Zombie Thrifts and Banks

According to voodoo, the term "zombie" refers to the supernatural power that enters and reanimates a dead body. Under the voodoo banking and thrift regulation of the 1980s, federal deposit insurance was the supernatural power that entered insolvent banks and thrifts to create **zombie depository institutions.** Government guarantees in the form of unbooked intangible assets are the lifeblood of zombie banks and thrifts. However, because the accounting identity applies to both booked and unbooked entries, the unbooked liabilities resulted in the de jure insolvency of the FSLIC and the de facto insolvency of the FDIC, sticking taxpayers with a

---

[14] These M&A transactions, as reported by O'Rourke ([1988], p. 20), include only 100 percent takeover deals.
[15] Information in this section is from the *American Banker* (July 23, 26, 29, 1996).

$160 billion tab (excluding interest) for the S&L mess. Although federal bank regulators created these living dead, they did not want to keep the zombies forever. Accordingly, they sought to get them back in the private sector as quickly as federal resources and bureaucratic redtape permitted, a process that offered healthy banks and thrifts the opportunity to acquire zombie banks or thrifts or both.[16]

The big zombie takeover of the 1990s was Fleet/Norstar's acquisition of the failed Bank of New England. In the late 1980s, NCNB (now NationsBank) and Banc One made substantial inroads in Texas's banking markets through acquisitions of zombie banks in that state. *Mergers and Acquisitions* (May/June, 1991) portrayed Banc One's acquisition pattern as follows:[17]

> With banking operations concentrated in Ohio and Michigan, Banc One leveraged the troubles of Texas banks to penetrate that state through acquisitions. Most were executed through federal assistance, including Banc One Texas, Dallas, which was formed from parts of the failed MCorp and Bright Bank Dallas. Banc One also bought a small banking organization in its home state, Metropolitan Bancorp, and added investment banking capabilities with Meuse, Rinker, Chapman, Endres, & Brooks. (p. 38)

Although the problems of large banks and thrifts garner most of the financial headlines, the numerous small banks and thrifts with financial difficulties offered acquisition opportunities for community banks. For example, Simoff [1991] reported that during the spring of 1991 the Resolution Trust Corporation (RTC) announced the sale of 34 S&L branches in Iowa. Twenty-six of the offices, with $475 million in deposits, were purchased by 19 independently owned community banks, 12 of which had less than $100 million in total assets.

On balance, the demise of about one-half of the nation's 3,000 S&Ls, with over 20,000 offices, created plenty of opportunities for community banks to acquire the offices of zombie thrifts. Two attractive features of RTC-arranged takeovers were the right of the acquiring bank to reprice all existing deposit contracts after 14 days and the continuation of data processing under RTC management until a conversion could be arranged, typically a three-to-four-year task. Simoff [1991] concluded: "The RTC thrift disposition process offers community banks the most financially compelling manner to enhance their service delivery capabilities, growth opportunities, and market diversification" (p. 7).

Monday-Morning Quarterbacking

Looking backwards, *Business Week* (January 15, 1990) classified and described its view of the best and worst merger deals of the 1980s across all industries. Two banking deals made the lists. Wells Fargo's acquisition of Crocker National for $1.1 billion in 1986 was seen as one of the best deals. In contrast, RepublicBank's acquisition of InterFirst in 1987 for $387 million was seen as one of the worst deals. The Republic deal was so bad that the resulting organization, First Republic, was declared insolvent in 1988 and taken over by NCNB (now NationsBank) with financial assistance from the FDIC.

---

[16] Regarding red-tape delays, it took the FDIC almost seven years (1984–1991) to complete the reprivatization of Continental Bank (formerly Continental Illinois, bailed out by the FDIC in 1984), and by 1996 the books had yet to be closed on the costs of the bailout.

[17] In 1990, M&A deals in banking totaled $9.5 billion ("M&A Almanac: 1990 Profile"). Across all industries, banking ranked first in number of deals and fourth in total value of deals. Banc One Corp. of Columbus, Ohio was the fourth-most-active acquirer in 1990, with 13 deals.

It will be interesting to see if Wells Fargo can generate the same rave reviews for its 1996 acquisition of First Interstate.

Bank Divestitures[18]

As part of corporate restructuring, the banking industry has been a leader in divestiture activity. For example, in 1995, banks completed 104 divestitures (4.7% of the 2,239 divestitures) worth $3 billion. The number of deals ranked third whereas the dollar value was not in the top ten, where telecommunications ranked first ($33.4 billion) and electric, gas, and water utilities ranked tenth ($4.6 billion).

Both distressed and viable banks use divestitures to raise cash. The ailing Bank of New England Corporation had two divestitures that ranked in the top 25 for 1990. The sale of its credit-card business to Citicorp for $828 million ranked as the 15th largest deal, and the sale of its leasing operations to Bank of Tokyo for $592.5 million ranked 24th. (The Bank of Tokyo's purchase was the 25th-largest foreign acquisition of a U.S. interest and the largest one in the banking industry.) Despite these divestitures, Bank of New England could not generate enough cash to save itself, because it was closed on January 6, 1991, and later bought by Fleet/Norstar in April of 1991.

BANK MERGER-AND-ACQUISITION (M&A) STRATEGIES

Megamergers such as the Chase–Chemical and the Wells–First Interstate deals make the boldest financial headlines and generate the largest fees for deal makers. Less dramatic but equally important are the numerous other transactions that account for the bulk of the consolidation of the banking industry. To highlight these other transactions, this section explores the **M&A strategies** employed by three superregional banks: Banc One (Columbus, Ohio), KeyCorp (Albany, New York), and SunTrust (Atlanta). In addition, we look at M&A strategies for community banks.

Banc One (Columbus, Ohio)

During the early 1990s, Banc One (Columbus, Ohio) moved into the elite group of 10 largest banks in the United States. Its acquisition strategy, described by one analyst as "the best in the country," follows four basic steps (Svare ([1990], pp. 19-20)):

- Find banks with good asset quality in attractive markets
- Make a nondilutive offer
- Allow the affiliated institution considerable autonomy
- Significantly enhance earnings of the new affiliate

Banc One implements this strategy by centering on three lines of business: (1) bank operations, which focus on high-profit-margin products, market diversity and balance, affiliate autonomy, and centralized support; (2) technology, which focuses on product enhancement, maintaining a leading edge, and fee income; and (3) affiliations, which focus on value added, increased market diversity, future profitability, and management pool.

---

[18] The data in this section are from "M&A Almanac 1995." *Mergers and Acquisitions* (March/April), 1996.

From 1990 through 1994, Banc One's rapid growth and high performance were fueled by buying lower-priced rivals. By 1995, however, John B. McCoy, Banc One's CEO, announced to 135 of his key managers that the bank's growth-by-acquisition strategy was unlikely to be able to sustain itself. With core earnings growth stagnating, McCoy was not optimistic, because, as he explained to his troops: "We don't have a compelling vision that's widely shared" (Pare [1995]). In contrast, Dick Kovacevich, CEO of Norwest, has a vision, but it's not a pretty one: "The banking industry is dead, and we ought to just bury it" (ibid). What he means by the "banking industry" is taking deposits and making loans. That traditional franchise has indeed been decimated. To survive, banks need to build on the remaining franchise value by carving out particular niches (e.g., credit cards) and by expanding into new areas (e.g., securities, insurance, and other financial services).

KeyCorp and Interstate Banking: "Hit 'em where they ain't"

When it comes to name recognition of major U.S. banks, KeyCorp (Cleveland, Ohio, and Albany, New York) does not come to mind. Nevertheless, Wilke [1991] described KeyCorp, with offices from Alaska to Maine, as a potential preview of nationwide banking. Based on *Business Week's* "Bank Scoreboard" for 1990, Key-Corp ranked 36th, with total assets of $19.3 billion and total deposits of almost $16 billion, all of which were gathered from domestic markets. More importantly, its total market value of equity (as of March 28, 1991) was $1.3 billion, so it ranked 34th and generated an equity-to-asset ratio of 6.73 percent. Although KeyCorp's loan portfolio of $12.7 billion ranked 28th in size in 1990, its quality was top grade, with a charge-off rate of only 0.7 percent, nonperforming assets of only 1.3 percent, and no highly levered transactions (HLTs). With five-year average EPS growth of 10.5 percent and a dividend yield of 4.44 percent, KeyCorp's stock price more than doubled, from about $15 per share in 1985 to over $30 per share in 1991.

Panel A of Table 19-4 reflects KeyCorp's acquisition strategy of "hitting 'em where they ain't" (i.e., where there ain't much competition, as in Alaska, Idaho, Utah, Wyoming, and Maine). However, as Panel B shows, such a geographically diverse operation is expensive to run because KeyCorp has a ratio of operating expenses to tax-equivalent revenue of 66.5 percent, highest of the 11 banks shown. Nevertheless, as long as KeyCorp maintains its loan quality, it should have adequate net interest income to cover its overhead.

Because KeyCorp hits 'em where they ain't, it has numerous locations in small towns. One of the keys to the company's success is that it believes in local banking and the kind of homespun management that seems to make a difference in small towns. Wilke ([1991], p. A5) illustrates KeyCorp's approach with the following story. When Rockland, Maine, was having financial difficulties with its annual Lobster Festival, KeyCorp contributed $3,000, whereas out-of-state banks did nothing. Ed Kolmosky, Rockland's Cadillac dealer, describes KeyCorp's manager in Rockland as follows: "(He) grew up here, and he's active in the Rotary and in the community. He's not just passing through."

How has KeyCorp been doing lately? By December 31, 1995, KeyCorp had total assets of $66.3 billion and ranked as the 14th-largest BHC in the United States. From August 1995 to August 1996, KeyCorp's stock traded at a high of $40.375 and a low of $30.625. On August 2, 1996, its *P/E* was 11 and its dividend yield was 3.8 percent ($1.52 per annum). One of KeyCorp's marketing efforts has focused on redesigning ATMs to make them more fun to use. For example, visitors

TABLE 19-4 KeyCorp: A Preview of Interstate Banking

Panel A. Geographic Presence

State	Branches
New York*	290
Maine	94
Oregon	79
Washington	41
Idaho	39
Utah	34
Wyoming	28
Alaska	18

*Does not include branches to be acquired with purchase of Goldome Savings Bank.

Panel B. Operating Efficiency

Comparison of various banks with 1990 assets of $10 billion to $25 billion, ranked by efficiency ratio (gross operating expenses as a percent of fully taxable equivalent revenue)

Bancorp Hawaii	56.49%
U.S. Bancorp	60.04
Signet Banking	61.77
Comerica	62.61
Crestar Financial	63.46
Corestates Financial	64.35
Meridian Bancorp	64.54
Cominion Bankshares	64.54
Midlantic	64.66
Manufacturers National	65.08
KeyCorp	66.52

Sources: Adapted from data reported in *The Wall Street Journal* (May 31, 1991), p. A5, for Panel A, and by Keefe, Bruyette & Woods, Inc. for Panel B.

to Cleveland's Rock and Roll Hall of Fame will encounter an ATM that looks and plays like a jukebox.

SunTrust: Bucking the Merger Trend[19]

SunTrust Banks of Atlanta, an earlier product of a merger of equals between Trust Company of Georgia and Sun Banks of Florida, has taken a decidedly different approach to merger mania. In 1994, analysts were saying that the best thing SunTrust ($46.5 billion in assets) could do would be to merge with Wachovia Corporation ($45 billion in assets) of Charlotte. According to the analysts, the marriage would gener-

---

[19] This section draws on Cline [1996].

ate a $300 million cost savings and unite two of the best franchises in the Southeast. SunTrust's response was to initiate its "Growth Project," a three-year plan (1995–1997) to boost revenues without resorting to outside acquisitions. The key ingredients in SunTrust's recipe for merger-free revenue growth include the following:

- Hire 1,500 sales-oriented employees
- Reduce back-office staff
- Ratchet up supermarket branching
- Standardize sales systems
- Build up capital markets group
- Invest in new technology

Cline [1996] describes the plan, which applies to six critical business lines (e.g., credit cards, which until recently were not a high-profile business at SunTrust), as similar to the reengineering efforts at other U.S. banks. In general, these efforts have focused on streamlining branch-delivery systems and upgrading technology. Although SunTrust experienced record earnings in 1995, they were attributed, in part, to financial engineering associated with stock buybacks, tight expense control, and a lower tax rate compared to that of 1994. Unwilling to go the merger route to boost earnings, SunTrust looked inward and came up with its "Growth Project."

Banks Enter the Free-Agent Market Looking for Nonbanking Franchise Value

In professional sports such as football, baseball, and basketball, owners and fans want franchise players (e.g., Michael Jordan)—those that can deliver a championship. Two alternative ways to attempt to develop a championship team are (1) building from scratch using the draft or farm teams and (2) buying up pricey free agents. Bankers face a similar strategic choice: Do they build new franchise value from scratch or do they enter the pricey free-agent market and attempt to buy it? Unfortunately, bankers are not free to buy any business that they think might add value because they cannot enter businesses prohibited by federal bank regulators. Historically, these opportunities have been restricted to businesses/products defined by the Federal Reserve as "closely related to banking."

With declining franchise value in the traditional business of funding loans with deposits, it seems less than wise, and perhaps only a stopgap measure, to attempt to expand this business segment. The solution is to find new sources of franchise value. Because banking, investments, and insurance seem to be the core businesses for the prototype financial-services firm of the future, banks need to enter those businesses that will best complement their existing core banking franchise. The dilemma with this strategy is competing against recognized leaders such as Prudential in insurance and Merrill Lynch in investments.

Three examples illustrate how some banks have attempted to enter the free-agent market to attempt to gain franchise value.[20] First, in 1996, First American Corp., a $9.7 billion BHC based in Nashville, acquired Invest Financial Corp., a leading provider of brokerage services to banks. Invest, which operates sales programs for one-third of the 3,000 banks that now sell mutual funds, annuities, and other investments, is known as a third-party marketer. It provides banks with licensed brokers, a menu of investment products, and the know-how to identify potential customers.

---

[20] In order of presentation, these deals were reported in the *American Banker* on March 29, 1996 and May 24, 1996.

In another deal announced in 1996, First Union of Charlotte, North Carolina, paid $900 million for USL Capital Corp., the railcar-leasing subsidiary of Ford Motor Company. The transaction, which was the second largest in North America, gave First Union a fleet of 44,000 railcars spread over some 300 clients. Because some banks have been involved in leasing for years, this deal was not new for banking, but it was new for First Union.

The third example focuses on the M&A business itself. Some banks, such as Chase Manhattan, Union Bank of Switzerland, and J. P. Morgan, have hired or groomed M&A teams (the draft or farm-team approach) whereas others, such as Bankers Trust, KeyCorp, and National Westminster, have bought M&A businesses outright (the free-agency approach). On May 22, 1996, Bankers Trust announced its purchase of Wolfensohn and Co. to form a new merger advisory business. The acquisition approach frequently encounters culture clashes and potential runoff of clients and valued employees. Compared to building a business from scratch, however, the buyer does not have to wait for the business to develop.

Community Banks and Thrifts: They Get Gobbled But They Also Gobble

In the gobble-or-be-gobbled world of bank consolidation, community banks and thrifts might look like ducks in a shooting gallery. Although many of them have been gobbled up, others are doing some gobbling of their own. Many of those that were gobbled during the 1980s and early 1990s were "wounded ducks" (aka "zombies") that were acquired with financial assistance from the FDIC or the FSLIC (defunct since 1989). With the profitability of banks and thrifts restored in the mid-1990s, most of the remaining ducks are healthy and looking either to fly alone (remain independent) or find a mate (merge).

Beginning in the 1990s, thrifts began to acquire community banks. For example, from 1990 through 1996, some 60 community banks (30 in 1996 alone) were taken over by thrift institutions. Before the 1990s, it was mainly commercial banks that gobbled other banks and thrifts. Thrifts are interested in buying community banks to obtain instant market shares in commercial and consumer lending while limiting start-up costs.

Community banks and thrifts merge for the same reasons that larger banks do: to improve operating efficiency, enhance revenue growth, broaden product lines, expand their markets, and build up size and value. In addition, they merge among themselves to retain their homespun appeal, which is why they are dubbed "community banks," and for those that are not looking to be bought out, to remain independent. Regarding the autonomy factor, one analyst says, "Most of these guys want to control their own destiny, but they'll sell at the right price" (Goldfield [1996]).

The mergers among big banks have created opportunities for community banks to "cherry pick" discarded branches and small-business customers who might feel displaced. In a 1996 survey of businesses' concerns about interstate banking, the Treasury Management Association discovered that businesses are worried about the following:[21]

- Fewer local banks (16 percent)
- Fewer customized services (18 percent)

---

[21] As reported in the *American Banker* (March 25, 1996), pp. 1, 5. Figures in parentheses are responses to the survey, in which multiple answers were allowed.

- Less responsive to community (26 percent)
- Decline in customer service (28 percent)

Because small-business banking is regarded as a "people business," community banks have an opportunity to fill this void for customers that feel displaced by mergers that gobble up their local banks. However, as illustrated by the case of KeyCorp, big banks that maintain local managers and give them some degree of autonomy can alleviate the concerns of managers of small businesses.

Mergers among big banks that involve overlapping geographic markets (e.g., Wells Fargo's acquisition of First Interstate) create opportunities for community banks to obtain the unwanted branches of the resulting bank. In some cases, the branches might still be coveted, but they are sold to satisfy antitrust concerns. In addition, big banks, even if they are not involved in merger mania but simply looking to dump some brick and mortar, contribute to the supply of branches for sale.

On balance, community banks that are looking to expand have had good opportunities to buy the branches of big banks. In cases where branch systems are not unbundled for sale, however, community banks are at a disadvantage. For example, when Wells Fargo was looking to sell 61 of its California branches, the winner of the competitive bidding was H. F. Ahmanson & Co., the parent of $50.5 billion Home Savings of America and the biggest thrift in the United States. The price was $206 million, a premium of 8.11 percent, not for 61 brick-and-mortar branches per se but for the portfolio of $1.3 billion in loans funded by $2.5 billion in deposits. One losing bidder regarded the price paid as "rich" compared to the 4 percent premium paid in similar type transactions in the recent past.[22]

Does the merger mania among big banks concern community bankers? Based on results of survey in 1996, 752 community bankers revealed they are concerned about the following competitors:

- Credit unions (78%)
- Brokerage/securities firms (63%)
- Other community banks (60%)
- Mutual-fund companies (52%)
- Regional/money-center banks (41%)
- Farm-credit banks (40%)

Although community bankers are not unconcerned about their bigger brethren, more of them expressed worry about other community banks and nonbank competitors than megabanks.

REASONS/HYPOTHESES FOR BANK MERGERS[23]

Why do firms merge? Finance theory suggests that mergers, like other investment decisions, should occur because they are positive net-present-value projects that increase the wealth or market value of the acquiring firm's shareholders. The increase

---

[22] As reported in the *American Banker* (March 29, 1996), pp. 1, 4. On March 26, the *American Banker* also reported that a consortium of California community banks submitted a bid, one of at least nine that were received. Justice Department misgivings and divergent computer systems were only two of the obstacles faced by the consortium.

[23] This section and the next one draw on Hawawini and Swary [1990], especially chapters 2 (pp. 23–36) and 8 (pp. 209–214), and on Roll [1986].

in wealth could come from the synergy of the merger or from a transfer of wealth from bondholders to shareholders with firm value unchanged or both. Because not all managers are motivated to maximize shareholder wealth, they may make policy decisions that benefit their own self-interest—called the manager-utility-maximization hypothesis. If the manager's utility function depends on firm size, risk, or compensation, then the manager will attempt to increase size, reduce risk, or increase compensation accordingly. Because larger firms tend to pay higher compensation to their top managers, one way to maximize executive compensation is to maximize the size of the firm.

Another behavioral explanation of the motivation for merger activity focuses on Roll's [1986] hubris hypothesis. Because *hubris* means "overweening pride or self-confidence" (arrogance), the hypothesis suggests that the managers of the bidding firm are so cocky about their ability to find undervalued firms that they overbid for target firms.[24] Moreover, because their hubris (arrogance or conceit) clouds the facts of the valuation process, they continue to attempt to acquire firms, and when successful, they continue to overpay.

In a Modigliani-and-Miller context, if mergers do create value, then we can think of their doing so by changing tax liabilities, changing contracting costs, or changing investment incentives. More specifically, the size, timing, or riskiness of future cash flows of the merged firms must exceed the cash flows of the separate firms for the merger to be a positive net-present-value project. Specific hypotheses related to the objective of maximizing shareholder wealth include the following:

1. The *information hypothesis* contends that the bidders have private information about the targets that permits them to identify undervalued firms. In banking, for example, correspondent banks may have private information about respondent banks.

2. The *market-power hypothesis* claims that the acquiring firm (by gaining monopoly power through horizontal mergers) can raise product prices after buying up competitors.

3. The *synergy hypothesis* focuses on cost reductions or synergies related to economies of scale or scope, lower distribution or marketing costs, or elimination of redundant assets. Acquisition-based cost cutting has been a major driver of bank mergers in the 1990s.

4. The *tax hypothesis* claims that reduced tax liabilities drive mergers. Although taxes are a cost of doing business, the tax hypothesis is viewed as a financial synergy rather than a cost-reducing synergy.

5. The *inefficient-management hypothesis* contends that firms with inept managers are potential takeover targets because the existing managers are not maximizing the value of the firm.

6. The *earnings-diversification hypothesis* argues that the acquiring firm wants to diversify earnings in an attempt to generate higher levels of cash flow for the same level of total risk. This approach substitutes reductions in business risk (earnings fluctuations) for greater financial risk (leverage).

If Banks Are Different or Special, Then Bank Mergers Might Be Different or Special

In perfect capital markets firms have no incentive to diversify because shareholders can do it better themselves. The lack of diversity in banks' portfolios, caused in part by restrictive regulations, creates concentrations of risk. The *diversification*

---

[24] An alternative reason for overbidding, called the "winner's curse," can result from an auction with only a few bidders. Pettway and Trifts [1985] and Giliberto and Varaiya [1989] report evidence of overbidding for failed banks auctioned by the FDIC in P&A transactions.

hypothesis claims that mergers can be beneficial because of diversification gains that reduce the risk of the combined firms below that of the weighted-average risk of the separate firms.

In addition to regulation, deposit insurance also makes banks unique. Thus, an additional motivation for bank mergers and acquisitions, the *deposit-insurance hypothesis,* contends that banks might merge in an attempt to increase the value of their deposit-insurance put option, assuming that an increase in the value of deposit insurance increases shareholder value. Another way to see this strategy is to say that a bank wants to become big enough to benefit from the government's too-big-to-fail (TBTF) policy. The way that the deposit-insurance hypothesis differs from other (suboptimal) managerial hypotheses is that it stipulates that acquiring banks will be willing to pay more for riskier, more profitable banks whose returns are highly correlated with the acquirer's returns. In the post-FDICIA era of prompt corrective action and more effective risk-based capital requirements, it would seem to be more difficult to implement a policy of maximizing risk to exploit the deposit-insurance put option or to attempt to become TBTF or too-big-to-liquidate.[25]

A COST-BENEFIT FRAMEWORK FOR ANALYZING BANK MERGERS AND ACQUISITIONS

Many bank analysts, regulators, and academics see consolidation as the best way of revitalizing the banking industry. According to Myers, however, "Mergers are tricky; the benefits and costs of proposed deals are not always obvious." To this academic view, *Business Week* ([April 22, 1991], p. 77) adds a poignant point with a Special Report entitled: "If Mergers Were Simple, Banking's Troubles Might Be Over." This section presents a framework for analyzing bank mergers and acquisitions. The focal point of the analysis is a cost-benefit rule that emphasizes determining values and premiums. This kind of analysis is important for both acquirers (bidders) and acquirees (targets).

The *benefit* of a bank merger can be stated as the difference between (1) the total present value of the merged banks and (2) the sum of their present values if they do not merge. This definition of benefit emphasizes the economic value of the bank merger with the value-estimation process being similar to a capital-budgeting problem in financial management. Letting V represent present value, the benefit, B, is

$$B = V_{\text{Bank 1\&2}} - V_{\text{Bank 1}} - V_{\text{Bank 2}} \qquad \textbf{(19-2)}$$

The fact that $V_{\text{Bank 1\&2}}$ is greater than the sum of $V_{\text{Bank 1}} + V_{\text{Bank 2}}$ is, of course, what makes mergers potentially worthwhile. The reasons or hypotheses for mergers were explained earlier.

Given Equation (19-2), the *cost* of the merger can be defined as the difference between the amount paid for Bank 2 and its value as a separate bank. Letting $P_{\text{Bank 2}}$ represent the payment to the owners of Bank 2, the cost of the merger, C, is

$$C = P_{\text{Bank 2}} - V_{\text{Bank 2}} \qquad \textbf{(19-3)}$$

---

[25] Benston, Hunter, and Wall [1995] report that they find little evidence to suggest that mergers among publicly traded banks in the early to mid-1980s were attempts to exploit deposit insurance. Their results are consistent with an earnings-diversification hypothesis.

Estimating C depends critically on how merger benefits are shared between the owners of Bank 1 and Bank 2 and on how the merger is financed (e.g., cash or common stock or some combination of the two). From the point of view of the acquired firm, Bank 2, the cost represents the "premium" paid for the bank (i.e., rearranging Equation (19-3), $P_{\text{Bank 2}} = V_{\text{Bank 2}} + C$, where C is the premium). The managers of Bank 2 will, of course, want to maximize the premium, whereas the managers of Bank 1 will want to minimize it (i.e., the cost). The give and take of the negotiation process will determine the size of C.

Combining Equations (19-2) and (19-3), Bank 1 should merge with Bank 2 if the benefit exceeds the cost, that is,

$$B - C = (V_{\text{Bank 1\&2}} - V_{\text{Bank 1}} - V_{\text{Bank 2}}) - (P_{\text{Bank 2}} - V_{\text{Bank 2}}) > 0 \qquad \textbf{(19-4)}$$

Rearranging terms, the net gain $(B - C)$ can also be expressed as

$$B - C = V_{\text{Bank 1\&2}} - V_{\text{Bank 1}} - P_{\text{Bank 2}} > 0 \qquad \textbf{(19-5)}$$

In words, the net gain from the merger of Bank 1 with Bank 2 will be positive if the present value of the resulting entity, Bank 1&2, is greater than the present value of Bank 1 plus the price paid for Bank 2, where the price of Bank 2 is its present value plus the purchase premium. The net gain $(B - C)$ can be regarded as the net present value (NPV) of the merger. It is obvious from Equation (19-5) that the stockholders of Bank 1 gain when the strictly positive condition holds (i.e., $B - C > 0$).

A Numerical Example

The four inputs required to conduct the **cost-benefit analysis** just described are

1. $V_{\text{Bank 1\&2}}$ = the synergistic present value of the combined banks
2. $V_{\text{Bank 1}}$ = the present value of bank 1
3. $V_{\text{Bank 2}}$ = the present value of bank 2
4. C = the purchase premium or cost of the merger

Given these values, it is a simple matter to plug the figures into Equation (19-5) and crank out the answer. The art of the analysis lies in coming up with estimates of the four inputs. If all bank stocks were traded in efficient markets, the market values of the acquiring and acquired banks would be equal to their present values and half of the problem would be solved. However, the purchase premium and value of the resulting consolidated bank still would be unknown.

The process of the merger cost–benefit analysis can be illustrated mechanically using the constant-growth model as the value-determining mechanism. Although this approach is a simplistic representation of the real world, it provides some interesting insights. Later in this chapter more realism is introduced. The example is summarized in Table 19-5. In this hypothetical situation, Bank 1 sees Bank 2 as a desirable merger partner because it is a low-risk bank (as reflected by $k = 0.10$) with growth opportunities ($g = 0.05$ is judged to be low). The acquisition of Bank 2 is expected to result in a $1.00 increase in the dividend paid by Bank 1&2 and an increase of 0.01 in its growth rate. The synergistic effect or benefit of the merger (from Equation 19-2) is $20 million (= 100 − 50 − 30). Given that $V_{\text{Bank 2}}$ = $30 million, and assuming a cash transaction, the breakeven purchase price to be paid by Bank 1 is $50 million. Alternatively, the breakeven cost of the merger (from Equation 19-3) is $20 million (i.e., this is the maximum premium that Bank 1 should be willing to pay for Bank 2). If it is assumed that the benefits of the mergers are shared equally by the owners of both banks, then the purchase price would be $40 million, with a cost or premium of $10 million.

TABLE 19-5   A Hypothetical Merger Cost-Benefit Analysis Using the Constant-Growth Model

Variable	Bank 1	Bank 2	Bank 1&2
Expected dividend (D_1)	$2.00	$1.50	$3.00
Capitalization rate (k)	.12	.10	.12
Growth rate (g)	.08	.05	.09
Share price ($P_0 = D_1/(k - g)$)	$50	$30	$100
Number of shares outstanding (N)	1,000,000	1,000,000	1,000,000[a]
Total market value ($V - P_0 \times N$)	$50,000,000	$30,000,000	$100,000,000

Cost-Benefit Analysis[b]

$$B - C = (V_{\text{Bank 1\&2}} - V_{\text{Bank 1}} - V_{\text{Bank 2}}) - (P_{\text{Bank 2}} - V_{\text{Bank 2}}) > 0$$

$$= (100 - 50 - 30) - (P_{\text{Bank 2}} - 30) > 0$$

$$= 20 - P_{\text{Bank 2}} + 30 > 0$$

$$= 50 - P_{\text{Bank 2}} > 0$$

Breakeven purchase price = 50

Breakeven cost or purchase premium = 50 − 30 = 20

[a]Assumes a cash transaction.
[b]Millions of dollars.

The example in Table 19-5 assumes that the merger is a cash transaction. Suppose, however, that the owners of Bank 2 would prefer not to be faced with the payment of a capital-gains tax.[26] If the same effective purchase price was negotiated, then a stock exchange of four shares of Bank 1 for every five shares of Bank 2 would be transacted.[27] Thus, immediately after the exchange of stock but before the synergy occurred, a shareholder with 100 shares of Bank 2 would find the value of his holdings increasing from $3,000 (= $30 × 100) to $4,000 (= $50 × 80). However, after the synergistic benefits are realized, the value of the investor's 80 shares of Bank 1&2 will be $4,480 (= $56 × 80).[28] If the market values of Bank 1 and Bank 2 *before* the merger are estimated correctly, then, because of the exchange of stock, part of the benefits generated by the merger will accrue to Bank 2's shareholders, because they now own 44.4 percent (= 800,000/1,800,000) of Bank 1&2. The true cost of the merger, therefore, cannot be determined from Equation (19-3). The relevant formula when the acquisition is financed by common stock is

$$C = \theta V_{\text{Bank 1\&2}} - V_{\text{Bank 2}} \qquad \textbf{(19-6)}$$

where θ (theta) is the proportion of Bank 1&2 owned by Bank 2's shareholders. With $\theta = .444$, the cost of the merger is $14.4 million, that is,

$$C = .444(100) - 30 = 14.4$$

Because the $4.4 million is greater than the cost of the merger when it is a cash acquisition, the implication is that Bank 1's shareholders should be indifferent between

[26] This assumes, of course, that they purchased their shares for less than $40 per share.

[27] Note that $40 million in cash is equal to 800,000 shares valued at $50 per share.

[28] The per share value of $56 is determined as follows. With 1.8 million shares outstanding after the exchange and with total expected dividend payments constant at $3 million, the expected per share dividend is $1.67. Other things being equal, $P_0 = 1.67/(.12 - .09) = 55.67$, or approximately $56. Total value is unchanged at $100 million ($\approx$ $56 × 1.8 million).

an offering of $14.4 million in cash and a stock offering worth $10 million before the merger announcement. From Equation (19-6), it is clear that the larger the benefits generated by the merger, the greater the cost of the 800,000-share offer.

In the case of an acquisition financed by common stock, the focal point of the cost-benefit calculation is essentially an attempt to estimate the market value of the acquired bank's shares *after* the merger is announced and consummated. When this occurs, the price of Bank 2's stock rises to roughly $56. Of course, this assumes that the market evaluates the benefits of the merger the same way that Bank 1 has (i.e., total benefits of $20 million). After the market has reacted to the merger, the cost of the acquisition is easy to determine:

$$C = \$55.67\,(800{,}000) - \$30{,}000{,}000$$
$$= \$44{,}536{,}000 - \$30{,}000{,}000$$
$$= \$14{,}536{,}000$$

which approximately equals the $14.4 million just discussed.

Estimating the Cost of a Bank Merger: Further Considerations

Two basic points have been established: (1) The cost of a merger is the difference between the price paid for the acquired bank and its value as a separate entity, and (2) the cost calculation is a relatively simple one when the merger is a cash transaction. However, suppose that the true or intrinsic value of the acquired bank is different from its market price or value around the time of the merger. Such a situation could arise because rumors of the impending merger drive the market price of the stock above its intrinsic or present value. In this case, Equation (19-3) would be become

$$C = (P_{\text{Bank 2}} - MP_{\text{Bank 2}}) + (MP_{\text{Bank 2}} + V_{\text{Bank 2}}) \qquad \textbf{(19-7)}$$

where MP stands for *market price*. The first term on the right-hand side of Equation (19-7) represents the premium paid over the market value of Bank 2, whereas the second term represents the difference between the market and intrinsic values. When $MP_{\text{Bank 2}} = V_{\text{Bank 2}}$, Equation (19-7) reduces to Equation (19-3). Suppose now, continuing with the example of the previous section, that rumors of the proposed merger force the price of Bank 2's stock up from $30 to $35 per share. Using Equation (19-7), the cost of the merger, assuming a cash transaction, is $15 million, that is,

$$C = (45 - 35) + (35 - 30)$$
$$= 15$$

This cost is $5 million higher than the "rumorless" cost. Thus, a merger rumor is good news for the seller but bad news for the buyer.

Cash versus Stock Financing

In a cash transaction, the payment to the owners of the acquired bank is independent of whether or not the merger is a synergistic one. In other words, because they receive their money up front, their reward does not depend on the success of the merger. Thus, in a cash transaction, the cost of the merger can be estimated using Equation (19-3), which does not include the benefits of the merger. In contrast, if common-stock financing is employed, the cost of the merger is determined by Equation (19-6), which includes the benefits, because they are shared with the owners of the acquired bank. Moreover, the greater the merger benefits are, the greater is the cost of stock financing, other things equal. One factor of stock financing is that it lessens the effect of over- or underevaluation of the acquired bank. For example, suppose that Bank 1 was too generous with its four-for-five exchange with Bank 2. The market will then penalize the resulting bank, and Bank 2's shareholders will have to absorb some of the penalty. In the opposite situation, that of underevaluation of Bank 2, the benefits will be spread over all the shareholders, much to the chagrin of Bank 1's shareholders but to the joy of Bank 2's shareholders. Thus, from the acquiring bank's point of view, a cash (stock) transaction is favored if the acquired bank is undervalued (overvalued). The opposite is true from the acquired bank's perspective.

If Mergers Were Simple, Banking's Troubles Might Be Over

Many analysts see consolidation as *the* way to revitalize the banking industry. Nevertheless, *Business Week* attempts to make the case, in agreement with Myers's statement that "mergers are tricky," that mergers are not simple. The chairman and CEO of Chemical Bank says, "It's a tough, agonizing thing to do." Since then, Chase Manhattan and Chemical have merged to become the largest bank in the United States. Although the Chase–Chemical merger was expected to generate shareholder gains from reductions in staff (private benefits), the deal added substantially to New York City's unemployment (social cost) and raised concerns about branch closings. As a result, many special-interest groups are worried about the consequences of bank consolidation in terms of downsizing and access to banking services. As KeyCorp has shown, however, a bank can be a nationwide organization and still be responsive to the needs of the local communities it serves.

Regarding banking's brick-and-mortar distribution system, Furash says,

> The industry is caught in a difficult transition period. It has this very expensive distribution system, and the consumer is saying, "I don't care about it." And yet the industry can't walk away, because of old myths about what it means. Politicians demand that you put branches in places to serve the poor. Their model of how you serve the poor is based on that and not on what kind of services the poor really need. (Marshall [1996], p. 2)

Finding Out about Your Merger Partner's RAIDS after You Merge

During the last half of the 1980s and early 1990s, numerous regional banks merged, some of them in deals called "mergers of equals." The deals in the 1980s created banking companies referred to as "superregional banks." For example, in the Southeast, Trust Company merged with Sun Banks to form SunTrust; First Atlanta and Wachovia combined to form First Wachovia (name changed to Wachovia in 1991); and C&S, running away from NCNB's hostile takeover attempt, merged with Sovran to form C&S/Sovran, which for a short time was called Avantor. C&S/Sovran was later acquired by NCNB to form NationsBank. Some analysts are skeptical that mergers of equals can be successful because corporate cultures and decision making are difficult to combine.

In the C&S/Sovran deal, C&S was caught with its merger pants around its ankles because its partner turned up with RAIDS—Regionally Acquired Income Deficiency Syndrome. Sovran's RAIDS was caused by problems with its portfolio of commercial-real-estate loans in the Washington, DC, area. King [1991] reported that C&S's chairman and stockholders were upset and one long-time shareholder went so far as to say that the bank "was sold a bill of goods." In addition, C&S's

chairman, Bennett A. Brown, said that if C&S had known about the problems, "We would have gone back to the table to renegotiate."

Although mergers can indeed be tricky, buyers need to do their homework before they buy, *caveat emptor*. When C&S and Sovran merged in 1990, the real-estate gun had already been smoking, especially in New England. Analysts at C&S were asleep at the switch for not doing adequate due diligence on Sovran's port-folio of commercial-real-estate loans. C&S's shareholders got one share of the new company for each share of C&S stock whereas Sovran shareholders got 1.23 shares for each share of Sovran.

ALTERNATIVE VALUATION METHODS

The cost–benefit analysis presented in the previous section has a present-value for-mation. Although this is the conceptually correct method for determining value, in practice estimating future cash flows and the appropriate discount or capitalization rate is a difficult task. As a result, bankers have developed rules of thumb designed to determine the premium that should be offered for a potential merge candidate's stock. The premium is usually expressed as a percentage of some base such as book value or earnings per share. This section presents and illustrates the alternative methods for developing bank-merger terms.[29]

The Book-Value Approach

The **book-value approach** for determining **merger premiums** and exchange ratios has intuitive appeal because value commonly is thought of in book-value terms. Thus, for example, if Bank 1 has a book value of $100 and Bank 2 has a book value of $50 per share, then one share of Bank 1 would exchange for two shares of Bank 2, assuming no premium. If the shareholders of Bank 2 require a 100 percent premium on book value, the exchange ratio would be one-for-one. The formula for determining book-to-book premiums is

$$\text{Premium} = \frac{B_{\text{Bank 1}}(ER) - B_{\text{Bank 2}}}{B_{\text{Bank 2}}} \qquad \textbf{(19-8)}$$

where

$$B_{\text{Bank 1}} = \text{book value per share of Bank 1 (the acquiring bank)}$$
$$ER = \text{the exchange ratio of Bank 1 for Bank 2}$$
$$B_{\text{Bank 2}} = \text{the book value per share of Bank 2 (the acquired bank)}$$

The numerator of the formula is simply the difference between book value received, $B_{\text{Bank 1}}(ER)$, and book value sold, $B_{\text{Bank 2}}$. To illustrate, using the previous data, the premium is

$$\frac{100(1) - 50}{50} = 1.0 \text{ or } 100 \text{ percent}$$

Alternatively, given the premium (P), the exchange ratio is given by

$$ER = \frac{B_{\text{Bank 2}}(1 + P)}{B_{\text{Bank 1}}} \qquad \textbf{(19-9)}$$

---

[29] The first three techniques presented in this section are those suggested by Darnell [1973].

By definition, the book values used in Equations (19-8) and (19-9) are the differences between the banks' total assets and total liabilities divided by the number of shares outstanding. In practice, however, it is common to use *adjusted* book values to account for asset quality, loan-loss reserves, the maturity risk of fixed-rate assets, potential contingent liabilities, and other factors. From the balance-sheet identity $K = A - L$, where K represents unadjusted book value, and using asterisks (*) to denote adjusted figures, adjusted book value is defined as $K^* = A^* - L^*$. To illustrate, suppose that Bank 2's unadjusted book value is $50 = 600 - 550$ ($ millions). However, if the bank has poor asset quality estimated at 10 and contingent liabilities also estimated at 10, then $K^* = 590 - 560 = 30$. With 1,000,000 shares outstanding, the adjusted book value is $30 per share compared to the unadjusted figure of $50 per share. Adjusted book values are important because they represent lower bounds in the valuation process.

The book-value approach is the most widely used method of calculating merger premiums. It focuses on the bid price of the acquiring bank relative to the book value of the acquired bank. The advantages of the approach are (1) book values are easily understood and calculated (like the payback period in capital-budgeting analysis), (2) book values are stable compared to market values, and (3) book values are isolated from the capriciousness of the stock market. The major disadvantage of the book-value approach is that it does not consider market value, which is the price that investors should mainly be concerned about. Because market value reflects the so-called going-concern value of a bank, it is preferred to book value.

Market-to-Book Premiums

Because investors should be concerned about market value, which is a reflection of a stock's present value, a natural approach is to look at **market-to-book premiums.** In this approach, the market price of the acquiring bank is substituted for its book value. Letting MP represent market price, Equation (19-8) becomes

$$\text{Premium} = \frac{MP_{\text{Bank 1}}(ER) - B_{\text{Bank 2}}}{B_{\text{Bank 2}}} \qquad \textbf{(19-10)}$$

To illustrate, if $MP_{\text{Bank 1}} = \$80$ and $ER = 1$, then, continuing with the previous example, the premium is

$$P = \frac{80(1) - 50}{50} = 0.6 \text{ or } 60 \text{ percent}$$

In this approach, the ER formula is

$$ER = \frac{B_{\text{Bank 2}}(1 + P)}{MP_{\text{Bank 1}}} \qquad \textbf{(19-11)}$$

Terry and Sexton [1975] claim that market-to-book premiums in the range of 150 to 200 percent are normal.

The difficulty with using market value is that only several hundred banks or BHCs have shares that are actively traded, which leaves roughly 8,000 banks whose stocks are traded in thin markets. Unless the acquiring bank is actively traded on at least a regional exchange, the market-to-book approach probably is unreliable. Because the prices of inactively traded shares tend to be biased upward, it is difficult to trade a substantial number of shares without a major price movement.

The EPS Approach

A third approach is to focus on income-to-income premiums. This technique compares EPS received with EPS sold. The premium formula for this approach is

$$\text{Premium} = \frac{EPS_{\text{Bank 1}}(ER) - EPS_{\text{Bank 2}}}{EPS_{\text{Bank 2}}} \qquad \textbf{(19-12)}$$

For example, with $EPS_{\text{Bank 1}} = \$4.00$, $EPS_{\text{Bank 2}} = \$2.00$, and $ER = 1/2$, the premium is zero. The ER formula for this approach is

$$ER = \frac{EPS_{\text{Bank 2}}(1 + P)}{EPS_{\text{Bank 1}}} \qquad \textbf{(19-13)}$$

Bank stock specialists who favor the EPS approach contend that the relative sizes of the banks' income streams are important in determining their value for exchange purposes. However, the earnings approach, which requires uniform accounting practices across banks, considers neither the *timing* nor the *riskiness* of the income stream. In addition, current EPS may not be a good indicator of a bank's future earning power.

Terry and Sexton [1975] have suggested using a weighted average of either historical or forecasted EPS in place of current earnings. The historical approach should be a better indication of past performance whereas the pro forma approach should be a better indicator of future performance. To illustrate the historical approach, consider the following weighting scheme and historical EPS data:

Period	Weight	Bank 1's EPS	Bank 2's EPS
t	.500	$5.00	$1.00
$t-1$	.200	4.00	2.00
$t-2$	.125	3.00	3.00
$t-3$	.100	2.00	4.00
$t-4$	.075	1.00	5.00
	1.000		

Bank 1's weighted-average EPS is $3.95, whereas Bank 2's is $2.04. Given a premium of 100 percent, the exchange rate using the weighted averages is approximately 1.0 (i.e., 4.08/3.95). In contrast, if current earnings are used (i.e., period t EPS), the ER is 0.4 (i.e., 2/5). On a *pro forma* basis, consider the following example:

Period	Weight	Bank 1's EPS	Bank 2's EPS
$t+1$	.500	$5.25	$1.50
$t+2$	.200	5.50	2.00
$t+3$	.125	5.75	2.50
$t+4$	.100	6.00	3.00
$t+5$	.075	6.25	3.50
	1.000		

With a premium of 100 percent, the ER using the weighted averages, which are $5.52 for Bank 1 and $2.02 for Bank 2, is .73 (i.e., 4.04/5.52), whereas the ER using current EPSs is still 0.4. If the income-to-income approach is used, a weighted-average scheme is preferred; however, the basic criticisms of the EPS approach are not eliminated.

The Price-Earnings Approach

Price-earnings or **P/E ratios** reflect the value that a bank's earnings (EPS) command in the marketplace. This approach requires, of course, that the shares be traded in efficient markets; otherwise the P/E ratios will be unreliable. The premium formula in this situation is[30]

$$\text{Premium} = \frac{(MP/EPS)_{\text{Bank 1}}(ER) - (MP/EPS)_{\text{Bank 2}}}{(MP/EPS)_{\text{Bank 2}}} \qquad \textbf{(19-14)}$$

Solving for *ER,* the exchange ratio is given by

$$ER = \frac{(MP/EPS)_{\text{Bank 2}}(1 + P)}{(MP/EPS)_{\text{Bank 1}}} \qquad \textbf{(19-15)}$$

If Bank 1 has a *P/E* ratio of 12.5 and Bank 2 has one of 7.5, then with a one-for-one *ER* the premium is 67 percent. If the premium is 100 percent, then *ER* would be 1.2, or six shares of Bank 1 for every five shares of Bank 2.

The Market-Value Approach

The market-value approach focuses on relative market values or prices for determining premiums and exchange ratios. By deleting the EPSs from Equations (19-14) and (19-15), the premium and ER formulas are established. Like the P/E approach, this method requires that both the acquiring and acquired banks have actively traded stocks.

The Core-Deposits Approach

The **core-deposits approach** focuses on paying premiums for *core deposits,* defined as demand deposits (excluding public funds), savings deposits, and fixed-rate time deposits. Banks with a substantial base of core deposits are desirable merger partners because of the relatively low cost of their funds. However, with the reduction of core deposits as Regulation Q was phased out, such banks have become harder to find. This structural change in deposit composition tends to make interstate banking less attractive and therefore may reduce the demand for merger partners.

THE NATURE OF THE ACQUISITION PREMIUM

The acquisition premium is the difference between the acquisition cost and the appraised or fair market value of the acquired net worth, where net worth, of course, is simply the difference between the market value of *booked* assets and the market value of *booked* liabilities. (Since a booked item is simply one that appears on the balance sheet, an "unbooked" item does not appear on the balance sheet.) For example, if the acquisition cost is $10 million and the market value of net worth is

---

[30] The P/E ratio is written as *MP/EPS* in Equations (19-14) and (19-15), because *MP* was used for market price in Equations (19-10) and (19-11).

estimated to be $7 million, the difference of $3 million is the acquisition premium. It represents the price paid for the unbooked intangible assets. If part (or all) of the acquisition premium can be allocated to specific, identifiable intangible assets, the premium is allocated based on fair market value of those assets. The balance of the premium, if any, is considered to be goodwill. Continuing with the previous example, if two-thirds of the premium of $3 million can be assigned to specific intangible assets (eg., core deposits), then the premium is so allocated, with the balance of $1 million going to goodwill. For tax purposes, the allocation of the premium between identifiable intangible assets and goodwill is crucial because the former is amortizable for tax purposes, and therefore affects cash flow, whereas the latter is not amortizable for tax purposes.

Intangible Assets and the Separability Issue

Intangible assets are defined as nonphysical assets that either involve rights, often ill-defined, against outsiders in general or represent anticipated future benefits that may not attach to a specific physical asset.[31] The words "ill-defined" and "may not attach" clearly indicate that some intangible assets may *not* be identifiable. Intangible assets are classified as either *identifiable* or *unidentifiable*. The financial assets held by a bank are intangible assets that are easily identified (e.g., loans and securities). Unidentifiable intangible assets are in the nature of goodwill/going-concern value and for banks include such factors as the quality of management, customer relations, market presence, charter value, the deposit-insurance guarantee, trade name, reputation, and so on. In the aggregate, these factors are, in essence, what the buyer receives for the acquisition premium. In banking, where entry and exit are tightly controlled, a bank's charter, which gives it the right to do business as a bank (i.e., to both accept demand deposits and make commercial loans), is by far its most important intangible asset. Moreover, today (and since 1933) it is virtually impossible to obtain a bank charter without simultaneously being accepted for deposit insurance.[32] Thus, the bank charter and deposit-insurance guarantee are inextricably interwoven into the fabric of U.S. banking. Because it is impossible to separate the two, they will be referred to together as the **charter-insurance contract,** with charter-insurance value used to indicate the present value of the contract. The charter-insurance contract is a perpetual agreement that is terminated either by the issuer through a declaration of insolvency or by the issuer through merger with another bank.

With the charter-insurance contract as its foundation, a bank can build its market presence, establish customer relations, and hope to build a trade name and reputation associated with the commercial-banking industry. Because commercial banks are the kingpins of the FSI in the United States, the charter-insurance contract represents a unique and scarce resource. Although the reregulated and more competitive environment of the FSI in the 1980s and early 1990s diminished some of the *market power* of the charter-insurance contract, it still is a fundamental ingredient of the package of intangible assets held by an established bank. If this is true, then why should an institution that already has a charter-insurance contract want to acquire another one? The critical linkage is that the contract at the "retail level" (i.e., consumers and small businesses) is tied to a *local* geographic market.

[31] Egginton [1982], p. 28.

[32] National banks are required to join the Federal Reserve System, and all Fed member banks must be insured by the FDIC. Moreover, most states will *not* grant a charter without the FDIC's prior approval of insurance for the proposed bank.

Two ways exist to enter such markets: (1) by *de novo* entry or (2) by acquisition of an existing bank. The latter, of course, is more desirable from the potential entrant's perspective because it eliminates a competitor and starts the entrant at the asset and liability values of the acquired bank. In contrast, a *de novo* entrant starts from scratch and faces an additional competitor. (The Justice Department is assigned the task of protecting consumer interests from anticompetitive behavior in such markets.)

Studies of local banking markets indicate that such markets are more monopolistic than competitive.[33] The highly valued charter-insurance contract is due to the monopoly power found in these markets. Moreover, because monopoly power means control over price and the power to earn "excess" or "abnormal" profits, it represents a dominant market position. As Horngren [1984] states: "Goodwill is fundamentally the price paid for 'excess' or 'abnormal' earning power" (p. 555). Moreover, he notes that goodwill is originally generated internally and gives as an example, "a happy combination of advertising, research, management talent, and timing [that] may give a particular company a dominant market position for which another company is willing to pay dearly. This ability to command a premium price for the *total business* is goodwill" (p. 555, emphasis added). For a bank, the *total business* is built on the foundation of the charter-insurance contract, with customer relationships, reputation, and so on providing the finishing touches.

To focus on the separability issue more closely, consider the following T-account or simple balance sheet, which lists both booked and unbooked assets for a hypothetical bank.

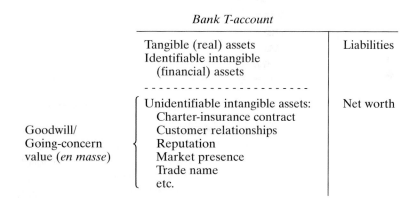

Bank T-account

The dashed line separates the identifiable and unidentifiable assets. Unidentifiable intangible assets *en masse* account for the **goodwill/going-concern value** of the bank, where *going concern* (i.e., established business) refers to the ability of a business to generate earnings without interruption because of a change in ownership. Because of the perpetual nature of the charter-insurance contract and because the contract is the heart of the bank's goodwill/going-concern value, the *en masse* package of unidentifiable intangible assets must be regarded as having an indefinite life.

Focusing on the T-account, it is easy to see why depository institutions that have been technically insolvent have still traded for positive values in the marketplace. That is, unbooked values have accounted for the difference. In particular, the deposit-insurance guarantee has been exploited. When the market value of an

---

[33] Heggestad [1979] presents a summary of the literature. The block quote at the bottom of page 837 offers further insight.

insured institution's net assets declines, the value of the charter-insurance contract takes on added value. Understanding the nature of unidentifiable intangible assets is a key to understanding the nature of the acquisition premium.

ACCOUNTING METHODS: PURCHASE VERSUS POOLING OF INTERESTS

The revaluation of assets, the recognition of intangibles, and the treatment of goodwill (discussed in the previous section) are considerations that arise from the use of **purchase accounting.** Two distinct methods exist to account for business combinations: (1) **pooling of interests,** which does *not* revalue assets or liabilities and (2) purchase accounting, which does.[34] These two methods, however, are not alternatives, and management is not free to select one over the other. Business combinations that do not meet the criteria for pooling-of-interest accounting must use the purchase method. The criteria for pooling of interests and the differences between purchase and pooling of interest are described in Table 19-6. Looking at acquisitions in the Sixth Federal Reserve District, Koch and Baker [1983] found that of the 139 combinations analyzed, 54 percent used pooling of interest and 46 used purchase accounting. They discovered that most of the acquisitions using the pooling method involved the establishment of a one-bank holding company (OBHC) through the purchase of a bank. The popularity of the OBHC (see chapter 15) is linked to the pooling method because it permits a transfer of ownership from the bank to the holding company without the stockholders incurring any tax liability. Recall that tax considerations have been a major factor in the establishment of BHCs.

In a nutshell, the accounting criteria for pooling are (1) independence, (2) continuity of interest, and (3) absence of planned transactions. The advantages of pooling include simple accounting, stock-for-stock exchanges, and regulatory considerations. The disadvantages are possible difficulty of achievement, dilution, and the retention of historical values. The advantages of the purchase method are greater flexibility in negotiations, avoidance of ownership dilution, and the opportunity to revalue assets. The disadvantages are difficult accounting, the effects on future earnings, and the controversial handling of goodwill and other intangibles.

The effects of pooling versus purchase with respect to capital adequacy (as measured by the capital-to-asset ratio), *EPS, ROA,* and *ROE* are illustrated by the following example:[35]

	Buyer	*Seller*
Total assets	$1,000 M	$100 M
Total equity	$ 50 M	$ 8 M
Net income	$ 10 M	$1.2 M
Shares outstanding	5 M	
Earnings per share	$2.00	
Stock price	$10/share	

---

[34] The accounting standards have been spelled out in Accounting Principles Board (APB) Opinions No. 16 and No. 17 established in October 1970. In 1973, the APB was succeeded by the Financial Accounting Standards Board (FASB). The latest FASB pronouncement in this area is Statement No. 72, "Accounting for Certain Acquisitions of Banking or Thrift Institutions" (February 1983).

[35] *Planning Bank Mergers and Acquisitions,* Ernst & Whinney [1984], pp. 5–11.

TABLE 19-6 Purchase Accounting versus Pooling-of-Interests Accounting

Pooling-of-Interests Criteria	*Purchase vs. Pooling of Interests*

Conditions for pooling-of-interest method—(*all* must be met or it is a "purchase")

A. Combining companies criteria:
  1. Subsidiaries or divisions of another corporation (if within two years before the plan of combination is initiated) are not allowed.
  2. Each of the combining companies is *independent* of the other combining companies.
    a. Thus no more than 10 percent of any company can be held as intercorporate investments prior to the initiation of the plan of combination.

B. Combining of interests criteria:
  1. The combination must be completed within one year after the plan is initiated.
  2. After the date the plan of combination is initiated, the issuing corporation issues *voting common stock* in exchange for at least 90 percent of the *voting common stock* of another combining company.
  3. Ratio of interest or predecessor owners must remain the same.
  4. "Voting rights" must remain the same, thus no "voting trusts" are allowed.
  5. "Contingent buyouts" not allowed (e.g., based on future earnings of either parent or sub, etc.).

C. Absence of "planned transactions" criteria:
  1. No future "buyout" agreements allowed (for example, through treasury stock, to dissident shareholders).
  2. The combined corporation cannot guarantee loans on stock issued in the combination, thus allowing some previous stock owners to get cash (in effect "sell") from their stock.
  3. The combined corporation does not intend to plan or dispose of a significant part of the assets of the combining companies within two years after combination, except for disposals of duplicated facilities.

The fundamental differences between the pooling and purchase methods are,

1. In a "purchase," the net income of a newly acquired subsidiary will be included in consolidated net income *from the date of acquisition.* In a "pooling," net income of the subsidiary for the *entire year* is added to consolidated net income regardless of the date of "pooling."

2. In a "purchase," only retained earnings from the date of acquisition are included in consolidated retained earnings. In a "pooling," *all* acquired retained earnings of the subsidiary are added to consolidated retained earnings.

3. In a "purchase," net book values of a newly acquired company are adjusted to acquisition date fair values. In a "pooling," net book values of the "pooled" companies remain the same.

4. In a "purchase," any difference between the amount paid for the subsidiary and the fair value of assets acquired would result in positive and negative goodwill that should be amortized over a period not to exceed 40 years. In a "pooling," no consolidated goodwill is created.

5. In a "purchase" where newly issued stock was exchanged for a newly purchased company, the shareholders' equity would be increased by the *fair market value* of the stock issued. In a pooling when new stock is issued for a newly acquired "pooled corporation," the shareholders' equity is increased by the total *net book value* of the newly pooled corporation.

Source: Koch and Baker [1983], p. 17.

The effects of pooling versus purchase on the relevant financials are as follows:

		Buyer Combined	
	Buyer	*Pooling*	*Purchase*
Capital/assets	5%	5.3%	4.6%
EPS	$2.00	$1.75	$1.85
ROA	1%	1.02%	.85%
ROE	20%	19.3%	18.5%

The pooling transaction is based on an exchange of shares of 1.75 times book, whereas the purchase transaction is based on the buyer paying $14 per share for the target corporation with the same exchange ratio (i.e., 1.75 times book). To get the financial statements for the buyer combined under the pooling method, simply add or pool the respective numbers together (i.e., total assets = $1,100, capital = $58, net income = $11.2, and shares outstanding = 6.4 = 5 + 1.75 × 8).[36] For the purchase transaction, the accounting is more complicated. In this example, it works out as total assets = $1,088, capital = $50, net income = $9.25, and shares outstanding = 5. The lower asset total is due to the revaluation to market values. The $12 million "hit" is amortized against earnings over a 16-year period. Thus, net income is reduced by $12/16 = $.75 million, hence the figure of $9.25 million. In the purchase transaction, the stock price stays at $10 per share, whereas in the pooling method the dilution reduces it to $9.06 = $58/6.4.

REGULATORY CONCERNS: SAFETY, STABILITY, AND STRUCTURE

Because trade-offs existed between safety and stability on the one hand and banking structure (competitiveness) on the other, the regulatory objectives of safety, stability, and structure are not easily achieved. With respect to mergers, the concerns about safety and stability have come to dominate concerns about structure. For example, prior to the banking crisis of the 1980s and early 1990s, a merger between two money-center banks in the same city, as in the marriage of Chase and Chemical, would have been unthinkable. Today, such a transaction is viewed as one way of revitalizing the banking system. Moreover, because money-center banks operate in a worldwide market, the relevant geographic market is so broad that the combination of two such institutions would not adversely affect worldwide concentration and competition. However, as mentioned above, social and political pressures may restrict how bank consolidation in major cities is achieved. In its 1989 *Annual Report* (p. 15), the FDIC stated,

> As a result of changes in the competitive environment for financial services over the past decade, the FDIC adopted a new policy on bank merger transactions that replaces a policy adopted in 1980. The new policy clarifies the standards that the FDIC will use in assessing whether a proposed bank merger would have anticompetitive effects or create other concerns that would warrant denial of an application. When analyzing the level of competition in a particular market, the FDIC will consider not just bank services but also equivalent products offered by other types of competitors, such as thrifts, credit unions and securities firms.

The last sentence officially recognizes what has been a market reality for years (i.e., that a narrow definition of the bank product market was obsolete). This recognition lays the foundation for the approval of mergers between banks in the same geographic market (e.g., the Chase–Chemical marriage). Although the federal banking agencies (Fed/OCC/FDIC) don't always march to the same drummer, when it comes to the merger parade, they are marching in unison. Moreover, it is unlikely, political and social pressures notwithstanding, that the Justice Department would challenge such a merger as anticompetitive. If one of the merger partners was financially distressed, a challenge would be even more unlikely.

Chapter Summary

Banking reregulation and thrift failures initiated a wave of bank mergers during the 1980s and early 1990s. For different reasons, related to revenue growth, cost

---

[36] These figures and the ones that follow are in millions.

cutting, and **corporate restructuring,** the merger wave continued in the 1990s and is expected to persist into the twenty-first century. Megamergers, as illustrated by the combination of Chase Manhattan Corporation and Chemical Banking Corporation (announced in August 1995, completed in April 1996, and resulting in Chase becoming the nation's largest bank), have been an important part of this merger wave. Many analysts see the future structure of banking in terms of a barbell shape with a few megabanks, such as the new Chase Manhattan, with over $300 billion in assets, on one end, and numerous small banks on the other end. In addition, many analysts see consolidation as *the* way to revitalize the banking industry.

The **financial-services industry** (FSI) in the United States used to be compartmentalized, meaning that commercial banks, savings banks, investment banks/securities firms, insurance companies, and other financial-services firms (FSFs) were separated. Although we are unlikely to see, even in the twenty-first century, a completely homogenized FSI consisting only of generic FSFs, consolidation is occurring within segments of the FSI and across it. Mergers have accounted for the bulk of the contraction in the number of commercial banks. The once clublike atmosphere of banking has even been shaken by hostile takeovers. The laissez-faire approach to financial economics contends (and the evidence suggests) that takeovers are good for the economy because they assure that a firm's assets are controlled by managers who can use them most efficiently.

This chapter has focused on the battle for **corporate control** in banking with particular emphasis on mergers and acquisitions. Along with some of the deals and deal makers of the 1980s and 1990s, a framework for analyzing bank mergers and acquisitions was presented. **Reasons/hypotheses for mergers** were analyzed and evidence regarding market reactions to the announcements of various kinds of bank/BHC corporate restructurings were summarized. In some cases, these market reactions differ from those observed for nonfinancial firms.

The basic condition for determining the net gain from a merger is to compare the synergistic value of the combined banks ($V_{\text{Bank 1\&2}}$) to the sum of the values of the acquiring bank ($V_{\text{Bank 1}}$) plus the price paid for the acquired bank ($P_{\text{Bank 2}}$). As expressed in equation (19-5), the condition for a cash sale is:

$$B - C = V_{\text{Bank 1\&2}} - V_{\text{Bank 1}} - P_{\text{Bank 2}} > 0$$

In a stock transaction, $P_{\text{Bank 2}}$ is replaced by $\theta V_{\text{Bank 1\&2}}$.

Although the net-present-value (NPV) approach is the conceptually correct method for evaluating bank mergers, in practice, rules of thumb have been developed because of the difficulty (or lack of skill or laziness) in estimating future cash flows and an appropriate discount rate. These rules of thumb are expressed in the various formulas for exchange ratios and premiums, based on such measures as book values, *EPS* ratios, and market values.

Key Words, Concepts, and Acronyms

- Bank holding company
- Banking companies
- Banking structure ("barbell")
- Book-value approach
- Cash versus stock financing (of merger)

- Charter-deposit insurance contract
- Consolidation
- Core deposits
- Corporate control and restructuring
- Cost–benefit analysis
- EPS approach

- Financial-services firm (FSF)
- Financial-services industry (FSI)
- Goodwill/going-concern value
- Hostile takeover
- Independent bank

- Intangible assets (identifiable versus unidentifiable)
- Interstate banking
- Investment bankers (M&A activity)
- M&A strategies (e.g., Banc One and KeyCorp)
- Market-to-book premiums

- Merger of equals
- Merger premium
- Mergers and acquisitions (M&A)
- Multibank holding company (MBHC)
- Multistate MBHC
- One-state MBHC
- Net gain or benefit (from merger)

- Poison pills
- Pooling-of-interest accounting
- Price-earnings approach
- Purchase accounting
- Reasons/hypotheses for mergers
- Regional interstate banking
- Zombie banks and thrifts

Review/Discussion Questions

1. On October 17, 1995, Eugene A. Ludwig, Comptroller of the Currency, told the Committee on Banking Financial Services of the U.S. House of Representatives that "consolidation of the banking industry . . . is a healthy part of the restructuring of the financial-services industry that has occurred over the last several years and that will continue for many more." Do you agree or disagree that this trend is "healthy"? What has happened to the number of banking companies, banks, branches, and offices during the 1980s and 1990s?

2. How are the following two sentences related?
   a. There's a constant market for a small, start-up bank.
   b. The big banks don't need a whole bunch of chiefs.

   How do these two statements mesh with the view that the banking structure of the future will have a barbell shape? Describe this barbell shape.

3. In the future, how many banks are likely to be competing in a town? A rural county? A metropolitan area? A state? A region? In the nation? On a worldwide basis?

4. "In the mid-1980s, if you could spell and had $5 million, they'd give you a charter." How did these criteria change in the 1990s and what are they likely to be in the twenty-first century?

5. The president of a start-up bank notes that the bank's officers have plowed their savings into it; they own some 10 percent of the stock. He adds: "We've got a lot at risk. So we're not going to make stupid decisions." What conclusions, if any, do you draw about corporate governance from this situation? By the way, the president of the bank put up $350,000 of his own money to help get the bank started.

6. What is a poison pill? Why do they exist? Should a community bank, such as the one discussed in the previous question, or any bank have a poison pill?

7. Do you have a hard or a soft view of what a corporation should be? How is this view likely to affect your opinion of takeovers? Why do laissez-faire financial economists favor takeovers? How are takeovers, corporate control, and restructuring related?

8. Who are the major M&A deal makers in banking and in the FSI? How do investment bankers attempt to prevent takeovers?

9. On April 21, 1987, the U.S. Supreme Court upheld an Indiana statute blocking hostile takeovers. Other states have enacted or attempted to enact similar laws. Should hostile takeovers be banned? Where do you stand?

10. Contrast and compare the acquisition strategies of Banc One, KeyCorp, and SunTrust.

11. Evaluate the following statements made in 1995:
    a. Consolidation could well make the banking industry more productive. But merging and slashing expenses give only a short-lived boost to earnings. Eventually the merger boom will peak, if for no other reason than that deals will get too expensive. Recently banks have been bidding for one another at more than two times book value, well above the multiple of 1.5 that prevailed just three years ago. And in the end, these bigger banks will still be stuck with the same problem—fewer and fewer people who need them.

    b. I wouldn't be surprised if in five years investors are talking about the breakup value of NationsBank.

12. Are community banks and thrifts only gobbled or do they do some gobbling of their own?

13. What social and political problems might affect bank consolidation in major cities in the United States? Should these factors be relevant to whether two banking firms should be allowed to merge? What is the FDIC's policy with respect to bank mergers? What role will the objectives of bank regulation play in how the merger game is likely to be played in the 2000s?

14. Summarize the reasons/hypotheses for mergers and the empirical evidence regarding market reactions to the announcements of BHC corporate restructurings. How does the empirical evidence compare with that for nonfinancial firms?

15. What is RAIDS, and what can acquiring banks do about it? Describe the three-way relation among NCNB, C&S, and Sovran.

16. *Business Week* in its issue of April 22, 1991 (p. 78), speculated on the following possible bank mergers and potential benefits:

> *Chemical Bank and Manufacturers Hanover.* Because the marriage of these two money-center banks could generate a cost savings of $800 million in overhead a year, it looks like a deal made in heaven. Moreover, the deal would result in the second-largest retail franchise in the New York City area behind Citicorp.

> *J. P. Morgan and Chase Manhattan.* The linkage of these two money-center banks would combine their long lists of blueblood clients to build a stronger corporate franchise than either has separately. In addition, Chase's retail network would supply core deposits (i.e., stable, lower-cost sources of funding).

> *Wells Fargo and Security Pacific.* This West Coast deal would create the biggest retail network in California, pushing BankAmerica into second place. More importantly, the projected cost savings would be in the range of $500 million to $1 billion annually.

> *BankAmerica and First Interstate.* Although BankAmerica failed to win the bid for Bank of New England, a deal closer to home might be a better way to start its founder's dream of a truly national franchise. Like the Wells–Security deal, this marriage would produce another large California bank, and give BA needed southern exposure.

> *NCNB and C&S/Sovran.* In 1989, NCNB attempted a hostile takeover of C&S, which led C&S to seek shelter with Sovran. Thus, it's unlikely that C&S would welcome another overture from NCNB with open arms. However, Sovran's weak portfolio of commercial real-estate loans in the Washington DC, area has soured the C&S/Sovran deal a bit; see King [1991]. Nevertheless, *Business Week* projects that an NCNB and C&S/Sovran combination would be a formidable one with almost 2,000 offices from Baltimore to Key West. In addition, NCNB also has a heavy presence in Texas.

Determine whether or not any of these forecasted deals came to fruition and, if not, whether any of the banks involved were in other major deals.

Problems

1. Given the following chart and information, write a brief event-study report regarding Bank of New York's bid for Irving Trust. On September 25, 1987, Bank of New York offered $80 per share, or $1.4 billion, for Irving Trust. On November 20, 1987, Bank of

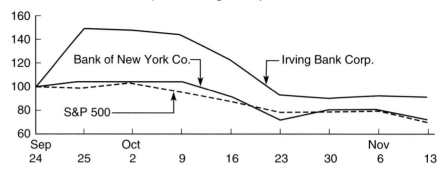

Sept. 24 closing share prices = 100

New York revised its offer downward to $68 per share, or $1.2 billion. Play Paul Harvey and determine "the rest of the story" of this hostile takeover attempt.

2. Bank X, which is valued at $50 million, wants to merge with Bank Y. The managers of Bank X predict a synergistic value of $75 million for the resulting bank; what is the maximum cash price they should be willing to pay for Bank Y? What is the maximum price if stock financing is used and the shareholders of Bank Y end up with 10 percent of the shares of the new bank?

3. Given the following information, determine the number of shares that you, as the buyer, would be willing to exchange for Bank A and Bank B in separate transactions.[37]

	Buyer	*Bank A*	*Bank B*
Deposits (000,000)	$750.9	$24.5	$21.7
Equity (000,000)	$62.3	$1.4	$2.1
Net operating income (000)	$7,125	$208	$223
Shares outstanding (000)	3,000	50	39
EPS	$2.37	$4.16	$5.72
Market price per share	$32	NA	NA
Book value per share	$20.77	$28.00	$53.85

4. Big Bank and Little Bank have the following financial characteristics:

	Big Bank	*Little Bank*
Total assets	$10,000 B	$100 M
Total equity	$550 M	$7 M
Net income	82.5 M	$1.2 M
Shares outstanding	12.2 M	.7 M
EPS	$6.76	$1.71
Stock price	$45/share	$10/share

Assuming an exchange ratio 1.5 times book, calculate the combined financials for a pooling and a purchase transaction ($15 paid per share) of Little Bank by Big Bank. In the purchase transaction, assume that a $20 million "hit" must be absorbed and that it is amortized against earnings over a ten-year period. Also compare the individual and combined financials with respect to *ROE, ROA* and *EM.*

---

[37] These data are slightly adjusted figures from Terry and Sexton [1975], Table 2, p. 89.

5. On July 15, 1991, Chemical Banking and Manufacturers Hanover announced a megamerger of equals with Manufacturers shareholders receiving 1.14 shares of Chemical for each share of Manufacturers. Use the following June 30, 1991, data (in billions of dollars, unless otherwise indicated) to compute the resulting company, which will be called Chemical Banking and since has merged with Chase Manhattan (1996). Assume that a minimum of 6,200 jobs are eliminated.

	Chemical Banking	+	*Manufacturers Hanover*	=	*Chemical Banking*
Total assets	$74.13		$61.33		
Loans	45.55		38.52		
Total deposits	48.90		39.26		
Retail deposits	26.78		13.96		
Common equity	3.08		2.94		
Total equity	3.99		3.72		
Branches	432		228		
Employees	27,000		18,000		

6. Use the accompanying chart to evaluate how the shareholders of Wells Fargo benefited from their company's acquisition of First Interstate on April 1, 1996. Is your conclusion consistent with the announcement effect of mergers?

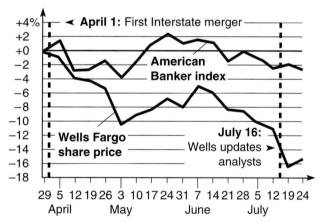

Sources: ILX Systems Inc., *American Banker.* Used by permission.

STOCK-MARKET REACTIONS TO MERGER ANNOUNCEMENTS

The hypotheses reviewed in the text suggest specific stock-market reactions to the announcements of proposed mergers. The two behavioral (non-wealth-maximizing) hypotheses predict that the share price of the bidding firm should fall whereas the share price of the target firm should rise. In these transactions, no value is created because gains are offset by losses. In contrast, the wealth-maximizing hypotheses suggest that the share price of the target firm will rise and that the share price of the bidder will not drop. In these transactions, the value created accrues to the owners of the target firm. If the market for corporate control is efficient, then competition among potential bidders will produce this result (i.e., merger price = real economic value of target firm). However, if merger announcements contain other signals about the bidding firm, then its share price could rise or fall. The problem is that the explicit signal (i.e. the merger announcement) is confounded by other implicit signals (e.g., about the bidding firm's investment opportunities or growth options). Roll [1988] summarizes the problem this way: "the [announcement of a] bid is a 'polluted' information item. The bidding firm is an activist, unlike the target firm, and its actions can be interpreted in the market as conveying more than just information about the takeover per se" (p. 243, insert mine).

Empirical Evidence on Bank Merger Announcements

Using event-study methods, Hawawini and Swary [1990] analyzed 118 bank mergers from 1970 through 1987. They found that the share prices of target banks rose during the week of the announcement on average by 11.5 percent after adjustment for risk. Inconsistent with the wealth-maximizing hypothesis, however, they also found that the share prices of the bidding banks fell, on average, by about 1.5 percent. Nevertheless, the bank mergers they analyzed resulted in a net increase in aggregate wealth.

Because not all bank mergers are approved by regulators, some announced mergers may not be consummated (e.g., First Bank System's attempt in 1995 to acquire First Interstate). Given this uncertainty, bank merger announcements can be described as partially anticipated events. In this context, Hawawini and Swary found that for mergers approved by the Federal Reserve share prices of the target banks rose, on average, by an additional 1.7 percent during the week of the regulatory approval. In contrast, for denials the share price of the target banks fell, on average, by 7.3 percent.

Hawawini and Swary also tested for different wealth effects for intrastate and interstate bank mergers. For intrastate bank mergers, they found a net creation of value to the shareholders of the target banks. In contrast, for interstate bank mergers they found no net gains but a transfer of wealth from the shareholders of the bidding banks to those of the target banks. On the surface, it would seem that capital markets have not recognized interstate banking as beneficial.

Because average results can obscure the diversity of market reactions across states, however, Hawawini and Swary took a closer look at the effects of interstate banking. In doing so, they concluded that the states that permitted unrestricted national entry, which were the ones with the most adverse economic conditions (such as Texas and Arizona), experienced positive market reactions to interstate-banking legislation, suggesting market expectations of positive potential gains from interstate banking in those states.

Using a sample of bank mergers for the period December 1981 through July 1986, Benston, Hunter, and Wall [1995] find no evidence to support the deposit-insurance (put-option) hypothesis. Although their results are consistent with the earnings-diversification hypothesis and with mergers having net-cash-flow advantages, they do not rule out that some mergers might have been undertaken in an attempt to increase the value of deposit insurance. The passage of FDICIA (1991) and other banking reforms would seem to make such attempts in the future futile.

Cornett and De [1991] found significant and positive stock price reactions to announcements of interstate bank mergers by both bidding and target banks. They studied 152 cases over the years 1982 to 1986. Because the positive excess returns to bidders has not been found in studies of nonfinancial firms or banks before, they attributed the result to the "release of a positive signal concerning capital quality and the synergies experienced in bank mergers . . ." (p. 293). They also found evidence that "the increase in potential competition associated with the allowance of nationwide returns and the acquisition of failed banks do not have an impact on bidder bank announcement period returns" (ibid.).

Baradwaj, Fraser, and Furtado [1990] compared market reactions to hostile and nonhostile bank takeovers. They found that the shareholders in target banks in hostile takeovers received significantly higher abnormal returns than those in nonhostile mergers. In both cases, however, they found that the bidding banks experienced negative abnormal returns. Moreover, because the negative abnormal returns were similar, the total positive wealth effects in hostile bank takeovers exceeded those in nonhostile ones. They also found that banks that attract hostile offers tend to be poorer performers in terms of profitability.

Regarding the financial characteristics of acquiring and acquired banks in nonhostile interstate acquisitions, Meric, Leveen, and Meric [1991] found differences that they attributed to consumer banking (e.g., acquiring banks had higher ratios of consumer loans to total assets, but they acquired banks with a high level of consumer operations). Their finding is consistent with the theory that the driving force behind interstate banking is the expansion of consumer franchises.

Slovin, Sushka, and Polonchek [1991] studied the valuation effects associated with the announcements of 23 BHC sale-and-leaseback agreements and 110 divestitures covering the years 1974 to 1988. They found results that differ significantly from those for nonfinancial firms. Specifically, the announcement of BHC sale-and-leasebacks generated negative excess returns whereas the announcement of BHC divestitures generated returns close to zero. In contrast, announcements of these two forms of corporate restructurings for nonfinancial firms have generated positive market responses. They conjecture that the difference in results can be attributed to bank capital regulation, which constrains the flexibility of bank managers and makes it difficult for them to undertake corporate restructuring based on economic efficiency. They regard this lack of managerial flexibility as one of the economic costs of bank capital regulation.

Selected References

Atkinson, Bill. [1991]. "After Bank of New England, What's Next?" *American Banker* (May 13), pp. 1 and 14.

"Bank Consolidation: Strategies for the Next Wave." [1996]. Chicago: Bank Administration Institute.

"Bank Mergers: A Giant Gnome?" [1996]. *The Economist* (April 13), p. 70.

Baradwaj, Babu G., Donald R. Fraser, and Eugene P. H. Furtado. [1990]. "Hostile Bank Takeover Offers." *Journal of Banking and Finance* (December), pp. 1229–1242.

Beatty, Randolph P., Anthony M. Santomero, and Michael Smirlock. [1987]. *Bank Merger Premiums: Analysis and Evidence*. New York: Salomon Brothers Center/New York University.

Bellanger, Serge. [1996]. "Choose Your Partners: The Era of Banking Consolidation." *Bankers Magazine* (March/April), pp. 19–23.

Benston, George J., William C. Hunter, and Larry D. Wall. [1995]. "Motivations for Bank Mergers and Acquisitions: Enhancing the Deposit Insurance Put Option versus Earnings Diversification." *Journal of Money, Credit, and Banking* (August), pp. 777–788.

"Best and Worst Deals of the 1980s." [1990]. *Business Week* (January 15), pp. 52–57.

Blanden, Michael, Anthony Rowley, Allan Sauderson, Leeslie de Quillacq, David Lane, and Stephen Timewell. [1995]. "More Weddings." *Banker* (October), pp. 23–29.

Born, Jeffery A., Robert A. Eisenbeis, and Robert S. Harris. [1988]. "The Benefits of Geographical and Product Expansion in the Financial Services Industry." *Journal of Financial Services Research* (January), pp. 161–182.

Brealey, Richard, and Stewart Myers. [1981]. *Principles of Corporate Finance*. New York: McGraw Hill, pp. 657–684.

Bremner, Brian, William Glasgall, and Kelley Holland. [1995]. "Tokyo Mitsubishi Bank: Big, Yes. Bad, No." *Business Week* (April 10), p. 40.

Bullington, Robert A., and Arnold E. Jensen. [1981]. "Pricing a Bank." *Bankers Magazine* (May–June), pp. 94–98.

Chault, Robert, and Matthew A. Troxell. [1982]. "Some Effects of Purchase Accounting." *American Banker* (January 7), pp. 4–6.

Cline, Kenneth. [1996]. "Bucking Merger Trend, SunTrust Looks Inward for Revenue Growth." *American Banker* (January 24), pp. 1, 4–5.

Copeland, Thomas, and J. Fred Weston. [1988]. *Financial Theory and Corporate Policy*. Reading, MA: Addison-Wesley.

Cornett, M. M., and S. De. [1991]. "Common Stock Returns in Corporate Takeover Bids: Evidence from Interstate Bank Mergers." *Journal of Banking and Finance* (April), pp. 273–295.

Crovitz, L. Gordon. [1973]. "Bank Mergers: Prices Paid to Marriage Partners." *Business Review*, Federal Reserve Bank of Philadelphia (July), pp. 16–25.

———. [1990]. "Can Takeover Targets Just Say No to Stockholders?" *The Wall Street Journal* (March 7), op-ed page.

Darnell, Jerome C. [1973]. "Merger Guidelines from the Phillipsburg National Bank Case." *Magazine of Bank Administration* (June), pp. 30–33.

Deogun, Nikhil. [1996]. "Back to the Fray: Displaced by Mergers, Some Bankers Launch Their Own Start-Ups." *The Wall Street Journal* (March 4), pp. A1, A3.

Egginton, Don A. [1982]. *Accounting for the Banker*. London: Longman Group.

Gabriel, Frederick. [1996]. "Not Much to Bank On; Mergers Bruise Firms that Count on Banks." *Crain's New York Business* (January 1), p. 3.

Garino, David P. [1981]. "Banks Grab Footholds Out of State, Betting that Restrictions Will End." *The Wall Street Journal* (February 2), Section 2, p. 35.

Giliberto, Michael S., and Hikhil P. Varaiya. [1989]. "The Winner's Curse and Bidder Competition in Acquisitions: Evidence from Failed Bank Auctions." *Journal of Finance* (March), pp. 59–76.

Goldfield, Robert. [1996]. "Small Banks Leap on Merger Bandwagon." *Business Journal-Portland* (March 1), p. 1.

Hawawini, Gabriel, and Itzhak Swary. [1990]. *Mergers and Acquisitions in the U.S. Banking Industry: Evidence from the Capital Markets.* Amsterdam: North-Holland.

Heggestad, Arnold A. [1979]. "Market Structure, Competition, and Performance in Financial Industries: A Survey of Banking Studies." In Franklin R. Edwards, ed., *Issues in Financial Regulation.* New York: McGraw-Hill, pp. 449–490.

Helm, Leslie, and Judith H. Dobrzynski. [1988]. "Meet Mike Jensen, the Professor Merger Mania." *Business Week* (February 8), pp. 66–67.

Hill, Miriam. [1995]. "Banking on Mergers; Relaxed Federal Rules, Need to Upgrade Systems Giving Bankers the Itch to Make Acquisitions." *Plain Dealer* (July 30), p. 1H.

Horngren, Charles. [1984]. *Introduction to Financial Accounting.* Englewood Cliffs, NJ: Prentice Hall.

"Interstate Banking: Mergers and Acquisitions in the Southeast under Regional Reciprocity." [1984]. New York: First Boston Research (March 21).

Jayaratne, Jith, and Christine Hall. [1996]. "Consolidation and Competition in Second District Banking Markets." *Current Issues in Economics and Finance* 2, Federal Reserve Bank of New York.

Jensen, Michael C. [1986]. "The Takeover Controversy: Analysis and Evidence." *Midland Corporate Finance Journal* (Summer), pp. 6–32.

King, Jim. [1991]. "Earnings Anger C&S Chairman, Stockholders." *Atlanta Constitution* (April 17), pp. B1 and B8.

Klinkerman, Steve. [1991]. "BankAmerica Emerges As Suitor for First City." *American Banker* (May 13), pp. 1 and 9.

Koch, Donald L., and Robert M. Baker. [1983]. "Purchase Accounting and the Quality of Bank Earnings." *Economic Review* (April), Federal Reserve Bank of Atlanta, pp. 14–22.

Koltveit, James M. [1983]. *Accounting for Banks.* New York: Matthew Bender.

Kraus, James R. [1995]. "Savings, Technology, and Clout Drove Chase-Chemical Merger." *American Banker* (August 29), p. 1.

Kreuzer, Teresa. [1987]. "Who Owns the Big Banks?" *Bankers Monthly* (August), pp. 43–46.

Ludwig, Eugene A. [1995]. "Testimony before the Subcommittee on Financial Institutions of the Committee on Banking and Financial Services of the U.S. House of Representatives," October 17. Comptroller of the Currency, Washington, DC.

"M&A Almanac: 1990 Profile." [1991]. *Mergers and Acquisitions* (May/June), pp. 36–53.

Mankowski, Cal. [1996]. "Giant U.S. Bank Mergers Reflect Efficiency Drive." *Reuters, Limited* (April 1).

Marshall, Jeffrey. [1996]. "Interview: Firebrand in Navy and Gray." *U.S. Banker* (http://banking.com/usbanker/art9.htm), p. 2.

Martin, Michael J. [1975]. "Bank Holding Company Acquisitions of Mortgage Banking Firms." *Mergers & Acquisitions* (Fall), pp. 19–26.

Matthews, Gordon. [1988]. "Despite the Crash, 1987 Was a Year for Mergers." *American Banker* (January 12), pp. 1, 14.

Meehan, John. [1991]. "If Mergers Were Simple, Banking's Troubles Might Be Over." *Business Week* (April 22), pp. 77–79.

Meeks, G. [1977]. *Disappointing Marriage: A Study of the Gains from Mergers.* London: Cambridge University Press.

Meric, Gulser, Serpil S. Leveen, and Ilhan Meric. [1991]. "The Financial Characteristics of Commercial Banks Involved in Interstate Mergers." *Financial Review* (February), pp. 75–90.

Myers, Stewart C. [1976]. "Introduction: A Framework for Evaluating Mergers." In Stewart C. Myers, ed., *Modern Developments in Financial Management.* New York: Praeger, pp. 633–645.

Nader, Ralph. [1995]. "Bank Mergers Skip Along, Right Past the Customers." *The New York Times* (November 12), p. 11.

Neely, Walter P. [1987]. "Banking Acquisitions: Acquirer and Target Shareholder Returns." *Financial Management* (Winter), pp. 66–74.

Nugent, Marguerite. [1996]. "Bank Mega-Mergers Limited Outside U.S.—Analysts." *Reuter Asia-Pacific Business Report* (March 29).

O'Rourke, Daniel. [1988]. "Bank versus Bank: The Hostile Takeover (and How to Fight It)." *Bank Administration* (January), pp. 16–19.

Pare, Terence P. [1995]. "Clueless Bankers; Merger Mania Can't Mask the Fact that America's Banks are Becoming Dinosaurs. Longtime Customers Simply Don't Need Them Anymore. There is a Survival Strategy, but Bankers Haven't got a Clue." *Fortune* (November 27), pp. 150–160.

Pettway, Richard, and Jack W. Trifts. [1985]. "Do Banks Overbid When Acquiring Failed Banks?" *Financial Management* (Summer), pp. 5–15.

Planning Bank Mergers and Acquisitions. [1984]. *Visual Aid Supplement.* New York: Ernst & Whinney.

Pound, John, and Gregg Jarrell. [1987]. "Hostile Takeovers and the Regulatory Dilemma: Twenty-Five Years of Debate." *Midland Corporate Finance Journal* (Summer), pp. 224–238.

Rappaport, Alfred. [1979]. "Do You Know the Value of Your Company?" *Mergers & Acquisitions* (Spring), pp. 12–17.

Rea, Alison. [1995]. "Top 25 U.S. Banks Seen Being Hit with More Mergers." *Reuters, Limited* (November 6).

Roll, Richard. [1986]. "The Hubris Hypothesis of Corporate Takeover." *Journal of Business* (April), pp. 197–216.

———. [1988]. "Empirical Evidence on Takeover Activity and Shareholder Wealth." In John Coffee, ed., *Knights, Raiders, and Targets.* New York: Oxford University Press, pp. 241–252.

Ross, Stephen A., and Randolph W. Westerfield. [1988]. *Corporate Finance.* St. Louis: Times Mirror/Mosby Publishing.

Silber, William L., and Roy C. Smith. [1995]. "A Bigger Bank Isn't Necessarily Better." *International Herald Tribune* (September 1), editorial page.

Simoff, Paul L. [1991]. "RTC Thrifts May Be Good Bet for Small Banks." *American Banker* (May 8), pp. 4 and 7.

Sloan, Allan. [1996]. "Deals: Take This Job and Cut It, How Wells Fargo Won the Battle of Banks." *Newsweek* (February 5), p. 47.

Slovin, M. B., M. E. Sushka, and J. A. Polonchek. [1991]. "Restructuring Transactions by Bank Holding Companies: The Valuation Effect of Sale-and-Leasebacks and Divestitures." *Journal of Banking and Finance* (April), pp. 237–255.

Spong, Kenneth. [1990]. *Banking Regulation: Its Purposes, Implementation, and Effects.* Kansas City: Federal Reserve Bank of Kansas City.

Statistics on Banking. (various issues). Washington, DC: FDIC.

Stern, Joel. [1987]. "The Future of Commercial Banking: A Roundtable Discussion." *Midland Corporate Finance Journal* (Fall), pp. 22–49.

Svare, J. Christopher. [1990]. "Acquiring for Growth and Profit: The Banc One Experience." *Bank Management* (November), pp. 18–24.

Terry, Ronald, and Merrill C. Sexton. [1975]. "Valuation of Banks in Acquisition." *Bankers Magazine* (Summer), pp. 86–89.

"Thrifts and Other Acquisition Targets." *ABA Banking Journal* (March 1990), pp. 58–63.

Varian, Hal R. [1988]. "Symposium on Takeovers." *Journal of Economic Perspectives* (Winter), pp. 3–82.

Wilke, John R. [1991]. "Nationwide Banking Is Getting a Preview at Growing KeyCorp." *The Wall Street Journal* (May 31), pp. A1 and A5.

Yellen, Janet L. [1995]. "Testimony before the Subcommittee on Financial Institutions and Consumer Credit of the Committee on Banking and Financial Services of the U.S. House of Representatives" (October 17). Board of Governors of the Federal Reserve System.

Contents

LEARNING OBJECTIVES

■ To understand the globalization of banking and the financial-services industry (FSI)

■ To understand why U.S. financial-services firms dominate world markets

■ To understand the delivery systems of international banking

■ To understand banks' exposure to sovereign (country) risk

■ To understand banks' exposure to foreign-exchange (cross-currency) risk

■ To understand bank asset-liability management (ALM) in a global context

■ To understand the role of foreign banks in the United States

CHAPTER THEME

Although international banking has developed over many centuries, the recent surge in international trade of goods and services has quickened the pace of the globalization of the financial-services industry (FSI). The international debt crisis of the 1980s and the collapse of communism in the 1990s created opportunities for new visions of financing for less-developed countries and for economies in transition. Although foreign-exchange risk and country (or sovereign) risk complicate international banking, the fundamental principles of financial management that guide a bank's domestic operations also apply to its foreign operations. From a business perspective, large banking companies traditionally have focused mainly on "global wholesale finance," including investment or merchant banking. Recently, however, some banks have expanded their retail operations overseas. International banking and financial markets such as the Eurodollar and foreign-currency markets are among the most competitive in the world. The anchor rate of international money markets is the London Interbank Offered Rate, or LIBOR.

KEY CONCEPTS, IDEAS, AND TERMS

- Americanization
- Country (sovereign or cross-border) risk
- Delivery systems of international banking
- Eurocurrency market
- Foreign banks (in the United States)
- Foreign-exchange (FX or FOREX) market
- Foreign-exchange (cross-currency) risk
- Global asset-liability management (ALM)
- Globalization

- International banking
- International debt crisis
- Investment (merchant) banking

- Less-developed country (LDC)
- Net exposure in a currency

- Off-balance-sheet activities (OBSAs)
- U.S. banks with foreign offices

GLOBALIZATION OF BANKING AND FINANCIAL SERVICES

> *International banking will continue to increase in importance, but it will also become even more complex. The quality of people will be a decisive factor.*
>
> —WILFRIED GUTH
> *Deutsche Bank, Frankfurt*

A **global financial system** is the institutional setting that has been developing for many years to accommodate international trade and the worldwide production of goods and services. **Technology** and the dissemination of **information** and ideas have been the driving forces for globalization in both the real sector, where goods and services are produced, and the financial sector, where institutions and markets facilitate the financing of the real sector. These changes have dramatically altered the nature of output, especially in the United States, from the physical (e.g., manufacturing) to the conceptual (e.g., services).

In a nutshell, the information revolution is transforming the world. In *The Twilight of Sovereignty,* Walter Wriston, who reigned as the chairman of Citicorp for 17 years, until his retirement in 1984, captures this theme and more with his broader view of the information revolution. The heart of his vision, which builds on the massive amount and the speed of transmission of information, is the following:

> The perception of what constitutes an asset, and what it is that creates wealth is shifting dramatically. Indeed, the new source of wealth is not material, it is information, knowledge applied to work to create value. The pursuit of wealth is now largely the pursuit of information to the means of production (p. xii).

Since 1992, when Wriston wrote these words, the Internet has increased the volume of information that is easily available and the speed with which it can be accessed. Wriston sees the "information age" producing decentralized democracies and prosperity. The title of Wriston's book follows from his conclusion that the information revolution leads to cooperation and coalitions, like the European Community, and to the collapse of repressive regimes, like the former USSR, hence *The Twilight of Sovereignty.* He claims that information has always been society's great equalizer, and he stresses three aspects of the information revolution:

- The relationship between countries and power, and how in today's information age it is difficult to act alone either politically or economically (e.g., to control a country's money supply)
- The reduction of the importance of middle managers to businesses as information technology replaces paper pushers
- The reduction of the importance of natural resources in favor of knowledge (although it is difficult to measure) as a country's major source of power

The second point has been an important factor in our analyses of bank technology (chapter 18) and of bank mergers as the primary means of consolidation in the FSI (chapter 19).

On balance, the information revolution and the resulting globalization have been good for the United States because they place a premium on innovativeness and ability to adapt to change, which Wriston and others consider strengths for the United States. The next section explores how well U.S. bankers have adapted to the information revolution and the globalization of banking and the FSI.

GLOBALIZATION OR AMERICANIZATION?

In 1981, Arturo Porzecanski [1981] of Morgan Guaranty Trust Company claimed that "The heyday of overseas banking already has passed the U.S. institutions and the international financial role played by American banks is likely to be diminished still further in coming years" (p. 5). During the 1980s, overseas banking in the United States did take a big hit mainly due to the **international debt crisis.** Since then, however, many U.S. financial-services firms, including large commercial banks, have witnessed a resurgence in their international activities. A unified Western Europe and the collapse of communism in Central and Eastern Europe have played major roles in this rebirth.

By 1996, Sesit [1996] offered this proposition in *The Wall Street Journal:* The globalization of finance is really nothing more than the **Americanization** of finance. The following evidence was offered in support:

- Seven of the top 10 merger advisors worldwide are American firms, and two others are partly American-owned businesses.
- The top four global underwriters of stock offerings in the past three years (1993–1995) have been American firms.
- Goldman Sachs & Co., the leading underwriter of global stock offerings in 1995, won the job of coordinator of the privatization of Deutsche Telekon (the world's largest such deal at the time) and landed the lead role in the biggest-ever equity offerings in Denmark, Mexico, Singapore, Spain, and Sweden.
- J. P. Morgan & Co. guided Hoechst AG, a German chemical firm, in its $7.1 billion takeover of Marion Merrell Dow. The deal was the biggest trans-Atlantic acquisition of 1995. J. P. Morgan also advised Credito Italiano SpA in its successful hostile takeover of Credito Romagnolo SpA. The target company was advised by Goldman Sachs and Morgan Stanley.
- In August 1995, Merrill Lynch became the first non-Swiss company to lead-manage a Swiss-franc bond issue for a Swiss company.

Absent from Sesit's list but worthy of mention is the dominance of the world's derivatives markets by five American banks (listed in alphabetical order): BankAmerica, Bankers Trust, Chase Manhattan-Chemical, Citicorp, and J. P. Morgan.

Six important factors explain why U.S. financial-services firms dominate world markets:

1. They operate in highly competitive domestic markets that serve to sharpen skills and stimulate innovation
2. English is the language of banking and finance
3. Sophisticated bank technology and modern tools of risk management are the modus operandi of U.S. financial-services firms
4. The U.S. regulatory environment is usually conducive to financial innovation
5. The acceptance by U.S. governments, businesses, households, and educators of free capital markets as efficient allocators of financial resources
6. A U.S. culture that encourages and rewards competitive spirit and innovation

On balance, a strong case can be made that the globalization of banking and financial services is nothing more than the Americanization of these activities, which reaffirms the view of Wriston and others that innovativeness and the ability to adapt to change are keys to leadership in the information age.

THE ROLE OF BANK SIZE IN THE TWENTY-FIRST CENTURY

Conspicuous by its absence in the previous discussion of U.S. financial firms dominating world markets was any mention of size as a requirement for that leadership. Wriston says that information is society's great equalizer. Because banks are entities that establish networking relationships through which they collect, store, process, and transmit information for their own accounts and those of their customers, they have the potential to continue to be the equal of any financial-services firms, domestic or foreign. Table 20-1 shows the world's 10 largest banks as of December 31, 1995. Conspicuous by its absence is any U.S. bank on the list. As the memo item shows, the United States did have the 19th (Chase/Chemical), 28th (Citicorp), 33rd (BankAmerica), 42nd (NationsBank), and 43rd (J. P. Morgan) largest banks in the world. Safety is more important than mere size, however. The last column in Table 20-1 shows, based on the Bank for International Settlement (BIS) capital ratio (i.e., risk-based capital requirements), that although the major U.S. banks are not the largest, they are the safest in terms of international capital

TABLE 20-1   The Worlds' Ten Largest Banks, December 31, 1995 (dollar amounts in billions)

Rank	Total Assets	Equity Capital	BIS Capital Ratio(%)
1. Bank of Tokyo-Mitsubishi Ltd[a]	$797	$26.1	8.46/9.20
2. Deutsche Bank, AG	502	18.9	10.10
3. Sanwa Bank Ltd.	500	17.7	9.12
4. Sumitomo Bank Ltd.	499	18.2	9.20
5. Dai-Ichi Kangyo Bank Ltd.	498	19.2	9.40
6. Fuji Bank Ltd.	486	15.4	8.36
7. Sakura Bank Ltd.	477	16.1	8.37
8. Norinchukin Bank	429	3.2	NA (9.25 in 1994)
9. Credit Agricole Mutuel	384	20.6	10.50
10. Industrial Bank of Japan	361	12.4	8.59
Memo (U.S. banks):			
19. Chase Manhattan/Chemical[a]	302	21.0	12.68/12.10
28. Citicorp	255	19.6	12.33
33. BankAmerica	230	20.2	11.48
42. NationsBank	186	12.8	11.58
43. J. P. Morgan	185	10.4	13.00

Note: Except for Deutsche Bank (Germany) and Crédit Agricole (France), the other top 10 banks are located in Japan. [a]Pro forma based on mergers in 1996. BIS = Bank for International Settlement (risk-based capital ratio; chapter 13 provides details). For merged banks' pro formas, the BIS capital ratio could be calculated.

Source: Adapted and compiled from data reported in *American Banker* (August 5, 1996), p. 8.

standards. Moreover, they have been able to combine this safety with innovativeness and efficiency in the mid-to-late 1990s.

For U.S. money-center or multinational banks, the mid-to-late 1990s are in sharp contrast to the 1980s and early 1990s. In 1982, Citicorp and BankAmerica ranked first and second on the list of the world's largest banks. The next 10 years were tumultuous for both organizations and for U.S. banking in general. In fact, more than one analyst questioned whether BOA and Citi might survive. Although neither of the banks was very safe, efficient, or profitable over this period, they both continued to be innovative. Along with other major banks throughout the world, the biggest problem Citicorp and BOA faced was the LDC debt crisis (LDC = less-developed countries), which began with Mexico's debt moratorium in 1982. It wasn't until 1987, however, when Citicorp bit the LDC bullet with a $3 billion provision for loan losses directed at Brazilian debt, that the light at the end of the LDC tunnel was not seen as an oncoming train.

The LDC Debt Crisis in Retrospect

The LDC debt crisis represents an interesting period in the history of U.S. and world banking. The international banker's rule for handling the LDC debt crisis was

> A rolling loan gathers no loss.

To understand this rule, you need to know that to keep LDC loans current (i.e., not in technical default) banks would lend LDCs money just for that purpose. Walter Wriston (not retired until 1984) defended the practice by saying, "Countries don't go bankrupt." Christine Bogdanowicz-Bindert of Shearson Lehman Brothers retorted, "Countries don't go bankrupt, but bankers who lend to them do."[1] Thanks to the federal safety net, no U.S. money-center banks went bankrupt as a result of the LDC debt crisis of the 1980s.

To see that a rolling loan *does* in fact gather potential loss, we need to distinguish between accounting and economic loan values. Consider a ten-year loan for $100 million with a 10 percent rate of interest.[2] Assuming a balloon repayment of principal, the annual interest payment is $10 million. With a rolling loan, the banker lends the borrower $10 million to make the first interest payment. From an accounting perspective, the loan is technically current, but the real or economic indebtedness has risen to $110 million. To make the next interest payment on a rolling basis requires $11 million, and the indebtedness rises to $121 million. After a decade of this charade, the total debt outstanding is $100(1.1)^{10}$, or $259.37 million. The power of compound interest has doomed the borrower whereas the lender has been pouring good money after bad. For a floating-rate loan in an environment of hyperinflation, not uncommon for LDC loans made during the 1970s and 1980s, the situation is even worse.

Closing the Barn Door before the LDC Horse Got Out[3]

The international debt crisis (i.e., the LDC debt crisis) was precipitated by some horrendously bad banking practices. The tale woven by a former lending officer and presented in Box 20-1 gives one indication of how bad the practice was

---

[1] The last two quotes are from Mayer [1987], p. 1, whereas the adage comes from banking folklore.
[2] This example is similar to Makin's [1984], pp. 150–151.
[3] This section draws on Makin [1984], chapter 7, pp. 129–153.

| BOX 20-1

LDC LENDING: AN INSIDER'S VIEW[a]

It is 1978. Thanks to the venal, repressive regime of President Ferdinand Marcos of the Philippines, I am safely and happily roosting in one of Manila's best hotels, the Peninsula. I am about to set in motion a peculiar and idiosyncratic process that will result in a $10 million loan to a Philippine construction company, a bedfellow of the Marcos clan—a loan that will soon go sour. I am unaware that any of this is going to happen as I enter the lobby of the Peninsula on my way to dinner, still trying to digest the live octopus that a Taiwanese bank served me last night, and attempting to remember exactly what it was they wanted and why they had gone to so much trouble.

International banking is an interesting business anyway, but what makes it rather more interesting in this case—both to me and to the hapless Ohioans whose money I am selling—is that I am 25 years old, with one and a half years of banking experience. I joined the bank as a "credit analyst" on the strength of an MA in English. Because I happened to be fluent in French, I was promoted 11 months later to loan officer and assigned to the French-speaking Arab countries of North Africa, where I made my first international calls. This is my third extended trip, and my territory has quickly expanded. I have visited 28 countries in six months.

I am far from alone in my youth and inexperience. The world of international banking is now full of aggressive, bright, but hopelessly inexperienced lenders in the mid-twenties. They travel the world like itinerant brushmen, *filling loan quotas*, peddling financial wares, and living high on the hog. Their bosses are often bright but hopelessly

inexperienced 29-year-old vice presidents with wardrobes from Brooks Brothers, MBAs from Wharton or Stanford, and so little credit training they would have trouble with a simple retail installment loan. *Their* bosses, sitting on the senior loan committee, are pragmatic, nuts-and-bolts bankers whose grasp of local banking is often profound, the product of 20 or 30 years of experience. But the senior bankers are fish out of water when it comes to international lending. Many of them never wanted to lend overseas in the first place, but were forced into it by the internationalization of American commerce; as their local clientele expanded into foreign trade, they had no choice but to follow them or lose the business to the money-center banks. So they uneasily supervise their underlings, who are the hustlers of the world financial system, the tireless pitchmen who drum up the sort of loans to Poland, Mexico, and Brazil that have threatened the stability of the system they want to promote.

"And now for the rest of the story . . ."[b]

The loan was eventually made after being partially guaranteed by the Philippines' largest bank. However, after 18 months the loan was on nonaccrual status and it was rescheduled. By the summer of 1983, the bank had received only a fraction of the debt and the guarantee was never called. Since October 1983, the Philippines had declared a moratorium on its external debt of $25 billion until 1985. In 1980, the banker changed jobs and moved to a West Coast bank at twice the salary. He quit shortly after that and turned from banking to writing.

---

[a] S. C. Gwynne, "Adventures in the Loan Trade." *Harper's* (September 1983), pp. 22–26.
[b] Makin [1984], p. 149.

out in the field. In this section, we focus on risk management and lending philosophy at the corporate level.

The key message of portfolio theory is diversification. The ultimate way to reduce risk is to find projects whose returns are unrelated or, ideally, move in opposite directions. The latter is illustrated by the situations of undertakers and life insurance companies; their returns move in opposite directions. International lending to LDCs was frequently in the form of umbrella loans to the governments of the countries. With the funds dispersed by the government over a wide range of projects, the country's loan portfolio presumably was diversified. The banks, however, had lost control over the creditworthiness of the borrowers within the country. Thus, they were running the risk of getting diversified but risky loans *within* the countries. Once the return is negative, it is small consolation to know that it is also stable. Another form of diversification that the banks tried to achieve was by lending across countries, such as oil exporters (e.g., Mexico and Venezuela) and oil importers (e.g., Brazil and Argentina). Unfortunately, because all of these countries were still in the LDC portfolio, there were certain risks that were not diversifiable (e.g., the propensity for these governments to be wasteful intermediaries and to resort to the inflation tax to reduce the burden of internal debt).

The terms of LDC loans were dominated in dollars at floating interest rates without any collateral. Because governments never go bankrupt because they have the power to tax, there presumably was no need for collateral. The first two terms were designed to protect against foreign inflation and domestic inflation, respectively. These terms were stacked against both the borrower *and* the lender; neither could win. The banks were making these loans without any control over their quality and *before* they had the funding (i.e., liability management). With LIBOR plus pricing, they simply bought OPEC dollars in the Eurocurrency market at the going rate of interest, marked them up, and sent them to the borrower. When U.S. inflation and interest rates took off in 1980 and 1981, LDC borrowers were rolled into higher and higher interest rates that would require massive debt reschedulings.

Stock-Market Reactions to Events Associated with the International Debt Crisis

The international debt crisis generated numerous event studies dealing with the stock market's reaction to announcements of debt moratoriums, loan-loss provisions, and loan syndications to LDCs.[4] The initial studies focused on the market's reaction to Mexico's debt moratorium in August 1982. Somewhat surprisingly, the results were mixed and conflicting (Musumeci and Sinkey [1990a] provide a recap). In February 1987, when Brazil announced its debt moratorium, the environment had changed (i.e., greater disclosure requirements, the development of secondary markets for LDC debt, investor experience with the debt crisis, etc). Although the market reacted negatively to Brazil's announcement, there was no evidence of mispricing or investor contagion.

Following Brazil's debt moratorium, in May 1987 Citicorp announced a $3 billion provision for loan losses for LDC debt. The market reacted positively to this corporate restructuring, and other banks with exposure to LDC debt were rewarded in partial anticipation that they would follow Citicorp's lead, which they did. When the other banks actually did announce their provisions, they were given the balance of their market reward, indicating the absence of a free-rider problem (Musumeci and Sinkey [1990b]).

Predating the international debt crisis, Megginson, Poulsen, and Sinkey [1995] found that the market reacted negatively to the announcements of syndicated LDC loans made to Latin American borrowers at the time the loans were made (i.e., over the years 1969 to 1985). Because the market treated these announcements

---

[4] Megginson, Poulsen, and Sinkey [1995] and Musumeci and Sinkey [1990a and 1990b] provide examples of such studies.

as negative net-present-value projects, why were the banks making the loans? Four potential explanations include the following:

- Bank managers' preferences for the accounting model of the firm, with its emphasis on current EPS, an approach that would lead lenders to focus on origination fees rather than cash flows over the life of the loan (Box 20-1)

- The absence of an effective market for corporate control of banking companies that would permit the accounting model to flourish (hostile takeovers had not yet occurred in banking, chapter 19)

- Political pressure on U.S. banks to make loans to developing countries with the implicit guarantee that the lenders were protected by the U.S. federal safety net provided by deposit insurance and the discount window (e.g., the too-big-to-fail doctrine)

- Restricted information flows that inhibited the ability of the market to fully evaluate the NPV of syndicated loans to LDCs

BARRIERS TO ENTRY FOR A WORLDWIDE PLAYER

Table 20-2 shows a geographic breakdown of the world's 200 largest banks, as of December 31, 1995. With 48 banks in the top 200, Japan held $8.3 trillion, or 34.2 percent of the market. Japan, Germany, and the United States, with a total of 101 banks in the largest 200, accounted for 56.5 percent ($14.1 trillion) of the assets held by the 200 institutions. Ten countries with 148 institutions held $21 trillion in assets (93.25% of market share).

U.S. banks (commercial and investment) have been able to dominate world financial markets without being the largest institutions in the world. Nevertheless,

TABLE 20-2   Geographic Breakdown of the World's 200 Largest Banks

Country	Assets 1995 (billions)	Market Share of 200	Number of Banks in 200
Japan	$ 8,259	34.21%	48
Germany	3,337	11.28	21
United States	2,404	11.00	32
France	2,022	7.55	9
United Kingdom	1,298	5.90	8
Italy	930	3.85	10
Switzerland	846	3.50	4
Netherlands	675	2.80	3
Belgium	663	2.75	7
Canada	589	2.44	6
Top Ten	$21,023	93.25%	148
18 others	3,120	6.75	52
Total 200	$24,143	100.00%	200

Note: The 18 other countries (in alphabetical order) include Australia, Austria, Brazil, Denmark, Finland, Greece, India, Ireland, Israel, Korea, Luxembourg, Mexico, Portugal, Singapore, Spain, Sweden, Taiwan, and Thailand.

Source: Adapted and compiled from data reported in *American Banker* (August 5, 1996), p. 16.

to be a major player on a worldwide basis requires some critical mass of assets and capital to be able to attract the skilled personnel and build the requisite technological foundation to compete in highly competitive and sophisticated international markets. Bankers Trust of New York, which is only the 77th-largest bank in the world but a major player in global wholesale finance, even after its derivatives debacles of 1994, *only* had total assets of $103.5 billion (1995). Two other New York City banks, Bank of New York (122nd in the world) and Republic New York (146th in the world), which are about one-half the size of Bankers Trust, are involved in international banking but not to the extent of Bankers Trust. Being in the right spot (NYC) and having an asset base of $43 billion (Republic) can be regarded as a good foundation for launching into international banking.

Let's consider the five U.S. banks (Bankers Trust, BankAmerica, Chase Manhattan, Citicorp, and J. P. Morgan) that rule the world of derivatives (Bennett [1993]). Because only one of these (Chase/Chemical) is among the world's 25 largest banks, size may not be the appropriate proxy for barriers to entry. With four of the five banks located in NYC, the real-estate adage location, location, location (in the money capital of the world) might be an important consideration. On a global basis, however, intellectual and reputational capital might be the most critical constraints. Combining these factors with an accounting, legal, regulatory, and technical environment conducive to financial innovation suggests why U.S. banks dominate the worldwide market for financial services, including derivatives, commercial and investment banking, and M&A activities.

GLOBALIZATION AND SYSTEMIC (CREDIT) RISK

Globalization and consolidation mean that financial systems are more interconnected. Computer technology means that billions of dollars of transactions can be conducted instantaneously within countries and across borders. Modern tools of risk management mean the underlying risks associated with commodity prices, interest rates, and exchange rates can be hedged; these same tools, however, can be used to speculate.[5] On balance, although the efficiency of global financial markets is a fantastic development, that same efficiency has the capability of transmitting mistakes at the same pace as error-free transactions.

At one time or another, we have all encountered the dreaded statement: The computer is down. Think about how the computer being down can pyramid depending on which computer or computer network is down. It is one problem, mainly customer inconvenience, if the computer controls an ATM; a bigger problem, however, if it controls a regional, national, or international ATM network but still just customer/traveler inconvenience. Suppose a POS system crashes, then both customers and businesses are affected. But what if it is the large dollar payments system that goes down? Will the world economy come to a halt? Will financial panic ensue?

Systemic credit risk focuses on the default risk of all firms in the economy; in contrast, firm-specific credit risk is the default risk of individual firms. If contagion exists, then the default of one firm leads to the collapse of the economy. Contagion

---

[5] Stevenson [1992] reports that many observers think that during the European currency crisis of September 1992, speculators played a major role in the monetary problems of Great Britain, Italy, and Spain. The GAO (General Accounting Office [1996a]) reports on Mexico's financial crisis.

in banking occurs when a deposit run at one bank spreads to other banks, resulting in a liquidity crisis for the financial system.

Alan Greenspan [1996], chairman of the Board of Governors of the Federal Reserve System, preaches that as international financial markets continue to expand, central bankers must have twin objectives:

- Fostering macroeconomic stability
- Maintaining safe-and-sound financial institutions that can take advantage of stability while exploiting the advantages of new technological advances (p. 6)

With the dynamics of globalization, the first objective has been directed to the increased threat of systemic risk. Greenspan suggests that the way to control systemic risk is not to attempt to suppress market forces and technological change but to use technology to contain them. Individual institutions can use technology to develop better risk-management systems, improve internal controls (absent in the collapse of Barings Bank and the derivatives debacles involving Bankers Trust), and to increase the efficiency and safety of the payments system (i.e., move closer to real-time settlement).

To protect against a meltdown of the financial system, central banks have adopted what Greenspan calls "catastrophic financial insurance coverage," which in the United States is simply the federal safety net consisting of FDIC deposit insurance and the Fed as lender of last resort. Properly managed, one device or the other can do the job, but the United States has both, neither of which worked very well in the 1980s. When public subsidies are mismanaged, they can be very costly to taxpayers, as illustrated by the $160 billion (excluding interest) S&L mess in the United States. Table 20-3 shows the deposit-insurance plans adopted by the United States and selected other countries. During the 1990s, French and Japanese central bankers had to assure market participants that their governments stood behind Crédit Lyonnais (France's largest bank) and the 10 largest city (commercial) banks in Japan, which were plagued by commercial-real-estate problems worse than those experienced by U.S. banks.

Greenspan [1996] argues that a government safety net, whether in the United States, France, or Japan, should be "reserved for only the rarest of disasters, triggered, at most, a handful of times per century" (p. 9). When financial institutions are given blanket protection, regulatory discipline is lost and moral-hazard behavior encouraged. The dilemma, in theory, is to balance, based on a bank's cost of capital, the responsibility for risk bearing between the private sector and the gov-

TABLE 20-3   Bank Deposit-Insurance Plans across Selected Countries: Level of Protection

Country	Maximum per Depositor	$ Equivalent	Membership
United States	$100,000	100,000	Compulsory
Britain	90% of protected deposits, up to maximum of £20,000	31,000	Compulsory
France	FFr400,000	79,000	Compulsory
Germany	Up to 30% of a bank's liable capital	NA	Voluntary
Japan	Yen 10 million	93,000	Compulsory
Switzerland	SFr30,000	25,000	Voluntary

Source: Office of the Comptroller of the Currency.

ernment. Any financial institution that cannot earn the economy's minimum risk-adjusted return should not be propped up by public support. Beyond that minimum return, a trade-off exists: If governments/central bankers do not absorb some financial risk, bank leverage will be limited, the financial sector reduced, and economic growth restricted; on the other hand, an overprotected banking and financial system promotes inefficiency, excessive risk taking, and other problems at taxpayers' expense.

On balance, Greenspan [1996] concludes that central bankers must absorb the "most extreme risks" to permit a globalized financial system to operate effectively. At the same time, normal operating and financial risks must remain in the private sector and not benefit from public subsidy.

THE DELIVERY SYSTEMS OF INTERNATIONAL BANKING

To deliver international banking services to existing customers or to tap international banking markets for growth opportunities, banks can employ one or more of the following alternative organizational forms:

1. Correspondent-Bank Relationships

This approach is the least costly way of providing international services for customers. Basically, it is a defensive position designed to provide a full menu of banking services without substantial investment. The opportunity for expansion is limited, however, with this approach.

2. International Department

As the base for home operations, this department is a prerequisite for expansion into international banking. The size of the department will determine the required investment and personnel requirements. A general package of services for multinational customers is the basic objective here. This vehicle provides some flexibility, direct control over operations, and the opportunity to exert pressure on correspondents for better service. Because of the broad range of services provided by international departments and because of their special operations, accounting, and personnel requirements, they are frequently referred to as "a bank within a bank."

3. Participations/Loan Syndications

This vehicle offers an opportunity for loan expansion without extensive foreign investment or travel. Loan participations or syndications usually are organized by money-center banks but not guaranteed by them. They enable new banks in the international market to "get their feet wet" (e.g., in terms of evaluating international loans) and to become known in the marketplace.

4. Representative Offices

This form of delivery system focuses on establishing contacts and providing information to the home office. Representative offices, whether foreign or domestic, are not permitted to gather deposits or make loans. A representative office can serve as a test vehicle for a future overseas branch without incurring the costs of establishing a full-service branch.

5. Overseas Branches

This approach permits a high degree of flexibility and control over the provision of international services, access to the Eurocurrency markets, and ability to attract new business. The investment costs are, of course, substantial, especially if a worldwide network is desired. Foreign taxes usually must be paid.

6. Edge Act and Agreement Corporations

These subsidiaries are in effect out of state international departments. They carry out the function of an international branch within the United States. Edge and agreement corporations are permitted to engage only in foreign banking and investment activities. Edge Act corporations are chartered by the Fed, whereas *agreement corporations* are state-chartered companies that agree to operate under the same Fed regulations that apply to Edges. As a result of the International Banking Act of 1978, Edge Act banks were permitted to establish branches. Recently, some banks have been establishing networks of Edge offices as a means of preparing for geographic deregulation in the United States.

7. Foreign Affiliates

These entities may be either majority owned or minority owned. They have the potential to provide a variety of financial services and joint ventures. To illustrate, in 1965, Mellon National Bank of Pittsburgh made a major foray into international banking by purchasing a substantial equity interest in the Bank of London and South America (BOLSA). BOLSA offered Mellon an opportunity to gain access to (*a*) the London money and foreign-exchange markets, (*b*) markets in Spain, Portugal, and Latin America, and (*c*) an experienced group of international bankers and operational procedures.[6]

8. International Banking Facilities (IBFs)

On December 3, 1981, the Fed granted U.S. banks the right to carry on their Eurocurrency business at home by establishing "free-trade" zones for international banking within the United States. Access to the IBFs is limited to individual non-U.S. residents, foreign corporations, foreign banks, and foreign subsidiaries of U.S. corporations. IBFs are not required to have offices separate from domestic facilities, but they must have a separate set of books. Deposits in IBFs were not subject to Regulation Q interest-rate ceilings, but they do count in determining FDIC deposit-insurance assessments. IBFs are not permitted to accept deposits from or make loans to U.S. residents, and they cannot be used to finance activities in the United States. Deposits in IBFs are required to stay on the books for at least two days, and the deposit instruments are not permitted to be negotiable. To encourage the establishment of IBFs, some states, such as California, Florida, Georgia, and New York, have passed laws making IBF deposits exempt from state and local income taxes. However, banks still are subject to federal income tax on earnings attributed to IBFs. The effect of IBFs on the Eurocurrency market has been mainly a distributional one, shifting some deposits into U.S. free-trade zones.

Recent data show the dominant international delivery system for U.S. banks to be foreign branches. Although they number about 2,500 or so, only some 200 commercial banks are players in international banking. In terms of claims on un-

---

[6] See Lees [1974], pp. 76–77.

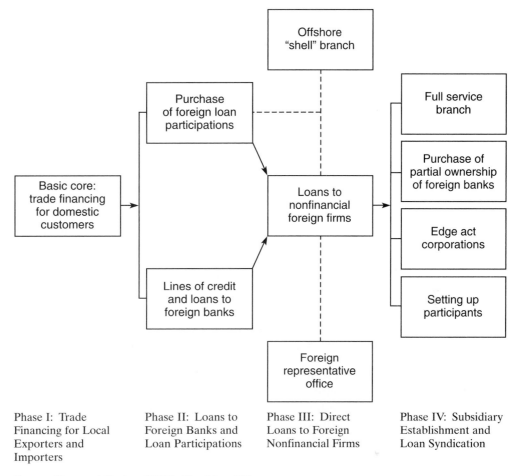

| Phase I: Trade Financing for Local Exporters and Importers | Phase II: Loans to Foreign Banks and Loan Participations | Phase III: Direct Loans to Foreign Nonfinancial Firms | Phase IV: Subsidiary Establishment and Loan Syndication |

Source: Baer and Garlow (1977), Chart 2, p. 130.

FIGURE 20-1 **The Phases of International Growth**

related parties, foreign branches generate more than one-half of total claims, followed by main offices (including IBFs) and foreign subsidiaries.

The way in which a bank's international operations might develop is depicted in Figure 20-1. This schematic, which is from Baer and Garlow [1977], views the pattern of growth as consisting of four phases. Alternatively, we could view the phases as various stages in the life cycle of a bank's international delivery system. In Phase I, the basic core of international operations is established in terms of providing trade financing for local exporters and importers. In Phase II, the bank moves into making loans to foreign banks and into loan participations. In Phase III, loans to nonfinancial foreign firms are started as offshore facilities are established and market contracts made. In Phase IV, the bank moves into establishing subsidiaries and organizing foreign loan syndications. In this phase, the bank's international department takes on a stature similar to that of the international division of a money-center bank.

INTERNATIONAL BANKING MARKETS

International banking markets perform a financial-intermediation function similar to that of domestic banking markets. That is, the banks in these markets gather deposits from surplus-spending units and lend them to deficit-spending units. The basic difference between international or external banking and domestic or internal banking is that international banking occurs across national boundaries, whereas domestic banking occurs within a country. For example, a U.S. bank may gather deposits in its London branch and lend them in Japan through its Tokyo branch. Thus, foreign exchange risk and foreign-country risk, which are not relevant for domestic banking, are important considerations in international banking.

The Eurocurrency Market

Multinational banks operate mainly in the international money market or the **Eurocurrency market.** A Eurocurrency is a claim in that currency held by a nonresident of the currency's country of origin. The Eurodollar is the major Eurocurrency. In general, a **Eurodollar** is a U.S. dollar claim arising from a dollar-denominated deposit, note, or bond held by a nonresident of the United States. The major instruments of international banking are Eurodollar deposits and loans. A Eurodollar deposit is a dollar-denominated deposit located in a bank or branch outside the United States. A Eurodollar loan is a dollar-denominated loan made by a bank or branch located outside the United States. The essence of international banking or Eurobanking is to bid for Eurodollar CDs or time deposits of $100,000 or more and to make Eurodollar loans with the proceeds.

To facilitate the expansion of their assets, multinational banks frequently engage in interest-arbitrage transactions. That is, they borrow funds in one foreign currency and country and make loans in another currency and country. For example, a bank might gather petrodollar deposits in the Middle East and lend them to developing nations in Africa or Asia. The existence of these arbitrage situations is due to substantially different interest rates across countries. The objective of these arbitrage transactions is to maximize the interest-rate spreads, given the bank's risk preferences.

The process of credit expansion in Eurocurrency markets may involve the redepositing of the original deposit in a series of banks before a loan to a nonbank customer is actually made. Of course, until the loan is made, credit expansion has not occurred. To estimate the size of the Eurocurrency market in terms of credit-generating capacity, interbank deposits must be netted out. The size of the (net) Eurocurrency market is estimated to be over $1 trillion. The interbank redepositing of funds takes place in the interbank market. Funds in this market trade on the basis of the receiving bank's size, reputation, and creditworthiness, as in the domestic market for federal funds and large CDs. The spread in the interbank market is narrow, around .25 percent, commensurate with the risk. However, high-risk institutions have to pay larger risk premiums or go without interbank funding.

The base or anchor rate in the Eurocurrency market is the **London Interbank Offer Rate** (LIBOR). LIBOR represents the rate at which leading multinational banks in London are willing to lend to each other. The flow of funds from an initial deposit to a loan, on the basis of markup pricing, is illustrated by the following example:

Transaction	Price (Rate, %)	Premium (%)
Initial Eurodollar deposit	6.000 (LIBOR)	—
First interbank deposit[a]	6.125	0.125
Second interbank deposit[a]	6.375	0.250
Third interbank deposit[a]	6.875	0.500
Eurodollar loan	9.000	2.125

[a] The interbank deposits are also called *bank placements.*

The markups or premiums on interbank deposits or placements are relatively small because the costs and risks are minimal. In contrast, Eurodollar loans are more costly to administer and typically more risky; thus, they require a larger markup. These loans are made on a floating-rate basis, with adjustments made every three to six months, depending on the maturity of the underlying liability instrument (time deposit).

The use of LIBOR-plus pricing in the Eurocurrency markets is functionally equivalent to the use of prime rate-plus pricing in the U.S. domestic market. In addition to markup pricing, the use of commitment fees is an integral part of Eurocurrency pricing arrangements. These fees, which are subject to competitive pressures, typically range in size from 0.25 to 0.5 percent, with payment required at the time the commitment is made. The U.S. banking practice of compensating balances is not employed in Eurocurrency markets or in domestic European banking markets.

Because of the unrestricted nature of the Eurocurrency market, competition is intense for both loans and deposits. Relative to domestic markets, international markets are more efficient, as evidenced by the higher deposit rates and lower loan rates observed. As a result, profit margins and spreads are thinner. The size of a particular segment of the Eurocurrency market (e.g., Eurodollars) can be viewed as being determined by the interest spread that multinational banks are willing to accept.

Like the foreign-exchange market, the Eurocurrency market is not restricted to a particular location; it is a mechanism for transferring funds that knows no boundaries. The assets of the foreign branches of U.S. banks are divided fairly evenly among three general areas including the United Kingdom, South America and the Caribbean Basin, and other locations (e.g., Continental Europe, Asia, and Africa).

To summarize, the Eurocurrency market has a number of important characteristics. First, it is basically a wholesale market. Large CDs are the basic liability instrument, with loan participations frequently used to facilitate denomination intermediation into large loans. Second, the international and domestic money markets are competing sectors in the global market for financial assets and liabilities. Third, the Eurocurrency market is an unregulated one that is not subject to restrictions such as reserve requirements or deposit-insurance fees. This fact makes the international-banking sector particularly attractive to U.S. banks because they are more heavily regulated than other banks. Fourth, the Eurocurrency market is more competitive than domestic financial markets. As a result, profit margins and interest spreads are thinner because deposit rates must be higher and loan rates lower to compete with domestic financial institutions. And, fifth, the risk analysis required in Eurocurrency markets is more complex because of foreign-exchange risk and foreign-country risk,[7] factors which are not critical in domestic financial markets. However, in Eurocurrency markets, it is possible to separate these risks. On balance, Eurocurrency markets link the various currencies and countries of the world into a global financial market.

The Foreign-Exchange Market

The Eurocurrency market should not be confused with the **foreign-exchange market.** In the foreign-exchange market, one currency is traded for another, in the Eurocurrency market, international-banking activities take place (i.e., gathering

---

[7] These risks are discussed later in the chapter.

deposits and making loans, usually in Eurodollars). Like the Eurocurrency market, the foreign-exchange market has no central marketplace and transactions are made by telephone or telex. The foreign-exchange market exists because of trade between countries with *different* currencies. That is, exporters prefer not to hold foreign currencies. They want to be paid in their *national* currency. Current quotations for the major exchange rates are available in daily publications such as *The Wall Street Journal* or from major financial institutions. The quoted rates are wholesale ones for amounts of $1 million or more as traded among major banks. Retail transactions typically provide fewer units of foreign currency per dollar.

The foreign-exchange market is dominated by giant commercial banks, domestic and foreign. To provide foreign-exchange services to their customers, these banks take a position (i.e., hold inventories) in the major currencies of the world. Some U.S. banks do this by keeping deposits with foreign banks. In addition to providing for customers' foreign currency needs in either the *spot* or *forward* markets,[8] banks trade for their own account in the foreign-exchange market.

The importance of foreign-exchange income to the major U.S. banks with extensive overseas operations is reflected by the fact that it accounts for 10 percent to 60 percent of their overseas operating income. Foreign-exchange income consists of two components: (1) trading profits or losses and (2) translation gains or losses. The latter refers to gains or losses on all monetary items on the balance sheet as a result of adjustments for exchange-rate movements.[9] The total gain or loss due to revaluation of the balance sheet is entered on the income-expense statement as a gain or a loss. The sum of the translation gain or loss plus the trading profits or losses equals total foreign-exchange income. The variability of foreign-exchange income is a good indicator of the risk involved in foreign-exchange operations. In general, the net international income of the multinational BHCs is highly volatile. In some cases, however, this volatility moves in the opposite direction of total net income, and the overall effect is a stabilizing one.

Coordinated Use of the Eurocurrency and Foreign-Exchange Markets

Interest-arbitrage transactions in the Eurocurrency market can be protected against foreign-exchange risk through the use of the forward-exchange market. The idea is to hedge the exchange risk by using forward-exchange contracts to insure the profitability of the arbitrage transaction. In this context, exchange gains or losses should not be treated as exchange-trading gains or losses, but as adjustments to the interest earnings of the arbitrage transactions.[10] For example, if a Eurodollar loan that nets 1 percent has a corresponding exchange loss on the forward contract of 0.4 percent of the loan, then the net profitability of the arbitrage transaction is 0.6 percent. Forward-exchange contracts can be used to hedge both Eurocurrency interest-arbitrage transactions and spot foreign-exchange transactions. This approach provides protection against unfavorable movements in exchange rates; but, at the same time, it eliminates the possibility of windfall profits due to favorable movements in exchange rates.

---

[8] Transactions in the spot market are for immediate delivery (i.e., usually within two business days), whereas transactions in the forward market are for future delivery at an exchange rate established when the forward contract is signed. The forward market provides a mechanism for hedging against foreign-exchange risk. The concept is identical to using the futures market to hedge against interest-rate risk.

[9] The Financial Accounting Standards Board requires these adjustments as a result of its 1976 ruling, FASB-8.

[10] See Johnson and Lewis (1975), p. 83.

The Eurobond Market

The Eurobond market is the international market for long-term debt; it is *not* the long-term segment of the Eurocurrency market. Eurobonds are similar to domestically issued bonds except that they are not subject to the legal restrictions of the countries in whose currencies the bonds are denominated, provided that the bonds are sold mainly to nonresidents. The most popular currency for Eurobonds is the U.S. dollar. Eurobonds are placed simultaneously in various countries through syndicates of investment or merchant bankers. In terms of dollar-equivalent volume, the Eurobond market is about one-tenth the size of the Eurocurrency market. Compared to the Eurocurrency and foreign-exchange markets, the Eurobond market is of minor importance to international commercial banking.

THE CROSS-BORDER AND CROSS-CURRENCY RISKS OF INTERNATIONAL BANKING

Let's define **international banking** as engaging in financial activities that involve cross-border and **cross-currency** risks. The activities, whether on or off the balance sheet, are for the most part the same whether we are dealing with domestic or international banking. Specifically, they involve traditional commercial banking: accepting deposits and making loans on the balance sheet and arranging contingent commitments off the balance sheet. In addition, without a Glass-Steagall prohibition in the international arena, U.S. multinational banks engage more freely in **investment banking,** which in many foreign countries is called **merchant banking.**

Domestic commercial banking is less complicated than international or cross-currency/cross-border banking because only one currency and one political regime exists. Imagine how much more complicated (and risky) U.S. banking would be if it had to deal with 50 independent political states, each with their own currency. The principles of banking and risk management would not be any different, but dealing with the risks of 50 different currencies and 50 different sovereignties would complicate the analyses. Nevertheless, as the Western European model shows, the task can be managed. To make it even more manageable, however, the European Community is attempting to develop a monetary union—in effect, a United States of Europe.

Figure 20-2 presents a useful 2×2 matrix that categorizes international banking activity.[11] The matrix should be read from the point of view of the country where the bank is located. The northwest cell of the matrix (labeled A) captures "domestic positions." Banks without any international banking activities, such as the thousands of community banks in the United States, engage only in banking with residents in domestic currency. The remaining cells ($B + C + D$) capture international positions either in domestic currency with nonresidents (B) or in foreign currency with residents (C) and nonresidents (D).

Banking with nonresidents in domestic currency (B) is referred to as "traditional foreign positions" because of the "traditional" or historical role of banks providing domestic currency facilities for financing foreign trade. This practice involves keeping corresponding balances with foreign banks. Community banks

---

[11] The matrix and descriptions that follow are from the Monetary and Economics Department of the Bank for International Settlements, Basle (August 1995).

Bank's Assets and Liabilities

	With residents	With nonresidents
In domestic currency	A	B
In foreign currency	C	D

A = domestic positions
B = traditional foreign positions
C + D = Foreign-currency positions
B + D = external or cross-border positions
B + C + D = international positions

Source: Adapted from Monetary and Economics Department of the Bank for International Settlements, Basle (August 1995), p. 4.

FIGURE 20-2 **Categories of International Banking Activity**

typically use their domestic correspondent banks to tap foreign currency markets for their customers.

Foreign-currency positions ($C + D$), such as Eurocurrency, reflect those assets and liabilities denominated in foreign currency conducted with both residents and nonresidents. With the development of offshore-banking facilities, especially in the United States and Japan, the distinction between C and D has become blurred. As a result, the term "international bank credit," which covers business in both domestic and foreign currencies with nonresidents and business in foreign currencies with residents, has increased in use.

Bank business with nonresidents generates external or cross-border positions ($B + D$) in either domestic or foreign currency. The Bank for International Settlement (BIS) collects this information for two purposes: to improve the recording of balance-of-payments transactions (for statistical purposes) and to gauge the extent of banks' involvement in balance-of-payments financing (for analytical purposes).

COUNTRY (SOVEREIGN CREDIT) RISK

According to Walter Wriston, "Countries don't go bankrupt." Sometimes, however, countries cannot or will not repay their bank loans, and that is bad news for banks. The LDC debt crisis discussed above is a classic example. Another famous example is Lenin's decision in 1916, following the Russian Revolution, not to honor the Czar's bonds (Lindsey [1996]). The price of that decision was that Communist Russia (the USSR) was not able to borrow in world capital markets for 80 years. In February 1996, Russia announced the first international underwriting of its government bonds since 1916. According to Lindsey [1996], Lenin probably did not take his decision to default lightly but as a rational calculation of costs and benefits. By repudiating Russia's debt, he freed financial resources to continue the revolution and feed the population. The globalization of financial markets and its accompanying imposition of discipline make it less likely that a Lenin-type decision in the twenty-first century would be in favor of repudiation. That is, the costs of being cut off from access to international credit and the consequences for the capacity to trade are likely to exceed the benefits of repudiation.

The uncertainty about repayment of cross-border loans is called **country or sovereign risk,** and it is, of course, a credit or default risk. Cross-border loans also involve exchange-rate or cross-currency risk. In addition, depending on how the loan is priced (fixed versus floating rate), the lender also may face interest-rate risk. Because interest rates are driven in part by inflationary expectations, a country's record for monetary discipline becomes an important consideration. The interaction between interest-rate risk and default risk must also be considered. For example, floating-rate LDC loans hampered the ability of LDCs to repay their debts in an inflationary environment.

As noted in our analyses of domestic default risk (chapters 2, 6, 10–12), deflation (of energy, farm, and commercial-real-estate prices) has been much more lethal as a destroyer of bank credit quality than inflation. With central bankers focused on controlling inflation through monetary discipline, this cause of credit difficulties is often overlooked. For example, the worldwide decline in energy and farm prices was a major cause of financial difficulties in LDCs, not to mention the financial havoc wreaked on the energy and farm belts of the United States. On balance, a bank does not have to be directly engaged in international banking for its operations to be affected by the international economy.

Whenever a financial institution transacts business across a national border or in a foreign currency, it is directly exposed to transfer and convertibility risks, another way of describing country risk, which also is called *political risk.* Even though foreign borrowers may be willing and able to repay their debts, exchange controls may prevent loans from being repaid because of the inability of borrowers to obtain and transfer currency. Alternatively, borrowers, including countries, may exhibit an unwillingness to repay their debts and may take the position that their loans should be restructured or renegotiated, as many LDCs did in the 1980s.

Country credit risk, like domestic credit risk, is manifested in the form of nonperforming assets. If a U.S. bank is not paid within 90 days, for whatever reason, the loan or asset must be placed on a cash basis, and interest previously accrued but not paid must be deducted from current earnings. Because nonaccrual loans adversely affect bank earnings, they can also adversely affect a bank's equity capital, other things being equal. In a nutshell, country risk can reduce shareholder wealth.

In credit analysis, the lender's job is to attempt to determine the probability that a loan, domestic or foreign, will be repaid. The five Cs of credit analysis apply to countries as well as businesses and individuals. Recall them as

- Character (reputation)
- Capacity (cash flow)
- Capital (real net worth)
- Collateral (security)
- Conditions (vulnerability to economic fluctuations)

The only difference in credit scoring between domestic and foreign loans is that foreign loans are more complex to analyze because of cross-currency risk and sovereign risk. If borrowers' cash flows and collateral asset values are sensitive to exchange rates, in addition to movements in input/output prices, interest rates, and government policies, modeling borrowers' repayment abilities requires complex contingent-pricing frameworks.

Application of Classification Techniques

From a statistical point of view, the development of a credit-scoring model for countries is similar to the approach used to develop a credit-scoring model for consumers or a bankruptcy-prediction model for firms (see chapter 10). In the country-risk area, "good" and "bad" observations can be separated on the basis of whether borrowers have ever rescheduled their debt. Because these groups should be distinct and identifiable, the application of binomial-response techniques like MDA, probit, or logit would be appropriate (see Altman, Avery, Eisenbeis, and Sinkey [1981]). The next step would be to develop a set of variables capable of discriminating between the groups and predicting which countries are likely to reschedule debt in the future. The types of variables typically used in such models are (1) international reserves/imports, (2) the debt service ratio, (3) IMF reserve position/imports, (4) exports/GNP, and (5) the inflation rate. In general, balance-of-payments statistics and other financial data are employed.

The supervisory approach to foreign lending employs statistical indicators for limited screening purposes in identifying high-risk countries. The purpose of the technique is to flag countries that have large current account deficits, heavy external debt service, or low international reserve positions. Given these country ratings, a bank's exposure to a country can be evaluated more thoroughly and accurately. As always, however, the use of statistical classification models must be tempered by the judgment of the financial manager in making risk–return decisions or by the judgment of the regulator in making safety-and-soundness decisions.

FOREIGN-EXCHANGE (CROSS-CURRENCY) RISK

Banks incur **foreign-exchange risk** in two ways: (1) by holding long or short positions in foreign currencies arising from dealer or trader activities, and (2) by holding assets and liabilities denominated in foreign currencies that are not equal. When a bank's net exposure is different from zero (long > 0, short < 0), it either gains or loses from unexpected changes in exchange rates. The more volatile exchange rates are, the more risky such exposures are. **Net exposure** (NET) in a foreign currency (FX) can be expressed as:

$$NET = [A(FX) - L(FX)] + NTP(FX) \qquad \text{(20-1)}$$

where

$$A(FX) = \text{book assets denominated in foreign currency } FX$$
$$L(FX) = \text{book liabilities denominated in foreign currency } FX$$
$$NTP(FX) = \text{the net trading position in foreign currency } FX$$
$$= FX \text{ bought} - FX \text{ sold}$$

The net booked position $[A(FX) - L(FX)]$ is akin to the maturity or duration gap position discussed with reference to the management of interest-rate risk (chapter 5). Foreign financial assets and liabilities are similar to domestic financial assets (securities, loans, and interbank deposits) and liabilities (deposits, CDs, interbank loans), except that they are denominated in a foreign currency.

Net trading positions arise from buying and selling currencies for customers and for the bank's own account. Banks engage in four major trading activities: They conduct two different activities for their customers: the buying and selling of foreign currency (1) to facilitate international trade and (2) to permit investment in foreign financial and real assets. Banks trade for their own account by buying or selling foreign currency either (3) to hedge or (4) to speculate. Closely related to these four trading activities is the supplying of risk-management services to corporate customers and high-net-worth individuals (e.g., Ross Perot) through the use of currency and interest-rate derivatives. The objective is to generate fee income. However, if the risk accepted by the bank is not "laid off" or offset by a counter-balancing transaction, then the bank is speculating that its view of future currency and interest-rate movements will be more accurate than the customer's forecast. In such a situation, serious ethical questions (chapter 17) arise about conflicts of interest and bank-customer relationships.

Banks that are matched or balanced ($NET = 0$) have immunized a particular foreign-currency portfolio from unexpected changes in FX. A bank's overall net position requires that the net positions across all FX be aggregated. When $NET = 0$, no foreign-exchange risk exists. When $NET > 0$, the position is described as "net long," which is vulnerable to unexpected depreciation in the value of the foreign currency (FX). When $NET < 0$, the position is described as "net short," which is vulnerable to unexpected appreciation in the value of the foreign currency (FX). The gain or loss ΔV in a particular foreign-currency position can be expressed as

$$\Delta V = NET \times [S(t) - S(t - 1)] \tag{20-2}$$

where

$S(t)$ = the spot foreign-exchange rate at time t and

$S(t - 1)$ = the spot foreign-exchange rate at time $t - 1$

If $NET = 0$ or if exchange rates do not vary, then no FX risk exists. Net exposure equal to zero requires a joint condition that $A(FX) = L(FX)$ and $NTP = 0$, or that a long position in one activity offsets a short position in the other. This kind of hedge would be accomplished on the balance sheet. If for business or other reasons a bank could not achieve an on-balance-sheet hedge, it could use off-balance-sheet techniques using currency derivatives such as futures, forwards, options, and swaps to hedge (or to speculate).

The following example illustrates equations (20-1) and (20-2) for FX BANCO, a Mexican bank whose domestic currency is the peso but which has exposure to the U.S. dollar (in millions) such that

$$NET = \$100 - \$90 + \$10 = \$20$$

and

$$\Delta V = \$20 \times [7.7519(\text{pesos/\$}) - 7.8493(\text{pesos/\$}] = -1,947,787 \text{ pesos}$$

Given the long dollar position, BANCO is exposed to a decline in the value of the dollar vis-à-vis the peso. When the dollar depreciates or becomes cheaper to Mexicans, BANCO loses 1,947,787 pesos, or $251,266, at an *FX* of 7.7519 pesos to the dollar.[12] BANCO had two ways to prevent the loss: set $NET = 0$ on its balance

---

[12] The number of units of a local currency (peso in this case) that can be exchanged for one unit of foreign currency ($) is called a *direct quote;* the number of units of foreign currency ($) that can be exchanged for one unit of local currency is called an *indirect quote.*

sheet or use currency derivatives to hedge its exposure (e.g., shorting the dollar in the futures market).

BANK ASSET-LIABILITY MANAGEMENT (ALM) IN A GLOBAL CONTEXT

Because the business of banking is the measuring, managing, and accepting of risk, the heart of bank financial management is risk management. One of the most important risk-management functions in banking is asset-liability management or ALM (chapter 5). It is the coordinated management of a bank's balance sheet to allow for alternative interest-rate, liquidity, and prepayment scenarios. When a bank has a global book or balance sheet, which can be viewed as the sum of its domestic book plus its foreign book, then it must also be prepared for alternative exchange-rate scenarios. Three techniques of **global ALM** are

- On-balance-sheet matching of assets and liabilities in terms of repricing (interest-rate risk) and net exposure to foreign currencies (exchange-rate risk)
- Off-balance-sheet hedging of one or more on-balance-sheet risks (foreign-exchange, interest-rate, and credit risks)
- Securitization, which removes risk from the balance sheet by selling assets (This technique, however, has limited applicability in global ALM because securitization has been confined mainly to U.S. markets.)

Allowing for alternative foreign-exchange, interest-rate, liquidity, and prepayment scenarios is the stuff of global ALM. Clearly, it is more complex than managing a domestic book.

Although the objective of ALM should be to add value to the bank, and although bank managers need to think of ALM in such a context, global ALM tends to focus on two variables: (1) an accounting measure expressed in dollar form as equation (20-1), but in aggregate form to capture the gain or loss from all major currency exposures, and (2) an economic measure expressed as the market value of (bank or portfolio) equity (MVE). The latter, of course, aligns with the economic model of the firm whereas the former aligns with the accounting model of the firm.

To conceptualize the effects of exchange-rate risk on bank value, let's reintroduce the notion of a risk profile (chapter 5). Consider a bank whose foreign book is exposed to only one FX and that is net long based on equation (20-1). It is vulnerable to unexpected depreciation in the value of the foreign currency. When a bank is net short it is vulnerable to unexpected appreciation in the value of the foreign currency. The gain or loss ΔV in a particular currency position can be expressed as equation (20-2). Here, however, we are concerned with the change in the value of the bank's equity. Figure 20-3 shows the **risk profiles** for a bank that is net long in FX (Panel A) and for a bank that is net short in FX (Panel B).

Faced with the problem of multiple currencies, the simple risk profiles in Figure 20-3 do not capture the enormous task of global ALM in a multinational bank. Suffice it to say, however, that if the books/portfolios in all foreign currencies are matched, or if not matched then hedged, then the bank's value will be immunized against unexpected changes in foreign currencies, all other things being equal. In terms of equation (20-1), global ALM managers focus on balancing assets and liabilities in a particular currency and hedging major imbalances; in contrast, foreign-currency traders attempt to generate trading profits while restricting their exposures

Panel A. A bank net long in FX

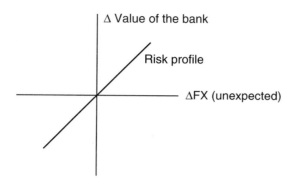

Panel B. A bank net short in FX

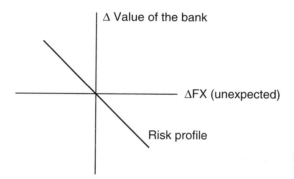

FIGURE 20-3 Global ALM and Bank Risk Profiles

to something less than Leeson proportions.[13] With proper internal controls, banks can prevent rogue traders from betting and busting the bank as in the case of Barings Bank of London.

As a practical matter and from a strategic-planning perspective (chapter 4), the goal of global ALM may be expressed as maintaining a competitive ROA or ROE or ensuring that the bank has adequate capital, both financial and reputational. The strong capital-adequacy positions of major U.S. banks are captured by the BIS capital ratios in Table 20-1. In addition, strategic choices regarding international products, markets, and company structure need to be linked to global ALM. Practical aspects of global ALM focus on the rates, volumes, and mixes of exchange-rate sensitive assets and liabilities over the short run. Simulation models permit global ALM managers to estimate the effects of different portfolio strategies and different exchange-rate scenarios on accounting and economic variables.

U.S. COMMERCIAL BANKS WITH FOREIGN OFFICES

The go-go era for international activity for U.S. multinational banks was the late 1960s and the early 1970s, when recycling petrodollars was a big game. International banking activity slowed down considerably during the mid-1970s when the

---

[13] Nick Leeson [1996] was the rogue trader in Singapore whose enormous derivatives exposures resulted in huge losses that caused the failure of Barings Bank of London.

1974 credit crunch, the REIT crisis, and failures of the Bankhaus Herstatt of Germany and Franklin National Bank of New York raised some concerns about safety and soundness below the top tier international banks. Following this setback, international banking activity picked up again, only to be flattened by a series of events, including the international debt crisis of the 1980s, Continental Illinois's liquidity crisis and bailout in 1984, and the massive bank restructurings associated with bad loans related to LDCs, highly leveraged transactions (HLTs), and commercial real estate.

As we have seen in previous chapters, off-balance-sheet activities (OBSAs) grew substantially in the 1980s and 1990s. These activities are the domain mainly of the largest banks, such as BankAmerica, Bankers Trust, Chase Manhattan, Citicorp, and J. P. Morgan. Many OBSAs are international banking activities, including foreign-exchange transactions, international money transfers, documentary letters of credit, Euronote issuance facilities, Eurocommercial paper, and derivatives, especially swaps based on exchange rates or interest rates or both. During the years 1993 to 1995, derivatives had a temporary reputational setback (i.e., no systemic risk) because isolated cases revealed lack of internal controls at both buyers and sellers (banks) of these contracts. Four of the most notorious cases involved Metalgesselschaft (Germany), Procter & Gamble (U.S.), Bankers Trust (New York), and Barings Bank (London/Singapore). Clearly, the problems were truly international in their dispersion, although they were not systemic or related in any way.

Although only about 500 or so U.S. banks hold any derivatives contracts, even fewer banks have foreign operations. As of December 31, 1995, only 200 U.S. commercial banks, 2 percent of the population of 9,941 banks, had foreign offices. Although the percentage is about the same, the number of banks with foreign offices is down from 235 at mid-year 1990. Consolidation among major banks explains the decline. Asset growth at foreign offices of U.S. banks is up, however, and it has outstripped domestic asset growth. For example, from the end of 1990 to the end of 1995, assets in foreign offices grew at 8.5 percent per annum compared to domestic growth of only 4.9 percent. At year-end 1995, total assets in foreign offices were $585 billion compared to total industry assets of $4.3 trillion.

The differences between domestic and international/foreign banking for U.S. banks are captured succinctly by the abbreviated income-expense statements shown in Table 20-4. Both dollar amounts and ratios relative to total assets are presented. Three ratios, which capture the heart of traditional commercial banking, tell the story:

- Net interest margin—lower in international markets because of greater competition
- Provision for loan loss—lower in international markets because of better loan quality
- Burden (net noninterest income)—lower in international markets because operations are more efficient (lower noninterest expense), because of less dependency on brick-and-mortar branches and fewer personnel

A brief comment on each of these financial characteristics provides further insight regarding the major differences between domestic and international banking:

A lower NIM is not, of course, what international bankers want, but it is what international markets dictate. Unlike domestic deposit markets, international bankers cannot tap low-cost core deposits to fund their asset portfolios. In addition, competition and stronger credit quality dictate lower (safer) loan rates.

The wholesale nature of international banking is a major reason for its superior loan quality compared to that of domestic banking (e.g., the high loss rates associated with credit-card loans, for which banks are handsomely rewarded; chapter

TABLE 20-4	Abbreviated Income-Expense Statements Comparing Foreign and Domestic Banking Operations of U.S. Banks, December 31, 1995			
	All Commercial Banks		**Foreign Offices of Banks**	
Item	*$ Millions*	*% of Assets*	*$ Millions*	*% of Assets*
Interest income	302,663	7.02	44,927	7.67
Interest expense	148,441	3.44	33,474	5.72
Net interest income	154,222	3.58	11,453	1.95
Provision for loan loss[a]	12,550	0.29	836	0.14
Noninterest income	82,440	1.91	11,282	1.93
Noninterest expense	149,670	3.47	13,479	2.30
Net income[b]	48,835	1.13	5,664	0.97
Memo:				
Burden	−67,230	−1.56	−2,197	−0.37

Note: [a]PLL includes allocated transfer risk. [b]Net income does not equal the sum of the previous items because the statement is abbreviated. Burden = net noninterest income = (noninterest income − noninterest expense). Total assets are $4.3 trillion (all banks) and $585 billion (foreign offices).

Source: Statistics on Banking [1995], Table RI-1, p. C-18, FDIC.

11). Figure 20-4 shows how loan-loss provisions have varied for the United States, Britain, France, and Japan over the years 1989 to 1995. The trend in PLL for Japanese banks explains why they have had major financial difficulties during the 1990s.

Bankers running domestic operations would give their eyeteeth for the burden ratios obtained by foreign offices. Note that the driver here is not higher noninterest or fee income per dollar of assets (they are almost identical) but greater cost efficiency. In international banking markets, the wholesale nature of transactions does not dictate a physical presence vis-à-vis brick and mortar; they do, however, dictate a reputational presence. U.S. money-center banks have long been noted for their reputational capital, and more recently, as Table 20-1 shows, for their strong capital positions (BIS ratios).

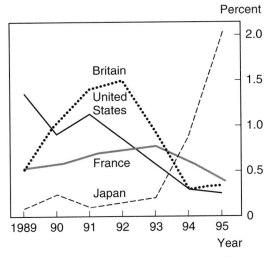

Primary source: IBCA. *Secondary source: The Economist* [1996], August 10, p. 58.

FIGURE 20-4 **Loan-Loss Provisions across Four Major Countries, 1989–1995 (as a percentage of total assets)**

International Banking: Traditional Money-Center Banks versus Superregional Banks

International or global banking is obviously not important to the day-to-day operations of the 20,000 or so community banks, thrifts, and credit unions in the United States. When these institutions need international banking services for their customers, they can go through large correspondent banks or direct customers to international institutions. The major U.S. players in global banking are the traditional money-center banks such as BankAmerica, Bankers Trust, Chase Manhattan, Citicorp, and J. P. Morgan. The new superregional banks such as NationsBank and Banc One do not have the international presence of the traditional money-center banks. To illustrate the differences, the next two sections compare the international operations of a money-center bank (Citicorp) with a superregional bank (NationsBank).

Citicorp: A Worldwide Player in the FSI

As a global financial-services firm, Citicorp views itself as serving two constituencies: individuals and institutions. As Table 20-5 shows, Citicorp's loan portfolio of almost $166 billion at year-end 1995 (64% of its total assets) consisted of $94 billion in offices outside the United States (57% of its total loan portfolio and 36% of its total assets). Its consumer loans are almost evenly divided between domestic ($55 billion) and foreign ($51 billion) business. In both sectors, consumer loans are dominated by installment and revolving credit ($32 billion in each). Citicorp's massive credit-card operations drive its global consumer business.

In contrast to its global balance in consumer lending, the bulk of Citicorp's commercial loans are held in offices outside the United States ($42 billion, 70% of commercial loans and 16% of total assets). Three out of every four dollars of Citicorp's foreign commercial loans are commercial-and-industrial (C&I) loans, compared to only one out of every two dollars on the domestic side. The imbalance between the consumer and commercial businesses across domestic and foreign markets reflects the greater development of capital markets in the United States, where direct-finance substitutes in the form of commercial paper and corporate bonds have displaced bank C&I lending.

To finance its $257 billion in total assets, Citicorp relies mainly on deposits held in offices outside the United States, where it raised $117 billion (45% of assets) at year-end 1995. Ninety-three percent of these deposits ($109 billion) were interest-bearing funds—lower-cost transactions accounts are scarcer items in foreign markets. Citicorp held $13 billion in non-interest-bearing deposits and $37 billion in interest-bearing deposits in U.S. offices at year-end 1995. It is interesting to note that Citicorp's loan-to-deposit ratio, a traditional measure of liquidity and safety, was 99 percent at year-end 1995. The ratio for funds in U.S. offices was 118 percent, compared to 90 percent for funds in offices outside the United States. Since Citicorp's operations are not traditional in any sense, don't put too much stock in these figures. The nature of the business of funding loans for multinational banks is to rely extensively on nondeposit sources of funding to supplement traditional deposit gathering. For example, at year-end 1995, Citicorp held $16 billion in purchase funds, $17 billion in long-term debt, and $10 billion in other liabilities. Adding these sources to its deposits generates a ratio of loans to deposits + purchased funds of 78 percent [165/(167 + 43)]. In terms of liquidity and liability management, Citicorp has the ability to tap money and capital markets, both domestic and foreign (chapter 11).

TABLE 20-5   Citicorp's Loan Portfolio: In U.S. Offices versus Offices Outside the United States

In Millions of Dollars at Year-End	1995	1994
Consumer Loans		
In U.S. offices		
Mortgage and real estate[abc]	$ 22,604	$ 21,089
Installment, revolving credit, and other	32,429	29,523
Lease financing	—	32
	55,033	50,644
In offices outside the United States		
Mortgage and real estate[ad]	18,240	16,830
Installment, revolving credit, and other	32,521	29,303
Lease financing	765	732
	51,526	46,865
	106,559	97,509
Unearned income	(916)	(909)
Consumer loans—net	$105,643	$ 96,600
Commercial Loans		
In U.S. offices		
Commercial and industrial[e]	$ 9,509	$ 10,236
Mortgage and real estate[a]	4,681	5,616
Loans to financial institutions	365	297
Lease financing	3,239	3,271
	17,794	19,420
In offices outside the United States		
Commercial and industrial[e]	32,966	27,120
Mortgage and real estate[a]	1,901	1,995
Loans to financial institutions	4,229	3,263
Governments and official institutions	2,180	3,265
Lease financing	1,098	934
	42,374	36,577
	60,168	55,997
Unearned income	(169)	(177)
Commercial loans—net	$ 59,999	$ 55,820

[a]Loans secured primarily by real estate.

[b]Includes $3.8 billion in 1995 and $4.0 billion in 1994 of commercial real estate loans related to community banking and private banking activities.

[c]Includes $3.0 billion and $1.7 billion of residential mortgage loans held for sale and carried at the lower of aggregate cost or market value as of December 31, 1995, and 1994, respectively.

[d]Includes $2.5 billion in 1995 and $2.4 billion in 1994 of loans secured by commercial real estate.

[e]Includes loans not otherwise separately categorized.

Source: Citicorp Annual Report [1995], p. 54.

At year-end 1985 Citicorp's gross consumer loans in domestic offices totaled $49 billion compared to only $11 billion in foreign offices. Over the next 10 years, consumer loans in domestic offices grew at an annual rate of only 1.2 percent, whereas consumer loans in foreign offices grew at a rate of 16.7 percent. On the commercial side, Citicorp originated $21 billion in loans in domestic offices and $37.6 billion in foreign offices. Over the next 10 years, commercial loans in domestic offices decayed at an annual rate of 1.6 percent, whereas those in foreign offices grew at a rate of 1.2 percent. These trends are indicative of where growth opportunities lie. As capital markets continue to develop both in the United States and outside it, the prospect of lending to major corporations will continue to dim. Accordingly, banks will have to look at the middle market and small businesses for commercial-lending opportunities. On the consumer side the relevant question is how long double-digit growth can be maintained.

To replace lost on-balance-sheet business, major banks like Citicorp have turned to **derivatives** and the provision of risk-management services as potential growth businesses. Table 20-6 shows the derivative and foreign-exchange contracts held by Citicorp at year-end 1995. These instruments can be used for trading, dealing, or hedging (called end-user contracts in the case of ALM hedging). In the case of Citicorp, end-user contracts for hedging on-balance-sheet risks are relatively small at only 4.8 percent of foreign-exchange products ($58 billion of $1.2 trillion) and 13.7 percent of interest-rate products ($156 billion of $1.1 trillion). Thus, the bulk of Citicorp's derivatives businesses, mainly conducted by Citibank, are designed to generate trading profits and fees from the provision of risk-management services. For 1995, Citicorp reported noninterest revenue of $8.7 billion compared to $3 billion for 1985, annual growth of 11 percent. In contrast, interest revenue grew at an annual rate of only 1.7 percent, from $19.5 billion for 1985 to $23 billion for 1995. These differences in accounting flows reflect the differences in the underlying balance-sheet characteristics described above.

TABLE 20-6   Derivative and Foreign-Exchange Contracts Held by Citicorp

In Billions of Dollars at Year-End	*Notional Principal Amounts*		*Balance Sheet Credit Exposure*[a]	
	1995	*1994*	*1995*	*1994*
Interest rate products				
Futures contracts	$145.2	$175.2	$ —	$ —
Forward contracts	295.2	561.3	0.6	0.6
Swap agreements	431.9	367.5	9.1	6.0
Purchased options	105.9	110.2	1.2	1.7
Written options	158.1	105.7	—	—
Foreign exchange products				
Futures contracts	1.1	0.1	—	—
Forward contracts	983.5	1,153.0	12.2	14.9
Cross-currency swap agreements	35.2	33.8	2.0	2.2
Purchase options	93.7	63.6	1.8	1.3
Written options	88.2	66.2	—	—
Commodity and equity products	38.0	28.0	0.9	0.8
			27.8	27.5
Effects of master netting agreements[b]			(11.7)	(7.0)
			$16.1	$20.5

[a]There is no balance sheet credit exposure for futures contracts because they settle daily in cash, and none for written options because they represent obligations (rather than assets) of Citicorp.

[b]Master netting agreements mitigate credit risk by permitting the offset of amounts due from and to individual counterparties in the event of counterparty default.

Source: Citicorp Annual Report [1995], p. 57.

The phenomenal growth of derivatives is captured by looking at the trend in interest-rate swaps. On December 31, 1985, Citicorp reported interest-rate swaps of $36.4 billion (notional value or the underlying principal amount, which is not reflective of actual credit-risk exposure—see Table 20-6). By year-end 1995, interest-rate swaps had grown to $432 billion, an annual rate of expansion of 28 percent. Citicorp estimated the balance-sheet credit exposure of these contracts to be $9.1 billion, or 46 percent of its equity capital. After adjusting for master netting agreements, Citicorp's net credit exposure for all derivative and foreign-exchange contracts at year-end 1995 was $16.1 billion (Table 20-6), or 82 percent of its equity capital.

U.S. Superregional Banks: Not Yet Worldwide Players

Although superregional banks such as Banc One (Columbus, OH), KeyCorp (Cleveland, OH), and NationsBank (Charlotte, NC) have made it into the ranks of the largest banks in the United States, they are not major players on a global basis. We use NationsBank to illustrate how U.S. superregional banks pale in relation to Citicorp and other traditional money-center banks when it comes to presence on the international scene.

At year-end 1995, NationsBank had slightly less than $13 billion in foreign time deposits, which funded 6.9 percent of its total assets of $187 billion. Its foreign loans were even smaller at $2.2 billion, only 1.1 percent of its total assets. In terms of derivatives, NationsBank held $788 million (notional value) of interest-rate contracts as a dealer but only $157 million in foreign-exchange contracts as a dealer. NationsBank also held $24.3 billion in interest-rate swaps as part of its ALM (end-user). Its credit-risk exposure across all derivatives-dealer positions was $3.8 billion, or 30 percent of shareholders' equity.

To summarize, the dominant U.S. players in multinational banking are still the traditional money-center banks such as BankAmerica, Bankers Trust, Chase Manhattan, Citicorp, and J. P. Morgan. Although some new banking companies (superregionals) have become multibillion-dollar institutions, they have not yet become major multinational players.

FOREIGN BANKS IN THE UNITED STATES[14]

Foreign banks from 68 countries play a substantial role in the U.S. financial-services industry (FSI). Almost all of the 50 largest banks in the world (excluding U.S.-owned banks) have commercial banking operations in the United States. Panel A of Table 20-7 shows the various organizational forms that foreign banks use to tap U.S. markets and the total assets held by each type of entity. The table also provides additional insight regarding the delivery systems for international banking discussed earlier in this chapter. Branches and agencies of foreign banks are the most popular organizational form, with 559 in existence at year-end 1994. These entities held $750 billion in assets and accounted for about one-third of business lending in the United States. As of June 30, 1995, Bank of Tokyo was the top foreign lender to U.S. businesses ($15.7 billion) whereas Mitsubishi Bank held the most assets ($50.3 billion in six U.S. offices). Since then, Bank of Tokyo and Mitsubishi merged

---

[14] This section draws on General Accounting Office [1996a], Kraus and Cacace [1996], and Phillips [1995].

TABLE 20-7   The Operations of Foreign Banks in the United States

Panel A. *The Organizational Forms Used by Foreign Banks Operating in the United States and their Assets, December 1994 (dollars in billions)*

Forms of Organization	Number	Assets
Branches and agencies	559	$750
Subsidiary banks	97	165
Commercial lending companies	4	1
Edge Act corporations	11	1
Representative offices	250	0
Total, U.S. offices	921	$917
Shell branches, managed by U.S. offices	142	293[a]
Total	1,063	$1,210

Note: Numbers may not add to total because of rounding.

[a] Of the $293 billion, $113 billion represented claims on U.S. addresses other than to related depositories, $84 billion represented claims on related depositories in the United States, $12 billion represented claims on U.S. addresses denominated in currencies other than U.S. dollars, and $85 billion represented claims on non-U.S. addresses.

Source: Federal Reserve.

Panel B. *Sources and Uses of Funds in Foreign Branches, Agencies, and Shell Branches, December 1994 (dollars in billions)*

Sources/Uses of Funds	Funds Raised	Funds Used	Difference
Transactions with customers with U.S. addresses	$357	$475	−$118
Transactions with customers with non-U.S. addresses	340	190	150
Transactions with customers whose locations are unknown	162	218	−56
Transactions with parent bank and related depositories	184	160	24

Source: Call report data.

on 1 April 1996 to form the largest bank in the world, Bank of Tokyo-Mitsubishi Ltd., as shown in Table 20-1.

Overall, foreign banks operated 1,063 various organizational forms controlling over $1.2 trillion in assets, which account for almost one out of every four dollars of U.S. banking assets. Excluding shell branches, the total assets held by foreign banks operating in the United States have grown from about $20 billion at year-end 1972 to over $900 billion at year-end 1994. The annual growth of 19 percent suggests why foreign banks like to operate in the United States. Foreign banks operating in the United States are subject to the same rules and regulations as U.S. banks and have access to the same opportunities—the policy of national treatment. For example, under the Riegle-Neal Interstate Banking and Branching Efficiency Act of 1994, a foreign bank may acquire subsidiary banks nationwide on the same basis as a U.S. bank holding company. Moreover, any U.S. bank subsidiary controlled by a foreign bank may branch to the same extent as other U.S. banks (i.e., nationwide).

Panel B of Table 20-7 shows the sources and uses of funds by the branches, agencies, and shell branches of foreign banks operating in the United States as of

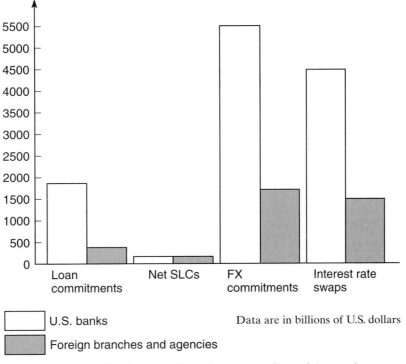

U.S. banks

Foreign branches and agencies

Data are in billions of U.S. dollars

Primary source: Bank call reports. *Secondary source:* General Accounting
Office [1996], Figure 2-3, p. 33.

**FIGURE 20-5 Selected Bank Off-Balance-Sheet Activities at Foreign Branches
and Agencies Compared to U.S. Banks, December 1994**

year-end 1994. Based on transactions with customers with U.S. addresses, foreign
banks ran a deficit, because uses exceeded sources by $118 billion. Sources of funds
from customers with non-U.S. addresses and from the parent organization and related depositories financed the shortfall. In addition to on-balance-sheet activities,
foreign branches and agencies engage in off-balance-sheet activities (OBSAs). For
selected derivatives contracts, Figure 20-5 compares the extent of these activities
with those of U.S. banks and reveals why the major U.S. banks rule the world of
derivatives. The chart also shows that credit-related OBSAs (e.g., loan commitments and standby letters of credit, SLCs) pale in relation to FX commitments and
interest-rate swaps.

EFFICIENCY AND INNOVATION
IN INTERNATIONAL BANKING MARKETS

Necessity, as the adage goes, is the mother of invention. Banking and finance, of
course, focus on the profitable application of inventions, or innovations. In efficient
markets, opportunities for innovations are unrestricted. Because international financial markets are among the most competitive and efficient in the world, they
present numerous opportunities for innovation. For example, the international
debt crisis created opportunities for new visions of commercial financing for less
developed countries (LDCs) whereas the collapse of the USSR created opportunities

for intermediaries and capital markets to finance economies in transition from central planning to market-driven allocations. In addition, the development and phenomenal growth of derivatives have been for the most part aimed at international markets and led by commercial banks in the United States.

The internationalization or globalization of financial institutions and markets is one of the most interesting and topical areas of banking and finance. Anticipated advances in technology and financial innovations promise to keep this area an interesting and topical one for many years to come.

Chapter Summary

This chapter assumes that the fundamental principles of financial management that guide a bank's international operations are no different from those applied to its domestic operations. Although the analysis certainly is more complex because of the need to consider cross-border and cross-currency risks, the analytical tools are the same. In this regard, international banking and finance simply focuses on the financial management of a more complex set of risk-return relationships (e.g., as in **global ALM**) than the one found in domestic banking and finance. The important international banking markets are the **Eurocurrency, foreign-exchange, and derivatives markets.**

The major U.S. banks, as exemplified by BankAmerica, Bankers Trust, Chase Manhattan, Citicorp, and J. P. Morgan, are multinational corporations that depend heavily on international markets for gathering deposits, making loans, supplying investment or merchant banking services, and trading and dealing derivatives. Because the Glass-Steagall Act, which separates commercial and investment banking in the United States, does not apply to the international activities of U.S. banks, investment banking (or merchant banking as it is called in the U.K. and other European countries) plays an important role in the international business of major U.S. banks. The dominant role that major U.S. commercial and investment banks have played in the **globalization** of the financial-services industry supports the argument that the phenomenon is simply the **Americanization** of world financial markets. Globalization is of course a two-way street and the U.S. policy of **national treatment** of foreign banks has created opportunities for foreign banks to play a major role in U.S. banking and financial markets. Although global wholesale finance captures the traditional business focus of the world's largest banks, global retail banking is increasing in importance.

A global financial system is the institutional setting that has been developing for many years to accommodate the worldwide production of goods and services. **Technology** and the dissemination of **information** and ideas have been the driving forces for globalization in both the real sector, where goods and services are produced, and the financial sector, where institutions and markets facilitate the financing of the real sector. These changes have dramatically altered the nature of output, especially in the United States, from the physical (e.g., manufacturing) to the conceptual (e.g., services).

Key Words, Concepts, and Acronyms

- Americanization
- Country (sovereign or cross-border) risk
- Cross-currency risk
- Delivery systems of international banking
- Derivatives
- Eurocurrency market
- Eurodollar

- Floating-rate loan (LIBOR-linked)
- Foreign banks (in the United States)
- Foreign-exchange (FX) market
- Foreign-exchange (cross-currency) risk
- Global ALM
- Global financial system
- Globalization
- Information
- International banking
- International debt crisis
- Investment banking
- Less-developed country (LDC)
- London interbank offer rate (LIBOR)
- Merchant banking
- National treatment (policy of)
- Net exposure in a currency
- Off-balance-sheet activities (OBSAs)
- Risk profile
- Technology
- The Twilight of Sovereignty
- U.S. commercial banks with foreign offices

Review/Discussion Questions

1. What is a global financial system and what have been the forces driving its development?

2. Who wrote *The Twilight of Sovereignty?* What is the heart of the author's vision of the future? Do you agree or disagree with it?

3. What are some reasons why U.S. financial-services firms dominate world markets? Are we witnessing globalization of world financial markets or simply the Americanization of these markets?

4. Regarding the dominance of U.S. commercial and investment banks in world markets, evaluate and comment on the following:

   > Some Europeans rebel at the "barbarity" of spartan American business mores, which include power breakfasts and banned alcohol at lunch. One Dutch student says: Americans work too hard; they work six, seven days a week. When they go out to dinner, they take their beepers; when it goes off, they go back to their offices.

5. Consider the following statistics:

   - In 1980, the U.S. federal-funds market (i.e., the domestic interbank loan market) was $74 billion; by 1995, it had more than doubled, to $170 billion, an annual growth of 5.6 percent. The international bank lending market, with a volume of $5.8 trillion (June 1995), dwarfs the U.S. federal-funds market.

   - In 1995 turnover in the foreign-exchange market was estimated at $1.2 trillion per day, almost double the 1989 figure.

   - On 31 March 1995 the notional amount of outstanding OTC derivatives was $41 trillion.

   Do you draw a doomsday scenario from these facts? Why or why not? What are the risks? Be sure to distinguish between firm-specific and systemic credit risk. What are the twin objectives of central bankers according to Greenspan? What is his suggestion for controlling systemic risk?

6. How do domestic and international banking differ? Use Figure 20-2 and Table 20-4 in your explanation.

7. What are the various delivery systems of international banking?

8. Briefly but carefully distinguish among the Eurocurrency market, the foreign-exchange market, and the Eurobond market. What is a Eurodollar? What is the base or anchor rate in the Eurocurrency market? Describe how loans and deposits are priced in this market.

9. How did the U.S. stock market react to the following events associated with LDC lending: (1) the announcement of loans to LDCs prior to 1982? (2) the announcements of the Mexican and Brazilian debt moratoriums? (3) the announcement of Citicorp's $3 billion loan-loss provision in 1987? What did other large banks throughout the world do after Citicorp's announcement?

10. Recall the epigram from the beginning of this chapter by Wilfried Guth of Deutsche Bank, Frankfurt: "International banking will continue to increase in importance, but it will also become even more complex. The quality of people will be a decisive factor."
    a. Why will international banking continue to increase in importance?
    b. Is international banking any more complex than domestic banking?
    c. Focusing on the "quality of people," discuss Rick Leeson (former trader for the defunct Barings Bank), the derivatives salespersons at Bankers Trust during 1993 and 1994, and the importance of internal controls in any organization.

11. The globalization of financial markets and its accompanying imposition of discipline make it less likely that a Lenin-type decision in the twenty-first century would be in favor of repudiation of a country's debt. Distinguish between a "debt moratorium" (e.g., Mexico and Brazil in the 1980s) and a repudiation of debt. How have Cuba and Iraq fared in the international community in terms of access to international credit and what have been the consequences for their capacity to trade?

12. How important is size (total assets) in international banking? What does BIS stand for and how do U.S. banks fare under its BIS capital standards? What are those capital requirements?

13. In 1989, Congress passed the International Development and Finance Act of 1989, which required regulators to monitor the level of bank reserves while giving them flexibility to deal with specific situations (i.e., forbearance). In addition, the regulators are to review the reserve levels of U.S. banks for potential losses from loans to highly indebted countries. Based on the reviews, the banking agencies are to advise banks about the adequacy of their reserves in light of the type of loan, the collateral, the existence of World Bank/IMF assistance programs for the country, and the bank's capital adequacy and earnings prospects. Finally, the act requires the federal banking agencies to report to Congress annually on the actions taken under the law. Do we need such a law? Are the managers and directors of major banks not capable of doing these things?

14. What role do foreign banks play in the United States? How many U.S. banks have foreign offices? What is the U.S. policy of "national treatment"?

15. What are the sources of foreign-exchange risk for a bank? How can net exposure be measured and what can a bank do about it? Draw risk profiles for banks that are net long and net short.

16. Compare domestic ALM with global ALM.

17. The differences between domestic and international/foreign banking for U.S. banks are captured succinctly by three ratios. What are they and why do they differ?

18. Distinguish between merchant banking and investment banking. Which one does Glass-Steagall prohibit in the United States? Does the law apply to overseas operations of U.S. banks?

Problems

1. Your bank lends a developing country $100 million. The loan has a balloon payment of principal due in five years. Interest payments are due annually at a rate of LIBOR plus 5 percent. When the country cannot make the first payment, the bank lends it the interest to keep the loan current. This charade goes on until the loan's maturity. What is the country's indebtedness to the bank at the end of each of the five years? Assume that LIBOR tracks the following annual pattern: 6 percent, 7 percent, 8 percent, 9 percent, 10 percent. How is this contract likely to be settled?

2. The accompanying chart shows the basis-point spread over LIBOR on syndicated loans to British companies. What does the trend in the spread tell you? Write a brief essay about your conclusion in which you demonstrate your understanding of LIBOR,

basis points, and syndicated loans. Find LIBOR for 1990 through 1995 and calculate the approximate interest rate on such loans. How do these rates compare with the prime rate in the United States over the same time period? What conclusions do you draw?

3. Given the following interest rates

Large U.S. CDs

Maturity	LIBOR	U.S. T-bills	Primary Market	Secondary Market
One month	5.9375%	NA	5.63%	5.85%
Three months	6.0625	5.46%	5.71	5.95
Six months	6.1875	5.65	5.81	6.00
One year	6.3735	NA	6.08	NA

LIBOR is the average for dollar deposits in the London market based on quotations at five major banks. The primary CD rate is an average of the top rates paid by major New York banks on issues of negotiable CDs. T-bill rates are from the Treasury auction of May 28, 1991.

a. Calculate and discuss the risk structures found in these data.

b. Calculate the forward rates embodied in these term structures and discuss their implications.

4. Currency-trading profits play an important role in the revenues of U.S. multinational banks. Consider the following data:

Banking Company	Foreign-Exchange Revenues	As % of Total Revenues
Bankers Trust	$425 million	13.6%
Morgan	309 million	9.7
Chase/Chemical	422 million	7.3
Citicorp	657 million	4.5
First Chicago	102 million	4.1

Calculate the total revenues for these BHCs and discuss how well diversified you think their earnings streams are. Are foreign-exchange bets like bets on interest rates? Should a federal safety net guaranteed by U.S. taxpayers support such transactions?

5. South Korean bank holds a net long position in U.S. dollars equal to $1,500,000. The current spot exchange rate is $1 = 770 won. If the spot exchange rate changes to $1 = 780 won, what is the gain or loss from the net long position? If spot exchange rate changes to $1 = 760 won, what happens?

6. Won-Ton Bank has a net short position in U.S. dollars of $1,500,000. If the U.S. dollar appreciates from $1 = 770 won to $1 = 780 won, what is the net gain or loss incurred by the bank?

7. Assume that a South Korean bank borrows $10 million in long-term deposits with a one-year maturity. It uses the proceeds to make loans denominated in won with a one-year maturity. The exchange rate is $1 = 770 won. If deposits cost 8 percent and loans return 15 percent, what risks does the bank face? What is the bank's net interest income and the net return on the loan?

a. Suppose the U.S. dollar appreciates to $1 = 900 won. What happens to the bank?

b. Suppose the U.S. dollar depreciates to $1 = 600 won. What happens to the bank in this case?

8. Your bank reports the following positions in assets and liabilities denominated in foreign currencies at the end of the past month.

	Assets	Liabilities
U.S. dollars	23,674,800	34,298,200
German marks	8,030,650	6,794,500
British pounds	3,326,550	1,198,280

The spot exchange rates for won (won per 1 unit of foreign currency) are

	S(t)	S(t − 1)
U.S. dollars	770	720
Deutsche mark	540	500
British pound	1220	1300

a. Calculate the net exposure in each currency.
b. Calculate the gain or loss for each position as a result of changes in the spot rates during the past month.
c. How might the bank hedge its on-balance-sheet exposure?

9. Shearson Lehman Brothers calculates a Developing Country Debt Index as a weighted average of the outstanding commercial bank debt to the countries. Given the information below, complete the last column by determining the market value of the outstanding debt during 1987. Given these market values, why might banks be reluctant to write off any LDC debt? In 1987 Peru's debt traded in the market at between 0 and 19 percent of its face value whereas Romania's debt ranged between 81 and 89 percent. What would your write-off strategy be comparing Peru with Romania? What events happened in 1987 that might explain the drop in the index from 66.7 to 48.1? If during the first two months of 1988, the index had values of 47.3 and 45.3 on a face amount of 284.4, what was the market value of the outstanding debt? Determine the change in the value of the debt from January 1986 to February 1988, if the index was 73.3 in January 1986 with a face amount of 274.8.

Month	Index	Face amount of indexed debt ($B)	Market value
January	66.7	279.4	
February	66.3	279.4	
March	64.8	279.4	
April	62.7	281.8	
May	62.6	281.8	
June	61.7	281.8	
July	58.7	281.8	
August	54.6	281.8	
September	47.9	281.8	
October	44.6	281.8	
November	45.3	281.8	
December	48.1	281.8	

10. Given the following data ($ millions), find *NIM* and *ROA*, and *PLL* and burden as a percentage of assets. Compare your results with the data in Table 20-4.

> Interest income = 13,220
> Interest expense = 7,773
> *PLL* = 382
> Noninterest income = 3,078
> Noninterest expense = 5,163
> Net income = 1,950
> Total assets = 187,298

APPENDIX

EXCHANGE RATES, INTEREST RATES, AND INFLATION

The various relationships among exchange rates, interest rates, and inflation rates across countries make international banking and finance a complex area.[15] Application of the Fisher effect, the expectations theory, and the concept of parity to international financial management can establish some basic relationships to reduce the degree of this complexity.

The Fisher Effect

Because the nominal or money rate of interest equals the real rate of interest plus the expected rate of inflation (i.e., the Fisher effect), differences in nominal interest rates across countries can be traced to one or both of these components. In a perfect international capital market, real rates would be the same across countries and differences in nominal interest rates could be explained by differences in the expected rates of inflation. Given the unrestricted nature of the Eurocurrency markets, real rates of interest are more likely to be equal in these markets than they are in domestic financial markets. In the absence of taxes, market imperfections, and government regulations, differences in interest rates across countries can be attributed to differences in expected rates of inflation.

The Expectations Theory

In the pure-expectations theory of the term structure of interest rates, a one-to-one correspondence between expected short-term spot rates and forward rates of interest is established. The expectations theory applied to the foreign-exchange market provides a similar linkage between the spot market and the forward market. That is, on average, the forward exchange rate is equal to the expected spot exchange rate. Alternatively, the difference between the forward rate (*F*) and the spot

---

[15] For an excellent and more detailed discussion of these relationships, see Brealey and Myers [1981], pp. 685–708. This appendix draws on their exposition.

rate (S) equals the expected change in the spot rate. Expressed as a percentage change, the relationship is[16]

$$\frac{F_{t+1} - S_t}{S_t} = \frac{F(S_{t+1}) - S_t}{S_t} \qquad \text{(20-A1)}$$

Multiplying by S_t and adding S_t to both sides of Equation (20-A1), the basic expectations-theory relationship for the foreign-exchange market is

$$F_{t+1} = E(S_{t+1}) \qquad \text{(20-A2)}$$

If the one-to-one correspondence depicted in Equation (20-A2) holds, then international bankers (and others) can ensure their interest-arbitrage transactions and foreign-exchange commitments in the forward market at a fair price. To the extent that nonexpectational elements (e.g., risk, transactions costs) distort the one-to-one correspondence, the forward rate can be either above or below the expected spot rate. In this case, the price of the forward contract includes either a premium or a discount on the price of the "insurance."

The Theory of Interest-Rate Parity

The fundamental principle of the theory of interest-rate parity is that a foreign rate of interest covered for exchange risk should be equal to the domestic interest rate. In the unrestricted Eurocurrency market, interest-rate parity tends to be the rule rather than the exception. In contrast, in restricted domestic markets, the existence of taxes and government regulations leads to differences in interest rates between countries even after coverage for exchange risk. Arbitrage fails to eliminate the existence of covered interest-rate differentials between countries because the potential profits are taxed away or because the actual capital flows are restricted.

In technical terms, the interest-rate-parity theory requires that the interest rate–foreign exchange relationship between two countries results in the equality of the interest agio and the exchange agio (see footnote 2). *Interest agio* is simply the interest-rate differential between two countries as an equilibrium condition; interest-rate parity guarantees that any gains arising from interest-rate differentials will be wiped out by losses from coverage against exchange risk in the forward market.

To illustrate the interest-rate-parity concept, consider the following example for country A and country B. The one-year interest rate in A is 8 percent; in B, it is 10 percent. The spot exchange rate is two of A's dollars for one of B's dollars (i.e., $S_{A/B} = 2$). The one-year forward exchange rate is $F_{A/B} = 1.9636$. Will a bank in country A be better off investing \$1 million in A or B? A loan in country A will produce a gross return of \$80,000 (= \$1,000,000 × .08) in A-dollars. A loan in country B will produce a return of \$50,000 (= \$500,000 × .10) in B-dollars. With the principal (\$500,000) and interest (\$50,000) of the loan in B covered by the forward contract at $F_{A/B} = 1.9636$, the value of the proceeds in A-dollars is \$1,080,000 (= \$550,000 × 1.9636), which equals the proceeds from the loan in A.

The agio equilibrium condition for interest-rate parity is

$$\text{Interest Agio} = \text{Exchange Agio} \qquad \text{(20-A3)}$$

---

[16] The LHS of Equation (20-A1) is called the *foreign-exchange agio* or simply the *exchange agio. Agio* refers to the premium or discount paid for the exchange of one currency for another.

In symbols, the condition is

$$\frac{(r_A - r_B)}{(1 + r_B)} = \frac{(F_{A/B} - S_{A/B})}{S_{A/B}} \qquad \text{(20-A3')}$$

Using the data from the example, the agio values are

$$\frac{(0.8 - .10)}{1.10} = \frac{(1.9636 - 2.0)}{1.9636}$$

$$-0.18 = -0.18$$

In words, the interest-rate advantage of investing in country B is offset by the forward discount in the exchange rate. If the flow of funds is from country B to country A, then the interest-rate *disadvantage* would be made up by the forward *premium* in the exchange rate. In this situation, the agio condition is

$$\frac{(.10 - .08)}{1.08} = \frac{(.50927 - .5000)}{.5000}$$

$$.0185 = .0185$$

The Law of One Price

Suppose that you could buy ATMs in Tokyo for $40,000 each and sell them to U.S. bankers for $50,000 each. If no one recognized this profitable opportunity, you could get rich quickly. Unfortunately, other shrewd businesspersons will recognize this opportunity and bid up the price of ATMs in Tokyo and perhaps cut the price of the ATMs they sell in the United States. In equilibrium, arbitrage will ensure that the dollar prices of ATMs in Japan and the United States will be equal. If the dollar/yen exchange rate is .005 (i.e., 200 yen = $1), the original disequilibrium ATM situation can be expressed as

$$\text{Yen Price of ATM} \times \$ \text{ Price of Yen} = \$ \text{ Price of ATM}$$

$$8 \text{ Million Yen} \times .005 = \$50,000$$

$$\$40,000 < \$50,000$$

In the equilibrium ATM price is $45,000 and the exchange rate is fixed, the price of an ATM in Japan will be 9 million yen. This equilibrium process is referred to as the *law of one price.* In general, it states that

$$\frac{\text{Foreign Currency}}{\text{Price of Product}} \times \frac{\text{Price of Foreign}}{\text{Currency}} = \frac{\text{Domestic Price}}{\text{of Product}} \qquad \text{(20-A4)}$$

or, alternatively, that

$$\text{Price of Foreign Currency} = \frac{\text{Domestic Price of Product}}{\text{Foreign Currency Price of Product}} \qquad \text{(20-A4')}$$

Applied to the price level in a country, the law of one price is known as the *theory of purchasing-power parity.*

By definition, the price of foreign currency (i.e., the exchange rate) is equal to the ratio of domestic to foreign product prices. From the previous example, in equilibrium, the ratio of domestic ATM prices is .005 = 45,000/9,000,000. Suppose now that 10 percent inflation is expected in the United States but only 5 percent inflation is expected in Japan. In equilibrium, the expected exchange rate will be .005238 = 49,500/9,450,000. In words, the dollar is expected to depreciate against the yen because of the higher expected rate of U.S. inflation. The important implication of the law of one price is that the expected change in the spot exchange rate is linked to the expected difference in inflation rates. Using previous notation and the following symbols, I = inflation rate, $\$$ = dollar, and Y = yen, this equilibrium condition can be expressed as

$$\frac{E(I_\$ - I_Y)}{1 + I_Y} = \frac{E(S_{\$/Y}) - S_{R/Y}}{S_{\$/Y}} \tag{20-A5}$$

Using data from the previous example, an illustration is

$$\frac{(.10 - .05)}{1.05} = \frac{(.005238 - .005)}{.005}$$

$$.0476 = .0476$$

The important empirical implication of Equation (20-A5) is that the best estimate of the expected change in the spot exchange rate is the expected differential in the inflation rates.

Recapitulation

Four fundamental financial or economic concepts have been applied in this appendix. (1) the Fisher effect, (2) the expectations theory, (3) interest-rate parity, and (4) the law of one price (purchasing-power parity). These models provide a basic foundation for understanding the relationships among exchange rates, interest rates, and inflation. Once these basic principles are mastered, the complexity of international banking and finance becomes much more manageable.

Selected References

Altman, Edward I., Robert B. Avery, Robert A. Eisenbeis, and Joseph F. Sinkey, Jr. [1981]. *Application of Classification Techniques in Business, Banking, and Finance.* Greenwich, CT: JAI Press.

Baer, Donald, and David Garlow. [1977]. "International Banking in the Sixth District." *Economic Review* Federal Reserve Bank of Atlanta (November/December), pp. 127–134.

Bennett, Rosemary. [1993]. "The Six Men Who Rule World Derivatives." *Euromoney* (August), pp. 45–49.

"BIS Statistics on International Banking and Financial Market Activity." [1995]. Monetary and Economic Department, Bank for International Settlement, Basle (August).

Brealey, Richard, and Stewart Myers. [1981]. *Principles of Corporate Finance.* New York: McGraw-Hill.

Citicorp Annual Report. [Various years]. New York: Citicorp.

Dombrowski, Peter. [1996]. *Policy Responses to the Globalization of American Banking.* Pittsburgh: University of Pittsburgh Press.

Fisk, Charles, and Frank Rimlinger. [1979]. "Nonparametric Estimates of LDC Repayment Prospects." *Journal of Finance* (March), pp. 429–438.

"Foreign Banks: Assessing Their Role in the U.S. Banking System." [1996]. United States General Accounting Office, Report to the Ranking Minority Member, Committee on Banking, Housing, and Urban Affairs, U.S. Senate (February).

General Accounting Office. [1996a]. *Foreign Banks: Assessing Their Role in the U.S. Banking System.* (February), GAO/GGD-96-25, Washington, DC.

General Accounting Office. [1996b]. *Mexico's Financial Crisis.* (February), GAO/GGD-96-56, Washington, DC.

Greenspan, Alan. [1996]. Board of Governors of the Federal Reserve System. Remarks at the Eighth Frankfurt International Banking Evening, Frankfurt am Main, Germany (May 7).

Gwynne, S. C. [1983]. "Adventures in the Loan Trade." *Harper's* (September), pp. 22–26.

Honeygold, Derek. [1989]. *International Financial Markets.* New York: Nichols Publishing.

Johnson, Howard G., and J. James Lewis. [1975]. "Keep Control of Foreign-Exchange Operations." *The Bankers Magazine* (Spring), pp. 79–83.

Jones, Geoffrey, ed. [1990]. *Banks as Multinationals.* London: Routledge.

J. P. Morgan. [1995]. *Annual Report.* New York.

Kraus, James R., and Michael Cacace. [1996]. "Foreign Banks Jump Back into U.S. Lending." *American Banker* (February 28), pp. 1, 14.

Lees, Francis. [1974]. *International Banking and Finance.* London: Macmillan.

Leeson, Nick. [1996]. *Rogue Trader: How I Brought Down Barings Bank and Shook the Financial World.* Boston: Little, Brown.

Lindsey, Lawrence B. [1996]. "The Political Economy of Sovereign Risk." Board of Governors of the Federal Reserve System, Remarks to the Global Treasury Summit, Palm Beach, FL (February 16).

Madrid, Raul L. [1990]. *Overexposed: U.S. Banks Confront the Third World Debt Crisis.* Washington, DC: Investor Research Responsibility Center.

Makin, John H. [1984]. *The Global Debt Crisis.* New York: Basic Books.

Mayer, Martin. [1987]. "Under the Mexican Hat." *American Banker* (December 31), pp. 1, 11.

Megginson, William. [1997]. "Understanding and Accessing Financial Markets." *Corporate Finance Theory.* Reading, MA: Addison-Wesley, pp. 388–464.

Megginson, William, Annette Poulsen, and Joseph F. Sinkey, Jr. [1995]. "Syndicated Loan Announcements and the Market Value of the Banking Firm." *Journal of Money, Credit, and Banking* (May), pp. 457–475.

Musumeci, James J., and Joseph F. Sinkey, Jr. [1990a]. "The International Debt Crisis, Investor Contagion, and Bank Security Returns in 1987: The Brazilian Experience." *Journal of Money, Credit, and Banking* (May), pp. 209–220.

Musumeci, James J., and Joseph F. Sinkey, Jr. [1990b]. "The International Debt Crisis and Bank Loan-Loss-Reserve Decisions: The Signalling Content of Partially Anticipated Events." *Journal of Money, Credit, and Banking* (August), pp. 370–387.

NationsBank. [1995]. *Annual Report.* Charlotte, NC.

Phillips, Susan M. [1995]. "Foreign Bank Participation in U.S. Financial Services Reform." Address at Foreign Banks in the United States: Economic, Supervisory, and Regulatory Issues, a conference sponsored by the OCC (July 13), Washington, DC.

Porzecanski, Arturo. [1981]. "The International Financial Role of United States Commercial Banks: Past and Future." *Journal of Banking and Finance* (March), pp. 5–16.

Rogoff, Kenneth. [1996]. "The Purchasing-Power-Parity Puzzle." *Journal of Economic Literature* (June), pp. 647–668.

Sesit, Michael R. [1996]. "Top Dogs: U.S. Financial Firms Seize Dominant Role in the World Markets." *The Wall Street Journal* (January 5), pp. 1, 6.

Sinkey, Joseph F., Jr. [1993]. Review of *The Twilight of Sovereignty: How the Information Revolution Is Transforming Our World* by Walter B. Wriston. *Journal of Banking and Finance* 17, pp. 764–766.

Stevenson, Richard W. [1992]. "Europe Weaker Currencies Fall." *The New York Times* (September 22), p. C2.

"Survey of International Banking." [1996]. *The Economist* (April 27), pp. 1–38 (insert).

Wriston, Walter. [1992]. *The Twilight of Sovereignty: How the Information Is Transforming the World.* New York: Scribner.

Glossary

AAA "Triple A" is the highest credit rating assigned to a borrower, for which full payment of principal and interest is expected at maturity.

Accounting model of the firm A simple valuation framework in which a firm's equity value is the product of its earnings per share (EPS) and the industry P/E ratio, that is, $P = EPS \times P/E$.

Accounting ratios Performance figures derived from accounting data and used to evaluate the financial soundness of an organization, e.g., return on assets (ROA = net income/average assets).

Accrual basis A method of accounting in which expenses are recognized when incurred and revenues are recognized as earned. Accrual accounting differs from cash-basis accounting where expenses and revenues are recognized when cash changes hands.

Accrued interest Interest earned but not paid on an asset such as a bond or certificate of deposit.

Acquisition, development, and construction (ADC) loans Funding used to get real-estate projects started.

Active investment management A practice used mainly by larger banks of speculating on future interest rates, providing dealer and market-making services, and hedging, dealing, and selling interest-rate derivatives.

Activity charge Fee assessed a bank account to cover servicing cost (e.g., a personal checking account with lots of checks written and ATM transactions versus a business account with lots of deposits [credit-card transactions and checks] and checks written).

Adjustable-rate mortgage (ARM) A loan contract with a variable rate of interest usually tied to some index or base rate but constrained by annual and lifetime caps to protect the borrower.

Adversely classified assets Loans and other assets with a higher degree of default risk than normal, classified by bank examiners as "substandard" (lowest risk), "doubtful" and "loss" (highest risk).

Affiliate A bank or nonbank subsidiary owned or controlled by the parent company of a bank holding company.

Affinity (credit) card A credit card that is "co-branded" between a bank and a party that bank customers are expected to have an identity with or have an "affinity" for, such as a particular sports team, university, or product.

Agency An arrangement similar to a trust. Unlike a trust, however, the title to the property does not pass to the agent but remains in the name of the principal. More generally, the relation between a principal and another party (agent).

Agency theory Deals with the analysis and resolution of conflicts of interest between principals and agents.

All-in cost Total cost, whether explicit or implicit.

Allocated transfer risk reserve (ATRR) The portion of a bank's ALLL reserved for losses to foreign borrowers ("country risk") as required by the International Lending Supervision Act of 1983. Transfer risk refers to the uncertainty regarding a borrower's ability to raise foreign exchange to service external debt.

Allowance for loan and lease losses (ALLL) A bank's loan-loss reserve or estimate of its expected loan losses. A contra-asset account deducted from gross loans to get net loans.

American Bankers Association (ABA) The national trade association for commercial banks in the U.S.

Americanization The view that globalization of financial services simply is paramount to Americanization.

Amortization The repaying or servicing of a loan with periodic payments of principal and interest over the life of the loan.

Annual clean-up A short period in which a business borrower has to be "out of the bank" while the relationship (e.g., line of credit) is reevaluated.

Annual percentage rate (APR) the cost of consumer credit, expressed as an annual percentage rate, that captures the effective cost of borrowing and permits comparison shopping.

Arbitrage The simultaneous buying and selling of an asset in two different markets such that a profit is guaranteed. In banking, funding an earning asset with a lower cost source of funds generates a positive "arbitrage" spread.

Asset-backed security A financial instrument representing a claim to the cash flows provided by a pool of underlying assets.

Asset-based lending The use of assets such as inventory, accounts receivable, or other nonreal-estate assets as security or collateral for a loan.

Asset liability management committee (ALCO) A senior management committee responsible for the coordinated management of a bank's rate-sensitive assets and rate-sensitive liabilities such that the volatility of net interest income or the market value of equity is minimized.

Asset liquidation The sale of assets at "fire-sale" prices. Also, a process in which the FDIC attempts to recover the maximum value from the assets of failed financial insured depositories.

Asset quality Reflection of a bank's credit risk—the major uncertainty a bank faces and the "A" in CAMEL. In a world of securitization, the modern view of asset quality is captured by the value or price a loan commands in the marketplace as opposed to probability of loan repayment— the two standards are, of course, directly related.

Asset sensitive A bank is said to be asset sensitive if it maintains a positive maturity gap position (RSA > RSL) or a negative duration gap.

Asset utilization (AU) Ratio of a bank's total revenue or gross income to average total assets—a measure of the ability of assets to generate revenue, where ROA = PM × AU.

Automated clearinghouse (ACH) An electronic funds transfer facility for the clearing and settling of payments among financial institutions. ACH entries are substitutes for checks.

Automated teller machine (ATM) An electronic funds transfer device for convenience transactions such as deposits, withdrawals, and balance inquiry. Later generations of ATMs perform more sophisticated services.

Automation The use of computers and other mechanical means to perform tasks previously performed by humans, especially important in bank consumer lending.

Balance sheet A financial statement that reports an entity's assets, liabilities and net worth at a point in time.

Balance-sheet management A three-stage framework for analyzing a bank's financial management. The first stage involves looking at the management of assets, liabilities, and capital. The second stage focuses on particular areas, both on and off the balance sheet. In stage three, the balance sheet is viewed as generating the income-expense statement.

Bank-examination process On- and off-site inspections by federal (OCC, FDIC, Fed) and state banking agencies to assess bank safety, soundness, and performance, especially in terms of loan quality relative to its capital. The bank-examination process traditionally has been an on-site inspection but is moving more and more toward off-premises computer analyses.

Bank holding company An organization that owns one or more banks.

Banking companies Together independent banks and bank holding companies (BHCs) are referred to as "banking companies."

Banking structure The number of firms in the banking industry, the evolution of which could be a "barbell" of large and small banks.

Bank Insurance Fund (BIF) Deposit insurance fund (DIF) for commercial banks. DIF = BIF + SAIF.

Bank performance It can be measured by accounting or market standards. Return on assets is a widely accepted accounting measure of the profitability of a bank's total assets; price-earnings and market-to-book ratios combine market and accounting information of bank value to measure performance.

Bankruptcy costs The expected costs of financial distress. As a firm uses more debt, the probability of bankruptcy rises and the expected costs of financial distress increase.

Bankruptcy prediction Use of statistical models or artificial intelligence to attempt to identify future bankrupts, both corporate and personal.

Base lending rates Anchor rates such as prime, federal funds, or LIBOR used for pricing loans.

Basis point (bp or b.p.) Term used to describe certain pricing aspects of financial contracts, e.g., the cost of funds is LIBOR plus 100 bp. Since one basis point equal 1/100 of one percent or 0.01% or 0.0001, 100 bp equal 1% or 0.01.

BBB/Baa This rating and above designate investment grade securities, which banks are permitted to hold.

Beta In the capital-asset-pricing model, beta represents an estimate of systematic or market risk of an asset. It captures the extent to which a stock's return moves with the return on the market portfolio.

Board of Governors of the Federal Reserve System The primary policymaking and administrative body of the Federal Reserve System.

Bond ratings Grades assigned to securities that reflect their underlying credit quality.

Bond valuation A bond is valued by discounting the stream of coupon payments and the subsequent principal repayment at a required rate of return that reflects the going rate of interest on obligations of similar risk and maturity.

Book value accounting A method of valuation based on historical cost, not market value. Except for certain investment securities, bank assets are carried at book value or historical cost.

BOPEC rating system Fed framework for evaluating bank holding companies in which B = bank, O = other subs, P = parent, E = earnings, and C = capital. BOPEC builds on CAMEL.

Borrower-information continuum A spectrum that runs from low-information, high-cost borrowers to high-information, low-cost borrowers.

Bridge bank If the FDIC needs additional time to resolve a failed bank, it may set up a bridge bank to be operated by existing or newly appointed management under federal supervision. The bridge bank is designed to give potential bidders time to value the situation.

Brokered deposits Funds acquired through national markets in which investment bankers (acting as money brokers) provide a third party to the normal two-party transaction.

Brokered trading Brokered trading involves agents bringing together buyers and sellers. Brokered trading usually takes place on an organized exchange.

Bullet loan A term loan with a balloon payment at maturity.

Burden Noninterest income minus noninterest expense, which for most banks is negative. Hence it is a "burden" to the bank.

Business units Separate divisions within a bank that serve distinct functions. For example, a large bank may have a retail unit (a provider of funds), a wholesale unit (a user of funds), and a treasury-and-trading unit (an intermediary within the bank responsible for centralized risk management).

Cap A contract, for which the buyer pays a fee, to protect against rising input prices, e.g., an interest-rate cap to protect against the rising cost of funds above a certain rate, called the strike rate. At rates above the strike, the seller pays the buyer the difference between the actual rate and the strike rate.

Capacity One of the five Cs of creditworthiness. It captures a borrower's cash flow or ability to service debt.

Capital One of the five Cs of creditworthiness. It captures the borrower's net worth or ownership at risk.

Capital adequacy The ability to absorb the unanticipated losses associated with the various risks of banking.

Capital markets A market where long-term financial claims and services are traded. The existence of a capital market serves to smooth consumption patterns to meet personal preferences.

Capital structure A firm's mix of debt and equity.

Cash-basis loan A nonperforming loan in which payments are recorded only when they are actually received rather than when they are due (accrual accounting).

Cash flow The difference between cash inflow (dollars received) and cash outflow (dollars paid out). A major source of loan repayment.

Cash-flow liquidity The difference between a bank's sources (liquid assets available over the next 30 days) and uses (short-term liabilities due over the next 30 days) represents a bank's liquidity position.

Cash-flow model of FDIC Framework for analyzing the operations of the FDIC beginning with two revenues (insurance premiums and investment income) and two costs (operating and insurance losses).

Caux Principles The first international code of ethics for business established by the Caux Round Table.

Character One of the five Cs of creditworthiness. It captures the borrower's willingness to repay as opposed to financial ability—"good citizens stand ready to repay their debts."

Charter-insurance contract An intangible asset for a bank that represents the combined value of the bank's right to do business (the charter) and its government-supplied guarantees (deposit insurance and the discount window).

Charter value An unbooked intangible asset that is part of a bank's goodwill/going concern value.

Classification models Statistical devices used to attempt to separate observations into two or more groups, e.g., bankruptcy-prediction models.

Closure rule A standard that a bank must meet or be faced with closure, e.g., market value of equity > 0.

Collateral One of the five Cs of creditworthiness. It captures the assets promised as security for a loan.

Commercial and industrial (C&I) loans Business loans made by banks.

Commercial bank Legally and narrowly an institution that accepts demand deposits and makes commercial loans.

Commercial banking Business of gathering deposits to fund loans. It is separate from investment banking as required by the Glass-Steagall Act of 1933.

Commercial letter of credit An agreement in which a bank definitely commits to finance a transaction.

Commercial paper Unsecured short-term debt instruments issued by major corporations, a corporate IOU.

Commercial real estate (CRE) Real estate used for business or nonresidential purposes. CRE loans created problems for many banks and S&Ls during the late 1980s and early 1990s.

Common law A legal system based upon rules deduced, mainly by judges, from the customs and institutions of the people and related to their sociopolitical/economic conditions.

Common stock A security granting its owner the right to share in the residual interests of the firm (the remaining assets after all claimants have been satisfied).

Communications firms Business that provide networking relationships through which information is collected, stored, processed, and transmitted. In this regard, banks are similar to communications firms.

Community bank A local or independent bank operating in a limited geographic market. All banks below the 1,000 largest.

Comparative-statics experiment An analytical technique used in economics and finance to measure the effect of a change or shock to a system by comparing one equilibrium to another equilibrium.

Compensating balance The percentage of a borrower's loan that must be kept on deposit with the bank as additional compensation for a loan or other services provided.

Component DCF analysis A method of valuing real estate in which properties are first grouped by use or by industry. The cash flows from each group or component are then evaluated by discounted-cash-flow or DCF analysis.

Computer simulation A technique (e.g., of ALM) for estimating future outcomes based on alternative scenarios.

Conditions (economic) One of the five Cs of creditworthiness. It captures the borrower's downside vulnerability or ability to repay under financial distress.

Confidence function A model of the public's confidence in the banking system that can be expressed as a function of information quality, stability of earnings, government guarantees, and net worth.

Conflict resolution A view of ethics as consisting of a set of normative guidelines directed toward resolving conflicts of interest, so as to enhance societal well-being.

Consolidated balance sheet A financial statement net of intercompany funds. A BHC can be viewed as a consolidated portfolio consisting of three components: bank subsidiaries, nonbank subsidiaries, and the parent company.

Consolidation In an industry, the decline in the number of firms due to mergers, failures, or reduced entry. The total number of banks has been declining and market power is becoming concentrated among a smaller group of banks.

Construction and land development One of the major areas for which banks make real-estate loans.

Consumer installment credit Installment financing for households in the form of automobile loans, revolving loans (mainly credit cards), and other loans.

Contestable market Markets that adapt through entry and exit to permit customer demand to be served at a minimum cost.

Contingent-commitment banking The promise of an extension of credit on a conditional basis, a form of off-balance-sheet banking.

Convenience function A primary factor for determining the selection of a financial institution. It can be modelled as a function of geographic reach, products supplied, costs of accessing the firm's facilities, and quality of services generated by the firm.

Convenience user Credit-card user who pays monthly balances in full every month and never incurs any finance charges, as opposed to credit users.

Convexity The curvature of a price-yield relation or deviation from a straight line. Since the normal price-yield relation is convex to the origin, a callable bond or an asset with prepayment risk exhibits "negative convexity" or becomes concave at relatively low interest rates when bonds are called and loans refinanced.

Core capital Tier 1 capital consisting of common stockholders' equity, noncumulative preferred stock, and minority interest in the equity of consolidated subsidiaries less goodwill. Core capital must equal or exceed four percent of risk-weighted assets.

Core deposits Lower cost and more stable sources of funding for a bank that are gathered in local markets. Small-denomination accounts of less than $100,000.

Corporate control The market for buying and selling companies.

Corporate restructuring Actions of a firm designed to improve efficiency and protect against hostile takeovers. Such restructuring includes dividend cuts, reorganizations, and stock buy-backs.

Cost-benefit analysis A framework for decision-making based on expected costs and benefits, e.g., in mergers.

Cost complementarities The extent to which the costs of producing a particular financial service or product may vary with the output levels of other products or services.

Cost dispersion The notion that banks of similar size may have substantially different average costs per dollar of assets.

Cost function An expression for the total cost of producing output. It is a function of input quantities and input prices.

Cost of capital The opportunity cost of capital for the firm's existing assets.

Country risk Exposure to transfer and/or convertibility risk.

Credit analysis The process of investigating a borrower's creditworthiness, e.g., with respect to the five Cs of character, capacity, capital, collateral, and conditions.

Credit application The first step in the credit-granting process.

Credit check Actions taken by a lender to verify that information supplied by potential borrowers is accurate.

Credit enhancer A participant in the asset-securitization process that provides a guarantee or letter of credit to enhance the creditworthiness of a pool of assets.

Credit extension One of the building blocks of financial engineering and consisting of bonds, loans, and private placements.

Credit memo A written statement, prepared by a commercial lender, evaluating a potential borrower's management, operations, market, and financial performance.

Credit quality Estimation of the quality of a bank's assets as in the A = asset quality of CAMEL.

Credit risk Credit or default risk refers to the probability of borrowers not repaying their loans. It can be measured by the market value of the loan, where a deep discount means greater credit risk. Since a majority of a bank's assets are in the form of loans, credit risk is the major risk a bank faces.

Credit scoring A statistical model used by lenders to analyze consumer-credit applications by assigning scores to potential borrowers based on such characteristics as age, income, stability of employment, etc. Each borrower's score is compared to a cutoff score to gauge creditworthiness.

Credit union A not-for-profit financial institution which offers financial services to its members, who share a common bond or affiliation such as the same employer.

Cross hedge Hedging the price or rate risk of one asset with the price or rate of a different asset or a synthetic contract, e.g., hedging a LIBOR-based loan with a T-bill futures contract.

Cross-selling A marketing strategy for getting bank customers to use more than just basic loan and deposit services to generate noninterest (fee) income.

Customer relationship A traditional part of any business including banking. Banks attempt to enhance such relationships by cross-selling and providing new and innovative products and services.

Debt capital Bank debt such as notes and debentures that is treated as regulatory capital when measuring capital adequacy.

Debt-equity model A method of valuing real estate in which the present value of a property equals the present value of existing leases (debt) and the present value of future leases (equity).

Decomposition (ROE) analysis A multi-stage method of analyzing financial data for any firm. The first stage links accounting return on equity (ROE) with return on assets (ROA) and the equity multiplier (EM) such that ROE = ROA × EM. In the second stage, return on assets is split into the product of profit margin (PM) and asset utilization (AU). Stage three involves a detailed examination of the components of PM and AU.

Default-risk structure (of interest rates) The relationship between bond yields and default risk.

Delegated monitoring By engaging in indirect finance, the saver, as a depositor, does not have to monitor the financial condition and performance of the borrower. This task is delegated to the intermediary which serves as the delegated monitor or engages in delegated monitoring.

Delivery risk The notion of a BHC/bank as a "deliverer of financial services" suggests the concept of delivery risk. This risk can be separated into four components: (1) technological risk, (2) affiliation risk, (3) operating-efficiency risk, (4) market-strategy risk.

Delivery systems Methods and devices for getting financial services to customers in either domestic or foreign markets.

Deposit insurance fund The federal deposit insurance fund is a combination of the Bank Insurance Fund (BIF) and the Savings Association Insurance Fund (SAIF).

Deposit Insurance National Bank (DINB) A bank chartered and run by the FDIC for up to two years to resolve a failed bank and ensure banking services to a community.

Deposit payoff A failure-resolution method in which the FDIC pays off the insured depositors and liquidates the assets of the failed bank.

Deposit transfer A failure-resolution method in which the FDIC transfers insured deposits to another viable bank.

Depository institutions Depository institutions, which include commercial banks, savings-and-loan associations, savings banks, and credit unions, raise loanable funds by accepting deposits from households, businesses, and governments.

Deposit-rate ceiling Limits on interest rates financial institutions could offer depositors. Prior to their removal, deposit-rate ceilings restricted the ability of financial institutions to attract funds and contributed to disintermediation during periods of high interest rates.

Deposits The major component of a bank's liabilities. Two ways to classify deposits are: (1) domestic vs. foreign or (2) interest-bearing (such as money-market accounts) vs. noninterest-bearing (certain types of checking accounts).

Derivatives Securities or assets that "derive" their value from the value of an underlying interest rate, currency, or commodity price.

Differential-income model A method of valuing real estate in which a property's present value is the sum of two perpetuities representing existing and future loans.

Diffusion process A way of viewing how innovations spread throughout society, e.g., by distinguishing between invention and innovation.

Direct finance The direct flow of funds from a surplus-spending unit (SSU) to a deficit-spending unit (DSU).

Direct public offering A firm engages in a direct public offering when it attempts to sell its securities directly to investors without the services of an underwriter.

Disclosure The practice of making private information available for decision-making.

Discrimination (ordinary use) Discrimination in the sense of prejudging.

Disinformation The unethical practice of not supplying the truth, the whole truth, and nothing but the truth.

Disintermediation The loss of traditional sources and uses of bank funds to new institutions or instruments. Bank deposits lost to mutual funds and bank business loans lost to commercial paper are important examples.

Diversification An attempt to control risk by holding assets providing less than perfectly correlated returns.

Divestiture The selling of a business or subsidiary.

Dividend-investment plan A program in which a shareholder agrees to accept a stock dividend in lieu of a cash dividend.

Dividend-payout ratio Dividend per share (DPS) divided by earnings per share (EPS).

Dividend yield Annual dividend divided by share price.

Double leverage The concept of passing parent company debt down to a bank subsidiary as an infusion of bank equity.

Dual banking The joint chartering, regulating, and supervising of commercial banks at the federal (national bank) and state (state bank) levels.

Duration The average life of a security, or the effective time to repricing. Technically, the time-weighted, present value of a financial instrument's cash flows.

Dynamic gap A bank's gap position viewed over several periods, the opposite of static gap at one point in time.

Earning assets Bank assets that generate either interest income or fees or both. Earning assets can be defined as: total assets − cash − fixed assets − other nonearning assets or loans and leases, investments, federal funds sold, interest-bearing deposits with other banks, and earning assets.

Economic discrimination Economic decision-making is based on opportunity cost or the value of an alternative forgone action—the "next best" alternative. This kind of "discrimination" is, in fact, the heart of financial management.

Economic failure A bank is considered an economic failure if its economic or real net worth is negative. This event can precede regulatory failure or closure.

Economic model of the firm It states that firm value equals the present value of future cash flows discounted at an interest rate reflecting the riskiness of the flows.

Economic net worth Net worth measured on a market-value basis. By closing a bank at the moment its economic net worth is exhausted, remaining asset values cover all liabilities and the deposit insurer incurs no losses.

Efficient market An allocation of resources such that it is not possible to make someone better off without making someone else worse off (Pareto optimality).

Efficient markets Mechanisms that quickly and accurately incorporate all relevant information into the price of a security.

Electronic banking (e-banking) Electronic-based banking services provided by devices such as ATMs, POSs, ACHs, and the Internet.

Electronic data interchange (EDI) Electronic communication of transactions among business and financial institutions that replaces paper devices.

Electronic funds transfer system (EFTS) A device for transferring funds with electronic images rather than paper devices such as ATMs, ACHs, or POSs.

Electronic money (e-money) The images or electronic impulses of electronic banking that replace currency and checks. E-money completes the evolution of money from the concrete to the ethereal.

Equity approach to valuing banks A method of valuing banks that equates equity value with forecasted free cash flow to equityholders, discounted at the cost of equity.

Equity multiplier (EM) Ratio of total equity capital to total assets, a measure of bank leverage or the "yeast" that raises ROA to ROE, that is, $ROE = ROA \times EM$. Reciprocal of EM is the ratio of equity capital to total assets.

Ethical guidelines Moral, institutional, and legal standards for decision-making.

Ethics The discipline dealing with what is good or bad and with moral duty and obligation.

Etymology The linguistic history of a word. The etymology of the word bank suggests the two basic functions that banks perform: the safekeeping and transactions functions. Safekeeping refers to the bank as a place to store savings. The transactions function refers to banks providing a means of payment for buying goods and services.

Eurobond market The international market for long-term debt.

Eurocurrency market The international money market. A Eurocurrency is a claim in that currency held by a non-resident of the currency's country of origin.

Failure-resolution methods The choices available to the FDIC for dealing with a failed bank. The FDIC has two basic failure-resolution methods: a deposit payoff or a purchase-and-assumption transaction.

FDIC Improvement Act (FDICIA) Law passed in 1991 to improve deposit insurance with, among other things, a requirement of "prompt corrective action" (PCA) of problem-bank situations.

Federal Deposit Insurance Corporation (FDIC) Federal agency that insures bank deposits up to $100,000 per account.

Federal Reserve ("the Fed") The central bank in the United States and chief regulator of bank holding companies and state member banks.

Federal safety net The government guarantee provided by deposit insurance and access to the Federal Reserve's discount window.

Fed funds rate The rate at which banks lend funds to each other for overnight use.

Fed wire A nationwide Federal Reserve facility used mainly for large-denomination transfers between financial institutions; the Fed guarantees these transactions.

Fee income Revenues earned by banks for originating and servicing loans and providing other services including off-balance-sheet activities.

Finance charge As defined by Truth-in-lending Regulation Z, the finance charge refers to "all charges payable directly or indirectly by the borrower and imposed directly or indirectly by the lender as an incident to or as an extension of credit."

Financial engineering Procedures for constructing financial contracts with unique cash flows.

Financial futures/forward contract A binding agreement between two parties to exchange (buy and sell) a stated amount of a financial asset at a specified price on a specified date. Futures are exchange-traded contracts while forwards are over-the-counter (OTC) contracts.

Financial innovation The development of new products, services, contracts, and delivery systems.

Financial intermediary An institution that channels funds from surplus-spending units (SSUs) to deficit-spending units (DSUs).

Financial risk The uncertainty or variability in earnings due to debt financing. More debt means more financial risk.

Financial-services firm (FSF) A business such as a bank, brokerage firm, or a financial subsidiary of a nonfinancial corporation that supplies financial services.

Financial-services industry (FSI) The aggregation of firms that supply financial services and products. The FSI includes traditional institutions such as banks, thrifts, credit unions, and real-estate and insurance firms as well as nonfinancial corporations engaged in the production and delivery of financial services and products.

Financial system Its primary function is resource allocation. To accomplish this task, financial systems perform six basic or core functions: clear and settle payments; aggregate (pool) and disaggregate wealth; transfer resources over time, space, and industries; accumulate, process, and disseminate information for decision-making purposes; provide ways for managing uncertainty and controlling risk; and provide ways for dealing with incentive and asymmetric-information problems that arise in financial contracting.

Fisher effect The idea that nominal interest rates equal the real interest rate plus a premium for expected inflation, including a cross-product term to capture the effect of expected inflation on the real rate.

Five Cs of creditworthiness Character, capacity (cash flow), capital (net worth), collateral, and conditions (economic).

Flat yield curve A yield-maturity relation in which rates are the same regardless of maturity. Mainly a theoretical construct that permits "the" interest rate to exist. Flat curves are approximated in the real world when rates are in transition from low to high or vice versa.

Floating-rate loan A loan with a variable interest rate tied to the prime rate, LIBOR, or some other index.

Floor A contract, for which the buyer pays a fee, to protect against falling output prices, e.g., an interest-rate floor to protect against falling revenues on uses of funds below a certain rate, called the strike rate. At rates below the strike, the seller pays the buyer the difference between the actual rate and the strike rate.

Forbearance Actions taken by lenders when borrowers show signs of loan default. Forbearance includes actions such as loan renewals and workout situations. Bank regulators also have been known to act with forbearance with respect to bank capital adequacy.

Foreign banks Banks operating in a country that were chartered outside the country in which they are operating.

Foreign-exchange market A market, dominated by the largest commercial banks, where one currency is traded for another.

Foreign-exchange risk The uncertainty associated with unexpected changes in the value of foreign currencies. Also called cross-currency risk.

Foreign-exchange transaction Attempts by banks to make money based on the spread between the currencies they buy and sell.

Forward contract An obligation to buy or sell a specified asset at a set price at a particular date in the future.

Fragmentation (of lending) Separation of traditional lending into its component parts of originate, fund, service, and monitor with selling replacing funding due to securitization.

Franchise value The value of the rights and privileges associated with a franchise. An individual or a group holding a franchise acquires the rights to be and exercise the powers of a corporation.

Fraud A conscious misrepresentation or concealment of the truth with an intent to benefit by causing another party to rely on the untruth to his or her detriment. A major cause of bank failures.

Functional cost analysis (FCA) A cost-accounting technique that attempts to assign costs of production to alternative business functions as in the Fed's FCA survey of commercial banks.

Funding The means of raising cash to invest in earning assets. Banks fund their assets with deposit and nondeposit liabilities.

Gap (maturity) The difference between rate-sensitive assets (RSAs) and rate-sensitive liabilities (RSLs) over a particular maturity horizon.

Gap management The technique of attempting to control the difference between rate-sensitive assets and rate-sensitive liabilities. Gap management focuses on net interest income (NII = interest income − interest expense). The gap formula (ΔNII = Δr × gap) highlights how changes in interest rates affect a bank's income.

Garn-St. Germain Act of 1982 Legislation designed to permit insured depositories to compete with money-market mutual funds, to expand thrift investment powers, and to give federal regulators more power to deal with troubled depositories.

Global asset-liability management The coordinated management of a bank's domestic and foreign balance sheets or "books."

Globalization The internationalization of financial institutions and markets, referred to some analysts as Americanization.

Goodwill An unbooked intangible asset representing the amount in excess of book value paid by one firm to acquire another.

Government guarantee Explicit and implicit promises made by the government with respect to financial backing. For example, the explicit promise of deposit insurance is up to a maximum of $100,000 per account; the implicit promise is one of 100 percent deposit insurance.

Guarantor A participant in the process of asset securitization that wholly or partially insures the securities. Insurance companies usually perform this function.

Hedging A counterbalancing transaction in derivatives markets designed to minimize risk in the cash or spot market.

Hidden action A type of principal-agent problem. The most common hidden action is the efforts of the agent. Conflicts occur because the agent often derives little utility from the efforts while the principal wants the agent to exert maximum effort on the principal's behalf.

Hidden capital Hidden or "unbooked" capital is the difference between accounting net worth and economic net worth. Hidden capital has two sources: (1) differences between the market and book values of items on the balance sheet and (2) neglected off-balance-sheet items.

Hidden information A principal-agent problem that occurs when the agent has information unknown to the principal (asymmetric information).

Home banking A service delivery system that permits bank customers to complete routine banking transactions over home computers or, to a lesser extent, over the telephone.

Home equity loan Credit secured by the equity value in a borrower's home.

Horizontal development A stage in the creation of value in real estate in which the infrastructure (roads, utilities, permits, etc.) needed to support the building phase is prepared.

Horizontal merger A combination of two firms in the same industry as opposed to a vertical merger (acquiring a supplier or distributor).

Hostile takeover An unwelcomed attempt by one firm to acquire another.

Humped yield curve A yield-maturity relation in which the short-term segment of the curve has an inverted U-shape. It occurs when interest rates are high by historical standards.

Hunters Bankers who specialize in selling banking products and services—they "hunt" for customers as opposed to "skinners" who evaluate creditworthiness.

Immunization A process in which a bond investor balances price risk and coupon reinvestment risk such that they are offsetting.

Implicit interest Noncash payments used by banks to attract depositors or reward borrowers. Examples include more branches, longer hours, merchandise premiums, or "free" services.

Implicit pricing The charging of nonmonetary fees. For example, implicit deposit insurance fees result from examination and supervision by regulators.

Incentive-compatible contracts A set of contracts (explicit and implicit) designed to promote the "common good" that leaves individual stakeholders unable to gain an advantage from other members of the group, even if they violate the "rules of the game."

Incentive compensation An attempt to reward managers for adding economic value to their firm. Incentive compensation is often tied directly to the value of the firm's stock.

Income-expense statement A financial statement that reports a firm's profitability over some time period by subtracting all expenses from all income.

Independent bank A bank not affiliated with a holding company, usually a community bank.

Indirect finance Funds transferred from a surplus-spending unit (SSU) to a financial intermediary which passes the funds on to a deficit-spending unit (DSU).

Information processor Financial institutions can be thought of as information processors because they send information signals to the market through their credit-granting and pricing decisions.

Information quality The accuracy and timeliness of information flows from the borrower to the lender.

Information technology The foundation for the advancement of the information revolution has been computer technology applied to the collecting, processing, storing, and transmitting of information.

Innovation The profitable application of an invention. Induced innovation is generated by outside forces while autonomous innovation just happens (not triggered by external stimuli).

Insolvency Negative net worth or inability to pay bills (cash-flow insolvency).

Installment loan A type of consumer loan made by commercial banks in which the borrower repays the loan by making periodic monthly payments.

Institutional investors The dominant participants in securities markets. They buy and sell securities for institutions such as pension funds, insurance companies, and nonfinancial corporations.

Institutionalization The increased participation of institutions in banking and financial markets, especially mutual funds and pension funds over recent years.

Intangible assets Nonphysical assets that either involve rights against outsiders in general or represent anticipated future benefits that may not attach to a specific physical asset.

Interchange fee Fee paid by one bank to another for handling and process costs and risk-bearing, e.g., in credit-card, ATM, and debit-card transactions.

Interest-rate cap An interest-rate option that provides the holder protection against an increase in interest rates.

Interest-rate collar An interest-rate option that is a combination of an interest-rate cap and an interest-rate floor.

Interest-rate cycle The movement of interest rates over the business cycle from trough to peak and back to trough.

Interest-rate floor An interest-rate option designed to protect earning assets against a decline in interest rates.

Interest-rate forecasting The attempts by a bank to forecast the speed of future movements in interest rates. Interest-rate forecasting is an important component of asset-liability management.

Interest-rate futures A contract giving the holder the right to buy or sell a financial instrument at a specific price at a given future date. A tool for hedging interest-rate risk.

Interest-rate risk The exposure to unexpected changes in interest rates. The degree of this risk can be measured by a bank's gap, the difference between rate-sensitive assets and rate-sensitive liabilities. Interest-rate risk has two components: price risk and reinvestment risk.

Interest-rate-risk products Financial contracts, developed by financial engineering, for use in the management of interest-rate risk.

Interest-rate swap An exchange of interest payments between two parties based on an underlying notional principal and specified interest rates (fixed and floating).

Internal capital generation rate The rate at which a bank can build its internal equity capital through retained earnings or undivided profits without the need for external equity. This rate equals the product of the bank's ROE and its earnings-retention rate.

Internal rate of return (IRR) A measure of a project's profitability that equates the present values of cash inflows and outflows. A bond's IRR is its yield to maturity.

International banking Banking across national boundaries that involves the accepting and measuring of sovereign and foreign-exchange risks.

International debt crisis Uncertainty during the 1980s associated with repayment of loans by less-developed countries to major banks, especially U.S. lenders.

Internet The World Wide Web (WWW) or communications linkage of computers among business, households, and governments. The system for the ultimate in electronic banking.

Invention An unfolding technological opportunity.

Inverted yield curve A yield-maturity relation in which short-term rates are higher than long-term rates. A yield curve with a negative slope occurs when interest rates are at historically high levels.

Investment bank An organization that specializes in the raising of capital through the issuance of new securities in the primary market and the bringing together of buyers and sellers of existing securities in the secondary market.

Investment banking Business of advising, underwriting, and distributing securities. In the United States, this business is separate from commercial banking as required by the Glass-Steagall Act of 1933.

Investment-grade securities Securities with a BBB/Baa rating or better.

Investment services Bank operating services related to investments including securities processing, bond services, annuities and institutional, corporate, and personal trust services.

Jurisdictional tangle (that boggles the mind) A description of U.S. bank regulation suggested by Arthur Burns, a former Chairman of the Board of Governors of the Federal Reserve.

Keiretsu The Japanese model of bank-industry linkage or cross shareholdings in which corporate control is based on continuous surveillance and monitoring by mangers of affiliated firms and banks.

Land assemblage The collecting of adjoining locations to allow the development of large real estate projects.

Lead steers Sophisticated investors who focus on economic value and ensure that securities are properly priced.

Lease portfolio A portfolio of leases, in-place and speculative.

Lending process (traditional) Component parts consist of originate, fund, service, and monitor.

Less-developed country (LDC) A country with a low level of economic development as characterized by low income GDP, high population growth, high unemployment, excessive inflation, and dependency on commodity exports. The LDC or international debt crisis of the 1980s resulted in huge financial losses for major banks, especially in the United States.

Leverage The use of debt financing by a firm. Its use in banking can be captured by the equity multiplier, EM = assets/equity.

Liability sensitive A bank is said to be liability sensitive if it has a negative gap position (RSL > RSA) or a positive duration gap.

Line of credit A commitment by a lender to supply a specified amount of funds over a specified period.

Liquidity premium A premium required by investors to hold long-term securities due to the uncertainty about future interest rates.

Liquidity risk The uncertainty about a bank's ability to meet its obligations as they come due including both deposit withdrawals and loan demand.

Loan broker A party that works with realtors to originate loans as an independent contractor for a financial institution.

Loan charge-off A loan "written off" as uncollectible.

Loan commitment A formal arrangement whereby a bank agrees to lend a customer a specified amount of money at an agreed-upon rate.

Loan-loss reserve An allowance or contra-asset account maintained on a bank's balance sheet that reflects the bank's estimate of potential loan losses.

Loan packager A participant in the process of asset securitization that specializes in the underwriting of securities.

Loan participation An arrangement between banks to share loans and the underlying risks.

Loan policy A written statement that provides a framework for the organization and control of bank lending. The loan policy usually consists of five major components: (1) general policies, (2) specific loan categories, (3) miscellaneous loan policies, (4) quality control, (5) committees.

Loan purchaser A participant, usually a subsidiary or separate trust, in the process of asset securitization that buys assets from originating banks.

Loan surveillance Monitoring the loan portfolio to determine the credit risk of outstanding loans.

London InterBank Offered Rate (LIBOR) The base rate at which major banks in London lend to each other, and the standard for pricing international financial contracts.

Loss-control instruments Guarantors such as FDIC and lenders can monitor asset values, restrict assets, and use risk-based pricing to manage their businesses.

Loss-sharing A deposit-insurance concept in which the insurer and the insuree share losses in the event of failure.

Macrohedge Strategies designed to hedge a firm's overall balance sheet.

Managing value Activities designed to maximize firm value (based on discounted cash flows).

Marked-to-market Restating the value of an asset or contract to reflect the market value of the asset or the value of the underlying asset. In a margin account, an adverse price movement requires the holder of a long position to contribute additional funds while favorable price movements permit the holder to withdraw cash.

Market discipline The notion that managers, knowing that the market closely monitors their actions, are encouraged to make value-maximizing decisions.

Market failure Inability to achieve Pareto optimality because of less-than-perfect market conditions.

Market-making A dealer is said to participate in market-making when it provides a market for the security issue after the underwriting is closed.

Market-segmentation theory An explanation of the term structure of interest rates that proposes that the forces of supply and demand in segmented markets determine the yields in these markets.

Market-strategy risk The uncertainty that a firm will fail to properly define its markets or fail to develop the financial services and products that create a demand or meet a need.

Market value For a firm, the product of the price per share and the number of shares outstanding.

Market-value accounting An accounting system whereby the market determines the value of assets and liabilities, as opposed to book value or historical cost.

Market value of (portfolio) equity The difference between the market value of assets and the market value of liabilities.

Matched book or funding A macro situation in which a bank's rate-sensitive assets and rate-sensitive liabilities are paired (zero gap) or a micro position in which a particular asset is funded with a particular liability of matching or similar duration.

Merchant banking The European name for investment banking.

Merchant discount Bank fee charged merchants for processing credit-card receivables, e.g., a 2% fee means the merchant receives $98 for $100 of receivables.

Mergers and acquisitions (M&A) One of the major businesses of investment bankers and large BHCs is to advise clients about M&A.

Microhedge Transactions designed to hedge individual components of the balance sheet.

Mix The composition of a bank's assets and liabilities, e.g., loan-to-asset ratio, loan-to-deposit ratio, or core deposits-to-total assets ratio.

Modified-expectations theory An explanation of the term structure of interest rates proposed by Hicks (1946). This theory holds that, because of uncertainty about future interest rates and bond prices, investors have to be paid a liquidity premium for bearing the interest-rate or maturity-risk of holding a long-term security.

Money-center banks The strongest, most powerful banks located in major financial centers such as New York, London, and Tokyo.

Money-market liabilities Bank liabilities that pay market rates and consisting of items such as large time deposits, federal funds purchased, and repurchase agreements.

Moral hazard Behavior induced by certain types of insurance, e.g., excessive risk-taking by banks because of mispriced deposit insurance.

Mortgage-backed security A security representing a share of a pool of securitized mortgage loans.

Multibank bank holding company (MBHC) A bank holding company that owns more than one bank.

Multistate MBHC An organization that owns more than one bank in more than one state.

Neal-Reigle Interstate Banking and Branching Efficiency Act of 1994 (IBBEA) Law that permitted interstate banking/branching in the United States on July 1, 1997.

Negligent misrepresentation A misrepresentation or concealment resulting from stupidity or negligence by a counterparty.

Net income The firm's earnings after all expenses have been deducted, including taxes and nonrecurring items.

Net interest income (NII) The difference between interest income and interest expense; it captures a bank's role as a pure intermediary.

Net interest margin (NIM) Net interest income divided by average earning assets or average total assets, a measure of a bank's intermediation profit rate before loan losses and operating or noninterest expenses.

Net loan charge-off Equals gross loan charge-offs minus recoveries. A gross charge-off is a loan written off as bad or uncollectible. Recoveries are subsequent cash collections from loans previously written off.

Net noninterest income Noninterest income minus noninterest expense, a bank's "burden" since for most banks this figure is negative.

Net present value (NPV) A measure of a project's profitability defined as the difference between the present value of future cash flows and the present value of expected costs or cash outflows.

Netting arrangements An agreement in which the parties involved only make net settlements at the end of the day—credits and debits are summed (netted) to generate a single journal entry.

Networking The linkage of computers and various periphery for conducting and approving financial transactions as in an ATM network.

Net worth Net worth or total equity capital is the difference between a bank's total assets and total liabilities. Book net worth is based on book or historical value. Real net worth is based on market values.

Nonaccrual asset An asset, especially a loan, that is nonperforming in terms of not accruing interest or principal, and for which a loan-loss reserve should be established.

Nonbank bank Organizations, also known as limited-service banks, which either accepted deposits or made commercial loans but did not do both—the legal definition of a commercial bank. In the process, they avoided regulation by the Federal Reserve. The loophole was closed in August 1987.

Nonbank subsidiary A subsidiary of a bank holding company engaged in nonbanking functions such as leasing, securities marketing, data processing, and insurance underwriting.

Noncurrent loan A contract for which payments are not current or past due.

Noninterest expense A bank's operating expense consisting primarily of salaries and wages, occupancy and equipment expense, and other operating expenses.

Noninterest income All income other than interest income from assets, e.g., fees and service charges.

Normal (shape) yield curve A yield-maturity relation in which short-term rates are lower than long-term rates, considered the "normal" curve with a liquidity premium for bearing interest-rate risk.

Notional amount or value The principal or face value of the underlying contracts in interest-rate swaps. Notional values are often used to express the volume of interest-rate swaps.

Objectives of bank regulation Safety, stability, and structure (competition).

Obligor The borrowers who make principal and interest payments to the loan originator.

Off-balance-sheet activity (OBSA) A transaction that is not recorded on a bank's balance sheet such as a loan commitment, line of credit, or derivatives activities in the form of futures, forwards, options, or swaps.

Office of the Comptroller of the Currency (OCC) Supervisor, regulator, and charterer of national banks.

Office of Thrift Supervision (OTS) Arm of U.S. Treasury Department responsible for regulation and supervision of S&Ls (formerly part of the Federal Savings & Loan Insurance Corp. or FSLIC).

One-state MBHC An organization that owns more than one bank but operates them in only one state.

Open-bank assistance Financial assistance provided by the FDIC to prevent the closing of an insured bank. The assistance may take the form of a cash infusion, facilitation of a merger, or facilitation of an acquisition by a bank holding company.

Operating-efficiency risk The uncertainty of inefficient bank or bank holding company operations and subsequent reduced streams of earnings.

Operating services Services that banks usually sell to corporate customers including securities processing, bond services, trust services, and cash management.

Opportunity cost The value of an alternative forgone action—the "next best" alternative.

Option A financial contract that provides the holder the right (but not the obligation) to buy or sell an asset at a specified price.

Option-adjusted spread A method of analyzing the risk and return for mortgage-backed securities. The option approach adjusts for both the timing and level of potential prepayment.

Option-pricing model Sophisticated model for valuing options based on five key parameters: exercise price, time to expiration, value of the underlying asset, expected price variability, and the short-term interest rate. Applied to the pricing of deposit insurance.

Originator A bank with the expertise and reputation to evaluate credit risk and initialize loans.

Outsourcing Hiring an outside party to perform a function that could be performed internally.

Ownership issue A major issue in the financial-services industry is whether nonfinancial corporations should be permitted to own commercial banks.

Parent company The head of a holding company that either partially or wholly owns the subsidiaries of the company, e.g., Citicorp, the parent company, owns Citibank.

Passive casualty-insurance model Traditional view of the FDIC as operating the passive business of underwriting casualty insurance.

Passive management A relatively inactive investment policy followed by most smaller banks, e.g., a staggered investment strategy with spaced maturities that generate a steady flow of liquidity for a bank.

Pass-through finance Arises from indirect finance when assets are pooled, packaged, and sold as securities to investors. The underlying cash flows pass-through from the borrower to the servicer to the investor.

Pass-through security When assets are securitized, the ownership of the assets and the cash flows pass-through to the investors.

Past-due loans Loans with payments not made as of the scheduled payment date, e.g., 90 or 180 days past due.

Payments system The mechanism used by banks to process payments for goods and services on behalf of their customers. It links the real and financial sectors of the economy.

Pay-through security A type of asset-backed security in which the interest and principal payments are split into payment tranches.

Perfectly competitive markets A capital market is considered perfectly competitive if (1) all participants have free and equal access to the market and no one controls prices, (2) the relevant information is free and widely available, (3) no market impediments or taxes exist. If these conditions hold, security prices accurately and quickly reflect all available information and capital markets are said to be efficient.

Pledging requirements Collateral that must be supplied for certain transactions. Pledging requirements are typically met by supplying U.S. Treasury securities or municipal obligations as collateral to be held by a third-party trustee.

Poison pill A measure designed to make it harder (more expensive) for a would-be suitor to acquire a target company. The poison pill permits current shareholders to buy shares at a discount, say 50 percent, from the company, which can make the task of buying the entire company prohibitively expensive.

Pooling of interest A method of accounting for business combinations in which the assets and liabilities of the combined firm are stated on the same basis as the books of the component companies without revaluation.

Portfolio A collection of financial assets. A commercial bank can be thought of as a portfolio of earning assets, consisting mainly of loans, and deposits (negative assets).

Portfolio-risk premium A risk premium attached to the rate of interest charged a borrower based on a loan's correlation with the existing loans in the bank's portfolio.

Portfolio theory The selection of alternative groups of securities based upon their risk-return characteristics as reflected in the portfolio's expected return and the variability of that return.

Preferred habitat theory An explanation of the term structure of interest rates, developed by Modigliani and Sutch (1966), which states that policy-determined or regulatory-induced risk aversion leads investors to hedge their balance sheets by staying in their preferred maturity habitat.

Preferred stock Capital stock to which preferences or special rights are attached, usually with respect to dividends and liquidation.

Prepayment risk Uncertainty regarding the life of a loan due to the borrower's option to refinance and therefore prepay the loan.

Price-earnings (P/E) ratio The ratio of market price to earnings per share (EPS > 0), a reflection of a company's relative worth. Since high P/E ratios translate into low required rates of return (E/P ratios), they are preferred, all other things being equal.

Price-fixing building blocks Arrangements designed to lock in or fix prices on commodities, currencies, or interest rates. They consist of forward contracts, futures contracts, and swaps.

Price-insurance building blocks Options contracts. Call options ensure the holder that the price paid for an asset will not exceed a pre-specified exercise price. Put options ensure that an asset can be sold at a price no lower than a prearranged exercise price.

Price risk The uncertainty associated with unfavorable changes in the price of an asset, e.g., a fixed-income security due to changes in interest rates.

Prime rate A benchmark interest rate used by banks for pricing loans. A bank's best customers usually have alternative sources of funding and therefore negotiate discounts from the prime rate.

Private (deposit) insurance Deposit insurance provided by the private sector, instead of by the government.

Probability of default The probability a borrower will fail to repay a loan.

Problem bank A bank that may require financial assistance from the FDIC in the future. The FDIC maintains a problem-bank list of banks with financial difficulties and consisting of three classes: (1) OP—other problem, (2) SP—serious problem, (3) PPO—potential payoff.

Product expansion A trend in banking in which banks are engaging in new activities and offering new products and services. Bank holding companies have begun to expand into insurance, real estate, and investment banking.

Profitable loan contract rate The rate of interest charged on loans after adjusting for portfolio risk and default risk.

Profit margin (PM) Ratio of net income to total revenue or gross income, a measure of profitability, where $ROA = PM \times AU$.

Prompt corrective action (PCA) Provision of FDICIA (1991) calling for problem-bank situations to be resolved quickly with PCA.

Purchase accounting A method of accounting for business combinations which results in the revaluation of assets, the recognition of intangibles, and the allowance for goodwill. Management is not free to choose the method of accounting for business combinations—certain criteria define which technique to follow.

Purchase-and-assumption (P&A) transaction The FDIC's major technique for resolving failed banks in which a viable bank assumes some of the assets and all the liabilities of the failed bank and pays a premium for the package.

Purchased funds Managed liabilities or "hot money" consisting of large negotiable CDs (domestic or foreign) and federal funds.

Put-call parity A relationship between puts and calls (both with the same exercise price). It states that a portfolio composed of a long position in a call and a short position in a put is equivalent to a long position in a forward contract.

Rate-sensitive asset (RSA) An asset that reprices or matures within a specific (short) time frame such as 90, 180, or 360 days.

Rate-sensitive liability (RSL) A liability that reprices or matures within a specific (short) time frame such as 90, 180, or 360 days.

Real-estate investment trust (REIT) A specialized business focused on the management of income-producing real estate or lending to developers.

Real-estate lending Loans secured by one–four family, multifamily, or nonfarm, nonresidential property.

Recourse A contingent claim that may remain with banks that have securitized or sold assets. If any of the securitized assets default, the seller (the bank) is responsible for the losses. Under current banking law, assets cannot be removed from the balance sheet if recourse is offered to the investor.

Regional bank A bank that operates in a regional market.

Regulatory dialectic A struggle model to explain the ongoing battle between regulators and regulatees as a clash between thesis and antithesis, leading to a synthesis which becomes the next thesis, etc.

Regulatory interference The process through which banking authorities attempt to correct a perceived unsafe or unsound banking practice. Major instruments in this process include capital regulation, cease-and-desist orders, and the threat of termination of deposit insurance.

Regulatory risk The risk that unforeseen regulatory action will damage the firm's profitability.

Reinvestment risk The risk that the intermediate cash flows (e.g., coupon or loan payments) will have to be reinvested at interest rates lower than the asset's yield to maturity at the time of purchase.

Repurchase agreement (repo or RP) A short-term sale of a security under agreement to repurchase it. Although 24 hours is the typical maturity, term repos can be arranged. Repos are an instrument of liability management used to raise funds. The countervailing transaction is a reverse repo. The difference between the sale and repurchase price represents the cost to the seller of the security (the purchaser of the funds) and the return to the lender.

Reputational capital The value of an organization's good name and standing in the marketplace.

Resolution Trust Corporation (RTC) Organization established by FIRREA (1989) to dispose of the assets of failed S&Ls. After 1996, remaining assets were to be transferred to SAIF.

Retained earnings The undivided profits or accumulated earnings of the business.

Return on assets (ROA) Ratio of net income to average total assets, the best accounting measure of a bank's overall performance or profitability, where $ROA = PM \times AU$ and $ROE = ROA \times EM$.

Return on equity (ROE) Ratio of net income to average equity capital, a measure of profitability from shareholders' perspective, where $ROE = ROA \times EM$.

Return-on-equity (ROE) decomposition analysis An accounting framework for analyzing a firm's performance. It begins with $ROE = ROA \times EM$, then $ROA \times PM \times AU$, and so on.

Returns to scale A means of expressing how output changes when inputs are changed. For example, a process exhibits increasing returns to scale when output changes by a larger percentage than the percentage change in inputs.

Reverse repurchase agreement (reverse repo or RP) A short-term purchase of a security under agreement to resale it. Although 24-hours is the typical maturity, term repos can be arranged. Repos are an instrument of asset/liquidity management used to employ funds. The countervailing transaction is a repo. The difference between the purchase and resale price represents the return to the purchaser of the security (the seller of the funds) and the cost to the borrower.

Risk The uncertainty associated with some event or outcome.

Risk-adjusted return The rate of return on a loan after adjusting for expected and unexpected loan losses.

Risk arbitrage A chance to increase the expected rate of return for a given level of risk.

Risk-based capital requirements The idea that banks with riskier assets should be required to maintain higher levels of capital.

Risk-based deposit insurance Deposit insurance in which the explicit price increases as the bank's riskiness increases.

Risk-free rate The rate of return on a default-free loan.

Risk index A measure to identify risky banks defined as $[E(ROA) + CAP]/\sigma_{ROA}$. The lower the index is, the riskier the bank is.

Risk of liquidity management It consists of a price element and a quantity element. The price factor refers to the price at which assets can be sold and the rate at which liabilities can be acquired. The quantity factor focuses on whether or not assets exist that can be sold and whether or not funds can be acquired in the marketplace at any cost.

Risk premium A payment paid for the greater default risk of a risky bond.

Risk profile A graph showing the relationship between a company's change in value compared to the change in a key underlying variable such as an input or output price, e.g., ARBL and LRBA pictures for a bank, where the underlying variable is the change in interest rates.

Sale-and-leaseback The sale of an asset to a second party who, in turn, leases the asset back to the user.

Savings Association Insurance Fund (SAIF) Fund to protect deposits in savings associations (up to $100,000) and operated by the FDIC. DIF = BIF + SAIF.

Scale economies A firm is said to benefit from economies of scale if its average cost of production, in the long run, declines as output increases.

Scope economies Economies of joint production exist when the cost of producing two products jointly is less than the costs of producing the two products separately. The existence of economies of scope is attributed to interproduct or cost complementarities.

Securitization The selling of assets (usually loans) packaged as securities, a major innovation in financial markets.

Separability issue Refers to the fact that a bank charter is virtually impossible to obtain without simultaneously being accepted for deposit insurance. The bank charter and deposit insurance guarantee are inextricably interwoven into the fabric of U.S. banking.

Separation of banking and commerce As stipulated by the Glass-Steagall Act (1933), the merging of financial and nonfinancial firms is prohibited.

Separation of commercial and investment banking A provision of the Glass-Steagall Act (1933) that separates these two activities. The separation is increasingly being eroded by commercial banks forays into investment banking. Original intent was to promote bank safety by prohibiting banks from participating in the speculative ventures associated with investment banking.

Services subsidiary A separate subsidiary (as part of a bank holding company) established to handle information and transactions processing at a wholesale level.

Servicing A function in the loan process which entails collecting payments, dispersing proceeds, reporting to investors, and other such activities.

Skinners Bankers who evaluate the financial data of potential borrowers and estimate the borrower's creditworthiness. "Green eyeshades" in old accounting jargon; today, spreadsheet jockeys.

Small business lending Financing for businesses with less than $5 million in assets or firms below "middle-market companies." Such businesses are important engines of economic growth.

Sources of loan repayment Cash flow, sale of assets, or another source of financing.

Specialness argument A line of thinking that says that commercial banks play a special role in the economy and, therefore, require special regulatory treatment.

Speculator An individual or organization willing to bear greater risk in pursuit of higher profits in financial markets.

Spilled milk A section of *The Journal of Commercial Bank Lending* in which lenders share their experiences in dealing with problem loans.

Spot price The price at which an asset can be bought today.

Spread account An escrow account established as a reserve against potential losses on securitized loans.

Spread management The management of the difference between lending and borrowing rates.

Standard deviation (σ) A common measure of risk in finance. It captures the dispersion, variability, or uncertainty of a distribution of returns, e.g., σ_{ROA} as used in the risk index.

Statement of cash flows A financial statement which details the cash inflows and outflows of an organization and designed to assist users in understanding the differences between net income and cash flows and to segment noncash investing and financing transactions.

Statement of sources and uses A financial statement, replaced by the statement of cash flows, which identified where a firm generated (sources) and spent (uses) its cash.

Static gap A bank's gap position at a single point in time; in contrast, dynamic gap looks at several periods.

Statistical market value accounting model (SMVAM) A model to measure a firm's hidden capital by regressing $MVE = a + b(BVE) + e$. The joint hypothesis of SMVAM is: $[a = 0, b = 1]$, in which case $MVE = BVE$ and no hidden capital exists.

Stock repurchase A stock repurchase refers to a firm buying back its equity from current stockholders.

Stored liquidity An internal source of funds in which liquid assets are stored on a bank's balance sheet. The liquidity is generated when assets are converted to cash.

Strategic planning The process of planning for alternative futures. Three critical questions for planners are: (1) Where is the organization today?, (2) Where is the organization going?, and (3) How is the organization going to get there?

Structural arbitrage Adaptive changes in a firm's organizational form designed to lighten its tax and regulatory burdens.

Subordinated notes and debentures Debt that is of lower priority than senior debt. Holders of subordinated debt are paid only following payment to more senior debtholders.

Superregional bank A bank which operates in several states or regions.

Supervision-by-risk program Approach to bank supervision that focuses on the risks of banking and how well banks manage them.

Supplemental capital Tier 2 capital consists of allowance for losses on loans; cumulative perpetual, long-term and convertible preferred stock; perpetual debt and other hybrid securities; intermediate-term preferred stock; and term subordinated debt.

Supremacy of equity The concept that common equity is viewed as the dominant determinant of bank stock value.

Surety A guarantee of debt repayment or fulfillment of contractual obligation, e.g., the trilateral performance bond of deposit insurance.

Swap A contract calling for the exchange of one asset, price, or interest rate for another. In an interest-rate swap, net interest payments are exchanged based on rates (e.g., fixed vs. floating) applied to an underlying notional amount or principal.

Synthetic contract or instrument An arrangement created by combining basic financial building blocks. For example, an interest-rate swap is simply a portfolio of forward contracts.

Synthetic portfolio A combination of securities that provide payoffs identical to those of another ("straight") security. Since the synthetic portfolio provides the same payoffs as the straight security, the two should be priced the same.

Systems approach The use of credit-analysis methodologies such as artificial intelligence and credit-scoring as an alternative to the traditional loan officer's appraisal of individual applicants.

Systems integration The linking of separate computer systems to provide more complete, unified reporting.

Taxable securities Securities that provide income subject to taxation.

Tax-equivalent yield The effective rate of return on tax-exempt securities.

Tax-exempt securities Securities whose returns are not subject to taxation. Municipal securities are tax-exempt at the federal level while Treasury securities are tax-exempt at the state level.

Tax Reform Act of 1986 Tax legislation that reduced the tax advantage provided banks for holding municipal obligations. The law denied any deduction for interest expense incurred to purchase or carry tax-exempt securities.

Tax shield Since interest on debt is tax-deductible, the interest expense provides a "shield" to protect income from taxes.

Technological risk The risk of technological obsolescence. Due to their increasing reliance on electronics, automation, and telecommunications, banks are becoming more prone to technological risk.

Temporary investments A bank's most liquid assets: interest-bearing balances due from depository institutions, federal funds sold and reverse repos, and short-term investment securities.

Terms of lending Conditions specified in a loan contract such as interest rate, maturity, collateral, down payment, etc.

Trading-account security Assets held for "trading" purposes include U.S. Treasury securities, U.S. government agency and corporate obligations, state and municipal securities, CDs, and commercial paper. They must be marked-to-market.

Tranche It represents the division of cash flows and maturities of the various assets underlying an asset-backed security. Investors in different tranches bear different levels of risk.

Transfer pricing The determination of the charge or "price" paid for funds transferred within a bank from one business unit to another.

Treasury bills Short-term government securities sold at a discount through a competitive-bidding process.

Trilateral performance bond A guarantee or surety arrangement involving three parties, which in the case of deposit insurance the parties are: the depositor, the bank, and the FDIC.

Trust A fiduciary relation between a principal and an agent in which the agent holds property for the benefit and use of the principal. The basic trust products that banks offer include estates, personal trust, employee benefits, corporate trusts and personal and corporate agencies.

Trustee A participant in the process of asset securitization who receives the principal and interest payments from the loan originator and "passes through" the cash flow to the investors.

Truth-in-lending disclosure The basic information that lenders must disclose in lending agreements. The key items include the annual percentage rate (APR) and the finance charge.

Twilight of sovereignty View and book title by Walter Wriston, who for 17 years reigned as the chairman of Citicorp until his retirement in 1984, of how the information revolution is transforming the world.

Value What an asset is worth, as in fair market value, or to appraise what an asset is worth.

Value additivity The basic notion that the value of the whole is equal to the sum of the parts.

Value creation (in real estate) Five stages: land assemblage, horizontal development, vertical development, leasing/sales, and management.

Value maximization The objective of management is to make decisions so that shareholders' wealth or the value of the firm is maximized.

Variable-rate loan A loan with an interest rate that varies according to market conditions based on some index or rate such a Treasury rate, the prime rate, or LIBOR.

Vendor A party that supplies services to another party. With the outsourcing of many banking functions, the role of vendors has increased.

Videotex The generic term to describe home information retrieval systems.

Virtual banking 24-hour banking for any service, potentially on the Internet. ATMs were the first generation of virtual banking.

Visa The association owned by member financial institutions that licenses various Visa products, the most popular of which is its credit card. Prior to 1977, Visa was known as BankAmericard.

Wall Street The heart of the world's financial markets is the financial district on Wall Street in lower Manhattan or New York City.

Watch list A list of "problem banks" maintained by banking agencies (e.g., FDIC) or private rating firms.

Weekly reporting banks Large commercial banks, numbering about 300, that report their assets and liabilities to the Federal Reserve on a weekly basis.

Weighted average cost of funds (capital) A cost that reflects the operating, interest, or required return on all sources of funds weighted by respective portions of the balance sheet.

What-if analysis or scenario Managerial device for judging a firm's performance against alternative economic and competitive environments as in strategic planning or asset-liability management.

Wholesale banking A business focus centered on providing banking services to large corporations and institutional clients, private or public.

Wire transfer The transfer of funds by wire (e.g., Fed-wire or CHIPS), mainly for large dollar payments.

With recourse A transaction in which the buyer has recourse to the seller, thereby failing to remove the underlying risks of the sold asset from the seller's balance sheet.

Without recourse A transaction in which the buyer has no recourse to the seller, thereby removing all the underlying risks of the sold asset from the seller's balance sheet.

Working capital The current assets of a business, frequently used as collateral for asset-based lending or for sale in the case of factoring. Net working capital refers to the difference between current assets and current liabilities.

Workout situations Attempts to recover the bank's money from a borrower having financial difficulties. The workout agreement can be either a formal or informal arrangement.

Write down The process of marking loans, securities, and other assets to market value when that value is less the book value of historical cost.

Write off A charged-off asset such as a loan loss. If some value is later recovered, the gross write off is reduced by that amount and called the net write off or net charge off.

Yield curve A graphical depiction of the relationship between a bond's term to maturity and yield to maturity. It is constructed by plotting the yields on bonds which are identical, except for time to maturity.

Yield to call For a callable bond, the annualized return calculated for the earliest call date. This return is often reported for the yield to maturity of a callable bond.

Yield to maturity A bond's internal rate of return. It is the discount rate that equates the bond's promised payments of interest and principal with its price.

Zaibutsa A pre-WWII Japanese industrial conglomerate, one component of which was a major banking company that funds the entire organization. Known today as Keiretsu, but with weaker linkages than the traditional Zaibutsu. In the U.S. the separation of banking and commerce prohibits such an organization from existing.

Z-bond The last bond in a collateralized mortgage obligation (CMO) tranche. It pays no cash flows until all prior bonds have been retired.

Zero-coupon security A security with no interim cash flows (e.g., coupon payments) that sells at a discount from par value. The investor's return is solely in the form of price appreciation or a lump-sum interest payment.

Zero-floor limit Point-of-sale (POS) authorization whereby credit- or debit-card transactions require prior approval with respect to available funds, credit limit, stolen card, etc.

Zero gap The condition for a bank when its rate-sensitive assets (RSAs) equal its rate-sensitive liabilities (RSLs) for a given time period, e.g., three months.

Zombie banks and thrifts Economically insolvent banks and thrifts that remain in business because of government guarantees and regulatory forbearance. They were especially prevalent in the United States during the 1980s.

Author Index

Subject Index